# INTERNATIONAL ECONOMIC LAW

# INTERNATIONAL ECONOMIC LAW

By

## ASIF H. QURESHI

Professor of International Economic Law
School of Law
University of Manchester, Manchester, UK

Barrister
Quadrant Chambers
Fleet Street
London, UK

Editor-in-Chief
*Manchester Journal of International Economic Law*

AND

## ANDREAS R. ZIEGLER

Professor
Faculty of Law and Criminal Justice
University of Lausanne, Switzerland

**SWEET & MAXWELL**

THOMSON REUTERS

Published in 2011 by Sweet & Maxwell, 100 Avenue Road, London NW3 3PF
part of Thomson Reuters (Professional) UK Limited
(Registered in England & Wales, Company No 1679046.
Registered Office and address for service:
Aldgate House, 33 Aldgate High Street, London EC3N 1DL)

Typeset by Servis Filmsetting Ltd, Stockport, Cheshire
Printed in Great Britain by Ashford Colour Press, Gosport, Hants

*For further information on our products and services,
visit www.sweetandmaxwell.co.uk

No natural forests were destroyed to make this product;
only farmed timber was used and re-planted.

A CIP catalogue record for this book is available from the British Library.

ISBN 978 0 414 04615 3

Thomson Reuters and the Thomson Reuters logo are trademarks of Thomson
Reuters. Sweet & Maxwell ® is a registered trademark of Thompson Reuters
(Professional) UK Limited

Crown copyright material is reproduced with the permission of the Controller of
HMSO and the Queen's Printer for Scotland.

# FOREWORD TO THE FIRST EDITION

At a time when the economic troubles of banana producers in Central America can lead to trade wars which affect the livelihoods of woollen manufacturers in the Scottish Borders, one may ask whether there is any international economic law and if so whether it is effective. This book seeks to answer those questions. It surveys the several strands of burgeoning international economic law and binds them together in a coherent whole. The Scottish woollen manufacturer may not find within it a swift and effective remedy for the adverse economic consequences visited upon him as a result of foreign government action, but that is not the fault of the book. It is the result of international economic law being still at a developing stage and serves to illustrate the need for a book of this nature.

Commercial lawyers, whether employed by industry or government or in private practice, will find that this book contains a wide ranging account of the several international economic institutions that have been created in an attempt to bring order to international economic relations. The many references to conventions, reports and articles indicate the difficulty which lawyers not familiar with the learning in this field would have, in the absence of this book, in researching the topics covered by it. For the same reasons Dr Qureshi's work will be of great assistance to students of this area of the law.

Dispute resolution in international trade traditionally centres upon the private rights and obligations of one trader to another. However, where the source of a trader's economic problems is a foreign government's decision, the law of private rights and obligations may not always provide a remedy. This book sheds much needed light on the alternative international avenues which may be available to traders, financiers, investors and their associations to seek redress for the consequences of such decisions. Even where the present international economic institutions cannot provide a remedy, this book will enable the lawyer to understand more of the framework in which governmental decisions affecting international trade are taken and thereby improve his ability to protect the interests of the trader, financier and investor in the future.

April 1999
Nigel Teare Q.C.
4 Essex Court
Temple, London

(Now Sir Nigel Teare Q.C., Justice of the High Court, UK)

# FOREWORD TO THE SECOND EDITION

A new generation of globalisation seems to be emerging in the early 21st century, one that poses fresh challenges for developing countries. For many of these nations, expectations that globalisation would accelerate the development process were dashed by the disappointing development results of liberalisation and integration in the 1990s. It was increasingly recognised that greater economic integration alone was not addressing development concerns. Despite extensive trade liberalisation, many of the 50 least developed countries (LDCs) had not significantly reduced poverty, and some had experienced negative growth. Concern that the benefits of globalisation were being reaped at the cost of the poor, environmental degradation and workers' rights, found expression in broad protest movements in a new global civil society.

As a result, a number of important international initiatives were taken to ensure greater benefits from global economic co-operation, the most prominent of which was the adoption by world leaders in 2000 of the Millennium Development Goals (MDGs), to be achieved by 2015. Priorities began to shift, as reflected, for example, in international efforts to mobilise finance for development and to address the supply constraints and limited productive capacities of developing countries through aid for trade.

Paradoxically, this renewed emphasis on development comes not at a time of economic crisis, but at a time of sustained economic growth for a large number of developing countries. Ever since the early 2000s, the world economic environment has been extraordinarily propitious. Indeed, developing economies as a group have performed quite well in the past five years. Many African nations and other LDCs—34 of which are in Africa—have been growing at an annual average exceeding five per cent, marking considerable progress over the late 1990s. A distinctive characteristic of this new wave of globalisation is multipolarity, in which the South plays a major role. The new economic weight of some developing countries creates significant opportunities for the rest of the developing world. But because that weight is not equally distributed among them—and because their resource endowments vary greatly—policy diversity is of the essence.

There is, in fact, no room for complacency. Despite the economic success of the past five years, continued vigilance is required. The current broad-based economic expansion is subject to risks, which should be avoided through careful economic management. Another risk relates to the potential impact of higher energy prices, and to the possible reversal of recent upswings in commodity prices. There are also signs that the rise of the South is prompting protectionist reactions in developed economies. This could undermine the liberalization paradigm that fuelled globalisation until now, and threaten the propitious environment. In the meantime, looming issues such as the economic impact of climate change and migration pose new challenges for the global partnership for development.

From UNCTAD's perspective, an even more compelling reason for caution is that despite the unprecedented expansion of trade, not everyone is benefiting from globalisation. The old issue of "growth with equity" has resurfaced in a new context, adding urgency to the need to find ways of sharing the gains from globalisation. Certain countries, and certain segments of the population within countries, are being left out of the current growth bonanza and are often adversely affected by its consequences. In addition, many countries, especially the LDCs and some middle-income and transition economies, have been unable to translate growth into poverty reduction and broader human development. Progress towards the MDGs in sub-Saharan Africa continues to lag far behind, despite accelerated growth. While the implementation of the WTO's Uruguay Round agreements improved developing countries' access to the markets of developed countries, the reduction in tariff barriers has recently been accompanied by greater use of non-tariff measures, and new gains from multilateral trade agreements remain elusive. Similarly in the financial domain, the launching of the Heavily Indebted Poor Countries Debt Initiative in 1996 has not been able to address the range of external debt problems, and commitments to step up official development assistance have yet to be translated into scaled-up flows.

Accordingly, this new edition of *International Economic Law*, co-authored by two distinguished scholars, comes at a timely juncture. There is growing recognition that pro-development considerations must be placed at the centre of all international economic cooperation. And greater coherence is essential between and within the global trade, monetary and financial systems, which do not always take account of the differing needs of countries at varying stages of development. An equally important recognition is that in the absence of a rules-based, transparent and co-operative approach to globalisation, any chances for achieving developmental results through multilateralism could be lost to the narrower gains that might result from bilateral or regional initiatives. There must be coherence between the rule of law and the cause of development if economic co-operation and progress are to extend to all nations, peoples and citizens of our increasingly interconnected global community.

August 2007
Supachai Panitchpakdi
Secretary-General of UNCTAD

# FOREWORD TO THE THIRD EDITION

*International Economic Law* is now in its third edition. Its first edition, of which Professor Qureshi was the sole author, appeared as recently as 1999. The second edition—for the preparation of which Professor Qureshi was joined by another leading scholar, Professor Ziegler—needed, among other things, to address the Millennium Development Goals articulated in 2000. The impacts, positive and negative (especially for least developed countries) of globalisation were centre stage.

It is a tribute to the authors that they have now been able to publish a rapid third edition a mere four years after publication of the second. Very much has happened since 2007. At that time we were in an era of development, in the sense that there had been an extended period of economic growth for a large number of developing countries. We now find ourselves in an era, which we must expect to be extended, of economic crisis.

These changes, and all the many relevant events within the broad umbrella of "international economic law", have required all chapters to be revisited. Even as the authors have put aside elements that have become outdated, they have nonetheless had to expand virtually every chapter. The attentive reader will note not only an updated bibliography (there has recently been much innovative writing in the areas comprised in International Economic Law, especially perhaps on trade and investment), but also a special focus now on International Financial Law and on IMF surveillance. Everywhere the law has been brought up to date, important cases from a variety of jurisdictions included, new agreements and treaties put under scrutiny.

International Economic Law is a subject that contains other subjects within it. This book thus covers International Trade Law (including WTO activity, juridical and otherwise); International Financial Law (with special emphasis, fully updated, on the IMF); International Fiscal Law; International Investment Law; and International Development Law. What is occurring within these fields and, importantly, the relationships among them, is well presented and very informative. It hardly needs saying that in these stressful times developments within several of these topics are of the keenest interest.

Teachers will understand that International Economic Law comprises the entirety of the elements within this book. Others may turn to it for contemporary analysis of particular issues engaging their attention. The following aspects have particularly attracted my own attention.

The chapter on International Development Law—significantly updated and expanded since the last edition—has had to reflect the changes of the last few years in this area. The focus on developing countries' preoccupations with trade preferences and natonalisation has incrementally shifted to a more global interest in stability in commodity prices (with models for achieving this having had mixed success) and insistence on good governance. And in recent years, we have seen that human rights can no longer be perceived as a freestanding subject. It now finds its place—and is acknowledged by all concerned to need to find its place—within IMF investment assessments, where impressive structures to this end have in recent years been put in place; and within trade and development law more generally. That development should not take place save in a holistic context (human rights, respect for local culture) is now accepted; though the means to achieve those ends are to an extent still the subject of debate. In particular, the place of human rights within the vastly expanding area of International Trade Law (rather than as inimical to it) is especially marked. The literature has not failed to reflect this.

Recent writing, including by Professor Qureshi, has not failed to address the issue of whether one institutional vehicle can serve other purposes—for example, whether WTO practices suggest that it is a development, as well as a trade, institution.

One of the most burgeoning areas of practice and study in recent years has been that of International Investment Law. Throughout the book the authors keep up to date by noting how the social and political contexts have developed through time (and since the first edition). International Investment Law was especially related to capital flows from developed to developing states, with all the tensions that that reality entailed. Today "all states try to attract important foreign investment flows" (p.490). The legal framework covering this is diffuse, but the number of bilateral investment treaties—and the ICSID and other possibilities for arbitrating them—has grown exponentially. The reader will find much on the emergence of norms across institutions—BITs, EPAs, GATS, TRIPS and TRIMS, and many others.

Just as no domestic lawyer can today ignore the basics of International Law (impacting as it does on so much of national law), so all international lawyers today require some understanding of the world of international economic law. This book (which, incidentally, is very attractively presented) will provide that bridge. It will also be invaluable to the specialist.

Rosalyn Higgins
President of the International Court of Justice (2006–2009)

# PREFACE

This book focuses on that branch of Public International Law which is concerned with international economic relations between States. However, International Economic Law is also increasingly directly concerned with the individual, the trader, the investor, and the international financier. International commercial lawyers can no longer operate within the parameters of national legislation. They need to have a sense of that legislation in the context of International Economic Law.

Part One is concerned with some of the fundamental and introductory aspects of International Economic Law. Parts Two, Three, Four and Five comprise of an examination of the core spheres of the international economic order—namely International Monetary Law, International Trade Law, the International Law Relating to Factor Movement, International Taxation and International Development Law. This view of International Economic Law is taken here with the conviction that the disparate international economic phenomena need to be understood in the context of the totality of International Economic Law. The necessity to engage in legal analysis of the international economic order from a wider perspective is dictated not merely from the consequences of globalization, but also from the need to bring to bear the influences of the respective fields to each other, as well as to ensure balance and moderation to the liberal and welfare poles of the international economy.

However, such an approach is becoming increasingly difficult to formulate, given that the different branches of International Economic Law are expanding to such an extent as to require treatment in their own right. Consequently, the short-comings of this work are as much the authors' weaknesses, as those borne out of an attempt to host the different spheres in a single time/space dimension. Any strength however is entirely attributable to the various International Economic Law scholars in the different specialisms of the subject, on whom the authors here have had to rely as a result of having to take this particular approach.

We have not set out to de-construct International Economic Law; nor indeed have we tried to craft our own distinct perspective of it. With respect to the former, we should have—all disciplines need to. In relation to the latter, certainly a peg for academic credibility—our concern however has been that perspectives can be not so much illuminators as blinkers—and often driven by dogma. We have tried here to give the reader some sense of the various debates and trends in International Economic Law from a Public International Law stand-point—and hope dearly that the reader will unfold many of our own blinkers.

The second edition of this book was published eight years after the first edition, with Asif H Qureshi as the sole author. During this period the first edition established itself as one of the leading texts in International Economic Law. The second edition brought on board Professor Andreas Ziegler as a co-author, thus making the publication truly international. The second edition updated the treatment of the subject in the first edition, and added new chapters viz., International Labour Law and International Double Taxation Relief. Moreover, the text of the second edition was accompanied by materials. This innovation is continued in the third edition. The third edition comes just after four years of the publication of the second edition. However, the four years seem a decade—having witnessed many changes—in particular precipitated by the financial crisis and under the shadows of the Doha multilateral trade negotiations. Moreover, there has been considerable jurisprudence both in investment law and WTO law, as well as an increase in focus in investment law. Thus, the updating has been substantial and many parts of several chapters have been revised.

The authors reiterate their gratitude to all those whose assistance facilitated the first and second editions. The authors are grateful to successive genera-tions of readers, in particular postgraduate students, for their contribution to the value of this book. Individual and specific thanks are extended to Mianghi for her assistance and constant support in bringing the various editions to fru-ition; and to the editors of Sweet and Maxwell, in particular Nicola Thurlow, for their contribution and timely reminders about deadlines.

Asif H. Qureshi, Professor of International Economic Law
School of Law
University of Manchester, Manchester, UK
Barrister
Quadrant Chambers, Fleet Street, London, UK
Editor-in-Chief, *Manchester Journal of International Economic Law*

Andreas R. Ziegler
Professor, Faculty of Law and Criminal Justice, University of Lausanne,
Switzerland

Conjoint Professor, Faculty of Law
University of New South Wales, Sydney
Of Counsel, Blum & Grob Attorneys-at-law, Zurich

# ACKNOWLEDGEMENTS

Grateful acknowledgment is made to the following authors and publishers for permission to quote from their works:

The Canadian and American Secretariat for NAFTA, *http://www.nafta-sec-alena.org/*

European Union, *http://eur-lex.europa.eu*

International Labour Organization, *http://www.ilo.org*

International Monetary Fund, *http://www.imf.org/external/index.htm*

The New Press, *http://thenewpress.com/*

OECD, *http://www.oecd.org*

OECD (1998), *Tax Sparing; A Reconsideration*, OECD Publishing, *http://dx.doi.org/10.1787/9789264162433-en*

Publications Office of the European Union, *http://publications.europa.eu/index_en.htm*

United Nations, *http://www.un.org*

World Bank, *www.worldbank.org/publications*

World Trade Organization, *http://www.wto.org/*

While every care has been taken to establish and acknowledge copyright, and contact the copyright owners, the publishers tender their apologies for any accidental infringement. They would be pleased to come to a suitable arrangement with the rightful owners in each case.

# CONTENTS

# PART TWO: INTERNATIONAL MONETARY & FINANCIAL LAW AND THE IMF

# TABLE OF CASES

**Executive Board Decisions**

# TABLE OF TREATIES

# TABLE OF ABBREVIATIONS

| | |
|---|---|
| AB | Appellate Body |
| AD | Antidumping |
| ASEAN | Association of South East Asian Nations |
| BITS | Bilateral Investment Treaties |
| CERDS | Charter of Economic Rights and Duties of States |
| DSB | Dispute Settlement Body |
| DSU | Dispute Settlement Understanding |
| DTAs | Double Taxation Agreements |
| EC | European Community |
| ECOSOC | United Nations Economic and Social Council |
| EU | European Union |
| FAO | Food and Agriculture Organisation |
| FCNs | Friendship-Commerce-Navigation treaties |
| GA Res. | General Assembly Resolution |
| GATS | General Agreement on Trade in Services |
| GATT | General Agreement on Tariffs and Trade |
| IBRD | International Bank for Reconstruction and Development |
| ICAO | International Civil Aviation Organisation |
| ICC | International Chambers of Commerce |
| ICJ | International Court of Justice |
| ICSID | International Centre for Settlement of Investment Disputes |
| IDA | International Development Association |
| IDL | International Development Law |
| IEL | International Economic Law |
| IFAD | International Fund for Agriculture Development |
| IFA | International Fiscal Association |
| ILO | International Labour Organisation |
| IMCO | Intergovernmental Maritime Consultative Organisation, now known as the International Maritime Organisation (IMO) |
| IMF | International Monetary Fund |
| LCDs | Less Developed Countries |
| MAI | Multilateral Agreement on Investment |
| MFN | Most Favoured Nation (or m-f-n) |
| MDGs | Millennium Development Goals |
| MIGA | Multilateral Investment Guarantee Agency |
| NAFTA | North American Free Trade Agreement |
| NGOs | Non-Governmental Organisations |

| | |
|---|---|
| NIEO | New International Economic Order |
| OECD | Organisation for Economic Co-operation and Development |
| OIC | Organisation of Islamic Conference |
| SALs | Structural Adjustment Loans |
| SDR | Special Drawing Rights |
| SECALs | Sectoral Adjustment Loans |
| TRIPS | Trade-Related Intellectual Property Rights |
| TRIMS | Trade-Related Investment Measures |
| UN | United Nations |
| UNCLOS | United Nations Conference on Law of the Sea |
| UNCTAD | United Nations Conference on Trade and Development |
| UNDP | United Nations Development Programme |
| UNESCO | United Nations Educational Scientific and Cultural Organisation |
| UNIDO | United Nations Industrial Development Organisation |
| WIPO | World Intellectual Property Organisation |
| WTO | World Trade Organization |

# PART 1

# FOUNDATIONS OF INTERNATIONAL ECONOMIC LAW

CHAPTER 1

# NATURE AND SOURCES OF INTERNATIONAL ECONOMIC LAW

## INTRODUCTION[1]

The enquiry into the nature and sources of International Economic Law    **1–001**
(IEL) is a preliminary and fundamental one, yet its exposition is not straightforward. This is because the landscape of "International Economic Law" is
a broad one, involving a series of descriptions. These are neither self-evident
nor uncontroversial, and can be shaped and clarified according to the perspective from which they are viewed. Thus, immediately one is confronted
with the question, what comprises "international", "economic" and "law"?
As well as the underlying question, viz. which international economic order?
There is an undeniable relationship between understanding the nature and
sources of IEL and developing that understanding with a perspective of the
International Economic Order. IEL is a branch of law. Insight into both the
tree of which it is a branch, as much as the forest in which the tree is located,
is called for.

Insights into the international economic order may be developed from a
variety of standpoints,[2] viz. legal; economic[3]; political[4]; philosophical (e.g.

---

[1] For alternative general works on International Economic Law see, for example, J. Jackson
and W. Davey et al., *International Economic Relations*, 5th edn (West Publishing Company,
2008); A. Lowenfeld, *International Economic Law,* 2nd edn (OUP, 2008); D. Carreau and P.
Juillard., *Droit international économique* 4th edn (Dalloz, 2010).

[2] Asif H. Qureshi (ed.), *Perspectives in International Economic Law* (Kluwer Law International,
2002).

[3] See, for example, Bhandari and Sykes, *Economic Dimensions in International Economic Law*
(1997); R.A. Cass, *Economic Perspectives in International Economic Law*, Ch.15 in Qureshi
(2002).

[4] See, for example, P. Hirst and G. Thomson, *Globalization in Question* (Polity Press, 1996);J.E.
Spero et al., *The Politics of International Economic Relations* (1997); J.A. Frieden and Lake,
*International Political Economy* (Routledge, 2000); R. Wilkinson, *The Political Economy of
International Economic Law: A Neo-Gramscian Perspective* in Qureshi; J. Rehman, *"Islamic
Perspectives on International Economic Law"* in Qureshi (2002); and R.B. Shapiee, "A
Framework of Economic Siyar or Islamic International Economic Law: An Introduction"
(M.J.I.E.L. Vol.3 Issue 3, 2006), pp. 45–91.

distributive justice)[5]; goal orientated (e.g. the comparative advantage model; the New International Economic Order (NIEO))[6]; State centric; individual (human rights)[7]; institutional[8]; North/South; sustainable development[9]; feminist[10]; cultural[11]; historical[12]; contextual; conceptual.[13] One point is clear, whereas the international economic order cannot be understood merely from one standpoint alone, it is equally clear that it needs to be well understood from every single standpoint.

### The perspective of justice in IEL[14]

1–002    For a proper comprehension of IEL and its operations—especially from the view point of its development, the skeleton of IEL needs to be infused with the very essence of its being. It is not sufficient merely to understand the legal framework of IEL along with its rules. Its framework and its rules are driven by its purposes and objectives, and are operated, within the constitutional limits of IEL, by a sense of what IEL ought to be. Traditionally, one such facilitator of such a discourse, particularly close to IEL, is the notion of fairness or justice. This justice concern has been coupled in IEL with its economic underpinnings—viz., efficiency. The latter having less of a legal affinity as such, although enshrined in IEL. Thus, participants in IEL seek to evaluate and engage in the operation of IEL in terms of justice. IEL, as indeed any other legal order, calls for a methodology in its analysis, functioning and development. The lenses through which it is assessed need to be clarified, as much as the pre-conceptions contained therein.

    The fairness focus in IEL is particularly relevant, as the discipline is apparently and quintessentially concerned with allocative decisions, and as such

---

[5] See, for example, T.M. Franck, *Fairness in International Law and Institutions* (Oxford, Oxford University Press, 1995); Frank J. Garcia, "Global Justice and the Bretton Woods Institutions", *Journal of International Economic Law,* 10, 3, 2007, pp. 461–481.

[6] See, for example, Charter of Economic Rights and Duties of States General Assembly Resolution adopted on December 12, 1974; and K. Hossain (ed.), *Legal Aspects of the New International Economic Order* (London, Francis Pinter, 1980).

[7] M. Addo, *Human Rights Perspectives of International Economic Law* in Qureshi; A. Clapham, *Human Rights Obligations of Non-State Actors* (Oxford, Oxford University Press, 2006).

[8] See, for example, G.F. Thompson *"Perspectives on Governing Globalization"* in Qureshi (2002); and E. Kwakwa, *"Institutional Perspectives of International Economic Law"* in Qureshi (2002).

[9] See, for example, F. Weiss et al., *International Economic Law With a Human Face* (1998); Surya P. Subedi, *Sustainable Development Perspectives of International Economic Law* in Qureshi (2002).

[10] See, for example, M. Childs *"Feminist Perspectives on International Economic law"* in Qureshi (2002).

[11] See, for example, M. Hahn, "A Clash of cultures? The UNESCO Diversity Convention and International Trade Law", J.I.E.L. 2006 9:515–552; C. Beat Graber, "The New UNESCO Convention on Cultural Diversity: A Counterbalance to the WTO?" J.I.E.L. (2006) 9:553–574.

[12] F.N.N. Botchway, *Historical Perspectives on International Economic Law* in Qureshi (2002).

[13] See Asif H. Qureshi & Xuan Gao, *Critical Concepts in Law: International Economic Law* 6 Volumes (Routledge, 2010).

[14] Extract from Qureshi, "Perspectives in International Economic Law—An Eclectic Approach to International Economic Engagement", Ch.1, Section 4.6 in Qureshi (2002). See also T.M. Franck, *Fairness in International Institutional Law and Institutions* (Oxford, Oxford University Press, 1995); and Frank J. Garcia, "Global Justice and the Bretton Woods Institutions", *Journal of International Economic Law,* 10, 3, 2007, pp. 461–481.

has indeed been the facilitator for its review in its disparate fields. At the general level of Public International Law, the fairness methodology has been comprehensively mapped by Thomas Franck.[15] Indeed, Franck also offers a fairness discourse in IEL specifically in the fields of environment, development, trade, investment, and the law of the sea. More particularly he focuses on commodity agreements, expropriation and damages,[16] access to waters, and with respect to the disparities between developed and developing States.[17] In this endeavour Franck demonstrates the relevance of fairness through, for example, highlighting the functions of IEL as an allocator of resources, as a compensator, and indeed even the clarifier of the very resource being allocated.[18]

In the field of IEL fairness discourse is also to be found elsewhere, in the sphere of international taxation,[19] and in international trade,[20] both in terms of States as well as individuals. This fairness discourse, in the disparate fields of IEL, has an undeniable relevance, but it has not necessarily been rigorously and systematically pursued in all of IEL. One particular field where the justice analysis has not been as prominent as it might be is in the field of international monetary law viz., exchange control, exchange and interest rates, although the weighted voting system of the IMF and its stabilisation programmes have so been analysed.[21]

Fairness as expounded by Franck, from J. Rawls's theory of justice,[22] has two aspects—the substantive (distributive justice) and the procedural (right process).[23] The former concerning itself with the allocative criteria for the distribution of costs and benefits and its impact, and the latter with the formal processes involved in the enactment and enforcement of the allocative criteria. Fairness discourse is considered most pertinent to circumstances of "moderate scarcity",[24] and a fortiori IEL, given its function as an arbitrator/allocator between different claimants of scarce economic resources viz., opportunities for market access, and access to monetary, capital and natural resources. Fairness discourse also calls for a sense of community.[25] In IEL States, international and regional economic organisations, individuals and NGOs are

---

[15] See T.M. Franck, *Fairness in International Institutional Law and Institutions* (Oxford, Oxford University Press, 1995).

[16] Franck, *Fairness in International Institutional Law and Institutions* (1995), p.50.

[17] Franck (1995), p.415.

[18] Franck (1995), p.434.

[19] See, for example, K. Vogel, "Worldwide vs. source taxation of income—a review and re-evaluation of arguments", *INTERTAX* (1988).

[20] See, for example, J. Bhagwati and R. Hudec (eds), *Fair Trade and Harmonization* (Cambridge, MA, MIT Press, 1996); and A.H. Qureshi et al., *The Legal and Moral Aspects of International Trade* (London/New York, Routledge, 1998).

[21] See, for example, A.H. Qureshi, "Value aspects of IMF Conditionality" (1988) 28 *Indian Journal of International Law*.

[22] See J. Rawls, *Theory of Justice* (1972); J. Rawls, *The Law of Peoples* (1999). See also Philippe van Parijs, "International Distributive Justice" in Asif H. Qureshi & Xuan Gao, *Critical Concepts in Law: International Economic Law* Volume One (Routledge, 2010). Briefly, Rawls's theory of justice is constructed in an original position behind a 'veil of ignorance', wherein all concerned agree to equal rights to equal liberties (First principle of justice); and under the Second principle of justice as follows: (i) fair equality of opportunity; (ii) inequalities can be justified wherein there is a proportionate or more than proportionate advantage to the least advantaged (the Difference principle (also equated with the maximin rule)).

[23] Franck, *Fairness in International Institutional Law and Institutions* (1995), p.7.

[24] Franck (1995), p.9.

[25] Franck (1995), p.11.

participants in this community, pursuing shared goals of economic development, whilst recognising inter-dependence and inter-relationships. This is borne out by the widespread membership of the Bretton Woods institutions and their objectives as set out in their respective charters. Fairness discourse is concerned, both as between State entities (aggregated fairness), and as between individuals within the State as well as between generations (disaggregated fairness).[26] At the core of the fairness discourse in the context of IEL is set one particular principle that is of special note, i.e., Rawls' "maximin" principle.[27] According to this, for instance, inequality between States can be justified if there is a proportionate or more than proportionate advantage for every other State at the bottom of the distribution scale.[28] This is the non-egalitarian "equality" principle of fairness, which can rebut the presumption of equality.[29] This maximin principle somewhat mirrors the theory of comparative advantage in international economics.

Whatever one might comprehend of Franck's sense of fairness implicit in his thesis or indeed his assessment of international economic issues—there are mainly three points to note here with respect to his fairness discourse. First, for an effective IEL the substantive aspect of fairness (distributive justice) must be perceived to be fair.[30] Similarly, the relevant allocative criteria must command legitimacy through the rights process.[31] Secondly, that the theory of justice, at a minimum, provides a relevant analytical approach to IEL. Thirdly, the fairness discourse opens up the range of considerations with which to engage in IEL. However, by the same token it needs to be stressed here that fairness is a relative and subjective concept.

Finally, at the level of international negotiations and discourse fairness is an obvious tool in the apparatus of international persuasion. An understanding of the sense of justice of others is equally an aspect of negotiations. However, given that most discourse of fairness draws from theory, and is not in the real world popularly understood, it poses interesting challenges for its understanding and use.

**1-003**     From the legal standpoint, understanding IEL is complex, involving not merely expertise in Public International Law, but also simultaneously some awareness of the rudiments of international economics and politics. But importantly—particularly given globalisation, the international welfare enhancing focus, and the increasing web of international economic norms covering the disparate tentacles of international economic relations—the legal standpoint must be detached, international and holistic in character. It is no longer possible to analyse the international economic order through the channelled tunnels of the Bretton Woods institution, viz. the international trade, monetary and development lenses respectively. In the same manner as is evident in international economics that differing economic policy instruments are interlinked, so in IEL differing normative frameworks can be, and often are, linked. From the legal standpoint it is necessary to

---

[26] Franck (1995), p.12.
[27] The other principle of note being the principle of "no trumping".
[28] Franck (1995), p.18.
[29] Franck (1995), p.18.
[30] Franck (1995), p.13.
[31] Franck (1995), p.26.

cultivate a method of participating in the international economic order in a manner which partakes of *all* the international economic legal frameworks, including the international trade, monetary and development perspectives. Many of the nuts and bolts of the international economic order, such as the most-favoured-nation (MFN) principle;[32] non-violation complaints;[33] the network of bilateral, regional and multilateral treaties sometimes in the same economic field; coupled with concepts such as "sustainable development", increasingly call for an approach that is holistic in character in relation to the legal problems of international economic relations. Thus, the trend in IEL of orienting discourse in IEL from the bias of international trade is noticeable, and in danger of inhibiting such a holistic perspective.[34]

With such a holistic approach it is possible to better understand the international economic phenomenon; to contribute more effectively to the constituent parts of the international economic order; to avert the legal clashes; to avoid duplication and to cement the various parts of the international economic mosaic in a complementary and mutually more effective manner. In short, the legal standpoint must mirror the globalised economy and the substantive inter-linkages between monetary, trade and development policies.

## DEFINING INTERNATIONAL ECONOMIC LAW

The process of defining IEL is closely connected with the formulation and **1-004** maintenance of perspectives on IEL. As such, it can be fraught with the danger of conflating definitions with perspectives. There is therefore always the need to endeavour at revelation from a neutral standpoint. At a preliminary level the process of defining IEL mainly involves the following two questions, viz. what system of law or systems of law are involved? And what is the content of IEL?

### The system or systems of law?

From a formal legal perspective this is an important query. It sheds light **1-005** on the system of law that IEL belongs to. It is concerned with the question whether IEL partakes of the domestic legal system or the Public International Law system. In this context there has been a lively debate amongst international economic lawyers[35] which appears to continue.[36] At

---

[32] See, for example, Art.I of GATT 1994.
[33] See, for example, Art.XXIII of GATT 1994.
[34] See, for example, the first issue of the *Journal of International Economic Law* (1998) wherein all four main contributions relate to international trade in the context of the WTO.
[35] See, for example, *University of Pennsylvania Journal of International Economic Law* (1996).
[36] See E.-U. Petersmann, "The Future of International Economic Law: A Research Agenda" European University Institute, Florence, Department of Law Working Paper LAW 2010/06 and S. Charnovitz, "What is International Economic Law?" J.I.E.L.

first sight there appear to be two conceptions of IEL.[37] First, it is understood as a branch of Public International Law[38] (the narrow definition). Secondly, it is conceived of, particularly of late, as including all branches of law concerned with economic phenomena of international concern[39] (the broader definition). As between these two standpoints, there is in fact no fundamental difference to the extent that they converge. The broader definition does not deny Public International Law as being a source, it merely is not confined to it. It includes domestic law, including Private International Law and Transnational Business Law.[40] To the extent that Public International Law is accepted as a source, it is acknowledged that it has a domain that is concerned with economics. It is also accepted that the Public International Law of International Economic Relations is a different system of law from domestic law.

[37] But see H. Fox, "The definition and sources of International Economic Law" in (ed.), *International Economic Law and Developing States* (2002) BIICL at p.12, wherein the author contends that there are three groups of definitions. Hazel Fox's three-tiered categorisation of the definitional approaches to International Economic Law as focusing on the origins of the law, the content of the subject, and the objective to be achieved, respectively, is not adopted here. This is inter alia because the broader definition focusing on the content of the subject has been explained also with a baggage of built-in objectives. Further, her characterisation of the New International Economic (NIEO) movement as a process of defining international economic law rather than an attempt at shaping it, is to attribute a level of preoccupation amounting to an obsession to the advocates of the New International Economic Order (NIEO). The advocates of the NIEO are credited with blurring the conceptual difference between the process of defining a subject, and promoting through law desired policy objectives. This attribution is unfortunate.

[38] See, for example, G. Schwarzenberger, "The principles and standards of International Economic Law" (1966) *Recueil des Cours*, pp.1 and 7; P. VerLoren van Themaat, *The Changing structure of International Economic Law* (Netherlands, Brill, 1981), pp.9–11 and pp.287–290; K. Mortelmans, "The Interdependence of International, European and National Economic Law: The European Community Example", in P.V. Dijk et al., *Restructuring the international economic order: the role of law and lawyers* (1986), p.14; G. White, "Principles of International Economic Law: An Attempt to Map the Territory" in H. Fox (ed.), *International Economic Law And Developing States: Some Aspects* (London, British Institute of International and Comparative Law, 1988); D. Carreau, T. Flory and P. Julliard, *Droit International Economique*, 3rd edn (1990) p.45 (see also 1998 edition); I. Seidl-Hohenveldern, *International Economic Law*, 2nd edn (1992), p.1.

[39] See, for example, E-U Petersmann, "International Economic Theory and International Economic Law" in R. St. J. Macdonald, and Douglas M. Johnstone (eds), *The Structure and Process of International Law, Essays in Legal Philosophy, Doctrine and Theory* (The Hague/Boston/Lancaster, Martinus Nijhoff Publishers, 1983), p.239; E-U Petersmann, "The Future of International Economic Law: A Research Agenda", European University Institute, Florence, Department of Law Working Paper LAW 2010/06; J.H. Jackson, *The World Trading System* (1989), pp.21–22; and J.H. Jackson et al., *Legal Problems of International Economic Relations*, 3rd edn (1995); J.P. Trachtman, "Introduction: The International Economic Revolution"; L.S. Zamora, "Introduction: International Economic Law"; J.R. Paul, "The New Movements In International Economic Law", *The American University Journal of International Law & Policy* (1995) 10, fn.2; R.A. Brand, "Introduction: semantic distinctions in an age of legal convergence", *University of Pennsylvania Journal of International Economic Law* (1996) 17, fn.1.

[40] The idea of transnational law as the set of domestic and international norms applicable to specific international business transactions is originally associated with the writing of P. Caryl Jessup, such as *Transnational Law* (New Haven, 1956).

In fact the debate as to the definition of IEL is not entirely a definitional one alone, although it is framed as such. It is partly triggered by the fact that the description "International Economic Law" lends itself to a number of explanations. The controversy is about which body of law provides a complete description of the subject, as much as which one has a better claim to the description "International Economic Law". In the latter sense, the controversy may be described as a semantic one. In the former, the underlying debate is really about how international economic phenomena should be perceived and shaped. The emphasis is on the process of comprehension and the development of the international economic order. Thus, defining IEL in terms of Public International Law *may* give the impression of endorsing a State centric "Westphalian", "top-down" conception of IEL[41]; wherein IEL is driven in international fora from a member-driven perspective.[42] On the other hand, in the broader definition market-driven solutions and individual economic rights are taken into account.[43] The broader definition is referred to by E-U Petersmann as a "multilevel economic law perspective" with an emphasis on "public-private" partnerships.[44]

More specifically, the broader definition is justified by its advocates, mainly on the following grounds. First, it is asserted that the definition of the subject should not be grounded in the origins of the law, but rather should focus on its object.[45] To comprehend the phenomena relating to international economic relations the totality of the body of law is relevant, as is an appreciation of the inter-dependence of the various sources of law.[46] Secondly, it is contended that there is in fact a convergence of Public International Law and domestic law.[47] This is because the increasing economic relations between States and private parties has meant that States have become subject to domestic law as a consequence, through, for example, the development of the restrictive doctrine of State immunity[48] and common arbitration procedures.[49] Conversely, increasingly private parties have seen the application of Public International Law to their relations. Further, private parties are now more affected by Public International Law rules intended to regulate

---

[41] See E-U Petersmann, "The Future of International Economic Law: A Research Agenda", European University Institute, Florence, Department of Law Working Paper LAW 2010/06.

[42] E-U Petersmann, "The Future of International Economic Law: A Research Agenda", op cit.

[43] E-U Petersmann, "The Future of International Economic Law: A Research Agenda", op cit.

[44] E-U Petersmann, "The Future of International Economic Law: A Research Agenda", op cit.

[45] See, for example, K. Mortelmans, "The Interdependence of International, European and National Economic Law: The European Community Example", in P.V. Dijk et al., *Restructuring the international economic order: the role of law and lawyers* (Kluwer Law and Taxation Publishers, 1987), p.14.

[46] See, for example, E-U Petersmann, "Constitutional functions of Public International Economic Law" in Dijk (1986), p.49.

[47] Brand (1996).

[48] Under the restrictive doctrine of State Immunity, a State or government does not enjoy complete or absolute immunity from proceedings in the courts of another State. See the United Nations Convention on Jurisdictional Immunities of States and Their Property 2004.

[49] i.e. where the State and a private party are the litigants involved in the arbitration.

State powers. In this context they have become involved, it has been contended, with the process of creation, interpretation and the implementation
of Public International Law,[50] for example, through litigation in domestic
courts. Thirdly, it has been asserted that Public International Law should
be re-evaluated so that it governs both States and private parties, and that a
broader definition fulfils this function.[51] Fourthly, many of the private economic structures and transactions are ultimately of public and governmental
concern. They need to be regulated nationally. Given that they are regulated
nationally, they also become of international interest.[52] Finally, generally,
domestic law affects both inward and outward relations between States and
people. The policy formation processes involved in such domestic law should
therefore be better integrated internationally.[53] This is particularly so given
that Public International Law is not a complete system. It is therefore better
served by the forces and exigencies of the domestic order.[54]

In this book, however, it is the former approach, namely the perspective
of Public International Law, that will be cultivated. This is without prejudice to the different stand-points in the definitional discourse on IEL. This
is mainly because the particular definitions are formulated in a particular
context, and in accordance with their underlying function. There can therefore be no doctrinal differences as such. However, it is nevertheless necessary
to proffer certain observations. First, it is of importance that distinctions
between systems of law are maintained in order to facilitate clarity, to maintain the integrity of the legal systems, and to further their respective development—including that of Public International Law. Secondly, and relatedly,
the conflation of domestic law with International Law can serve to buttress
unduly the significance of the role of certain national economies, particularly
those which are more "sovereign" than others, and which have pronounced
national legislation in the economic sphere or affecting the economic sphere.[55]
Such "transplantation" of certain domestic legislation in what are in the end
economic issues of international concern can be likened in its effects to a form
of "disguised or covert extraterritorial" application of national legislation. It
is also to be noted that domestic law reflects national economic objectives.
In some important respects, IEL, especially IEL at its core (i.e. at the level of
international monetary, trade and development/ investment policy) is not in
harmony with some of the driving forces underpinning national economies.
Thirdly, the narrow definition of IEL has never been exclusive to the back-

---

[50] Brand (1996).
[51] Trachtman, (1995).
[52] Trachtman, (1995).
[53] Trachtman, (1995).
[54] Trachtman, (1995).
[55] A cynic might query whether, given that a large impetus for the broad approach originates
from the US, this was not a desire to arrogate the "boiler room of international relations"? See
J. Jackson, "International Economic Law: Reflections on the 'boiler room' of International
Relations" (1995) 10, fn.2 *The American University Journal of International Law and Policy*,
p.595.

ground and the context within which it operates—including domestic law. The function of International Law in domestic law, and the importance of the relationship between national and International Law, have never been denied. Finally, of course at a practical level the narrow approach is a useful way of demarcating and managing what is already a vast subject. In sum, focussing on IEL from a Public International Law perspective is not necessarily to look at the phenomenon from a "Westphalian" stand-point.[56]

If IEL is part of the system of Public International Law then is it a branch or a specialism of Public International Law? Or is it within the broad legal system of Public International Law *sui generis*, and a principal focus of the nation State? It has been contended that the caricature of IEL as a branch or specialism of International Law is fundamentally flawed.[57] Although it does not clearly appear to be as disputed that IEL is rooted in Public International Law. What is challenged mainly is its characterisation as a "specialism". One consequence of characterising IEL as a specialism is to marginalise it, despite its obvious centrality in international relations. Thus, Jackson asserts that some 90 per cent of International Law work relates to IEL.[58] IEL, it is contended, is not a specialism inter alia for the following reasons. First, both historically and currently, economic activity is central to government affairs[59] and International Law.[60] Secondly, International Law and an important component of IEL, viz. International Trade Law (ITL), are each underpinned by inconsistent assumptions, or fundamentally opposed assumptions.[61] Whereas International Law is based on the State and the notion of sovereignty, IEL (particularly International Trade Law) is based on the dictates of comparative advantage,[62] namely on promoting individual cross-border exchanges and specialisation.[63] Thirdly, whereas International Law is traditionally oriented towards defence and peace and economic self-sufficiency or mercantilism[64] the international economic system as reflected in the Bretton Woods institutions (i.e. the IMF, the WTO and the World Bank Group), is based on the market economy[65] and the promotion of global welfare, not so much the prevention of economic warfare.[66] Whereas mercantilism is about safeguarding

**1-006**

---

[56] Contra E-U Petersmann, "The Future of International Economic Law: A Research Agenda", op cit.

[57] D.M. McRae, "The contribution of International Trade Law to the Development of International Law", *Recueil des Cours*, Vol.1 (1996), pp.99–237.

[58] See J. Jackson, "Global economics and international economic law" in (1998) 1(1) *Journal of International Economic Law* 1–28 at 8.

[59] D.M. McRae (1996), pp.114 and 122.

[60] D.M. McRae (1998), p.121.

[61] D.M. McRae (1998), p.118.

[62] See for example Alan O. Sykes "Comparative advantage and the normative economics of international trade policy" in Asif H. Qureshi & Xuan Gao, *Critical Concepts in Law: International Economic Law* Volume Three (Routledge, 2010).

[63] D.M. McRae (1998), p.117.

[64] D.M. McRae (1998), p.126.

[65] D.M. McRae (1998), pp.126 and 137.

[66] D.M. McRae (1998), p.138.

national economic power, the theory of comparative advantage is concerned with increasing global economic welfare.[67] International trade law operates not so much to regulate how the actions of one State affect the interests of another State, but rather it is concerned with those State actions because they reduce economic welfare.[68] Fourthly, key features of Public International Law are not present in the same manner in the field of IEL. Thus, because of globalisation it is not possible to talk about the national economy.[69] Capital is no longer entirely domestic nor is the manufacturing process. States are increasingly less in control of their economies. Further, key aspects of the international economic regime—for example, non-discrimination rules such as the national treatment requirement and the MFN standard—do not so much reflect the notion of sovereign equality of States, but rather serve to ensure that market mechanisms operate unhindered.[70] Free trade undermines the notion of autonomous economies operating independently of each other. Accordingly, IEL (particularly International Trade Law) is defined as being concerned with those State measures that are taken at the border, or internally that inhibit the operation of the comparative advantage (specialisation and voluntary exchange) to function effectively.[71] International economic law is concerned with eliminating cross-border impediments.[72]

However, in this scheme the role of the State in economics is not disputed. States provide both a facilitative and regulatory infrastructure in the economic field.[73] Furthermore, the international economic system (particularly the international trade regime) also reflects the nation State model of International Law and politics. Thus, for example, the international mechanism for tariff reduction is based on reciprocity[74]; and some WTO systems such as anti-dumping, safeguard measures and intellectual property measures, are not entirely consonant with comparative advantage. In addition, the theory of comparative advantage is not without its shortcomings. Thus, comparative advantage is silent as to how the benefits of economic welfare are to be shared. The proposition that liberalisation enhances global welfare belies, it is contended, the question of *whose* welfare.[75] Further, comparative advantage can be tampered with by States through, for example, the operation of a strategic trade policy.[76] Thus, although there are two models through which IEL (particularly International Trade law) can be viewed (i.e.

---

[67] D.M. McRae (1998), p.143.
[68] D.M. McRae (1998), p.144.
[69] D.M. McRae (1998), p.128.
[70] D.M. McRae (1998), p.145.
[71] D.M. McRae (1998), at p.144.
[72] D.M. McRae (1998), at p.123.
[73] D.M. McRae (1998), at p.133.
[74] D.M. McRae (1998), at p.169.
[75] D.M. McRae (1998), at p.227.
[76] D.M. McRae (1998), p.155. In basic terms a strategic trade policy involves the nurturing of certain economically strategic industries.

the comparative advantage model and the State model) it has been contended that the comparative advantage model is gaining ground.[77]

There are a number of problems with the comparative advantage model **1–007** normally relied upon in IEL, although the central role of IEL cannot be denied. First, IEL is defined from the international trade paradigm. Thus, other aspects of international economic law are ignored and marginalised; for example, development. Further, notions of fairness/justice and culture are discounted. Secondly, the role and function of the State and the imprint of the State system on the international economic order is seriously underrated. Thirdly, in the comparative advantage model the theory of comparative advantage is considered to have been embraced by the international economic community in an absolute form and released into the system without any reigns. The international economic community, in adopting the theory of comparative advantage, is deemed to have triggered the logical inevitability of the consequences of the theory of comparative advantage. This attribution of the adoption of the theory of comparative advantage in an absolute sense is flawed. In fact, the canvas of IEL is painted by the painters from a variety of colour pots—including the comparative advantage pot. But it is the painters who determine the degree of its application to the canvas. The degree to which the international community applies the theory of comparative advantage is determined firmly by the international community. The State system and International Law are thus not opposed to comparative advantage. They at all material times control the degree to which its logic is activated into the international economic system. This is the daily discourse amongst Member States in the Bretton Woods institutions.

In conclusion, the particular approach preferred here is a global approach but within the broad spectrum of Public International Law. Essentially it comprises of the Public International Law analysis of the economic phenomena of international concern. This Public International Law perspective has a number of merits. It is detached from a national system and therefore more objective. At the same time, it can draw from national economic systems in a scientific manner. It is value-laden but in as much as it carries with it the values of the international economic community as a whole. It steers the processes involved in the development of IEL in a more transparent and democratic fashion. If necessary, national economic systems can be objects of deconstruction. They do not uncritically permeate the international scene. The role of the national systems is contained and put in perspective. This process of conflation of national and international is facilitated through the negotiation of international economic agreements. In addition, the Public International Law perspective also subjects the national economic system to international legal scrutiny. It affirms the role of law (contra power) and international economic organisations in the regulation of conflicting domestic economic policies and legislation. Finally, the analysis serves to emphasise

[77] D.M. McRae (1998), p.230.

the role of International Law and institutions in the pursuit of commonly agreed *international* goals. In short, the approach taken here is not so much "Westphalian" rather it is "internationalist".

### The content of International Economic Law?

**1-008**    The basic subject-matter (i.e. the problem requiring regulation) comprises the economic phenomena. It may be generally defined, and/or its coverage may be listed. A number of writers have engaged in the list approach. This is enlightening to the extent that it is illustrative. Thus, Jackson includes "trade, investment, services when they are involved in transactions that cross national borders, and those subjects that involve the establishment on national territory of economic activity of persons or forms originating from outside that territory".[78] However, the list approach on its own can have some shortcomings. First, where the list purports to be exhaustive it becomes problematic. Thus, Gillian White's[79] unquestioned approval of Schwarzenberger's description of IEL as illuminating is questionable. Schwarzenberger described the field as being concerned with "(1) the ownership and exploitation of natural resources; (2) the production and distribution of goods; (3) invisible international transactions of an economic or financial character; (4) currency and finance; (5) related services and (6) the status and organisation of those engaged in such activities".[80] However, he specifically excluded[81] labour, social, transport and intellectual property spheres. Such exclusion is an arbitrary legal construct which detracts from the inter-linkages between various disciplines. Indeed, for a lawyer to define the economic phenomena, particularly in the context of an exclusionary list, is to engage in insights into the dynamics of the international economic phenomena. Secondly, a list approach can be a means of articulating a value preference of the international economic system. Thus, there is a danger of implicit prioritisation of trade and investment issues as opposed to, for example, aid and technology transfer. Inevitably some of the preoccupations of the definer, the discipline from which the definition stems, and its political origins are going to colour the list and its order. It is to be noted that subsequent lists to that formulated

---

[78] J.H. Jackson et al., *International Economic Relations* (St. Paul, West Group, 2002), pp.193–194. See also J.R. Paul, *The American University Journal of International Law and Policy* (1995) 10, fn.2, p.609. He includes "subjects like international business transactions, private international law, international trade law, immigration law, European Communities law, comparative law, transnational litigation, international arbitration procedure, and aspects of banking, competition, employment, environmental, intellectual property, securities, tax, and telecommunications laws that regulate transnational transactions".

[79] White, "Principles of International Economic Law" in H. Fox (ed.), *International Economic Law And Developing States: Some Aspects* (1998).

[80] See G. Schwarzenberger, "The principles and standards of International Economic Law", (1966) 1 *Recueil Des Cours*, p.7. See also G. Schwarzenberger, *Economic World Order? A Basic Problem of International Economic Law* (Manchester, Manchester University Press, 1970), p.4.

[81] Schwarzenberger (1966), p.8.

by Schwarzenberger's are broader and non-exclusive. This expansive view of IEL has been fuelled both from academic[82] and political movements. There is now a general recognition that the globalisation of the world economy involves, inter alia, increasing interactions between various economic policies (especially structural, macroeconomic, trade, financial, investment and development).[83] Thus, the notion of "trade related" in international trade.[84] Moreover, economic development is no longer conceived purely in terms of economic development. Development now is a more integrated and holistic concept, involving the realisation of individual freedoms,[85] as well as the notion of sustainable development.[86]

General definitions[87] of the economic phenomena as comprising all aspects of Public International Law that relate to economics have been criticised as being too broad.[88] Indeed, they have been characterised as being so broad as to encompass all of International Law, given that most spheres of international relations have an economic dimension.[89] This assessment of the definition as being vacuous is however somewhat extreme. Certainly it identifies a relevant point of focus. It is not value-laden. It does not emphasise, for example, trade as opposed to development. It is dynamic in that the economic terrain has a relationship with the development of Public International Law. It is defining in that it identifies only that facet of economics that is of international concern. It is such that it does not preclude cognisance of the inter-linkages of the various national economic policy instruments, the relationship of the economic phenomena with external factors, and the advent of the globalised international economy. To deprecate the definition by contending that most aspects of international relations have an economic consequence is to deny that which is accepted, namely that various economic phenomena and various disciplines are interconnected; or at any rate to acknowledge such linkages only up to a limit.

There are few logical reasons why the breadth of international relations

---

[82] See J.R. Paul, "The new movements in international economic law", *The American University Journal of International Law and Policy* (1995) 10, fn.2 at pp.609 and 613, wherein the author mentions both value-neutral movements such as theorists in public choice theory, game or regime theory, and law and economics; and others, such as critical legal studies, feminism and law and society.

[83] See Uruguay Round Ministerial Declaration on the Contribution of the World Trade Organization to Achieving Greater Coherence in Global Economic Policy Making in WTO *The Results of the Uruguay Round of Multilateral Trade Negotiations, Legal Texts* (1995).

[84] Uruguay Round Ministerial Declaration.

[85] See Amartya Sen: *Development as Freedom* (OUP, 1999).

[86] See, for example, P. Sands, "International Law in the field of Sustainable Development", (1994) B.Y.I.L., p.303.

[87] See, for example, Van Themaat, *The Changing Structure of International Economic Law* (Netherlands, Brill, 1981), p.9. He states: ". . . international economic law can be described in overall terms as the total range of norms (directly or indirectly based on treaties) of public international law with regard to transnational economic relations".

[88] See J.H. Jackson et al., *International Economic Relations* (St. Paul, West Group, 2002), pp.193–194 and I. Seidl-Hohenveldern (1992), p.1.

[89] Jackson et al. (1998), pp.193–194.

cannot be analysed from an economic perspective, at any rate initially. From this starting-point it is possible to demarcate the core and the penumbra that informs it. Thus, to borrow a criterion,[90] the core of IEL comprises of that which is directly and obviously of an economic dimension; whereas the penumbra consists of those non-economic considerations (viz., social, human rights, environmental, political, cultural) which colour the development of the core. The preoccupations at the core of international economic relations are generally identified as relating to international trade in goods and services, international monetary relations, and the development and investment fields.[91] The range in the penumbra is however more extensive—indeed, potentially open-ended.

**1–009**    To epitomise, it is not for lawyers to define what is in the end not their discipline—i.e. the economic terrain. To do so is to go beyond a mere understanding of the context of the subject. It is to engage in speculation as to the actual dynamics and intricacies of the field. It is enough to define the perspective, and to have a sense of the subject. There is a general outline which has a core and a penumbra. In essence the terrain comprises of the economic phenomena which are or ought to be of international concern. The context of the economic phenomena is demarcated by the international value system.

Finally, there are two additions to the traditional discourse of the content of IEL which need to be noted here. IEL is not merely concerned with substantive IEL. IEL also has an institutional aspect, as well as a focus on the national legal system.

The national legal system as it pertains to the economic phenomena is germane not only because it is subject to IEL, but also because the exigencies of the domestic economic and legal system have a bearing on the development of IEL. Not only is the domestic system to enshrine international concerns, but the international dimension needs to take cognisance of it.

The significance of the national economic system lies in the manner in which it is created and implemented—including the manner in which IEL is incorporated in the domestic legal system. Thus, not only is transnational economic law and purely domestic economic law (including as they relate to the regulation of business, tax, intellectual property, competition, investment, environment, labour, banking, telecommunications, movement of goods and services) of concern, but so is the private International Law, national conflict resolution procedures, and the national administrative and legislative processes. Good governance at the national level is of increasing international concern, particularly to the extent that it affects the national and international economic system. Similarly, the manner of the reception of IEL in the domestic system is significant in terms of the efficient implementation of IEL.[92]

---

[90] S. Zamora, "Is there Customary International Economic Law?", *German Yearbook of International Law* (1989) 32, p.15, fn.9.

[91] Zamora (1989).

[92] See Ch.5.

**EXAMPLE: United Nations Conference on Trade and Development, SÃO PAULO CONSENSUS (June 25, 2004, Eleventh session São Paulo, June 13–18, 2004)**

. . . § 21. Good governance within each country and at the international level is essential for sustained growth and development. Sound economic policies, solid democratic institutions responsive to the needs of people and improved infrastructure are the basis for sustained economic growth, poverty eradication and employment creation. Freedom, peace and security, domestic stability, respect for human rights, including the right to development, the rule of law, gender equality, market-oriented policies, and an overall commitment to just and democratic societies are also essential and mutually reinforcing. Transparency in the financial, monetary and trading systems, and full and effective participation of developing countries in global decision-making, are essential to good governance and to development and poverty eradication. These basic factors need to be complemented by policies at all levels to promote investment, building of local capabilities, and successful integration of developing countries into the world economy. A crucial task is to enhance the efficacy, coherence and consistency of macroeconomic policies.[93]

**1-010**

The institutional aspects of IEL focus on the institutional framework involved in the creation, development, and implementation of the international economic order. Here the subject-matter is not so much economic in character but rather draws upon international institutional law as it relates to international economic relations. International economic organisations are a critical focal point in this constitutional setting. Herein such considerations as the manner of the decision-making processes involved in the organisation, the level of rule orientation in the various decision-making processes, and the capacity of the institution to facilitate the implementation of its agenda, both at the national and international level, are all critical.

## THE NATURE OF INTERNATIONAL ECONOMIC LAW

There are essentially two basic questions which shed light on the nature of IEL—namely, why do participants engaged in international economic relations obey IEL? And, what are the underlying goals of IEL?

**1-011**

### Why is IEL obeyed?

This question can have a bearing on important practical questions of law, as well as shedding light on the actual normative processes that determine international economic relations.[94] Thus, the question can have a bearing

**1-012**

---

[93] Extract from UN Conference on Trade and Development, SÃO PAULO CONSENSUS (June 25, 2004, 11th session São Paulo, June 13–18, 2004), *http://www.un.org.* (Accessed June 8, 2011).

[94] See, for instance, O. Schachter, "Towards a theory of international obligation" in M. Schewebel (ed.), *The effectiveness of International Decisions* (1971). (Extract published in J. Jackson, *International Economic Relations*, 3rd edn (1995), pp.246–251.

on both the prior question whether a particular IEL standard is binding, or the post normative query relating to compliance. Insights into the question can dictate better compliance techniques, as well as providing a criterion for distinguishing binding IEL norms.

The explanations as to why participants of Public International Law generally obey it are numerous, ranging from consent to sanctions.[95] This is the background that is also germane to IEL. However, the imprint of IEL to the debate also needs to be appreciated. Some factors have been particularly critical. First, given that the core of international economic relations is centred around "exchange" and its facilitation, and given that international economics is dominated by mercantilism and laissez-faire, the notion of reciprocity and its built-in sanction of withdrawal have been important considerations. Secondly, given that much of IEL is to be found in international agreements, the notion of consent is significant. Thirdly, the reality of the integrated character of international economic activity, and the linkages between various economic policy instruments, engender certain shared concerns and goals. The desire to achieve these is as much a reason for obedience, as self-interest. However, the impact of this factor may well be recent, although likely to develop, and sometimes muddied by the dogma of reciprocal rights and consent. This is because the international community's international economic consciousness has only of late woken, and like all states of consciousness always has room for development. Finally, there is something in the very nature of economic activity which calls for a measure of certainty and predictability. These objectives feature critically in the institution of law and cultivate an interest in obedience and an orderly framework. On the whole IEL has enjoyed a high degree of compliance.

### The goals of IEL?

1-013      The questions, what are the goals of the international economic order; and what they ought to be, are not without controversy. The international economic order does not have an overarching coherently constructed constitutional framework such that its goals can be easily read from it. In the same vein, the goals that it ought to pursue are informed by its multitude of stakeholders and independent analysts. In particular, the precise configuration of the economic and relevant non economic goals within national economic systems is a challenge. Be that as it may, the following may be observed with respect to the aims and objectives of the *international* economic order. These aims and objectives of the international economic order

---

[95] Schachter (1971), Oscar Schachter lists (I) consent; (II) customary practice; (III) juridical conscience; (IV) natural law; (V) social necessity; (VI) consensus of the international community; (VII) direct (or "stigmatic") intuition; (VIII) common purposes of the participants; (IX) effectiveness; (X) sanctions; (XI) systemic goals; (XII) shared expectations as to authority; (XIII) rules of recognition.

are not to be confused with those of the domestic order although they may coalesce and have a symbiotic relationship. Thus, the general goals of IEL are concerned with facilitating the development of individual economies and relevant units within those economies, whilst ensuring the overall economic development of the international economy (viz., the raising of standards of living, ensuring full employment, and the facilitation of growth in real income).[96] Herein are set the mechanisms of co-operation, co-ordination, conflict avoidance and resolution and liberalisation of economic borders. Additionally, specific international community goals have been adopted from time to time in response to certain long term problems requiring an international response, as for instance a development agenda.[97] These focus from the development of developing countries, in particular poverty reduction, to the taking into account of development levels in the implementation of international economic norms. Finally, in some measure and somewhat inevitably, the domestic ideals of national economic development inform and shape the international goals that drive or ought to drive the international economic order. Herein and of more recent origin has been the advent of the integration of certain value considerations in the pursuit of economic goals. Thus, the world's resources are to be optimally utilised, in line with the objectives of sustainable development and the preservation of the environment. Similarly, the notion of transnational economic rights as human rights is advanced, as indeed the realisation of human freedoms and human rights generally.

As increasingly international economic affairs become crystallised in multilateral accords, the goals of IEL become clearer and better articulated. Such goals so articulated have a bearing in the process of interpreting the text of multilateral economic instruments, as well as driving the international economic order.

## Sources of International Economic Law

There are essentially two dimensions to a consideration of the sources of IEL. **1-014** The actual formal sources of Public International Law; and the complexion of these sources in the context of IEL.

International Law, considered merely as a body of rules, comprises of those sources of law as enumerated in Art.38 (1) of the Statute of the International Court of Justice.

---

[96] See, for example, the preamble to the Marrakesh Agreement Establishing the World Trade Organization; Art.1 of the IMF Articles of Agreement; Art.55 of the Charter of the UN 1945.
[97] See, for example, the UN Millennium Development Goals. Resolution adopted by the UN GA September 2000 (A/55/L.2); and the Monterrey Consensus (UN International Conference on Financing for Development March 22, 2002).

**Article 38 of the Statute of the International Court of Justice:**

**1-015**

1. The Court, whose function is to decide in accordance with international law such disputes as are submitted to it, shall apply:

   (a) international conventions, whether general or particular, establishing rules recognized by the contesting states;

   (b) international custom as evidence of a general practice accepted as law;

   (c) the general principles of law recognized by civilized nations;

   (d) subject to the provisions of Article 59, judicial decisions and the teachings of the most highly qualified publicists of the various nations, as subsidiary means for the determination of rules of law.

2. This provision shall not prejudice the power of the Court to decide a case *ex aequo et bono* if the parties agree thereto.[98]

However, "International Law" is not defined universally merely as a body of rules alone. A broader conception of International Law is entertained by some. Whilst it includes the sources mentioned in Art.38, this broader perspective of law comprehends it as a process of decision making[99]; or to put it another way, as a process of communication.[100] Thus, according to Reisman, law involves a prescription, the authority to prescribe, and the power, the capacity and the willingness to render effective the prescription.[101] The emphasis here is on how decisions are formulated by relevant decision-makers, and arguably also on power. In IEL too the relevance of this theory of law in predicting decision-making needs to be explored. However, whatever one's standpoint as to the nature of International Law, the sources of law mentioned in Art.38 of the Statute of the International Court of Justice cannot be avoided.

**Conceptions of law and IEL as a process of decision-making[102]:**

**1-016**

Somewhat in the same vein conceptions of 'law' also have a role in determining IEL perspectives. Here too the undercurrents of positivism and natural law cannot be ignored—although their significance is by no means uniform through out IEL. Similarly, the view of law as a process rather than a set of rules, has equal relevance in IEL. Although no systematic analysis of it in such terms as such is evident, WTO panel decisions are one obvious source for such focus.

---

[98] Source: *http://www.icj-cij.org*. (Accessed June 8, 2011).

[99] See, for example, R. Higgins in *Problems and Process: International Law and How We Use It* (Oxford, Clarendon Press, 1994), p.15 wherein she states, "It is decision-making by authorised decision-makers, when authority and power coincide."

[100] W.M. Reisman, "International Law Making: A Process of Communication", Memorial Lecture of the World Academy of Art and Science, delivered at the Annual Meeting of the American Society of International Law, April 24, 1981, Washington, DC. Therein he states "prescriptive or law making communications. . .carry simultaneously three coordinate communication flows. . .The three flows may be briefly referred to as the policy content; the authority signal and the control intention."

[101] Reisman, "International Law Making" (1981).

[102] Extract from Qureshi (2002), Ch.1, Section 4.4.

The recent WTO Panel Report[103] on Sections 301–310 of the US Trade Act 1974 provides an interesting parallel with the deliberations of the International Court of Justice (hereinafter referred to as ICJ) in the Nuclear Test cases,[104] which have been the subject of some analysis from the view point of law as a process.[105] Briefly, in this case the EC alleged that Sections 301–310 of the US Trade Act were not in conformity with US obligations under the WTO—in particular, the obligation not to take action against Members of the WTO outside the WTO dispute settlement process, with respect to matters arising within the WTO framework. Faced with this allegation the Panel had a two-pronged function viz., to determine what the US law actually was; and the scope of the relevant WTO provision against which US legislative conformity was to be assessed. How did the Panel determine the US 'law' and the scope of the relevant WTO provision?

First and foremost the Panel recognised that it was confronted with a politically sensitive case[106] involving two major trading nations. Against this background the Panel took a restricted view of its mandate in the dispute.[107] Second, the Panel approached the task of determining the US law in the following manner. First, recognising that the enquiry relating to the US law was a question of fact as a matter of WTO jurisprudence, deference needed to be given to the US view as to the meaning of its own legislation.[108] Second, that in evaluating this 'fact' the Panel needed to take into account the wide-ranging diversity in the legal systems of the WTO members.[109] Finally, the Panel evaluated US law in terms of its end result. Indeed the Panel expressly stated that "it is the end result that counts not the manner in which it is achieved".[110] Thus, the Panel took into account not merely the statutory language, but also other institutional and administrative elements.[111] Employing this strategy, the Panel concluded that the statutory language of the US legislation, namely s.304, was such that it constituted prima-facie a violation of an Article of the WTO code. However, given that the statutory language needed to be considered in the light of other US institutional and administrative elements, the Panel took into account an administrative measure[112] which lawfully ensured that the deficiency (in terms of non-conformity with the WTO code) in the statutory language was removed.[113] Thirdly, the Panel in interpreting the WTO code expressly acknowledged that they were taking the teleological approach.[114] In particular, the Panel noted that the WTO provision in question was concerned with the mere existence of statutory power which might be used in a WTO inconsistent manner, (as was the case with the US statutory language), because such a power had a "chilling effect" on economic activities of individual

---

[103] WTO Panel Report on United States—ss.301–310 of the Trade Act of 1974 (WT/DS152/R) (December 1999).
[104] I.C.J. Reports, 1974.
[105] See, for example, Reisman, "International Lawmaking" (1981).
[106] WTO Panel Report (1997), p.11.
[107] WTO Panel Report (1999), p.12.
[108] WTO Panel Report (1999), p.13.
[109] WTO Panel Report (1999), p.15.
[110] WTO Panel Report (1999), p.15.
[111] WTO Panel Report (1999), p.15.
[112] WTO Panel Report (1999). Statement of Administrative Action submitted by the President and approved by the Congress. The Statement accompanied the US legislation implementing the results of the Uruguay Round.
[113] WTO Panel Report (1999), p.37.
[114] WTO Panel Report (1999), p.34.

operators,[115] and exerted an undue leverage on other members of the WTO.[116] Such an impact created for uncertainty—"certainty and predictability" being objectives of the WTO.[117] Finally, the Panel took account of US statements made during the Panel proceedings that determinations under the US legislation would be made consistently with the WTO code.[118] The Panel concluded that the US statements brought into an international setting statements of US trade policy made in a domestic context.[119] The statements were made solemnly, for the record, and with the intention that the Panel and the WTO membership would rely on it.[120] The effect of the statements inter alia was to provide a remedy for the breach in the statutory language.[121]

On an analysis of the Panel approach from the viewpoint of the New Haven School's perspective of law as a process using a communication model[122] the Panel could be found to have availed itself of this approach. Briefly, according to the New Haven communication model, law needs to satisfy three requirements viz., policy content; authority signal; and control intention.[123] With respect to the US law first, there is a policy content in the form of the administrative measure, although not contained in the relevant US Statute. According to the communication model, 'the policy content may not be directly expressed, but be embedded in the situation'.[124] Second, the policy content was accompanied by the authority signal. The administrative measure was made with authority. It was lawfully submitted by the US President to the US Congress and approved by it. Finally, the control intention was found by the Panel to exist. The Panel noted that the administrative measure originated from the administration—the very administration responsible for the implementation of the policy. Thus, the Panel found as a matter of fact that the administrative measure was effective.[125]

This appraisal by the Panel may be said to beg a number of questions. With respect to the Panel's decision on the question of WTO conformity did the Panel appreciate that there was a probability that a finding against the US would not have been accompanied by control intention, i.e. the Panel ruling would not have been effective were it to be made? Such a ruling may have brought the WTO system under serious strain, and the US would have been very reluctant to comply. Thus, did the Panel fudge the issue, inter alia by seizing upon the US statements made during the Panel proceedings, along with the US administrative statement, given that it faced a serious test to its own credibility and effectiveness as a judicial organ of the WTO, in issuing a Panel Report that the US might have repudiated? In this manner both the EU and the US could claim a victory.

This is an analysis, which is informed by the New Haven School's appraisal of the ICJ's reactions to the events in the Nuclear Tests case.[126] The Panel in the vein of the communication model, accompanied by its analysis of the

115 WTO Panel Report (1999), p.31.
116 WTO Panel Report (1999), p.34.
117 WTO Panel Report (1999), p.34.
118 WTO Panel Report (1999), p.41.
119 WTO Panel Report (1999), p.41.
120 WTO Panel Report (1999), p.43.
121 WTO Panel Report (1999), p.43.
122 Reisman, "International Law Making" (1981).
123 WTO Panel Report (1999), p.108.
124 WTO Panel Report (1999), p.108–109.
125 WTO Panel Report (1999), p.38.
126 Reisman, "International Law Making" (1991).

policy underpinning the relevant US and WTO provisions, could be argued to have applied in the field of IEL, the approach of law as a process, rather than a mere set of rules.

From the viewpoint of perspectives here, the WTO Panel decision may be considered significant because it is a pronouncement made by an important organ of the international economic system. However, equally it needs to be acknowledged that this particular Panel decision is not necessarily representative of all WTO and Appellate Body pronouncements. Certainly, the range of considerations taken into account by this particular Panel is wider than a rules based approach. And it begs the question whether the negotiators at the Uruguay Round were conscious that the rules for the international trading system they were agreeing to would in fact be the subject of such an interpretation.

## Conventional International Economic Law[127]

IEL derives mainly from agreements arrived at between States, either on a bilateral, regional or multilateral level. This is because treaties suit the exigencies of the international economic system, being efficient in norm creation, adaptable, and capable of generating detailed rules. International economic treaty practice has often progressed from bilateral to multilateral arrangements. However, the existence of a network of bilateral arrangements can also inhibit progression to a multilateral state because it involves the setting aside of a vast network of bilateral agreements. This is not necessarily, however, an overwhelming obstacle, and mechanisms to deal with such an inhibitor need to be explored further.

**1-017**

There are a number of problems that characterise this source of IEL. Some of the main problems may be described as follows. First, given the abundance of international agreements, there are serious questions as to the co-ordination of such obligations. A State may have entered into multilateral, regional and bilateral arrangements involving the same subject-matter. Indeed such arrangements are entered into against the background of General International Law (viz., Customary International Law and General Principles of Law) which further compounds the problem of conflicts. Thus, questions of conflict of norms[128] have been raised in relation to the WTO code and the IMF;[129]

---

[127] For a general background on the Law of Treaties useful chapters are found in the standard International Law works, for example, I. Brownlie, *Principles of Public International Law* (2008) or *Oppenheim's International Law* (1992). For more specialist treatment see, for example, the Vienna Convention on Succession of States in Respect of Treaties (1978); I. Sinclair, *The Vienna Convention On the Law Of Treaties*, 2nd edn (1984). See also the Vienna Convention on the Law of Treaties (1969); the Vienna Convention on the Law of Treaties Between States and International Organisations (1986); P. Reuter, *Introduction to the Law Of Treaties* (1995); A. Aust, Modern Treaty Law and Practice (2000).

[128] See for example J. Pauwelyn, *Conflict of norms in Public international Law* (CUP, 2003); ILC: *Fragmentation of international law: difficulties arising from the diversification and expansion of international law http://untreaty.un.org/ilc/guide/1_9.htm* in particular: *http://untreaty.un.org/ilc/texts/instruments/english/draft%20articles/1_9_2006.pdf.* (Accessed June 8, 2011).

[129] See, for example, the Argentinean contention in relation to its IMF obligations and its obligations under GATT 1994 (Argentina—Certain Measures Affecting Imports of Footwear, Textiles, Apparel and Other Items (WTO Panel Report 1997)).

the WTO code and environmental treaties[130] and customary international environmental law[131]; the WTO code and bilateral agreements, for example double taxation agreements,[132] and US/EC agreement on aircraft subsidies[133]; the WTO code and regional economic arrangements[134]; and the IMF and the European Monetary Union. When these conflicts arise International Law provides some guidance. Thus, with reference to conflicts as between the different sources of Public International Law, although in principle there is no set hierarchy, as between treaties and General International Law a treaty norm normally prevails with the exception of a *jus cogens*[135] or exceptionally when a later Customary International Law emerges.[136] This hierarchy as between sources is informed by such general legal principles as *lex specialis derogat generali* and *lex posterior derogat priori*. The conflict resolution as between treaties is also similarly informed by such general legal principles, including Article 103 of the UN Charter, under which obligations under the UN charter prevail over other treaty regimes. In some measure tensions between treaty norms in different treaties may be eased through the process of treaty interpretation under Art.31 VCLT, in particular Art.31(3)(c) of the VCLT. The international conflict resolution mechanisms are however not without their uncertainties and therefore there is the need to ensure at the outset the avoidance of conflicting obligations undertaken in different treaty arrangements.

Further, the particular feature of the MFN standard in international economic relations calls for an added vigilance by States when negotiating new commitments. For example, there is arguably a query in relation to the MFN commitments under the WTO code, and bilaterally agreed double taxation relief.[137] By the same token, a bilateral investment agreement with a MFN provision opens a State to more than the commitments proffered in the actual bilateral investment agreement.[138]

Secondly, the process of interpreting international economic agreements can be fraught with difficulties. These can stem from the language of the agreement itself (which can sometimes shelter differences of opinions

---

[130] See, for example, United States—Import Prohibition of Certain Shrimp and Shrimp Products. Panel and Appellate Body Ruling (1998) with reference to the *Convention* on International Trade in *Endangered Species* (1973 as amended 1979).

[131] See EC-Hormones (WTO AB 1998) with reference to the *precautionary principle*.

[132] See, for example, J. Fischer-Zernin, "GATT versus tax treaties? The basic conflicts between international taxation methods and the rules and concepts of GATT" (1987) JWT.

[133] *EC Aircraft* (WTO Panel 2010) with reference to *US/EC Agreement on Aircraft Subsidy 1992*

[134] See, for example, Brazil—Measures Affecting Imports of Retreaded Tyres (WTO AB 2007); and Turkey–Restrictions on Imports of Textile and Clothing Products (WTO AB, 1999).

[135] See Art.53 of the VCLT 1969: "A treaty is void if, at the time of its conclusion, it conflicts with a peremptory norm of general international law."

[136] See, for example, J. Pauwelyn, *Conflict of norms in Public international Law* (CUP, 2003) at p.133.

[137] Fischer-Zernin (1987).

[138] See, for example, A. Ziegler, "The Nascent International Law on Most-Favoured-Nation (MFN) Clauses in Bilateral Investment Treaties (BITs)" in *European Yearbook of International Economic Law*, 2010, Volume 1, Part 1, 77–101.

between States); from the institutional processes involved in interpreting an agreement in international economic institutions[139]; from the differences in interpretations of international agreements by national courts[140]; from the lack of agreement as to the particular national law to be applied which is conclusive of the meaning of a term in an international agreement[141]; and in the determination of the status of an international interpretation in national law. In particular, the mechanisms for the interpretation and implementation of international agreements often involve internalised mechanisms of interpretation and dispute resolution. These procedures can have a tendency to ensure a pragmatic rather than a strict rule-orientated solution. Further, given the multitude of international economic agreements and the various principles enunciated under General International Law, the interpretation process of a particular international economic agreement has to take into account the corpus of IEL as it governs the relations between the parties.[142]

---

**EXAMPLE: WTO Appellate Body Japan—Taxes on Alcoholic Beverages (AB-1996–2) WT/DS8/AB/R; WT/DS10/AB/R; WT/DS11/AB/R) October 4, 1996[143]**

... D. Treaty Interpretation

1-018

Article 3.2 of the *DSU* [Dispute Settlement Understanding] directs the Appellate Body to clarify the provisions of GATT 1994 and the other 'covered agreements' of the *WTO Agreement* 'in accordance with customary rules of interpretation of public international law'. Following this mandate, in *United States—Standards for Reformulated and Conventional Gasoline*,[144] we stressed the need to achieve such clarification by reference to the fundamental rule of treaty interpretation set out in Article 31(1) of the *Vienna Convention*. We stressed there that this general rule of interpretation 'has attained the status of a rule of customary or general international law'.[145] There can be no doubt that Article 32 of the *Vienna Convention*, dealing with the role of supplementary means of interpretation, has also attained the same status.[146]

---

[139] For example, both the IMF and the WTO employ political organs to engage in the process of interpretation.

[140] e.g. Art.VIII(2)(b) of the IMF Articles of Agreement.

[141] e.g. Art.3(2) of the OECD Model Tax Convention on Income and on Capital.

[142] See Art.31, s.3(c) of the Vienna Convention on the Law of Treaties 1969. For example, WTO Appellate Body European Communities—Trade description of sardines (WT/DS231/AB/R, September 26, 2002) and on this subject in general Marco Slotboom, *A Comparison of WTO and EC Law: Do Different Treaty Objectives and Purposes Matter for Treaty Interpretation* (London, 2006). See also ILC: *Fragmentation of international law: difficulties arising from the diversification and expansion of international law http://untreaty.un.org/ilc/guide/1_9.htm* in particular: *http://untreaty.un.org/ilc/texts/instruments/english/draft%20articles/1_9_2006.pdf.* (Accessed June 8, 2011)

[143] Extract from *WTO Appellate Body Japan—Taxes on Alcoholic Beverages (AB-1996-2) WT/DS8/AB/R; WT/DS10/AB/R; WT/DS11/AB/R)* October 4, 1996, *http://www.wto.org.* (Accessed June 8, 2011).

[144] Adopted May 20, 1996, WT/DS2/9.

[145] United States—Standards for Reformulated and Conventional Gasoline, adopted May 20, 1996, WT/DS2/9 at p.17.

[146] See, for example, Jiménez de Aréchaga, "International Law in the Past Third of a Century" (1978-I) 159 *Recueil des Cours*, p.1 at 42; *Territorial Dispute (Libyan Arab Jamahiriya/Chad)*,

Article 31, as a whole, and Article 32 are each highly pertinent to the present appeal. They provide as follows:

## ARTICLE 31

### General rule of interpretation

1. A treaty shall be interpreted in good faith in accordance with the ordinary meaning to be given to the terms of the treaty in their context and in the light of its object and purpose.

2. The context for the purpose of the interpretation of a treaty shall comprise, in addition to the text, including its preamble and annexes:

   (a) any agreement relating to the treaty which was made between all the parties in connexion with the conclusion of the treaty;

   (b) any instrument which was made by one or more parties in connexion with the conclusion of the treaty and accepted by the other parties as an instrument related to the treaty.

3. There shall be taken into account together with the context:

   (a) any subsequent agreement between the parties regarding the interpretation of the treaty or the application of its provisions;

   (b) any subsequent practice in the application of the treaty which establishes the agreement of the parties regarding its interpretation;

   (c) any relevant rules of international law applicable in the relations between the parties.

4. A special meaning shall be given to a term if it is established that the parties so intended.

## ARTICLE 32

### Supplementary means of interpretation

Recourse may be had to supplementary means of interpretation, including the preparatory work of the treaty and the circumstances of its conclusion, in order to confirm the meaning resulting from the application of Article 31, or to determine the meaning when the interpretation according to Article 31:

(a) leaves the meaning ambiguous or obscure; or

(b) leads to a result which is manifestly absurd or unreasonable.

Article 31 of the *Vienna Convention* provides that the words of the treaty form the foundation for the interpretive process: 'interpretation must be

*Judgment* (1994) I.C.J. Reports, p.6 at 20; *Maritime Delimitation ᴬᴺᴰ Territorial Questions between Qatar and Bahrain, Jurisdiction and Admissibility, Judgment* (1995) I.C.J. Reports, p.6 at 18; *Interpretation of the Convention of 1919 Concerning Employment of Women during the Night* (1932), P.C.I.J., Series A/B, No. 50, p.365 at 380; cf. the *Serbian and Brazilian Loans Cases* (1929), P.C.I.J., Series A, Nos. 20–21, p.5 at 30; *Constitution of the Maritime Safety Committee of the IMCO* (1960) I.C.J. Reports, p.150 at 161; "Air Transport Services Agreement Arbitration (United States of America v France)" (1963) *International Law Reports*, 38, p.182 at 235–243.

based above all upon the text of the treaty'.[147] The provisions of the treaty are to be given their ordinary meaning in their context.[148] The object and purpose of the treaty are also to be taken into account in determining the meaning of its provisions.[149] A fundamental tenet of treaty interpretation flowing from the general rule of interpretation set out in Article 31 is the principle of effectiveness (*ut res magis valeat quam pereat*).[150] In *United States—Standards for Reformulated and Conventional Gasoline*, we noted that '[o]ne of the corollaries of the 'general rule of interpretation' in the *Vienna Convention* is that interpretation must give meaning and effect to all the terms of the treaty. An interpreter is not free to adopt a reading that would result in reducing whole clauses or paragraphs of a treaty to redundancy or inutility'.[151]

### E. Status of Adopted Panel Reports

In this case, the Panel concluded that,

> . . . panel reports adopted by the GATT CONTRACTING PARTIES and the WTO Dispute Settlement Body constitute subsequent practice in a specific case by virtue of the decision to adopt them. Article 1(b) (iv) of GATT 1994 provides institutional recognition that adopted panel reports constitute subsequent practice. Such reports are an integral part of GATT 1994, since they constitute 'other decisions of the CONTRACTING PARTIES to GATT 1947'.[152]

Article 31(3)(b) of the *Vienna Convention* states that 'any subsequent practice in the application of the treaty which establishes the agreement of the parties regarding its interpretation' is to be 'taken into account together with the context' in interpreting the terms of the treaty. Generally, in international law, the essence of subsequent practice in interpreting a treaty has been recognized as a 'concordant, common and consistent' sequence of acts or pronouncements which is sufficient to establish a discernable pattern implying

---

[147] *Territorial Dispute (Libyan Arab Jamahiriya/Chad)*, *Judgment* (1994) I.C.J. Reports, p.6 at 20; *Maritime Delimitation and Territorial Questions between Qatar and Bahrain, Jurisdiction and Admissibility*, *Judgment* (1995) I.C.J. Reports, p.6 at 18.

[148] See, for example, *Competence of the General Assembly for the Admission of a State to the United Nations (Second Admissions Case)* (1950) I.C.J. Reports, p.4 at 8, in which the International Court of Justice stated: "The Court considers it necessary to say that the first duty of a tribunal which is called upon to interpret and apply the provisions of a treaty, is to endeavour to give effect to them in their natural and ordinary meaning and in the context in which they occur."

[149] That is, the treaty's "object and purpose" is to be referred to in determining the meaning of the "terms of the treaty" and not as an independent basis for interpretation: *Competence of the ILO to Regulate the Personal Work of the Employer* (1926) P.C.I.J., *Re Competence of Conciliation Commission* (1955) 22 *International Law Reports*, p.867 at 871; Series B, No.13, p.6 at 18; *International Status of South West Africa* (1962) I.C.J. Reports, p.128 at 336; Jiménez de Aréchaga, "International Law in the Past Third of a Century" (1978-I) 159 *Recueil des Cours*, p.1 at 44; Sinclair, *The Vienna Convention and the Law of Treaties*, 2nd edn (1984), p.130; Harris, *Cases and Materials on International Law*, 4th edn (1991), p.770; See, for example, Jennings and Watts, (eds), *Oppenheims' International Law*, 9th edn (1992) Vol.I, p.1273.

[150] See also (1966) *Yearbook of the International Law Commission*, Vol.II, p.219: "When a treaty is open to two interpretations one of which does and the other does not enable the treaty to have appropriate effects, good faith and the objects and purposes of the treaty demand that the former interpretation should be adopted."

[151] *United States—Standards for Reformulated and Conventional Gasoline*, WT/DS2/9, adopted May 20, 1996, p.23.

[152] Panel Report, para.6.10.

the agreement of the parties regarding its interpretation.[153] An isolated act is generally not sufficient to establish subsequent practice[154]; it is a sequence of acts establishing the agreement of the parties that is relevant.[155]

Although GATT 1947[156] panel reports were adopted by decisions of the CONTRACTING PARTIES,[157] a decision to adopt a panel report did not under GATT 1947 constitute agreement by the CONTRACTING PARTIES on the legal reasoning in that panel report. The generally-accepted view under GATT 1947 was that the conclusions and recommendations in an adopted panel report bound the parties to the dispute in that particular case, but subsequent panels did not feel legally bound by the details and reasoning of a previous panel report.[158]

We do not believe that the CONTRACTING PARTIES, in deciding to adopt a panel report, intended that their decision would constitute a definitive interpretation of the relevant provisions of GATT 1947. Nor do we believe that this is contemplated under GATT 1994. There is specific cause for this conclusion in the *WTO Agreement*. Article IX:2 of the *WTO Agreement* provides: "The Ministerial Conference and the General Council shall have the exclusive authority to adopt interpretations of this Agreement and of the Multilateral Trade Agreements". Article IX:2 provides further that such decisions "shall be taken by a three-fourths majority of the Members". The fact that such an "exclusive authority" in interpreting the treaty has been established so specifically in the *WTO Agreement* is reason enough to conclude that such authority does not exist by implication or by inadvertence elsewhere.

Historically, the decisions to adopt panel reports under Article XXIII of the GATT 1947 were different from joint action by the CONTRACTING PARTIES under Article XXV of the GATT 1947. Today, their nature continues to differ from interpretations of the GATT 1994 and the other Multilateral Trade Agreements under the *WTO Agreement* by the WTO Ministerial Conference or the General Council. This is clear from a reading of Article 3.9 of the *DSU*, which states:

> The provisions of this Understanding are without prejudice to the rights of Members to seek authoritative interpretation of provisions of a covered agreement through decision-making under the WTO Agreement or a covered agreement which is a Plurilateral Trade Agreement.

Article XVI:1 of the *WTO Agreement* and paragraph 1(b)(iv) of the language of Annex 1A incorporating the GATT 1994 into the *WTO Agreement* bring the legal history and experience under the GATT 1947 into the new realm of the WTO in a way that ensures continuity and consistency in a

---

[153] Sinclair, *The Vienna Convention on the Law of Treaties*, 2nd edn (1984), p.137; Yasseen, "L'interprétation des traités d'après la Convention de Vienne sur le Droit des Traités" (1976-III) 151 *Recueil des Cours*, p.1 at 48.

[154] Sinclair (1984), p.137, fn.24.

[155] *Yearbook of the International Law Commission* (1966) Vol.II, p.222; Sinclair (1984), p.138, fn.24.

[156] By GATT 1947, we refer throughout to the General Agreement on Tariffs and Trade, dated October 30, 1947, annexed to the Final Act Adopted at the Conclusion of the Second Session of the Preparatory Committee of the United Nations Conference on Trade and Employment, as subsequently rectified, amended or modified.

[157] By CONTRACTING PARTIES, we refer throughout to the CONTRACTING PARTIES of GATT 1947.

[158] *European Economic Community—Restrictions on Imports of Dessert Apples*, BISD 36S/93, para.12.1.

smooth transition from the GATT 1947 system. This affirms the importance to the Members of the WTO of the experience acquired by the CONTRACTING PARTIES to the GATT 1947—and acknowledges the continuing relevance of that experience to the new trading system served by the WTO. Adopted panel reports are an important part of the GATT *acquis*. They are often considered by subsequent panels. They create legitimate expectations among WTO Members, and, therefore, should be taken into account where they are relevant to any dispute. However, they are not binding, except with respect to resolving the particular dispute between the parties to that dispute.[159] In short, their character and their legal status have not been changed by the coming into force of the *WTO Agreement*.

For these reasons, we do not agree with the Panel's conclusion in paragraph 6.10 of the Panel Report that 'panel reports adopted by the GATT CONTRACTING PARTIES and the WTO Dispute Settlement Body constitute subsequent practice in a specific case' as the phrase 'subsequent practice' is used in Article 31 of the *Vienna Convention*. Further, we do not agree with the Panel's conclusion in the same paragraph of the Panel Report that adopted panel reports in themselves constitute 'other decisions of the CONTRACTING PARTIES to GATT 1947' for the purposes of paragraph 1(b)(iv) of the language of Annex 1A incorporating the GATT 1994 into the *WTO Agreement*.

However, we agree with the Panel's conclusion in that same paragraph of the Panel Report that *unadopted* panel reports 'have no legal status in the GATT or WTO system since they have not been endorsed through decisions by the CONTRACTING PARTIES to GATT or WTO Members'.[160] Likewise, we agree that 'a panel could nevertheless find useful guidance in the reasoning of an unadopted panel report that it considered to be relevant'.[161]

Finally, there are questions relating to the reception of international economic agreements into domestic law. State practice differs as to the status of international agreements in domestic law and the manner of their reception in domestic law. Indeed, the very viability of transforming international economic agreements into domestic law has spawned two schools of thought![162]  **1-019**

Conventional IEL is to be found in bilateral, regional and multilateral agreements. Examples of bilateral agreements are Friendship-Commerce-Navigation treaties (FCNs); Double Taxation Agreements (DTAs); Bilateral Investment Treaties (BITs). In 2009 there were some 5,939 such investment agreements.[163] Examples of regional agreements are mostly those which facilitate regional economic integration, e.g. free-trade agreements, and agreements for the establishment of customs unions. As of July 2010 there

---

[159] It is worth noting that the Statute of the International Court of Justice has an explicit provision, Art.59, to the same effect. This has not inhibited the development by that Court (and its predecessor) of a body of case law in which considerable reliance on the value of previous decisions is readily discernible.

[160] Panel Report, para.6.10.

[161] Panel Report, para.6.10.

[162] See Hilf and Petersmann, *National constitutions and International Economic Law* (Kluwer, 1993) and Jackson and Sykes, *Implementing the Uruguay Round* (Oxford, Oxford University Press, 1997).

[163] See UNCTAD World Investment Report 2010.

were some 474 regional integration agreements notified to the WTO. Chief examples of multilateral agreements comprise of those establishing the international economic organisations (e.g. the IMF, the WTO, the World Bank Group), and those arrived at under their framework.

### Customary International Economic Law

**1-020**   At one level Customary International Law provides the foundations and the background for the institutions of international economic relations.[164] Examples of such norms are those that pertain to freedom of communication,[165] for instance freedom of the high seas; diplomatic protection and international claims[166]; the principle of *pacta sund servanda* and the standards in relation to the treatment of aliens.[167] In this respect the role of Customary International Law is significant. However, in so far as the body of Customary International Economic Law is concerned this is mostly marginal.[168] The Customary IEL that does exist has been characterised as having three distinct features,[169] viz. negativity, extremity and ambiguity. Thus, generally the rules proscribe rather than prescribe, tend to be vague, and focus on extreme situations. As examples of Customary IEL, mention has particularly been made of the norms relating to expropriation,[170] international economic torts, economic warfare,[171] interference of the international monetary system,[172] and the requirement to consult and collaborate in international monetary matters.[173]

In addition to State practice generally, State treaty practice[174] in the economic field, and the practice of international economic organisations,[175] can give rise to the formation of Customary IEL. This may appear undemocratic in that the rules so formed bind non-parties to the agreements.[176] Generally, State treaty practice has been driven by the economically powerful States, as indeed have the activities of some international economic organisations.

The very establishment of the existence of customary norms can be fraught with difficulties. This is illustrated by the lack of consensus between

---

[164]  See, for example, G. White, "Principles of International Economic Law" in H. Fox (ed.), *International Economic Law And Developing States: Some Aspects* (1998), p.5.
[165]  White (1998), p.16.
[166]  White (1998), p.16.
[167]  See Jackson (1997), p.269.
[168]  See S. Zamora, "Is there customary international economic law?" (1989) 32 *German Yearbook of International Law*, p.41, fn.9.
[169]  Zamora (1989) p.41.
[170]  Jackson (1997), p.269. See also Zamora (1989), pp.23–33, fn.9.
[171]  G. Schwarzenberger "The principles and standards of International Economic Law", p.14. But see Zamora (1989), p.25.
[172]  R. Edwards, *International Monetary Collaboration* (1985), pp.647–55.
[173]  Edwards (1985).
[174]  The North Sea Continental Shelf Cases (1969) I.C.J. Reports.
[175]  Palitha. T.B. Kohona, *The Regulation of International Economic Relations Through Law* (1985), pp.89–90.
[176]  Zamora (1989).

developing and developed States as well as academics as to the nature and impact of certain UN General Assembly resolutions in the international economic field; [177] the impact of bilateral double taxation agreements on the development of international tax law;[178] and bilateral investment agreements on the development of customary international investment law.[179]

### General principles of law

The importance of this source to IEL was considered at one time even more limited to that of Customary IEL.[180] The International Economic Order may be said now to have evolved somewhat since then. Indeed, as the view was expressed even then, it may be contended it was formulated in somewhat strong terms. As Zamora points out[181] International Economic Organisations can and have promoted harmonisation and uniformity in domestic law.[182] This domestic development may in turn spawn the birth of General Principles of IEL at the international level. In 1966 when Schwarzenberger delivered his lectures[183] he considered this source to lend itself "too readily to abuse". Certainly in the interpretation and application of the principles there can be much latitude.

**1-021**

### Soft law

The phenomenon of soft law[184] has been variously described. At its core it refers to "rules" that command respect,[185] but are either not strictly

**1-022**

---

[177] e.g. the UN Charter on Economic rights and Duties of States, GA Resolution 3281 1974; and the Declaration on Permanent Sovereignty over Natural Resources, GA Res 1803 (XVII) 1962.

[178] See on the obligation to avoid double taxation, for example, R. S. Avi-Yonah, *International Tax as International Law* (CUO, 2007). Contra A. H. Qureshi 'The freedom of a State to legislate in fiscal matters under General International Law', *Bulletin for International Fiscal Documentation,* 41:1 (1987), p.14–21.

[179] See for example on whether the "fair and equitable" standard contained in bilateral investment agreements has become a norm of customary international law, S. Vasciannie, "The fair and equitable treatment standard in international investment law and practice", in *BYIL,*70 (1999), p.99–164.

[180] See Seidl-Hohenveldern (1992), p.36; G. Schwarzenberger, "Principles and Standards of International Economic Law" (1966) I *Recueil Des Cours,* pp.14–15.

[181] S. Zamora, "Economic Relations And Development" in O. Schacter and C. Joyner, *United Nations Legal Order* (American Society of International Law, 1995), Vol.I p.550.

[182] See, for example, Art.3 of the Uruguay Round Agreement On The Application Of Sanitary And Phytosanitory Measures; and Art.4 of the Uruguay Round Agreement on Technical Barriers to Trade.

[183] Schwarzenberger (1966).

[184] See generally, e.g. C. Chinkin, "The Challenge of Soft Law: Development and Change in International Law" (1989) 38 I.C.L.Q. 850; S.A. Voitovich, "Normative acts of the international economic organizations in international law-making" (1990) J.W.T., Vol.24, pp.21–38. See also J. Gold, *Interpretation: The IMF and International Law* (Kluwer International, 1996), Ch.4 and references therein.

[185] J. Gold, "Strengthening the soft international law of exchange arrangements" (1983) 77 A.J.I.L.

formulated,[186] and/or not strictly enforceable.[187] Soft law is not legally binding. It is an expression of a preference. Non-compliance is not considered a violation,[188] although compliance with it endows the relevant conduct with legitimacy.[189] However, failure to observe can lead to certain consequences. Further, the formation of soft law in relation to a certain matter takes it out of the domestic jurisdiction of a State.[190] An example of soft law is Article XXXVII of GATT 1994 which states inter alia in paragraph one:

> "The developed contracting parties shall to the fullest extent possible—that is, except when compelling reasons, which may include legal reasons, make it impossible—give effect to the following provisions: (a) accord high priority to the reduction and elimination of barriers to products currently or potentially of particular export interest to less-developed contracting parties. . .".

The notion of "soft" is as much a reference to a rule as to the manner of its enforcement. In so far as the soft-law indicia of the rule are concerned, these have been described as having any one or more of the following elements: vagueness[191]; imprecision[192]; recommendatory language;[193] strictly formulated obligations in a binding instrument but undermined by exceptions;[194] and strictly formulated obligations but contained in recommendatory non-binding instruments, for example, UN General Assembly Resolutions, Guidelines and Codes of Conduct.[195] In addition to these indicia, the requirements for soft law to exist have been stated to comprise of a common intent, and an acceptance of the legitimacy of their promulgation.[196]

The soft-law indicia relating to the enforcement apparatus include any or all of the following: waivers from compliance,[197] flexible or haphazard enforcement,[198] compliance mechanisms that de-emphasise the role of law and jurists.[199] However, it seems some measure of policing is necessary.[200]

**1–023**        Although soft law is not strictly law, it has many positive assets. It is in fact

---

[186] See Seidl-Hohenveldern (1992), pp.42–45; and Zamora, "Economic Relations and Development" in O. Schacter and C. Joyner, *United Nations Legal Order* (1995), *American Society of International Law*, Vol.I at p.540.

[187] Seidl-Hohenveldern (1992).

[188] Gold (1996), p.301.

[189] Gold (1996) and see also Baade, "The legal effects of codes for multinational enterprises" (1979) 22 G.Y.I.L. at pp.39–40.

[190] Gold (1996).

[191] Gold (1996).

[192] Gold (1996).

[193] Gold (1996).

[194] Gold (1996).

[195] White (1998), p.10.

[196] J. Gold, "Strengthening the soft international law of exchange arrangements" (1983) 77 A.J.I.L., p.443.

[197] Zamora (1995).

[198] Zamora (1995).

[199] Seidl-Hohenveldern (1992). An example would be the Trade Policy Review Mechanism of the WTO.

[200] Seidl-Hohenveldern (1995).

both a sophisticated normative framework, as well as a pre-legal or legislative apparatus. It is a method for experimenting and experience building, and a formula for encapsulating compromises.[201] Soft law can shape opinion and practice, and thereby assist in the formation of General International Law. Thus, when soft law codes are incorporated in national legislation,[202] given force in judicial practice, form a basis of treaty practice, the elements necessary for the development of General International Law are triggered into operation. Compliance with it on a voluntary basis on its own, however, cannot bring directly the emergence of Customary International Law, since the compliance is not engaged in out of a sense of legal obligation.[203]

There are in international economic relations certain matters that are more effectively served through soft law, either because of the delicacy involved, or because the nature of the object of regulation is such that it does not, or cannot lend itself to strict legal regulation. Thus, soft law provides a diplomatically more palatable method for regulating State conduct, as well as a method for States to undertake international obligations.

Although, the advantages of soft law have been variously rehearsed—some specific mention of the problems associated with this form of "law" needs to be made. Firstly, soft law can be a deliberate device to minimise and cloak firm law purely for political reasons. The political reasons may not be sound. In such a situation "soft law" is not so much a second-best solution but rather a facilitator for the postponement of firm law. Secondly, soft law can involve convoluted jargon in order to avoid legal obligations. In this sense, it does not promote clarity. Thirdly, soft law interpretations can be liberal and thus could result in a higher degree of burden. Fourthly, soft law is static—it does not benefit from authoritative interpretations and clarifications that are consequent upon the processing of firm law through adjudication. Finally, soft law can be a more potent instrument of power—given, for example, the latitude in interpretation, and the flexibility in avoiding legal and constitutional constraints through soft-law characterisations. Such considerations provide a safe harbour for non-transparent power-oriented *modus operandi*—both at the national and international levels.

### The subsidiary means for the determination of International Economic Law

The sources of IEL may be determined by judicial decisions and the teachings     **1-024**
of the most highly qualified publicists of various nations.[204]

Judicial decisions include those of national and international courts. In IEL the jurisprudence of the WTO has made a significant impact in the

---

[201] Gold (1983), p.301.
[202] Zamora (1995).
[203] Seidl-Hohenveldern (1995), p.45. See also cited therein H.W. Baade, "The Legal Effects of Codes of conduct for Multinational Enterprises", in H. Horn (ed.), *Legal Problems of Codes of Conduct for Multinational Enterprises* (BV Kluwer Deventer, 1980).
[204] Art.38(1)(d) of the Statute of the International Court of Justice.

development of international trade law and generally IEL, with over 186 cases litigated since 1995.[205]In the same vein there have been until the end of 2009 some 164 concluded investment disputes, mostly under the auspices of ICSID.[206] At the regional economic integration level too there is much judicial activity with some 8267 total number of cases between 1952 to 2009 considered by the European Court of Justice alone[207]; and approximately some 105 completed cases under the auspices of NAFTA between 1989 to 2010.[208] This amount of judicial activity is likely to continue, in particular because of the increasing number of free trade agreements and the establishment of arbitration systems to service those agreements.

In International Law there is no binding system of precedent.[209] The WTO Appellate Body however recently came close to confirming such a system,[210] albeit in the framework of the WTO. Moreover, there is evidence of reliance on the jurisprudence within the different economic regimes operating in international economic relations. Furthermore, although technically arbitration decisions are not considered to be authoritative sources of interpretation, because the decision is shaped by the specific terms of the arbitration,[211]in practice such decisions do contribute to the clarification of IEL.

The International Court of Justice is considered as not having played a significant role in the development of IEL.[212] This is partly because international economic organisations have internalised their interpretative and dispute settlement mechanisms. Thus, the IMF[213] and the WTO[214] have internal dispute settlement and interpretative mechanisms. However, the fragmented nature of IEL may well provide an overarching constitutional role to the International Court.

Further, in international economic relations the general approach to dispute resolution has been pragmatic rather than rule-orientated. Thus, both the IMF and the WTO interpretative mechanisms are reliant not on their judicial organs for interpretation, but on the political organs of the respective institutions. Similarly, the WTO dispute settlement mechanism is geared to achieving a positive and mutually acceptable solution.[215] Although, it should be noted that the WTO dispute settlement procedures are now frequently used, well-developed and the outcomes tend to be rule-orientated.

---

[205] See WTO Annual Report 2010.
[206] See UNCTAD WIR 2010.
[207] See European Court of Justice Annual Report 2009 (CVRIA).
[208] See *http://www.nafta-sec-alena.org/en/StatusReportResults.aspx*. (Accessed June 8, 2011).
[209] See Art.59 of the Statute of International Court of Justice.
[210] United States—Final Anti-Dumping Measures on Stainless Steel from Mexico (WT/DS 344/AB/R (2008)).
[211] See Seidl-Hohenveldern (1995), p.36.
[212] Zamora (1995), p.553.
[213] Art.XXIX of the IMF Articles of Agreement.
[214] Art.IX of the Marrakesh Agreement Establishing The World Trade Organization.
[215] See WTO Understanding On Rules And Procedures Governing The Settlement Of Disputes.

The process involved in determining the relevant practice and consensus in the identification of Customary International Economic norms involves judges and scholars.[216] These are unrepresentative, if informed, forces. Further, traditionally a significant majority of publicists in the field have been from developed States. Publicists, no matter their origins, can bring to their field their own particular perspectives.[217]

**Perspectives on the role of the International Court of Justice in the development of International Economic Law[218]:**

Of late there has been much ado about the role of the WTO dispute settlement mechanism and ICSID[219] in the development of international trade and investment law. The importance of the ICJ on the other hand seems to have been eclipsed in this evaluation of the contribution of conflict resolution mechanisms to international economic relations. Thus, E-U Petersmann observes that it is doubtful whether the ICJ can assume a more active role in the settlement of international economic disputes.[220] Such an analysis not only brings at the forefront pessimism about the role of the ICJ in international economic relations, but also may beg the question whether underlying it are value judgements about the importance of the disparate spheres of international economic relations serviced by the various judicial institutions other than the ICJ.

This pessimism is expressed despite Karel Wellens exhaustive study of the ICJ in the context of international economic disputes in which he[221] concludes that the assumption about the Court's incapability and/or unwillingness to deal in a satisfactory way with economic disputes is completely unfounded[222]; and that the court does provide suitable judicial remedies for economic disputes.[223]

There may not be an inconsistency here, in that Petersmann's pessimism does not cast doubt on the actual ability or capacity of the ICJ as such to deal with international economic disputes. His focus is on the frequency of the future role of the ICJ in IEL. Yet one cannot but feel that there is an underlying pessimism here that goes beyond mere frequency of the use of the ICJ. Indeed, it would not be far fetched to attribute this pessimism expressed to the general role of the ICJ as such in the international economic sphere. Thus,

**1-025**

---

[216] See, for example, Zamora (1995).

[217] See, for example, M. Lachs, *The Teacher in International Law* (1982); and A.H. Qureshi, "Editorial Control and International Law" in *The Political Quarterly* (1990), Vol.61, No.3, p.328.

[218] The following is an extract from "Perspectives in International Economic Law—An eclectic approach to International Economic Law" in Qureshi (2002).

[219] International Center for the Settlement of Investment Disputes.

[220] See E-U Petersmann, "Dispute Settlement in International Economic Law—Lessons for Strengthening International Dispute Settlement in Non-Economic Areas", *Journal of International Economic Law* (1999), pp.189–248.

[221] See, for example, G. Jaenicke, "International trade conflicts before the Permanent Court of Justice and the International Court of Justice" in Petersmann and Jaenicke, *Adjudication of international trade dispute in International and National Economic Law* (Fribourg, University Press, 1992); and K. Wellens, *Economic Conflicts and Disputes before the World Court (1922–1995)* (The Hague/London/Boston, Kluwer Law International, 1996).

[222] Wellens (1996), pp.253–254.

[223] Wellens (1996).

Petersmann does not delve the role that the ICJ might play in this sphere. Unfortunately, however, Karel Wellens exhaustive study does not adequately touch upon this question either. Instead, the author is preoccupied in his work somewhat extensively with negating the assumption that the court is incapable and/or unwilling to deal in a satisfactory fashion with economic conflicts. Yet there are sound reasons for an evaluation of the ICJ in terms of its role in international economic relations, that go beyond merely confirming its capacity to have a role, or that touch on the frequency of its user—although of course such factors feature in an appraisal of this nature.

**1–026**    Thus, the fact that States have on a number of occasions taken disputes involving IEL to the ICJ has been documented, as indeed have the reasons for and the reluctance of States to resort to it in this sphere.[224] However, the pessimism with which the future role of the ICJ has been regarded does however need to be questioned. In an international economic order that is increasingly becoming fragmented both in the context of its disparate fields, as well as in terms of regional developments, the ICJ has an important constitutional role in this order, along side its normal adjudicatory function. In this constitutional role may well rest an important setting for the safeguard of differing perspectives in IEL.

In the first instance, at a very fundamental level the ICJ serves in a number of ways to guard and facilitate some of the principal substantive and procedural pillars upon which international economic relations rest upon; and which are founded, inter alia, upon General International Law. First, the Court has a role in ensuring certain basic freedoms without which international commerce and investment would not be possible. Thus, the ICJ has frequently been instrumental in clarifying the circumstances when international communication and navigation systems ought to be unhindered.[225] Second, the Court has an essential function in clarifying questions of basic State economic sovereignty—particularly in the context of rights over territorial and maritime resources. Thus, the Court has frequently been asked to clarify competing claims of sovereignty over natural resources[226] and the demarcation of boundaries, especially maritime zones, with important economic significance for States. Third, the Court has a role in identifying the circumstances which entitle the State in the economic sphere to make a claim on the international plane on behalf of different national and transnational entities. In this respect, the ICJ at least on two occasions has had the opportunity to clarify when diplomatic protection may be afforded by a State on behalf of its nationals, whose economic interests have been affected by the actions of another State.[227] Thus, the ICJ enunciated the requirement of 'genuine link' for a nationality to be recognised on the international plane[228]; and in recognising the institution of the corporation, the Court stated that generally a State may not exercise diplomatic protection on behalf of national shareholders, and that the right of diplomatic protection where a corporation's interests are

---

[224] Wellens (1996).
[225] For example the Corfu Channel Case (Merits) (1949) I.C.J. Reports; and the Case Concerning Right of Passage Over Indian Territory (1960).
[226] See, for example, North Sea Continental Shelf Cases (1967) I.C.J. Reports. Fisheries Jurisdiction Case (1974) I.C.J. Reports; Aegean Sea Continental Shelf Case (1978) I.C.J. Reports; Case Concerning Delimitation of the Maritime Boundary in the Gulf of Maine Area (1984); Case Concerning certain Phosphate Lands in Nauru (1992) I.C.J. Reports.
[227] *Nottebohm (Liechstein v Guatemala)* (1953) I.C.J. Reports and Case Concerning the Barcelona Traction Light & Power Company Limited (Second Phase) (1970) I.C.J. Reports.
[228] *Nottebohm* Case.

affected rest with the national State of the corporation.[229] Significantly, in arriving at these decisions the Court both addressed the question of the implications of any particular course of action for international relations, as well as the need to ensure that diplomatic protection is available at all material times. Thus, in one case the Court stated that 'the adoption of the theory of diplomatic protection of shareholders as such would open the door to competing claims on the part of different States, which could create an atmosphere of insecurity in international economic relations'.[230] At the same time the Court did not close the possibility of claims being brought on behalf of shareholders completely. Similar concerns may be reflected in the Court's decision that diplomatic protection can only be availed, even if on behalf of a corporation, where the general requirement in International Law of exhaustion of local remedies is satisfied.[231]

Second, the Court despite the presence of other mechanisms of conflict resolution in the international economic sphere, is still an important judicial organ of the international economic order, as much as that of the United Nations; and in that context also has a constitutional role in IEL. Firstly, the Court services many international economic treaties, which refer to it in the event of the need for conflict resolution; as well as international economic organisations for advisory opinion.[232] Thus, the ICJ has been involved in examining compliance with bilateral Friendship, Commerce and Navigation agreements—particularly as they relate to investment standards for the benefit of multinational corporations.[233] These are a significant genre of bilateral agreements, which have been the basis for determining the nature of commercial relations between States, although the modern versions of these agreements tend not to refer to the ICJ.[234] Similarly, States have availed themselves of the ICJ to resolve disputes arising from bilateral agreements (other than FCNs or BITs) dealing with specific economic issues, for example a loan agreement,[235] the construction of river locks for the development of hydroelectricity and improved navigation.[236] Second, in an international economic order that is characterised by different bilateral, regional and multilateral legal regimes, there are bound to occur conflicts and tensions arising from the different sources of obligations. The ICJ has an undoubted role here. Indeed, there are examples of its role in this context.[237] Third, the Court has a function in the resolution of disputes that draw from the rights of States under General International Economic law. Thus, there is evidence that States have resorted to the Court for the resolution of economic disputes falling outside treaty provisions.[238]

Finally, the ICJ has a law determining function in the context of General International Economic law. Thus, the court has been instrumental in

**1–027**

---

[229] *Barcelona Traction* Case.

[230] *Barcelona Traction* Case.

[231] Case Concerning Elettronica Sicula S.P.A (ELSI) (1989) I.C.J. Reports.

[232] See Wellens (1996), p.62 where he lists ILA, ICAO, UNESCO, IMO, IMF, UNIDO IDA and IFC.

[233] See, for example, *ELSI* case; Case Concerning Oil Platforms (1996) I.C.J. Reports.

[234] See, for example, E-U Petersmann (1999), p.204.

[235] Case of Certain Norwegian Loans (1957) I.C.J. Reports.

[236] Case Concerning Gabcikovo-Nagymaros Project (1997) I.C.J. Reports.

[237] For example Case of the Free Zones of Upper Savoy & the District of Gen (1929) (1930) and (1931) P.C.I.J.

[238] Ahmadou Sadio Diallo (*Republic of Guinea v Democratic Republic of the Congo*), ICJ Press Communiqué 2000/28.

confirming certain fundamental principles of IEL, for example the right to development, the right to environmental protection, and the principle of sustainable development.[239] Similarly, it has provided clarification of certain basic concepts, for example the meaning of 'commerce' at the international level is considered to include more than just the purchase and sale of goods.[240] Further, this law determining function, in the context of determining whether treaty norms serving different spheres of IEL have transformed into Customary International Economic Law, is more authoritatively performed by the ICJ than those disparate and specialist international economic judicial organs servicing such economic regimes.

Thus, the ICJ's role in international economic relations is fundamental, overarching and above all constitutional in international economic relations. Such a role cannot be usurped by other judicial systems, no matter how successful their practice and critical their determinations. This constitutional role is particularly evident in its guardianship of fundamental principles and procedures, in its function in the development of international economic norms, and in its advisory and conflict resolving role for and between different legal regimes—as well as its function as a judicial system for the residual international economic problems not adequately covered by the existing multilateral monetary, trade and development regimes. However, this attribution of a 'constitutional' role to the ICJ in international economic relations is not of course to deny the various shortcomings of this court, which have been well documented.

This constitutional role of the ICJ has an important function in facilitating the airing of different perspectives in international economic relations. First, the ICJ provides a forum for outsiders not part of the existing trade/monetary/development and investment regimes. Secondly, the court is a reservoir for the nurturing of new perspectives in international economic relations not otherwise effectively catered for in existing regimes. Thirdly, it facilitates the trumping of the existing trade/monetary/development and investment regimes—where there are sound external reasons for such trumping.

Finally, and related, the court has a role in checking the excesses of existing legal regimes. This can be the case despite appearances of exclusive and autonomous dispute settlement systems. Thus, Article IX of the Marrakesh Agreement Establishing the WTO states that the Ministerial Conference and the General Council 'have exclusive authority to adopt interpretations'. However, what is not clear nevertheless is whether this organ of the WTO can make the final[241] definitive judgement with respect to questions of interpretations. Is 'exclusive' used in terms of the WTO organs alone, or in an objective and wider sense? If it is the latter then the WTO, nor the members of the WTO, can usurp the jurisdiction of the ICJ—for it is for the ICJ to determine its jurisdiction. Further, Article IX refers only to questions of interpretation. It does not cover non-interpretation issues, such as disputes not involving questions of interpretation. Similarly, Article I of the WTO Dispute Settlement Understanding refers to the Understanding as applying to 'disputes'. It does not refer to the Understanding as applying 'exclusively' or to 'all' disputes. Further, under Article 17(14) of the Understanding the Appellate Body Report is to be 'unconditionally accepted by the parties'. However, unconditional acceptance of the report by the parties does not

---

[239] (*Republic of Guinea v Democratic Republic of the Congo*).

[240] Case Concerning Oil Platforms (1996) I.C.J. Reports.

[241] Contra Art.XXIX(b) of the IMF Articles of Agreement which refers to the Decision of the Board of Governors as being "final" with respect to questions of interpretation.

necessarily imply that they are precluded from obtaining an external determination whilst having accepted the report. Similarly, unconditional acceptance relates to the parties—it does not cover non-parties. In the same vein, under Article 23 of the Understanding Members are enjoined to seek redress under the Understanding, but the Understanding is not given in this context an exclusive function. Further, Article 23 of the Understanding refers to the 'Members' not making determinations of violations. It does not refer to external (international) judicial organs making determinations. Thus, it would not be safe to regard judicial organs within the different international economic legal regimes as having exclusive and final decision-making authority in all conceivable matters—unless perhaps it is very clearly stated, but then no drafter can possibly conceive of all the variety of issues that may one day impinge on the treaty drafted.'

## The politics of the sources of International Economic Law

There has been much ado about the sources of Public International Law, as indeed there has been somewhat of the sources of IEL. However, there has been little analysis of the strategic role the sources play and have been made to play in international economic relations. Some observations are tentatively made here. **1-028**

There has been in the background a discernable pattern of legal evolution in international economic relations that begins historically from General International Law, progresses into bilateral agreements and then metamorphoses into multilateral structures. This three-tiered evolution will, it is suggested, in time transform further leading to the further integration of the disparate multilateral structures in international economic relations. Indeed, this process of transformation will also engulf the processes of regional economic integration. There is at one level nothing remarkable here. This is a process after all that is mirrored elsewhere in other fields of international relations; and is consistent with the degree of maturity the international economic community inherits through time.

However, this apparent pattern belies the power politics of international economic relations. Upon closer scrutiny the pace of the evolution in the disparate international economic fields is different. Indeed, the legal techniques and structures vary in the disparate international economic fields. Thus, in international monetary law where the weight of State power is diverse, soft law has played a role in the maintenance of a certain power ratio. Soft law, it may be argued, can be an instrument of obfuscation, discretion and the maintenance of power structures. In international trade law on the other hand, there is more clarity. Soft law has not been as dominant—the instrument of treaty has been more significant. Further, the environment of international trade is rule-orientated. There is in trade relatively more equality between States, and there are as such fewer vested interests to safeguard. More equality however, but not complete equality, which is why there is a preference for rule orientation, not the strict rule of law. In both the trade and the monetary fields multilateralism has been affected. There was some overall mutual interest in the establishment of such frameworks. Another difference between monetary and trade law of note is the difference in the development of dispute settlement mechanisms. In international trade under the WTO the dispute settlement mechanism is now well-structured. In the monetary field dispute settlement mechanisms are barely present. Similarly, in the investment field soft law has played a different role. It has been used as an instrument to bring long-term changes. But general legislative attempts either by way of soft law or through multilateralism have not been very successful. Thus, the absence of a multilateral agreement on investment at any rate thus far. Instead, the approach in the investment field has been contractual, as evidenced by the hundreds of bilateral investment agreements that characterise the regulation of international investment. Whereas States have in the investment field at a bilateral level agreed upon certain matters, when it has come to those same proposals at the multilateral level, they have been reluctant to proffer their consent. Interestingly, in the international taxation field States have evolved a hybrid system, between multilateralism and bilateralism. Thus, the international community is confronted with a network of bilateral double taxation agreements mainly set against a model double taxation convention crafted by like-minded States. Finally, where neither bilateral nor multilateral progress has been achieved, the more economically powerful participants have simply tried to apply on an extraterritorial basis their own national legislation, for example, in the anti-trust and environment fields.

To conclude, the manner in which the sources of IEL are used have a power dimension and strategic aspects. Indeed, even the manner in which these sources are elucidated, for example with or without a positivist or natural orientation, serve the goals of certain interest groups better than others. Non-active strategists of the sources of IEL need to wake up; as indeed should the legal texts be understood in this light.

### THE PARTICIPANTS AND THEIR ROLE IN THE DEVELOPMENT OF IEL

1-029    IEL concerns itself in varying degrees with the relationships between State participants, between individual participants, between the State and the individual, between the State and international economic organisations, and as between international economic organisations. The participants are those entities which have economic rights and duties under the international economic system. They have a recognised personality which entitles them to operate on the international plane. The ranges of entitlements varies, and depend on the kind of participants involved. Thus, entitlements involve being able to enter into international economic agreements; being able to enforce international economic agreements; becoming beneficiaries of international economic agreements; being able to participate in dispute settlement mechanisms involving economic rights.

There are mainly three participants—although with varying degrees of personality. First, given the perspective here, the primary subjects are States. It is State action or inaction that is the object of international economic regulation. Equally it is States which have been critically responsible for the development of IEL. Some States have of course made a greater imprint than others. Thus, the role of economically powerful States needs to be acknowledged. This is particularly so given that a significant body of international economic norms are generated from international financial institutions, and institutions whose modus operandi is characterised by reciprocity. In such circumstances those States or Regional Economic Organisations which command the strings in the financial organisations, and which have more to offer in terms of trade concessions, will almost inevitably have a greater role in the shaping of the development of IEL.

The manner in which States have participated in the development of IEL is varied, and does not simply embrace activities as a member of one of the multilateral international economic organisations. First, States have formed informal economic groupings wherein important consultations take place and from which important initiatives can arise.[242] Such consultations sometimes take place in the face of formal democratic international institutional structures for such consultations. For example the G 20 has been critical in leading an international response to the recent global financial crisis and not the IMF. Secondly, States also operate through what have been described as informal "governmental networks".[243] These are networks of like minded governmental departments and agencies. For example in the banking field is the Basle Committee comprising central bank officials of mainly G–10 countries.[244] Important proposals and practices that originate in these groupings then find their way into the international legislative processes. Governmental networks are not accountable.[245] They operate in secrecy, informally, selectively, and are unrepresentative, being composed of technocrats.[246] Thirdly, States operate through more formal institutions such as the OECD and UNCTAD, representing broadly developed and developing country interests. Important legislative initiatives have arisen from these institutions—particularly the OECD. However, such organisations whilst catering for the divergence of international economic interests can distort the development

---

[242] For example the G 20; the G.7 (France, Germany, Japan, UK, US, Canada and Italy) and observers and the Chair of the Commission and Council of the EU; and G–77 (some 140 developing countries).

[243] Ann-Marie Slaughter Harvard Law School speaking on "The regulation of the international economy: what role for the State?" at ILA Conference, Oxford University (April 1998) titled The role of law in international politics.

[244] See C. Freeland, "The work of the Basle Committee", Ch.19 in R.C. Effros, *Current Legal Issues Affecting Central Banks*, (1994) Vol.2 IMF. Another example of the practice of governmental networking can be found in the taxation field—the practice being described by Sol Piccioto as the "internationalization of tax administration". See S. Piccioto, *International Business Taxation* (Weidenfeld & Nicholson, 1992), in particular see Ch.10.

[245] Slaughter (1998).

[246] Slaughter (1998).

of IEL. Finally, some States operate in international economic organisations by unilaterally giving to their membership rights a kind of a gloss. This is done through national legislation directed at international economic organisations. Thus, US legislation specifically directs that US representatives in international organisations promote certain US economic and foreign policy, *despite* the particular organisation's own mandate.[247]

The second category of participants comprises the international economic organisations. These organisations can be considered as actors in the system, although they are not in a strict sense the beneficiaries of the international economic regulation as the other two are. In reality the personality enjoyed by international economic organisations generally tends to be coterminous with their membership—in legal analysis they possess a distinct personality of their own, and this personality increasingly will expand so as to accord greater independence to these institutions.

**1-030**    There are a variety of international organisations with varying degrees of involvement in the economic sphere. Some have jurisdiction in economic matters alone,[248] such as the IMF, whereas others are involved in the economic field, along with other matters, for example the UN.[249] International economic organisations, particularly those in the UN system,[250] have played a critical role in the development of the international economic order. However, the UN itself has not been as significant as the Bretton Woods institutions.[251] This is because the international community has been better disposed to legislative changes when they feature in specialist fields.[252] In turn specialist international economic organisations have been free from wider political constraints, so as to be able to pioneer changes in the international economic system.[253]

International Economic organisations have played their role in the development of IEL in two principal ways. First, some of them have critically provided basic constitutional frameworks in specific fields of international economic relations. This they have done by focusing on the fundamental

---

[247] See, for example, Pub.L. 96–389 (1980), Sec.33 in relation to IMF Conditionality and basic human needs.

[248] e.g. the UN (including its committees and commissions, viz. United Nations Economic and Social Council (ECOSOC); Economic Commission For Africa; Economic and Social Commission For Asia and the Pacific; Economic Commission for Europe; Economic Commission for Latin America; and Economic Commission for Western Asia; Commission on Transnational Corporations); UN Specialised Agencies (e.g. FAO; IFAD; IBRD; IDA; IFC; ICAO; IMCO; IMF; ILO; UNIDO, WIPO); WTO (its predecessor was treated as a de facto specialised agency of the UN (see Zamora (1995)); Organisations created by the UN General Assembly, viz. UNCTAD; UNDP and WFC; OECD.

[249] See Arts 1 and 55 of the UN Charter. Art.1 states inter alia: "The purposes of the United Nations are. . .(3) To achieve international co-operation in solving international problems of an economic. . . character." Art.55 states inter alia: ". . .the United Nations shall promote: (a) higher standards of living, full employment, and conditions of economic and social progress and development; (b) solutions of international economic, social, health and related problems."

[250] For an excellent exposition on this see Zamora (1995).

[251] Zamora (1995).

[252] Zamora (1995).

[253] Zamora (1995).

aspects of their respective spheres, by the provision of a legislative and enforcement system, and by ensuring a universal or near-universal membership. The organisations which have played particularly such a role are the Bretton Woods institutions. Secondly, and more particularly, the international economic organisations, both through their operational activities (e.g. lending, technical assistance, dissemination of information),[254] and rule generating processes (norm creation and enforcement)[255] have either played a direct legislative function, or have contributed to it over a period of time. Although the operational functions are not apparently concerned with norm creation, they can in fact have an impact in that respect[256]—particularly in bringing changes in domestic legislation (e.g. IMF conditionality).

International Economic Organisations are not strictly sources of IEL. Their legislative function is enacted through the format of the traditional sources of International Law.[257] To borrow Zamora's analysis[258] the legislative processes engaged in by international economic organisations are mainly five-fold. First, international economic organisations have been instrumental in spawning international agreements.[259] Secondly, both through the practice of international economic organisations, *qua* international economic organisations, and the evidence of practice of States and their intentions[260] within these organisations, Customary IEL can and does develop. It should be noted here that the impact the practice of international economic organisations can make on the development of Customary IEL[261] is constrained by the mandate accorded to them by their members, by the reluctance of States to accord too wide a mandate, and by the number of its members.[262] Thirdly, international economic organisations have contributed to bringing about harmonisation of domestic legislation,[263] and thereby to the development of Customary International Law and General Principles of Law. Fourthly, international economic organisations have contributed to the development of soft law, particularly through the passing of resolutions and the establishment of codes of conduct. Finally, international economic organisations generate internal administrative rules, as well as rules concerning their relationship with Member States.

International economic organisations in their role as facilitators of the development of IEL suffer from a certain overall lack of co-ordination. They have a narrow specialist approach to international economic affairs, given

---

[254] Zamora (1995), p.504.

[255] Zamora (1995).

[256] Zamora (1995).

[257] See Art.38 of the Statute of the International Court of Justice.

[258] Zamora (1995).

[259] e.g. the GATT and *The Results of the Uruguay Round of Multilateral Trade Negotiations* 1994.

[260] e.g. UN General Assembly Resolutions.

[261] Zamora (1995), p.545 and Kohona (1985), pp.89–90. See also White (1998), at pp.8–9.

[262] According to Seidl-Hohenveldern (1992), p.79 only the UN enjoys objective personality.

[263] See, for example, J.O. Honnold, "International Unification of Private Law" in Schacter and Joyner (1995).

international economic relations are increasingly globalised, and national and international economic policies increasingly interlinked. Further, some international economic organisations are, simply put, undemocratic institutionally, and operate systems of interpretation that are in fact legislative in character.[264] This state of affairs has led to a recent call for a Global Economic Coordination Council.[265]

**1-031**     *The Stiglitz Report* **(2010): pp. 126–127.**

The variety of international institutions and organizations with specific mandates requires an overarching, inclusive body with an integrated view of the economic problems confronting the world and the adequacy of existing institutional arrangements and institutions, including their mandates, policies, instruments, and governance for addressing the economic challenges facing the world today. A globally representative forum, which we call the Global Economic Coordination Council, that addresses areas of concern in the functioning of the global economic system in a comprehensive and sustainable way must be created.

**1-032**     The third category of participants comprises individuals.[266] The role of the individual in IEL is more pronounced now, given its liberal trade and investment focus. This focus emphasises individual rights; the power of multinational companies, and their accompanying responsibilities; and the increasing entrenchment of domestic remedies for individuals in relation to internationally arrived at standards, along with access to international dispute settlement mechanisms.[267] Individuals here include corporate entities.

To the extent that individuals can be described as participants, they are accepted to that extent as being subjects of International Law.[268] Individuals are participants not only because they are the ultimate beneficiaries of the system, but also because they have rights and duties conferred upon them

---

[264] See, for example, in relation to Gold (1983).

[265] See *The Stiglitz Report: Reforming the International Monetary and Financial Systems in the Wake of the Global Crisis. Joseph E Stiglitz and Members of a UN Commission of Financial Experts* (The New Press, 2010)

[266] Gold (1983). See also, for example, Kokkini-Iatridou, D. and P.J.I.M de Waart, "Legal personality of Multinationals in International Law" (1983) N.Y.I.L. 14:87–131, I. Seidl-Hohenveldern, *Corporations in and under International Law* (1987); Seidl-Hohenveldern (1992), Ch.II; and N. Schrijver, *Sovereignty Over Natural Resources* (Cambridge University Press, 1997), p.8.

[267] For example, the availability of judicial review of administrative decisions affecting international trade under the WTO code of conduct (see WTO *The Results of the Uruguay Round Of Multilateral Trade Negotiations* (1994)). See also, for example, the procedures under the World Bank Convention on the International Settlement of Investment Disputes between States and National of Other States; under the 1982 UN Convention on the Law of the Sea (s.6 of Pt XI of UNCLOS); and the World Bank Convention Establishing the Multilateral Investment Guarantee Agency (MIGA). See also, for example, Kokkini-Iatridou and de Waart, "Economic disputes between States and Private parties: some legal thoughts on the institutionalization of their settlement" (1986) N.I.L.R. 33:289–333.

[268] See Seidl-Hohenveldern (1992), p.11. See also *Barcelona Traction, Light And Power Co* Case (1970) I.C.J. Reports.

directly. This is clear where such rights and duties are conferred through the instrument of international agreements.[269] It has been contended, however, even in the absence of such agreements, that the procedural bar suffered by individuals in not being able to directly invoke IEL in national or international courts does not rob the individual of the status as a participant.[270]

Finally, account needs to be taken of the role of non-governmental organisations[271] (NGOs) in the development of international economic relations. In the sense that participants have been described here, they are possibly the weakest candidates to fit into such a description. However, there is much advocacy for their increased participation in the affairs of international economic organisations.[272] Through their participation international economic organisations can be made more responsive, representative and effective. Thus, it is contended that NGOs form a "connective tissue" connecting international decision-makers with their ultimate constituencies.[273] States are not necessarily the ideal representatives of public opinion.[274] They can ignore minority opinions.[275] NGOs represent communities of interest cutting across jurisdictions, and thus increase representation[276] in international economic organisations. NGOs are able to draw attention to trans-boundary problems which governments sometimes fail to address.[277] Further, NGOs provide good competition for governments in policy analysis and advice.[278] In addition, they also act as watch dogs over governmental practices in international organisations.[279] In fact, NGOs are increasingly playing a part in the process of decision-making in international economic organisations such as the WTO,[280] World Bank[281] and the OECD[282]—although this is more at the level of exchanging of views and observing proceedings.

---

[269] Seidl-Hohenveldern (1992), p.13.

[270] Higgins (1994), Ch.3.

[271] On defining non-governmental organisations see, for example, S. Charnovitz, "Two Centuries of Participation: NGOs and International Governance" (1997) 18 *Mich Journal of International Law* 183.

[272] See, for example, D.C. Esty, "Non-Governmental Organizations At The World Trade Organization: Cooperation, Competition, Or Exclusion", *Journal of International Economic Law* 1 (1998), p.123 and references therein. See also J. Bhagwati, *In Defence of Globalization*, (OUP, 2004), pp.36–48.

[273] Esty (1998), p.126.

[274] Esty (1998).

[275] Esty (1998), p.131.

[276] Esty (1998), p.131.

[277] Esty (1998), p.124.

[278] Esty (1998).

[279] Esty (1998), p.134.

[280] Esty (1998) and see, for example, Art.V, para.2 of the Marrakesh Agreement Establishing the World Trade Organization. The Article specifically allows the General Council of the WTO to make arrangements for consultation and co-operation with NGOs. See also Director-General Renato Ruggiero's statement on enhanced co-operation with NGOs of July 17, 1998 WTO Press/107.

[281] Esty (1998) and see also, for example, P. Nelson, *The World Bank and non-governmental organizations* (New York, St. Martins and Houndmills, Macmillan Press, 1995).

[282] Esty (1998), and see also, for example, R.H. Housman, "Democratizing international trade decision-making" (1994) 27 Cornell Int'l.L.L.J. 699.

There are, however, some difficulties with NGO participation in international economic organisations.[283] First, and importantly, there are questions revolving around the degree of representation they actually enhance in international fora. Thus, it is not clear how NGOs can be identified and whether they are representative of their constituency. Secondly, there is generally a deficit in NGOs and their resources around the North/South divide of the international community. Thus, increasing the representation already enjoyed by developed States. Thirdly, NGOs have their own agenda and can distort international decision-making along the lines of their special interests. Further, NGOs already have the opportunity to lobby their respective governments at the national level.

---

[283]  Esty (1998).

### CHAPTER 2

# ECONOMIC SOVEREIGNTY

## INTRODUCTION

A fundamental role of modern International Economic Law comprises the **2-001** re-configuring of a State's economic sovereignty, such that it both better reflects the reality of human, economic, social, political, and environmental relationships across the international community; and enhances the overall capacity of States and the international community to manage global threats, such as climate change, protectionism and violations of human rights.[1] This role is set against the historical foundations of IEL wherein a State's economic sovereignty forms the basis for its internal and external economic relations. Both of these domains form the subject-matter of IEL as it is developing. As such the concept of sovereignty is critical to an understanding of IEL and its development. And herein lie some of the central problems of the subject. The relationship of IEL and State economic sovereignty, including the place of economic sovereignty in international economic relations, is increasingly being informed and clarified by international agreements and globalisation. This has led to the observation that sovereignty has "lost much of its normative or descriptive meaning".[2] Yet key international economic institutions such as the IMF and the WTO, remain very much "member/sovereignty driven". Thus, the nature and concept of economic sovereignty remains a focus of considerable discourse—particularly theoretical.

Sovereignty, it is claimed, has different meanings, dimensions and attributes.[3] Its correct understanding depends on the context in which it is used.[4] Thus,

---

[1] See Matti Koskenniemi, "What use for sovereignty today?" *Asian Journal of International Law,* 1 (2011), pp 61–70 at p.61. See also M. K. Lewis & S. Frankel (ed), *International Economic Law and National Autonomy* (CUP, 2010).

[2] See Matti Koskenniemi, "What use for sovereignty today?" *Asian Journal of International Law,* 1 (2011), pp 61–70 at p.62.

[3] See, for example, D. Sarooshi, *International Economic Organizations and their Exercise of Sovereign Powers* (Oxford, Oxford University Press, 2005), p.1 and J. Jackson, *Sovereignty, the WTO, and Changing Fundamentals of International Law* (Cambridge, Cambridge University Press, 2006), p.58.

[4] Sarooshi (2005), p.1.

according to Dan Sarooshi the concept of sovereignty "being inherently unstable and in a constant state of having its core criteria subject to contestation and change has the consequence that there is no single, or indeed authoritative, definition that can be given to the concept".[5] Sovereignty thus has been described variously—as "an essentially contested concept",[6] referring "to questions about the allocation of power; normally 'government decision-making power'".[7] At its core sovereignty is said to focus on "the monopoly of power".[8]

Moreover, discourse on loss of sovereignty needs to be set against a clear background of the sense in which the concept of "sovereignty" is being used (for example, formal or substantive). In particular, it has been contended that State sovereignty needs to be distinguished from the question of the degree of "freedom of State action".[9] Thus, with reference to the measure of a loss of State sovereignty, sovereignty can be understood as irrevocably lost where, for example, there is no possibility of withdrawal from an international economic organisation (irrevocable-based narrow conception of sovereignty); or revocably lost, where, for example, there is a possibility of withdrawal from an international economic organisation (revocability-based conception of sovereignty).[10] In both circumstances the State's freedom of action is affected but in the latter case there is no loss of sovereignty as such but rather simply its revocable delegation.[11] This distinction between freedom of State action and formal sovereignty involves a narrow conception of sovereignty. Loss of sovereignty however can also be understood in the sense where the State can ex post veto a decision of an international economic organisation (veto-based conception of sovereignty) or where State action is hindered in any manner (expansive concept of sovereignty).[12] In short, the concept of sovereignty can be open-ended. Moreover it can be an emotive response set against the ambiguities of General International Law, and the philosophical differences as to the nature of law and the State. Indeed, it can be informed by vested economic standpoints.

## ECONOMIC SOVEREIGNTY[13]

**2-002**   Economic sovereignty, in a nutshell, is both descriptive of the totality of the economic powers of a State, as well as its equal status in international

---

[5] Sarooshi (2005), pp.6–7.
[6] Sarooshi (2005), p.3.
[7] Jackson (2006), p.72.
[8] Jackson (2006), p.59.
[9] K. Raustiala, "Rethinking the Sovereignty Debate in International Economic Law" (2003) J.I.E.L. 6 (4), 841–878 at p.846.
[10] Raustiala (2003), p.846–847.
[11] Raustiala (2003), p.846.
[12] Raustiala (2003), p.847.
[13] On sovereignty and equality generally see, for example, *Oppenheim's International Law*, 9th edn, Ch.2 and references therein; L. Wildhaber, "Sovereignty and International Law" in

economic relations. In this framework, State sovereignty connotes juridical independence from the authority of the other participants in international economic relations, under International Law; and as constrained and augmented by the principle of equality as between States. Thus, Art.2 (1) of the UN Charter specifically affirms the sovereign equality of States.[14] Similarly, the principle of equality and independence has been affirmed in various UN resolutions in the economic field, as well as judicial decisions.[15]

In Public International Law the sovereignty and equality of States have been described as basic constitutional doctrines of the law of nations.[16] In IEL too, sovereignty and equality feature as basic constitutional doctrines. Sovereignty in the international economic sphere relates mainly to a State's permanent resources, to its economic system and to the rules of engagement in international economic relations. Further economic sovereignty encapsulates, as a corollary to the notions of equality and independence, both State rights and duties.

The demarcation of a State's economic sovereignty is not an exercise without controversy. A commendable attempt was made in the 1970s by the developing countries in an attempt to craft a new international economic order (NIEO).[17] In particular, stress was placed on the permanent sovereignty

R. St J. MacDonald and D.M. Johnstone (eds), *The Structure and Process of International Law* (1983) at 425; and V. Pechota, "Equality: Political Justice in an Unequal World" in *The Structure and Process of International Law* (1983), p.453; S. Waller and A. Simon, "Analysing Claims of Sovereignty in International Economic Disputes" (1985) 7 Northwestern J.of Intl L 1–4; and A.V. Lowe, "The problems of extraterritorial jurisdiction: economic sovereignty and the search for a solution" (1985) 34 I.C.L.Q. 724; I. Seidl-Hohenveldern, *International Economic Law* (1992); C. Schreuer, "The waning of the Sovereign State: Towards a New Paradigm for International Law?" (1993) 4 Eur.J.IntL L 447–471; Specifically on economic sovereignty see, for example, N. Schrijver, *Sovereignty over natural resources* (Cambridge, Cambridge University Press, 1997) and references therein; B. Kingsbury, "Sovereignty and Inequality" (1998) E.J.I.L. Vol.9, No.4, p.599; J. Jackson, "The great 1994 sovereignty debate: United States acceptance and implementation of the Uruguay Round Results", in *Essays in Honor of Louis Henkin* (1998); K Raustiala, "Rethinking the Sovereignty Debate in International Economic Law" (2003) J.I.E.L. 6 (4), 841–878; D. Sarooshi, *International Organizations and their Exercise of Sovereign Powers* (Oxford, Oxford University Press, 2005); J.H. Jackson, *Sovereignty, the WTO, and Changing Fundamentals of International Law* (Cambridge, Cambridge University Press, 2006); M. Koskenniemi, *From Apology to Utopia* (Cambridge and New York, Cambridge University Press, 2006) pp.192–263; W. Shan, P. Simons and D. Singh (eds), *Redefining Sovereignty in International Economic Law* (Forthcoming; Hart, 2007).

[14] See also Declaration On Principles Of International Law Concerning Friendly Relations And Co-operation Among States in Accordance With The United Nations Charter 1970 in Annex to GA Res 2625 (XXV).

[15] See, for example, Declaration on the Principles of International Law Concerning Friendly Relations And Co-operation Among States in Accordance with the Charter of the UN 1970; and principle (b) and Arts 1 and 10 of General Assembly Resolution 3281 (XXIX) 1974, Charter of Economic Rights And Duties of States (hereinafter referred to as CERDS). See also, for example, the decision of Max Huber in the Island of Palmas Case (1928) 2 UN Rep. Int'L Arb.Awards 829.

[16] I. Brownlie, *Principles of Public International Law*, 5th edn (Oxford, Oxford University Press, 1998), p.289.

[17] See CERD and the GA Resolution of 1962 on Permanent Sovereignty over Natural Resources (GA Res 1803) (1962). See also, for example, P. Verloren Van Themaat, *The*

over natural resources of the State.[18] Preoccupation with sovereignty was a consequence of the process of decolonisation and the attainment of independence. It was intended to deal with the inequitable arrangements inherited from the colonial era to regulate foreign economic interests within the State, and to participate more effectively in the development of IEL.[19] This attempt by the South to demarcate the contours of economic sovereignty was considered particularly controversial by developed States as it touched on sensitive questions, such as the right of States to expropriate foreign property and the consequent payment of compensation; the question of the standard of treatment of foreigners—(i.e. whether foreigners should be accorded the national standard of treatment or a minimum universal standard); and the devolution of rights and responsibilities upon State succession (specially the question whether a newly independent State started with a clean slate in terms of its international treaty obligations).[20] Developed countries reacted by stressing the principle of *pacta sunt servanda*.[21] Whilst the undercurrents of the NIEO continue,[22] there is now also a new emphasis on responsibilities of States, particularly in terms of the environment and the framework of the agenda for sustainable development.[23]

2-003    **EXAMPLE: Resolution adopted by the UN General Assembly 55/2. United Nations Millennium Declaration, 8th plenary meeting, September 8, 2000[24]**

*The General Assembly*

*Adopts* the following Declaration:

---

*Changing Structure of International Economic Law* (1981), Ch.IV; S.K. Chatterjee, "The Charter of Economic Rights and Duties of States: An evaluation after 15 years" (1991) 40 I.C.L.Q., p.669; and R.L. Barsh, "A Special Session of the UN General Assembly Rethinks the Economic Rights and Duties of States" (1991) 85 A.J.I.L., p.192 on the declaration for the co-ordination of national and international economic policies of the UN General Assembly of the 18th Special Session 1990 (UN Doc.A.A/S-18/14 (1990).

[18] See N. Schrijver, *Sovereignty over natural resources* (Cambridge, Cambridge University Press, 1997).

[19] Schrijver (1997).

[20] Schrijver (1997), especially Chs 9 and 10.

[21] Schrijver (1997).

[22] See Asif H. Qureshi "Critical Concepts in the New International Economic Order and its Impact on the Development of International Economic Law—A Tribute to the Call for a NIEO", M.J.I.E.L. Volume 7, Issue 3, 2010. pp.3–10.

[23] See the 1992 Rio Declaration on Environment and Development arising out of the UN Conference on Environment & Trade (1992) 31 I.L.M., p.874. See also, for example, M.C.W. Pinto, "The Legal Context: Concepts, Principles, Standards and Institutions", F. Weiss et al.., *"Towards International Economic Law with a Human Face"* (The Hague, Kluwer Law International, 1998); G.K. Ginther et al. (eds), *Sustainable Development and Good Governance* (Boston, Kluwer Academic, 1995); and P. Sands, "International Law in the field of Sustainable Development" (1994) B.Y.I.L., pp.303–381; D. French *International Law & Policy of Sustainable Development*, (MUP, 2005); C Voight, *Sustainable Development as a Principle of International Law* (Martin Nijhoff, 2009); D Tladi, *Sustainable Development in International Law*, (Pretoria University Law Press, 2007).

[24] Extract from Resolution adopted by the General Assembly 55/2. United Nations Millennium Declaration, 8th plenary meeting, September 8, 2000, *http://www.un.org*. (Accessed June 8, 2011).

**United Nations Millennium Declaration**

**I. Values and Principles**

4. We are determined to establish a just and lasting peace all over the world in accordance with the purposes and principles of the Charter. We rededicate ourselves to support all efforts to uphold the sovereign equality of all States, respect for their territorial integrity and political independence, resolution of disputes by peaceful means and in conformity with the principles of justice and international law, the right to self-determination of peoples which remain under colonial domination and foreign occupation, non-interference in the internal affairs of States, respect for human rights and fundamental freedoms, respect for the equal rights of all without distinction as to race, sex, language or religion and international cooperation in solving international problems of an economic, social, cultural or humanitarian character.

5. We believe that the central challenge we face today is to ensure that globalization becomes a positive force for all the world's people. For while globalization offers great opportunities, at present its benefits are very unevenly shared, while its costs are unevenly distributed. We recognize that developing countries and countries with economies in transition face special difficulties in responding to this central challenge. Thus, only through broad and sustained efforts to create a shared future, based upon our common humanity in all its diversity, can globalization be made fully inclusive and equitable. These efforts must include policies and measures, at the global level, which correspond to the needs of developing countries and economies in transition and are formulated and implemented with their effective participation.

6. We consider certain fundamental values to be essential to international relations in the twenty-first century. These include:

   • **Freedom.** Men and women have the right to live their lives and raise their children in dignity, free from hunger and from the fear of violence, oppression or injustice. Democratic and participatory governance based on the will of the people best assures these rights.

   • **Equality.** No individual and no nation must be denied the opportunity to benefit from development. The equal rights and opportunities of women and men must be assured.

   • **Solidarity.** Global challenges must be managed in a way that distributes the costs and burdens fairly in accordance with basic principles of equity and social justice. Those who suffer or who benefit least deserve help from those who benefit most.

   • **Tolerance.** Human beings must respect one other, in all their diversity of belief, culture and language. Differences within and between societies should be neither feared nor repressed, but cherished as a precious asset of humanity. A culture of peace and dialogue among all civilizations should be actively promoted.

   • **Respect for nature.** Prudence must be shown in the management of all living species and natural resources, in accordance with the precepts of sustainable development. Only in this way can the immeasurable riches provided to us by nature be preserved and passed on to our descendants. The current unsustainable patterns of production and consumption must be changed in the interest of our future welfare and that of our descendants.

- **Shared responsibility.** Responsibility for managing worldwide economic and social development, as well as threats to international peace and security, must be shared among the nations of the world and should be exercised multilaterally. As the most universal and most representative organization in the world, the United Nations must play the central role.

7. In order to translate these shared values into actions, we have identified key objectives to which we assign special significance.

## II. Peace, security and disarmament

(Section omitted)

## III. Development and poverty eradication

11. We will spare no effort to free our fellow men, women and children from the abject and dehumanizing conditions of extreme poverty, to which more than a billion of them are currently subjected. We are committed to making the right to development a reality for everyone and to freeing the entire human race from want.

12. We resolve therefore to create an environment—at the national and global levels alike—which is conducive to development and to the elimination of poverty.

13. Success in meeting these objectives depends, *inter alia*, on good governance within each country. It also depends on good governance at the international level and on transparency in the financial, monetary and trading systems. We are committed to an open, equitable, rule-based, predictable and non-discriminatory multilateral trading and financial system.

14. We are concerned about the obstacles developing countries face in mobilizing the resources needed to finance their sustained development. We will therefore make every effort to ensure the success of the High-level International and Intergovernmental Event on Financing for Development, to be held in 2001.

15. We also undertake to address the special needs of the least developed countries. In this context, we welcome the Third United Nations Conference on the Least Developed Countries to be held in May 2001 and will endeavour to ensure its success. We call on the industrialized countries:

- To adopt, preferably by the time of that Conference, a policy of duty- and quota-free access for essentially all exports from the least developed countries;

- To implement the enhanced programme of debt relief for the heavily indebted poor countries without further delay and to agree to cancel all official bilateral debts of those countries in return for their making demonstrable commitments to poverty reduction; and

- To grant more generous development assistance, especially to countries that are genuinely making an effort to apply their resources to poverty reduction.

16. We are also determined to deal comprehensively and effectively with the debt problems of low- and middle-income developing countries, through various national and international measures designed to make their debt sustainable in the long term.

17. We also resolve to address the special needs of small island developing States, by implementing the Barbados Programme of Action and the outcome of the twenty-second special session of the General Assembly rapidly and in full. We urge the international community to ensure that, in the development of a vulnerability index, the special needs of small island developing States are taken into account.

18. We recognize the special needs and problems of the landlocked developing countries, and urge both bilateral and multilateral donors to increase financial and technical assistance to this group of countries to meet their special development needs and to help them overcome the impediments of geography by improving their transit transport systems.

19. We resolve further:

- To halve, by the year 2015, the proportion of the world's people whose income is less than one dollar a day and the proportion of people who suffer from hunger and, by the same date, to halve the proportion of people who are unable to reach or to afford safe drinking water.

- To ensure that, by the same date, children everywhere, boys and girls alike, will be able to complete a full course of primary schooling and that girls and boys will have equal access to all levels of education.

- By the same date, to have reduced maternal mortality by three quarters, and under-five child mortality by two thirds, of their current rates.

- To have, by then, halted, and begun to reverse, the spread of HIV/ AIDS, the scourge of malaria and other major diseases that afflict humanity.

- To provide special assistance to children orphaned by HIV/AIDS.

- By 2020, to have achieved a significant improvement in the lives of at least 100 million slum dwellers as proposed in the 'Cities Without Slums' initiative.

20. We also resolve:

- To promote gender equality and the empowerment of women as effective ways to combat poverty, hunger and disease and to stimulate development that is truly sustainable.

- To develop and implement strategies that give young people everywhere a real chance to find decent and productive work.

- To encourage the pharmaceutical industry to make essential drugs more widely available and affordable by all who need them in developing countries.

- To develop strong partnerships with the private sector and with civil society organizations in pursuit of development and poverty eradication.

- To ensure that the benefits of new technologies, especially information and communication technologies, in conformity with recommendations contained in the ECOSOC 2000 Ministerial Declaration, are available to all.

**IV. Protecting our common environment**

21. We must spare no effort to free all of humanity, and above all our children and grandchildren, from the threat of living on a planet irredeemably spoilt by human activities, and whose resources would no longer be sufficient for their needs.

22. We reaffirm our support for the principles of sustainable development, including those set out in Agenda 21, agreed upon at the United Nations Conference on Environment and Development.

23. We resolve therefore to adopt in all our environmental actions a new ethic of conservation and stewardship and, as first steps, we resolve:

- To make every effort to ensure the entry into force of the Kyoto Protocol, preferably by the tenth anniversary of the United Nations Conference on Environment and Development in 2002, and to embark on the required reduction in emissions of greenhouse gases.

- To intensify our collective efforts for the management, conservation and sustainable development of all types of forests.

- To press for the full implementation of the Convention on Biological Diversity and the Convention to Combat Desertification in those Countries Experiencing Serious Drought and/or Desertification, particularly in Africa.

- To stop the unsustainable exploitation of water resources by developing water management strategies at the regional, national and local levels, which promote both equitable access and adequate supplies.

- To intensify cooperation to reduce the number and effects of natural and man-made disasters.

- To ensure free access to information on the human genome sequence.

**V. Human rights, democracy and good governance**

24. We will spare no effort to promote democracy and strengthen the rule of law, as well as respect for all internationally recognized human rights and fundamental freedoms, including the right to development.

25. We resolve therefore:

- To respect fully and uphold the Universal Declaration of Human Rights.

- To strive for the full protection and promotion in all our countries of civil, political, economic, social and cultural rights for all.

- To strengthen the capacity of all our countries to implement the principles and practices of democracy and respect for human rights, including minority rights.

- To combat all forms of violence against women and to implement the Convention on the Elimination of All Forms of Discrimination against Women.

- To take measures to ensure respect for and protection of the human rights of migrants, migrant workers and their families, to eliminate the increasing acts of racism and xenophobia in many societies and to promote greater harmony and tolerance in all societies.

- To work collectively for more inclusive political processes, allowing genuine participation by all citizens in all our countries.

- To ensure the freedom of the media to perform their essential role and the right of the public to have access to information.

### VI. Protecting the vulnerable

26. We will spare no effort to ensure that children and all civilian populations that suffer disproportionately the consequences of natural disasters, genocide, armed conflicts and other humanitarian emergencies are given every assistance and protection so that they can resume normal life as soon as possible.

We resolve therefore:

- To expand and strengthen the protection of civilians in complex emergencies, in conformity with international humanitarian law.

- To strengthen international cooperation, including burden sharing in, and the coordination of humanitarian assistance to, countries hosting refugees and to help all refugees and displaced persons to return voluntarily to their homes, in safety and dignity and to be smoothly reintegrated into their societies.

- To encourage the ratification and full implementation of the Convention on the Rights of the Child and its optional protocols on the involvement of children in armed conflict and on the sale of children, child prostitution and child pornography.

### VII. Meeting the special needs of Africa

(Section omitted)

### VIII. Strengthening the United Nations

(Section omitted). . .

A State's economic sovereignty can be conceived as having two dimensions— an internal and an external domain.[25]

---

[25] A State's external and internal sovereignty are not exclusive zones, and whereas there is an essential relationship and overlap between the two, for analytical purposes such a categorisation is useful.

## THE INTERNAL DOMAIN OF ECONOMIC SOVEREIGNTY

**2-004**    In general terms, internal sovereignty has been aptly described as the power of a State freely and autonomously to organise itself, and to exercise a monopoly of legitimate power within its territory.[26] An important aspect of this sovereignty is the right to development, which is a recognised principle of International Law.[27] More specifically, the following basic and interconnected propositions may be proffered in relation to the internal aspect of economic sovereignty under General International Economic Law:

- a State has permanent sovereignty over its natural resources[28];
- a State has sovereignty over the non-natural resources or economic activities within its territorial jurisdiction—including its human resources[29];
- a State has the inalienable right to choose and conduct its own economic system, i.e. it has the right of economic self-determination and governance[30]; and
- a State has the right of non-interference in its economic affairs through the threat or use of force.[31]

The first two propositions are essentially descriptive of the sovereignty over the economic resources of a State. These have traditionally been divided into two categories—viz., natural resources (e.g. land, wildlife, natural resources etc)[32]; and the non-natural resources (e.g. labour, cultural wealth, services, viz., financial services). This internal domain of sovereignty, comprising of a State's natural and non-natural resources, has also been described in terms of a State's personal sovereignty, territorial sovereignty, and its functional sovereignty.[33] The personal

---

[26] Wildhaber (1983), p.436.

[27] See Separate Opinion of Vice-President Weeramantry in Case Concerning Gabeikovo-Nagymaros Project (Hungary/Slovakia) (1997) I.C.J. Reports; and Isabella Bunn, *The Right to Development and International Economic Law: Legal and Moral Dimensions* (Oxford, Hart Publishing, 2008).

[28] See, for example, General Assembly Resolution of 1962 On Permanent Sovereignty over Natural Resources, Resolution 1803 (XVII); Art.2 of CERDS; Art.1 of the International Covenant on Economic, Social and Cultural Rights (1966); and SS. Lotus, The PCIJ, Ser.A, No.1 (1923); Brownlie (Oxford, Oxford University Press, 2003). See also Schrijver (1997), p.3.

[29] Art.1, para.1 of CERDS; and see, for example, Schrijver (1997), p.19.

[30] See, for example, Art.1 of CERDS; Art.1 of the International Covenant On Economic, Social And Cultural Rights (1966; and Declaration On Principles Of International Law Concerning Friendly Relations And Co-operation Among States in Accordance With The United Nations Charter 1970. See also Nicaragua Case (1986) I.C.J. Reports 186; Schrijver.

[31] See, for example, Art.1 of CERDS and Art.2(7) of the UN Charter; and Declaration On Principles Of International Law Concerning Friendly Relations And Co-operation Among States in Accordance With the United Nations Charter 1970.

[32] See Schrijver (1997), pp.16–19.

[33] See, for example, R.S.J. Martha, "Extraterritorial taxation in International Law" in K.M. Meessen (ed.), *Extraterritorial Jurisdiction in Theory and Practice* (Kluwer Law International, 1996), p.22.

sovereignty relates to the power a State has over its national subjects (natural and juridical) wherever they may be.[34] Territorial sovereignty refers to the power of a State within its territory over persons and its natural and non-natural resources. Functional sovereignty is a limited kind of sovereignty over specific designated regions,[35] in relation to the sea[36] for example, the continental shelf, the exclusive economic zone, the seabed and the sub-soil of the high seas; in relation to air-space, the flight information region of a State as designated by the International Civil Aviation Organisation. The latter two propositions relating to economic self-determination and non-interference are essentially about the ability of a State to organise its natural and non-natural wealth within its territory.

There has been much discourse both as between States and by way of academic commentary in relation to a State's sovereignty over its natural resources, it being an important economic resource. In relation to the rights of a State over its natural resources, Nico Schrijver based on a study of the sources of IEL lists the principal rights as follows[37]:

- the possession, use and freedom to dispose its natural resources[38];

- the free determination and control of the prospecting, exploration, development, exploitation, use and marketing of natural resources[39];

- the management and conservation of the State's natural resources pursuant to its national developmental[40] and environmental policies[41];

- the regulation of foreign investment, including regulation over the

---

[34] Martha (1996).

[35] Martha (1996).

[36] See the Law of the Sea Convention 1982.

[37] Schrijver (1997), p.391.

[38] See Schrijver, Ch.9. See also references therein, particularly Principle III of UN 1970 Declaration on Principles of International Law; Art.I of the 1966 Human Rights Covenants; Art.21 of the 1981 African Charter on Human and Peoples' Rights; Art.21.1 of the 1992 Biodiversity Convention; Texas Award (1977) 53 I.L.R., p.389; *Liamco v Libya* (1981) 62 I.L.R., p.140; *Kuwait v Aminoil* (1982) 21 I.L.M., pp.976–1053.

[39] See Schrijver (1997), Ch.9. See also references therein particularly UN GA Resolutions 626 (VII) 21 Dec 1952, 1803 (XVII), 2158 and 3171; para.4(e) of the NIEO Declaration, GA Res 3201 (1974); GA Res 523 (VI); 1958 Convention on the Continental Shelf; Art.77.1 of the 1982 Convention on the Law of the Sea; Art.25 of the International Covenant on Civil and Political Rights; International Covenant on Economic Social & Cultural Rights; Art.18 of the 1994 of the Energy Charter Treaty; Fisheries Jurisdiction Cases (1974) I.C.J. Reports; *Kuwait v Aminoil* (1982) 21 I.L.M., pp.1019–27.

[40] See Schrijver (1997), Ch.9. See also references therein particularly GA Resolutions 626 (VII), 1803 (XVII); Art.7 CERDS; Pt IV of GATT 1994; 1992 Climate Change Convention; *Saudi Arabia v Aramco Oil Co* (1958) (1963) 27 I.L.R. 117; *Kuwait v Aminoil* (1982) 21 I.L.M.; Code of Conduct of Liner Conferences (1974) 13 I.L.M., pp.917–47.

[41] See Schrijver (1997), Ch.9. See also references therein particularly Principle 21 of the 1972 Stockholm Declaration arising from the UN Conference on the Human Environment 1972 (Action plan for international co-operation and development) (1972) 11 I.L.M., p.1416; 1992 Rio Declaration on Environment and Development (1992) 31 I.L.M., p.874; Art.193 of the 1982 UN Convention on the Law of the Sea; Ozone Layer Convention (1985); Climatic Change and Biodiversity Convention (1992); Desertification Convention (1994); Art.19–3 of the Energy Charter Treaty (1994).

admission of foreign investment and the activities of foreign investors, including the outflow of capital[42]; and

• the right to nationalise or expropriate property, of both nationals and foreigners.[43]

In relation to the responsibilities of a State in the exercise of its permanent sovereignty over its natural resources Nico Schrijver identifies in particular the following duties.[44] First, the requirement that the exercise of sovereignty over economic resources must be for national development and the well-being of the inhabitants as a whole.[45] This requirement is as yet an expectation. There does not appear to be strong evidence that it is a rule of International Law as such.[46] Secondly, a requirement of respect for the rights and interests of the indigenous people. There appears to be some recognition of such a requirement.[47] The rights of the indigenous people are, however, ultimately subject to the discretion of the State.[48] Thirdly, an expectation to co-operate towards global development[49]—and par-

---

[42] See Schrijver (1997), Ch.9. See also references therein particularly ICC Guidelines for International Investments (1972); OECD Declaration & Guidelines for Multinational Enterprises (1976); Draft UN Code of conduct on TNCs (1990) UN Doc E/1990/94, June 12, 1990; GA Resolutions 1803 (XVII), 2158 (XXI), 3281 (XXIX), and 3201; Art.12 of the Havana Charter (1948); 1987 ASEAN Investment Agreement (1988) 27 I.L.M.; Art.258 Lome IV Convention; para.9 of Notes & Comments to Art.1 (b) of 1967 OECD Draft Convention on the Protection of Foreign Property (1968) 71 I.L.M.; 1973 Agreement on Arab Investment; Art.101.2 of NAFTA; Art.18.3 of Energy Charter Treaty 1994; World Bank Guidelines in World Bank Group *Legal framework for the treatment of foreign investment* Vols I and II (hereinafter referred to as World Bank Guidelines); Art.12 of the 1985 MIGA Convention; ELSI Case (1989) I.C.J. Reports; and the various Bilateral Investment Agreements (BITS).

[43] See Schrijver (1997), Ch.9. See also references therein particularly GA Resolutions 1803, 3171, 3201, 3281; NAFTA; Energy Charter Treaty (1994); Chorzow Factory Case (1928) P.C.I.J.; Anglo-Iranian Oil Co (1951–1952); *Texaco v Libya* (1982) 17 I.L.M.; *Lianco v Libya* (1981) 20 I.L.M.; *Kuwait v Aminoil* (1982) 21 I.L.M.

[44] Schrijver (1997), Ch.10.

[45] See Schrijver (1997), Ch.10. See also references therein particularly, for example, UN General Assembly Resolutions 523 (VI), 626 (VII), 1803, and 2692 (XXV); Art.21(1) of the African Charter of Human and Peoples' Rights, adopted June 27, 1981, entered into force October 21, 1986, 21 I.L.M.; 1968 African Convention on the Conservation of Nature and Natural Resources; 1978 Treaty for Amazonian Co-operation; 1985 ASEAN Agreement on the Conservation of Nature & Natural Resources.

[46] Schrijver (1997), Ch.10, p.311.

[47] See Schrijver (1997), Ch.10. See also references therein particularly, for example, UN Draft Declaration on the Rights of Indigenous Peoples UN Doc E/CN.4/Sub.2/1993/29, August 23, 1993; Principle 22 of the Rio Declaration on Environment & Development. UN Doc.A/Conf. 151/26, Vol III, August 13, 1992; Vienna Declaration adopted by the World Conference on Human Rights, UN Doc A/Con.157/23, para.20; ILO Conventions No.107 concerning the Protection and Integration of Indigenous and other Tribal and Semi-Tribal Populations in Independent Countries (1957) 328 U.N.T.S. 247; ILO Convention No.169 Concerning Indigenous and Tribal Peoples in Independent Countries (1989) 28 I.L.M.; Amazon Declaration (1989) 28 I.L.M., pp.1303–1305; 1992 Biodiversity Convention; 1994 International Tropical Timber Agreement; 1994 Desertification Convention; 1994 Energy Charter Treaty; Western Sahara Case (1995) I.C.J. Reports; World Bank Guidelines on Indigenous Peoples (1992).

[48] Schrijver (1997), p.319.

[49] See Schrijver (1997), Ch.10. See also references therein particularly, for example, UN Resolutions 837 (IX), 1314 (XIII); 1514 (XV), 2626 (1970) and 3281 (XXIX); UN Charter

ticularly to assist developing States.[50] However, this is an expectation which is to be distinguished from an actual requirement to assist in development.[51] Fourthly, there is a duty relating to the preservation of the environment—a requirement of conservation and the sustainable use of natural wealth and resources.[52] The norms here are more developed in terms of damage to the environment of other States. Thus, there is a clear obligation not to damage the environment of other States.[53] In addition, there is now a recognised principle of sustainable development under International Law, born out from UN resolutions, treaty practice, and the legal systems and cultures of the world.[54] Fifthly, there is a progressive development of a requirement that natural resources that cut across boundaries (i.e. trans-boundary natural resources e.g. water, oil, gas, and fish resources) ought to be shared equitably. At a minimum, at any rate, there is an obligation to recognise the rights of others in relation to trans-boundary resources, along with a duty to consult in matters affecting the resources.[55] This obligation, however,

chapter IX; the agreements establishing the Bretton Woods Institutions (IMF. WTO, World Bank Group); 1994 Energy Charter Treaty; 1982 UN Convention on the Law of the Sea.

[50] See Schrijver (1997), Ch.10. See also references therein particularly, for example, Arts 69 and 70 of the 1982 UN Convention on the Law of the Sea; and Phillippe Cullet, "Differential Treatment in International law: Towards a New Paradigm of Inter-state Relations" (1999) E.J.I.L. Vol.10, No.3, p.549.

[51] Schrijver (1997), pp.323–324.

[52] See Schrijver (1997), Ch.10. See also references therein particularly, for example, General Assembly Resolutions 1831 (XVII), Art.30 of chapter III of 3281 (XXIX) CERDS, 35/7 (1980), 36/6, 37/7 World Charter for Nature 1982, 3129 (1973), 3201 NIEO Declaration (1974), 3326 (XXIX), 2995 (XXVII); the Stockholm Declaration on the Human Environment (1972) especially Principles 2, 13 and 21; 1940 Washington Convention on Nature Protection & Wildlife Preservation in the Western Hemisphere 161 UNTS; African Convention on the Conservation of Natural Resources; Apia Convention on Conservation of Nature in South Pacific (1976); 1978 Treaty for Amazonian co-operation, the Amazon Declaration (1989) 28 I.L.M.; ASEAN Agreement on the Conservation of Nature & Natural Resources (1985) 15 E.P.L.; Single European Act (1987); Treaty of Maastricht (1992); Convention on Wetlands of International Importance Especially as Waterfowl Habitat and 1982 Protocol (1971) 11 I.L.M.; UNESCO Convention for the Protection of the World Cultural and Natural Heritage (1972) 11 I.L.M.; International Convention on International Trade in Endangered Species of Wild Fauna and Flora (CITIES) (1973) 12 I.L.M.; Convention on the Conservation of Migratory Species of Wild Animals (1979) 19 I.L.M.; Convention on Biological Diversity (1992) 31 I.L.M.; UN Framework Convention on Climate Change (1992) 31 I.L.M.; UN Convention to Combat Desertification in those Countries Experiencing Serious Drought and/or Desertification, Particularly in Africa (1994) 33 I.L.M.; Art.1 of the Constitution of the FAO (1945); 1982 Convention on the Law of the Sea; International Tropical Timber Agreement (1983); International Tin Agreement (1977); Lome IV Convention (1989) and Protocol 10 on Sustainable Management of Forest Resources; NAFTA; Energy Charter Treaty (1974); Marrakesh Agreement Establishing the WTO; Trail Smelter Arbitration (1938/1941); Lac Lanoux Arbitration (1957); Nuclear Tests Cases (1974) and (1995) I.C.J. Reports; Nuclear Weapons Opinion (1996) I.C.J. Reports.

[53] See Schrijver (1997), p.336.

[54] See Separate Opinion of Vice-President Weeramantry in Case Concerning Gabikovo-Nagymaros Project (Hungary/Slovakia) (1997). See Ch.17, below.

[55] Schrijver (1997), Ch.10, p.338. See also references therein particularly, for example, GA Resolution 3281 (XXIX); UN Environment Programme—Principles of Conduct in the Field of the Environment for the Guidance of States in the Harmonious Utilization of Natural Resources Shared by Two or More States (1978); Action for the Environmentally Sound Management of the Common Zambizi River System (1988) 27 I.L.M.; River Oder Case

does not constitute a requirement to share jurisdiction, or engage in a system of common management of trans-boundary natural resources.[56] Although there is an orientation in the development of IEL to embrace joint development, equitable use and the conservation of transboundary resources.[57] Finally, there is a requirement to fairly treat foreign investors—particularly those involved in a State's natural resources.[58] There are a number of aspects to this. First, there are general and basic obligations affirming State observation of International Law and international agreements.[59] Secondly, there are obligations relating to the expropriation and nationalisation of foreign property. Thus, the nationalisation or expropriation must be for public purpose,[60] non-discriminatory,[61] accompanied by compensation[62] and due process.[63]

---

(1927) P.C.I.J.; Lac Lanoux Award (1957); United States—Import of Certain Shrimps and Shrimp Products (WTO 1998).

[56] Schrijver (1997), p.338.

[57] Schrijver (1997), p.339.

[58] Schrijver (1997), Ch.10, p.344. See also references therein, particularly, for example, General Assembly Resolutions 837 (IX), 1314 (XIII), 1803 (XVII), Art.2 of 3281 (XXIX); Art.1 of Human Rights Covenants (1966); African Charter on Human & People's Rights (1981); UN Convention on the Law of the Sea (1982); ICSID Convention 1965; OIC Investment Treaty (1981); ASEAN Investment Treaty (1987); Energy Charter Treaty (1994); Bilateral Investment Treaties (see Schrijver, p.342); Barcelona Traction Case (1970) I.C.J. Reports; Draft UN Code of Conduct on Transnational Corporations, UN Doc E/1990/94; World Bank Guidelines (1992).

[59] Schrijver (1997), Ch.10, p.344 and references therein.

[60] Schrijver (1997), Ch.10. See also references therein particularly, for example, General Assembly Resolution 1803, 3201 (NIEO Declaration); Art.1 of the 1952 Protocol 1 to the European Convention for the Protection of Human Rights & Fundamental Freedoms (1950); American Convention on Human Rights (1969); African Charter on Human and People's Rights (1981); OECD Draft Convention on the Protection of Foreign Property (1967); Inter-Arab Investment Agreement (1980); OIC Investment Agreement (1981); ASEAN Investment Agreement (1987); Energy Charter Treaty (1994); NAFTA (1992); Bilateral Investment Agreements (see Schrijver, p.345); German Investments in Polish Upper Silesia Case (1926) P.C.I.J.; Chorzów Factory Case (1928) P.C.I.J.; BP v Libya (1973) 53 I.L.R. 297; Kuwait v Aminoil (1982) 21 I.L.M.; Iran–US Claims Tribunal—the American International Group case (1983), the INA Corporation case (1985), and the Amoco case (1987); ALI Third Restatement of the US Foreign Relations Law (1987).

[61] Schrijver (1997), Ch.10. See also references therein particularly, for example, Inter-Arab Investment Agreement (1980); OIC Agreement (1981); ASEAN Investment Agreement (1987); NAFTA; Energy Charter Treaty (1994); Bilateral Investment Agreements (see Schrijver, p.348); BP v Libya (1973) 53 I.L.R. 297; Amoco Case (1987) 15 Iran-US. C.T.R. 189; (1988) I.L.M.; ICC Guidelines; ALI Third Res of US Foreign Relations Law—s.712; Draft UN Code of Conduct on TNCs; World Bank Guidelines (1992).

[62] Schrijver (1997), Ch.10. See also references therein, particularly, for example, 1962 Declaration on Permanent Sovereignty (UN Gen Rees 1803); Art.1 of the First Protocol to the Council of Europe Convention; Art.21–2 of the American Convention on Human Rights (1969); Bilateral Investment Agreements; Mavrommatis Jerusalem Concessions Case (1925) P.C.I.J., Series A, No.5 (1925); German Interests in Polish Upper Silesia Case (1926) P.C.I.J., Series A, No.7 (1926), p.32; Chorzow Factory Case (1928) P.C.I.J. Series, No.17 (1928); Spanish Zones of Morocco Case (1923) RIAA (1949); Shufeldt Claim (1930) RIAA (1949); Temple of Preah-Vihear I.C.J. Re. (1962); BP Award 62 I.L.R.; Kuwait v Aminoil (1982) I.L.M.; American International Group Inc v Iran (1983 AIG Award 4 Iran-US CTR); Ebrahimi Case, Iran-US Claims Tribunal, (1994); ICC Guidelines Draft UN Code of Conduct on TNCS; ALI Third Restatement; World Bank Guidelines 1992.

[63] Schrijver (1997), Ch.10, p.344. See also references therein particularly, for example, OECD Draft Convention on the Protection of Foreign Property (1967); Inter-Arab Investment

In conclusion, a State's permanent sovereignty over its natural resources can no longer be considered in isolation. The exclusivity of the principle of permanent sovereignty has gradually been eroded by the development of international environmental law[64]and human rights, in particular in terms of basic human needs.[65] This integration has found succour in the principle of sustainable development.[66]

There is not much evidence of a systematic evaluation and focus on the constraints on a State's sovereignty over its non-natural resources. This is possibly in part because the areas covered are disparate, and there has not been an easily identifiable single homogenous development having a bearing on this dimension of a State's sovereignty. Some important in-roads can be traced however. These are mainly at the level of Conventional International Law—for example in the field of labour standards and related human rights[67]; intellectual property rights, and activities over the outer space.[68] Further, much of the international developments in relation to natural resources would, to the extent that they are relevant, also presumably have a bearing on a State's non-natural resources and activities.

One particular problem of note relating to sovereignty over non-natural **2-005** resources and activities, concerns those economic processes and activities which cannot easily be located in a particular State, and thus give rise to conflicts of sovereignty and jurisdiction.[69] This is a problem that has arisen in, for example, in the determination of an "economic process" for the purposes of determining the location of a tax subsidy[70]; and generally in the determination

---

Agreement (1980); ASEAN Investment Treaty; NAFTA (1992); Energy Charter Treaty (1994); Bilateral Investment Agreements (see Schrijver, p.360); Special Copper Tribunal Decision on the Question of Excess of Profits of Nationalized Copper in Chile (1972) 11 I.L.M.

[64] Schrijver (1997), p.377.

[65] See for example. A. Follesdal, "Sustainable development, State Sovereignty and International Justice" January 20, 2011 available at *http://papers.ssrn.com/sol3/papers.cfm?abstract_id=1744103* (Accessed June 8, 2011); E-U Petersmann, *The future of International Economic Law: A Research Agenda, European University Institute Working Paper LAW 2010/06;* and A Peters, *"Humanity as the Alpha and Omega of sovereignty"* in E.J.I.L. 20)2009),513, at 544 cited by E-U Petersmann ibid at p.26.

[66] Schrijver (1997), p.377. See Separate Opinion of Vice-President Weeramantry in Case Concerning Gabeikovo-Nagymaros Project (Hungary/Slovakia) (1998) I.C.J. Reports.

[67] See, for example, L.A. Compa and S.F. Diamond (eds), *Human rights, labour rights, and international trade* (Philadelphia, University of Pennsylvania Press, 1996).

[68] It is to be noted that a State's sovereignty over economic activities in its outer space appears to be severely limited. Thus, States can place satellites over the outer space of other States. (See Treaty On Principles Governing The Activities Of States In The Exploration And Use Of Outer Space, Including The Moon And Other Celestial Bodies (1979) I.L.M.; and R. Jennings and A. Watts (eds), *Oppenheim's International Law*, 9th edn (1992), Ch.7.)

[69] For example, the taxation of electronic commerce.

[70] See, for example, GATT Panel reports relating to the Income Tax Practices of France, Belgium and the Netherlands in BISD, 23rd Supplement; and United States—Tax Treatment for "Foreign Sales Corporations" (WT/DS108/AB/R,2000); United States—Tax Treatment for "Foreign Sales Corporations" Recourse to Art.21.5 of the DSU by the European Communities (WT/DS108/AB/RW,2000). See also J. Fisher-Zernin, "GATT versus tax treaties? The basic conflicts between international taxation methods and the rules and concepts of GATT" (1987) J.W.T.; A.H. Qureshi and R. Grynberg, "United States Tax Subsidies Under

of the source of a particular revenue item for the purposes of tax liability.[71] Thus, for example in the case of interest, is it located where the debtor resides, where the loan is made available, or the residence of the creditor?

The sovereignty of a State in terms of its ability to determine its economic system is considered inalienable,[72] but it is of course de facto subject to the impact of the globalised economy. Further, given developments in the international economic order there is now a question of the extent to which this inalienable domain at the level of General International Economic Law is intact. How much freedom do States have to engage with the domestic economy in a particular fashion? In particular, is market economy the order of the day? It has been suggested, for example, that there is now in fact a comparative advantage model of IEL wherein the State has withered away.[73] Certainly, some of the practices of the Bretton Woods institutions would tend to suggest such a development. However, whether they lead to the development of a norm of Customary International Economic Law still remains to be seen. In the first place these are multilateral agreements which still do not enjoy full universal membership of the international community, and are in the end examples of Conventional International Law practice. Secondly, both the IMF and the WTO tend to focus mainly on external economic relations on the whole. In the case of the IMF, it has both a past and on-going record of memberships of States with non-market orientated systems. Certainly, the IMF Articles of Agreement do not stipulate a particular economic system as a condition of membership. Finally, key components of State authority necessary for economic self-determination still elude multilateral control, for example the power and manner of State taxation.

International concerns in relation to individual economic human rights have a bearing[74] also on the question of the ability of a State to design its own economic system and its market orientation. The status of the individual's economic human rights as a legal constraint to the State's exercise of its economic sovereignty is apparent, although the nature of the individual's economic human rights is not necessarily clear. It is not very clear, for example, if there is a human right to own property,[75] let alone the right of foreigners to acquire foreign property. In the view of one commentator the only reason

---

Domestic International Sales Corporation, Foreign Sales Corporation and Extraterritorial Income Exclusion Act Legislation Within the Framework of the World Trade Organization", J.W.T. Vol.36, No.5, October 2002, pp.979–99.

[71] See, for example, K. Vogel, "Worldwide vs. source taxation of income—a review and re-evaluation of arguments" (1988) *INTERTAX*.

[72] See Art.1 of CERDS.

[73] See D.M. McRae, "The contribution of International trade Law to the Development of International Law" (1996) *Recueil des Cours*.

[74] See, for example, M. Hilf and E. Petersmann (eds), *National Constitutions and International Economic Law* (1993). See also Arts 17 and 23 of the Universal Declaration of Human Rights (UN Doc.A/811); Arts 3, 6, 7, 8 and 15 International Covenant On Economic, Social And Cultural Rights.

[75] See I. Seidl-Hohenveldern, *International Economic Law* (The Hague, Kluwer, 1987), p.132 (see also 1992 edn) wherein he points to the obiter dictum in the Barcelona Traction Case

for the existence of the State is to facilitate maximum individual economic rights.[76] However, this view may be controversial for some, although the traditional Western negative view that human rights are confined to civil and political rights appears to be softening up.[77] However, at present generally there are few limits under general IEL on the power of a State to restrict and regulate the economic activities of its citizens[78]; including its taxing capacity.

Finally, interference of an economic character in the political or economic affairs of another State appears not to be prohibited. Thus, the introduction of subsidised goods in the economy of another State, the erosion of another State's tax incentives through the credit method of double taxation relief, the control of prices of goods sold in another country, are all practices that are not prohibited under General International Law.[79] Indeed, it has been contended that financial support of another candidate in a foreign election is not considered to be an objectionable interference.[80] Similarly, there is a practice of interference in another State through wireless transmission and remote sensing by satellite, albeit along with a right to jam by the target State.[81]

### The internal domain of economic sovereignty and International Economic Organisations

A State's internal sovereignty is increasingly impacted upon by global governance (i.e. the phenomenon of norm generation by international economic organisations directed at the domain of a State's internal sovereignty). Thus, the IMF, the WTO and the World Bank Group in particular are said to impact upon national economic decision-making. This generation of governance has evoked discourse in terms of the erosion of State sovereignty and freedom of State action.

**2-006**

One seminal work which seeks to question this perception of erosion of State economic sovereignty as a consequence of State participation in international economic organisations is that of Karl Raustiala.[82] The author points out that discourse on erosion of sovereignty in this context must be set against a clearly set out concept of sovereignty.[83] Moreover, it must take into account the reality of globalisation which has meant that State sovereignty is already considerably diminished.[84] The traditional autonomy in economic affairs that the State enjoyed on its own can no longer be achieved in a world

---

(1970) I.C.J. Report where the court appears not to have considered the right to own property as a basic human right.

[76] See Petersmann and Hilf (1993), Ch.1.

[77] R. Higgins, *Problems and Process* (Oxford, Clarendon Press, 1994), p.99.

[78] See Petersmann (1993), p.31.

[79] But note the US view when the practices affect the US (the effects doctrine see above).

[80] See Seidl-Hohenveldern (1987), p.103 basing his observation on *ITTSA v OPIC* (1974) 13 I.L.M., p.1346.

[81] I. Seidl-Hohenveldern (1987), pp.106–108.

[82] Raustiala.

[83] Raustiala (2003), p.844.

[84] Raustiala (2003), p.857.

order with fluid economic borders, as a consequence of interdependence in international relations and technological advances.[85] Thus, at one level it is contended that sovereignty through membership of international economic organisations is not affected (although State freedom of action may be circumscribed) given that a State can always withdraw from the organisation or alternatively engage the option of ex post veto of the decisions of the international organisation.[86] More significantly, it is contended, that international organisations play in fact a "sovereignty-strengthening" role.[87] This is mainly for the following reasons. First, decisions that were formerly made at the national level are made at the international level more objectively without the "rent-seeking" influence of vested parties on relevant decision makers in government, at the level of the State.[88] In this manner, popular sovereignty is better served and State goals are better achieved. Secondly, it is contended that international economic organisations actually serve to equip States to preserve their economic sovereignty against some of the negative influences of globalisation.[89]

Karl Raustiala's conclusions are sound and need to be taken seriously. However, there is a premise here that some of the globalisation resulting in the erosion of State economic sovereignty is not attributable to the very fact of membership in international economic organisations, and the role of these organisations in international economic relations. Moreover, "rent-seeking" can take place also in international organisations—not to mention the phenomenon of "State rent-seeking" within international economic organisations.

## THE EXTERNAL DOMAIN OF ECONOMIC SOVEREIGNTY

**2-007**    The domain of a State's external economic sovereignty is concerned with its international economic status and capacity to operate externally. This status and capacity is one of independence and equality in relation to other subjects under International Law.[90]

The notion of sovereign equality is particularly important in a discourse relating to the external domain of a State's economic sovereignty. This is because it is the domain where the question of "equality" has to be addressed more frequently in various forms. Sovereign equality is a juridical construct, and can be a factual condition, as well as an aspiration. Juridically, sovereign

---

[85] Raustiala (2003), p.860.
[86] Raustiala (2003), p.846.
[87] Raustiala (2003).
[88] Raustiala (2003), p.864.
[89] Raustiala (2003), p.863.
[90] See Wildhaber (1983), p.437.

equality can have two components. It is a requirement for equality, but can also imply equal treatment under similar conditions.

As a requirement for equality it implies in particular the following[91]:

- All States are equal under International Law. All States enjoy the same level of protection under it.

- All States enjoy the same capacity to acquire rights and assume obligations.

- All States have an equal capacity to bring international claims and have equal standing in procedures for conflict resolution.

- All States are entitled to respect and consideration before the law as States.

- Where there is differential treatment this is to be justified on relevant and objective criteria.

As a requirement for equal treatment under similar conditions equality can imply differential treatment. According to Phillippe Cullet,[92] differential treatment "refers to instances where the principle of sovereign equality is sidelined to accommodate extraneous factors, such as divergences in levels of economic development or unequal capacities to tackle a given problem".[93] This is a helpful description although it controversially implies that differential treatment is not the consequence of sovereign equality rather a consequence of its displacement. It is not clear whether this was really the intention of the author given his general analysis of differential treatment.

Although in international economic relations differential treatment is normally based on levels of economic development (viz., per capita GNP), differential treatment can also be based on other grounds for instance share of international trade, resources under the territorial sovereignty of a State, and geographical location.[94] The differential treatment can take different forms, for instance non-reciprocity in international trade negotiations, different implementation periods, technical assistance or aid.[95] Thus, differential treatment can be substantive and procedural.[96]

According to Phillipe Cullet, differential treatment is to be distinguished **2-008** from the giving of charity.[97] Differential treatment is accorded on the basis

---

[91] Wildhaber (1983), pp.463–465.
[92] Phillippe Cullet, "Differential Treatment in International Law: Towards a New Paradigm of Inter-state Relations" (1999) E.J.I.L., Vol.10. No.3, pp.549–582.
[93] Cullet (1999), p.551.
[94] Cullet (1999), p.556.
[95] Cullet (1999), p.552.
[96] Cullet (1999).
[97] Cullet (1999), p.558.

of some form of objective criteria and is intended to empower weaker participants.[98] Its basis can be grounded on notions of justice (distributive justice),
equity and, in particular, the principle of equality—especially substantive
equality.[99] Raj Bhala[100] on the other hand constructs a theological framework within which differing types of differential treatment may be encompassed. Thus, he suggests that differential treatment can be understood in
terms of: Homiletic Rules (Exhortation to developed States); Mortification
Rules (surrender of rights or forbearance in exercising them); Merciful
Rules; and Almsgiving (gratis transfer). There is no serious divergence here
between the two authors apart from Almsgiving. But, as Bhala asserts, these
theological rules are not exclusive and differential treatment may partake of
elements of all four rules. In other words differential treatment may encompass Almsgiving. Moreover his explanation is as much normative—directed
at motivations for differential treatment as it is about explaining their true
character. To the extent of the former there would appear to be no serious
divergence between the two authors. There is still however here a lingering
question namely, although Almsgiving may take the form of differential
treatment, can certain types of differential treatment be properly described
as charitable acts?

The objectives of differential treatment have been described as follows[101]:

- to facilitate substantive equality in an international system based on
  formal equality;

- to enable States to co-operate; and

- to facilitate better and effective implementation.

Thus, differential treatment, it is claimed, enables co-operation amongst
States because of the principle of solidarity and partnership in international
relations[102]; redistributive policies which serve the interests of developed
States, for example the securing of access to primary resources in developing
countries, and ensuring a growing market in developing countries for exports
from developed States.[103]

Although differential treatment has existed in the international system
as a principle for decades,[104] its real significance emerged after the Second
World War during the period after decolonisation and the emergence

---

[98]  Cullet (1999), p.558.
[99]  Cullet (1999), p.555. See also, for example, T.M. Franck, *Fairness in International Law and Institutions* (Oxford, Oxford University Press, 1997), especially Chs 1, 13 and 14; R. Bhala, *Trade, Development, and Social Justice* (Durham, Carolina Academic Press, 2003).
[100] See Bhala (2003).
[101] Bhala (2003), pp.552–553.
[102] Bhala (2003), p.558.
[103] Bhala (2003), p.560.
[104] Bhala (2003), p.564. Cullet (1999) gives the example of reservation in multilateral agreements as an instance of the principle.

of developing States; and the integration of the international economic system.[105] Thus, there have been various international instruments in the international economic and environmental spheres wherein differential treatment provisions are to be found. The advent of this principle in particular is to be attributed to (i) developing countries' increased bargaining position in certain international organisations, for example the WTO; and (ii) where the self-interest of developed States is served,[106] for example in the environmental sphere.

**EXAMPLE: WTO, Annex 1a, GATT 1994, Part VI of GATT 1947[107]**

Part IV: Trade and Development                                          **2-009**

**Article XXXVI: Principles and Objectives**

1.* The contracting parties,

    (a) recalling that the basic objectives of this Agreement include the raising of standards of living and the progressive development of the economies of all contracting parties, and considering that the attainment of these objectives is particularly urgent for less-developed contracting parties;

    (b) considering that export earnings of the less-developed contracting parties can play a vital part in their economic development and that the extent of this contribution depends on the prices paid by the less-developed contracting parties for essential imports, the volume of their exports, and the prices received for these exports;

    (c) noting, that there is a wide gap between standards of living in less-developed countries and in other countries;

    (d) recognizing that individual and joint action is essential to further the development of the economies of less-developed contracting parties and to bring about a rapid advance in the standards of living in these countries;

    (e) recognizing that international trade as a means of achieving economic and social advancement should be governed by such rules and procedures—and measures in conformity with such rules and procedures—as are consistent with the objectives set forth in this Article;

    (f) noting that the CONTRACTING PARTIES may enable less-developed contracting parties to use special measures to promote their trade and development;

agree as follows.

2. There is need for a rapid and sustained expansion of the export earnings of the less-developed contracting parties.

3. There is need for positive efforts designed to ensure that less-developed

---

[105] Bhala (2003), p.564.
[106] Bhala (2003), p.574.
[107] *http://www.wto.org.* (Accessed: June 8, 2011).

contracting parties secure a share in the growth in international trade commensurate with the needs of their economic development.

4. Given the continued dependence of many less-developed contracting parties on the exportation of a limited range of primary products,* there is need to provide in the largest possible measure more favourable and acceptable conditions of access to world markets for these products, and wherever appropriate to devise measures designed to stabilize and improve conditions of world markets in these products, including in particular measures designed to attain stable, equitable and remunerative prices, thus permitting an expansion of world trade and demand and a dynamic and steady growth of the real export earnings of these countries so as to provide them with expanding resources for their economic development.

5. The rapid expansion of the economies of the less-developed contracting parties will be facilitated by a diversification* of the structure of their economies and the avoidance of an excessive dependence on the export of primary products. There is, therefore, need for increased access in the largest possible measure to markets under favourable conditions for processed and manufactured products currently or potentially of particular export interest to less-developed contracting parties.

6. Because of the chronic deficiency in the export proceeds and other foreign exchange earnings of less-developed contracting parties, there are important inter-relationships between trade and financial assistance to development. There is, therefore, need for close and continuing collaboration between the CONTRACTING PARTIES and the international lending agencies so that they can contribute most effectively to alleviating the burdens these less-developed contracting parties assume in the interest of their economic development.

7. There is need for appropriate collaboration between the CONTRACTING PARTIES, other intergovernmental bodies and the organs and agencies of the United Nations system, whose activities relate to the trade and economic development of less-developed countries.

8. The developed contracting parties do not expect reciprocity for commitments made by them in trade negotiations to reduce or remove tariffs and other barriers to the trade of less-developed contracting parties.*

9. The adoption of measures to give effect to these principles and objectives shall be a matter of conscious and purposeful effort on the part of the contracting parties both individually and jointly.

### Article XXXVII: Commitments

1. The developed contracting parties shall to the fullest extent possible—that is, except when compelling reasons, which may include legal reasons, make it impossible—give effect to the following provisions:

    (a) accord high priority to the reduction and elimination of barriers to products currently or potentially of particular export interest to less-developed contracting parties, including customs duties and other restrictions which differentiate unreasonably between such products in their primary and in their processed forms;*

    (b) refrain from introducing, or increasing the incidence of, customs duties or non-tariff import barriers on products currently or potentially of particular export interest to less-developed contracting parties; and

(c) (i) refrain from imposing new fiscal measures, and

(ii) in any adjustments of fiscal policy accord high priority to the reduction and elimination of fiscal measures, which would hamper, or which hamper, significantly the growth of consumption of primary products, in raw or processed form, wholly or mainly produced in the territories of less-developed contracting parties, and which are applied specifically to those products.

2. (a) it is considered that effect is not being given to any of the provisions of subparagraph (*a*), (*b*) or (*c*) of paragraph 1, the matter shall be reported to the CONTRACTING PARTIES either by the contracting party not so giving effect to the relevant provisions or by any other interested contracting party.

(b) (i) CONTRACTING PARTIES shall, if requested so to do by any interested contracting party, and without prejudice to any bilateral consultations that may be undertaken, consult with the contracting party concerned and all interested contracting parties with respect to the matter with a view to reaching solutions satisfactory to all contracting parties concerned in order to further the objectives set forth in Article XXXVI. In the course of these consultations, the reasons given in cases where effect was not being given to the provisions of subparagraph (*a*), (*b*) or (*c*) of paragraph 1 shall be examined.

(ii) As the implementation of the provisions of subparagraph (*a*), (*b*) or (*c*) of paragraph 1 by individual contracting parties may in some cases be more readily achieved where action is taken jointly with other developed contracting parties, such consultation might, where appropriate, be directed towards this end.

(iii) The consultations by the CONTRACTING PARTIES might also, in appropriate cases, be directed towards agreement on joint action designed to further the objectives of this Agreement as envisaged in paragraph 1 of Article XXV.

3. The developed contracting parties shall:

(a) make every effort, in cases where a government directly or indirectly determines the resale price of products wholly or mainly produced in the territories of less-developed contracting parties, to maintain trade margins at equitable levels;

(b) give active consideration to the adoption of other measures* designed to provide greater scope for the development of imports from less-developed contracting parties and collaborate in appropriate international action to this end;

(c) have special regard to the trade interests of less-developed contracting parties when considering the application of other measures permitted under this Agreement to meet particular problems and explore all possibilities of constructive remedies before applying such measures where they would affect essential interests of those contracting parties.

4. Less-developed contracting parties agree to take appropriate action in implementation of the provisions of Part IV for the benefit of the trade of other less-developed contracting parties, in so far as such action is consistent with their individual present and future development, financial and trade needs taking into account past trade developments as well as the trade interests of less-developed contracting parties as a whole.

5. In the implementation of the commitments set forth in paragraph 1 to 4 each contracting party shall afford to any other interested contracting party or contracting parties full and prompt opportunity for consultations under the normal procedures of this Agreement with respect to any matter or difficulty which may arise.

## Article XXXVIII: Joint Action

1. The contracting parties shall collaborate jointly, with the framework of this Agreement and elsewhere, as appropriate, to further the objectives set forth in Article XXXVI.

2. In particular, the CONTRACTING PARTIES shall:

   (a) where appropriate, take action, including action through international arrangements, to provide improved and acceptable conditions of access to world markets for primary products of particular interest to less-developed contracting parties and to devise measures designed to stabilize and improve conditions of world markets in these products including measures designed to attain stable, equitable and remunerative prices for exports of such products;

   (b) seek appropriate collaboration in matters of trade and development policy with the United Nations and its organs and agencies, including any institutions that may be created on the basis of recommendations by the United Nations Conference on Trade and Development;

   (c) collaborate in analysing the development plans and policies of individual less-developed contracting parties and in examining trade and aid relationships with a view to devising concrete measures to promote the development of export potential and to facilitate access to export markets for the products of the industries thus developed and, in this connection, seek appropriate collaboration with governments and international organizations, and in particular with organizations having competence in relation to financial assistance for economic development, in systematic studies of trade and aid relationships in individual less-developed contracting parties aimed at obtaining a clear analysis of export potential, market prospects and any further action that may be required;

   (d) keep under continuous review the development of world trade with special reference to the rate of growth of the trade of less-developed contracting parties and make such recommendations to contracting parties as may, in the circumstances, be deemed appropriate;

   (e) collaborate in seeking feasible methods to expand trade for the purpose of economic development, through international harmonization and adjustment of national policies and regulations, through technical and commercial standards affecting production, transportation and marketing, and through export promotion by the

> establishment of facilities for the increased flow of trade information and the development of market research; and
>
> (f) establish such institutional arrangements as may be necessary to further the objectives set forth in Article XXXVI and to give effect to the provision of this Part.

The question whether there is now a widespread State practice such that there is a legally binding customary norm of International Law to accord differential treatment is considered still a matter of debate, indeed dispute.[108] Many differential treatment provisions in treaty law are couched in soft law or hortatory fashion.[109] In international environmental law the principle seems more established, although in a limited context. However, even here it is considered as not yet having gained the currency of a customary International Law norm.[110] According to Phillipe Cullet, it is doubtful whether there is now clear State practice affirming the principle of deferential treatment as a customary norm of International Law.

**2-010**

Unfortunately, despite Phillipe Cullet's excellent work in this field there is still more room for rigorous analysis on the legal status of the principle of differential treatment in IEL.[111] The prevailing conclusion that there is no such binding principle in general International Law is arrived at with more caution than normal in the inferences to be drawn from the building blocks of IEL. It is necessary to examine more closely domestic State practice, as it is to examine differential treatment in the framework of the disparate fields of international economic law. There is now arguably a substantial body of material, based on State and bilateral practice[112]; UN General Assembly resolutions[113]; regional economic agreements[114]; multilateral agreements,[115] which in their totality continue to place the question of the status of differential treatment as a general principle of IEL, very much on the international agenda.

---

[108] Bhala (2003), pp.575 and 576.

[109] Bhala (2003).

[110] Bhala (2003), p.579.

[111] Aside from Phillipe Cullet's work cited above see also, for example, Y. Abdulqawi, *Legal Aspects of Trade Preferences for Developing States: A Study in the influence of Development Needs on the Evolution of International Law* (The Hague/Boston, M. Nijhoff, 1982); and Verwey, "The Principle of Preferential Treatment for Developing Countries" (1983) 23 Indian J.Intl Law 343.

[112] For example in the field of taxation double taxation agreements based on the UN Model Double Taxation Convention between Developed and Developing Countries, 2001; and domestic tax legislation which accords differential treatment to developing countries viz., unilateral tax sparing provisions (see for example V. Thuronyi, *Tax Law Design & Drafing* Volume 2 (IMF, 1998) at p.1016).

[113] See, for example, Arts 4, 8, 9, 10, 11, 13, 14, 17, 18, 19, 20, 22, 24, 25, 26, 28, 29 and 30 of CERDS.

[114] See, for example, Lome IV Convention 29 I.L.M.

[115] See, for example, the IMF, WTO and the World Bank Group. See also international environmental agreements for example Preamble to the Agreement Establishing the WTO; Principles 2 and 11 of the Rio Declaration on the Environment and Development and United States—Import of Certain Shrimp and Shrimp Products WTO (1998).

### Voting in International Economic Organisations as an Aspect of External Sovereignty

**2-011**  The disparity between the legal condition and the economic condition of the state has given rise to some tension in international economic relations. The tension has been generated by the endeavour of developing States to liberate themselves from "inequality", and the anxiety of developed States in some of the processes involved in such an aspiration. This tension has been particularly evident in the processes of decision making in international economic organisations. Indeed, the manner of such State participation in international economic organisations provides a good measure and insight generally into the external aspects of State sovereignty.

The voting strength of a State in the decision making processes of international economic organisations is a good measure of external economic sovereignty. Both the condition of one State one vote and the aspiration of one state one vote, has given rise to much political unease amongst developed States, who form a voting minority under such circumstances. The debate, however, as to the appropriate manner of decision making in international economic organisations has become unduly distracted by the perceived need to react to the claims by developing States of equality in voting strength based on sovereign equality. Furthermore, there is a barely disguised correlation between the perceptions of jurists and those of their nation's. This does beg the question whether the jurists have shown the independence of mind and detachment that their vocation calls for. Thus, religiously it has been pointed out that whereas a State may well have juridical sovereign equality, a distinction needs to be made between it and material sovereignty. From this distinction, between substance and form, has gone on the argument that the formal equality is in fact meaningless.[116]

Such reasoning is emotive and extreme in the manner in which it is formulated. The doctrine of sovereign equality is significant. It is not merely in its own right an established doctrine of statehood in International Law, but critically is an articulation of the basic human rights of individuals whatever

---

[116] See, for example, G. Schwarzenberger, "The principles and standards of international economic law" (1966) *Recueil des Cours* pp.27 and 31: "Without a minimum of political, economic or military de facto independence, de jure independence is meaningless."; and P.V. Van Themmaat, *The Changing Structure of International Economic Law* (Netherlands, Brill, 1981) p.267: ". . . legal independence without a sufficient degree of economic independence is worth little"; Seidl-Hohenveldern (1987), p.23 wherein he states: "One may see a certain logical inconsistency in the fact that developing countries, on the one hand rely on the notion of sovereign equality, which thanks to the 'one vote one State' rule grants them a comfortable two-thirds majority in the United Nations General Assembly, while stressing, on the other hand, the obvious fact that they do not enjoy the same wealth and power as those developed States, in order to obtain special treatment."; R.A. Klein, quoted in Jackson, *Legal Problems of International Economic Relations*, 3rd edn (1995), p.260: ". . . there is a gross disproportion between voting power and real power. The smallest and financially weakest States, representing economic minority of the total population in the organization possess a majority of the votes. . .All this is manifestly unjust.".

their origins. The State is not a mere artificial construct; it comprises in the end an aggregate of individuals.[117] To deprecate the principle of sovereign equality in this context in so scathing a manner is to undermine the basic human rights of the individuals in developing States in the manner in which they have a stake in multilateral institutional governance that affects them. The International Law on human rights has evolved in such a manner that its development can only have reinforced the doctrine of sovereign equality of States.

It is of course self-evident that just as individuals are different in their economic status, so are States. This does not undermine the validity of the doctrine of sovereign equality of States, nor the significance of such a legal principle. The debate as to how votes are to be distributed in international economic organisations is one which largely focuses on how voting practices in such organisations might be. There is however a legal paradox which needs to be pointed. This is that where States in an economic organisation agree to work towards objectives of that organisation, against the background of relevant criteria as set out in the constitution of the respective organisation, differences in voting status encapsulate notions of working practices which may not necessarily conform to those set out in the agreement, and the spirit with which the agreement is entered into. Of course States enter into membership of an organisation consenting to the differential status in their voting status (where that is the case); and therefore the laden consideration in the difference of voting is implicitly part of the agreement. It is however ultimately subject to the express provisions of the agreement. There is therefore, at a minimum, a legal responsibility in the exercise of the differential voting prowess. Thus, the differential vote must be exercised in a manner that gives due respect and consideration to the notion of sovereign equality of States.

Arguments in favour of differential voting structures in international **2-012** economic organisations emphasise political realism, and the objective of ensuring the effective functioning of an organisation along the lines of its objectives.[118] It would appear that such arguments echo the notion of law as a process of decision-making, rather than as a body of rules. Such perspectives are to be discerned when it comes to voting, even by jurists with a traditional rule-based conception of law.

The issue here with differential participation in international economic organisations is as much an absolute one, as it is one of degree and emphasis. Of course it is self-evident that States are predisposed to perpetuating their self interest. But it does not logically, irrefutably and automatically follow from this that international economic organisations will not function effectively if they do not mirror this reality. The considerations that motivate

---

[117] V. Pechota, "Equality: political Justice in an unequal world" (1993), p.453.
[118] See S. Zamora, "Voting in International Economic Organizations" (1980) Vol.74 A.J.I.L., p.566.

the modern State into action are complex, and cannot be reduced to mere self-interest. In this civilised era, States are not mere automatons responding to perceived self-interest. There is a domain of a civilised perspective that differentiates the modern State from its predecessor, which thought nothing of conquests through brute force. Some of the debate on voting has been conducted in ignorance of this rational domain of the State.

The distribution of voting rights is a complex issue, and depends on the subject-matter and the circumstances involved. The debate cannot be conducted at the level of generalities. In some situations a voting formula that does not reflect the sovereign equality of States is not appropriate. This is particularly so where the decisions involved are legislative in character, and where the particular State interest is not directly relevant. Thus, it has been rightly pointed out that on a technical issue there is no reason why the vote of a US expert should be higher than that of a Swiss or Luxembourg expert.[119] In other circumstances there might be a case for differentiation, provided it is based on objective and relevant criteria.

Voting power in international economic organisations can take the form of one state one vote. This reflects the sovereign equality of States—at any rate at a formal level. This is the case in the WTO. It appears to have been accepted by developed Members of the WTO (although with some rancour) because trade concessions are negotiated and not voted upon; decision making is in practice through a consensus mode; and the system generally is fairly dependent in its implementation on the economic strength of the parties involved.[120] One State one vote seems to be more a characteristic of international bodies which are involved in recommendatory activities, such as UNCTAD.[121] These organisations influence the development of the law but do not actually bind members.

2-013       EXAMPLE: Marrakesh Agreement Establishing the World Trade
            Organization (WTO Agreement (1994))[122]

            . . .

            **Article IX Decision-Making**

            1. The WTO shall continue the practice of decision-making by consensus
               followed under GATT 1947. Except as otherwise provided, where a
               decision cannot be arrived at by consensus, the matter at issue shall be
               decided by voting. At meetings of the Ministerial Conference and the

[119] See *Towards a New Bretton Woods, Challenges for the World Financial and Trading System* (Report by a Commonwealth Study Group, 1983); and R. Gerster, "Proposals for voting reform with the International Monetary Fund" (1993) J.W.T. See also H.G. Schermers and N.M. Blokker, *International Institutional Law*, 3rd revised edn (1995), para.792 (see also 4th edition, 2004).
[120] Zamora (1980), p.591.
[121] Zamora (1980), p.589.
[122] *http://www.wto.org* (footnotes not included). (Accessed June 8, 2011).

General Council, each Member of the WTO shall have one vote. Where the European Communities exercise their right to vote, they shall have a number of votes equal to the number of their member States which are Members of the WTO. Decisions of the Ministerial Conference and the General Council shall be taken by a majority of the votes cast, unless otherwise provided in this Agreement or in the relevant Multilateral Trade Agreement.

2. The Ministerial Conference and the General Council shall have the exclusive authority to adopt interpretations of this Agreement and of the Multilateral Trade Agreements. In the case of an interpretation of a Multilateral Trade Agreement in Annex 1, they shall exercise their authority on the basis of a recommendation by the Council overseeing the functioning of that Agreement. The decision to adopt an interpretation shall be taken by a three-fourths majority of the Members. This paragraph shall not be used in a manner that would undermine the amendment provisions in Article X.

3. In exceptional circumstances, the Ministerial Conference may decide to waive an obligation imposed on a Member by this Agreement or any of the Multilateral Trade Agreements, provided that any such decision shall be taken by three fourths (4) of the Members unless otherwise provided for in this paragraph.

   (a) A request for a waiver concerning this Agreement shall be submitted to the Ministerial Conference for consideration pursuant to the practice of decision-making by consensus. The Ministerial Conference shall establish a time-period, which shall not exceed 90 days, to consider the request. If consensus is not reached during the time-period, any decision to grant a waiver shall be taken by three fourths4 of the Members.

   (b) A request for a waiver concerning the Multilateral Trade Agreements in Annexes 1A or 1B or 1C and their annexes shall be submitted initially to the Council for Trade in Goods, the Council for Trade in Services or the Council for TRIPS, respectively, for consideration during a time-period which shall not exceed 90 days. At the end of the time-period, the relevant Council shall submit a report to the Ministerial Conference.

4. A decision by the Ministerial Conference granting a waiver shall state the exceptional circumstances justifying the decision, the terms and conditions governing the application of the waiver, and the date on which the waiver shall terminate. Any waiver granted for a period of more than one year shall be reviewed by the Ministerial Conference not later than one year after it is granted, and thereafter annually until the waiver terminates. In each review, the Ministerial Conference shall examine whether the exceptional circumstances justifying the waiver still exist and whether the terms and conditions attached to the waiver have been met. The Ministerial Conference, on the basis of the annual review, may extend, modify or terminate the waiver.

5. Decisions under a Plurilateral Trade Agreement, including any decisions on interpretations and waivers, shall be governed by the provisions of that Agreement.

**2-014**    A particular feature of international economic organisations however is the system of weighted voting.[123] Under this system voting rights are distributed amongst States according to a set criteria—normally intended to reflect the economic weight of the State, and/or its contribution to the organisation and its economic interest. The actual formula used can differ, and normally all States have a number of initial equal votes (to reflect the notion of equality), which are then supplemented by additional votes, according to the particular formula for weighted voting. In the formulation and application of the criteria used to determine weighted voting, there can be an interplay of political considerations.[124] The IMF, World Bank, regional development banks, IFAD, international commodity councils, and regional economic organisations such as the EU, all have a system of weighted voting in one form or another.[125] According to one commentator[126] weighted voting is a feature of "task-orientated" international economic organisations. In order to function efficiently these organisations need to be certain that the members involved will participate in the implementation of the decisions taken.

> **EXAMPLE: Articles of Agreement of the International Monetary Fund[127]**
>
> **2-015**    **Article XII—Organization and Management**
>
> *Section 1. Structure of the Fund*
>
> The Fund shall have a Board of Governors, an Executive Board, a Managing Director, and a staff, and a Council if the Board of Governors decides, by an eighty-five percent majority of the total voting power, that the provisions of Schedule D shall be applied.
>
> *Section 2. Board of Governors*
>
> (a) All powers under this Agreement not conferred directly on the Board of Governors, the Executive Board, or the Managing Director shall be vested in the Board of Governors. The Board of Governors shall consist of one Governor and one Alternate appointed by each member in such manner as it may determine. Each Governor and each Alternate shall serve until a new appointment is made. No Alternate may vote except in the absence of his principal. The Board of Governors shall select one of the Governors as Chairman.
>
> (b) The Board of Governors may delegate to the Executive Board authority to exercise any powers of the Board of Governors, except the powers conferred directly by this Agreement on the Board of Governors.
>
> (c) The Board of Governors shall hold such meetings as may be provided for by the Board of Governors or called by the Executive Board. Meetings

---

[123] See, for example, J. Gold, "Weighted Voting Power in the Fund: Some Limits" in *Legal and Institutional Aspects of the International Monetary System: Selected Essays* (Washington, IMF, 1979), p.292; and Schermers and Blockker (1995).

[124] See Schermers and Blokker (1995), para.799.

[125] See Schermers and Blokker (1995), para.799.

[126] Zamora (1980), p.588.

[127] Source: *http://www.imf.org*. (Accessed June 8, 2011).

of the Board of Governors shall be called whenever requested by fifteen members or by members having one-quarter of the total voting power.

(d) A quorum for any meeting of the Board of Governors shall be a majority of the Governors having not less than two-thirds of the total voting power.

(e) Each Governor shall be entitled to cast the number of votes allotted under Section 5 of this Article to the member appointing him.

(f) The Board of Governors may by regulation establish a procedure whereby the Executive Board, when it deems such action to be in the best interests of the Fund, may obtain a vote of the Governors on a specific question without calling a meeting of the Board of Governors.

(g) The Board of Governors, and the Executive Board to the extent authorized, may adopt such rules and regulations as may be necessary or appropriate to conduct the business of the Fund.

(h) Governors and Alternates shall serve as such without compensation from the Fund, but the Fund may pay them reasonable expenses incurred in attending meetings.

(i) The Board of Governors shall determine the remuneration to be paid to the Executive Directors and their Alternates and the salary and terms of the contract of service of the Managing Director.

(j) The Board of Governors and the Executive Board may appoint such committees as they deem advisable. Membership of committees need not be limited to Governors or Executive Directors or their Alternates.

*Section 3. Executive Board*

(a) The Executive Board shall be responsible for conducting the business of the Fund, and for this purpose shall exercise all the powers delegated to it by the Board of Governors.

(b) The Executive Board shall consist of Executive Directors with the Managing Director as chairman. Of the Executive Directors:

  (i) five shall be appointed by the five members having the largest quotas; and

  (ii) fifteen shall be elected by the other members.

For the purpose of each regular election of Executive Directors, the Board of Governors, by an eighty-five percent majority of the total voting power, may increase or decrease the number of Executive Directors in (ii) above. The number of Executive Directors in (ii) above shall be reduced by one or two, as the case may be, if Executive Directors are appointed under (c) below, unless the Board of Governors decides, by an eighty-five percent majority of the total voting power, that this reduction would hinder the effective discharge of the functions of the Executive Board or of Executive Directors or would threaten to upset a desirable balance in the Executive Board.

(c) If, at the second regular election of Executive Directors and thereafter, the members entitled to appoint Executive Directors under (b)(i) above do not include the two members, the holdings of whose currencies by the Fund in the General Resources Account have been, on the average over

the preceding two years, reduced below their quotas by the largest absolute amounts in terms of the special drawing right, either one or both of
such members, as the case may be, may appoint an Executive Director.

(d) Elections of elective Executive Directors shall be conducted at intervals
of two years in accordance with the provisions of Schedule E, supplemented by such regulations as the Fund deems appropriate. For each
regular election of Executive Directors, the Board of Governors may
issue regulations making changes in the proportion of votes required to
elect Executive Directors under the provisions of Schedule E.

(e) Each Executive Director shall appoint an Alternate with full power
to act for him when he is not present. When the Executive Directors
appointing them are present, Alternates may participate in meetings but
may not vote.

(f) Executive Directors shall continue in office until their successors are
appointed or elected. If the office of an elected Executive Director
becomes vacant more than ninety days before the end of his term,
another Executive Director shall be elected for the remainder of the term
by the members that elected the former Executive Director. A majority
of the votes cast shall be required for election. While the office remains
vacant, the Alternate of the former Executive Director shall exercise his
powers, except that of appointing an Alternate.

(g) The Executive Board shall function in continuous session at the principal
office of the Fund and shall meet as often as the business of the Fund
may require.

. . .

### Section 5. Voting

(a) Each member shall have two hundred fifty votes plus one additional vote
for each part of its quota equivalent to one hundred thousand special
drawing rights.

(b) Whenever voting is required under Article V, Section 4 or 5, each
member shall have the number of votes to which it is entitled under (a)
above adjusted

(i) by the addition of one vote for the equivalent of each four hundred
thousand special drawing rights of net sales of its currency from the
general resources of the Fund up to the date when the vote is taken,
or

(ii) by the subtraction of one vote for the equivalent of each four
hundred thousand special drawing rights of its net purchases under
Article V, Section 3(b) and (f) up to the date when the vote is taken,

provided that neither net purchases nor net sales shall be deemed at any
time to exceed an amount equal to the quota of the member involved.

(c) Except as otherwise specifically provided, all decisions of the Fund shall
be made by a majority of the votes cast.

**2-016**    A weighted voting system is at one level not egalitarian. On the other hand,
it is so substantively, in that it purports to take cognisance of relevant differences in differentiating between States. The doctrine of sovereign equality

would imply the need to differentiate between States in the allocation of rights and duties according to their respective conditions.[128] Although it may be added that this is truer in so far as burdens are concerned but not necessarily an imperative with respect to rights.

There are essentially two levels of arguments both grounded in equality that have been proffered against systems of weighted voting. First, issue is taken with the criteria involved not so much the differential treatment. Potentially there can be a number of considerations included in the weighting criteria—e.g. population, national income, financial contribution, interest in subject-matter, and levels of exports or imports. The components for the criteria normally purport to have some relationship with the functions of the organisation in question. Secondly, premium is put on formal equality because of the danger that differential voting treatment can be the slippery route to the enactment of a subjective differential system. Such a system in the domestic context has been rejected, namely when blacks, women and non-property owners were franchised. Indeed, in domestic systems of voting, individuals are not barred as a consequence of their lack of education, lack of economic weight, life expectancy, or on occasions even absence of residence.

Another form of voting is "bloc" voting. In this situation, the economic sovereignty of a State is being assimilated with "like-minded" States. Thus, in the Common Fund for Commodities[129] the votes are distributed as between developing States, developed States, Eastern European States and China. Generally, in International Commodity Agreements the votes are divided as between the exporters and importers.[130] In the WTO, the EU has the number of votes of its membership.[131] In block voting, internally in the block, State sovereignty is constrained, externally in relation to outsiders, it is enhanced.

In a number of international economic organisations, e.g. the WTO and the IMF, decisions are arrived at through consensus. Here, a decision is formed, unless it is formally challenged by a member.[132] Only if a decision cannot be arrived at through consensus, is a decision made the subject of voting. In this situation, the knowledge of the voting framework of the organisation, and the economic weight underpinning opinions proffered, can have as potent an effect as, for example, a formal weighted voting system. Moreover, it has been observed[133] that consensus decision-making "does not

---

[128] See Zamora (1980), p.573 and Kelsen, "The Principle of Sovereign Equality of States as a basis for International Organization" (1944) 53 Yale L.J. 207 quoted therein. See also Franck (1995).

[129] See Schermers and Blokker (1995), para.805 (see also now the fourth edition—2003); and UNCTAD, Fundamental Elements of the Common Fund, para.24.

[130] Zamora (1980), p.582.

[131] See Art.IX of the Marrakesh Agreement Establishing The World Trade Organization.

[132] See, for example, fn.1 to Art.IX of the Marrakesh Agreement Establishing the World Trade Organization.

[133] Claus-Dieter Ehlermann & L Ehring 'Decision-Making in the World Trade Organization: Is the consensus practice of the World Trade organization adequate for making, revising and implementing rules on international trade?' J.I.E.L., 8:1 (2005),51–75.

provide for equality (in terms of decision and influence) because not every Member has the same ability to maintain vetoes".

Finally, mention should be made of the effect of majority vote requirements, and some of the procedures adopted in voting, in terms of the discourse on a State's sovereignty. First, majority requirements can impact on individual and group sovereignty.[134] Thus, a special or high majority requirement allows a small minority of States a high stake in the decision making process.[135] Second, where voting is open, by way (for example) of a show of hands, or roll-call, where members are asked in succession for their votes and this is then recorded, the safeguard of anonymity is lost, and external influences on economic sovereignty may take place.

---

[134] Zamora (1980), p.595.
[135] But see J. Jaconelli, "Majority Rule and Special Majorities" in *Public Law* (Sweet & Maxwell, 1989), p.587. The author points out that in a qualified majority provision equality is not violated in a formal sense.

### CHAPTER 3

# EXTRATERRITORIAL JURISDICTION IN THE ECONOMIC SPHERE

## GENERALLY

A State's economic jurisdiction refers to its exercise of power over persons, **3-001** property and economically relevant events and transactions, in the framework of its legal system. The State exercises this power by prescribing a code of conduct through legislative, administrative and judicial measures. Such prescriptive exercise of power is generally referred to as *legislative jurisdiction*. A State further exercises its power in order to ensure the implementation of its legislative jurisdiction through enforcement measures (e.g. gathering evidence, imposing sanctions, viz. appropriation of property, imposition of penalties, awarding of damages, imprisonment, denial of entry into the country, etc.). This is referred to as its *enforcement jurisdiction*. A State's jurisdiction is considered to be an aspect of its *sovereignty*[1]—an attribute of its sovereignty. The demarcation of the extent of a State's economic jurisdiction, in particular *extraterritorial*, is the function of International Law. A State exercises extraterritorial jurisdiction when its legislative and/or enforcement jurisdiction impacts on persons and/or events outside its territory.

In IEL the State is not the only entity vested with jurisdiction in the economic sphere. Regional economic organisations (such as the European Union) are also vested with the power to prescribe and enforce economic laws.[2] Although their powers are derived from their respective constitutions—both those powers expressly stipulated, and those inherent, are

---

[1] See R. Jennings and A. Watts, *Oppenheim's International Law* (1992) 9, p.456 (Vol.1, Pt 1). But see Succession in Taxes (Czechoslovakia) Case Supreme Administrative Court of Czechoslovakia (1925) cited in A.H. Qureshi, *Public International Law of Taxation* (London/ Boston, Graham and Trotman, 1994), p.72 where sovereignty and jurisdiction did not coincide but the court nevertheless held that Czechoslovakia had fiscal jurisdiction; R.S.J. Martha in K.M. Meessen (ed.), *Extraterritorial Jurisdiction in Theory and Practice*, (Kluwer Law International, 1996) at p.22. See also I. Brownlie, *Principles of Public International Law*, 5th edn (Oxford, Oxford University Press, 1998), p.300.

[2] M. McDougal and W.M. Reisman, *International Law in Contemporary Perspective*, 3rd reprint (Mineda, Foundation Press, 1981), p.1271. (See also now 2nd edn, 2004).

subject to International Law. The analysis on jurisdiction however has been mainly framed in terms of the State, but is equally relevant to regional economic organisations.

Generally, jurisdictional problems in the economic field arise as a consequence of the globalisation of the international economy, and the multi-jurisdictional character of the international economic order. Thus the possibility of cross-border transactions, the phenomenon of multinational companies, the "locational" diversity of decision making in international business, and the ease in international transfers of funds, are but some of the factors which have contributed to an expansive exercise of jurisdiction by States—particularly extraterritorially, given the de-centralised character of international economic regulation. In addition, of relevance in this context is the very existence of the various national economies; the competition between them; and the general propensity of some legal systems to export their legislation. Indeed, the exercise of extraterritorial jurisdiction by States in the economic sphere has been described as "nearly inevitable".[3]

More particularly, there are a number of reasons why a State exercises its legislative jurisdiction in the economic sphere. Generally, in relation to matters arising within the territory, jurisdiction is exercised for the following reasons[4]:

- to engage in the use of its economic resources and in the design of its economic system;

- to derive optimal use of its resources; and

- to ensure the efficient functioning of the economic system (e.g. competition rules).

**3-002**   In relation to matters arising extraterritorially, it is generally recognised that there should not be an absolute prohibition in the exercise of legislative jurisdiction.[5] Specifically, States engage in legislative jurisdiction in the economic sphere extraterritorially, for the following reasons[6]:

- to protect territorially based economic resources and systems from external influence;

- to protect its resources and economic system from outflows of resources;

---

[3] C. Ryngaert, *Jurisdiction in International Law,* (OUP, 2008) at p.187.
[4] For a general description of why States engage in the exercise of jurisdiction see McDougal and Reisman (1981), p.1273.
[5] See McDougal and Reisman (1981), p.1275 asserted albeit in the context of the federal system of States in the US.
[6] McDougal and Reisman (1981).

- to ensure that the legitimate economic interests of nationals whilst abroad are protected;

- to ensure access to common economic interests, e.g. the oceans and the outer space;

- to competitively engage in the international economy;

- to protect common economic interests and resources;

- to protect the international economic system;

- to cover deficiencies in the economic regulatory framework of other States; and

- to enforce International Law (e.g. human rights).

The exercise of extraterritorial jurisdiction has led to clashes of jurisdictional authority amongst States; undermines the sovereign equality and independence of States; and is characterised by a "democratic deficit".[7] Moreover, it has been described as "a form of regulatory imperialism";[8] which has contributed to a "chaotic"[9] framework of international business. The dangers of the exercise of extraterritorial jurisdiction, prevalent in international economic relations, have been considered by one commentator, albeit as long ago as 1982, as potentially posing a greater threat than concerns over tariffs, quotas and exchange rates.[10] This is somewhat of an exaggeration, but nevertheless the significance of the problem for the functioning of the international economy is highlighted.

The unilateral and regulatory transplanting character of the exercise of extraterritorial jurisdiction can also be found in other forms of inter-state economic relations. Thus, some bilateral and regional economic agreements, though consensual, are not necessarily set on equal economic terms. These can act as conduits for the transplanting extraterritorially of legislation, as for instance in the case of the EU, the *acquis communautaire*,[11] and the European Neighbourhood Policy (ENP) launched in 2004,[12] which impacts on non-EU members in their dealings with the EU.

There is by no means a universally accepted conception of what constitutes extraterritorial exercise of jurisdiction.[13] Certainly, the term should not be

---

[7] See C. Ryngaert (2008) at p.190.

[8] W Grassl, "Between a Rock and a Hard Place: Transnational Firms Under the Extraterritorial Application of National Law", (2008) at: *http://www.consultorium.com/docs/Between%20 a%20Rock%20and%20a%20Hard%20Place.pdf.* (Accessed June 8, 2011).

[9] W. Grassl (2008).

[10] See Legal Advisor of the US Department of State, Davis R. Robinson, June 30, 1982 in Department of State *Cumulative Digest of United States Practice in International Law (1981–1988) II* (1994), p.1326.

[11] See, for example, the GATT, *Trade Policy Review-EC, Report of the Secretariat* (1993).

[12] See *http://ec.europa.eu/world/enp/welcome_en.htm* (Accessed June 8, 2011) .

[13] A. Nollkaemper, "The existence and scope of rights to protect environmental values in other

assumed as given, and the question of its meaning should be addressed in any analysis. There is no doubt that the exercise of legislative or enforcement jurisdiction beyond the territorial borders is covered. Thus, legislation prescribing conduct outside the territory would fall under this definition. However, there is some query as to whether control within the territory (without legally prescribing conduct abroad) but with extraterritorial implications is covered.[14] The US has argued, for instance, that merely denying access to its own market to foreign imports, is in fact a measure directed at its own domestic market, and therefore intra-territorial.[15] This argument, however, has been rejected in the WTO.

Much has been written on jurisdiction generally.[16] Much has been written on the extraterritorial exercise of jurisdiction, particularly focusing on US claims of extraterritorial jurisdiction in the economic field, especially in terms of its anti-trust legislation or economic sanctions.[17] There are, however, some problems and controversies that surround the development of the international principles on the allocation of jurisdiction between States under General International Law. There are a number of reasons for this. First, the principles of jurisdictional allocation that have evolved thus far are not complete. This is inter alia because Customary International Law, as a source, does not lend itself well to the enunciation of positive allocative rules. Secondly, much of the deliberation in the field stems from national court decisions, and the deliberations of affected national publicists in International Law. Such decisions and writings arguably can be parochial in their analysis of the competence of the jurisdiction of their States.[18] National decisions often avoid being grounded in International Law, latching on instead to

States through the use of trade measures", Ch.9 in F. Weiss et al. (eds), *Towards International Economic Law with a Human Face* (The Hague, Kluwer, 1998) at p.188. See also US arguments in the United States—Import of Certain Shrimp and Shrimp Products, WTO Appellate Body (1998) (hereinafter referred to as the *Shrimps* Case).

[14] See, for example, Nollkaemper (1998).

[15] *Shrimps* case. See also Nollkaemper (1998), p.188.

[16] See particularly, for example, F. Mann, "The doctrine of jurisdiction in International Law" (1964) 111 *Recueil des cours*, and "The doctrine of International Jurisdiction revisited after twenty years" (1984) 186 *Recueil des cours*; M. Akehurst, "Jurisdiction in International Law" (1972–1973) B.Y.I.L.See, for example, Bowett, "Jurisdiction: changing problems of authority over activities and references" (1982) 53 B.Y.I.L.; B. Bowett in Macdonald and Johnstone (eds), *The structure and process of International Law* (1983), pp.555–580; C.J. Olmstead (ed.), *Extraterritorial Applications of Laws and Responses Thereto* (Oxford, ESC Publishing, 1984); Henkin (1989) 216 *Recueil des cours* iv, pp.277–330; *Oppenheim's International Law* (1992), pp.456–498 and references therein; K.M. Meessen (ed.) (1996); C. Ryngaert (2008); IBA: Report of the Task Force on Extraterritorial Jurisdiction (2009) at *http://tinyurl.com/taskforce-etj-pdf* (Accessed Jan 8, 2011).

[17] See, for example, Cynthia Wallace "'Extraterritorial' Discovery: Ongoing Challenges for Antitrust Litigation in an Environment of Global Investment," J.I.E.L. (2002) 353–392; and C. Ryngaert, "The Limits of Substantive International Economic Law: In Support of Reasonable Extraterritorial Jurisdiction", in Eric Claes, Wouter Devroe and Bert Keirsbilck, eds., *Facing the Limits of the Law*, (Berlin, Heidelberg, Springer, 2009), pp. 237–252.

[18] See, for example, *Oppenheim's International Law* (1992), p.457.

domestic law.[19] Thirdly, the analysis on jurisdictional questions can reflect philosophical differences as to the nature of International Law, the State and sovereignty. Finally, there is a tendency to ignore the fact that jurisdictional problems in the disparate economic fields are different in character.

The allocative principles of jurisdiction under International Law, such as they are, are grounded in the notion of State sovereignty. They derive from the practice of States in their assertions of jurisdiction, and thus of freedom of action, particularly as to matters within the territory. In relation to the domestic sphere, a State is sovereign,[20] although the scope of "domestic" is a function of International Law.[21] Thus, what alien labour force a State may allow in its territory, and what kind of currency it may circulate in its economy, are matters that pertain to the State's domestic sphere. The domestic sphere of a State's jurisdiction is not necessarily coterminous with its territory as such, although it does relate to internal matters. On the other hand, a State's territory is a basic ground of legislative jurisdiction. A State's legislative jurisdiction in its domestic sphere, as much as its legislative jurisdiction over its territory, is however underpinned by the fact that a State's enforcement jurisdiction is territorial. A State cannot enforce its economic code in the territory of another State.[22]

**3-003**

A State's legislative jurisdiction is not generally confined to its territory. Indeed, it has been asserted that a State is presumed to have legislative jurisdiction, even extraterritorially, unless there is a prohibitory rule of International Law.[23] Although it is accepted universally that a State's legislative jurisdiction may extend beyond its territory, a general presumption of legitimacy of State action, particularly as it relates to extraterritorial matters, as enunciated in the *Lotus* case,[24] has been maligned somewhat, particularly by European jurists.[25] This is because the presumption is perceived as reflecting an extreme positivistic view of International Law, and the dangers for the international system that it is supposed to pose.[26] The criticisms emphasise that a State's legislative jurisdiction is restrained by the doctrine of sovereign equality of States. However, it is suggested that critics of the

---

[19] For example, at least twice the US Supreme Court when the opportunity arose failed to consider principles of legislative jurisdiction under International Law. See *Morrison v National Australian Bank* (US Supreme Court June 2010); and *Barclays Bank PLC V Franchise Tax Board* (US Supreme Court, 1994).

[20] Art.2(7) of the UN Charter.

[21] See, for example, *Tunis-Morocco Nationality Decrees* case (1923) P.C.I.J. Rep; and *Nottebohn* case (1955) I.C.J. Reports.

[22] The *SS Lotus* case (1923) P.C.I.J.

[23] The *SS Lotus* case (1923) P.C.I.J.

[24] The *SS Lotus* case (1923) P.C.I.J. W. Estey, "The Five Bases of Extraterritorial Jurisdiction and the Failure of the Presumption Against Extraterritoriality", Hastings, *International and Comparative Law Review* (1997) 21 (1).

[25] See, for example, R. Higgins, *Problems & Process* (Oxford, Clarendon Press, 1994), p.77.

[26] See, for example, G. Fitzmaurice, "The General Principles of International Law considered from the standpoint of the rule of law" (1957) *Recueil des Cours*; A.V. Lowe, "International Law issues arising in the pipeline dispute: the British position" (1984) 27 G.Y.I.L., p.56.

*Lotus* presumption exaggerate the level of criticism of the presumption,[27] and often fail to point out that there are in fact divergent views on the subject.[28] It is not statistically proven that the *Lotus* presumption has been widely criticised, as is religiously suggested by some writers.[29] The view proffered by Judge Rosalyn Higgins, that it is dangerous to rely on the *Lotus* presumption because it stems from a decision that is now dated, is dissented from.[30] At the very least the decision carries more weight than pronouncements by writers. Indeed, it was relied upon recently in the International Court in its consideration of a State's universal jurisdiction in the criminal sphere.[31]

The principal grounds[32] upon which legislative jurisdiction has been claimed are on the basis of territorial presence (territorial jurisdiction)[33]; the nationality of the individual (nationality jurisdiction or personal jurisdiction),[34] including in certain circumstances the residence of the individual[35]; the protection of vital national interests, viz. security, integrity and independence, (protective jurisdiction); the protection of universal interests (universal jurisdiction)[36]; and the protection of the interests of the State from the effects of actions taken abroad (effects doctrine, especially important in competition law). These grounds are not mutually exclusive. Although formulated in the context of a State's criminal jurisdiction they are equally relevant in relation to civil matters—particularly given that ultimately civil jurisdiction is enforced through criminal sanctions.[37] Not all of the grounds are, however, universally considered to be valid under International Law. The passive personality principle and the effects doctrine, historically mainly claimed by the US, are considered to be controversial, whereas the other grounds are well

---

[27] See, for example, M. Shaw, *International Law*, 4th edn (Cambridge, Cambridge University Press, 1997), p.461.

[28] Reliance on the *Lotus* case is in fact significant. See, for example, G. Schwarzenberger, "The principles of international economic law" (1966) *Recueil des cours*; H. Kindred, *International Law—Chiefly as Interpreted and Applied in Canada*, 4th edn (1987); I.A. Shearer, *Stark's International Law*, 11th edn (1994), p.184; M. Dixon, *International Law*, 2nd edn, p.115; R.S.J. Martha, "Extraterritorial taxation in International law" in Meessen (1996); H.G. Maier, "Jurisdictional Rules in Customary International Law" in Meessen (1996).

[29] See, for example, A.V. Lowe (1984).

[30] R. Higgins (1994), p.77.

[31] See Case Concerning the Arrest Warrant of April 11, 2000—*Congo v Belgium* (2002) I.C.J. Reports.

[32] See the Harvard Research on International Law: "Jurisdiction with respect to crime", 29 A.J.I.L. Supplement 1 (1935).

[33] Territorial presence includes objective territorial presence and subjective territorial presence. Objective territorial presence occurs when an offence or act terminates within the territory. The subjective territorial principle relates to an offence or act being initiated within the territory but terminating outside the territory.

[34] However, where the national is not resident and if there is a conflict with the domestic law of the State of the residence the nationality jurisdiction is ousted. See Mann (1964), p.254. Normally, the competence to regulate the behaviour of a national is based on the *active* personality principle, while the protection of a national (especially abroad) is based on the *passive* personality principle.

[35] See, for example, *Oppenheim's International Law* (1992), p.469.

[36] Confined to universally recognised crimes.

[37] See, for example, Brownlie, *Principles of Public International Law*, 5th edn (Oxford, Oxford University Press, 1996), p.302.

established under International Law.[38] With respect to the effects doctrine, there is latterly evidence of a more widespread use of some form of an "effects tests" being used by States to determine the extraterritorial reach of their competition laws.[39] In the context of international economic relations the territorial, nationality and the effects doctrine have been the more frequent grounds upon which States have rested their jurisdiction.

There have been a number of attempts at discerning the underlying princi-  **3-004**
ple behind the bases of jurisdiction adumbrated above. However, such general principles as are enunciated need to be considered with some caution. This is because the law of jurisdiction does not necessarily lend itself to generalities. This is the assumption in the quest for an underlying normative principle for the exercise of legislative jurisdiction. The correct approach to the problem of identifying the underlying basis under International Law for the exercise of legislative jurisdiction must take cognisance of the context and underlying economic subject-matter in question.[40] The subjects in question are varied, and include for example taxation, anti-trust and export control. In turn, the economic subjects may be dealt with as criminal and/or as civil matters. However, the scope of a State's jurisdiction in the criminal and civil field correspond.[41]

As a general principle underlying the law of jurisdiction, particularly in relation to civil matters, it has been asserted that a State may only exercise its legislative jurisdiction when it is substantially affected.[42] Similarly, it has been contended that a State can only exercise its legislative jurisdiction when there is a reasonable connection (or link) between it and the subject or object of regulation.[43] Both these principles purport to emphasise the doctrine of sovereign equality of States. That there are however such general underlying principles is not without controversy.[44] In the alternative, it is maintained that a State generally enjoys freedom in the exercise of its legislative jurisdiction; but that this general freedom is constrained, by the prohibition that a State may not enforce its jurisdiction extraterritorially; by the obligation to observe the requirement under International Law of a minimum standard towards foreigners[45]; and possibly more controversially by the prohibition of the abuse by a State of its jurisdictional rights under International Law.[46]

---

[38] See, for example, *Oppenheim's International Law* (1992), pp.456–498.
[39] See IBA: Report of the Task Force on Extraterritorial Jurisdiction (2009) at p.72.
[40] For a similar view see Andrea Bianchi at p.100 in Karl M. Meeson (ed.) (1996). I am indebted to Andrea Bianchi for pointing out an inaccuracy here in the previous edition footnote (Letter to the author dated August 21, 1999).
[41] See, for example, M. Dixon, *International Law* (Oxford, Oxford University Press, 2005), Ch.6.
[42] See McDougal and Reisman (1981), p.1274.
[43] Mann (1964).
[44] See, for example, M. Dixon, *International Law* (Oxford, Oxford University Press, 2005), Ch.6; A.H. Qureshi, "The Freedom of a State to Legislate in Fiscal Matters under General International Law" (1987) 41 *Bulletin for International Fiscal Documentation*, p.14; C. Ryngaert, (2008) Ch.5.
[45] Qureshi (1987). See also F. Francioni in Meesen (1996), p.125.
[46] See R.S.J. Martha in Meesen (1996), p.28, advocating the doctrine of abuse of rights in the jurisdictional field. See, also *Oppenheim's International Law* (1992), p.407.

The international principles on State jurisdiction have developed exclusively against the background of *terra firma*. Therefore, the straightforward application of these principles to cyberspace is a modern challenge. Indeed, the governance of the internet and jurisdictional allocation with respect to activities on the internet based on *terra firma* principles is widely acknowledged as problematic,[47] giving rise to clashes of jurisdiction and extraterritoriality. The different spheres of the law have, however, approached the internet differently in accordance with their specific policy goals.[48] Thus, in the field of taxation the OECD has advocated application of the same jurisdictional principles as apply to conventional taxation to electronic commerce[49]—in particular, that States should take into account fiscal sovereignty, fair sharing of the tax base and avoid double taxation and non-taxation. However, clashes of jurisdiction and extraterritoriality can surface. Governance of the internet to safeguard national public policy and values can either be based on the territoriality principle (i.e. the subjective territoriality principle where the act or information flow originates from), or the effects doctrine.[50] With respect to the former, this approach is considered as too restrictive as it displaces the jurisdiction of the State where the impact is felt. On the other hand, the effects doctrine is too wide as it involves compliance with the laws of all States.[51] One suggestion has been to allow jurisdiction based on the notion of "targeting" i.e. "the activity must be intended to have effects within the territory of the State asserting jurisdiction—it is so to speak a "tighter version of the effects doctrine".[52] This suggestion, however, is *lex fernada*. That said, the internet, it has been observed, also has developed its own normative system in some spheres, designed by the online community, for example with respect to the resolution of e-Bay disputes contracted out to a private enterprise,[53] or Google taking off their search engine websites that appear to be harmful in terms of virus or malware to its visitors.

## Specifically

**3-005**  States exercise extraterritorial jurisdiction in a number of economic spheres to achieve the goals of those sectors; or spheres which impact on the flow of

[47] See, for example, U Kohl, "*Jurisdiction and the Internet: a study of regulatory competence over online activity*", (CUP, 2007); T. Schultz, "Carving up the internet jurisdiction, legal orders, and the private/public international law interface", E.J.I.L. (2008); B. Maier, "How has the law attempted to tackle the borderless nature of the internet?" *International Journal of Law and Information Technology* (2010) Vol 18, No.2.

[48] B. Maier (2010).

[49] OECD: Electronic Commerce: Ottawa Taxation Framework Conditions (1998).

[50] See T. Schultz, E.J.I.L.,(2008).

[51] See T. Schultz, E.J.I.L.,(2008).

[52] See T. Schultz, E.J.I.L.,(2008).

[53] See T. Schultz, E.J.I.L.,(2008).

international economic transactions. Indeed, States employ economic sanctions to achieve non-economic ends. Potentially, therefore, the need for the exercise of extraterritorial jurisdiction is open-ended. These claims of extraterritorial jurisdiction over transnational economic transactions and entities have been made under various grounds of prescriptive jurisdiction—including the effects doctrine. In each of the economic spheres, the State's interest has had elements mainly of protection, acquisition and regulation. The extraterritorial systems intended essentially to protect the operation of the economy have been the least objectionable. Systems that have been wealth acquiring, and those particularly that have had a substantial extraterritorial normative impact, have aroused the most controversy. The following are the principal instances of the exercises of extraterritorial jurisdiction with an economic dimension, particularly by the US.[54]

## Taxation[55]

The object of the extraterritorial reach of fiscal authority has been both wealth-acquiring, as well as to ensure that the domestic tax base is not undermined through tax avoidance and evasion. Thus, the primary aim of extraterritorial fiscal jurisdiction is not normative. The extraterritorial element of the jurisdiction can arise in a number of ways. The following are some of the main permutations[56]:

**3-006**

1. tax liability on the basis of nationality, domicile or residence of the individual on worldwide income; despite the fact that the source of the income is located in another State;

2. in the computation of domestic source income and foreign source income;

3. in the attribution of income to a domestic taxpayer;

---

[54] See American Law Institute: *US Restatement Of The Law, Third, Foreign Relations Law of the United States* (1987). For discussion on problems of extraterritoriality in relation to bribery and corruption, and insolvency see Chs 4 and 6 of IBA: Report of the Task Force on Extraterritorial Jurisdiction (2009) at *http://tinyurl.com/taskforce-etj-pdf.* (Accessed June 8, 2011).

[55] See paras 411–413 of the US Restatement of the Law (1987). See also A.H. Qureshi, "The Freedom of a State to Legislate in Fiscal Matters under General International Law", *Bulletin for Fiscal Documentation* 16–21 (1987); R.S.J. Martha, *The Jurisdiction to Tax in International Law* (Kluwer, 1989); A.H. Qureshi, *The Public International Law of Taxation* (Kluwer, 1994); R.S.J. Martha, "Extraterritorial Taxation in International Law", Ch.II in K.M. Meeson (ed.), *Extraterritorial Jurisdiction in Theory and Practice* (Kluwer 1996); R. J. Jeffrey, *The Impact of State Sovereignty on Global Trade and International Taxation* (Kluwer Law International:1999). For a more economic analysis of jurisdictional issues see Vogel, "Worldwide vs. Source Taxation of Income—a Review and Re-evaluation of Arguments", Pts I, II, and III in *INTERTAX* (1988); A. Schindel & A. Atchabahian General Report, *Source and Residence* Cahiers de Droit Fiscal International , 90a (2005) 21–99.

[56] See American Law Institute, *US Restatement Of The Law, Third, Foreign Relations Law of the United States* (1987).

4. computation for tax purposes of the profits of an enterprise within the jurisdiction, that is part of a multinational enterprise, in a manner so as to take into account the overall profits of the multinational enterprise, (i.e. the profits made by the parent or subsidiary company located outside the jurisdiction, as the case may be); but only to the extent of the contribution made by the enterprise located within the jurisdiction to the making of the overall profits.[57] This method of computation involves ignoring the separate identity of the parent and subsidiary companies;

5. taxation of the undistributed income of certain foreign entities which can be attributed to beneficiaries within the State;

6. taxation of transactions that terminate within the State, or otherwise have a substantial connection with it;

7. taxation of services performed outside the State but utilised within the State;

8. inheritance and allied taxes imposed on the basis of the relationship of the individual with the State (e.g. nationality or domicile), regardless of the location of the property in question.

Most conflicts of fiscal jurisdiction are resolved through bilateral double taxation agreements between States. These double taxation agreements are normally based on either of two model double taxation agreements, viz. the OECD Model Tax Convention on Income and Capital, and the UN Model Double Taxation Convention between Developed and Developing Countries, (adopted 2001). Nevertheless, there are occasions when States engage in the application of extraterritorial taxation, or their tax system has an extraterritorial impact. In such circumstances, under General International Law, the State has jurisdiction if the claim is within the personal, territorial or functional sovereignty of the State, provided there is no prohibitive rule of International Law denying the exercise of fiscal jurisdiction.[58] Further, in such circumstances it is contended, even when there is jurisdiction as a consequence of a fiscal attachment arising from the personal/territorial/ functional sovereignty of the State, the scope of the tax (i.e. the extent of the fiscal liability) is dependent on the kind of attachment.[59] However, this view is not universally shared.[60] It is maintained that where a State has prescriptive

---

[57] This method of calculation is known as the Unitary method of taxation. See A.H. Qureshi, "Unitary taxation and General International Law" in *Bulletin for International Fiscal Documentation*, February 1987, Vol.41, pp.56–64. Contra Martha in Meesen (1996), p.28, wherein he maintains that this is not a matter of excess of jurisdiction but possibly a matter of abuse of rights. See also R.S.J. Martha, *The Jurisdiction to Tax in International Law* (1996).

[58] See *Lotus* case, P.C.I.J., Series No.10; and R.S.J. Martha in Meesen (1996), p.27 and Qureshi (1987).

[59] See Martha (1996), p.22.

[60] See Qureshi (1987).

fiscal jurisdiction (for example, by reason of the nationality or residence of the taxpayer, or because of the presence within the territory of the economic activity) the scope or amount of the tax liability is unlimited in the absence of a rule of International Law to the contrary.[61] Where the fiscal claim is outside the personal, territorial or functional sovereignty of the State, there are two conflicting schools of thought. On the one hand it is asserted that if there is no prohibitive rule of International Law, then subject to the limitation that a State may not exercise its fiscal enforcement jurisdiction outside its territory, and subject to the entitlement of foreigners to receive a minimum standard of treatment under International Law, a State may validly formulate such a fiscal prescriptive jurisdiction.[62] On the other hand, however, it is asserted that in such circumstances a State may exercise its prescriptive jurisdiction, provided only if there is a permissive rule of International Law allowing for such an exercise of jurisdiction.[63]

### Regulation of anti-competitive conduct abroad[64]

States and regional economic organisations have regulated conduct of an anti-competitive nature occurring abroad or originating domestically, and   **3-007**

---

[61] Qureshi (1987).

[62] See Qureshi (1987) and now Case Concerning the Arrest Warrant of April 11, 2000—*Congo v Belgium* (2002) I.C.J. Reports. But contra Martha (1996), p.27.

[63] See Martha (1996), p.27.

[64] See para.415, *US Restatement of the Law* (1987). See fn.43 in *Oppenheim's International law* (1992) for references on the extraterritorial application of anti-trust laws. See also generally on jurisdictional questions in the economic field, for example, R.Y. Jennings, "Extraterritorial jurisdiction and the US Anti-trust laws" (1957) 33 B.Y.I.L.; J. Atwood et al., Brewster, *Anti-trust and American Business Abroad* (1981); A.V. Lowe, "Blocking extraterritorial jurisdiction; the British Protection of Trading Act, 1980" (1981) 75 A.J.I.L., p.257; Huntley (1981) 30 I.C.L.Q. 213 and 21; A.V. Lowe (ed.), *Extraterritorial Jurisdiction* (Cambridge, Grotius, 1983); Castel, "The extraterritorial effects of anti-trust laws" (1983), 179 *Receuil des Cours*; Lowenfield (1981) 75 A.J.I.L. 629; W. Knighton, and D.Rosenthal, *National Laws and International Commerce* (Routledge et al. and Chatham House, 1982); A.H. Herman, *Conflicts of national laws with international business activity: Issues of Extraterritoriality* (British–North American Committee, 1982); C. Olmstead (ed.), *Extraterritorial Application of Law and Responses thereto* (Oxford, ESC Publishing, 1984); Meesen, "Antitrust jurisdiction under Customary International Law", (1984) 78 A.J.I.L., p.783; A.V. Lowe, "Extraterritorial jurisdiction and the Structure of International Law", in H. Fox (ed.), *International Economic Law and Developing States* (1988), Ch.III; L. Kramer, "Extraterritorial Application of American Law After the Insurance Antitrust Case: A reply to Professors Lowenfeld & Trimble" (1995) 89 A.J.I.L., p.750; A.D. Neale and M.L. Stephens, *International Business And National Jurisdiction* (Oxford, Clarendon Press, 1988); Trimble P.R., "The Supreme Court and International Law: the demise of Restatement Section 403" (1995) 89 A.J.I.L., p.53; A.F. Lowenfeld, "Conflict, Balancing of Interest, and the Exercise of Jurisdiction to prescribe: Reflections of the Insurance Antitrust Case" (1995) 89 A.J.I.L.; A. Lowenfeld, "Jurisdictional issues before national courts: the Insurance Antitrust case", Ch.1 in K.M. Meessen (ed.), *Extraterritorial jurisdiction in theory and practice* (1996); P. Torremans, "Extraterritorial application of EC and US Competition Law" (1996) 21 *European Law Review*, p.280; Y. Ohara, "New US Policy on the Extraterritorial Application of Antitrust Law and Foreign Responses", in Meesen (1996); W. Pengilley, "The extraterritorial impact of US Trade Laws Is it not time for 'ET' to 'Go Home'?", *World Competition* (1997), 20 (3) March, pp.17–55; Andreas Weitbrecht, "National Control

which has a bearing on the domestic consumers and producers within the national economy. The regulation is aimed at private conduct abroad, that is intended to undermine the market conditions within the territory, and that does have such an effect. Where the anti-competitive conduct affects the economy of a third State, prescriptive jurisdiction is generally not exercised. Thus, the exercise of extraterritorial prescription is not intended to enforce internationally a particular market philosophy, but rather is protective of the integrity of the economic system within. The kind of extraterritorial conduct considered to be anti-competitive can take different forms. For example:

- Agreement or conduct abroad, by individuals or corporations, whether or not nationals, that involves the fixing of prices of goods and services that are available within the jurisdiction.

- Agreement or conduct abroad, by individuals or corporations, whether or not nationals, of an anti-competitive nature, that interferes with the domestic production of goods and services.

- Agreement or conduct abroad, that is restrictive of imports, exports, or the domestic supply of goods and services.

- Mergers and acquisitions of companies, resulting for example in the elimination of competition between domestic subsidiaries,[65] or resulting in a dominant market position, either domestically or world-wide. Such results can occur in mergers and acquisitions involving, for example,[66] either (i) domestic acquirer or a foreign target; or (ii) domestic target and a foreign acquirer; or (iii) foreign acquirer and a foreign target both of which have domestic subsidiaries; or (iv) domestic acquirer and domestic target (specially of a foreign domestic subsidiary).

- Joint ventures abroad in a manner that inhibits domestic competitors from competing in the market abroad.[67]

The prescriptive jurisdiction with extraterritorial impact, regulating anti-competitive conduct, is particularly engaged in by the US,[68] and is grounded

---

over International Mergers and Acquisitions" in Meesen (1996); A. Douglas Melamed, "International Cooperation in Competition Law and Policy: What can be achieved at the bilateral, regional, and multilateral levels" (1999) J.I.E.L. 423–433; C. Day Wallace, "Extraterritorial' Discovery: Ongoing challenges for anti trust litigation in an environment of global investment" (2002) J.I.E.L. 2.5 353; Dietmar Baetge, 'The Extraterritorial Reach of Antitrust Law between Legal Imperialism and Harmonious Coexistence', in Eckart Gottschalk, Ralf Michaels, Gisela Ru¨ hl and Jan von Hein (eds), Conflict of Laws in a Globalized World (Cambridge, Cambridge University Press, 2007).

[65] See Neale and Stephens (1981), p.105.
[66] Weitbrecht (1996), p.183.
[67] Neale and Stephens (1981), p.107.
[68] Sherman (Anti-trust Act) 1890.

in the effects doctrine. In a nutshell, the US assumes prescriptive jurisdiction under the effects doctrine in relation to conduct abroad, whether or not engaged by persons within its allegiance, when the conduct outside the territory has or is intended to have substantial effect within the territory.[69] This exercise of prescriptive jurisdiction is moderated by the requirement that its exercise should be reasonable.[70] The effects doctrine is justified under International Law by its proponents on the basis that the prescriptive jurisdiction is presumed to be legitimate, given the absence of a prohibitive rule of International Law to the contrary.[71] It is also justified with reference to the territorial principle. In this respect the argument runs as follows. Control over a State's territory is under International Law a prerequisite to statehood.[72] Control over territory, it is contended, includes control over the events that affect that territory, and thus the assertion of jurisdiction falls under the objective territorial principle.[73]

**Restatement (Third) of Foreign Relations Law of the United States**

§ 402. BASES OF JURISDICTION TO PRESCRIBE Subject to § 403, a state has jurisdiction to prescribe law with respect to (1). . . (c) conduct outside its territory that has or is intended to have substantial effect within its territory;

§ 403. LIMITATIONS ON JURISDICTION TO PRESCRIBE (1) Even when one of the bases for jurisdiction under § 402 is present, a state may not exercise jurisdiction to prescribe law with respect to a person or activity having connections with another state when the exercise of such jurisdiction is unreasonable.

(2) Whether exercise of jurisdiction over a person or activity is unreasonable is determined by evaluating all relevant factors, including, where appropriate: (a) the link of the activity to the territory of the regulating state, i.e., the extent to which the activity takes place within the territory, or has substantial, direct, and foreseeable effect upon or in the territory;

    (b) the connections, such as nationality, residence, or economic activity, between the regulating state and the person principally responsible for the activity to be regulated, or between that state and those whom the regulation is designed to protect;

    (c) the character of the activity to be regulated, the importance of regulation to the regulating state, the extent to which other states regulate such activities, and the degree to which the desirability of such regulation is generally accepted. (d) the existence of justified expectations that might be protected or hurt by the regulation;

---

[69] See *US v Aluminum Co of America* (1945) 148 F.2d 416; *Timberlane Lumber Co v Bank of America* (1976) 549 F.2nd 597; *Mannington Mills Inc v Congoleum Corp* (1979) 595 F.2nd 1287; *Hartford Fire Insurance Co v California* (1993) 113 S Ct 2891; and the ALI Third Restatement of Foreign Relations Law, paras 402 and 403.

[70] ALI Third Restatement of Foreign Relations Law, paras 402 and 403.

[71] *SS Lotus (France v Turkey)* (1927) P.C.I.J.

[72] See H.G. Maier in Meesen (1996), p.67.

[73] See H.G. Maier in Meesen (1996) where the author cites the *Lotus* case for this contention.

(e)  the importance of the regulation to the international political, legal, or economic system; (f) the extent to which the regulation is consistent with the traditions of the international system; (g) the extent to which another state may have an interest in regulating the activity; and (h) the likelihood of conflict with regulation by another state.

(3)  When it would not be unreasonable for each of two states to exercise jurisdiction over a person or activity, but the prescriptions by the two states are in conflict, each state has an obligation to evaluate its own as well as the other state's interest in exercising jurisdiction, in light of all the relevant factors, including those set out in Subsection (2); a state should defer to the other state if that state's interest is clearly greater.

However, the effects doctrine has not been generally recognised. Its status as a legitimate basis of jurisdiction is considered controversial, and opposed by the UK.[74] The objective territorial principle it is maintained does not apply because that basis operates only where a constituent part of an offence takes place within the territory. In the effects doctrine on the other hand, the impact or the repercussion of the offence is territorial, not the offence nor a constituent part of it.[75] Anti-competitive conduct originating abroad is also the subject of regulation by the EU,[76] and other States, including major developing States.[77] However, in the case of the EU, reliance on the effects doctrine has been avoided for a long time. Rather, the entities engaging in such conduct have either been found to have a territorial presence, through the presence of their subsidiaries[78]; or through a factual finding of the actual implementation within the EU[79] of the activities in question (i.e. the conspiracy) originating outside, under a somewhat stretched notion of the objective territorial principle.[80] Thus, in practice in terms of end results the EU approach in competition law has not been very dissimilar to the US.[81] Indeed, more recently the European Court of Justice (Court of First Instance) has stated that the application of the Merger Regulation to a merger between companies located outside EU territory was "justified under public international law when it is foreseeable that a proposed concentration will have an immediate and substantial effect in the Community".[82]

---

[74]  See *Oppenheim's International Law* (1992), p.474. Contra Day Wallace, "Extraterritorial' Discovery: Ongoing Challenges for Antitrust Litigation in an Environment of Global Investment" (2002) J.I.E.L. 353–392 at p.353 wherein the author states: ". . . the 'effects doctrine' (or its equivalent) is generally accepted as applicable to international competition/antitrust cases. . .".

[75]  See *Oppenheim's International Law* (1992).

[76]  See Art.85 (1) of the EEC Treaty.

[77]  See commentary to para.415 of the US Restatement of the Law (1987).

[78]  The *Dyestuff* case (*ICI v Commission* (1972) E.C.R. 619).

[79]  As opposed to the effect of the act.

[80]  The *Wood Pulp* case (*A. Ahlstrom Oy v Commission* (1988) 4 C.M.L.R. 901). See M. Shaw, *International Law*, 4th edn, p.490. See also, for example, Lange and Sandage, "The Wood Pulp Decision and its Implications for the scope of EC Competition Law" (1989) 26 C.M.L.R.

[81]  See for example C. Ryngaert (2008) at p.231.

[82]  See Judgment of the Court of First Instance of March 25, 1999 in Case T–102/96 *Gencor Ltd v Commission* [1999] E.C.R. II-0753, at paras 89–92. See also Commission Decision, COMP/

## Regulation of transactions in securities[83]

A State may want to exercise jurisdiction to regulate conduct[84] occurring   **3-008**
abroad, involving transactions in securities related to its internal securities
market, when that conduct has or is intended to have substantial effect on
its securities market. The exercise of jurisdiction would be over those who
buy and sell in such a market; and on holdings of such securities by nationals
or residents. Such prescriptive jurisdiction is exercised by the US, and has
not raised as much concern and jurisdictional conflict, as for example, the
anti-trust field. The national regulation is not concerned with effect on third-
country securities market.[85] Thus, the regulation is intended to protect the
market conditions in the securities market, and the value of securities, within
the State. It is not intended to export a particular economic philosophy
abroad as such. The kind of extraterritorial conduct, the subject of regulation, involves, for example:

- insider trading, whether or not by nationals, through for example the
  use of foreign bank secrecy legislation;

- misrepresentation, whether or not by nationals; and

- market manipulation whether or not by nationals.

Where there is an extraterritorial impact of the regulations in relation to
the trading, market-making and influencing of the price of securities in the
domestic securities market, the basis for such prescriptive legislation would
appear to be founded on the effects doctrine[86]—although there could well
be other less contentious grounds which may be more appropriate in the
circumstances.

---

M220, General Electric/Honeywell, OJ 2001 L 48/1, aff'd Case T-210/01, *General Electric v
Com'n* [2005] ECR II-5575.

[83] See para.416 of *US Restatement of the Law* (1992). See also Lowenfeld (1979) *Recueil des
Cours* 163, ii p.311; Haseltine (1987) I.C.L.Q. 36 pp.307–328; references in fn.41, p.474 in
*Oppenheim's International Law* (1992), particularly A.J. Steven, 63 A.J.I.L.; Loomis and
Grant, "The US Securities and Exchange Commission, Financial Institutions outside the US
and extraterritorial application of the US Securities Laws" (1978) J. Comp.Corp.L & Sec Reg
3; U. Bosh, "Extraterritorial rules on banking and securities", Ch.X in Meesen (1996); S.J.
Choi, "The dangerous extraterritoriality of American Securities Law", *Northwestern Journal
of International Law and Business* 17 (1996), pp.207–241.

[84] e.g. trading in securities abroad; market-making and exercising an influence on the price of the
securities. See U. Bosh (1996).

[85] *Morrison v National Australia Bank Ltd* (US Supreme Court, 2010). See also Knox,
John H., The Unpredictable Presumption Against Extraterritoriality (January 11, 2011).
Southwestern University Law Review, Forthcoming; Wake Forest University Legal Studies
Paper No. 1739967. Available at SSRN: *http://ssrn.com/abstract=1739967*. (Accessed June 8,
2011).

[86] See, for example, Ulrich Bosh (1996), p.212.

### Regulation to affirm ownership of property[87]

**3-009**  States have from time to time found the need to affirm and claim the ownership of property connected to it, located extraterritorially. This has been done, in times of emergency, to protect the ownership of property of its nationals during enemy occupation.[88] It has also been done in times of peace, as part of a general assertion of State ownership of property or that of its nationals; and to protect and prevent the illegal transferring of assets of national interest. More specifically, the following are some examples of such affirmations of ownership:

- nationalisation of corporations with assets abroad;

- nationalisation of rights of shareholders of corporations with foreign assets;

- transfer of title to the State in case of illegal exportation of art treasures; and

- measures aimed at persons, including those from third countries, engaged in trafficking (e.g. buying/selling) with property confiscated from its nationals, by another confiscating State.[89]

---

[87] See I. Seidl-Hohenveldern, *International Economic Law*, 2nd revised edn (1992), pp.116–127. In relation to Intellectual Property Rights see, for example, J.C. Gingburg, "Extraterritoriality and multiterritoriality in copyright infringement" (1997) *Virginia Journal of International Law* 37, pp.587–602.

[88] See Seidl-Hohenveldern (1992), p.118, citing the Netherlands government in exile's nationalisation of property of its national during the German occupation of the Netherlands.

[89] See, for example, J. Ratchik, "Cuban Liberty and the Democratic Solidarity Act of 1995", *American University Journal of International Law and Policy*, Vol.II, No.2; the US Cuban Liberty and Democratic Solidarity (Libertad) Act of 1996(known as the Helms-Burton Act). See note on the Helms-Burton Act by A.F. Lowenfeld in (1996) 90 A.J.I.L., p.419; B.M. Clagett, "Title III of the Helms-Burton Act is consistent with International Law" (1996) 90 A.J.I.L. 434; M.P. Gibney, "The Extraterritorial Application of United States Law and the Protection of Human Rights: Holding Multinational Corporations to Domestic and International Standards" (1996) *Temple International and Comparative Law Journal* 10 pp.123–145; R.L. Muse, "A Public International Law Critique of the Extraterritorial Jurisdiction of the Helms-Burton Act (Cuban Liberty and Democratic Solidarity (Libertad) Act of 1996", *The George Washington Journal of International Law and Economics* (1996/97) 30: pp.207–270; A.V. Lowe, "US extraterritorial jurisdiction: the Helms Burton and D'Amoto Acts" (1997) I.C.L.Q. 46 (2) pp.378–390; B. Stern, "Can the US set rules for the world? A French view" (August 1997) J.W.T., Vol.31, Number 4; P.K. Chudzicki, "The European Union's Response to the Libertad Act and the Iran-Libya Act: Extraterritoriality without Boundaries" (1997) *Loyola University Chicago Law Journal* 28 (3) pp.505–550; W.S. Dodge, "The Helms-Burton Act and Transnational Legal Process" (1997) *Hastings International and Comparative Law Review* 20 (4) pp.713–728; L. Gierbolini, "The Helms-Burton Act: Inconsistency with International Law and Irrationality at Their Maximum" (1997) *Journal of Transnational Law and Policy* 6, pp.289–332; J. Brett Busby, "Jurisdiction to Limit Third-country Interaction with Sanctioned States: the Iran and Libya Sanctions and Helms-Burton Acts" (1998) *Columbia Journal of Transnational Law* 36 (3) pp.621–658; C. Franken, "The Helms-Burton Act: Force or Folly of the World's Leaders?" (1998) *Minnesota Journal of Global Trade* 7 (1): pp.157–177; C.T. Graves, "Extraterritoriality and Its Limits: the Iran and Libya Sanctions Act of 1996", (1998) *Hastings International and Comparative Law Review* 21(3), pp.715–741;

Generally, it appears that there is sufficient State practice which precludes the recognition of the extraterritorial effects of nationalisation in peace time.[90] A State's territorial sovereignty implies that it has monopoly of power in its territory such that a foreign nationalising State cannot usurp its power to affect the transfer of title within its territory. However, in the case of nationalisation accompanied by adequate compensation in accordance with international norms, the extraterritorial effects of the nationalisation measure is recognised by the foreign State where the assets are located.[91] A nationalising State, may avoid usurping the power of another State in determining title to property within its jurisdiction, by simply nationalising the shareholder's rights as opposed to the corporate entity itself, thus not affecting the title to the assets abroad which would remain in the same company.[92] Where this is not accompanied by compensation however the extraterritorial impact of the measure is not recognised.[93] The corporation is in such a circumstance severed, and has a split personality.[94] The assets in the nationalising State belong to the corporate shareholder. This would be the nationalising State as the sole shareholder. On the other hand, the assets abroad belong to the original shareholders in proportion to their share holdings.[95]

Where a State, in order to safeguard its cultural heritage, prescribes measures which render illegal the export of national art treasures, and thus prevents the transfer of title to property the extraterritorial effect of the measure should, in principle, be recognised. However, this desideratum does not appear to be born out by State practice.[96]

Of late, the US has directed its prescriptive jurisdiction against nationals of third States, trafficking[97] in property confiscated by Cuba from US nationals, in 1959. The measures are enforced through the imposition in the US of severe penalties such as treble damages at the instigation of US citizens whose property was confiscated[98]; including denial of entry into the US.[99] In this manner the legislation has an extraterritorial impact. The US based the extraterritorial reach of the legislation on the effects doctrine.[100] Several

---

L.K. Treat, "An Unreasonable Act: the Extraterritorial Reach of the Cuban Liberty and Democratic Solidarity Act and Its Practical Implications" (1997) *New York International Law Review* 10, pp.77–100; C Ryngaert, 'Extraterritorial export controls (Secondary Boycotts)' *Chinese Journal of International Law*, Volume 7, Issue 3, (2008) pp.625–658.

[90] Seidl-Hohenveldern (1992), pp.118–119.
[91] Seidl-Hohenveldern (1999), p.121.
[92] Seidl-Hohenveldern (1999), p.121.
[93] Seidl-Hohenveldern (1999), p.121.
[94] Seidl-Hohenveldern (1999), p.125.
[95] Seidl-Hohenveldern (1999), p.125.
[96] Seidl-Hohenveldern (1999), p.120.
[97] Trafficking defined in very broad terms as ". . . selling; transferring; buying; leasing. . .engaging in a commercial activity; using or otherwise benefiting from confiscated property". See Title III of the Helms-Burton Act.
[98] See Title III of the Helms-Burton Act.
[99] See Title IV of the Helms-Burton Act.
[100] See s.301 of the Helms-Burton Act.

other arguments have been advanced in justification. It has been claimed, for example,[101] that the US measures enforce the prohibition in International Law on confiscation; prevents the transfer of title of confiscated property; underlines the fundamental human right of ownership of property, and the entitlement to compensation in the event of compensation; supplements lack of legislation in other States; and generally merely stipulates the price for commercial relations with the US. However, the US measure has given rise to much concern and severely criticised. Particularly, it has been contended[102] that the measure undermines the sovereignty of third States in matters of economic and foreign policy; is contrary to the principle of sovereign equality and self-determination; is based on the controversial effects doctrine; stretches the effects doctrine, by focusing on conduct of nationals of third States, when the effect is in fact caused by the actions of the Cuban State, and by taking into account the effects of actions too many decades ago. This policy has also led to problems with regard to the treatment of property rights of foreigners and thereby inconsistencies with the US' obligations under various agreements of the WTO.[103] The US has so far somewhat blunted the impact of the extraterritorial reach of the Act by maintaining a suspension of Title III of the Act.[104]

**EXAMPLE: WTO DISPUTE SETTLEMENT: DISPUTE DS38—United States—The Cuban Liberty and Democratic Solidarity Act[105]**

**3-010**

On 3 May 1996 the European Communities requested consultations with the United States concerning the Cuban Liberty and Democratic Solidarity (LIBERTAD) Act of 1996 and other legislation enacted by the US Congress regarding trade sanctions against Cuba. The EC claims that US trade restrictions on goods of Cuban origin, as well as the possible refusal of visas and the exclusion of non-US nationals from US territory, are inconsistent with the US obligations under the WTO Agreement.. . .The European Communities requested the establishment of a panel on 3 October 1996. The DSB established a panel at its meeting on 20 November 1996. At the request of the EC, dated 21 April 1997, the Panel suspended its work. The Panel's authority lapsed on 22 April 1998, pursuant to Article 12.12 of the DSU.

---

[101] See, for example, Clagett (1996).

[102] See, for example, A.V. Lowe (1997) 46(2) I.C.L.Q. 378–390 and F. Lowenfeld (1996) 90 A.J.I.L. 419. See also opinion expressed by the Inter-American Juridical Committee of the Organisation of American States, describing the US exercise of jurisdiction as being contrary to International Law (1996) 35 I.L.M.

[103] WTO Dipsute DS 176 US—Appropriations Act s.211; *European Communities v United States, Panel Report* circulated: August 6, 2001; *Appellate Body Report* circulated: January 2, 2002 and WTO Dispute DS38—United States—The Cuban Liberty and Democratic Solidarity Act.

[104] These waivers in the interest of national security and transition to democracy in Cuba have been through six monthly letters by the incumbent Presidents addressed to the US Senate. The latest letter has been signed by President Obama dated January 11, 2011 suspending operation of Title III for six months beyond February 1, 2011.

[105] Source: WTO Secretariat—Dispute Settlement Gateway, *http://www.wto.org*. (Accessed June 8, 2011).

**Regulation in the monetary and financial spheres[106]**

Various aspects of a State's monetary and financial law have an extrater-   **3-011**
ritorial dimension. First, States exercise jurisdiction in order to protect their
vital monetary interests. The principal example of such conduct that is regulated involves the counterfeiting of its currency abroad.[107] States also protect
their currency reserves through exchange control restrictions, by imposing
obligations on residents for conduct that takes place abroad.[108] The jurisdictional basis for such regulation is grounded on personal jurisdiction, on
the basis that the non-national resident has sufficient close connection with
the State, so as to warrant the exercise of jurisdiction.[109] Further, under
General International Law, a State can, as a general rule, impose exchange
control regulations.[110] Although, there is now some suggestion that this
position may have changed, and that under Customary International Law
certain types of restrictions on the transfer of money may not be permitted,
for example, transfers of current transactions and repatriation of foreign
capital made on the understanding of eventual repatriation.[111] In addition,
members of the IMF are required not to enforce an exchange contract,
wherever formed, that is inconsistent with the exchange restrictions of any
Member State of the IMF, imposed consistently with the IMF Articles of
Agreement.[112]

Secondly, a State's involvement in its monetary system can have serious
implications abroad. Thus, the external effects of the valuation of a State's
currency are recognised.[113] States have also tried to divest completely the
value of their currency abroad.[114] However, as a general rule, the international effects of the changes in the external value of a currency, under General
International Law, do not bring about violations of international norms,
because of the recognition of the principle of nominalism under International
Law.[115]

---

[106] See F. Mann (1964) *Recueil des Cours* III, Section 7; Ulrich Bosch "Extraterritorial rules
on banking and securities", Ch.X in Meessen (1996); and C. McLachlan, "Extraterritorial
orders affecting bank deposits", Ch.III in Meesen (1996); F. Mann, *The Legal Aspect Of
Money*, 4th edn (see now C. Proctor, *The Legal Aspects of Money*, 6th edn (Oxford, Oxford
University Press, 2005); C.Tietje and M.Lehmann, 'The Role and Prospects of International
Law in Financial Regulation and Supervision' *Journal of International Economic Law* 13(3)
(2010), 663–682.

[107] See, for example, *Oppenheim's International Law* (1996), p.471. See also Convention on the
Suppression of Counterfeiting Currency 1929.

[108] For example, in the UK certain offences can be committed by UK residents abroad in violation of the UK Exchange Control Act 1947 (see also *Oppenheim's International Law* (1996),
p.469; Mann (1982), p.428; and Art.VIII (2) (B) of the IMF Articles of Agreement).

[109] Oppenheim's International Law (1996); Mann (1982).

[110] Mann (1982), p.471. (See now Proctor et al. *The Legal Aspects of Money*, 6th edn (Oxford,
Oxford University Press, 2004.)

[111] Mann (1982), p.472.

[112] Art.VIII 2 (b) of the IMF Articles of Agreement.

[113] Mann (1982), p.468.

[114] Mann (1982), p.474.

[115] Mann (1982), pp.467 and 468.

Finally, there are also some issues arising either from State legislation, or from private litigation, which raise questions of extraterritorial jurisdiction which are specific to the financial sector. Thus, it is now generally recognised that a bank should be globally supervised by the home regulator in relation to its capital adequacy, management and business practices.[116] This has been particularly apparent after the recent (2007–2009) financial crisis. Thus, banks are required to comply, for example, with reporting requirements arising from money laundering legislation, those relating to securities held on account of customers, and to grant supervisory access to necessary information, which may have extraterritorial implications.[117] Moreover, given that financial products are essentially rooted in the domestic legal system but also traded internationally, these products are inherently extraterritorial in their "reach and effect".[118] Thus, they raise problems associated with extraterritorial legislation including transactions costs, as in competition law.[119] These extraterritorial financial and monetary aspects of domestic legislation need co-ordination between different States. One unilateral approach in terms of banking has been through conditioning the entry and operation of foreign and domestic banking, to supervisory mechanisms with extraterritorial reach.[120]

Further, private litigation resulting in attachments and injunctions with respect to foreign deposits also raise questions of jurisdiction.[121] Thus, in civil proceedings interim relief based on personal jurisdiction of the defendant or a third party is given in most jurisdictions, including the UK,[122] with extraterritorial effect.[123]

### Regulation of international transport and movement of people

**3-012**    The regulation of international transport is an interest that is universal, and of course critical to the functioning of the international economy. Where the interest of the international community as a whole is seriously affected, on the basis of the universal principle, a State may exercise jurisdiction. Thus,

---

[116] See, for example, Bosh (1996), p.200; T.C. Baxter and J.J. De Saram, "BCCI: The lessons of banking Supervision", Ch.19 in *Current Legal Issues Affecting Central Banks*, Vol.4, IMF; Basle Committee Banking Regulations and Supervisory Practices, revised Concordat (1983), and Supplement to the Concordat (1990); Core Principles for Effective Banking Supervision, Basle Committee on Banking Supervision, Basle September 1997, *http://www.bis.org/publ/bcbs30a.pdf*. (Accessed June 8, 2011).

[117] Bosh (1996), p.200 and Core Principles for Effective Banking Supervision, Basle Committee on Banking Supervision, Basle September 1997, *http://www.bis.org/publ/bcbs30a.pdf*. Accessed June 8, 2011. See also, for example, US Foreign Bank Supervision Enhancement Act of 1991.

[118] C.Tietje and M.Lehmann (2010) at p.670.

[119] C.Tietje and M.Lehmann (2010) at p.678.

[120] Bosh (1996), p.200.

[121] See, for example, C. McLachlan (1996).

[122] Practice Direction Ex P Mareva Injunctions and Anton Piller Orders July 28, 1994. See C. McLachlan (1996).

[123] See C. McLachlan (1996).

wherever the conduct occurs, piracy[124] and hijacking[125] are offences over which all States can have jurisdiction.

States also need to control the movement of people entering and departing their territory for political, economic, social and security reasons. To protect this flow, certain regulation is introduced which may also have extraterritorial effect. This regulation is based on the protective principle, where there is a violation, for example, of immigration legislation.[126]

### Regulation relating to branches and affiliated corporations located outside the jurisdiction[127]

Commercial enterprises within a State frequently maintain interests abroad **3-013** through branches or affiliated companies.[128] This interest is one of ownership and control. In turn, the State needs to maintain a corresponding interest on foreign extensions of domestic commercial enterprises, in order effectively to police their commercial operations within its territory. In the case of a branch located outside the territory, there is of course a legal unity in the identity of the corporation located within the territory and its branch. In the case of a subsidiary located abroad, the legal relationship is not there. Under International Law the nationality of a corporation is that of the State in which it is incorporated.[129]

Generally, in the case of branches located extraterritorially of corporations based within the State, a certain limited exercise of jurisdiction is exercised. In the case of an affiliated company located extraterritorially, jurisdiction is exercised in more exceptional circumstances than a branch.

The exact nature of regulation involved varies, but is generally connected with international transactions, and relationships connected with the parent company or the State of the parent company, rather than purely domestic issues involving the branch or affiliated company. Thus, the regulation can relate to international transactions linked to the parent company, for example, export/import, foreign exchange, auditing and transborder investment. It can relate to State supervisory functions, for example, imposing reserve requirements or interest rates or lending limits on branches of banks; the obtaining of documents from foreign branches and affiliated companies for tax and criminal proceedings; preventing the obtaining of contracts by bribing foreign government officials. Generally, the regulation does not focus

---

[124] See in relation to the international community's response to piracy across Somalia: The IMO Action Plan to Promote the 2011 World Maritime Day theme: Piracy IMO Orchestrating the Response 03/02/201. *http://www.imo.org/MediaCentre/SecretaryGeneral/SpeechesByTheSecretaryGeneral/Pages/piracyactionplanlaunch.aspx.* (Accessed June 8, 2011).

[125] Jurisdiction has also been claimed on the grounds of passive personality.

[126] See *Oppenheim's International Law* (1996), p.471.

[127] See para.414 of *US Restatement of the Law* (1987).

[128] i.e. corporate entities which have either a parent subsidiary relationship or a subsidiary parent relationship.

[129] See Barcelona Traction (Second Phase) (1970) I.C.J. Reports.

on domestic issues of the branch or subsidiary, for example, health and safety practices.

The jurisdiction over the foreign affiliated company is exercised either through directions aimed at the domestic corporation, or when necessary directly at the foreign affiliated company, to further important national interests or programmes. The regulation of the foreign entity is established inter alia to prevent a foreign country from depriving a parent company and its State from control over all its operations. One manner in which a foreign State re-enforces its jurisdiction over a commercial enterprise present in its territory is by requiring the foreign enterprise to incorporate locally. Normally, a subsidiary is directed through commands addressed at nationals from the parent company working in the subsidiary company.[130] In some cases, a completely foreign company has been the subject of jurisdiction where it has been using technology of the State claiming jurisdiction.

**3-014**      The jurisdictional bases of particular relevance here are the territoriality, nationality and the effects doctrine. Two general questions are, however, posited given the independent legal character of the affiliated companies. The first question relates to the circumstances under International Law which permit the lifting of the corporate veil. The second question relates to the relationship between a State's enforcement jurisdiction and its prescriptive jurisdiction. Both lines of inquiry are relevant in any justification for the exercise of jurisdiction on corporate entities abroad. To a certain extent answers are also dependent on which side of the "*Lotus*"[131] controversy are the standpoints. The lifting of the corporate veil is not absolutely prohibited under International Law, although there would appear to be a presumption that the separate entity of a foreign subsidiary exempts it from the jurisdiction of the parent company's State.[132] In the first instance a State may disregard the legal entity it created, where there is no foreign involvement.[133] Secondly, where there is foreign involvement by way of investment in the country the corporate veil may be pierced in the circumstances where it is pierced in domestic practice, for example, to prevent the misuse of the privileges arising from the legal personality, for example, fraud, the protection of third parties such as creditors or purchasers, or the prevention of the evasion of legal obligations.[134] Thirdly, the corporate veil may be pierced in any other circumstances despite the foreign involvement, provided that in doing so no obligation towards another State under International Law is being violated. As a corollary to this the corporate

---

[130] According to the Reporters Notes to the *US Restatement* (1987) it is not clear what the position would be if there are not nationals working in the foreign affiliate.

[131] *S.S. "Lotus"* (1927) P.C.I.J. Series A.No.10, 18–19.

[132] See H.G. Mair in Meesen (1996), p.64.

[133] See, for example, D. Greig, *International Law* (London, Butterworths, 1970), p.397.

[134] See *Barcelona Traction* case (1970) I.C.J. Reports, para.58. See also F. Mann (1984) *Recueil des Cours*, Vol.III, p.63.

veil may also be pierced where there are overriding national interests.[135] These principles are borne out by the *Barcelona Traction* case. The case is not authority for the rather absolute proposition attributed to it by F. Mann that as a matter of International Law parent and subsidiary are each subject to the exclusive jurisdiction of their respective sovereigns.[136] The lifting of the corporate veil may have a role in the establishment of jurisdiction,[137] although it may not necessarily be a general means of acquiring jurisdiction. Further, in any event, a parent company is present within the territorial jurisdiction of the State in its capacity as a share-holder or as directors,[138] and has a connection by reason of its interest in the company as a shareholder.[139]

The next question relates to the measure of enforcement through an intra-territorial connection permitted under International Law. There are mainly two views here underpinned by the *Lotus* controversy. First, it is maintained that generally there are no prohibitions in International Law in relation to the measure of enforcement jurisdiction exercised through a territorial pres-ence. Moreover, it has also been asserted, somewhat controversially that "an act by one state in the territory of another is contrary to international law only where there is a usurpation of the sovereign powers of the latter by the former".[140] This view proffered by Cynthia Wallace does not appear to accord with the principle in the *Lotus* case that a State may not exercise enforcement jurisdiction outside its territory. Secondly, it is maintained that there must be a measure of correlation between the nature of the connection and the degree of enforcement.[141] Thus, it is asserted that a State may not achieve a result through its enforcement jurisdiction on a matter over which it does not have legislative jurisdiction.[142] This debate continues. Although whatever the view,

---

[135] Greig (1970), p.398.

[136] Mann (1984), p.56.

[137] See also the ALI Restatement (1987), para.414, para.(I) of commentary. See also Case 48/69, *Imperial Chemical Industries Ltd v Commission* (1972) E.C.R. 619, 662; Case 6/72, *Europemballage Corp and Continental Can Co, Inc v Commission* (1973) E.C.R. 215; Case 6 and 7/73, *Instituto Chemioterapico Italiano SpA and Commercial Solvents Corp v Commission* (1974) E.C.R 223, 253–55.

[138] See W. Park, in C.J. Olmstead (ed.), *Extraterritorial application of laws and responses thereto* (Oxford, ESC Publishing, 1984), p.145.

[139] The *situs* of a share for tax purposes at any rate is located in the State of the residence of the Company. I.L.R. 42, p.409.

[140] C. Day Wallace (2002) 353–392 p.358, relying on M. Akehurst (1972–1973) 46 B.Y.I.L., p.146.

[141] See, for example, A.R. Albrecht, "The taxation of aliens under International Law" (1952) B.Y.I.L., p.156; F. Mann, "The doctrine of International Jurisdiction Revisited After Twenty Years" (1984) *Recueil des Cours* (III) p.29.

[142] Mann (1984), p.146. Contra C. Day Wallace (2002), 353–392, p.360: "The Lotus case dem-onstrates, then the somewhat arbitrary nature of the linkage of enforcement with prescriptive jurisdiction. . . It is not, then, far removed to reason that, just as a state having jurisdiction to prescribe a rule of law does not necessarily have jurisdiction to enforce it in all cases, the enforcement of a rule, where jurisdiction is established (through, for example, veil-lifting), ought not to have to rely in all cases solely on the power to prescribe a rule of law within the foreign territory in question."

the relevance of the conflicting legislation in the other State, and the requirement of actual control over events abroad, is recognised.

### Regulation of the environment[143]

**3-015**  States regulate conduct in the environmental field that has an extraterritorial effect. Such claims to extraterritorial jurisdiction are closely linked to
international economic issues—especially international trade. In particular
three extraterritorial effects are of note.[144] First, and most importantly, is
the claim to export environmental standards extraterritorially, through the
regulation of international trade, in the form of a denial of entry of products
that contravene certain environmental standards.[145] Secondly, high environmental standards in certain States has induced the relocation of certain
industries into developing countries, referred to as "polluting tourism".[146]
Here the concern has been in terms of the "duty" of the exporting State to
export environmental responsibilities so as to deal with the local lacuna in
environmental standards.[147] Finally, there is the increasing national practice
of prohibiting the import of environmentally noxious substances.[148]

The extent of a State's extraterritorial jurisdiction in the environmental
field under General International Law needs to be considered against the
background of the various multilateral environmental agreements, and the
normative framework under the WTO. Not only do some of these authorise
regulation with extraterritorial consequences,[149] but they also pose conflicts
between environmental and trade objectives, particularly in the context of the

---

[143] H.L. Thaggert, "A closer look at the Tuna-Dolphin Case: 'Like Products' and 'Extraterritorial-
jurisdictionality' in the Trade and the Environment Context", in J. Cameron et al. (eds),
*Trade and the Environment: The Search for Balance* (1994) Vol.1; GATT Panel decisions
on United States Restrictions on Import of Tuna (1991), Vol.30, I.L.M.; and (1994) Vol.33
I.L.M.; B. Kingsbury, "The Tuna-Dolphin Controversy, The World Trade Organization,
and the Liberal Project to Re conceptualize International Law" (1994) Vol.5, Yb.Int'l Env.l;
F. Francioni, "Extraterritorial application of environmental law", Ch.VI in Meesen (1996);
See, for example, A. Nollkaemper, "The existence and scope of rights to protect environmen-
tal values in other States through the use of trade measures", Ch.9 in F. Weiss et al. (eds),
*Towards International Economic Law with a Human Face* (1998); United States—Import of
Certain Shrimp and Shrimp Products, WTO Appellate Body (1998) (hereinafter referred
to as the *Shrimps* case); Brazil—Measures Affecting Imports of Retreaded Tyres, WTO
Appellate Body (2007).
[144] Francioni (1996), p.122.
[145] But see OECD, *Report on Trade and Environment*, 1995. See also GATT Panel Report,
United States—Restrictions on Imports of Tuna (1991), GATT (unadopted) (1991) 30
I.L.M.; and GATT Panel Report, USA—Restriction on Imports of Tuna (1994) (unadopted)
(1994) 33 I.L.M.; United States—Standards For Reformulated And Conventional Gasoline.
United States—Import Prohibition of Certain Shrimp Products, WTO Appellate Body
Report (1998).
[146] See F. Francioni (1996), p.122 and OECD, Report on Trade and Environment (1995).
[147] F. Francioni (1996), p.124 and see references therein to T. McGarity, "Bhopal and the
Export of Hazardous Technologies" (1985) 20 Texas Intl L.J. 333.
[148] F. Francioni (1996), p.122.
[149] For example, the Convention on the International Trade in Endangered Species; Protocol
on Substances that deplete the Ozone Layer (1987); Basle Convention on Transboundary
Movement of Hazardous Waste (1989) cited at Francioni (1996), p.129.

precise interpretation of the environmental safeguard exceptions under the GATT 1994.[150] However, the emphasis here is the General International Law framework of the jurisdictional limits.

Under General International Law the key grounds of relevance for the exercise of prescriptive jurisdiction may be the territorial principle, the nationality principle, the effects doctrine, and the universal principle, where global environmental interests are at stake, for example the ozone layer and the need to preserve biodiversity.[151] Amongst these, however, both the effects doctrine and the universal principle are controversial. Certainly, the unilateral imposition of national environmental standards extraterritorially is prohibited under General International Law.[152] The sovereign right of a State to formulate its own environmental policy (as long as there are no trans-boundary effects), in accordance with its socio-economic circumstances is acknowledged.[153] It should be noted though, that it has been contended that there is now an international practice that is beginning to take shape, wherein environmental standards are being applied on an extraterritorial basis. The observation is based on State practice, as evidenced in national legislation advancing extraterritorial claims of jurisdiction in the environmental field,[154] particularly in relation to the sea and marine resources[155]; multilateral treaty practice[156]; and UN General Assembly resolutions.[157] However, the evidence as to the *opinio juris* necessary for a binding customary international norm is yet to be found.[158]

---

[150] See Art.XX (b) and (g) of GATT 1994; and GATT Panel Reports, viz. United States—Restrictions on Imports of Tuna (1991) GATT (unadopted) (1991) 30 I.L.M.; and GATT Panel Report, USA—Restriction on Imports of Tuna (1994) (unadopted) (1994) 33 I.L.M.; and WTO Panel and Appellate Body Reports United States—Standards For Reformulated And Conventional Gasoline; United State—Import Prohibition of Certain Shrimp Products, WTO (1998).

[151] Francioni (1996), p.123. See also reference therein to B. Doos, "Environmental issues requiring international action", in Lang, Neuhold and Zemanek (eds), *Environmental Protection and International Law* (London/Dordrecht/Boston, Graham and Trotman/M. Nijhoff, 1991).

[152] See, for example, E.M. Hirzon in Meesen (ed.) (1996), p.136. See also 1992 Rio Declaration on Environment and Development (UNCED) (specially Principles 2, 11 and 12); Agenda 21 adopted by UNCED 1992; Principle 21 of the 1972 Stockholm Declaration on the Human Environment; OECD Report on Trade and Environment (1995). See also GATT Panel decisions on United States restrictions on Import of Tuna (1991), (1991) 30 I.L.M.; and (1994) 33 I.L.M.; United States—Import of Certain Shrimp and Shrimp Products, WTO (1998).

[153] See, for example, 1992 Rio Declaration on Environment and Development and the *Shrimps* case (Panel Report), p.289. See also the Appellate Body Report (1998).

[154] See, for example, the State practice described by Nollkaemper (1998) viz., Austrian Federal Law for the labelling of tropical timber and tropical products and for the creation of a quality mark for timber and timber products from sustainable exploitation, BGB/309/1992; EC eco-labeling scheme—Council Regulation 880/92 OJ (1992) L99; Dutch Government's Policy Paper on Tropical Rainforest (1992); US Wild Bird Conservation Act 1992; US Federal Meat Inspection Act, Vol.21 U.S.C (1994).

[155] See, for example, Canada's Arctic Water Pollution Act 1970; the US Marine Mammals Protection Act (MMPA) 1972 (as variously amended); New Zealand 1991 legislation prohibiting pelagic drift nets referred to by Francioni (1996).

[156] For example, the 1989 Wellington Convention on the prohibition of pelagic drifnets; the 1990 Noumea Protocol cited by Francioni (1996).

[157] Francioni (1996), p.131.

[158] Francioni (1996), p.131. See also WTO *Shrimps* case.

In relation to internationally agreed environmental standards, where that standard relates, for example, to a global environmental threat, there is some suggestion that extraterritoriality may have a place, provided certain conditions are met.[159] Thus, it has been suggested that the measure should be proportionate, necessary in the sense that there are no other "intra-territorial" means of dealing with the hazard[160]; non-discriminatory; transparent; and taking into account the special conditions and development capacity of developing nations.[161] The existence of internationally agreed environmental standards, it is contended, takes the matter outside the exclusive domestic jurisdiction of a State.[162] However, the importance of serious bilateral/multilateral negotiations prior to the application of unilateral extraterritorial measures, where the matter is a transboundary one, and where there is a nexus involved with the State applying the measure, has been emphasised as a matter of law and precondition.[163] Further, it has also been suggested that extraterritorial environmental policies based on a violation of an international agreement could also be analysed as countermeasures.[164]

### Regulation to enforce foreign policy

**3-016**     States have exercised jurisdiction in order to enforce their foreign policy, through regulating the conduct of private economic participants both within and outside the jurisdiction, with extraterritorial effect. This has been done through the prohibition of exports whether or not nationals, including foreign affiliated companies and branches controlled by domestic companies.[165] A further device of ensuring continued State control abroad has been to impose re-export (or user) conditions on certain goods of domestic

---

[159] E.M. Hirzon (1996), p.134; Nollkaemper (1998), p.195, and D. Esty, *Greening the GATT: Trade, Environment & the Future* (1994). See also *Shrimps/Turtle* case WTO Appellate Body Report (1998); and A.H. Qureshi, "Extraterritorial shrimps, NGO's, and the WTO Appellate Body" (1999) I.C.L.Q.

[160] Hirzon (1998), p.134.

[161] Hirzon (1998), p.134 and Agenda 21 of 1992 UNCED.

[162] See Nollkaemper (1996), p.195. See also *Nicaragua v US* (1986) I.C.J. Reports, para.258.

[163] See *Shrimps* case Panel Report (1998), p.292. This part of the Panel decision seems to have been confirmed by the Appellate Body upon appeal. See Appellate Body Report WTO (1998). See also A.H. Qureshi "Extraterritorial Shrimps, NGOs, and the WTO Appellate Body" (1999) I.C.L.Q.

[164] See Nollkaemper (1998), p.196.

[165] See, for example, s.8 of the US Export Administration Act 1979, and the Iran and Libya Sanctions Act of 1996 (known as the D'Amata Act). See also, for example, R. Edwards, "Extraterritorial application of the US Iran Assets Control Regulations" (1981) 75 A.J.I.L., p.870; H. Moyer and L. Mabry, "Export controls as instruments of foreign policy: the history, legal issues and policy lessons of three recent cases" (1983) 15 L & Pol.Int.Bus, p.1; D. Vagt, K. Meesen, P. Kuyper and J. Basedow in (1984) 27 G.Y.I.L.; A.V. Lowe, "International Law issues arising in the pipeline dispute: the British position" (1984) 27 G.Y.I.L. 55–71; Lowe, "Public International Law and the Conflict of Laws" (1984) 33 I.C.L.Q., p.515; J. Bridge, "The law and policies of US Foreign Policy Export Controls" (1984) 4 *Legal Studies*, p.2; H.G. Maier in Meesen (1996), Ch.IV; H.G.A. Bianchi, "Extraterritoriality and export controls: some remarks on the alleged antinomy between European and US approaches" (1992) 35 G.Y.I.L. 366–434, K. Meesen (ed.), *The International Law of Export Control* (1992);

origin.[166] Thus, such assets even though owned and controlled by foreign corporations, when of military or technological significance, if passed on to third parties, are subject to such regulation. Prescriptive jurisdiction has been enforced intra-territorially, through such sanctions, as damages, denial of entry into the country, and denial of the right to engage in international trade (i.e. import and export) with the country.

Generally export controls applied to foreign subsidiaries, and non-resident non-nationals, are regarded as extraterritorial and contrary to international norms.[167] Similarly, jurisdiction over goods on the basis of their origin, once they are outside the territory, is not recognised under International Law.[168]

## RESPONSES TO EXTRATERRITORIAL EXERCISES OF JURISDICTION[169]

To date, States have responded to the various jurisdictional conflicts in a variety of ways. Domestically, States have various internal options to manage the unilateral exercise of extraterritorial jurisdiction. First, there is the option of restraint through reasonable engagement in extraterritorial exercise of jurisdiction. Thus, the US engages a "reasonableness" test in the application of its legislation extraterritorially when based on the effects doctrine. Secondly, it is a generally recognised principle of interpretation of domestic statutes that unless expressly stated there is a "presumption against the extraterritorial application of domestic legislation. This was reiterated in the recent US Supreme Court decision in *Morrison v National Australia Bank Ltd*.[170] Thirdly, national legislators and domestic courts are also bound by "a presumption against the extension of statutes beyond limits set by the international law of legislative jurisdiction, or a presumption against extrajurisdictionality".[171] These principles of legislative jurisdiction under International Law, such as they are, partake of Customary International

**3-017**

Lowe, "US extraterritorial jurisdiction: the Helms-Burton and D'Amoto Acts" (1997) I.C.L.Q.

[166] See, for example, US Export Administration Regulations. Such exercises of jurisdiction have been described by W. Pengally (1997) 20(3) *World Competition* 17–55 (March) as the "contractual submission theory".

[167] See, for example, *Oppenheim's International Law* (1996), p.471; V. Lowe, "US extraterritorial jurisdiction: the Helms-Burton and D'Amota Acts" (April 1997) I.C.L.Q. See also C.Ryngaert, *Chinese Journal of International Law* (2008).

[168] See A. Bianchi in K. Meesen (1996), p.95. (I am grateful to Andrea Bianchi for correcting a previous inaccuracy in this footnote of the first edition.) See also C. Ryngaert, *Chinese Journal of International Law* (2008).

[169] See, for example, A. D. Melamed, "International Cooperation in Competition Law and Policy: What can be achieved at the bilateral, regional, and multilateral levels" (1999) J.I.E.L. 423–433.

[170] US Supreme Court (June 24, 2010).

[171] See John H. Knox, The Unpredictable Presumption Against Extraterritoriality (January 11, 2011). Southwestern University Law Review, Forthcoming; Wake Forest University Legal Studies Paper No. 1739967. Available at SSRN: *http://ssrn.com/abstract=1739967*.

Law, and therefore would be directly applicable in most jurisdictions adhering to the doctrine of incorporation with respect to General International Law.[172] Fourthly, States at the receiving end of extraterritorial jurisdiction have some unilateral mechanisms to undermine the foreign exercise of jurisdiction, through, for example, prohibitions on the production of evidence and documents to the State exercising extraterritorial jurisdiction[173]; unilateral mechanisms to thwart the objectives of the foreign extraterritorial legislation completely, through, for example, blocking legislation essentially prohibiting compliance with overseas extraterritorial requirements in certain fields[174]; unilateral mechanisms to recapture losses sustained as a consequence of any extraterritorial exercise of jurisdiction, by allowing for the recovery of losses incurred overseas within the jurisdiction.[175] Finally, at the international level there is the option of diplomacy; bilateral agreements[176]; regional,[177] multilateral[178] efforts including multilateral harmonisation of relevant laws; and through litigation.[179]

Of late there have been several proposals for a better management of jurisdictional conflicts between States. First, of note is the suggestion made by C. Ryngaert that there should be a rule-based framework of jurisdic-

---

(Accessed June 8, 2011); and John H. Knox, "A presumption against extrajurisdictionality", 104 Am.J.Int'L.351 (2010).

[172] See Ch. 4 below.

[173] See, for example, the Australian Foreign Proceedings (Prohibition of Certain Evidence) Act of 1976; the UK Protection of Trading Interests Act of 1980. See W. Pengally (1997), p.40 lists other States with similar legislation, e.g. UK, New Zealand, South Africa, Canada, Belgium, Denmark, Finland, France, Germany, Italy, the Netherlands, the Philippines and Sweden.

[174] See, for example, Australian Foreign Judgement (Restriction of Enforcement) Act of 1979 and The Foreign Proceedings (Excess of Jurisdiction) Act 1984; UK Protection of Trading Interests Act 1980. There are some 20 countries with blocking statutes (see P. Bovey, in Meesen (ed.) (1996), p.157).

[175] See, for example, the UK Protection of Trading Interests Act 1980.

[176] For example, in tax Double Taxation Agreements; in anti-trust for example the USA—Australia Agreement Relating to Cooperation on Anti-Trust Matters (1982) I.L.M. 21; Memorandum of Understanding between the Government of the United States of America and the Government of Canada as to Notification, Consultation and Cooperation with respect to the Application of National Antitrust Laws, (1984) 23 I.L.M. 275; Agreement Regarding the Application of Competition Laws between the US and EU (as rectified) (1995) O.J.L. 95/45.

[177] See, for example, NAFTA Art.1501.

[178] Not many. But see, for example, the OECD Decision of 1976 (as amended 1991) on Intergovernmental Consultation Procedures on the guidelines for Multinational Enterprises. This has not been frequently used (see Bovey (1996), p.158). See also in the sphere of competition OECD Council recommendations, for example, OECD Guiding Principles for Regulatory Quality and Performance (2005); OECD Best Practices for Formal Exchange of Information Between Competition Authorities in Hard Core Cartel Investigations (2005); OECD Recommendations of the Council Concerning Merger Reviews (2005); OECD Recommendations of the Council Concerning Structural Separation in Regulated Industries (2001); OECD Recommendations of the Council Concerning Effective Action Against Hard Core Cartels (1998); OECD Recommendations of the Council Concerning Cooperation between member Countries on anticompetitive practices affecting international trade (1995).

[179] By, for example, resorting to the WTO dispute settlement mechanism, if this was an option.

tion under which unilateral exercises of jurisdiction are managed.[180] Under this framework there would be transnational networks which would facilitate consultation between courts, regulators and private actors before the exercise of unilateral extraterritorial jurisdiction. Ryngaert advocates that this is a relatively better option than substantivism. Substantivism in his discourse comprises "an international *jus commune* of substantive rules and procedures"[181]—to be equated essentially with the process of harmonisation of laws. This is mainly because according to Ryngaert the process by which substantivism is arrived involves an inter-play of power; and therefore the powerful States have a greater influence in the outcome of multilateral negotiations for harmonisation of laws in accordance with their interests.[182] Moreover, the overall costs involved at the multilateral level (including the time involved in arriving at an agreement) are greater than those involved in the exercise of unilateral jurisdiction.[183] Ryngaert's assertions are however somewhat generalised. Thus, multilateral negotiations are more nuanced now in terms of the play of the power dynamics, with developing countries increasingly acting in groups. Additionally, the multilateral forum must surely blunt the force of the unilateralist. Moreover, the efficiency argument needs more clarification. Thus, W Grassl using Game Theory concludes that co-operating on a legal regime "is the most efficient option or, as the economist would say, it is Pareto-superior".[184] The assertion therefore that substantivism in the long run is not the better approach is not without controversy.

Secondly, the International Bar Association in a recent study recommends a number of possible approaches to resolving the problem of extraterritoriality. These are summarised as follows:[185]

"(a)  creating a legal hierarchy or other test to determine which state has priority;

(b)  encouraging states to adopt discretionary doctrines to refrain from exercising jurisdiction in certain circumstances (i.e., no legal hierarchy, but consideration of doctrines such as reasonableness and comity to temper the use of extraterritorial jurisdiction);

(c)  establishing methods of mutual recognition and cooperation between multiple states with jurisdiction (i.e., no legal hierarchy, but systems to encourage cooperation between states to avoid jurisdictional conflicts); and

---

[180]  See C. Ryngaert, "The Limits of Substantive International Economic Law: In Support of Reasonable Extraterritorial Jurisdiction", in Eric Claes, Wouter Devroe and Bert Keirsbilck, eds., Facing the Limits of the Law, (Berlin, Heidelberg, Springer, 2009), pp. 237–252.

[181]  C. Ryngaert (2008) at p.194.

[182]  C. Ryngaert (2009) at p.238.

[183]  C. Ryngaert (2009) at p.2343.

[184]  W. Grassl (2008) at p.8.

[185]  IBA: Report of the Task Force on Extraterritorial Jurisdiction (2009) at p.26.

(d) encouraging harmonisation of laws (i.e. no legal hierarchy, but encouraging convergence in the substance of laws to reduce the problems caused by jurisdictional conflicts)."

The responses to the problem of extraterritoriality thus far have in practice generally been of a unilateral or bilateral character in the absence of harmonisation, and have tended to be ad hoc, responding to new developments. There is also generally a marked absence of active participation in the jurisdiction discourse from the developing States' perspectives. These perspectives may differ according to the economic sphere involved. They need to be understood. From the standpoint of democracy all the participants in international economic relations need to have a voice in the development of jurisdictional principles. Further, such development should be transparent and multilateral. The multilateral approach can be sector specific, as well as general. Thus, an authoritative multilateral general clarification of some core jurisdictional principles may be in order. In conjunction with this there may be a case for the establishment of an international institutional mechanism facilitating resolution of jurisdictional issues.

### CHAPTER 4

# RELATIONSHIP BETWEEN NATIONAL AND INTERNATIONAL ECONOMIC LAW

## INTRODUCTION

The relationship between national and IEL is multifaceted, integrationist **4-001** and dynamic. It is multifaceted in that the enquiries involved in considering the relationship are varied; integrationist in its provision of an interface between national and IEL; and dynamic both in terms of the scope and pace of the relationship. Hitherto the primary focus of this relationship in IEL has been through the international trade paradigm,[1] particularly in terms of the status of international economic obligations at the national and international levels respectively. This focus is a useful model for a general examination of the relationship between national and IEL, provided it is informed by the knowledge that it does not necessarily provide a complete snap-shot of the relationship issues.

The relationship between national and IEL involves a number of processes, viz. formulation of foreign economic policy, implementation of international economic obligations and legal scrutiny of national economic measures. These processes are not necessarily exclusive; and may be analysed from an international or a domestic perspective. The aspects of the formulation process involve the procedures facilitating the formation of national foreign

---

[1] See, for example, J. Jackson, "Status of treaties in domestic legal systems: a policy analysis" (1992) 86 A.J.I.L. 310, 315–319; M. Hilf and E-U Petersmann (eds), *National Constitutions and International Economic Law*, Kluwer (1993); E-U Petersmann, "The Future of International Economic Law: A Research Agenda", EUI Working Paper LAW 2010/06; J. Jackson and A. Sykes, *Implementing the Uruguay Round* (Oxford University Press, 1997); T. Cottier and K.N. Schefer, "The relationship between World Trade Organization, National and Regional Law" (1998) *Journal of International Economic Law*, Vol.1; P. Eeckhout, "The domestic legal status of the WTO Agreements: Interconnecting Legal Systems" (1997) 34 C.M.L.R. 11, 40–42. For general works on the relationship between national and International Law, see, for example, Jacobs and Roberts (eds), *The Effect of Treaties in Domestic Law* (London: Sweet & Maxwell, 1987); S.R. Riesenfeld and F.M. Abbott (eds), *Parliamentary participation in the making and operations of treaties: a comparative study* (Dordrecht: Martinus Nijhoff, 1994); M. Leigh and M.R. Blakeslee (eds), *National Treaty Law and Practice* (Washington D.C.: American Society of International Law, 1995).

economic policy and legislation; the procedures and structures involved in the translation at the international level of national foreign economic policy, through the negotiation and acceptance of international economic commitments; and the substantive content of the normative fraemwork. The processes involved in implementation are concerned with the procedures of policing, and enforcement of IEL at the national level. The processes involved in legal scrutiny focus on the status of national law at the international level, and the status of IEL at the national level. The processes of implementation and scrutiny are closely related. To the extent that these processes are internal to the State, they nevertheless feature in the relationship of national and IEL, given that they are the internal response to international economic affairs.

The relationship between national and IEL has traditionally been State-centered and therefore top-down.[2] However, human rights developments call for a more cosmopolitan, multi-level, citizen oriented, bottom up approach.[3] Thus, the discourse on the relationship between national and IEL is concerned with establishing what the relevant considerations are in the determination of the various formulation, implementation and legal scrutiny processes. It is grounded in considerations relating to constitutional safeguards in the national foreign economic relations field, as well as the efficacy of IEL. Thus, it is concerned with the doctrine of separation of powers as it relates to national foreign economic policy and practice; good governance in the national foreign economic policy and practice, viz. the rule of law, transparency, accountability, democratic processes, due process, non-discrimination, proportionality; economic efficiency; and human rights.

## FORMULATION: PROCESS AND SUBSTANCE

4-002    Generally, the formulation process involved in national foreign economic policy and practice tend to be primordial, lacking in constitutional safeguards, and inducing an inefficient manner of engagement in international economic relations.[4] Thus, there are few effective constitutional checks on the government, such as separation of power, democratic participation in policy formation, due process, transparency, proportionality, and non-discrimination.[5] In the field of international trade in particular, constitutional principles of separation of legislative and executive powers are not

---

[2] See E-U Petersmann, "The Future of International Economic Law: A Research Agenda", EUI Working Paper LAW 2010/06.

[3] E-U Petersmann, "The Future of International Economic Law: A Research Agenda", EUI Working Paper LAW 2010/06

[4] See E-U Petersmann, "National constitutions and international economic law" in Hilf and Petersmann (1993) Ch.1, p.8. See also K Meesen, "Governmental decision-making in the World Economy", *European Yearbook of International Economic Law* (2011).

[5] Petersmann (1993).

prominent.[6] For example, in the US, the executive's power of entering into self-executing treaties having direct effect in the domestic legal system, is not subject to effective constitutional controls—especially legislative.[7] Thus, the US executive has in the past at any rate engaged in negotiating VERs[8] without legislative involvement.[9] Similarly, in the EU, the mandate for its external economic relations is broadly drafted,[10]and somewhat removed from the ordinary citizens of its member States.

**EXAMPLE: CONSOLIDATED VERSIONS OF THE TREATY ON EUROPEAN UNION AND THE TREATY ON THE FUNCTIONING OF THE EUROPEAN UNION[11]**

**4-003**

**(2010/C 83/01)EN 30.3.2010 Official Journal of the European Union C 83/1**

**TITLE II COMMON COMMERCIAL POLICY**

*Article 206* (ex Article 131 TEC)

By establishing a customs union in accordance with Articles 28 to 32, the Union shall contribute, in the common interest, to the harmonious development of world trade, the progressive abolition of restrictions on international trade and on foreign direct investment, and the lowering of customs and other barriers. EN 30.3.2010 Official Journal of the European Union C 83/139

*Article 207* **(ex Article 133 TEC)**

1. The common commercial policy shall be based on uniform principles, particularly with regard to changes in tariff rates, the conclusion of tariff and trade agreements relating to trade in goods and services, and the commercial aspects of intellectual property, foreign direct investment, the achievement of uniformity in measures of liberalisation, export policy and measures to protect trade such as those to be taken in the event of dumping or subsidies. The common commercial policy shall be conducted in the context of the principles and objectives of the Union's external action.

2. The European Parliament and the Council, acting by means of regulations in accordance with the ordinary legislative procedure, shall adopt the measures defining the framework for implementing the common commercial policy.

3. Where agreements with one or more third countries or international organisations need to be negotiated and concluded, Article 218 shall apply, subject to the special provisions of this Article.

   The Commission shall make recommendations to the Council, which

---

[6] Petersmann (1993), p.34.
[7] Petersmann (1993), p.29.
[8] Voluntary Export Restrictions.
[9] Petersmann (1993), p.36.
[10] Petersmann (1993), p.36. See Arts 206 and 207 of The Lisbon Treaty.
[11] *http://eur-lex.europa.eu/LexUriServ/LexUriServ.do?uri=OJ:C:2010:083:FULL:EN:PDF* (Accessed June 8, 2011).

shall authorise it to open the necessary negotiations. The Council and the Commission shall be responsible for ensuring that the agreements negotiated are compatible with internal Union policies and rules.

The Commission shall conduct these negotiations in consultation with a special committee appointed by the Council to assist the Commission in this task and within the framework of such directives as the Council may issue to it. The Commission shall report regularly to the special committee and to the European Parliament on the progress of negotiations.

4. For the negotiation and conclusion of the agreements referred to in paragraph 3, the Council shall act by a qualified majority.

   For the negotiation and conclusion of agreements in the fields of trade in services and the commercial aspects of intellectual property, as well as foreign direct investment, the Council shall act unanimously where such agreements include provisions for which unanimity is required for the adoption of internal rules.

   The Council shall also act unanimously for the negotiation and conclusion of agreements:

   (a) in the field of trade in cultural and audiovisual services, where these agreements risk prejudicing the Union's cultural and linguistic diversity;

   (b) in the field of trade in social, education and health services, where these agreements risk seriously disturbing the national organisation of such services and prejudicing the responsibility of Member States to deliver them.

5. The negotiation and conclusion of international agreements in the field of transport shall be subject to Title VI of Part Three and to Article 218. EN C 83/140 Official Journal of the European Union 30.3.2010

6. The exercise of the competences conferred by this Article in the field of the common commercial policy shall not affect the delimitation of competences between the Union and the Member States, and shall not lead to harmonisation of legislative or regulatory provisions of the Member States in so far as the Treaties exclude such harmonisation.

## TITLE III COOPERATION WITH THIRD COUNTRIES AND HUMANITARIAN AID

### CHAPTER 1

### DEVELOPMENT COOPERATION

*Article 208* (ex Article 177 TEC)

1. Union policy in the field of development cooperation shall be conducted within the framework of the principles and objectives of the Union's external action. The Union's development cooperation policy and that of the Member States complement and reinforce each other.

   Union development cooperation policy shall have as its primary objective the reduction and, in the long term, the eradication of poverty. The Union shall take account of the objectives of development cooperation in the policies that it implements which are likely to affect developing countries.

> 2. The Union and the Member States shall comply with the commitments
> and take account of the objectives they have approved in the context of
> the United Nations and other competent international organisations.

In terms of the substance of the policy, in particular, domestic systems do     **4-004**
not recognise the importance of the transnational economic rights of the
individual[12] as a human right.[13] Thus, in common with most States, in the
US the individual's right to engage in international trade is considered a
privilege, rather than a right.[14] Yet individual transnational economic rights
are human rights, and such rights are acknowledged within federations and
regional economic organisations.[15] The transnational economic rights of
the individual are a bundle of rights related to an open, liberal international
economic system. The rights embrace, for example, in the field of trade, the
right to import and export goods and services; in the monetary field, the
right to remit currencies and exchange currencies; in the development field
the right to be involved in IMF and World Bank conditionalities; in the
field of international taxation, the right not to be double taxed; in the field
of investment, the right to be accorded appropriate compensation upon the
expropriation of property situated abroad and the right to repatriate profits.
National constitutions do not provide effective mechanisms to safeguard
these rights. Similarly, domestic systems do not provide effective mechanisms
which ensure that foreign economic policy is subjected to cost-benefit analysis taking the interests of consumers, the general welfare of the community,
and the economic interests of all the participants as a whole.[16]

In his seminal work E-U Petersmann,[17] in describing the importance
of constitutional safeguards in the context of national foreign economic
policy-making and practice, suggests that there should be a constitutional guarantee of the individual's transnational economic rights, both
on grounds of individual liberty and economic efficiency.[18] This right, he
asserts, should inter alia be guaranteed to the individual, through the direct
invokability of international economic norms which are designed to ensure
transnational economic rights.[19] Government limitations on individual liberties should have a legal basis, and must be necessary and proportionate.
The executive's power to constrain individual liberty must be accompanied
by precise criteria as to use of its discretionary power in foreign economic
affairs. Restrictions on individual rights must have a basis in parliamentary legislation. There should be separation of power to protect against
concentrations of uncontrolled power in a single authority. Delegation of

[12] i.e. the rights of the individual, for example, to import and export.
[13] Petersmann (1997).
[14] Petersmann (1997), p.17.
[15] Petersmann (1997), p.10.
[16] Petersmann (1997).
[17] Petersmann (1993), Ch.1, pp.29, 30, 31, 42, 48, and 49.
[18] Peteersmann (1993), pp.8 and 39.
[19] Petersmann (1993), p.7.

powers must be limited, and accompanied with guidelines. Broad discretion enhances the opportunities for rent-seeking. There should be due process, and judicial protection of individual rights, for example, through the availability of judicial review processes of government restrictions on transnational economic rights. Policy formation must be transparent and democratically arrived at.

The traditional justifications for wide discretionary governmental powers in the field of national foreign economic policy and practice was set against the background of a lack of prohibition on the use of force in International Law; in mercantilism and the primacy of national interests; in adversarial State relations; and a belief that foreign policy (including national foreign economic policy) is best left to those knowledgeable about such affairs in the Government.[20] However, foreign economic policy no longer operates within such parameters. In particular, the case for such unchecked discretionary national foreign economic policy is not weighty any longer, given that foreign economic policy in the globalized economy is intricately connected with individual welfare[21] and international welfare. Further, better communication and education has meant that the individual is sometimes even better informed than government—in particular NGOs.

**EXAMPLE: Judgment of the Court of December 12, 1972—International Fruit Company NV and others v Produktschap voor Groenten en Fruit—Reference for a preliminary ruling: College van Beroep voor het Bedrijfsleven—Netherlands—Joined cases 21 to 24–72[22]**

**4-005**

1. By decision of 5 May 1972, received at the Court Registry on 8 May 1972, the College van beroep voor het bedrijfsleven referred to the Court, under Article 177 of the EEC Treaty, two questions relating to the interpretation of that article and to the validity of certain regulations adopted by the Commission.

2. The first question invites the Court to rule whether the validity of measures adopted by the institutions of the Community also refers, within the meaning of Article 177 of the EEC Treaty, to their validity under international law.

. . .

18. It therefore appears that, in so far as under the EEC treaty the Community has assumed the powers previously exercised by member states in the area governed by the General Agreement [GATT 1947], the provisions of that agreement have the effect of binding the community.

19. It is also necessary to examine whether the provisions of the General Agreement confer rights on citizens of the Community on which they can rely before the courts in contesting the validity of a Community measure.

---

[20] Petersmann (1993), p.9.
[21] Petersmann (1993).
[22] [1972] E.C.R. 1219.

20. For this purpose, the spirit, the general scheme and the terms of the General Agreement must be considered.

21. This agreement which, according to its preamble, is based on the principle of negotiations undertaken on the basis of 'reciprocal and mutually advantageous arrangements' is characterized by the great flexibility of its provisions, in particular those conferring the possibility of derogation, the measures to be taken when confronted with exceptional difficulties and the settlement of conflicts between the contracting parties.

22. Consequently, according to the first paragraph of Article XXII 'each contracting party shall accord sympathetic consideration to, and shall afford adequate opportunity for consultation regarding, such representations as may be made by any other contracting party with respect to. . .All matters affecting the operation of this agreement'.

23. According to the second paragraph of the same Article, 'the contracting parties'—this name designating 'the contracting parties acting jointly' as is stated in the first paragraph of Article xxv—'may consult with one or more contracting parties on any question to which a satisfactory solution cannot be found through the consultations provided under paragraph (1)'.

24. If any contracting party should consider 'that any benefit accruing to it directly or indirectly under this agreement is being nullified or impaired or that the attainment of any objective of the agreement is being impeded as a result of', inter alia, 'the failure of another contracting party to carry out its obligations under this agreement', article xxiii lays down in detail the measures which the parties concerned, or the contracting parties acting jointly, may or must take in regard to such a situation.

25. Those measures include, for the settlement of conflicts, written recommendations or proposals which are to be 'given sympathetic consideration', investigations possibly followed by recommendations, consultations between or decisions of the contracting parties, including that of authorizing certain contracting parties to suspend the application to any others of any obligations or concessions under the general agreement and, finally, in the event of such suspension, the power of the party concerned to withdraw from that agreement.

26. Finally, where by reason of an obligation assumed under the General Agreement or of a concession relating to a benefit, some producers suffer or are threatened with serious damage, article xix gives a contracting party power unilaterally to suspend the obligation and to withdraw or modify the concession, either after consulting the contracting parties jointly and failing agreement between the contracting parties concerned, or even, if the matter is urgent and on a temporary basis, without prior consultation.

27. Those factors are sufficient to show that, when examined in such a context, article xi of the general agreement is not capable of conferring on citizens of the community rights which they can invoke before the courts. . .

However, the arguments propounded by Petersmann reflect an individualist view of the world. In his view, the only reason for the State to exist is the **4-006** individual, and the maximisation of individual liberty. On the other hand, the international society is premised on a plural State system. Developing economies, as well as transitional economies, need to be more interventionist and therefore are concerned with the individual's transnational economic rights from this perspective. Further, some States, particularly Islamic, may be perceived as less wedded ideologically to absolute notions of individual liberty. In addition, it has been contended that liberal economic theory should not be thrust upon nations but rather should be promoted through persuasion.[23]

The translation, shaping, and articulation of national foreign economic policy at the international level, takes place through the negotiation and acceptance of international economic commitments. The structures through which the national negotiators operate; the identity of the national negotiators involved, and their precise mandate has a bearing on the direction of the negotiations at the international level.[24] Thus, negotiations can be influenced by the identity and composition of the negotiators, who in turn can be influenced by particular national interest groups[25]; the level of power of the negotiators, given the credibility of the negotiators is contingent upon their mandate[26]; the mechanisms or lack thereof to ensure that the executive pursues the concerns of the legislature[27]; the checks or lack thereof to ensure that the executive negotiators are not being influenced by a bureaucracy which may have its own agenda to follow[28]; and finally the procedures and likelihood for the acceptance or ratification of the international economic commitments negotiated.

In this respect the structure of the interface between regional economic organisations (RIOs) and federal systems, and their respective constituents, has a particular bearing on the negotiation of international economic commitments. Thus, in such systems the individual States of the federation and members of the RIO can affect the negotiations in two ways. First, given that they generally do not have a right to veto the outcome of the final negotiations, they tend to restrict at the outset the competence of the central authorities, where possible.[29] For example, the precise mandate of the European Commission representing the EU in negotiating international trade agreements used to be shared with individual members of the EU in the field of services and intellectual property rights[30] prior to the Lisbon Treaty. Although there was a duty to co-operate in the negotiation of international agreements in this field, such a shared competence carried with it the possi-

---

[23] J.H. Jackson, "National Constitutions, Transnational Economic Policy and International Law: Some Reflections" in M. Hilf and E-U Petersmann (eds), *National Constitutions and International Economic Law* (Deventer, Kluwer, 1993), pp.569–576 at 575.
[24] See Jackson and Sykes (1997).
[25] Jackson and Sykes (1997), Ch.13.
[26] Jackson and Sykes (1997), Ch.13.
[27] Jackson and Sykes (1997), p.459.
[28] Jackson and Sykes (1997), p.459.
[29] Jackson and Sykes (1997), Ch.13.
[30] See ECJ Opinion 1/94.

bility of restraint. Despite the closing of this gap in services and intellectual property rights now, some competences are still shared post the Lisbon Treaty, for example the agricultural and fisheries sectors.[31]Further, generally differences between individual members and the Commission as to the direction of international negotiations can handicap the negotiators, particularly if the non-members have knowledge of those differences.[32] Secondly, the negotiators have to bear in mind that the eventual ratification and implementation of the outcome of the negotiations may depend ultimately on the individual States and members.[33]

In conclusion, at the international level many of the concerns in relation to the formulation and substance of national foreign economic policy and practice have in fact been taken up by international organisations. Thus, the IMF and World Bank Group through their consultation procedures and conditionalities have pushed for good governance practices at the national level in the economic sphere. A similar thrust can be discerned in the practice of the WTO—particularly through its Trade Policy Review Mechanism directed at the manner in which national foreign trade policy is arrived at.

## IMPLEMENTATION AND LEGAL SCRUTINY

The relationship between national and IEL inevitably leads to a focus on the status of IEL in the domestic system, and conversely the status of domestic law at the international level. This focus essentially involves scrutiny of the national legal system from different perspectives.          **4-007**

First, there is the question relating to the status of international economic agreements within the domestic legal systems. This is the more complex issue arising from the fact that IEL leaves it to domestic systems the manner in which IEL should be adopted within the State.[34] The precise status of international economic agreements within the domestic system has a bearing on the effectiveness of the implementation of the international economic agreement—whether bilateral or multilateral. It also has a bearing on the degree of adherence to certain fundamental international economic norms; and on the discretion in foreign economic policy formulation by the executive and the legislature. This is of particular significance given that in IEL, State

---

[31] See Art.4(2) of the Consolidated Versions of the Treaty on European Union and the Treaty on the Functioning of the European Union

[32] See P. van den Bossche, Ch.2, in Jackson and Sykes (1997), p.68.

[33] See P. van den Bossche, Ch.2, in Jackson and Sykes (1997). See now however also Article 218 of Consolidated Versions of the Treaty on European Union and the Treaty on the Functioning of the European Union which sets out the procedure for the conclusion of agreements under the common commercial policy. These now involve substantially the European Council and Parliament.

[34] See, for example, Jackson and Sykes (1997), Ch.13.

practice in relation to treaties is prevalent, whereas Customary International Economic norms are at a minimum.

The status of IEL within the domestic system is dependent upon the approach adopted by it to the system of International Law. The practice of States in this regard is not uniform. At a theoretical level, three models of the relationship have been formulated.[35] First, under monism, International Law and domestic law are part of the same system; and here International Law prevails over domestic law, where there is a conflict, without further ado.[36] Secondly, under dualism International Law and domestic law operate separately. International Law in the domestic system operates only if specifically applied by the State through, for example, legislation.[37] Domestic law overrides International Law. Finally, under an intermediate position between monism and dualism, is the theory that International Law and domestic law are two different systems.[38] Thus, no question of International Law overriding domestic law arises, given that they are different systems of law. Each is supreme in its respective sphere.[39]

The language and theory of the models is however mirrored in the adherence under domestic law to the doctrines of incorporation and transformation. Basically, under the doctrine of incorporation International Law norms are without further ado part of the domestic legal system. They have direct effect in the national legal system. Under the doctrine of transformation, International Law is part of domestic law only if it has been specifically transformed into the domestic legal system, normally through legislation.

**4-008**     The three theoretical models provide some insight into State practice in relation to the status of IEL in the domestic sphere. However, the practice of States does not necessarily comfortably fit exactly in the models.[40] It varies as between General International Law and Treaties. It also varies in the degree to which States adhere to any particular theoretical framework. As a general rule, in most States Customary International Law is incorporated into the domestic system without further ado, provided it does not conflict with domestic legislation.[41] In relation to treaties however, the position is more complex. In most common law States generally, treaties have to be transformed through legislation to be part of the domestic legal system.[42] In civil law systems, the practice in relation to treaties is not uniform. In some

---

[35] See, for example, M. Shaw, *International Law*, 4th edn (Cambridge, Grotious, 1997), p.100.
[36] Shaw, p.100.
[37] Shaw, p.100.
[38] Shaw (1997), p.102 (and see now 5th edition). See also, for example, Fitzmaurice, "The general principles of international law considered from the standpoint of the rule of law" (1957) 92 Hague *Recueil*, II.
[39] Shaw (1997).
[40] Shaw (1997), p.127.
[41] Shaw (1997), p.127.
[42] Shaw (1997), p.120. See, in the UK, for example, *Trendtex Trading Corporation v Central Bank of Nigeria* (1977) 2 W.L.R. 356; and *Maclaine Watson v Department of Trade and Industry* (1988) 3 W.L.R. 1033.

States, for example, the Netherlands, in relation to treaties the doctrine of incorporation applies.[43] In Germany, the doctrine of incorporation applies but subject to the constitution.[44] In France, the doctrine of incorporation applies to a stated category of treaties only.[45] In the US, generally treaties are on the same par as domestic legislation subject to the rule that the later in time prevails. More specifically, the doctrine of incorporation applies to self-executing treaties,[46] subject to subsequent US legislation.[47] In Russia, treaties are part of the domestic system without further ado.[48] In Korea, the doctrine of incorporation is followed but foreigners can only invoke the treaty provision in domestic Korean courts if their own systems allow for a similar remedy.[49]

Whatever the status of IEL in the domestic sphere, this much is clear in most States that there is a presumption that domestic legislation is to be interpreted in such a manner as to avoid conflict with International Law.[50] This would cushion somewhat the full impact of the lack of adherence to the doctrine of incorporation, where this is the case.

The case for direct applicability of international economic agreements is by no means clear cut. There are mainly two schools of thought.[51] The advocates of direct applicability advance a number of reasons—Ernst-Ulrich Petersmann being a principal proponent of this school. The case essentially is founded on a monist model of the relationship between International Law and national law; on the need for constitutional safeguards for the transnational economic rights of individuals, coupled with a firm belief in the merits of international economic agreements. More particularly, the following inter alia are the arguments proffered. First, it facilitates the involvement of private participants, the administration and the courts in the enforcement of international commitments through domestic redress, without the reliance on the exercise of governmental discretion for redress at the international level.[52] Direct applicability enhances the powers of the court in relation to the executive and the legislative branches of government.[53] It facilitates individual transnational economic rights. In this manner a correcting mechanism is in place for government and market failures.[54] Moreover, it is contended that there are savings in the costs of the legislative processes foregone.[55] This may

---

[43] Shaw (1997), p.123.
[44] Shaw (1997).
[45] Shaw (1997).
[46] Shaw (1997), p.118. See also Art.VI of the US Constitution; and for example *Linder v Portocarrero*, 747 F.Supp 1452.
[47] Shaw (1997), p.120.
[48] Shaw (1997), p.126.
[49] See Moon-Soo Chung in Jackson and Sykes (eds) (1997), p.393.
[50] Chung (1997).
[51] But see also P. Eckhout (1997). Also referred to in Cottier and Schefer (1998).
[52] Jackson and Sykes (1997), p.462. See also Cottier and Schefer (1998), p.91.
[53] See Cottier and Schefer (1998), p.111.
[54] Petersmann (1993).
[55] Jackson and Sykes (1997), p.461.

be of particular note for developing States. Secondly, it facilitates better State execution of international commitments; and reigns in the power of economic blocks.[56] With respect to better execution, the calls for direct effect to be given to those clarifications of treaty provisions, that have been enunciated through international due process, in an international judicial forum, need to be heeded. It is contended that in such a situation any doubts about the content of the particular provision, coupled with the binding character of the agreement, should trump any concerns over direct effect.[57]

The case against direct applicability, led by John Jackson, is founded mainly on a concern for democratic processes and an emphasis on State rights in international economic relations. In particular the advantages for denying direct applicability inter alia are stated to be as follows. First, ensuring transformation facilitates and re-inforces democratic legitimisation of international agreements entered into by the executive.[58] Transformation prevents the executive from legislating without the involvement of the legislature.[59] However, it should be noted that international agreements are ratified by the legislature, and the executive responsible for the negotiations are elected individuals. Further, the empowering of private parties, the court and administrators that direct effect facilitates, alters the internal constitutional balance of power between the legislator, the executive and the judiciary.[60] Secondly, transformation facilitates the clarification of ambiguities contained in international agreements, and adjustments to the international bargain, according to local traditions.[61] Thirdly, direct applicability precludes the occurrence of an "efficient breach".[62] Where an agreement is directly applicable, a court may not show the degree of flexibility in its application that a government might. This argument of efficient breach originates from economic analysis of IEL, stemming from a cost-benefit analysis of the detriment to the interests of parties abroad as a consequence of a breach, and the advantages gained domestically. It is concluded that where the detriment is minimal, but the political advantages at home substantial, a breach may be a viable proposition![63] The possibility of minor breaches is considered a better option than the rejection of the international agreement altogether. It is thought that mandatory direct applicability will drive major economic powers from participating in international agreements completely.[64] Fourthly, direct applicability of an international agreement on a unilateral basis, where other partner States do not similarly engage, can create an imbalance in the distribution of the level of burden of international

---

[56]  Jackson and Sykes (1997), Ch.13. See also Cottier and Schefer (1998), p.120.
[57]  Cottier and Schefer (1998), p.101, and see, for example, Eickhout (1997).
[58]  Jackson and Sykes (1997), p.462.
[59]  Shaw (1997), p.110.
[60]  Cottier and Schefer (1998), p.121.
[61]  Jackson and Sykes (1997), p.462.
[62]  Jackson and Sykes (1997), p.462.
[63]  Jackson and Sykes (1997), p.462.
[64]  Cottier and Schefer (1998), pp.98 and 120.

commitments, arising from the international agreement.[65] However, it should be noted that this is a mercantilist argument.[66] Fifthly, direct applicability can inhibit future amendments of the international agreement.[67] Sixthly, direct applicability may not be suitable for developing countries which may need to be more interventionist in their economies. Seventhly, direct applicability does not ensure that national courts will in fact faithfully interpret and apply the international agreement. Further, multiple court decisions could lead to a multiplicity of interpretations. These interpretations could be legislative in character.[68] In addition, the national judges and lawyers may not have sufficient expertise in the international economic field concerned.[69] Eighthly, direct applicability binds a government to legislative change, whilst taking away the option instead to grant temporary compensation and being subjected to sanctions at the international level.[70] Ninthly, the major beneficiaries of direct applicability are multinational corporations. Individuals do not generally have the resources to bring such actions.[71] Finally, non-direct applicability allows a State maximum use of the sharp edge of IEL to pressure foreign States into behaving in a certain manner, whilst allowing the fact of non-direct applicability to act as a form of a shield in internal affairs.[72] Non-direct applicability affirms the domestic discretion of the State in foreign economic policy-making.

In conclusion, not only is the status of IEL at the domestic level left to the discretion of States, but that those States which engage in that discretion do so taking into account policy considerations. Thus, there are policy arguments involved in establishing the precise relationship between IEL and national law. This is not only evident in the varying permutations of the operation of the doctrine of incorporation practised by States,[73] but also the differing practice within a State in relation to different disciplines within IEL. Thus, for example, in the US Double Taxation Agreements are considered self-executing and directly invocable by private parties in courts[74]; as have traditionally been trade agreements,[75] for example Friendship, Commerce and Navigation treaties.[76] However, the US Uruguay Round Agreements

---

[65] Cottier and Schefer (1998).

[66] Cottier and Schefer (1998), p.120.

[67] Cottier and Schefer (1998).

[68] Cottier and Schefer (1998), p.121.

[69] Cottier and Schefer (1998), p.98.

[70] Cottier and Schefer (1998), p.120.

[71] Cottier and Schefer (1998), p.122.

[72] Cottier and Schefer (1998), p.111.

[73] viz. some treaties have direct effect and override national law; some treaties have the same status as national law; some treaties have direct effect but can only be invoked by a certain category of individuals in domestic courts.

[74] See, for example, R.L. Kaplan, *Federal Taxation of International Transactions* (St. Paul, Minn., West Group, 1988) at p.393. See also, for example, *Reid v Covert* (1957) 354 US 1, 77 S.CT 1222, 1L.ED 1148 and *Restatement (Third) of Foreign Relations Law of the US*, para.115.

[75] Cottier and Schefer (1998), p.107.

[76] Cottier and Schefer (1998).

Act expressly excludes the direct applicability of it in US courts. Similarly, the differing conclusions as to the character of certain international economic agreements in terms of their self-executing nature, must also shed some insight into the policy considerations underpinning those conclusions.[77]

**EXAMPLE: U.S. Congress: Uruguay Round Agreements Act[78]**

**4-009**       . . .

### SEC. 102. RELATIONSHIP OF THE AGREEMENTS TO UNITED STATES LAW AND STATE LAW.

(a) RELATIONSHIP OF AGREEMENTS TO UNITED STATES LAW.—

   (1) UNITED STATES LAW TO PREVAIL IN CONFLICT.—No provision of any of the Uruguay Round Agreements, nor the application of any such provision to any person or circumstance, that is inconsistent with any law of the United States shall have effect.

   (2) CONSTRUCTION.—Nothing in this Act shall be construed—

      (A) to amend or modify any law of the United States, including any law relating to—

         (i) the protection of human, animal, or plant life or health,

         (ii) the protection of the environment, or

         (iii) worker safety, or

      (B) to limit any authority conferred under any lawof the United States, including section 301 of the Trade Act of 1974, unless specifically provided for in this Act.

(b) RELATIONSHIP OF AGREEMENTS TO STATE LAW.—

   (1) FEDERAL-STATE CONSULTATION.—

      (A) IN GENERAL.—Upon the enactment of this Act, the President shall, through the intergovernmental policy advisory committees on trade established under section 306(c)(2)(A) of the Trade and Tariff Act of 1984 (19 U.S.C. 2114c(2)(A)), consult with the States for the purpose of achieving conformity of State laws and practices with the Uruguay Round Agreements.

      (B) FEDERAL-STATE CONSULTATION PROCESS.—The Trade Representative shall establish within the Office of the United States Trade Representative a Federal-State consultation process for addressing issues relating to the Uruguay Round Agreements that directly relate to, or will potentially

---

[77] See, for example, EU Council Decision Dec.94/800/EC, December 22, 1994, OJ, L336/2; *International Fruit Company* case (1972) E.C.R. 1219; ECJ in the *Banana* Case, Case C–280/93, *Germany v Council (Bananas)* (1994) E.C.R. I–4973; *R. v Comptroller of Patents, Designs and Trade ex parte Lenzing AG v Courtauld (Fibres) Ltd* (1996) R.P.C. 245; contra Supreme Court of Korea decisions, for example the Sup.C.Decn.Nos.85nu 448 (1987) and 91 nu 10763 cited by Chung (1997), p.373.

[78] H.R. 5110, 103d Cong., 2d Sess., became Pub. L. No. 103–465, 108 Stat. 4809.

have a direct effect on, the States. The Federal-State consultation process shall include procedures under which—

(i) the States will be informed on a continuing basis of matters under the Uruguay Round Agreements that directly relate to, or will potentially have a direct impact on, the States;

(ii) the States will be provided an opportunity to submit, on a continuing basis, to the Trade Representative information and advice with respect to matters referred to in clause (i); and

(iii) the Trade Representative will take into account the information and advice received from the States under clause (ii) when formulating United States positions regarding matters referred to in clause (i).

The Federal Advisory Committee Act (5 U.S.C. App.) shall not apply to the Federal-State consultation process established by this paragraph.

(C) FEDERAL-STATE COOPERATION IN WTO DISPUTE SETTLEMENT.—

(i) When a WTO member requests consultations with the United States under Article 4 of the Understanding on Rules and Procedures Governing the Settlement of Disputes referred to in section 101(d)(16) (hereafter in this subsection referred to as the 'Dispute Settlement Understanding') concerning whether the law of a State is inconsistent with the obligations undertaken by the United States in any of the Uruguay Round Agreements, the Trade Representative shall notify the Governor of the State or the Governor's designee, and the chief legal officer of the jurisdiction whose law is the subject of the consultations, as soon as possible after the request is received, but in no event later than 7 days thereafter.

(ii) Not later than 30 days after receiving such a request for consultations, the Trade Representative shall consult with representatives of the State concerned regarding the matter. If the consultations involve the laws of a large number of States, the Trade Representative may consult with an appropriate group of representatives of the States concerned, as determined by those States.

(iii) The Trade Representative shall make every effort to ensure that the State concerned is involved in the development of the position of the United States at each stage of the consultations and each subsequent stage of dispute settlement proceedings regarding the matter. In particular, the Trade Representative shall—

(I) the State concerned not later than 7 days after a WTO member requests the establishment of a dispute settlement panel or gives notice of the WTO member's decision to appeal a report by a dispute settlement panel regarding the matter; and

(II) the State concerned with the opportunity to advise and assist the Trade RepH. R. 5110—9 resentative in the preparation of factual information and argumentation for any written or oral presentations by the United States in consultations or in proceedings of a panel or the Appellate Body regarding the matter.

(iv) If a dispute settlement panel or the Appellate Body finds that the law of a State is inconsistent with any of the Uruguay Round Agreements, the Trade Representative shall consult with the State concerned in an effort to develop a mutually agreeable response to the report of the panel or the Appellate Body and shall make every effort to ensure that the State concerned is involved in the development of the United States position regarding the response.

(D) NOTICE TO STATES REGARDING CONSULTATIONS ON FOREIGN SUBCENTRAL GOVERNMENT LAWS.—

(i) Subject to clause (ii), the Trade Representative shall, at least 30 days before making a request for consultations under Article 4 of the Dispute Settlement Understanding regarding a subcentral government measure of another WTO member, notify, and solicit the views of, appropriate representatives of each State regarding the matter.

(ii) In exigent circumstances clause (i) shall not apply, in which case the Trade Representative shall notify the appropriate representatives of each State not later than 3 days after making the request for consultations referred to in clause (i).

(2) LEGAL CHALLENGE.—

(A) IN GENERAL.—No State law, or the application of such a State law, may be declared invalid as to any person or circumstance on the ground that the provision or application is inconsistent with any of the Uruguay Round Agreements, except in an action brought by the United States for the purpose of declaring such law or application invalid.

(B) PROCEDURES GOVERNING ACTION.—In any action described in subparagraph (A) that is brought by the United States against a State or any subdivision thereof—

(i) a report of a dispute settlement panel or the Appellate Body convened under the Dispute Settlement Understanding regarding the State law, or the law of any political subdivision thereof, shall not be considered as binding or otherwise accorded deference;

(ii) the United States shall have the burden of proving that the law that is the subject of the action, or the application of that law, is inconsistent with the agreement in question;

(iii) any State whose interests may be impaired or impeded in the action shall have the unconditional right to intervene in the action as a party, and the United States shall be entitled to amend its complaint to include a claim or cross-claim concerning the law of a State that so intervenes; and

    (iv) any State law that is declared invalid shall not be deemed to have been invalid in its application during any period before the court's judgment becomes final and all timely appeals, including discretionary review, of such judgment are exhausted.

(C) REPORTS TO CONGRESSIONAL COMMITTEES.—At least 30 days before the United States brings an action described in subparagraph (A), the Trade Representative shall provide a report to the Committee on Ways and Means of the House of Representatives and the Committee onFinance of the Senate—

    (i) describing the proposed action;

    (ii) describing efforts by the Trade Representative to resolve the matter with the State concerned by other means; and

    (iii) if the State law was the subject of consultations under the Dispute Settlement Understanding, certifying that the Trade Representative has substantially complied with the requirements of paragraph (1)(C) in connection with the matter.

Following the submission of the report, and before the action is brought, the Trade Representative shall consult with the committees referred to in the preceding sentence concerning the matter.

(3) DEFINITION OF STATE LAW.—For purposes of this subsection—

    (A) the term 'State law' includes—

        (i) any law of a political subdivision of a State; and

        (ii) any State law regulating or taxing the business of insurance; and

    (B) the terms 'dispute settlement panel' and 'Appellate Body' have the meanings given those terms in section 121.

(c) EFFECT OF AGREEMENT WITH RESPECT TO PRIVATE REMEDIES.—

    (1) LIMITATIONS.—No person other than the United States—

        (A) shall have any cause of action or defense under any of the Uruguay Round Agreements or by virtue of congressional approval of such an agreement, or

        (B) may challenge, in any action brought under any provision of law, any action or inaction by any department, agency, or other instrumentality of the United States, any State, or any political subdivision of a State on the ground that such action or inaction is inconsistent with such agreement.

    (2) INTENT OF CONGRESS.—It is the intention of the Congress through paragraph (1) to occupy the field with respect to any cause of action or defense under or in connection with any of the Uruguay

Round Agreements, including by precluding any person other than the United States from bringing any action against any State or political subdivision thereof or raising any defense to the application of State law under or in connection with any of the Uruguay Round Agreements—

(A) on the basis of a judgment obtained by the United States in an action brought under any such agreement;or

(B) on any other basis.

(d) STATEMENT OF ADMINISTRATIVE ACTION.—The statement of administrative action approved by the Congress under section 101(a) shall be regarded as an authoritative expression by the United States concerning the interpretation and application of the Uruguay Round Agreements and this Act in any judicial proceeding in which a question arises concerning such interpretation or application.

## SEC. 103. IMPLEMENTING ACTIONS IN ANTICIPATION OF ENTRY INTO FORCE; REGULATIONS.

(a) IMPLEMENTING ACTIONS.—After the date of the enactment of this Act—

(1) the President may proclaim such actions, and

(2) other appropriate officers of the United States Government may issue such regulations, as may be necessary to ensure that any provision of this Act, or amendment made by this Act, that takes effect on the date any of the Uruguay Round Agreements enters into force with respect to the United States is appropriately implemented on such date. Such proclamation or regulation may not have an effective date earlier than the date of entry into force with respect to the United States of the agreement to which the proclamation or regulation relates.

(b) REGULATIONS.—Any interim regulation necessary or appropriate to carry out any action proposed in the statement of administrative action approved under section 101(a) to implement an agreement described in section 101(d) (7), (12), or (13) shall be issued not later than 1 year after the date on which the agreement enters into force with respect to the United States.

. . .

**4-010**   The question of the relationship of national law with International Law at the international level is relatively less complex, but nevertheless arises in a number of circumstances. The first principle of importance to note is that international agreements are binding on the parties.[79] Secondly, the domestic law of a State at the international level is not a defence to non-performance.[80] Non-conformity of national law gives rise to international responsibility.

---

[79]  See, for example, Art.26 of the Vienna Convention on the Law of Treaties 1969.
[80]  Vienna Convertion, Art.27.

Thirdly, national law can be viewed at the international level in a number of ways.[81] It can serve as evidence of fact providing insight into the conformity of national law with IEL. It can also provide evidence of State practice. One question that has given rise to some comment, at any rate in international trade, is the precise level of scrutiny national measures should give rise to at the international level when these have been the subject of domestic judicial deliberation—viz., the standard of review. Should international judicial organs, when examining a national measure for conformity with International Law, merely review a domestic decision examining national measures for compatibility with International Law, for its objectivity,[82] or review it *de novo* so as to replace its own judgment with that of the national decision-maker?

---

[81] See, for example, India—Patent Protection for Pharmaceutical and Agricultural Chemical Products. Report of the Appellate Body (1997).
[82] See, for example, Art.17.6 of The Agreement on Implementation of Article VI of the General Agreement on Tariffs and Trade 1994.

PART 2

# INTERNATIONAL MONETARY LAW

### Chapter 5

# INTERNATIONAL MONETARY & FINANCIAL LAW AND THE IMF[1]

## The Role of Law

The role of law in international monetary relations has been misunderstood, **5-001** maligned and malnourished. Yet not only is there an essential function for the institution of law in international monetary relations, but an understanding of it is fundamental to an insight into international economic relations. The role of law is misunderstood because law has been strictly equated with "rules", and the inadequacy of rules so defined, to the resolution of certain international monetary problems, viz. exchange rates and balance of payments adjustment. Thus, the often quoted sentiment expressed by Keynes[2] that "the most difficult question to determine is how much to decide by rule and how much to leave to discretion". But this sentiment properly analysed is not so much about a choice between regulation and non-regulation, as it is about the particular nature of the regulatory approach to international monetary matters. Law is an institution and offers a variety of regulatory techniques—including discretion in decision-making, and the conditions necessary for the proper exercise of such discretion.

Further, it is not proven (this is implicit from Keynes's statement) whether

---

[1] IMF internet address: *http://www.imf.org*. For general works on international monetary law, see, for example, D. Carreau, *Soverainete et cooperation monetaire internationale* (Paris, Cujas, 1970); B. Tew, *The evolution of the International Monetary System* (London: Hutchinson & Co, 1977); R.W. Edwards, *International Monetary Collaboration* (Transnational Publishers,1985); J. Gold, *Legal and Institutional Aspects of the International Monetary System*, Vols 1 and 2 IMF; A.B. Altshuler, *International Monetary Law* (Moscow: Progress Publishers, 1988); Association International de Droit Economique, *Droit et monnaie: Etats et espace monetaire transnational*, (Dijon, France, 1988); M.Giovanoli (ed.), *International Monetary Law* (Oxford, Oxford University Press, 2000); R.M. Lastra, *The Legal Foundations of International Monetary Stability* (Oxford, Oxford University Press, 2006); M. Giovenoli & D .Devos (ed.), *International Monetary and Financial Law* (OUP, 2010); A.H.Qureshi & Gao (ed),*International Economic Law: Critical Concepts in Law* (Routledge, 2010. Volume II).

[2] See, for example, H. James, *International Monetary Cooperation since Bretton Woods* (Oxford: Oxford University Press, 1996), p.37; and J. Gold, The Rule of law in the International Monetary Fund IMF, *Pamphlet Series* No.32, p.4.

the institution of law cannot in fact provide a normative framework that takes into account the specific need in certain aspects of international monetary affairs of confidentiality, of discreetness, of a certain degree almost of necessary "non-transparency" in the application of a code of conduct. In the regulation of exchange rates, for example, the focus of IMF disciplines on the underlying economic conditions producing exchange rate stability rather than exchange rate stability as such, is not only a substantive response to regulating exchange rates, but can also be regarded as a legal response to regulating what is possible,[3] and what is fundamental.

Secondly, the role of law has been maligned, particularly by economists who have hitherto been the chief architects of the system; and by lawyers who have been blinded by the technicalities of the field, and whose construction of the institution of the law, is possibly narrow and arguably questionable. Thus, a preoccupation with rules has contributed to the focus on hard law. Yet it is clear that a principal characteristic of international monetary law is the positive role played by soft law. Similarly, notions of the techniques of law enforcement have a bearing on the question of the role of law. The techniques of enforcement in the international context are multifaceted. They can be subtle and apparently lacking in the use of traditional sanctions—and yet be effective. Thus, it is dangerous to carry into the international field an outlook of law enforcement that is grounded in the domestic framework.

**5-002**    Thirdly, the role that law can play has been malnourished. Of particular note is the inability of the international community to come to a consensus in relation to some aspects of international monetary and financial problems; an ineffective or non-transparent enforcement system in particular with respect to developed States, giving rise to cynicism; the existence of institutional flaws which bend in favour of power; and finally, the deliberate cloaking and minimisation of the role of law by States in monetary matters—especially developed countries. This is manifest through the elaborate constructions of soft law rather than firm law that characterise IMF jurisprudence. Thus, a former US Under Secretary for International Affairs in the Department of Treasury acknowledged openly that it was the US policy to avoid legally enforceable arrangements in international monetary relations.[4]

The character of the international monetary order, much of which is set under the IMF framework, is shaped inter alia by the nature of the particular monetary problem; the consensus as to the solution; the capacity of the international community to enforce; and the state of international monetary relations. Such considerations combine to beg a number of questions relating to the nature of the role of law in international monetary relations, viz. is soft law or hard law the appropriate instrument of regulation in a given

---

[3] See Art.IV of the IMF Articles of Agreement.
[4] J. Gold, *Interpretation: The IMF and International Law* (Kluwer Law International, 1996), p.399; and D.C. Mulford, "Non-legal arrangements in International Economic Relations" (1991) *Virginia Journal of International Law*, Vol.31 pp.437–446.

situation; should there be a preordained rule based system, or should monetary decision-making be based on co-ordination; are international monetary problems better resolved through an international or regional monetary framework; should international monetary matters be managed or regulated; should international monetary changes be brought about through legislation, or through interpretation of existing instruments; and finally should international monetary disputes be resolved through mechanisms of interpretation of international instruments, or through discreet dispute settlement mechanisms. In all such juxtapositions, there is either an orientation towards law or an undermining of it.

Firstly, at the core there are a number of monetary problems that can be regulated through a traditional rule-based approach, for example, exchange restrictions. Hard law functions here. Essentially, the main source of this hard law is to be found in the Articles of Agreement of the IMF. Few norms in the monetary field are to be found in General International Law. However, the number of such regulated monetary problems, where a predetermined decision-making process can function, is considered by at least one commentator as being minimal.[5] Such pessimism needs to be treated with some caution—as it is a generalisation and an exaggeration. The role of hard law in international monetary matters depends as much on the nature of the monetary problem involved, as the degree of international consensus present—including the availability of mechanisms for such consensus to emerge.

Secondly, for a variety of reasons—including diplomacy, the need for flexibility and the absence of consensus—soft law has provided an important modus operandi in international monetary matters. Thus, the instrument of the stand-by arrangement was created as a non-contractual instrument because developed States did not wish to appear to be obligated to the IMF when resorting to it for its assistance. Soft law is non-binding. It can serve as a compromise between differing positions or as a substitute where there is inadequate experience in a particular field. Because it is non-binding, non-conformity with soft law does not constitute a breach of the Articles of Agreement of the IMF; nor can the *ultra vires* doctrine be properly applied. However, one important consequence of the development of soft law is that the matters which it is concerned with, can no longer be regarded as being within the exclusive domestic jurisdiction of a State.[6]

Thirdly, and perhaps in the international monetary field more so, there are a range of monetary problems which do not for a variety of reasons lend themselves well to regulation in a predetermined manner. Such problems are better dealt with through co-ordination of monetary policies. However, co-ordination requires the setting up of the necessary conditions in order to facilitate it. Co-ordination can be conceived of as entailing synchronisation

---

[5] See K.O. Pohle, "You can't robotize policy making", *The International Economy*, October/November 1987, pp.20,22, quoted in James (1996), p.442.

[6] Gold (The Hague/London, Kluwer Law International, 1996), Ch.4.

or the joint formulation of monetary policy.[7] It can also mean, however, co-operation or both. International co-ordination in the sense of synchronisation is not without its shortcomings. It can lead through joint action to the simultaneous expansion and contraction of the world economy.[8]

5-003    International co-ordination, in the sense of co-operation, is less prone to bringing about cyclical changes based on mistaken premises. Co-operation which stems from mutually compatible monetary policies rather than necessarily similar policies is considered the preferred option.[9] This form of co-ordination, which is rooted in co-operation, requires inter alia a high degree of mutual awareness of the interaction of monetary policies.[10] In this respect individual State and global economic surveillance has a critical role to play in engendering awareness and co-operation.

It has been observed that the international monetary system is characterised by a trend, beginning from the provision of rules, to a system based on cooperation.[11] Indeed, it has even been suggested that increased information has displaced the role in some respects of the legal or quasi-legal framework.[12] Whilst the point being made is clear and at one level accurate, from the legal perspective it is somewhat controversial. In the first instance, it is arguably somewhat naive to suggest that heightened consciousness alone can engender monetary co-operation. States are critically influenced by self-interest in the monetary field as in any other field. Secondly, whilst not denying the importance of information and transparency, in fact what is increasingly enmeshed is peer pressure through co-operative arrangements, particularly through IMF surveillance exercises.

Thirdly, international monetary regulation can take place at the regional and/or the international level. There are certain monetary issues which may well lend themselves to a regional framework, and certainly there are examples of regional monetary co-operation.[13] They have, however, been described as second-best solutions,[14] and have certain drawbacks. Thus, regional monetary arrangements are more rules-based.[15] They can therefore be inflexible in the manner in which they respond to the international economy.[16] Further, international surveillance of regional monetary arrangements can be difficult.[17] In addition, in such arrangements political considerations are more prone to permeate and distort market conditions. For example, Greece, in the context of the EC, was afforded favourable balance of pay-

---

[7] James (1996), p.466.
[8] James (1996), p.465.
[9] James (1996), p.465. See also IMF World Economic Outlook April 1986, p.17.
[10] James (1996), p.465.
[11] James (1996), p.586.
[12] James (1996).
[13] For example, the Communnaute Financiere Africaine and the European Monetary System.
[14] See, for example, James (1996), p.469.
[15] James (1996), p.472.
[16] James (1996).
[17] James (1996), p.471.

ments support under the EC Community Loan Mechanism in 1981 for its part in not obstructing the process of European integration.[18]

Fourthly, there is the regulatory approach promoted through the international framework and directed at the national level. This is done through, for example, IMF conditions attached to its loans, along with the IMF codes and standards, implemented through IMF loan conditions and surveillance exercises. Here, law has an aspect in terms of substantive norms and institution building[19] at the national level. Thus, national monetary institutions need to be designed so as to respond appropriately to market conditions. For example, central banks should operate independently of the Government.[20]

**The Role of Fund in Governance Issues[21]**                            **5-004**

> 2. The Fund contributes to promoting good governance in member countries through different channels. First, in its policy advice, the Fund has assisted its member countries in creating systems that limit the scope for ad hoc decision making, for rent seeking, and for undesirable preferential treatment of individuals or organizations. To this end, the Fund has encouraged, inter alia, liberalization of the exchange, trade, and price systems, and the elimination of the direct credit allocation. Second, Fund technical assistance has helped member countries in enhancing their capacity to design and implement economic policies, in building effective policy-making institutions, and in improving public sector accountability. Third, the Fund has promoted transparency in financial transactions in the government budget, central bank, and the public sector more generally, and has provided assistance to improve accounting, auditing, and statistical systems in all these ways, the Fund has helped countries to improve governance, to limit the opportunity for corruption and to increase the likelihood of exposing instances of poor governance, in addition, the Fund has addressed specific issues of poor governance, including corruption, when they have been judged to have a significant macroeconomic impact.

Fifthly, there is an important, if not often appreciated distinction between   **5-005**
the role of law, and the role of management in international monetary relations. Whereas in relation to law, questions as to its nature, the level at which it operates and its institutions are all relevant—there is additionally another dimension to the operation of the international monetary framework—namely its management. This is a distinct question—and distinct from the Keynesian dichotomy between rule and discretion. The international monetary system requires both a normative framework and within that framework

---

[18] James (1996), p.477.
[19] See, for example, IMF Executive Board decision adopting guidelines covering the role of the IMF in issues of governance 1997. IMF, *Selected Decisions* (2005), p.62. See for a report in IMF *Survey* Vol.26, No.15 (1997).
[20] James (1996), p.609. See also R.C. Effros, *Current Legal Issues Affecting Central Banks*, IMF (1995), Ch.15.
[21] Guidance Note EBS/97/125, July 2, 1997 in IMF *Selected Decisions* (2005), p.62, *http://www.imf.org*. (Accessed June 8, 2011).

the immediate management of monetary affairs. The international monetary system is dynamic—in addition to having an engine, it needs to be driven and steered. This management function is performed at the international level mainly by the IMF. But key stakeholders in addition have arrogated to themselves such a function independently of the IMF—somewhat outside the framework of the system. This is seen, for example, in the form of the personalised summit diplomacy[22] of the Groups of Twenty, Ten, Seven and Five[23]—in particular latterly the Group of Twenty.[24] Notable examples of the results of this form of diplomacy are the Declaration of the Group of Seven on Strengthening the Architecture of the International Monetary System[25]; and the various G 20 Declarations to deal with the 2008 financial crisis.[26] The G 20 has been prominent in responding to the recent financial crisis, although outside the framework of the IMF and led essentially by developed countries. Management decisions are also taken at the regional and national levels.

Finally, developments in the international monetary field have been brought about more through the interpretative processes of the IMF, rather than the legislative process prescribed under the Articles of Agreement of the IMF. The processes of amending the IMF Articles of Agreement are more cumbersome, but more democratic. On the other hand, the interpretative process affords much flexibility, and is rooted in the existing power structure of the IMF. Further, it is operated through a policy-making organ assisted with the sole legal advice of the legal advisor of the Fund, rather than through a judicial process involving an effective appellate procedure.[27] The conflation of the interpretative process with the legislative process has prompted Joseph Gold to call for independent scrutiny of the legislative and interpretative processes.[28] Similarly, there is no well-structured dispute settlement mechanism in the framework of the IMF. Disputes are resolved essentially through the interpretative processes.

The role of lawyers in the international monetary field is a difficult one, particularly for the lawyer outside the IMF. This is mainly because of the

---

[22] James (1996), p.265.
[23] On Group of Five see J. Gold, "The group of five in international monetary arrangements" in Cheng and Brown (eds), *Contemporary Problems of International Law: Essays in honour of Georg Schwarzenberger*, (London: Stevens, 1988). On G20 see for example Martinez-Diaz, Leonardo, The G20 After Eight Years: How Effective a Vehicle for Developing-Country Influence? (October 2007). Brookings Global Economy and Development Working Paper No. 12. Available at SSRN: *http://ssrn.com/abstract=1080280* (Accessed June 8, 2011); and Zaring, David T., International Institutional Performance in Crisis (March 17, 2010). Chicago Journal of International Law, Vol. 10, No. 2, 2010. Available at SSRN: *http://ssrn.com/abstract=1573660* (Accessed June 8, 2011); C. Schmucker & K Gnath, "From G8 to the G20:Reforming the Global Economic Governance System" *European Yearbook of International Economic Law,* (2011).
[24] See *www.g20.org.* Accessed June 8, 2011.
[25] October 30, 1998. Published on the IMF website *http://www.imf.org.* (Accessed June 8, 2011).
[26] See the G20 Summit outcomes held in Washington in 2008, in London and Pittsburgh in 2009, and in Toronto and Seoul in 2010.
[27] Gold (1996).
[28] Gold (1996), p.599.

excessive secrecy that surrounds much of activities of the IMF—particularly in the context of accessing documentation. Thus, the minutes of the Executive Board relating to the First, Second and Third amendment are only available to insiders in the IMF involved in the interpretation of the IMF Articles.[29] Inside the Fund the lawyers have a key function, particularly in the advice they proffer to the Executive Board. The Legal Counsel of the IMF has a monopoly in the advice given to the Executive Board, particularly in the context of the interpretation of the IMF Articles of Agreement. This advice is not subject to review or external scrutiny. Such a condition has prompted Joseph Gold to suggest for an effective appellate procedure in the case of the interpretative process in the IMF; more transparency in the legal advice given, such that it can be scrutinised through different legal perspectives, either external or internal.[30]

To conclude, the role of law in international monetary relations appears to be consciously minimal and possibly subverted. This is unlike other fields of international economic relations, for example, international trade under the WTO framework, where the pendulum between law and diplomacy has swung towards law. This state of affairs begs the question whether international monetary relations are really so different that law should be de-emphasised.

## LEARNING INTERNATIONAL MONETARY LAW

International Monetary Law is like visiting an exhibition of "minimal art" at a very expensive art gallery. This is how many students feel when they encounter International Monetary Law—cheated because it appears minimal. And yet such visitors, if educated in advance, surely would have a more enlightened insight into this "minimal art". There is no doubt that there is a specific need to address the question of how international monetary law should be appreciated. There is the need at the outset to understand that whereas the phenomenon of the international monetary order may appear minimal—with care the traces of law can be understood; the nuances of order discerned; and the art of international monetary law appreciated. International monetary order does not emphasise black-letter law, legal relations and dispute settlement. The vocabulary of law, obligation, agreement, breach, legislation and even dispute settlement are frequently avoided. International monetary law needs to be understood with an outlook of law that takes into account the specifics of international monetary relations, in particular the need inter alia to serve economics and economists. International monetary problems

**5-006**

---

[29] Gold (1996), p.180.
[30] See Gold (1996), p.601. He suggests there should be two legal advisors in the Fund—one to check/react to the advice given by the other (see Gold (1996), p.597).

need to be approached imaginatively, with an awareness of the role played by informal and non-legal arrangements.[31]

In addition to the cultivation of a certain outlook for an understanding of the international monetary system, some insight into the analytical tools with which to appraise the international monetary phenomenon is needed. These must be set against the background of the aims and objectives of the international monetary order. In particular, the international monetary phenomenon must exhibit the indicia of an order—viz. (i) an effective norm creating machinery; (ii) an effective enforcement machinery; (iii) mechanisms facilitating monetary relations; (iv) comprehensiveness and integrity in the system and its code of conduct; (v) mechanisms integrating it into the wider international economic order. In addition, there should be evidence of good governance principles in the institutions of the system; recognition of the exigencies of international monetary relations; recognition of a member's sovereignty; and generally, a critical analytical approach to evaluation. Further, international monetary law, which revolves mostly around the IMF, needs to be evaluated from the perspective of the broader corpus of Public International Law, particularly the law of treaties, immunities, State succession, sovereignty and sovereign equality.[32]

Finally, it should be noted that, formerly at any rate, much of the legal appraisal of the international monetary order comes from sources within the IMF, in particular from legal advisors based in the Fund. The works, particularly of Joseph Gold, provide a wealth of insight in this field. However, care needs to be taken in their evaluation. Legal advisors of the IMF are contractually and otherwise constrained in the insights they provide through their writing.[33] In this respect, it is to be noted only much after his retirement[34] that Gold publicly acknowledged the monopoly of influence the Legal Counsel of the IMF enjoyed in the advice given to the IMF Executive Board, and the need for some form of check on this.

## INTERNATIONAL MONETARY AND FINANCIAL PROBLEMS

5-007    International monetary problems are varied, and arise not only from State and individual action, but also as a consequence of the international normative framework itself. International monetary problems arise essentially as a consequence of the inter-linkages within the global economy, and the need for a liberal world trading system. Thus, financial transactions between

---

[31]  Gold (1996), p.400.

[32]  See E. Denters, *Law and Policy of IMF Conditionality* (The Hague/London, Kluwer Law International, 1996), p.17.

[33]  For a similar observation see also Denters (1996), p.20.

[34]  In his latest book *Interpretation: The IMF and International Law*, buried in the last pages in a chapter titled "Some Retrospection and Some Insights".

States, and between individuals in different States, can only be facilitated effectively within the context of some kind of an international framework. In an inter-dependent world, State and individual action in the monetary field has consequences for other economies, and individual transactions. Thus, an under-valued currency can contribute to an increase in exports but result in more expensive imports. Furthermore, individual financial transactions across borders, particularly capital flows, if not managed in an orderly fashion, can undermine State monetary policy and international monetary collaboration.

Elucidating international monetary problems in a comprehensive manner can be complex. First, monetary problems are related to other issues with their own specific regulatory regimes, for example, financial, development and trade. This has the consequence of regime fragmentation distracting from a holistic approach to relevant problems. Thus, the concept of the "international monetary system" within the context of the mandate of the IMF has been described as being[35]:

"limited to official arrangements relating to the balance of payments—exchange rates, reserves, and regulation of current payments and capital flows—and is different from the international *financial* system. While the financial sector is a valid subject of scrutiny, it is a second order activity, derived from the potential impact on the stability of the international monetary system."

| | |
|---|---|
| **IMF:** *The Fund's* **Mandate—The** *Legal Framework* **Prepared by the Legal Department** | **5-008** |

(In Consultation with the Strategy, Policy and Review Department) Approved by Sean Hagan

February 22, 2010

21 ***The International Monetary System.*** References to the "international monetary system" were introduced into the Articles in the context of the Second Amendment. Although not defined in the Articles, the term was discussed extensively in the Fund's work on international monetary reform in the 1960s and early 1970s, including the work that led to the Second Amendment.14 The relevant sources reveal that, while the objectives and benefits of a stable international monetary system are relatively broad, the elements of the system itself are rather specific, and consist of four elements:

14 A study in the Fund's 1965 *Annual Report* is of particular note.

• The rules governing exchange arrangements between countries and the rates at which foreign exchange is purchased and sold;

[35] IMF: *The Fund's* Mandate—An *Overview* Prepared by the Strategy, Policy, and Review Department (In consultation with the Legal Department) Approved by Reza Moghadam January 22, 2010 available at *http://www.imf.org/external/np/pp/eng/2010/012210a.pdf.* (Accessed June 8, 2011).

- The rules governing the making of payments and transfers for current international transactions between countries;

- The rules governing the regulation of international capital movements; and

- The arrangements under which international reserves are held, including official arrangements through which countries have access to liquidity through purchases from the Fund or under official currency swap arrangements.

22. Several important features of the concept of the international monetary system should be noted. First, and consistent with the Fund's status as an inter-governmental organization, it deals entirely with official arrangements and rules in place among member countries, including the relevant provisions of the Fund's Articles. Arrangements between private parties (e.g., banks) fall outside of its scope although, as discussed below, the design of official policy is necessarily informed by an analysis of private actions and incentives.

Second, the concept deals solely with rules at the international rather than the domestic level. Accordingly, a member's domestic financial sector policies do not form part of the international monetary system. Third, and consistent with the two previous points, the international *monetary* system is different from the international *financial* system. The terms "monetary" and "financial" both appear in the Fund's Articles and, under the rules of interpretation, the use of different terms indicates that the drafters intended the terms to have different meanings.15 Importantly, the meaning of the term "monetary" (which normally refers to a means of payment) becomes clearer when read in conjunction with the term "international": "international monetary" matters are matters relating to a country's external payments— i.e., the balance of payments.

**5-009**   International financial problems (including the financial crisis of 2008) are concerned essentially with the operation of the global financial market, wherein private entities and financial institutions, for example banks, engage in financial dealings in the private sector.[36] The financial sector is concerned with such spheres of the economy as banking, insurance, securities, financial intermediaries, corporations and central bank operations. The normative framework of international financial law is concerned both with the allocation as between States of jurisdiction with respect to cross-border financial operations, including allocation as between multilateral and national governance; as well as substantive governance in terms of its functioning, for example accounting practices, disclosure requirements, lending practices,

---

[36] There have been a number of textbooks and monographs lately on International Financial Law. See for example: Sol Picciotto, *Regulating Global Corporate Capitalism (International Corporate Law and Financial Market Regulation)* (Cambridge, 2011); Mario Giovanoli and Diego Devos (Eds), *International Monetary and Financial Law: The Global Crisis* (OUP, 2010); Colin Bamford, *Principles of International Financial Law* (OUP, 2011); Avgouleas, E. *Governance of Global Financial Markets: The Law, The Economics, The Politics.* (CUP, 2011).

and good governance including anti-corruption and money-laundering.[37] Thus, the underlying objectives of international financial law have been described as being concerned with the prevention and management of an international financial crisis; along with measures to ensure transparency and the integrity of the global financial markets.[38] These objectives however so described may be considered minimalist and skewed in favour of the financial sector.

The governance of the international financial system falls not only within the framework of the international monetary system as it affects it but is said to be set within the "international financial architecture". The concept of the "international financial architecture" is "generally understood as encompassing the rules, guidelines and other arrangements governing international financial relations as well as the various institutions, entities and bodies through which such rules, guidelines and other arrangements are developed, monitored and enforced."[39] In the circumstances governance in the international financial architecture is fragmented as between multilateral institutions (for example, IMF, BIS, and G 20) and national and non-governmental organisations (for example, IASC[40]). Moreover, the regulatory regime is mostly of a soft law character; and its various institutional settings raise questions with respect to its democratic credentials.[41] In sum, there is a fragmentation of governance within the international monetary and financial sectors—in particular, arising from the lack of clear mandate of the IMF over the international financial sector. This has given rise to calls for the amendment of the IMF articles to clearly include this sector so as to facilitate effective IMF surveillance of this sector.[42]

Secondly, economists are not *at idem* with the model of relationships of     **5-010** the various economic systems which cause international monetary problems. Harold James makes the point succinctly when he states:

"Economists first developed a multiplicity of different mathematical models of the interrelationships of the world economy. Then they began to worry about the consequences of a coordination exercise based on the 'wrong' model."[43]

---

[37] See for example M Giovanoli, "A new architecture for the global financial market" in M Giovanoli (ed.), *International Monetary Law: Issues for the New Millennium*, (OUP, 2000).

[38] See M. Giovanoli in Mario Giovanoli and Diego Devos (Eds), *International Monetary and Financial Law: The Global Crisis* (OUP, 2010)

[39] See M. Giovanoli, "A new architecture for the global financial market" in M. Giovanoli (ed.), *International Monetary Law: Issues for the New Millennium*, (OUP, 2000) citing A. Crockett, "Thoughts on the New Financial Architecture" *in Essays in Honour of Max Fry* (London, 2000).

[40] i.e. The International Accounting Standards Committee (IASC).

[41] See, for example, M. Giovanoli, "A new architecture for the global financial market" in M. Giovanoli (ed.), *International Monetary Law: Issues for the New Millennium*, (OUP, 2000).

[42] See Committee on IMF Governance Reform Final Report (2009) *http://www.imf.org/external/np/omd/2009/govref/032409.pdf*. (Accessed June 8, 2011).

[43] James (1996), p.463.

Finally, the demarcation between what are purely domestic and international monetary issues is not easy to make; and is compounded by the disposition on the part of States to interpret their monetary sovereignty in an expansive manner.

International monetary problems can be considered from different standpoints. First, they can be analysed from the perspective of international trade liberalisation.[44] Here the monetary obstacles relate to constraints in the facilitation of international financial payments and transactions, viz. the lack of the provision of international liquidity (money), and currency exchange control regulations on the one hand, and those which because of their function in connecting different economies and consequential repercussions need to be regulated, viz. currency exchange rate fluctuations and balance of payments disequilibrium. A balance of payments disequilibrium can lead to the State being unable to pay its debts. Where a sovereign State is in debt and is unable to repay its foreign debts its assets internally cannot be seized, and those located abroad can be considerably protected through the application of the doctrine of sovereign immunity.[45] There is no single international procedure along the lines of a bankruptcy court dealing with all types of sovereign debts in International Law.[46] In the circumstances, these are some of the core international monetary problems of exchange control, currency fluctuation and balance of payments adjustment which confront the international community. Secondly, international monetary problems can be analysed from the perspective of international investment and capital market liberalisation. These objectives involve ensuring orderly capital liberalisation; interest rate co-ordination; banking supervision; transparency and generally good governance in domestic monetary policy and practice. These partake of some of the new monetary challenges that confront the international community. They have not traditionally featured as a preoccupation of the IMF but relate to spheres with which the IMF is increasingly getting concerned with in a more direct manner. Finally, there are general institutional or constitutional problems within which the international monetary system operates, for example ensuring the operation of the Special Drawing Rights as a major reserve currency; ensuring good governance in international monetary institutions; designing effective mechanisms for the surveillance of national economies and the global economy, so as to pre-empt and resolve national and global economic crisis circumstances; establishing a comprehensive international monetary system.

These same international monetary problems can also be examined from different levels. Thus, for example, at the level of individual participants

---

[44] See Art.1 of the IMF Articles of Agreement.

[45] See F.P. Gianviti, "Resolution of Sovereign Liquidity Crisis: Basic Concepts and Issues", in R.C. Effros (ed.), *Current Legal Issues Affecting Central Banks*, Vol.5 (Washington D.C., International Monetary Fund, 1998).

[46] H. Morais, "Legal framework for dealing with sovereign debt defaults", in Effros Vol.5 (1998).

within an economy, there are a host of matters, which if not nationally managed and internationally co-ordinated, can have consequences for other economic systems, participants within those systems and indeed the management of the international monetary system. For example, the advent of the Euromarkets; open stock markets; derivatives markets[47]; the exchange markets; capital liberalisation[48]; cross-border electronic banking[49]; money laundering[50]; and unsupervised banking operations,[51] all have implications for other economic systems. In the case of competing private credit facilities available for governments generally on an unconditional basis, the advice in connection with balance of payments adjustment proffered by international institutions such as the IMF is undermined.

At the level of the State there are a number of aspects of State activity which impinge on international monetary relations. First, there is the internal institutional framework. Here, the focus is on good governance issues that impinge on the formulation and operation of economic policy and practice in general and the monetary sphere in particular.[52] Essentially, good governance is used here to describe the operation of the rule of law, efficiency, transparency and accountability in the public sector.[53] Secondly, a State's national economic policy, either through action, inaction or mismanagement has an impact on such macroeconomic variables as the inflation rate, interest rate and capital liberalisation. Such economic variables have consequences for the national economy, and also impact on other economic systems. Indeed, the larger the economy, the more repercussions there are for outside economic systems. Thus, high interest rates in developed countries have a bearing on the cost of international credit, and increases the burden of debt servicing on the part of developing States. A greater degree of global co-ordination here has been called for.[54]

**5-011**

At the international level there are a number of flaws in the international monetary system. The character of an international monetary system is bestowed upon the international community under the framework of the IMF. But the IMF at any rate traditionally has not dealt with international monetary problems in a comprehensive manner—although it does have a principal role that is increasingly developing. There is no international monetary

---

[47] See E.T. Patrikis and D. Gland, "Derivatives activities of banking institutions: Initiatives for supervision and enhanced disclosure" in Effros Vol.5 (1998).
[48] See, for example, Ch.X, IMF *Annual Report* (1998).
[49] See, for example, R. Bhala "Cross-border electronic banking: perspectives on systemic risk and sovereignty", in Effros (1998) Vol.5.
[50] See, for example, M.F. Zelden, "Money laundering: Legal Issues" in R.C. Effros, *Current Issues Affecting Central Banks*, (1994) Vol.2.
[51] See, for example, Effros (1998) Vol.5, "Dealing with banks in distress", Chs 8, 9, 10, and 11; and R. Effros (ed.), *Current Legal Issues Affecting Central Banks*, (1997) Vol.4, Chs 17 and 18.
[52] See IMF Executive Board guidelines covering the role of the IMF in issues of governance mentioned in IMF *Survey* Vol.26, No.15 (August 1997).
[53] IMF *Survey* (August 1997).
[54] See, for example, James (1996), p.326. See also R.W. Edwards, "International Monetary Law: The next twenty-five years", *Vanderbilt Journal of Transnational Law* (1992) Vol.25 p.219.

convention which comprehensively deals with the monetary and financial spheres.[55] Consequently, initiatives in the monetary field have emerged from diverse sources such as groups of States,[56] in particular the G 20; and organisations with a regional orientation.[57] Further, the IMF itself has institutional flaws, particularly in the manner of its decision making processes. The Fund itself is constrained by international politics despite its approach at the national level to decouple economic and monetary policy making from the influence of domestic politics. Its development is affected by national and regional interests. For example, it has been suggested that the role of SDRs has been inhibited by US fears of the undermining of the role of the dollar as an international currency.[58] Similarly, the effectiveness of IMF policing of monetary policy has been affected by monetary integration in Europe.[59]

Of late, the international monetary and financial system has been confronted with a number of financial crisis viz., the financial crisis in Southeast Asia in mid-1997, the Russian crisis in 1998, and the recent 2008 global financial crisis,[60] sparked off in particular by the US sub-prime mortgage lending. These various episodes of crisis, in particular the 2008 global financial crisis, have served to give a particular focus to international monetary problems. The events in the past have highlighted not merely country problems, but also weaknesses in the international monetary system arising from the challenges of globalisation,[61] in particular lack of transparency; weak financial systems; piecemeal opening of capital accounts; lack of institutional structures to facilitate private sector involvement in monetary crisis management; and lack of regulations and structures to deal with global forms of financial intermediation.[62] With reference to the 2008 global financial crisis it has been pointed out that it "has exposed fundamental problems, not only in national regulatory systems affecting finance, competition, and corporate governance, but also in the international institutions and arrangements created to ensure

---

[55] F.A. Mann, *The Legal Aspect of Money*, (Oxford, Oxford University Press, 1982), p.463.
[56] For example, Groups of Ten, Seven and Five.
[57] For example, the Bank For International Settlements (BIS) .
[58] James (1996), p.271.
[59] James (1996), p.489.
[60] G20: Declaration Summit on Financial Markets and the World Economy November 15, 2008: "Root Causes of the Current Crisis — (3) During a period of strong global growth, growing capital flows, and prolonged stability earlier this decade, market participants sought higher yields without an adequate appreciation of the risks and failed to exercise proper due diligence. At the same time, weak underwriting standards, unsound risk management practices, increasingly complex and opaque financial products, and consequent excessive leverage combined to create vulnerabilities in the system. Policy-makers, regulators and supervisors, in some advanced countries, did not adequately appreciate and address the risks building up in financial markets, keep pace with financial innovation, or take into account the systemic ramifications of domestic regulatory actions (4)4. Major underlying factors to the current situation were, among others, inconsistent and insufficiently coordinated macroeconomic policies, inadequate structural reforms, which led to unsustainable global macroeconomic outcomes. These developments, together, contributed to excesses and ultimately resulted in severe market disruption."
[61] See *IMF Survey* (October 1998).
[62] *IMF Survey* (October 1998).

financial and economic stability".[63] In particular, the 2008 crisis highlighted the lack of clarity in the IMF mandate with respect to the financial sector, the ineffectiveness of IMF surveillance, the inadequacy of IMF funds to cope with a crisis of high magnitude, the manner of governance in the IMF, and the fragmentation in the monetary and financial disciplines including governance in the financial sector.

## Monetary Sovereignty and Sources of International Monetary and Financial Law

At the level of General International Law few monetary norms have developed[64]; and therefore a State's monetary sovereignty is fairly extensive.[65] A State is entitled to regulate its own currency.[66] Indeed, a State's monetary affairs are considered to be prima facie within its domestic jurisdiction,[67] and are understood to include[68]:     **5-012**

> "1. The power to issue notes and coins. . .
>
> 2. The power to regulate money (to dictate laws and regulations that affect the external or internal dimension of money), the banking system (regulation of credit) and the payment system (clearing and settlement).
>
> 3. The power to control the money supply and interest rates (monetary policy). . .
>
> 4. The power to control the exchange rate and to determine the exchange regime (exchange rate policy). . .
>
> 5. The power to impose exchange and capital controls. . .."

In the same vein, a State is free under General International Law to decide on the degree of trade and investment liberalisation it desires in the financial

---

[63] The Stiglitz Report: Reforming the International Monetary & Financial Systems in the wake of the global crisis.(The New Press, 2010) p.1.

[64] See, for example, R.W. Edwards, Jr., "International Monetary Law: The next twenty-five years" in *Vanderbilt Journal of Transnational Law* (1992) Vol.25, p.210. See also J. Gold, "The Rule of Law in the International Monetary Fund", IMF *Pamphlet Series* No.32, p.2; J. Gold, "The International Monetary Fund and International Law: An introduction", IMF *Pamphlet Series* No.4 (1965); and J. Gold, "Special Drawing Rights: Character and Use", IMF *Pamphlet Series* No.13 (1970).

[65] See, for example, T. Treves, "Monetary Sovereignty Today" in Giovanoli (2000), Ch.5; Lastra (2006), Ch.1; and F Gianviti, "Current legal aspects of monetary sovereignty" in *Current Developments in Monetary and Financial Law* 4 (2005), 3–16.

[66] Lastra (2006), Ch.1, and see *Serbian & Brazilian Loans* cases (1929) P.C.I.J.

[67] Lastra (2006), Ch.1, p.19.

[68] Lastra (2006), Ch.1, p.22.

sector, as well as the nature of the substantive regulation in this sector within its jurisdiction.[69]

The essentially permissive character of a State's monetary sovereignty under General International Law is accompanied by disciplines which are largely treaty based. The Articles of Agreement of the IMF play a central role in this respect. Indeed, they have been described as providing the basic constitution of the international monetary system.[70] This is because the Articles cover the core of international monetary problems; provide an international forum in monetary matters; and facilitate the development of international monetary law.[71] Further, this premier role is reinforced by the "central bank of central banks"[72] role of the IMF. The IMF is considered as a central bank of central banks, because it acts as a lender of last resort for States, it creates liquidity (i.e. supply of money) through the SDR facility; it manages the international monetary system; it is engaged in information collection and dissemination; and finally because it has regulatory powers over national monetary policy.[73] This regulatory power is exercised by the IMF through the surveillance[74] it engages in the national and international systems, and through the balance of payments adjustment programmes (conditionality), when a member seeks the financial assistance from the Fund.

In the international financial sector, the regulatory sources have been outlined as comprising[75]the international financial institutions, such as the IMF (crisis management and development of standards and their enforcement); the World Bank and regional development banks ((in terms of development of the financial sector and its governance), BIS (standard setting, supervision and forum for co-ordination), the OECD (standard setting), the WTO (liberalisation in the sector); the various groupings of countries, in particular the G 20 (crisis management, standard setting and reform); the sector specific groups of regulators, for example, the Basel Committee on Banking Supervision located in BIS, International Organization of Securities Commissions (IOSCO based in Spain), the International Association of Insurance Supervisors (IAIS—secretariat in BIS), the International Association of Deposit Insurers (IADI, with its secretariat in BIS), the Committee on the Global Financial System

---

[69] See, for example, M. Giovanoli, "A new architecture for the global financial market" in M. Giovanoli (ed.), *International Monetary Law: Issues for the New Millennium*, (OUP, 2000).

[70] J. Gold, "The Rule of Law in the International Monetary Fund", IMF *Pamphlet Series* No.32 (1980), pp.13–17.

[71] Gold (1980).

[72] F. Gianviti, "International Monetary Law", in R.C. Effros, *Current Legal Issues Affecting Central Banks* (1994) Vol.2, p.1.

[73] Gianviti (1994).

[74] See Art.IV of the IMF Articles of Agreement.

[75] See for an excellent account M Giovanoli, "A new architecture for the global financial market" in M. Giovanoli (ed.), *International Monetary Law: Issues for the New Millennium*, (OUP, 2000). On the role of the IMF in the financial sector see Rosa M. Lastra, "The Role of the IMF as a Global Financial Authority", *European Yearbook of International Economic Law* (2001).

(CGFS, based in BIS), the Committee on Payment & Settlement Systems (CPSS, located in BIS), the Financial Stability Board (FSB, an umbrella organisation to coordinate activities as between various institutions and sources, secretariat located in BIS); the professional bodies, for example, the International Accounting Standards Committee (IASC, in London), the International Swaps and Derivatives Association (ISDA, in New York), the International Securities Market Association (ISMA, in Zurich). These sources, along with the nature of the law emanating there from, raise the following questions.[76] How can co-ordination of the various normative efforts in the international financial sector be appropriately institutionalised multilaterally so that there is clear overarching oversight, and leadership? For example, should there be a New Global Financial Authority?[77] How can the disparate sources be imbued with democratic legitimacy? Thus, the majority of developing States are not represented in standard setting organisations nor are developing countries well represented in the FSB.[78] Moreover, such institutions as the IASB and the IOSCO are not politically accountable even though they delve in standard setting with respect to cross-border concerns.[79] What underlying principles should shape the international financial normative framework? For instance should the concerns of the financial sector be pre-eminent? And finally whether the existing soft law approach needs to be revisited?

Although the IMF is the premier institution in the monetary sphere, mention must also be made of other institutions which carry weight in the shaping of international monetary norms. Of particular note in this context is the Bank for International Settlements (BIS).[80] BIS has acquired particular importance and prominence because of the 2008 financial crisis. The BIS originally was a club for the central banks of industrialised countries (i.e. the Group of Ten) but has now broadened its horizons to include some developing and Eastern European countries.[81] The BIS in many respects performs competing functions to that of the IMF but has a particular focus on financial matters. It acts essentially as an institution for central banks, and

---

[76] See M. Giovanoli, "A new architecture for the global financial market" in M. Giovanoli (ed.), *International Monetary Law: Issues for the New Millennium*, (OUP, 2000).

[77] See The Stiglitz Report (New Press, 2010) at p.136.

[78] See The Stiglitz Report (New Press, 2010) at p.137.

[79] See The Stiglitz Report (New Press, 2010) at p.139.

[80] See *http://www.bis.org/*. (Accessed June 8, 2011). See also, for example, M. Giovanli, "The Role of the BIS in International Monetary Cooperation and Its Tasks Relating to the ECU" in R.C. Effros (ed.), *Current Legal Issues Affecting Central Banks* (1992) Vol.1, Ch.3.

[81] As of March 2011, 56 institutions currently have rights of voting and representation at General Meetings: the central banks or monetary authorities of Algeria, Argentina, Australia, Austria, Belgium, Bosnia and Herzegovina, Brazil, Bulgaria, Canada, Chile, China, Croatia, the Czech Republic, Denmark, Estonia, Finland, France, Germany, Greece, Hong Kong SAR, Hungary, Iceland, India, Indonesia, Ireland, Israel, Italy, Japan, Korea, Latvia, Lithuania, Macedonia (FYR), Malaysia, Mexico, the Netherlands, New Zealand, Norway, the Philippines, Poland, Portugal, Romania, Russia, Saudi Arabia, Serbia, Singapore, Slovakia, Slovenia, South Africa, Spain, Sweden, Switzerland, Thailand, Turkey, the United Kingdom and the United States, plus the European Central Bank.

as a forum for international monetary and financial co-operation. Thus, the BIS has been instrumental in the crafting of codes of conduct in the banking sector involving, for instance minimum standards for capital adequacy that domestic authorities are encouraged to implement through domestic measures. The latest in these set of standards is Basel III: International Regulatory Framework for Banks in response to the 2008 financial crisis, aimed at strengthening regulation, supervision and risk management in the banking sector. Furthermore, as of March 31, 2010, some 130 central banks and other international institutions, "made use of BIS financial services."[82] The BIS also acts as a secretariat to a number of other financial institutions in particular the Financial Stability Board set up in 2009 as part of the package of international responses to the 2008 financial crisis.

**Selected Articles of the Statute of the Bank for International Settlements (of January 20, 1930; text as amended on June 27, 2005)[83]**

**5-013**

**Article 3**

The objects of the Bank are: to promote the co-operation of central banks and to provide additional facilities for international financial operations; and to act as trustee or agent in regard to international financial settlements entrusted to it under agreements with the parties concerned.

**Article 21**

The Board shall determine the nature of the operations to be undertaken by the Bank. The Bank may in particular:

   a) buy and sell gold coin or bullion for its own account or for the account of central banks;

   (b) hold gold for its own account under earmark in central banks;

   (c) accept the custody of gold for the account of central banks;

   (d) make advances to or borrow from central banks against gold, bills of exchange and other short-term obligations of prime liquidity or other approved securities;

   (e) discount, rediscount, purchase or sell with or without its endorsement bills of exchange, cheques and other short-term obligations of prime liquidity, including Treasury bills and other such government short-term securities as are currently marketable;

   (f) buy and sell exchange for its own account or for the account of central banks;

   (g) buy and sell negotiable securities other than shares for its own account or for the account of central banks;

   (h) discount for central banks bills taken from their portfolio and rediscount with central banks bills taken from its own portfolio;

---

[82] See BIS, *The BIS in Profile* February 2011, *http://www.bis.org*. (Accessed June 8, 2011).
[83] *http://www.bis.org.*

(i) open and maintain current or deposit accounts with central banks;

(j) accept:

    (i) deposits from central banks on current or deposit account;

    (ii) deposits in connection with trustee agreements that may be made between the Bank and Governments in connection with international settlements;

    (iii) such other deposits as in the opinion of the Board come within the scope of the Bank's functions.

The Bank may also:

(k) act as agent or correspondent of any central bank;

(l) arrange with any central bank for the latter to act as its agent or correspondent. If a central bank is unable or unwilling to act in this capacity, the Bank may make other arrangements, provided that the central bank concerned does not object. If in such circumstances it should be deemed advisable that the Bank should establish its own agency, the sanction of a two-thirds majority of the Board will be required;

(m) enter into agreements to act as trustee or agent in connection with international settlements, provided that such agreements shall not encroach on the obligations of the Bank towards third parties; and carry out the various operations laid down therein.

### Article 23

The Bank may enter into special agreements with central banks to facilitate the settlement of international transactions between them. For this purpose it may arrange with central banks to have gold earmarked for their account and transferable on their order, to open accounts through which central banks can transfer their assets from one currency to another and to take such other measures as the Board may think advisable within the limits of the powers granted by these Statutes. The principles and rules governing such accounts shall be fixed by the Board.

### Article 24

The Bank may not:

(a) issue notes payable at sight to bearer;

(b) 'accept' bills of exchange;

(c) make advances to Governments;

(d) open current accounts in the name of Governments;

(e) acquire a predominant interest in any business concern;

(f) except so far as is necessary for the conduct of its own business, remain the owner of real property for any longer period than is required in order to realise to proper advantage such real property as may come into the possession of the Bank in satisfaction of claims due to it.

### Financial Stability Board Charter (2009). Selected Articles     5-014

Having regard to:

(1) the initial mandate given to the Financial Stability Forum by the Finance

Ministers and Central Bank Governors of the Group of Seven (20 February 1999); (2) the broadened mandate given by the Heads of State and Government of the Group of Twenty (London Summit, 2 April 2009, "Declaration on Strengthening the Financial System"); (3) the call of the Heads of State and Government of the Group of Twenty to re-establish the Financial Stability Board "with a stronger institutional basis and enhanced capacity" (London Summit, 2 April 2009, "Declaration on Strengthening the Financial System"); and Recognising the need to promote financial stability by developing strong regulatory, supervisory and other policies and fostering a level playing field through coherent implementation across sectors and jurisdictions.

We, the Members of the Financial Stability Board, have set forth the following Charter:

## I. General provisions

### Article 1. Objectives of the Financial Stability Board

The Financial Stability Board (FSB) is established to coordinate at the international level the work of national financial authorities and international standard setting bodies (SSBs) in order to develop and promote the implementation of effective regulatory, supervisory and other financial sector policies. In collaboration with the international financial institutions, the FSB will address vulnerabilities affecting financial systems in the interest of global financial stability.

### Article 2. Mandate and tasks of the FSB

(1) As part of its mandate, the FSB will:

    (a) assess vulnerabilities affecting the global financial system and identify and review on a timely and ongoing basis the regulatory, supervisory and related actions needed to address them, and their outcomes;

    (b) promote coordination and information exchange among authorities responsible for financial stability;

    (c) monitor and advise on market developments and their implications for regulatory policy;

    (d) advise on and monitor best practice in meeting regulatory standards;

    (e) undertake joint strategic reviews of the policy development work of the international standard setting bodies to ensure their work is timely, coordinated, focused on priorities and addressing gaps;

    (f) set guidelines for and support the establishment of supervisory colleges;

    (g) support contingency planning for cross-border crisis management, particularly with respect to systemically important firms;

    (h) collaborate with the International Monetary Fund (IMF) to conduct Early Warning Exercises; and

    (i) undertake any other tasks agreed by its Members in the course of its activities and within the framework of this Charter.

(2) The FSB will promote and help coordinate the alignment of the activities of the SSBs to address any overlaps or gaps and clarify demarcations in light of changes in national and regional regulatory structures relating

to prudential and systemic risk, market integrity and investor and consumer protection, infrastructure, as well as accounting and auditing.

**Article 3. Consultation**

In the development of the FSB's medium- and long-term strategic plans,
principles, standards and guidance, the FSB will consult widely amongst
its Members and with other stakeholders including private sector and non-
member authorities. The consultation process will include regional outreach
activities to broaden the circle of countries engaged in the work to promote
international financial stability.

Finally, to note is that not only is soft law prevalent in international financial    **5-015**
law,[84] it is also an important source in international monetary law[85] under the
framework of the IMF.

## INSTITUTIONAL ASPECTS OF THE IMF

The IMF was created in 1945, to alleviate the economic problems of the inter-    **5-016**
war years and the challenge of post-war reconstruction,[86] as a consequence of
the Bretton Woods conference held at Bretton Woods, New Hampshire,[87] in
1944. It was established as part of a trilogy of multilateral institutions dealing
with monetary, trade and development issues respectively. These institutions now comprise of the IMF, the World Bank Group and the WTO. The
blue-print for the IMF was shaped mainly by a combination of two different
plans—namely the British plan,[88] whose architect was J.M. Keynes; and the
US proposal[89] designed by H.D. White. The text of the Articles of Agreement
of the IMF is closer to the White Plan.[90]

The primary objective of the IMF is to facilitate growth in international
trade.[91] This primary objective is secured mainly through[92]: (i) the provision

---

[84] See M. Giovanoli, "A new architecture for the global financial market" in M. Giovanoli (ed.),
*International Monetary Law: Issues for the New Millennium*, (OUP, 2000).

[85] See, for example, J. Gold, *Interpretation: The IMF and International Law* (Kluwer Law
International, 1996), pp.301–401.

[86] For the historical aspects of the IMF see, for example, J.K. Horsefield, *The International
Monetary Fund 1945–1965. Twenty Years of International Monetary Cooperation* (1969)
Vols.1–3 IMF; M.G. de Vries, *The International Monetary Fund 1966–1971:The system under
stress* (1976) Vols 1–2 IMF; M.G. de Vries, *The International Monetary Fund 1972–1978;
Cooperation on Trial* (1985) Vols 1–3 IMF.

[87] i.e. the UN Monetary and Financial Conference, Bretton Woods, New Hampshire, USA
between July 1–22, 1944.

[88] Proposals for an International Clearing Union.

[89] United and Associated Nations Stabilization Fund.

[90] See, for example, G.M. Meier, *Problems of a World Monetary Order* (Oxford, Oxford
University Press, 1982).

[91] Art.1 (ii) of the IMF. Growth is an objective not purpose of the IMF. The IMF does not have
jurisdiction in the field of economic growth as such. See Gold (1996), pp.481–502.

[92] Art.1 of the IMF Articles of Agreement.

of a code of conduct to ensure stable exchange rates, and the elimination of restrictions on payments for current account transactions; (ii) the availability of international liquidity, and financial discipline in order to correct balance of payments disequilibrium; and (iii) the medium of a forum for consultation and collaboration. In this manner the IMF promotes high levels of employment, real income and the development of productive resources.[93]

**IMF Articles of Agreement[94]**

**5-017**    **Article I—Purposes**

The purposes of the International Monetary Fund are:

  (i)  To promote international monetary cooperation through a permanent institution which provides the machinery for consultation and collaboration on international monetary problems.

 (ii)  To facilitate the expansion and balanced growth of international trade, and to contribute thereby to the promotion and maintenance of high levels of employment and real income and to the development of the productive resources of all members as primary objectives of economic policy.

(iii)  To promote exchange stability, to maintain orderly exchange arrangements among members, and to avoid competitive exchange depreciation.

 (iv)  To assist in the establishment of a multilateral system of payments in respect of current transactions between members and in the elimination of foreign exchange restrictions which hamper the growth of world trade.

 (v)  To give confidence to members by making the general resources of the Fund temporarily available to them under adequate safeguards, thus providing them with opportunity to correct maladjustments in their balance of payments without resorting to measures destructive of national or international prosperity.

 (vi)  In accordance with the above, to shorten the duration and lessen the degree of disequilibrium in the international balances of payments of members.

The Fund shall be guided in all its policies and decisions by the purposes set forth in this Article.

**5-018**    The Articles of Agreement of the IMF have been amended five times, the most recent being February 18, 2011. The primary objective of the first amendment, which took effect in July 1969, was to create a new international reserve asset, i.e. the Special Drawing Right. The second amendment, which took effect in April 1978, was mainly concerned with introducing a new system of exchange rates. The third amendment came into effect in November 1992, and was intended to improve upon the mechanisms for

---

[93]  Art.1 of the IMF Articles of Agreement. See also Gold (1996), p.186.
[94]  *http://www.imf.org.* (Accessed June 8, 2011).

ensuring compliance with IMF obligations. Of late there had been some talk of a fourth amendment in order to ensure jurisdiction over capital transactions.[95] The Fourth amendment came into effect on August 10, 2009 providing for a special one-time SDR allocation in order to make SDR allocations more equitable as between members. The fifth amendment which came into effect on February 18, 2011 is mainly intended to bring certain "quota and voice" reforms, thus realigning the voting powers of certain countries in particular emerging economies so as to better reflect changes in the international economy; and to increase the voting power and participation of low income countries. A sixth amendment of the Articles (not yet effective) has also been proposed (viz., the investment authority amendment) intended to broaden Fund authority to invest.[96]

Membership of the IMF comprises States; and this membership is nearly universal.[97] It is restricted to States. Each State is a separate member; and is individually responsible for its obligations under the Articles of Agreement of the IMF.[98] This is the case even where there is regional monetary integration and there is one common currency.[99] Thus, the special position accorded to the EU in the WTO is not formally accorded to it in the IMF.

The legal norms of the Fund comprise[100]: (1) the Articles of Agreement; (2) By-Laws[101]; (3) Resolutions of the Board of Governors; (4) Decisions of the Executive Board; and (5) Directives of the Managing Director. Broadly, this topography of the legal norms also comprises a hierarchy, with the Articles of Agreement being paramount.

The development of the normative framework of the IMF is facilitated in a number of ways.[102] First, there is provision of the mechanism for amending the Articles of Agreement.[103] Amendment is, however, difficult process, given that it involves 85 per cent of the total votes. There have nevertheless been latterly a number of amendments. Secondly, there are what have been described as built-in variation powers,[104] wherein the Articles allow for certain specified variations in given circumstances.[105] Thirdly, there are enabling provisions, which are broader than variation powers. Enabling provisions can facilitate the creation of general norms[106]; authorise the making of recommendations

---

[95] See IMF *Survey* October 9, 1995, p.299.

[96] See Report of the Executive Board to the Board of Governors on the proposed amendment of the Articles of Agreement of the IMF to expand the investment authority of the IMF April 7, 2008. *http://www.imf.org/external/np/pp/eng/2008/040908b.pdf.* (Accessed June 8, 2011).

[97] As of March 2011 it had 187 members.

[98] See F.P. Gianviti, "Developments at the International Monetary Fund", in Effros (ed.), *Current Legal Issues Affecting Central Banks* (1995) Vol.3 p.11.

[99] Gianviti (1995).

[100] See J. Gold, *The Rule of Law in the International Monetary Fund*, IMF (1980).

[101] See Art.XII s.2 (g) of the Articles of Agreement of the IMF.

[102] See Gold (1980).

[103] Art.XXVIII (a) of the Articles of Agreement of the IMF.

[104] Gold (1980), p.19.

[105] For example, Art.V, s.7 (c) in relation to the basic period for repurchase.

[106] Art.IV, s.2 (c).

and guidelines[107]; or authorise the operation of predetermined normative regimes.[108] Fourthly, the Articles of Agreement authorise the adoption by the IMF of rules.[109] The rules are to be formulated in order to facilitate the general operation and conduct of business of the IMF. They are in this context operational, rather than significant.

5-019     The Fund also has at its disposal opportunities of contact between itself and members, which have important norm generating impacts on the international monetary framework. Thus, under the Articles of Agreement there are various obligations on members to collaborate with the Fund.[110] Further, the Fund has particularly used its surveillance authority in the context of exchange rates,[111] and its conditionality in the context of the balance of payments stabilisation programmes,[112] to inject new counsel to members. These techniques are, however, internalised mechanisms of norm generation involving technocrats; and subject to decision-making processes that involve the weight of less than 85 per cent of the total voting power within the Fund.

The IMF has international legal personality,[113] and thus is able to engage in external relations in furtherance of its purposes. Internally, the organisation of the IMF, in hierarchical order, can be sketched as in the diagram below.[114]

The Board of Governors consists of one Governor and one Alternate appointed by each member.[115] Governors are normally Ministers of Finance or Governors of Central Banks. The Board of Governors has delegated most of its powers to the Executive Board. It meets normally once a year, unlike the WTO plenary organ viz., the WTO Ministerial Conference, which meets every two years.

The Executive Board consists of Executive Directors. However, unlike the Board of Governors, not every Executive Director is appointed by every member. Normally, five of the Executive Directors are appointed by the five members who have the largest quotas; and 15 others are elected by the rest of the membership which is not eligible to appoint.[116] The process whereby some Executive Directors are appointed is now the subject of a package of Quota and Governance reforms approved by the Board of Governors in December

---

[107] See, for example, Art.IV, ss. 2(c) and 3(b).
[108] For example, Art.IV, s.4 Sch.D.
[109] See Art.XII, s.2 (g).
[110] Art.IV, s.1.
[111] Art.IV, s.3 (a).
[112] Art.V, s.3 of the Articles of Agreement of the IMF.
[113] Art.IX of the Articles of Agreement of the IMF.
[114] See Art.XII of the Articles of Agreement of the IMF.
[115] Art.XII, s.2.
[116] Art.XII, s.3 (b). The elections of Executive Directors take place every two years. A two year tenure it has been suggested is not a long enough tenure for a director to perform effectively (See IEO: Governance of the IMF: An evaluation (2008)). Hitherto the five members entitled to appoint have been: US, UK, Japan, France and Germany. China, Russia, Saudi-Arabia also have one executive Director but these are elected.

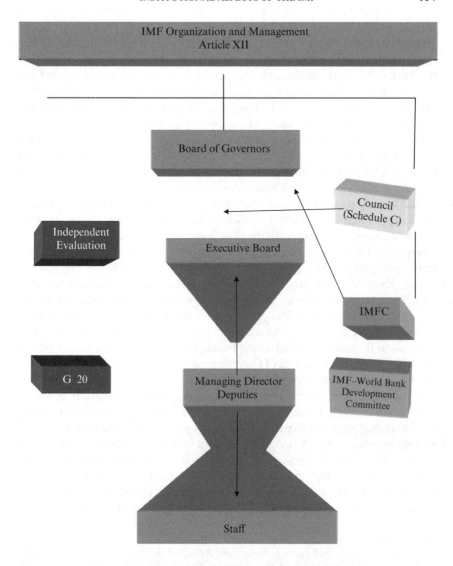

2010, so as to establish an all-elected Executive Board.[117]The Executive Board is a smaller organ, consisting normally of 21 Executive Directors. The number of elected Executive Directors can be increased. In 2011, for example, there are a total of 24 Executive Directors. The December 2010 proposed Quota and Governance Reform calls for the maintenance of an Executive Board of the size of 24. The constituencies which the elected directors represent are established through a principle of voluntary constituency

[117] See IMF Quota and Governance Reforms approved by the IMF Board of Governors December 15, 2010 (upon acceptance by at least three-fifths of IMF members representing 85 percent of the total voting powering the IMF).

formation.[118] Generally, the Executive Directors have a civil service background rooted in Central Banks and Ministry of Finances of member countries, and are predominantly economists by vocation. However, given that the work of the IMF increasingly focuses on development, including elimination of poverty, the need to draw from development and planning ministries also has been highlighted.[119] The tenure of an appointed Executive Director can be terminated at any time. The tenure of an elected Executive Director however can only be terminated after the lapse of the two years for which he is elected.[120] Executive Directors are subject to a personal ethical code of conduct which deals with such matters as harassment, conflicts of interests and the protection of confidential information.[121]

**5-020**    The Managing Director acts as the chairperson of the Executive Board, and is appointed by it. However, there is little transparency in the selection of the Managing Director with the post normally reserved for a European.[122] There have been recent calls for the appointment of the Managing Director to be open and on merits.[123]

The Executive Director acts as a representative of the member that appointed them, or the group of members who elected them. However, the Executive Director is also an official of the Fund,[124] and is not in legal analysis a representative.[125] As such, the Executive Directors have dual allegiance—to the members, and to the Fund. The Executive Board is in principle accountable to the Board of Governors, although there are no established mechanisms for such accountability.[126]

It is envisaged in addition to the existing organs that a Council would be established to supervise the management and adaptation of the international monetary system, if the Board of Governors so decide.[127] The Council would feature in between the Board of Governors and the Executive Board.[128] For the present, however, instead of the Council, the International Monetary and Financial Committee of the Board of Governors (IMFC) has been established. This Committee meets twice a year and deliberates on important questions of policy. It consists of 24 IMF Governors, Ministers, or other offi-

---

[118] See IMF: IMF Quota and Governance Reform: Elements of an Agreement Prepared by the Finance, Legal, and Strategy, Policy, and Review Departments Approved by Andrew Tweedie, Sean Hagan, and Reza Moghadam October 31, 2010 paragraph 13 *http://www.imf.org/external/np/pp/eng/2010/103110.pdf.* (Accessed June 8, 2011).

[119] See The Stiglitz Report (New Press, 2010) at p.135.

[120] Art.XII, s.3 (d).

[121] See Executive Board Decision 12239–(00/71) July 14, 2000 as amended.

[122] See IEO: Governance of the IMF: An evaluation (2008) Ch. 4.

[123] Committee on IMF Governance Reform Final Report (2009) *http://www.imf.org/external/np/omd/2009/govref/032409.pdf* (Accessed June 8, 2011).

[124] See Art.IX, s.8. See also R. Gerster, "Accountability of Executive Directors in the Bretton Woods Institutions" (1993) J.W.T., Vol.7, No.6, pp.87–116.

[125] Gold (1996), p.179.

[126] See IEO: Governance of the IMF: An evaluation (2008) para 38.

[127] See Art.XII and Sch.D.

[128] J. Gold, *Interpretation: The IMF and International Law* (Kluwer Law International, 1996), p.xxvii.

cials of comparable rank. The 24 Governors in the IMFC reflect the model of representation in the Executive Board. However, the IMFC can only advise the Board of Governors. Its communications do not carry legal weight.[129] In these circumstances, a call for the activation of the Council has been made.[130] The Council would in particular be able to provide strong strategic leadership, as its membership would comprise of Ministers or individuals of comparable ranking; as well as clarity in representation given that its members would be able to split the votes of their constituency. Along with the IMFC, there is also the IMF–World Bank Development Committee. This committee is composed of 24 members, also generally finance ministers or others of comparable rank, representing the membership of the IMF and the World Bank. It meets generally at the same time as the IMFC. The Development Committee advises the Board of Governors of the World Bank and the IMF on development related issues.[131] Both the IMFC and the Development Committee proffer advice indirectly to the IMF Executive Board. In practice however in the IMF it is "seen as primarily occupied with the work of the World Bank and receives scant attention from the" IMF.[132]

In 2001, the IMF set up the Independent Evaluation Office with the objective of conducting independent and objective evaluation of IMF policies and activities.[133] As of March 2011 it has conducted some 18 evaluations on different aspects of Fund activity, including its institutional aspects. The Fund, however, has not implemented all of the reform suggestions made, including the activation of the Council. **5-021**

The distribution of functions and powers as between the various organs of the IMF are variously set out in the Articles of Agreement. However, it is felt that there is lack of clarity of the respective roles of the Executive Board, the management and the IMFC.[134] Those powers that are not expressly set out are vested in the Board of Governors.[135] In particular, the Board of Governors has exclusive decision-making authority in relation to the admission of new members, the adjustment of quotas and the allocation and cancellation of SDRs. The Board of Governors meets twice a year. The Executive Board has the responsibility of conducting the normal business of the Fund, and functions in a continuous session.[136] Its powers include those that are set out

---

[129] See IEO: Governance of the IMF: An evaluation (2008) Ch.4.
[130] See Committee on IMF Governance Reform Final Report (2009)
[131] See, for example, *http://www.imf.org/external/about/govstruct.htm* (Accessed June 8, 2011).
[132] See IEO: Governance of the IMF: An evaluation (2008) Ch. 4.
[133] See "Making the IMF's Independent Evaluation Office Operational: A Background Paper", August 7, 2000 and "IMF Executive Board Report to the IMFC on the Establishment of the Independent Evaluation Office and its Terms of Reference", September 12, 2000. See also "Terms of Reference for the Director and Terms and Conditions of Appointment for Director and Employees of the Independent Evaluation Office—Report by Evaluation Group" (EBAP/01/31, April 17, 2001). (Source of this note *http://www.IMF.org* (Accessed June 8, 2011)).
[134] See IEO: Governance of the IMF: An evaluation (2008) para.17.
[135] Art.XII, s.2.
[136] Art.XII, s.3 (g).

in the Articles of Agreement, and those that are delegated to it by the Board of Governors.[137] The Executive Board is involved in the preparation of the work for the Board of Governors, and also prepares the recommendations to be considered by the Board of Governors for adoption. Thus, the Executive Board performs both strategic (legislative) as well as operational (executive) functions. In practice, the Managing Director proposes new initiatives to the Executive Board.[138]Given the mixed responsibility of the Executive Board it has been suggested that its functions should be re-configured such that it is able to play a more strategic and supervisory role rather than be too weighed with operational matters.[139]

The decision-making process in the Fund normally is through consensus. In practice, important decisions are arrived at only when there is widespread agreement. Indeed, where there is overt opposition, from those who do not have a blocking voting power, then the decision is not normally arrived at.[140] In the Executive Board, the rule is that unless a formal vote is called for by an Executive Director, the Chairman is to ascertain the sense of the meeting with reference to those with the voting strength to carry the motion through.[141] However, when there is voting, this is done through a system of weighted voting.[142]

5-022      The IMF was one of the first international organisations after the Second World War to have a system of weighted voting. Basically, in such a system, votes are allocated to reflect the economic strength of a member in the international economic system, and its contribution to the IMF resources. In this manner, the different interests of members are catered for—i.e. the interests of creditor and debtor members, and the interests and perspectives arising from different levels of development. The votes allocated under the weighted voting system to a member comprise "its basic votes and its quota-based votes". The basic votes allocated are intended to reflect the notion of sovereign equality of members. The basic votes originally allocated were a set of fixed votes viz., 250 votes. However, since the quota determined for each member can be adjusted,[143] and has been increased over the years,[144] the

---

[137] Art.XII, s.XII.
[138] See IMF: Committee on IMF Governance Reform Final Report (2009) at p.8.
[139] Committee on IMF Governance Reform Final Report (2009)
[140] Gold (1996), p.231.
[141] Gold (1996), p.231 and Rule C-10 of the Rules and Regulations (Executive Board).
[142] Art.XII, s.5 of the Articles of Agreement of the IMF. See also, e.g. J. Gold, "*Voting and Decisions in the International Monetary Fund: An Essay on the Law and Practice of the Fund*" (IMF 1972); J. Gold, *Legal and Institutional Aspects of the International Monetary System: Selected Essays* (IMF 1979), Vol.I, Ch.7.
[143] See Art.III, s.2. A general review of quotas is to take place at intervals of not more than five years.
[144] For example, the Ninth General Review of Quotas by the Board of Governors resulted in a 50% increase of quotas. The 14th General Review of Quotas (part of the 2010 package of Quota and Governance Reforms) which when it becomes effective will result in 100 per cent increase in total quotas along with some realignments in line with the changing weight of individual member's economy.

proportion of basic votes to the total number of votes declined considerably.[145] Indeed, with some members its value became de minimis in relation to its quota based votes.[146] Therefore, effective as of February 2011, as part of the Voice and Quota Reform of 2008, to "ensure that the ratio of the sum of the basic votes of all members to the sum of the total voting power of all members remains constant"[147] the basic votes of each member is to comprise "the number of votes that results from the equal distribution among all the members of 5.502 per cent of the aggregate sum of the total voting power of all the members".[148] The basic votes of members have therefore been increased so as to reflect a constant and more sensible relationship with their quota-based votes. The quota-based votes of a member comprise "the number of votes that results from the allocation of one vote for each part of its quota equivalent to one hundred thousand' special drawing rights" (SDRs).[149]

A member's quota describes its share of contribution and level of entitlement to benefits. Each member when joining the Fund is allocated a quota.[150] A member's quota is calculated according to economic criteria intended to reflect the relative economic size of a member. The IMF articles do not set out a quota formula and over the years the quota formula has evolved and continues to do so. The current formula arising out of the 2008 Quota and Voice Reform is based on a weighted average of GDP "(weight of 50 per cent), openness (30 per cent), economic variability (15 per cent), and international reserves (5 per cent)."[151] This formula is the subject of review which is to complete in January 2013. The old formula took into account such factors as its GDP; its international reserves; its current payments; the variability of current (export) receipts; and the ratio of current receipts to GDP.[152] In addition to economic criteria, political considerations may also enter into the calculation of the quota. However, the determination of quota is done on a

---

[145] See R. Gerster, "Proposals for voting reform within the International Monetary Fund", (1993) J.W.T. See also, for example, W. Gianaris, "Weighted voting in the International Monetary Fund and the World Bank" (1990–1991) *Fordham International Law Journal*, Vol.14; R. Jeker, "Voting rights of less developed countries in the IMF" (1978) J.W.T. 12(3).

[146] Gold (1996), p.440.

[147] Reform of Quota and Voice in the International Monetary Fund: Board of Governors Resolution 63-2, effective April 28, 2008.

[148] Article XII, Section 5(a) of the IMF Articles of Agreement as amended March 2011.

[149] Art.XII, s.5 (a) as amended. SDRs are an international reserve asset and a unit of account (see Ch.8 further).

[150] Art.III.

[151] See IMF IMF Quotas March 3, 2011. See also IMF Quota and Voice Reform—Key Elements of a Potential Package of Reforms Prepared by the Quotas and Voice Working Group1 Approved by David Burton February 26, 2008 *http://www.imf.org/external/np/pp/eng/2008/022608.pdf.* (Accessed June 8, 2011).

[152] See Eighth General Review of Quotas. See also IMF *Survey* (September 1997), Vol 26. Original member's quota was determined by the Bretton Woods formula. This has since been revised in 1963 and in the early 1980s.

non-discriminatory basis, so that a new member's quota is comparable to an existing IMF member's quota with a similar economic profile.[153]

The voting rights of a member can be affected in two circumstances. First, where there has been a failure to fulfil any of the obligations of the Fund, the Fund may suspend a member's voting rights.[154] Secondly, where in the context of a member using Fund resources[155] which results in a member purchasing another currency or which results in an increase of sales of a member's currency,[156] then there is a corresponding adjustment of votes, with the member whose currency has been borrowed acquiring more votes, and the member who has borrowed suffering a reduction of votes. This adjustment of votes, however, is only for the purposes of voting involved in decision-making relating to waiver of the conditions of use of Fund resources,[157] or a declaration of ineligibility to use Fund resources.[158]

**5-023**    The Articles of Agreement require different voting majorities for different types of decisions. Important questions involving institutional or policy changes, or changes affecting membership rights, viz. changes in quotas[159]; and the establishment of the Council[160] require, an 85 per cent majority. It has been suggested that this category of important concerns should be widened, in particular to include the question of the appointment of the Managing Director[161]; and the threshold brought from 85 per cent to 70–75 per cent.[162] For general operational reforms, such as changes in rates of charges,[163] a 70 per cent majority is required. For all other decisions, unless special majorities have been specifically provided, the decisions of the Fund are to be arrived at by a majority of the votes cast.[164] The effect of the qualified voting requirements is to moderate the influence of the weighted voting system, and to increase the influence of the larger economically more powerful members, for example, the US. Where this results in an effective veto it has been suggested that this qualified vote should be eliminated.[165] However, the institution of special majorities can also increase the influence of developing countries (as well as other groups) provided they act as a group.

Every Executive Director has the number of votes allotted to the group of members who elected him,[166] or the member which appointed him.[167]

---

[153] See *IMF Survey* (Supplement) (September 1998).
[154] See Art.XXVI, s.2(b) and Art.XII, s.3 (i).
[155] i.e. under Art.V.
[156] Art.XII, s.5(b).
[157] Art.V, s.4.
[158] See Art.V, s.5.
[159] Art.III, s.2(c).
[160] See Art.XIII, s.1.
[161] See p.133 of The Stiglitz Report (New Press, 2010).
[162] Committee on IMF Governance Reform Final Report (2009)
[163] See Art.V, s.8(a), (b), (d).
[164] See Art.XII, s.5(c).
[165] See p.133 of The Stiglitz Report (New Press, 2010).
[166] Art.XII, s.3 (i) (iii).
[167] Art.XII, s.3 (i) (i).

Thus, Executive Directors have different voting powers. In contrast, at the Board of Governors, each governor has the number of votes allotted to the member which appointed him. A governor has no constituency of membership. However, it is the Executive Director who casts his/her votes, and not the votes of the member or members of his/her constituency,[168] although the numbers of votes he/she can cast are the number of votes of his/hers constituency. Given this manner of voting, it has been suggested the Executive Director is not the representative of his constituency.[169] Moreover, the tenure of elected Executive Directors cannot be terminated by their constituency. In addition, the Executive Directors cannot split the votes of their constituency. Whilst this has the disadvantage of subverting the dissenting votes, it also has the effect of enhancing the power and influence of Executive Directors.[170] However, some directors appear to suffer from a "chilling effect" in the IMF which deters them from being critical of the management of the IMF for "fear of negative repercussions".[171]

The Articles of Agreement do not provide guidance as to how Executive Directors should decide on voting.[172] Executive Directors may decide on the basis of their own judgment, or through sounding their constituency. Where there are divergent views, Executive Directors may orally express those views of the members of their constituency. The freedom of Executive Directors in casting their vote, coupled with the dual allegiance of Executive Directors, both to the Fund and their constituency, has led one observer to conclude that there is an "institutionalised bias against public accountability of the Executive Directors in the IMF".[173] Further, it is to be noted, where a category of a member, for example, a developing member, finds itself grouped in another constituency of a different category of members, for instance with a majority of developed members, then because Executive Directors cannot split votes, there is a likelihood that the effect of the developing member's vote is lost.[174] An appointed Executive Director's continued tenure is dependent on the attitude of the appointing member. Therefore, in practice, an appointed Executive Director will reflect the appointing member's views in the deliberations of the Executive Board. Moreover, the average size of a constituency of an elected Executive Director is about ten, making his/her job demanding in representing the entire constituency.[175]

Governance in the IMF has been the subject of much criticism and suggestion for reform, in particular of late precipitated by the 2007/8 financial **5-024**

---

[168] See Gold (1996), p.260.
[169] Gold (1996).
[170] Gold (1996), p.129.
[171] IEO: Governance of the IMF: An evaluation (2008) para.28.
[172] Gold (1996), p.10.
[173] Gerster, "Accountability of Executive Directors in the Bretton Woods Institutions" (1993) JWT, Vol.27, No.6, pp.87–116.
[174] Gerster (1993).
[175] See IEO: Governance of the IMF: An evaluation (2008) Ch.3.

crisis.[176] One basis for evaluating IMF governance has been through the prisms of "effectiveness, efficiency, accountability, and voice".[177] The principal dimensions of governance that have excited particular focus pertain to "power-sharing" (quota and voice), decision-making (including decision-making and implementation structures) and the IMF mandate.[178] The decision-making processes involved in the IMF have been the subject of much criticism, particularly from developing countries.[179] In the first place the weighted voting system is considered to be undemocratic and non-egalitarian. Its relevance in relation to all types of decision making is particularly questioned.[180] Some reforms have been suggested.[181] These focus on increasing votes including basic votes, and increasing representation of numbers on the Executive Board of elected Executive Directors. Thus, the criteria to determine quotas could be made more objective, and include considerations such as population.[182] However, it is to be noted that the recent calls for realignment of quotas so as to better reflect the global economic realities, in particular the weight of emerging economies, seem to emphasise economic considerations in this share allocation without as much emphasis with respect to concerns of justice.

[176] See in particular three recent reports commissioned by the IEO, IMF and the UN viz., IEO: Governance of the IMF: An evaluation (2008) and references therein; IMF: Committee on IMF Governance Reform Final Report (2009) (Committee chaired by Trevor Manuel, Minister of Finance, South Africa under the auspices of the IMF. *http://www.imf.org/external/np/omd/2009/govref/032409.pdf* (Accessed June 8, 2011); and The Stiglitz Report (commissioned by the UN) published by New Press 2010.

[177] IEO: Governance of the IMF: An evaluation (2008).

[178] IMF: Committee on IMF Governance Reform Final Report (2009)

[179] See, for example, R.M. Jeker, "Voting rights of less developed countries in the IMF" (1978) 12(3) J.W.T.L. 218–227 (May/June); Report of the Independent Commission on International Development Issues Under the Chairmanship of Willy Brandt, North–South, A Programme for Survival (1980); E. Osieke, "Majority voting systems in the international Labour Organisation and the International Monetary Fund" (April 1984) I.C.L.Q. 33, pp.381–408; W.N. Gianaris, "Weighted Voting in the International Monetary Fund and the World Bank" (1990–1991) *Fordham International Law Journal* 14 No.4, pp.910–945; J. Head, "Suspension of debtor countries' voting rights in the IMF: an assessment of the third amendment to the IMF charter" (Spring 1993) *Virginia Journal of International Law* 33 No.3, pp.591–646; J. Head, "Suspension of debtor countries' voting rights in the IMF: an assessment of the third amendment to the IMF charter" (Spring 1993) *Virginia Journal of International Law* 33 No.3, pp.591–646; R. Gerster, "Proposals for voting reform within the International Monetary Fund" (June 1993) J.W.T. 27 No.3, pp.121–136; R. Gerster, "Accountability of executive directors in the Bretton Woods institutions" (December 1993) J.W.T. 27 No.6, pp.87–116; A. Bichsel, "The World Bank and the International Monetary Fund from the perspective of the Executive Directors from Developing countries" (December 1994) J.W.T. 28 No.6, pp.141–167.

[180] See, for example, France in 1955 referred to by Gold (1996), p.123. See also Commonwealth Study Group Towards a new Bretton Woods (1983) at p.57, paras 4–45.

[181] See, for example, R.M. Jeker, "Voting rights of less developed countries in the IMF" (1978) J.W.T. 12(3), pp.218–227. R. Gerster, "Proposals for voting reform within the International Monetary Fund" (1993) J.W.T. See also A.H. Qureshi, *Indian Journal of International Law* (1988), Vol.28 Nos.3 and 4, p.481. See also IMF: Committee on IMF Governance Reform Final Report (2009).

[182] R. Gerster (1993) J.W.T., p.126. See also, for example, L.H. Officer, "Are international monetary fund quotas unfavourable to less-developed countries? A normative historical analysis" (June 1991) *Journal of International Money and Finance* 10 (2), pp.193–213.

Further, the level of accountability of Executive Directors, as well as the manner of decision-making by Executive Directors has been particularly queried.[183] This is inter alia for the following reasons. First, it has been contended that good governance requires access by individuals and non-governmental organisations, to participate in the affairs of the IMF.[184] Executive Directors do not account for themselves to the legislators of their constituencies.[185] Secondly, Executive Directors are not appointed by national representative bodies.[186] Thirdly, the lack of guidance as to how Executive Directors should engage in decision-making, allows them a considerable element of discretion.[187] Fourthly, national legislatures have little role in monitoring and participating in Fund affairs.[188] Many of the decisions are actually made by the Central Banking authorities.[189] The lack of transparency in some Fund decision-making processes makes it difficulty to obtain relevant information.[190] For example, Fund surveillance activities are not accompanied by automatic publication of the conclusions of the consultations.[191] Fund operations are not reported in national legislatures.[192] This reduces the possibility of generating interest and discussion on monetary matters. Finally, the practice of decision-making through consensus (i.e. arriving at a decision through the sense of the meeting) is not necessarily conducive to full and effective participation of all the membership. The culture of consensus can in fact harbour, as one observer has commented, an "expression of powerlessness".[193]

The Fund has, in particular in response to the recent 2008 financial crisis, responded to criticisms of its governance, including decision-making processes and its determination of quotas, through a series of measures in 2008 viz., the IMF Quota and Voice Reform,[194] and in 2010 viz., Quota and Governance Reforms.[195]Briefly, the 2008 Quota and Voice Reform include reform of the quota formula, ad hoc quota increases to align the quotas of certain emerging economies to global economic realties (in 2006 and 2008), increase in quotas based on new quota formula, increase in basic votes and change in the formula in their allocation; and two additional alternate

---

[183] See R. Gerster, "Accountability of Executive Directors in the Bretton Woods Institutions" (1993) J.W.T., Vol.27 No.6, pp.87–116. See also G7 October 1998, Work Program on Strengthening the Architecture of the International Monetary System.

[184] R. Gerster (1993) J.W.T.

[185] See IEO: Governance of the IMF: An evaluation (2008).

[186] R. Gerster (1993) J.W.T.

[187] R. Gerster (1993).

[188] R. Gerster (1993).

[189] R. Gerster (1993).

[190] R. Gerster (1993). See also IEO: Governance of the IMF: An evaluation (2008) Ch.3 para. 30 wherein it is observed that IMF "disclosure policies and practices could be strengthened to match best practice among international organization."

[191] R. Gerster (1993). As of 1998 they are published, but only where a member country so requests. See *IMF Economic Reviews*: Press Information Notices.

[192] R. Gerster (1993).

[193] R. Gerster (1993).

[194] Effective 2011.

[195] Not yet in effect.

executive directors for African constituencies. However, the increase in quotas resulting from the Quota and Voice Reform are considered marginal in their impact[196]; and the revision of the quota formula is considered not sufficient for good governance purposes as it "actually shifts voting weight to industrial countries a the expense of middle-and low-income ones."[197] Moreover, the percentage increase of around 5.5 per cent in the basic votes is not considered sufficient given that in 1944 when the first basic votes were allocated the basic votes constituted 11.3 per cent of the total voting share of the then 44 members of the IMF.[198] The 2010 Quota and Governance Reform involves a doubling of quotas, adjustment of quotas, completion of quota formula review by January 2013, reduction in European representation in Executive Board by two, an all-elected Executive Board, and the possibility of a second Alternate Executive Director for multi-constituency countries.

5-025      These recent changes are a step in the right direction. Some of these, however, are slow and staggered and still others suggested in recent influential reports remain to be made. Moreover, the institutional changes within the IMF need to be considered in the framework of the family of international economic institutions, and the multitude of concerns that affect the global economy. From this external vantage, reform of the IMF has to be set against the perceived need of a global economic institution, such as the Global Economic Coordination Council (GECC) suggested in the Stiglitz Report.[199]

Finally, of note are some constitutional constraints on the substantive nature of Fund decisions. The decisions by the organs of the Fund must be consistent with the law of the Fund. In particular, the last sentence of Art.1 has been read to require the exclusion of non-economic considerations.[200] However, the Fund is required to have due regard for decisions of the UN Security Council under Arts 41 and 42 of the UN Charter.[201] The Fund however is only bound to pay due regard. Thus, it can provide financial assistance to a member condemned by the UN Security Council.[202] In addition, the Fund is required to respect the domestic, social and political policies of members and to pay due regard to the circumstances of the member in exercising surveillance over exchange rate arrangements.[203] In relation to conditionality the Fund is required to pay due regard to the domestic social and political objectives, the economic priorities and the circumstances of

---

[196] See p.133 of The Stiglitz Report (New Press, 2010).
[197] See p.133 of The Stiglitz Report (New Press, 2010).
[198] See p.133 of The Stiglitz Report (New Press, 2010).
[199] See Ch 4 of The Stiglitz Report (New Press, 2010).
[200] Compare this however with Art.IV, s.10 of the IBRD which specifically excludes political or non-economic considerations.
[201] See Art.VI of the Agreement Between the United Nations and the International Monetary Fund in IMF, *Selected Decisions of the IMF*, 22nd Issue (1997).
[202] See, for example, E. Denters, *Law and Theory of IMF Conditionality* (Kluwer Law International, 1996), p.167.
[203] Art.IV, s.3.

the member.[204] The former injunction has been construed as being of more weight. Generally, the Articles of Agreement do not discriminate as between the members. Finally, the principle of reciprocity has no application in the context of the Fund.

## INTERPRETATION AND DISPUTE SETTLEMENT[205]

In the IMF, the function of interpretation and the mechanism of dispute settlement is somewhat conflated. There is no express mention of mechanisms for dispute settlement, either as between the IMF and a member, or as between members. The explanation for this lies in the belief that all complaints raise questions of interpretation, and therefore the fairly comprehensive provisions in the Articles of Agreement dealing with interpretation would suffice.[206] In addition, there is a perception of a certain lack of a litigious disposition amongst the membership of the IMF.[207] Such a perception may well be controversial, given that members are not so disposed, often because of political expediency, a sense of helplessness in the light of the dispute settlement mechanism, and general lack of expertise in the international monetary field.

**5-026**

There is some debate as to whether the interpretative function embraces questions of fact. It is contended that whereas the distinction between law and fact is clear in theory, it is not so easy to make in practice. Further, it has been observed by Gold that the IMF has the mandate to settle all questions of fact and law in order to perform its functions.[208]

However, if the interpretative mechanism proves to be inadequate in dealing with the settlement of disputes there are existing mechanisms contained in the Articles of Agreement and the subordinate law of the IMF which may be invoked. Thus, it is always open, for example, for a member to raise a matter with the Executive Board or the Board of Governors.[209]

In the practice of the Fund, there are two types of interpretative decisions, viz. formal and informal interpretations. The procedure for formal interpretations is set out in Art.XXIX. Basically, any question of interpretation may be raised in the first instance with the Executive Board for its decision.[210] Where the decision of the Executive Board is considered to be unsatisfactory, then the matter can be referred to the Board of Governors. This reference

---

[204] para.4 of IMF Guidelines on Conditionality: EB Decision No. 12864–(02/102), September 25, 2002.

[205] Generally on interpretation see J. Gold, *Interpretation: The IMF and International Law* (Kluwer Law International, 1996).

[206] Gold (1996), p.36.

[207] Gold (1996), p.163.

[208] Gold (1996), p.311.

[209] Gold (1996).

[210] Art.XXIX.

must be within three months. The decision of the Board of Governors is final. Where a question is referred to the Board of Governors, it is to be considered by a Committee of Interpretation of the Board of Governors. In this committee each member is to have one vote.[211] This committee has not been set up. This has been mainly because of the reluctance of developed members to establish it, given the absence of the operation of the weighted voting system.[212] It has been suggested that the inability to establish this Committee constitutes a breach of Art.XXIX.[213] Interpretative decisions of the Executive Board involve weighted voting, but there are no special majorities required. In contrast an amendment of the Articles involves an 85 per cent majority. A degree of fairness in the process of interpretation is injected not only by allowing an appeal to the Board of Governors, but also by ensuring that where a question particularly affects a member not entitled to appoint an Executive Director, then that member may send a representative to the Executive Board.[214] In this manner, the problems arising from the inability of the elected Executive Director to split the votes of his constituency are resolved.

5-027    The formal interpretative process does not partake of a judicial proceeding. Therefore there are no timetables, nor is there the need for pleadings and affidavits, etc. The procedure for a formal interpretation does not apply to the subordinate law of the IMF, namely the By-Laws of the Board of Governors, Rules and Regulations of the Executive Board, and resolutions based on these subsidiary sources.[215]

The Fund has made few authoritative interpretative decisions. In all thus far there have been approximately 12, which were made before the First Amendment.[216] The reasons for these formal interpretations are varied. They have one thing in common however. They have all proved to be of advantage to the IMF in enhancing its powers and protecting its interests.[217] Since then most interpretative decisions have been informal. The departure from the formal mode to the informal approach appears to have been as a consequence of the advantage of flexibility in informality.[218] Informal decisions can be more easily arrived at and are more adaptable.[219] The informal interpretative decisions are endowed with a degree of legitimacy through the existence of the formal interpretative procedure.[220] This is because the greater power in the form of the authoritative interpretation mechanism justifies the exist-

---

[211] Art.XXIX.
[212] Denters (1996), p.202.
[213] Denters (1996).
[214] Gold (1996), p.6. See also Art.XXIX (a) and XII, s.3(j). See also s.19 of the IMF By-Laws of the Board of Governors.
[215] Gold (1996), p.59.
[216] Gold (1996), p.50.
[217] Gold (1996), p.90.
[218] Gold (1996), p.91.
[219] Gold (1996), p.163
[220] Gold (1996), p.3.

ence of the lesser informal process.[221] Further, the authority to adopt rules and regulations in order to conduct the business of the Fund also implies authority for informal interpretations.[222] Informal decisions, in addition, are binding, because they are arrived at in a decision making process set against the structure of the voting power of members; and the fact that members are bound to collaborate with the Fund.[223] Interpretative decisions, whether formal or informal, are binding on members; and where the interpretation is not binding on national court as a consequence of national law, then the member is obliged to make the interpretation binding.[224] An informal interpretation arrived at by the Board of Governors is not final, and can be challenged through the formal mode of interpretation.[225]

The Fund interpretative process is internalised, i.e. the Fund engages in auto-interpretation. Interpretation is not considered externally. Such a system involves the Fund acting as a judge in its own affairs. The main reason for a system of auto-interpretation is the financial character of the rights and obligations of members.[226] Of course the fact that the treaty is complex has a bearing, but this is of less significance. Auto-interpretation has the consequence that those engaged in the interpretation have the necessary expertise in the field, especially of the origins and development of the purposes of the organisation, as set out in the Fund law. Further, given that the Articles require a teleological approach to interpretation,[227] it is more likely that the internal officers of the Fund are going to be disposed to such an approach in order to give effect to the objectives set out in the Articles of Agreement.[228] It has been contended that in international financial organisations in particular, questions are best settled by the policy-making organs of the organisation rather than through an adjudicative process.[229] It is to be noted, however, that this practice has now been followed in the World Trade Organization as well in so far as its legislative interpretative process is concerned.[230] Such a manner of interpretation gives greater flexibility in interpretation and ensures that decisions will carry the weight of the consent of the membership.

The Articles are to be interpreted with a teleological approach.[231] Such **5-028** an approach to interpretation is legislative in character. It is dictated by the constitutional character of the Articles[232]; and the special direction in the last sentence of Art.1, wherein are set out the purposes of the IMF, and a

[221] Gold (1996), p.169.
[222] Gold (1996), p.170.
[223] Gold (1996), pp.39–40.
[224] See Art.XXXI, s.2(a).
[225] Gold (1996), p.225.
[226] Gold (1996), p.16.
[227] Gold (1996), p.19. See also Art.I, last sentence.
[228] Gold (1996), p.15.
[229] Gold (1996), p.217 quoting I. Shihata.
[230] See Art.IX (2) of the Marrakesh Agreement Establishing the WTO.
[231] Gold (1996), p.19. See also Art.1.
[232] Gold (1996), p.172.

direction in essence that the teleological approach is followed. However, the teleological approach is not a synonym for pragmatism. The approach is dependent upon the purposes of the IMF as set out in the Articles. It is not an approach that undermines the rule of law, and that merely responds on an ad hoc basis to problems.[233] For such an approach, the purposes set out in Art.1 of the Articles of Agreement are germane. However, other purposes of the Fund are also to be found stated elsewhere in the Articles and are equally relevant. Further, the purposes set out in Art.1 are interdependent, and may even conflict.[234] Thus, the teleological approach is, it is suggested, not licence for any course of action on the part of the IMF. In this respect, issue is taken with Joseph Gold when he states[235]:

"Every action of the IMF every day expresses or implies some interpretation of its law. . .Even if an action is not itself a decision of the one or the kind, or is not expressly justified by reference to a decision of either kind, the action will imply a view about the meaning of some element or elements in the IMF's law. . . . All actions of the IMF are quintessentially interpretative."

Gold does make a number of qualifications to this, however. He points out that where a decision has been arrived at by the Executive Board, even an interpretative decision, that decision is not one that establishes the agreement of the parties as stipulated in the Vienna Convention on the law of Treaties, because the Executive Board's decision is not a decision of the representatives of the membership.[236] Further, he does concede that it is possible at all material times to evaluate the consistency of practice with the Articles of Agreement of the IMF.[237]

The interpretative approach adopted within the IMF is not in full conformity with internationally recognised principles of treaty interpretation.[238] The IMF practice does not follow the letter of the guidelines on treaty interpretation set out in the Vienna Convention on the Law of Treaties. Supplementary means are given more weight. This departure from the Vienna Convention is not deliberate.[239] The traveau preparatoire is considered an important aid to interpretation, and is always referred to in the interpretation process.[240] In the practice of the IMF the traveaux preparatoire includes, according to Joseph Gold,[241] (i) the Proceedings and Documents of the Bretton Woods Conference as published by the US State Department; (ii) Minutes of the Executive Board on amendments of the Articles and Decisions of the IMF's

---

[233] Gold (1996), p.176.
[234] Gold (1996), p.20 quoting H.D. White.
[235] Gold (1996), p.3.
[236] Gold (1996), p.193.
[237] Gold (1996), p.217.
[238] Gold (1996), p.176. See Arts 31–32 of the Vienna Convention On the Law of Treaties 1969.
[239] Gold (1996), p.176.
[240] Gold (1996), p.180.
[241] Gold (1996), p.184.

organs; (iii) Reports or Communiqués by organs and other bodies within the structure of the IMF; (iv) IMF Official Histories, available minutes and commentaries of national delegations, collected papers and reminiscences of leading negotiators, hearings and debates of member's legislatures.

Under an agreement between the IMF and the UN,[242] the IMF has the authority to request an advisory opinion from the ICJ on any legal question within the scope of the Fund's activities.[243] Thus far, however, no opinion has been sought. Probable reasons include the fact that reference would undermine the Fund's own authority in the field of interpretation. Further, the ICJ may be less inclined to follow the teleological approach, not to mention the slow process involved in the deliberations of the ICJ.[244] However, it has been suggested that some questions, for example relating to State succession, may well be better left to the ICJ.[245]

Finally, in the context of dispute settlement, the existence of the Arbitral Tribunal[246] to deal with disputes after withdrawal of a member from the IMF; and the Administrative tribunal dealing with employment issues within the organisation, are to be noted.

## Enforcement—Generally

The Fund has a range of techniques by which it ensures compliance with its codes of conduct. Some of these techniques are specific to particular codes of conduct or operation in question—for example, the vehicle of IMF Conditionality upon the use of the resources of the Fund; and IMF surveillance exercises in the context of a member's exchange rate and exchange control policies. In general, however, the following play a particular part in enforcement. First, the judgment of peers. The Fund can publish reports and is authorised to communicate its views to any member,[247] for example Reports on the Observance of Standards and Codes ROSCs. The Fund assists members at their request by providing ROSCs in spheres in which it has adopted standards and codes viz., accounting; auditing; anti-money laundering and countering the financing of terrorism (AML/CFT); banking supervision; corporate governance; data dissemination; fiscal transparency; insolvency and creditor rights; insurance supervision; monetary and financial policy transparency; payments systems; and securities regulation; and anti-money laundering and combating the financing of terrorism. Secondly, the

**5-029**

---

[242] Art.VIII of the Agreement between the UN and the IMF 1947.
[243] Art.VIII of the Agreement Between the United Nations and the International Monetary Fund in IMF, *Selected Decisions of the IMF*, 22nd Issue (1997).
[244] Gold (1996), p.244.
[245] Gold (1996), p.245.
[246] Art.XXIX of the IMF Articles of Agreement.
[247] Art.XII, ss.7 and 8.

Fund can declare a member ineligible to use its resources where a member has failed in its obligations,[248] as for instance Zimbabwe in 2001 for overdue financial obligations. Thirdly, the Fund can suspend the voting rights of a member where the member is persistent in failing its obligations, as for instance Liberia in 2003 for failing to implement IMF policy.[249] Finally, a member can be made to withdraw as a member from the Fund[250] as, for example, Czechoslovakia in 1954.

**5-030**     **Article XXVI, Section 2 of the IMF. Compulsory withdrawal**

a) If a member fails to fulfill any of its obligations under this Agreement, the Fund may declare the member ineligible to use the general resources of the Fund. Nothing in this Section shall be deemed to limit the provisions of Article V, Section 5 or Article VI, Section 1.

(b) If, after the expiration of a reasonable period following a declaration of ineligibility under (a) above, the member persists in its failure to fulfill any of its obligations under this Agreement, the Fund may, by a 70 percent majority of the total voting power, suspend the voting rights of the member. During the period of the suspension, the provisions of Schedule L shall apply. The Fund may, by a 70 percent majority of the total voting power, terminate the suspension at any time.

(c) If, after the expiration of a reasonable period following a decision of suspension under (b) above, the member persists in its failure to fulfill any of its obligations under this Agreement, that member may be required to withdraw from membership in the Fund by a decision of the Board of Governors carried by a majority of the Governors having 85 percent of the total voting power.

(d) Regulations shall be adopted to ensure that before action is taken against any member under (a), (b), or (c) above, the member shall be informed in reasonable time of the complaint against it and given an adequate opportunity for stating its case, both orally and in writing.

Despite the array of techniques at the disposal of the IMF, whilst its record in implementation of its code is generally impressive it is nonetheless not perfect. Its record particularly in relation to developed and politically important or powerful members appears to be poor. In this respect, two areas are of particular note as they relate to developed members, viz. surveillance operations in the field of exchange rate and its involvement with regional monetary integration processes. In the case of the latter, the Fund has now addressed the issue somewhat.[251] The Fund deals with States, not regional

---

[248] Art.XXVI, s.2 (a).

[249] Art.XXVI, s.2(b).

[250] Art.XXVI, s.2(c).

[251] See for the need to act, for example, R. Martha, "The Fund Agreement and the Surrender of Monetary Sovereignty to the European Community" (1993) 30 *Common Market Law Review* 749. See for the Fund's response to the problem, EB Decision No.12899–(02/119), December 4, 2002, & EB 11846-(98/125). See further Ch.6 below.

economic organisations. Each member of the EU is individually responsible in terms of its monetary policy to the IMF. Moreover, members of the IMF cannot undermine their IMF obligations through membership of a regional monetary integration process. The Articles of Agreement of the IMF allow for co-operative arrangements in the field of exchange arrangements[252] but they do not cater for the situation, as in the EMU, wherein there is a common currency envisaged.[253] Upon the establishment of a single currency, the participants in that system have one monetary policy—in particular exchange rate policy. It would not be in point in such circumstances for the IMF to deal with individual members of the EMU.[254] The Fund has therefore adopted various decisions to manage its relationships in relation to surveillance with different monetary unions.[255] In the case of an EMU member being subjected to IMF Conditionality also as a consequence of the use of its resources — the modalities could be complex both to prescribe and ensure compliance with Conditionality.[256] However, the Fund has managed to address the complexity as illustrated by the recent IMF lending to Greece in 2010. This would serve as a model in future similar cases.[257]

**Framework for Cooperation between the Fund, the European Commission, and the ECB**                                                                                                   **5-031**

Close cooperation between the three institutions is crucial in three areas:

Program design

The authorities' program represents a coordinated framework for policy adjustment and financing supported by the EC, the ECB and the IMF. Program discussions were conducted on a quadrilateral basis between the authorities and the three institutions, resulting in a unified and consistent set of macroeconomic and structural policy parameters. These are set out in the MEFP/TMU of the IMF and the MEFP/MoU of the EC (attached for information). The MEFP focuses on macroeconomic policies and selected structural measures, while the MoU covers the full structural reform agenda agreed between the authorities and the EC.

Program monitoring

Conditionality for Fund Board reviews is based on a standard quarterly framework of performance criteria and structural benchmarks. For the

---

[252] Art.IV 2 (b).
[253] Denters (1996), p.56.
[254] Denters (1996).
[255] See Surveillance over Monetary and Exchange Rate Policies: Members of Euro Area EB Decision 11846-(98/125); Modalities for Surveillance over Central African Economic and Monetary Union Policies in Context of Article IV Consultations with Member Countries (EB 13654-(06/1)); Modalities For Surveillance over Eastern Caribbean Currency Union Policies in Context of Article IV Consultations with Member Countries (EB: 13655-(06/1)); Modalities for Surveillance over West African Economic and Monetary Union Policies in Context of Article IV Consultations with Member Countries (EB: 13656-(06/1)).
[256] Denters (1996), p.63.
[257] See IMF *IMF Survey* May 2010.

EC, conditionality is based on an overall assessment of progress against the structural agenda in the MoU as well as the macroeconomic targets. The EC conducts this assessment in liaison with the ECB, and then makes a recommendation to the Euro Group committee of finance ministers, to approve the disbursement. Conditionality for both the IMF and EC is set on the basis of regular end-quarter test dates, with joint review missions consisting of IMF, EC and ECB staff and with disbursements intended to coincide to the extent possible in a fixed proportion of 3-8 between the Fund and the European financing mechanism, described next.

Financing arrangements

Bilateral support is provided by Greece's 15 partner eurozone countries, in ratio to their shares in ECB capital. The loans will be governed by a single loan agreement between Greece and the euro countries, signed by the EC on their behalf, covering the full three years of the program. The loans will have the same maturities as the Fund purchases, and will carry floating rate interest rates (3-month Euribor) plus a spread of 3 percentage points, rising to 4 percentage points for amounts outstanding beyond three years. Each drawing is subject to a one-off service charge of 0.5 percent. Greece has undertaken to draw on the IMF and EC facilities in a constant 3:8 ratio throughout the program period.

Source: IMF: Greece: Staff Report on Request for Stand-By Arrangement, May 2010.

## RELATIONS WITH OTHER INTERNATIONAL ORGANISATIONS

**5-032**    The IMF maintains relations with related international economic organisations. Thus, it cooperates with the World Bank Group, the WTO[258] and other international economic agencies, having entered into agreements with these organisations. The functions of the IMF and the World Bank increasingly coalesce. The World Bank's mandate mainly focuses on reconstruction, and development through specific projects. Here the emphasis is on microeconomic rather than macroeconomic variables.[259] The IMF has strayed, through its involvement in structural adjustment, into development and microeconomic issues. In turn the World Bank exceptionally offers structural adjustment loans. To deal with the smooth operations of the Fund and the World Bank both institutions have entered into a mutual understanding through the IMF–World Bank Concordat.[260] In addition, the two

---

[258] See Agreement Between the International Monetary Fund and the World Trade Organization in IMF, *Selected Decisions of the IMF*, 22nd Issue (1997).

[259] In general, the term "macroeconomic" carries the meaning of "globality and aggregation". It refers, for example, to the overall credit policy rather than the credit policy in a specific sector of the economy. Where the conditions are specific and particular for example focusing on the elimination of subsidies of a particular product they are referred to as being microeconomic. See M. Guitian, "Fund Conditionality: evolution of principles and practices", *IMF Pamphlet Series* No.38 (1981), p.35. See also Denters (1996), p.109.

[260] IMF–World Bank Concordat (SM/89/54, March 31,1989). See also Denters (1996), p.160.

institutions under the Concordat have emphasised the need to strengthen collaboration mechanisms in specific sectors, as for instance financial issues, through further elaboration of guidelines.[261] In essence, the institutions define their respective mandates in terms of macro and microeconomic variables and set out procedures for collaboration so as to avoid differing policy advice.[262] Thus, where the two institutions are engaged in operations which involve both their respective spheres there is particular evidence of collaboration. This is mostly in terms of balance of payments assistance involving structural adjustment, social safety nets in IMF Conditionality, and assistance to heavily indebted members.[263] More specifically, the two institutions have also been involved in co-operation in reducing debt burdens, reducing poverty, monitoring progress on the MDGs, and assessing financial stability.[264]

**IMF-World Bank Concordat 1989[265]**                                            **5-033**

9.  The Fund has among its purposes the promotion of economic conditions conducive to growth, price stability, and balance of payments sustainability and is required to exercise surveillance on a continual basis over the performance of its members as defined by Article IV. The Fund is empowered to provide temporary balance of payments financing to members to enable them to correct maladjustments in their balance of payments without resorting to measures destructive of national or international prosperity. Thus, the Fund has focused on the aggregate aspects of macroeconomic policies and their related instruments—including public sector spending and revenues, aggregate wage and price policies, money and credit, interest rates and the exchange rate. The Fund has to discharge responsibilities with respect to surveillance, exchange rate matters, balance of payments, growth-oriented stabilization policies and their related instruments. These are the areas in which the Fund has a mandate, primary responsibility, and a record of expertise and experience.

10. The Bank has the objective of promoting economic growth and conditions conducive to efficient resource allocation, which it pursues through investment lending, sectoral and structural adjustment loans. Thus, the Bank has focused on development strategies; sector and project investments; structural adjustment programs; policies which deal with the efficient allocation of resources in both public and private sectors; priorities in government expenditures; reforms of administrative systems, production, trade and financial sectors; the restructuring of state enterprises and sector policies. Moreover, as a marketbased institution, the Bank also concerns itself with issues relating to the creditworthiness of its members. In these areas, except for the aggregate aspects of the

[261] See IMF, *Annual Report* (1998). See IMF and World Bank Factsheet September 2010.
[262] See IMF–World Bank Concordat. See also Denters (1996), p.161.
[263] See IMF, *Annual Report* (1998) and IMF and World Bank Factsheet 2010.
[264] See IMF and World Bank Factsheet 2010.
[265] Source: *http://www.imf.org.* (Accessed June 8, 2011). See also the 2007 Joint Management Action Plan on World-Bank-IMF Collaboration (JMAP).

economic policies mentioned in the previous paragraph, the Bank has a mandate, primary responsibility, and a record of expertise and experience.

11. While it is important to strengthen the framework for collaboration and to reduce the risk of conflict and duplication, both the Bank and the Fund must be allowed to explore their legitimate concerns with regard to macroeconomic and structural issues and to take them into account in their policy advice and lending operations. The 1966 guidelines stipulate that views on matters clearly within the area of 'primary responsibility' of one or the other of the two institutions 'should be expressed to members only by or with the consent of that institution.' This provision remains appropriate. The procedures for enhanced collaboration spelled out below are designed to assure resolution of issues. It is, of course, equally important that borrowing countries be aware of the responsibility of the institution for policy advice in the areas of its primary responsibility.

**5-034**    Similarly, there is a close relationship between trade and monetary matters. In recognition of this, the Fund has produced guidelines for its staff to avoid conflict between the WTO and the IMF and duplication of focus.[266] Thus, Fund staff are advised to avoid recommending economic conditions under a balance of payments adjustment programme which would conflict with the member's WTO obligations. In order to strengthen further collaboration between the IMF and the WTO, the two institutions have entered into a co-operative agreement.[267] The agreement covers exchange of information between the organisations, attendance at meetings in areas of common interest, observer status to the WTO at the Annual Meetings of the Board of Governors, and the grounds for greater coherence in global policy-making.[268] However, the agreement does not resolve all questions of conflicting jurisdiction between them. This was highlighted in the WTO case in which Argentina argued that it had imposed a statistical tax at the instigation of the IMF under a balance of payments adjustment programme. But the WTO panel ruled that the tax was in violation of Art.VIII of GATT 1994; and nothing in the 1996 agreement between the IMF and the WTO excused Argentina's compliance with the requirements of GATT 1994.[269]

The relationship between the IMF and the UN is governed by a formal agreement.[270] The agreement inter alia provides for mutual co-operation in the field of exchange of information and reciprocal participation in

---

[266] See Guidelines/Framework for Fund Staff Collaboration with the WTO EB/CGATT/95/1 in *Selected Decisions of the IMF* online on IMF website.

[267] Fund–WTO Cooperation Agreement 1996 in *Selected Decisions of the IMF* (1997).

[268] See IMF, *Annual Report* (1997) for a summary of the agreement.

[269] See Argentina—Measures *Affecting Imports of Footwear Textiles, Apparel and Other Items*. Report of the Panel (1997) and Appellate Body Report (1998).

[270] Agreement Between the United Nations and the International Monetary Fund (1947) in *Selected Decisions of the IMF* .

some of the meetings of the plenary organs of the respective organisations of mutual concern. However, although the Fund is a specialised agency of the UN[271] it is required to function as an independent international organisation.[272]

---

[271] See Agreement Between the United Nations and the International Monetary Fund (1947); United Nations Convention on the Privileges and Immunities of the Specialized Agencies (1947) and Annex V (1949); and Articles 57 and 63 of the UN Charter.

[272] Art.1(2) of the Agreement Between the United Nations and the International Monetary Fund in IMF, *Selected Decisions of the IMF*.

### CHAPTER 6

# REGULATING EXCHANGE RATES & IMF SUREVEILLANCE

The origins of IMF surveillance are rooted in the regulation of exchange rates.[1] However, given that IMF surveillance has now evolved into a core function almost in its own right this chapter focuses both on exchange rates and surveillance respectively and together.

**6–001**

## EXCHANGE RATES—GENERALLY

The external value of a State's currency is the value of its relationship with the currencies of other nations—generally known as the exchange rate. Exchanges rates are influenced by the state of the national economy and

**6–002**

---

[1] On exchange rates see, for example, R.W. Edwards, Jr, *International Monetary Collaboration* (Transnational Publishers, 1985), Ch.11; W. Holder, "Exchange rate policies: the role and influence of the IMF" (1986) *American Society of International Law Proceedings* 29–35; J. Gold, "Exchange Rates", *International Law And Organization*, (American Bar Association, 1988); R.W. Edwards, "An 'interesting' provision concerning exchange rate arrangements", in W.F. Ebke and J.J. Norton et al. (eds), *Festricht in Honour of Sir Joseph Gold* (1990); IMF Independent Evaluation Office, *IMF's Advice on Exchange Rate Policy, Issues Paper* (June 2006); IMF Independent Evaluation Office, *Evaluation of IMF Exchange Rate Policy Advice (1999–2005)* (May 2007); RW Staiger & A. Sykes, "Currency manipulation' and World Trade', *World Trade Review* (2010), 9:4, 583-627. On IMF Surveillance see, for example, Rosa M. Lastra, "The Role of the IMF as a Global Financial Authority", *European Yearbook of International Economic Law* (2001); IEO: *Multilateral Surveillance* (2006); D. Lombardi & N. Woods, "The Politics of Influence—An analysis of IMF Surveillance", *Review of International Political Economy,* 15:5 (2008), 711–739; IMF: "Modernizing the Surveillance Mandate and Modalities" Prepared by the Strategy, Policy, and Review Department and the Legal Department Approved by R.Moghadam and S.Hagan, March 26, 2010 (Available on IMF website); IMF, *Financial Sector Surveillance and the Mandate of the Fund*, Prepared by the Monetary and Capital Markets Department and the Strategy, Policy, and Review Department, Approved by J.Viñals and R.Moghadam, March 19, 2010 (Available on IMF website); Robert Lavigne and Lawrence Schembri, *Strengthening IMF Surveillance: An Assessment of Recent Reforms*, Discussion Paper 2009–10, Bank of Canada; S. Hagan, "Enhancing the IMF's Regulating Authority", J.I.E.L. (2010) 13 (3):55; IEO: *IMF Performance in the Run-up to the Financial and Economic Crisis: IMF Surveillance in 2004–07* (2011) and IMF *IMF Fact Sheet—IMF Surveillance* (2011).

the influence of the international economy. In particular government fiscal[2] and monetary policy[3] has a bearing on the exchange rates. Further, in a globalized economy, exchange rate fluctuations have a domino effect both internally and internationally. Thus, if the exchange rate of the British currency is unduly high, foreigners wanting to buy British exports would have to pay more in their own currency to obtain British products. Similarly, where foreign debts are incurred in an appreciating currency then the value of the debt burden increases. Thus, exchange rates are of international concern.[4]

Of late, exchange rate stability has become of particular concern, because of the growth in international capital movement, elimination of exchange controls and the advent of regional economic and monetary integration.[5] Thus, the strength of the Euro, introduced in the EU, challenges the dominance of the US dollar as a principal global reserve currency. This circumstance would give rise to exchange rate volatility between the Euro and the dollar.[6]

As has been pointed out earlier, under General International Law a State has freedom to determine the value of its currency.[7] However, given that exchange rates impact on the international economic system, it is legitimate to enquire as to the extent to which the role of IEL has evolved, from the General International Law position, in the regulation of exchange rates, as well as the manner in which the existing structures can be improved.[8] In fact, given the troubled record of the regulation of exchange rates, this is one area of particular challenge for the lawyer. Effective exchange rate regulation has proved to be particularly elusive for the international community.

Considering briefly the chronology of international monetary relations, a gold standard operated at the beginning of the last century. Currency values were fixed by a number of States with reference to gold. During the inter-war years, the gold standard proved difficult to sustain, and so it was abandoned around the 1930s. Currency values were allowed to float according to market forces. With the advent of the IMF, under the original Articles of Agreement, a par value system was established. Under this system, essentially, members were obliged to establish and sustain a value of their currency, and permitted

---

[2] Fiscal policy is concerned with the raising of revenue through taxation; and the adjustment of the level of public expenditure.

[3] Monetary policy is concerned with the control of the supply of money and/or interest rates.

[4] See, for example, H.D. White, quoted in K. Horsefield (ed.), *The International Monetary Fund (1945–1965)*, Vol.III, p.60, wherein he is states: "Alterations off a currency affect other countries as well as the country making the change. It is therefore, only reasonable to demand that the other countries have the some say in the decision."

[5] See *IMF Survey*, Vol.26 (September 1997), p.7.

[6] See W. Muchan, *Financial Times*, September 9, 1997.

[7] Case Concerning the payment of various Serbian Loans issued in France (1927) P.C.I.J., ser.A, No.10, p.44 quoted in F. Mann, *The Legal Aspect of Money* (Oxford, Oxford University Press, 1982), p.465 (see also 6th edition).

[8] See J. Gold, *Exchange Rates* (Washington D.C., American Bar Association, Section of International Law and Practice, 1988), p.2.

deviations from that value only within certain limited margins.[9] The par value of a member's currency was fixed and expressed directly and indirectly in terms of gold.[10] The gold was referred to indirectly through the medium of the US dollar, of the gold weight and fineness of the US dollar in effect on July 1, 1944.[11] This was against the background of the practice of a number of States to fix the value of their currency in relation to the dollar. The US in turn maintained the value of the US dollar in terms of gold. In addition, the US had underwritten the par value system by declaring a willingness to buy and sell gold in transactions with foreign monetary authorities at the value of the US dollar in effect on July 1, 1944.[12] A member could change its par value under prescribed circumstances if it was suffering from a fundamental disequilibrium.

On August 15, 1971 the US unilaterally suspended its willingness to convert official holdings of the dollar into gold, and reneged on its commitment to maintain the par value of the dollar. Between 1971 and the time when the second amendment came into effect in 1978, there followed a temporary extra legal regime. Under the second amendment of the IMF Articles of Agreement a discretionary system of exchange rates was introduced. Under this system members have the choice of the system according to which the values of their exchange rates are determined.

## THE DISCRETIONARY SYSTEM OF EXCHANGE RATES UNDER THE IMF

The character of the current system of exchange rate regulation is essentially    **6–003** that of soft law.[13] This is because the normative framework is crafted in the form of guidelines, recommendations, and exhortations to endeavour to achieve certain objectives. Further, it is vaguely crafted, so as to make it difficult to ascertain a breach[14]; and the policing of the guidelines are conducted through a system based mainly on consultation. The character of the regulatory regime partakes of soft law because some of the norms touch upon domestic policies. Given that governments are reluctant to be subjected to external regulation in relation to their domestic sphere, a soft law approach in the circumstances is considered to be an appropriate manner of dealing with such reluctance. Further, the soft law approach is a good technique to build upon experience in the field.

---

[9] 1% margin. See Art.IV of the original IMF Articles of Agreement.
[10] Art.IV of the Original Articles of Agreement of the IMF.
[11] The first date of the Bretton Woods Conference. See Gold (Washington D.C.: American Bar Association, Section of International Law and Practice, 1988), p.28 and Art.IV of the original IMF Articles of Agreement.
[12] Letter by J.W. Snyder, Secretary of the US Treasury, addressed to Camill Gutt, IMF Managing Director—dated May 20, 1949. See Gold (Washington D.C., American Bar Association, Section of International Law and Practice, 1988), p.59.
[13] Gold (1988), p.104.
[14] Gold (1988).

The mandate of the IMF in relation to exchange rates is set out under Art.I (iii) of the IMF Articles of Agreement as follows:

"To promote exchange stability, to maintain orderly exchange arrangements among members, and to avoid competitive exchange depreciation."

Exchange rate stability, although set out as an objective under Art.I, has acquired a different meaning since the second amendment. The objective of exchange rate stability in the Article is a remnant of the original Articles. Any discussion of amending Art.I would open a Pandora's box; therefore it has remained, although not unscathed.[15] In reality the international community has moved away from a rigid focus on attaining exchange rate stability. Instead, the emphasis now is on economic stability which would be conducive to exchange rate stability.[16] The reference to exchange arrangements is a reference to the system which a member adopts to determine the value of its currency (e.g. floating, fixed or pegged to a certain currency). Such arrangements are to be orderly. Competitive exchange depreciation is a reference to the devaluation of currency, in response to the devaluation by another member of its currency, in a competitive manner.

Article IV of the IMF Articles is the key provision which gives effect to the objectives of the Fund in relation to exchange rates. In relation to exchange rate arrangements, in the first instance, a discretionary system of exchange arrangements has been designed, and this is the system which operates currently.[17] This system gives the members the freedom to establish their own exchange rate arrangement.[18] Under this system members have the choice of a number of exchange arrangements, viz. the pegging of the member's currency in terms of the Special Drawing Right, or another denominator, or another currency, or a composite of currencies; an arrangement under a regional monetary co-operative system; or the floating of the currency according to the exchange market rate.

A number of points need to be made about the discretionary arrangements. First, in accordance with Art.IV linking of exchange rates with gold is prohibited.[19] Secondly, a member, whilst not having to seek the approval of the Fund for the type of exchange arrangement chosen, must nevertheless inform the Fund of its choice.[20] Thirdly, the system of discretionary arrangements can be changed by a general exchange arrangement, provided there is an 85 per cent majority of the total voting power. However, this general arrangement would not detract from the freedom of members to have their

---

[15] Gold, J. *Exchange Rates. International Law and Organization* (Washington D.C.: American Bar Association, Section of International Law and Practice, 1988), p.12.
[16] Gold (1988), and see also Art.IV.
[17] Art.IV, s.2.
[18] Gold (1988), p.8.
[19] See also Gold (1988), p.115.
[20] Art.IV, s.2(a).

own exchange rate arrangement consistent with the purposes of the Fund and Art.IV.[21] The object of the provision of a general arrangement appears to be to give the Fund the opportunity to encourage a uniform system of exchange arrangements.[22] Some commentators have called for the IMF to use this enabling power to provide for a general exchange arrangement.[23] Finally, the discretionary system of exchange arrangements can also be replaced, assuming there is an 85 per cent majority of the total voting power, by a widespread system of exchange arrangements based on stable but adjustable par values, as set out in Schedule C of the Articles of Agreement of the IMF.[24] It appears that a member may, consistently with the purposes of the IMF and its obligations under Art.IV, after consultation with the Fund maintain an exchange arrangement not based on the par value system proposed under Sch.C.[25]

**Article IV Section 2 of IMF Articles of Agreement[26]**

**General exchange arrangements**                                     6–004

(a) Each member shall notify the Fund, within thirty days after the date of the second amendment of this Agreement, of the exchange arrangements it intends to apply in fulfilment of its obligations under Section 1 of this Article, and shall notify the Fund promptly of any changes in its exchange arrangements.

(b) Under an international monetary system of the kind prevailing on January 1, 1976, exchange arrangements may include (i) the maintenance by a member of a value for its currency in terms of the special drawing right or another denominator, other than gold, selected by the member, or (ii) cooperative arrangements by which members maintain the value of their currencies in relation to the value of the currency or currencies of other members, or (iii) other exchange arrangements of a member's choice.

(c) To accord with the development of the international monetary system, the Fund, by an eighty-five percent majority of the total voting power, may make provision for general exchange arrangements without limiting the right of members to have exchange arrangements of their choice consistent with the purposes of the Fund and the obligations under Section 1 of this Article.

Regardless of the particular exchange arrangement operating, a member   6–005
must fulfil certain obligations in relation to its exchange rates which are set out in Art.IV, s.I. These obligations are formulated essentially in soft terms,[27]

---

[21] Art.IV, s.2(c).
[22] Gold (1988), p.120.
[23] See R. Edwards, "An 'interesting' provision concerning exchange rate arrangements" in W.F. Ebke and J.J. Norton et al. (eds), *Festricht in Honour of Sir Joseph Gold* (Heidelberg, Verlag Recht und Wirtschaft GmbH, 1990), p.109.
[24] Art.IV, s.4.
[25] See Sch.C, para.3.
[26] Source: *http://www.imf.org.* (Accessed June 8, 2011).
[27] Thus, language such as "endeavour to", "seek to" and "avoid" is used.

and focus mainly on underlying economic, social and political conditions. Generally, a member is obligated to collaborate with the IMF and other members to assure orderly exchange arrangements; and to promote a stable system of exchange rates. It is not clear what is meant by orderly exchange arrangements.[28] A stable system of exchange rates is not to be confused with the maintenance of exchange rate stability, although it is directed at that objective. A stable system of exchange rates is not only descriptive of the whole process involved in the determination of exchange rates, but also of the quality of that process. It focuses on the underlying conditions, on the stability of the underlying economic and financial conditions; and on the responsiveness of/relationship of, the exchange rate to the underlying conditions. There is thus at present no legal obligation as such to maintain stable exchange rates.[29]

More specifically, a member is enjoined, under Article IV Section 1, as follows:

**Article IV of the IMF Articles of Agreement[30]**

**6–006**

**Obligations Regarding Exchange Arrangements**
**Section 1. General obligations of members**

Recognizing that the essential purpose of the international monetary system is to provide a framework that facilitates the exchange of goods, services, and capital among countries, and that sustains sound economic growth, and that a principal objective is the continuing development of the orderly underlying conditions that are necessary for financial and economic stability, each member undertakes to collaborate with the Fund and other members to assure orderly exchange arrangements and to promote a stable system of exchange rates. In particular, each member shall:

(i) endeavor to direct its economic and financial policies toward the objective of fostering orderly economic growth with reasonable price stability, with due regard to its circumstances;

(ii) seek to promote stability by fostering orderly underlying economic and financial conditions and a monetary system that does not tend to produce erratic disruptions;

(iii) avoid manipulating exchange rates or the international monetary system in order to prevent effective balance of payments adjustment or to gain an unfair competitive advantage over other members; and

(iv) follow exchange policies compatible with the undertakings under this Section.

**6–007**   The Fund has the mandate to adopt specific principles in order to guide its members in the formulation of correct exchange rate policies.[31] The Fund has enunciated few principles under this mandate. This is mainly because of

---

[28]  Gold (1988), p.102.
[29]  Mann (1982), p.514–515.
[30]  Source: *http://www.imf.org.* (Accessed June 8, 2011).
[31]  Art.IV, s.3.

the difficulty in formulating the correct economic theory of exchange rates. However, some guidance is given in the formulation of the policies. Thus, the policies must not be inconsistent with monetary cooperative arrangements. In addition, the principles must be formulated so as to pay due regard to the domestic social and political policies of the members including their particular circumstances. The domestic policies are not, however, given an overriding effect. Article IV Section 1 has been the subject of recent clarification by a 2007 Executive Board Decision under its Article IV Section 3 mandate.[32] With respect to the actual principles set out in Article IV Section 1, the decision makes clear the obligatory nature of Article IV Section 1 (iii) in contrast to its other provisions. Further clarification is provided in an Annex to the decision with respect to Article IV Section 1 (iii). The Annex sets out, to borrow a criminal law analogy, a mens rea and actus rea element to the prohibition on exchange rate manipulation. First, with respect to the mens rea, it emphasises that manipulation should be targeted in order to gain an unfair competitive advantage to secure fundamental exchange rate misalignment in the form of an undervalued exchange rate and to increase net exports. Secondly, with respect to the actus rea, the manipulation must actually affect the level of an exchange rate such as to result in a fundamental exchange rate misalignment in terms of its equilibrium level.[33] The 2007 decision also recommends intervention in the exchange market to counter disorderly conditions whilst taking into account the interests of other members. Moreover, generally exchange rate policies need to avoid resulting in external instability. These clarifications are accompanied by two principles of evidence, namely that there is a presumption of compliance with respect to the principles enunciated in the Decision and that a member will be given the benefit of a reasonable doubt in relation to the assessment of a fundamental exchange rate misalignment in the context of the application of Article IV Section (iii). In sum, the 2007 decision elaborates both on the circumstances when exchange rate policy should be engaged and when it should not be engaged. With respect to the latter the normative framework is obligatory.

Exchange rate manipulation has been much in the focus in international economic relations latterly, in particular as between the United States and China with respect to the Chinese foreign exchange policies pertaining to the RMB; and the perception that the currency is deliberately not being allowed to appreciate so as to give a competitive advantage to Chinese exports.[34] Staiger & A. Sykes conclude that it would be difficult to prove violation of the prohibition on manipulation (mens rea) given China's denial of such an intent; its alternative explanations; and the evidential principle in the 2007 EB Decision which give the member of the IMF the benefit of reasonable

---

[32] EB Decision No. 13919-(07/51), June 15, 2007

[33] See R W Staiger & A Sykes, "Currency manipulation' and World Trade', *World Trade Review* (2010), 9:4, 583–627 at p.591 quoting an IMF Staff Paper.

[34] See R. W. Staiger & A. Sykes, "'Currency manipulation' and World Trade", *World Trade Review* (2010), 9:4, 583–627 and references therein.

doubt.[35] In any event, it is pointed that even if it was possible to substantiate a claim of manipulation it would not be possible to impose any effective sanctions against China within the framework of the IMF.[36]

**6–008**      **EB Decision No. 13919-(07/51), June 15, 2007 (Extract-edited)**

Part II. Principles for the Guidance of Members' Policies Under Article IV, Section 1

13. Principles A through D below are adopted pursuant to Article IV, Section 3 (b) and are intended to provide guidance to members in the conduct of their exchange rate policies in accordance with their obligations under Article IV, Section 1. In accordance with Article IV, Section 3 (b), these Principles respect the domestic social and political policies of members. In applying these Principles, the Fund will pay due regard to the circumstances of members. Members are presumed to be implementing policies that are consistent with the Principles. When, in the context of surveillance, a question arises as to whether a particular member is implementing policies consistent with the Principles, the Fund will give the member the benefit of any reasonable doubt, including with respect to an assessment of fundamental exchange rate misalignment. In circumstances where the Fund has determined that a member is implementing policies that are not consistent with these Principles and is informing the member as to what policy adjustments should be made to address this situation, the Fund will take into consideration the disruptive impact that excessively rapid adjustment would have on the member's economy.

14. Principle A sets forth the obligation contained in Article IV, Section 1(iii); further guidance on its meaning is provided in the Annex to this Decision. Principles B through D constitute recommendations rather than obligations of members. A determination by the Fund that a member is not following one of these recommendations would not create a presumption that that member is in breach of its obligations under Article IV, Section 1.

A. A member shall avoid manipulating exchange rates or the international monetary system in order to prevent effective balance of payments adjustment or to gain an unfair competitive advantage over other members.

B. A member should intervene in the exchange market if necessary to counter disorderly conditions, which may be characterized inter alia by disruptive short-term movements in the exchange rate of its currency.

C. Members should take into account in their intervention policies the interests of other members, including those of the countries in whose currencies they intervene.

---

[35] R. W. Staiger & A. Sykes, "'Currency manipulation' and World Trade", *World Trade Review* (2010), 9:4, at p. 591–592.
[36] R. W. Staiger & A. Sykes, "'Currency manipulation' and World Trade", *World Trade Review* (2010), 9:4, at 592.

D. A member should avoid exchange rate policies that result in external instability.

15. In its surveillance of the observance by members of the Principles set forth above, the Fund shall consider the following developments as among those which would require thorough review and might indicate the need for discussion with a member:

(i) protracted large-scale intervention in one direction in the exchange market;

(ii) official or quasi-official borrowing that either is unsustainable or brings unduly high liquidity risks, or excessive and prolonged official or quasi-official accumulation of foreign assets, for balance of payments purposes;

(iii) (a) the introduction, substantial intensification, or prolonged maintenance, for balance of payments purposes, of restrictions on, or incentives for, current transactions or payments, or (b) the introduction or substantial modification for balance of payments purposes of restrictions on, or incentives for, the inflow or outflow of capital;

(iv) the pursuit, for balance of payments purposes, of monetary and other financial policies that provide abnormal encouragement or discouragement to capital flows;

(v) fundamental exchange rate misalignment;

(vi) large and prolonged current account deficits or surpluses; and

(vii) large external sector vulnerabilities, including liquidity risks, arising from private capital flows.

ANNEX

Article IV, Section 1(iii) and Principle A

1. Article IV, Section 1(iii) of the Fund's Articles provides that members shall "avoid manipulating exchange rates or the international monetary system in order to prevent effective balance of payments adjustment or to gain an unfair competitive advantage over other members." The language of this provision is repeated in Principle A contained in Part II of this Decision. The text set forth below is designed to provide further guidance regarding the meaning of this provision.

2. A member would only be acting inconsistently with Article IV, Section 1(iii) if the Fund determined both that: (a) the member was manipulating its exchange rate or the international monetary system and (b) such manipulation was being carried out for one of the two purposes specifically identified in Article IV, Section 1(iii).

(a) "Manipulation" of the exchange rate is only carried out through policies that are targeted at—and actually affect—the level of an exchange rate. Moreover, manipulation may cause the exchange rate to move or may prevent such movement.

(b) A member that is manipulating its exchange rate would only be acting inconsistently with Article IV, Section 1(iii) if the Fund were to determine that such manipulation was being undertaken "in order to prevent effective balance of payments adjustment or to gain an unfair competitive advantage over other members." In that regard, a member will only be considered to be manipulating exchange rates in order to gain an unfair competitive advantage over other members if the Fund determines both that: (A) the member is engaged in these policies for the purpose of securing fundamental exchange rate misalignment in the form of an undervalued exchange rate and (B) the purpose of securing such misalignment is to increase net exports.

3. It is the responsibility of the Fund to make an objective assessment of whether a member is observing its obligations under Article IV, Section 1 (iii), based on all available evidence, including consultation with the member concerned. Any representation made by the member regarding the purpose of its policies will be given the benefit of any reasonable doubt. (SM/07/183, Sup. 2, 6/19/07)

1 Decision No. 14175-(08/84), September 26, 2008, provides that the next review required by paragraph 21 shall be completed no later than September 26, 2011. (SM/08/287, Sup. 3, 9/2/08)

## SURVEILLANCE

**6-009**    The principal mechanism for the implementation of the regulatory jurisdiction of the Fund in relation to exchange rates is through IMF surveillance operations. Surveillance is described in various IMF literatures as a core function of the IMF.[37] Essentially, surveillance comprises of supervision/ overseeing/monitoring and consultation. It is based on the assumptions that the provision of information, peer pressure, and leverage of power are elements that contribute to effective influence and compliance.[38] A number of key international economic organisations engage in forms of surveillance operations in their respective spheres, as for instance the OECD and the WTO. From a legal perspective IMF surveillance raises questions relating to the IMF mandate, member sovereignty and the effectiveness of the IMF surveillance apparatus as a compliance measure.

IMF surveillance is conducted at the country, regional and global levels— although the bilateral and multilateral surveillance exercises comprise the principal surveillance activities of the Fund. In fact, amongst these surveillance at the bilateral level has been a major preoccupation. The Fund's authority to conduct surveillance is set out in Article IV of the IMF Agreement[39]; and the Executive Board Decision 2007 on Bilateral Surveillance over Member's Policies.[40] Thus, authority to conduct surveillance is found in the member's

---

[37]  See, for example, IEO *Multilateral Surveillance* (2006).
[38]  See D. Lombardi & N. Woods, "The Politics of Influence: AN analysis of IMF surveillance", *Review of International Political Economy,* 15:5 (2008),711–739.
[39]  See Art.IV, s.3(a) and (b).
[40]  EB Decision No. 13919-(07/51), June 15, 2007. There is no decision on multilateral surveillance although there have been calls for it.

obligation to collaborate[41] with the Fund in order to assure orderly exchange arrangements, and a stable system of exchange rates; as well as the express authority given to the Fund to exercise firm surveillance for such purposes.[42] The obligation to collaborate gives the Fund much room for the determination of the criteria for collaboration.[43] Similarly, a member is obliged to provide information to the Fund in order to facilitate surveillance, and to consult the Fund when requested.[44]

**Article IV Section 3 of the IMF Articles of Agreement. Surveillance over exchange arrangements[45]**

(a) The Fund shall oversee the international monetary system in order to ensure its effective operation, and shall oversee the compliance of each member with its obligations under Section 1 of this Article.

6-010

(b) In order to fulfil its functions under (a) above, the Fund shall exercise firm surveillance over the exchange rate policies of members, and shall adopt specific principles for the guidance of all members with respect to those policies. Each member shall provide the Fund with the information necessary for such surveillance, and, when requested by the Fund, shall consult with it on the member's exchange rate policies. The principles adopted by the Fund shall be consistent with cooperative arrangements by which members maintain the value of their currencies in relation to the value of the currency or currencies of other members, as well as with other exchange arrangements of a member's choice consistent with the purposes of the Fund and Section 1 of this Article. These principles shall respect the domestic social and political policies of members, and in applying these principles the Fund shall pay due regard to the circumstances of members.

The mandate for IMF surveillance at the bilateral level pertains to a member's exchange rate policies. This is essentially defined now in terms of external stability which forms "the organising principle"[46] for bilateral surveillance. Thus, the 2007 decision defines the surveillance mandate as pertaining to exchange rate policies as well as "monetary, fiscal, and financial sector policies (both their macroeconomic aspects and macroeconomically relevant structural aspects)" as they impinge on the member's external stability. A member's external stability is a reference to its balance of payments that is not disruptive of exchange rate movements. Bilateral surveillance thus involves the full range of economic policies and developments which impact on the balance of payments and exchange rate.

6-011

---

[41] See Art.IV, s.1.
[42] Article IV Section 3.
[43] See Gold (1988), p.101.
[44] Art.IV, s.3 (b).
[45] Source: *http://www.imf.org.* (Accessed June 8, 2011).
[46] See *http://www.imf.org/external/about/econsurv.htm.* (Accessed June 8, 2011).

**Decision No. 13919-(07/51), June 15, 2007 (Extract)**

6–012 *Part I. Principles for the Guidance of the Fund in its Bilateral Surveillance*

A.  The Scope of Bilateral Surveillance

4.  The scope of bilateral surveillance is determined by members' obligations under Article IV, Section 1. Members undertake under Article IV, Section 1 to collaborate with the Fund and other members to assure orderly exchange arrangements and to promote a stable system of exchange rates (hereinafter "systemic stability." Systemic stability is most effectively achieved by each member adopting policies that promote its own "external stability"—that is, policies that are consistent with members' obligations under Article IV, Section 1 and, in particular, the specific obligations set forth in Article IV, Sections 1 (i) through (iv). "External stability" refers to a balance of payments position that does not, and is not likely to, give rise to disruptive exchange rate movements. Except as provided in paragraph 7 below, external stability is assessed at the level of each member.

5.  In its bilateral surveillance, the Fund will focus on those policies of members that can significantly influence present or prospective external stability. The Fund will assess whether these policies are promoting external stability and advise the member on policy adjustments necessary for this purpose. Accordingly, exchange rate policies will always be the subject of the Fund's bilateral surveillance with respect to each member, as will monetary, fiscal, and financial sector policies (both their macroeconomic aspects and macroeconomically relevant structural aspects). Other policies will be examined in the context of surveillance only to the extent that they significantly influence present or prospective external stability.

6.  In the conduct of their domestic economic and financial policies, members are considered by the Fund to be promoting external stability when they are promoting domestic stability—that is, when they (i) endeavor to direct their domestic economic and financial policies toward the objective of fostering orderly economic growth with reasonable price stability, with due regard to their circumstances, and (ii) seek to promote stability by fostering orderly underlying economic and financial conditions and a monetary system that does not tend to produce erratic disruptions. The Fund in its surveillance will assess whether a member's domestic policies are directed toward the promotion of domestic stability. While the Fund will always examine whether a member's domestic policies are directed toward keeping the member's economy operating broadly at capacity, the Fund will examine whether domestic policies are directed toward fostering a high rate of potential growth only in those cases where such high potential growth significantly influences prospects for domestic, and thereby external, stability. However, the Fund will not require a member that is complying with Article IV, Sections 1(i) and (ii) to change its domestic policies in the interests of external stability.

7.  This Decision applies to members of currency unions, subject to the following considerations. Members of currency unions remain subject to all of their obligations under Article IV, Section 1 and,

accordingly, each member is accountable for those policies that are conducted by union-level institutions on its behalf. In its surveillance over the policies of members of a currency union, the Fund will assess whether relevant policies implemented at the level of the currency union (including exchange rate and monetary policies) and at the level of members are promoting the external stability of the union and will advise on policy adjustments necessary for this purpose. In particular, the Fund will assess whether the exchange rate policies of the union are promoting its external stability, and whether domestic policies implemented at the level of the union are promoting the domestic, and thereby external, stability of the union. Because, in a currency union, exchange rate policies are implemented at the level of the union, the principles for the guidance of members' exchange rate policies and the associated indicators set out in paragraph 15 of this Decision only apply at the level of the currency union. With respect to the conduct of domestic policies implemented at the level of individual members, a member of a currency union is considered by the Fund to be promoting the external stability of the union when it is promoting its own domestic stability. In view of the importance of individual members' balances of payments for the domestic stability of the member and the external stability of the union, the Fund's assessment of the policies of a member of a currency union will always include an evaluation of developments in the member's balance of payments.

B. The Modalities of Bilateral Surveillance

8. Dialogue and persuasion are key pillars of effective surveillance. The Fund, in its bilateral surveillance, will clearly and candidly assess relevant economic developments, prospects, and policies of the member in question, and advise on these. Such assessments and advice are intended to assist that member in making policy choices, and to enable other members to discuss these policy choices with that member. In the context of bilateral surveillance, the Fund will foster an environment of frank and open dialogue and mutual trust with each member and will be evenhanded across members, affording similar treatment to members in similar relevant circumstances.

9. The Fund's assessment of a member's policies and its advice on these policies will pay due regard to the circumstances of the member. This assessment and advice will be formulated within the framework of a comprehensive analysis of the general economic situation and economic policy strategy of the member, and will pay due regard to the member's implementation capacity. Moreover, in advising members on the manner in which they may promote external stability, the Fund shall, to the extent permitted under Article IV, take into account the member's other objectives.

10. The Fund's assessment and advice in the context of bilateral surveillance will be informed by, and be consistent with, a multilateral framework that incorporates relevant aspects of the global and regional economic environment, including exchange rates, international capital market conditions, and key linkages among members. The Fund's assessment and advice will take into account the impact of a member's policies on other members to the extent that the

member's policies undermine the promotion of its own external stability.

11. The Fund's assessment and advice in the context of bilateral surveillance will, to the extent possible, be placed in the context of an examination of the member's medium-term objectives and the planned conduct of policies, including possible responses to the most relevant contingencies.

12. The Fund's assessment of a member's policies will always include an evaluation of the developments in the member's balance of payments, including the size and sustainability of capital flows, against the background of its reserves, the size and composition of its other external assets and its external liabilities, and its opportunities for access to international capital markets.

**6–013**    Thus, in recent times surveillance has focussed on exchange rate, monetary and fiscal policies; the financial services sector; assessments of risks arising from large unpredictable capital flows; and institutional and structural issues.[47] Consultations have also included regional, social, industrial, labour market, trade, income distribution, environmental issues, to the extent that these impact on macroeconomic policies and performance[48]; and good governance including in that context implementation of IMF standards and codes. Moreover, despite a lack of a formal mandate in the IMF Articles of Agreement, IMF surveillance operations are also recognised to be an appropriate medium for fostering an open and liberal system of capital movements. Furthermore, as part of the surveillance exercise, the Fund may be able to request data on military expenditure, although at a highly aggregate level where necessary. The Fund may also discuss the expenditure, although at the invitation of the member.[49] Finally, bilateral surveillance exercises also encompass consultations in relation to a member's obligations involving exchange control regulations, under Arts VIII and XIV of the Articles of Agreement of the IMF.

With respect to the financial sector the current mandate of the IMF has two short-comings. First, it does not cover financial shocks which do not impact on the member's balance of payments.[50] Secondly, a member is not obliged to provide information pertaining to private parties in the financial sector. With respect to the mandate for multilateral surveillance Article IV Section 3(a) refers to the overseeing of the international monetary system. It

---

[47] IMF *Factsheet* (August 2006).

[48] See IMF *Survey*, Vol.26 (September 1996).

[49] See Concluding Remarks by the Acting Chairman Military Expenditure and the Role of the Fund Executive Board Meeting 91/138 October 2,1991 in *Selected Decisions of the IMF*, 30th Issue.

[50] See IMF The Fund's Mandate—The Legal Framework Prepared by the Legal Department (In Consultation with the Strategy, Policy and Review Department) Approved by Sean Hagan February 22, 2010. *http://www.imf.org/external/np/pp/eng/2010/022210.pdf.* (Accessed June 8, 2011). See also Rosa M. Lastra, "The Role of the IMF as a Global Financial Authority", *European Yearbook of International Economic Law* (2001).

does not refer to the international financial system.[51] Nor is there authority to gather information from private parties.

The "standards and codes" in the IMF which are the subject of surveillance, relate to "the institutional environment—the 'rules of the game'—within which economic and financial policies are devised and implemented;"[52] such that transparency and good governance[53] is promoted. These rules of the game are part of an overall strategy to strengthen the international monetary and financial system. The Fund has embarked on introducing a series of standards and codes of conduct in 12 different spheres in the public sector; as well as international standards, particularly in the domestic financial sector.[54] This focus is justified on the basis that such codes and standards have significant macro-economic implications. In establishing the guidelines for the promotion of good governance, the Executive Board has recognised that the role of the IMF should be confined to the economic aspects of good governance.[55]

**The Role of the Fund in Governance Issues-Guidance Note EBS/97/125, July 2, 1997[56]**                                     6–014

> 3. Building on the Fund's past experience in dealing with governance issues and taking into account the two Board discussions, the following guidelines seek to provide greater attention to Fund involvement in governance issues, in particular through:
>
> - a more comprehensive treatment in the context of both Article IV consultations and Fund-supported programs of those governance issues that are within the Fund's mandate and expertise;
>
> - a more proactive approach in advocating policies and the development of institutions and administrative systems that aim to eliminate the opportunity for rent seeking, corruption, and fraudulent activity;
>
> - an evenhanded treatment of governance issues in all member countries; and

---

[51] See IMF The Fund's Mandate—The Legal Framework Prepared by the Legal Department (In Consultation with the Strategy, Policy and Review Department) Approved by Sean Hagan February 22, 2010. *http://www.imf.org/external/np/pp/eng/2010/022210.pdf.* (Accessed June 8, 2011).

[52] IMF *Standards and* Codes: The Role of the IMF Fact Sheet September 2010 at *http://www.imf.org/external/np/exr/facts/sc.htm.* (Accessed June 8, 2011).

[53] Good governance has been defined by I. Shihata as: "the appropriate management of a country's resources, based upon rules, implemented by institutions, to ensure accountability. Proper governance also implies predictability, and legal due process which, in turn, assumes a government of laws and not a government of men" in "Human rights, development and international financial institutions" in *American University Journal of International Law* (1992) Vol.8, pp.27–37. See also J. Gold, *Interpretation: The IMF and International Law* (Kluwer Law International, 1996), p.503.

[54] See IMF Interim Committee Communiqué, "Strengthening the Architecture of the International Monetary System" in IMF *Annual Report* (1998). See also October 1998 G7 Declaration on Strengthening the Architecture of the International Monetary System.

[55] See IMF *Survey*, Vol.26 (August 5, 1997). Executive Board Decision adopting Guidelines Regarding Governance Issues.

[56] Source: *http://www.imf.org.* (Accessed June 8, 2011).

- enhanced collaboration with other multilateral institutions, in particular the World Bank, to make better use of complementary areas of expertise.

*Aspects of governance of relevance to the Fund*

5. Many governance issues are integral to the Fund's normal activities. The Fund is primarily concerned with macroeconomic stability, external viability, and orderly economic growth in member countries. Therefore, the Fund's involvement in governance should be limited to economic aspects of governance. The contribution that the Fund can make to good governance (including the avoidance of corrupt practices) through its policy advice and, where relevant, technical assistance, arises principally in two spheres:

   - *improving the management of public resources* through reforms covering public sector institutions (e.g., the treasury, central bank, public enterprises, civil service, and the official statistics function), including administrative procedures (e.g., expenditure control, budget management, and revenue collection);

   - supporting the development and maintenance of a transparent and stable economic and regulatory environment conducive to efficient private sector activities (e.g., price systems, exchange and trade regimes, banking systems and their related regulations).

6-015          **IMF Factsheet September 2010: Standards and Codes: The Role of the IMF[57]**

The IMF and the World Bank have recognized international standards in 12 areas, which may be divided into three groups:

(1) **Policy Transparency**: Standards in these areas were developed, and are assessed, by the IMF:

   - Data Transparency: IMF's Special Data Dissemination Standard (SDDS) and General Data Dissemination System (GDDS).

   - Fiscal Transparency: IMF's Code of Good Practices on Fiscal Transparency, complemented bythe Guide on Resource Revenue Transparency.

   - Monetary and Financial Policy Transparency: IMF's Code of Good Practices on Transparency in Monetary and Financial Policies.

(2) **Financial Sector Regulation and Supervision**: IMF efforts to promote financial system soundness rely on standards developed by a number of specialized institutions. These standards are typically assessed in the context of the joint IMF-World Bank Financial Sector Assessment Program (FSAP):

   - **Banking Supervision:** Basel Committee on Banking Supervision's Core Principles for Effective Banking Supervision.

   - **Securities:** International Organization of Securities Commission's Objectives for Securities Regulation.

---

[57] Source: *http://www.imf.org*. (Accessed June 8, 2011).

- **Insurance:** International Association of Insurance Supervisors' Insurance Supervisory Principles.

- **Payments Systems:** Committee on Payments and Settlements Systems' Insurance Supervisory Principles, complemented by Recommendations for Securities Settlement Systems for countries with significant securities trading.

- **Anti-Money Laundering and Combating the Financing of Terrorism:**Financial Action Task Force's (FATF) 40+9 Recommendations.

(3) **Market Integrity:** Standards in these areas have been developed by various institutions, including the World Bank. These are usually assessed by the World Bank:

- **Corporate Governance:** Organization of Economic Cooperation and Development's Principles of Corporate Governance.

- **Accounting:** International Accounting Standards Board's International Accounting Standards.

- **Auditing:** International Federation of Accountants' International Standards on Auditing.

- **Insolvency and Creditor Rights:** A standard based on the World Bank's Principles for Effective Insolvency and Creditor Rights Systems and the United Nations Commission on International Trade Law's Legislative Guide on Insolvency Law is being finalized.

These standards and codes of conduct are to be implemented and enforced    **6-016** through Art.IV surveillance exercises; IMF Conditionality, and IMF technical assistance. Moreover, the standards and codes can also be assessed specifically at the request of a member by the IMF and/or the World Bank. A summary of the assessment is then published in a *Report on the Observance of Standards and Codes* (ROSC).[58] In September 2010, in response to the 2008 financial crisis, the Fund made it mandatory for the Financial Sector Assessment Programme to be applied every five years to 25 jurisdictions "with systemically important financial sectors."[59]

The modalities of the bilateral country level surveillance are as follows. The surveillance is conducted through consultations between the Fund and the member on a regular annual basis. IMF staff holds annual bilateral meetings with the member in its home country. The Fund team involved in the country surveillance not only meets the governmental sector but also "other stakeholders such as parliamentarians and representatives of business, labour unions, and civil society".[60] Based on these meetings the IMF staff prepares a report which forms a basis for discussion at the Executive Board.[61] At the

---

[58] Standards and Codes: The Role of the IMF. IMF *Factsheet*—September 2010.
[59] See IMF *FSAP Factsheet* March 2011. (Accessed June 8, 2011).
[60] IMF *IMF Surveillance Factsheet* 2011.
[61] See IMF *Surveillance Factsheet*, August 2006.

end of every discussion the Chairman of the Board compiles a summary of the opinions expressed by the Executive Directors. This summing up is then communicated to the authorities of the member. In between the annual consultations, when developments warrant, consultations can also take place informally, and on a confidential basis, at the behest of the Managing Director. The consultations need to be informal and confidential because of the need not to exacerbate the exchange rates through adverse publicity or signal for action. As of 1997, the Executive Board's summing up is published where the member so requests (known as Public Information Notices).[62]

In addition to the regular surveillance exercises the Fund has also elaborated on certain events which may trigger surveillance in a decision of the Executive Board. Accordingly Fund surveillance can be actuated inter alia upon the occurrence of the following events[63]:

(i) protracted large-scale intervention in one direction in the exchange market;

(ii) official or quasi-official borrowing that either is unsustainable or brings unduly high liquidity risks, or excessive and prolonged official or quasi-official accumulation of foreign assets, for balance of payments purposes;

(iii) (a) the introduction, substantial intensification, or prolonged maintenance, for balance of payments purposes, of restrictions on, or incentives for, current transactions or payments, or (b) the introduction or substantial modification for balance of payments purposes of restrictions on, or incentives for, the inflow or outflow of capital;

(iv) the pursuit, for balance of payments purposes, of monetary and other financial policies that provide abnormal encouragement or discouragement to capital flows;

(v) fundamental exchange rate misalignment;

(vi) large and prolonged current account deficits or surpluses; and

(vii) large external sector vulnerabilities, including liquidity risks, arising from private capital flows.

The modalities of surveillance in relation to economic, monetary and currency unions under Art.IV involve IMF staff holding consultations with the regional institution responsible for the common monetary policy. This is

---

[62] See IMF *Economic Reviews*: Press Information Notices 1998. See IMF *Annual Report* (1998) and IMF *Survey* (September 1998); and Executive Board Decision No.11493–(97/45) in *Selected Decisions*, 30th Issue.

[63] Executive Board Decision No. 13919-(07/51), June 15, 2007.

accompanied with separate individual consultations with the Member States of the union.[64]

**MODALITIES FOR SURVEILLANCE OVER EURO-AREA POLICIES IN CONTEXT OF ARTICLE IV CONSULTATIONS WITH MEMBER COUNTRIES[65]**

The current frequency of Article IV consultations with individual euro-area countries, which are generally on the standard 12-month cycle, will be maintained.

There will be twice-yearly staff discussions with EU institutions responsible for common policies in the euro area. These discussions will be held separately from the discussions with individual euro-area countries, but are considered an integral part of the Article IV process for each member. The discussions with individual euro-area countries will be clustered, to the extent possible, around the discussions with the relevant EU institutions.

There will be an annual staff report and Board discussion on Euro-Area Policies in the Context of the Article IV Consultations with Member Countries, which will be considered part of the Article IV consultation process with individual members. In addition to monetary and exchange rate policies, the staff report will also cover from a regional perspective other economic policies relevant for Fund surveillance. Staff will report informally to the Board on the second round of discussions with EU institutions to provide adequate context for bilateral consultations with euro-area countries that do not coincide broadly with the annual Board discussion on the euro area.

There will be a summing up of the conclusion of the Board's annual discussion on Euro-Area Policies in the Context of the Article IV Consultations with Member Countries. It will be cross-referenced in the summing up for the Article IV consultations with euro-area countries at the conclusion of the Article IV process for each country. To the extent that the summing up for the euro area covers economic policies that apply to all EU member countries and that are considered relevant for Fund surveillance, the pertinent parts of the summing up for the euro area could also be referred to in the bilateral Article IV consultations with EU member countries that are not part of the euro area. (SM/02/359, 11/21/02).

**6-017**

With respect to the multilateral surveillance of the global economy, and the co-ordination of individual economic policy in that global context, the Fund oversees the international monetary system mainly through the Executive Board's twice-yearly publication titled *World Economic Outlook* (WEO)[66]; and the *Global Financial Stability Report (GFSR)*. The WEO focuses on important issues concerning the global economy, whereas the GFSR is more

---

[64] See Executive Board decisions on the modalities for surveillance over Euro-Area policies; Central African Economic and Monetary Union policies; Eastern Caribbean Currency Union policies; West African Economic and Monetary Union Policies in the context of Art.IV consultations with Member Countries in IMF *Selected Decisions*, 30th Issue (updated).

[65] Extract from Decision No.12899–(02/119), December 4, 2002, *http://www.imf.org*. (Accessed June 8, 2011).

[66] See IMF *Survey*, Vol.26 (September 1997).

focussed on the financial sector. The WEO discussions in the Executive Board are supplemented by the participation of the IMF's Managing Director in the policy discussions of the Group of Eight major industrial countries, where the Managing Director focuses on the global implications of G–8 economic policies and practices.[67]

**6-018**    As part of its effort to strengthen multilateral surveillance, the Fund has also now launched the Early Warning Exercises which take place on a semi annual basis. This initiative which came from the G20 in 2008 comprises a joint IMF-Financial Stability Board (FSB) exercise in assessing possible "vulnerabilities and triggers in the global economy that could precipitate systemic crisis."[68] Additionally, the G20 countries agreed at their 2009 Pittsburgh Summit to a Mutual Assessment Process (MAP) which involves the Fund at the request of the G20 assessing the progress in achieving the shared goals of the G20 countries.[69]

CONCLUSION

**6-019**    As a core IMF function surveillance engenders much expectation both in terms of its results as well as in terms of what it could potentially facilitate. Although its origins are specific, set essentially in exchange rates, its evolution is increasingly all-encompassing in the scope of its normative coverage, with calls for its mandate to be widened, along with the development of extra surveillance props forming a whole family of the IMF surveillance apparatus. Surveillance as an implementation tool is "metamorphosising" into a norm generating apparatus wherein the lines between regulation and enforcement are becoming blurred, albeit softly softly. Historically, the track record of IMF surveillance has been less than satisfactory. Thus the perception in the asymmetry of its influence has been widely expressed, and now empirically observed. First, the IEO in 2007[70] reported its ineffectiveness with respect to exchange rate surveillance as between 1999–2005, the period of its study. Recently, post the EB 2007 Decision on bilateral surveillance, the IEO observed with respect to the 2007/8 financial crisis, that the IMF "provided few clear warnings about the risks and vulnerabilities associated with the impending crisis before its outbreak".[71] Indeed, the IMF endorsed the very policies and practices which contributed to the crisis, of those countries such

---

[67]  See IMF *Survey*, Vol.26 (September 1997).

[68]  See IMF IMF-FSB Early Warning Exercise Fact Sheet 2010 at *http://www.imf.org/external/ np/exr/facts/ewe.htm.* (Accessed June 8, 2011).

[69]  IMF *Factsheet* The G20 Mutual Assessment Process (MAP), March 2011. *www.imf.org.* (Accessed June 8, 2011).

[70]  See IEO *IMF Exchange Rate Policy Advice* (2007) reported its ineffectiveness as between 1999–2005 with respect to exchange rate surveillance.

[71]  IEO *IMF Performance in the Run-Up to the Financial and Economic Crisis: IMF Surveillance in 2004–07* (2011).

as the US and UK, at the very "epicentre" of the crisis.[72] The IEO attributed this failure as follows[73]:

> "The IMF's ability to correctly identify the mounting risks was hindered by a high degree of groupthink, intellectual capture, a general mindset that a major financial crisis in large advanced economies was unlikely, and inadequate analytical approaches. Weak internal governance, lack of incentives to work across units and raise contrarian views, and a review process that did not 'connect the dots' or ensure follow-up also played an important role, while political constraints may have also had some impact."

The analysis with respect to multilateral surveillance is in the same vein. Thus, for example, multilateral surveillance also failed to pick up the impending 2007/8 financial crisis.[74] Further, in 2006 the IEO observed that multilateral surveillance was not "achieving its full potential", had a "low readership", and moreover did not achieve its "potential for peer pressure".[75]

In sum, surveillance will continue to be probed and developed further. The challenge for the legal stand point is to comprehend it as a normative and enforcement vehicle.

---

[72] IEO *IMF Performance in the Run-Up to the Financial and Economic Crisis: IMF Surveillance in 2004–07* (2011).

[73] IEO *IMF Performance in the Run-Up to the Financial and Economic Crisis: IMF Surveillance in 2004-07* (2011).

[74] IEO *IMF Performance in the Run-Up to the Financial and Economic Crisis: IMF Surveillance in 2004–07* (2011) para.6.

[75] IEO *Multilateral Surveillance* (2006).

CHAPTER 7

# EXCHANGE RESTRICTIONS & THE CODE FOR A MULTILATERAL SYSTEM OF PAYMENTS

## INTRODUCTION[1]

The "multilateral system of payments" is a reference to a system of payments **7-001** across national borders aimed mainly at restricting "exchange restrictions" for international trade. Exchange restrictions can relate to current account or capital account transactions. In essence, the multilateral system of payments under the IMF connotes a system of unhindered international transfers and payments, between residents of a country and non-residents, for "current international transactions". This agenda is expressed as a major purpose of the Fund, viz:.[2]

> "To assist in the establishment of a multilateral system of payments in respect of current transactions between members and in the elimination of foreign exchange restrictions which hamper the growth of world trade."

It is not very clear what is meant by "current international transactions". Clarification can be sought from the Fund.[3] The Articles shed some light by defining these as payments which are not made for the purpose of transferring capital.[4] They include[5]:

---

[1] See particularly, for example, J. Gold, "Use, Conversion, and Exchange of Currency Under the Second Amendment of the Fund's Articles", IMF *Pamphlet Series* No.23, (1978); R.W. Edwards Jr, *International Monetary Collaboration*, (Transnational Publishers, 1985), Ch.10; S. Silard, *Money and Foreign Exchange International Encyclopedia of Comparative Law* (1975) Vol.17, Ch.20; J. Gold, *The Fund Agreement in Courts* (1962; 1976; 1982; 1986; 1989) Vols 1–4 IMF; the IMF *Annual Reports* on *Exchange Arrangements and Exchange Restrictions*; and IMF *Article VIII Acceptance by IMF Members: Recent Trends and Implications for the Fund.* (Prepared by the Monetary and Financial Systems and Legal Departments. Approved by U. Baumgartner and S. Hagan (May 2006).) Available at *www.imf.org.* (Accessed June 8, 2011).
[2] Art.1 (IV) of the IMF Articles of Agreement.
[3] Art.XXX(d).
[4] See Art.XXX(d).
[5] Art.XXX(d).

(1)    all payments due in connection with foreign trade, other current business, including services, and normal short-term banking and credit facilities;

(2)    payments due as interest on loans and as net income from other investments;

(3)    payments of moderate amount for amortization of loans or for depreciation of direct investments; and

(4)    moderate remittances for family living expenses.

**7–002**    The dichotomy between capital and current in the Articles is not an economic but a legal one. The notion of capital in accounting or tax practice is different.[6] Capital movements comprise, for example, of financial flows connected with direct investment; portfolio investment; loans; transfers of bank deposits; purchases of life insurance policies; and transfers of personal savings by emigrants.[7]

The objective of a multilateral system of payments for current international transactions is achieved through a set of prohibitions and stipulations.[8] In particular, the system is characterised by "convertible currencies". Convertibility of currencies refers to the freedom of residents of a State to acquire and dispose currency, in exchange markets, for current international transactions. A member's currency is said to be convertible if it has undertaken the prohibitions and stipulations of the IMF, as set out in Art.VIII of the IMF Articles of Agreement. Essentially, a freely convertible currency is a currency which does not partake of any restrictions as to its holding, or the manner in which it can be exchanged for another currency, or transferred to non-residents, or as to how it may be used.[9]

However, there are in fact two systems of payments existing under the IMF for current international transactions. A member needs to make a choice upon joining the Fund as to which regime it wishes to maintain. First, there is the optimal regime which the IMF sets out to promote. This is the regime under Art.VIII, which purports to achieve the objectives of the IMF under Art.1 (IV). Secondly, there is a transitional regime—a second-best option under Art.XIV. Members have to notify the Fund at the outset, as to which regime they propose to be under.[10] In 2010 there were 167 acceptances under Art.VIII,[11] out of which 95 acceptances took place between 1992–2005.[12] This is to be contrasted with the situation in 1995 when there were some 73 members of the IMF which had restrictions on payments for

---

[6]  Edwards (1985), p.396.

[7]  See Edwards (1985), at p.449.

[8]  These are set out in Art.VIII of the IMF Articles of Agreement.

[9]  Edwards (1985), p.381.

[10]  Art.XIV.

[11]  July 2010: Source IMF.

[12]  See IMF *Article VIII Acceptance by IMF Members: Recent Trends and Implications for the Fund.* (Prepared by the Monetary and Financial Systems and Legal Departments. Approved by Ulrich Baumgartner and Sean Hagan (May 2006).) Available at *http://www.imf.org.* (Accessed June 8, 2011).

current international transactions.[13] The reasons for such a change in Art. VIII adherence is attributed to the success of IMF surveillance, the price imposed for acceding to the WTO and the EU; obligations imposed in bilateral and regional agreements on current-account convertibility; and generally the exigencies of globalisation.[14] Thus, most exchange restrictions on current account transactions have been eliminated by the majority of the membership of the IMF. Those exchange restrictions on current account transactions that remain are concerned with payments and transfers for current invisible transactions.[15]

"Exchange restrictions" relating to payments and transfers for international transactions, can take different forms. For example, a State measure can involve a prohibition, a limitation, an undue delay, or a special cost with respect to the purchase or transfer of foreign exchange.[16] The typical State with exchange controls[17] would have a currency that cannot be freely transferred to non-residents; that cannot be freely transferred to residents; and wherein residents cannot freely hold foreign currencies without permission.[18] Normally, the exchange regulations are enforced by ensuring the availability of foreign exchange through a process of applications to a governmental agency, such as the Central Bank. In addition to the actual exchange restrictions, States also monitor through reporting requirements, developments in the flow and availability of foreign exchange nationally. Such reporting requirements for statistical purposes are referred to as passive controls.[19]

| | |
|---|---|
| 20. **These exchange measures are mainly of three types**: (i) limits on payments for invisible transactions (i.e., travel, medical, and educational allowances); (ii) limits on transfers from nonresident accounts; and (iii) foreign exchange budget allocation systems. Some of the exchange measures are evidenced by the existence of nonsovereign external payments arrears. Existing MCPs arise | **7-003** |

---

[13] See IMF *Annual Report*: Exchange Arrangements and Exchange Restrictions (1995).

[14] See IMF *Article VIII Acceptance by IMF Members: Recent Trends and Implications for the Fund.* (Prepared by the Monetary and Financial Systems and Legal Departments. Approved by Ulrich Baumgartner and Sean Hagan (May 2006).) Available at *http://www.imf.org.* (Accessed June 8, 2011).

[15] See for example IMF Annual Report on Exchange Arrangements and Exchange Restrictions 2010; and Keith Jefferis *The Rationalization of Foreign Exchange Controls in Angola,* Southern Africa Global Competitiveness Hub (2008) *www.satradehub.org/assets/files/ RationalisationofForeignExchangeControlsinAngola.pdf.* (Accessed June 8, 2011).

[16] F. Gianviti, "International Monetary Law" in R.C. Effros, *Current Legal Issues Affecting Central Banks* (1994) Vol.2 IMF, p.7.

[17] Strictly speaking, "exchange control regulations" refer to those regulations which relate to the acquisition, holding or use of foreign exchange; or to the use of domestic or foreign currency in international payments or transfers. "Exchange restrictions" on the other hand is a narrower concept referring only to exchange measures which affect the making of payments and transfers for current international transactions. See, for example, H. Cisse (Legal Counsel at the IMF) in unpublished IMF background paper on Art.VIII titled "Concepts of exchange restriction and multiple currency practice under the Fund's Articles" November 21, 1994.

[18] Edwards (1985), p.382.

[19] Edwards (1985), Ch.10, p.389.

mainly from the use of special exchange rates for official transactions and the imposition of foreign exchange taxes and subsidies."[20]

**7–004**    States have an interest in maintaining exchange control regulations for a number of reasons. The principal reason is to encourage the use and allocation of foreign exchange towards attaining the objectives and priorities of the State. Normally, these State priorities are designed to ensure imports for the State, in particular of capital goods for industrial development and essential food supplies.[21] Competing foreign products and luxury items are the least of the priorities.[22] Currency regulations, such as multiple currency practices (MCPs), are used to discourage such low priority imports.[23] Further, in addition to generating impacts on trans-boundary flows, certain exchange rate regulations, such as multiple currency practices, can operate as instruments for the shaping of domestic policy objectives—for example as techniques for the imposition of taxes and for the according of subsidies to certain sectors of the economy.[24]

More specifically, a State may want to regulate the claims that foreigners can have over their economy.[25] One way in which foreigners can have a claim over the economy is by holding the currency of the economy. Thus, foreigners having holdings of the Pakistani Rupee have an equivalent claim over the Pakistani economy. To regulate this control over the economy, the authorities can, for example, restrict the transfer of its currency abroad; or only allow foreigners to open bank accounts in local banks subject to its permission. Secondly, a State may have an interest in seeing to it that the foreign exchange held by its residents is actually used optimally, in accordance with national priorities. An unmanaged situation could contribute to increased imports, and depreciate the value of the currency.[26] In this respect, States have used various restrictive measures, for example it may require its resident to sell to it any foreign currency acquired from export proceeds (Surrender requirements)[27]; or it may stipulate that its citizens can only retain a certain amount of the foreign currency held (Retention quotas)[28]; or it may prescribe

---

[20] Extract from IMF, *Article VIII Acceptance by IMF Members: Recent Trends and Implications for the Fund.* (Prepared by the Monetary and Financial Systems and Legal Departments. Approved by Ulrich Baumgartner and Sean Hagan (May 2006).) Available at *http://www.imf. org.* (Accessed June 8, 2011).

[21] Edwards (1985), Ch.10, p.387.

[22] Edwards (1985).

[23] Edwards (1985), p.396.

[24] Edwards (1985), p.396.

[25] See R. Edwards, *International Monetary Collaboration* (Dobbs Ferry, N.Y., Transnational Publishers, 1985), Ch.10.

[26] Edwards (1985).

[27] In 1995 there were 127 IMF members which had Surrender or Repatriation Requirements for Export Proceeds. Some of these countries had Art.VIII status. See IMF, *Exchange Arrangements and Exchange Restrictions Annual Report* (1995).

[28] On Retention quotas see Executive Board Decision No.201–(53/29). Retention quotas are discouraged where they lead to abnormal shifts in trade.

the currency in which its residents may receive payment (Currency prescription requirement).[29] The IMF regularly records the exchange control restrictions that its members maintain in an annual publication.[30]

Exchange control regulations inhibit and distort international trade.[31] Thus, the alternative manner of achieving the same objectives of exchange control restrictions is through the imposition of controls over a country's international trade. A State can restrict the nature and volume of its imports through the imposition of tariffs and import quotas. However, members of the IMF who are also members of the WTO have undertaken not to frustrate through trade action the provisions of the Articles of Agreement of the IMF.[32] Under GATT 1994, the WTO is to co-operate with the IMF so that both organisations are able to co-ordinate their policies in relation to exchange questions which are within the jurisdiction of the Fund, and in relation to quantitative restrictions and trade measures which are within the mandate of the WTO. Particularly, the WTO is to accept determinations in relation to the balance of payments positions of members.[33] Moreover, in addition to having adverse trade effects, exchange controls are difficult to administer, and involve costs.[34]

Exchange control legislation and its implementation differ amongst States. Every piece of legislation and practice needs to be examined against the background of the international monetary norms—in particular the IMF Articles of Agreement. However, there are other international regimes which may also have a bearing on State regulation in this sphere.[35]

### THE MULTILATERAL SYSTEM OF PAYMENTS UNDER ARTICLE VIII

As mentioned above, a majority of the membership of the IMF now fall **7-005** under this regime, which is a measure of the success of the IMF. The regime under Art.VIII applies as between members and not to transactions with non-members of the IMF. Article VIII countries are countries which have specifically undertaken the obligations under Art.VIII(2), (3) and (4). These undertakings are as follows.

---

[29] For example, Afghanistan, Angola, Barbados and Belarus (see IMF, *Exchange Arrangements and Exchange Restrictions* (1995)).
[30] See IMF, *Annual Report* on *Exchange Arrangements and Exchange Restrictions*.
[31] See for example Shang-Jin Wei & Zhiewei Zhang, "Collateral damage: Exchange controls and international trade." *Journal of International Money and Finance* Volume 26, Issue 5, September 2007, Pages 841–863.
[32] See Art.XV of GATT 1994.
[33] Art.XV of GATT 1994.
[34] Edwards (1985), p.396.
[35] See for example regional and bilateral payments arrangements. See also the OECD Code of Liberalisation for Current Invisible Operations (1961); the OECD Code of Liberalisation of Capital Movements (1961).

**Restrictions on the making of payments and transfers for current international transactions**

7-006    A member undertakes not to impose, without the approval of the Fund, restrictions on the making of payments and transfers for current international transactions.[36] Article VIII involves, in the first instance, the establishment of market mechanisms for payments and transfers for international transactions. The buying and selling of foreign currencies has to be under market conditions. Secondly, it involves ensuring that there are no undue delays or limits as a consequence of government action, preventing a resident from obtaining foreign exchange in order to make payments to non-residents to settle current international transactions. Undue delays in the availability or use of exchange that results from government action gives rise to payments arrears, and is considered to be a restriction under Art.VIII(2)(a).[37] The non-residents should be able to convert the local currency into a currency of their choice, and to transfer such holdings outside the jurisdiction. However, there is no restriction if there is a prohibition on the taking of national currency out of the country, so long as there is an exchange market for payments to be facilitated in another currency.[38] Further, a member may specify the currency to be used in the international transaction, as long as it is acceptable to the recipient, and does not add additional costs to the payer (prescription of currency[39]). For example, in 1995 in Zimbabwe, despite the country having an Art.VIII status, all payments by non-residents to residents had to be effected in denominated currencies.[40] Similarly, a government can insist that the payment or transfer is through a certain channel. For example, restricting the use of credit cards for international payments does not constitute a restriction, as long as other means of payment are available. Article VIII(2)(a) is concerned with the making, as opposed to the receipt of payments and transfers.[41] Therefore, currency surrender requirements in relation to foreign exchange received by residents, and the specifying of which currency can be received, are not restrictions.[42] Thus, in 1995 surrender requirements for export proceeds were to be found in a number of Art.VIII countries, e.g. Pakistan, Paraguay and Poland.[43]

Thirdly, the restrictions involved need to be currency restrictions, involving payments and transfers. Thus, import prohibitions on certain products are permissible. The test for the determination of what constitutes a currency restriction is whether it involves a direct governmental limitation on the avail-

---

[36] Art.VIII, s.2(a).
[37] See Executive Board Decision No.3153–(70/95) in IMF *Selected Decisions*, 22nd edn (1997).
[38] Edwards (1985), at p 391.
[39] Edwards (1985), at p.391.
[40] IMF, *Exchange Arrangements and Exchange Restrictions Annual Report* (1995).
[41] F. Gianviti in R.C. Effros (ed.), *Current Legal Issues Affecting Central Banks* (1994) Vol.2, p.7.
[42] Gianviti (1994).
[43] See IMF, *Exchange Arrangements and Exchange Restrictions Annual Report* (1995).

ability or use of exchange as such.[44] This involves an analysis not only of the governmental measure, but also its implementation. Thus, quantitative restrictions on imports have an indirect impact on limiting payments, and therefore are not currency restrictions. Similarly, whereas the prohibition on the use of credit cards abroad by residents whilst restrictive is not a limitation on the use of availability of foreign exchange if other means of payment are available. In the same manner, procedures to monitor exchange transactions are not limitations, as long as they do not result in delaying unduly the transactions. But where a class of company is prohibited from transferring dividends to non-residents, then there is a currency restriction, under Art.VIII(2)(a).[45] However, the requirement of filling an auditor's certificate, upon the transfer of the dividend, is permissible as long as it does not cause undue delay in the transfer.

The restriction must be a governmental restriction, in the form of its laws, regulations or administrative practices. Thus, non-governmental acts, for example, judicial orders as a consequence of private litigation, resulting in the forfeiture of assets, do not constitute exchange restrictions. The registration or licensing of international transfers and payments is acceptable, so long as they do not cause undue delay.

Fourthly, the exchange restrictions apply only to international transactions, and not to purely domestic transactions as between residents.[46] Finally, the non-residents who have acquired a currency of another Member State through current international transactions must be able to convert the currency into a currency of their choice, normally a freely usable currency.[47] A freely usable currency is defined as:[48]

"A freely usable currency means a member's currency that the Fund determines (i) is, in fact, widely used to make payments for international transactions, and (ii) is widely traded in the principal exchange markets."

Restrictions in the following circumstances are allowed. First, where foreign exchange is restricted to prevent the acquisition of forbidden imports.[49] Secondly, where foreign exchange restrictions are imposed on the use of a currency declared by the Fund to be scarce.[50] Thirdly, restrictions on exchange transactions with non-members, or with persons in their territories, provided they are not found to prejudice the interests of other members of the Fund, and are not contrary to its purposes.[51]

---

[44] Executive Board Decision No.1034–(60/27) in *Selected Decisions*.
[45] Edwards (1985), at p. 394.
[46] Cisse (1994).
[47] Cisse (1994).
[48] Art.XXX (f). See also Decision No.5719–(78/46) in *Selected Decisions* wherein freely usable currencies have been determined by the Fund as comprising, until further notice, the deutsche mark, French franc, Japanese yen, pound sterling, and the US dollar.
[49] See R. Edwards and J. Gold (1985), *The Fund Agreement in Courts* (3 Vols).
[50] See Art.VII, s.3(b).
[51] Art.XII.

The following are some examples of prohibited exchange restrictions:[52]

   (i) Restriction on availability of foreign exchange for tourist or business travel abroad, education, and family living expenses.

   (ii) No limits on availability of foreign exchange, but the authorities approve request for foreign exchange on a discretionary basis.

   (iii) Limits on the transferability of investment income by non-residents, e.g. limits on transfers of profits, dividends and interest; dividend balancing requirements wherein company allowed to transfer dividends only up to the amount of foreign exchange earnings of the company from exports.

   (iv) Foreign exchange quotas for certain categories of importers.

   (v) Exchange licence requirements for imports.

   (vi) Importers can only pay from their own foreign exchange earnings to pay for certain imports (own fund systems).

   (vii) Undue delays in availability or use of foreign exchange, giving rise to payments arrears.[53]

   (viii) Deposit requirements on tourist exchange requests.

   (ix) Where fixed weekly amounts of foreign exchange are allocated through auction, in such a manner that whatever the rate of exchange there will be unsuccessful bidders, with no alternative access to foreign exchange.[54]

**Discriminatory currency arrangements and multiple currency practices**

**7-007** A member undertakes not to engage in discriminatory currency arrangements or multiple currency practices, unless the Fund has given its approval for such practices.[55]

Multiple currency practices are also exchange restrictions, because they affect the making of payments for current international transactions.[56] However, they are nevertheless a discreet category, distorting international payments and transfers. A multiple currency practice occurs as a consequence of a governmental action, which must be directly related to exchange transactions, and result in a multiplicity of effective exchange

[52] The examples below are from measures found to have been exchange restrictions by the Fund set out in paper by Cisse (1994).
[53] Executive Board Decision No. 3153–(70/95) in IMF *Selected Decisions*.
[54] Exchange Auction System operating in Ghana in 1986.
[55] Art.VIII (3).
[56] See Executive Board Decision No.649–(57/33) in IMF *Selected Decisions*.

rates.[57] The notion of effective rate of exchange implies that if there are costs or subsidies so closely related to the exchange transactions, they must be considered as integral to the effective rate. For a multiple currency practice to occur the government action must result in a spread of more than two per cent between the buying and selling rates for spot exchange transactions.[58]

A multiple currency practice operated through an official exchange market may give rise to government revenue foregone or not collected,[59] and thus confer a benefit on the transaction with the lower exchange rate. This form of subsidy would by definition be specific in that it is targeted, having the consequence of affecting a certain sector[60] of the economy. Such a subsidy could be a prohibited subsidy[61] or an actionable subsidy.[62] In the circumstances a multiple exchange practice could give rise to the imposition of a countervailing measure under the WTO Subsidies code.[63]

The following are examples of prohibited multiple currency practices[64]:

(i)    Where a black market in foreign exchange is tolerated alongside the official exchange market, which results in spreads of more than two per cent between the two markets.[65]

(ii)   Where the buying and selling rates in the exchange market are different so as to result in a spread of more than two per cent between the buying and selling rates.[66]

(iii)  Officially managed exchange guarantee scheme for the benefit only of a certain category of traders, thus limiting access to a preferential rate of exchange to other traders.

(iv)   Different exchange rates for different transactions (e.g. commercial transactions, tourist transactions, and official transactions) resulting in spreads of more than two per cent between the rates.

(v)    Exchange taxes contingent upon transfer of exchange abroad. Tax is considered as part of the effective tax rate and therefore gives rise to multiple currency practice.

---

[57] Cisse (1994) and see also Executive Board Decision No.6790–(81/43) in IMF *Selected Decisions*.

[58] Executive Board Decision No.6790–(81/43), IMF *Selected Decisions*.

[59] See Art.1(a)(ii) of the Agreement on Subsidies and Countervailing Measures.

[60] Art.2(1)(c) of the Agreement on Subsidies and Countervailing Measures.

[61] Art.3(1)(b) of the Agreement on Subsidies and Countervailing Measures.

[62] Art.5 of the Agreement on Subsidies and Countervailing Measures.

[63] See also Edwards (1985), p.399.

[64] The examples below are from measures found to have been exchange restrictions by the Fund set out in paper by Cisse (1994).

[65] See Dominican Republic 1972 reported in IMF, *Annual Report on Exchange Arrangements and Exchange Restrictions* (1981).

[66] Executive Board Decision No.6790–(81/43) in IMF *Selected Decisions*.

(vi) Exporters allowed to retain foreign exchange and sell at a different rate than official rate (Retention quotas).

(vii) Where foreign exchange is available only through a foreign exchange auction and the amount available at auction is insufficient to meet the demand for foreign exchange for current payments.

(viii) Requirement of import deposits, so that the payers, resources are blocked for a certain period, limiting their ability to pay for imports. This also constitutes multiple currency practice because the import deposit is considered part of the effective exchange rate. Such a practice is also considered an exchange restriction.

(ix) Selective provision of exchange guarantees covering exchange risks.

(x) Subsidy or levy in certain sales and purchases of foreign exchange.

Discriminatory currency arrangements are practices which involve discrimination against other members. Thus, a discriminatory practice exists, when for example, local currency can only be transferred to residents of one State and not other states; or foreign exchange is made available on preferential terms to residents of some States, and not others.[67] Discriminatory practices are particularly to be found in bilateral payments arrangements, wherein the availability of foreign exchange is normally encouraged through the partner countries of the agreement.[68]

### Obligation to purchase as between monetary authorities

**7-008**    The member undertakes to buy balances of its currency held by another member, provided the holdings have been recently acquired as a result of current transactions, or because their conversion is needed in order to make payments for current transactions.[69]

This is an obligation to purchase as between monetary authorities, where there is no exchange market which could equally serve this function.[70] The holdings of the monetary authority of the foreign currency would however result from sales to it by private individuals. The monetary authority buying its own currency may do so by paying in SDRs, or in the currency of the requesting country. The object of this undertaking under Art.VIII(4) is to give confidence to non-residents as to the convertibility of the currency of the member which has undertaken Art.VIII obligations.

---

[67] Edwards (1985), Ch.10 at p.389.
[68] Edwards (1985), Ch.10 at pp.389 and 400.
[69] Art.VIII (4).
[70] Edwards (1985), p.422.

**Article VIII of the IMF Articles of Agreement—General Obligations of Members**[71]

### Section 1. Introduction

7-009

In addition to the obligations assumed under other articles of this Agreement, each member undertakes the obligations set out in this Article.

### Section 2. Avoidance of restrictions on current payments

(a) Subject to the provisions of Article VII, Section 3(*b*) and Article XIV, Section 2, no member shall, without the approval of the Fund, impose restrictions on the making of payments and transfers for current international transactions.

(b) Exchange contracts which involve the currency of any member and which are contrary to the exchange control regulations of that member maintained or imposed consistently with this Agreement shall be unenforceable in the territories of any member. In addition, members may, by mutual accord, cooperate in measures for the purpose of making the exchange control regulations of either member more effective, provided that such measures and regulations are consistent with this Agreement.

### Section 3. Avoidance of discriminatory currency practices

No member shall engage in, or permit any of its fiscal agencies referred to in Article V, Section 1 to engage in, any discriminatory currency arrangements or multiple currency practices, whether within or outside margins under Article IV or prescribed by or under Schedule C, except as authorized under this Agreement or approved by the Fund. If such arrangements and practices are engaged in at the date when this Agreement enters into force, the member concerned shall consult with the Fund as to their progressive removal unless they are maintained or imposed under Article XIV, Section 2, in which case the provisions of Section 3 of that Article shall apply.

### Section 4. Convertibility of foreign-held balances

(a) Each member shall buy balances of its currency held by another member if the latter, in requesting the purchase, represents:

(i) that the balances to be bought have been recently acquired as a result of current transactions; or

(ii) that their conversion is needed for making payments for current transactions.

The buying member shall have the option to pay either in special drawing rights, subject to Article XIX, Section 4, or in the currency of the member making the request.

(b) The obligation in (*a*) above shall not apply when:

(i) the convertibility of the balances has been restricted consistently with Section 2 of this Article or Article VI, Section 3;

(ii) the balances have accumulated as a result of transactions effected before the removal by a member of restrictions maintained or imposed under Article XIV, Section 2;

---

[71] Source: *http://www.imf.org*. (Accessed June 8, 2011).

> (iii) the balances have been acquired contrary to the exchange regulations of the member which is asked to buy them;
>
> (iv) the currency of the member requesting the purchase has been declared scarce under Article VII, Section 3(*a*); or
>
> (v) the member requested to make the purchase is for any reason not entitled to buy currencies of other members from the Fund for its own currency.

## THE TRANSITIONAL REGIME[72]

**7-010**   Members who have not undertaken the obligations under Art.VIII2(a) fall under the transitional regime. This category consists mainly of developing members. Under this arrangement, a member may maintain and adapt to changing circumstances the restrictions on payments and transfers for current international transactions that were effective on the date of membership of the member in question, notwithstanding the provisions of Art.VIII. However, members are enjoined to strive towards establishing the conditions to achieve the objective of a multilateral system of payments, and the elimination of foreign exchange restrictions. Indeed, a member is expected to withdraw its exchange control restrictions, as soon as the member's balance of payments condition allows it to do so.[73] The Fund has the authority in exceptional circumstances to represent to a member that conditions exist for the withdrawal of exchange restrictions maintained inconsistently with the Articles of Agreement of the IMF. Indeed, if the representations are not taken seriously then the Fund has the authority to declare the member ineligible to use the financial resources of the Fund.[74] Once a member accepts the obligations under Article VIII it cannot revert back to the transitional regime.

It will be noted that under the transitional regime new restrictions cannot be introduced; although existing restrictions can be maintained and adapted to changing circumstances. This begs the question what constitutes a new restriction,[75] as opposed to a mere adaptation of an existing restriction.[76]

The difference is one of degree and nature[77] and calls for an examination of the measure as a whole.[78] Where a restrictive measure merely affects the level

---

[72] Art.XIV.
[73] Art.XIV.
[74] See Arts XIV and XXVI, s.2(a) of the IMF Articles of Agreement.
[75] Art.VIII 2(a).
[76] Art.XIV, s.2.
[77] Cisse (1994).
[78] See Edwards (1985), p.424 and J. Gold, *Use, Conversion, and Exchange of Currency*, IMF *Pamphlet Series* No.23.

of existing restriction, rather than introduces a restriction into an activity previously unrestricted, then it probably is an adaptation covered under Art. XIV of the IMF Articles of Agreement.

**Article XIV of the IMF Articles of Agreement—Transitional Arrangements[79]**

**Section 1. Notification to the Fund**

Each member shall notify the Fund whether it intends to avail itself of the transitional arrangements in Section 2 of this Article, or whether it is prepared to accept the obligations of Article VIII, Sections 2, 3, and 4. A member availing itself of the transitional arrangements shall notify the Fund as soon thereafter as it is prepared to accept these obligations.

**7-011**

**Section 2. Exchange restrictions**

A member that has notified the Fund that it intends to avail itself of transitional arrangements under this provision may, notwithstanding the provisions of any other articles of this Agreement, maintain and adapt to changing circumstances the restrictions on payments and transfers for current international transactions that were in effect on the date on which it became a member. Members shall, however, have continuous regard in their foreign exchange policies to the purposes of the Fund, and, as soon as conditions permit, they shall take all possible measures to develop such commercial and financial arrangements with other members as will facilitate international payments and the promotion of a stable system of exchange rates. In particular, members shall withdraw restrictions maintained under this Section as soon as they are satisfied that they will be able, in the absence of such restrictions, to settle their balance of payments in a manner which will not unduly encumber their access to the general resources of the Fund.

## Approved restrictions

The introduction of new restrictions have to be approved by the Fund under Art.VIII. Generally, the Fund's approval normally depends on the measure being necessary; temporary; non-discriminatory; and without adverse effects on other members or the member's balance of payments.[80] Exchange restrictions for non-balance of payments reasons are not encouraged.[81] Insofar as multiple currency arrangements are concerned these have to be approved by the Fund, whether or not a member is under the Art.VIII or Art.XIV regime. The Fund does not normally approve discriminatory exchange restrictions.[82]

**7-012**

---

[79] Source: *http://www.imf.org*. (Accessed June 8, 2011).

[80] Executive Board Decision No.1034 and Executive Board Decision 6790 in IMF *Selected Decisions*. See also P. Francotte in R.C. Effros, *Current Legal Issues Affecting Central Banks* (IMF, 1992), p.22.

[81] Executive Board Decision No.1034 and Executive Board Decision 6790 in IMF *Selected Decisions*. See also P. Francotte in R.C. Effros, *Current Legal Issues Affecting Central Banks* (IMF, 1992), p.22.

[82] Executive Board Decision No.955–(59/45), in *Selected Decisions*, October 23, 1959.

**Article XIV of the IMF Articles of Agreement—Transitional Arrangements**[83]

**Section 3. Action of the Fund relating to restrictions**

7-013    The Fund shall make annual reports on the restrictions in force under Section 2 of this Article. Any member retaining any restrictions inconsistent with Article VIII, Sections 2, 3, or 4 shall consult the Fund annually as to their further retention. The Fund may, if it deems such action necessary in exceptional circumstances, make representations to any member that conditions are favorable for the withdrawal of any particular restriction, or for the general abandonment of restrictions, inconsistent with the provisions of any other articles of this Agreement. The member shall be given a suitable time to reply to such representations. If the Fund finds that the member persists in maintaining restrictions which are inconsistent with the purposes of the Fund, the member shall be subject to Article XXVI, Section 2(a).

## EXCHANGE RESTRICTIONS AND NATIONAL SECURITY

7-014    Where a member imposes restrictions on current payments and transfers solely for the preservation of national and international security, the member is required to notify the Fund wherever possible, before the imposition of such restrictions.[84] The member may continue with the restrictions, unless the Fund informs the member within 30 days after receipt of the notice of the restrictions that it is not satisfied that the restrictions are for the purposes of national or international security. This procedure is in fact designed to facilitate the imposition of restrictions for security purposes, given that it is difficult for the Fund to evaluate the security reasons proffered.

National or international security is not defined, although in investment disputes in ICSID arbitration the national security defence in bilateral investment agreements has been interpreted to include economic emergency.[85] It is unlikely that this interpretation would be followed in the IMF here, since the Fund already has mechanisms to deal with situations of economic emergency for its members. Indeed, the reasons why the disciplines on exchange controls were introduced in the first place may well have a bearing on this question. However, a member's determination of its national security interest is presumed to be appropriate unless the IMF challenges this.[86] Thus, the determination of a Member's security interest is very much the province of

---

[83]  Source: *http://www.imf.org*. (Accessed June 8, 2011).

[84]  Executive Board Decision No.144–(52/51) 1952 IMF *Selected Decisions*.

[85]  *Enron Corporation v Argentine Rep* (2007); *CMS Gas Transmission Co v Argentine Rep* (2005); *LG&E Energy Corp v Argentine Rep* (2006); *Sempra Energy International v Argentine Rep* (2007).

[86]  EB Decision Number 144 August 14, 1952:

"A member intending to impose restrictions on payments and transfers for current international transactions that are not authorized . . .. And that in the judgment of the member, are solely related to the preservation of national or international security, should whenever possible, notify the Fund before imposing such restrictions. . ... Unless the Fund informs the member within 30 days after receiving notice form the member that it is not satisfied that such

the Member imposing the restrictions on payments and transfers for current international transactions. The only substantive constraint by way of a safeguard in the invocation of this defence is that the imposition of exchange controls need to be "solely to preserve such security".[87]

> **21. A number of members have, in the past five years, introduced exchange controls in the context of recent international initiatives to combat terrorist-financing and money-laundering.**
>
> Some of these controls give rise to exchange restrictions that should be notified to the Fund pursuant to the procedures described in Decision No. 144-(52/51). The number of countries maintaining such restrictions has increased from 69 (37 percent of total reporting countries) in 2000 to 104 (54.5 percent of total reporting countries) in 2005. However, there would appear to be scope for improving the reporting of such measures to the Fund. There is evidence to suggest that not all such restrictions have been notified to the Fund. [Footnotes omitted][88]

7–015

## THE REGULATION OF CAPITAL MOVEMENTS[89]

The nature of international capital flows can be short or long term, as well as inwards or outwards.[90] An example of a short-term inflow would be portfolio investment, as for instance when a non-resident invests in the national stock market.[91] Whereas a short term outflow would take place, for instance when a resident invests in a pension investment offshore.[92] On the other hand,

7–016

---

restrictions arte proposed solely to preserve such security, the member may assume that the Fund has no objection to the imposition of the restrictions."

[87] IMF EB Decision Number 144 August 14, 1952.

[88] Source: IMF, *Article VIII Acceptance by IMF Members: Recent Trends and Implications for the Fund.* (Prepared by the Monetary and Financial Systems and Legal Departments. Approved by U. Baumgartner and S. Hagan (May 2006).) Available at *http://www.imf.org.* (Accessed June 8, 2011).

[89] See, for example, J. Gold, *International Capital Movements Under The Law of The International Monetary Fund*, IMF Pamphlet Series No.21 (1977); S. Fischer, "Capital Account Liberalization and the Role of the IMF" (1997) available on IMF website: *http://www.imf.org/external/np/apd/asia/FISCHER.htm*; see also, OECD Code of liberalisation of capital movement; G. Nelson, "Towards the increased international mobility of capital under the Articles of Agreement of the IMF", *Yale Studies in World Public Order* (Fall, 1978); C. Crawford Lichtenstein, "International jurisdiction over international capital flows and the role of the IMF: plus ca change...", M. Giovanoli (ed.), *International Monetary Law* (Oxford, Oxford University Press, 2000); IMF Independent Evaluation Report *The IMF's Approach to Capital Account Liberalization* (2005); A. Yianni & C. D. Vera, "The return of capital controls?" *Law and Contemporary Problems* Vol 73:357.

[90] Keith Jefferis, *The Rationalization of Foreign Exchange Controls in Angola,* Southern Africa Global Competitiveness Hub (2008) at p.5.

[91] Keith Jefferis, *The Rationalization of Foreign Exchange Controls in Angola,* Southern Africa Global Competitiveness Hub (2008) at p.5

[92] Keith Jefferis, *The Rationalization of Foreign Exchange Controls in Angola,* Southern Africa Global Competitiveness Hub (2008) at p 5.

foreign direct investment would comprise of a long term capital inflow; and a resident purchasing property abroad, would be an example of a long term outflow.[93]

Restrictions on capital movements at the moment can be imposed without the approval of the IMF.[94] Indeed, the Fund cannot require the removal of capital restrictions.[95] In the case of capital movements, national restrictions can relate both to inward or outward flows of different forms, unlike national restrictions on current transactions which focus essentially on outflows.[96]Thus, the kind of capital restrictions States impose can involve requiring governmental approval for direct and portfolio investment abroad; and the restricting of the lending of money to non-residents.[97] However, such restrictions as are imposed must not restrict or delay unduly payments and transfers for current transactions.[98] Nor should they result in the manipulation of exchange rates or the international monetary system, so as to hinder balance of payments adjustment or to gain an unfair competitive advantage over other members.[99] In regulating the control of capital, members are to pay due regard to the general purposes of the Fund.[100] Moreover, given the relationship between exchange rates and the stability of a member's balance of payments, the Fund has the mandate to engage a member in its surveillance exercises with respect to its capital restrictions. Thus, "the introduction or substantial modification for balance of payments purposes of restrictions on, or incentives for, the inflow or outflow of capital", give rise to consultations with the Fund; as do "large external sector vulnerabilities, including liquidity risks, arising from private capital flows".[101]

Over the years, the landscape of restrictions on capital movements both in terms of their efficacy and advocacy has been changing. First, the widespread acceptance of Article VIII commitments has undermined the efficacy of capital controls.[102] This is because, as has been pointed out "(1) some current transactions can substitute for capital account transactions that are otherwise restricted and (2) current transactions can create scope for disguised capital transactions through leads and lags or under- and over-

---

[93] Keith Jefferis, *The Rationalization of Foreign Exchange Controls in Angola,* Southern Africa Global Competitiveness Hub (2008) at p.5.

[94] Art.VI, s.3 and Executive Board Decision No.541–(56/39) in IMF *Selected Decisions of the IMF* 22nd Issue (1997).

[95] See IMF Independent Evaluation Report *The IMF's Approach to Capital Account Liberalization* (2005). Ch. 2.

[96] Keith Jefferis *The Rationalization of Foreign Exchange Controls in Angola,* Southern Africa Global Competitiveness Hub (2008) at p.5.

[97] Edwards (1985), p.450.

[98] See Art.VI,

[99] Art.IV. See also Edwards (1985), p.458

[100] Executive Board Decision No.541–(56/39) in IMF *Selected Decisions.*

[101] See Executive Board Decision No. 13919-(07/51), June 15, 2007.

[102] See *The IMF's Approach to Capital Account Liberalization* (2005) Ch. 2.

invoicing".[103] Secondly, in the same vein, the development of sophisticated financial instruments cannot have reinforced capital controls.[104] Thirdly, capital liberalisation found an impetus through regional,[105] bilateral[106] and multilateral[107] efforts.[108] Fourthly, there have been times, albeit in the past, when the IMF encouraged capital liberalisation through surveillance and in the process of imparting Fund resources, although there is no evidence that it required capital liberalisation as such.[109] Indeed, in the late 1990s the IMF Interim Committee endorsed the amendment of the IMF Articles to include the liberalisation of capital in an orderly and sustainable manner.[110] This proposal has now been abandoned. Finally, of late the Asian crisis, and more recently the 2008 financial crisis, has changed the focus from liberalisation to the regulation of capital liberalisation. Indeed, the current General Counsel of the IMF has observed[111]:

"It would be open for the Fund to establish policies pursuant to Article IV, Section 1 that provide guidance to members as to: (i) what conditions should be in place before a member liberalizes its capital account, and (ii) when the imposition of controls on outflows or inflows may be an appropriate response to balance of payments or macroeconomic pressures."

The arguments for liberalisation can briefly be stated as follows.[112] First, capital flows contribute to development. Secondly, the free availability of capital assists governments and individuals, by enabling them to borrow and lend in varied and sophisticated markets. On the other hand, capital liberalisation, particularly with respect to short term "foot-loose" capital[113] flows, generates risks for the financial system and the stability of the balance of payments.[114] The proposals for capital liberalisation have thus been qualified by the requirement that they should be orderly and sustainable. However, such incorporation of safeguards could become a means to validate restrictions on capital movements.[115] In the circumstances the debate on capital liberalisation is still not yet fully settled.

---

[103] See *The IMF's Approach to Capital Account Liberalization* (2005) Ch. 2.
[104] See *The IMF's Approach to Capital Account Liberalization* (2005) Ch. 2.
[105] OECD Code of Liberalization of Capital Movements (1961) and the European Communities Directives on Capital Account Liberalization.
[106] Bilateral Investment Agreements.
[107] GATS
[108] See *The IMF's Approach to Capital Account Liberalization* (2005) Ch. 2
[109] See *The IMF's Approach to Capital Account Liberalization* (2005).
[110] See IMF *Survey* (September 1997), Vol.26.
[111] S. Hagan, "Enhancing the IMF's regulatory authority" J.I.E.L. 13(3), 955–968 at 968.
[112] Fischer (1997).
[113] *Financial Times*, March 11, 1998.
[114] See, for example, S. Hagan, "Enhancing the IMF's regulatory authority" J.I.E.L. 13(3), 955–968 at 966.
[115] *Financial Times*, March 11, 1998.

**Article VI of the IMF Articles of Agreement—Capital Transfers[116]**

**Section 3. Controls of capital transfers**

7-017    Members may exercise such controls as are necessary to regulate international capital movements, but no member may exercise these controls in a manner which will restrict payments for current transactions or which will unduly delay transfers of funds in settlement of commitments, except as provided in Article VII, Section 3(*b*) and in Article XIV, Section 2.

**IMF Independent Evaluation Report: The IMF's Approach to Capital Account Liberalization (2005)[117]**

**Recommendations**

7-018    The evaluation suggests two main areas in which the IMF can improve its work on capital account issues.

> *Recommendation 1. There is a need for more clarity on the IMF's approach to capital account issues.* The evaluation is not focused on the arguments for and against amending the Articles of Agreement, but it does suggest that the ambiguity about the role of the IMF with regard to capital account issues has led to some lack of consistency in the work of the IMF across countries. This may reflect the lack of clarity in the Articles, but with or without a change in the Articles it should be possible to improve the consistency of the IMF's country work in other ways. For example:

> • *The place of capital account issues in IMF surveillance could be clarified.* It is generally understood that while under current arrangements the IMF has neither explicit mandate nor jurisdiction on capital account issues; it has a responsibility to exercise surveillance over certain aspects of members' capital account policies. However, much ambiguity remains on the scope of IMF surveillance in this area. The clearest statement of the basis for surveillance of capital account issues is embodied in the 1977 Executive Board decision calling for surveillance to consider certain capital account restrictions introduced for balance of payments purposes, but the qualification limiting the scope to balance of payments reasons is too restrictive to cover the range of capital account issues that surface in the IMF's country work. On the other hand, the broader statement of the IMF's surveillance responsibility, found in the preamble to Article IV, is too wide to serve as an operational guide to surveillance on capital account issues. There would be value if the Executive Board were formally to clarify the scope of IMF surveillance on capital account issues. Such a clarification would recognize that capital account policy is intimately connected with exchange rate policy, as part of an overall macroeconomic policy package, and that in many countries capital flows are more important in this respect than current flows; capital controls can be used to manipulate exchange rates or to delay needed external adjustment; and a country's capital account policy creates externalities for other countries. Capital account policy is therefore of central importance to surveillance.

---

[116]  Source: *http://www.imf.org.* (Accessed June 8, 2011).
[117]  Source: *http://www.imf.org.* (Accessed June 8, 2011).

- *The IMF could sharpen its advice on capital account issues, based on solid analysis of the particular situation and risks facing specific countries.* Given the limited evidence that exists in the literature on the benefits or costs of capital account liberalization in the abstract, the IMF's approach to any capital account issue must necessarily be based on an analysis of each case. . .

- *The Executive Board could issue a statement clarifying the common elements of agreement on capital account liberalization.* At present, there remains considerable uncertainty among many staff members on what policy advice to provide to individual countries. . .

*Recommendation 2. The IMF's analysis and surveillance should give greater attention to the supply-side factors of international capital flows and what can be done to minimize the volatility of capital movements.* The IMF's policy advice on managing capital flows has so far focused to a considerable extent on what recipient countries should do. While this is important, it is not the whole story. As discussed in the evaluation report, the IMF's recent analyses have given greater attention to supply-side factors, including the dynamics of boom-and-bust cycles in emerging market financing. The IMF has also established an International Capital Markets Department (ICM) as part of an effort to better understand global financial markets; it participates actively in the work of the Financial Stability Forum, which was established to monitor potential vulnerabilities in global financial markets; and it has proposed a Sovereign Debt Restructuring Mechanism (SDRM), encouraged the use of collective action clauses (CACs), and has attempted to place limitations on countries' access to IMF resources in a crisis, in an effort to reduce the perceived moral hazard that may have led capital markets to pay insufficient attention to the risks of investing in developing countries and contributed to the boom-and-bust cycles of capital movements. These are important and welcome initiatives, but the IMF has not yet fully addressed issues of what, if anything, can be done to minimize the volatility of capital flows by operating on the supply side—as yet, little attention seems to be paid to supply-side risks and potential mitigating actions in the industrial countries that are home to the major global financial markets. . .

## IMPLEMENTATION

There are a number of ways in which the Fund encourages compliance with **7-019** its mandate for a multilateral system of payments. Non-compliance can have several consequences. First, a report may be prepared by the Managing Director for the attention of the Executive Board. Secondly, a member may be declared ineligible to use Fund resources.[118] Thirdly, a member's voting and related rights can be suspended.[119] Fourthly, when considering a request for financial assistance the Fund must examine a member's exchange restrictions,

---

[118] Art.XXVI.
[119] Art.XXVI.

and may address the question of compliance in its decision to accord assistance. In practice, the Fund has allowed the use of its resources to members imposing non-approved exchange restrictions. However, the Fund normally engages in approval of such restrictions whilst approving the use of its resources. The Fund has also included conditions (known as performance criteria) relating to the imposition of exchange restrictions, upon the use of its resources, when a member has resorted to it for financial assistance, resulting in the interruption of the further use of resources. Fifthly, a member who falls under the transitional regime has to undergo annual consultations with the Fund arising from the restrictions. These consultations are subsumed under the Art. IV consultations relating to exchange rates. Sixthly, a Member is obliged to furnish information to the Fund at all material times as to its exchange control regulations.[120] Seventhly, members are encouraged to co-operate as between themselves through mutual agreement to render more effective exchange control regulations made consistently with the IMF Articles.[121]

### Extraterritorial implementation[122]

**7-020**    The Fund ensures that exchange control restrictions made in violation of the IMF Articles of Agreement are not given effect to within the jurisdiction of Member States. Thus, Art.VIII 2(b) states:

> "Exchange contracts which involve the currency of any member and which are contrary to the exchange control regulations of that member maintained or

---

[120] Art.VIII, s.5.

[121] Art.VIII 2(b).

[122] J. Gold, *The Fund Agreement in Courts* (1962; 1976; 1982; 1986; 1989), Vols1–4 IMF; J.S. William, "Extraterritorial enforcement of exchange control regulations under the International Monetary Fund Agreement" (Winter 1975) *Virginia Journal Of International Law* No.15:319–396; S.C A Obeyesekere, "International economic cooperation through international law: the IMF agreement and the recognition of foreign exchange control regulations" (1984) *German Yearbook of International Law* No.27, 142–195; D.M. Krasnostein, "The use of multi-currency and multi-international Jurisdiction stability agreements under Article VIII(2)(b) of the International Monetary Fund Articles of Agreement" (Fall 1985) *Syracuse Journal of International Law and Commerce* 12, No.1:15–58; G.B. Schwab, "The unenforceability of international contracts violating foreign exchange regulations: Article VIII, Section 2(b) of the International Monetary Fund Agreement" (Summer 1985) *Virginia Journal of International Law* No.25:967–1005; W.F. Ebke, "Article VIII, Section 2(b), International Monetary Cooperation, and the Courts", in *Festsrift in Honor of Sir Joseph Gold*; W.F. Ebke and J.J. Norton (eds) et al. (1990), p.63; A.T. Marks, "Exchange control regulations within the meaning of the Bretton Woods Agreement: a comparison of judicial interpretation in the United States and Europe" (Summer 1990) *International Tax And Business Lawyer* (Calif) 8, No.1:104–138; O. Sandrock, "Are disputes Over the Application of Article VIII, Section 2(b) of the IMF Treaty Arbitrable?" in W.F. Ebke and J.J. Norton (eds), *Festschrift in Honor of Sir Joseph Gold* (Heidelberg: Verlag Recht und Wirtschaft GmbH, 1990), p.351; F. Gianviti, "The Fund Agreement in the Courts" in R.C. Effros (ed.), *Current Legal Issues Affecting Central Banks* (1992) Vol.1 IMF, p.1; Seidl-Hohenveldern, "Article VIII, Section 2(b) of the IMF Articles of Agreement and Public Policy" in Ebke and Norton (eds), p.379; W.F. Ebke, "Article VIII, Section 2(b) of the IMF Articles of Agreement and international capital transfers: perspectives from the German Supreme Court" (Fall 1994) *International Lawyer* (Chicago, Ill), 28, No.3:761–7711.

imposed consistently with this Agreement shall be unenforceable in the territories of any member."

Article VIII, s.2(b) imposes an obligation on members to ensure under their domestic law that effect is given to it.[123] It creates essentially a departure from the general position that national courts, when confronted with a dispute as between private parties, with an international dimension, will not normally as a matter of national public policy take cognisance of or enforce the public law[124] of another State. Thus, courts following the Anglo-American tradition normally do not enforce the exchange control, revenue, or criminal legislation of another foreign State. National courts on the other hand do recognise foreign law which regulates private relationships between parties. Article VIII, s.2(b) puts a gloss to the general practice by preventing the ground of public policy from stopping a party enforcing an exchange contract, under foreign exchange control regulations enacted consistently with IMF Articles.[125] An unenforceable contract, however, is not to be confused with a void contract.

It is to be noted that the obligation under Art.VIII(2)(b) is in fact minimal. Article VIII(2)(b) imposes an obligation on members not to render ineffective another member's exchange control regulations. It does not impose a positive duty to enforce other member's exchange control regulations. In this sense the obligation is minimal. However, it nevertheless ensures that the consensus *ad idem* represented in the Articles of Agreement is in fact implemented, albeit at the national level in the national courts, and that private parties engaged in international transactions all receive a uniform treatment.

The exchange control regulations mentioned in Art.VIII, s.2(b) relate to the acquisition, holding or use of foreign exchange; or to the use of currency, whether foreign or domestic, in international payments and transfers.[126] Further, the reference is to such regulations as are maintained and imposed consistently with the Articles of Agreement of the IMF. The term "regulation" here is broader than the allusion to "restriction" in Art.VIII, s.2(a).[127] The relevant regulations are the regulations in force at the time of the proceedings.[128] The regulations comprise as follows:

(i) Capital controls regulations.[129]

(ii) Restrictions authorised under the Articles and/or approved by the Fund.[130]

---

[123] Gianviti (1994), p.8.

[124] i.e. the law which serves the State's economic or political purposes.

[125] Decision No.446-4 in IMF *Selected Decisions.*

[126] Francotte (1992), p.16.

[127] Gianviti (1994), p.11.

[128] Francotte (1992), p.21.

[129] Art.VI, s.3. According to Edwards (1985), p.480 reference to exchange control regulations includes reference to monetary controls on capital movements.

[130] Art.VIII, s.2(a).

(iii)  Restrictions under the transitional regime.[131]

(iv)  Restrictions on non-members.[132]

(v)  Restrictions relating to a scarce currency.[133]

(vi)  Exchange controls for security reasons.[134]

**7-021**    Article VIII 2(b) has given rise to a number of problems of interpretation in national courts. However, despite this, the provision has been the subject of an IMF clarification on only one occasion. The explanation for such minimal clarification on the part of the Fund has been summarised by Gold as follows.[135] First, the Fund is reluctant, to act as an Appellate Court for national courts. Secondly, members in the Fund are generally reluctant to request interpretations of the IMF Articles. Thirdly, the Articles do not permit the national courts direct access to the Fund. However, the Fund has concluded that it would be prepared to advise whether particular national exchange control regulations are "maintained or imposed consistently with the Fund Agreement".[136] The Fund has in fact responded to many enquiries in relation to matters pending before domestic courts.[137] Fourthly, Art.VIII, s.2(b) involves technical legal questions involving private parties. This does not accord well with the character of the Executive Board which is an intergovernmental body concerned with the affairs of States, rather than individuals. The reasons so adumbrated need however to be considered critically. Many of the reasons proffered, for example, have not prevented other international economic organisations from taking a different course of action.

The basic purpose underlying Art.VIII, s.2(b) is clarified by the Fund in its interpretation of the provision as follows[138]:

> "Parties entering into exchange contracts involving the currency of any member of the Fund and contrary to exchange control regulations of that member which are maintained or imposed consistently with the Fund Agreement will not receive the assistance of the judicial or administrative authorities of other members in obtaining the performance of such contracts. That is to say, the obligations of such contracts will not be implemented by the judicial or administrative authorities of member countries, for example by decreeing performance of the contracts or by awarding damages for their non performance."

It is clear from this that Art.VIII, s.2(b) is concerned with executory contracts. Further, it is concerned with denying assistance in the implementation of such contracts. In addition, the provision applies to both Art.VIII and Art. XIV members.

---

[131]  Art.XIV.
[132]  Art.XI.
[133]  Art.VIII, s.3.
[134]  Francotte (1992), p.17.
[135]  Gold, *The Fund Agreement in Courts*, Vol.II, pp.7–8.
[136]  Executive Board Decision No.446–4 in IMF *Selected Decisions*.
[137]  Gianviti (1994), p. 9.
[138]  Executive Board Decision No.446–4 in IMF *Selected Decisions*.

National courts should consider, in particular the following, when confronted with interpreting the provision. First, they should take notice that the provision is part of an international agreement and therefore needs to be interpreted in that light. Effect should be given to the purposes of the IMF. Secondly, courts should strive for uniformity in interpreting the provision. This is in order to give effect to the consensus *ad idem* represented in the agreement; to ensure uniformity in the obligations as between the members; and to facilitate equality of treatment of litigants.[139] Finally, courts should take on board the fact that if they gave effect to Art.VIII, s.2(b) contrary to its requirements, then the Member State will be in breach of its treaty obligations.[140] A member is required to ensure that it has taken all the necessary steps nationally to enable it to carry out its obligations under the Articles.[141]

National courts have in fact not demonstrated uniformity in interpretation—for several reasons. First, there is the obvious difficulty in having access to foreign judgments. In this respect Gold's three volumes in the field[142] were of particular significance, but some years have passed since the last volume. Secondly, national courts tend to be tainted with judicial conservatism and national policy considerations. In contrast, opinions of jurists in relation to the provision tend to be more liberal and international in their outlook.

**7-022**

Of the several aspects of Art.VIII 2(b) that are not clear one particular aspect needs special highlighting. The meaning of "exchange contracts", which is at the heart of the provision, is a source of some ambiguity. National courts have interpreted this provision in different ways. Although it is clear that the reference here is to contracts, and not, for example tortuous acts.[143] It is the meaning of "exchange" that is not clear. There are basically three different interpretations. First, there is the narrow, literal interpretation wherein exchange is defined as referring to the exchange of means of payments, i.e. contracts for the exchange of currency of a State against another State.[144] This is the practice followed in the US[145] and the UK.[146] Thus, in the UK the House of Lords described it as referring to[147]:

---

[139] J. Gold, *Fund Agreement in Courts*, Vol.3.
[140] Edwards (1985), p.478. See also Art.XXXI, s.2(a) of the Articles of Agreement of the IMF.
[141] Edwards (1985), p.478.
[142] Gold, *Fund Agreement in Court*, Vols1–3.
[143] See Edwards (1985), p.479, and F. Mann, *The Legal Aspect of Money* (Oxford, Oxford University Press, 1992), p.373.
[144] First proposed by Nussbaum in "Exchange control and the International Monetary Fund" in *Yale Law Journal* (1949–1950).
[145] See, for example, *Banco do Brasil, SA v AC Israel Commodity Co Inc* (1963) 239 N.Y.S. 2d 872; *Zeevi v Grindlays Bank (Uganda) Ltd* (1975) 371 N.Y.S. 2d 892s; *Libra Bank Ltd v Banco Nacional de Costa Rica* (1983) 570 F.Sup.870.
[146] Gianviti (1994), p.10. See also for the practice of UK courts, for example, *Wilson, Smithett & Cope Ltd v Terruzzi* (1976) 1 All E.R. 817; and *United City Merchants (Investments) Ltd v Royal Bank of Canada* (1982) 2 All E.R. 720.
[147] *United City Merchants (Investment Ltd) v Royal Bank of Canada* (1983) 1 A.C. 168; *Wilson, Smithett & Cope Ltd v Terruzi* (1976) 1 Q.B. 683; and *Mansouri v Singh* (1986) 2 All E.R. 619;

". . . contracts to exchange currency of one country for another as well as monetary transactions in disguise".

The narrow interpretation reflects a certain disdain for exchange control regulations, given the objectives of the IMF. The narrow interpretation undermines the enforceability of exchange restrictions. On the other hand, it can be argued that the effective enforcement of exchange restrictions made consistently with IMF Articles would ensure their early demise. It has been suggested that the narrow interpretation is so restrictive that it is in reality of no consequence in the courts of the UK and the US.[148] Under this approach exchange controls relating to international loans are not affected.[149] The staff at the IMF take the view that the narrow interpretation is not in conformity with Art.VIII, s.2(b) properly interpreted.[150]

A much broader interpretation, and one followed by French[151] and German courts,[152] defines exchange contracts as any contracts which affect a State's foreign exchange reserves, or balance of payments. The problem with this approach is that it is difficult to apprehend a test of "affecting the balance of payments" that can be suitable for use in a court of law.[153]

**7-023**    A broader interpretation is preferred by most jurists,[154] including former[155] General Counsels of the IMF. Significantly the Fund staff advocate a broad intermediate definition of exchange contracts as follows[156]:

> "a contract that provides for either a payment or transfer of foreign exchange or an international payment or transfer (i.e. a payment between a resident and a non-resident, or a transfer of funds from one country to another)."

This definition is broad enough to cover a contract providing for payment in foreign exchange as between residents, and international loans.[157]

The different meanings attached to "exchange contracts" have a knock on effect on other aspects of Art.VIII, s.2(b), in particular the meaning of

---

*Batra v Ebrahim* (1982) 2 Lloyd's Rep; *Overseas Union Insurance v AA Mutual International Insurance* (1988) 2 Lloyd's Rep. 63. See also Mann (1992), p.380.

[148] Gianviti (1994).

[149] Francotte (1992), p.19.

[150] Francotte (1992), p.19.

[151] See, for example, *Soc. Daiei Motion Picture v Zavicha Paris*, May 14, 1970, (1974) R.C.D.I.P., p.486.

[152] Gianviti (1994), p.10. See also for a German case Court of Appeal of Berlin, Decision of July 8, 1974, No.138, as translated by Mann (1992).

[153] Francotte (1992), p.19.

[154] See Mann (1992); Gianviti, "La control des changes etranger devant le juge national", in *Revue critique de droit international prive* (1980) (R.C.D.I.P.). See also Gianviti, "Reflections sur l'article VIII, section 2b des statute du *Fonds monetaire international*" (1973); Edwards (1985).

[155] Gold, *The Fund Agreement in the Courts* (Washington D.C.: IMF, 1962, 1976, 1982, 1986, 1989), Vols1–4; and F. Gianviti.

[156] Francotte (1992), p.19.

[157] Francotte (1992).

"involving the currency". In the framework of the narrow interpretation "involving the currency" refers to the involvement of the currency the subject-matter of the exchange.[158] Such an interpretation would restrict the benefit of Art.VIII, s.2(b) to the few States whose currencies are widely used.[159] On the other hand in the context of the broader interpretation a member's currency is involved if the member's balance of payments or exchange resources are affected. This however is not a precise legal criterion. The Fund staff consider a currency to be involved if either[160]:

> "(1)  one of the parties to the contract was a resident of that country. . .or
> (2)  the contract is to be performed with assets located in that country's territory."

In conclusion, Art.VIII, s.2(b) has given rise to a number of problems in its interpretation. Whilst not all of these have been highlighted here,[161] it is clear that so minimal an obligation has managed to generate so much literature and diverse case law. There is indeed the need here for authoritative clarifications.

---

[158] Gianviti (1973).
[159] Francotte (1992).
[160] Francotte (1992), p.21.
[161] They have been examined in the literature is some detail elsewhere. See references in fn.102 above on extraterritorial implementation.

### CHAPTER 8

# INTERNATIONAL LIQUIDITY AND THE SDR

## INTRODUCTION[1]

The provision of "international liquidity" refers to the reserve assets or **8–001** reserve currency at the disposal of monetary authorities in order to finance potential balance of payments deficits.[2] Reserve assets or reserve currencies refer to currencies which monetary authorities and international institutions are willing to hold and use in international trade. A reserve currency is a currency, which in economic analysis is relatively stable; is issued by a State holding a significant share of world trade; has an exchange market; and is convertible.[3] Such criteria broadly correspond with the definition of a freely usable currency defined in the IMF Articles of Agreement.

---

[1] On SDRs see, for example, J. Gold, *Special Drawing Rights*, IMF *Pamphlet Series* No.13 (1970); J. Gold, *Special Drawing Rights: The Role of Language*, IMF *Pamphlet Series* No.15 (1971); J.J. Polak, "Some reflections on the nature of *Special Drawing Rights*", IMF *Pamphlet Series* No.16 (1971); W. Habermeier, "*Operations and Transaction in SDRs*: The first basic period", IMF *Pamphlet Series* No.17 (1973); J.J. Polak, "*Valuation and rate of interest of the SDR*", IMF *Pamphlet Series* No.18 (1974); .A. Chrystal, "International money and the future of the SDR", in *Essays in International Finance*, (June 1978) No.128, Princeton University; J.J. Polak, "*Thoughts on an International Monetary Fund Based Fully on the SDR*", IMF *Pamphlet Series* No.28 (1979); J. Gold, "Development of the SDR as reserve asset, unit of account, and denominator: a survey" (1981) *Journal of International Law and Economics*, 16:1–64; K. L.Ward, "The SDR in transport liability conventions: some clarification" (October 1981) *Journal of Maritime Law and Commerce*, 13:1–20, R.W. Edwards, *International Monetary Collaboration* (1985), Ch.5; W.L. Coats et al., "The SDR system and the issue of resource transfers", Reprints in *International Finance* (December 1990) No.180: 1–30, Princeton University; W. Coats, "Developing a market for the official SDR", in R.C. Effros (ed.), *Current Legal Issues Affecting Central Banks* (IMF 1992); F. Gianviti in R.C. Effros, *Current Legal Issues Affecting Banks* (1998), Vol.5; P.B. Clark and J.J. Polak, "International Liquidity and the Role of the SDR in the International Monetary System", IMF *Staff Papers* (2004), Vol.51, No.1.

[2] See, for example, G. Meier, *Problems of a world monetary order*, 2nd edn (Oxford, Oxford University Press, 1982), p.55; and J.M. Fleming, "The Fund and International Liquidity", IMF *Staff Papers* (1964).

[3] G. Bannock and R. Baxter et al., *Dictionary of Economics* (Penguin Books, 1984).

**8–002**     **Article XXX (f) of the IMF Articles of Agreement[4]**

A freely usable currency means a member's currency that the Fund determines

(i) is, in fact, widely used to make payments for international transactions, and

(ii) is widely traded in the principal exchange markets.

**8–003**   The availability of international liquidity is critical for the operation of a State's economy and indeed the functioning of the global economic system. International liquidity is concerned with the relationship of the volume of money with the volume of economic transactions at any given time.[5] The focus on the condition of this relationship begs the question as to the necessary volume and velocity of money for a desired level of economic activity.[6] The question of international liquidity is thus concerned with the adequacy of a State's reserve assets. Broadly, a measurement of this adequacy can be ascertained inter alia through a focus on the ratio of reserves to imports— although the accuracy of this measure has been questioned.[7] It can also be considered by focusing on actual borrowing levels, and symptoms of inadequacy such as increases in import restrictions or barter trade.[8]

The problem of the adequacy of a State's reserves arises as long as the objective of maintaining a stable currency is being pursued. Where the currency is allowed to freely float, then the adequacy of the liquidity is governed by market forces. The question of the adequacy of liquidity can be dealt with in a number of other ways, including import restrictions and the increase of the volume of liquidity through international borrowing. However, import restrictions are not an internationally acceptable manner of dealing with shortages of liquidity. Similarly, increasing the volume of liquidity can be burdensome and inflationary.

Before the creation of the Special Drawing Rights (SDR) under the framework of the IMF, international liquidity was dependent inter alia on a number of factors. First, gold—but this is and was an unreliable source for obvious reasons. Secondly, reserve currencies, from deficit reserve countries, viz., the US dollar. However, such reliance could be dangerous as a deficit correction by the respective reserve-currency State would affect the value of the reserve currency. Thirdly, resources from the IMF, although a significant proportion of these are conditional. Finally, the availability of currency swap arrangements between monetary authorities. These tend to be for short durations and need to be negotiated. Despite this range of resources albeit with shortcomings, international liquidity proved to be inadequate, and contrasted with the increase in international trade, during the period leading up

---

[4] Source: *http://www.imf.org.* (Accessed June 8, 2011).
[5] Edwards (1985), p.167.
[6] Edwards (1985), p.167.
[7] IMF Institute Manual INST/86–IX/9–3. Not available publicly.
[8] See, for example, IMF *Annual Report* (1989), p.21.

to the establishment of the SDRs. Thus, international liquidity had a finite aspect which was particularly ominous against the background of the par value system. In recent times, the problem of international liquidity, has been described in a sense as not existing anymore[9] given the discretionary system of exchange rates and the floating character of reserve currencies; the increase in Art.VIII members, thus facilitating the availability and circulation of reserve currencies; and capital market liberalisation. However, such market induced corrections and resource supplies have a cost attached to them.

## THE SPECIAL DRAWING RIGHT

The inadequacy of international liquidity led to calls from various quarters for a new reserve asset.[10] Indeed, the call for an international reserve asset the quantum of which was not determined in an unpredictable and irrelevant fashion related to the requirements of international trade—and was made as early as 1948, by J.M. Keynes at the Bretton Woods Conference.[11] Thus, the raison d'être for a new reserve asset was to provide for the objective regulation of the quantum of international liquidity aligned to the needs and conditions of the international economy, set against a system of fixed exchange rates.

**8–004**

In 1964, the Group of Ten approved the formation of a Study Group on the creation of a reserve asset.[12] This resulted in the publication of a report,[13] which persuaded the Group of Ten to engage in the deliberate creation of an unconditional reserve asset, on the basis of a collective judgment of world reserves. The creation of such a reserve asset was considered to be a major responsibility of the industrialised States. In 1969, the Articles of Agreement of the IMF were amended, so as to establish the Special Drawing Rights Facility.

There is some debate as to the nature of SDRs. Thus, it has been contended that the SDR is a form of money[14]—international fiat money, i.e. legal money not covered by gold; paper money that must be accepted as legal tender. The SDR has the attributes of money, i.e. it is a means of payment; a store of value; and a unit of account. On the other hand, it is contended that the SDR

---

[9] P.B. Clark and J.J. Polak, "International Liquidity and the Role of the SDR in the International Monetary System", IMF *Staff Papers* (2004), Vol.51, No.1.

[10] See, for example, R. Triffin, *Gold and the Dollar Crisis: The Future of Convertibility* (New Haven, Yale University Press, 1960); "The adequacy of monetary reserves", IMF *Staff Papers* (October 1953), Vol.III No.2, p.181.

[11] United Nations Monetary And Financial Conference 1948.

[12] IMF Institute Manual INST/86–IX/9–3, chapter on Special Drawing Rights. Not available publicly.

[13] Group of Ten Report of the Study Group on the Creation of Reserve Assets: Report to the Deputies of the Group of Ten 1965. See also Edwards (1985), p.169.

[14] Shuster, *The Public International Law of Money* (Oxford, Clarendon Press, 1973), Ch.IX.

is a credit, recorded in the IMF books in favour of participating members. The better view, however, seems to be that it is in fact sui generis.[15] Members receive SDRs without having to give real resources in return.

### Allocation and cancellation of the SDRs

**8–005** The Fund has the mandate to allocate and cancel SDRs, to participants in the Special Drawing Rights Department, in order to supplement existing reserve assets as and when the need arises.[16] A participant may, however, opt out of an allocation.[17] The SDR facility is administered by the Special Drawing Rights Department in the IMF.[18] Initially, SDRs are intended to supplement (not replace)[19] existing reserve assets.

> **Article XV of the IMF Articles of Agreement—Special Drawing Rights**
>
> **Section 1. Authority to allocate special drawing rights20**
>
> **8–006** To meet the need, as and when it arises, for a supplement to existing reserve assets, the Fund is authorized to allocate special drawing rights to members that are participants in the Special Drawing Rights Department.

However, the long-term objectives were to make the SDR the principal reserve asset of the international monetary system.

> **Article XXII of the IMF Articles of Agreement—General Obligations of Participants[21]**
>
> **8–007** In addition to the obligations assumed with respect to special drawing rights under other articles of this Agreement, each participant undertakes to collaborate with the Fund and with other participants in order to facilitate the effective functioning of the Special Drawing Rights Department and the proper use of special drawing rights in accordance with this Agreement and with the objective of making the special drawing right the principal reserve asset in the international monetary system.

**8–008** This long-term objective, however, does not reflect the reality since the establishment of the SDR. This is because the share of SDRs in terms of total world reserve assets is small—indeed in recent times the "share of SDRs in total world reserve assets has declined to about 1 per cent".[22]

In all its decisions in relation to SDRs, the Fund is to meet the long-term

---

[15] Shuster (1973); and J. Gold, "Special Drawing Rights, Character and Use", IMF *Pamphlet Series* No.13 (1970), p.28. See also Edwards (1985), p.172.

[16] Art.XV, s.1.

[17] Art.XVIII, s.2 (e).

[18] Art.XVI, s.1.

[19] IMF Institute Manual INST/86–IX/9–3, p.5. Not available publicly.

[20] Source: *http://www.imf.org*. (Accessed June 8, 2011).

[21] Source: *http://www.imf.org*. (Accessed June 8, 2011).

[22] See Clark and Polak (2004).

global needs of the international community in a manner that will promote the attainment of the IMF purposes, and avoid economic stagnation and deflation, as well as excess demand and inflation in the world.[23] The Fund does not take short-term global needs into account here, because it is difficult to arrive expeditiously at decisions in relation to SDRs. In any event, it is not clear if a decision in relation to SDR allocation, for example, would have an immediate impact on the global economy. Further, SDR allocative decisions are based on assessments of the global economy and its requirements, and not in relation to individual members of the IMF.

**Article XVIII of the IMF Articles of Agreement—Allocation and Cancellation of Special Drawing Rights**

**Section 1. Principles and considerations governing allocation and cancellation[24]**

(a) In all its decisions with respect to the allocation and cancellation of special drawing rights the Fund shall seek to meet the long-term global need, as and when it arises, to supplement existing reserve assets in such manner as will promote the attainment of its purposes and will avoid economic stagnation and deflation as well as excess demand and inflation in the world."

8-009

Although the Articles of Agreement give some indication as to the circumstances of SDR allocative decisions, there is in fact no agreed objective indicator for assessing the adequacy of existing amounts of international reserves.[25] Judgments as to the need can vary as between deficit and surplus members.[26] The decision to allocate and cancel SDRs is to be arrived at through a collective decision. The allocative decisions are to be made for basic periods of five years' duration.[27] Proposals for the allocation or cancellation of SDRs are to be initiated by the Managing Director of the IMF in accordance with the IMF Articles.[28] The proposal needs to be agreed by the Executive Board, before it is sent to the Board of Governors for its decision. An SDR allocative decision requires an 85 per cent majority of total voting powers.

8-010

The SDR allocations are expressed as a percentage of quotas and allocated uniformly.[29] The allocations are phased over the course of the basic period in annual instalments. The phased introduction of the SDRs ensures a steady expansion or contraction of SDRs.[30] Thus far there have been three general allocations—one during 1971–1973 (SDR 9.3 billion), another during 1979–1981 (SDR 12.1 billion), and a third on August 28, 2009 (for the ninth

[23] Art.XVIII.
[24] Source: *http://www.imf.org.* (Accessed June 8, 2011).
[25] IMF Institute Manual INST/86–IX/93. Not available publicly.
[26] IMF Institute Manual INST/86–IX/93. Not available publicly.
[27] Art.XVIII.
[28] Art.XVIII, s.4.
[29] Art.XVIII, s.2(b).
[30] Gold (1970), p.18.

basic period)[31] in response to the 2008 financial crisis. Furthermore, given that members who joined the IMF since 1981 (some one-fifth of the IMF membership) did not have any SDR allocations, as they joined the Fund after the 1981 allocation[32] a special allocation on September 9, 2009 has been made on grounds of equity to remedy this non-allocation. The IMF Board of Governors had adopted in 1997 a resolution approving a one-time special SDR equity allocation.[33] This one-time allocation has now been implemented upon the Fourth Amendment of the Articles of Agreement of the IMF becoming effective.[34] The third general SDR allocation is by far the largest, comprising of SDR 161.2 billions. Together the general and special SDR allocations in 2009 amount to SDR 204 billion. Thus, the total amount of SDR allocations in 2009 increased SDR allocations from SDR 21.4 billion to SDR 204 billion (equal to $324.1 billion).[35] In addition, the Eleventh General Review of Quotas has resulted in 1998 in an increase of 45 per cent of IMF quotas,[36] and thus raising the total allocation of SDRs as well. No quota increases were proposed in the Twelfth and Thirteenth General Review of Quotas. The Fourteenth General Review of Quotas was completed in December 2010 and once approved by the members will result in a 100 per cent increase of quotas.

### Users and uses

**8–011**     The SDR facility is restricted to members of the IMF who have specifically undertaken all the obligations of a participant in the Special Drawing Rights Department.[37] In addition, the IMF may prescribe certain designated holders of SDRs who are not members of the Fund, or who are members but not participants in the SDR facility, or institutions which perform central bank functions and other official entities.[38] As of 2011 there are some 16 prescribed institutional holders.[39] These other holders can use SDRs amongst themselves or other IMF members, but cannot be recipients of SDR allocations. The fund may prescribe terms and conditions for the participation in the

---

[31]  See Board of Governors Resolution 64-3 (2009).
[32]  IMF *Survey*, Vol.26 (September 1997).
[33]  IMF *Survey*,Vol.26 (October 1997).
[34]  See IMF *Factsheet* Special Drawing Rights March 31, 2011.
[35]  See IMF *Factsheet* Special Drawing Rights March 31, 2011.
[36]  See Board of Governors Resolution January 30, 1998, No.53–2, IMF *Annual Report* (1998).
[37]  Art.XVII.
[38]  Art.XVII.
[39]  The prescribed institutional holders include: Bank For International Settlements; Andean Reserve Fund; East Caribbean Currency Authority; Nordic Investment Bank; International Fund for Agricultural Development; Arab Monetary Fund; International Bank for Reconstruction and Development; the International Development Association; Central Bank of West African States; Bank of Central African States; Islamic Development Bank; Asian Development Bank; East African Development Bank; Eastern Caribbean Central Bank; African Development Bank and the African Development Fund; Central Bank of Europe. See footnote one to Decision No. 6486-(80/77) S,1. April 18,1980 and *IMF Press* No.00/59, November 15, 2000.

Special Drawing Facility of the designated holders.[40] The IMF itself may hold SDRs.[41] However, only participants may be allocated SDRs, whereas other holders and the IMF do not receive allocations of SDRs.

SDR allocations are made across the membership in an unconditional manner. The holding of SDRs can be used to obtain freely usable currency from other participants. This can occur in two circumstances. First, a participant can obtain an equivalent amount of freely usable currency from a participant designated by the Fund to accept the SDRs.[42] This designation method is not frequently used. In designation transactions the special drawing rights are expected to be used only if the member has a need as a consequence of its balance of payments, or its reserve position or developments in its reserves.[43] Participants are to notify the Fund of such a need. However the use of SDR is not subject to challenge on that basis, although if there is user for a non-authorised purpose, the Fund may make representations to the participant.[44] Transactions in SDRs cannot be engaged in solely in order to change the composition of the member's reserves.[45] The designated participant is obliged to provide a freely usable currency.[46] However, this obligation does not extend beyond the point at which the designated participant's holdings of SDRs exceed the point at which its holdings of SDRs in excess of its net cumulative allocation, are equal to twice its net cumulative allocation.[47] Effectively this means that the obligation does not extend beyond three times the participants SDR allocation. It is open to the designated participant to accept a higher amount of SDRs, if it so wishes. The Fund's mandate to designate has a key role in guaranteeing the usability of the SDR.[48] The Fund designates a member participant on the basis essentially of a three-pronged criteria, viz. economic, equitable and operational.[49] Thus, participants will be designated if their balance of payments or reserve position is strong; in a manner so as to promote over a period of time a balanced distribution of SDR holdings amongst all the participants; and, for example, to reduce negative holdings of SDRs.

Secondly, a participant is entitled to obtain an equivalent amount of freely usable currency from another participant by mutual agreement.[50] This is the more usual method of exchanging SDRs. Members can enter into such agreements in all circumstances. There is no balance of payments

[40] Art.XVII, s.3(ii). See also Executive Board Decision No.6484–(80/77)S April 18, 1980 in IMF *Selected Decisions*.
[41] Art.XVII, s.2.
[42] Art.XIX.
[43] Art.XIX.
[44] Art.XIX, s.3.
[45] Art.IX.
[46] Art.XIX, s.4.
[47] Art.XIX, s.4(a).
[48] Executive Board Decision No.6209–(79/124)S in IMF *Selected Decisions*.
[49] IMF Institute Manual INST/86–IX/9–3. Not available publicly. See also Art.XIX, s.5 and Executive Board Decision No.6209–(79/124)S in IMF *Selected Decisions*.
[50] Executive Board Decision No.6209–(79/124)S.

need requirement, nor is there the need for Fund authorisation.[51] In addition to exchanging SDRs for currency, the Fund is empowered to extend the use of the SDR, under prescribed conditions as between participants.[52] The Fund has under this mandate extended the use of the SDR for the following purposes:

(i)   by agreement with another participant to settle a financial obligation with it[53];

(ii)  by agreement with another participant to make a loan of SDRs to it[54];

(iii) by agreement with another participant, to pledge SDRs in order to secure the performance of a financial obligation with it[55];

(iv)  by agreement with another participant, to transfer SDRs to the other participant in order to secure the performance of a financial obligation to the other participant[56];

(v)   by agreement to use SDRs in swap operations between participants[57];

(vi)  by agreement with another participant to use SDRs in forward operations[58]; and

(vii) by agreement with another participant to use SDRs in donations.[59]

Of late the amount of SDR transactions, in volume and rate, have been more substantial through the process of agreement rather than through designation.[60] This is a consequence of the steps taken in the Second Amendment to make the SDR more attractive.[61]

### Checks and balances

8-012    The Articles of Agreement of the IMF contemplate a balanced distribution of SDRs amongst its participant membership, by expecting those members which use SDRs to maintain a certain level of holdings of SDRs, through the reconstitution of their SDR holdings. Reconstitution as a requirement has,

---

[51] IMF Proposed Second Amendment to the Articles of Agreement of the International Monetary Fund—A Report by the Executive Directors to the Board of Governors (1976).
[52] Art.XIX, s.2.
[53] Executive Board Decision No.6000–(79/1)S in IMF *Selected Decisions*.
[54] Executive Board Decision No.6001–(79/1)S in IMF *Selected Decisions*.
[55] Executive Board Decision No.6053–(79/34)S in IMF *Selected Decisions*.
[56] Executive Board Decision No.6054–(79/34)S in IMF *Selected Decisions*.
[57] Executive Board Decision No.6336–(79/178)S in IMF *Selected Decisions*.
[58] Executive Board Decision No.6337–(79/178)S in IMF *Selected Decisions*.
[59] Executive Board Decision No.6437–(80/37)S in IMF *Selected Decisions*.
[60] W. Coats, *Developing a Market for the official SDR* (1992), p.26.
[61] Coats (1992).

however, been abrogated,[62] but there is still an expectation that participants will pay due regard to the desirability of pursuing over time a balanced relationship between holdings of SDRs and other reserves. The abrogation of the reconstitution requirements has been criticised by one author on the grounds that confidence in the SDR could be undermined, if as a consequence of a lack of reconstitution the SDRs become concentrated in the possession of a few participants.[63]

It can be seen thus that the Articles of Agreement provide for mechanisms to ensure that the SDR is a viable and credible financial instrument. For example, there are limitations as to the user of the SDR, as there are provisions which ensure that the SDR is accepted (e.g. through designation). In addition, the Articles also provide that failure to observe the obligations in relation to the SDR facility would result in suspension of rights in using the SDRs.[64]

### Valuation, interest and charges

The SDR is valued with reference to a basket of four currencies[65]—currently the US dollar; the Japanese yen; the pound sterling; and the euro.[66] This basket of currencies is reviewed every five years. The four currencies are determined according to those currencies of members whose exports of goods and services during a specified five-year period were the largest in value; and which have been determined by the IMF to be freely usable currencies.[67] Each of the four currencies in the basket is in turn weighted. The percentage weights of each of the currencies reflect the value of the balances held at the end of each year by the monetary authorities of other members, and the value of the exports of goods and services of the issuer of the currency over the prescribed five year period.[68] It will be noted that the SDR is valued in terms of the currencies of certain key economies. The value of the SDR is thus influenced by events in these economies. Unfortunately, the Fund has relatively little influence over these key economies.[69]

Interest is earned by participants on holdings of SDRs when the holdings

**8-013**

---

[62] Executive Board Decision No.6832–(81/65)S in IMF *Selected Decisions.*

[63] Edwards (1985), p.212.

[64] Art.XXIII.

[65] Art.XV, s.2 and Decision No.12281–(00/98), October 11, 2000, as amended by Decision No.13595–(05/99), November 23, 2005, effective January 1, 2006.

[66] The euro, upon the launch of the economic and monetary union in Europe (EMU) on January 1, 1999, replaced the currency amounts of the Deutsch mark and French franc. See Decision No. 12281-(00/98), October 11, 2000 as amended.

[67] Decision No.12281–(00/98), October 11, 2000, as amended by Decision No.13595–(05/99), November 23, 2005, effective January 1, 2006.

[68] Decision No.12281–(00/98), October 11, 2000, as amended by Decision No.13595–(05/99), November 23, 2005, effective January 1, 2006.

[69] See also Edwards (1985), p.220.

are in excess of the participant's net allocation.[70] Conversely charges are paid by participants when holdings of the participant are below that of its net allocation.[71] The interest and charges are determined in SDRs[72]; and the rates are the same.[73] Only participants pay charges. The interest is calculated with reference to the weighted average interest rates on short-term assets of the four countries whose currencies feature in the SDR valuation basket,[74] as determined on a weekly basis.

SUCCESS OF THE SDR?

**8-014** The role of the SDR as a reserve asset has been limited. Its history has been disappointing and it has failed to emerge as a genuine major international reserve unit.[75] There are several reasons for this. First, there has been the difficulty in arriving at the allocative decision as a consequence of inflationary concerns, along with the voting requirements for such a decision. Secondly, of note are the built-in SDR constraints, for instance the restricted ownership of SDRs to the exclusion of the private sector.[76] Currently it can be held and traded only by official entities. Moreover, the SDR as a reserve asset competes with other reserve currencies given that its establishment was not accompanied by the displacement of other reserve currencies. This is reinforced by the increase in the number of Art. VIII members, and increased capital liberalisation amongst States. Thirdly, some of the underlying reasons for the very establishment of the SDR are no longer present.[77] Thus, the demise of the par value system and its replacement with a discretionary system that tolerates floating regimes has taken away the heat from the concern for the adequacy of international reserves.[78] Finally, the lack of success of the SDR is also attributable in part to vested "reserve currency state interests". Thus, the US succeeded during the negotiations in relation to the Second Amendment, to ensure low interest rates for SDR's, in order to block any speedy movement out of the dollar and into the SDR.[79]

Yet the need to strengthen the role of the SDR is still recognised by the

---

[70] Art.XX, s.1.
[71] Art.XX, s.2. See also Executive Board Decision No.7116–(82/68) in IMF *Selected Decisions*.
[72] Art.XX, s.5.
[73] Art.XX, s.3.
[74] Rule T–I.
[75] James (1996), p.171.
[76] James (1996).
[77] See P.B. Clark and J.J. Polak, "International liquidity and the role of the SDR in the International Monetary System", IMF *Staff Papers* (2004) Vol.51, No.1.
[78] Clark and Polak (2004).
[79] H. James, *The International Monetary Cooperation* (Oxford, Oxford University Press, 1996), p.271.

international community.[80] Thus, the use of the SDR can be expanded, for example, it can be made available in exchange for a wider range of currencies, and the list of its uses could be expanded. Similarly, the list of official holders could be expanded and its use could also be extended to private users. Further, the SDR has a potential function in the transfer of resources to developing countries. This is the view taken by developing countries,[81] and was discussed at the UN International Conference on Financing for Development, Monterrey, Mexico, 2002. Further, to deal with concerns relating to inflation and the undermining of adjustment processes as a consequence of SDR allocations, it has been suggested that SDR allocations be accompanied by better surveillance.[82]

The prospect of the SDR becoming the principal reserve asset of the international monetary system in the near future is still slim.[83] However, the 2009 allocations of the SDR are indeed significant developments.

---

[80] See, for example, Group of 24 Communiqué in IMF *Survey* (October 1997) Vol.26.
[81] See, for example, James (1996), p.166. See also de Vries, *International Monetary Fund 1966–1971*, Vol.I, p.85.
[82] IMF *Annual Report* (1989).
[83] See, for example, IMF *Annual Report* (1997), p.34.

### Chapter 9

# IMF FINANCING FOR BALANCE OF PAYMENTS ADJUSTMENT

## Introduction

States facing balance of payments problems need to adjust their payments **9-001** disequilibrium through financing from a reserve currency and/or economic disciplines (e.g. reducing government spending, adjusting exchange rates and combating inflation). The IMF performs a significant role in both reserve currency financing and implementation of economic disciplines (known as IMF Conditionality) when called upon for its assistance by a member. This chapter focuses mainly on the apparatus of IMF funding for balance of payments purposes. Chapter 10 on the other hand concentrates on the nature of IMF Conditionality mainly within a legal framework.

One of the purposes of the IMF is:

"To give confidence to members by making the general resources of the Fund temporarily available to them under adequate safeguards, thus providing them with opportunity to correct maladjustments in their balance of payments without resorting to measures destructive of national or international prosperity.

In accordance with the above to shorten the duration and lessen the degree of disequilibrium in the international balances of payments of members."[1]

The Fund has interpreted this function to enable it to address a variety of balance of payments problems.[2] Thus, the main functions of lending have been to facilitate adjustment arising from internally and externally generated shocks; to prevent crisis situations from occurring; and finally, as has been its traditional role, to act as a catalyst for lending from other sources.[3] This funding is not directly for development purposes as such. That is a role that

---

[1] Art.1(V) and (VI) of the IMF Articles of Agreement, *http://www.imf.org*. (Accessed June 8, 2011).

[2] See IMF: Lending by the IMF at *http://www.imf.org/external/about/lending.htm*. (Accessed June 8, 2011).

[3] See IMF: Lending by the IMF at *http://www.imf.org/external/about/lending.htm*. (Accessed June 8, 2011).

has been reserved for the World Bank Group. Thus, the Fund is not concerned with project financing, although it has responded to certain development related balance of payments problems.

BALANCE OF PAYMENTS PROBLEM

**9-002**  There is no definition in Fund law of what constitutes a country's "balance of payments". There is some evidence to suggest it might have been deliberate, given the difficulty in arriving at a satisfactory definition.[4] The general assumption is that the reference is to an accounting balance,[5] concerned with a State's accounting balance, i.e. the national account, with a record of the economic transactions during a given period, between its "residents" and "residents" of the rest of the world. This is confirmed in an authoritative Fund publication on balance of payments itself.[6] This publication is issued as a guide to members when making their regular reports on their balance of payments.

> **2.12** *The balance of payments is a statistical statement that summarizes transactions between residents and nonresidents during a period. It consists of the goods and services account, the primary income account, the secondary income account, the capital account, and the financial account.* Under the double-entry accounting system that underlies the balance of payments, each transaction is recorded as consisting of two entries and the sum of the credit entries and the sum of the debit entries is the same.[7]

The balance of payments comprises of different accounts recording different types of economic transactions. The Current Account comprises the goods and services account, which reflects the difference between exports and imports in goods and services; as well as the primary income account and secondary income account.[8] The primary income account "shows amounts payable and receivable in return for providing temporary use to another entity of labor, financial resources, or nonproduced nonfinancial assets".[9] The secondary income account comprises transfer payments. These comprise of transactions which have no quid pro quo, e.g. aid. The balance in the

---

[4]  See J.K. Horsefield, *The IMF 1945–1965* (Washington D.C.: IMF, 1969) Vol.II, p.581.
[5]  See also Executive Board Decision No.71–2 in *Selected Decisions of the IMF*, 22nd Issue (1997).
[6]  See *IMF Balance of Payments and International Investment Position Manuel*, 6th edn (Washington D.C., IMF, 2009).
[7]  IMF *Balance of Payments and International Investment Position Manuel*, 6th edn (Washington D.C., IMF, 2009) para.212.
[8]  IMF *Balance of Payments and International Investment Position Manuel*, 6th edn (Washington D.C., IMF, 2009) para.214.
[9]  IMF *Balance of Payments and International Investment Position Manuel*, 6th edn (Washington D.C., IMF, 2009) para.214.

current account is referred to as the current account balance.[10] The capital account is a record of capital transactions consisting of "nonproduced non financial assets" and liabilities—essentially, representing its wealth or capital as opposed to its income, and includes capital transfers between residents and non-residents. The financial account is a record of the "net acquisition and disposal of financial assets and liabilities" for example, portfolio investment.

The balance that is of principal concern is the balance of payments on current account. From an accounting point of view, as a matter of double-entry book-keeping, this account always balances, since it is axiomatic that a country cannot spend what it cannot afford. The disequilibrium that is expressed as of concern in the Articles of Agreement, is with reference to an economic balance in the Current Account, within the overall balance of payments.[11] Economic transactions in this balance may be classified as follows. One class of transaction is viewed as representing the national income of the State. The other constitutes of settlement[12] items which operate to finance any deficit or shortage that may arise in the first class of transactions. These settlement items are also in a sense a measure of the wealth or capital of the State. The critical point of balance is between these two types of transactions. Underlying the division lays the basic fact that a State cannot, for a long period, allow its expenditure to exceed its income.

The nature of this disequilibrium that is of concern is a deficit, and from the perspective of the Fund's mandate, one that partakes of a temporary balance of payments problem.[13] It is in this sense also that economists conceive of equilibrium and disequilibrium.[14]

> "The Executive Directors of the International Monetary Fund interpret the Articles of Agreement to mean that authority to use the resources of the Fund is limited to use in accordance with its purposes to give temporary assistance in financing balance of payments deficits on current account for monetary stabilization operations."[15]

The balance of payments is not entirely an economic phenomenon. It is in fact, as Machlup puts it, disequilibrium with "built-in-politics" or "disguised politics".[16] Further, economists are divided as to the correct method          **9-003**

---

[10] IMF *Balance of Payments and International Investment Position Manuel*, 6th edn (Washington D.C., IMF, 2009) para.215.

[11] Executive Board Decision No.71–2 in *Selected Decisions of the IMF*.

[12] See, for example, G. Meir, *International Economics: The Theory of Policy* (Macmillan, 1980), p.138.

[13] Executive Board Decision No.102–(2/11) February 13, 1952 in *Selected Decisions of the IMF*.

[14] See, for example, A.P. Thirlwell, *Balance of Payments Theory and the UK Experience* (London, The Macmillan Press, 1980), p.5.

[15] Pursuant to Decision No.71–2, September 26, 1946, *http://www.imf.org*. (Accessed June 8, 2011).

[16] F. Machlup, *International Monetary Economics* (London, Allen & Unwin, 1970), Ch.V, p.110.

of analysing the balance of payments. The difference of opinion is between conceiving equilibrium in a normative sense, and in a value free sense.[17] By equilibrium in a normative sense is meant a conception of a desired balance of payments equilibrium that includes certain objectives, e.g. levels of inflation and employment. These objectives are based on value judgments as to what is a desirable state of affairs. The equilibrium is normative because with regard to these objectives it "dictates" a certain course of action.[18] In contrast, balance of payments equilibrium in a value free sense is an equilibrium which does not have incorporated therein other value derived objectives; and is concerned solely with balancing the account. The point of interest for the lawyer is whether the concept as used in the Articles is purely neutral and descriptive, or in fact evaluative and normative.

The Articles of Agreement refer to equilibrium with a normative orientation. The equilibrium is normative because it tends to urge a course of action that is infused with social goals.[19] However, the precise social goals incorporated formally into the concept of equilibrium by the Articles of Agreement and generally in the Fund law are somewhat elusive. Article 1(v) sheds some light in its proscription of a current account equilibrium, resulting from national measures that are destructive of national or international prosperity. A current account equilibrium by force of abstention that is detrimental to "national and international prosperity" will constitute a balance of payments disequilibrium or problem.

The objectives of "national and international prosperity" in Art.I(V) encapsulate the aims of the Fund, as stated in Art.1, and the Agreement as a whole. They may also, however, incorporate a wider set of objectives to include, for example, inflation, employment, growth, the absence of restrictions over capital transaction,[20] the equitable distribution of wealth, and even arguably sustainable development. These however are not identical to those stipulated as such in Art.1. Thus, although the guidance contained in Art.1(V) of measures destructive of national and international prosperity infuses some clarity into the equilibrium conditions, it is nevertheless also of panoramic scope. It raises the question whether States have delegated to the IMF such a *carte blanche* of social objectives to legislate—through the Fund's notion of balance of payments equilibrium.

**9-004**     Given that the precise balance and optimum level of the equilibrium conditions is not clear, the determination of the existence of a balance of payments problem can be a matter of judgment, as much as statistical data. The

[17] A.P. Thirlwall, *Balance of Payments Theory*, 2nd edn (London, Macmillan, 1982), p.30.
[18] See, for example, G. Meir International Economics (1980) at p.144; A.P. Thirlwell (1982), p.20.
[19] Machlup (1970), pp.111–112.
[20] See, for example, T. Killick, *Extent, Causes and Consequences of Disequilibria in Developing Countries. ODI Working Paper*, No.1; Meier (1980), p.145; M. Guitian, "Fund Conditionality. Evolution of Principles and Practices", IMF *Pamphlet Series* No.38, p.25; J. Williamson, *The lending policies of the IMF* (Washington D.C., Institute for International Economics, 1982), p.11.

exercise of the judgment must, however, be set within the parameters of the potential of the particular economy, its economic characteristics, and importantly the stage of its economic development. Thus, the levels of employment, inflation and economic growth acceptable will vary according to the different States involved—in particular their level of development. In addition to the judgmental element infused by the "normative conditions" of the balance of payments, the assessment of the balance of payments statistical data also needs to be accompanied by a qualitative appraisal of the State's economy, set against the background of any special circumstances which may have a bearing on the interpretation of the statistics; and in the light of developments in the national and international economy.[21]

The circumstances that constitute balance of payments problems are also revealed through the various decisions of the Fund establishing special financial facilities for different types of balance of payments problems.[22] These special policies are in response in some measure to the dictates of normative conditions infused in the Fund concept of balance of payments problem. Thus, the Extended Fund Facility emphasises the objective of development. Similarly, the late Compensatory Financing Facility[23] focused on fluctuations in the cost of cereal imports in response to "basic needs", to alleviate the possible hardship resulting from the lack of accessibility to an essential commodity.

The further emergence of special facilities would be directed at the normative goals with which the Fund's concept of equilibrium is infused. This is the pressure point for countries to realise some of their social goals. The establishment of special facilities will, albeit haphazardly, lead to further elucidation of the Fund's concept of balance of payments equilibrium.

Insofar as the actual presentation of the balance of payments account is concerned, two points may be made. First, the statistics involved may not necessarily accurately reflect the true state of the transactions involved. There may be inaccuracies or misrepresentations. Secondly, the selection of the items and their classification, particularly in borderline cases, is very often a matter of judgment. Thus, it can be difficult to determine items which are compensatory and those which are not.[24]

Generally the causes of balance of payments problems are varied. They may be due to external reasons, e.g. terms of trade shocks such as increase in price of oil; acts of God; currency speculation; or indeed a global financial crisis. Alternatively (or in conjunction) they may be internal, e.g. due to

---

[21] See IMF *Balance of Payments and International Investment Position Manuel*, 6th edn (Washington D.C.: IMF, 2009). See also *IMF Balance of Payments and International Investment Manual* (2007). See also P. Host-Madsen, IMF *Pamphlet Series* No.9, p.16.

[22] See, for example, the Executive Board Decisions establishing the non-concessional facilities, viz. the Extended Fund facility; Supplemental Reserve Facility; and the Compensatory and Contingency Financing Facility; and the concessional facilities for low-income countries, viz. the Poverty Reduction and Growth Facility (PRGF) and Exogenous Shocks Facility.

[23] Now abolished. See Decision No. 14282-(09/29), March 24, 2009.

[24] See, for example, Meir (1980), p.138; and the IMF *Balance of Payments and International Investment Position Manuel*, 6th edn (Washington D.C., IMF, 2009).

economic mismanagement, viz. incorrect exchange rate policy, misguided tax incentives, inappropriate investment policy, excessive imports, falling commodity prices, outward flight of capital, post conflict circumstances, economic transitions to market based economic systems, poverty reduction and sovereign debt reduction.[25] They may be temporary, e.g. short-term cyclical drop in exports; or permanent—due to structural disorders in the economy. The symptoms of balance of payments disequilibrium can be inflation, excessive aggregate demand, and fiscal imbalance, i.e. excessive public expenditure.

## FINANCING FOR BALANCE OF PAYMENTS DISEQUILIBRIUM

**9-005**     Financial assistance for balance of payments adjustment is available from a number of sources, including the IMF. Sources other than the IMF, include commercial banks operating in the euro-currency market[26]; official lenders such as development banks; central bank swaps; regional assistance, for example from the EU; the issuing of bonds in a foreign currency; and country loans, increasingly for example from China.[27] Development bank financing normally is long term, and involves typically project financing. Central bank swaps, on the other hand, tend to be very short term.[28]

However, despite these other sources, there is still an important need for an international institution, such as the IMF, to be involved in balance of payment adjustment. The IMF is well placed to arrive at informed decisions as to the State of an economy, and to ensure the implementation of corrective economic policies. Further, it enjoys the confidence of the private sector in its approach to balance of payments problems, so as to act as a catalyst for private sources of financing.[29] In addition, non-IMF/non-official sources of funding can raise some concerns, from which the fund does not suffer.[30] First, financing may not be available to all States; and when it is it may delay adjustment, because it is not necessarily accompanied by the rigours of financial and economic discipline that must accompany the financing of balance of payments disequilibrium. Secondly, such financing is determined on the basis of an imperfect understanding of the state of an economy. Further, a lack of co-ordination amongst lenders can distort the behaviour of lenders, and their perception of borrowers. Thirdly, only a premier multilateral lending institu-

---

[25] E. Denters, *Law and Policy of IMF Conditionality* (The Hague, Kluwer Law International, 1996), p.5. See also IMF: Lending by the IMF at *http://www.imf.org/external/about/lending. htm.* (Accessed June 8, 2011).

[26] A Euro-currency market is a market wherein currencies are available on a commercial basis. The currencies traded are not the currencies of the State where they are made available.

[27] i.e. a form of fixed interest security.

[28] P.R. Mason and M. Mussa, "The role of the IMF", IMF *Pamphlet Series* No.50 (1995), p.23.

[29] Mason and Mussa (1995).

[30] Mason and Mussa (1995).

tion such as the IMF can raise the large amounts that can be necessary to address modern global challenges such as the recent financial crisis. Finally, the difficulty of enforcing loan contracts against sovereign borrowers can inhibit private sovereign lending.

The IMF makes financial resources available to its members on a temporary and individual basis, upon a request by a member for such assistance, in order to alleviate the member's balance of payments disequilibrium.[31] Depending on eligibility the assistance can be availed either on a non-concessional or concessional basis. Moreover, the normal apparatus for the imparting of the Fund's resources is through a Stand-by or similar arrangement.

The Regular Facilities (viz., non-concessional lending) are made available through the General Resources Account, whereas the concessional assistance for developing members is made through the Poverty Reduction and Growth Trust.[32] The manner and conditions under which the financial resources are made available through the various facilities varies according to the source and account from which they are made available.[33]

## THE OPERATION OF THE GENERAL RESOURCES ACCOUNT

The General Resources Account from which the non-concessional financial resources are made available to a member comprises:                                                    **9-006**

   (i)  currencies of the Fund's members (including securities);

  (ii)  SDR holdings; and

 (iii)  gold.

The sources of revenue of the General Resources Account are primarily subscriptions and borrowed resources. The Fund has borrowed from the major industrialised countries under the General Arrangements to Borrow (GAB).[34] The GAB is essentially a line of credit from 11 industrialised States made under certain conditions. The Executive Board has also approved another borrowing arrangement (the New Arrangements to Borrow (NAB)),[35] under which some 39 members[36] stand ready to lend to the IMF, in order to deal with a situation that impairs the international monetary system, or that

---

[31] Arts 1 (V) and (VI). See also Art.V.

[32] See EB Decision 14354-(09/79), July 23, 2009, effective January 7, 2010.

[33] See below.

[34] Established in 1962. See also Art.VII, s.1 and Executive Board Decision No.1289–(62/1) as amended in *Selected Decisions*. The GAB has been renewed for another five years from 2008.

[35] Executive Board Decision No.11428–(97/6) January 1997 as amended. NAB became effective in 1998. Renewed for another five years from 2008.

[36] See IMF Factsheet IMF Standing Borrowing Arrangements April 2011.

threatens its stability. It should be noted here that the capacity of the IMF to borrow is not limited to borrowing from members, non-Member States or other official sources.[37]

Financial resources are made available at the initiation of a member by way of a drawing.[38] Drawings may be made under the Regular Facilities or Special Policies; where applicable through a Stand-by or similar arrangement. The drawing is made by way of a purchase and the Fund supplies by selling, normally freely usable currencies.[39] The purchasing by the member and the selling of the same by the Fund is in exchange for an equivalent amount of the member's own currency.[40] The exchanged currency of the drawing member is owned absolutely by the Fund. The whole operation is known as a transaction[41] and results in an increase of the Fund's holdings of the drawing member's currency, and a decrease in its holdings of currencies that are drawn.

Although the entitlement to purchase is at the initiative of the member, the member cannot without more proceed to purchase. The member has to make a request for a purchase and represent that it has a need to make the purchase because of its balance of payments or reserve position or developments in its reserves.[42] The Fund determines "whether the proposed purchase would be consistent with the provisions" of the Agreement "and the policies adopted under it".[43] The actual purchase or sale transaction is conducted by a process of debiting and crediting the Fund and the member's accounts respectively. The computation of the value of the currencies exchanged is in terms of SDR, i.e. the exchange rate between the two currencies that corresponds to their exchange rates in terms of SDRs. Ultimately, the exchanges involved in a transaction reflect the market exchange rates.[44]

Drawings can take place through an immediate/direct drawing, or under the framework of an arrangement between the IMF and the member such as a Stand-by or similar arrangement.[45] An immediate drawing is where a purchase is facilitated immediately, i.e. not by way of an available future line of credit. A "Stand-by arrangement" is defined as a decision of the Fund by which a member is given an assurance that the member will be able without more to enter into a purchase, sale or exchange, transaction provided the member makes these in accordance with stipulated terms.[46] A Stand-by arrangement

---

[37] IMF *Survey* (September 1997).
[38] Generally, to draw is to receive money. See Collins, *English Gem Dictionary* (London/Glasgow, Collins, 1966).
[39] Art.V, ss.2(a) and 3(b), (d) and (e).
[40] But see Ch.10, below.
[41] Art.XXX(h).
[42] Art.V, s.3(II).
[43] Art.V, s.3(c).
[44] Art.V, s.10(a).
[45] Executive Board Decision No.102–(5211) February 1952; Guidelines on Conditionality; Stand-By Arrangements Decision No.12865–(02/102) September 25, 2002 as amended. See also Art.V, s.2(3)(a).
[46] Art.XXX(b). See also Ch.10, below.

is normally embodied in two documents,[47] viz. the Stand-by arrangement and the Letter of Intent. Members may also submit Side Letters containing confidential information.[48] The Letter of Intent contains both the request for a drawing by the member, and also the member's adjustment programme that it proposes to follow. The Letter of Intent emanates from the Member State. The response of the Fund is contained in a document known as the Stand-by or similar arrangement, as the case may be. This is a decision of the Fund to grant the request and incorporates the Letter of Intent by reference.

### Guidelines on Conditionality[49]

10. Members program documents. The authorities policy intentions will be described in documents such as a Letter of Intent (LOI), or a Memorandum on Economic and Financial Policies (MEFP) that may be accompanied by a Technical Memorandum of Understanding (TMU). These documents will be prepared by the authorities, with the cooperation and assistance of the Fund staff, and will be submitted to the Managing Director for circulation to the Executive Board. The documents should reflect the authorities policy goals and strategies. In addition to conditions specified in these documents, members requesting the use of Fund resources may in exceptional cases communicate confidential policy understandings to the Fund in a side letter addressed to the Managing Director and disclosed to the Executive Board. In all their program documents, the authorities should clearly distinguish between the conditions on which the Fund's financial support depends and other elements of the program. Detailed policy matrices covering the broader agenda should be avoided in program documents such as LOIs and MEFPs unless they are considered necessary by the authorities to express their policy intentions.

**9-007**

The cost of purchase, in addition to the price for the exchange of the monetary assets, involves a charge imposed by the Fund.[50] Different kinds of charges are made, viz.:

**9-008**

- service charge[51];

- periodic charge[52];

- commitment charge on Stand-by and similar arrangements[53]; and

- special charges on the occasion of overdue repurchases.[54]

---

[47] EB 14407-(09/105), October 26, 2009.
[48] EB Decision No. 12067-(99/108), September 22, 1999.
[49] Decision No.12864–(02/102) September 25, 2002 as amended, *http:www//imf.org*. (Accessed June 8, 2011).
[50] Art.V, s.8.
[51] Art.V, s.8(a)(i) and Rule 1–1, IMF, *By-Laws Rules and Regulations*.
[52] Art.V, s.2(b).
[53] Art.V, s.8(a)(ii).
[54] Executive Board Decision No.8433–(86/175) in IMF *Selected Decisions*.

The level of charges levied varies according to the facilities under which a purchase is made.

The purchase, sale or exchange transaction is entered into under an obligation by the member to repurchase the Fund's holdings of its currency that result from the purchase, and that are subject to charges, not later than five years after the date of the purchase.[55] The Fund has discretion to allow longer periods of re-purchase.[56]

A member earns remuneration, i.e. interest, if the member has a creditor position in the Fund. Essentially, a member has a creditor position when the level of the member's currencies held by the Fund is less than the normal balance[57] of the member's currency the Fund should be holding.

In order to understand the purchase, sale or repurchase transaction it is necessary to understand the relationships between a member's quota, its subscription and the tranche system of calibration. Quotas determine the amount of access to financial resources in the General Resources Account.[58] The Board of Governors are to review every five years the need for a general review of quotas with a view to adjustment[59] in the light of global economic changes. The Fourteenth General Review of Quotas was completed in December 2010 which when approved and implemented will result in 100 per cent increase in quotas. A member's quota is equal to its subscription in the IMF.[60] Each member is required to pay a subscription upon joining the Fund, and augment its subscription every time there is a general quota review. The composition of a member's subscription to the Fund comprises 75 per cent of its own currency, and 25 per cent in the form of SDRs or other currencies.

By juxtaposing a member's quota and its subscription the Fund calibrates a member's access and the terms of access to the resources, through the measure of tranches. The tranches or segments run every 25 per cent. The first tranche is known as the reserve tranche, and the rest as credit tranches. A reserve tranche is defined as a purchase by a member which does not cause the Fund's holdings of the member's currency in the General Resources Account to exceed its quota.[61] Essentially, it is the first 25 per cent tranche of the member's quota which corresponds to the 25 per cent of its subscription, which is in the form of SDRs and other currencies held by the Fund.

---

[55] Art.V, s.7(c).

[56] Art.V, s.7(g).

[57] Art.V, s.9.

[58] See Art.III. See also Ch.5 on the determination of a member's quota.

[59] Art.III, s.2. See IMF *Factsheet*, March 2011.

[60] Art.III of the IMF Articles of Agreement.

[61] Article XXX of the IMF: "(c) Reserve tranche purchase means a purchase by a member of special drawing rights or the currency of another member in exchange for its own currency which does not cause the Fund's holdings of the member's currency in the General Resources Account to exceed its quota, provided that for the purposes of this definition the Fund may exclude purchases and holdings under: (iii) other policies on the use of its general resources in respect of which the Fund decides, by an eighty-five percent majority of the total voting power, that an exclusion shall be made".

The reserve tranche is considered to be part of a member's reserves because it represents the country's own currency in its subscription to the Fund, and therefore a member is able to draw on it at any time. The Fund cannot challenge the propriety of the user in the context of consistency with the Articles of Agreement. There is no obligation to repay nor are periodic charges imposed. This framework applies to all the membership availing itself of the Fund's resources generally unless otherwise stated. The tranches may be considered both as measures and as descriptions of the Fund's financial facilities.

The amount of the currency a member may draw may be either a reserve tranche purchase, or if not, one that would not cause the Fund's holdings of a member's currency to exceed 200 per cent of its quota.[62] The Fund has discretion to waive this upper quantitative limit and has exercised that discretion in relation to its various facilities. Generally, the conditions attached to drawings from the first credit tranche tend to be mild, whereas the conditions that accompany the upper credit tranche drawings tend to be more severe. A member may make a drawing from the upper credit tranches either immediately, or through the medium of Stand-by or extended arrangements.

## THE NON-CONCESSIONAL FACILITIES

The non-concessional financial resources available under the Regular **9-009** Facilities of the IMF for alleviating balance of payments problems of members are the normal "windows" through which the Fund makes available its resources to its membership. These facilities do not partake of preferential terms for low-income countries. Over the years these facilities have responded to various economic and non-economic concerns impacting on a member's balance of payments. In 2009, the facilities were further re-organised as part of the Fund's efforts to respond to global developments impacting on the demand of its resources, including the financial crisis.

Normally the drawings in the credit tranches are made available through Stand-by arrangements. A Stand-by arrangement is described in IMF literature as one of the non-concessional facilities for short-term balance of payments problems, although the Stand-by or similar arrangement can also be descriptive of the apparatus through which the Fund imparts its resources. The normal period for a Stand-by arrangement is between 12–18 months, but the period can be extended up to three years.[63]

---

[62] Article V Section 3: '(iii) the proposed purchase would be a reserve tranche purchase, or would not cause the Fund's holdings of the purchasing member's currency to exceed two hundred percent of its quota;..'
[63] See Decision No.12865–(02/102) September 25, 2002.

**STAND-BY ARRANGEMENTS[64]**

**9-010**

1. A representation of need by a member for a purchase requested under a stand-by arrangement will not be challenged by the Fund.

2. The normal period for a stand-by arrangement will range from 12 to 18 months. If a longer period is requested by a member and is considered necessary by the Fund to enable the member to implement its adjustment program successfully, the stand-by arrangement may extend beyond this range, up to a maximum of three years.

3. Phasing and performance clauses will be omitted in stand-by arrangements within the first credit tranche. They will be included in all other stand-by arrangements but will apply only to purchases outside the first credit tranche. For an arrangement within the first credit tranche, a member may be required to describe the general policies it plans to pursue, including its intention to avoid introducing or intensifying exchange and trade restrictions.

**9-011**    For special balance of payments problems identified[65] by the Fund in addition to the Stand-by arrangement, assistance is made available through Special Policies or Facilities. The special non-concessional assistance now mainly comprises the Flexible Credit Line[66] (FCL) and the Precautionary Credit Line[67] (PCL), both of which focus on crisis situations; the Trade Integration Mechanism (TIM) focusing on trade-related balance of payments problems[68]; and finally the Extended Fund Facility (EFF), which focuses on development related balance of payments problems.[69] The Stand-by, the EFF and the TIM have been available for some time, whereas the crisis related facilities are very recent developments.

**IMF Non-concessional Facilities:**

**9-012**    **FLEXIBLE CREDIT LINE (fcl) ARRANGEMENTS:** 1. The Fund decides that resources in the credit tranches may be made available under a Flexible Credit Line (FCL) arrangement, in accordance with the terms and conditions specified in this Decision. 2. An FCL arrangement shall be approved upon request in cases where the Fund assesses that the member (a) has very strong economic fundamentals and institutional policy frameworks, (b) is implementing-and has a sustained track record of implementing-very strong policies, and (c) remains committed to maintaining such policies in the future, all of which give confidence that the member will respond appropriately to the balance of payments difficulties that it is encountering or could encounter. In addition to a very positive assessment of the member's policies by the Executive Board in the context of the most recent Article IV consultations,

---

[64] Decision No.12865–(02/102) September 25, 2002, as amended *http://www.imf.org*. (Accessed June 8, 2011).

[65] Art.V, s.3(a). See below on the Regular and Special Facilities.

[66] EB Decision No. 14283-(09/29), March 24, 2009.

[67] See 2010 IMF Press Release No. 10/321.

[68] EB Decision No. 13229-(04/33), April 2, 2004, as amended.

[69] EB Decision 14287-(09/29), March 24, 2009.

the relevant criteria for the purposes of assessing qualification for an FCL arrangement shall include: (i) a sustainable external position; (ii) a capital account position dominated by private flows; (iii) a track record of steady sovereign access to international capital markets at favorable terms; (iv) a reserve position that is relatively comfortable when the FCL is requested on a precautionary basis; (v) sound public finances, including a sustainable public debt position; (vi) low and stable inflation, in the context of a sound monetary and exchange rate policy framework; (vii) the absence of bank solvency problems that pose an immediate threat of a systemic banking crisis; (viii) effective financial sector supervision; and (ix) data transparency and integrity. 3. In light of the qualification criteria set out in paragraph 2 of this Decision, and except for the review requirement specified in paragraph 5 of this Decision, FCL arrangements shall not be subject to performance criteria or other forms of ex-post program monitoring. 4. There shall be no phasing under FCL arrangements and, accordingly, the entire amount of approved access will be available to the member upon approval of an FCL arrangement. A member may make one or more purchases up to the amount of approved access at any time during the period of the FCL arrangement, subject to the provisions of this Decision. The Fund shall not challenge a representation of need by a member for a purchase requested under an FCL arrangement. Extracts from EB Decision No. 14283-(09/29), March 24, 2009

**EXTENDED FUND FACILITY:** I.(i) The Executive Directors have been considering the establishment of an extended facility for members that would enable the Fund to give medium-term assistance in the special circumstances of balance of payments difficulty that are indicated in this decision. The facility, in its formulation and administration, is likely to be beneficial for developing countries in particular.

(ii) The Executive Directors have noted the studies prepared by the staff, including SM/74/58 ("Extended Fund Facility," March 8, 1974), and especially paragraphs 12 to 16 of that memorandum, in which certain situations to which an extended facility could apply, are described as follows:(a) an economy suffering serious payments imbalance relating to structural maladjustments in production and trade and where prices and cost distortions have been widespread;(b) an economy characterized by slow growth and an inherently weak balance of payments position which prevents pursuit of an active development policy. Extracts from EB Decision 14287-(09/29), March 24, 2009.

**TRADE INTEGRATION MECHANISM:** 1. The Fund is prepared to provide financial assistance to members that are experiencing balance of payment difficulties as a result of trade liberalization measures undertaken by other countries. Such assistance shall be made available: (i) in the upper credit tranches under a Stand-by Arrangement, (ii) under the Extended Fund Facility, or (iii) under the Poverty Reduction and Growth Facility, and shall be subject to the general access limits established from time to time under such policies. Liberalization measures undertaken by other members would normally be limited to measures introduced either (i) under a WTO agreement or (ii) on a nondiscriminatory basis. 2. Financing under this decision may be provided to address the existing or anticipated balance of payments difficulties identified in paragraph 1 either at the time of the approval of an arrangement or completion of a program review under such an arrangement, upon the Fund's determination that the member is implementing economic adjustment policies that are designed to address the identified balance of payments problems. Extracts from EB Decision No. 13229-(04/33), April 2, 2004, as amended

**The IMF Precautionary Credit Line (PCL):** The new PCL is available to a wider group of members than those that qualify for the FCL. In practice, qualification is assessed in five broad areas, namely: (i) external position and market access, (ii) fiscal policy, (iii) monetary policy, (iv) financial sector soundness and supervision, and (v) data adequacy. While requiring strong performance in most of these areas, the PCL permits access to precautionary resources to members that may still have moderate vulnerabilities in one or two of these dimensions. Features of the PCL include: • Streamlined ex post conditions designed to reduce any economic vulnerabilities identified in the qualification process, with progress monitored through semi-annual program reviews. • Frontloaded access with up to 500 percent of quota made available on approval of the arrangement and up to a total of 1000 percent of quota after 12 months. Extract from 2010 IMF Press Release No. 10/321

The FCL has a pre-set qualification criteria focussing on members with "very strong fundamentals". It does not have normal access limits and the financial resources are available up-front. Thus, there is no conditionality as such. This facility is in response to the recent financial crisis to enable members to prevent a crisis or to respond to it. However, it will be noted the pre-set qualification is fairly stringent excluding many members. The PCL on the other hand, intended for crisis prevention alone, has a relatively less stringent pre-qualification requirement, as it focuses on "sound fundamentals" as opposed to "very strong fundamentals". Up to 1000 per cent of a member's quota is potentially available although only 500 per cent of this is available up-front. The rest is available subject to conditionality. The TIM makes available assistance under any of the non-concessional facilities to a developing member suffering from a balance of payments problem that is trade related viz., consequent upon multilateral trade liberalisation, where it has lost preferential access to certain markets, or where it has suffered price increases from food imports resulting from the elimination of agricultural subsidies.[70] It is not clear whether the TIM is not available for trade related balance of payments problems that arise from regional (contra multilateral) integration agreements given that these are discriminatory although arise as an exception under the WTO. Moreover, of note is that TIM is specific to two types of problems alone arising from multilateral trade liberalisation. Drawings under an extended arrangement can be made through the Extended Fund Facility for development related balance of payments problems. Extended arrangements are for longer periods than Stand-by arrangements—normally three years, involving larger amounts, and longer repayment periods.[71]

**9-013**     The Fund has also designed special policies on the manner in which the regular facilities or parts thereof may be used. First, there is provision for

---

[70]  *http://www.imf.org/external/about/lending.htm.* (Accessed June 8, 2011).
[71]  EB Decision No.4377–(74/114).

emergency assistance in the form of quick outright purchases in the event of natural disasters, such as floods, earthquakes, or hurricanes, which cannot be dealt with without serious implications for a member's external reserves.[72] Secondly, there is the provision for emergency assistance for post-conflict countries,[73] viz where the member's institutional and administrative capacity has been disrupted as a consequence of a conflict but nonetheless there remains a sufficient capacity for planning and policy implementation; and where there is an urgent balance of payments need.[74] This assistance is accompanied by an expectation that the member would engage thereafter in an adjustment programme under an upper-credit tranche Stand-by or extended arrangement, or an arrangement under the enhanced structural adjustment facility (ESAF).[75] The policies on emergency assistance are supplemented by the establishment of an emergency procedure for financial access under the framework of the Emergency Financing Mechanism,[76] so as to facilitate a rapid response from the Fund for member's facing crises in their external accounts. The natural disaster and post-conflict facilities have now been transformed into one Special Policy.[77]

In addition to these special policies there have been other facilities set up in the past but which are no longer available, for example the Systemic Transformation Facility, which was intended to assist members in the transition from a planned economy to a market-based economy[78]; the Buffer Stock Financing Facility intended to assist in the financing of contributions to international commodity stabilisation funds; the Oil Facility to assist in responding to international oil price rises; Compensatory and Contingency Financing Facility to address "balance of payments difficulties arising out of (i) temporary export shortfalls or (ii) excess costs of cereal imports"; and the Supplementary Reserve Facility set up to deal with the risk of contagion posing a potential threat to the international monetary system.

## Concessional Facilities

Concessional lending is made available on special terms to developing members facing difficult balance of payments circumstances (known as Concessional Facilities).[79] In 2010, reflecting the changing needs of low **9-014**

---

[72] See EB Meeting 82/16 February 10, 1982 and EB Decision No.12341–(00/117) November 28, 2000.
[73] EBM/95/82. See also Decision No.12341–(00/117) November 28, 2000.
[74] EBM/95/82. See also Decision No.12341–(00/117), November 28, 2000.
[75] EBM/95/82.
[76] EBM/95/85 in *Selected Decisions of the IMF*.
[77] EB Decision No.12341–(00/117) November 28, 2000.
[78] See also the Enlarged Access Policy and the Supplementary Financing Facility decision in IMF *Selected Decision*.
[79] See Art.V, s.12(ii).

income countries, the IMF re-organised the concessional facilities. These now comprise mainly the Extended Credit Facility (ECF)[80]; the Standby Credit Facility (SCF)[81]; the Rapid Credit Facility (RCF) set up under a newly established Poverty Reduction and Growth Trust.[82] The lending under these facilities is highly concessional, with no to minimal interest charges and higher lending amounts. Each of the facilities has its own particular balance of payments focus. Thus, the ECF is aimed at medium to longer term balance of payments problems. The SCF resembles[83] a non-concessional Stand-by arrangement with a short-term focus arising from domestic or external shocks. The RCF makes upfront lending available for urgent financial needs arising from post-conflict or other fragile circumstances.[84] In sum, the nature of the lending terms have been designed to respond to the global environment under which low income countries engage in the management of their balance of payments account—in terms of the level of access, the concessional nature of the terms, the time framework of the lending schedule, the timing of the availability of the funding, and the causes of the balance of payments difficulties. The various facilities embrace a diverse set of circumstances to reflect the differing kinds of problems faced by the diverse body of low income countries. The critical question is whether they are comprehensive enough in their identification of the diverse balance of payments problems faced by low-income countries; whether they are adequate in terms of amounts and whether the conditionality accompanying them is appropriate.

**IMF Concessional Facilities: Facilities set up under the Poverty Reduction and Growth Trust: ECF; SCF;RCF**

**9-015**     *Annex: Instrument to Establish the Poverty Reduction and Growth Trust*

*Introductory Section*

To help fulfill its purposes, the International Monetary Fund (here-inafter called the "Fund") has adopted this Instrument establishing the Poverty Reduction and Growth Trust (hereinafter called the "Trust"), which shall be administered by the Fund as Trustee (hereinafter called the "Trustee"). The Trust shall be governed by and administered in accordance with the provisions of this Instrument.

Section I. *General Provisions*

Paragraph 1. *Purposes*

The Trust shall assist in fulfilling the purposes of the Fund by providing:

(a) loans on concessional terms (hereinafter called "Trust loans") to low-income developing members that qualify for assistance under this Instrument, in order to:

---

[80] The ECF replaced the Poverty Reduction and Growth Facility.
[81] The SCF replaced the high access part of the Exogenous Shocks Facility's.
[82] EB Decision 14354-(09/79), July 23, 2009, effective January 7, 2010.
[83] IMF *Factsheet IMF Support for Low-Income Countries,* March 2011.
[84] IMF *Factsheet IMF Support for Low-Income Countries,* March 2011.

(i) support programs under the **Extended Credit Facility** (hereinafter called the "ECF") that enable members with a protracted balance of payments problem to make significant progress toward stable and sustainable macroeconomic positions consistent with strong and durable poverty reduction and growth;

(ii) support programs under the **Standby Credit Facility** (hereinafter called the "SCF") that enable members with actual or potential short-term balance of payment needs to achieve, maintain or restore stable and sustainable macroeconomic positions consistent with strong and durable poverty reduction and growth;

(iii) support policies under the **Rapid Credit Facility** (hereinafter called the "RCF") of members facing urgent balance of payment needs so as to enable them to make progress towards achieving or restoring stable and sustainable macroeconomic positions consistent with strong and durable poverty reduction and growth; and (iv) for a transitional period, support programs under the Exogenous Shocks Facility that help members to resolve their balance of payments difficulties whose primary source is a sudden and exogenous shock in a manner consistent with strong and durable poverty reduction and growth; and

(b) grants, for a transitional period, to subsidize post-conflict and/or natural disaster emergency assistance purchases under Decision No. 12341-(00/117) made by low-income developing members as of January 7, 2010, through transfers to the Post-Conflict and Natural Disaster Emergency Assistance Subsidy Account for PRGT Eligible members annexed to Decision No. 12481-(01/45) ("the ENDA/EPCA Subsidy Account"). Extracts from: EB Decision 14354-(09/79), July 23, 2009, effective January 7, 2010

The distinctive feature of these facilities is that they are available, unlike the facilities under the General Resources Account, only to low-income members. "Low-income countries" are defined essentially as those which are eligible for the World Bank's IDA loans and suffering from a protracted balance of payments problem.[85]

The resources from the Trust derive from loans and donations. The assistance is made available in the form of a loan, and not under a purchase, sale or repurchase transaction.[86] The loan is made in a freely usable currency, and the interest is to be paid in a freely usable currency or US dollars. The loan made under an ECF arrangement is accompanied by a Poverty Reduction Strategy Paper (PRSP), a document akin to the Letter of Intent in a Stand-by arrangement.

---

[85] For a list of the members eligible see list annexed to Decision 8240–(86/56) SAF as amended.
[86] See Executive Board Decision No.8759 ESAF December 18, 1987 as amended in *Selected Decisions of the IMF*.

### DEBT REDUCTION ASSISTANCE

**9-016**    The IMF supports the debt-reduction efforts of its indebted members in a number of ways. First, the Fund assists members in formulating adjustment programmes under Stand-by and extended arrangements that will facilitate rescheduling arrangements with commercial creditors in the framework of the London Club[87] and under the auspices of the Paris Club with official creditors.[88] In particular, the Fund has an established policy under which provision for support for debt and debt service reduction is available within the framework of Stand-by or extended arrangements.[89] Similarly, the Fund makes available an enhanced surveillance procedure[90] to a member at its request, to enable the Fund to monitor the member's macroeconomic and structural[91] policies, normally at the time of Art.IV consultations, on the basis of an economic policy programme. The procedure is intended to assist a member in its relations with commercial banks and official creditors.

**9-017**    **Summing Up by the Chairman-Biennial Review of the Fund's Surveillance Policy Executive Board Meeting 93/15, January 29, 1993. . .[92]**

The Executive Board agreed that the criteria relating to enhanced surveillance set out on pages 28 and 29 of SM/92/234 (below) would be appropriate. In sum, these provide that the procedures, which would normally be initiated by the authorities in the context of Article IV discussions, would involve submitting a quantified annual economic program, generally formulated with the assistance of the staff, and also half-yearly reports to the Board; both the Article IV reports (as appropriately modified) and the half-yearly reports could be made available to creditors. Application of the procedures would be approved by the Executive Board until the next Article IV consultation or for a 12-month period.

**9-018**    More recently the Fund has established the Policy Support Instrument (PSI).[93] Under this an eligible member can submit to the Fund an economic programme which the Fund will approve and oversee its implementation.

---

[87] Deals with restructuring of loans made by commercial banks to governments. See, for example, H. Morais, "Legal framework for dealing with sovereign debt defaults", in R. Effros (ed.), *Current Legal Issues Affecting Central Banks* (Washington D.C., IMF, 1998) Vol.5.

[88] The Paris Club is an informal group of OECD government creditors under the French Finance Ministry assisting in the restructuring of official debts. See, for example, Morais (1998).

[89] See "The Chairman's Summing Up on External Debt Management Policies", Executive Board Meetings 79/106 and 79/107, July 6, 1979 and Executive Board Meeting 79/121, July 23, 1979.

[90] See "Summing Up by the Chairman—Biennial Review of the Fund's Surveillance Policy", Executive Board Meeting 93/15, January 29, 1993.

[91] Refers to the infrastructure of the economy.

[92] Source: *http://www.imf.org.* (Accessed June 8, 2011).

[93] See EB Decision No.13561–(05/85) October 5, 2005. See also A.A. Eleso, "Understanding the Policy Support Instrument of the IMF" (2006) M.J.I.E.L., Vol.3, Issue 2, pp.44–66.

Engagement in the PSI is intended to act as a signal to potential private and multinational donors of the sound economic policies being pursued by the Member. The PSI is not accompanied with any financial assistance from the IMF. Thus, in 2005 the IMF approved Nigeria's request for a PSI which in turn enabled Nigeria to restructure its debts with its Paris Club creditors.[94]

### POLICY SUPPORT INSTRUMENT-FRAMEWORK[95]

*General*

1. Upon request, the Fund will be prepared to provide the technical services described in this Decision to members that are eligible for assistance under the Poverty Reduction and Growth Trust (PRGT), i.e., included in the list of members annexed to Decision No. 8240-(85/56), as amended, and that: (a) have a policy framework focused on consolidating macroeconomic stability and debt sustainability, while deepening structural reforms in key areas in which growth and poverty reduction are constrained; and (b) seek to maintain a close policy dialogue with the Fund, through the Fund's endorsement and assessment of their economic and financial policies under a Policy Support Instrument (PSI).

2. A PSI is a decision of the Executive Board setting forth a framework for the Fund's assessment and endorsement of a member's economic and financial policies. A PSI may be approved for a duration of one to three years, and may be extended up to an overall maximum period of four years.

**9-019**

Secondly, for heavily indebted poor countries (HIPCs), the Fund, in conjunction with the World Bank, has set up a programme of action to assist HIPCs so as to reduce their external debt burden levels to such a level as to enable them to service their debt through export earnings, aid and capital inflows.[96] The HIPC initiative is open to members eligible for PRGF-ESF and IDA funds; and following a programme of adjustment or reform. The HIPC initiative is financed through loans and grants under a Trust for Special Poverty Reduction and Growth Operations for the Heavily Indebted Poor Countries and Interim ECF Subsidy Operations (PRG-HIPC TRUST).[97] The IMF HIPC initiative is intended to run in conjunction and in parallel with initiatives for debt rescheduling from official creditors and other bilateral and commercial creditors. To date there have been some 36 countries that have had approved debt reduction packages.[98]

**9-020**

---

[94] See Eleso (2006).
[95] Extract from Decision No.13561–(05/85) October 5, 2005.
[96] See IMF Survey (September 1997) and Executive Board Decision No.11436–(97/10), as amended.
[97] Executive Board Decision No.11436–(97/10) as amended.
[98] IMF Debt Relief Under the Heavily Indebted Poor Countries (HIPC) Initiative *Factsheet,* March 2011.

**Paragraph 2.** *Purposes*

**9-021**    The Trust shall assist in fulfilling the purposes of the Fund by providing balance of payments assistance to low-income developing members by:

(a) making grants ("Trust grants") and/or loans ("Trust loans") to eligible members that qualify for assistance under the terms of this Instrument for purposes of the Initiative; and

(b) subsidizing the interest rate on interim PRGF operations to PRGF-eligible members.[99]

**How the HIPC Initiative works[100]**

**9-022**    **First step: decision point.** To be considered for HIPC Initiative assistance, a country must fulfill the following four conditions: 1) be eligible to borrow from the World Bank's International Development Agency, which provides interest-free loans and grants to the world's poorest countries, and from the IMF's Extended Credit Facility, which provides loans to low-income countries at subsidized rates. 2) face an unsustainable debt burden that cannot be addressed through traditional debt relief mechanisms.

3) have established a track record of reform and sound policies through IMF- and World Bank supported programs4) have developed a Poverty Reduction Strategy Paper (PRSP) through a broad-based participatory process in the country. Once a country has met or made sufficient progress in meeting these four criteria, the Executive Boards of the IMF and World Bank formally decide on its eligibility for debt relief, and the international community commits to reducing debt to a level that is considered sustainable. This first stage under the HIPC Initiative is referred to as the decision point. Once a country reaches its decision point, it may immediately begin receiving interim relief on its debt service falling due.

**Second step: completion point.** In order to receive full and irrevocable reduction in debt available under the HIPC Initiative, a country must:1) establish a further track record of good performance under programs supported by loans from the IMF and the World Bank.2) implement satisfactorily key reforms agreed at the decision point 3) adopt and implement its PRSP for at least one year. Once a country has met these criteria, it can reach its completion point, which allows it to receive the full debt relief committed at decision point.

**9-023**    The HIPC initiative is now augmented with the Multilateral Debt Relief Initiative (MDRI).[101] Both initiatives have been established under Art.V, s.2(b) of the IMF Articles. The MDRI initiative includes countries eligible for the HIPC Initiative, and is intended to further the UN Millennium Development Goals. Under the MDRI full debt relief is given with respect to debt outstanding to the IMF as of December 31, 2004.

---

[99]  Extract from Executive Board Decision No.11436–(97/10) as amended.
[100]  IMF Debt Relief Under the Heavily Indebted Poor Countries (HIPC) Initiative *Factsheet,* March 2011.
[101]  See Decision No.13588–(05/99) MDRI November 23, 2005, effective January 5, 2006.

**"How is the IMF implementing the MDRI?**

In deciding to implement the MDRI, the IMF Executive Board modified the **9-024** original G-8 proposal to fit the requirement, specific to the IMF, that the use of the IMF's resources be consistent with the principle of uniformity of treatment. Thus, it was agreed that all countries with per-capita income of US$380 a year or less (whether HIPCs or not) will receive MDRI debt relief financed by the IMF's own resources through the MDRI-I Trust. HIPCs with per capita income above that threshold will receive MDRI relief from bilateral contributions administered by the IMF through the MDRI-II Trust.

MDRI relief covers the full stock of debt owed to the IMF at end-2004 that remains outstanding at the time the country qualifies for such relief. There is no provision for relief of debt disbursed after January 1, 2005."[102]

## LEGAL CHARACTERISATION OF THE UNDERLYING TRANSACTION WITHIN WHICH IMF FINANCING IS SET

There are mainly two aspects to this focus. First, whether in legal analysis **9-025** a drawing under the General Resources Account is a "loan". Secondly, whether the drawing results in an international agreement between the IMF and the member. Although both questions appear to have been resolved in the IMF jurisprudence, it is nevertheless of importance to reflect upon some of the assumptions underlying the IMF characterisations, and the policy considerations that have led to those conclusions.

### Is a drawing under the General Resources Account a "loan"?

There are no official IMF interpretations on this point. Successive legal advis- **9-026** ers from the IMF Legal Department have maintained in their writings that the purchase, sale or repurchase transaction is not in legal analysis a loan.[103]

---

[102] IMF MDRI *Factsheet,* March 2011, *http://www.imf.org.*
[103] See, for example, J.E.S. Fawcett, "The Place of Law in an International Organization" (1960) XXXVI B.Y.I.L. 32, 339; J.E.S. Fawcett, "The IMF and International Law" (1964) XL B.Y.I.L. 33, 68; J.E.S. Fawcett, "Trade and Finance in International Law" (1968) 1 R.D.C. 219, 233; J. Gold, *The International Monetary Fund and International Law,* IMF *Pamphlet Series* No.4 (1965), p.23; J. Gold, *The Stand-by Arrangement of the International Monetary Fund* (1970), p.7; J. Gold, *Financial Assistance by the International Monetary Fund,* IMF *Pamphlet Series* No.27 (1980), p.10; J. Gold, "Balance of Payments Transactions of the International Monetary Fund" in R.S. Rendell (ed.), *International Financial Law: Lending Capital, Transfers and Institutions* (1980), Ch.1; J. Gold, "Transformations of the IMF" (1981) 20(2) *Colombia Journal of International Law* 227; S.A. Silard, "Money and Foreign Exchange" (1975) *International Encyclopedia of Comparative Law,* Vol.XVII (*State and Economy*), Ch.20, p.97; G.R. Delaume, *Legal Aspects of International Lending and Economic Development Financing* (Oobbs Ferry, N.Y., Oceana, 1967), p.98; F. Gianviti, "The International Monetary Fund and External Debt" (1989) *Recueil Des Cours* Vol.III, p.225.

Outside observers have absorbed such conclusions.[104] They have however all conceded that the transaction in economic analysis is a loan.[105]

The transaction has the economic effect of a loan because there is an imbalance in the contribution made by the requesting member to the Fund. The excess in contribution by the Fund is the financial assistance a member receives. To the economist, to purchase is to use Fund resources currently, with an obligation to repay (repurchase) in future. Charges are like interest rates.[106] The transaction is a loan in the economic sense however only in so far as the drawings are beyond the reserve tranche.

The principal reasons why the transaction is not considered in legal analysis a loan have been variously asserted as follows[107]:

- the purchasing member pays with an equivalent amount of its own currency for currency it purchases at market value;
- the Articles of Agreement avoid the language of a loan;
- the selling by the Fund of a member's currency can have the effect of terminating a member's obligations to repurchase; and
- a loan is necessarily a contractual transaction.[108]

However, it is maintained here that not only is a drawing in economic analysis a loan but it is so in legal analysis also. First, there is no equivalence in the "value" of the currencies exchanged. The exchange is made by reference to the market exchange rate, but only as a guide in calibrating the amount of assistance entitled. The fact that the market rate is used does not imply that there is equality in the value of the exchange as such. The worth of the currency "purchased" is significantly more. The quality and characteristics it has are not the same as the member's own currency. It is precisely because of this difference in "value", that the member resorts to the Fund, and not outside. Further, the rates of the charges imposed by the Fund can be less than the market interest rates.[109] In addition, Art.V, s.4 of the IMF Articles of Agreement formally acknowledges this imbalance, by authorising the Fund

---

[104] See, for example, A. Nussbaum, *Money in the Law—National and International* (Brooklyn: The Foundation Press Inc, 1950), Ch.3, p.537; F. Mann, "Money in Public International Law" (1959) 1 R.D.C., Ch.II, pp.23–25; L. Focsaneanu, "Les Aspects Juridique du System Monetaire International" (1968) *Journal du Droit International* Paris, Clunet, 95, 239, 253; D. Carreau, *Soverainete et Cooperation Monetaire International* (Paris), pp.405–406; D. Carreau, et al., "Chronique de Droit International Economique" (Paris, 1968) *Annuaire Francais de Droit International*, pp.554-563; R.M. Lastra, *Legal Foundations of International Monetary Stability* (Oxford, Oxford University Press, 2006), p.410.

[105] See, for example, Delaume (1967).

[106] IMF *Pamphlet Series* No.37 at p.31.

[107] IMF *Pamphlet Series* No.37 at p.31.

[108] J. Gold, *Interpretation: The IMF and International Law* (Kluwer Law International, 1997), p.369.

[109] Rules and Regulations of the International Monetary Fund: I—CHARGES IN RESPECT OF GENERAL RESOURCES ACCOUNT TRANSACTIONS AND REMUNERATION

to require a pledge as collateral security of assets that are of sufficient value in the Fund's view to protect the Fund's interests—over and above the currency obtained of the member—where a waiver of IMF conditions is asked for.

In reality the member does not "pay" in its own currency. It "exchanges" its own currency in lieu of the currency sought. A sale transaction normally involves payment by money.[110] An exchange or barter is where there is no money involved.[111] Whether the transaction is a sale or an exchange or barter is to be considered by ascertaining whether the member's currency is operating as money on the international plain. In other words, does the member's currency function as money, that is to say, as a medium of exchange, or is it the object of commercial intercourse?[112]

At the international level, a member resorting to the IMF has a currency that has lost, or is losing vis-à-vis the currency sought, the function as a medium of exchange. It is for this reason that the member is resorting to the Fund. In view of this, to maintain that the member's currency is operating as a medium of exchange in its particular dealing with the Fund is illusory. Some support may be sought for this in Art.V, s.3(b). This Article does not refer to a member "paying" in an equivalent amount of its own currency; rather it refers to the member engaging in an "exchange" of equivalent amount of its own currency.

Conversely, the money acquired by the member is money, and not a commodity. To reiterate, a "commodity" is defined as that which is the object of commercial intercourse, and money is that which functions as a medium of exchange.[113] If what is involved is money then the transaction is a loan. If it is a commodity then it is not a loan, as a loan transaction involves the use of money. The question "what is money" is generally a legal one.[114] Money is a creature of the State, or more accurately here, "the legal basis for the definition of the basic monetary unit of Fund members"[115] is International Law. In fact, money can have a varying degree of legal character.

The international economy lacks a currency of its own as such.[116] SDRs **9-027** approximate somewhat but they are as yet underdeveloped, and of limited use. Money on the international plain is that which is accepted as such by States. Because of the lack of an international currency, States are forced to use certain national currencies as substitutes.[117] Money on the international

---

[110] See, for example, F. Mann, *The Legal Aspects of Money* (Oxford, Oxford University Press, 1982), p.1.

[111] See, for example, F. Mann, *The Legal Aspects of Money* (Oxford, Oxford University Press, 1982), p.1.

[112] See, for example, F. Mann, *The Legal Aspects of Money* (Oxford, Oxford University Press), p.191.

[113] Mann (1982), Ch.1; and A. Nussbaum, *Money in the Law. National and International* (1950).

[114] J.M. Keynes, *Pure Theory of Money* (London, Macmillan), Vol.I, Ch.I, p.13. See also Knapp, *The State Theory of Money* (London, Macmillan), Ch.1.

[115] H. Aufricht, "The Fund Agreement and the Legal Theory of Money" (1959) 9–10 *Osterreichische Zeitschrift fur Offentliches recht* 26, 32–33.

[116] See, for example, Mann (1982) Pt IV, Ch.XXI, p.531.

[117] See, for example, Mann (1982) Pt IV, Ch.XXI, p.531.

terrain is not entirely a creature of law as it is in the municipal law—it is, however, heading in that direction and does have a certain measure of legal quality. This quality has been bestowed by the Fund to the foreign exchange Member States seek from the Fund. This foreign exchange has a specific quality. It must be a freely usable currency.[118] In a practical sense this money transposes the function domestic money performs at the municipal level on the international plain.[119] Foreign money within the domestic jurisdiction is money where it functions as such i.e. as a medium of exchange.[120] There is no reason why the freely usable currency on the international level should not be classified as money, if it functions in the same way. The currency obtained by a State from the Fund amounts to receipt of purchasing power. Purchasing power is the essence of money.[121]

On the international terrain the foreign currency is operating as a medium of exchange. It cannot be bought as a commodity, since this would involve paying in money i.e. money on the international plain. There is no money other than the foreign exchange here—therefore there is nothing with which to pay. The foreign currency that is tendered is a medium of exchange. In a loan transaction money operates as a medium of exchange. Further, money is exchanged for the promise or obligation to repay (repurchase)—in money and not in the form of a commodity. The obligation to repurchase is central to the revolving character of the use of Fund resources, and is inextricably tied to the availability of the resources.[122] Thus, use by a member of Fund resources other than "reserve tranche purchases" constitutes money use, and the repurchase is a repayment of money, i.e. money at the international level, in the form of freely usable currency, and not a commodity. A drawing member repays the Fund currency, normally freely usable currency that is acceptable to the Fund.

If the currency purchased and the currency returned (in the purchase) was a commodity, then the transaction would be barter, and not a purchase or sale transaction. This is because for the purposes of a sale transaction, money is the medium of exchange. The drawing is not however a barter. "Barter" is defined as the "simultaneous exchange of commodities against commodities", while a sale is the "simultaneous exchange of commodities against a specified amount of money".[123] The fact that the Articles of Agreement describe the transaction as a "sale" transaction is recognition that there is indeed money that is involved in the transaction—or else as stated above, the whole transaction would be a reversible barter transaction.

Secondly, whilst the obligation to repurchase can be extinguished,[124] for

---

[118] Art.XXX (f) of the IMF Articles of Agreement.
[119] See, for example, S.A. Silard, *Money and Foreign Exchange in International Encyclopaedia of Comparative Law* (State and Economy, 1975), Vol.XVII, Ch.20.
[120] Mann (1982), pp.179–219.
[121] Mann (1982), Ch.I, p.26.
[122] Art.V, s.7 of the IMF Articles of Agreement.
[123] H. Aufricht, "The Fund Agreement and the Legal Theory of Money" (1959) 9–10 *Osterreichiche Zeitschrift fur offentliches recht* 26, 32–33.
[124] See Art.V, ss.7 and 8(b).

example by the Fund selling the member's currency in other transactions—this does not detract from the fact that there is an obligation to repurchase—albeit one that may be discharged. In the same way an obligation to repay in a loan transaction may be waived without affecting the character of the transaction.

Thirdly, all analysis stems from a literal interpretation of Art.V. The assumption implicit is that this problem of characterisation is exclusively a matter of treaty interpretation.[125] The relevant question, however, relates to the overall consequence of the transaction, and its characterisation in International Law. This task involves an evaluation of all the relevant factors; and Art.V is in this overall scheme only one factor. In this context, there are two issues of particular note. First, what is a loan? Secondly, what is a loan in International Law?

The concept of the loan exists both in law and economics—however it **9-028** does not exist in isolation in economic analysis. Not only is there a core of meaning common to the disciplines—but the disciplines are interdependent in their conception. This is because, if the etymology of "loan" is investigated, it will be found that the transaction is rooted in the institution of the law. In economic analysis a loan normally has the following characteristics[126]: (i) a promise; (ii) to allow at present the use of financial resources i.e. the benefit; (iii) with an obligation to pay in future; (iv) normally with interest (i.e. the price for the use of the resources currently). Thus, first there is the "promise" to allow the use and an "obligation" to return. Secondly, the subject-matter is "money"—a creature of the law.[127]

Applying this common analysis a member is receiving from the Fund that benefit which is of the essence of a loan, namely the present use of foreign currencies. This benefit is enough to alter the complexion of the transaction from a sale (which is more of a value for value affair, without an obligation to reverse) to a loan (where the member is receiving in the first instance more from the Fund than it has contributed in economic terms). The Fund is imparting purchasing power to the member of a kind that the member is not imparting to the Fund. In a loan transaction too, purchasing power is imparted without at that time a similar reciprocal qualitative consideration flowing the other way.

There is no explicit definition in the IMF Articles of Agreement of a loan. However, Art.VII, s.1 does contain reference to "borrow", "loan" and "lend", in the context of the Fund replenishing its holdings of currencies.

---

[125] Art.31(4) of the Vienna Convention on the Law of Treaties 1969 only allows the parties to attribute a special meaning to a term, it does not allow them through linguistic juggling to change the true character of a transaction.

[126] See, for example, J.M. Keynes, *Treatise on Money—The pure theory of money* (London, Macmillan), Vol.1; A. Gilpin, *Dictionary of Economic Terms*, 3rd edn (Butterworths, 1973); J.L. Hanson, *A Dictionary of Economics and Commerce*; *The McGraw-Hill Dictionary of Modern Economics*, 6th edn (Trans-Atlantic Publications, 1986); Soloan and Zurcher, *A Dictionary of Economics* (Barnes & Noble, 1965).

[127] G.F. Knapp, *The State Theory of Money* (London, Macmillan, 1924), Ch.1.

This Article is two-pronged. Art.VII, s. 1(i) refers explicitly to the Fund "borrowing". Article VII, Section 1(ii) requires the member to sell its currencies to the Fund for SDRs held in the General Resources Account. Juridically, there is no difference between Art.VII s. 1(i) and (ii). Both amount to a loan. This is confirmed in the Executive Board decision relating to the General Agreement to Borrow (GAB),[128] wherein both limbs of Article VII, s.1 are characterised as referring to a loan. Procedurally, the operations in the GAB bear a marked resemblance to the exchange transactions in Art.V.

**9-029**     The meaning of a "loan" in International Law is well established. A loan in national systems has a fairly standard sense.[129] Thus, under the general principles of law recognised by nations[130] a "loan" is defined in terms of a promise to allow for the use of money presently, under an obligation to return at a future date on specified terms. The position under Customary International Law is the same. Evidence of Customary International Law in this connection may be found by an analysis of international loan agreements,[131] multilateral treaties establishing machinery for financing States,[132] and State practice itself. Similarly, international disputes[133] involving loans[134]; and the deliberations of jurists,[135] have all proceeded on this established conception of a loan.

Finally, the attitude and practice of States when approaching the IMF for assistance is formulated in terms of a loan characterisation of an IMF drawing.[136] Indeed, national legislation relating to IMF drawings uses the vernacular of "loan".[137]

In conclusion there is no material distinction between the conception of a loan in International Law, and in economic analysis. Use of Fund resources under the General Resources account amounts to a loan in International Law. The fact that there is no international money in the strict chartalist[138]

---

[128] Executive Board Decision No.1289–(62/1) as amended in *Selected Decisions,* 22nd Issue (1997).

[129] See, for example, *Chitty on Contracts*, 29th edn (Sweet & Maxwell, 2006) *(Specific Contracts)*; G. Sanagen, *Words and Phrases. Legal Maxims*, 3rd edn (Canada, Carswell, 2005), Vol.2 at p.426; Dalloz, *Dictionaire de droit* (1966), p.372; German Civil Code (607-B.G.B).

[130] Art.38(1)(c) of the ICJ.

[131] See, for example, Agreement between the Government of Denmark and the Government of Kenya on a Danish Government loan to Kenya in *UN Treaty Series* (1974); Exchange of Notes concerning an Interest Free Loan by the Government of the UK. . .to the Government of the Republic of Honduras, 1980.

[132] For example, IBRD.

[133] See Art.38(1)(d) of the Statute of the ICJ.

[134] For example, *Brazilian Loans* Case (1929) P.C.I.J. Reports Series A, No.21; and Certain Norwegian Loans (1957) I.C.J. Reports.

[135] See, for example, Nussbaum (1950), p.139.

[136] See, for example, *travaux preparatoires* of the US Amendment to authorise consent to an increase in the US quota in the IMF.96 Congress, Second Session on HR 5970 (February/March/April 1980).

[137] See for example s.30(a) of the US Public Law 95-435 Congressional Record July 31, 1978, H 7548; and s.53 of the International Monetary Fund Act 1979.

[138] See F. Mann (1982), p.13. He states: "Only those chattels are money to which such character has been attributed by law, i.e. by or with the authority of the State. This is the State or

sense has not precluded in the past the existence of international loans. The money component of the International Law definition of a loan has been assumed to exist, because of the existence of something that has functioned as money on the international level.

Insofar as the matter is a question of interpretation, Art.V must be interpreted in the context of the Articles of Agreement, and generally Fund law as a whole.[139] Article V of the Agreement is plagued with the vernacular of sale—the ordinary meaning of which is obvious. But this is not conclusive of the issue, as the reality as reflected in the Articles as a whole, and all the circumstances surrounding the text, does not reflect this classification.[140] Article V is not a definition of the legal nature of the use of Fund resources. It describes merely the mode, or the manner in which the use of Fund resources is to be conducted. It is the form through which the resources of the Fund are to be made available under Art.1(V).

**9-030**

The focal point of analysis for the purposes of determining the legal nature of the use of Fund resources is Art.1(V). Article 1(V) encapsulates a purpose of the Fund. It directs the Fund to make "available" its resources "temporarily" to give confidence to members. "Available" is not a neutral term, but has the definite positive sense of "help", "benefit" and "afford value". This sense is reinforced by the fact that the availability is designed to instil confidence, and the use of the word "making" which emphasises the positive sense of "imparting" value or benefit (over that which is received). In a sale transaction, there is at least a measure of equality in the values exchanged. Therefore, "availability" is not consistent with a sale as the Fund would not in theory be "imparting value", it would be exchanging it. Availability is more consonant with loan. In a loan value is being imparted.

The provisions of Art.1(V) are thus consistent with the analysis that the use of Fund resources amount to a loan in law. "Availability" is not consistent with a sale transaction. A sale transaction does not constitute financing. "Loan" is synonymous with "financing". The Fund has in its decisions referred to the use of Fund resources as assistance in financing balance of payments deficits.[141] Assistance by way of financing is not the same as an exchange transaction. Assistance is a characteristic of loan, and not sale. The availability of a loan is done by the mode of a sale transaction. The fact that the sale transaction is indeed a mode is borne out by the fact that Art.V is titled "Operations and Transactions". This interpretation is in accordance with the purposes of the Articles of Agreement.[142] It is reinforced by the fact

---

Chartalist theory of money".

[139] See Art.31 of the Vienna Convention on The Law of Treaties 1969.

[140] See McNair, *The Law of Treaties*, 2nd edn (Oxford, Oxford University Press, 1961), Ch.XX at p.367 wherein he cites the example of "mother" in the text of a will of a man which was interpreted in court as being a reference to his wife because his wife was referred to as mother in family circles.

[141] See, for exampl, Executive Board Decision No.71–72 September 26, 1946 in *Selected Decisions of the* IMF (1997).

[142] Art.31 of the Vienna Convention on the Law of Treaties 1969.

that the Fund has the mandate to grant loans to member countries. This mandate, which derives from Art.1, has been relied upon in the establishment of the concessional lending facilities under the PRGT and previously the PRGF. Indeed, the Fund has had no qualms in crafting the concessional facilities expressly in terms of loans.[143]

**9-031**     It is difficult to comprehend fully the intentions of the original drafters, as there is some difficulty in accessing historical material, not in the public domain. Some support for the characterisation of the transaction as a loan is to be found in the Fund's basic *travaux preparatoires*.[144] Further support may be invoked from the Keynes Plan.[145] The Keynes Plan involved "bancor" an international currency, and the use of this currency was to be in the form of overdrafts—with collateral of gold, foreign or domestic currency, or government bonds, where the debit reached half of a member's quota. The US White Plan[146] was however antithetical to the notion of overdraft or loan and contemplated the use of Fund resources through the mechanism of purchase, sale or repurchase as set out in the Articles of Agreement. However, the major objectives of the Keynes Plan were achieved in the form of the Stabilisation Fund (proposed under the White Plan) and were considered by UK experts as technical set ups, capable of performing precisely the same functions.[147] The Stabilisation Fund was formulated in terms of a sale transaction to secure US Congressional approval. It was not actuated by sound legal reasoning. It was to avoid the spectacle of a credit creating agency, with unlimited credit, and an inability to press for corrective balance of payments policies of members.[148] By the same token the non-loan characterisation served the interests of States, reluctant to humble themselves when the need arose, to a process which openly involved the soliciting of an external loan.[149]

Finally, a loan characterisation is often associated with the existence of an international agreement. This association leads to the apprehension that the Fund would be robbed of its authority to engage in auto-interpretation of its affairs, and open it to external justiciability. But the legal form of the loan need not necessarily be an agreement. Whilst loan transactions are normally imbued with the complexion of an agreement, a loan may also exist in legal analysis even in the absence of a strict agreement. Thus, the obligation to allow the current use of finance and the obligation to repay—the constituent

---

[143] See EB Decision establishing PRGT: 14354-(09/79), July 23, 2009, effective January 7, 2010.
[144] *Proceedings and Documents of the UN Monetary and Financial Conference*, Vols I and II, US Department of State Publication 2866, Document 396.
[145] J.K. Horsefield, *The IMF 1945–1965* (Washington D.C.: IMF, 1969), Vol.III.
[146] Horsefield, "Preliminary Draft Outline of a Proposal for an International Stabilization Fund of the United and Associated Nations" (1969).
[147] Horsefield (1969), Vol.III at p.129.
[148] Horsefield (1969), p.142: "US Questions and Answers on IMF June 10, 1944".
[149] J. Gold, *Interpretation: The IMF and International Law* (Kluwer Law International, 1996), p.368.

elements of a loan—may draw their force, for instance, from a decision of the Fund, from unilateral undertakings, or from the Articles of Agreement.

The characterisation of the underlying transaction accompanying Conditionality is not merely of academic interest. A significant part of the Fund's regulatory functions venture through this channel, and this clarity is aimed at their very constitutionality. The consequences that flow from a variation in characterisation are multi-faceted. First, there may be implications within the member's jurisdiction. Characterisation as a loan may necessitate the invocation of a different piece of legislation, or may even necessitate approval by a relevant constitutional organ. This is not a difficulty that should be circumvented by an incorrect diagnosis. Indeed, since an external loan taken by a State is an important decision, and a loan from the Fund with all its ramifications still more, there is a case for detracting from the present obfuscation by the Fund for the benefit of a member. Good governance and the need for democratic participation endorse this standpoint. Secondly, although the nature and extent of the obligations arising from the transaction may not significantly differ according to the characterisation, in the event of a default or breach the nature of the characterisation could be of relevance. Considerations that operate in the event of a default in a loan transaction may be distinct from those in the event of a breach in a sale transaction.

### Does the drawing take the form of an international agreement?

Underlying this question lie policy considerations. On the one hand there is **9-032** a desire to attribute "consensus" to something as important as a drawing. By the same token there are the consequences of appearing to have become bound by an international agreement, which militates against such a characterisation. This reflects a national standpoint. On the other hand, there is a tendency within the Fund to be didactic, and the desire to keep the Fund's affairs internalised. Set against this background, there are mainly two schools of thought relating to the characterisation of the form of a drawing. First, the unilateral perspective which emphasises the role of the Fund in the process of a drawing. Secondly, the bilateral school which emphasises the consensual character of the drawing.

From the unilateral perspective,[150] a drawing whether by way of a direct drawing, or a stand-by or similar arrangement, takes the form of a decision of the Fund.[151] It is not an international agreement.[152] Violations of the decision

---

[150] J. Gold, IMF *Pamphlet Series* No.11, pp.59–61; J. Gold, IMF *Pamphlet Series* No.4 (1965), pp.25–26; J. Gold, *Stand-by Arrangements* IMF (1970), p.3; J. Gold, IMF *Pamphlet Series* No.27, p.17; J. Gold, IMF *Pamphlet Series* No.35, p.43; S.A. Silard, "The Legal Aspects of Development Financing in the 1980s. The role of the IMF", *The* (1982) 32(1) *American University Law Review* 89; V. Van Themat, *The Changing Structure of International Economic Law* (T.M.C. Asser Institute, 1981), p.166; E. Denters, *Law and Policy of IMF Conditionality* (Kluwer Law International, 1996), pp.8 and 99.

[151] Art.XXX(b) of the IMF Articles of Agreement.

[152] Guidelines on Conditionality EB Decision No.12864–(02/102) September 25, 2002.

do not constitute breaches of an international agreement. This is because the Fund does not have the intention to create legal relations, necessary for an international agreement to arise.

From the bilateral perspective, the drawing is a binding international agreement independent of the basic treaty, viz. the Articles of Agreement of the IMF.[153] In other words, a drawing results in an international agreement between the Fund and the drawing member within the framework of the Articles of Agreement, but independent of it. The reason why such agreements are not registered under Art.102 of the UN Charter is because in the case of an immediate drawing the agreement is wholly executed after the drawing; and in the case of the Stand-by or similar arrangement, the arrangement is of a temporary character, and therefore is not an agreement which is required to be registered.[154]

Are the Fund's pronouncements conclusive and exhaustive of the issue? As noted earlier, Article XXX(b) defines a "Stand-by arrangement" as a decision of the Fund. The definition does not include the Letter of Intent.[155] It refers only to the response of the Fund to the request made by way of the Letter of Intent. Article XXX(b) is in a sense axiomatic.[156] The Fund is an artificial entity and responds to a request at the initiative of a member. The Fund is directed to examine the request, and if necessary set out terms, for a grant. The Fund's modus operandi in these circumstances can only be by way of a decision. Article XXX(b) characterises a process that is internal to the Fund. The act characterised is one that is a prelude to another. The decision is not an end in itself. It is in fact a decision to grant a Stand-by arrangement. Thus, if the parties were willing, they are not precluded from treating the Stand-by documents as an agreement.[157] Article XXX(b) is indecisive as to the nature of the relationship arising between the Fund and the member once the decision is made.

In para.9 of the Guidelines to Conditionality 2002 it is stated:

---

[153] D. Summers et al., "Conflict Avoidance in International Loans and Monetary Agreements" (1956) 21 *Law and Contemporary Problems* 463, 478; J.E.S. Fawcett, "The Place of Law in an International Organization" (1960) XXXVI B.Y.I.L. 321, 339; I. Detter, *Law-making by International Organizations* (Stockholm, Norstedt & Soners, 1965), p.115; J.E.S. Fawcett, "Trade and Finance in International Law" (1968) R.D.C. 219, 236; G.H. Alexandrowicz, *The Law-Making Functions of the Specialized Agencies of the UN* (Sydney, Angus & Robertson, 1973), p.123; D. Carreau et al., *Droit International Economique*, 2nd edn (1988), p.137; Schuster, *The Public International Law of Money*, p.196. For a characterisation as a de-facto or gentleman's agreement see E. Lauterpacht, "Gentleman's Agreements" in F.A. Mann and W. Flume (eds), *International Law and Economic Order* (Muenchen, Beck,1977), p.383; and F. Roessler, "Law, de facto Agreements and Declarations of Principle in International Economic Relations" (1978) 21 *German Yearbook of International Law* 27–58.

[154] Fawcett (1960).

[155] J. Gold, IMF *Pamphlet Series* No.35, p.1.

[156] Lazar Focsaneanu, "Le droit international monetaire selon de deuxieme amendement aux statuts du fond monetaire international" (1978) 105 *Journal du droit international*, Clunet 805, 862.

[157] J. Gold, IMF *Pamphlet Series* No.35.

### Guidelines on Conditionality

9. **Nature of Fund arrangements.** A Fund arrangement is a decision of        **9-033**
the Executive Board by which a member is assured that it will be able
to make purchases or receive disbursements from the Fund in accordance with the terms of the decision during a specified period and up to a
specified amount. Fund arrangements are not international agreements
and therefore language having a contractual connotation will be avoided
in arrangements and in program documents. Appropriate consultation
clauses will be incorporated in all arrangements.[158]

This statement is interpreted as meaning that the Fund has no *animus cont-*        **9-034**
*rahendi* when approving an arrangement such as a Stand-by arrangement.[159]
The decision appears to be conclusive of the issue. But there are some points
that may nevertheless be made. First, the agreement falls short of deeming
the arrangements from not being agreements. Secondly, from one standpoint
it may be asserted that the decision in fact expresses the view of the Fund as
to the character of Stand-by arrangements.[160] As a legal conclusion, para.9
of the Guidelines on Conditionality is not an interpretation of the Articles
of Agreement by the Fund, under its powers of interpretations[161]—and
therefore arguably it is open to challenge. Indeed Gold characterises para.3
of the March 2, 1979 Decision (which is similarly worded to para.9 of the
Guidelines on Conditionality 2002[162]) as soft law, that is not binding on the
Executive Board.[163]

The characterisation may be challenged on the following grounds. First,
the question whether an IMF "arrangement" such as a Stand-by arrangement, is an international agreement, has to be decided with reference to the
relevant International Law norms on international agreements; and is a
query that transcends the Fund's exhortations. The Fund's stand is only a
factor to be taken into account, which may or may not conclusively shed light
on the issue. This seems to be appreciated by Gold in his acknowledgement
that the March 2, 1979 Decision (the predecessor Decision to the current
Executive Board Decision titled Guidelines on Conditionality) is not beyond
controversy.

Secondly, the positive assertion that an arrangement is a decision of
the Fund would be an interpretative decision, as the Fund is attributing a
meaning to an "arrangement"—a terminology and creature of the Articles of
Agreement. However, the negative assertion that Fund arrangements are not
international agreements is not an interpretative decision. It is not directed
at elucidating the meaning of an "arrangement" strictly speaking. Instead,
it focuses primarily on international agreements. It sheds a light, albeit in a

---

[158] Decision No.12864-(02/102) September 25, 2002.
[159] J. Gold, IMF *Pamphlet Series* No.35, p.12. See also Gold (1996), p.360.
[160] See, for example, J. Gold, IMF *Pamphlet Series* No.31.
[161] See Art.XXIX of the Articles of Agreement of the IMF.
[162] Decision No.12864–(02/102)September 25, 2002.
[163] Gold (1996), p.375.

negative sense, on the character of international agreements. The question whether or not a Fund arrangement is an international agreement has to be answered by considering the juridical nature of an international agreement. The two are inextricably linked but in so far as the proposition is put in a negative way, it focuses mainly on international agreements. Paragraph 9 of the Guidelines on Conditionality is in fact a deliberation on international agreements. What is an international agreement is not a question that comes under the "interpretative jurisdiction" of the Fund, though the Fund may express its opinion. To the extent that it is an opinion, albeit expressed in the form of a decision, it is open to query.

**9-035**     What constitutes an international agreement between a Member State and the IMF needs to be answered with reference to the Vienna Convention on the Law of Treaties between States and International Organizations.[164] Against this background, elements of a Fund arrangement can arguably be construed as partaking of an international agreement. The designation as a decision is not conclusive.[165] The same would apply to a direct drawing.

There are three essential elements in an agreement governed by International Law[166]—viz. (1) capacity, (2) consensus *ad idem* and (3) intention to create legal relations. The first two present little difficulty. There is no doubt that the Fund has capacity to enter into international agreements, to further its purposes.[167] There is no doubt either that there is the necessary consensus *ad idem* between the parties. The Fund treats every request separately, and responds individually to each request. The drawings do not merely arrange for the execution of existing provisions in the Articles of Agreement of the IMF or policies formulated under Fund law. The terms are offered *de novo* on the occasion of each drawing.[168] The Fund "arrangement" is a consensual arrangement,[169] which takes a form akin to an Exchange of Notes.[170] In both a direct drawing and a Stand-by or similar arrangement there is consensus *ad idem*, and it occurs *de novo*. The *de novo* theory is consistent with normal

---

[164] Vienna Convention on the Law of Treaties between States and International Organisations (1986).

[165] See Vienna Convention on the Law of Treaties between States and International Organisations (1986), Art.2.

[166] See, for example, C. Osakwe, "The concept and forms of treaties concluded by international organizations" in K. Zemanek (ed.), assisted by L. R. Behrmann, *Agreements of International Organizations and the Vienna Convention on the Law of Treaties* (Wien, Springer, 1971), pp.165, 190.

[167] See, for example, J.E.S. Fawcett, "Trade and finance in International Law" (1968) I R.D.C. I, 219, 231 and Art.IX of the IMF Articles of Agreement.

[168] In the context of the UN treaty practice see R. Higgins, *The Development of International Law through the Political Organs of the United Nations* (Oxford, Oxford University Press, 1963), p.288, n.31; Detter (1965), p.176; J.M. Van Wouw, "Formal aspects of the Technical Assistance Agreements concluded by the UN Family or Organizations" in K. Zemanek (ed.), *Agreements of International Organizations and the Vienna Convention on the Law of Treaties*.

[169] J. Gold, IMF *Pamphlet Series* No.35.

[170] See for a description of exchange of notes for example J.D. Meyers, "The Names and Scope of Treaties" (1957) 51 A.J.I.L. 590.

municipal banking practice with regard to overdrafts.[171] The existence of the *animus contrahendi* is the major stumbling block in the characterisation of a Fund arrangement as an international agreement.

Before considering the issue from this perspective it is necessary for the purposes of analysis to differentiate between three basic types of norms that result from a drawing. These may be termed as "the core obligations", "the inner Conditionality" and the "outer Conditionality". The core obligations involve obligations on the part of the Fund that are very closely attached to the use of Fund resources. They comprise, on the one hand, the basic under-taking by the Fund to allow the drawing, or grant the assurance tendered in a Stand-by or similar arrangement upon request, for the requisite amount, in the requisite currency, during the specified period; and on the other hand, the member's obligations to repurchase, to pay charges, and such closely allied obligations. The "inner Conditionality" comprises those economic or financial policies that are formulated as concrete, enforceable undertakings. The inner Conditionality comprises mainly (not necessarily exclusively) of performance criteria. Performance criteria are economic prescriptions that are formulated in an arithmetic or other objective manner. They are generally macroeconomic in character, and limited to purchases beyond the first credit tranche; and to those matters necessary to implement specific provisions of the Articles of Agreement or policies adopted under them.

**Guidelines on Conditionality**

11(b).  Performance criteria. A performance criterion is a variable or measure whose observance or implementation is established as a formal condition for the making of purchases or disbursements under a Fund arrange-ment. Performance criteria will apply to clearly-specified variables or measures that can be objectively monitored by the staff and are so critical for the achievement of the program goals or monitoring implementation that purchases or disbursements under the arrangement should be inter-rupted in cases of nonobservance. The number and content of perform-ance criteria may vary because of the diversity of circumstances and institutional arrangements of members.[172]

**9-036**

The "outer Conditionality" consists of obligations by a Member State nor-mally involving general economic aims and objectives of the member that are less easily formulated in objective terms. They indicate the general trend in which the economy will proceed or is expected to proceed. The core and inner Conditionality are contained in the Stand-by document. A sense of this "outer Conditionality" is reflected in part of para.10 of the Guidelines on Conditionality.

**9-037**

---

[171] See, for example M. Megrah and F.R. Ryder, *Paget's Law of Banking*. Contra Denters (London: Butterworths, 1982), p.101 where he argues that under Art.V, s.3(b) a member is already entitled to a drawing under certain conditions. The stand-by arrangement merely summarises those conditions.

[172] Decision No.12864–(02/102) September 25, 2002.

**9-038**

10. Members program documents. The authority's policy intentions will be described in documents such as a Letter of Intent (LOI), or a Memorandum on Economic and Financial Policies (MEFP) that may be accompanied by a Technical Memorandum of Understanding (TMU). These documents will be prepared by the authorities, with the cooperation and assistance of the Fund staff, and will be submitted to the Managing Director for circulation to the Executive Board. The documents should reflect the authority's policy goals and strategies. In addition to conditions specified in these documents, members requesting the use of Fund resources may in exceptional cases communicate confidential policy understandings to the Fund in a side letter addressed to the Managing Director and disclosed to the Executive Board. *In all their program documents, the authorities should clearly distinguish between the conditions on which the Fund's financial support depends and other elements of the program. Detailed policy matrices covering the broader agenda should be avoided in program documents such as LOIs and MEFPs unless they are considered necessary by the authorities to express their policy intentions.*[173]

(Emphasis added)

**9-039** The following points may be made. First, in so far as the period prior to the Fund decisions[174] relating to Fund arrangements is concerned, the arguments for contending that Fund arrangements entered into during this period, were international agreements, as maintained by a former Legal Counsel of the IMF, J.E.S Fawcett, carry weight. Secondly, the Fund pronouncements purporting to negate the *animus contrahendi* are concerned only with "arrangements", and not with immediate drawings. Thus, the arguments for the characterisation of an immediate drawing as an international agreement have more weight.[175] Thirdly, the core obligations are binding and there is no disagreement on this.[176] There is, however, disagreement as to the source of the obligation. Joseph Gold contends that these derive from the Articles of Agreement or Fund decisions.[177] But as is suggested in relation to these it is possible that the consensus is *de novo*. The lack of intention to create legal relations on the part of the Fund as indicated in its 1979 EB Decision and subsequently reiterated in the September 2002 Guidelines on Conditionality, assuming such an intention can be read, relates it is suggested to the spheres of Conditionality and not the core obligations. With regard to the consensus on the core obligations, there is an intention to create legal relations. The thrust of the lack of the *animus contrahendi* is directed at the outer Conditionality. In this respect, the reasons formulated for the lack of an intention are

---

[173] Decision No.12864–(02/102) September 25, 2002.
[174] i.e. the 1968 and 1979 Executive Board decisions purporting to negate the intention to create legal relations.
[175] Gold (1996), p.366. See also J.E.S. Fawcett, "The International Monetary Fund and International Law" (1964) XL B.Y.I.L. 339.
[176] See, for example, J. Gold, IMF *Pamphlet Series* No.35, at p.27.
[177] See, for example, J. Gold, IMF *Pamphlet Series* No.35, at p.27.

pertinent. They are described inter alia as follows[178]: (1) public opinion in relation to Conditionality; (2) to encourage use of Fund arrangements so as to facilitate application of Conditionality more effectively and with speed; (3) the problems of determining objectively breaches of Conditionality; (4) avoidance of the stigma of violation of an international agreement in the event of a breach; (5) flexibility with regard to Conditionality as it avoids the need for parliamentary approval; allows the member at anytime to opt out of the arrangement without legal implications of breaches[179]; avoidance of conflicting obligations with other international organisations. Historically, the reason for the denial of *animus contrahendi* lies in the reluctance of the major developed members in entering into a binding agreement with the Fund which could lead to determinations of violations.[180]

To conclude, there are persuasive reasons why an IMF "arrangement" whether in the form of a Stand-by or similar arrangement, or an immediate drawing, may be characterised as an international agreement. The agreement characterisation is particularly so in relation to the core obligations. The decision theory is unilateral in character and reserves to the Fund the right to revoke the decision by way of another decision. The consensus theory characterises the drawing as bilateral and thus commits the Fund to the drawing.

### The underlying character of the concessional facilities for low-income countries

The availability of funds under the PRGT[181] is through the means of a loan **9-040** under a programme of adjustment and reform. The Executive Board decision establishing the Trust facilities expressly refers to "loans". Moreover, there is no express denial of intention to create legal relations under the decision. There are several reasons for this. First, it may be because Art.V, s.3(b) does not apply.[182] Secondly, under this facility the Fund did not have currency to exchange.[183] Thirdly, the reasons why the loan agreement characterisation was not originally followed may have been forgotten.[184] Fourthly, the safeguards incorporated in the non-loan non-agreement characterisation may now appear "archaic legalism, or even worse, unaccountable legalisms".[185] Fifthly, the members affected may be too weak to be able to worry about the safeguards to their reputations to which the IMF showed sensitivity in the past.[186] Finally, the loan agreement category may have been contrived

[178] J. Gold, IMF *Pamphlet Series* No.35, at p.27. See also Gold (1996), pp.363–364.
[179] Gold (1996), p.363; see also Denters (1996), p.102.
[180] See Gold (1996), p.371 in n.125 therein.
[181] EB Decision: 14354-(09/79), July 23, 2009, effective January 7, 2010
[182] Denters (1996), p.120 and Gold (1996), pp.369–370.
[183] Gold (1996), p.370.
[184] Gold (1996), p.374.
[185] Gold (1996), p.374.
[186] Gold (1996), p.374.

simply because of the scarcity in the legal categories available for such transactions.[187]

Broadly, the ECF, SCF and RCF facilities under the PRGT whilst not involving the same exact terminology as in Stand-by arrangements involve the same concepts. Thus, in both the ECF and SCF there has to be an "arrangement", and in the case of the RCF a "Letter". However, although the transaction is characterised as a "loan", the decision refers to "arrangements" which has the effect that the IMF does not actually treat departures as breaches of contract. What merely transpires, as in Fund arrangements, is that further disbursements are withheld. Thus, in practice the agreement is dealt with in accordance with the rules of the organisation.[188]

---

[187] Gold (1996), p.374.
[188] See also Denters (1996), p.120.

CHAPTER 10

# THE NATURE OF IMF CONDITIONALITY

## INTRODUCTION[1]

There are compelling reasons for a legal analysis of Conditionality. Foremost **10-001** amongst these is the potency of Conditionality itself. The financial discipline it encapsulates impinges on the very nerve centres of a State. This fact in itself is enough to alert the lawyer. The function of the lawyer is to police Conditionality within the framework of the international economic order and to counsel and assist in its formulation and implementation. Further, the treatment of Conditionality as technical economic prescriptions to alleviate a balance of payments maladjustment obscures the very important fact that the system it engenders is underpinned by political and ideological choices.[2] The effect it produces is concerned with the allocation of benefits and burdens, both within a State and within the international community at large, and therefore raises questions of distributive justice. The role of the lawyer is to shed light on these rights and burdens, and indeed to be involved in their proper dissemination on a *de lege ferenda* level. Finally, Conditionality has been the subject of much criticism from economists as well as political economists.[3] The task for the lawyer is to consider the extent to which these are properly "justiciable".

[1] On legal aspects of IMF Conditionality see generally A.H. Qureshi, *The International Legal Theory of IMF Conditionality—An alternative approach* PhD thesis, University of London, 1985; the works of Sir Joseph Gold in particular IMF *Pamphlet Series* Nos 27, 31; E. Denters, *Law and Practice of IMF Conditionality* (Kluwer Law International, 1996); Sorel, J.M., "Sur quelques aspects juridique de la conditionalite du F.M.I et leur consequence (1996) 7(1) *European Journal of International Law* 42–66; O. Eldar, "Reform of IMF Conditionality: A Proposal for Self-imposed Conditionality" (2005) 8(2) J.I.E.L. 509–554.

[2] See, for example, A.H. Qureshi, "Value aspects of IMF Conditionality" (July–December 1988) *Indian Of International Law* Vol.28; J. Harrigan, "Alternative concepts of Conditionality" (October 1988) *Manchester Papers on Development* Vol.IV No.4., pp.451–71; A. Carty, "Liberal economic rhetoric as an obstacle to the democratization of the world economy" (July 1988) *Ethics*, Vol.98, No.4;R W Stone, "The scope of IMF Conditionality", *International Organization* (2008: CUP);A Buira, 'An analysis of IMF Conditionality", UNCTAD G-24 Discussion Paper No.22 (August 2003).

[3] See, for example, C. Payer, *The Debt Trap: The International Monetary Fund and the Third World* (Harmondsworth, Penguin, 1974), C. Pirzio-Biroli, "Making sense of IMF Conditionality" (1983) *Journal of World Trade* 119; M. Lucas, "The International Monetary

Moreover, the significance of IMF Conditionality lies not only in the extent of the in-road it makes in a member's economy but also the number of members that in practice come under its purview and that potentially could. In practice historically, IMF Conditionality has been mainly concerned with developing countries, although the recent financial crisis has somewhat shaken this premise. Furthermore, the Fund has also been able to assist countries going through transition from a planned economy to a market economy, as well as the so-called Asian tiger economies. According to the IMF, some four out of five of its members have at some point or other availed themselves of IMF assistance,[4] including the UK and more recently Greece and Ireland. As of April 2010 there were some 21 Standby Arrangements, 2 Extended Arrangements, and 3 Flexible Credit Line arrangements, 30 Extended Credit Facility arrangements/Exogenous Shock Facility.[5] In the circumstances, Conditionality has been described as a "tool to promote good policies", "serves as substitute for collateral", and "encourages investment".[6] That said, the work of the IMF on Conditionality has been very controversial, in particular for not achieving its objectives.[7] Indeed, before the recent financial crisis in 2007 there was a decline in the use of Fund resources attributable to negative perceptions of it. The financial crisis however in 2008 resulted in a sharp rise in demand for Fund resources,[8] and highlighted the inadequacy of Fund resources to respond to the magnitude of the crisis.

A number of empirical studies have cast doubt on the actual impact of IMF stabilisation programmes—including their very design and implementation aspects.[9] Thus, the Fund's performance as a catalyst for further funding has been questioned.[10] And according to one measure successfully completed programmes in the 90's declined below 30 per cent.[11] Against this background and the potency of IMF Conditionality Ariel Buira raises a number

Fund's Conditionality and the International Covenant of Economic, Social, and Cultural Rights: an Attempt to Define the Relation" in (1992) 25(1) *Revue Belge De Droit International* 104–35; B. Trubitt, "IMF Conditionality and Options for Aggrieved Fund Members" (1987) 20(4) *Vanderbilt Journal of Transnational Law* 665–697; A Buira, "An analysis of IMF Conditionality", UNCTAD G-24 Discussion Paper No.22 (August 2003).

[4] IMF: Lending by the IMF at *http://www.imf.org/external/about/lending.htm*. (Accessed June 8, 2011).

[5] IMF Annual Report 2010 Appendix Table II.2.

[6] See, for example, R.M. Lastra (2006), p.417.

[7] See, for example, A. Buira, "An analysis of IMF Conditionality", UNCTAD G-24 Discussion Paper No.22 (August 2003).

[8] See IMF Lendign by the IMF at *http://www.imf.org/external/about/lending.htm#changing*. (Accessed June 8, 2011)

[9] See T. Killick, The Impact of IMF Stabilization Programmes in Developing Countries, *ODI, Working Paper* No.7, p.37; A. Buira, "An analysis of IMF Conditionality" UNCTAD G24 Discussion Paper No.22 August 2003). With reference to events in Russia see *Financial Times* September 17, 1998. See also IMF IEO, *Evaluation of the Prolonged Use of Fund Resources* (2002).

[10] A. Buira, "An analysis of IMF Conditionality" UNCTAD G24 Discussion Paper No.22 (August 2003).

[11] A. Buira, "An analysis of IMF Conditionality" UNCTAD G24 Discussion Paper No.22 (August 2003).

of very pertinent questions which deserve being highlighted even though they raise political concerns. The questions are relevant for legal analysis from an International Law perspective of IMF Conditionality. The questions he posits are set out as follows[12]:

1) Can programme ownership by a country be made compatible with externally imposed conditionality? Can externally imposed policies or values become internalized in recipient countries?
2) Is conditionality compatible with democracy?
3) To what extent is (IMF) conditionality power without responsibility?
4) Should economic policy decisions that affect all be taken outside the domestic political process?
5) Are the transparency and accountability of governments, which the (IMF) consider essential to good governance, compatible with conditionality?
6) When conditionality is coercive, can governments be held domestically accountable and responsible for the effects of policies imposed from outside? Are governments accountable to, their electorate, or to some external institutions wherein they are under-represented?
7) Since the political viability of an adjustment programme is related to the depth of a crisis, to the actions of the government and to the amount and timeliness of external support, when can inadequate financial support by the international community be considered responsible for it?
8) Governments and the (IMF) are prepared to intervene in the affairs of third countries, but are they prepared to take political responsibility for he policies or measures they sponsor?
9) Since the majority of programmes are not completed successfully what, if any, are the consequences for the staff and for the Fund of imposing programmes that fail more often than not?
10) Should liberalisation of the markets take place before liberalization of the State?

The Fund makes available its resources to a member subject to certain conditions, referred to as IMF Conditionality.[13] The conditions prescribed by the Fund upon the use of its resources derive from the stated objectives in Art.1(V) and 1(IV). More specifically, the authority for Conditionality derives from the requirement on the part of the Fund to "adopt adequate safeguards" for the use of its resources.[14] The conditions that govern the use of the general resources are tabulated in sub-sections of Art.V, s.3. The Article directs the Fund to formulate policies on the use of its general resources, that will assist members to solve their balance of payments problems, in a manner consistent with the provisions of the Agreement, and that

**10-002**

---

[12] A. Buira, "An analysis of IMF Conditionality" UNCTAD G24 Discussion Paper No.22 (August 2003).

[13] A programme of action subject to Conditionality is also referred to as an adjustment or stabilisation programme.

[14] See Art.1(V). See also J. Gold, IMF *Pamphlet Series* No.31, p.2; and E. Denters, *Law and Policy of IMF Conditionality* (Kluwer Law International, 1996), pp.7 and 26. Contra T. Killick, *IMF Stabilisation Programmes* ODI Working Paper No.6, pp.3–4.

will establish adequate safeguards for the temporary use of the resources of the Fund.

**Article V Section 3 of the IMF Articles of Agreement.**[15]

Conditions governing use of the Fund's general resources

**10-003**

(a) The Fund shall adopt policies on the use of its general resources, including policies on stand-by or similar arrangements, and may adopt special policies for special balance of payments problems, that will assist members to solve their balance of payments problems in a manner consistent with the provisions of this Agreement and that will establish adequate safeguards for the temporary use of the general resources of the Fund.

(b) A member shall be entitled to purchase the currencies of other members from the Fund in exchange for an equivalent amount of its own currency subject to the following conditions:

   (i) the member's use of the general resources of the Fund would be in accordance with the provisions of this Agreement and the policies adopted under them;

   (ii) the member represents that it has a need to make the purchase because of its balance of payments or its reserve position or developments in its reserves;

   (iii) the proposed purchase would be a reserve tranche purchase, or would not cause the Fund's holdings of the purchasing member's currency to exceed two hundred percent of its quota;

   (iv) the Fund has not previously declared under Section 5 of this Article, Article VI, Section 1, or Article XXVI, Section 2(*a*) that the member desiring to purchase is ineligible to use the general resources of the Fund.

(c) The Fund shall examine a request for a purchase to determine whether the proposed purchase would be consistent with the provisions of this Agreement and the policies adopted under them, provided that requests for reserve tranche purchases shall not be subject to challenge.

**10-004** The mandate for Conditionality relating to assistance through the concessional facility is also set against the background of Arts 1 and V. It is also specifically elaborated in the Fund decision establishing the Poverty Reduction and Growth Trust (PRGT),[16] which refers to programmes involving macroeconomic and structural adjustment.[17] Further, the IMF in administering the PRGT is to apply the same rules as apply to the operations of the General Resources Account.[18] This has been interpreted to mean that to the extent

---

[15] Source: *http://www.imf.org*. (Accessed June 8, 2011).

[16] See EB Decision 14354-(09/79), July 23, 2009, effective January 7, 2010.

[17] See EB Decision No.8759–(87/176) as amended.

[18] See s.VII, para.1(b) of the EB Decision No.8759–(87/176) as amended 14354-(09/79), July 23, 2009. effective January 7, 2010. See also Denters (1996), p.45.

applicable the principles in relation to Conditionality under the General Resources Account also apply in the administration of the PRGT.

Although, the Fund has the mandate to formulate Conditionality, Conditionality itself as such is not defined in the Articles of Agreement.[19] However, the Articles of Agreement and Executive Board decisions explicitly recognise the concept of Conditionality,[20] and do specifically refer to "conditions".[21] Thus, Fund law provides a framework within which Conditionality is formulated and applied.[22] The various decisions of the Fund[23] shed light on the nature and kind of Conditionality. Further insight is provided by the individual Fund stabilisation programmes. These constitute the actual practice of the Fund and members in the process of the application of Conditionality. In this practice, which although individual in character, it is possible to discern some trends. In the premises, Conditionality may be said to have the attributes of a legal term of art.[24] It can be defined as the policies adopted by the Fund on the use of its resources to assist members to solve their balance of payments problems in a manner consistent with the provisions of the Articles of Agreement and that will establish adequate safeguards for the temporary use of the resources of the Fund.[25]

**GUIDELINES ON CONDITIONALITY[26]**

A. Principles

1. Basis and purpose of conditionality. Conditions on the use of Fund resources are governed by the Fund's Articles of Agreement and implementing decisions of the Executive Board. Conditionality-that is, program-related conditions-is intended to ensure that Fund resources are provided to members to assist them in resolving their balance of payments problems in a manner that is consistent with the Fund's Articles and that establishes adequate safeguards for the temporary use of the Fund's resources.

**10-005**

The policies are of two kinds—viz. financial Conditionality, e.g. the amount of assistance, repurchase obligations, charges, etc.; and economic Conditionality, normally macroeconomic in character, e.g. reduction of food subsidies, devaluation, credit ceiling, public sector borrowing and

**10-006**

---

[19] J. Gold, IMF *Pamphlet Series* No.31, p.2.

[20] Art.V, s.3. See also, for example, EB Decision No.12864–(02/102), Guidelines on Conditionality (2002); and the Operational Guidance to IMF Staff on the 2002 Conditionality Guidelines Revised—January 25, 2010 *http://www.imf.org/external/np/pp/eng/2010/012510a. pdf.* (Accessed June 8, 2011).

[21] Art.V, s.3. See also Guidelines on Conditionality (2002) & Operational Guidance 2010.

[22] Contra J. Gold, IMF *Pamphlet Series* No.27, p.20.

[23] See decisions set out in *Selected Decisions of the IMF.*

[24] Contra J. Gold, IMF *Pamphlet Series* No.31, p.2.

[25] See also, for example, M. Guitian, IMF *Pamphlet Series* No.38, p.1.

[26] EB Decision No.12864–(02/102) September 25, 2002 as revised, *http://www.imf.org.* (Accessed June 8, 2011).

expenditure targets, tax reforms,[27] international reserves, external debt, the pricing system, exchange rate, interest rates and commodity processes that affect public finances, good governance and foreign trade.[28] Further, the policies may be general or special. The general policies relate to drawings on the credit made available in the non-concessional facilities (also known as credit tranches to describe the levels of credits). The special policies are designed specifically for a type of balance of payments problem.[29] Generally, the financial conditions can vary according to the type of policy, as can the economic conditions. The economic conditions vary according to the circumstances of the drawing member and the nature of the balance of payments problem. The process of formulation of policies, whether special or general, is a continuing one, and may take place either in abstract or in response to an individual request. Where it is articulated in abstract, in the form of guidelines contained in decisions of the Fund, the Fund cannot derogate from the tenor of that decision in individual cases. A key guide to Conditionality is the Executive Board Decision of September 25, 2002.[30] In this decision the Fund has set out certain principles according to which IMF Conditionality is to be formulated and prescribed. These guidelines, which are supplemented with operational guidelines,[31] are applied generally whatever the form of balance of payments assistance.[32]

## THE NATURE OF CONDITIONALITY

**10-007** Conditionality can be conceived of as comprising those policies the Fund management requires to be included in the member's programme of action[33]; or as comprising the standards that are applied by the Fund in evaluating a member's balance of payments adjustment programme.[34] From an analysis of the Articles of Agreement and the Decisions of the Fund[35] the normative quality of Conditionality is affirmed by the former perception. Given that Conditionality is by and large tailor-made to individual circumstances, its

---

[27] C. Pirzio-Biroli, "Making sense of IMF Conditionality Debate" (April 1983) J.W.T., pp.115–116.

[28] On trade-related assistance and conditionality see *Trade-Related Balance of Payments Adjustments—Fund Support* EB Decision No.13229–(04/33), April 2005. See also G7 October 1998 Work Program on Strengthening the Architecture of the International Monetary System.

[29] For example, the Extended Fund Facility.

[30] See Guidelines on Conditionality EB Decision No.12864, September 25, 2002.

[31] Operational Guidance to IMF (2010).

[32] Denter (1996), p.46. See also para.1(b), s.VII of Executive Board Decision No.8759–(87/176) ESAF as amended in *Selected Decision of the IMF*.

[33] See, for example, T. Killick, IMF Stabilisation Programmes *ODI Working Paper* No.6 (1982), p.1.

[34] See J. Gold, IMF *Pamphlet Series* No.39, p.3.

[35] See Art.V, s.3(a) and (b); and Guidelines on Conditionality.

characterisation as a standard is somewhat misleading. The reference to "adoption by the Fund" of policies, as set out in the Articles,[36] correctly reflects the circumstances wherein the Fund mission generally travel to the requesting member country with a Letter of Intent already drafted,[37] but one which is subject to negotiation. However, it needs to be acknowledged that the Fund now has tried to address this criticism in the revision of the Guidelines on Conditionality by stressing the national ownership of the economic programme.

The policies and the use of Fund resources have a complementary function in the attainment of a common objective. The use of the resources must be in such a manner as to support and/or further the policies adopted.[38] To this extent the manner of the use is prescribed by the policies. However, in fact the member has considerable latitude within the framework of the Articles and the policies.

The Fund assistance must be of a temporary character for the financing of balance of payments deficits on current account.[39] This time framework is related to the time of the use of the Fund resources. However, the Fund has over the years stretched the notion of "temporary" in order to deal with the problems of development, by allowing for repeated stand-by arrangements, and by creating special facilities for longer periods of time, in particular the Concessional Facilities.[40] Such prolonged use can stretch between seven to ten years and beyond, for example the Philippines with 23 programmes between 1962 and 2000.[41] One view advanced has been stated as follows:

> "The fundamental objectives of the IMF, as set out in Article I of the Articles of Agreement, are sufficiently broad that they could encompass such an expanded role. However, this raises the basic question of where a legitimate adaptation of roles ends, and where inappropriate 'mission creep' begins."[42]

The policies must be such as to assist a member in its balance of payments problems, so as to shorten the duration or lessen the degree of disequilibrium.[43] Similarly, the policies must be directed at the solution of balance of payments problems. Thus, one commentator has observed, perhaps controversially, that the Articles do not provide a basis for action on the rate of inflation or on development strategy, except to the extent that they impinge

---

[36] Art.V, s.2(a).
[37] See T. Killick, *The Quest for Economic Stabilisation. The IMF and the Third World* (New York, St. Martins Press, 1984), p.285.
[38] See Art.V, s.3(b)(1) and Art.I(V).
[39] Executive Board Decision No.71–2 in *Selected Decisions*.
[40] Denters (1996), p.125. IMF IEO *Evaluation of the Prolonged Use of Fund Resources* (2002). See also for example the ECF arrangement under the PRGT EB Decision: 14354-(09/79), July 23, 2009, effective January 7, 2010.
[41] IMF IEO, *Evaluation of the Prolonged Use of Fund Resources* (2002).
[42] Source: IMF IEO, *Evaluation of the Prolonged Use of Fund Resources* (2002).
[43] Art.I (VI).

upon the balance of payments disequilibrium.[44] In the same vein it has been suggested that the Articles do not give the Fund a mandate to promote basic human needs, and the improvement of income distribution.[45] A more realistic approach by the IMF Independent Evaluation Office has been as follows:

> "Political considerations are unavoidable in an institution governed by the votes of its shareholder governments. However, these considerations should be taken into account in a transparent manner—with decisions and accountability clearly at the level of the Executive Board."[46]

The balance of payments problem may be a balance of payments problem strictly speaking, or a potential balance of payments problem, or a balance of payments problem involving its reserve position or developments in its reserves.[47] The latter conditions which fall short of immediate balance of payments problem are included to accommodate the practice of Stand-by arrangements as originally conceived. However, whereas the reserve position of a member or the developments in its reserves are contemplated as grounds for applications for the use of the resources, the member may not generally use the resources of the Fund to meet a sustained outflow of capital.[48]

The policies must be such as to safeguard the revolving character of Fund resources. The safeguards in fact connote considerations more akin to those within the contemplation of a banker or lender—directed primarily at the return of the money. These safeguards must be adequate, but the primary emphasis is on the objective of stabilisation. There must be a judicious blend that insures the objective of stabilisation as the primary goal, with adequate safeguards for the resources as a subsidiary, though nevertheless an important consideration.[49] Indeed one observer[50] has gone further and stated that the Fund should not give "priority to the goal of achieving a prompt external adjustment to permit a prompt recovery of the resources lent by the Fund—over the objectives of the Fund as written out in its Articles of Agreement" viz., "the promotion and maintenance of high levels of employment and real income and to the development of the productive resources of all members as primary objectives of economic policy". The Fund's financial Conditionality contains a significant strand of the safeguard requirement. Examples include

---

[44]  T. Killick, IMF Stabilisation Programmes *ODI Working Paper* No.6 at p.4.

[45]  See C.D. Finch, "Adjustment policies and conditionality" in J. Williamson (ed.), *IMF Conditionality* at p.77.

[46]  IMF IEO, *Evaluation of the Prolonged Use of Fund Resources* (2002), see *http://www.imf.org.* (Accessed June 8, 2011).

[47]  Art.V, s.3(b).

[48]  Art.VI, s.1.

[49]  See I.S. Friedman, "Private Bank Conditionality: Comparison with the IMF and the World Bank" in J. Williamson (ed.), *IMF Conditionality* (Washington D.C., Institute for International Economics, 1983), p.115.

[50]  A. Buira, "An analysis of IMF Conditionality", UNCTAD G-24 Discussion Paper No.22 (August 2003).

performance criteria, consultation clauses, phasing of drawings, the instrument of the stand-by arrangement, and repurchase obligations.

### Design and Content of Conditionality

Conditionality can operate at two stages. First, in the form of a prior action, **10-008**
where it is a condition precedent to the use of Fund resources. Secondly, it
is attached to the use of Fund resources and forms an integral part of the
drawing.

Authority to prescribe prior actions stems from Art.V, s.3 and generally
Fund law.[51] Prior actions are a type of Conditionality and must be prescribed
within limits.

"11(a). Prior actions. A member may be expected to adopt measures prior **10-009**
to the Fund's approval of an arrangement, completion of a review,
or the granting of a waiver with respect to a performance criterion
when it is critical for the successful implementation of the program
that such actions be taken to underpin the upfront implementation
of important measures. In reaching understandings on prior actions,
the Fund will also take into account the strain that excessive reliance
upon such actions can place on member's implementation capacity. The Managing Director will keep Executive Directors informed
in an appropriate manner of the progress of discussions with the
member."[52]

Moreover, in extreme cases where a prior action emanates from the wrong **10-010**
organ, and/or if it is contrary to the express provisions of the Articles of
Agreement, then the matter could be submitted to the Executive Directors,
or the Board of Governors for a decision. Thus, the setting of a non-
macroeconomic political variable as a prior action, such as defence reduction
or the signing of a nuclear non-proliferation treaty could be controversial.[53]

Only those corrective measures seem to be contemplated which if disclosed
in advance would prejudice the implementation and efficiency of the stabilisation contemplated. Prior actions comprise chiefly of devaluation, but may
also include tax increases, expenditure cuts, and rises in interest rates. If such
conditions were formulated as conditions they may leak, and thus contribute
to speculation and thereby exacerbate the economic situation.[54] Prior actions
are not generally incorporated in the Letter of Intent or the stand-by arrangement. However, Letters of Intent may contain reference to measures taken
before the start of a stabilisation programme.[55] It is also now possible to set

---

[51] See, in particular, para.11 of the Guidelines on Conditionality (Decision No.12864–(02/102),
September 25, 2002).
[52] Decision No.12864–(02/102) September 25, 2002.
[53] Contra Denter (1996), p.110.
[54] See Williamson (1983), p.633.
[55] See, for example, W.A. Beveridge and M.R. Kelly, "Fiscal content of Financial Programs
supported by Stand-by Arrangements in the Upper Credit Tranches 1969–78", IMF (1980)
27(2) *Staff Papers*.

out in exceptional circumstances "confidential policy understandings" in a side letter addressed to the Managing Director and disclosed under special circumstances to the Executive Board.[56]

**10-011**

4. Members requesting the use of Fund resources are encouraged to include all policy undertakings in letters of intent. Side letters will be used sparingly and only in those circumstances which the authorities consider, and management agrees, require such exceptional communication.

5. The use of side letters to keep certain understandings confidential can be justified only if their publication would directly undermine the authorities' ability to implement the program or render implementation more costly. Accordingly, their use will normally be limited to cases in which the premature release of the information would cause adverse market reaction or undermine the authorities' efforts to prepare the domestic groundwork for a measure.

6. While there is no presumption that particular kinds of measures would be conveyed in a side letter rather than a letter of intent, some matters that could in some cases be considered for inclusion in side letters would be: (i) exchange market intervention rules; (ii) bank closures; (iii) contingent fiscal measures; and (iv) measures affecting key prices.[57]

**10-012**   The significance of a prior action is primarily in the context of enforcement. However, since the device of a prior action has a built-in enforcement aspect, i.e. the consequence of non-observance results in the denial of use, the question of its legal character has little significance for the fund. On the other hand, from the requesting member's point of view, the legal character of a prior action may be of importance, both in the context of negotiating a stabilisation programme; and post facto, where for instance, the Fund having imposed a prior action relents on its promise, or insists on compliance with further prior actions. The Fund in these circumstances may well have a mandate stemming from other provisions of the Articles of Agreement to influence the requesting member's behaviour.[58] However, the Fund in undermining an expectation that it engenders may raise the question whether it is acting in breach of a general duty to act in good faith.[59] Further, the doctrine of estoppel[60]; and the instrument of a binding unilateral declaration[61] as

---

[56] See Guidelines on Conditionality para.10. See EB Decision on Side Letters and the Use of Fund Resources Decision No.12067–(99/108) September 22, 1999.

[57] Decision No.12067–(99/108) September 22, 1999.

[58] For example under Art.IV or XIV consultations.

[59] See, for example Schwarzenberger and Brown, *A Manual of International Law*, 6th edn (Abingdon: Professional Books, 1976), pp.7, 23, 27, 444–445 and p.118; and J. Gold, IMF *Pamphlet Series* Nos 35, 28–29.

[60] See, for example B. Cheng, *General Principles of Law* (London: Stevens, 1953), Ch.5; I.C. MacGibbon, "Estoppel in International Law" (1958) 7 I.C.L.Q. 468–513; G. Schwarzenberger, *International Law*, Vol.I, 3rd edn. See Shaw, *International Law*, 4th edn (Cambridge: Cambridge University Press, 1997), pp.350–352; I. Sinclair, "Estoppel and Acquiescence" in A.V. Lowe and M. Fitzmaurice (eds), *Fifty Years of the International Court of Justice* (Cambridge University Press, 1996), p.104.

[61] *Nuclear Tests Case (Australia v France)*, Judgment of December 20, 1974, I.C.J. Reports, pp.267–8. See also *Nicaragua* case (1986) I.C.J. Reports; and *Burkina Fasa v Mali* case

facets of the principle of good faith,[62] may reinforce the question whether the Fund could be precluded from acting contrary to its declared intentions. Indeed, the two derivatives of the general principle of good faith could involve a positive obligation on the Fund to implement the undertaking it tendered to the requesting State; or possibly involve a duty of restitution. The Fund's undertaking is not undermined by the Fund's declaration that its "arrangements" are not international agreements.[63] In the circumstances, any capricious refusal amounting to bad faith, to approve a request on the terms agreed, would be a breach of the undertaking tendered by the Fund.

In general, Conditionality is progressively stringent according to the level of the drawing. In reserve tranches the member enjoys the overwhelming benefit of any doubt. The Fund does not challenge the member's representation of need for balance of payments purposes.[64] The Fund's attitude towards drawings under the first tranche is liberal but drawings in the higher tranches require substantial justification.[65] Of late, in order to prevent and respond effectively to crisis situations, the Fund has made provision for up-front financing of large amounts without Conditionality although with stringent pre-qualification requirements.

Within the economic parameters of Conditionality, there are nevertheless guide posts which need to be followed in its formulation. These are to be discerned from the Articles of Agreement, the Executive Board Decisions,[66] and generally from International Law. The Guidelines on Conditionality offer the following principles. First, the primary responsibility for the design and implementation of Conditionality must be within the ownership of the member (ownership of programme).[67] Secondly, the policies must be adapted so as to pay due regard to the domestic social and political objectives of the member in question, the circumstances of the member, including the causes of the balance of payments problems (circumstances of Member).[68] This injunction guards against the Fund usurping the domestic social and political choices available to the member. Moreover, it is reinforced by the emphasis on the role of the Fund at a macroeconomic rather than at the microeconomic level.[69] However, the Fund is under no obligation to create an economic environment conducive to a member realising its domestic social and political objectives; its economic priorities and an environment dictated by

---

(1986) I.C.J. Reports. See also, for example, J.-D. Sicault, "Du Caractère Obligatoire des Engagements Unilateraux en Droit International Public" (1979) 83 *Revue Generale de Droit International Public* 634–88; A.P. Rubin, "The International Legal Effects of Unilateral Declarations" (1977) 71 *American Journal of International Law* 1–30.

[62] Mac Gibbon (1958), p.468.

[63] Para.9 of the Guidelines on Conditionality.

[64] See Art.V, s.3(b)(ii) and (c).

[65] See IMF *Annual Reports* of the Executive Directors (1963), p.16. See also *Annual Reports*, 1953, 1955, 1959, 1961, and 1962 and *Selected Decisions* above.

[66] In particular the Guidelines on Conditionality.

[67] Para.3 of the Guidelines on Conditionality.

[68] Para.4 of the Guidelines on Conditionality.

[69] Denter (1996), p.115. See para.6 of the Guidelines on Conditionality.

its individual circumstances.[70] Thirdly, the overriding purpose of the policies is the balance of payments equilibrium whilst fostering sustainable economic growth (focus on programme goals).[71] Fourthly, the conditions must be applied parsimoniously i.e., they must be critical, necessary, under the control of the member; and in general must be formulated in macroeconomic or structural terms—specially the performance criteria (parsimony).[72] However, there is no precise definition of what constitutes a macroeconomic target. The macroeconomic variables and structural measures must, however, be within the Fund's core areas of responsibility. Some measures can fall into a grey area and then there can be conflict, for example in relation to wages.[73] Some microeconomic involvement of the Fund exceptionally can be justified. This is because of the need to consider not only the general symptoms of balance of payments problems but also the underlying causes for the problem which may well be microeconomic.[74]

**10-013**    However, there are considerable difficulties in the Fund involving itself at the microeconomic level.[75] First, the Fund does not have the necessary expertise in this field, and its involvement may well interfere with the World Bank operations. Secondly, it is more difficult to formulate and monitor the observation of microeconomic performance criteria. Finally, the level of intrusion in the domestic affairs of a member's domestic and political affairs would generate resentment within the Member State's economy.

Fifthly, Conditionality must be such as not to intrude into the political affairs of the member.[76] This is not explicitly stated as such in the Guidelines on Conditionality but is implicit. Thus, Conditionality must be applied uniformly, in a non-discriminatory fashion, across the membership; and in accordance with the Fund's provisions and polices. However, where the level of political turmoil is such as to affect the capacity of a member to implement economic changes, there is some suggestion that in that event political considerations may well impact in the decision-making processes of the IMF.[77] Conditionality aimed at the reduction of excessive defence expenditure may be construed as political interference, and also characterised as being microeconomic.[78] It cannot, it seems, totally be ignored.[79] Indeed, although military expenditure has not been allowed to be the focus of performance criteria,

---

[70] See J. Gold, "Political considerations are prohibited by Articles of Agreement when the Fund considers requests for use of resources", IMF *Survey* (May 23, 1983), pp.146–148.

[71] Para.6 of the Guidelines on Conditionality.

[72] Para.7 of the Guidelines on Conditionality.

[73] Denters (1996), p.110.

[74] See, for example, Denters (1996), p.144.

[75] See, for example, Denters (1996), p.144.

[76] Art.1 of the IMF Articles of Agreement. See also paras 1, 6, 7, 8 of the Guidelines on Conditionality; and Gold (1983), pp.146–148.

[77] See Denters (1996), p.114 and reference therein to I.F. Shihata, *The World Bank in a Changing World* (Martinus Nijhoff, 1991), p.76.

[78] See, for example, Denters (1996), pp.10 and 139.

[79] Denters (1996), p.10.

or a condition for the use of Fund resources,[80] where there are sound grounds for economic reasons for its reduction the question whether a performance criteria requiring reduction in military expenditure is contrary to the Articles of Agreement is as yet undecided.[81] Similarly, Fund involvement in income distribution could also be considered as being political and microeconomic in character. By the same token, concern for human rights violations can open the Fund to the charge of political interference in the domestic affairs of the member. But violations which affect the implementation of an adjustment programme may be the concern of the IMF.[82]

To conclude, the Guidelines on Conditionality take particular account of a members' economic sovereignty by stressing national ownership of economic programmes; inculcating due regard to the particular circumstances of the member in the design of the economic programme; emphasising the inclusion of macroeconomic (as opposed to micro) conditions; ensuring parsimony in the prescription of Conditionality; discouraging cross-conditionality; and finally by reinforcing the conformity of Conditionality with the Articles of Agreement of the IMF and the uniform application of Conditionality amongst members.

**Guidelines on Conditionality[83]:**

'A. Principles                                                                              **10-014**

1. Basis and purpose of conditionality. Conditions on the use of Fund resources are governed by the Fund's Articles of Agreement and implementing decisions of the Executive Board. Conditionality—that is, program-related conditions—is intended to ensure that Fund resources are provided to members to assist them in resolving their balance of payments problems in a manner that is consistent with the Fund's Articles and that establishes adequate safeguards for the temporary use of the Fund's resources.

2. Early warning and prevention. Conditionality is one element in a broad strategy for helping members strengthen their economic and financial policies. Through formal and informal consultations, multilateral surveillance including the World Economic Outlook and discussions of capital market developments, advice to members on the voluntary adoption of appropriate standards and codes, and the provision of technical assistance, the Fund encourages members to adopt sound economic and financial policies as a precaution against the emergence of balance of payments difficulties, or to take corrective measures at an early stage of the development of difficulties.

---

[80] See Concluding Remarks by the Acting Chairman Military Expenditure and the Role of the Fund Executive Board Meeting 91/138 October 2, 1991 published in *Selected Decisions*.

[81] Gold, *Interpretation* (1996), pp.498–499.

[82] See, for example, Denters (1996), pp.11, 175–176. See also M. Cogen, "Human rights prohibition of political activities and the lending policies of World Bank and the IMF" in P. de Waart et al. (eds), *International Law and Development* (Dordrecht/Boston/London, Martinus Nijhoff, 1988), p.379.

[83] Decision No. 12864–(02/102) September 25, 2002 as amended.

3. Ownership and capacity to implement programs. National ownership of sound economic and financial policies and an adequate administrative capacity are crucial for successful implementation of Fund-supported programs. In responding to members' requests to use Fund resources and in setting program-related conditions, the Fund will be guided by the principle that the member has primary responsibility for the selection, design, and implementation of its economic and financial policies. The Fund will encourage members to seek to broaden and deepen the base of support for sound policies in order to enhance the likelihood of successful implementation.

4. Circumstances of members. In helping members to devise economic and financial programs, the Fund will pay due regard to the domestic social and political objectives, the economic priorities, and the circumstances of members, including the causes of their balance of payments problems and their administrative capacity to implement reforms. Conditionality and program design will also reflect the member's circumstances and the provisions of the facility under which the Fund's financing is being provided. The causes of balance of payments difficulties and the emphasis to be given to various program goals may differ among members, and the appropriate financing, the specification and sequencing of policy adjustments, and the time required to correct the problem will reflect those and other differences in circumstances. The member's past performance in implementing economic and financial policies will be taken into account as one factor affecting conditionality, with due consideration to changes in circumstances that would indicate a break with past performance.

5. Approval of access to Fund resources. The Fund will ensure consistency in the application of policies relating to the use of its resources with a view to maintaining the uniform treatment of members. A member's request to use Fund resources will be approved only if the Fund is satisfied that the member's program is consistent with the Fund's provisions and policies and that it will be carried out, and in particular that the member is sufficiently committed to implement the program. The Managing Director will be guided by these principles in making recommendations to the Executive Board with respect to the approval of the use of Fund resources by members.

6. Focus on program goals. Fund-supported programs should be directed primarily toward the following macroeconomic goals:

   (a) solving the member's balance of payments problem without recourse to measures destructive of national or international prosperity; and

   (b) achieving medium-term external viability while fostering sustainable economic growth.

7. Scope of conditions. Program-related conditions governing the provision of Fund resources will be applied parsimoniously and will be consistent with the following principles:

   (a) Conditions will be established only on the basis of those variables or measures that are reasonably within the member's direct or indirect control and that are, generally, either (i) of critical importance for achieving the goals of the member's program or for monitoring the implementation of the program, or (ii) necessary for the implementation of specific provisions of the Articles or policies adopted under them. In general, all variables or measures that meet these criteria will be established as conditions.

(b) Conditions will normally consist of macroeconomic variables and structural measures that are within the Fund's core areas of responsibility. Variables and measures that are outside the Fund's core areas of responsibility may also be established as conditions but may require more detailed explanation of their critical importance. The Fund's core areas of responsibility in this context comprise: macroeconomic stabilization; monetary, fiscal, and exchange rate policies, including the underlying institutional arrangements and closely related structural measures; and financial system issues related to the functioning of both domestic and international financial markets.

(c) Program-related conditions may contemplate the member meeting particular targets or objectives (outcomes-based conditionality), or taking (or refraining from taking) particular actions (actions-based conditionality). The formulation of individual conditions will be based, in particular, upon the circumstances of the member.

8. Responsibility of the Fund for conditionality. The Fund is fully responsible for the establishment and monitoring of all conditions attached to the use of its resources. There will be no cross-conditionality, under which the use of the Fund's resources would be directly subjected to the rules or decisions of other organizations. When establishing and monitoring conditions based on variables and measures that are not within its core areas of responsibility, the Fund will, to the fullest extent possible, draw on the advice of other multilateral institutions, particularly the World Bank. The application of a lead agency framework, such as between the Fund and the Bank, will be implemented flexibly to take account of the circumstances of members and the overlapping interests of the two institutions with respect to some aspects of members policies. The Fund's policy advice, program design, and conditionality will, insofar as possible, be consistent and integrated with those of other international institutions within a coherent country-led framework. The roles of each institution, including any relevant conditionality, will be stated clearly in Fund-related program documents.

The IMF, like the WTO, is set within and against the background of **10-015** International Law. Therefore IMF Conditionality is not only informed by the Fund's internal law but it is also subject to external influences which the Fund needs to take into account in its formulation. The degree to which the IMF can be influenced is dependent inter alia upon the extent to which the Fund is bound by such sources; or the degree to which the interpretation of IMF Articles of Agreement is informed by applicable relevant International Law norms[84] impacting on IMF Conditionality. First, there is the notion of sustainable development.[85] In the context of Conditionality, three forms of

---

[84] See Art.31 of the Vienna Convention on the Law of Treaties 1969.
[85] See Ch.2 above. See also, for example, World Commission on Environment and Development, *Our Common Future* (Oxford, Oxford University Press, 1987), p.43; and W. Lang (ed.), *Sustainable Development and International Law* (Kluwer Law International, 1995).

concerns have been identified from this requirement.[86] First, that present consumption must not be financed through debts which future generations must
honour. Secondly, there is the need for such a level of investment in education and health so that future generations are not confronted with problems
arising from a lack of such investment. Finally, the exploitation of natural
resources must not create an ecological debt for future generations. The
actual impact that sustainable development has on Fund decision making is
dependent on the scope and binding character of sustainable development as
a requirement of International Law, and its role in the normative conditions
of a balance of payments equilibrium.[87] Indeed, sustainable development
may be implicit in the requirement in the Articles of Agreement that Fund
polices should not act as "measures destructive of national or international
prosperity."[88] Moreover, the Guidelines on Conditionality now specifically
refer to the "fostering of sustainable economic growth."[89] Further, given
that sustainable development features in the work and operations of some
international organisations[90] the IMF is bound to co-operate with these
organisations operating in related fields,[91] although within the framework
of its mandate. Secondly, there is the question of the relevance of international agreements emphasising the enjoyment of human rights, in particular
in the context of Conditionality the 1966 Covenant on Economic, Social
and Cultural Rights. The 1966 Covenant places on parties to the agreement
obligations in relation to the socio-economic welfare of citizens, for example,
the right to employment, fair labour conditions, social security, adequate
health and education facilities.[92] The view from the Fund in relation to the
Covenant appears to be that the IMF is not a party to it.[93] However, the
Covenant considerations are not entirely irrelevant. This is because of the
requirement under Art.1 of the IMF Articles to avoid measures destructive of
national prosperity; the requirement to have due regard to social and politi-

---

[86] Denters (1996), p.146; and UNDP *Human Development Report* (1992).
[87] See above, Ch.9.
[88] Art 1.
[89] See para.6 of Guidelines on Conditionality.
[90] See, for example, the preamble to the Marrakesh Agreement Establishing The World Trade
Organization.
[91] See Art.X of the Articles of Agreement of the IMF and para.8 of the Guidelines on
Conditionality as amended.
[92] See Denters (1996), p.180. The author refers to Arts 6, 7, 9, 12 and 13 of the 1966
International Covenant on Economic, Social and Cultural Rights and also other instruments for example the UN Universal Declaration of Human Rights (1948); UN Declaration
on Social Progress and Development (1969); the Charter of Economic Rights and Duties
of States (1974); the Declaration on International Economic Cooperation; the Vienna
Declaration and Programme of Action (1993); Agenda for Development (1994); and the
Declaration and Programme of Action of the World Summit for Social Development
(1995). See also M. Lucas, "The International Monetary Fund's Conditionality and the
International Covenant on Economic, Social and Cultural Rights: an attempt to define
the relation" (1992) 1 *Revue Belge de Droit International* 104–35; and M.C.R. Craven, *The
International Covenant on Economic, Social, and Cultural Rights* (Oxford, Oxford University
Press, 1995).
[93] See Denters (1996), p.181.

cal objectives of the member;[94] and the expectation in other international agreements[95] that parties to it will co-operate to achieve the objectives of the Agreement.[96] In some Member States, the Executive Director to the Fund is expected to work towards the promotion of socioeconomic objectives in adjustment programmes.[97]

Finally, the Fund has come under considerable criticism, particularly in the past, for stressing demand management and showing a lack of concern for the socio-economic consequences on the lesser off.[98] The Fund has responded to this by calling for a consideration of growth and structural reforms in adjustment programmes.[99] Thus, the IMF focuses on exchange rate and interest rates with growth in mind. Similarly, the IMF adjustment programmes attempt to deal with distortions that hamper export growth and efficiency in government spending.[100] Further, the Fund has recognised that socioeconomic factors need to be taken into account in adjustment pro-grammes, and these are discussed with the member by the Fund mission.[101] Thus, IMF missions are involved in discussing the establishment of social safety nets targeted at the neediest groups.[102]

### Conditionality: Hard Law or Soft Law?

For the purposes of establishing the legal character of IMF Conditionality, the three-tiered distinction between the core obligations, the inner and outer Conditionality mentioned earlier[103] is important. It is contended that the inner Conditionality is binding and generally the outer Conditionality is not.     **10-016**

### Letters of Intent[104]

The Letter of Intent expresses Conditionality at two levels. First, it sets out the broad objectives of the programme. These are the purposes of the arrangement, formulated in general terms. The objectives identify specific economic areas of action. Secondly, the specific measures to implement the objectives are stated. These are the policies of the arrangement to implement     **10-017**

---

[94] See Guidelines on Conditionality, para.4.

[95] For example Art.2 of the Covenant on Civil and Political Rights (1966).

[96] See Denters (1996), pp.183–184.

[97] See Denters (1996), p.187; and US International Development and Finance Act of 1989, Public Law 101–240: Title V, 541(d)(1), 103 Stat.2518 and Title III, 302, 103 Stat 2501.

[98] See Denters (1996), pp.117 and 152; G-24 "Supplement on the Group of 24 Deputies Report", IMF *Survey* (August 10, 1987); and G.A. Cornia et al. (eds), *Adjustment with a Human Face* (Oxford, Oxford University Press, 1987), Vol.1.

[99] See IMF *Annual Reports* (1988) and (1998); and Denters (1996), p.127. See also para.6 of the Guidelines on Conditionality.

[100] IMF *Survey* (September 1997), Vol.26.

[101] See Denters (1996), pp.135–136. See also IMF *Annual Report* (1989), p.37; and IMF *Annual Report* (1998).

[102] IMF *Survey* (September 1997) Vol.26; and IMF *Annual Report* (1998).

[103] See Ch.9 para.9-033.

[104] Or a Memorandum on Economic and Financial Policies (MEFP) or Technical Memorandum of Understanding (TMU).

the objectives. They are often very specific and detailed. The objectives and policies comprise the economic conditions. In addition, the Letter of Intent contains provisions as to the financial Conditionality. Further, Letters of Intent normally contain a clause which restates existing obligations under the Articles of Agreement generally.

As a prerequisite to ascertaining the binding character of Conditionality, it is necessary to examine if there are actually any "obligations" or "undertakings", as opposed for example to mere declarations of aspirations, contained in the Letter of Intent. The obligations are conditions that are to be implemented by the Member State requesting the drawing. As such they must be clear, certain, govern specific behaviour, and have the quality of being enforceable. Not every assertion would necessarily amount to a condition. This process of examination involves interpreting the Letter of Intent.

The need for construction arises particularly because the Letter of Intent is not in the traditional sense a formal legal document as such. The content of the Letter of Intent is not necessarily set out chronologically or indeed to be found in a single document.[105] It may be accompanied, for example, by a side letter. Thus, the Letter of Intent may contain a number of paragraphs which deal with the past state of the economy, the problems within the economy, the political objectives of the Government and the circumstances leading up to the request. The individual objectives of the programme may in turn be preceded by the past and current state of affairs regarding them, and the difficulties envisaged in implementing them. Further, the objectives and policies may not be stated as such but may have to be fathomed from the general tenor of the letter as a whole—including any attached annexes.

**10-018**    However, the Letter of Intent does betray a certain measure of legal character. Thus, standardised language and clauses are to be found. This can be attributed to the legal expertise of the fund, and its involvement in its formulation. Further, the Letter of Intent also reflects the complex of opposing forces operating during the negotiations of the programme—particularly the interest of the requesting state to minimise and camouflage any commitments tendered.

First, in relation to the objectives stated in a Letter of Intent. These on their own, whilst they influence the behaviour of a State in a general sense, by indicating a trend, do not in themselves constitute conditions that may be justiciable in law. They are too broad, vague and lack certainty. Indeed, they are not expressed as undertakings. Rather they constitute explanations as to the purpose of the programme. They are in the true sense objectives, and are expressed as priorities of the government or objectives of the programme. They indicate the desired direction of the programme. These objectives must be consistent with the Articles of Agreement, and may embrace also other

---

[105] For example, in the case of the Jamaican Extended Arrangement of May 10, 1979, there were three annexes. These were (1) the Letter of Intent; (2) a Memorandum of Economic Policy; (3) a Technical Memorandum of Understanding.

objectives not expressly stated in Art.1. Thus, frequently the objective of reducing inflation is found in the programme even though this objective is not expressly stated in Art.1.

Secondly, the policies in the Letter of Intent designed to implement the objectives of the programme would seem to approximate closest to obligations/ conditions. They are generally more specific and impinge directly upon the conduct of the requesting State. However, the policies do not form a homogeneous group that may be analysed as either amounting to obligations or not. The policies need to be analysed further individually to ascertain whether there is any concrete "undertaking" in fact tendered. They are variously expressed, and their normative character is to be determined primarily with reference to the language used.

The policies expressed may be categorised in order of the degree of their normative quality. First, there are statements of measures already undertaken. The measures may have been IMF prior actions. The actions already undertaken indicate how the government is minded to conduct its policies in future.

The statements of measures already undertaken must be true. There is here an obligation on the part of the member concerned to tender correct information regarding measures taken, arising from the general duty on the part of the drawing member to act in good faith—quite apart from any general obligations arising under the Articles of Agreement to co-operate with the Fund. In addition, the Fund may challenge any representation made that is false under Art.V, s.3(c). The Fund has also decided that where there has been misreporting, the member will be called upon to take corrective action in relation to a drawing made under such circumstances, either by repurchase or by the use of its currency in transactions or operations of the Fund, unless the Fund decides otherwise.[106] However, the non-complying purchase does not constitute a violation,[107] and only gives rise to an expectation to repurchase.[108]

### MISREPORTING AND NONCOMPLYING PURCHASES IN THE GENERAL RESOURCES ACCOUNT-GUIDELINES ON CORRECTIVE ACTION[109]

In some cases, it has been found that a member has made a purchase in the General Resources Account that it was not entitled to make under the terms of the arrangement or other decisions governing the purchase (a "noncomplying purchase"). The purchase was permitted because, on the basis of the information available to it at the time, the Fund was satisfied that all performance criteria or other conditions applicable to the purchase under the terms of the relevant decision had been observed, but this information later proved to be incorrect. When such a case arises in the future, the member will be

**10-019**

---

[106] Executive Board Decision No.7842-(84/165) in *Selected Decisions*.
[107] Gold (1996), p.374.
[108] Gold (1996), p.374 and see also para.3 of Executive Board Decision No.7842–(84/165) as amended.
[109] Decision No.7842–(84/165), November 16, 1984, as amended by Decision No.12249–(00/77) July 27, 2000.

called upon to take corrective action regarding a noncomplying purchase, to the extent that it is still outstanding, either by repurchase or by the use of its currency in transactions and operations of the Fund, unless the Fund decides that the circumstances justify the member's continued use of the purchased resources. Steps should also be taken to improve the accuracy and completeness of the information to be reported to the Fund by the member in connection with its use of the Fund's general resources, and to define performance criteria and other applicable conditions in a manner that would facilitate accurate reporting.

**10-020**   Secondly, there are express representations that indicate the Government's state of mind, and the likely trend of future conduct. These are representations which, although indicative of a State's economic policy, do not if properly analysed constitute concrete undertakings. They are more in the nature of assertions descriptive of the Government's state of mind, rather than actual promises regarding future conduct. The statements indicate the Government's perception of an economic situation, and how it may be minded to tackle the problem.

Thirdly, there are statements which apparently profess future course of conduct, but given the manner of their formulation do not in fact amount to positive unqualified, final and specific enforceable undertakings of future conduct.[110] Further, given the choice of language in the context of an agreement, there is no intention to be bound by the representations made. However, there may be an expectation that the member will act in good faith with regard to these policies.[111]

Fourthly, there are statements regarding future conduct as intentions of the Government.[112] The point of importance is that the measures are not positively stated as undertakings. It is not stated that the Government will, but rather that the Government intends to. Given this formulation there is no actual undertaking tendered by the State concerned, since an expression of what the State intends to do is merely descriptive of a future course of conduct contemplated, and not promissory. The State is not undertaking to take measures in the future, it is merely articulating what at the time of writing the Letter it intends to do in the future. However, given the circumstances in which the intentions are tendered, particularly the fact that they are addressed "bilaterally"—specifically to another entity—the intentions so articulated are not devoid of consequences. First, there is an obligation

---

[110] For example "we expect that we will be able to mobilise the additional foreign exchange required" or "the government will make every effort to speed up the execution of the projects" or "the government will consider raising contributions to the social security schemes".

[111] See, for example, J. Gold, "The Legal character of the Fund's Stand-by Arrangements and Why it Matters", IMF *Pamphlet Series* No.35.

[112] See, for example, "the Government intends to introduce immediately legislation to prohibit access by the health institutions, including the Hospital Fund, to short-term bank credit" or "the Government intends to restore immediately legislation to prohibit access by the health institutions, including the Hospital Fund, to short-term bank credit".

that the intention stated is actually contemplated at the time of its being expressed, and that there are reasonable grounds for holding that intention.[113] If this is not the case then the State concerned would in fact be tendering a misrepresentation. This could amount to a breach of an obligation of good faith, and could involve the member in having to take corrective measures for the misreporting.[114] However, in the absence of the intention being made performance criteria, there is, it is suggested, no obligation to adhere to the course of action stipulated in the future—provided of course the deviation is bona fide.

Finally, there are definitive policy undertakings in concrete terms. These **10-021** are categorical statements of measures that will be taken.[115] The language used is promissory. Generally only the performance criteria and consultation provisions appear to fall under this category. Other provisions are found to be expressed in the "the government will. . ." form, but these have to be analysed to ascertain if there is in fact any concrete substantive specific enforceable undertaking.

There are some other provisions that are expressed in promissory language, but which when analysed in fact are too vague and general, so as not to contain any enforceable specific undertaking.[116] Such provisions lack concrete obligatory character even though expressed in promissory language, because they are not specific and detailed enough. They cannot be enforced. However, some undertakings may nevertheless be found that are not performance criteria.

In conclusion, the actual obligations or undertakings given by the Member State have to be ascertained by an analysis of the Letter of Intent, and upon the construction of the language used. This is now recognised by J. Gold when he states[117]:

> ". . . it is necessary to be cautious about defining the Stand-by arrangement as an informal instrument, or as an instrument of law, or an instrument that does not have legal consequences. The Stand-by arrangement is too complex an instrument to be adequately described by any of those slogans. . .A better approach is to understand the character of the terms to be found in a Stand-by arrangement because they fall into various categories."

Generally, in the context of the whole Letter of Intent the actual concrete **10-022** undertakings are, in practice, very few. Those that are found, including any performance criteria, will have to be assessed against the background

---

[113] *Edgington v Fitzmaurice* (1885) 29 Ch.D 459 at 483 per Bowen L.J: "The state of a man's mind is as much a fact as the state of his digestion."
[114] Executive Board Decision No.7842–(84/165) in *Selected Decisions*.
[115] See, for example, "the Government will. . .".
[116] See, for example, "the Government will pursue policies that will stimulate production and exports and maintain the appropriate balance between demand and supply".
[117] Gold (1996), p.398.

of the economy as described in the Letter of Intent, and the reasons and cir-cumstances surrounding the measures.

On this analysis, a Letter of Intent is primarily a process of self-appraisal and rationalisation on the part of the Government, rather than an instrument containing undertakings as such. Indeed, it is conceivable that Letters of Intent may exist without any actual normative content in legal analysis—so far as the economic Conditionality is concerned.

The next step in the enquiry is to consider the legal character of those undertakings found in the Letter of Intent. It is suggested that the preceding analysis into the existence of an undertaking is not thoroughly conducted by most commentators. The emphasis is on the issues arising from the second stage of the inquiry. This is particularly true of Gold's former characterisa-tion of the stand-by arrangement.[118] There was a tendency to treat the Letter of Intent as a monolithic whole—without clearly distinguishing between the types of policies in the Letters of Intent.[119]

Some undertakings are to be found in Letters of Intent, and they are expressed in promissory language, and properly analysed do form positive undertakings. The Letter of Intent emanates from the Member State, and there would appear to be little to prevent it from using promissory language to take upon itself positive concrete undertakings. The decisive element in this context is the intention to be bound. This intention to be bound may be evident in the language used by the member. There is nothing to prevent a member from entertaining such an intention.

In the alternative, the undertakings in the Letter of Intent may amount to binding unilateral declarations[120] where there is an intention to be bound on the part of the member. It is not possible to generalise about the inten-tions of the members.[121] The Fund's negation of an intention to contract,[122] if it can be discerned at all with regard to the undertakings in question, has no bearing on the question whether the member has the requisite inten-tion for a binding unilateral declaration. The Fund may not usurp the prerogative of a member to formulate such an intention. What the Fund's negation may amount to is a waiver of compliance with the undertakings. Or alternatively, the Fund may refuse to hold the member bound by its declaration.[123]

---

[118] See Gold, IMF *Pamphlet Series* No.35.

[119] This is the case also with Denters (1996), p.99.

[120] *Nuclear Tests Case (Australia v France)*, Judgment of December 20, 1974, I.C.J. Reports, 267–68. See also *Nicaragua* case (1986) I.C.J. Reports; and *Burkina Fasa v Mali* case (1986) I.C.J. Reports. See also, for example, J.D. Sicault, "Du Caractère Obligatoire des Engagements Unilateraux en Droit International Public" (1979) 83 *Revue Generale de Droit Internationale Public* 634–88; A.P. Rubin, "The International Legal Effects of Unilateral Declarations" (1977) 71 *American Journal of International Law*, 1–30. Contra Denters (1996), p.99; and Gold (1996), p.367.

[121] This is what Gold does (see Gold (1996), p.367).

[122] J. Gold, IMF *Pamphlet Series* No.35, p.25. See also Guidelines on Conditionality, para.9 and Art.XXX(b).

[123] Gold (1996), p.367.

From the perspective that the Letter of Intent is not part of a binding agreement or a binding unilateral declaration, non-compliance with the terms of the Letter of Intent does not constitute an unlawful act.[124] The drawings already made, according to this view are not held illegally, and do not have to be returned or repurchased. However, the resources would have to be returned or repurchased if there was a non-complying purchase as a consequence of misreporting, or the member was using the resources contrary to the purposes of the IMF.[125] Further, if the conditions are not fulfilled, all that happens is that further drawings cannot be made. The member cannot be obliged to implement the unfulfilled conditions.

### The Fund "arrangement"

The Fund arrangement is more formal than the Letter of Intent. They are very precise, detailed and standardised. Precedents of stand-by and extended arrangements are set out in the Executive Board Decisions of the Fund.[126] The Conditionality in the arrangement is expressed in two ways. First, the Conditionality in the Letter of Intent is incorporated into the arrangement by reference to the Letter of Intent. However, the Stand-by or similar document differentiates between its own provisions, and the policies and objectives set out in the Letter of Intent. Secondly, the Conditionality is expressly stated in the provisions of the arrangement. The provisions of the arrangement comprise the economic and financial Conditionality. The financial Conditionality is set out in detail. However, the economic Conditionality is confined to a restatement of the policies in the Letter of Intent. The broad objectives stated in the Letter of Intent are not stated in the arrangement. Indeed, the arrangement document seems to be confined to stating those policies which are performance criteria.

**10-023**

The arrangement is confined to those policies in the Letter of Intent that form the inner Conditionality in the Letter of Intent. Additionally, the stand-by document contains provisions with regard to the financial Conditionality, and the provisions relating to the phased use of the Fund resources. The document is a formal document, drafted in a legal manner and the provisions contained are all formulated in precise concrete, specific and obligatory a manner. The normative content of the arrangement is beyond doubt.

Although the Fund's arrangement is considered a binding decision of the Fund,[127] for the reasons given previously the stand-by document may also

---

[124] See, for example, Denters (1996), p.100.
[125] See Executive Board Decision No.7842–(84/165) (November 16, 1984) in *Selected Decisions of the IMF* above. See also Art.V, s.5.
[126] See Executive Board Decision No.10464–(93/130) in *Selected Decisions of the Fund* above.
[127] Art.XXX(b).

be characterised, albeit controversially, as a contractual arrangement, with respect to the undertakings determined.

### DOCTRINE OF ULTRA VIRES AND THE PRINCIPLE OF DÉTOURNEMENT DE POUVOIR

**10-024**    The doctrine of *ultra vires* in the context of international organisations is generally accepted,[128] as is the principle of *détournement de pouvoir*.[129] Generally, *ultra vires* in the context of international organisations refers to the situation where an international organisation is operating beyond its powers. The principle of *détournement de pouvoir* is related but refers to the situation where the international organisation exercises the power that it is vested with in a manner other than that contemplated.[130] Both principles are accepted as general principles of law.[131] That Conditionality may be subject to such principles is also accepted.[132] The doctrine of *ultra vires* is confined exclusively to the regulation of the inner Conditionality. This is because only these are binding, and therefore capable of constituting acts that are *ultra vires*. However, even here not all the inner Conditionality may be subject to the doctrine of *ultra vires*. Where the inner Conditionality is binding only by reason of the State involved, because it is part of a binding unilateral declaration and not adopted by the Fund, conformity with the Fund law is not called for. A prerequisite of the application of the doctrine of *ultra vires* in this context involves an act of the Fund. Where the binding character is by reason of a binding decision or agreement then the doctrine of *ultra vires* operates, as there is, in one form or another, an act of the Fund.

The inner Conditionality that is subject to the *ultra vires* doctrine is binding, until it is successfully invalidated.[133] The ground of *ultra vires* involves a question of interpretation of the Articles of Agreement. Therefore, the matter would be raised in the first instance with the Executive Board, with the possibility of appeal to the Board of Governors. The decision of the Board of Governors would be final.

The *ultra vires* doctrine in the context of the inner Conditionality involves the consideration of the inner Conditionality in accordance with the

---

[128] See for example E. Osieke (1983) 77(2) "The legal validity of Ultra Vires Decisions of International Organisations", A.J.I.L.; B. Trubitt, "IMF Conditionality and options for aggrieved Fund members" (1987) 20 *Vanderbilt Journal of Transnational Law*, n.4.

[129] See J.E.S. Fawcett, "Detournment de Pouvoir by International Organizations" (1957) 33 *British Year Book of International Law* 311–316. See also Gold (1996), p.532.

[130] Gold (1996), p.532.

[131] Gold (1996), p.532.

[132] E. Osieke, *The Constitutional Character of International Organizations with particular reference to the ILO, ICAO and IMF* University of London PhD thesis, April 1974 (unpublished). See also Denters (1996), p.193 and Gold (1996), p.532.

[133] Osieke (1983), p.239.

Articles of Agreement and Fund decisions—in particular the Guidelines on Conditionality. The doctrine has a more pronounced impact in the context of the inner financial Conditionality, than the inner economic Conditionality. However, generally, the doctrine has in practice some limitations—unless there is an overt infusion of blatant political and/or non-economic considerations.[134] As long as the objectives and policies, in particular the inner Conditionality is pre-eminently economic in complexion directed at the balance of payments, the Fund has considerable latitude.

First, as has been seen, the Letter of Intent contains certain objectives and policies. The objectives set in the Letter of Intent are those objectives which the member tenders of its own initiative. They are the objectives of the programme. These objectives may or may not be similar to those objectives of the Fund, as set in out in Art.1, so long as they are not inconsistent with these. The stand-by decision is to be interpreted in the light of these objectives and is in support of them. Thus, the scope of the inner Conditionality is broadened by this infusion of objectives of the requesting member. If the objectives of the member are not directed immediately at the balance of payments problem—still no question of *ultra vires* arises, as the member will have consented to these, and their binding force derived from this consent. **10-025**

Secondly, the balance of payments problems in Art.V, involve not just a balance of payments disequilibrium per se but also other "equilibrium objectives" of an economic character, e.g. inflation, unemployment, trade restrictions etc. Furthermore, Art.I is not an exclusive list of the Fund objectives and policies. These are to be ascertained having regard to the Articles of Agreement as a whole. In addition, the Fund in formulating the policies under Art.V must have regard to the provisions of the Articles of Agreement generally. The Articles of Agreement generally impose a host of considerations upon a Member State that the Fund has to take into account in formulating its policies. Thus, Art.IV, s.I invites a Member State to consider "the development of the orderly underlying conditions that are necessary for financial and economic stability".

Thirdly, the Fund is directed in all its policies and decisions to be guided by the purposes set out in Art.1. These purposes are of panoramic scope. They embrace a variety of economic objectives, and are subject to a number of interpretations. The decision of the ICJ in the *Expenses* case[135] applied to this situation raises a presumption that any action taken in fulfilment of one of the stated purposes in Art.1 of the IMF Articles of Agreement is not *ultra vires*. In the context of Art.1, given the scope and generality of the Articles this presumption has serious implications.

Fourthly, on the basis that performance criteria, that does not repeat the obligations under the Articles, is not obligatory as a consequence of the Articles, or as a consequence of the existence of an international agreement **10-026**

---

[134] Contra T. Killick, IMF Stabilisation Programmes *ODI. Working Paper* No.6, p.4.
[135] (1962) I.C.J. Reports, p.168.

qua the stand-by arrangement, the Fund has much latitude in the range of performance criteria it can prescribe, as long as it is directed at the balance of payments and the purposes of the IMF.[136] In practice, the Fund has included trade liberalisation provisions as performance criteria even though trade is not within the Fund's regulatory jurisdiction as such.[137] Indeed, in October 1997 the Executive Board approved of a staff report advocating trade-related Conditionality.[138] The doctrine of *ultra vires* has more of a bearing, in the context of legally binding conditions.[139]

Fifthly, it was suggested by Gold[140] that the March 2, 1979 Executive Board Decision (predecessor of the current Guidelines on Conditionality 2002) which sets out the guidelines on Conditionality for the Executive Board to observe is not binding. The guidelines are mere "guidelines". Therefore there are no grounds for the application of the *ultra vires* doctrine. Although there is some merit in this soft-law characterisation of the March 2, 1979 decision, there are two concerns in relation to it which need to be noted. First, although expressly set out as "guidelines" the question nevertheless can be posed whether such a characterisation need necessarily be read literally. Secondly, even if it can be read literally does it necessarily characterise all the provisions of the decision, even those formulated in a firm manner. Thirdly, if indeed the decision merely sets out guidelines, then it does rob somewhat the legal force to the paragraph in the decision which characterises a Fund "arrangement" as a decision of the Fund!

Finally, the *ultra vires* doctrine has limitations because of a presumption of validity,[141] arising as a consequence of the fact that the Executive Board, which deliberates on a request for a drawing—is also the organ responsible for interpreting the Articles of Agreement—subject to an appeal to the Board of Governors.[142] Where the *ultra vires* is not blatant, the force of the presumption is strong. Where there is a substantial deviation, the implication may be unfounded. Further, because of the exclusive and internal power of interpretation (auto-interpretation) operating in the Fund, the decisions of the Executive Board cannot be effectively challenged in reality.[143]

**10-027**     From this perusal, it is evident that the Fund possesses a whole breadth of economic objectives for which it can formulate policies. In a sense, what is being asserted is, provided there is a balance of payments problem, and there

---

[136] Gold (1996), p.355.
[137] Gold (1996), p.355. But see Voluntary Declaration on Trade and Other Current Account Measures. Executive Board Decision No.4254–(74/75) in *Selected Decisions of the IMF*. The declaration, however, has not yet come into effect. See Gold (1996), p.357.
[138] See IMF *Survey* (Supplement Sept 1998) See also G7 October 1998 Work Program on Strengthening the Architecture of the International Monetary System. See also Decision No.13229–(04/33), April 2, 2004.
[139] Gold (1996).
[140] Gold (1996), p.375.
[141] See H. Schermers, *International Institutional Law* (The Netherlands, Sitjhoff & Noordhoff, 1980), Ch.12 at p.896 in the context of the World Bank.
[142] Art.XXIX.
[143] See Gold (1996), p.605.

are significant objectives and policies directed at this problem—this situation acts as a catalyst for the Fund to pursue other lateral economic objectives which it has a mandate to pursue under the Articles of Agreement, as long as these are consonant with the balance of payments equilibrium per se. These lateral objectives need not necessarily impinge on the balance of payments directly in a positive way, so long as they are subordinate to the main object. In addition, the difficulty in practice in isolating and identifying with precision the objectives and policies, in apportioning their contribution or lack of contribution to the balance of payments, poses severe difficulties for legal argumentation in the field.

In conclusion, however, whilst there are practical considerations which militate against the application of the doctrine of *ultra vires* in connection with the inner Conditionality, the doctrine is not without complete force. Indeed, even in the context of economic inner Conditionality, it serves to oust political considerations from infusion into Conditionality. Thus, the last sentence of Art.I forbids the Fund from taking political considerations into account, by requiring the Fund to be guided in all its policies and decisions by the purposes set forth in Art.I.[144] Further, even where it is in practice difficult to assert—it is nevertheless an instrument that operates as a check whilst leaving the economists with considerable latitude necessary to develop Conditionality.

## Enforcement Machinery for Conditionality[145]

The enforcement of Conditionality is double-edged—with built-in safeguards, as well as external sanctions. In the first instance, the actual monitoring of compliance is not done by the Executive Board but by the IMF staff.[146]  **10-028**

First, enforcement takes place by the very terms of the arrangement—a form of an internalised enforcement machinery. In this respect, prior actions, performance criteria, phasing of the use of resources and consultation clauses are critical. Such terms are an integral part of the inner Conditionality, and are concerned with its implementation, as distinct from their binding nature.

> "11  Monitoring of performance. The implementation of the member's understandings with the Fund may be monitored, in particular, on the basis of prior actions, performance criteria, program and other reviews, and other variables and measures established as structural benchmarks or indicative targets."[147]  **10-029**

---

[144] J. Gold, "Political considerations are prohibited by the Articles of Agreement when the Fund considers requests for use of resources", IMF *Survey* May 23, 1998, p.146.
[145] IMF *Pamphlet Series* No.32.
[146] Denters (1996), p.170.
[147] Decision No.12864–(02/102) September 25, 2002.

**10-030**   Where there is a departure from a performance criteria then the member is unable to make further drawings under the arrangement, without further consultations with the Fund. Departures from performance criteria are not, according to one view,[148] considered to be breaches of legal obligations, unless there is a departure from the provisions of the Articles of Agreement. They are merely departures which result in the interruption of the drawings.

**10-031**   (b)   Performance criteria. A performance criterion is a variable or measure whose observance or implementation is established as a formal condition for the making of purchases or disbursements under a Fund arrangement. Performance criteria will apply to clearly-specified variables or measures that can be objectively monitored by the staff and are so critical for the achievement of the program goals or monitoring implementation that purchases or disbursements under the arrangement should be interrupted in cases of nonobservance. The number and content of performance criteria may vary because of the diversity of circumstances and institutional arrangements of members.
*Decision No. 12864-(02/102) September 25, 2002*

**10-032**   Phasing is the practice of the Fund whereby drawings are allowed to be made in instalments only. It has been described as "the iron fist in a kid glove" which prevents a member from abusive use of Fund resources.[149] The mechanism of phasing is included only in stand-by arrangements beyond the first credit tranche.

Review provisions are included in all arrangements. This enables the Fund to review progress in the implementation of the stabilisation programme from time to time.[150] The consultation can take place through visits and the sending of information.[151] The review is conducted by the Executive Board and may focus on, in addition to the performance criteria, on "indicative targets" and "structural benchmarks" where these are set.

**10-033**   (c)   Reviews. Reviews are conducted by the Executive Board.

(i)   Program reviews. Program reviews provide a framework for an assessment of whether the program is broadly on track and whether modifications are necessary. A program review will be completed only if the Executive Board is satisfied, based on the member's past performance and policy understandings for the future, that the program remains on track to achieve its objectives. In making this assessment, the Executive Board will take into consideration, in particular, the member's observance of performance criteria, indicative targets, and structural benchmarks, and the need to safeguard Fund resources. The elements of a member's program that will be taken into account for the completion of a review will be specified as fully

---

[148] Gold (1996), p.353.
[149] Denters (1996), p.112. This may be somewhat an optimistic description given recent examples of abuses, e.g. Russia.
[150] Guidelines on Conditionality, para.11(c).
[151] Denters (1996), p.111.

and transparently as possible in the arrangement. Arrangements will provide for reviews to take place at a frequency appropriate to the member's circumstances. Reviews are expected to be held every six months, but substantial uncertainties concerning major economic trends or policy implementation may warrant more frequent monitoring. In cases of major delays in the completion of a review, the Managing Director will inform Executive Directors in an appropriate manner.

(ii) Financing assurances reviews. Where the Fund is providing financial assistance to a member that has outstanding sovereign external payments arrears to private creditors or that, by virtue of the imposition of exchange controls, has outstanding non-sovereign external payments arrears, the Executive Board will conduct a financing assurances review to determine whether adequate safeguards remain in place for the further use of the Fund's resources in the member's circumstances and whether the member's adjustment efforts are undermined by developments in creditor-debtor relations. More specifically, every purchase or disbursement made available after the approval of the arrangement will, while such arrears remain outstanding, be made subject to the completion of a financing assurances review. Financing assurances reviews may also be established where the member has outstanding arrears to official creditors.

(d) Other variables and measures. In monitoring the implementation of a member s program, the Fund may also examine variables and measures established as indicative targets and structural benchmarks. The same principles governing the scope of conditions set out in paragraph 7 apply to these variables and measures as well as to other program-related conditions.

(i) Indicative targets. Variables may be established as indicative targets for the part of an arrangement for which they cannot be established as performance criteria because of substantial uncertainty about economic trends. As uncertainty is reduced, these targets will normally be established as performance criteria, with appropriate modifications as necessary. Indicative targets may also be established in addition to performance criteria as quantitative indicators to assess the member's progress in meeting the objectives of a program in the context of a program review.

(ii) Structural benchmarks. A measure may be established as a structural benchmark where it cannot be specified in terms that may be objectively monitored or where its non-implementation would not, by itself, warrant an interruption of purchases or disbursements under an arrangement. Structural benchmarks are intended to serve as clear markers in the assessment of progress in the implementation of critical structural reforms in the context of a program review.[152]

Secondly, the internalised enforcement measures are set against the back-ground of the specific enforcement regime found in the Articles of Agreement **10-034**

---

[152] Decision No.12864–(02/102) September 25, 2002.

and Executive Board Decisions other than the Guidelines on Conditionality. First, the Fund may under Art.XII(8) publish an adverse report in relation to the member's monetary or economic conditions, and developments which lead to a serious disequilibrium in the international balance of payments of members.

**10-035**     **Article XII of the IMF Articles of Agreement. Section 8.**

Communication of views to members The Fund shall at all times have the right to communicate its views informally to any member on any matter arising under this Agreement. The Fund may, by a seventy percent majority of the total voting power, decide to publish a report made to a member regarding its monetary or economic conditions and developments which directly tend to produce a serious disequilibrium in the international balance of payments of members. If the member is not entitled to appoint an Executive Director, it shall be entitled to representation in accordance with Section 3(j) of this Article. The Fund shall not publish a report involving changes in the fundamental structure of the economic organization of members.[153]

**10-036**     Secondly, the Fund has a series of measures at its disposal in the event of overdue payments and misreporting. Overdue payments obligations are a breach of an obligation to the Fund.[154] They can result in the imposition of special charges[155]; and a denial of new requests for the use of Fund resources.[156] More importantly, the Fund has set out a clear time-scale for remedial measures, which at its inception includes a limitation on the further use of Fund resources, progresses to a declaration of no co-operation; and finally to the ultimate sanction of compulsory withdrawal during a period lasting up to 24 months.[157] Examples of members declared ineligible to use Fund's general resources include Liberia, Sudan, Vietnam and Guyana because of overdue financial obligations in the General resources account.[158] Where there has been a purchase on the basis of misreporting the Fund can ask for corrective measures, for example a repurchase.[159] Thirdly, under Art.V, s.5 where the Fund is of the opinion that a member is using the general resources of the Fund in a manner contrary to the purposes of the Fund, it may in the first instance draw the matter to the attention of the member. After this it may (i) limit the use of the resources of the Fund; and if still not satisfied with the member's response it may (ii) after giving reasonable notice to the member, declare the member ineligible to use the resources of the Fund. Art.V, s.5,

---

[153] Source: *http://www.imf.org.* (Accessed June 8, 2011).
[154] See EBM 89/100 and 89/101, July 27, 1989, as amended by Decision No.12546–(01/84) August 22, 2001.
[155] See Executive Directors Decision No.8165–(85/189) as amended in *Selected Decisions*; and Art.V(8).
[156] EBM/84/54 *Selected Decisions of the IMF.*
[157] Procedures for Dealing with Overdue Financial Obligations to the Fund, July 27 1989 in *Selected Decisions of the Fund.*
[158] Arts 5, s.V, and XXVI, s.2.
[159] Executive Board Decision No.7842–(84/165).

as is evident, is an example of a soft-law approach to the occurrence of a delict.[160] Thus, before a declaration of ineligibility several steps must be taken, viz. the sending of a report, limitation of the use of the resources, continuation of the period of limitation, notice that a declaration of ineligibility is in prospect.[161] Article V, s.5 does not reduce use of Fund resources contrary to the purposes of the Fund as a legal violation of the provisions of the Articles of Agreement; nor does it provide for a penalty, although it does provide for a remedy in the event of the Fund's resources being used contrary to its purposes.[162] The reasons why the vernacular of violation and penalty is avoided lie in the difficulty of formulating and implementing criteria for a violation. Such an exercise involves judgement, which the IMF would have been able to exercise, but considered best withheld.[163]

**Article V, Section 5 of the IMF Articles of Agreement:**

Ineligibility to use the Fund's general resources:                                 **10-037**

Whenever the Fund is of the opinion that any member is using the general resources of the Fund in a manner contrary to the purposes of the Fund, it shall present to the member a report setting forth the views of the Fund and prescribing a suitable time for reply. After presenting such a report to a member, the Fund may limit the use of its general resources by the member. If no reply to the report is received from the member within the prescribed time, or if the reply received is unsatisfactory, the Fund may continue to limit the member's use of the general resources of the Fund or may, after giving reasonable notice to the member, declare it ineligible to use the general resources of the Fund.[164]

In addition, under Art.VI, where a member uses the Fund's general resources     **10-038**
to meet a large or sustained outflow of capital—the Fund may declare the member ineligible to use the resources of the Fund. Finally, under Art.XXVI, where a member fails to fulfil any of its obligations under the Articles of Agreement of the IMF, the Fund may declare the member ineligible to use the resources of the Fund. If the member persists the Fund may suspend the voting rights[165] of the member e.g. Sudan and Zaire in 1994. If the member still persists then the member may be required to withdraw from membership in the Fund by a decision of the Board of Governors.

---

[160] Gold (1996), p.343.
[161] Gold (1996).
[162] Gold (1996).
[163] Gold (1996), p.344.
[164] Source: *http://www.imf.org*. (Accessed June 8, 2011).
[165] See Art.XXVI of the IMF Articles. See also J. Head, "Suspension of debtor countries' voting rights in the IMF Charter" (1993) *Virginia Journal of International Law* 591–646.

# PART 3

# INTERNATIONAL TRADE LAW

### CHAPTER 11

# INTERNATIONAL TRADE AND THE WTO

## THE ROLE OF LAW

International trade involves the flow of goods (trade in goods) and services **11-001** (trade in services) across national frontiers. International trade law, at any rate traditionally, has been concerned mainly with domestic trade legislation focusing at the interface of domestic borders regarding goods, services and trade-related policies. As such, international trade law plays a significant role in the shaping of international trade relations as between States. This law is on the whole characterised by rules, and a substantial and growing case law. There is thus not much difficulty in identifying the general corpus of international trade jurisprudence—despite its complexity and detailed character. However, by no means is it easy to comprehend, given that it has evolved, rather than been the subject of specific design as such. Thus, the picture of clarity that rules evoke is only partial. Further, the regime is plagued with exceptions; and suffers from overlapping legal regimes, both from within the discipline, as well as the potential of conflicts with extraneous disciplines. In addition, in its treatment of the concerns of developing States it tends to engage in soft law; in its institutional and enforcement regimes it has on occasions pandered to its power-orientated clientele; and in its substantive concerns the developed States have not been ignored. Yet of all the branches of International Economic Law international trade law is the most developed, and one of the most sophisticated. This state of affairs has been set against the background of a movement in international trade from a non-judicious alliance of law with pragmatism, to a judicious blend of law and pragmatism. The future orientation promises to be closer to law, and augmented by transparency.

International trade law or World Trade Law has been painted as one of the most significant branches of international economic law by some of its key enlighteners. This was particularly true with regard to the term World Trade Law after the establishment of the World Trade Organization in 1995 as the first truly global multilateral international organisation in this field. Certainly, trade in international economic relations is a key sphere of concern for developed States. From that vantage such an attribution of significance is clear. However, such prioritisation is to a certain extent politically premised. For the vast majority of States, which comprise developing States, development is surely more of significance. To the extent that development can be export induced (export-induced or export-led growth), the two may be heavily interrelated.[1] Obviously, the examples of Germany and Japan in the nineteenth century and after World War II as well as more recently an important number of Asian and Latin American countries, including most recently China and Brazil, are normally referred to as examples. However, be that as it may, the significance of the role of law in international trade is also an attribute of the fact that international trade requires the clarity and predictability of an orderly system. It lends itself to a predetermined decision-making process. Further, both the need for greater international trade, and the advent of globalisation call for a supranational regime ensuring co-operation, order and harmonisation. In addition, because international trade is about market access[2] to trade, it involves according the "concession" of market access to other States. As such, international trade has a built-in enforcement mechanism, which not only serves it well in its implementation and development, but also is a powerful tool for legislating in allied spheres. Finally, the success of the normative regime is also to be attributed to the fact that important developed state interests are served by its development. Thus, much of the development of the international trade order in the 20th century has been driven by the initiatives, and caprice of the US.

At the level of general International Law few norms regulating international trade can be discerned. There are no restraints on a State engaging in protectionist foreign trade practices. A State can define the terms upon which it accords access to foreign trade to its market. This is because, historically, States engaged in international trade with zeal,[3] thus ensuring a permissive international trade framework.

**11-002**       This permissive regime has now been supplanted in 1994/5 by the World Trade Organization (WTO), which provides the basic "constitutional" framework, facilitating the development of international trade law. The WTO provides an executive, legislative and enforcement apparatus for a code of conduct regulating international trade policies and practices of nation States. The scope of this regulatory regime is no longer confined to cross-border aspects of international trade. It encompasses internal aspects which have a bearing on international trade. However, not all States are members of

---

[1] See Asif H. Qureshi "International Trade for Development: the WTO as a Development Institution?" 43:1 *Journal of World Trade*, (February 2009) p.173 – 188

[2] See John Mo, "The mystery of market access" *Journal of World Intellectual Property,*3.2 (2000) p.225– 47.

[3] Mercantilism can be summarised as a nationalistic policy which promotes exports and inhibits imports so as to ensure high levels of foreign exchange reserves. See for example B. Hoekman and M. Kostecki, *The Political Economy of the World Trading System* (Oxford University Press, Oxford, 1995), p.2.

the WTO. Further, by its own terms of reference the WTO framework tolerates regional integration processes which are subject to a different regulatory
regime; as well as differential burdens of disciplines in accordance with the
level of development of States. In addition, the WTO regime does not cover
all aspects of international trade. Some of the spheres not covered are governed by other multilateral or bilateral regimes, including soft-law codes of
conduct. Indeed, in the international trade sphere there are other institutions
which also play a role in the development of international trade, for example,
the United Nations Conference on Trade and Development (UNCTAD),
the World Intellectual Property Organization (WIPO) and the International
Labour Organization (ILO).[4] To a certain extent, the parameters of the normative framework of international trade can only be mapped against a clear
notion of the phenomenon of international trade.

Another important development is due to the fact that already since the
1950s members of the GATT and later the WTO have engaged in preferential trade agreements (PTA): European Economic Community (EEC) 1957,[5]
European Free Trade Agreement (EFTA) 1960, first Agreements between
the EEC and States in Africa, the Caribbean and the Pacific (ACP countries) 1975[6] etc. These agreements were originally mostly concluded between
countries of a particular region, hence the term "regional trade agreements"
(RTAs) normally used in the GATT and WTO context. Today it is more
and more common that these agreements are concluded simply between two
parties (bilateral agreements) irrespective of their geographic constellation.
Despite their preferential character (which contradicts the most-favoured-
nation (MFN) principle of the trade agreements under the WTO and therefore the very spirit of the multilateral trading system) they are exceptionally
acceptable under Art. XXIV GATT (with regard to trade in goods) and Art.
V GATS (with regard to services).[7]

While the conclusion of the Uruguay Round of Multilateral Trade negotiations (Marrakesh Agreements of 1994) and the creation of the WTO as of
January 1, 1995 were generally greeted as an important step for the strengthening of the multilateral trading system, they were also accompanied by a
new wave of regional trade agreements coming into force: North American
Free Trade Agreement (NAFTA) 1993/4,[8] the European Economic Area
(EEA) 1992/4,[9] and Mercosur 1991, etc. For many developed States, their
trade relations are these days predominantly governed by bilateral agreements while the WTO remains fundamental for certain developing states and

---

[4] On the role of labour standards in international trade negotiations and with regard to migratory flows see Ch.15.

[5] Now integrated into the European Union.

[6] Now in the process of being phased out and replaced by so-called Economic Partnership
Agreements (EPAs)—see below.

[7] See Ch.12 for details regarding these provisions.

[8] See L.A. Glick, "*Understanding the North American Free Trade Agreement*", Alphen aan den
Rijn [u.a.], Kluwer Law International, 2010

[9] See E. Méndez Pinedo, "EC and EEA Law" *Groningen: Europa Law Publ.*, (2009).

for the time being also for the trade relations between traditional and new trading powers (USA-EU-Japan-Russia-China-India). As an example one can mention Mexico, which has managed to conclude free trade agreements with the United States (NAFTA 1994), the European Union (2000)[10] and Japan (2004) and thereby assures its market access to these traditionally important markets for its car production. There is ongoing debate on the interrelationship of the multilateral and the preferential system and whether they are mutually supportive or whether the increase of regional agreements in recent years leads to a loss of interest in the multilateral system and an increase of power-play by rich countries.[11]

**11-003** The role of the lawyer in international trade has a number of facets. The lawyer has a function not only in its elucidation and development, but also has the responsibility of enlightenment in an objective manner. Where the enlighteners are acknowledged they carry with them the responsibility of not plugging their own governmental policy interests. At the practising level the international trade lawyer performs mainly two functions. First, in advising States and NGOs private lawyers can now participate in WTO dispute settlement processes involving State litigation.[12] Many governments do not have in-house international trade lawyers. Further, the lawyer has a role in assisting in the submissions put forward by NGOs in international trade disputes between States to WTO dispute panels.[13] Secondly, at the national level the lawyer has a role in advising exporters and domestic producers particularly. This is performed by applying international trade law to national systems, both in domestic processes where this is possible, for example through judicial review of administrative decisions on trade or anti-dumping proceedings; as well as a prelude to inter-State intervention at the international level in the WTO dispute settlement forum. Thus, it is not enough to have knowledge of international trade law. This needs to be supplemented with knowledge of domestic trade regimes (particularly of those regimes applying important policy tools in this area, such as trade remedies.[14] Where the national legal system of another State is involved, it may call for liaising with foreign lawyers.

International trade law needs to be understood with some background

---

[10] See M. Cremona, "The European Union and regional trade agreements", *European Yearbook of International Economic Law*, 1(2010), 245 – 268.

[11] See for a detailed analysis of the various aspects of RTAs: L. Bartels et al. (eds), *Regional Trade Agreements and the WTO Legal System* (Oxford, Oxford University Press, 2006), S. Lester, (ed.), *Bilateral and Regional Trade Agreements*. (Cambridge, Cambridge Univ. Press, 2009) and R. Senti, Regional trade agreements in the world trade order. European yearbook of international economic law, 1(2010), p. 227–243; W.-M. Choi, "Aggressive regionalism in Korea-U.S. FTA", *Journal of International Economic Law*, 12 (2009), 3, p.595–615.

[12] EC-Regime for the Importation, Sale, and Distribution of Bananas, Report of the Appellate Body (1997), confirmed in *Indonesia—Certain Measures Affecting the Automotive Industry, Panel Report adopted 23 July 1998*. A growing number of law firms in Geneva, Washington and Brussels are specialising in WTO dispute settlement and related consulting services.

[13] See United States—Import Prohibition of Certain Shrimp and Shrimp Products. Appellate Body Report (1998).

[14] See Ch.12 on these tools.

of its economic underpinnings—particularly the theory of comparative advantage. At the same time some of the pragmatism that is embellished in the international trade order can only be understood with some political insight. Further, it needs to be noted that the elucidation of international trade law is dominated by American and European jurists. Often the commentators are advisers to respective governments, or have had insights into the operation of the WTO. Their analysis, therefore, whilst being invaluable, needs to be approached with some caution where it is too rosy-eyed or underpinned by national policy objectives and perspectives.

## INTERNATIONAL TRADE PROBLEMS

International trade problems[15] are varied, but by no means are they all clearly identifiable, or perceived universally as trade problems. They are problems, however, of international concern because national foreign trade policy impacts upon foreign producers, exporters and consumers. Similarly, national foreign trade policy can be destructive of national prosperity, and as such of international interest. It is estimated that the bill in 1995 to the OECD taxpayer for maintenance of trade protection in the agricultural sector alone was $145 billion, and $190 billion to the OECD consumers![16] In a sense, like the balance of payments problem, there is a case for a State to maintain its international trade relations in a manner that is not destructive of national and international prosperity. Without international constraints on the manner in which national foreign trade policies are conducted, a situation reminiscent of the 1930s wherein States conducted their policies in a beggar-thy-neighbour fashion, would resurface. In such a situation States tried to obtain through their national foreign trade practices economic advantage at the expense of other nations, by restricting imports (protectionism) and inflicting subsidised goods on other nations.[17] In turn other States would retaliate in a similar manner, thus seriously inhibiting international trade. During the recent financial crisis it could be shown that a number of States were tempted to take protectionist measures—and would probably have taken even more of them without existing WTO (and RTA) obligations.[18]

**11-004**

---

[15] See particularly F. Roessler, "The Scope, Limits and Function of the GATT Legal System" (1985) 8(3) *The World Economy*, p.287–298; A. Dunkel and F. Roessler, "The ranking of trade policy instruments under the GATT Legal System" in G. *Ladreit de Lacharrière et la Politique Juridique Extérieure de la France* (Masson, Paris, 1989); I. Arake and G. Marceau; "GATT/WTO code of conduct—The legal management of international trade relations" in WTO Documentation for the regional seminar on dispute settlement procedures and practices for Asian Developing Countries February 1998, Bali, Indonesia.

[16] See President of the UK Board of Trade Mansion House Speech April 7, 1998.

[17] Roessler (1985).

[18] See C. Dordi, "A new 'protectionist era' in the aftermath of the economic and financial crisis?", *Diritto Pubblico Comparato ed Europeo*, (2010) 1 233-242.

A State engages in its foreign trade policy through the use of national trade policy instruments. The range of these trade instruments is wide—as long as there are no treaty obligations (WTO, RTAs etc.) limiting their use. These measures are particularly famous with regard to trade in goods but today they are also increasingly important with regard to trade in services as the latter's importance is rising. Thus, first, a State may impose quantitative restrictions, i.e. limits on the amount or value of a product that can be imported into the country, or exported from the country. Such quantitative restrictions or quotas may be global or allocated amongst exporting nations. In the area of services a prohibition to buy services from certain foreign suppliers (e.g. health services) has similar effects. Secondly, a State may impose tariffs. A tariff is a duty, a form of an indirect tax, paid on a product upon its import (import tariff). Some countries apply also export tariffs—often to benefit domestic producers with regard to the availability of cheap inputs into their production process. Tariffs are not available normally to discourage the import of services, but discriminatory tax treatments (just as in the case of trade in goods) can have a similar effect. Thirdly, a State may enter into "Voluntary Export Restraint" arrangements (i.e. VERs, also referred to as "orderly marketing arrangement"; OMAs) with a supplying State or with suppliers.[19] These are arrangements to restrict imports, normally implemented by the exporting nation through export licences. Fourthly, a State may impose, intentionally or otherwise, non-tariff barriers. These are barriers other than tariffs, and strictly include quantitative restrictions. However, in the international trade vernacular quantitative restrictions and other non-tariff barriers are normally further distinguished. Non-tariff barriers are potentially open-ended and can take various forms. Thus, a State may accord a subsidy to a particular industry and thereby distort trade flows. Subsidies can be of different kinds, and can be directed at different activities, for example, a production subsidy or an export subsidy. Similarly, States impose administrative measures at the border. These can relate, for instance, to the valuation of the goods (customs valuation), the determination of the origins of the goods (rules of origin), or the according of import licences. These border measures can involve unnecessary delays or the payment of bribery and thereby reduce trade flows. Further, a State may impose disguised restrictions on trade, for example, unnecessary or onerous technical specifications or standards (technical barriers to trade, often referred to as TBTs). Measures ostensibly introduced for the protection of human, animal or plant life will often also reduce trade flows; they are normally referred to as sanitary and phytosanitary measures (SPS measures). In addition, a State may channel its trade through State trading enterprises which may not, for example import, or procure domestically, on a competitive basis. Fifthly, States have been known to abuse legitimate responses (i.e. trade remedies) to trade from other

---

[19]  See D. Kitt, "Whaᴅs wrong with volunteering? The Futility of the WTOᴅs Ban on voluntary export restraints", *Columbia Journal of Transnational Law*, 47 (2009) 2 359–386.

States. Examples are the use of anti-dumping duties when a product is considered to have been cheaply exported or a countervailing duty when a good is considered to have been unduly subsidised by the exporting government. Sixthly, States impose discriminatory regulations and taxes once goods and services are inside the territory. Finally, States sometimes engage in the discriminatory enforcement of domestic policies, e.g. industrial policy (assisting a particular industry); intellectual property rights, and competition policy.[20]

At the core, international trade problems arise when States use the trade policy instruments at their disposal against goods and services from abroad, and use them particularly in a manner that is discriminatory, that distorts or inhibits trade by making imports less competitive, and/or is protectionist. The trade policy instruments all raise varying degrees of problems for international trade and the domestic economy.[21] They can be evaluated not only in terms of their impact on the flow of international trade, but also in terms of the costs to the domestic importer and consumers. For example, from an economic standpoint, production subsidies are economically less costly than tariffs, quotas and VERs.[22] Tariffs, quotas and VERs affect both the capacity of an industry as well as the price of goods and services; whilst production subsidies only affect the capacity of the industry. Tariffs, whilst affecting the domestic price of the imports do not decouple the relationship of domestic prices with international prices. On the other hand this is the effect of quotas. Where there is a de-coupling of the price relationship with international prices, consumers suffer with higher domestic prices. Further, quotas are normally imposed through administrative measures, whereas tariffs are legislated. There is therefore more transparency in the imposition of tariffs than quotas. VERs are the least economically sound. They are secret arrangements and economically benefit the exporters more.[23] Thus, the greater and the more obvious the trade distortion resulting from a trade policy instrument, the more forefront its position in the classification of trade barriers.[24] From this standpoint, the classification of trade instruments may be ranked as follows (beginning with the worst measure): quantitative restrictions; tariffs; discriminatory practices; non-tariff barriers (e.g. State trading; customs procedures); unfair trade practices (e.g. subsidies); and trade-related aspects of other measures (e.g. intellectual property rights and investment protection).

The international trade problem discourse is premised mainly on David **11-005** Ricardo's economic theory of comparative advantage[25]; and the political

---

[20] See, for example, Arake and Marceau (1998).

[21] Dunkel and Roessler (1985).

[22] Dunkel and Roessler (1985).

[23] Dunkel and Roessler (1985).

[24] For an examination of economic, political and legal ranking of trade policy instruments see, for example, F. Roessler "The constitutional function of the multilateral trade order" in M. Hilf and E-U Petersmann, *National Constitutions and International Economic Law* (Kluwer Law International, 1993).

[25] See D. Ricardo, *The Principles of Political Economy* (1817); Alan O Sykes, "Comparative advantage and the normative economics of international trade policy" J.I.E.L.,1.1 (1998)

theory of the transnational economic rights of the individual.[26] From both of these premises the case for liberal trade is articulated. Ricardo's theory has been described by Paul Krugman as[27] "truly, madly, deeply difficult. But it is also utterly true, immensely sophisticated—and extremely relevant to the modern world".

One particular reason for the difficulty in understanding the theory of comparative advantage, especially for lawyers, is that the idea is grounded in mathematical models, and is often explained in the rather simplistic form of a two-country scenario, with each engaged in the production of two different commodities. In essence, the theory of comparative advantage predicts that barriers to trade and discrimination in trade, particularly in the long run, do not contribute positively to the economic welfare of the national and the international economy. A State should specialise and export in that product (product A) in which it has a cost advantage comparative to another State, and import in that product (product B) where the cost advantage is relatively smaller, even where the State had an absolute cost advantage in products A and B. Where there is such a specialisation and trade, then there will be an overall increase in world production of the products in question. Such trading benefits the consumer (in choice and price), and provides a competitive stimulus to local enterprises. Thus, comparative advantage provides for an efficient allocation of world resources and increased choices for the consumer.

Accordingly, the political trade theory is often premised on the rights of an individual to freely import and export products and services.[28] It is contended that such rights are human rights and should be recognised as such. This argument is based on the liberal premise that the primary task of the State is to maximise individual liberty and choices.[29]

Both the economic and political arguments for free trade and a liberal world economic order are set against a series of assumptions, and are not without adversarial comment. However, be that as it may, there are also other reasons why restrictions for international trade are called for, although not necessarily all the time justifiably. Thus, arguments for trade restrictions can be grounded, inter alia, in mercantilism; concerns about domestic employment and industry, particularly infant industry; national security; cultural homogeneity; revenue through tariffs; correction of market imperfections; protection of domestic concerns such as the environment, and human

---

49–82. See also, for example, C.P. Kindleberger, *International Economics*, 5th edn (1973); M.J. Trebilcock and R. Howse, *The Regulation of International Trade*, 3rd edn (London, Routledge, 2005), p.3.

[26] See Hilf and Petersmann (1993).

[27] P. Krugman, "Ricardo's difficult idea—why intellectuals don't understand comparative advantage" in G. Cook (ed.), *The Economics and Politics of International Trade* (1998).

[28] See E-U Petersmann, "National Constitutions and International Economic Law" in Hilf and Petersmann (1993) and more recently E-U Petersmann, "Human rights, constitutionalism and international economic law in the 21st century", (Oxford, Hart, 2011).

[29] See E-U Petersmann, "National Constitutions and International Economic Law" in: Hilf and Petersmann (1993).

or animal welfare, etc. Normally, the advocates for trade restrictions are the import competing enterprises, which tend to be vociferous and organised because the burden imposed by liberalisation is focused on them.[30] However, the benefits of trade liberalisation on the other hand are dispersed, but individually small amongst the disorganised consumers. They consequently are less vociferous in their call for trade liberalisation.[31]

## THE WTO—INSTITUTIONAL ASPECTS

The World Trade Organization (WTO)[32] was operational on January 1, 1995. It was created as a consequence of the results of the Uruguay Round of          **11-006**

[30] B. Hoekman and M. Kostecki, *The Political Economy of the World Trading System*, 2nd edn (Oxford, Oxford University Press, 2001), p.27.

[31] B. Hoekman and M. Kostecki, *The Political Economy of the World Trading System*, 2nd edn (Oxford, Oxford University Press, 2001), p.27.

[32] This section is based on work published in A.H. Qureshi, *World Trade Organization: Implementing International Trade Norms* (Manchester: Manchester University Press, 1996). For relevant GATT panel decisions see the GATT Analytical Index (1995) and now the WTO Analytical Index as provided online by the WTO Secretariat. For a more detailed elucidation of the code see specialist books on international trade for example J. Jackson, *The World Trading System* (MIT, 1997); E. McGovern, *International Trade Regulation* (Globefield Press (loose-leaf)); P. Van den Bossche, *The Law and Policy of the World Trade Organization* (Cambridge, Cambridge University Press, 2005); M.J. Trebilcock and R. Howse, *The Regulation of International Trade*, 3rd edn (London, Routledge, 2005); P. Macrory, A.E. Appleton and M.G. Plummer (eds), *The World Trade Organization—Legal, Economic and Political Analysis* (Berlin, Springer, 2005); see also the series of commentaries by R. Wolfrum and P. T. Stoll (General Editors), *Max-Planck Commentaries on World Trade Law*, Vol.3 (The Hague, Martinus Nijhoff Publishers) (various volumes); M. Matsushita, T. Schoenbaum, P. Mavroidis, *The World Trade Organization*, 2nd edn (Oxford, Oxford University Press, 2006); M. Rafiqul Islam, *International Trade Law of the WTO* (Oxford, Oxford University Press, 2006); P. T. Stoll and F. Schorkopf, *WTO—World Economic Order, World Trade Law* (Nijhoff, 2006); B. M. Hoekman and P. C. Mavroidis, *World Trade Organization (WTO): Law, Economics, and Politics* (Global Institutions, Routledge, 2007); J. Wouters, B. de Meester, *The World Trade Organization : A Legal and Institutional Analysis* (Mortsel, Intersentia, 2007); D. C. K. Chow and T. J Schoenbaum, *International Trade Law: Problems, Cases, and Materials* (Aspen Publishers, 2008); K. Kennedy, *International Trade Regulation: Readings, Cases, Notes, and Problems* (Aspen Publishers, 2008); R. Bhala, *Dictionary of International Trade Law* (Newark NJ, LexisNexis, 2008); R. Bhala, *International Trade Law: interdisciplinary theory and practice*, 3rd edn. (Newark NJ, LexisNexis, 2008); P. C. Mavroidis, *The General Agreement on Tariffs and Trade,* 2nd edn. (Oxford, Oxford University Press, 2008); P. van den Bossche, *The Law and Policy of the World Trade Organization*, 2nd edn. (Cambridge University Press, 2008); S. Lester, B. Mercurio, A. Davies, and K. Leitner, *World Trade Law: Text, Materials and Commentary* (Oxford, Hart Publishing, 2008); A. Guzman and J.H.B. Pauwelyn, *International Trade Law* (Aspen Publishers, 2009); D. Bethlehem, D. McRae and R. Neufeld (eds), *The Oxford Handbook of International Trade Law* (Oxford University Press, Oxford, 2009); P. C. Mavroidis, G. A. Bermann and M.Wu, *The Law of the World Trade Organization (WTO): Documents, Cases & Analysis* (American Casebook West Publishers 2010). See also collected works on WTO issues, for example, J. Bhagwati and R. Hudec (eds), *Fair Trade and Harmonization* (1996); A. Krueger (ed.), *The WTO as an International Organization* (1998); A.H. Qureshi et al. (eds), *The Legal and Moral Aspects of International Trade* (London: Routledge, 1998). On negotiating history see, for example, T.P. Stewart (ed.), *The GATT Uruguay Round: A Negotiating History (1986–1992)* (Kluwer Law International,

Multilateral Trade Negotiations (MTN), which took place under the framework of the General Agreement on Tariffs and Trade (GATT) of 1947[33]—namely the WTO predecessor international trade regime. The multilateral trade negotiations leading to the establishment of the WTO were launched in 1986 as a consequence of the GATT Ministerial Meeting at Punta del Este, Uruguay.[34] The so-called Uruguay Round of multilateral trade negotiations, much of which took place in Geneva, was the eighth of such multilateral trade liberalisation negotiation rounds.[35] Its distinctive feature has been that not only did it ensure further liberalisation of international trade like previous rounds, but it resulted in the metamorphosis of the GATT into a fully fledged institution, viz. the WTO. At the Ministerial Meeting in Marrakesh the Final Act ("Final Act") was signed on April 15, 1994.

The establishment of the WTO on January 1, 1995 has placed the international trading system on a firm institutional footing. For the first time, the pillars of the international trading system rest on a full-fledged international organisation, with international legal personality. The international community was denied the existence of GATT 1947 as an organisation, though it did operate de facto as such. A key player in international trade, viz. the US, contributed to this denial, by opposing successive attempts at the creation of an international trade organisation. This was done by the US to the ITO (International Trade Organisation) Charter drafted at the Havana Conference in 1948, and later the draft proposal for the Organization for Trade Cooperation (OTC), under a 1955 GATT Review Session, to provide an institutional framework for GATT. The significance of the very establishment of the WTO qua an international organisation is best measured against the fundamental shift that has taken place from the approach by the international community and indeed the US, to the institution of the de facto GATT

---

1993); J. Croome, *Reshaping the World Trading System: A History of the Uruguay Round*, 2nd rev. edn (The Hague, Kluwer Law International, 1999). See further on institutional and doctrinal issues, for example, F. Roessler, "The Agreement Establishing the World Trade Organization", in J.H.J. Bourgeois, F. Berrod and E. Gippini Fournier (eds), *The Uruguay Round Results—A European Lawyer's Perspective* (Brussels, European Interuniversity Press, 1995); J. Jackson, *The World Trade Organization—Constitution and Jurisprudence* (London, RIIA, 1998). For a particular emphasis of the constitutional functions of the WTO see E-U Petersmann, *Reforming the World Trading System: Legitimacy, Efficiency and Democratic Governance* (Oxford, Oxford University Press, 2005) D.Z. Cass, *The Constitutionalization of the World Trade Organization: Legitimacy, Democracy, and Consistency in the International Trading System* (Oxford, Oxford University Press, 2005); J.H. Jackson, *Sovereignty, the WTO and Changing Fundamentals of International Law* (Cambridge: Cambridge University Press, 2006); and E-U Petersmann, "*Human rights, constitutionalism and international economic law in the 21st century*" (Oxford, Hart, 2011).

[33] See Art.XXVIII *bis* of GATT 1947.

[34] See the Punta del Este Declaration 1986.

[35] The first round took place in 1947 in Geneva; the second round at Annecy, France in 1949; the third round at Torquay, England in 1950; the fourth round at Geneva in 1956; the fifth round, the Dillon round, in Geneva in 1960, named in honour of US Under-Secretary of State Douglas Dillon; the sixth round, the Kennedy round in Geneva in 1964; the seventh round, the Tokyo round, in Geneva in 1973. In November 2001, already under the WTO, was launched the Doha (Development) Round in Doha, Qatar (see final section of this chapter).

1947. The WTO as an institution is now more effectively able to administer the international trade code of conduct, to liaise with other international economic organisations (e.g. the World Intellectual Property Organization (WIPO) or the International Monetary Fund (IMF)), and to offer more effective legislative and enforcement mechanisms. This is particularly evidenced by the prolific use of the WTO dispute settlement mechanism,[36] and the continuing international discourse on further trade liberalisation proposals.

### Purposes and objectives

The Marrakesh Agreement (establishing the World Trade Organization) of 1994 sets out the purposes and objectives of the WTO, along with its institutional framework. The purposes and objectives of the WTO can be discerned from the preamble to the WTO Agreement.[37]    **11-007**

**WTO Agreement: Preamble**    **11-008**

The *Parties* to this Agreement,

**Recognizing** that their relations in the field of trade and economic endeavour should be conducted with a view to raising standards of living, ensuring full employment and a large and steadily growing volume of real income and effective demand, and expanding the production of and trade in goods and services, while allowing for the optimal use of the world's resources in accordance with the objective of sustainable development, seeking both to protect and preserve the environment and to enhance the means for doing so in a manner consistent with their respective needs and concerns at different levels of economic development,

   **Recognizing** further that there is need for positive efforts designed to ensure that developing countries, and especially the least developed among them, secure a share in the growth in international trade commensurate with the needs of their economic development,

   **Being desirous** of contributing to these objectives by entering into reciprocal and mutually advantageous arrangements directed to the substantial reduction of tariffs and other barriers to trade and to the elimination of discriminatory treatment in international trade relations,

   **Resolved**, therefore, to develop an integrated, more viable and durable multilateral trading system encompassing the General Agreement on Tariffs and Trade, the results of past trade liberalization efforts, and all of the results of the Uruguay Round of Multilateral Trade Negotiations,

   **Determined** to preserve the basic principles and to further the objectives underlying this multilateral trading system,

   **Agree** as follows:. . .

---

[36] See Ch.13.
[37] See, for example, I. Sinclair, *The Vienna Convention on the Law of Treaties*, 2nd edn (Manchester, Manchester University Press, 1984), p.130 and D. Shanker, "The Vienna Convention on the Law of Treaties, the dispute settlement system of the WTO and the Doha Declaration on the TRIPs Agreement" *Journal of World Trade*, 36 (2002) 4, 721–772. See also United States—Import Prohibition of Certain Shrimp And Shrimp Products, Report of the Panel and the Appellate Body (1998).

**11-009**    These purposes and objectives shed light not only on the Agreement
establishing the WTO but are also relevant to the interpretation of the
other Uruguay Round Agreements which are an integral part of the
WTO Agreement.[38] The primary purposes of the WTO relating to trade
liberalisation are three-fold: to ensure the reduction of tariffs and other
barriers to trade, and the elimination of discriminatory treatment in
international trade relations, and a rule-oriented trading environment
(Including dispute settlement).[39] The WTO is to ensure these primary
purposes regarding multilateral trade relations in order to facilitate in the
economies of Member States higher standards of living, full employment,
growing volume of real income and effective demand, and an expansion of
production and trade in goods and services. These national objectives correspond to those of other international organisation, e.g. the International
Monetary Fund (IMF).[40]

There are however three main qualifications to the pursuit of these
national objectives. First, national objectives must be pursued in a manner
that is consistent with the optimal use of the world's resources. Thus, the
rationale of the theory of comparative advantage may be stated to be
embedded in the preamble of the agreement establishing the WTO. This
is because the emphasis is on the optimal use of the world's resources. By
specialising in the production of those goods in which a Member State has
a comparative cost advantage and trading in those goods in which such
advantage is relatively less, the world's resources are optimally used and
maximised.

Secondly, account must be taken of the need for sustainable development[41]
and the protection and preservation of the environment. This requirement
reinforces the first. It is, however, contingent upon the respective circumstances of a particular member and its level of economic development. Thus,
environmental policies are to be formulated with reference to their appropriateness to the conditions prevailing in each Member State—presumably
both in terms of actual needs and economic means".[42] Further, sustainable
development objectives need to be approached on a multilateral rather than
unilateral basis—especially as they relate to the integration of environmental

---

[38]  Art. II of the Marrakesh Agreement.

[39]  See Preamble to the Marrakesh Agreement Establishing the World Trading Organization.

[40]  Although, the reference in the IMF Articles of Agreement relating to employment, refers to
the promotion and maintenance of high levels of employment, as opposed to full employment. See Art.I (II) of the IMF Articles of Agreement.

[41]  See, for example, G. Handl, "Sustainable Development: General Rules versus Specific
Obligations" in W. Lang (ed.), *Sustainable Development and International Law* (1995); World
Commission on Environmental and Development, *Our Common Future* (Oxford, Oxford
University Press, 1987); D. French, *International Law and Policy of Sustainable Development*
(Manchester University Press, 2005); C. Voigt, *Sustainable development as a principle of inter-
national law*, (Leiden [u.a.], Martinus Nijhoff Publishers, 2009); G. P. Sampson, "The WTO
and sustainable development", *World Trade Review*, 7 (2008), 2, 467–471.

[42]  See United States—Import Prohibition Of Certain Shrimp And Shrimp Products, Report of
the Panel and Appellate Body (1998).

concerns into trade issues.[43] Thus formulated sustainable development and environmental concerns arguably are like a basket full of holes to draw water from a well! This basket is of course in form a political compromise between developed and developing countries.

Thirdly, it is stipulated in the preamble that the objectives are to be pursued so as to ensure that developing countries, especially the least developed, obtain a level of share in the growth of international trade that reflects the needs of their economic development. This is not so much a statement that the international trading system must fairly allow all members to share in the growth of international trade according to their respective contribution to it, though doubtless that is implicit, but rather that in so far as developing and least developed members are concerned positive efforts are to be made to ensure that they secure a share in the growth of international trade that reflects the needs of their respective economic development. Herein is the articulation of the differential and more favourable treatment standard as it relates to developing members. At the same time, one should not forget that the complexity of the WTO—coverage and institutional set-up—make it increasingly difficult for developing countries to participate fully in the organisation.[44]  **11-010**

To sum up, one might perhaps state, albeit somewhat cynically, that the ideals of the WTO as articulated in the preamble of the Marrakesh Agreement have been driven by the politics of international economic relations of an era, rather than necessarily from a sense of a vision of the world order and the condition of mankind as a whole.

**Functions**

The functions of the WTO may be described as follows. First, the WTO provides a substantive code of conduct directed at the reduction of tariffs and other barriers to trade, and the elimination of discrimination in international trade relations. Secondly, the WTO provides the institutional framework for the administration of the substantive code. It provides an integrated structure for the administration of all past (and future) trade agreements, including the agreements under the Uruguay Round of Multilateral Trade Negotiations. Thirdly, the WTO ensures the implementation of the substantive code. It provides a forum for dispute settlement in international trade matters, and conducts surveillance of national trade policies and practices in order to prevent disputes and contribute to increased transparency and efficiency. Fourthly, the WTO acts as a medium for the conduct of international  **11-011**

---

[43] See United States—Import Prohibition Of Certain Shrimp And Shrimp Products, Report of the Panel and Appellate Body (1998).

[44] G.A. Berman and P. Mavroidis (eds), *WTO Law and Developing Countries* (Cambridge, Cambridge University Press, 2007) and R. Grynberg (ed.), *WTO at the Margins—Small States and the Multilateral Trading System* (Cambridge, Cambridge University Press, 2006); see also C. Thomas (ed.), *Developing countries in the WTO legal system.* (Oxford [u.a.], Oxford Univ. Press, 2009).

trade relations amongst Member States, both bilaterally and multilaterally. Particularly, the WTO is to act as a forum for the negotiation of further trade liberalisation, and improvement in the international trading system.[45] Finally, the WTO is expected to engage in the achievement of greater coherence in global economic policy-making by co-operating with the IMF and the World Bank Group,[46] but also other institutions and actors. This must imply an acknowledgement that in international economics trade is but a component, and that the WTO mandate in trade is constrained by this function.

## Organisational structure

11-012    **The organisational structure of the WTO is as follows:**

**The Ministerial Conference, which is the highest organ, is to meet at least once every two years. It is composed of representatives of all the members—normally Ministers of Trade or otherwise in charge of the trade policy of a Member. The Ministerial Conference has supreme authority over all matters (Art.IV:1 WTO Agreement). The General Council is composed of the representatives of all the members—normally country trade delegates based in Geneva. The General Council is in session between the meetings of the Ministerial Council. In essence it is the real engine of the WTO, and has all the powers of the Ministerial Conference when that body is not in operation. The General Council also acts as the Dispute Settlement Body, and the Trade Policy Review Body (Art.IV:2–4 WTO Agreement).**

The Council for Trade in Goods, the Council for Trade in Services and the Council for Trade-Related Aspects of Intellectual Property Rights (TRIPS) have been established with specific spheres of responsibility, arising from respective agreements defining their tasks[47] (Art.IV:5 WTO Agreement).

## Decision-making

11-013    A central question in relation to any international organisation is the manner in which decisions are arrived at. Unlike the IMF or the World Bank there is no weighted voting at the WTO as such. Formally, all members have equal

---

[45] See Art.III of the Marrakesh Agreement.
[46] Art. III of the Marrakesh Agreement.
[47] The Council for Trade in goods is to be responsible for the functioning of the following agreements: GATT 1994; Agreement on Agriculture; Agreement on Sanitary and Phytosanitary Measures; Agreement on Textiles and Clothing; Agreement on Technical Barriers to Trade; Agreement on Trade-related aspects of investment measures; Agreement on Implementation of Article VI of GATT; Agreement on Implementation of Article VII of the GATT; Agreement on Preshipment Inspection; Agreement on Rules of Origin; Agreement on Import Licensing Procedures; Agreement on Subsidies and Countervailing Measures; Agreement on Safeguards. The Council for Trade in Services is to be responsible for the General Agreement on Trade in Services. The Council for Trade-Related Aspects of Intellectual Property Rights is to be responsible for the Agreement on Trade-Related Aspects of Intellectual Property Rights.

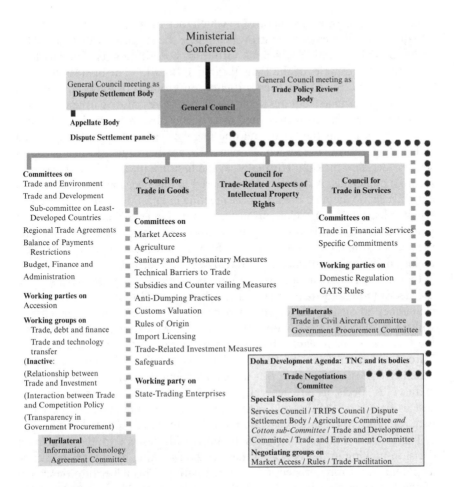

votes. Voting prowess is not dependent on a member's contribution to international trade, or its contribution to the budget of the WTO. Prima facie, thus the decision making process is democratic. Regrettably, Professor John Jackson has described this democratic form of majority voting as "majority voting by sometimes irresponsible one-nation one-vote procedures".[48] This is a highly regrettable and unjustifiable slur on the voting habits of States. Presumably, the reference is to the majority developing members. It is one thing to argue for a voting system which reflects all interests adequately, it is another to characterise as irresponsible the voting habits, albeit sometimes, of developing members. Developed members equally can vote sometimes irresponsibly in a weighted voting system.

Similarly, the characterisation by Hoekman and Kostecki of the WTO

---

[48] See J. Jackson, *The World Trade Organization. Constitution and Jurisprudence* (R.I.I.A., 1998), p.57.

Council as "an unwieldy structure" in which each member is represented with an equal voice[49] is equally controversial; as is the suggestion that the WTO emulate the IMF and World Bank Group by constituting its Council along the lines, for example, of the IMF Executive Board.[50] The operation of the IMF Executive Board has been criticised on grounds of good governance; and good governance requires democratic and representative organisations.

However, be that as it may, and a detached observer would not be surprised to learn that the "one vote one member" system has been qualified in the WTO, through a system known also in other organisations as "consensus" decision-making. Normally, in the first instance, decision-making is through consensus. A decision is considered to have been arrived at through consensus if no member present at the meeting in question formally objects to the proposed decision.[51] Consensus decision-making can facilitate maximum participation in decision-making, thus allowing a greater say to developing members through the formation of coalitions.[52] Further it avoids the formality and divisiveness attached to a system based on formal voting.

**11-014**    In the event that a decision cannot be arrived at by consensus, then the decision-making takes place through voting. However, the ability of a member to sustain an objection depends on the member's capacity to withstand objections to its objection.[53] At the Ministerial Conference and the General Council each Member State has one vote. In the case of the European Union (EU), the EU is to have the number of votes equal to its Member States. Although it is a distinctive member itself, it does not have extra votes. Decisions are generally arrived at when there is a majority vote cast in favour of the decision. Thus, the normal voting system is designed with reference to the votes cast and not the majority of the membership.[54]

There are a number of points to note with respect to the system of decision-making in the WTO.[55] First, decision-making by consensus can be as potent as a formal system of weighted voting. This is because the mood of the forum in question will be influenced implicitly by the weight of the opinions proffered by the economically more dominant members. In a sense, decision-making by consensus can be regarded as decision-making through latent weighted voting. Professor John Jackson suggests that this manner of decision-making wherein members defer to economically more power-

---

[49] See Hoekman and Kostecki (1995), p.54.
[50] Hoekman and Kostecki (1995), p.54 and J. Schott and J. Buurman, *The Uruguay Round: an assessment* (Washington D.C., Institute for International Economics, 1994).
[51] Art.IX of the Marrakesh Agreement.
[52] See Hoekman and Kostecki (2001), pp.56–60. See also Claus-Dieter Ehlermann & L Ehring, "Decision-making in the World Trade Organization:is the consensus practice of the World Trade Organization adequate for making, revising and implementing rules on international trade?" J.I.E.L., 8:1 (2005), pp.51–75.
[53] See Claus-Dieter Ehlermann & L. Ehring (2005).
[54] Art.IX (I) of the Marrakesh Agreement.
[55] See also B. Mercurio, "The WTO and its institutional impediments", *Melbourne Journal of International Law*, 8 (2007) 1, 198–232.

ful members under the consensus framework of decision-making formed a customary practice under GATT,[56] and therefore should prevail under the WTO in the light of Art.XVI(1) of the Marrakesh Agreement. This Article states inter alia that the WTO "shall be guided by the decisions, procedures and customary practices followed by the CONTRACTING PARTIES[57] to GATT 1947 and the bodies established in the framework of GATT 1947". This analysis of Professor Jackson is controversial for the following reasons. First, there is no evidence of such a practice. Certainly, Professor Jackson does not substantiate his claim. The reasons why members engage in certain types of decision-making is complex. To establish deference to economically powerful members as a motive for decision-making needs actually to be proven and would be difficult to substantiate. Further, the assertion that there is the likelihood of such deference is not the same as it actually transpiring. Secondly, Art.XVI (1) refers to the practices of the Contracting Parties and the GATT bodies. It does not refer to the individual practice of Member States or contracting parties. Finally, to suggest that the WTO Charter actually enshrines servility on the part of certain members may be offensive to those members.[58]

Secondly, because consensus decision-making requires a higher degree of consensus amongst the membership present it can be a slower mechanism for bringing about change.[59] However, this has to be weighed against the value of winning as much consent as possible from the membership in question.

Thirdly, the voting can be through a show of hands. Thus, for example, **11-015** the hand of the Bangladesh delegate is lifted in full view of the US delegate. Again, in a sense, the decision-making, albeit through "one member one vote", can have the same effect as a weighted voting system.

Fourthly, some sense of the de facto influences in decision-making need to be taken aboard. One particular factor of note is the relationship of a member's contribution towards the expenses of the WTO and influence in decision-making. Broadly, the contribution a member makes towards the expenses of the WTO reflects, inter alia, a member's share of the total international trade of the WTO membership.[60] Although the level of contribution or share of international trade is not intended formally to have a bearing on decision-making, it cannot be without significance. There is an interesting question in this respect as to the relationship of posts in the WTO Secretariat, and the nationality profile of its staff—particularly in key positions. Certainly, some of the process involving the appointment of the Appellate Body judges

---

[56] See Jackson (1998), p.46.
[57] Under GATT 1947, the Contracting Parties written in capital letters referred to all the parties taken as a whole, thereby constituting a kind of treaty organ.
[58] On the role of Art.XVI:1 WTO in general see also Japan—Taxes on Alcoholic Beverages, WT/DS 8, 10, 11 /AB /R, AB. Report adopted on November 1, 1996.
[59] Hoekman and Kostecki (2001), p. 57.
[60] Art.VII of the Marrakesh Agreement. See also, "World Trade Organization: WTO analytical index". (Geneva, World Trade Organization; Cambridge [u.a.]).

involved the advancement of national nominees on grounds of the share of world trade of the respective national State.[61]

### Legislative and constitutional changes and relationships

**11-016** The constitution of the WTO allows for changes in international trade law to take effect so that the WTO can respond effectively to the exigencies of international trade relations. This is done through provisions allowing, under specified circumstances, for individual waivers of obligations; authoritative interpretative decisions; amendments of the agreements arrived at under the Uruguay Round of Trade Negotiations[62]; decisions of the organs of the WTO; and through the negotiation of new agreements.

However, special voting procedures and arrangements apply to each of these respective "legislative" mechanisms. Thus, a waiver of an obligation imposed upon a member under any of the Uruguay Round agreements is to be given only in exceptional circumstances, for a limited period, and subject to constant review.[63] Waiver decisions are thus to be interpreted with great care, taking into account the fact they are subject to strict disciplines.[64] Further, decisions as to a waiver are to be arrived at by the Ministerial Conference, and only in the event of a three-fourth majority of the membership votes. In this manner, the integrity of the international trading system is guarded, whilst avoiding rigidity.

Proposals to amend provisions of the agreement may be made by any member to the Ministerial Conference or the General Council. The voting requirements and the effect of the amendment differ according to the nature of the amendment.[65] Thus, generally, in the absence of a consensus decision, amendment decisions are to be arrived at by a two-thirds majority vote. However, amendments relating to Arts I (MFN), II (Tariff concessions) of GATT 1994; Art. IX (Decision-making) of the Agreement Establishing the WTO; Art.II:1 (MFN) of GATS and Art.4 (MFN) of the Agreement on TRIPS can only be made by the acceptance of all the members.[66] Generally, amendments are binding only in relation to those members that have accepted them.[67] However, members who have not accepted an amendment can be invited by the Ministerial Conference, by a two-thirds majority, to accept the amendment or withdraw from the Agreement, or remain a

---

[61] See, for example, the EU argument for having two EU judges rather than one as is the case on the grounds that EU share of world trade represented 45% of the total world trade. See *Financial Times* (November 1, 1995). The new distribution of world trade among emerging economies and traditional stakeholder will certainly lead to further pressures on this system.

[62] See General Council, WT/L/641 December 8, 2005 Amendment of the TRIPS Agreement, Decision of December 6, 2005.

[63] See Art.IX(3) and (4) of the Marrakesh Agreement.

[64] European Communities—Regime for the importation, sale and distribution of bananas. Report of the Appellate Body (1997).

[65] See Art.X of the Marrakesh Agreement.

[66] Art.X(2) of the Marrakesh Agreement.

[67] Art.X(3) of the Marrakesh Agreement.

member only with the consent of the Ministerial Conference.[68] It is thought that such pressure is unlikely to be brought against the key international trade players.[69] As of 2011 there has been only one formal amendment under para.1 of Art.X of the Marrakesh Agreement.[70] Interestingly enough, the amendment could not enter into force as the WTO members did not proceed in sufficient number to ratification. For the time being the content of the amendment is guaranteed through a waiver—a temporary decision not to apply an existing WTO rule.[71]

---

**Amendment of the TRIPS Agreement – Decision of 6 December 2005**                    **11-017**
**(GENERAL COUNCIL/WT/L/641/8 December 2005)**

The General Council;

*Having regard* to paragraph 1 of Article X of the Marrakesh Agreement Establishing the World Trade Organization ("the WTO Agreement");

*Conducting* the functions of the Ministerial Conference in the interval between meetings pursuant to paragraph 2 of Article IV of the WTO Agreement;

*Noting* the Declaration on the TRIPS Agreement and Public Health (WT/MIN(01)/DEC/2) and, in particular, the instruction of the Ministerial Conference to the Council for TRIPS contained in paragraph 6 of the Declaration to find an expeditious solution to the problem of the difficulties that WTO Members with insufficient or no manufacturing capacities in the pharmaceutical sector could face in making effective use of compulsory licensing under the TRIPS Agreement;

*Recognizing*, where eligible importing Members seek to obtain supplies under the system set out in the proposed amendment of the TRIPS Agreement, the importance of a rapid response to those needs consistent with the provisions of the proposed amendment of the TRIPS Agreement;

*Recalling* paragraph 11 of the General Council Decision of 30 August 2003 on the Implementation of Paragraph 6 of the Doha Declaration on the TRIPS Agreement and Public Health;

*Having* considered the proposal to amend the TRIPS Agreement submitted by the Council for TRIPS (IP/C/41);

*Noting* the consensus to submit this proposed amendment to the Members for acceptance;

*Decides* as follows:

1. The Protocol amending the TRIPS Agreement attached to this Decision is hereby adopted and submitted to the Members for acceptance.

2. The Protocol shall be open for acceptance by Members until 1 December 2007 or such later date as may be decided by the Ministerial Conference.

---

[68] Art.X of the Marrakesh Agreement.
[69] Jackson (1998), p.45.
[70] General Council, WT/L/641 December 8, 2005 Amendment of the TRIPS Agreement, Decision of December 6, 2005. See also para.12–046.
[71] See below.

3.  The Protocol shall take effect in accordance with the provisions of paragraph 3 of Article X of the WTO Agreement.

[. . .]

AMENDMENT OF THE TRIPS AGREEMENT – SECOND EXTENSION OF THE PERIOD FOR THE ACCEPTANCE BY MEMBERS OF THE PROTOCOL AMENDING THE TRIPS AGREEMENT, *DECISION OF 17 DECEMBER 2009* (**WT/L/785 21 DECEMBER 2009**)

The General Council,

*Conducting* the functions of the Ministerial Conference in the interval between meetings pursuant to paragraph 2 of Article IV of the Marrakesh Agreement establishing the World Trade Organization (the "WTO Agreement");

*Having regard to* paragraph 2 of the Decision of the General Council of 6 December 2005 on the Amendment of the TRIPS Agreement (the "TRIPS Amendment Decision") and paragraph 3 of the Protocol Amending the TRIPS Agreement (the "Protocol")[72], which provide that the Protocol shall be open for acceptance by Members until 1 December 2007 or such later date as may be decided by the Ministerial Conference;

*Recalling* that the General Council, by its decision of 18 December 2007 (the "2007 Extension Decision")[73], initially extended the period for acceptances of the Protocol by Members until 31 December 2009 or such later date as may be decided by the Ministerial Conference;

*Recalling also* that, pursuant to paragraph 3 of the TRIPS Amendment Decision and paragraph 4 of the Protocol, the Protocol shall take effect and enter into force in accordance with the provisions of paragraph 3 of Article X of the WTO Agreement;

*Noting* that acceptance of the Protocol by two thirds of the Members in accordance with paragraph 3 of Article X of the WTO Agreement is taking longer than initially foreseen;

*Having considered* the proposal to further extend the period for acceptances of the Protocol submitted by the Council for TRIPS (IP/C/54);

*Decides* as follows:

The period for acceptances by Members of the Protocol Amending the TRIPS Agreement referred to in paragraph 2 of the TRIPS Amendment Decision and paragraph 3 of the Protocol, and extended by the 2007 Extension Decision, shall be further extended until 31 December 2011 or such later date as may be decided by the Ministerial Conference.

**11-018**   The obligations of members may differ not only according to whether or not they have accepted a particular amendment, but also according to whether or not a member has consented to the application of a particular Uruguay Round agreement or agreements[74] as between itself and another member at

[72] WT/L/641.
[73] WT/L/711.
[74] i.e. the Marrakesh Agreement Establishing the WTO and the Multilateral Agreements on Trade in Goods; GATS; TRIPS, and the Understanding on Rules and Procedures Governing the Settlement of Disputes.

the time of becoming a member. In such an event the agreement or agreements in question are not binding as between the two members.[75]

### Interpretation[76]

Insofar as interpretative decisions are concerned, the Ministerial Council **11-019** and the General Council have exclusive authority to adopt interpretative decisions.[77] The two organs are, however, to act on the advice of the relevant Council under whose remit the relevant agreement falls. Interpretative decisions are to be arrived at by a three-fourth majority of the membership votes. The interpretative decisions are to be in accordance with customary rules of interpretation of public International Law.[78]

The GATT *acquis* is incorporated expressly,[79] and also flow from Arts 31[80] and 32[81] of the Vienna Convention on the Law of Treaties. Thus, the aids to interpretation include, inter alia, the *travaux préparatoires* of the agreements under the Uruguay Round; the subsequent practice of the WTO; the decisions and customary practices followed by the Contracting Parties to GATT 1947 and the bodies established under the GATT 1947[82]; and the

---

[75] Art.XIII of the Marrakesh Agreement. For non-application of GATT see Art.XXXV of GATT 1994. See also L. Wang, "Non-application in the GATT and the WTO", J.W.T. Vol.28 No.2, p.49.

[76] A.H. Qureshi, *Interpreting WTO Agreements: Problems and Perspectives* (Cambridge, Cambridge University Press, 2006); and I. V. Damme. *Treaty Interpretation by the WTO Appellate Body* (OUP, 2009) and R. R. Babu, "Interpretation of the WTO agreements, democratic legitimacy and developing nations", *The Indian Journal of International Law*, 50(2010) 1, 45–90. See also J. Pauwelyn, *Conflict of Norms* (2003); M. Panizzon, *Good faith in the Jurisprudence of the WTO* (Hart Publishing, 2006).

[77] Art.IX of the Marrakesh Agreement.

[78] See Art.3(2) of the Understanding on rules and procedures governing the settlement of disputes. See also Arts 31–33 of the Vienna Convention On The Law Of Treaties 1969.

[79] Art.XVI of the Marrakesh Agreement.

[80] Art.31 of the Vienna Convention on the Law of Treaties states: (1) A Treaty shall be interpreted in good faith in accordance with the ordinary meaning to be given to the terms of the treaty in their context and in the light of its object and purpose. (2) The context for the purpose of the interpretation of a treaty shall comprise, in addition to the text, including its preamble and annexes: (a) any agreement relating to the treaty which was made between the parties in connection with the conclusion of the treaty; (b) any instrument which was made by one or more parties in connection with the conclusion of the treaty and accepted by the other parties as an instrument related to the treaty. (3) There shall be taken into account, together with the context: (a) any subsequent agreement between the parties regarding the interpretation of the treaty or the application of its provisions; (b) any subsequent practice in the application of the treaty which establishes the agreement of the parties regarding its interpretation; (c) any relevant rules of international law applicable in the relations between the parties. (4) A special meaning shall be given to a term if it is established that the parties so intended.

[81] Art.32 of the Vienna Convention on the law of Treaties states: "Recourse may be had to supplementary means of interpretation, including the preparatory work of the treaty and the circumstances of its conclusion, in order to confirm the meaning resulting from the application of article 31 or to determine the meaning when the interpretation according to article 31: (a) leaves the meaning ambiguous or obscure; or (b) leads to a result which is manifestly absurd or unreasonable."

[82] Art.XVI of the Marrakesh Agreement. See also US—Standards for Reformulated and Conventional Gasoline, WT/DS2/AB/R, Report of the AB adopted on May 20, 1996, Section III B.

principles of the Havana Charter.[83] However, Panel Reports adopted by the GATT Contracting Parties and the WTO Dispute Settlement Body do not constitute subsequent practice as understood under Art.31 of the Vienna Convention.[84] This is because the GATT Panel Reports, even when adopted, did not amount to an agreement of the parties regarding interpretation of the GATT. The Report bound only the parties to the dispute. Similarly, in the context of the WTO the fact that exclusive interpretative authority is reserved for the Ministerial Conference and the General Counsel precludes such authority from existing by implication or by inadvertence elsewhere.[85] However, adopted decisions under GATT should be taken into account where relevant to any dispute given they are part of the GATT *acquis* specifically incorporated under the Marrakesh Agreement.[86] However, such decisions are not binding. Unadopted GATT panel reports have no legal status in GATT or the WTO. However, a dispute settlement panel may nevertheless resort for guidance to such reports if relevant.[87] Resorting for guidance is not, however, the same as reliance—which is not permitted.[88]

Three points are of particular note insofar as the interpretative function is concerned. First, it is not clear what constitutes an "interpretative" decision. Secondly, the authority to interpret the agreements is vested with political organs. This has the advantage of attuning interpretative decisions with the general consensus of the membership at any given time, and thus allowing for a teleological approach to interpretation of the agreements. In this manner the prospects of compliance with such interpretative decisions is also enhanced. However, the process arguably could result in a form of creeping legislation, which could undermine the original undertakings given by the members, despite the edict that interpretative decisions are not to undermine the amendment provisions.[89] Finally, interpreting the WTO normative framework is complex, involving a variety of sources as aides to interpretation—including for example not only the *travaux préparatoires* but also subsequent practice and agreements on interpretation, as well as any relevant rules applicable as between the members—including bilateral or multilateral agreements. Thus, for example bilateral and multilateral environmental treaties can put a gloss on the trade obligations of the parties. On this basis, the Appellate Body has confirmed that WTO rules must not be interpreted in clinical isolation of public International Law.[90] In addition, reference can be

---

[83] Art.XXIX of the GATT 1994. See also "World Trade Organization: WTO analytical index", (Geneva: World Trade Organization; Cambridge [u.a.]).
[84] See Japan—Taxes on Alcoholic Beverages. Report of the Appellate Body (1996).
[85] See Japan—Taxes on Alcoholic Beverages. Report of the Appellate Body (1996).
[86] Art.XVI of the Marrakesh Agreement.
[87] Art.XVI of the Marrakesh Agreement.
[88] Argentina—Measures Affecting Imports of Footwear, Textiles, Apparel And Other Items. Report of the Appellate Body (1998).
[89] Art.XI(2) of the Marrakesh Agreement.
[90] Appellate Body Report, *US—Gasoline*, DSR 1996:I, 3, at 16–17: "That direction reflects a measure of recognition that the *General Agreement* is not to be read in clinical isolation from

made to Art.31(3)(c) of the Vienna Convention on the Law of Treaties, which calls for treaties to be interpreted in accordance with any relevant rules of International Law applicable in the relations between the parties.

## Membership and accession

Membership of the WTO is open to any State, or separate customs territory which has autonomy over the conduct of its external commercial relations and in matters covered under the WTO and the multilateral trade agreements. Membership is open on such terms as are agreed as between the WTO and the State or the Customs territory.[91] Further, under Art.XXXIII of GATT 1994 accession by a government is permitted, so that an entity that is not a State can also be a party to the agreement.[92] An important example is the membership of the European Union (EU) as it is in charge of the common commercial policy of its members.                                    **11-020**

However, an application for membership is not a mere formality. Application for membership has to be negotiated.[93] The decision to approve accession to the WTO is to be taken by a two-thirds majority of the members of the WTO.

It should also be noted that membership of the WTO implies acceptance of all multilateral agreements as contained in the Annexes 1–3 of the WTO Agreement (single undertaking). However, Annex 4 of the WTO Agreement contains a number of Agreements which are referred to as Plurilateral Trade Agreements that are only binding on those members that have explicitly accepted them. In so far as accession to these Plurilateral Trade Agreements[94] is concerned, participation in those agreements is dependent upon the terms of the respective agreement in question.[95]

The procedures adopted in the consideration of an application for accession briefly are as follows.[96] The WTO establishes a Working Party to consider the application.[97] The applicant is requested to submit a Memorandum on its Foreign Trade Regime. WTO members are then invited to pose questions to

public international law". On this also G. Goh and A. R. Ziegler, "A real world where people live and work and die". *Journal of World Trade*, 32 (1998) 5, 271–290

[91] Arts XII, XI and XIV of the Agreement Establishing the WTO and Art.XXXIII of GATT 1994. See also the Decision on the Acceptance of and Accession to the Agreement Establishing the World Trade Organization. For an interesting article in the area see G. Patterson, "The GATT: Categories, Problems And Procedures Of Membership" (1992) 1(7) *Columbia Business Law Review* 7. See also K. Jones, "The political economy of WTO accession, *World Trade Review*, 8(2009), 2, 279–314

[92] See also "World Trade Organization: WTO analytical index". (Geneva, World Trade Organization; Cambridge [u.a.]).

[93] See Art.XII of the Marrakesh Agreement.

[94] These are agreements that bind only those members that are party to them. See Art.II(3) of the Marrakesh Agreement.

[95] Art.II(3) of the Marrakesh Agreement.

[96] World Trade Organization: WTO analytical index. (Geneva, World Trade Organization; Cambridge [u.a.]).

[97] World Trade Organization: WTO analytical index. (Geneva, World Trade Organization; Cambridge [u.a.]).

the applicant based on the information provided in the Memorandum which is circulated to them for this purpose. Parallel with the work of the Working Party on accession, tariff negotiations are held between the applicant and interested members of the WTO. Upon the completion of tariff accession negotiations, the schedule of tariff concessions is annexed to the report by the Working Party and the draft Decision and Protocol of Accession. All of these are than submitted to the Council for adoption.

Thus, the Working Party is essentially involved in establishing the trade and tariff concessions and commitments that the applicant would be prepared to give as the price of its entry into the WTO in return for the benefits it would receive from the membership.[98] In the practice of GATT, members have negotiated entry into the system on the basis of some sort of reciprocity[99] between the tariff and non-tariff concessions offered by the State negotiating accession and other interested members. The reciprocity relates to the benefits in terms of trade flow which would ensue as a consequence of the commitments given. They are referred to as market access commitments. There is no express stipulation in the WTO code that such negotiations must be on the basis of reciprocity.[100] The calculation of reciprocity in the tariff concession negotiations is a complex exercise and not necessarily precise. Calculation of reciprocity in the context of non-tariff concessions, and its interaction with tariff concessions is an even more complex affair.[101] There is a fair amount of judgement involved in arriving at a reciprocal arrangement. In the case of developing countries the expectation of reciprocity is subject to it being consistent with the developing country's individual development, financial and trade needs or administrative and institutional capabilities.[102]

The accession negotiations are conducted from a number of standpoints— and not merely market access. The standpoints may be summarised as follows:

1. Ensuring the appropriate price of entry into the system (i.e. market access).

2. Ensuring that the acceding member accepts the application of the common code of conduct amongst the members of the WTO (i.e. the application of the WTO code).

3. Ensuring that the member at the time of entry enters with a foreign trade regime that is consistent with the WTO code.

[98] World Trade Organization: WTO analytical index. Geneva, World Trade Organization; Cambridge [u.a.].

[99] See J. Michael Finger, "A diplomat's economics: Reciprocity in the Uruguay Round negotiations" *World Trade Review,*4.1 (2005), 27–40.

[100] However, Art.XXVIII *bis* does refer to reciprocity but in the context of multilateral trade negotiations.

[101] See, for example, Jackson (1989), p.123; and World Trade Organization: WTO analytical index. (Geneva, World Trade Organization; Cambridge [u.a.]).

[102] See Art.XI(2) of the Marrakesh Agreement and Art.XXXVI(8) of GATT 1994.

4. Ensuring that the acceding member will be able to continue complying with the WTO code.

The criteria against which the Working Party evaluates the applicant State's case for entry does not appear to be transparent. It is not clearly stated anywhere in the WTO code. At its core it is synonymous with the WTO code and ensuring acceptable market access commitments. As such it is concerned with the foreign trade regime of the State in question. However, in practice the review seem to be fairly wide, focusing on the general state of the economy and on economic matters which strictly arguably are not within the remit of the WTO code. Non-economic considerations, for example, human rights reported in the press[103] as conditions for entry, if made, are made outside the WTO framework. There is no current method in the framework of the WTO to ensure that political considerations do not permeate the decision-making at this level.

These particular conditions accepted in the accession process can also be enforced through the dispute settlement process against the particular member after accession.[104]

| DISPUTE DS363: China — Measures Affecting Trading Rights and Distribution Services for Certain Publications and Audiovisual Entertainment Products (Official Summary by the WTO Secretariat, available online) | 11-021 |

On 10 April 2007, the United States requested consultations with China concerning: (1) certain measures that restrict trading rights with respect to imported films for theatrical release, audiovisual home entertainment products (e.g. video cassettes and DVDs), sound recordings and publications (e.g. books, magazines, newspapers and electronic publications); and (2) certain measures that restrict market access for, or discriminate against, foreign suppliers of distribution services for publications and foreign suppliers of audiovisual services (including distribution services) for audiovisual home entertainment products.

[. . .]

The United States claims that in relation to the two above-mentioned categories of measures possible inconsistencies with the Protocol of Accession, [. . .] arise as follows:

Regarding trading rights, the measures at issue appear not to allow all Chinese enterprises and all foreign enterprises and individuals the right to import the products into the customs territory of China. It also appears that foreign individuals and enterprises, including those not invested or registered in China, are accorded treatment less favourable than that accorded to enterprises in China with respect to the right to trade. Accordingly, the measures at issue appear to be inconsistent with China's obligations under the provisions

---

[103] For example, in the context of the US attitude to the membership of the People's Republic Of China. See also for the EU, H. Zimmermann, "How the EU negotiates trade and democracy". *European Foreign Affairs Review*, 13 (2008), 2, 255–280.

[104] See China—Measures Affecting Trading Rights and Distribution Services for Certain Publications and Audiovisual Entertainment Products, Report of the Appellate Body (December 21, 2009 DS 363).

of paragraphs 5.1 and 5.2 of Part I of the Protocol of Accession, as well as China's obligations under the provisions of paragraph 1.2 of Part I of the Protocol of Accession (to the extent that it incorporates commitments in paragraphs 83 and 84 of the Report of the Working Party on the Accession of China). Furthermore, to the extent that the measures at issue impose prohibitions or restrictions other than duties, taxes or other charges, on the importation into China of the Products, these measures appear to be inconsistent with China's obligations under Article XI:1 of the GATT 1994.

[. . .]

On 21 December 2009, the Appellate Body report was circulated to Members. With respect to China's measures pertaining to films for theatrical release and unfinished audiovisual products, the Appellate Body upheld the panel's conclusions that Article 30 of the Film Regulation and Article 16 of the Film Enterprise Rule are subject to these provisions are inconsistent with China's trading rights commitments in its Accession Protocol and Accession Working Party Report. The Appellate Body also upheld the Panel's conclusion that Article 5 of the 2001 Audiovisual Products Regulation and Article 7 of the Audiovisual Products Importation Rule are inconsistent with China's obligation, in paragraph 1.2 of China's Accession Protocol and paragraph 84(b) of China's Accession Working Party Report, to grant in a non-discretionary manner the right to trade.

### Relationship with other international organisations

**11-022**    The WTO is not a specialised UN agency.[105] Thus, it does not have an agreement with the UN creating such a relationship. However, the WTO engages actively in relations with other international organisations[106] and is explicitly required to co-operate with the IMF and the World Bank group.[107] To this effect, it has negotiated agreements with the IMF and the World Bank establishing the manner of co-operation as between the two organisations.[108]

The WTO has a particular relationship with the IMF given that trade and monetary matters impinge upon each other. Thus, the WTO and the IMF are to cooperate specially in co-ordinating policies with regard to exchange questions.[109] Further, in matters of monetary reserves, balance of payments or foreign exchange the WTO is to consult with the IMF and accept its findings—especially in the application of the safeguard restrictions for balance

---

[105] See, for example, Jackson (1998), p.52. See also WT document WT/GC/W/10 cited by Jackson (1998).

[106] See, for example, W. Benedek, "Relations of the WTO with other international organizations and NGOs" in F. Weiss et al. (eds), *International Economic Law With A Human Face* (The Hague: Kluwer Law International, 1998), V. Hrbatá, "No international organization is an Island. . . the WTO's relationship with the WIPO" *Journal of World Trade*, 44 (2010) 1, 1–47 and R. L. Okediji, "WIPO-WTO relations and the future of global intellectual property norms". *Netherlands Yearbook of International Law*, 39 (2008), 69–125.

[107] Art.III of the Marrakesh Agreement.

[108] See the Agreement between the IMF and the WTO 1996 in WT/L/195; and the Agreement Between the International Bank For Reconstruction and Development and the WTO 1996 in Annex I WT/GC/W/431.

[109] Art.XV of GATT 1994.

of payments purposes.[110] Further, a member is expected not to frustrate through trade measures the intent of the provisions of the IMF Articles of Agreement.[111] Finally, a member of the WTO is expected to be a member of the IMF and if not it is under an obligation to enter into a special exchange agreement with the WTO.[112]

The WTO also has the mandate to enter into arrangements for consultation and co-operation with other international organisations,[113] and non-governmental organisations concerned with matters related to the WTO.[114] Thus, the WTO has joined forces with WIPO to assist developing countries in trade-related aspects of intellectual property rights[115]; and it also co-operates with UNCTAD, especially in the framework of the jointly managed International Trade Centre (ITC) in Geneva. Similarly, the WTO has addressed the question of the role of NGOs in WTO-related matters by having a plan for enhanced cooperation with them. In essence this involves more participation of NGOs in the deliberations of the work of the WTO, in the form, for example, of briefings for NGOs and circulation of NGO documents to members.[116] In recent years, the WTO has undertaken important steps to provide NGOs with more information about its policies and better access to documents and representatives, e.g. through organising the annual WTO Public Forum and establishing an NGO Contact Point.

---

**Guidelines for arrangements on relations with Non-Governmental Organizations (WT/L/162, 23 July 1996)**

11-023

*Decision adopted by the General Council on 18 July 1996*

> I. Under Article V:2 of the Marrakesh Agreement establishing the WTO "the General Council may make appropriate arrangements for

---

[110] Art.XV of GATT 1994.

[111] See Art.XV of GATT 1994.

[112] Art.XV of GATT 1994.

[113] See Art.V of the Marrakesh Agreement. An important example are the relations between the WTO and the Codex Alimentarius Commission, established by the World Health Organization (WHO) and the Food and Agriculture Organization (FAO), with regard to sanitary and phytosanitary (SPS) measures; see J. Ewers, "Dueling risk assessments: why the WTO and codex threaten U.S. food standards", *Environmental Law*, 30 (2000) 2, 387–412 and Ch.13 on this issue.

[114] Art.V(2) of the Marrakesh Agreement. See for proposals for greater NGO participation at the WTO for example: D.C. Esty, "Non-governmental organizations at the World Trade Organization: Cooperation, competition, or exclusion" (1998) 1 *Journal of International Economic Law* 123–147 and M. Slotboom, "Participation of NGOs before the WTO and EC tribunals" *World Trade Review*, 5 (2006) 1, 69–101 as well as J. A. Lacarte, "Transparency, public debate and participation by NGOs in the WTO", *Journal of International Economic Law*, 7 (2004) 3, 683–686.

[115] See WTO Press Release July 21, 1998.

[116] See July 16, 1998 WTO Press Release. On July 18, 1996 the General Council further clarified the framework for relations with NGOs by adopting a set of guidelines (WT/L/162) which "recognizes the role NGOs can play to increase the awareness of the public in respect of WTO activities".

consultation and cooperation with non-governmental organizations concerned with matters related to those of the WTO".

II. In deciding on these guidelines for arrangements on relations with non-governmental organizations, Members recognize the role NGOs can play to increase the awareness of the public in respect of WTO activities and agree in this regard to improve transparency and develop communication with NGOs.

III. To contribute to achieve greater transparency Members will ensure more information about WTO activities in particular by making available documents which would be derestricted more promptly than in the past. To enhance this process the Secretariat will make available on on-line computer network the material which is accessible to the public, including derestricted documents.

IV. The Secretariat should play a more active role in its direct contacts with NGOs who, as a valuable resource, can contribute to the accuracy and richness of the public debate. This interaction with NGOs should be developed through various means such as inter alia the organization on an ad hoc basis of symposia on specific WTO-related issues, informal arrangements to receive the information NGOs may wish to make available for consultation by interested delegations and the continuation of past practice of responding to requests for general information and briefings about the WTO.

V. If chairpersons of WTO councils and committees participate in discussions or meetings with NGOs it shall be in their personal capacity unless that particular council or committee decides otherwise.

VI. Members have pointed to the special character of the WTO, which is both a legally binding intergovernmental treaty of rights and obligations among its Members and a forum for negotiations. As a result of extensive discussions, there is currently a broadly held view that it would not be possible for NGOs to be directly involved in the work of the WTO or its meetings. Closer consultation and cooperation with NGOs can also be met constructively through appropriate processes at the national level where lies primary responsibility for taking into account the different elements of public interest which are brought to bear on trade policy-making.

**11-024**     With regard to dispute settlement, the Appellate Body has decided that NGOs can make submissions in a trade dispute (*amicus curiae briefs*) to a panel—although it is open to the panel to accept or reject such submissions.[117] Similarly, a member party to a dispute may adopt as part of its own submissions information and advice compiled by NGOs.[118]

---

[117] United States—Import Prohibition Of Certain Shrimp and Shrimp Products. Report of the Appellate Body (1998).
[118] United States—Import Prohibition Of Certain Shrimp and Shrimp Products. Report of the Appellate Body (1998). See Ch.13 on dispute settlement in general.

**Conclusions**

In conclusion, the institutional framework of the WTO can be said to provide    **11-025** a basic, but by no means complete, constitutional framework for the international trading system.[119] The system provides for a legislative machinery in the field of international trade, for a dispute settlement apparatus, a surveillance mechanism, and an administrative structure. The constitutional structure appears to be sufficiently flexible, so as to be responsive within its limits to the exigencies of international trade relations. Further, the place of the WTO in the context of the wider international economic order is acknowledged. Thus, the WTO is to co-operate with the IMF and World Bank Group in order to facilitate greater coherence in global economic policy-making.[120] However, the international apparatus[121] for greater coherence in this respect has not been able to deal effectively with conflicting obligations of members arising, for example, from membership of the IMF and the WTO.[122] Thus, in a recent WTO Panel and Appellate Body Report, Argentina's contention that its statistical tax although in violation of Art.VIII of GATT 1994, was in fact imposed to meet IMF commitments, did not succeed in absolving it from its WTO commitments.[123] Although the Appellate Body held that the precise nature and extent of the Argentinean commitments undertaken in relation to the IMF were not clear and proven it added that the 1996 Agreement between the IMF and the WTO did not make provision for substantive rules for the resolution of conflicts between obligations under the IMF and the WTO of a member.[124]

There are a number of stress points at the level of the basic constitution. First, the purposes and objectives of the WTO are arguably limited in scope. Secondly, the WTO does not appear to have any effective mechanism to ensure that the development of international trade regulation in future will be responsive to the needs of the international trading system as objectively determined, rather than by the influence of international lobbyists. Thirdly, it is contended that the WTO, independent of the volition of its membership, has a fairly rudimentary international personality. Finally, the creation of

---

[119] See also B. Mercurio, "The WTO and its institutional impediments", *Melbourne Journal of International Law*, 8 (2007) 1, 198–232.

[120] Art.III(5) of the Marrakesh Agreement.

[121] i.e. the Agreement Between the IMF and the WTO (1996) (see particularly Art.III:5 of the Agreement); the Declaration on the Relationship of the World Trade Organization with the International Monetary Fund; and the 1994 Declaration on the Contribution of the World Trade Organization to Achieving Greater Coherence in Global Economic Policy Making. See D. Ahn, "Linkages between international financial and trade institutions". *Journal of World Trade*, 34 (2000) 4, 1–35 and D.E. Siegel, "Legal aspects of the IMF/WTO relationship", *the American Journal of International Law*, 96 (2002) 3, 561–599

[122] See Argentina—Measures Affecting Imports of Footwear, Textiles, Apparel and other Items. Report of the Panel (1997).

[123] See Argentina—Measures Affecting Imports of Footwear, Textiles, Apparel and Other Items. Report of the Panel (1997). See also the Appellate Body Report (1998).

[124] See Argentina—Measures Affecting Imports of Footwear, Textiles, Apparel and Other Items. Report of the Panel (1997). See also the Appellate Body Report (1998).

the WTO has not been negotiated *de nouveau* but has emerged rather from the GATT. Thus, the WTO inherits some of the shortcomings of the former institution. Indeed, past GATT practice is to have a bearing on future WTO conduct.[125] Further, from a technical perspective, the substantive law under the framework of the WTO has not been codified. The international trading system still comprises of a mosaic of different international agreements. This not only creates for complexity; but can potentially give rise to conflicts or inconsistencies as between agreements. There will doubtless be institutional changes in the WTO in future. On January 17, 2005, the WTO Secretariat presented a Report entitled "The Future of the WTO", the so-called "Sutherland Report". This report addressed several institutional issues, with recommendations to reform the way the organisation works and how decisions are made.[126]

With regard to the multilateral trade negotiations in general, the conclusion of the Uruguay Round had been followed a number of negotiations on left-overs, especially in the area of services (Financial services, Telecommunications)[127] until 1997. In a number of areas a so-called "built-in agenda" foresaw automatically further negotiations. At the Singapore Ministerial in 1996 the so-called Singapore issues were identified for further negotiations[128] besides the remaining liberalisation and negotiation endeavours, but the Seattle Ministerial of 1999 was considered a complete disaster in view of the absence of consensus between WTO members and riots in the streets. Only in 2001 was launched the so-called Doha Round in Doha (Qatar). It was referred to as a Development Round in view of the continued lack of integration of developing countries into the world trading system. A particular emphasis was laid on market access for developing countries, especially in the area of agriculture.[129] The Ministerial Conference of Cancun (2003) was not considered a success and only the following Ministerial Conference in Hong Kong in 2005 gave renewed hope of concluding a round in the near future by limiting the negotiations to a number of key issues. Due to the lack of consensus about the kind of tariff cuts (especially in the agricultural sector, but also with regard to industrial goods) and market openings (especially in the field of services) that were needed for a balanced result, the negotiations were suspended again in July 2006 and only resumed a few months later with the hope to reach a breakthrough at some point in 2007. Another ministerial meeting was held in July 2008. On this occasion a so-called July 2008 package was presented in order to allow for the conclusion of the negotiations. The

---

[125] Art.XVI of the Marrakesh Agreement.

[126] The report was written by a Consultative Board set up by the WTO Director General at that time, Dr. Supachai Panitchpakdi. The Group was chaired by Peter Sutherland, a former Director-General of GATT and the WTO, Peter Sutherland. See also, A. V. Bogdandy, "The 'Sutherland Report' on WTO reform", *World Trade Review*, 4 (2005) 3, 439–447.

[127] For example, the so-called Reference Paper; in this respect see Mexico—Measures Affecting Telecommunications Services, Panel Report adopted on June 1, 2004.

[128] See Ch.12.

[129] See Ch.12.

July 2008 package was considered as a stepping stone on the way to concluding the Doha Round. According to the WTO Secretariat, the main task before WTO members was to settle a range of questions that would shape the final agreement of the Doha Development Agenda. Consultations took place in Geneva among a group of ministers who were considered representing all interests in the negotiations. As a result the so-called "modalities" of the negotiations in agricultural and non-agricultural goods were revised. These are formulas and other methods to be used to cut tariffs and agricultural subsidies, and a range of related provisions. Nevertheless, the result was a document that was considerably more complicated than formulas alone. But the aim remained still to strike a deal to enable governments to open their markets and reduce trade-distorting subsidies. The results were more consultations and negotiations but no meaningful results were achieved. On April 29, 2011 WTO ambassadors endorsed Director-General Pascal Lamy's plan[130] to consult delegations in Geneva and ministers around the world in the search for a different way of achieving a breakthrough in the Doha Development Agenda negotiations. There are now more and more voices calling for the official termination (without results) of the negotiations in view of the lack of political will among WTO members to make meaningful concessions. At the same time many Members fear that such a step would further weaken the WTO as a multilateral institution and enhance the tendency of countries around the world to seek bilateral agreements.[131]

**WTO—Trade Negotiations Committee (TN/C/W/58, 15 April 2011)**

Open Letter on the WTO Doha Round Negotiations

**11-026**

15 April 2011

The attached letter has been received from the delegation of Australia on behalf of the delegations of Australia, Chile, Colombia, Costa Rica, Hong Kong China, Indonesia, Korea, Malaysia, Mexico, New Zealand, Norway, Singapore, Switzerland with the request that it be circulated to all WTO members.

We represent a group of WTO Members at varied stages of development, from different regions of the globe. We are united, however, in our

---

[130] On April 21, 2011 the negotiating chairs circulated documents representing the product of the work in their negotiating groups. An accompanying report was issued by the Chair of the Trade Negotiations Committee, Pascal Lamy. Director-General Pascal Lamy, in his cover note to the documents, said that for the first time since the Round was launched in 2001 "Members will have the opportunity to consider the entire Doha package". He says the picture is "impressive" in the significant progress achieved so far, but also "realistic" in what it shows on the remaining divides. He asked Members to think hard about "the consequences of throwing away ten years of solid multilateral work" and called on members to "use the upcoming weeks to talk to each other and build bridges".

[131] See R. Senti, "Regional trade agreements in the world trade order", *European Yearbook of International Economic Law*, 1 (2010), 227–243.

determination that for the sake of all countries the Round now needs to be brought quickly to a successful conclusion.

We are deeply concerned that despite the great deal of effort and energy through intensified work in the last few months, there has been very little progress in the Doha negotiations.

We are now in a very difficult situation and our ability to conclude the Round this year might seriously be in question.

We want to work with all Members to ensure that every effort is made to conclude the Round. We believe that a deal is achievable. We believe a deal is also worth fighting for, both in its own right, and in the longer-term interests of the multilateral trading system upon which we all so heavily rely. The Round's significant contribution to development must also be at the forefront of our thinking.

We are not prepared to stand by with such important stakes in play. We are committed to continue to work across all areas of the negotiations and with all Members to bring an ambitious and balanced conclusion to the negotiations. We are prepared to show further flexibility and to contribute to the successful conclusion of the Round this year. We call on all Members to do the same.

[. . .]

## REGIONAL AGREEMENTS

**11-027**    The increasing number of regional agreements contain normally only rudimentary institutional provisions. The management of the bilateral trade relations takes often place in a joint committee or a trade commission which holds regular meetings in order to tackle problems, discusses necessary amendments or future liberalisation objectives (e.g. NAFTA Free Trade Commission under Art.2001 of the NAFTA Agreement of 1992[132]; the Association Committee in the Agreement establishing an association between the European Community (now officially the EU) and its Member States, of the one part, and the Republic of Chile, of the other part of 2002). For more technical questions they regularly establish a number of special bodies, e.g. sub-committees.

The exact relationship to other agreements and, in particular, to the WTO is usually only addressed in a very superficial way. It is very common in this type of agreement to simply confirm the existing rights and obligations under existing multilateral agreements (including the WTO). Existing older bilateral agreements, however, are normally terminated except if they contain rules that may not be (entirely) transferred into the new agreement. From the view point of the WTO, obviously, the existence of a bilateral agreement cannot

---

[132] Of particular fame and rather exceptional is the NAFTA-related Commission of Environmental Cooperation, see C.Wold, "Evaluating NAFTA and the Commission for Environmental Cooperation". *Saint Louis University: Saint Louis University Public Law Review*, 28 (2008) 1, 201–252

change the rights and obligations of third parties to the latter—i.e. under the WTO. The dispute settlement organs of the WTO cannot, therefore, accept an argument that a specific violation of the WTO agreements towards a third Party should be justified because there is a duty to behave in a particular way under a bilateral or regional agreement[133]—except if the WTO itself provides for such an exception. At the same time, it is debated to what extent more specific rules in a bilateral agreement can taken be into account among two or more WTO members that have agreed on such rules outside of the WTO. This applies also to the availability of different dispute settlement mechanisms—which potentially can lead to so-called "forum-shopping".[134] Of particular interst in this respect were a number of cases between Mexico and the United States generally referred to as "soft drink cases" or sweetener cases where the difficult relationship between NAFTA and WTO became evident.[135]

**NAFTA Chapter Twenty: Institutional Arrangements and Dispute Settlement Procedures[136]**                                                11-028

Section A —Institutions

**Article 2001: The Free Trade Commission**

1. The Parties hereby establish the Free Trade Commission, comprising cabinet-level representatives of the Parties or their designees.

2. The Commission shall:

    (a)  supervise the implementation of this Agreement;

    (b)  oversee its further elaboration;

---

[133] In Brazil—Measures Affecting Imports of Retreaded Tyres (DS 332) the Appellate Body (Report of 3 December 2007) reversed the Panel's findings that the MERCOSUR exemption and imports of used tyres through court injunctions (i) would not result in the Import Ban being applied in a manner that constituted "arbitrary discrimination", and (ii) would lead to "unjustifiable discrimination" and a "disguised restriction on international trade" only to the extent that they result in import volumes that would significantly undermine the achievement of the objective of the Import Ban. The Appellate Body determined that the assessment of whether discrimination is arbitrary or unjustifiable should be made in the light of the objective of the measure, and found that the MERCOSUR exemption, as well as the imports of used tyres under court injunctions, had resulted in the Import Ban being applied in a manner that constituted arbitrary or unjustifiable discrimination and a disguised restriction on international trade within the meaning of the chapeau of Art.XX.

[134] See K. Kwak and G. Marceau, "Overlaps and Conflicts of Jurisdiction Between the WTO and RTAs". *Conference on Regional Trade Agreements World Trade Organisation*, K.Kwak & G. Marceau (2002). "Overlaps and Conflicts of Jurisdiction Between the WTO and RTAs". *Conference on Regional Trade Agreements World Trade Organisation* (2002). See also T. Cottier, "The relationship between World Trade Organization law, national and regional law", *Journal of International Economic Law*, 1 (1998) 1, 83–122. See also R. Leal-Arcas, "Choice of jurisdiction in international trade disputes", *Minnesota Journal of International Law*, 16 (2007), 1, 1–59.

[135] See W.J. Davey, "The soft drinks case". *World trade review*, 8(2009), 1, 5–23 and F. Rössler, "Mexico—tax measures on soft drinks and other beverages (DS308)", *World Trade Review*, 8 (2009), 1, 25–30.

[136] Source: *http://www.nafta-sec-alena.org*.

(c) resolve disputes that may arise regarding its interpretation or application;

(d) supervise the work of all committees and working groups established under this Agreement, referred to in Annex 2001.2; and

(e) consider any other matter that may affect the operation of this Agreement.

3. The Commission may:

(a) establish, and delegate responsibilities to, ad hoc or standing committees, working groups or expert groups;

(b) seek the advice of non-governmental persons or groups; and

(c) take such other action in the exercise of its functions as the Parties may agree.

4. The Commission shall establish its rules and procedures. All decisions of the Commission shall be taken by consensus, except as the Commission may otherwise agree.

5. The Commission shall convene at least once a year in regular session. Regular sessions of the Commission shall be chaired successively by each Party.

## Article 2002: The Secretariat

1. The Commission shall establish and oversee a Secretariat comprising national Sections.

2. Each Party shall:

(a) establish a permanent office of its Section;

(b) be responsible for

(i) the operation and costs of its Section, and

(ii) the remuneration and payment of expenses of panelists and members of committees and scientific review boards established under this Agreement, as set out in Annex 2002.2;

(c) designate an individual to serve as Secretary for its Section, who shall be responsible for its administration and management; and

(d) notify the Commission of the location of its Section's office.

3. The Secretariat shall:

(a) provide assistance to the Commission;

(b) provide administrative assistance to

(i) panels and committees established under Chapter Nineteen (Review and Dispute Settlement in Antidumping and Countervailing Duty Matters), in accordance with the procedures established pursuant to Article 1908, and

(ii) panels established under this Chapter, in accordance with procedures established pursuant to Article 2012; and

(c) as the Commission may direct

    (i) support the work of other committees and groups established under this Agreement, and

    (ii) otherwise facilitate the operation of this Agreement."

## AGREEMENT BETWEEN JAPAN AND THE UNITED MEXICAN STATES FOR THE STRENGTHENING OF THE ECONOMIC PARTNERSHIP (17 September 2004)

*Article 165 Joint Committee*

1. The Joint Committee composed of representatives of the Governments of the Parties shall be established under this Agreement.

2. The functions of the Joint Committee shall be:

    (a) reviewing the implementation and operation of this Agreement and, when necessary, making appropriate recommendations to the Parties;

    (b) considering and recommending to the Parties any amendments to this Agreement;

    (c) by mutual consent of the Parties, serving as a forum for consultations referred to in Article

152;

    (d) supervising the work of all Sub-Committees established under this Agreement;

    (e) adopting:

      (i) modifications to Annexes referred to in Articles 8 and 37;

      (ii) the Uniform Regulations referred to in Article 10;

      (iii) an interpretation of a provision of this Agreement referred to in Articles 84 and 89;

      (iv) the Rules of Procedure referred to in Article 159; and

      (v) any necessary decisions; and

    (f) carrying out other functions as the Parties may agree.

3. The Joint Committee may:

    (a) establish and delegate its responsibilities to Sub-Committees for the purposes of the effective

implementation and operation of this Agreement; and

    (b) take such other action in the exercise of its functions as the Parties may agree.

4. The following Sub-Committees shall be established on the date of entry into force of this Agreement:

    (a) Sub-Committee on Trade in Goods.

    (b) Sub-Committee on Sanitary and Phytosanitary Measures.

    (c) Sub-Committee on Technical Regulations, Standards and Conformity Assessment Procedures.

(d) Sub-Committee on Rules of Origin, Certificate of Origin and Customs Procedures.

(e) Sub-Committee on Cross-Border Trade in Services.

(f) Sub-Committee on Entry and Temporary Stay.

(g) Sub-Committee on Government Procurement.

(h) Sub-Committee on Cooperation in the Field of Trade and Investment Promotion.

(i) Sub-Committee on Cooperation in the Field of Agriculture.

(j) Sub-Committee on Cooperation in the Field of Tourism.

Other Sub-Committees may be established as the Parties may agree.

5. The Joint Committee shall establish its rules and procedures.

6. The Joint Committee shall meet alternately in Japan and Mexico at the request of either Party.

*Article 166 Communications*

Each Party shall designate a contact point to facilitate communications between the Parties on any matter relating to this Agreement.

*Article 167 Relation to Other Agreements*

1. The Parties reaffirm their rights and obligations under the WTO Agreement.

2. Nothing in Chapters 3, 7 and 8 shall be construed to prevent either Party from taking any necessary action as may be authorized by Article 22 of the Understanding on Rules and Procedures Governing the Settlement of Disputes in Annex 2 to the WTO Agreement, as may be amended.

3. The Convention on Commerce between Japan and the United Mexican States signed at Tokyo on January 30, 1969 shall expire upon the date of entry into force of this Agreement.

### CHAPTER 12

# INTERNATIONAL TRADE LAW: SUBSTANTIVE RULES

## INTRODUCTION

The substantive rules under the WTO framework[1] partake more of a code **12-001** than the provision of a detailed regulatory system in the sphere of international trade that States need to adopt.[2] Interestingly, in view of the relatively detailed set of rules contained in the WTO Agreement and its annexes, most bilateral and regional trade agreements will either follow the same regulatory approach or only modify it in certain respects. These changes are sometimes entitled WTO plus elements.[3] On the whole, a relatively homogenous set of substantive rules regulating international trade has evolved that is often referred to as "trade disciplines". At the same time, the differences in the specific rules are increasingly criticised as leading to a "spaghetti bowl" of agreements that is neither transparent nor business-friendly in view of the many different rules. The objectives of transparency, predictability and non-discrimination as pillars of the WTO system are thus endangered by the developments relating to bilateral and regional agreements. This holds particularly true for exporters from developing countries.[4]

---

[1] Emphasis in this chapter will be put on the rules of the WTO, as despite their increasing number, many regional agreements are directly inspired by the WTO disciplines and language. Rules from RTAs will be highlighted, however, when they constitute important examples going beyond the WTO *acquis* or may lead to incompatibilities.

[2] This updated chapter is based on material originally included in Ch.2 of A.H. Qureshi, *The World Trade Organization—Implementing International Trade Norms* (Manchester, Manchester University Press, 1996). The examination of the code here is a general one; and does not purport to be detailed or exhaustive. In this section only the relevant WTO Panel and Appellate Body Reports have been mentioned. For relevant literature and materials on GATT 1947 and the WTO in general refer to the literature referred in Ch.11, n.28; in addition on GATT 1994 see R. Bhala, *Modern GATT Law: a Treatise on the General Agreement on Tariffs and Trade* (London, Sweet & Maxwell, 2005) and P.C. Mavroidis, The General Agreement on Tariffs and Trade (Oxford, Oxford University Press, 2005).

[3] See J. Ya Qin, "'WTO-Plus' Obligations and Their Implications for the World Trade Organization Legal System" (2003) 37 *Journal of World Trade* 483 – 522.

[4] See C. Agu, "Multilateralism, regionalism and the paradox of the 'spaghetti bowl' in developing countries" *Aussenwirtschaft, Zürich,* 64(2009), 3, 293–316 and M. L. Abugattas,

The rules prescribe the framework within which national trade legislation may be formed, as well as guidance for national legislation. Generally, the rules do not prescribe substantive provisions in the field of trade, nor are they directly concerned with harmonising national legislation relating to trade as such. Where the rules do make provision for substantive norms, and harmonisation, these are limited to furthering the trade liberalisation objectives of the WTO, and are minimalist. Further, the very essence of the WTO code is such that it is driven by a particular perspective—namely trade liberalisation. As such, the code is not concerned with the totality of trade issues. The WTO mainly focuses on the interface of national trade legislation, rather than the national legislation itself. Thus, the non-discrimination edict in the code prescribes the uniform application of the national standard, but not the content of that standard. Similarly, the disciplines in relation to standards focus not so much on the content of the standards, but rather on basic principles which should govern the formulation of the standards. However, within its remit the WTO code is a code for State conduct, in the sense that it provides generally comprehensively for the necessary rules to ensure trade liberalisation. And whilst it encompasses a spectrum of norms, ranging from the mere hortatory, the "soft", the permissive, to the mandatory—it includes sufficient mandatory prescriptions so as to cloak the code with the force of International Law.

Essentially, the WTO code is aimed at securing access to foreign markets. This market access[5] is ensured mainly by eliminating quantitative restrictions; reducing tariff and non-tariff barriers; eliminating all forms of discrimination in government regulation; providing for the protection of intellectual property rights; ensuring predictable and transparent governmental regulations; and through disciplines which aim at ensuring fair competition. These are the objectives of trade liberalisation. Generally, the burden of these objectives is graduated according to the level of development of a member. The focus of the code is three-fold, viz. border measures; intra-territorial measures impinging on disciplines at the border; and finally the trade-related sphere.

**12-002**      The international trading system has evolved in response to a number of factors. Historically, it draws, inter alia, from GATT 1947 and the amendments and agreements arising from the various rounds of trade negotiations.[6] Politically, the system has been shaped in response to national and international lobbies, particularly from the developed States. From an international

---

*Swimming in the spaghetti bowl: challenges for developing countries under the "new regionalism"* (New York NY [ u.a.], United Nations, 2004).

[5] See J. Mo, "The mystery of market access", *Journal of World Intellectual Property,* 3:2 (2000), p.225–247 and K. Bagwell, "It's a question of market access", *The American journal of international law,* 96 (2002) 56–76 as well as J.D. Southwick, "Addressing market access barriers in Japan through the WTO", *Law and Policy in International Business,* 31 (2000) 3, 923–976.

[6] GATT trade rounds: 1947 (Geneva); 1949 (Annecy, France); 1951 (Torquay, England); 1956 (Geneva); 1960–1961 (Geneva, the Dillon Round); 1964–1967 (Geneva, the Kennedy Round); 1973–1979 (Geneva, the Tokyo Round); 1986–1993 (Geneva, the Uruguay Round), 2001 (Doha Development Round).

perspective, the limits of the international legal system have had a bearing. Because the international trading system has evolved thus in this piecemeal and diverse fashion, it is lacking somewhat in internal coherence; and is incomplete as a general framework.[7]

The WTO code is particularly significant for two reasons. First, the code of conduct is significant because the GATT 1947 disciplines and commitments have been strengthened and clarified; and the coverage of the code has been extended to include disciplines which hitherto had escaped regulation, for example services, agriculture and textiles—albeit in varying degrees. Secondly, it sets the stage for an integrated approach to international economic issues, albeit from the standpoint of trade. An integrated approach involves a recognition that international economic issues cannot be reduced to distinct subjects, e.g. trade, or in relation to monetary or development matters. The issues cannot be considered in isolation from the rest of the international economic order—or indeed from political aspects. Thus, the inclusion in the code of the trade-related aspects of intellectual property rights, and the trade-related aspects of investment measures; the stage-setting for the inclusion of trade-related aspects of the environment; the establishment of the Trade Policy Review Mechanism as a focus, inter alia, on the inter-linkages between various economic policies; and the edict that the WTO is to co-operate with the IMF and the World Bank Group with a view to achieving greater coherence in global economic policy making[8] all represent the modus operandi of an integrated approach. Indeed, such has been the perception of this integrated approach that discussion for the inclusion in the remit of the WTO of such matters as trade and environment[9];

---

[7] Although certain principles such as the MFN and national treatment standards have evolved over the last couple of centuries. See Andreas R. Ziegler, "The Nascent international law on Most-Favoured-Nation (MFN) Clauses in Bilateral Investment Treaties (BIT's)", *European Yearbook of International Economic Law*, 1 (2010), 77–101

[8] Art.III(5) of the Agreement Establishing the WTO.

[9] See the Marrakesh Ministerial Decision on Trade and Environment and the work of the WTO Committee on Trade and Environment. See also, for example, K. Anderson and R. Blackhurst (eds), *The Greening of World Trade Issues* (New York, Harvester Wheatsheaf, 1992); E-U Petersmann, *International and European Trade and Environmental Law after the Uruguay Round* (London, Kluwer Law International, 1995); M. Schlagenhof, "Trade Measures Based on Environmental Processes and Production Methods" (1995) 29(6) *Journal of World Trade* 123; C. Tietje, "Voluntary Eco-labelling Programmes and Questions of State Responsibility in the WTO/GATT Legal System" (1995) 29(5) *Journal of World Trade* 123–58; OECD Report on Trade and Environment to the OECD Council at Ministerial Level (OECD, Paris, 1995); J. Adams, "Globalisation, Trade and Environment" in *Globalisation and Environment: Preliminary Perspectives* (OECD, 1997); S.W. Chang, "GATTing a Green Trade Barrier—Eco-labelling and the WTO Agreement on Technical Barriers to Trade" (1997) 31(1) J.W.T. 137–60; R. Eglin, "Trade and Environment in the World Trade Organisation" (1995) 18(6) *The World Economy* 769–80; M.J. Ferrantino, "International Trade, Environmental Quality and Public Policy" (1997) 20(1) *The World Economy* 43–72; M.A. Cole, A.J. Rayner and J.M. Bates, "Trade Liberalisation and the Environment: The Case of the Uruguay Round" (1998) 21(3) *The World Economy* 337–48; R. Quick and C. Lau, "Environmentally Motivated Tax Distinctions and WTO Law: The European Commission's Green Paper on Integrated Product Policy in Light of the 'Like Product-' and 'PPM-' Debates" (2003) 6. *Journal of International Economic Law* 419–58; G. Sampson and J. Whalley (eds), *The WTO, Trade and*

trade and culture,[10] trade and investment[11]; and trade and competition[12] are under way; and calls for the inclusion in the remit of the WTO of such matters

*the Environment* (E. Elgar, 2005); G.P. Sampson, *The WTO and Sustainable Development* (United Nations University Press, 2005); N. Bernasconi-Osterwalder with D. Magraw et al. (eds), *Environment and Trade: a guide to WTO jurisprudence* (Earthscan, 2006); A. Goyal, *The WTO and International Environmental Law: Towards a conciliation* (Oxford, Oxford University Press, 2006); D.A. Gentile, "International trade and the environment", *Fordham Environmental Law Review*, 19 (2009), 1, 195–230; and M. S. Blodgett, "The environment and trade agreements" *Hastings International and Comparative Law Review*, 33(2010), 1, 1–19.

[10] M.E. Footer and C.B. Graber, "Trade liberalization and cultural policy" (2003) 3 *J. Int. Economic Law* 115–44; M. Hahn, "A Clash of Cultures? The UNESCO Diversity Convention and International Trade Law" (2006) *J. Int. Economic Law* 515–52; C. Beat Graber, "The New UNESCO Convention on Cultural Diversity: A Counterbalance to the WTO?" (2006) 9 *Journal of International Economic Law* 553–74; T. Voon, *Cultural Products and the World Trade Organization* (Cambridge, Cambridge University Press, 2007); M. Burri Nenova, "Trade and culture in international law", *Journal of World Trade*, 44(2010) 1, 49–80.

[11] See, for example, "Trade and foreign direct investment", Ch.4; WTO Annual Report (1996); WTO Report (1998) of the Working Group on the Relationship Between Trade and Investment to the General Council, WT/WGTI/2, December 8, 1998; T.L. Brewer and S. Young, "Investment Issues at the WTO: the architecture of rules and the settlement of disputes" (1998) 1 *J. Int. Economic Law* 457–70; D. Collins, "A new role for the WTO in international investment law" *Connecticut Journal of International Law*, 25.2009 (2010), 1, S.1–35

[12] As a consequence of the December 1996 Singapore Ministerial Conference, a Working Group to study the interaction between trade and competition policy was established. See in particular, for example, "Special Study on Trade and Competition Policy" in WTO Annual Report (1997), Ch.4; UNCTAD World Investment Report (1997); WTO Report (1998) of the Working Group on the Interaction Between Trade and Competition Policy to the General Council, WT/WGCP/2 December 8, 1998; Organisation for Economic Co-operation and Development, Trade and competition: from Doha to Cancún Paris (OECD, 2003). See also, for example, J.H. Jackson, "Editorial. Introducing a group of articles on competition policy" (1992) 2 *Journal of International Economic Law* 399–401; P. Lloyd, and G. Sampson, "Competition and Trade Policy: Identifying the Issues After the Uruguay Round" (1995) 18 *The World Economy* 681–705; E-U Petersmann, "International competition rules for governments and for private business" (1996) 30(3) J.W.T. 37; P. Nicolaides, "For a World Competition Authority" (1996) 30(4) J.W.T. 131–46; C. Morgan, "Competition policy and anti-dumping—is it time for a reality check?" (1996) 30(5) J.W.T. 61–89; M.J. Trebilcock, "Competition policy and trade policy: mediating the interface," (1996) 30(4) J.W.T. 71–106; B. Hoekman, "Competition policy and the global trading system" (1997) 20(4) *World Economy* 383–406; C.P. Mavroidis, and S.J. Van Siclen, "The Application of the GATT/WTO dispute Resolution System to Competition Issues" (1997) 31(5) J.W.T. 5–48; A. Mattoo, and A. Subramanian, "Multilateral Rules on Competition Policy: A Possible Way Forward?" (1997) 31 (5) J.W.T. 95–115; E. Hope and P. Maeleng, *Competition and Trade Policies:Coherence or Conflict?* (Routledge, 1998); M.-C. Malaguti, "Restrictive business practices in International Trade and the role of the World Trade" (1998) 32(3) J.W.T. 117–151; R. Pitofsky, "Competition policy in a global economy—today and tomorrow" (1999) 2 *Journal of International Economic Law* 403–11; F. Roessler, "Should principles of competition policy be incorporated into WTO law through non-violation complaints?" (1999) 2 *Journal of International Economic Law* 413–21; A.D. Melamed, "International cooperation in competition law and policy: what can be achieved at the bilateral, regional, and multilateral levels" (1999) 2 *Journal of International Economic Law* 423–33; P.M. Smith, "A long and winding road: trips and the evolution of an international competition framework" (1999) 2 *Journal of International Economic Law* 435–40; M.E. Janow, "The Work of the International Competition Policy Advisory Committee to the Attorney General and the Assistant Attorney General for Antitrust" (1999) 2 *Journal of International Economic Law* 441–44; D.K. Tarullo, "Competition policy for global markers" (1999) 2 *Journal of International Economic Law* 445–55; E.M. Fox, "Competition Law and the Millennium Round" (1999) 2 *Journal of International Economic Law* 665–80; Ig.G. Bercero and S.D. Amarasinha, "Moving the Trade and Competition Debate Forward" (2001) 4 *Journal of International Economic Law* 481–506; R.D. Anderson and P. Holmes, "Competition Policy and the Future of the Multilateral Trading System" (2002) 5 *Journal*

as labour[13] and human rights[14] and trade and taxation[15]—not to mention a general questioning of the traditional Bretton Woods demarcations.

*of International Economic Law* 531–63; E.M. Fox, "The WTO's First Antitrust Case—Mexican Telecom: A Sleeping Victory for Trade and Competition" (2006) 9 *Journal of International Economic Law* 271–92; M.D. Taylor, *International Competition Law: A New Dimension for the WTO?* (Cambridge University Press, 2006); B. Sweeney, "Export Cartels: Is there a need for Global Rules?", *Journal of International Economic Law Advance Access* published on February 14, 2007: (2007) 10 *Journal of International Economic Law* 87–115; D.J. Gerber, "Competition law and the WTO" *Journal of International Economic Law*, 10 (2007), 3, 707–724; G. Sacerdoti, "Competition issues in the global economy and the WTO Regulation of World Trade" *Anuário brasileiro de direito internacional,* 4 (2009), 2, 68-80.

[13] See Ch.15 and, for example, D. Rodrik, "Labor standards in International Trade: Do they matter and what do we do about them?" in R.Z. Lawrence, J. Whalley and D. Rodrik, Emerging agenda for global trade: High Stakes for developing countries Policy Essay No.20, Overseas Development Council, Washington (USA); E. De Wet Erika, Labour standards in the globalized economy: The inclusion of a social clause in the General Agreement on Tariffs and Trade/World Trade Organization, Discussion Paper, DP/76/1994 (ILO, International Institute for Labour Studies, Geneva, 1994); D. Ehrenberg, "The labor Link: Applying the International Trading System to Enforce Violations of Forced and Child Labor" (1995) 20(2) *The Yale Journal of International Law* 361–417; J.A. De Castro, Trade and Labour Standards: (Using the wrong instruments for the rights cause, UNCTAD, Discussion Paper, No.99 (May 1995); A. Sapire, "The interaction between labour standards and international trade policy" (1995) 18 *The World Economy* 6; S.S. Golub, International labor standards and international trade. IMF Working Paper WP/97/37 (Washington D.C., April, 1997); OECD, Trade and Labour Standards. A review of the Issues (Paris, Organization for Economic Cooperation and Development, 1995); WTO, Singapore Ministerial Declaration (Ministerial Conference, Singapore, December 9–13, 1996), WT/MIN(96)/DEC, December 18, 1996; P. Waer, "Social clauses in international trade—the debate in the European Union" (1996) 30 J.W.T. 4; H. Ward, "Common but Differentiated Debates: Environment, labour and the World Trade Organization" (1996) 45 *International and Comparative Law Quarterly* 592–632; F. Weiss, "Internationally Recognized Labour Standards and Trade" (1996) *Legal Issues of European Integration* 161–78; B.A. Langille, "Right ways to think about international labour standards" (1997) 31 *Journal of World Trade* 4; J.S. Mai, "Core Labour Standards and Export Performance in Developing Countries (1997) 20 *The World Economy* 6; N. Haworth and S. Hughes, "Trade and International Labour Standards: Issues and Debates over a Social Clause" (1997) 39(2) *The Journal of Industrial Relations* 179–95; K.E. Maskus, "Should Core Labour Standards Be Imposed Through International Trade Policy", Policy Research Working Paper, 1817, The World Bank Development Research Group, August 1997; E-U Petersmann, "The WTO constitution and human rights" (2000) 3 *Journal of International Economic Law* 19–25; C. McCrudden and A. Davies, "A perspective on trade and labor rights" (2000) 3 *Journal of International Economic Law* 43–62; T. Cottier, "Trade and Human Rights: A Relationship to Discover" (2002) 5 *Journal of International Economic Law* 111–32; P. Macklem, "Labour Law Beyond Borders" (2002) *Journal of International Economic Law* 605–45; C. Lopez-Hurtado, "Social Labelling and WTO Law" (2002) 5 *Journal of International Economic Law* 719–46; C. Thomas, "Trade-Related Labor and Environment Agreements?" (2002) 5 *Journal of International Economic Law* 791–819, S.M.H. Razavi, "Labour standards and WTO" *The journal of World Investment & Trade*, 11 (2010) 5, 879–898.

[14] See, for example, the discussion of the results of the Uruguay Round in the British Parliament (House of Commons) June 14, 1994 *Hansard* Issue Number 1658; T. Cottier, J. Pauwelyn and E. Burqui, *Human Rights and International Trade* (Oxford, Oxford University Press, 2005); J. Harrison, *The Human Rights Impact of the World trade Organisation* (Hart Publishing, 2007). Also B. Konstantinov, "Human rights and the WTO", *Journal of world trade*, 43 (2009) 2, 317–338 and E-U Petersmann, "Human rights, international economic law and constitutional justice", *European Journal of International Law*, 19 (2008) 5, 955–960.

[15] See, for example, A.H. Qureshi, "TRIT—a new WTO code of conduct on trade-related aspects of international taxation?" in A. Qureshi et al. (eds), *The Legal and Moral Aspects of International Trade Volume III* (London, Routledge, 1998); M. Daly, "WTO rules on direct taxation" (2006) 29 (5) *World Economy* 527–57.

Some of these areas were identified in the Singapore Ministerial Meeting (1996) of the WTO as the so-called "Singapore Issues". Four working groups were set up, namely investment protection,[16] competition policy,[17] transparency in government procurement[18] and trade facilitation[19]; but due to the problems during the Doha Development Round most of these negotiations were abandoned (with the exception of trade facilitation) or given little priority after the 2003.

## THE FRAMEWORK OF THE WTO CODE

12-003    The WTO code focuses on three distinct spheres, viz. goods, services and trade-related aspects of intellectual property rights (TRIPS).[20] Each of these spheres is governed by distinct legal regimes—namely, the General Agreement on Tariffs and Trade (GATT) 1994 and the Multilateral Agreements on Trade; the General Agreement on Trade in Services (GATS); and the TRIPS Agreement.[21] More particularly, in the sphere of goods, the basic agreement comprises GATT 1994.[22] This agreement is further reinforced, elaborated and even sometimes deviated from, through a number of agreements. These relate to specific sectors—namely, agriculture and textiles; to standards, i.e. health regulations for farm products (known as sanitary and phytosanitary measures), and product standards (known as technical barriers to trade); to "fair" competition—namely, anti-dumping duties and countermeasures relating to subsidies; to the re-enforcement of disciplines at the border, namely customs valuation methods, preshipment inspection requirements, rules of origin, and import licensing; to the trade-related aspects of investment measures; and finally, to safeguard measures to protect domestic producers. These agreements,[23] together with GATT 1994, are known as the Multilateral Agreements on Trade in Goods. The agreements need to be considered in conjunction with the market access commitments of the

---

[16] See Ch.14.
[17] See below on parallel developments in RTAs.
[18] See below on parallel developments in RTAs.
[19] See below.
[20] Discussions to include competition issues or investment have not led to further negotiations for the time being, see below.
[21] Trade-related Aspects of Intellectual Property Rights.
[22] The provisions of GATT 1947 have been re-enacted as GATT 1994, and include certain subsequent instruments entered into under the GATT 1947. See Annex 1A of the Marrakesh Agreement Establishing the WTO.
[23] i.e. the Agreement on Agriculture; Agreement on Sanitary and Phytosanitary Measures; Agreement on Textiles and Clothing; Agreement on Technical Barriers to Trade; Agreement on Trade-Related Aspects of Investment Measures; Agreement on Implementation of Article VI of the General Agreement on Tariffs and Trade; Agreement on Implementation of Article VII of the General Agreement on Tariffs and Trade; Agreement on Preshipment Inspection; Agreement on Rules of Origin; Agreement on Import Licensing Procedures; Agreement on Subsidies and Countervailing Measures; Agreement on Safeguards.

respective members, which are contained in the member's schedules of commitments. In the event of a conflict between GATT 1994 and the Multilateral Agreements on Trade, the provisions of the latter prevail.[24] In the field of services the basic agreement comprises of GATS. This is accompanied by a number of annexes focusing on some specific sectors of services, along with the schedules of market access commitments of the members. In the sphere of intellectual property rights the main obligations are exclusively to be found in the TRIPS.

The Multilateral Agreements on Trade in Goods; GATS; TRIPS; the Understanding on Rules and Procedures Governing the Settlement of Disputes (DSU); and the Trade Policy Review Mechanism (TPRM) are also collectively known as the "Multilateral Trade Agreements".[25] These agreements are to be distinguished from the agreements known as the Plurilateral Agreements.[26] Save from the Plurilateral Agreements, the Multilateral Trade Agreements along with the Marrakesh Agreement Establishing the WTO form in combination a single undertaking.[27] Because the other multilateral agreements are an integral part of the Marrakesh Agreement,[28] the members are in fact parties to a single undertaking under a single treaty instrument.[29] All the members are bound by the Marrakesh Agreement and the agreements that form an integral part of it.[30] In view of the recent problems to conclude the Doha Development Round, there are increasingly voices calling for negotiations of new plurilateral agreements on certain aspects negotiated during this round where at least a certain number of members seem to have reached consensus.[31]

The Plurilateral Agreements bind only their signatories. Of the original four Plurilateral Agreements only two are still in force: one on trade in civil aircraft; the other on government procurement. Of these two, especially the latter, known as government procurement agreement (GPA), is of increasing interest for developed States that form the bulk of its members. But a number of developing states have also started negotiations for accession to the GPA. Often this is due to their bilateral trade negotiations with developed States which are already members of the GPA and have a strong desire to see their preferential trading partners becoming parties to the GPA.[32]

---

[24] See interpretative note to Annex 1A of to the Agreement Establishing the WTO.

[25] See Art.II of the Marrakesh Agreement Establishing the World Trading Organization.

[26] Originally these included the Agreement on Trade in Civil Aircraft; the Agreement on Government Procurement; the International Dairy Arrangement; and the International Bovine Meat Agreement.

[27] Art.II of the Marrakesh Agreement Establishing the WTO.

[28] Art.II(2) of the Marrakesh Agreement.

[29] Brazil—Measures Affecting Desiccated Coconut. Report of the Appellate Body (1997).

[30] Art.II(2) of the Marrakesh Agreement.

[31] See below in the Conclusions of this Chapter.

[32] See S. Arrowsmith, "Reviewing the GPA: The Role and Development of the Plurilateral Agreement After Doha" (2002) 5 *Journal of International Economic Law* 761–90 and V. Rege, "Transparency in Government Procurement Issues of Concern and Interest to Developing Countries" (2001) 35 *Journal of World Trade* 489–515. See also S. Arrowsmith, "Government procurement in the WTO", (The Hague [u.a.], Kluwer Law Internat, 2003).

## Government Procurement

**12-004**   While the WTO Agreements on Goods and the GATS focus on the opening of markets and trade for private consumers, an increasing part of all goods and even more so services has been consumed by the State in recent years. This is normally related to the development of infrastructure and social security. Transport networks and infrastructure, energy and telecommunication infrastructure is often provided for by the State despite recent attempts in many States to liberalise these sectors. This still holds mostly true for defence expenditures. At the same time, education and health services (including caring for the elderly) are often provided for by the State.

It is therefore not surprising that in recent decades States have undertaken attempts to assure that such goods and services are procured (Government or Public Procurement) in a way that does not undermine the liberalization of trade. Results are the GPA and an increasing number of bilateral agreements including procurement rules. While originally only developed States seemed ready to accept binding rules in this regard, there is an increasing attempt to "convince" emerging economies and developing States to do so—a political fact often criticised by NGOs.[33]

The GPA and these bilateral agreements follow similar rules. They normally require States to organise the procurement according to certain transparent rules, to prefer the commercially most interesting offer and to provide competitors with remedies against negative decisions. In order to find a balance between the administrative burden resulting from these requirements and the benefits of undistorted procurement, international agreements normally provide for certain thresholds and exceptions that allow procurement without following these rules (distinction between covered procurement and uncovered procurement).

**12-005**   **United States signed the Dominican Republic-Central America-United States Free Trade Agreement (CAFTA-DR), signed on 5 August 2004**

*Chapter Nine—Government Procurement*

*Article 9.1: Scope and Coverage*

1. This Chapter applies to any measure, including any act or guideline of a Party, regarding covered procurement.

2. For purposes of this Chapter, covered procurement means a procurement of goods, services, or both:

---

[33] See P.Wang, "China›s accession to the WTO government procurement agreement", *Journal of international economic law*, 12 (2009) 3, 663–706 and A. Barua, (ed.), "The WTO and India" (New Delhi, Orient BlackSwan, 2010).

(a) by any contractual means, including purchase, rental, or lease, with or without an option to buy, build-operate-transfer contracts, and public works concession contracts;

(b) listed and subject to the conditions specified in:

    (i) Annex 9.1.2(b)(i), which shall apply between the United States and each other Party;

    (ii) Annex 9.1.2(b)(ii), which shall apply between the Central American Parties; and

    (iii) Annex 9.1.2(b)(iii), which shall apply between each Central American Party and the Dominican Republic;

(c) that is conducted by a procuring entity; and

(d) that is not excluded from coverage.

3. This Chapter does not apply to:

(a) non-contractual agreements or any form of assistance that a Party or a state enterprise provides, including grants, loans, equity infusions, fiscal incentives, subsidies, guarantees, cooperative agreements, government provision of goods and services to persons or to state, regional, or local governments, and purchases for the direct purpose of providing foreign assistance;

(b) purchases funded by loans or grants made to a Party, including an entity of a Party by a person, international entities, associations, or another Party or a non- Party, to the extent that the conditions of such assistance are inconsistent with this Chapter;

(c) acquisition of fiscal agency or depository services, liquidation, and management services for regulated financial institutions, and sale and distribution services for government debt;

(d) hiring of government employees and related employment measures;

(e) any good or service component of any contract that is awarded by a procuring entity that is not listed in Sections A through C of Annexes 9.1.2(b)(i), 9.1.2(b)(ii), and 9.1.2(b)(iii); and

(f) purchases made under exceptionally advantageous conditions that only arise in the very short term, such as unusual disposals by companies that normally are not suppliers, or disposals of assets of businesses in liquidation or receivership.

4. Each Party shall ensure that its procuring entities comply with this Chapter in conducting any covered procurement.

5. Where a procuring entity awards a contract in a procurement that is not covered by this Chapter, nothing in this Chapter shall be construed to cover any good or service component of that contract.

6. No procuring entity may prepare, design, or otherwise structure or divide any procurement in order to avoid the obligations of this Chapter.

7. Nothing in this Chapter shall prevent a Party from developing new procurement policies, procedures, or contractual means, provided they are not inconsistent with this Chapter.

*Article 9.2: General Principles*

1. With respect to any measure covered by this Chapter, each Party shall accord to the goods and services of another Party, and to the suppliers of another Party of such goods and services, treatment no less favorable than the most favorable treatment the Party or procuring entity accords to its own goods, services, and suppliers.

2. With respect to any measure covered by this Chapter, no Party may:

   (a) treat a locally established supplier less favorably than another locally established supplier on the basis of degree of foreign affiliation or ownership; or

   (b) discriminate against a locally established supplier on the basis that the goods or services offered by that supplier for a particular procurement are goods or services of another Party.

3. For purposes of paragraphs 1 and 2, determination of the origin of goods shall be made in a manner consistent with Chapter Four (Rules of Origin and Origin Procedures).

4. With respect to covered procurement, a procuring entity shall not seek, take account of, or impose offsets in any stage of a procurement.

5. Paragraphs 1 and 2 do not apply to measures respecting customs duties or other charges of any kind imposed on or in connection with importation, the method of levying such duties or charges, other import regulations, including restrictions and formalities, or measures affecting trade in services other than measures specifically governing procurement covered by this Chapter.

*Article 9.3: Publication of Procurement Measures*

Each Party shall promptly:

 (a) publish any law or regulation, and any modification thereof, relating to procurement;

 (b) make publicly available any procedure, judicial decision, or administrative ruling of general application, relating to procurement; and

 (c) on request of a Party, provide to that Party a copy of a procedure, judicial decision, or administrative ruling of general application, relating to procurement [. . .]

## THE LIBERALISATION OF INTERNATIONAL TRADE IN GOODS

**The general obligations**

**12-006**  The general framework driving the liberalisation of trade in goods[34] is founded on five important principles, viz. the prohibition on quantitative restrictions; the prohibition on undermining tariff commitments undertaken;

---

[34] The classification of obligations that follows is not intended to be mutually exclusive.

the prohibition on acting inconsistently with the most-favoured-nation (MFN) standard; the prohibition on acting inconsistently with the national treatment (NT) standard; and the requirements of transparency.

First, the general rule is that quantitative restrictions on the importation and exportation of products are prohibited.[35] This rule is a traditional component of the GATT 1947 and a regular feature of regional trade agreements.[36] The quantitative restriction may be complete or partial. When the restriction is partial it is known as a quota. Measures having such effects may include import or export licences when not freely granted, or other measures operating similarly. Embargoes and economic sanctions (e.g. approved by the UN Security Council) are normally governed by special rules relating to security issues.[37]

Secondly, whilst tariffs are generally tolerated under the WTO code,[38] successive rounds of trade negotiations have resulted in a general reduction of tariff rates. The Uruguay Round of Multilateral Trade Negotiations accomplished a 40 per cent reduction of tariffs.[39] Accordingly, Member States can impose tariffs on goods, but only to the extent of the rate of the duty that they have agreed upon (i.e. the "bound" rate). The tariff concessions are contained in the respective member's schedule of tariff concessions. The schedules are annexed to the Uruguay Round Marrakesh Protocol, and are an integral part of GATT 1994. A member is obliged to accord to the trade of the other members' treatment no less favourable than that agreed upon in its schedule of concessions.[40] Generally, the tariff reductions either came immediately into effect, or were phased up to ten years after the entry into force of the Agreement establishing the WTO.[41]

---

[35] Basic provision: Art.XI of GATT 1994. See also Arts XIII and IV of GATT 1994. See European Communities—Regime For The Importation, Sale and Distribution of Bananas, Appellate Body Report (1997); Japan—Measures Affecting Agricultural Products, Report of the Panel (1998). See also Canada—Periodical, Appellate Body Report adopted on July 30, 1997; India—Quantitative Restrictions on Imports of Agricultural, Textile and Industrial Products, AB Report adopted September 22, 1999.

[36] See, for example, the concept of quantitative measures used in the Treaty on the Functioning oft he European Union; see C. Barnard, *The Substantive Law of the EU* (Oxford [u.a.], Oxford Univ. Press, 2010).

[37] Art. XXI GATT (Security exceptions); see on this issue A. Emmerson, "Conceptualizing security exceptions", *Journal of International Economic Law*, 11 (2008) 1, 135–154.

[38] See Art.II GATT 1994, and Understanding on the Interpretation of Article XVII of the General Agreement On Tariffs and Trade 1994. See European Communities—Customs Classification of Certain Computer Equipment, Appellate Body Report (1998); Argentina—Measures Affecting Imports of Footwear, Textiles, Apparel and Other Items. Report of the Panel (1997), and the Report of the Appellate Body (1998); European Communities—Regime For the Importation, Sale And Distribution of Bananas, Report of the Appellate Body (1997). In general on tariff reduction M. Baccetta, "Industrial tariff liberalization and the Doha Development Agenda" (Geneva World Trade Organization, 2003) and A. Hoda, *Tariff Negotiations and Renegotiations under the GATT and the WTO* (Cambridge [u.a.], Cambridge Univ. Press, 2002).

[39] See the Marrakesh Declaration of April 15, 1994.

[40] Art.II(1)(a) of GATT 1994. See P. Gallagher, *A Handbook on Reading WTO Scheduels* (Cambridge, Cambridge University Press, 2007).

[41] Art.2 of the Uruguay Round Protocol to The GATT 1994.

Any other duties or charges levied upon bound tariff items are to be recorded also in the tariff schedule.[42] Such other duties or charges shall not exceed the levels at which they existed on the date of entry into force of the Agreement Establishing the WTO. In this manner other duties or charges also become bound, along with the bound tariff items. The tariff schedules of all countries constitute an integral part of the WTO agreement. They are normally based on the Harmonized Commodity Description and Coding System (HS) of tariff nomenclature, an internationally standardised system of names and numbers for classifying traded goods developed and maintained by the World Customs Organization (WCO). They were last revised in 2007. The codes are standard up to six digits, the most detailed level that can be compared internationally. States can go further and add sub-categories (tariff lines). The information on bound rates is based on the WTO's Consolidated Tariff Schedules (CTS) database.[43]

**12-007**

**Harmonized System (HS): Chapter 87 Vehicles other than railway or tramway rolling-stock, and parts and accessories thereof**

| Heading | H.S. Code | |
|---|---|---|
| 87.01 | | Tractors (other than tractors of heading 87.09). |
| | 8701.10 | Pedestrian controlled tractors |
| | 8701.20 | Road tractors for semi-trailers |
| | 8701.30 | Track-laying tractors |
| | 8701.90 | Other |
| 87.02 | | Motor vehicles for the transport of ten or more persons, including the driver. |
| | 8702.10 | With compression-ignition internal combustion piston engine (diesel or semi-diesel) |
| | 8702.90 | Other |
| 87.03 | | Motor cars and other motor vehicles principally designed for the transport of persons (other than those of heading 87.02), including station wagons and racing cars. |
| | 8703.10 | Vehicles specially designed for travelling on snow; golf cars and similar vehicles —Other vehicles, with spark-ignition internal combustion reciprocating piston engine: |
| | 8703.21 | Of a cylinder capacity not exceeding 1,000 cc |
| | 8703.22 | Of a cylinder capacity exceeding 1,000 cc but not exceeding 1,500 cc [. . .] |

---

[42] See Understanding on the Interpretation of Article II:1(b) of the General Agreement on Tariffs and Trade 1994.

[43] See D. Rovetta, "Some reflections on customs classification and the harmonized system as tools for interpreting the schedules of commitments under GATT Article II", *Legal issues of economic integration*, 36(2009) 1 7–22 and D. Yu, "The harmonized system" (Geneva, WTO, 2008).

**Example: Brazil—Bound Concessions at the HS 6-digit subheading level (WTO Secretariat, 2011)**

| HS subhdg | Binding Status (B/U) | Number of TL[1] | Number of AV duties[2] | Average of AV Duties | Minimum AV Duty | Maximum AV Duty | Duty Free TL (%) | Number of Non-AV Duty |
|---|---|---|---|---|---|---|---|---|
| 870110 | B | 2 | 2 | 32.5 | 30 | 35 | 0 | 0 |
| 870120 | B | 3 | 3 | 30 | 20 | 35 | 0 | 0 |
| 870130 | B | 2 | 2 | 32.5 | 30 | 35 | 0 | 0 |
| 870190 | B | 2 | 2 | 32.5 | 30 | 35 | 0 | 0 |
| 870210 | B | 2 | 2 | 35 | 35 | 35 | 0 | 0 |
| 870290 | B | 2 | 2 | 35 | 35 | 35 | 0 | 0 |
| 870310 | B | 1 | 1 | 35 | 35 | 35 | 0 | 0 |
| 870321 | B | 1 | 1 | 35 | 35 | 35 | 0 | 0 |
| 870322 | B | 2 | 2 | 35 | 35 | 35 | 0 | 0 |

**12-008**

In regional and bilateral agreements the elimination over time and subsequent prohibition of customs tariffs is the rule.[46] This is also requested by Art. XXIV GATT with regard to "substantially all the trade" among the members of a RTA. In reality this obligation leads most of the time only to a limited reduction, with long transitional periods (phasing out) and a number of exceptions—normally products considered being of strategic importance or sensitive. Typical examples for such exceptions are the automotive production of a country or the agricultural sector. As these tariff preferences apply only to the goods originating in the partner country, the definition of what constitutes an "originating good" through rules of origin is particularly important.[47]

**12-009**

**AGREEMENT BETWEEN JAPAN AND THE UNITED MEXICAN STATES FOR THE STRENGTHENING OF THE ECONOMIC PARTNERSHIP (17 September 2004)**

*Chapter 3      Trade in Goods*

*Section 1      General Rules*

*[. . .]*

*Article 4 Classification of Goods*

The classification of goods in trade between the Parties shall be in conformity with the Harmonized System.

*Article 5 Elimination of Customs Duties*

1. Except as otherwise provided for in this Agreement, each Party shall eliminate or reduce its Customs Duties on originating goods designated

---

[44] TL = Tariff Line.

[45] AV = ad valorem: a tariff rate charged as percentage of the price.

[46] See for the EU, C. Barnard, *The Substantive Law of the EU* (Oxford [u.a.], Oxford Univ. Press, 2010).

[47] See W.-M. Choi, "Defragmenting fragmented rules of origin of RTAs", *Journal of International Economic Law*, 13 (2010) 1, 111–138 and S. Inama, *Rules of Origin in International Trade* (Cambridge [u.a.], Cambridge Univ. Press, 2009).

for such purposes in its Schedule in Annex 1, in accordance with the terms and conditions set out therein.

2. Except as otherwise provided for in this Agreement, neither Party shall increase any Customs Duty on originating goods from the level provided for in its Schedule in Annex 1.

*Note:* The term "level" means the level of Customs Duty that shall be implemented by each Party in accordance with its Schedule and does not mean the Base Rate specified in such Schedule.

[. . .]

4. The Parties shall consult to consider further steps in the process of liberalization of trade between the Parties in respect of originating goods set out in the Schedule in Annex 1, in light of the result of the multilateral trade negotiations under the World Trade Organization (WTO).

5. Any amendment to the Schedules as a result of the consultations referred to in paragraph 3 or 4 above shall be approved by both Parties in accordance with their respective legal procedures, and shall supersede any corresponding concession provided for in their respective Schedules.

**12-010**  This elimination of customs tariffs between the parties is typical for free trade areas or zones, customs unions and common markets. In a customs union it is accompanied by the creation of a common external customs tariff—an exercise which requires a harmonization of the existing external customs tariffs and therefore is more ambitious.[48] Examples for such customs unions are the Customs Union between the EU and Turkey[49] or the Customs Union between Switzerland and Liechtenstein. Some economic integration schemes go even further and attempt the creation of a common market (normally not only for goods) which requires additional measures to eliminate obstacles to trade like the harmonization of rules. The most famous examples are the European Union's internal market, Mercosur or the Common Market for Eastern and Southern Africa (COMESA)[50].

**12-011**  **Treaty Establishing a Common Market between the Argentine Republic, the Federal Republic of Brazil, the Republic of Paraguay and the Eastern Republic of Uruguay (of 26 March 1991)**

*CHAPTER I Purposes, Principles and Instruments*

Article 1

The States Parties hereby decide to establish a common market, which shall be in place by 31 December 1994 and shall be called the "common market of the southern cone" (MERCOSUR).

---

[48] See Laurence W. Gormley, *EU Law of Free Movement of Goods and Customs Union* (Oxford [u.a.], Oxford Univ. Press, 2009).
[49] See S. Krauss, "The European Parliament in EU external relations: the customs union with Turkey", *European Foreign Affairs Review*, 5 (2000) 2, 215–237.
[50] See L. Dirar, "Common market for Eastern and Southern African countries", *African Journal of International and Comparative Law*, 18 (2010) 2, 217–232.

This common market shall involve:

> The free movement of goods, services and factors of production between countries through, inter alia, the elimination of customs duties and non-tariff restrictions on the movement of goods, and any other equivalent measures;
>
> The establishment of a common external tariff and the adoption of a common trade policy in relation to third States or groups of States, and the co-ordination of positions in regional and international economic and commercial forums;
>
> The co-ordination of macroeconomic and sectoral policies between the States Parties in the areas of foreign trade, agriculture, industry, fiscal and monetary matters, foreign exchange and capital, services, customs, transport and communications and any other areas that may be agreed upon, in order to ensure proper competition between the States Parties;
>
> The commitment by States Parties to harmonize their legislation in the relevant areas in order to strengthen the integration process. [. . .]

*Article 5*

During the transition period, the main instruments for putting in place the common market shall be:

a) A trade liberalization programme, which shall consist of progressive, linear and automatic tariff reductions accompanied by the elimination of non-tariff restrictions or equivalent measures, as well as any other restrictions on trade between the States Parties, with a view to arriving at a zero tariff and no non-tariff restrictions for the entire tariff area by 31 December 1994 (Annex I);

b) The co-ordination of macroeconomic policies, which shall be carried out gradually and in parallel with the programmes for the reduction of tariffs and the elimination of non-tariff restrictions referred to in the preceding paragraph;

c) A common external tariff which encourages the foreign competitiveness of the States Parties;

d) The adoption of sectoral agreements in order to optimize the use and mobility of factors of production and to achieve efficient scales of operation.

Thirdly, a member may not discriminate as between WTO members in relation to like products originating from members or in relation to like products destined for different member countries.[51] This prohibition of discrimination as between other members is known as the most-favoured-nation treatment (MFN).[52] The discrimination relates to any advantage, favour, privilege or    **12-012**

[51] See Art.I of GATT 1994. See, for example, Indonesia—Certain Measures Affecting the Automobile Industry, Report of the Panel (1998).

[52] See EC—Bananas III (Art.21.5), Panel Report adopted on April 12, 1999 and Canada—Certain Measures Affecting the Automotive Industry, AB Report adopted June 19, 2000. More recently European Communities—Conditions for the Granting of Tariff Preferences to Developing Countries, AB Report adopted on April 20, 2004.

immunity with respect to a like product, in relation to customs duties and charges of any kind imposed on the importation or exportation of a like product[53]; or in relation to international transfer of payments for exports or imports; or in relation to any rules and formalities connected with the import or export of a product. The most important exception to the MFN standard is the possibility to form free trade areas (FTA) and Customs Unions (CU) under Art.XXIV GATT and Art.V GATS.[54] In order to balance the negative effects from such preferential agreements (trade diversion)[55] against the potentially positive effects (trade creation) a number of conditions must be fulfilled.[56]

Fourthly, a member is required to accord national treatment to all products, whether imported or domestic.[57] This national treatment (NT) standard is broken down into a number of discrete obligations.[58] First, internal taxes, regulations and requirements in relation to the internal sale, transportation, distribution, use or the content of the product are not be applied in such a

---

[53] The distinction between a customs tariff and an internal charge is not always simple. In China—Measures Affecting Imports of Automobile Parts the the Appellate Body (DS 339, 340, 342, Report of December 15, 2008) upheld the Panel's characterization of the specific charge as an "internal charge" (Article III:2), rather than as an "ordinary customs duty" (first sentence, Article II:1(b)), because, after considering the characteristics of the measure, the Panel had properly ascribed legal significance to, inter alia, the fact, that the obligation to pay the charge accrues internally, after auto parts enter China. The Appellate Body rejected China's argument that the Harmonized System (HS) serves as relevant context for determining this question.

[54] See, for example, Turkey—Textiles, AB Report adopted on November 19, 1999 on whether a specific measure is necessary for the establishment of a customs union.

[55] See, for example, A.F. Ghoneim, "Rules of Origin and Trade Diversion: The Case of the Egyptian-European Partnership Agreement" (2003) 37 *Journal of World Trade* 597–621 and A. D. Tarlock, "The strange career of the Dormant Commerce Clause and international trade law in the Great Lakes anti-diversion regime", *Michigan State Law Review*, (2006) 5, Special issue, 1375–1397.

[56] See below with regard to the exceptional character of these preferential arrangements. See also P. Hilpold, "Regional integration according to Article XXIV GATT", *Max Planck yearbook of United Nations law*, 7 (2003), 219–260 and R. Islam, "Preferential trade agrements and the scope of GATT Article XXIV, GATS Article V and the enabling clause", *Netherlands International Law Review*, 56 (2009) 1, 1–34.

[57] See Art.III of GATT 1994. See, for example, Japan—Taxes on Alcoholic Beverages, Appellate Body Report (1996); Japan—Measures Affecting Consumer Photographic Film and Paper (1998); Indonesia—Certain Measures Affecting the Automobile Industry, Report of the Panel (1998); Korea—Taxes On Alcoholic Beverages, Report of the Panel (1998) and Report of the Appellate Body (1999).

[58] See also D.H. Regan, "Further Thoughts on the Role of Regulatory Purpose under Article III of the GATT" (2003) 37 *Journal of World Trade* 737–60 and O.K. Fauchald, "Flexibility and Predictability Under the World Trade Organization's Non-Discrimination Clauses" (2003) 37 *Journal of World Trade* 443–82; P. M. Gerhart & M.S. Baron, "Understanding national treatment" *Indiana International & Comparative Law Review*, 14:3 (2003–2004),505–552; R. Pillai, "National Treatment and WTO Dispute Settlement" (2002) 1(3) *World Trade Review* 321–43. See also, for example, M. Melloni, *The Principle of National Treatment in the GATT* (Bruxelles, Bruylant, 2005); G. Verhoosl, *National Treatment and WTO Dispute Settlement* (Hart Publishing, 2002); Gaetan Verhoosl, *National Treatment and WTO* (Hart Publishing, 2002).

manner so as to accord protection to domestic production of like products.[59] Protectionism through the application of internal taxes and regulations is to be avoided. Secondly, the internal taxes and charges should not be discriminatory. This national treatment has been interpreted to entail an obligation to provide equality of competitive conditions for like imported products in relation to domestic products.[60] Thus, the trade effects of the tax differential are not relevant.[61] What is significant is the equality of competitive relationship between the imported and domestic products.[62] Discrimination under the NT standard is prohibited, irrespective of whether it is direct or indirect (de facto).[63] An intention to protect a domestic industry is not necessary.[64]

**WTO Dispute Settlement: India – Additional and Extra-Additional Duties on Imports from the United States (DS 360, Appellate Body Report of 30 October 2008) (Summary by WTO Secretariat available online)**     **12-013**

On 6 March 2007, the United States requested consultations with India with respect to "additional duties" or "extra additional duties" that India applies to imports from the United States, which include (but are not limited to) wines and distilled products (HS2204, 2205, 2206 and 2208.

The Appellate Body reversed the Panel's finding that the United States had failed to establish that the Additional Duty and the Extra-Additional Duty were inconsistent with Art. II:1(a) and II:1(b) [GATT]. The Appellate Body explained that it did not see a textual or other basis for the Panel's conclusion that "inherent discrimination" is a relevant or necessary feature of charges

---

[59] See Art.III of GATT 1994. See, for example, Japan—Taxes on Alcoholic Beverages, Appellate Body Report (1996); Japan—Measures Affecting Consumer Photographic Film and Paper (1998); Indonesia—Certain Measures Affecting the Automobile Industry, Report of the Panel (1998); Korea—Taxes On Alcoholic Beverages, Report of the Panel (1998) and Report of the Appellate Body (1999); Mexico—Tax Measures on Soft Drinks and Other Beverages, AB Report adopted March 24, 2006.

[60] See, for example, Japan—Taxes on Alcoholic Beverages, Report of the Appellate Body (1996); and Canada—Certain Measures Concerning Periodicals, Report of the Appellate Body (1997); see also Korea—Measures affecting Imports of Fresh, Chilled and Frozen Beef, WT/DS161/AB/R, WT/DS169/AB/R, AB Report adopted on January 10, 2001, para.135 and following and India—Measures Affecting the Automotive Sector, AB Report adopted April 5, 2002.

[61] See, for example, Japan—Taxes on Alcoholic Beverages. Report of the Appellate Body (1996); and Canada—Certain Measures Concerning Periodicals. Report of the Appellate Body (1997); see also Korea—Measures affecting Imports of Fresh, Chilled and Frozen Beef, WT/DS161/AB/R, WT/DS169/AB/R. AB Report adopted on January 10, 2001, para.135 et seq., and India—Measures Affecting the Automotive Sector. AB Report adopted April 5, 2002.

[62] See, for example, Japan—Taxes on Alcoholic Beverages. Report of the Appellate Body (1996); and Canada—Certain Measures Concerning Periodicals. Report of the Appellate Body (1997); see also Korea—Measures affecting Imports of Fresh, Chilled and Frozen Beef, WT/DS161/AB/R, WT/DS169/AB/R. AB Report adopted on January 10, 2001, para.135 et seq., and India—Measures Affecting the Automotive Sector. AB Report adopted April 5, 2002.

[63] See Canada—Certain Measures affecting the Automotive Industry, WT/DS139/AB/R, WT/DS142/AB/R, AB Report adopted on June 19, 2000, para.77 and following.

[64] See Japan—Taxes on Alcoholic Beverages, Report of the Appellate Body (1996), Section H.2.(c).

covered by Art. II:1(b). The Appellate Body further found that the Panel erred in its interpretation of the two elements of Art. II:2(a), that is "equivalence" and "consistency with Art. III:2". In particular, the Appellate Body disagreed with the Panel's conclusion that the term "equivalent" does not require any quantitative comparison of the charge and internal tax. Instead, the Appellate Body considered that the term "equivalent" calls for a comparative assessment that is both qualitative and quantitative in nature. Moreover, the Appellate Body clarified that the element of "consistency with Art. III:2" must be read together with, and imparts meaning to, the requirement that a charge and a tax be "equivalent". The Appellate Body considered that the Additional Duty and Extra-Additional Duty would be inconsistent with Art. II:1(b) to the extent that they result in the imposition of duties in excess of those set forth in India's Schedule of Concessions.

**12-014**  The term "like product" has been frequently used in the GATT 1994. Its precise scope can vary according to the context in which the term is to be found. Generally problems in its interpretation are to be considered on a case-by-case basis.[65] "Like product" can mean either "similar" or "identical" product. The reference is to the product not the producer.[66] Factors to be taken into account in determining whether a product is like or similar include: the product's end use in a given market; consumers' tastes and habits (which can vary from country to country); the product's properties, nature and quality.[67] Further, similar tariff classification nomenclature[68] can be a useful indicator of likeness.[69] The use of the term "like products" is not the same when it is used in different articles of the agreements. Sometimes it relates to a narrower concept, sometimes to a more flexible one.[70] But the way

---

[65] See the 1970 Working Party Report on Border Tax Adjustments L/3464, adopted on December 2, 1970, BISD 18S/97. See also United States—Standards for Reformulated and Conventional Gasoline, Appellate Body Report (1996). See also D.H. Regan, "Regulatory Purpose and 'Like Products' in Article III:4 of the GATT (With Additional Remarks on Article III:2)" (2002) 36 *Journal of World Trade* 443–78.

[66] See the 1970 Working Party Report on Border Tax Adjustments L/3464, adopted on December 2, 1970, BISD 18S/97. See also United States—Standards for Reformulated and Conventional Gasoline. Report of the Appellate Body (1996). See also D.H. Regan, "Regulatory Purpose and 'LikeProducts' in Article III:4 of the GATT (With Additional Remarks on Article III:2)" (2002) 36 *Journal of World Trade* 443–478.

[67] See the 1970 Working Party Report on Border Tax Adjustments L/3464, adopted on December 2, 1970, BISD 18S/97. See also United States—Standards for Reformulated and Conventional Gasoline Panel Report (1996) and Canada—Periodical, Appellate Body Report adopted on July 30, 1997.

[68] For example, nomenclature based on the Customs Cooperation Council Nomenclature or the nomenclature based on the harmonised system.

[69] For example, nomenclature based on the Customs Cooperation Council Nomenclature or the nomenclature based on the harmonised system. See also S. Charnovitz, "Belgian Family Allowances and the challenge of origin-based discrimination" (2005) 4(1) *World Trade Review* 7–26.

[70] The AB has used the picture of an accordion; see Japan—Taxes on Alcoholic Beverages, Report of the Appellate Body (1996), Section H.1.(a). See also Won-Mog Choi, "Like Products" in *International Trade Law: Towards a Consistent GATT/WTO Jurisprudence* (Oxford, Oxford University Press, 2003).

a product has been produced (processes and production methods (PPM[71]), e.g. environmental concerns) or the legal context (labour standards, etc.) in which it was produced is not to be taken into account regarding the "likeness" of products.[72] But the question whether a product is more dangerous for human health than another product is clearly a factor when determining whether a product is a like product or not.[73] The question whether the grey energy contained in a product should allow for a different treatment (e.g. taxation) remains controversial—in particular in view of current attempts to fight against climate change.[74]

**WTO Dispute Settlement: Mexico – Tax Measures on Soft Drinks and Other Beverages (DS 308, Summary by WTO Secretariat available online)** 12-015

On 16 March 2004, the United States requested consultations with Mexico concerning certain tax measures imposed by Mexico on soft drinks and other beverages that use any sweetener other than cane sugar.

The tax measures concerned include: (i) a 20 percent tax on soft drinks and other beverages that use any sweetener other than cane sugar ("beverage tax"), which is not applied to beverages that use cane sugar; and (ii) a 20 percent tax on the commissioning, mediation, agency, representation, brokerage, consignment and distribution of soft drinks and other beverages that use any sweetener other than cane sugar ("distribution tax").

The US considers that these taxes are inconsistent with Article III of GATT 1994, in particular, Article III:2, first and second sentences, and Article III:4 thereof. . ..

On 7 October 2005, the Report of the Panel was circulated to Members. 1. The Panel found: The soft drink tax and the distribution tax, as imposed on imported sweeteners and on imported soft drinks and syrups, are inconsistent with Article III:2 of GATT 1994. 2. The soft drink tax, the distribution tax and the bookkeeping requirements, as imposed on imported sweeteners, are inconsistent with Article III:4 of GATT 1994.

Finally, under Art.X of GATT 1994 there is a specific obligation on the part of members to publish all trade and trade-related measures.[75] This 12-016

---

[71] See S. Charnovitz, "The law of environmental 'PPMs' in the WTO- Debunking the Myth of Illegality", *Yale Journal* (2002) 27 Yale J. Int'l L. p. 59.

[72] But this may be relevant under the exception clause of Art.XX GATT, e.g. with regard to environmental concerns see United States—Import Prohibition of Certain Shrimp and Shrimp Products—AB-1998-4—Report of the Appellate Body. See also R. Quick and C. Lau, "Environmentally Motivated Tax Distinctions and WTO Law: The European Commission's Green Paper on Integrated Product Policy in Light of the 'Like Product-' and 'PPM-' Debates" (2003) 6 *Journal of International Economic Law* 419–58.

[73] See EC—Measures affecting Asbestos and Asbestos-Containing Products, WT/DS135/AB/R, AB Report adopted on April 11, 2001. See also G.A. Berman and P. Mavroidis (eds), *Trade and Human Health and Safety* (Cambridge: Cambridge University Press, 2006).

[74] See J. De Cendra, "Can emissions trading schemes be coupled with border tax adjustments?" *Review of European Community & international environmental law*, 15(2006) 2, 131–145.

[75] See, for example, Japan—Measures Affecting Consumer Photographic Film & Paper (1998). See G. H. Addink, "The transparency principle in the framework of the WTO", *Jurnal Hukum Internasional Indonesian Journal of International Law*, 6 (2009) 2, 232–243.

requirement of transparency engenders a measure of certainly, predictability and accountability of governmental measures.

After several years of exploratory work, WTO Members formally agreed to launch negotiations on trade facilitation in July 2004, on the basis of modalities contained in Annex D of the so-called "July package" of 1998.[76] Under this mandate, Members are directed to clarify and improve GATT Article V (Freedom of Transit), Article VIII (Fees and Formalities connected with Importation and Exportation), and Article X (Publication and Administration of Trade Regulations). The negotiations also aim to enhance technical assistance and capacity building in this area and to improve effective cooperation between customs and other appropriate authorities on trade facilitation and customs compliance issues.

### The obligations in relation to customs and allied procedures[77]

12-017    The obligations under the WTO code in relation to quantitative restrictions and tariffs can be undermined through customs and allied procedures. National customs and allied procedures can be crafted so as to have similar effects as quantitative and tariff restrictions. Thus, for example by determining the value of an imported product by a particular method or by attributing its origins to a particular State, the authorities of a country can affect the tariff commitments undertaken, or its obligations not to impose quantitative restrictions.

There are no general principles as such specifically enunciated in relation to customs and allied procedures. The approach adopted is a disparate manner of dealing with the various issues identified as being problematic. The underlying principles from the disparate disciplines may be stated as follows. That customs and allied procedures must not be discriminatory. They must not operate as disguised protectionist measures, and thus undermine the integrity of quantitative and tariff commitments. Further, the procedures must be transparent, and their application must be subject to principles of due process.

The principal disciplines in this field are as follows. First, in relation to customs valuation the rules are contained in the Agreement on Implementation of Art.VII. Customs valuation is the process of estimating the value of imported goods by the customs authority of the importing country—normally with a view to applying import restrictions, for example, for the purposes of levying ad valorem duties on imported goods.[78] Article VII of the GATT 1994 is concerned with ensuring an objective and

---

[76] See above.
[77] See Arts VII; VIII; IX of GATT 1994.
[78] Art.15 of the Agreement On Implementation of Art.VII of GATT 1994. See S. Rosenow, *A handbook on the WTO Customs Valuation Agreement*, (Cambridge [u.a.], Cambridge University Press, 2010) and M. E. Murphy, "The intersection of transfer pricing and customs valuation", *International Trade Law & Regulation*, 15 (2009) 5, 149–156.

uniform basis for the valuation of imported products. The Agreement on Implementation of Art.VII (Customs Valuation Code; CVC) supplements Art.VII of GATT 1994. It provides for greater uniformity, certainty and fairness in the process of customs valuation. The primary basis for customs valuation specified under the Agreement is the "transaction value"[79] of the imported goods. This is defined broadly as the price actually paid or payable at the time of sale for export to the country of importation.[80] If the transaction value cannot be determined in accordance with Art.1, for example where the buyer and seller are related, then alternative methods of valuation are set out in the Agreement.[81] Similar rules exist in most RTAs, often by simply referring to the WTO.

Secondly, all fees and charges in connection with the importation or exportation of products are to be levied only up to the cost of the services rendered.[82] This includes fees and charges relating inter alia to statistical services, licensing and documentation.[83] Further, the fees and charges are not to accord indirect protection to domestic products, or comprise an imposition of a tax character. Penalties for minor breaches of customs requirements are to be of a reasonable character. Generally members are urged to have customs formalities that are simple and reasonable.[84]

**12-018**

Thirdly, the application of a number of the provisions of GATT 1994 necessitates the determination of the origins of a particular product (e.g. in the imposition of anti-dumping duties and quantitative restrictions where these are authorised). This need to ascertain the source of a product arises both in the application of the code to trade on a non-preferential basis, as well as in the context of preferential trade relations, where these are authorised under the code. In order to accord preferential treatment in trade it is necessary to distinguish the source of the product so as to target the member the subject of the preferential treatment. Similarly, where authorised restrictions are to be imposed in a discriminatory manner—it is necessary to ascertain the source. The WTO disciplines concerned with rules of origin are to be found in the Agreement on Rules of Origin.[85]

---

[79] Art.1 of the Agreement on Implementation of Art.VII of GATT 1994.

[80] Art.1 of the Agreement on Implementation of Art.VII of GATT 1994.

[81] See Arts 2, 3, 5, 6 and 7. These refer to the transaction value of identical goods; the transaction value of similar goods; deductive value; computed value; fall-back method.

[82] See Art.VIII of GATT 1994. Argentina—Measures Affecting Imports of Footwear, Textiles, Apparel and other items. Report of the Panel (1997), and Report of the Appellate Body (1998).

[83] Art.VIII of GATT 1994.

[84] See also *Organisation for Economic Co-operation and Development: Cutting red tape*. (Paris, OECD, 2006).

[85] See Art.IX of GATT 1994. See, for example, M. Hirsch, "The asymmetric incidence of rules of origin—will progressive and cumulation rules resolve the problem?" (1988) 32 (4) *Journal of World Trade* 441–54; "Preferential Rules of Origin and WTO disciplines with specific reference to the US practices in the textiles and apparel sectors" (2005) 32(1) *Legal Issues of Economic Integration* 25–63; O. Cadot, A. Estevadeordal, A. Swa-Eisemam and T. Verdier (eds), *The Origin of Goods: Rules of Origin in Regional Trade Agreements* (Oxford, Oxford University Press, 2006), W.M. Choi, "Defragmenting fragmented rules of origin of RTAs".

Rules of origin refer to the criteria applied by a member in order to determine the origins of goods.[86] The Agreement is concerned mainly with the criteria for the determination of rules of origin in the context of non-preferential trade relations between members. In this context, more specifically, the rules are germane to the operation of the most-favoured-nation standard under Arts I, II, III, XI and XIII[87] of GATT 1994; the application of anti-dumping and countervailing duties under Art.VI; the imposition of safeguard measures under Art.XIX; the requirements of marks of origin under Art. IX; the imposition of discriminatory tariff quotas; and the conduct of government procurement, and compilation of trade statistics.[88]

**12-019**     The Agreement envisages as a principal regulatory technique the harmonisation of rules of origin by the Ministerial Conference, in conjunction with the World Customs Organization (WCO).[89] The WCO is an international organisation concerned with technical customs rules and practices.[90] The programme of harmonisation commenced upon the establishment of the WTO, and was originally scheduled to be completed in July 1998. While substantial progress was made in that time in the implementation of the HWP, it could not be completed due to the complexity of issues. Some basic guidelines for the harmonisation are set out under Art.9 of the agreement. The basic criterion is that the origin of a good is to be determined according to where the good has been wholly obtained; or where more than one country is involved, the country where the last substantial transformation has taken place. Further positive (i.e. what indicates origin, rather than what does not), coherent and objective standards are to be established. In addition, the rules of origin should not themselves be such as to partake the functions of trade policy instruments. They should not be trade-restrictive, or disruptive of international trade; and should be administered in a consistent, impartial and reasonable fashion. For the transitional period, before the establishment of harmonised rules of origin, certain disciplines are prescribed.[91] These on the whole mirror the basic guidelines for harmonisation.

The annex[92] to the agreement contains some basic disciplines in so far as preferential trade regimes (i.e. contractual or autonomous preferential trade

---

*Journal of International Economic Law*, 13(2010) 1, 111–138 and S. Inama, *Rules of Origin in International Trade* (Cambridge [u.a.], Cambridge Univ. Press, 2009). See also United States—Rules of Origin for Textiles and Apparel Products, Panel Report adopted on July 21, 2003.

[86] Art.1 of the Agreement on Rules of Origin.

[87] See EC—Bananas III (Art.21.5), Panel Report adopted on April 12, 1999.

[88] EC—Bananas III Art.1.

[89] EC—Bananas III—Art.9.

[90] See the Convention establishing a Customs Co-operation Council, Brussels, 1950157 UNTS 129, Since 1994 called the World Customs Organizations (WCO) headquartered in Brussels.

[91] See the Convention establishing a Customs Co-operation Council, Brussels, 1950157 UNTS129.

[92] See the Convention establishing a Customs Co-operation Council, Brussels, 1950157 UNTS129.

arrangements within the framework of GATT) are concerned. They are, however, minimalist. Essentially, the Member State is enjoined to craft its regulations in a clear and non-retroactive fashion. Further, the standards are to be couched in a positive form. Most RTAs contain very specific Rules of Origin. These are often of great importance in view of the specific production patterns of certain industries in certain countries.

**AGREEMENT BETWEEN JAPAN AND THE UNITED MEXICAN STATES FOR THE STRENGTHENING OF THE ECONOMIC PARTNERSHIP (17 September 2004)** *Chapter 4 Rules of Origin* 12-020

*Article 22 Originating Goods*

1. Except as otherwise provided for in this Chapter, a good shall be an originating good where:

   (a) the good is wholly obtained or produced entirely in the Area of one or both Parties, as defined in Article 38;

   (b) the good is produced entirely in the Area of one or both Parties exclusively from originating materials;

   (c) the good satisfies the requirements set out in Annex 4, as well as all other applicable requirements of this Chapter, when the good is produced entirely in the Area of one or both Parties using non-originating materials; or

   (d) except for a good provided for in Chapters 61 through 63 of the Harmonized System, the good is produced entirely in the Area of one or both Parties, but one or more of the non-originating materials that are used in the production of the good does not undergo an applicable change in tariff classification because:

       (i) the good was imported into a Party in an unassembled or a disassembled form but was classified as an assembled good pursuant to Rule 2(a) of the General Rules for the Interpretation of the Harmonized System; or

       (ii) the heading for the good provides for and specifically describes both the good itself and its parts and is not further subdivided into subheadings, or the subheading for the good provides for and specifically describes both the good itself and its parts; provided that the regional value content of the good, determined in accordance with Article 23, is not less than 50 percent, unless otherwise provided for in Annex 4, and that the good satisfies all other applicable requirements of this Chapter.

2. For the purposes of this Chapter, the production of good using non-originating materials that undergo an applicable change in tariff classification and satisfying other requirements, as set out in Annex 4, shall occur entirely in the Area of one or both Parties and every regional value content of a good shall be entirely satisfied in the Area of one or both Parties.

Fourthly, in order to ensure that preshipment requirements do not become 12-021 obstacles to international trade, it is necessary to impose obligations both on the member requiring preshipment inspection, as well as the exporting member, i.e. the country from where the goods are being exported. Preshipment inspection refers to the activities carried out by private-sector companies in the territory from where the goods are exported. The activities relate to such matters as the verification of the quality, the quantity, and the price of goods to be exported. The preshipment activities are conducted by specialised private companies on behalf of the State where the goods are imported. The Agreement on Preshipment Inspection[93] for the first time brings to regulation this area of activity. Preshipment inspection is mainly stipulated by developing countries to compensate for their own inadequate customs facilities; and is aimed at preventing fraud e.g. through over-invoicing or undervaluation. Over-invoicing results in outward flight of foreign exchange and undervaluation results in loss of customs revenue. In the absence of disciplines relating to preshipment inspection, the activities of the preshipment companies could result in thwarting the expectations of the exporters for example through revisions of prices and delays in inspections.[94]

The obligations in relation to preshipment activities in so far as they concern the importing member are as follows. First, preshipment activities are to be conducted in a non-discriminatory and objective fashion, so as to apply equally to all exporters, and without discriminating in favour of like domestic products.[95] Secondly, the quality and quantity inspections required should be in accordance with the standards agreed by the seller and buyer, or in the absence of such agreed standards, relevant international standards. Thirdly, the preshipment inspection entities are to treat as confidential information received in the course of the inspection. Further, certain kinds of information of a trade sensitive nature, for example, processes for which a patent is pending, are not to be requested.[96] Fourthly, the preshipment inspection entities are to verify prices according to guidelines set out in the agreement. Essentially, the prices are to be compared with identical or similar goods offered for export from the same country of exportation around the same time.[97] Finally, unreasonable delays in the inspection and in the announcement of the deliberations of the entity conducting the preshipment inspection are to be avoided.

Exporter members are to ensure that their laws and regulations concerning

---

[93] See GATT, The Results of the Uruguay Round Of Multilateral Trade Negotiations 1994. See also, for example, Patrick Low Preshipment Inspection Services World Bank Discussion Papers (1995).

[94] See V. Rege, "Developing country participation in negotiations leading to the adoption of the WTO", Agreements on Customs Valuation and Preshipment Inspection *World Competition*, 22 (1999) 1, 37–117 and E. Rome, "The background, requirements, and future of the GATT/WTO Preshipment Inspection Agreement", *Minnesota Journal of Global Trade*, 7 (1998) 2, 469–507.

[95] Art.2 of the Agreement On Preshipment Inspection.

[96] Agreement On Preshipment Inspection Art.2.

[97] Agreement On Preshipment Inspection Art.2.

preshipment inspection activities are applied in a non-discriminatory manner, and are transparent.[98]

Fifthly, there are obligations to prevent import licensing procedures from distorting international trade. These are to be found in the Agreement on Import Licensing Procedures.[99] Import licences are permits for the importation of a particular product. They can be obtained by applying to a relevant designated administrative body in the country of import. States may have import licensing procedures for a variety of reasons—including the administration of quantitative restrictions, tariff quotas and the monitoring of the flow of particular imports. Import licensing is thus broadly defined under the Agreement to include such practices.[100] The code identifies basically two types of licences i.e. automatic or non-automatic licences.

The scheme of the Agreement is as follows. First, there are general disciplines in relation to import licences. Secondly, there are additional disciplines in relation to automatic import licensing arrangements. Finally, there are disciplines in relation to non-automatic import licensing arrangements. None of the disciplines, however, is concerned with import licensing rules as such.[101] The disciplines in the Agreement are concerned with import licensing procedures and their administration.

The general disciplines prescribe that the administration of the licensing regime is in conformity with GATT 1994.[102] The import licensing arrangements should not unduly distort or be restrictive of international trade; and must be neutral, fair and transparent. The application forms should be simple, and reasonable time for submission must be given to the importer. Applications should not be refused for minor errors in documentation, value, quantity or weight of the product. Generally, the disciplines in the Agreement are intended to ensure that the licensing system is coherent; based on sound economic principles; and such that the importer is not subjected to undue burdens.

Finally, goods are to be allowed to be transported freely through a member country.[103] Where the goods are in transit they are not to be subject to customs duties. Any charges, regulations or formalities in connection with transit that are authorised, are to be applied on a non-discriminatory basis.

---

[98] Agreement On Preshipment Inspection Art.3.

[99] See European Communities—Regime for the importation, sale and distribution of bananas. Report of the Appellate Body (1997). See also European Communities—Measures Affecting the Importation of Certain Poultry Products. Report of the Panel (1998).

[100] See Art.1.1 of the Licensing Agreement. See also European Communities—Regime for the importation, sale and distribution of bananas. Report of the Appellate Body (1997).

[101] European Communities—Regime for the importation, sale and distribution of bananas. Report of the Appellate Body (1997).

[102] Art.1(2) of the Licensing Agreement.

[103] See Art.V of GATT 1994. See on the current problems relating to the transit of generic drugs (treated below) under the TRIPs Agreement: European Union and a Member State—Seizure of Generic Drugs in Transit (DS408 and DS 409) and S.P. Kumar, "Border Enforcement of IP Rights Against in Transit Generic Pharmaceuticals: An Analysis of Character and Consistency" (April 15, 2009), *European Intellectual Property Review*, Forthcoming. Available at SSRN: *http://ssrn.com/abstract=1383067* (Accessed June 8, 2011).

### The obligations in relation to non-tariff barriers

**12-022**  Non-tariff barriers[104] take a variety of forms and disguises. Potentially, they comprise an open-ended category. There is however no general approach adopted in order to deal with non-tariff barriers as such. The regulation is through special disciplines in relation to specific types of non-tariff barriers identified. Two particular areas have been of particular focus—namely State trading activities, and the setting of standards, for example in the interest of health and safety, which goods have to satisfy to be eligible for marketing.

First, although State trading on its own is not prohibited, nevertheless the manner of the conduct of such entities can be the subject of WTO disciplines.[105] Generally, where a member maintains a State trading enterprise, the enterprise must not discriminate in the exportation or importation of products, or be compelled from so discriminating. Further, the enterprise is to take into account commercial considerations in its decision making.[106] This requirement however does not apply where the imports are of products for the immediate or ultimate governmental consumption.[107]

In addition, these general disciplines are further reinforced, albeit in a plurilateral agreement (viz. the Agreement on Government Procurement[108]), focusing specifically on government procurement, i.e. the import or purchase by government for its own consumption. The Agreement applies to government procurement of products and services above a certain specified amount.[109] It provides that legislation and requirements should not result in discrimination, both as between domestic and foreign suppliers, and as between foreign supplier.[110] Normal rules of origin are to be applied.[111] Further, provision is made for rules in relation to tendering procedures[112] in order to ensure objective and non-discriminatory processing of tenders; and generally so that the procedures do not act as barriers to international trade. Certain provisions of the agreement do not apply to defence contracts.[113]

---

[104] i.e. barriers other than quantitative restrictions, customs and allied procedures, and obligations in relation to trade-related measures. See in particular Arts X; XVII and XX of GATT 1994. See R. L. P. De Andrade, "The positive consequences of non-tariff barriers", *Journal of World Trade*, 43 (2009) 2 363–378.

[105] See Art.XVII of GATT 1994, and the Understanding on the interpretation of Article XVII of GATT 1994 set out in GATT The results of the Uruguay Round of multilateral negotiations.

[106] See Art.XVII para.b.

[107] See Cottier, Thomas [Hrsg.], *State Trading in the Twenty-first Century* (Ann Arbor, Mich, Univ. of Michigan Press, 1998).

[108] See above the section on the framework of the GPA and for further details see S. Arrowsmith, "Towards a multilateral agreement on transparency in government procurement" (1998) 47(4) I.C.L.Q. 793–816; B.M. Hoekman and P.C. Mavroidis (eds), *Law and Policy in Public Purchasing: the WTO Agreement on Government Procurement* (Ann Arbor, University of Michigan Press, 1997).

[109] See Art.1 of the Agreement On Government Procurement.

[110] Agreement On Government Procurement Art.III.

[111] Agreement On Government Procurement Art.V.

[112] Agreement On Government Procurement; see for example Arts VII, VIII, XI, XII and XIII.

[113] Agreement On Government Procurement Art.XXIII.

Secondly, the disciplines in relation to standards[114] are set out in two dis- **12-023** tinct agreements, viz., the Agreement on the Application of Sanitary and Phytosanitary Measures,[115] and the Agreement on Technical Barriers to Trade.[116]

The Agreement on Sanitary and Phytosanitary Measures (SPS Agreement)[117] supplements Art.XX(b) of GATT 1994. Under Art.XX(b) of the GATT, and the preamble to the Agreement, a member country may introduce measures that are necessary to protect human, animal or plant life or health. Sanitary and phytosanitary measures are defined widely[118] to include all relevant laws and requirements that affect international trade, and which protect human, animal or plant life or health within the territory from external risks—such as pests, disease carrying organisms, and diseases carried by animals and plants. These measures are particularly aimed at agricultural products, such as plants, fruits and meat produce. All such standards are to be developed and applied in accordance with the Agreement.[119]

The sanitary and phytosanitary (SPS) measures must be based on scientific principles,[120] and not be arbitrary. They need to be founded on an assessment of the risks to human, animal or plant life or health, as appropriate to the

[114] See, for example, E. McGovern, "Standards and technical regulations as barriers to trade: regulating regulations", Ch.14 in A.H. Qureshi et al., *The Legal and Moral Aspects of International Trade* (1998); W.S. Atkins, *Consultants Technical Barriers to Trade* (1998). See also G. Marceau, J.P. Trachtman, "The Technical Barriers to Trade Agreement, the Sanitary and Phytosanitary Measures Agreement, and the General Agreement on Tariffs and Trade A Map of the World Trade Organization Law of Domestic Regulation of Goods" (2002) 36 *Journal of World Trade* 811–81; G.A. Bermann and P.C. Mavroidis (eds), *Trade and Human Health and Safety* (Cambridge, Cambridge University Press, 2006); M. Du, "Reducing product standards heterogeneity through international standards in the WTO", *Journal of World Trade*, 44 (2010) 2, 295–318.

[115] See EC Measures Concerning Meat And Meat Products (Hormones), Report of the Appellate Body (1998); Australia—Measures Affecting Importation of Salmon, Report of the Appellate Body (1998); Japan—Measures Affecting Agricultural Products, Report of the Panel (1998). See also, for example, D. Robert, "Preliminary assessment of the effects of the WTO on Sanitary and Phytosanitary Trade Regulations" (1998) 1(3) *Journal of International Economic Law* 377–406.

[116] R.J. Zedals, "The environment and the technical barriers to trade agreement. Did the reformulated gasoline panel miss a golden opportunity?" (1997) 44(6) *Netherlands International Law Review* 186–208.

[117] See, for example, J. Scott, *WTO Agreement on Sanitary and Phytosanitary Measures: a commentary*, Oxford Commentaries on the GATT/WTO Agreements (Oxford, Oxford University Press, 2006). See also G. Mayeda, "Developing Disharmony? The SPS and TBT Agreements and the Impact of Harmonization on Developing Countries" (2004) 7 *Journal of International Economic Law* 737–64; Bermann and Mavroidis (2006); C. Button, *The Power to Protect Trade, Health and Uncertainty in the WTO* (Hart Publishing, 2004); M. Matsushita, "Foodsafety Issues under WTO Agreements" (2005) 2(2) M.J.I.E.L. 7–17; L. Gruszczyński, Regulating health and environmental risks under WTO law.—Oxford [u.a.], Oxford Univ. Press, 2010.

[118] See para.1 of Annex A of the Agreement on SPS.

[119] This applies also to the regulation of new areas of technology like genetically modified organisms; see EC—Approval and Marketing of Biotech Products, WT/DS291-293.

[120] See Japan—Measures Affecting Agricultural Products, AB Report adopted March 19, 1999; see also A. Green and T. Epps, "The WTO, Science, and the Environment: Moving Towards Consistency" (2007) 10 *Journal of International Economic Law* 285–316; G. Goh, "Tipping the Apple Cart: The Limits of Science and Law in the SPS Agreement after Japan—Apples"

circumstances.[121] The measures must be based on international standards or guidelines where these exist,[122] although members are at liberty to formulate measures of a higher standard.[123] Where a member is involved in defining the level of standard, however, these must be based on scientific justification,[124] and accompanied by an assessment of risk.[125] Further, the measures must not unjustifiably discriminate between members, or constitute disguised restrictions on international trade.[126]

In addition, the control, inspection and approval procedures necessary for the implementation of the sanitary and phytosanitary measures must conform to certain basic norms, for example, they must not result in undue delay, and must be reasonable.

The Agreement thus attempts to avoid that SPS measures create unnecessary barriers to trade, whilst at the same time ensuring the right and indeed the duty of members to afford protection to the life and health of their people.[127] This endeavour is accompanied by safeguards to prevent the use of such measures in arbitrary, discriminatory or trade protective manner.[128]

**12-024**    **Article 5: Assessment of Risk and Determination of the Appropriate Level of Sanitary or Phytosanitary Protection (SPS Agreement)[129]**

1. Members shall ensure that their sanitary or phytosanitary measures are based on an assessment, as appropriate to the circumstances, of the risks to human, animal or plant life or health, taking into account risk assessment techniques developed by the relevant international organizations.

2. In the assessment of risks, Members shall take into account available scientific evidence; relevant processes and production methods; relevant inspection, sampling and testing methods; prevalence of specific diseases or pests; existence of pest- or disease-free areas; relevant ecological and environmental conditions; and quarantine or other treatment.

(2006) 40 *Journal of World Trade* 655–86 or Ca. Button, *The Power to Protect: Trade, Health and Uncertainty in the WTO* (Hart Publishing, 2004).

[121] See Art.5 of the Agreement on the Application of Sanitary And Phytosanitory Measures. See EC—Measures Concerning Meat And Meat Products (Hormones) Report of the Appellate Body (1998) and Australia—Salmon (Art.21.5) Panel Report of February 18, 2000 (DS18).

[122] Art.3 of the Agreement. The requirement is to base on international standards and guidelines not conform to. See also EC Measures Concerning Meat and Meat Products (Hormones) Report of the Appellate Body (1997).

[123] Art.3(3) of the Agreement. See also A. Laowonsiri, "Application of the precautionary principle in the SPS Agreement", *Max Planck Yearbook of United Nations Law*, 14 (2010), 565–623.

[124] Art.3(3) of the Agreement.

[125] Art.5 of the Agreement and EC Measures Concerning Meat And Meat Products (Hormones). Report of the Appellate Body (1998) and Japan—Measures Affecting the Importation of Apples, AB Report adopted on December 10, 2003.

[126] See M. Du, "Standard of review under the SPS Agreement after EC-Hormones II" *The International and Comparative Law Quarterly*, 59 (2010) 2, 441–459.

[127] EC Measures Concerning Meat And Meat Products (Hormones) Report of the Appellate Body (1997).

[128] EC Measures Concerning Meat And Meat Products (Hormones) Report of the Appellate Body (1997).

[129] Source: *http://www.wto.org*. (Accessed June 8, 2011).

3. In assessing the risk to animal or plant life or health and determining the measure to be applied for achieving the appropriate level of sanitary or phytosanitary protection from such risk, Members shall take into account as relevant economic factors: the potential damage in terms of loss of production or sales in the event of the entry, establishment or spread of a pest or disease; the costs of control or eradication in the territory of the importing Member; and the relative cost-effectiveness of alternative approaches to limiting risks.

4. Members should, when determining the appropriate level of sanitary or phytosanitary protection, take into account the objective of minimizing negative trade effects.

5. With the objective of achieving consistency in the application of the concept of appropriate level of sanitary or phytosanitary protection against risks to human life or health, or to animal and plant life or health, each Member shall avoid arbitrary or unjustifiable distinctions in the levels it considers to be appropriate in different situations, if such distinctions result in discrimination or a disguised restriction on international trade. Members shall cooperate in the Committee, in accordance with paragraphs 1, 2 and 3 of Article 12, to develop guidelines to further the practical implementation of this provision. In developing the guidelines, the Committee shall take into account all relevant factors, including the exceptional character of human health risks to which people voluntarily expose themselves.

6. Without prejudice to paragraph 2 of Article 3, when establishing or maintaining sanitary or phytosanitary measures to achieve the appropriate level of sanitary or phytosanitary protection, Members shall ensure that such measures are not more trade-restrictive than required to achieve their appropriate level of sanitary or phytosanitary protection, taking into account technical and economic feasibility.(3)

7. In cases where relevant scientific evidence is insufficient, a Member may provisionally adopt sanitary or phytosanitary measures on the basis of available pertinent information, including that from the relevant international organizations as well as from sanitary or phytosanitary measures applied by other Members. In such circumstances, Members shall seek to obtain the additional information necessary for a more objective assessment of risk and review the sanitary or phytosanitary measure accordingly within a reasonable period of time.

8. When a Member has reason to believe that a specific sanitary or phytosanitary measure introduced or maintained by another Member is constraining, or has the potential to constrain, its exports and the measure is not based on the relevant international standards, guidelines or recommendations, or such standards, guidelines or recommendations do not exist, an explanation of the reasons for such sanitary or phytosanitary measure may be requested and shall be provided by the Member maintaining the measure.

**WTO Dispute Settlement: Australia — Measures Affecting the Importation of Apples from New Zealand (DS 367, Appellate Body Report of 29 November 2010) (Summary by WTO Secretariat available online)**

On 27 March 2007, Australia's Director of Animal and Plant Quarantine determined a policy for the importation of apples from New Zealand:

"Importation of apples can be permitted subject to the Quarantine Act 1908, and the application of phytosanitary measures as specified in the Final import risk analysis report for apples from New Zealand, November 2006".

On 31 August 2007, New Zealand requested consultations with Australia concerning measures imposed by Australia on the importation of apples from New Zealand. New Zealand considers that these restrictions are inconsistent with Australia's obligations under the SPS Agreement, and in particular Articles 2.1, 2.2, 2.3, 5.1, 5.2, 5.3, 5.5, 5.6, 8 and Annex C.

[. . .]

The Appellate Body upheld the panel's finding that the 16 measures at issue, both as a whole and individually, constituted SPS measures within the meaning of Annex A(1) and were covered by the SPS Agreement. The Appellate Body also upheld the panel's finding that the 16 measures were not based on a proper risk assessment and, accordingly, were inconsistent with Articles 5.1 and 5.2 of the SPS Agreement and that, by implication, those measures were also inconsistent with Article 2.2 of the SPS Agreement.

The Appellate Body reversed the panel's finding that Australia's measures regarding fire blight and ALCM were inconsistent with Article 5.6 of the SPS Agreement, but it found itself unable to complete the legal analysis as to what level of protection would be achieved by New Zealand's proposed alternative measures for fire blight and ALCM. Additionally, the Appellate Body reversed the panel's finding that New Zealand's claims of undue delay pursuant to Annex C(1)(a) and Article 8 of the SPS Agreement were outside the panel's terms of reference. The Appellate Body then completed the legal analysis and found that New Zealand had not established that the 16 measures at issue were inconsistent with Australia's obligations under these provisions of the SPS Agreement.

## AGREEMENT BETWEEN JAPAN AND THE UNITED MEXICAN STATES FOR THE STRENGTHENING OF THE ECONOMIC PARTNERSHIP (17 September 2004)

### Article 12 Reaffirmation of Rights and Obligations

The Parties reaffirm their rights and obligations relating to sanitary and phytosanitary (hereinafter referred to in this Chapter as "SPS") measures under the Agreement on the Application of Sanitary and Phytosanitary Measures in Annex 1A to the WTO Agreement, as may be amended.

### Article 13 Enquiry Points

Each Party shall designate an enquiry point which is able to answer all reasonable enquiries from the other Party regarding SPS measures referred to in Article 12 and, if appropriate, to provide their relevant information.

### Article 14 Sub-Committee on SPS Measures

1. For the purposes of the effective implementation and operation of this Section, a Sub-Committee on SPS Measures (hereinafter referred to in this Article as "the Sub-Committee") shall be established pursuant to Article 165.

2. The Sub-Committee shall meet at such venue and times as may be agreed by the Parties.

3. The functions of the Sub-Committee shall be:

(a) exchange of information on such matters as occurrences of SPS incidents in the Parties and non-Parties, and change or introduction of SPS-related regulations and standards of the Parties, which may, directly or indirectly, affect trade in goods between the Parties;

(b) notification to either Party of information on potential SPS risks recognized by the other Party;

(c) science-based consultation to identify and address specific issues that may arise from the application of SPS measures with the objective of obtaining mutually acceptable solutions;

(d) discussing technical cooperation in relation to SPS measures;

(e) consulting cooperative efforts between the Parties in international fora in relation to SPS measures;

(f) reporting the findings of the Sub-Committee to the Joint Committee; and

(g) carrying out other functions which may be delegated by the Joint Committee pursuant to Article 165.

4. The Sub-Committee may, if necessary, establish ad hoc technical advisory groups as its subsidiary bodies. The groups shall provide the Sub-Committee with technical information and advice at the request of the Sub-Committee.

*Article 15 Non-Application of Chapter 15*

The dispute settlement procedure provided for in Chapter 15 shall not apply to this Section.

The Agreement on Technical Barriers to Trade (TBT) builds upon the provisions of an earlier text negotiated during the Tokyo Round (TBT Code).[130] Essentially, it facilitates the development of international standards to promote international trade, whilst ensuring that the standards themselves do not become obstacles.[131] It applies to all products—industrial and agricultural, but not to sanitary and phytosanitary measures as defined in the Agreement on Sanitary and Phytosanitary Measures. The Agreement refers to technical regulations and standards. Technical regulations are mandatory regulations pertaining to product characteristics, related processes and production methods. Technical standards are similar measures, but which are not mandatory. They originate from a recognised body which makes provision for such standards.[132]

**12-025**

---

[130] See M.M.Du, "Domestic regulatory autonomy under the TBT agreement", *Chinese Journal of International Law*, 6 (2007) 2, 269–306.

[131] See EC—Trade Descriptions of Sardines, WT/DS231/AB/R, AB Report adopted on October 23, 2002, para.274. See H. Zúñiga Schroder, "Definition of the concept 'international standard' in the TBT agreement" *Journal of World Trade*, 43 (2009) 6, 1223–1254.

[132] See Annex 1 to the Agreement on Technical Barriers To Trade.

The main stipulations of the Agreement are as follows. First, the technical regulations and standards must not discriminate between products of national origin and products of foreign origin, and between products of foreign origin. Secondly, the technical regulations and standards must not result in unnecessary obstacles to international trade. Thirdly, the technical regulations and standards must be necessary and based on scientific requirements. The technical regulations and standards may be crafted to fulfil inter alia national security requirements, the prevention of deceptive practices, protection of human health or safety, animal or plant life or health, or the environment.[133] Where international standards exist members should base their regulations and standards on them.[134] Fourthly, the technical regulations and standards should pertain to product performance rather than the design or descriptive characteristics of the product.[135]

**12-026**

**Article 2: Preparation, Adoption and Application of Technical Regulations by Central Government Bodies (TBT Agreement)[136]**

With respect to their central government bodies:

2.1 Members shall ensure that in respect of technical regulations, products imported from the territory of any Member shall be accorded treatment no less favourable than that accorded to like products of national origin and to like products originating in any other country.

2.2 Members shall ensure that technical regulations are not prepared, adopted or applied with a view to or with the effect of creating unnecessary obstacles to international trade. For this purpose, technical regulations shall not be more trade-restrictive than necessary to fulfil a legitimate objective, taking account of the risks non-fulfilment would create. Such legitimate objectives are, inter alia: national security requirements; the prevention of deceptive practices; protection of human health or safety, animal or plant life or health, or the environment. In assessing such risks, relevant elements of consideration are, inter alia: available scientific and technical information, related processing technology or intended end-uses of products.

2.3 Technical regulations shall not be maintained if the circumstances or objectives giving rise to their adoption no longer exist or if the changed circumstances or objectives can be addressed in a less trade-restrictive manner.

2.4 Where technical regulations are required and relevant international standards exist or their completion is imminent, Members shall use them, or the relevant parts of them, as a basis for their technical regulations except when such international standards or relevant parts would be an ineffective or inappropriate means for the fulfilment of the legitimate objectives pursued, for instance because of fundamental climatic or geographical factors or fundamental technological problems.

---

[133] See Art.2 of the Agreement on Technical Barriers to Trade.
[134] See Art.2 of the Agreement on Technical Barriers to Trade.
[135] See Art.2 of the Agreement on Technical Barriers to Trade.
[136] Source: *http://www.wto.org*. (Accessed June 8, 2011).

2.5 A Member preparing, adopting or applying a technical regulation which may have a significant effect on trade of other Members shall, upon the request of another Member, explain the justification for that technical regulation in terms of the provisions of paragraphs 2 to 4. Whenever a technical regulation is prepared, adopted or applied for one of the legitimate objectives explicitly mentioned in paragraph 2, and is in accordance with relevant international standards, it shall be rebuttably presumed not to create an unnecessary obstacle to international trade.

2.6 With a view to harmonizing technical regulations on as wide a basis as possible, Members shall play a full part, within the limits of their resources, in the preparation by appropriate international standardizing bodies of international standards for products for which they either have adopted, or expect to adopt, technical regulations.

2.7 Members shall give positive consideration to accepting as equivalent technical regulations of other Members, even if these regulations differ from their own, provided they are satisfied that these regulations adequately fulfil the objectives of their own regulations.

2.8 Wherever appropriate, Members shall specify technical regulations based on product requirements in terms of performance rather than design or descriptive characteristics.

2.9 Whenever a relevant international standard does not exist or the technical content of a proposed technical regulation is not in accordance with the technical content of relevant international standards, and if the technical regulation may have a significant effect on trade of other Members, Members shall:

  2.9.1 publish a notice in a publication at an early appropriate stage, in such a manner as to enable interested parties in other Members to become acquainted with it, that they propose to introduce a particular technical regulation;

  2.9.2 notify other Members through the Secretariat of the products to be covered by the proposed technical regulation, together with a brief indication of its objective and rationale. Such notifications shall take place at an early appropriate stage, when amendments can still be introduced and comments taken into account;

  2.9.3 upon request, provide to other Members particulars or copies of the proposed technical regulation and, whenever possible, identify the parts which in substance deviate from relevant international standards;

  2.9.4 without discrimination, allow reasonable time for other Members to make comments in writing, discuss these comments upon request, and take these written comments and the results of these discussions into account.

2.10 Subject to the provisions in the lead-in to paragraph 9, where urgent problems of safety, health, environmental protection or national security arise or threaten to arise for a Member, that Member may omit such of the steps enumerated in paragraph 9 as it finds necessary, provided that the Member, upon adoption of a technical regulation, shall:

  2.10.1 notify immediately other Members through the Secretariat of the particular technical regulation and the products covered, with a brief

> indication of the objective and the rationale of the technical regula-
> tion, including the nature of the urgent problems;
>
> 2.10.2 upon request, provide other Members with copies of the technical
> regulation;
>
> 2.10.3 without discrimination, allow other Members to present their com-
> ments in writing, discuss these comments upon request, and take
> these written comments and the results of these discussions into
> account.
>
> 2.11 Members shall ensure that all technical regulations which have been
> adopted are published promptly or otherwise made available in such
> a manner as to enable interested parties in other Members to become
> acquainted with them.
>
> 2.12 Except in those urgent circumstances referred to in paragraph 10,
> Members shall allow a reasonable interval between the publication of
> technical regulations and their entry into force in order to allow time
> for producers in exporting Members, and particularly in developing
> country Members, to adapt their products or methods of production to
> the requirements of the importing Member."

**12-027**    The Agreement contains a code of good practice for the preparation, adoption and application of standards.[137] Members are obliged to ensure that their
Central government, local government and non-governmental standardising
bodies accept and abide by the code of good practice.[138] The Code reflects
the provisions of the Agreement. Essentially, it prescribes that the regulations should be non-discriminatory; should not constitute obstacles to international trade unduly; and should reflect internationally agreed standards.
Further, the standards should pertain to product performance, rather than
design or descriptive characteristics.

The Agreement also governs the actual procedures involved for the assessment of conformity to the regulations and standards by the Central
Government Bodies.[139] Thus, such procedures must not be discriminatory,
and/or constitute unnecessary obstacles to trade. The assessment must be
expeditious. The parties concerned must be protected for any necessary confidentiality involved; and their legitimate commercial interests. Members
are urged to recognise and accept the results of assessment of conformity
carried out by another member's central government bodies.

### The obligations in relation to "unfair trade practices"

**12-028**    Unfair trade practices[140] are practices the effect of which is felt not so much at
the border, but in the domestic market. The perpetrators of the practices may

---

[137] Annex 3 of the Agreement on Technical Barriers to Trade.
[138] Art.4 of the Agreement on Technical Barriers To Trade.
[139] See Art.5 of the Agreement on Technical Barriers to Trade.
[140] See Arts VI and XVI of GATT 1994. See also A. S. Smbatian, "Common economic space
and some thoughts on protection of the Russian market against unfair trade", *Journal of*

be private traders or States. The practices are perceived to affect the ability of competitors to compete "fairly". In other words, the practices are considered to affect the free-market conditions of the economy. There is some disagreement as to whether the practices in question are in fact "unfair" as such.[141] WTO law does not expressly identify the barriers as "unfair" trade practices. It, however, focuses on subsidies and dumping, which have been considered as unfair trade practices in certain domestic systems. Sometimes the measures taken against dumping and unfair subsidies are categorised as "trade remedies" or trade defence measures.[142] These measures are normally highly controversial as they can be easily abused. It is therefore often an objective of certain States to eliminate (or limit) their use through RTAs—and ultimately in the WTO.[143]

First, the disciplines in relation to subsidies are contained in the Agreement on Subsidies and Countervailing Measures[144] (SCM Agreement). This Agreement supplements Arts XVI and VI of GATT 1994; and builds upon the Tokyo Round of Agreement on Subsidies and Countervailing Duties.[145] A subsidy is defined as a financial contribution

---

*World Trade*, 39 (2005) 5, 937–948 and R.M. MacLean, *EU Trade Barrier Regulation— Tackling Unfair Foreign Trade Practices* (London, Thomson Sweet & Maxwell, 2006).

[141] See, for example, J. Jackson, *The World Trading System* (MIT Press, 1997); and M.J. Trebilcock and R. Howse, *The Regulation of International Trade*, 3rd edn (London: Routledge, 2005), Chs 8, 9 and 10.

[142] This terminology is especially common in North America, e.g. Canada and the United States where safeguard measures are sometimes also included into this category although they are treated as a separate type of measures in this book. See also D.P. Steger, "Appellate Body Jurisprudence Relating to Trade Remedies" (2001) 35 *Journal of World Trade* 799–823; R.O. Cunningham and T.H. Cribb, "Dispute Settlement Through the Lens of 'Free Flow of Trade': A Review of WTO Dispute Settlement of US Anti-Dumping and Countervailing Duty Measures" (2003) 6 *Journal of International Economic Law* 155–70; R. Tiago Juk Benke, "List of WTO Dispute Settlement Cases on 'Trade Remedies': USA as Respondent" (2003) 6 *Journal of International Economic Law* 171–4; de Lima-Campos, "Nineteen Proposals to curb abuse in antidumping and countervailing duty proceedings" (2005) 39(2) J.W.T.; see also on a combined measure United States—Continued Dumping and Subsidy Offset Act of 2000 (Byrd Amendment, AB Report adopted on January 27, 2003).

[143] See T. Voon, "Eliminating trade remedies from the WTO", *International & Comparative Law Quarterly*, 59 (2010) 3, 625–667 and D. S. Beckford, Trade remedies within the CARICOM Single Market and Economy.—In: West Indian Law Journal, 32 (2007), 1, p. 13–50.

[144] See Brazil—Measures Affecting Desiccated Cocunut. Appellate Body Report (1997); Indonesia—Certain Measures Affecting The Automobile Industry, Report of the Panel (1998). See also, for example, G. Kleinfeld and D. Kaye, "Red light, Green light/The 1994 Agreement on Subsidies and Countervailing Measures, Research and Development Assistance, and US policy" (1994) 28(6) J.W.T. 43–63; T. Collins-Williams and G. Salember, "International disciplines on subsidies, the GATT, the WTO and the future Agenda" (1996) 30(1) J.W.T. 5–17; W.K. Wilcox, "GATT-based protectionism and the definition of a subsidy" (1998) 16(16) *Boston University International Law Journal* 129–163; A. O'Brien,"Countervailing Low Wage Subsidies. A Counter to the Levelling of Labor Conditions" (1994) 4(2) *Transnational Law and Contemporary Problems* 826–72; M. Clough, "Subsidies & the WTO Jurisprudence" (2002) 8(4) Int.T.LR 109–17. See now M. Benitah, *The Law of Subsidies under the GATT/WTO System* (Kluwer Law International, 2001) and H. de Madrid, G.E. Luengo: *Regulation of Subsidies and State Aids in WTO and EC Law* (Kluwer Law International, 2007).

[145] i.e. the Agreement on Interpretation and Application of Articles VI, XVI and XXIII of the General Agreement On Tariffs And Trade (The Tokyo Round Agreement).

directly or indirectly by a government or public body within the territory of a member. It occurs when there is a direct transfer of funds; or when government revenue otherwise due is foregone; or where goods or services (other than general infrastructure) are made available.[146] A subsidy is also defined as occurring where an advantage is conferred as a consequence of any form of income or price support resulting in an increase of exports, or a reduction of imports.[147] To be relevant the subsidies must result in a benefit to the recipient. The definition of an export subsidy is further elaborated through an illustrative list.[148]

**12-029**    **Annex I: Illustrative List of Export Subsidies (SCM Agreement)[149]**

(a) The provision by governments of direct subsidies to a firm or an industry contingent upon export performance.

(b) Currency retention schemes or any similar practices which involve a bonus on exports.

(c) Internal transport and freight charges on export shipments, provided or mandated by governments, on terms more favourable than for domestic shipments

(d) The provision by governments or their agencies either directly or indirectly through government-mandated schemes, of imported or domestic products or services for use in the production of exported goods, on terms or conditions more favourable than for provision of like or directly competitive products or services for use in the production of goods for domestic consumption, if (in the case of products) such terms or conditions are more favourable than those commercially available(57) on world markets to their exporters.

(e) The full or partial exemption remission, or deferral specifically related to exports, of direct taxes(58) or social welfare charges paid or payable by industrial or commercial enterprises.(59)

(f) The allowance of special deductions directly related to exports or export performance, over and above those granted in respect to production for

---

[146] Art.1 of the Agreement on Subsidies and Countervailing Measures. See also Canada—Measures Affecting the Export of Civilian Aircraft, AB Report adopted on August 20, 1999 and Korea—Definitive Safeguard Measure on Imports of Certain Dairy Products, AB Report adopted October 27, 1999.

[147] Art.1 of the Agreement on Subsidies and Countervailing Measures and Art.XVI of GATT 1994.

[148] See Annex 1 of the Agreement. See also United States—Tax Treatment for "Foreign Sales Corporation", AB Report adopted on March 20, 2000 and United States—Tax Treatment for "Foreign Sales Corporations"—Recourse to Art.21.5 of the DSU by the European Communities, AB Report adopted on January 29, 2002. See also A.H. Qureshi and R. Grynberg, "United States Tax Subsidies under DISC, FSC and ETI legislation within the framework of the WTO" (2002) 36(5) *Journal of World Trade* 979–92, D. Coppens, "How much credit for export credit support under the SCM agreement?" *Journal of International Economic Law*, 12 (2009) 1, 63–113 and R. Soprano, "Doha reform of WTO export credit provisions in the SCM agreement", *Journal of World Trade*, 44 (2010) 3, 611–632.

[149] Source: *http://www.wto.org*. (Accessed June 8, 2011).

domestic consumption, in the calculation of the base on which direct taxes are charged.

(g) The exemption or remission, in respect of the production and distribution of exported products, of indirect taxes in excess of those levied in respect of the production and distribution of like products when sold for domestic consumption.

(h) The exemption, remission or deferral of prior-stage cumulative indirect taxes on goods or services used in the production of exported products in excess of the exemption, remission or deferral of like prior-stage cumulative indirect taxes on goods or services used in the production of like products when sold for domestic consumption; provided, however, that prior-stage cumulative indirect taxes may be exempted, remitted or deferred on exported products even when not exempted, remitted or deferred on like products when sold for domestic consumption, if the prior-stage cumulative indirect taxes are levied on inputs that are consumed in the production of the exported product (making normal allowance for waste).(60) This item shall be interpreted in accordance with the guidelines on consumption of inputs in the production process contained in Annex II.

(i) The remission or drawback of import charges58 in excess of those levied on imported inputs that are consumed in the production of the exported product (making normal allowance for waste); provided, however, that in particular cases a firm may use a quantity of home market inputs equal to, and having the same quality and characteristics as, the imported inputs as a substitute for them in order to benefit from this provision if the import and the corresponding export operations both occur within a reasonable time period, not to exceed two years. This item shall be interpreted in accordance with the guidelines on consumption of inputs in the production process contained in Annex II and the guidelines in the determination of substitution drawback systems as export subsidies contained in Annex III.

(j) The provision by governments (or special institutions controlled by governments) of export credit guarantee or insurance programmes, of insurance or guarantee programmes against increases in the cost of exported products or of exchange risk programmes, at premium rates which are inadequate to cover the long-term operating costs and losses of the programmes.

(k) The grant by governments (or special institutions controlled by and/or acting under the authority of governments) of export credits at rates below those which they actually have to pay for the funds so employed (or would have to pay if they borrowed on international capital markets in order to obtain funds of the same maturity and other credit terms and denominated in the same currency as the export credit), or the payment by them of all or part of the costs incurred by exporters or financial institutions in obtaining credits, in so far as they are used to secure a material advantage in the field of export credit terms.

Provided, however, that if a Member is a party to an international undertaking on official export credits to which at least twelve original Members to this Agreement are parties as of 1 January 1979 (or a successor undertaking which has been adopted by those original Members),

> or if in practice a Member applies the interest rates provisions of the relevant undertaking, an export credit practice which is in conformity with those provisions shall not be considered an export subsidy prohibited by this Agreement.
>
> (l) Any other charge on the public account constituting an export subsidy in the sense of Article XVI of GATT 1994."

**12-030**　The Agreement distinguished originally between prohibited subsidies, actionable subsidies and non-actionable subsidies (so-called "traffic light" approach). The original category of non-actionable subsidies was abolished as of 1999.[150] A prohibited or actionable subsidy has to be specific. The concept of specificity distinguishes between a general subsidy and one that relates to or is targeted at a specific enterprise, or a group of enterprises or industries.[151] A subsidy may be expressly stated to be specific, or in fact be specific. Prohibited subsidies are deemed to be specific.[152] Prohibited subsidies broadly are defined as subsidies that are contingent upon export performance[153] or subsidies conditional upon use of domestic over imported goods. Member States are enjoined not to accord a prohibited subsidy.[154] It is normally considered that WTO members have an obligation to stop the payment of subsidies ("withdraw")[155] if found in violation of this provision but no obligation to request the beneficiary of an unlawful subsidy to reimburse it.[156]

Actionable subsidies are subsidies that have an adverse trade effect on the interests of other members. Adverse trade effects are defined as occurring when there is an injury to a domestic industry of another member; when benefits (particularly bound concessions) under GATT 1994 are nullified or impaired; and/or when there is serious prejudice to the interests of another Member.[157] Actionable subsidies are not prohibited, but give rise to certain responses at the instance of another member where the subsidy causes or

---

[150] This category (along with a provision establishing a presumption of serious prejudice in respect of certain specified types of actionable subsidies) applied provisionally for five years ending December 31, 1999, and pursuant to Art.31 of the Agreement, could be extended by consensus of the SCM Committee. As of December 31, 1999, no such consensus had been reached.

[151] Art.2 of the Agreement on Subsidies and Countervailing Measures.

[152] Art.2 of the Agreement on Subsidies and Countervailing Measures.

[153] See Brazil—Aircraft, Appellate Body Report adopted on August 20, 1999 with regard to Art.3.1 ASCM.

[154] Art.3 of the Agreement on Subsidies and Countervailing Measures.

[155] See United States—Tax Treatment for "Foreign Sales Corporations"—Second Recourse to Article 21.5 of the DSU by the European Communities, AB Report adopted on March 14, 2006.

[156] See, however, the controversial Panel Report in Australia—Subsidies provided to Producers and Exporters of Automotive Leather, Recourse to Art.21.5, WT/DS126/RW Report adopted on February 11, 2000, Section 6.39 and the the related discussion on retrospective remedies; see Ch.13 (Section 2.10 Remedies) and G. Goh and A.R. Ziegler, "Retrospective Remedies in the WTO after Automotive Leather" (2003) 6 *Journal of International Economic Law* 545–64. See also Brazil—Aircraft, Appellate Body Report adopted on August 20, 1999 with regard to Art.4.7 ASCM.

[157] Art.5 of the Agreement on Subsidies and Countervailing Measures.

threatens material injury to its established domestic industry or in the establishment of a domestic industry.[158]

**WTO Dispute Settlement: European Communities — Measures Affecting Trade in Large Civil Aircraft (DS 316, Appellate Body Report of 18 May 2011) (Summary by WTO Secretariat available online)**

On 6 October 2004, the United States requested consultations with the Governments of Germany, France, the United Kingdom, and Spain (the "member States"), and with the European Communities ("EC") concerning measures affecting trade in large civil aircraft.

According to the request for consultations from the United States, measures by the EC and the member States provide subsidies that are inconsistent with their obligations under the SCM Agreement and GATT 1994. The measures include: the provision of financing for design and development to Airbus companies ("launch aid"); the provision of grants and government-provided goods and services to develop, expand, and upgrade Airbus manufacturing sites for the development and production of the Airbus A380; the provision of loans on preferential terms; the assumption and forgiveness of debt resulting from launch and other large civil aircraft production and development financing; the provision of equity infusions and grants; the provision of research and development loans and grants in support of large civil aircraft development, directly for the benefit of Airbus, and any other measures involving a financial contribution to the Airbus companies. The subsidies in question include those relating to the entire family of Airbus products (A300 through the A380)

The United States further notes that certain launch aid provided for the A340 and A380 appear to be illegal export subsidies in contravention of certain provisions of Article 3 of the SCM Agreement.

The United States is further concerned that the measures appear to be causing adverse effects to US in a manner contrary to the provisions of Articles 5 and 6 of the SCM Agreement.

[. . .]

The Appellate Body [. . .] upheld the Panel's finding that certain subsidies provided by the European Union and certain Member state governments to Airbus are incompatible with Article 5(c) of the *SCM Agreement* because they have caused serious prejudice to the interests of the United States. The principal subsidies covered by the ruling include financing arrangements (known as "Launch Aid" or "Member state financing") provided by France, Germany, Spain, and the UK for the development of the A300, A310, A320, A330/A340, A330-200, A340-500/600, and A380 LCA projects. The ruling also covers certain equity infusions provided by the French and German governments to companies that formed part of the Airbus consortium. Additionally, it covers certain infrastructure measures provided to Airbus [. . .]. The Appellate Body found that the effect of the subsidies was to displace exports of Boeing single-aisle and twin-aisle LCA from the European Union, Chinese, and Korean markets and Boeing single-aisle LCA from the Australian market. Moreover, the Appellate Body confirmed the Panel's determination that the subsidies caused Boeing to lose sales of LCA in the campaigns involving the A320 (Air Asia, Air Berlin, Czech Airlines, and easyJet), A340 (Iberia, South African

---

[158] Art.VI of GATT 1994. See Ch.4 below.

Airways, and Thai Airways International), and A380 (Emirates, Qantas, and Singapore Airlines) aircraft.

However, for different reasons, the Appellate Body excluded certain measures from the scope of the finding of serious prejudice. [. . .]

Moreover, the Appellate Body disagreed with the Panel's views on when subsidies can be considered as being *de facto* contingent upon anticipated export performance. Consequently, the Appellate Body reversed the Panel's findings that the financing provided by Germany, Spain and the UK to develop the A380 was contingent upon anticipated exportation and thus a prohibited export subsidy under Article 3.1(a) and footnote 4 of the *SCM Agreement*. The Appellate Body also rejected the United States' cross-appeal of the Panel finding that it had not been established that certain other member State financing contracts constituted prohibited export subsidies. As a consequence, the Appellate Body reversed the Panel's recommendation that the European Union withdraw prohibited subsidies within 90 days. The Appellate Body also found that the United States' claims regarding an alleged unwritten launch aid/member State financing programme were outside its jurisdiction. In addition, the Appellate Body reversed the Panel's findings regarding the rate of return that a market lender would have demanded for launch aid/member State financing loans because they were not based on an objective assessment; but found that a benefit was conferred even on the basis of the European Union's calculations. Finally, with respect to the actionable subsidies that have been found to cause adverse effects to the interests of the United States, the Panel's recommendation that the European Union "take appropriate steps to remove the adverse effects or . . . withdraw the subsidy" stands.

**12-032**  Secondly, the disciplines governing the responses to dumping are contained in the Agreement on Implementation of Art.VI, generally referred to as Agreement on Anti-dumping (AD).[159] The Agreement on Anti-dumping

---

[159] See, for example, G.Z. Marceau, Anti-dumping and anti-trust issues in free trade areas (Oxford, Oxford University Press, 1994); K. Steele (ed.), *Anti-dumping under the WTO: a comparative review* (1996); D. Palmeter, "A commentary on the WTO Anti-dumping code" (1996) 30(4) J.W.T. 43–69; B.M. Hoekman and P.C. Mavroidis, "Dumping, Anti-dumping and Anti-Trust" (1996) 30(1) J.W.T. 27–52; B.M. Hoekman, "Dumping, Antidumping and Antitrust" (1996) 30(1) J.W.T. 27–53; E. Vermulst, "Adopting and Implementing Anti-Dumping Laws: Some suggestions for Developing Countries" (1997) 31(2) J.W.T. 5–24; E. Vermulst and N. Komuro, "Anti-dumping disputes in the GATT/WTO—navigating dire straits" (1997) 31(1) J.W.T. 5–44; E. Vermulst, *The WTO Anti-Dumping Agreement: A Commentary*, Oxford Commentaries on the GATT/WTO Agreements (Oxford, Oxford University Press, 2005); P.J. Lloyd, *Anti-dumping Actions and the GATT System* (Trade Policy Research Centre, London, 1997); See also Guatemala—Anti-dumping Investigation Regarding Portland Cement From Mexico, Reports of the Panel and Appellate Body (1998); United States—Anti-Dumping Duty on Dynamic Random Access Memory Semiconductors (DRAMS) of one Megabit or Above from Korea, Panel Report (1999); B. Lindsey, "The US Antidumping Law" (2000) 34 *Journal of World Trade* 1–38; A.H. Qureshi, "Drafting Anti-Dumping Legislation; Issues and Tips" (2000) 34 J.W.T. 19–32; J.B. Kim, "Fair Price Comparison in the WTO Anti-dumping Agreement Recent WTO Panel Decisions against the 'Zeroing' Method" (2002) 36 J.W.T. 39–56; C.P. Bown, B. Hoekman and C. Ozden, "The pattern of US antidumping: the path from initial filing to WTO dispute settlement" (2003) 2(3) *World Trade Review* 349–71; D.K. Tarullo, "Paved with good intentions: the dynamic effects of WTO review of anti-dumping action" (2003) 2(3) *World Trade Review* 373–93; G. Horlick and E. Vermust, "The 10 major problems with the Anti-dumping Instrument: an

is founded on Art.VI of GATT 1994; and builds upon the Tokyo Round Agreement on Dumping. Dumping may be described as the introduction of products by private parties into the economy of another State at a price below its cost or domestic price. The practice of dumping thus is essentially a price discrimination phenomenon. More specifically, dumping is defined as the sale into the market of another member of a product at less than its normal value.[160] Generally, the normal value is a reference to the price charged in the domestic market of the exporter. The normal value can be established with reference to the price of a like product in the domestic market, or in the absence of such a sale in the domestic market with reference to the price of a like product sold to the market of a third country. A "like product" is defined as a product that is identical, or in the absence of such a product another product which has similar characteristics.[161] Where no such comparison can be made then the normal value is constructed with reference to the cost of production in the country of export, plus a margin for profits.

A particular problem that has occupied the WTO members and led to a plethora of cases in recent years concerned the so-called "zeroing".[162] Zeroing refers to a controversial methodology used by the United States for calculating anti-dumping duties. In order to compare the prices of the good in the country of origin and the price in the United States over time the United States sets at zero the negative differences (i.e. in cases where the price in the United States is higher than the price in the home market). This obviously leads to a calculation where the positive price differences resulting from higher domestic prices do not fully enter into the resulting figures while any situation where the US price is actually lower does. This device used by the United States leads to increasing, often substantially, the exporter's margin of dumping and thus the amount of anti-dumping duty to be paid. The United States has been condemned several times by the WTO Appellate Body but still refuses to comply (DS294, DS 322, DS350).

---

attaempt at synthesis" (2005) 39(1) J.W.T. 67–73; J. Czako, J. Human and J. Miranda, *A Handbook on Anti-Dumping Investigations* (Cambridge, Cambridge University Press, 2003); Y. Luo, "*Anti-dumping in the WTO, the EU and China*", Alphen aan den Rijn, Kluwer Law Internat., 2010; H. Andersen, "*EU Dumping Determinations and WTO Law*", Alphen aan den Rijn, Kluwer Law Internat. [u.a.], 2009.

[160] Art.2 of the Agreement on the implementation of Article VI of GATT 1994.

[161] Art.2 of the Agreement on the implementation of Article VI of GATT 1994. Art.2(6).

[162] See, for example, T. S. Voon, "The End of Zeroing? Reflections Following the WTO Appellate Body's Latest Missive" (March 19, 2009). U of Melbourne Legal Studies Research Paper No. 378; U of Melbourne Legal Studies Research Paper No. 378. Available at SSRN: *http://ssrn.com/abstract=1365543* (Accessed June 8, 2011); T.J. Prusa, "A one-two punch zeroing", *World trade review*, 8 (2009) 1, 187–241.

**12-033**        **Part I: Article 2 Determination of Dumping (WTO Agreement on Anti-dumping, footnotes omitted)[163]**

2.1  For the purpose of this Agreement, a product is to be considered as being dumped, i.e. introduced into the commerce of another country at less than its normal value, if the export price of the product exported from one country to another is less than the comparable price, in the ordinary course of trade, for the like product when destined for consumption in the exporting country.

2.2  When there are no sales of the like product in the ordinary course of trade in the domestic market of the exporting country or when, because of the particular market situation or the low volume of the sales in the domestic market of the exporting country, such sales do not permit a proper comparison, the margin of dumping shall be determined by comparison with a comparable price of the like product when exported to an appropriate third country, provided that this price is representative, or with the cost of production in the country of origin plus a reasonable amount for administrative, selling and general costs and for profits.

2.2.1  Sales of the like product in the domestic market of the exporting country or sales to a third country at prices below per unit (fixed and variable) costs of production plus administrative, selling and general costs may be treated as not being in the ordinary course of trade by reason of price and may be disregarded in determining normal value only if the authorities determine that such sales are made within an extended period of time in substantial quantities and are at prices which do not provide for the recovery of all costs within a reasonable period of time. If prices which are below per unit costs at the time of sale are above weighted average per unit costs for the period of investigation, such prices shall be considered to provide for recovery of costs within a reasonable period of time.

2.2.1.1  For the purpose of paragraph 2, costs shall normally be calculated on the basis of records kept by the exporter or producer under investigation, provided that such records are in accordance with the generally accepted accounting principles of the exporting country and reasonably reflect the costs associated with the production and sale of the product under consideration. Authorities shall consider all available evidence on the proper allocation of costs, including that which is made available by the exporter or producer in the course of the investigation provided that such allocations have been historically utilized by the exporter or producer, in particular in relation to establishing appropriate amortization and depreciation periods and allowances for capital expenditures and other development costs. Unless already reflected in the cost allocations under this sub-paragraph, costs shall be adjusted appropriately for those non-recurring items of cost which benefit future and/or current production, or for circumstances in which costs during the period of investigation are affected by start-up operations.

[163] Source: *http://www.wto.org*. (Accessed June 8, 2011).

2.2.2 For the purpose of paragraph 2, the amounts for administrative, selling and general costs and for profits shall be based on actual data pertaining to production and sales in the ordinary course of trade of the like product by the exporter or producer under investigation. When such amounts cannot be determined on this basis, the amounts may be determined on the basis of:

(i) the actual amounts incurred and realized by the exporter or producer in question in respect of production and sales in the domestic market of the country of origin of the same general category of products;

(ii) the weighted average of the actual amounts incurred and realized by other exporters or producers subject to investigation in respect of production and sales of the like product in the domestic market of the country of origin;

(iii) any other reasonable method, provided that the amount for profit so established shall not exceed the profit normally realized by other exporters or producers on sales of products of the same general category in the domestic market of the country of origin.

2.3 In cases where there is no export price or where it appears to the authorities concerned that the export price is unreliable because of association or a compensatory arrangement between the exporter and the importer or a third party, the export price may be constructed on the basis of the price at which the imported products are first resold to an independent buyer, or if the products are not resold to an independent buyer, or not resold in the condition as imported, on such reasonable basis as the authorities may determine.

2.4 A fair comparison shall be made between the export price and the normal value. This comparison shall be made at the same level of trade, normally at the ex-factory level, and in respect of sales made at as nearly as possible the same time. Due allowance shall be made in each case, on its merits, for differences which affect price comparability, including differences in conditions and terms of sale, taxation, levels of trade, quantities, physical characteristics, and any other differences which are also demonstrated to affect price comparability. In the cases referred to in paragraph 3, allowances for costs, including duties and taxes, incurred between importation and resale, and for profits accruing, should also be made. If in these cases price comparability has been affected, the authorities shall establish the normal value at a level of trade equivalent to the level of trade of the constructed export price, or shall make due allowance as warranted under this paragraph. The authorities shall indicate to the parties in question what information is necessary to ensure a fair comparison and shall not impose an unreasonable burden of proof on those parties.

2.4.1 When the comparison under paragraph 4 requires a conversion of currencies, such conversion should be made using the rate of exchange on the date of sale, provided that when a sale of foreign currency on forward markets is directly linked to the export sale involved, the rate of exchange in the forward sale shall be used. Fluctuations in exchange rates shall be ignored and in an investigation the authorities shall allow exporters at least 60 days to have adjusted their export prices to reflect sustained movements in exchange rates during the period of investigation.

2.4.2 Subject to the provisions governing fair comparison in paragraph 4, the existence of margins of dumping during the investigation phase shall normally be established on the basis of a comparison of a weighted average normal value with a weighted average of prices of all comparable export transactions or by a comparison of normal value and export prices on a transaction-to-transaction basis. A normal value established on a weighted average basis may be compared to prices of individual export transactions if the authorities find a pattern of export prices which differ significantly among different purchasers, regions or time periods, and if an explanation is provided as to why such differences cannot be taken into account appropriately by the use of a weighted average-to-weighted average or transaction-to-transaction comparison.

2.5 In the case where products are not imported directly from the country of origin but are exported to the importing Member from an intermediate country, the price at which the products are sold from the country of export to the importing Member shall normally be compared with the comparable price in the country of export. However, comparison may be made with the price in the country of origin, if, for example, the products are merely transshipped through the country of export, or such products are not produced in the country of export, or there is no comparable price for them in the country of export.

2.6 Throughout this Agreement the term "like product" ("produit similaire") shall be interpreted to mean a product which is identical, i.e. alike in all respects to the product under consideration, or in the absence of such a product, another product which, although not alike in all respects, has characteristics closely resembling those of the product under consideration.

2.7 This Article is without prejudice to the second Supplementary Provision to paragraph 1 of Article VI in Annex I to GATT 1994.

**12-034**    Both dumping and subsidies can give rise to certain responses at the behest of the member where the dumping or subsidised exports are taking place. These responses by the member may be triggered by the initiation, through a written application, of a private party, i.e. the domestic industry, for an investigation into the dumping or subsidy, with a view to the imposition of anti-dumping or countervailing measures on the relevant imported goods, so as to offset the impact of the dumping or subsidy.[164] In both cases, before a response can be formulated there has to be a determination of dumping or a subsidy as the case may be, and a determination of injury. The agreements provide guidance as to how the investigations into dumping and subsidies should take place, including how the injury to the domestic industry as a con-

---

[164] Art.2 of the Agreement on the implementation of Article VI of GATT 1994; Arts 5 and 11 of the Agreement on Subsidies and Countervailing Measures.

sequence of the dumping or subsidy is to be established. This is particularly so as to ensure that the responses do not themselves become instruments of trade barriers. At the same time, the Appellate Body has stated that the same trade practices cannot be subject to "double remedies", that is, the offsetting of the same subsidization twice through the concurrent imposition of anti-dumping duties and countervailing duties. The Appellate Body found that "double remedies" are inconsistent with the requirement in Article 19.3 of the SCM Agreement that countervailing duties be levied in the appropriate amounts in each case.[165]

The range of specific remedies at the disposal of an importing member in response to a subsidised import depends upon the type of subsidy involved. Broadly, in the case of a prohibited subsidy or an actionable subsidy an importing member has two options. It may impose countervailing duties,[166] or through the Dispute Settlement procedures seek the withdrawal of the subsidy or impose appropriate countermeasures.[167] Both of these options may be exercised in parallel—but in so far as dealing with the effect of a subsidy on the domestic market is concerned, only one form of relief is available, i.e. the importing member cannot impose countermeasures and countervailing duties simultaneously.[168] In the case of a non-actionable subsidy causing adverse effects, no countervailing duty may be imposed. However, the Committee on Subsidies and Countervailing Measures may recommend modification of the subsidy programme, or authorise countermeasures.[169] Voluntary undertakings, for example to eliminate or limit the subsidy may also be elicited from the exporting member, after a preliminary determination of a subsidy and consequential injury, in lieu of the continuation of the countervailing duty proceedings.[170]

The principal form of response to dumping is the anti-dumping duty imposed on the dumped imported good. A member may also impose provisional measures where necessary, for example a duty[171] or require a cash deposit[172]—but only where a preliminary affirmative determination of dumping and injury has been made. A member may accept from an exporter, in lieu of the imposition of anti-dumping duties or provisional measures, a price undertaking, or an undertaking to cease the export of the product in

---

[165] United States—Definitive Anti-Dumping and Countervailing Duties on Certain Products from China, AB Report of 11 March 2011.
[166] "Countervailing duties" are defined under Art.10 of the Agreement on Subsidies and Countervailing Measures as special duties "levied for the purpose of offsetting any subsidy bestowed directly or indirectly upon the manufacture, production or export of any merchandise, as provided for in paragraph 3 of Article VI of GATT 1994".
[167] Arts 4 and 7 of the Agreement on Subsidies and Countervailing Measures.
[168] See Agreement on Subsidies and Countervailing Measures Art.10.
[169] Agreement on Subsidies and Countervailing Measures Art.9.
[170] Agreement on Subsidies and Countervailing Measures Art.18.
[171] Art.7 of the Agreement on Implementation of Article VI of the General Agreement On Tariffs And Trade.
[172] Agreement on Implementation of Article VI of the General Agreement On Tariffs And Trade.

question. Such undertakings can only be obtained however after a preliminary affirmative determination of dumping and injury has been made.[173]

**12-035**     **United States – Peru Trade Promotion Agreement, signed on 12 April 2006**

*Chapter 8 Trade Remedies*

*Section B: Antidumping and Countervailing Measures*

1. Each Party retains its rights and obligations under the WTO Agreement with regard to the application of antidumping and countervailing duties.

2. No provision of this Agreement, including the provisions of Chapter Twenty-One (Dispute Settlement), shall be construed as imposing any rights or obligations on the Parties with respect to antidumping or countervailing duty measures.

### Obligations in relation to certain trade-related measures

**12-036**     This category is descriptive of measures which do not strictly or directly partake of the character of trade measures as such, but which can impact upon international trade.[174] For example, in theory it might include competition measures which nullify or impair the benefits members are entitled to under GATT.[175] There is no general approach to dealing with such trade-related measures in the WTO yet. The development of this field is piecemeal, and is likely to evolve further. Especially RTAs contain more and more rules in this respect that may (or may not) one day influence the WTO.

Competition rules have been discussed in the WTO, but the negotiations have been terminated without any results.[176] Many bilateral and regional agreements do create specific procedures for the cooperation of competition authorities and address at least certain highly dangerous anti-competitive practices. At the same time, it is rather common to exclude the competition rules from the general dispute settlement mechanisms of these agreements to avoid a "second-guessing" regarding the decisions by domestic competition authorities by an international arbitral tribunal.

---

[173] Agreement on Implementation of Article VI of the General Agreement On Tariffs And Trade: Art.8. See European Communities—Anti-Dumping Duties on Imports of Cotton-Type Bed Linen from India, AB Report adopted on March 12, 2001 or United States—Laws, Regulations and Methodology for Calculating Dumping Margins ("Zeroing") AB Report adopted on May 9, 2006 and Mexico—Definitive Anti-Dumping Measures on Beef and Rice, Complaint with Respect to Rice, AB Report adopted on December 20, 2005.

[174] See Arts III, XI and XX(d) of GATT 1994.

[175] It was contended in the TPRM exercise involving the EC (now EU) that where a member of the WTO neglects to maintain competition laws which result in nullification or impairment of benefits than recourse may be had to the WTO Dispute Settlement Procedures. See GATT Trade Policy Review—EC 1993.

[176] See G. Sacerdoti, "Competition issues in the global economy and the WTO Regulation of World Trade" *Anuário Brasileiro de Direito Internacional*, 4 (2009) 2, 68–80 and D.J. Gerber, "Competition law and the WTO", *Journal of International Economic Law*, 10 (2007) 3, 707–724.

**AGREEMENT BETWEEN JAPAN AND THE UNITED MEXICAN STATES FOR THE STRENGTHENING OF THE ECONOMIC PARTNERSHIP (17 September 2004)**

*Chapter 12 Competition*

*Article 131 Anticompetitive Activities*

Each Party shall, in accordance with its applicable laws and regulations, take measures which it considers appropriate against anticompetitive activities, in order to facilitate trade and investment flows between the Parties and the efficient functioning of its market.

*Article 132 Cooperation on Controlling Anticompetitive Activities*

1. The Parties shall, in accordance with their respective laws and regulations, cooperate in the field of controlling anticompetitive activities.

2. The details and procedures of cooperation under this Article shall be specified in an implementing agreement.

*Article 133 Non-Discrimination*

Each Party shall apply its competition laws and regulations in a manner which does not discriminate between persons in like circumstances on the basis of their nationality.

*Article 134 Procedural Fairness*

Each Party shall implement administrative and judicial procedures in a fair manner to control anticompetitive activities, pursuant to its relevant laws and regulations.

*Article 135 Non-Application of Article 164 and Chapter 15*

Article 164 and the dispute settlement procedure provided for in Chapter 15 shall not apply to this Chapter.

**ECONOMIC PARTNERSHIP AGREEMENT between the CARIFORUM States, of the one part, and the European Community and its Member States, of the other part (signed on 15 October 2008)**

*TITLE IV TRADE-RELATED ISSUES*

*CHAPTER 1 Competition*

*Article 125 Definitions*

For the purposes of this Chapter:

1. "Competition Authority" means for the EC Party, the "European Commission"; and for the CARIFORUM States one or more of the following Competition Authorities as appropriate: the CARICOM Competition Commission and the Comisión Nacional de Defensa de la Competencia of the Dominican Republic;

2. "enforcement proceeding" means a proceeding instituted by the competent Competition Authority of a Party against one or more undertakings with the aim of establishing and remedying anti-competitive behaviour;

3. "competition laws" includes:

(a) for the EC Party, Articles 81, 82 and 86 of the Treaty establishing the European Community, and their implementing regulations or amendments;

(b) for the CARIFORUM States, Chapter 8 of the Revised Treaty of Chaguaramas of 5 July 2001, national competition legislation complying with the Revised Treaty of Chaguaramas and the national competition legislation of The Bahamas and the Dominican Republic. Upon entry into force of this Agreement and thereafter, the enactment of such legislation shall be brought to attention of the EC Party through the CARIFORUM-EC Trade and Development Committee.

## Article 126 Principles

The Parties recognise the importance of free and undistorted competition in their trade relations. The Parties acknowledge that anti-competitive business practices have the potential to distort the proper functioning of markets and generally undermine the benefits of trade liberalisation. They therefore agree that the following practices restricting competition are incompatible with the proper functioning of this Agreement, in so far as they may affect trade between the Parties:

(a) agreements and concerted practices between undertakings, which have the object or effect of preventing or substantially lessening competition in the territory of the EC Party or of the CARIFORUM States as a whole or in a substantial part thereof;

(b) abuse by one or more undertakings of market power in the territory of the EC Party or of the CARIFORUM States as a whole or in a substantial part thereof.

## Article 127 Implementation

1. The Parties and the Signatory CARIFORUM States shall ensure that within five years of the entry into force of this Agreement they have laws in force addressing restrictions on competition within their jurisdiction, and have established the bodies referred to in Article 125(1).

2. Upon entry into force of the laws and the establishment of the bodies referred to in paragraph 1, the Parties shall give effect to the provisions of Article 128. The Parties also agree to review the operation of this Chapter after a confidence-building period between their Competition Authorities of six years following the coming into operation of Article 128.

## Article 128 Exchange of information and enforcement cooperation

1. Each Competition Authority may inform the other Competition Authorities of its willingness to cooperate with respect to enforcement activity. This cooperation shall not prevent the Parties or the Signatory CARIFORUM States from taking autonomous decisions.

2. With a view to facilitating the effective application of their respective competition laws, the Competition Authorities may exchange non-confidential information. All exchange of information shall be subject to the standards of confidentiality applicable in each Party and the Signatory CARIFORUM States.

3. Any Competition Authority may inform the other Competition Authorities of any information it possesses which indicates that anti-competitive business practices falling within the scope of this Chapter are taking place in the other Party's territory. The Competition Authority of each Party shall decide upon the form of the exchange of information in accordance with its best practices. Each Competition Authority may also inform the other Competition Authorities of any enforcement proceeding being carried out by it in the following instances:

   (i) The activity being investigated takes place wholly or substantially within the jurisdiction of any of the other Competition Authorities;

   (ii) The remedy likely to be imposed would require the prohibition of conduct in the territory of the other Party or Signatory CARIFORUM States;

   (iii) The activity being investigated involves conduct believed to have been required, encouraged or approved by the other Party or Signatory CARIFORUM States.

*Article 129 Public enterprises and enterprises entrusted with special or exclusive rights, including designated monopolies*

1. Nothing in this Agreement prevents a Party or a Signatory CARIFORUM State from designating or maintaining public or private monopolies according to their respective laws.

2. With regard to public enterprises and enterprises to which special or exclusive rights have been granted, the Parties and the Signatory CARIFORUM States shall ensure that, following the date of the entry into force of this Agreement, there is neither enacted nor maintained any measure distorting trade in goods or services between the Parties to an extent contrary to the Parties interest, and that such enterprises shall be subject to the rules of competition in so far as the application of such rules does not obstruct the performance, in law or in fact, of the particular tasks assigned to them.

3. By derogation from paragraph 2, the Parties agree that where public enterprises in the Signatory CARIFORUM States are subject to specific sectoral rules as mandated by their respective regulatory frameworks, such public enterprises shall not be bound or governed by the provisions of this Article.

4. The Parties and the Signatory CARIFORUM States shall progressively adjust, without prejudice to their obligations under the WTO Agreement, any State monopolies of a commercial nature or character, so as to ensure that, by the end of the fifth year following the entry into force of this Agreement, no discrimination regarding the conditions under which goods and services are sold or purchased exists between goods and services originating in the EC Party and those originating in the CARIFORUM States or between nationals of the Member States of the European Union and those of the CARIFORUM States, unless such discrimination is inherent in the existence of the monopoly in question.

5. The CARIFORUM-EC Trade and Development Committee shall be informed about the enactment of sectoral rules provided for in paragraph 3 and the measures adopted to implement paragraph 4.

*Article 130 Cooperation*

1. The Parties agree on the importance of technical assistance and capacity-building to facilitate the implementation of the commitments and achieve the objectives of this Chapter and in particular to ensure effective and sound competition policies and rule enforcement, especially during the confidence-building period referred to in Article 127.

2. Subject to the provisions of Article 7 the Parties agree to cooperate, including by facilitating support, in the following areas:

   (a) the efficient functioning of the CARIFORUM Competition Authorities;

   (b) assistance in drafting guidelines, manuals and, where necessary, legislation;

   (c) the provision of independent experts; and

   (d) the provision of training for key personnel involved in the implementation of and enforcement of competition policy.

**12-038**    While the WTO code does not contain comprehensive investment rules,[177] it contains rules on trade-related investment measures (i.e. TRIMS). TRIMS are investment measures which impact on international trade.[178] For example a State may require an investor to make use of local inputs in its production (known as local content requirements); or a it may compel an investor to export a certain proportion of its production (known as export performance requirements); or it may require that an enterprise's use of imported products bears a relationship with its use of domestic products for export (trade balancing requirement). These are governed by the Agreement on Trade-Related Investment Measures (TRIMs).[179] An illustrative list of trade-related investment measures is set out in an annex to the Agreement. Essentially the Agreement ensures that TRIMS are not used in such a manner so as to undermine the provisions of Art.III of GATT 1995 (i.e. the national standard), and Art. XI of GATT 1994 (i.e. the elimination of quantitative restrictions).

**12-039**    **Annex: Illustrative List (TRIMs Agreement)[180]**

1. TRIMs that are inconsistent with the obligation of national treatment provided for in paragraph 4 of Article III of GATT 1994 include those which are mandatory or enforceable under domestic law or under

---

[177] See Ch.14 and D. Collins, "A new role for the WTO in international investment law", *Connecticut Journal of International Law*, 25.2009 (2010) 1, S.1–35

[178] See C. Curtiss, "Agreement on trade-related investment measures" *The Comparative Law Yearbook of International Business*, 25 (2003), 233–255 and J. F. Dennin, "Trade-related investment measures", *the Comparative Law Yearbook of International Business*, 23 (2001) 129–191.

[179] Indonesia—Certain Measures Affecting The Automobile Industry, Report of the Panel (1998).

[180] Source: *http://www.wto.org*. (Accessed June 8, 2011).

administrative rulings, or compliance with which is necessary to obtain an advantage, and which require:

(a) the purchase or use by an enterprise of products of domestic origin or from any domestic source, whether specified in terms of particular products, in terms of volume or value of products, or in terms of a proportion of volume or value of its local production; or

(b) that an enterprise's purchases or use of imported products be limited to an amount related to the volume or value of local products that it exports.

2. TRIMs that are inconsistent with the obligation of general elimination of quantitative restrictions provided for in paragraph 1 of Article XI of GATT 1994 include those which are mandatory or enforceable under domestic law or under administrative rulings, or compliance with which is necessary to obtain an advantage, and which restrict:

(a) the importation by an enterprise of products used in or related to its local production, generally or to an amount related to the volume or value of local production that it exports;

(b) the importation by an enterprise of products used in or related to its local production by restricting its access to foreign exchange to an amount related to the foreign exchange inflows attributable to the enterprise; or

(c) the exportation or sale for export by an enterprise of products, whether specified in terms of particular products, in terms of volume or value of products, or in terms of a proportion of volume or value of its local production."

Furthermore, trade-related aspects of monetary measures may distort **12-040** trade.[181] Generally, the WTO and Member States are obliged to consult and co-operate with the IMF on matters which have a bearing on the latter's jurisdiction. In particular, members are obligated not to frustrate the provisions of GATT 1994 through exchange measures, nor to undermine the Articles of Agreement of the IMF through trade measures. In recent years, the developments with regard to exchange rates have motivated several WTO members to ask for more action within the WTO regarding exchange rates. Most recently, on May 18, 2011 a Brazilian proposal for the WTO to examine the impact of currency exchange rates on international trade was introduced.

Finally, the WTO code incorporates the goals of development[182] (i.e.

---

[181] See Art.XV of GATT 1994. R.Staiger & A.Sykes "Currency manipulation and world trade" *World Trade Review* (2010), 9:4, 583–627, M.U. Killion, "China's foreign currency regime" the Kagan Thesis and legalification of the WTO Agreement—*Minnesota Journal of Global Trade*, 14 (2004) 1, 43–89 and M.R. Leviton, "Is it a subsidy? An evaluation of China's currency regime and its compliance with the WTO" *University of California, Berkeley, Calif., / Los Angeles Campus: UCLA Pacific Basin Law Journal*, 23 (2005/06), 2, 243–267.

[182] See, for example, Pt IV of GATT 1994 and Decision of the Contracting Parties of November 28, 1979 on Differential and More Favourable Treatment, Reciprocity and Fuller Participation of Developing Countries. See also Uruguay Round Decision on Measures in Favour of Least-Developed Countries; and the Uruguay Round Decision on Measures Concerning the Possible Negative Effects of The Reform Programme on Least-Developed

the trade related aspects of economic development) into trade policy in a number of ways. In this context, a distinction is made between developing members, least-developed members, and members undergoing transition from a planned economy to a market economy. However, no clear criteria have been established with respect to these categories.[183] Article XVIII of GATT 1994 defines developing countries as comprising those economies which support low standards of living and are in their early stages of development. This, however, is imprecise.[184] In the context of the subsidies code however a clearer criteria is indicated drawing on the United Nations definition of least-developed countries. In addition the distinction between different classes of developing countries (least developed countries, emerging economies etc.) becomes increasingly important.

Of particular note of this inclusion of development concerns are the following. First, developed members are authorised to accord differential and more favourable treatment to developing countries, without at the same time extending such treatment to developed countries.[185] This authority has spurned the introduction of a number of preferential systems accorded to developing members by some developed members (Generalized Systems of Preferences: GSP). Some governments have used this to encourage recipient countries to respect labour, human, environmental and good governance rights and rules (e.g. the EU through its GSP+ scheme).[186]

Secondly, developing members amongst themselves are allowed to accord

and Net Food-Importing Developing Countries. See also, for example, M. Rom, "Some early reflections on the Uruguay Round Agreement as seen from the viewpoint of a developing country" (1994) 28(6) J.W.T. 5–30; M Pangestu, "Special and Differential Treatment in the Millenium", *The World Economy*, 23:9 (2000), 1285–1302; R. Bhala, *Trade, Development and Social Justice* (Carolina Academic Press, 2003); R Zhang, "Food security; Food trade regime and food aid regime", J.I.E.L., 7:3 (2004) 565–584; Y.S. Lee, *Reclaiming Development in the World Trading System* (Cambridge, Cambridge University Press, 2006); G.A. Bermann (eds), *WTO Law and Developing Countires* (Cambridge, Cambridge University Press, 2007); UNCTAD, "Aid for Trade: Cool aid or Kool-aid?" G-24 Discussion Paper Series, No.48, 2007; A. H. Qureshi, "International Trade for Development: the WTO as a Development Institution?" 43:1 *Journal of World Trade*, (February 2009) 173–188.

[183] See, for example, G. Verdirame, "The definition of developing under GATT and other International Law" (1996) *German Yearbook of International Law*.

[184] See, for example, G. Verdirame "The definition of developing under GATT and other International Law" (1996) *German Yearbook of International Law*, p.175.

[185] See, for example, Pt IV of GATT 1994 and Decision of the Contracting Parties of November 28, 1979 on Differential and More Favourable Treatment, Reciprocity and Fuller Participation of Developing Countries. See also for example A. Yusuf, *Legal Aspects of Trade Preferences for Developing States* (The Hague, Martinus Nijhoff, 1982).

[186] Council Regulation (EC) No732/2008 of July 22, 2008 applying a scheme of generalised tariff preferences for the period from January 1, 2009 to December 31, 2011 and amending Regulations (EC) No 552/97, (EC) No1933/2006 and Commission Regulations (EC) No 1100/2006 and (EC) No964/2007. See L. Gruszczyński, "EC incentive arrangements for sustainable development and good governance (GSP Plus) and WTO law", *The Polish Yearbook of International Law*, 28.2006/08(2009), 219–235 and J. Orbie, "The new GSP+ beneficiaries", *European Foreign Affairs Review*, 14 (2009), Special Issue, 663–681.

favourable treatment to each other.[187] Thirdly, the different levels of economic development in the undertaking of the disparate WTO code obligations is taken into account; as is the need to facilitate the development of developing economies acknowledged. Furthermore the world's resources are to be used optimally in accordance with the objective of sustainable development.[188] The measures range from exempting developing countries from certain spheres of regulation or countermeasures, for example in the field of subsidies[189] and safeguard measures[190]; to facilitating technical assistance to developing members[191]; and according longer time-periods to implement particular provisions of the WTO code. Finally, there are certain authorisations in the WTO code to facilitate governmental assistance for economic development[192] mainly for the benefit of developing members[193] to enable them to implement programmes of economic development. Thus, such members may, in order to establish a particular industry (infant industry), resort to protection through the imposition of tariffs, having negotiated modifications of concessions in their respective schedules; or deviate from other provisions of GATT 1994. A developing member may also impose quantitative restrictions on imports for balance of payments purposes, to deal with the demand for imports generated by the programme for economic development.

In view of the remaining problems relating to the integration of developing countries into the world trading system, the Doha Ministerial Meeting declared the Doha Round of multilateral trade negotiations to be a "Development Round" (Doha Development Round). Throughout the negotiations it proved difficult to have a common understanding of what this should implicate for the negotiations, especially with regard to market access of developing countries in developed states.[194] A particular problem remained the treatment of emerging

---

[187] See, for example, Pt IV of GATT 1994 and Decision of the Contracting Parties of November 28, 1979 on Differential and More Favourable Treatment, Reciprocity and Fuller Participation of Developing Countries.

[188] See preamble to the Final Act of the Uruguay Round.

[189] See Art.27 of the Agreement on Subsidies and Countervailing Measures.

[190] See Art.9 of the Agreement on Safeguards.

[191] See, for example, Art.11 of the Agreement on Technical Barriers to Trade; Art.9 of the Agreement on the Application of Sanitary and Phytosanitary Measures; Art.23 of the Agreement On Implementation Of Article VII of the GATT 1994; Art.67 of TRIPS.

[192] Art.XVIII of GATT 1994; and see also The Understanding on the Balance of Payments Provisions of the General Agreement on Tariffs and Trade 1994.

[193] i.e. mainly members the economies of which can only support low standards of living, and are in the early stages of development. See Art.XVIII (1) of GATT 1994.

[194] See P. Sutherland, "The Doha Development Agenda: Political Challenges to the World Trading System—A Cosmopolitan Perspective" (2005) 8 *Journal of International Economic Law* 363–75; F. Ismail, "A Development Perspective on the WTO July 2004 General Council Decision" (2005) 8 *Journal of International Economic Law* 377–404; B. Hoekman, "Operationalizing the Concept of Policy Space in the WTO: Beyond Special and Differential Treatment" (2005) 8 *Journal of International Economic Law* 405–24; D. McRae, "Developing Countries and 'The Future of the WTO'" (2005) 8 *Journal of International Economic Law* 603–10; J.P. Trachtman, "The Missing Link: Coherence and Poverty at the WTO" (2005) 8 *Journal of International Economic Law* 611–22; H. Hohmann (ed.), *Agreeing and Implementing the Doha Round of the WTO* (Cambridge, Cambridge University Press, 2007).

economies with regard to their market opening potential. At the end of May 2011 trade diplomats in Geneva had to admit that a conclusion of the Doha Development Round in 2011 was not feasible. While they originally aimed at still preparing a special package of measures for developing countries, including market access for least-developed countries and in the cotton sector,[195] this idea had to be abandoned on July 26, 2011. According to a WTO press release, the Director-General proposed to focus on ideas on how to proceed afterwards in order to end the paralysis of the organisation's ability to negotiate.[195]

**Emergency measures**

**12-041**  There are a number of measures in the Code which allow for the imposition of temporary trade restrictions in an emergency.[196] First, emergency measures are authorised to deal with the sudden influx of imports of a particular type. The disciplines in the exercise of these measures (known as safeguard measures in the context of the GATT and now the WTO) are to be found in the Agreement on Safeguards.[197] The Agreement on Safeguards supplements Art.XIX of GATT 1994. Briefly, a member may apply safeguard measures in the form of tariffs or quantitative restrictions, to a product if the member determines, in accordance with the Agreement, that a product is being imported in its territory in such increased quantities in relation to domestic production of the product so as to cause serious injury to the domestic industry producing the product, or a directly competitive product.[198] Certain States have a tendency to include safeguard measures in the category of

---

[195] See E. Kessie, "The Doha development agenda at a crossroads", *European Yearbook of International Economic Law*, 1 (2010), 361–390 and S. Cho, "The demise of development in the Doha Round negotiations", *Texas International Law Journal*, 45 (2009/10) 3, 573–601.

[196] See Arts XII, XVIII, XIX and XXI GATT 1994.

[197] See Korea—Definitive Safeguard Measure on Imports of Certain Dairy Products, AB Report adopted January 12, 2000 and Argentina—Safeguard Measures on Imports of Footwear, AB Report adopted on January 12, 2000; United States—Definitive Safeguard Measures on Imports of Wheat Gluten from the European Communities, AB Report adopted on January 19, 2001; United States—Definitive Safeguard Measures on Imports of Certain Steel Products, AB Report adopted on December 10, 2003; see for example G.D. Holliday, "The Uruguay Round Agreement on Safeguards" (1995) J.W.T.; A.O. Sykes, *The WTO Agreement on Safeguards: A Commentary*, Oxford Commentaries on the GATT/WTO Agreements, (Oxford, Oxford University Press, 2006); F. Spadi, "Discriminatory Safeguards in the Light of the Admission of the People's Republic of China to the World Trade Organization" (2002) 5 *Journal of International Economic Law* 421–43; Y.S. Lee, "Safeguard Measures: Why Are They Not Applied Consistently With the Rules? Lessons for Competent National Authorities and Proposal for the Modification of the Rules on Safeguards" (2002) 36 J.W.T. 641–73; Y.S. Lee, *Safeguard Measures in World Trade: The Legal Analysis* (Kluwer Law International, 2003); F. Mueller, "Is the GATT Article XIX 'Unforeseen Developments Clause' Still Effective Under the Agreement on Safeguards" (2003) 37 J.W.T. 1119–51; J. Pauwelyn, "The Puzzle of WTO Safeguards and Regional Trade Agreements" (2004) 7 *Journal of International Economic Law* 109–42; A.O. Sykes, "The Persistent Puzzles of Safeguards: Lessons from the Steel Dispute" (2004) 7 *Journal of International Economic Law* 523–64; A.O. Sykes, "The Fundamental Deficiencies of the Agreement on Safeguards: A Reply to Professor Lee" (2006) 40 J.W.T. 979–96; M.J. Hahn, "Balancing or Bending? Unilateral Reactions to Safeguard Measures" (2005) 39 J.W.T. 301–26.

[198] Section 2 para.1 of the Agreement On Safeguards.

"trade remedies" (i.e. the United States) or "trade defence" instruments (e.g. in the European Union). This is justified if one looks at the actual "political" use of safeguard measures to provide protection to certain sectors—but in principle they do not relate to "unfair trading" and are thus rather specific exceptions. It should be noted that developed States and increasingly also emerging economies[199] have a strong tendency to increase the use of such measures in times of economic and political crisis to satisfy domestic requests for protection—even in cases where they do seem justified.[200]

| Article 2: Conditions (WTO Safeguards Agreement, footnote omitted)[201] | 12-042 |

1. A Member may apply a safeguard measure to a product only if that Member has determined, pursuant to the provisions set out below, that such product is being imported into its territory in such increased quantities, absolute or relative to domestic production, and under such conditions as to cause or threaten to cause serious injury to the domestic industry that produces like or directly competitive products.

2. Safeguard measures shall be applied to a product being imported irrespective of its source."

Thus, safeguard measures are in fact trade restrictions, imposed for certain **12-043** specific periods, in response to fairly traded imports. Consequently, where a member proposes or maintains a safeguard measure it must endeavour to maintain a substantially equivalent level of concessions and other obligations to that existing between it and exporting members prior to the safeguard measure.[202] Generally, the measures are to be directed against all imports of the product, irrespective of the source (i.e. in a non-discriminatory manner) (parallelism).[203] Members are expressly prohibited from entering into voluntary export restraint arrangements, orderly marketing arrangements, or any other similar export or import arrangements.[204]

Secondly, Member States may impose restrictions to safeguard their balance of payments,[205] where there is an imminent threat to, or serious decline in, the

---

[199] See *International Trade Centre: Business guide to trade remedies in Brazil*. (Geneva, Internat. Trade Centre, 2009).

[200] See *Conference on Trade and Development: The global economic crisis*. (New York [u.a.], United Nations, 2009).

[201] Source: *http://www.wto.org* (accessed June 8, 2011).

[202] Agreement On Safeguards section III. See also M.R. Nicely, "Article 8 of the WTO Safeguards Agreement" *St. John's Journal of Legal Commentary*, 23 (2008) 3, 699–763.

[203] See United States—Definitive Safeguard Measures on Imports of Circular Welded Carbon Quality Line Pipe from Korea, Appellate Body Report adopted on March 8, 2002.

[204] Agreement On Safeguards section IV. They are often referred to as "grey area measures"; see, for example, Y.S. Lee, "Revival of Grey-Area Measures? The US–Canada Softwood Lumber Agreement: Conflict with the WTO Agreement on Safeguards" (2002) 36 *Journal of World Trade* 155–65.

[205] See Art.XII of GATT 1994; and the Understanding on the Balance-of-Payments Provisions of the General Agreement on Tariffs and Trade 1994. See above on the cooperation with the IMF, as well as U. C. Ukpabi, "Juridical substance or myth over balance-of-payment" *Michigan Journal of International Law*, 26 (2005) 2, 701–736.

country's monetary reserves; or to facilitate a reasonable rate of increase in the country's reserves, where the monetary reserves are very low.

Finally, members may impose restrictions to prevent or relieve critical shortages of foodstuffs, or other products of importance to the exporting country[206]; and for essential national security reasons.[207]

Bilateral and regional agreements often confirm the availability of safeguards as foreseen in the WTO but introduce additional possibilities for bilateral safeguards with respect to the increased inflow of goods under the RTA. It is controversial whether an obligation not to apply multilateral safeguards available under the WTO against preferential trading partners is compatible with the obligations of a WTO member.[208]

**12-044**    **Economic Partnership Agreement between the CARIFORUM States, of the one part, and the European Community and its Member States, of the other part (signed on 15 October 2008)**

*PART II TRADE AND TRADE-RELATED MATTERS*

*TITLE I TRADE IN GOODS*

[. . .]

*CHAPTER 2 Trade defence instruments*

*Article 24 Multilateral safeguards*

1. Subject to the provisions of this Article, nothing in this Agreement shall prevent the Signatory CARIFORUM States and the EC Party from adopting measures in accordance with Article XIX of the General Agreement on Tariffs and Trade 1994, the Agreement on Safeguards, and Article 5 of the Agreement on Agriculture annexed to the Marrakech Agreement Establishing the World Trade Organization. For the purpose of this Article, origin shall be determined in accordance with the non-preferential rules of origin of the Parties or Signatory CARIFORUM States.

2. Notwithstanding paragraph 1, in the light of the overall development objectives of this Agreement and the small size of the economies of the CARIFORUM States, the EC Party shall exclude imports from any CARIFORUM State from any measures taken pursuant to Article XIX of the GATT 1994, the WTO Agreement on Safeguards and Article 5 of the Agreement on Agriculture.

---

[206] See, for example, Art.XI(2)(a) of GATT 1994 .

[207] Art.XXI of GATT 1994. See R. Chand, *International trade, food security and the response to the WTO in South Asian countries* (Helsinki, Finland, UNU World Inst. for Development Economics Research (UNU/WIDER), Oct. 2006) and Carmen G. Gonzalez, "Trade liberalization, food security, and the environment" *Transnational Law & Contemporary Problems*, 14 (2004) 2, 419–498.

[208] See J. M. Finger, *Safeguards and Antidumping in Latin American Trade Liberalization* (Washington, DC, World Bank, 2006); D. S. Beckford "Trade remedies within the CARICOM Single Market and Economy", *West Indian Law Journal*, 32 (2007) 1, 13–50.

3. The provisions of paragraph 2 shall apply for a period of five years, beginning with the date of entry into force of the Agreement. Not later than 120 days before the end of this period, the Joint CARIFORUM-EC Council shall review the operation of those provisions in the light of the development needs of the CARIFORUM States, with a view to determining whether to extend their application for a further period.

4. The provisions of paragraph 1 shall not be subject to the Dispute Settlement provisions of this Agreement.

*Article 25 Safeguard clause*

1. Notwithstanding Article 24, after having examined alternative solutions, a Party may apply safeguard measures of limited duration which derogate from the provisions of Article 15 or 16 as the case may be, under the conditions and in accordance with the procedures laid down in this Article.

2. Safeguard measures referred to in paragraph 1 may be taken where a product originating in one Party is being imported into the territory of the other Party in such increased quantities and under such conditions as to cause or threaten to cause:

   (a) serious injury to the domestic industry producing like or directly competitive products in the territory of the importing Party; or

   (b) disturbances in a sector of the economy, particularly where these disturbances produce major social problems, or difficulties which could bring about serious deterioration in the economic situation of the importing Party, or

   (c) disturbances in the markets of like or directly competitive agricultural products [3] or in the mechanisms regulating those markets.

3. Safeguard measures referred to in this Article shall not exceed what is necessary to remedy or prevent the serious injury or disturbances, as defined in paragraph 2. Those safeguard measures of the importing Party may only consist of one or more of the following:

   (a) suspension of the further reduction of the rate of import duty for the product concerned, as provided for under this Agreement,

   (b) increase in the customs duty on the product concerned up to a level which does not exceed the customs duty applied to other WTO Members, and

   (c) introduction of tariff quotas on the product concerned.

4. Without prejudice to paragraphs 1 to 3, where any product originating in one or more Signatory CARIFORUM State(s) is being imported in such increased quantities and under such conditions as to cause or threaten to cause one of the situations referred to under paragraphs 2(a), (b) and (c) to one or several of the EC Party's outermost regions, the EC Party may take surveillance or safeguard measures limited to the region or regions concerned in accordance with the procedures laid down in paragraphs 6 to 9.

5. (a) Without prejudice to paragraphs 1 to 3, where any product originating in the EC Party is being imported in such increased quantities and under such conditions as to cause or threaten to cause one of the situations referred to under paragraphs 2(a), (b) and (c) to a

Signatory CARIFORUM State, the Signatory CARIFORUM State concerned may take surveillance or safeguard measures limited to its territory in accordance with the procedures laid down in paragraphs 6 to 9.

(b) A Signatory CARIFORUM State may take safeguard measures where a product originating in the EC Party is being imported into its territory in such increased quantities and under such conditions as to cause or threaten to cause disturbances to an infant industry producing like or directly competitive products. Such provision is only applicable for a period of 10 years from the date of entry into force of this Agreement. Measures must be taken in accordance with the procedures laid down in paragraphs 6 to 9.

6.

(a) Safeguard measures referred to in this Article shall only be maintained for such a time as may be necessary to prevent or remedy serious injury or disturbances as defined in paragraphs 2, 4 and 5.

(b) Safeguard measures referred to in this Article shall not be applied for a period exceeding two years. Where the circumstances warranting imposition of safeguard measures continue to exist, such measures may be extended for a further period of no more than two years. Where the CARIFORUM States or a Signatory CARIFORUM State apply a safeguard measure, or where the EC Party apply a measure limited to the territory of one or more of its outermost regions, such measures may however be applied for a period not exceeding four years and, where the circumstances warranting imposition of safeguard measures continue to exist, extended for a further period of four years.

(c) Safeguard measures referred to in this Article that exceed one year shall contain clear elements progressively leading to their elimination at the end of the set period, at the latest.

(d) No safeguard measure referred to in this Article shall be applied to the import of a product that has previously been subject to such a measure, for a period of at least one year since the expiry of the measure.

7. For the implementation of paragraphs 1-6, the following provisions shall apply:

(a) Where a party takes the view that one of the circumstances set out in paragraphs 2, 4 and/or 5 exists, it shall immediately refer the matter to the CARIFORUM-EC Trade and Development Committee for examination.

(b) The CARIFORUM-EC Trade and Development Committee may make any recommendation needed to remedy the circumstances which have arisen. If no recommendation has been made by the CARIFORUM-EC Trade and Development Committee aimed at remedying the circumstances, or no other satisfactory solution has been reached within 30 days of the matter being referred to the CARIFORUM-EC Trade and Development Committee, the importing party may adopt the appropriate measures to remedy the circumstances in accordance with this Article.

(c) Before taking any measure provided for in this Article or, in the cases to which paragraph 8 applies, as soon as possible, the Party or the signatory CARIFORUM State concerned shall supply the CARIFORUM-EC Trade and Development Committee with all relevant information required for a thorough examination of the situation, with a view to seeking a solution acceptable to the parties concerned.

(d) In the selection of safeguard measures pursuant to this Article, priority must be given to those which least disturb the operation of this Agreement.

(e) Any safeguard measure taken pursuant to this Article shall be notified immediately to the CARIFORUM-EC Trade and Development Committee and shall be the subject of periodic consultations within that body, particularly with a view to establishing a timetable for their abolition as soon as circumstances permit.

8. Where exceptional circumstances require immediate action, the importing party concerned, whether the EC Party, the CARIFORUM States or a Signatory CARIFORUM State as the case may be, may take the measures provided for in paragraphs 3, 4 and/or 5 on a provisional basis without complying with the requirements of paragraph 7. Such action may be taken for a maximum period of 180 days where measures are taken by the EC Party and 200 days where measures are taken by the CARIFORUM States or a Signatory CARIFORUM State, or where measures taken by the EC Party are limited to the territory of one or more of its outermost regions. The duration of any such provisional measure shall be counted as a part of the initial period and any extension referred to in paragraph 6. In the taking of such provisional measures, the interest of all parties involved shall be taken into account. The importing party concerned shall inform the other party concerned and it shall immediately refer the matter to the CARIFORUM-EC Trade and Development Committee for examination.

9. If an importing party subjects imports of a product to an administrative procedure having as its purpose the rapid provision of information on the trend of trade flows liable to give rise to the problems referred to in this Article, it shall inform the CARIFORUM-EC Trade and Development Committee without delay.

10. Safeguard measures adopted under the provisions of this Article shall not be subject to WTO Dispute Settlement provisions.

## Exceptions

Like all sustainable codes, the WTO code contains exceptions to its general **12-045** rules. In this sense it is not an absolute code. Rather, it is adaptable to reflect both the variegated character of the international economic society, and national circumstances. In this context, to reflect the diversity of the international economic community, there are three main broad categories of exceptions to the MFN standard.[209] First, there is the exception

---

[209] See Arts XIV, XXIV and Pt IV of GATT 1994.

relating to preferential arrangements that have existed mainly for historical reasons, normally in relation to former colonies or between neighbouring countries.[210] Secondly, there are preferential arrangements for the benefit of developing members, either on a bilateral basis as between developed and developing countries, or on a unilateral basis offered by a developed member, or preferential arrangements as between developing countries.[211] The preferences in these two categories relate mainly to preferential market access conditions accorded to developing members. Finally, there is the exception relating to customs unions,[212] free trade areas and allied arrangements.[213] A customs union is basically an arrangement where trade restrictions are eliminated in relation to substantially all the trade as between the members, and where the external trade restrictions of the members of the Union with respect to non-members are substantially the same.[214] A free-trade arrangement on the other hand is an arrangement where trade restrictions on substantially all the trade as between the members are eliminated, but where the members maintain control of their external foreign trade regime in relation to non-members of the arrangement.[215] The process of such economic integration must not result in higher external trade barriers for non-members.[216] These arrangements escape the application of the GATT MFN standard, but unless specifically exempted, the other disciplines of the WTO code apply to the arrangements, both as between the members of the arrangements and outside members. The amount of international trade that escapes the full rigour of the WTO code under this exception is considerable.[217]

To reflect national priorities and aspirations the WTO code entertains certain deviations from the norm—particularly from the general prohibition

---

[210] See Art.1(2) of the GATT 1994.

[211] See Pt IV of the GATT 1994, and the Tokyo Round Decision of November 28, 1979 (L/4903) Differential And More Favourable Treatment Reciprocity And Fuller Participation Of Developing Countries.

[212] See, for example, K. Anderson and R. Blackhurst, *Regional Integration and the Global Trading System* (New York: Harvester Wheatsheaf, 1993); P. Demaret, J.F. Bellis and G.G. Jiminez (eds), *Regionalism and Multilateralism After the Uruguay Round* (Brussels: European Interuniversity Press, 1997); Sungjoon Cho, "Breaking the barrier between regionalism and multilateralism", *Harvard International Law Journal*, 42:2 (2001), 419–465.

[213] Art.XXIV of the GATT 1994; and the Understanding on the Interpretation of Art.XXIV of GATT 1994.

[214] See Art.XXIV(8) of GATT 1994. The most famous customs union is probably the European Community with its common customs tariff. See also K. Chase, "Multilateralism compromised: the mysterious origins of GATT Art. XXIV" (2006) 5(1) *World Trade Review* 1–30.

[215] Chase (2006). As the members of a free trade area do not adopt a common external customs tariff for all members, they relies on preferential rules of origin (RO) to distinguish products originating within the free trade area (tariff-free) and those having non-preferential origin (subject to MFN treatment). On RO in general see above.

[216] Art.XXIV(5) of GATT 1994.

[217] See L. Bartels, "Interim agreements under Article XXIV GATT" *World Trade Review*, 8 (2009) 2, 339–350 and D. Ahn, "Foe or friend of GATT Article XXIV", *Journal of International Economic Law*, 11(2008) 1, 107–133.

on the imposition of quantitative restrictions.[218] Article XX GATT contains general exceptions while Art.XXI GATT deals with security exceptions.[219]

First, a member may apply certain restrictions to protect its internal value system. Thus, for example, a member may impose restrictions necessary to protect its public morals; or impose restrictions for the protection of its national treasures of artistic, historic or archaeological value[220]; or introduce measures necessary to ensure compliance with certain national regulations not inconsistent with GATT 1994.

Secondly, a member may impose certain restrictions to preserve and protect its tangible and intangible wealth and its economic system. Thus, for example, a member may impose restrictions necessary to conserve exhaustible natural resources[221]; necessary to protect human, animal or plant life or health; necessary to protect intellectual property rights; relating to the control of the flow of gold and silver[222]; and to ensure the marketing of commodities in international trade.[223] To prevent abuse in the application of these exceptions, certain conditions have been included. Thus, the national restrictions or measures must not be unjustifiably discriminatory. Further, they should not constitute disguised restrictions on international trade or be arbitrary. These general conditions are included in the so-called *chapeau* of Art.XX GATT.[224]

Of particular importance is the question whether a measure is "necessary", where this is a prerequisite under Art. XX GATT. Normally means that it must be the least trade-restrictive measure, i.e. no less GATT-inconsistent measure is available to achieve a given goal.[225] This may involve a "weighing and balancing [of] a series of factors which prominently include the contribution made by the compliance measure to

---

[218] See Arts XI(2) and XX of GATT 1994. See United States—Standards fro Reformulated and Conventional Gasoline, Report of the Appellate Body (1996); United States—Import Of Certain Shrimp And Shrimp Products, Appellate Body Report (1998); Canada—Certain Measures Concerning Periodicals, Report of the Appellate Body (1997). See also, for example, S. Charnorotz, "The moral exception in trade policy" (1998) 38(4) *Virginia Journal of International Law* 689–745; B. McGrady, "Necessity exceptions in WTO law", *Journal of International Economic Law*, 12 (2009) 1, 153–173.

[219] See A. Emmerson, "Conceptualizing security exceptions", *Journal of International Economic Law*, 11 (2008) 1, 135–154.

[220] Art.XX of GATT 1994. See N.F. Diebold, "The morals and order exceptions in WTO law", *Journal of International Economic Law*, 11 (2008) 1, 43–74.

[221] See United States—Standards For Reformulated And Conventional Gasoline. Report of the Appellate Body (1996). The AB considered clean air to be an exhaustible natural resource in the sense of Art.XX (g) GATT.

[222] See further for other exceptions listed in Art.XX of GATT 1994 .

[223] Art.XI(2) of GATT 1994.

[224] On the character of the chapeau see, for example, United States—Import Prohibition of Certain Shrimp and Shrimp Products—AB-1998-4—Report of the Appellate Body, paras 158 and following, and United States—Import Prohibition of Certain Shrimp and Shrimp Products—Recourse to Article 21.5 of the DSU by Malaysia, AB Report adopted November 21, 2001.

[225] See Dominican Republic—Measures Affecting the Importation and Internal Sale of Cigarettes, AB Report adopted on May 19, 2005.

the enforcement of the law or regulation at issue, the importance of the common interests or values protected by the law or regulation, and the accompanying impact on the law or regulation on imports or exports".[226] Alternatives must only be considered if they are "reasonably available", i.e. not excessively expensive.[227]

**12-046**        **Article XX: General Exceptions (GATT 147)[228]**

Subject to the requirement that such measures are not applied in a manner which would constitute a means of arbitrary or unjustifiable discrimination between countries where the same conditions prevail, or a disguised restriction on international trade, nothing in this Agreement shall be construed to prevent the adoption or enforcement by any contracting party of measures:

(a) necessary to protect public morals;

(b) necessary to protect human, animal or plant life or health;

(c) relating to the importations or exportations of gold or silver;

(d) necessary to secure compliance with laws or regulations which are not inconsistent with the provisions of this Agreement, including those relating to customs enforcement, the enforcement of monopolies operated under paragraph 4 of Article II and Article XVII, the protection of patents, trade marks and copyrights, and the prevention of deceptive practices;

(e) relating to the products of prison labour;

(f) imposed for the protection of national treasures of artistic, historic or archaeological value;

(g) relating to the conservation of exhaustible natural resources if such measures are made effective in conjunction with restrictions on domestic production or consumption;

(h) undertaken in pursuance of obligations under any intergovernmental commodity agreement which conforms to criteria submitted to the CONTRACTING PARTIES and not disapproved by them or which is itself so submitted and not so disapproved;

(i) involving restrictions on exports of domestic materials necessary to ensure essential quantities of such materials to a domestic processing industry during periods when the domestic price of such materials is held below the world price as part of a governmental stabilization plan; *Provided* that such restrictions shall not operate to increase the exports of or the protection afforded to such domestic industry, and shall not depart from the provisions of this Agreement relating to non-discrimination;

(j) essential to the acquisition or distribution of products in general or local short supply; *Provided* that any such measures shall be consistent with

---

[226] Korea—Measures affecting Imports of Fresh, Chilled and Frozen Beef, WT/DS161/AB/R, WT/DS169/AB/R, AB Report adopted on January 10, 2001, para.164.

[227] With regard to services see US—Measures affecting the Cross-Border Supply of Gambling and Betting Services, WT/DS285/AB/R, AB Report adopted on April 20, 2005, para.308.

[228] Source: *http://www.wto.org*. (Accessed June 8, 2011).

> the principle that all contracting parties are entitled to an equitable share
> of the international supply of such products, and that any such meas-
> ures, which are inconsistent with the other provisions of the Agreement
> shall be discontinued as soon as the conditions giving rise to them have
> ceased to exist. The CONTRACTING PARTIES shall review the need
> for this sub-paragraph not later than 30 June 1960.

Finally, from a national sectoral standpoint, in certain circumstances, a **12-047**
member may impose import restrictions on agricultural or fisheries product,
for example, to reinforce governmental measures controlling the domestic
market in like products[229]; and to control the production of animal-based
domestic produce.

### Special regimes for certain special sectors

Two key areas of international trade have been the subject in the past of **12-048**
privileged regimes, mainly as a consequence of national protectionist forces.
These comprise traditionally the agriculture and the textiles sectors. The
Agreement on Agriculture[230] and the Agreement on Textiles and Clothing[231]
were special regimes created during the Uruguay Round which essentially
tried to bring these two sectors into the general fold of the WTO code.

Prior to the establishment of the WTO, the agriculture sector escaped
international regulation either as a consequence of exceptions or waivers to
general international trade regulations, or through international breaches.[232]
In general terms, the Agreement on Agriculture provides for a free-market
orientation in the sector, and in that light a regulatory framework. More specifically, the basic objectives of the Agreement are to secure the dismantling
of barriers to trade in the field of agriculture; the reduction of support to

---

[229] See Art.XI(2) of GATT 1994.
[230] See, also for example, T.E. Josling, *Agriculture in the GATT* (Basingstoke, Macmillan, 1996);
F. Delcros, "The Legal Status of Agriculture in the World Trade Organization State of
Play at the Start of Negotiations" (2002) 36 *Journal of World Trade* 219–53; R. Aggarwal,
"Dynamics of Agriculture Negotiations in the World Trade Organization" (2005) 39
*Journal of World Trade* 741–61; and J.A. McMahon, *The WTO Agreement on Agriculture:
A Commentary*, Oxford Commentaries on the GATT/WTO Agreements (Oxford, Oxford
University Press, 2006). See also European Communities—Measures Affecting Certain
Poultry Products, Report of the Panel (1998); European Communities—Regime for the
importation, sale and distribution of bananas, Report of the Appellate Body (1997); Japan—
Measures Affecting Agricultural Products (1998).
[231] For clarification on Art.6 of the Agreement on Textiles and Clothing see United States—
Restrictions on Imports of Cotton and Man-made Fibre Underwear. Report of the Appellate
Body (1997); United States—Measure Affecting Imports of Woven Wool Shirts and Blouses
from India. Report of the Appellate Body (1997). See also, for example, C. Jimenez Cortes,
*GATT, WTO and the Regulation of International Trade in Textiles* (Aldershot, Ashgate,
1997).
[232] The agricultural sector was originally also regulated by two plurilateral agreements resulting
from the Uruguay Round, namely the International Dairy Agreement and the International
Bovine Agreement. These agreements provided mainly for international structures in their
respective fields to facilitate co-operation and co-ordination of policies, including price stabilisation. See BISD 26S/91 and BISD 26Sboth were terminated in 1997.

domestic producers; and the establishment of a fair system of export competition. These objectives are limited by two considerations. First, the regulatory framework applies to agricultural products specified in Annex 1 to the agreement. Secondly, it binds a member only to the extent of its commitments specified in Pt IV of each member's schedule, in so far as domestic support and export subsidies are concerned.

More specifically the basic obligations under the Agreement are as follows. First, a member is committed not to provide a domestic producer support in excess of that specified in its schedule.[233] Secondly, a member is committed not to provide export subsidies in excess of that specified in its schedule, and in conformity with the Agreement.[234] Thirdly, a member is required to convert into ordinary customs duties certain quantitative restrictions, variable import levies, minimum import prices, discretionary import licensing, non-tariff measures maintained through State Trading Enterprises,[235] voluntary export and similar measures.[236] Finally, a member is bound by the tariff concessions and other market access commitments specified in its schedule.[237]

WTO members agreed to initiate further negotiations for continuing the agricultural trade reform process one year before the end of the implementation period of the 1994 Agreement on Agriculture, i.e. by the end of 1999. These talks began in early 2000 under the original mandate of Article 20 of the Agriculture Agreement. Throughout the Doha Round they constituted one of the major stumbling blocks for the conclusion of negotiations, mostly due to the absence of consensus between developed countries protecting their domestic agricultural sector and competitive exporters of agricultural products (like Brazil, Argentina, Australia, New Zealand etc.).[238]

Like the agricultural sector, the textile sector had been operating under a special international regime until the end of the Uruguay Round in 1994. The object of the Agreement on textiles and clothing was to integrate the regulation of international trade in this sphere into the general WTO framework. The Agreement set the mechanisms by which the integration of this sector, hitherto governed by the Multi-Fibre Arrangement, was to be achieved. In effect the thrust of the agreement was on how the transition of this sector

---

[233] See Agreement On Agriculture Art.3.

[234] The value of direct export subsidies are to be reduced to a level 36% below the 1986–1990 base period level over a six-year implementation period. The quantity of subsidised exports are to be reduced by 21% over a six-year period. In the case of developing countries the reductions are two-thirds those of developed members over a 10-year period. No reduction commitments apply to least-developing country members. See the Marrakesh Protocol GATT 1994.

[235] See Canada—Measures Relating to Exports of Wheat and Treatment of Imported Grain, AB Report adopted on September 27, 2007.

[236] Art.4.

[237] Art.4.

[238] See B.H. Malkawi, "Sustainable agriculture within WTO law and Arab countries", *International Trade Law & Regulation*, 17 (2011) 1, 1–9; R.M. Ortiz, (ed.), *Agricultural subsidies in the WTO Green Box*, (Cambridge [u.a.], Cambridge Univ. Press, 2009); B. Connor, *Agriculture in WTO law*, London (Cameron May, 2007).

into the GATT regime was to be achieved. Basically all restrictions (i.e. all unilateral quantitative restrictions, bilateral arrangements and other measures having a similar effect) other than those specifically excluded under the Agreement, were to be brought into conformity with GATT 1994, within one year following the entry into force of the Agreement, or are to be phased out according to an approved programme[239] over a 10-year period. Accordingly, the Agreement on Textiles and Clothing (ATC) and all restrictions thereunder was terminated on January 1, 2005.[240] The expiry of the 10-year transition period of ATC implementation meant that trade in textile and clothing products is no longer subject to quotas under a special regime outside normal WTO/GATT rules but is now governed by the general rules and disciplines embodied in the multilateral trading system. However, the accession of China to the WTO and the fact that this country is today's most competitive exporter of textiles and footwear led to specific measures against this country, mostly based on specific safeguard measures provided for in China's accession agreement, starting in 2005.[241] Against other textile exporters the application of trade remedies or safeguard measures remains also likely. In this logic the use of narrow rules of origin to limit textile imports under RTAs is also understandable.[242]

## THE LIBERALISATION OF INTERNATIONAL TRADE IN SERVICES

The Agreement on Trade in Services (GATS) provides for the liberalisation of trade in the field of services.[243] It is novel in bringing this new area into the          **12-049**

---

[239] Art.3 of the Agreement on Textiles and Clothing.

[240] See E. Vermulst and P. Mihaylova, "EC Commercial Defence Actions against Textiles from 1995 to 2000: Possible Lessons for Future Negotiations" (2001) 4 *Journal of International Economic Law* 527–55; D. Audet, "Smooth as Silk? A First Look at the Post MFA Textiles and Clothing Landscape" (2007) 10 *Journal of International Economic Law* 267–84; J. Mayer, "Not Totally Naked: Textiles and Clothing Trade in a Quota-free Environment" (2005) 39 J.W.T. 393–426.

[241] See F. Spadi, "Discriminatory Safeguards in the Light of the Admission of the People's Republic of China to the World Trade Organization" (2002) 5 *Journal of International Economic Law* 421–43 and S.J. Kim, K.A. Reinert and G.C. Rodrigo, "The Agreement on Textiles and Clothing: Safeguard Actions from 1995 to 2001" (2002) 5 *Journal of International Economic Law* 445–68.

[242] See A. Barua, (ed.) *The WTO and India.* (New Delhi Orient BlackSwan, 2010) and A. Qureshi, "Preferential rules of origin and WTO disciplines with specific reference to the US practice in the textiles and apparel sectors", *Legal Issues of Economic Integration*, 32 (2005) 1, 25–63.

[243] See, for example, GATS 2000: opening markets for services: the General Agreement on Trade in Services, (1998) Official Publication of the European Communities; M. Johnson, "Developments in the services sector: the GATS", Ch.10 in A.H. Qureshi et al. (eds), *The Legal and Moral Aspects of International Trade* (London, Routledge, 1998); W. Yi, "Most-favoured-nation treatment under the General Agreement on Trade in Services—And its application in Financial services" (1996) 30(1) J.W.T.; A. Matoo, "National treatment in the GATS—corner-stone or pandora's box?" (1997) 31(1) J.W.T.; M. Bronckers, and P. Larouche, "Telecommunications Services and the WTO" (1997) 31 J.W.T.; W. Zdouc, "WTO dispute

remit of an international organisation in the context of liberalisation. Two types of obligations are enunciated—i.e. general obligations and disciplines (Pt II), and specific commitments (Pt III). Further, the Agreement provides for the specifics of a particular service sector by the provision of annexes to the GATS.[244] The general obligations cover all measures affecting trade in services,[245] and all types of services. The specific commitments are confined to the particular service sector commitments members have undertaken in their respective schedules.[246]

The Agreement applies to measures affecting trade in services.[247] Trade in services is defined as the supply of a service in any sector, other than in the course of governmental authority. The kind of supply envisaged is wide, and encompasses supply from one Member State to the territory of another Member State (i.e. a cross-border supply)[248]; the supply from within the territory of one Member State to the service consumer of another Member State (i.e. consumption abroad e.g. tourism[249]); the supply from within the territory of a Member State through a commercial presence (i.e. commercial presence e.g. through a subsidiary or a branch); or the presence of natural persons in the territory of any other member[250] (i.e. movement of persons).

### Article I: Scope and Definition (GATS)[251]

"...

**12-050**

2. For the purposes of this Agreement, trade in services is defined as the supply of a service:

   (a) from the territory of one Member into the territory of any other Member;

   (b) in the territory of one Member to the service consumer of any other Member;

   (c) by a service supplier of one Member, through commercial presence in the territory of any other Member;

settlement practice relating to the GATS" (1999) 2 *Journal of International Economic Law* 295–346; WTO, *A Handbook on the GATS Agreement* (Cambridge University Press, 2005); N. Munin, Legal guide to GATS.—Alphen aan den Rijn : Kluwer Law International, 2010 See also European Communities—Regime for the importation, sale and distribution of bananas, Report of the Appellate Body (1997) and US—Measures affecting the Cross-Border Supply of Gambling and Betting Services, WT/DS285/AB/R, AB Report adopted on April 20, 2005.

[244] i.e. the Annex on Financial Services; the Annex on Telecommunications; Annex On Air Transport Services.
[245] Art.1(1) of GATS.
[246] Art.XX.
[247] Art.I.1 of GATS.
[248] See, for example, S. Wunsch-Vincent, The Internet, cross-border trade in services, and the GATS: lessons from US–Gambling (2006) 5(3) *World Trade Review* 319–55.
[249] See GATT—News of the Uruguay Round Of Multilateral Negotiations. April 5, 1994.
[250] See Art.I of the General Agreement On Trade In Services.
[251] Source: *http://www.wto.org*. (Accessed June 8, 2011).

> (d) by a service supplier of one Member, through presence of natural persons of a Member in the territory of any other Member.
>
> . . ."

The general obligations are as follows. First, the most-favoured-nation principle is prescribed in relation to measures pertaining to trade in services.[252] Thus, each member is to grant unconditionally to services and service suppliers of any other member the same treatment as it accords to the services and service suppliers of other members. This standard, however, is subject to certain exceptions. For example, the MFN standard does not preclude members from entering into economic arrangements in which trade in services are liberalised amongst members; or to enter into labour market integration Agreements.[253] Members may also specify MFN exemptions in relation to specific services. Secondly, there must be full transparency in so far as measures pertaining to services are concerned.[254]

**12-051**

Thirdly, the Council for Trade in Services is to ensure by designing appropriate disciplines, that qualification requirements and procedures technical standards and licensing arrangements do not constitute unnecessary barriers to trade.[255] Members are encouraged to recognise unilaterally, or through agreement, the education and experience or certification obtained in other member countries. The member is required not to accord recognition of such qualifications in a discriminatory fashion; and to base where appropriate recognition upon multilaterally agreed criteria.[256]

Fourthly, members are to ensure that monopoly suppliers of services within their territory do not act in a manner that is inconsistent with the most-favoured-nation standard, or specific commitments given by the member.[257] In the same vein a member is required to enter into consultation, upon the request of another member, to eliminate business practices of suppliers which restrain and restrict trade in services.[258]

**Article XVI: Market Access (GATS, footnotes omitted)[259]**

**12-052**

> 1. With respect to market access through the modes of supply identified in Article I, each Member shall accord services and service suppliers of any other Member treatment no less favourable than that provided for

---

[252] See Art.II GATS. See EC—Bananas III (Article 21.5), Panel Report adopted on April 12, 1999.

[253] GATS Art.V and V *bis*. See also Annex on Art.II.

[254] GATS Art.III.

[255] GATS Art.VI para.4.

[256] GATS Art.VII.

[257] GATS Art.VIII. See also M. Krajewski, "Public Services and Trade Liberalization: Mapping the Legal Framework" (2003) 6 *Journal of International Economic Law* 341–67; R. Adlung, "Public Services and the GATS" (2006) 9 *Journal of International Economic Law* 455–85.

[258] GATS Art.XI.

[259] Source: *http://www.wto.org*. (Accessed June 8, 2011).

under the terms, limitations and conditions agreed and specified in its Schedule.

2. In sectors where market-access commitments are undertaken, the measures which a Member shall not maintain or adopt either on the basis of a regional subdivision or on the basis of its entire territory, unless otherwise specified in its Schedule, are defined as:

(a) limitations on the number of service suppliers whether in the form of numerical quotas, monopolies, exclusive service suppliers or the requirements of an economic needs test;

(b) limitations on the total value of service transactions or assets in the form of numerical quotas or the requirement of an economic needs test;

(c) limitations on the total number of service operations or on the total quantity of service output expressed in terms of designated numerical units in the form of quotas or the requirement of an economic needs test;(9)

(d) limitations on the total number of natural persons that may be employed in a particular service sector or that a service supplier may employ and who are necessary for, and directly related to, the supply of a specific service in the form of numerical quotas or the requirement of an economic needs test;

(e) measures which restrict or require specific types of legal entity or joint venture through which a service supplier may supply a service; and

(f) limitations on the participation of foreign capital in terms of maximum percentage limit on foreign shareholding or the total value of individual or aggregate foreign investment.

**12-053**    The following obligations apply where a member has given specific commitments in relation to measures affecting trade in services. An outright prohibition of a specific activity for which a commitment has been made can result in a violation of Art.XVI GATS.[260] Such commitments are made in a countries schedule with regard to specific sectors according to the Services Sectoral Classification List[261] :

**12-054**    **WTO Services Classification: SECTORS AND SUB-SECTORS[262]**

1. BUSINESS SERVICES

A. Professional Services

   B. Computer and Related Services

   C. Research and Development Services

---

[260] See US—Measures affecting the Cross-Border Supply of Gambling and Betting Services, WT/DS285/AB/R, AB Report adopted on April 20, 2005.

[261] MTN.GNS/W/120 of July 10, 1991. See also US—Measures affecting the Cross-Border Supply of Gambling and Betting Services, WT/DS285/AB/R, AB Report adopted on April 20, 2005.

[262] Source: *http://www.wto.org*. (Accessed June 8, 2011).

    D. Real Estate Services

    E. Rental/Leasing Services without Operators

    F. Other Business Services

2. COMMUNICATION SERVICES

    A. Postal services

    B. Courier services

    C. Telecommunication services

    D. Audiovisual services

    E. Other

3. CONSTRUCTION AND RELATED ENGINEERING SERVICES

    A. General construction work for buildings

    B. General construction work for civil engineering

    C. Installation and assembly work

    D. Building completion and finishing work

    E. Other

4. DISTRIBUTION SERVICES

    A. Commission agents' services

    B. Wholesale trade services

    C. Retailing services

    D. Franchising

    E. Other

5. EDUCATIONAL SERVICES

    A. Primary education services

    B. Secondary education services

    C. Higher education services

    D. Adult education

    E. Other education services

6. ENVIRONMENTAL SERVICES

    A. Sewage services

    B. Refuse disposal services

    C. Sanitation and similar services

    D. Other

7. FINANCIAL SERVICES

    A. All insurance and insurance-related services

    B. Banking and other financial services (excl. insurance)

    C. Other

8. HEALTH RELATED AND SOCIAL SERVICES (other than those listed under 1.A.h-j.)

    A. Hospital services

    B. Other Human Health Services

    C. Social Services

    D. Other

9. TOURISM AND TRAVEL RELATED SERVICES

    A. Hotels and restaurants (incl. catering)

    B. Travel agencies and tour operators' services

    C. Tourist guides services

    D. Other

10. RECREATIONAL, CULTURAL AND SPORTING SERVICES (other than audiovisual services)

    A. Entertainment services (including theatre, live bands and circus services)

    B. News agency services

    C. Libraries, archives, museums and other cultural services

    D. Sporting and other recreational services

    E. Other

11. TRANSPORT SERVICES

    A. Maritime Transport Services

    B. Internal Waterways Transport

    C. Air Transport Services

    D. Space Transport

    E. Rail Transport Services

    F. Road Transport Services

    G. Pipeline Transport

    H. Services auxiliary to all modes of transport

    I. Other Transport Services

12. OTHER SERVICES NOT INCLUDED ELSEWHERE"

**12-055**    First, each member is required not to accord treatment to other members that is less favourable than that provided for under the terms and conditions specified in the member's schedule[263]; or treatment that is less favourable than that accorded to its own like services and service suppliers (i.e. national treatment).[264]

[263] GATS Art.XVI.
[264] GATS Art.XVII.

Secondly, unless specified otherwise in the member's schedule, the member is not to impose any limit on the number of service suppliers, or the total value of service transactions, or the number of service operations, or the number of natural persons who may be employed in a particular service sector, or the type of legal entity through which the service may be supplied, or the extent of foreign capital participation (i.e. quantitative restrictions).[265]

Thirdly, where a Member State has given specific commitments in a particular sector of services, than the domestic measures affecting trade in services are to be administered in an objective and reasonable manner.[266] In addition, where an application is required in order to facilitate the supply of a service, the application must be processed without delay.

Some restrictions on the supply of services can be imposed in specified circumstances. First, restrictions to correct a member's balance-of-payments equilibrium are permitted provided they are consistent with the Articles of Agreement of the IMF, are non-discriminatory, transparent and temporary.[267] Secondly, the most-favoured-nation stipulation, market access commitments and the national standard do not apply to government procurement of services.[268] Thirdly, there are certain restrictions that may be placed by a member, to protect for instance public morals, human, animal or plant life; to prevent fraud; to ensure privacy,[269] and in the interests of national security.[270] A member may also impose or enforce restrictions that undermine the national treatment standard in order to ensure effective and equitable collection of direct taxes in respect of services of suppliers of other members. Further, a member may also adopt measures inconsistent with the most-favoured-nation standard, provided these are consequential upon the member's participation in agreements on the avoidance of double taxation.[271] Finally, restrictions may be imposed to prevent measures affecting natural persons seeking access to a member's employment market.[272]

A number of matters have been left for further negotiations, and a framework has been provided for this purpose. Thus, for example, the areas to be negotiated further are safeguards,[273] and subsidies.[274] The Agreement

---

[265] GATS Art.XVI.
[266] GATS Art.VI.
[267] GATS Art.XII.
[268] GATS Art.XIII.
[269] GATS Art.XIV.
[270] GATS Art.XIV *bis*.
[271] GATS Art.XIV.
[272] GATS Annex on Movement of Natural Persons Supplying Services under the Agreement. See Ch.15.
[273] GATS Art.X; see Adlung, Rudolf "Negotiations on safeguards and subsidies in services" *Journal of International Economic Law*, 10 (2007) 2, 235–265 and P. Poretti, *The Regulation of Subsidies within the General Agreement on Trade in Services of the WTO* (Alphen aan den Rijn [u.a.], Kluwer Law International, 2009).
[274] GATS Art.XV. See also Art.XIX.

also provides for further negotiations to liberalise trade in the services sector generally.

In general the liberalisation of services markets remains relatively modest. Only developed States have made major bindings under the WTO—and even here they do usually not include commitments with regard to mode 4 (movement of natural persons).[275] In the Doha Round developed countries have requested emerging economies to open their services markets for foreign competition, in particular also with regard to mode 3 (commercial presence)—this implies to access for foreign investors in services sectors.[276] In addition, many RTAs include enhanced commitments with regard to services, in particular where commercial presence is needed.[277]

**12-056**      **Economic Partnership Agreement between the CARIFORUM States, of the one part, and the European Community and its Member States, of the other part (signed on 15 October 2008)**

*TITLE II INVESTMENT, TRADE IN SERVICES AND E-COMMERCE*

*CHAPTER 2  Commercial presence*

*[. . .]*

*Article 67 Market access*

1. With respect to market access through commercial presence, the EC Party and the Signatory CARIFORUM States shall accord to commercial presences and investors of the other Party a treatment no less favourable than that provided for in the specific commitments contained in Annex IV.

2. In sectors where market access commitments are undertaken, the measures which the EC Party and the Signatory CARIFORUM States shall not maintain or adopt either on the basis of a regional subdivision or on the basis of their entire territory, unless otherwise specified in Annex IV, are defined as:

    (a) limitations on the number of commercial presences whether in the form of numerical quotas, monopolies, exclusive rights or other commercial presence requirements such as economic needs tests;

    (b) limitations on the total value of transactions or assets in the form of numerical quotas or the requirement of an economic needs test;

    (c) limitations on the total number of operations or on the total quantity of output expressed in terms of designated numerical units in the form of quotas or the requirement of an economic needs test [10];

    (d) limitations on the participation of foreign capital in terms of maximum percentage limit on foreign shareholding or the total value of individual or aggregate foreign investment; and

---

[275] See Ch.15.

[276] See Ch.14.

[277] See C. Fink, "East Asian free trade agreements in services", *Journal of International Economic Law*, 11 (2008) 2, 263–311.

(e)  measures which restrict or require specific types of commercial presence (subsidiary, branch, representative office) [11] or joint ventures through which an investor of the other Party may perform an economic activity.

### Article 68 National treatment

1. In the sectors where market access commitments are inscribed in Annex IV and subject to any conditions and qualifications set out therein, with respect to all measures affecting commercial presence, the EC Party and the Signatory CARIFORUM States shall grant to commercial presences and investors of the other Party treatment no less favourable than that they accord to their own like commercial presences and investors.

2. The EC Party and the Signatory CARIFORUM States may meet the requirement of paragraph 1 by according to commercial presences and investors of the other Party, either formally identical treatment or formally different treatment to that they accord to their own like commercial presences and investors.

3. Formally identical or formally different treatment shall be considered to be less favourable if it modifies the conditions of competition in favour of commercial presences and investors of the EC Party or of the Signatory CARIFORUM States compared to like commercial presences and investors of the other Party.

4. Specific commitments assumed under this Article shall not be construed to require the EC Party or the Signatory CARIFORUM States to compensate for inherent competitive disadvantages which result from the foreign character of the relevant commercial presences and investors.

### Article 69 Lists of commitments

The sectors liberalised by the EC Party and by the Signatory CARIFORUM States pursuant to this Chapter and, by means of reservations, the market access and national treatment limitations applicable to commercial presences and investors of the other Party in those sectors are set out in lists of commitments included in Annex IV.

### Article 70 Most-favoured-nation treatment

1. With respect to any measures affecting commercial presence covered by this Chapter:

    (a)  the EC Party shall accord to commercial presences and investors of the Signatory CARIFORUM States a treatment no less favourable than the most favourable treatment applicable to like commercial presences and investors of any third country with whom it concludes an economic integration agreement after the signature of this Agreement;

    (b)  the Signatory CARIFORUM States shall accord to the commercial presences and investors of the EC Party a treatment no less favourable than the most favourable treatment applicable to like commercial presences and investors of any major trading economy with whom they conclude an economic integration agreement after the signature of this Agreement.

2. When a Party or a Signatory CARIFORUM State concludes a regional economic integration agreement creating an internal market or requiring the parties thereto to significantly approximate their legislation with a view to removing non-discriminatory obstacles to commercial presence and to trade in services, the treatment that such Party or Signatory CARIFORUM State grants to commercial presences and investors of third countries in sectors subject to the internal market or to the significant approximation of legislation is not covered by the provision of paragraph 1 [12].

3. The obligations set out in paragraph 1 shall not apply to treatment granted:

(a) under measures providing for recognition of qualifications, licences or prudential measures in accordance with Article VII of the GATS or its Annex on Financial Services,

(b) under any international agreement or arrangement relating wholly or mainly to taxation, or

(c) under measures benefiting from the coverage of an MFN exemption listed in accordance with Article II.2 of the GATS.

4. For the purpose of this provision, a "major trading economy" means anydeveloped country, or any country accounting for a share of world merchandise exports above 1 % in the year before the entry into force of the economic integration agreement referred to in paragraph 1, or any group of countries acting individually, collectively or through an economic integration agreement accounting collectively for a share of world merchandise exports above 1,5 % in the year before the entry into force of the economic integration agreement referred to in paragraph 1. [13]

5. Where any Signatory CARIFORUM State becomes party to an economic integration agreement with a third party referred to in paragraph 1(b) and that agreement provides for more favourable treatment to such third party than that granted by the Signatory CARIFORUM State to the EC Party pursuant to this Agreement, the Parties shall enter into consultations. The Parties may decide whether the concerned Signatory CARIFORUM State may deny the more favourable treatment contained in the economic integration agreement to the EC Party. The Joint CARIFORUM-EC Council may adopt any necessary measures to adjust the provisions of this Agreement.

TRADE-RELATED ASPECTS OF INTELLECTUAL PROPERTY RIGHTS (TRIPS)

**12-057** The Agreement on Trade-Related Aspects of Intellectual Property Rights, including Trade in Counterfeit Goods (TRIPS Agreement)[278] focuses on the

---

[278] See, for example, M. Blakeney, *Trade Related Aspects of Intellectual Property Rights—A Concise Guide to the TRIPs Agreement* (1996); UNCTAD The TRIPS Agreement and developing countries (1997) Report on TRIPS Agreement; Sodipo, Bankole Piracy and Counterfeiting: GATT, TRIPs and developing countries (1997); F. Wooldridge, *TRIPS and Enforcement* (1997); D. Gervais, *The Trips Agreement* (1998); J. Watal, "The Trips

interface between the protection of intellectual property rights and international trade. International disciplines in the field of intellectual property rights still found their way into the WTO code, despite the existence of the World Intellectual Property Organization (WIPO). This was mainly because the WTO offered a more effective implementation process.[279] Essentially, the lack of intellectual property protection can deter international trade and investment, as indeed can the over-protection of these rights. Hitherto the subject of intellectual property rights was within the domain of WIPO. In this light the objectives of the Agreement are mainly three-fold. First, to reduce distortions and impediments to international trade caused by the nature of national intellectual property protection afforded within member countries. In this context the Agreement establishes a certain minimum of protection of intellectual property rights in Member States. Secondly, conversely it is intended to ensure that the intellectual property protection afforded does not itself distort or impede international trade.[280] Thirdly, the protection of intellectual property rights should contribute to the promotion of technological innovation, and assist in the transfer and dissemination of technology.[281]

The categories of intellectual property rights covered are as follows: copyright and related rights[282]; trademarks[283]; geographical indications[284]; industrial designs[285]; patents[286]; and the protection of undisclosed information.[287] In addition, the Agreement regulates certain anti-competitive practices in contractual licences.[288]

The Agreement incorporates and reinforces, to the extent necessary, the provisions of certain international conventions in the field of intellectual property. This it does in a three-pronged fashion. First, certain provisions from these conventions are required, and/or encouraged to be adopted in national

---

Agreement & Developing Countries" (1998) J.W.I.P; F.M. Abbott, Editorial. "The enduring enigma of TRIPS: a challenge for the world economic system" (1998) 1 *Journal of International Economic Law* 497–521; A. Otten, "Implementation of the TRIPS agreement and prospects for its further development" (1998) 1 *Journal of International Economic Law* 523–36, C.A. Primo Braga and C. Fink, "Reforming intellectual property rights regimes: challenges for developing countries" (1998) 1 *Journal of International Economic Law* 537–54; C. Correa, *Trade Related Aspects of Intellectual Property Rights—A Commentary on the TRIPS Agreement* (Oxford, Oxford University Press, 2007). See also India—Patent Protection for Pharmaceutical and Agricultural Chemical Products. Report of the Appellate Body (1997); Indonesia—Certain Measures Affecting The Automobile Industry, Report of the Panel (1998).

[279] See F.M. Abbott, "Distributed governance at the WTO-WIPO: an evolving model for open-architecture integrated governance" (2000) 3 *Journal of International Economic Law* 63–81.

[280] See preamble to the Agreement On Trade-Related Aspects Of Intellectual Property Rights, including Trade in Counterfeit Goods (hereinafter referred to as TRIPS).

[281] TRIPS Art.7.

[282] See Arts 9–14 of TRIPS.

[283] TRIPS Arts 15–21.

[284] TRIPS Arts 22–24.

[285] TRIPS Arts 25–26.

[286] TRIPS Arts 27–38.

[287] TRIPS Art.39.

[288] TRIPS Art.40.

legislation.[289] Secondly, each member is to accord to the nationals of other members treatment no less favourable than that accorded to its own nationals in relation to intellectual property rights.[290] Thirdly, each member is to accord the most-favoured-nation treatment unconditionally to the nationals of all other members.[291] In addition to this general framework the Agreement also sets out a framework for the enforcement of the intellectual property rights which the members are to introduce in their domestic system.[292] There has been since the start of the negotiations of the TRIPs Agreement during the Uruguay Round an ongoing debate whether the inclusion of these rules and the level of protection were adequate.[293] In general, it was considered that a balance had been found between the various interests of WTO members. However, in recent years many developed countries have started to introduce higher standards (WTO plus or TRIPS plus) in their bilateral agreements—often involving developing countries. This has led to new criticism regarding the protection of IPRs and their impact on development.

**12-058**

**Economic Partnership Agreement between the CARIFORUM States, of the one part, and the European Community and its Member States, of the other part (signed on 15 October 2008)**

*Section 2　Intellectual property*

**Subsection 2　Standards concerning intellectual property rights**

**Article 145 Geographical indications**

**A. Protection in the country of origin**

1. Nothing in this Agreement shall require the EC Party and the Signatory CARIFORUM States to protect in their territories geographical indications that are not protected in their country of origin.

2. The Signatory CARIFORUM States shall establish a system of protection of geographical indications in their respective territories no later than 1 January 2014. The Parties shall cooperate through the CARIFORUM-EC Trade and Development Committee in accordance with the provisions of Article 164(2)(c) towards the development of geographical indications in the territories of the CARIFORUM States. To this end, and within six months from the entry into force of the Agreement, the CARIFORUM States shall submit to the consideration of the CARIFORUM EC Trade and Development Committee a list of prospective Geographical Indications originating in the CARIFORUM States for its discussion and comments.

---

[289] See Canada—Patent Protection of Pharmaceutical Products, WT/DS114/R, Panel Report adopted on April 7, 2000.

[290] TRIPS Art.3.

[291] TRIPS Art.4.

[292] See Ch.4 below.

[293] See P. Acconci, "The implementation of the patent regulation of the TRIPs Agreement and the protection of non-trade values", *Problemi e Tendenze del Diritto Internazionale Dell'Economia*, (2011), 803–828.

[...]

*Article 147 Patents*

A. International agreements

1. The EC Party shall comply with:

   (a) The Patent Cooperation Treaty (Washington, 1970, last modified in 1984);

   (b) The Patent Law Treaty (Geneva, 2000);

   (c) The Budapest Treaty on the International Recognition of the Deposit of Micro-organisms for the Purposes of Patent Procedure (1977, amended in 1980).

2. The Signatory CARIFORUM States shall accede to:

   (a) The Patent Cooperation Treaty (Washington, 1970, last modified in 1984);

   (b) The Budapest Treaty on the International Recognition of the Deposit of Micro-organisms for the Purposes of Patent Procedure (1977, amended in 1980).

3. The Signatory CARIFORUM States shall endeavour to accede to the Patent Law Treaty (Geneva, 2000).

A major issue of the discussion of the TRIPS Agreement during the first ten years of its existence was due to the fact that the increased patent protection it provides in many countries coincided with the AIDS/HIV epidemic. The claim from developing countries that "access to essential medicines" or generally "public health" was endangered overshadowed[294] the functioning of the TRIPS Agreement. As a result, several decisions were taken and declarations[295] were made by the parties in this respect, leading inter alia to an amendment of the TRIPS Agreement regarding the availability of compulsory licences. Here, the requirement that such licenses be only issued to procure medicines for the local market was waived.[296]    **12-059**

---

[294] See also P. Lamy, "Trade-Related Aspects of Intellectual Property Rights—Ten Years Later" (2004) 38 *Journal of World Trade* 923–34.

[295] Most notably Ministerial Conference, Declaration on the TRIPS Agreement and Public Health, November 14, 2001, WT/MIN(01)/DEC/W/2 which led to the amendment of December 6, 2005. See in this regard D. Matthews, "WTO Decision on Implementation of Paragraph 6 of the Doha Declaration on the TRIPS Agreement and Public Health: A Solution to the Access to Essential Medicines Problem?" (2004) 7 *Journal of International Economic Law* 73–107.

[296] Amendment of the TRIPS Agreement, Decision of December 6, 2005, WT/L/641 of December 8, 2005. See Ch.11 on the amendment procedure. See, for example, F.M. Abbott, "The Doha Declaration on the TRIPS Agreement and Public Health: Lighting a Dark Corner at the WTO" (2002) 5 *Journal of International Economic Law* 469–505; M.G. Bloche, "Introduction: Health and the WTO" (2002) 5 *Journal of International Economic Law* 821–23; M.G. Bloche, "WTO Deference to National Health Policy: Toward an Interpretive Principle" (2002) 5 *Journal of International Economic Law* 825–48; H. Grabowski, "Patents, Innovation and Access to New Pharmaceuticals" (2002) 5 *Journal of International Economic Law* 849–60; A.R. Chapman, "The Human Rights Implications of Intellectual Property Protection" (2002) 5 *Journal of International Economic Law* 861–82; P.J. Hammer,

But also with regard to the access to drugs the new RTAs including TRIPS plus elements are often criticised for introducing higher standards that undermine the balance agreed upon in the WTO.[297] For example, the intellectual property rules in the Central America Free Trade Agreement (CAFTA) provide pharmaceutical companies with monopoly protections that allow them to market some drugs without competition by less costly generics. A recent study examined availability of certain drugs in Guatemala and found that CAFTA intellectual property rules reduced access to some generic drugs already on the market and delayed new entry of other generics because Article 15:10 goes considerably beyond what the TRIPS Agreement provides in Article 39.3. Some drugs protected from competition in Guatemala will become open for generic competition in the United States before generic versions will be legally available in Guatemala.[298]

**12-060**   **WTO: TRIPS: AGREEMENT ON TRADE-RELATED ASPECTS OF INTELLECTUAL PROPERTY RIGHTS**

**PART II – Standards concerning the availability, scope and use of Intellectual Property Rights**

**SECTION 7: PROTECTION OF UNDISCLOSED INFORMATION**

*Article 39*

1. In the course of ensuring effective protection against unfair competition as provided in Article 10*bis* of the Paris Convention (1967), Members shall protect undisclosed information in accordance with paragraph 2 and data submitted to governments or governmental agencies in accordance with paragraph 3.

2. Natural and legal persons shall have the possibility of preventing information lawfully within their control from being disclosed

---

"Differential Pricing of Essential AIDS Drugs: Markets, Politics and Public Health" (2002) 5 *Journal of International Economic Law* 883–912; F.M. Scherer and J. Watal, "Post-TRIPS Options for Access to Patented Medicines in Developing Nations" (2002) 5 *Journal of International Economic Law* 913–39; H. Sun, "Reshaping the TRIPS Agreement Concerning Public Health: Two Critical Issues" (2003) 37 *Journal of World Trade* 163–97. G. Shaffer, "Recognizing Public Goods in WTO Dispute Settlement: Who Participates? Who Decides?: The Case of Trips and Pharmaceutical Patent Protection" (2004) 7 *Journal of International Economic Law* 459–82; H. Sun, "The Road to Doha and Byond—Some Reflections on the TRIPS Agreement and Public Health" (2004) E.J.I.L. 123 et seq.; H.P. Hestermeyer *Human Rights and the WTO: The Case of Patents and Access to Medicines* (Oxford University Press, 2007); M.T. Islam, "TRIPS Agreement and public health", *International Trade Law & Regulation*, 17 (2011) 1, 10–38 and B. Boidin, "L' accès des pays pauvres aux médicaments et la propriété intellectuelle", *Revue Internationale de Droit Économique*, 24 (2010) 3, 325–350.

[297] See B. Lindstrom, "Scaling back TRIPS-plus", *New York University: New York University Journal of International Law & Politics*, 42 (2010) 3, 917–980; M. Turk, "Bargaining and intellectual property treaties". *New York University: New York University Journal of International Law & Politics*, 42 (2010) 3, 981–1029; p. Frankel, "Challenging TRIPS-plus agreements", *Journal of International Economic Law*, 12 (2009) 4, 1023–1065; S.K. Sell, "TRIPS-Plus free trade agreements and access to medicines", *Liverpool Law Review*, 28 (2007) 1, 41–75.

[298] E.R. Shaffer and J. E, Brenner, A Trade Agreement's Impact On Access To Generic Drugs, *Health Aff,* September 2009, vol. 28 no. 5. 957–968.

to, acquired by, or used by others without their consent in a manner contrary to honest commercial practices (**10**) so long as such information:

(a) is secret in the sense that it is not, as a body or in the precise con-figuration and assembly of its components, generally known among or readily accessible to persons within the circles that normally deal with the kind of information in question;

(b) has commercial value because it is secret; and

(c) has been subject to reasonable steps under the circumstances, by the person lawfully in control of the information, to keep it secret.

3. Members, when requiring, as a condition of approving the marketing of pharmaceutical or of agricultural chemical products which utilize new chemical entities, the submission of undisclosed test or other data, the origination of which involves a considerable effort, shall protect such data against unfair commercial use. In addition, Members shall protect such data against disclosure, except where necessary to protect the public, or unless steps are taken to ensure that the data are protected against unfair commercial use.

**United States signed the Dominican Republic-Central America-United States Free Trade Agreement (CAFTA-DR), signed on 5 August 2004**

*Chapter Fifteen   Intellectual Property Rights*

*[. . .]*

*Article 15.10: Measures Related to Certain Regulated Products*

1. (a) If a Party requires, as a condition of approving the marketing of a new pharmaceutical or agricultural chemical product, the submis-sion of undisclosed data concerning safety or efficacy, the Party shall not permit third persons, without the consent of the person who provided the information, to market a product on the basis of (1) the information, or (2) the approval granted to the person who submitted the information for at least five years for pharmaceutical products and ten years for agricultural chemical products from the date of approval in the Party.15[299]

(b) If a Party permits, as a condition of approving the marketing of a new pharmaceutical or agricultural chemical product, third persons to submit evidence concerning the safety or efficacy of a product that was previously approved in another territory, such as evidence of prior marketing approval, the Party shall not permit third persons, without the consent of the person who previously obtained such approval in the other territory, to obtain authorization or to market a product on the basis of (1) evidence of prior marketing approval in the other territory, or (2) information concerning safety or efficacy

---

[299] Where a Party, on the date it implemented the TRIPS Agreement, had in place a system for protecting pharmaceutical or agricultural chemical products not involving new chemical entities from unfair commercial use that conferred a period of protection shorter than that specified in para.1, that Party may retain such system notwithstanding the obligations of para.1.

that was previously submitted to obtain marketing approval in the other territory, for at least five years for pharmaceutical products and ten years for agricultural chemical products from the date approval was granted in the Party's territory to the person who received approval in the other territory. In order to receive protection under this subparagraph, a Party may require that the person providing the information in the other territory seek approval in the territory of the Party within five years after obtaining marketing approval in the other territory.

(c) For purposes of this paragraph, a new product is one that does not contain a chemical entity that has been previously approved in the territory of the Party.

(d) For purposes of this paragraph, each Party shall protect such undisclosed information against disclosure except where necessary to protect the public, and no Party may consider information accessible within the public domain as undisclosed data. Notwithstanding the foregoing, if any undisclosed information concerning safety and efficacy submitted to a Party, or an entity acting on behalf of a Party, for purposes of obtaining marketing approval is disclosed by such entity, the Party is still required to protect such information from unfair commercial use in the manner set forth in this Article.

2. Where a Party permits, as a condition of approving the marketing of a pharmaceutical product, persons, other than the person originally submitting safety or efficacy information, to rely on evidence or information concerning the safety and efficacy of a product that was previously approved, such as evidence of prior marketing approval in the territory of a Party or in another country, that Party:

(a) shall implement measures in its marketing approval process to prevent such other persons from marketing a product covered by a patent claiming the previously approved product or its approved use during the term of that patent, unless by consent or acquiescence of the patent owner; and

(b) shall provide that the patent owner shall be informed of the request and the identity of any such other person who requests approval to enter the market during the term of a patent identified as claiming the approved product or its approved use.

12-061   Apart from the negotiation of more ambitious TRIPS plus elements in RTAs, a second tendency has been to negotiate multilateral solutions among "willing" States outside of the WTO—but also outside of WIPO. In particular, the negotiations of an Anti-Counterfeiting Trade Agreement (ACTA) between 2006 and 2010 led to important controversies on the systemic consequences of such an approach and the transparency and legitimacy of the approach chosen. The main objective of the negotiations was to strengthen enforcement measures regarding IPR infringements—an area where many developed States seem not satisfied with the level achieved in the WTO/

TRIPS[300]. Examples of additional or more restrictive rules can be found with regard to the use of the internet or transhipments (of generic drugs for example). Here there are important overlaps with the existing TRIPs regime and diverging interpretations on WTO members' obligations exist.[301]

The Anti-Counterfeiting Trade Agreement (ACTA) was opened for signature on May 1, 2011, following its adoption by participants in its negotiations on April 15, 2011.[302] On March 10, 2010, the European Parliament adopted a resolution[303] criticising the ACTA with 663 in favour of the resolution and 13 against, arguing that "in order to respect fundamental rights, such as the right to freedom of expression and the right to privacy" certain changes in the ACTA content and the process should be made. On June 23, 2010 a group of 90 academics released a public declaration regarding the proposed rules saying "that the terms of the publicly released draft of ACTA threaten numerous public interests, including every concern specifically disclaimed by negotiators."[304]

ANTI-COUNTERFEITING TRADE AGREEMENT (TEXT AS OPENED FOR SIGNATURE ON 15 APRIL 2011)    **12-062**

[. . .]

ARTICLE 16: BORDER MEASURES

1. Each Party shall adopt or maintain procedures with respect to import and export shipments under which:

   (a) its customs authorities may act upon their own initiative to suspend the release of suspect goods; and

   (b) where appropriate, a right holder may request its competent authorities to suspend the release of suspect goods.

---

[300] See H.G. Ruse-Khan, "From TRIPS to ACTA: Towards a New 'Gold Standard' in Criminal IP Enforcement?" (April 19, 2010); C. Geiger (ed.), *Criminal Enforcement of Intellectual Property: A Blessing or a Curse?*, Edward Elgar, 2010; Max Planck Institute for Intellectual Property, Competition & Tax Law Research Paper No. 10-06. Available at SSRN: *http://ssrn.com/abstract=1592104*. (Accessed June 8, 2011).

[301] See European Union and a Member State—Seizure of Generic Drugs in Transit (DS408 and DS 409) and S. P. Kumar, Border Enforcement of IP Rights Against in Transit Generic Pharmaceuticals: An Analysis of Character and Consistency (April 15, 2009), European Intellectual Property Review, Forthcoming. Available at SSRN: *http://ssrn.com/abstract=1383067*. (Accessed June 8, 2011).

[302] The text as made available online by the European Commission can be found at: *http://trade.ec.europa.eu/doclib/docs/2011/may/tradoc_147937.pdf*. (Accessed June 8, 2011).

[303] European Parliament Resolution of March 10, 2010 on the transparency and state of play of the ACTA negotiations, available online at: *http://www.europarl.europa.eu*. (Accessed June 8, 2011).

[304] Urgent ACTA Communique—International Experts Find that Pending Anti-Counterfeiting Trade Agreement Threatens Public Interests, June 23, 2010, American University Washington College of Law, Washington, D.C., available online at: *http://www.wcl.american.edu/pijip/go/acta-communique*. (Accessed June 8, 2011).

2. A Party may adopt or maintain procedures with respect to suspect in-transit goods or in other situations where the goods are under customs control under which:

   (a) its customs authorities may act upon their own initiative to suspend the release of, or to detain, suspect goods; and

   (b) where appropriate, a right holder may request its competent authorities to suspend the release of, or to detain, suspect goods.

### G8—STATEMENTS ON RESPONSIBLE LEADERSHIP FOR A SUSTAINABLE FUTURE: RESPONSIBLE LEADERSHIP FOR A SUSTAINABLE FUTURE – 2009 (L'AQUILA SUMMIT, JULY 8, 2009)

1. WE, THE LEADERS OF THE GROUP OF EIGHT MEETING IN L'AQUILA,. [. . .]

57. INNOVATION CAN BE PROMOTED VIA AN EFFECTIVE INTELLECTUAL PROPERTY RIGHTS SYSTEM. THE INCREASING USE OF IPR AT THE INTERNATIONAL LEVEL HAS MADE IP A KEY COMPONENT IN SECTORS AS DIVERSE AS TRADE, INDUSTRIAL POLICY, PUBLIC HEALTH, CONSUMER SAFETY, ENVIRONMENT PROTECTION AND THE INTERNET. WE ACKNOWLEDGE THE CENTRAL ROLE THAT THE WORLD INTELLECTUAL PROPERTY ORGANISATION (WIPO) PLAYS IN FOSTERING AN INTEGRAL VISION AND COHERENT DEVELOPMENT OF THE INTERNATIONAL IP SYSTEM. WE ALSO REAFFIRM THE IMPORTANCE OF PATENT COOPERATION TREATY AND GLOBAL PATENT HARMONISATION SUCH AS SUBSTANTIVE PATENT LAW TREATY (SPLT) AND ACKNOWLEDGE THE EXPANSION OF INTERNATIONAL PATENT COLLABORATION INCLUDING WORK-SHARING INITIATIVES SUCH AS THE PATENT PROSECUTION HIGHWAY.

58. COUNTERFEITING AND PIRACY CONTINUE TO POSE A THREAT TO THE GLOBAL ECONOMY, PUBLIC HEALTH AND WELFARE. FOR THIS REASON, WE WELCOME THE RESULTS OF WORK CARRIED OUT BY OUR EXPERTS, AS REFLECTED IN THE G8 INTELLECTUAL PROPERTY EXPERT GROUP REPORT OF DISCUSSION. WE STRESS THE IMPORTANCE OF ENHANCED, INCLUSIVE, AMBITIOUS INTERNATIONAL COOPERATION TO TACKLE COUNTERFEITING AND PIRACY. THE NEGOTIATIONS FOR THE ANTI-COUNTERFEITING TRADE AGREEMENT (ACTA), WHICH THE PARTICIPANTS SHOULD SEEK TO AGREE AS SOON AS POSSIBLE, REPRESENT AN IMPORTANT OPPORTUNITY TO STRENGTHEN STANDARDS FOR ENFORCEMENT OF IPR. WITH THE SAME AIM, WE WILL CONTINUE STRENGTHENING BILATERAL AND MULTILATERAL COOPERATION AMONG CUSTOMS AUTHORITIES THROUGH INFO IPR AND INFORMATION EXCHANGE CONSIDERING THE MODEL ARRANGEMENT AND CAPACITY BUILDING AT THE WORLD CUSTOMS ORGANISATION (WCO). MOREOVER, WE ENCOURAGE GOVERNMENTS AND BUSINESSES TO PARTICIPATE IN THE ONGOING WORK OF THE OECD AS IT EXAMINES FURTHER THE ECONOMIC IMPACTS OF COUNTERFEITING AND PIRACY IN PHASE III OF ITS STUDY.

### THE CHALLENGES AHEAD

**12-063**   There is no doubt the WTO code will expand. It will do so because there is a built-in agenda for further negotiations in a number of the Uruguay Round

Multilateral Trade Agreements. It will do so because of the pressure for inclusion of certain trade-related issues.[305] It will do so because of the need to accommodate to technological changes that confront the international trading system, for example electronic commerce.[306] And finally it will do so to keep abreast with innovations in trade barriers that emerge. In this normative growth the WTO needs to take particular care that its members can keep pace with its changes, and that there is symmetry in the interests of its members that it responds to.

At the same time, the recent years have shown that the achievements of the Uruguay Round were so comprehensive that it took considerable time for members to make the necessary adjustments in their domestic systems: Considerable tensions arose from the implementation of specific areas. The controversies especially relating to the adjustments to the TRIPS Agreement (e.g. access to medicine) or to the new textile regime (combined with China's accession to the WTO) show that ambitious liberalisation goals put the system under strain. The inclusion of new areas (investment, competition, etc.) becomes therefore even more difficult, especially where compensation opportunities in traditional areas (market access for agricultural goods, opening of the services markets including mode 4) are missing due to domestic resistance.[307]

There are even voices who argue that more use should be made of variable geometry; i.e. allowing certain Member States to conclude new agreements not necessarily binding all members. This could be done through new plurilateral agreements outside the single undertaking of the WTO.[308]

---

[305] For example, Trade and Environment; Trade and Investment; and Competition and Trade. See the work of the WTO Working Parties in each of these spheres and the literature quoted in the respective sections of this Chapter.

[306] See, for example, WTO Report Electronic Commerce and the Role of the WTO (1998). See A.D. Mitchell, "Towards compatibility: the future of electronic commerce within the global trading system", *Journal of International Economic Law*, 4 (2001) 4, 683–723.

[307] See also Ch.15 on this point as well as S. Chaudhuri, A. Mattoo and R. Self, "Moving People to Deliver Services: How Can the WTO Help?" (2004) 38 *Journal of World Trade* 363–93.

[308] See T. Cottier, "From Progressive Liberalization to Progressive Regulation in WTO Law" (2006) 9 *Journal of International Economic Law* 779–821; R.Z. Lawrence, "Rulemaking Amidst Growing Diversity: A Club-of-Clubs Approach to WTO Reform and New Issue Selection" (2006) 9 *Journal of International Economic Law* 823–35; C. VanGrasstek and P. Sauvé, "The Consistency of WTO Rules: Can the Single Undertaking Be Squared with Variable Geometry?" (2006) 9 *Journal of International Economic Law* 837–64; F. Pagani, "Are Plurilateral Trade Agreements Possible Outside of the World Trade Organization?" (2006) 40 *Journal of World Trade* 797–812.

CHAPTER 13

# INTERNATIONAL TRADE LAW: ENFORCEMENT

## INTRODUCTION

In International Institutional Law[1] enforcement has a wide meaning so    **13-001**
as to embrace all manner of techniques that facilitate implementation.[2]
Essentially, the techniques are concerned with the realisation of the application of the WTO code at the international level.[3] They include techniques
that pre-empt non-compliance as well as those which correct non-compliance.
There are a variety of techniques through which the WTO code of conduct
is and can be implemented.[4] However, in accordance with the practice
generally of international economic organisations, there are two principal
methods of ensuring implementation, which are particularly institutionalised in the WTO framework, and are of note. These comprise of the WTO
Dispute Settlement (DS) Mechanism and the WTO Trade Policy Review
Mechanism (TPRM); the former embracing surveillance and supervision
techniques and the later conflict resolution mechanisms.

---

[1] This updated chapter is based on work published originally in A.H. Qureshi, *The World Trade
Organization: Implementing International Trade Norms* (Manchester: Manchester University
Press, 1996).

[2] See, for example, H.G. Schermers, *International Institutional Law*, 3rd edn (1995), p.684 (see
also 4th edn, Martinus Nijhoff); P. Sands and P. Klein, *Bowett's Law of international institutions*, (London, Sweet & Maxwell, 2009).

[3] See Ch.4 for the (limited) role of domestic courts in the application of WTO law. See also
T. Cottier and K.N. Schefer, "The relationship between World Trade Organization law,
national and regional law" (1988) 1 *Journal of International Economic Law* 83–122 and
M. Schaefer, "Are private remedies in domestic courts essential for international trade
agreements to perform constitutional functions with respect to sub-federal governments?"
*Northwestern Journal of International Law & [and] Business*, 17 (1996/97) 2/3, 609–652.
The WTO Agreement as such does not require direct effect of its provisions at the domestic
level, see also US—Section 301–310 of the Trade Act of 1974, WT/DS152/R, Panel Report
adopted on December 22, 1999, Section 7.72.

[4] See, for example, Qureshi (1996), Ch.3.

## Dispute Settlement

**13-002**   One of the most significant of achievements in the institutional field arising from the results of the Uruguay Round has been the establishment of a sophisticated dispute settlement mechanism under the framework of the WTO.[5] Although, the WTO dispute settlement machinery is in many respects

---

[5] P. Pescatore, W. Davey et al. (eds), *Handbook of GATT Dispute Settlement* (Transnational Juris Publications, 1991/1995); A. Bogdandy, "The non-violation procedure of Article XXIII:2, GATT" (1992) J.W.T. 95–111; P. Pescatore, "The GATT Dispute Settlement Mechanism" (1993); J.W.T.; R. Hudec, *Enforcing International Trade Law* (Butterworths, 1993); R. Hudec et al., "A statistical profile of GATT Dispute Settlement Cases: 1948–1989" (1993) 2 *Minnesota Journal of Global Trade* 1–113; P.T.B. Kohona, "Dispute Resolution under the World Trade Organization. An overview" (1994) (28) (2) J.W.T. 23–47; E.U. Petersmann, "The Dispute Settlement System of the World Trade Organization and Evolution of the GATT Dispute Settlement System Since 1948" (1994) 31 *Common Market Law Review* 1157–1244; N. Komuro, "The WTO Dispute Settlement Mechanism" (1995) 29(2) J.W.T. 5–95; E. Vermulst and B. Driessen, "An overview of the WTO dispute settlement system and its relationship with the Uruguay Agreements" (1995) 29(2) J.W.T. 131–61; M. Lucas, "The role of private parties in the enforcement of the Uruguay Round Agreements" (1995) 29(5) J.W.T. 181–206; D.M. Schwarz, "WTO Dispute Resolution Panels: Failing to protect against conflicts of interest" (1995) 10(2) *AM.U.J.Int'L.L & Policy* 955–995; J. Bello, et al., "GATT Dispute Settlement Agreement: Internationalisation or elimination of Section 301" (1995) 26(3) *The International Lawyer* 795–802; C. Reitz, "Enforcement of the General Agreement on Tariffs and Trade" (1996) 17(2) *University of Pennsylvania Journal of International Economic Law* 555–603; S. Croley and J. Jackson, "WTO dispute procedures, standard of review, and deference to national governments" (1996) 90(2) A.J.I.L. 193–213; E-U Petersmann, *The GATT/WTO Dispute Settlement System. International Law, International Organization and Dispute Settlement* (Kluwer Law International, 1996); C. Thomas, "Litigation process under the GATT Dispute Settlement System—Lessons for the World Trade Organization ?" (1996) 30(2) J.W.T. 53–81; R.S.J. Martha, "World Trade Disputes Settlement and The Exhaustion Of Local Remedies" (1996) 30(4) J.W.T. 107–130; J.H. Bello, "The WTO Dispute Settlement Understanding: less is more" (1996) 90(3) A.J.I.L. 416–418; R.S.J. Martha, "Presumptions and burden of proof in world trade law" (1997) 14(1) J.W.T. 67–98; L. Wang "Are trade disputes fairly settled?" (1997) 1 J.W.T. 59–72; J. Jackson, *The World Trade Organization. Constitution and Jurisprudence* (RIIA, 1998), Ch.4; J. Jackson, "Dispute Settlement and the WTO.Emerging Problems" (1998) 1(3) *Journal of International Economic Law* 329–351; S. Cho, "GATT non-violation issues in the WTO framework:are they the Achilles' Heel of the dispute settlement process?" (1998) 39(2) *Harvard International Law Journal* 311–55; E-U Petersmann, "From the Hobbesian International Law of Coexistence to Modern Integration Law: The WTO Dispute Settlement System" (1998) 1(2) *Journal of International Economic Law* 175–198; A. Chua, "Reasonable expectations and non-violation complaints in GATT/ WTO jurisprudence" (1998) J.W.T. 27–50; A. Chua, "The precedential effect of WTO Panel and Appellate Reports" (1998) II(1) *Leiden Journal of International Law* 45–61; R. Bhala, "The power of the Past: Towards De Jure Stare Decisis in WTO Adjudication" (Trilogy) (2001) *George Washington International Law Review* 873–978; T.J. Schoenbaum, "WTO dispute settlement: praise and suggestions for reform" (1998) 47 I.C.L.Q. 647–658; R. Behboodi "Legal reasoning and the international law of trade" (1998) J.W.T. 55–99; D.P. Steger and S.M. Hainsworth, "World Trade Organization Dispute Settlement: The first three years" (1998) 1(2) *Journal of International Economic Law* 199–226; Y. Iwasawa, "WTO Dispute Settlement as Judicial Supervision" (2002) 5 *Journal of International Economic Law* 287–305; C. Carmody, "Remedies and Conformity under the *WTO Agreement*" (2002) 5 *J. Int. Economic Law* 307–29; F. Ortino and E-U Petersmann, "*The WTO Dispute Settlement System 1995–2003*" (Kluwer Law International, 2004); W.J. Davey, "The WTO Dispute Settlement System: The First Ten Years" (2005) 8 *Journal of International Economic Law* 17–50; R. Yerxa and B. Wilson, "*Key Issues in WTO Dispute Settlement The First Ten Years*"

really a reorganisation of the previous GATT dispute settlement machinery, it is nevertheless sufficiently innovative as to be distinguished from it. The previous regime was characterised by delays, fragmentation of dispute settlement mechanisms, blocking of adoption by the GATT Contracting Parties of decisions by dispute settlement panels, and the non-availability of an appellate system. The contribution of the WTO dispute settlement machinery to the international trade system is amply demonstrated by the number of successfully resolved trade disputes that have taken place since its establishment, involving both developed and developing members. Amongst its key features are its near-automatic jurisdiction over trade disputes, its efficient and well-developed adjudicatory and appellate system, and generally its rule-orientated approach.

The dispute settlement machinery provides for security and predictability in the trading system.[6] This it does mainly in the following manner. First, it preserves the rights and obligations of the members as stated in the WTO code. This objective is reinforced by the express stipulation that the recommendations and rulings arising from the conflict resolution mechanisms cannot add or diminish the rights and obligations agreed by the members under the code.[7] Secondly, it facilitates clarification of the provisions of the WTO code in an orderly fashion in accordance with the rules of interpretation under customary international law.[8] Finally, it provides that members are not to make determinations of violations under the WTO code, except through recourse to the mechanisms under the Understanding.[9] This is a measure which brings the use of unilateral measures deployed by States, such as s.301 of the US trade law, under the framework of the Understanding. It is clearly stipulated that the WTO authorisation must be sought before the suspension of trade concessions or other obligations (trade sanctions).[10]

---

(Cambridge, Cambridge University Press, 2005); M.T. Grando, "Allocating the Burden of Proof in WTO Disputes: A Critical Analysis" (2006) 9 *Journal of International Economic Law* 615–56; G. Sacerdoti, A. Yanovich and J. Bohanes et al., *The WTO at Ten: The Contribution of the Dispute Settlement System* (Cambridge, Cambridge University Press, 2006); J. Gomula, "Precedential effect of WTO decisions" *The Global Community*, (2008) 1, 295–318.

[6] Art.3 of the Understanding on Rules And Procedures Governing the Settlement of Disputes in GATT. The Results of the Uruguay Round of Multilateral Trade Negotiations (1994) (hereinafter referred to as the Understanding).

[7] Art.3 of the Understanding.

[8] Art.3 of the Understanding.

[9] Art.23(2)(a) of the Understanding.

[10] See United States—ss. 301–310 of the Trade Act of 1974 AB Report adopted January 27, 2000; United States—Import Measures on Certain Products from the European Communities, AB Report adopted on January 10, 2001; on this issue also B.P. McGivern and C.M. Walles, "The Right to Retaliate under the WTO Agreement" (2000) 34 *Journal of World Trade* 63–84 and H. Spamann, "The Myth of 'Rebalancing' Retaliation in WTO Dispute Settlement Practice" (2006) 9 *Journal of International Economic Law* 31–79; M. Putra Iqbal, "Preventing retaliation in trade by harmonizing the SPS measures", *Jurnal Hukum Internasional Indonesian Journal of International Law*, 7(2010) 2, 215–241; B. Mercurio, "Why compensation cannot replace trade retaliation in the WTO Dispute Settlement Understanding", *World Trade Review*, 8 (2009) 2, 315–338; R. Malacrida, "Towards sounder and fairer WTO retaliation", *Journal of World Trade*, 42 (2008) 1, 3–60.

### The dispute settlement framework

**13-003**    The WTO dispute settlement framework is set out principally in the Understanding on Rules and Procedures Governing The Settlement of Disputes (DSU; the Understanding), Annex 2 to the WTO Agreement.[11] The Understanding is intended to be a comprehensive framework for conflict resolution in the field of international trade under the auspices of the WTO. As such it provides for a variety of mechanisms for the resolution of trade disputes between Member States. Further, the Understanding establishes a single integrated structure for conflict resolution in relation to the various trade agreements under the Uruguay Round—including trade in services and intellectual property rights.

A Dispute Settlement Body (DSB) has been established to administer the rules and procedures under the Understanding.[12] The DSB and the General Council are essentially coterminous, but acting in different capacities. The DSB may, however, have its own chairman, and may have different rules of procedures. The General Council is to meet as appropriate in order to discharge the functions of the DSB according to the Understanding.[13] The DSB is responsible for the administration of the dispute settlement rules and procedures under the Understanding.[14] The administrative charge of the DSB includes important decision making functions. Thus, the DSB is empowered to establish panels, adopt panel and appellate body reports, authorise the use by members of sanctions, and monitor the implementation of rulings and recommendations.

The WTO provides ample information on the disputes that have been tackled under the dispute settlement mechanisms. On its website, the WTO has established a "Dispute settlement gateway". It allows to search for cases according to various criteria (complainant, respondent, topic, articles of the agreements concerned, etc.). The cases under the GATT 1947 (until 1994) are also available.[15] For all cases there are summaries and for important cases the Secretariat provides one-page summaries of key findings of the AB in the respective dispute which is especially useful for long reports.

**13-004**    In addition, the WTO Appellate Body has established a "Repertory of Reports and Awards 1995–2005". It was initially developed as an internal research tool to assist the Appellate Body Secretariat in carrying out its duty to provide legal support to Appellate Body Members. It allows to search

---

[11] See Arts XXII and XXIII of GATT 1994; and the Understanding. See also in conjunction with the Understanding, Rules of Conduct For The Understanding On Rules And Procedures Governing The Settlement of Disputes WT/DSB/RC/W/1 (November 1996); and Working Procedures For Appellate Review, WT/AB/WP/3 (February 1997).

[12] Art.2 of the Understanding.

[13] Art.IV(3) of the Marrakesh Agreement Establishing the World Trade Organization (hereinafter referred to as the Marrakesh Agreement).

[14] Art.2 of the Understanding.

[15] *http://www.wto.org/english/tratop_e/dispu_e/dispu_e.htm.* (Accessed June 8, 2011).

for specific subjects and to find references to the relevant paragraphs of the reports.[16] A more recent version (1995–2010) exists in print.[17]

Furthermore, the "WTO Analytical Index—Guide to WTO Law and Practice" is the authoritative guide to the interpretation and application of findings and decisions of WTO panels, the WTO Appellate Body and other WTO bodies. It contains all the relevant references for each single article of all the agreements. A convenient and concise way to get an overview over the finding in all disputes that have led to Panel and/or Appellate Body Reports is a collection regularly published by the WTO Secretariat entitled "WTO Dispute Settlement: One-Page Case Summaries 1995–Sept 2009".[18]

"WorldTradeLaw.net" is a commercial service (but available at most universities). It provides, inter alia, a Dispute Settlement Commentary (DSC) service—a comprehensive legal research tool for WTO dispute settlement. Features include summary and analysis of all reports and arbitrations; up-to-date keyword index; and a database of dispute settlement tables and statistics.[19] A comprehensive updated statistical review of all WTO dispute settlement cases by the same authors is published once a year in the Journal of International Economic Law (JIEL).[20]

The "Integrated Database of Trade Disputes for Latin America and the **13-005** Caribbean" is a service run by the Economic Commission for Latin America and the Caribbean (ECLAC).[21] It contains ample information on WTO disputes involving countries from that region, but also under regional agreements like Mercosur, NAFTA, the Andean community etc.

There are normally annual reviews of the case law of the WTO Appellate Body (and other regional trade regimes) in specialised journals, such as the *Journal of International Economic Law* (J.I.E.L.), and publications commenting specifically on the case law.[22]

Finally, it is now easier to find cases where domestic courts address international trade law—although these cases remain scarce for the reasons described earlier.[23] A database on "International Law in Domestic Courts"—a commercial service—also contains cases from domestic jurisdictions (normally of last resort) making reference to the WTO and RTAs.[24]

---

[16] *http://www.wto.org/english/tratop_e/dispu_e/repertory_e/repertory_e.htm.* (Accessed June 8, 2011).

[17] WTO Appellate Body, Repertory of Reports and Awards 1995–2010, 4th edn, Geneva, WTO.

[18] WTO, WTO Dispute Settlement: One-Page Case Summaries 1995–2009 (2010 edn), Geneva, 2010, also online at *http://www.wto.org.* (Accessed June 8, 2011).

[19] *http://www.worldtradelaw.net/.* Accessed June 8, 2011.

[20] For 2006 K. Leitner and S. Lester, "WTO Dispute Settlement 1995–2006—A Statistical Analysis" (2007) 10 *Journal of International Economic Law* p. 165–79.

[21] *http://idatd.eclac.cl/controversias/index_en.jsp.* (Accessed June 8, 2011).

[22] In particular: B. Stern, Ruiz Fabri (eds), *La jurisprudence de l'OMC/The Case Law of the WTO* (The Hague, Martinus Nijhoff Publishers, several volumes starting in 2004), several volumes; and H. Horn and P. Mavroidis (eds), *The WTO Case Law of. . .* (annually; several volumes, Cambridge, Cambridge University Press, several volumes starting 2003).

[23] See Ch.4.

[24] See *http://www.oxfordlawreports.com/About#aboutildc.* (Accessed June 8, 2011).

### Access to dispute settlement procedures

**13-006**Access under the dispute settlement framework is available only to members of the WTO.[25] Private parties cannot be directly involved in instigating proceedings at the WTO. The obligations imposed under the WTO code apply to Member States. However, private parties can request their respective governments to initiate a complaint.[26] Thus, there are an important number of WTO disputes where the underlying interests of specific companies are clearly known.[27] The WTO code does not appear to provide for national mechanisms, for example judicial review, at the disposal of private parties, to facilitate the scrutiny of governmental decisions in this respect. The decision whether or not to bring proceedings against another member is a matter pertaining to a member's foreign trade policy. A government may not bring proceedings for a variety of reasons.[28] First, it may consider it not in its general interest to bring proceedings in the light of the relations it wants to cultivate with the offending Member State. Secondly, the Government may not want a clear ruling because it may be engaging in similar conduct in a different context. Thirdly, the particular private interests may not have sufficient leverage over governmental discretion.[29] At the same time, WTO members do not have to show a specific legal interest in asking for consultation under the WTO.[30]

As the WTO practice currently stands there is no requirement for the exhaustion of local remedies before proceedings are brought at the WTO.[31] However, a number of commentators had originally advocated the exhaustion of local remedies rule despite that ruling.[32] This they have done mainly

[25] See, for example, P. Grané, "Remedies Under WTO Law" (2001) 4 *Journal of International Economic Law,* p.755–72.
[26] Panel Discussion moderated by P.C. Mavroidis published in "Is the WTO Dispute Settlement Mechanism Responsive to the Needs of the Traders? Would a system of direct action by private parties yield a better result?" (1998) J.W.T. 147–165 and F.A.S. Albashar, "Reforming the WTO dispute settlement system", *The Journal of World Investment & Trade,* 11(2010) 3, 311–373.
[27] See, for example, Japan—Measure affecting Consumer Photographic Film and Paper, Panel Report adopted on April 22, 1998, WT/DS44/R also known as the Kodak–Fuji case with reference to the two competing companies involved.
[28] See W. Davey in "Is the WTO Dispute Settlement Mechanism Responsive to the Needs of the Traders? Would a system of direct action by private parties yield a better result?" (1998) J.W.T. 147–165 and F.A.S. Albashar, "Reforming the WTO dispute settlement system", *The Journal of World Investment & Trade,* 11 (2010) 3, 311–373.
[29] See W. Davey in "Is the WTO Dispute Settlement Mechanism Responsive to the Needs of the Traders? Would a system of direct action by private parties yield a better result?" (1998) J.W.T. 147–165.
[30] See European Communities—Regime for the Importation, Sale and Distribution of Bananas, WT/DS27/AB/R, Report of the AB adopted on September 25, 1997, paras 132–36.
[31] This was decided in a GATT Panel Report. See United States—Anti-Dumping on Gray Portland Cement and Cement Clinker from Mexico GATT, Doc.ADP/82, 72. The issue is of particular relevance in the context of diplomatic protection and investment law, see Ch.14.
[32] See, for example, R.S.J. Martha, "World Trade Disputes Settlement and the Exhaustion of Local Remedies" (1996) 30(4) J.W.T. 107–130; E-U Petersmann, "The dispute settlement system of the World Trade Organization and the evolution of the GATT dispute settlement

on the following grounds. First, a number of the Uruguay Round agreements are concerned with private rights, e.g. intellectual property rights. Secondly, a number of the agreements provide for judicial review procedures domestically. Finally, given that the exhaustion of local remedies rules is a rule of customary International Law, it has bearing in the process of interpretation of the WTO code. According to a customary International Law rule of treaty interpretation account is to be taken of any relevant rules of International Law applicable in the relations between the parties.[33]

Members can be represented by private lawyers in panel[34] and appellate proceedings.[35] However, the private lawyers can only appear as part of the member's delegation. They must be responsible to the Government they are representing, and respect the confidentiality of the proceedings.[36] The assistance of private counsel is a generally accepted practice[37] insofar as seeking legal advice and involvement in written proceedings are concerned. The involvement of private lawyers has been allowed particularly to facilitate full participation in dispute settlement proceedings by developing members; and to reinforce the Appellate Body's mandate to focus on questions of law or legal interpretation arising in panel reports.[38] Mention should also be made of the Advisory Centre on WTO Law (ACWL), an intergovernmental organisation (independent from the WTO) set up in 2001 in Geneva by certain WTO members to provide legal advice on WTO law, support in WTO dispute settlement proceedings and training in WTO law to developing countries, in particular to least developed among them (LDCs), and to customs territories and countries with economies in transition.[39]

As private parties in general, NGOs cannot bring proceedings at the

---

system since 1948" (1994) CML.Rev. 1157–1244; K.C: Kennedy, "Parallel proceedings at the WTO and under NAFTA" 19, *The George Washington International Law Review*, 39 (2007) 1, 47–87.

[33] See Art.31 of the Vienna Convention on the Law of Treaties 1969. See also G. Marceau, "Conflicts of Norms and Conflicts of Jurisdictions The Relationship between the WTO Agreement and MEAs and other Treaties" (2001) 35 J.W.T. 1081–1131; L. Bartels, "Applicable Law in WTO Dispute Settlement Proceedings" (2001) 35 J.W.T. 499–519 and Joost Pauwelyn, *Conflict of Norms in Public International Law* (Cambridge, Cambridge University Press, 2003) and K.C: Kennedy, "Parallel proceedings at the WTO and under NAFTA chapter 19", *The George Washington International Law Review*, 39 (2007) 1, 47–87.

[34] See Korea—Taxes on Alcoholic Beverages. Panel Report (1998).

[35] See European Communities—Regime for the Importation, Sale and Distribution of Bananas. Report of the Appellate Body (1997). See also R.S.J. Martha, "Representation of Parties in World Trade Disputes" (1997) 31 J.W.T. 84–86. See also D.W. Layton, J.O. Miranda, "Advocacy before World Trade Organization Dispute Settlement Panels in Trade Remedy Cases" (2003) 37 J.W.T. 69–103.

[36] See Korea—Taxes on Alcoholic Beverages. Panel Report (1998).

[37] See European Communities—Regime for the Importation, Sale and Distribution of Bananas. Report of the Appellate Body (1997). See also R.S.J. Martha, "Representation of Parties in World Trade Disputes" (1997) 31 J.W.T. 84–96.

[38] See European Communities—Regime for the Importation, Sale and Distribution of Bananas. Report of the Appellate Body (1997).

[39] K. Van der Borght, "The advisory center on the WTO law: advancing fairness and equality" (1999) 2 *Journal of International Economic Law* 723–28.

WTO.[40] They can, however, make submissions in disputes between members. The submissions of NGO's can be adopted as part of a member's submissions, or can be directly placed in dispute settlement proceedings (e.g. amicus curiae briefs).[41] Third countries can act similarly.[42] In the latter case it is for the dispute settlement panel to decide whether or not to accept the submission.[43]

### Jurisdiction

**13-007**  The jurisdiction of the DSB, under the institutional framework of the WTO, extends to the whole of the WTO code.[44] Thus, the remit of the DSB includes trade in goods, services and intellectual property rights, and is generally coterminous with the GATT 1994. Additionally, the DSB is also the forum for the settlement of disputes arising from the Agreement Establishing the WTO, and the Understanding itself. Thus, all disputes as between members, or as between members and the WTO, appear to have been internalised, i.e. subject to the provisions of the Understanding. Recourse to the International Court of Justice does not appear to be contemplated, even where a question of interpretation of the multilateral trade agreements is involved.[45] However, there remain many questions relating to the exact relationship between the WTO dispute settlement system and recourse to bilateral mechanisms contained in regional trade agreements such as NAFTA.[46]

---

[40]  See Ch.11 on the role of civil society and NGOs in the WTO system in general. United States—Import Prohibition Of Certain Shrimp And Shrimp Products, Report of the Appellate Body (1998). See also, for example, p. Charnovitz, "Participation of non-governmental organizations in the WTO" (1996) 17(1) *University of Pennsylvania Journal of International Economic Law* 331–357; and D.C. Esty, "Non-governmental organizations at the World Trade Organization: Cooperation, Competition, or Exclusion" (1998) 1 *Journal of International Economic Law* 123–147.

[41]  See A.E. Appleton, "*Amicus curiae* submissions in the *Carbon Steel* case: another rabbit from the appellate body's hat?" (2000) 3 *Journal of International Economic Law* 691–99; "Issues of *Amicus curiae* submissions: note by the editors" (2000) 3 *Journal of International Economic Law* 701–06; G. Marceau and M. Stilwell, "Practical suggestions for *amicus curiae* briefs before WTO adjudicating bodies" (2001) *Journal of International Economic Law* 155–87; G.C. Umbricht, "An 'Amicus Curiae Brief' on Amicus Curiae Briefs at the WTO" (2001) 4 *Journal of International Economic Law* 773–94; G.A. Zonnekeyn, "The Appellate Body's Communication on Amicus Curiae Briefs in the Asbestos Case. An Echternach Procession?" (2001) 35 J.W.T. 553–63 and Y. Fukunaga, "Participation of private parties in the WTO dispute settlement processes", *Soochow Law Journal*, 4 (2007) 1, 99–130.

[42]  Morocco submitted an *amicus curia* brief in European Communities—Trade Description of Sardines, AB Report adopted on October 23, 2002.

[43]  See Art.13 of the Understanding; and United States—Import Prohibition Of Certain Shrimp And Shrimp Products, Report of the Appellate Body (1998).

[44]  Art.1 of the Understanding. Appendix 1 of The Understanding adumbrates the agreements covered. These are stated to include the following: Agreement Establishing the WTO; Multilateral Trade Agreements; and the Plurilateral Trade Agreements.

[45]  See Art.IX(2) of the Marrakesh Agreement.

[46]  See M. Matsushita below. An important precedent is the dispute between the United States on the alleged subsidisation of exports of softwood lumber which led to proceedings under both NAFTA and the WTO. In order to avoid conflict, on September 12, 2006, the Government of Canada and the Government of the United States of America signed the

The jurisdiction of the DSB is, however, limited in some important respects. First, the rules and procedures under the Understanding are subject to any special provisions in relation to dispute settlement in the various covered Uruguay Round trade agreements.[47] Secondly, the DSB is not empowered to adopt in abstract interpretations of the multilateral trade agreements or the Agreement Establishing the WTO. This function is reserved for the exclusive authority of the Ministerial Conference and the General Council.[48] Thus, the aim of the dispute settlement process is to settle disputes. The process is not intended to clarify the law outside the context of the dispute.[49] Thirdly, where a measure is no longer in force at the time of the dispute proceedings, a panel may well not consider the compatibility of the measure with the WTO code.[50] At the same time, the Appellate Body found that an unwritten rule or norm can be challenged as a measure of general and prospective application in WTO dispute settlement. It emphasised, however, that particular rigour is required on the part of a panel to support a conclusion as to the existence of such a "rule or norm" that is not expressed in the form of a written document. A complaining party must establish, through sufficient evidence, at least (i) that the alleged "rule or norm" is attributable to the responding Member; (ii) its precise content; and (iii) that it does have "general and prospective" application.[51] Fourthly, dispute proceedings may not relate to claims by a member not stated in the terms of reference of the dispute.[52]

Finally, the DSB is reliant considerably on the consent and willingness of the parties, particularly in ensuring the implementation of its determinations

Softwood Lumber Agreement, which entered into force, as amended, on October 12, 2006. See also William A. Kerr, "Greener Multilateral Pastures for Canada and Mexico Dispute Settlement in the North American Trade Agreements" (2001) 35 *Journal of World Trade* 1169–80; 41. M. Matsushita, "Governance of International Trade under WTO Agreements: Relationships between WTO Agreements and other Trade Agreements" (2004) 2 *Journal of World Trade* 185–210; G. Verhoosel, "The Use of Investor–State Arbitration under Bilateral Investment Treaties to Seek Relief for Breaches of WTO Law" (2003) 6 *Journal of International Economic Law* 493–506 and J. Pauwelyn, "Editorial Comment: Adding Sweeteners to Softwood Lumber: the WTO–NAFTA 'Spaghetti Bowl' is Cooking" (2006) 9 *Journal of International Economic Law* 197–206; M. L. Busch, "Overlapping institutions, forum shopping, and dispute settlement in international trade", *International Organization*, 61 (2007) 4, 735–761K.C: Kennedy, "Parallel proceedings at the WTO and under NAFTA chapter 19", *The George Washington International Law Review*, 39 (2007) 1, 47–87; F. Piérola "WTO dispute settlement and dispute settlement in the "North-South" Agreements of the Americas", *Journal of World Trade*, 41 (2007) 5, 885–908.

[47] See Art.1(2) and Appendix 2 of the Understanding.

[48] Art. IX of the Marrakesh Agreement.

[49] See Art.3.4 of the Understanding; and United States—Measures Affecting Imports of Woven Wool Shirts and Blouses from India.Report of the Appellate Body (1997).

[50] See Argentina—Measures Affecting Imports of Footwear, Textiles, Apparel and Other Items. Report of the Panel (1997). However, on several occasions panels have considered national measures that are no longer in force but this has not been the normal practice.

[51] United States—Laws, Regulations and Methodology for Calculating Dumping Margins ("Zeroing"), Report of the Apppellate Body of May 9, 2006.

[52] India—Patent Protection For Pharmaceutical And Agricultural Chemical Products. Report of the Appellate Body (1997).

(compliance phase).[53] Thus, the DSB in the final analysis ensures enforcement essentially through authorisation of retaliatory measures by the aggrieved member. In the same vein, the DSB itself cannot initiate complaints on behalf of the WTO. The DSB comprises an administrative structure for the dispute settlement framework. It is not a prosecuting authority.

### Interpretation

13-008  The process of interpretation[54] is to be in accordance with customary rules of interpretation of public International Law, as set out in Arts 31 to 32 of the Vienna Convention on the Law of Treaties.[55] This has been reiterated and followed on the whole in a number of WTO Appellate Reports.[56] The use of preparatory work however has been resorted to somewhat liberally, despite the fact that its use is limited under Art.32 of the Vienna Convention on the Law of Treaties.[57]

---

[53] See J.E. Kearns and S. Charnovitz, "Adjudicating Compliance in the WTO: A Review of DSU Article 21.5" (2002) 5 *Journal of International Economic Law* 331–52; Y. Fukunaga, "Securing Compliance Through the WTO Dispute Settlement System: Implementation of DSB Recommendations" (2006) 9 *Journal of International Economic Law* 383–426; Br. Wilson, "Compliance by WTO Members with Adverse WTO Dispute Settlement Rulings: The Record to Date" (2007) 10 *Journal of International Economic Law* 397–40; W. J. Davey, "Compliance Problems in WTO Dispute Settlement", *Cornell International Law Journal*, 42 (2009) 1, 119–1283.

[54] See above Ch.11. See also J. Pauwelyn, *Conflict of Norms in Public International Law* (Cambridge, Combridge University Press, 2003); A.H. Qureshi, *Interpreting WTO Agreements: Problems and Perspectives* (Cambridge, Cambridge University Press, 2006);. See also M.M. Slotboom, "Do Different Treaty Purposes Matter for Treaty Interpretation?: The Elimination of Discriminatory Internal Taxes in EC and WTO Law" (2001) 4 *Journal of International Economic Law* 557–79; M. Lennard, "Navigating by the Stars: Interpreting the WTO Agreements" (2002) 5 *Journal of International Economic Law* 17–89; N.P. Meagher, "The Sound of Silence: Giving Meaning to Omissions in Provisions of World Trade Organization Agreements—*A Note on the World Trade Organization Appellate Body Decision in* United States—Countervailing Duties on Certain Corrosion-Resistant Carbon Steel Flat Products from Germany" (2003) 37 *Journal of World Trade* 417–27; F. Ortino, "Treaty Interpretation and the WTO Appellate Body Report in *US—Gambling*: A Critique" (2006) 9 *Journal of International Economic Law* 117–48; M. Panizzon *Good Faith in the Jurisprudence of the WTO* (Hart Publishing, 2006); I. Van Damme *Treaty Interpretation by the WTO Appellate Body*. (Oxford [u.a.], Oxford Univ. Press, 2009); G. Abi-Saab, "The Appellate Body and treaty interpretation", *Treaty interpretation and the Vienna Convention on the Law of Treaties*, (2010), 99–109; and I. Van Damme, "Treaty interpretation by the WTO Appellate Body", *European Journal of International Law*, 21 (2010), 3, 605–648.

[55] Art.3 of the Understanding. See Art.31–32 of the Vienna Convention On the Law of Treaties 1969. See also for example, United States—Standards for Reformulated and Conventional Gasoline. Report of the Appellate Body (1996); and Japan—Taxes on Alcoholic Beverages. Report of the Appellate Body, European Communities—Customs Classification of Frozen Boneless Chicken Cuts, AB Report adopted on September 27, 2005. See also S. Shanker, "The Vienna Convention on the Law of Treaties, the Dispute Settlement System of the WTO and the Doha Declaration on the TRIPs Agreement" (2002) 36 *Journal of World Trade* 721–72.

[56] See also, for example, United States—Standards for Reformulated and Conventional Gasoline. Report of the Appellate Body (1996); and Japan—Taxes on Alcoholic Beverages. Report of the Appellate Body (1996); European Communities—Customs Classification of Frozen Boneless Chicken Cuts, AB Report adopted on September 27, 2005.

[57] Limited to where the meaning is ambiguous or obscure; or where it leads to a result which is manifestly absurd or unreasonable. See Jackson (1998), p.95.

**European Communities – Customs Classification of Frozen Boneless Chicken Cuts (DS 269, 286—Appellate Body Report of 12 September 2005) : Summary by the WTO Secretariat**

13-009

[In this dispute one of the questions was whether specific imports of poultry were to be considered as salted chicken or as frozen chicken—which was decisive for the applicable tariff duty. The AB had consequently to interpret the term "salted"]

*Interpretation of the term at issue "salted" in EC Schedule*

Ordinary meaning (VCLT Art. 31(1)): The Appellate Body upheld the Panel's finding that "in essence, the ordinary meaning of the term 'salted' . . . indicates that the character of a product has been altered through the addition of salt" and that "there is nothing in the range of meanings comprising the ordinary meaning of the term 'salted' that indicates that chicken to which salt has been added is not covered by the concession contained in heading 02.10 of the EC Schedule".

Context (VCLT Art. 31(2)): Having considered relevant context including explanatory notes to the EC schedule and the Harmonized System for Tariff Classification for the interpretation of the term "salted", the Appellate Body upheld the Panel's finding that the term "salted" in the relevant EC tariff commitment was not necessarily characterized by the notion of long-term preservation as argued by the European Communities, but rather encompassed both concepts, i.e. "preparation" and "preservation" by the addition of salt.

Subsequent practice (VCLT 31(3)(b)): The Appellate Body, reversing the Panel's interpretation and application of the concept "subsequent practice" within the meaning of Article 31(3)(b), provided its own interpretation of "subsequent practice" to the extent that the importing Member's practice alone could not constitute "subsequent practice". Consequently, it reversed the Panel's conclusion that the EC practice of classifying the products at issue under heading 02.10 between 1996 and 2002 amounted to "subsequent practice" within the meaning of VCLT 31(3)(b).

Circumstances of conclusion (VCLT 32): The Appellate Body upheld the Panel's conclusion that the supplementary means of interpretation considered under VCLT Art. 32 (including circumstances of conclusion at the time of tariff negotiations, such as EC's legislation on customs classification, the relevant judgments of the European Court of Justice and EC classification practice) confirmed that the products at issue were covered by the tariff commitment under heading 02.10 of the EC Schedule.

The process of interpretation has partially been decoupled from the "judicial" function with the requirement that the exclusive authority to adopt interpretations rests with the Ministerial Conference and the General Council.[58] Thus, the application by a dispute settlement panel of the provisions of an agreement involves interpretation.[59] A dispute panel is required to rule on the

13-010

---

[58] Art.IX of the Marrakesh Agreement.
[59] A.H. Qureshi, "Interpreting WTO Agreements for the Development Objective" (2003) 37 *Journal of World Trade* 847–82 and A.H. Qureshi, *Interpreting WTO Agreements: Problems and Perspectives* (Cambridge, Cambridge University Press, 2006). See also J. Pauwelyn, *Conflict of Norms* (Cambridge, Cambridge University Press, 2003).

conformity of the WTO code in the context of the facts in hand.[60] Similarly, the Appellate Body is required to consider issues of law covered in the panel report and legal interpretations developed by the panel.[61] The decoupling provision is not so much a denial of the interpretative function, but rather concerns the organ that may take the final decision on a question of interpretation. The question therefore is posed as to the differences between the adoption of panel and Appellate Body reports by the DSB, and the adoption by the General Council or the Ministerial Conference of a decision on a question of interpretation. There are essentially two differences. First, the General Council and the Ministerial Conference are formally political bodies. In reality however, the DSB is also political in its character. Secondly, the decision making in the General Council, insofar as this interpretative function is concerned, is to be arrived at by a three-fourths voting majority,[62] unlike decisions by the DSB which are through consensus.[63]

It should be noted, although the General Council is to act on the basis of a recommendation by the Council overseeing the functioning of the agreement in question,[64] it is not clear as to who would decide when an interpretation has been arrived at? Indeed, the distinction between the process of applying the WTO code, and interpreting it is not self-evident, nor defined in the WTO code. Can, for example, a party to a dispute delay the adoption of an Appellate Report by the DSB, by contending that the determination of the Appellate Body is not limited to issues of law covered in the panel report and legal interpretations developed by the panel?[65] There are no time-scales by which an interpretative decision is required to have been adopted, unlike the case with proceedings under the DSB. Indeed, to take the reasoning to its logical conclusion, there is also potentially the question of the distinction between an interpretation and an amendment. Different voting requirements exist insofar as amendments are concerned.[66] The decoupling of the interpretative function from the "judicial" forum has the merit of ensuring an "ambulatory" approach to the interpretation of the international agreement. Further, given that the decision carries with it the political force of the membership, the prospects of the implementation of the decision are better. In addition, it would seem appropriate that given interpretative decisions concern the membership at large, that such decisions should be more difficult to adopt, and that the membership should make a positive contribution to the decision-making.[67]

Thus, a member has a distinct right, distinct from the dispute settlement

---

[60] See Art.11 of the Understanding.
[61] See Art.17(6) of the Understanding.
[62] Art.IX(2) of the Marrakesh Agreement.
[63] Art.2(4) of the Understanding.
[64] Art.IX(2) of the Marrakesh Agreement.
[65] See Art.17(6) of the Understanding.
[66] See Art.X of the Marrakesh Agreement.
[67] Contra non-interpretative panel and Appellate decisions which are adopted by the BSB unless there is a decision by consensus not to adopt them.

procedures, to obtain an authoritative interpretation of the WTO code from the WTO.[68] However, there is a danger that interpretative decisions could have legislative characteristics for those members who are not amongst the three-fourths majority. Article IX of the Agreement Establishing the WTO does however stipulate that the interpretative process should not be used to undermine the amendment provisions in Art.X of the Agreement. In other words, the interpretative process must not result in disguised amendment of the WTO code. There has sometimes arisen criticism of the Appellate Body and Panels regarding their interpretations, usually describing their attitude as legal or judicial activism, but in general both have made proof of judicial constraint.[69]

**Decision-making**

Decisions by the DSB are to be arrived at through consensus.[70] Decisions are deemed to have been arrived at by consensus if no member present at the meeting of the DSB formally objects to the proposed decision. Thus, by consensus decision-making is meant that all panel and Appellate Reports will automatically be adopted by the DSB, unless there is a decision by consensus against the adoption of the reports. A so-called negative consensus is thus required to block the establishment of a panel or the adoption of panel or Appellate Body reports. Such a negative consensus in practice is difficult to occur. In a sense the individual right to veto the establishment of a panel and the adoption of a panel report, which existed in the context of GATT 1947, have been replaced by the collective right of veto. The integrity of the decisions arrived at by the members of the panels and the Appellate Body is preserved. It is however subject to a political veto through a consensus decision.

13-011

Thus, the DSB has almost automatic jurisdiction over a dispute without the need for a member's consent for the dispute to proceed for adjudication. This kind of jurisdiction is very significant in international relations given that a primary organ of the UN, viz. the ICJ, does not enjoy such a universal automatic jurisdiction.

**Dispute settlement methods**

There are a range of techniques available for conflict resolution under the Understanding.[71] The principal and most discussed technique is adjudication

13-012

---

[68] Art.3(9) of the Understanding.

[69] See also P.J. Kelly, "Judicial activism at the World Trade Organization", *Northwestern Journal of International Law & [and] Business*, 22 (2002) 3, 353–388; H.E. Zeitler, "'Good Faith' in the WTO Jurisprudence—Necessary Balancing Element or an Open Door to Judicial Activism?" (2005) 8 *Journal of International Economic Law* 721–58; M. Panizzon, *Good Faith in the Jurisprudence of the WTO* (Hart Publishing, 2006). See also C.-D. Ehlermann, "Six Years on the Bench of the 'World Trade Court': Some Personal Experiences as Member of the Appellate Body of the World Trade Organization" (2002) 36 *Journal of World Trade* 605–39.

[70] Art.2(4) of the Understanding.

[71] See C.-D. Ehlermann, "Tensions between the dispute settlement process and the diplomatic and treaty-making activities of the WTO" (2002) 1(3) *World Trade Review* 301–08.

through the panel process, subject to an appeal procedure. The other methods include consultation procedures, good offices, conciliation, mediation, and arbitration.[72] The emphasis in the deployment of all these techniques is on ensuring a "consensual" resolution between the members, rather than necessarily a rule orientated decision. However, there are a number of features in the Understanding which are designed to ensure the prominence of the rule of law.

Good offices, conciliation and mediation are available at any time, should the States so desire.[73] Provision is also made for the offer of good offices, conciliation or mediation by the Director-General, acting in an *ex officio* capacity.[74] Arbitration as an alternative means for resolving disputes is a facility also available to the parties if they so agree.[75] The parties to arbitration are to agree in advance to abide by the arbitration decision.[76] Some of the provisions of the Understanding, as they relate particularly to the implementation of recommendations and rulings, including compensation and suspension of concessions, apply to the arbitration proceedings.[77] Arbitration awards are to be consistent with the provisions of the WTO code.[78]

### Causes of action giving rise to the dispute settlement procedures

**13-013** The circumstances under which any of the conflict resolution mechanisms are available to a member are based on the rules originally mentioned in Arts XXII and XXIII of the GATT 1947 and now part of the GATT 1994.[79] There are essentially three causes of action. These provide a broad spectrum of grounds of action. First, there is what has become known as "the violation complaint", involving a violation of the WTO code. Essentially, under the violation complaint, the aggrieved party can have access to the available conflict resolution mechanisms where it is of the opinion that a benefit accruing to it under the agreements covered by the Understanding, is being nullified or impaired, or the attainment of an objective of the agreement in question is being impeded, as a consequence of the failure of another party to carry out its obligations under the agreement in question. Almost all disputes under the GATT and the WTO thus far have been violation complaints.[80]

In the event of a violation complaint there is a prima facie presumption that a benefit accruing to the complaining party is being nullified or impaired.

---

[72] See, for example, Y. Iwasawa, "Settlement of disputes concerning the WTO Agreement: various means other than panel procedures" in M.K. Young and Y. Iwasawa (eds), *Trilateral Perspectives on International Legal Issues: Relevance Of Domestic Law And Policy* (1996).
[73] Art.5 of the Understanding.
[74] Art.5(6) of the Understanding.
[75] Art.25 of the Understanding.
[76] Art.25(3) of the Understanding
[77] Art.25(4) of the Understanding.
[78] Art.3(5) of the Understanding.
[79] Art.3 of the Understanding.
[80] India—Patent Protection For Pharmaceutical And Agricultural Chemical Products. Report of the Appellate Body (1997).

The onus of disproving nullification and impairment of benefits under the agreement rests, therefore, on the member against whom the complaint has been brought.[81] However, in GATT practice this presumption proved to be irrefutable.[82] It has been contended that this practice will not necessarily be followed in the WTO, given that the presumption has been referred to specifically in the Understanding,[83] but this has not happened.

Secondly, there is the non-violation complaint,[84] not involving a violation of the code as such. Under this, the aggrieved party can have access to the available conflict resolution mechanisms, where it is of the opinion that a benefit accruing to it, under a covered agreement, is being nullified or impaired, or the attainment of an objective of the agreement in question is being impeded, as a consequence of the application by a member of any trade measure, whether or not it conflicts with the provisions of the agreement in question. Thus, in a non-violation complaint there is no need to evidence a violation or breach of the actual WTO code of conduct as such. However, the complainant has to demonstrate at the outset that there has been a nullification or impairment of benefits. This nullification or impairment must be the result of a trade measure or omission. It can include a trade measure applied by the member under an expressly stated exception or a waiver of the WTO code.[85] The onus of proof in a non-violation complaint lies with the complainant right from the outset.

The basis of the non-violation compliant is originally rooted mainly in the need to protect the reciprocal tariff concessions, negotiated amongst members under Art.II of GATT 1994, from being undermined by non-tariff or other policy measures.[86] The practice of GATT has been to confine the application of non-violation complaints to the protection of tariff bindings.[87] However, it

**13-014**

---

[81] Art.3(8) of the Understanding.

[82] See, for example, United States: Taxes on Petroleum and Certain Imported Substances, GATT BISD 34 Supp. 136 (1988).

[83] Art.3(8) of the Understanding. See Jackson (1998), p.71. See also, for example, R.S.J. Martha, "Presumptions and burden of proof in world trade law" (1997) 14(1) *Journal of International Arbitration* 67–98; J. Pauwelyn, "Evidence, proof and persuasion in WTO Dispute Settlement: Who bears the burden?" (1998) 2(1) *Journal of International Economic Law* 227–258; M.T. Grando, Evidence, proof, and fact-finding in WTO dispute settlement.— Oxford [u.a.], Oxford Univ. Press, 2009.

[84] See Chua (1998) and F. Roessler & P. Gappah, "A re-appraisal of non-violation complaints under the WTO dispute settlement procedures" in P.F.J. Macrory, A.E. Appleton & M Plummer (eds), *The World Trade Organisation: Legal, Economic and Political Analysi*, Vol 1, (Springer:2005), 1372–1387; C. Larouer, "WTO non-violation complaints", *Netherlands International Law Review*, 53 (2006) 1, 97–126.

[85] See, for example, US—Importation of Sugar (1990) GATT Panel Report BISD 37S/255; and US-Trade Measures Affecting Nicaragua (unadopted 1986) L/6053.

[86] India—Patent Protection for Pharmaceutical and Agricultural Chemical Products. Report of the Appellate Body (1997). See also E-U Petersmann, "Violation Complaints and Non-Violation Complaints in International Law" (1991) *German Yearbook of International Law* 175. See also L. Hsu, "Non-violation Complaints—World Trade Organization Issues and Recent Free Trade Agreements" (2005) 39 *Journal of World Trade* 205–37.

[87] See, for example, E-U Petersmann, "The dispute settlement system of the World Trade Organization and the evolution of the GATT system since 1948" (1994) 31 CML.Rev 1188.

is generally acknowledged that non-violation complaints may apply in other situations as well.[88] To sum up, normally for a non-violation complaint there has to be a governmental measure involved in the nullification or impairment of the benefit; it must impact on the competitive conditions established for the tariff bindings; and the interference in the competitive conditions must be unexpected.[89]

Non-violation complaints are possible for goods and services (under GATT for goods and market-opening commitments in services). However, for the time being, members have agreed not to use them under the TRIPS Agreement. There have thus far been only a handful of non-violation complaints. GATT panels faced with non-violation complaints have found nullification or impairment in only four out of fourteen cases where it was alleged[90]—although some of these non-violation complaints have been significant.[91] This caution is appropriate particularly where the WTO code contains inadequate or imprecise rules.[92]

Finally, there is what has been described as the "situation complaint". Here the aggrieved party can have access to the available conflict resolution mechanisms, where a benefit accruing to it under a covered agreement is being nullified or impaired, or the attainment of an objective of the agreement in question is being impeded, as a consequence of any situation (other than a violation, or the application of a measure whether or not in violation of the agreement in question). Situation complaints have not featured significantly in the practice of the GATT 1947 at all. In fact in the history of the GATT and the WTO thus far it has never been the basis for a recommendation or ruling of the GATT Contracting Parties or the Dispute Settlement Body.[93] It has however been argued upon in a small number of cases.[94] The adoption of a situation complaint panel report can be blocked by the member adversely affected.[95]

**13-015**     The availability of the violation, non-violation and situation complaints is not uniform throughout the Uruguay Round trade agreements. Thus, in

---

[88] See, for example, E-U Petersmann, "The dispute settlement system of the World Trade Organization and the evolution of the GATT system since 1948" (1994) 31 CML.Rev 1188. See also, for example, E. McGovern, *International Trade Regulation* (Exeter, Globefield Press, 1995), pp.2–272.

[89] B. Hoekman and M. Kostecki, *The Political Economy of the World Trading System* (Oxford, Oxford University Press, 1995), p.46.

[90] See India—Patent Protection for Pharmaceutical and Agricultural Chemical Products. Report of the Appellate Body (1997).

[91] See Jackson (1998), p.69; and, for example, EEC—Payments & Subsidies Paid to Processors and Producers of Oilseeds and Related Animal-Feed Proteins, GATT, BISD 26 Supp. (1980).

[92] See Jackson (1998), p.93.

[93] India—Patent Protection For Pharmaceutical And Agricultural Chemical Products Report of the Appellate Body (1997). See T. N. Samahon, TRIPs copyright dispute settlement after the transition and moratorium: nonviolation and situation complaints against developing countries, *Law and Policy in International Business*, 31 (2000) 3, 1051–1075.

[94] India—Patent Protection for Pharmaceutical and Agricultural Chemical Products Report of the Appellate Body (1997).

[95] See Art.26 of the Understanding.

GATS only violation and non-violation complaints are allowed. In TRIPS non-violation and situation complaints were not to be entertained for the initial period of five years of the agreement (Art.64.2 TRIPS). It has been extended since then. In both GATS and TRIPS there are no tariff bindings to protect, although in GATS there are commitments negotiated on a mutually advantageous basis.[96]

A member has a fairly wide discretion in deciding whether or not to bring proceedings.[97] This discretion however needs to be exercised in such a manner that the proceedings brought would be "fruitful". It is for the member to consider whether or not the proceedings would be fruitful. A member has an interest in bringing proceedings even if it is not an actual exporter of the goods or services or is a producer on a small scale. A member's interests may be affected because it has a potential export interest or because its internal market can be affected as a consequence of world supplies and prices of the goods or services in question. This sensitivity to the member's interests is particularly reinforced as a consequence of the increased interdependence in the global economy.[98]

**Panel System**

The cornerstone of the Understanding is the consultation and panel system. **13-016** From a general International Law perspective it resembles traditional arbitration but it contains a number of highly specific features due to the technicality of most trade disputes. In the first instance, States which have a grievance are enjoined to enter into consultations with each other, and to give sympathetic consideration to the representations made in this process.[99] Thus, consultations provide each party with an opportunity to understand each other's positions.[100] Strict time-periods for the consultation process have been set.[101] Requests for consultations are to be made in writing[102] but are to be confidential.[103] All consultations are to be notified to the DSB.[104] Resolution of disputes under the consultation process have to be consistent with the WTO code.[105] If however, the consultations do not lead to a constructive result, then the aggrieved party may ask for the establishment of a panel so that the matter can be adjudicated upon.[106] Most disputes are resolved in the consultation

---

[96] See Art.XIX and XXI of GATS. See also Petersmann (1994), p.1231.
[97] European Communities—Regime for the Importation, Sale and Distribution of Bananas. Report of the Appellate Body (1997).
[98] See European Communities—Regime for the Importation, Sale and Distribution of Bananas. Report of the Appellate Body (1997).
[99] Art.XXII of GATT 1994; and Art.4 of the Understanding.
[100] Art.4(2) of the Understanding.
[101] Art.4(3) of the Understanding.
[102] Art.4(4) of the Understanding.
[103] Art.4(6) of the Understanding.
[104] Art.4(4) of the Understanding.
[105] Art.3(5) of the Understanding.
[106] Art.4(7) of the Understanding.

stage. As of June 2007, there have been some 363 consultation requests. This makes the WTO dispute settlement mechanism the most successful peaceful dispute settlement mechanism in the history of International Law.

Before instigating a case for adjudication by a panel, an aggrieved member is required to consider whether in its judgement action under the dispute settlement procedures would in fact be fruitful.[107] It is not entirely clear as to what is meant by "fruitful". The reference may be interpreted as an invitation to consider the remedies or the solutions that the procedures will facilitate. Thus, the injunction appears to place a certain complexion on the character of availability of the dispute settlement procedures, viz. that the procedures are available in order to achieve positive action from the other party or parties to the dispute.[108] In this light availability of the dispute settlement procedures for declaratory purposes seem to be discouraged—although a member can always obtain an authoritative interpretation of a provision of the WTO code from the Ministerial Conference or the General Council.[109] Further, not only is there a preference for a solution which has a positive quality, but it must also be one which is acceptable to the parties, as well as being consistent with the WTO code. The invitation is to take into consideration the willingness of a member to agree to a solution. In the premises, this injunction to reflect is in effect an articulation of a diplomatic and pragmatic approach, as opposed to a strict rule based approach, to the resolution of disputes. Equally, however, it serves to discourage vexatious litigation.

When consultations fail, a complaining party has a right to the establishment of a panel for the adjudication of its complaint, unless the DSB decides by consensus not to establish a panel.[110] The panel shall be composed of well-qualified governmental and/or non-governmental individuals, persons who have served in a representative capacity in the WTO system or its Secretariat, and individuals who have taught or published on international trade law.[111] It is not clear what is meant by "well qualified". It is clear, however, that panellists need not have a legal background. Traditionally the majority of panellists have been former trade officials.[112] When serving as panellists, the members are to serve in their individual capacity, and not as representatives of their governments or organisation.[113] The impartiality of the panellists is ensured through the disclosure of relevant information by the panellists, and declarations made by them upon their appointment.[114] The Secretariat

---

[107] Art.3(7) of the Understanding.
[108] Art.3(7) of the Understanding.
[109] Art.3(9) of the Understanding.
[110] Art.6 of the Understanding.
[111] Art.8 of the Understanding.
[112] See A.W. Shoyer, "Panel Selection in WTO Dispute Settlement Proceedings" (2003) 6 *Journal of International Economic Law* 203–09 and M. L. Busch, "Does the WTO need a permanent body of panelists?", *Journal of International Economic Law*, 12 (2009) 3, 579–594.
[113] Art.8(9) of the Understanding.
[114] See Rules of Conduct for the Understanding And Procedures Governing the Settlement of

maintains an indicative list of panellists (roster), from which it proposes individuals.[115] Nationals of members whose governments are in dispute are not to serve on the panel, unless it is agreed otherwise.[116] The proposed panellists by the WTO Secretariat are not to be opposed by the parties to the dispute unless there are compelling reasons.[117] In practice the parties have considerable latitude in rejecting a proposed panellist, given that their agreement is necessary for the composition of the panel.[118] The panel is to consist of three persons, unless the parties to the dispute agree otherwise, in which case it will be five.[119] The present panel system has come under criticism on the grounds particularly that the panellists are part-time and therefore unable to fully keep abreast with developments in international trade. The EU has proposed for the setting up of a permanent group of panellists to hear trade disputes,[120] as it is already the case for the Appellate Body.

The panel must make an objective assessment of the matter before it.[121] **13-017** This involves an obligation to consider the evidence, and to arrive at conclusions on the basis of the evidence before it.[122] The panel should not deliberately disregard, or refuse to consider evidence before it.[123] It must not wilfully distort or misrepresent the evidence put to it.[124] The panel must act in good faith, and must not deny the parties due process of law or natural justice.[125] Insofar as the standard of review is concerned[126] the general GATT/WTO

Disputes WT/DSB/RC/W/1 (1996). See G. Marceau, "Rules on Ethics for the New World Trade Organization Dispute Settlement Mechanism" (1998) J.W.T. 57–97.

[115] Art.8(4) and (6) of the Understanding.

[116] Art.8(3) of the Understanding.

[117] Art.8(6) of the Understanding.

[118] See also B. Hoekman and M. Kostecki, *The Political Economy of the World Trading System* (Oxford: Oxford University Press, 1995), p.53 (see now 2nd edn, Ch.4). See also A.W. Shoyer, "Panel Selection in WTO Dispute Settlement Proceedings" (2003) 6 *Journal of International Economic Law* 203–09.

[119] Art.8(5) of the Understanding.

[120] See F. Williams in *Financial Times* (October 21, 1998). See for details W.J. Davey, "Mini-Symposium on the Desirability of a WTO Permanent Panel Body: Introduction" (2003) 6 *J. Int. Economic Law* 175–6; W.J. Davey, "The Case for a WTO Permanent Panel Body" (2003) 6 *Journal of International Economic Law* 177–86; T. Cottier, "The WTO Permanent Panel Body: a Bridge Too Far?" (2003) 6 *Journal of International Economic Law* 187–202; J.H.J. Bourgeois, "Comment on a WTO Permanent Panel Body" (2003) 6 *Journal of International Economic Law* 211–35.

[121] Art.11 of the Understanding. See also R.S.J. Martha, "Presumptions and burden of proof in World Trade Law" (1997) 14(1) *Journal of International Arbitration* 67–98; M. Lugard, "Scope of Appellate review: Objective Assessment of the Facts and Issues of Law" (1998) 1(2) *Journal of International Economic Law* 323.

[122] EC Measures Concerning Meat and Meat Products (Hormones). Report of the Appellate Body (1998).

[123] EC Measures Concerning Meat and Meat Products (Hormones). Report of the Appellate Body (1998).

[124] EC Measures Concerning Meat and Meat Products (Hormones). Report of the Appellate Body (1998).

[125] EC Measures Concerning Meat and Meat Products (Hormones). Report of the Appellate Body (1998).

[126] See, *United States—Investigation of the International Trade Commission in Softwood Lumber from Canada—Recourse to Article 21.5 of the DSU by Canada*, AB Report adopted on May

practice has been to consider *de novo* a case,[127] except where otherwise stipulated.[128]

The panel is to produce a final report within six months of its establishment; and in cases which require urgent consideration including cases involving perishable goods, the final report of the panel should be produced within three months.[129] The DSU does not explicitly address the question as of whether a panellist or a Member of the Appellate Body can dissent, i.e. formulate a minority view against the rest of the panel but in practice this has happened with regard to specific aspects of the findings.[130] In no case should the submission of the report to the members of the WTO exceed nine months.[131] Panel deliberations are to be confidential; and opinions expressed by individual panellists are to be anonymous.[132] No explicit guidance is provided as to how the panellists should arrive at a decision in the event of differing opinions amongst themselves. However, the panel is enjoined to consult on a regular basis with the parties to the dispute, and to give the parties adequate opportunity to develop a mutually satisfactory solution. The Panel is to issue an interim report for the consideration of the parties before a final report is recommended.[133] The parties may comment on the report and request that the panel review specific aspects of the interim report. The final report is to be adopted within sixty days of its issuance to the members at the DSB meeting.[134] However, the Final Report will not be adopted if one of the parties to the dispute formally notifies the DSB of its intention to appeal, or if it is decided by the DSB by consensus not to adopt the report.[135]

---

9, 2006; on this issue for example, S.P. Croley and J. Jackson, "WTO dispute procedures, standard of review, and deference to national governments" (1996) A.J.I.L. On the standard of review see also G.S. Desmedt, "Hormones: 'objective assessment' and (or as) standard of review" (1998) 1 *Journal of International Economic Law* 695–8; C.-D. Ehlermann and N. Lockhart, "Standard of Review in WTO Law" (2004) 7 *Journal of International Economic Law* 491–521; M. Oesch, "Standards of Review in WTO Dispute Resolution" (2003) 6 *Journal of International Economic Law* 635–59; M. Oesch, "*Standards of Review in WTO Dispute Resolution* (Oxford: Oxford University Press, 2003); H. Spamann, "Standard of Review for World Trade Organization Panels in Trade Remedy Cases: a Critical Analysis" (2004) 38 *Journal of World Trade* 509–55; R. Becroft, "The Standard of Review Strikes Back: the *US—Korea Drams* Appeal" (2006) 9 *Journal of International Economic Law* 207–17; M.M. Du, "Standard of review under the SPS Agreement after EC-Hormones II", *The International and Comparative Law Quarterly*, 59 (2010) 2, 441–459; A. T. Guzmán "Determining the appropriate standard of review in WTO Disputes" *Cornell international law journal*, 42 (2009) 1, 45–76.

[127] Petersmann (1994), p.1236.
[128] For example in the Agreement on Implementation of Art.VI of the GATT 1994.
[129] Art.12(8) of the Understanding.
[130] See M.K. Lewis, "The Lack of Dissent in WTO Dispute Settlement" (2006) 9 *Journal of International Economic Law* 895–931 and J. Flett, "Collective intelligence and the possibility of dissent", *Journal of International Economic Law*, 13 (2010) 2, 287–320. See European Communities—Measures Affecting the Importation of Certain Poultry Products, Panel Report circulated on March 12, 1998.
[131] Art.12(9) of the Understanding.
[132] Art.14 of the Understanding.
[133] Art.15 of the Understanding.
[134] Art.16(4) of the Understanding.
[135] Art.16(4) of the Understanding.

The panel proceedings have characteristics both of an adversarial system, as well as an inquisitorial system. They are not open to the public. This fact has drawn criticism on grounds of lack of transparency. However, it is defended inter alia on the basis of the confidential nature of some of the information involved.

## APPELLATE SYSTEM

A party may appeal to the Appellate Body (AB) with respect to the final panel report.[136] The permanent Appellate Body must be conceived like a permanent international court or tribunal although the WTO members have avoided this terminology. Its members are simply called Members of the Appellate Body although they act like international judges. A right of appeal from a panel report exists only on a point of law covered in the panel report and legal interpretation developed by the panel.[137] If as a consequence of the deliberations of the Appellate Body the panel findings need to be revisited the Appellate Body does not currently have the jurisdiction to remand the case back to the panel for the re-examination of the facts.[138] As of June 2007, the Appellate Body had issued 82 Reports, many of which were of paramount importance for the clarification of open questions under the WTO Code as established in 1994.

**13-018**

The Appellate Body has in its various deliberations, albeit on a piecemeal basis, tried to clarify what is a point of law. Thus, in one case it held that consideration of domestic law can serve as evidence of fact.[139] It can, however, also provide evidence of state practice; and of compliance or non-compliance with international obligations.[140] In another case the Appellate Body ruled that the question whether or not a panel has complied with the obligation to make an objective assessment of the facts[141] is a question of law.[142] Generally, however, most trade disputes do not involve much factual material, given that normally a member does not have to prove the trade effect of a trade measure.[143]

---

[136] Art.16(4) of the Understanding.

[137] Art.17(6) of the Understanding.

[138] See European Communities—Measures Affecting Asbestos and Asbestos-Containing Products, AB Report adopted on March 5, 2001; see for example D. Palmeter, "The WTO Appellate Body needs remand authority" (1998) 32(1) J.W.T. 41–4 or A. Yanovich and T. Voon, "Completing the Analysis in WTO Appeals: The Practice and its Limitations" (2006) 9 *Journal of International Economic Law* 933–50; J. McCall Smith, "WTO dispute settlement: the politics of procedure in Appellate Body rulings" (2003) 2(1) *World Trade Review* 65–100.

[139] See India—Patent Protection For Pharmaceutical And Agricultural Chemical Products. Report of the Appellate Body (1997).

[140] See India—Patent Protection For Pharmaceutical And Agricultural Chemical Products. Report of the Appellate Body (1997).

[141] Art.11 of the Understanding.

[142] EC Measures Concerning Meat and Meat Products (Hormones). Report of the Appellate Body (1998).

[143] See US—Taxes on Petroleum (1987) GATT 34S/136.

**13-019**      **Article 17 DSU: Appellate Review (footnotes omitted)[144]**

*Standing Appellate Body*

1. A standing Appellate Body shall be established by the DSB. The Appellate Body shall hear appeals from panel cases. It shall be composed of seven persons, three of whom shall serve on any one case. Persons serving on the Appellate Body shall serve in rotation. Such rotation shall be determined in the working procedures of the Appellate Body.

2. The DSB shall appoint persons to serve on the Appellate Body for a four-year term, and each person may be reappointed once. However, the terms of three of the seven persons appointed immediately after the entry into force of the WTO Agreement shall expire at the end of two years, to be determined by lot. Vacancies shall be filled as they arise. A person appointed to replace a person whose term of office has not expired shall hold office for the remainder of the predecessor's term.

3. The Appellate Body shall comprise persons of recognized authority, with demonstrated expertise in law, international trade and the subject-matter of the covered agreements generally. They shall be unaffiliated with any government. The Appellate Body membership shall be broadly representative of membership in the WTO. All persons serving on the Appellate Body shall be available at all times and on short notice, and shall stay abreast of dispute settlement activities and other relevant activities of the WTO. They shall not participate in the consideration of any disputes that would create a direct or indirect conflict of interest.

4. Only parties to the dispute, not third parties, may appeal a panel report. Third parties which have notified the DSB of a substantial interest in the matter pursuant to paragraph 2 of Article 10 may make written submissions to, and be given an opportunity to be heard by, the Appellate Body.

5. As a general rule, the proceedings shall not exceed 60 days from the date a party to the dispute formally notifies its decision to appeal to the date the Appellate Body circulates its report. In fixing its timetable the Appellate Body shall take into account the provisions of paragraph 9 of Article 4, if relevant. When the Appellate Body considers that it cannot provide its report within 60 days, it shall inform the DSB in writing of the reasons for the delay together with an estimate of the period within which it will submit its report. In no case shall the proceedings exceed 90 days.

6. An appeal shall be limited to issues of law covered in the panel report and legal interpretations developed by the panel.

7. The Appellate Body shall be provided with appropriate administrative and legal support as it requires.

8. The expenses of persons serving on the Appellate Body, including travel and subsistence allowance, shall be met from the WTO budget in accordance with criteria to be adopted by the General Council, based on recommendations of the Committee on Budget, Finance and Administration.

---

[144] Source: *http://www.wto.org*. Accessed June 8, 2011.

*Procedures for Appellate Review*

9. Working procedures shall be drawn up by the Appellate Body in consultation with the Chairman of the DSB and the Director-General, and communicated to the Members for their information.

10. The proceedings of the Appellate Body shall be confidential. The reports of the Appellate Body shall be drafted without the presence of the parties to the dispute and in the light of the information provided and the statements made.

11. Opinions expressed in the Appellate Body report by individuals serving on the Appellate Body shall be anonymous.

12. The Appellate Body shall address each of the issues raised in accordance with paragraph 6 during the appellate proceeding.

13. The Appellate Body may uphold, modify or reverse the legal findings and conclusions of the panel.

*Adoption of Appellate Body Reports*

14. An Appellate Body report shall be adopted by the DSB and unconditionally accepted by the parties to the dispute unless the DSB decides by consensus not to adopt the Appellate Body report within 30 days following its circulation to the Members. This adoption procedure is without prejudice to the right of Members to express their views on an Appellate Body report."

The Appellate Body[145] is to comprise seven individuals. These are appointed for a four-year period.[146] The composition of the Appellate Body is to reflect the membership of the WTO.[147] This has been interpreted in such a manner as to lead to three out of the seven being appointed from the largest trading powers, viz. US, EU and Japan. Further, the individuals appointed are to be persons of recognised authority, with evident expertise in law, international trade and the subject-matter of the covered agreements generally.[148] Such a rule is, of course, given the political dimension of the appointments difficult to enforce. Thus, it is to be noted that the background of individuals serving on the Appellate Body is not the same as those of panellists, in that there is emphasis on legal expertise. In addition, members of the Appellate Body should not be affiliated with any government. The impartiality of the appellate judges is ensured through relevant disclosures, and declarations made by them upon their appointment.[149] Unlike panellists,[150] however, at the appellate level, nationality is no bar in presiding over an appeal.

**13-020**

---

[145] The Appellate Body has formulated rules to govern its procedures. See Working Procedures for Appellate Review, WT/AB/WP/1, February 15, 1996.
[146] Art.17(2) of the Understanding.
[147] Art.15(2) of the Understanding
[148] Art.17(3) of the Understanding.
[149] See Working Procedures For Appellate Review WT/AB/WP/3 (1997). See G. Marceau (1998).
[150] See Art.8(3) of the Understanding.

At any given time in an appeal only three members preside.[151] The manner in which these three are picked is such as to prevent anyone from predicting which of the judges will preside in a given appeal. The rules stipulate that the division is to be selected "on the basis of rotation, whilst taking into account the principles of random selectivity, unpredictability and opportunity for all members to serve regardless of their origin".[152] Although only three serve on a particular appeal, the others are kept informed of the proceedings, and are expected to meet to discuss the appeal.[153] This is to ensure that the combined wisdom of the Appellate Body is brought to bear on the appeal, as well as continuity. Furthermore, in this manner the perspectives of all the divergent legal systems represented are taken into account.

In the same light as panel deliberations, the proceedings of the Appellate Body are to be confidential and the opinions of the individuals on the Appellate Body are to be anonymous.[154] The Appellate Body is to conclude its deliberations no later than 90 days from the date of notification of the appeal.[155] It may uphold, modify or reverse the legal findings and conclusions of the panel.[156] However, an Appellate Body does not have the mandate to remand a case back to a panel.[157] Therefore, its practice has been to consider the issues *de novo*, where it has reversed the panel's decision and is left with outstanding issues. An Appellate Report is to be adopted by the DSB and unconditionally accepted by the parties.[158] However, the DSB by consensus may decide not to adopt the Appellate Report, provided it does so within thirty days of the report being issued.[159]

To date the Appellate Body reports have been generally of high standard, providing much needed guidance on the interpretation of the WTO code. The Appellate Body has not only contributed to the development of international trade jurisprudence, it has also facilitated the WTO to respond to the exigencies of international trade developments, e.g. in the area of the involvement of civil society or environmental concerns.[160] The Appellate Body has also accepted that the WTO agreements should be interpreted in a way that protects the domestic power to regulate (sovereignty) where such discretion

---

[151] Art.17(1) of the Understanding.
[152] See para.6 of the Working Procedures for Appellate Review WT/AB/WP/3 (1997).
[153] See para.4 of the Working Procedures for Appellate Review WT/AB/WP/3 (1997).
[154] Art.17(10) and (11) of the Understanding.
[155] Art.17(5) of the Understanding.
[156] Art.17(13) of the Understanding.
[157] See, for example, United States—Standards for Reformulated and Conventional Gasoline Appellate Body Report (1996). See also, for example, D. Palmeter, "The WTO Appellate Body Needs Remand Authority" (1998) 32(1) *Journal of World Trade* 41–45.
[158] Art.17(14) of the Understanding.
[159] Art.17(14) of the Understanding
[160] For an evaluation of the Appellate Body thus far see R. Behboodi (1998).

exists[161] and that the interpretation of specific terms in the WTO agreements can change over time (evolutionary interpretation).[162]

Generally the Appellate Body reports try to achieve consistency in the interpretation and application of WTO law, thereby giving guidance to the Members and future panels. This creates a certain case-law even if the adopted reports bind only the parties at dispute and there is no rule of precedent as such. Members have therefore sometimes argued in appeals that a specific panel acted inconsistently with Art.11 of the DSU by "failing to follow well-established Appellate Body jurisprudence" on a specific the issue.[163] The Appellate Body accordingly sometimes expressed its deep concern over panels' "departing from" prior Appellate Body reports addressing the same legal issues.[164]

## Remedies

The sanctions available at the disposal of the panel and the Appellate Body are varied, and depend on whether or not the complaint is a violation complaint. The remedies available comprise of a recommendation or a ruling for the withdrawal of the offending trade policy measure; the authorisation to suspend trade concessions; and compensation. These remedies are not mutually exclusive. There is no provision for interim measures or for compensation for loss during the proceedings.[165] Two principles underpinning the sanctions regime can be particularly discerned. First, the objective of the removal of the inconsistent measure is paramount. Secondly, the principle that the redress must be proportional to the nullification or impairment must be observed.

**13-021**

In the event of a violation complaint, the recommendation may be that measures should be brought in conformity with the agreement in question or withdrawn. However, in the event of a non-violation or situation complaint, only a ruling and/or a recommendation may be made.[166] There is no obligation to withdraw the measure at issue. The recommendations cannot add or diminish the rights and obligations in the relevant agreement. In a non-violation complaint the panel or Appellate Body can recommend that a mutually satisfactory adjustment is sought through compensation.[167]

---

[161] European Communities—Measures concerning Meat and Meat Products (Hormones), WT/DS26 and WT/DS48, AB Report adopted on February 13, 1998; para.154; see also, for example, "Sovereignty Issues in the WTO Dispute Settlement—A 'Development Sovereignty' Perspective" in W. Shan (ed.), *Redefing Sovereignty* (Hart Publishing, 2007).

[162] US—Import Prohibition of Certain Shrimp and Shrimp Products, WT/DS58, AB Report adopted on November 6, 1998, paras 129–130.

[163] See, for example, Mexico's argument in *US – Stainless Steel (Mexico) (AB)*, para.154.

[164] *US—Stainless Steel (Mexico) (AB)*, para.161–62. See also A. Chua, "The precedential effect of WTO Panel and Appellate Reports" (1998) II(1) *Leiden Journal of International Law* 45–61; and J. Gomula, "Precedential effect of WTO decisions", *The Global Community*, (2008) 1, 295–318.

[165] See, for example, Jackson (1998), p.97.

[166] Art.26(1) of the Understanding.

[167] See Art.26.1(b) of the Understanding.

The Panel or Appellate Body Report must be implemented promptly.[168] If this is not possible the member concerned is to be given reasonable time to implement the recommendations, and is required to inform the DSB of its intentions in relation to the implementation of the recommendations.[169] However, insofar as the implementation of a panel recommendation and ruling is concerned, considerable latitude is built into the system. The member in effect is given a "reasonable period of time" to comply with the panel recommendations and rulings. The determination of what is "reasonable time" is, however, a time period that is proposed by the member in question, although subject to the approval of the DSB. Where this approval is not forthcoming the parties are to agree amongst themselves as to what is reasonable. If there is no agreement then the determination of a reasonable time must be arrived at through arbitration. The arbitrators are to be guided by the desideratum that a reasonable time should not normally exceed 15 months from the date of the establishment of the panel, unless there are particular circumstances justifying a longer or shorter period.[170] Thus, the reasonable time may be shorter or longer depending on the circumstances.[171] The reasonable time determined by the arbitrator is binding.[172] Despite this, however, the question whether the parties can subsequently to the arbitrators determination, legitimately decide on an extended time-framework has been posed and remains unclear.[173] Further, where there is disagreement as to whether there has been implementation in conformity with the Appellate or Panel Report recommendations there is some confusion as to whether the DSB has to refer the issue back to the original Panel, or if the aggrieved party can go ahead and request for the authorisation of the suspension of concessions.[174] In the US/EC banana dispute the DSB agreed to reconvene the Panel to examine whether EC implementation was in conformity with the original recommendation.[175] However, despite this the US has contended that it can request for retaliation against the EC.[176] The EC/US banana

---

[168] Art.21 of the Understanding.

[169] Art.21(3) of the Understanding.

[170] Art.21(3) of the Understanding. See, for example, Japan—Taxes on Alcoholic Beverages. Arbitration under Art.21(3)(c) (1997); European Communities—Regime For The Importation, Sale And Distribution Of Bananas. Arbitration under Art.21.3(c) (January 1998); EC Measures Concerning Meat and Meat Products (Hormones), Arbitration under Art.21.3(c) (1998).

[171] Art.21(3) of the Understanding.

[172] Art.21(3)(c) of the Understanding.

[173] See E-U Petersmann, "From the Hobbesian International Law of coexistence to modern integration law: the WTO dispute settlement system" (1998) *Journal of International Economic Law* 195 where he refers to the US/Japan bilateral agreement in the context of Japan—Taxes on Alcoholic Beverages (December1997).

[174] See in the context of the banana dispute between the US and the EC, *Financial Times*, January 15, 1999.

[175] Pursuant to Art.21.5 of the Understanding. See, for example, J.E. Kearns and S. Charnovitz, "Adjudicating Compliance in the WTO: A Review of DSU Article 21.5" (2002) 5 *Journal of International Economic Law* 331–52.

[176] See *Financial Times*, January 15, 1999.

dispute illustrates the potential of the extent to which the implementation of a recommendation can be dragged.[177]

This manner of negotiating compliance, whilst relying on ensuring compliance through the "willing" participation of the offending member party to the dispute, has its short-comings, in that it can enable in a creeping fashion, the "blocking" of the implementation of an adopted panel or appellate body report. There is the further need for reform here, perhaps by introducing a system of "supervised negotiations" of the implementation process under the auspices of the WTO. The case for such a procedure is more compelling where the dispute involves unequal parties. Small developing countries can hardly effectively retaliate against States whose exports are essential for their population in cases.[178] At the same time, big trading nations are less affected by sanctions as they do not depend on trade in a few strategic sectors.[179]

**13-022**

A member may receive payment of compensation and/or suspend concessions or other obligations in relation to the other member. However, these are only temporary measures, and available only in the event that the recommendation for the withdrawal of the offending trade measure is not implemented within a reasonable time. The payment of compensation is voluntary, and not mandatory. It is available until the withdrawal of the offending measure.[180] GATT/WTO practice has been not to order restitution,[181] even for customs duties and internal taxes illegally collected.[182] This is because

---

[177] See also K. Anderson, Peculiarities of retaliation in WTO dispute settlement (2002) 1(2) *World Trade Review* 123–34; W.J. Davey, "Compliance Problems in WTO Dispute Settlement", *Cornell International Law Journal*, 42 (2009) 1, 119–128; B. Wilson, "Compliance by WTO members with adverse WTO dispute settlement rulings", *Journal of International Economic Law*, 10 (2007) 2, 397–403.

[178] See below Section 12 and J. Lacarte-Muró and P. Gappah, "Developing countries and the WTO legal and dispute settlement system: a view from the bench" (2000) 3 *Journal of International Economic Law* 395–401; J.L. Pérez Gabilondo, "Developing Countries in the WTO Dispute Settlement Procedures Improving their Participation" (2001) 35 *Journal of World Trade* 483–88; M.E. Footer, "Developing Country Practice in the Matter of WTO Dispute Settlement" (2001) 35 *Journal of World Trade* 55–98; R. Bush, "Developing countries and GATT/WTO Dispute Settlement" (2003) 4 *Journal of World Trade*; C.P. Bown and B.M. Hoekman, "WTO Dispute Settlement and the Missing Developing Country Cases: Engaging the Private Sector" (2005) 8 *Journal of International Economic Law* 861–90; and C. Thomas (ed.), *Developing countries in the WTO legal system*. (Oxford [u.a.], Oxford Univ. Press, 2009).

[179] The EC did not comply with the Report in European Communities—Measures concerning Meat and Meat Products (Hormones), WT/DS26, WT/DS48, Report of the Appellate Body adopted on February 13, 1998 in view of the political situation in its Member States knowing that this would eventually lead to sanctions. See for example Brock, "Power paradoxes in enforcement and implementation of WTO Dispute Settlement Reports: Interdisciplinary approaches and new approaches" (2003) 37(1) *Journal of World Trade*; G. Shaffer, "How to make the WTO Dispute Settlement System Work for Developing Countries: Some Proactive Developing Strategies", Geneva: ICTSD Resource Paper No.5 (2003); R. Howse, *Global Governance by the Judiciary: the WTO Experiment with Appellate Review* (Hart Publishing, 2004); A.H. Qureshi, "Participation of developing countries in the WTO Dispute Settlement System" in F. Ortino and E-U Petersmann (eds), *WTO Dispute Settlement System 1995-2003* (Kluwer Law International, 2004), Ch.24, 475–98.

[180] Art.3(7) of the Understanding.

[181] See, for example, the Trondheim Panel Report (1992) BISD 39S/400.

[182] See Petersmann (1994), p.1178.

generally the WTO code focuses on expectations rather than trade effects; and the difficulty in calculating the damages suffered on a retroactive basis.[183] The question of retrospective remedies has been asked by legal writers but is generally answered in the negative and finds no basis in the legal texts and the practice resulting from the case law.[184] It should be noted though, that there is provision in GATT 1994, for the availability of domestic judicial review, so as to ensure the review and correction of administrative actions relating to customs matters.[185]

Where a member fails to negotiate an acceptable compensation, however, then the member may invite the DSB to authorise the suspension of concessions or other obligations under the relevant agreement.[186] The DSB is to authorise suspension upon a properly formulated request, unless the DSB decides by consensus to reject the request. Thus, the suspension of a concession is effectively automatic.[187] Such authorisation is given by the DSB only to the complainant member which has had a ruling in its favour. Non-parties to the dispute do not have the authority to suspend concessions or other obligations. The suspension of trade concessions or other obligations is to be on a discriminatory basis vis-à-vis the other member.[188] Suspending concessions can be counterproductive, as well as ineffective hence the calls for further reform for the dispute settlement system involving possibly fines and collective measures by all WTO members.[189]

---

[183] Petersmann (1994), p.1178.

[184] See G. Goh and A.R. Ziegler, "Retrospective Remedies in the WTO after *Automotive Leather*" (2003) 6 *Journal of International Economic Law* 545–64 with regard to Panel Report in Australia—Subsidies provided to Producers and Exporters of Automotive Leather, Recourse to Art.21.5, WT/DS126/RW Report adopted on February 11, 2000, Section 6.39. See also N. H. Yenkong, "The role of arbitrators in determining reasonable period of time and retrospective remedies in WTO dispute resolution", *The Journal of World Investment & Trade; Law, Economics, Politics*, 6 (2005) 4, 611–634.

[185] Art.X(3) of GATT 1994, and Petersmann (1994), p.1180.

[186] Art.22(1) of the Understanding.

[187] See Art.22(6) of the Understanding.

[188] Art.3(7) of the Understanding.

[189] See P. Grané, "Remedies Under WTO Law" (2001) 11 *Journal of International Economic Law* 755–72; O'Connor, "Remedies in the WTO dispute settlement system—the *Bananas and Hormones* Case" (2004) 2 J.W.T.; N.H. Yenkong, "Third Party rights and the concept of legal interest in WTO dispute settlement: extending participatory rights to enforcement rights" (2004) 5 *Journal of World Trade* 757–772; M. Bronckers and N. van den Broek, "Financial Compensation in the WTO: Improving the Remedies of WTO Dispute Settlement" (2005) 8 *J. Int. Economic Law* 101–26; B. O'Connor and M. Djordjevic, "Practical Aspects of Monetary Compensation: The *US—Copyright* Case" (2005) 8 *Journal of International Economic Law* 127–42. See also M. Rafiqul Islam, "Recent EU Trade Sanctions on the US to Induce Compliance with the WTO Ruling in the Foreign Sales Corporations Case: Its Policy Contradiction Revisited" (2004) 38 *Journal of World Trade* 471–89; A. Davies, Reviewing dispute settlement at the World Trade Organization: a time to reconsider the role/s of compensation? (2006) 5(1) *World Trade Review* 31–67; Y. Ngangjoh and R. Rios-Herran, "WTO dispute settlement system and the issue of Compliance: Multilateralizing the Enforcement Mechanism" (2004) 1(3) M.J.I.E.L. 15; R. Rios-Herran and M. Diego-Fernandez, "The reform of the WTO Dispute Settlement Understanding: A closer look at the Mexican Proposal" (2004) 1(1) M.J.I.E.L 15–30; I; G. Bercero and P. Garzotti, "DSU Reform—Why Have Negotiation to Improve WTO Dispute Settlement Failed so far and What Are the Underlying Issue?" (2005)

"Cross-sanctions" or "cross-retaliation" under different covered agree-     **13-023**
ments are allowed, subject to the following conditions.[190] The suspension
of concessions or other obligations should in the first instance relate to the
same sector in which there has been a violation or other nullification or
impairment. If this is not satisfactory then the complaining party may seek
the suspension of concessions or obligations in other sectors under the same
agreement. If even this is not satisfactory and the circumstances are serious
enough, then the complaining party may seek suspension of concessions and
obligations under another agreement. A member may ask for arbitration in
the event of an issue being taken with the kind or level of suspension of concession or other obligations. The suspension of concessions or other obligations are to be applied only until the measure found to be the violation has
been removed.[191]

A surveillance mechanism has been placed in relation to the implementation of panel recommendations or rulings.[192] The DSB is to monitor the
implementation of adopted panel reports; and the implementation of the
report is to be kept on the DSB agenda for a certain period of time. Further,
the member against whom the panel report has been made is required to
submit in writing to the DSB a progress report on the implementation of
the recommendations and rulings for DSB meetings for a certain period of
time. The merit of this surveillance, whilst undeniable from an enforcement
perspective, is of course dependent in the first instance on the quality of the
recommendation or ruling arrived. Given the reliance on the consent of the
parties to the dispute in the process of the formulation of panel reports, and
in the time schedule for the implementation of the recommendations and
rulings—the value of the surveillance exercise may in some respects be diminished thereby.

**Procedural aspects**

A number of the procedural aspects of the Understanding are of particular     **13-024**
note. First, the Understanding has at all stages time-schedules to ensure that
the proceedings are conducted and concluded in an expeditious manner.
Thus, the time for the adoption of the panel report or the adoption of the
Appellate Report by the DSB is stated not to exceed nine months where there
is no appeal, and 12 months where there has been an appeal.[193] Some concern
as to the appropriateness of some of the time schedules has been expressed.[194]
The time-frame for panel and Appellate Body deliberations have been considered to be short. The length of many reports and the frequency by which

---

6 *The Journal of World Investment & Trade* 847; M. Iynedjian, "Reform of the WTO Appeal
Process" (2005) 6(5) *The Journal of World Investment & Trade* 809.
[190] Art.22(3) of the Understanding.
[191] Art.22(8) of the Understanding.
[192] Art.21(6) of the Understanding.
[193] Art.20 of the Understanding.
[194] For example Davey (1998).

both Panels and the Appellate Body have to ask for extensions are certainly indicators of the complexity of many of the cases submitted.

Secondly, third-party interests are catered for in a number of ways. Thus, a third State which has a substantial trade interest affected may join the consultation process.[195] However, this right to join is not automatic. It is dependent upon the addressee of the request for consultation determining that the member has a "substantial interest". Similarly, a third party can join in the panel process, where it has a substantial interest. Thus, it can be heard by the relevant panel, and may make written submissions to it.[196] In the same vein, a third State with a substantial trade interest affected can make written submissions to the Appellate Body, and may be given the opportunity to be heard by the Appellate Body.[197] A third State, however, does not have an original right to appeal if no appeal has been made by the original party. Where a third State considers that the measure subject to the dispute nullifies or impairs benefits to which it is entitled, then it may have recourse itself to the dispute settlement procedure. Multiple complaints may also be brought provided they relate to the same subject-matter.[198] A single panel would in such circumstances be established, but the rights of the respective parties are not thereby to be impaired.

Thirdly, the Panels are given specific authority to seek information and expert opinion from any individual or body within the jurisdiction of a Member State.[199] This has been interpreted widely to mean not just "seek" but also receive.[200] The Panel must, however, notify the authorities of the Member State, where appropriate, of its intention to so seek information.[201] The Panel is able to receive information from NGOs[202] as well as the IMF.[203]

### Developing members

13-025 On the whole, the general consensus based on the frequency of user seems to be that the dispute settlement mechanism has not deterred developing

---

[195] Art.4(11) of the Understanding. See also Yenkong (2004).

[196] Art.10 of the Understanding.

[197] Art.17(4) of the Understanding; and Arts 18(2), 24 and 27 of the Working Procedures for Appellate Review (1997).

[198] Art.9 of the Understanding.

[199] Art.13 of the Understanding. See also EC Measures Concerning Meat And Meat Products (Hormones) Report of the Appellate Body (1997). See also See Turkey—Textiles, AB Report adopted on November 19, 1999 where the Panel asked the EC (which was not a party) for specific information regarding the case (Art.13.2 DSU).

[200] See United States—Import prohibition of certain shrimp and shrimp products, Report of the Appellate Body (1998). This is particularly important in respect of so-called *amicus curiae* briefs; see above.

[201] Art.13 of the Understanding.

[202] United States—Import Prohibition of Certain Shrimp and Shrimp Products.

[203] See Decision adopted by the General Council Concerning Agreements between the WTO and the IMF and the World Bank at its Meeting on November 7, 8 and 13, 1996 (WT/L/194, November 18, 1996). See also Argentina—Measures Affecting Imports of Footwear, Textiles, Apparel and Other Items, Appellate Body Report adopted April 22, 1998.

members from using it.[204] Indeed, developing country participation in the WTO system is more extensive than that in the previous GATT regime. In recent years a number of cases brought by emerging economies against the United States and the European Union in the area of agriculture have been greeted as symbols for the availability of the mechanism for developing countries.[205] At the same time, the complexity of many cases may deter certain developing countries from bringing cases to the WTO.

The Understanding contains special provisions relating to developing and least developing countries. First, in the case of a complaining developing member, the provisions of the Decision of Contracting Parties of the April 5, 1966[206] are available as an alternative to the corresponding provisions in the Understanding.[207] Essentially, the April 5, 1966 Decision facilitates the intervention by the Director-General where the consultations between the developed State and the developing State fails to result in a satisfactory solution. Secondly, where a developing and developed State are party to a dispute, then upon the request of the developing country there should be on the panel at least one panellist from a developing State.[208] Thirdly, where a developing member is involved, the consultation periods can be longer if the parties so agree.[209] In addition, a developing country is to be given sufficient time by the panel to prepare and present its case.[210] Fourthly, where a developing member is involved, the panel's report should specifically indicate the manner in which the standard of differential and more-favourable treatment for developing countries conceded in the agreement in question has been taken

---

[204] See, for example, K.O. Kufuor, "From the GATT to WTO—The developing countries and the reform of the procedures for the settlement of international disputes" (1997) 31(5) J.W.T. 117–146; P.E. Kuruvila, "Developing countries and the GATT/WTO Dispute Settlement Mechanism" (1997) 31(6) J.W.T. 171–208; L. Wang, "Are trade disputes fairly settled?" (1997) 1 J.W.T. 58; J. Lacarte-Muró and P. Gappah, "Developing countries and the WTO legal and dispute settlement system: a view from the bench" (2000) 3 *Journal of International Economic Law* 395–401; D. Ahn, "Korea in the GATT/WTO Dispute Settlement System: Legal Battle for Economic Development" (2003) 6 *Journal of International Economic Law* 597–633; A.H. Qureshi, "Participation of Developing Countries in the WTO Dispute Settlement System" in F. Ortino and E-U Petersmann, *The WTO Dispute Settlement System 1995–2003* (Kluwer Law International, 2004); S. Shoraka, "World Trade Dispute Resolution and Developing Countries: Constructing a Framework for Fairness in the context of the WTO law" (2006) 3(2) M.J.I.E.L. 2–43; and C.P. Bown, "Developing countries and enforcement of trade agreements", *Journal of World Trade*, 42 (2008) 1, 177–203.

[205] Especially DS246 European Communities—Conditions for the Granting of Tariff Preferences to Developing Countries, Appellate Body Report circulated on April 7, 2004; and DS267 United States—Subsidies on Upland Cotton (complainant Brazil), Appellate Body Report circulated on March 3, 2005. The second report, however, shows also that the interests of developing countries as a group are no longer identical in view of the their increasing heterogeneity. See also V. Mosoti, "Africa in the First Decade of WTO Dispute Settlement" (2006) 9 *Journal of International Economic Law* 427–53.

[206] GATT BISD 14S/18.

[207] Art.3(12) of the Understanding.

[208] Art.8(10) of the Understanding.

[209] Art.12(10) of the Understanding.

[210] Art.12(10) of the Understanding

into account in the panel report.[211] Fifthly, in the context of the surveillance of the implementation of recommendations and rulings, special attention is to be paid in so far as issues affecting developing countries are concerned.[212] The DSB is authorised to take into account further appropriate action. Sixthly, in the case of least developing members, the determinations by the panels and the Appellate Body must take into account the special circumstances of least-developed countries.[213] Developed members are enjoined in such circumstances to exercise due "restraint" in bringing matters under the dispute settlement mechanism.[214] Where nullification or impairment is found to result from a measure taken by a least developed member, the complaining party is invited to exercise due restraint in asking for compensation or the authorisation to suspend concessions or other obligations in the agreement in question. In addition, where at the consultation stage a solution is not found, the least-developed member may request the Director-General or the Chairman of the DSB for his or her good offices, conciliation and mediation, before a request for a panel is made.[215] Finally, provision is to be made by the Secretariat for special legal expertise to be made available from the WTO through its technical co-operation division to any developing member which so requests.[216]

The dispute settlement system offers a number of challenges for developing members. First, a significant number of the provisions in relation to developing and least developing countries are hortatory in character, and difficult to enforce. Secondly, the general consensual character of the process of adjudication allows for power-based solutions which could militate against the interests of developing countries. Thirdly, given that the system essentially relies on the capacity of the parties to the dispute to suspend concessions or obligations, the efficacy of such enforcement is contingent on the "quality" of the concessions and obligations vis-à-vis the other party. The system does not appear to allow a third Member State to retaliate on behalf of another member. In addition, a developing member runs the dangers of taking on a developed member which may retaliate in other spheres, or force a poor implementation agreement.[217] Finally, developing members despite provision for assistance from the WTO can have problems in having access to relevant expertise in order to engage in litigation.[218]

## Conclusions

13-026    A number of changes brought about by the Understanding are of particular note. First, the Understanding deals in important respects with one of the

---

[211] Art.12(11) of the Understanding.
[212] Art.21(2) of the Understanding.
[213] Art.24 of the Understanding.
[214] Art.24 of the Understanding.
[215] Art.24(2) of the Understanding.
[216] Art.27(2) of the Understanding.
[217] See, for example, Kufour (1997).
[218] See above the section on the Advisory Center on WTO Law (ACWL).

major shortcomings of the previous system by removing the veto of the complaining party from the very establishment of a panel and the adoption of the panel report. Secondly, the express characterisation of the Understanding as the exclusive framework for the resolution of conflict in the international trading system is significant. Thirdly, a wider array of dispute settlement techniques are made available. Fourthly, there has been a general improvement in the system as a whole with, for example, specified time schedules at all the stages of the conflict management, higher and more suitable qualifications of panellists, and a greater responsiveness to the particular exigencies of a dispute. Finally, the specific position of the developing and least-developed States is taken into account in a more developed and integrated fashion.

On the other hand, there are many provisions in the Understanding that lack precision and that could have been formulated in more concrete and enforceable terms. Generally, there is some need for transparency in the manner in which the dispute panels and the Appellate Body works. The most significant flaw in the system from an enforcement perspective, however, is that it is still reliant in important respects on the consent and initiative of the parties to the dispute. Thus, whilst the parties can no longer in most respects block the adoption of panel reports, there is still the possibility of delaying the implementation of panel decisions. There is a general absence of the availability of redress provisions independent of the parties to the dispute. In this respect some reforms can be suggested, for example, introducing a right of action by any member in the event of a breach; introducing a right of retaliatory action by third parties; introducing the right to transfer a retaliatory action to another member; compulsory compensation where developing members are concerned.

In conclusion, the Understanding provides a constitutional framework for the resolution of disputes in the field of international trade. It codifies some of the practice developed in this field over the years under the GATT 1947, and generally strengthens the system as a whole. Its merit as an enforcement mechanism cannot be fully evaluated without taking into account the other measures introduced in the Final Act. Thus, the very fact of the creation of an international organisation, the introduction of the Trade Policy Review Mechanism, and the institution of judicial review mechanisms for the benefit of private parties in some of the agreements in the Final Act—all have a bearing on enforcement. The Understanding probably is significant however not so much because of its actual content, even though that has much to commend it, but rather the climate and condition that it sets for the evolution of an effective dispute settlement mechanism.

Already the 1994 Ministerial Decision had said that dispute settlement rules should be reviewed by January 1, 1999 (DSU reform).[219] The Dispute

---

[219] See E-U Petersmann, "WTO Negotiators Meet Academics: The Negotiations on Improvements of the WTO Dispute Settlement System" (2003) 6 *Journal of International Economic Law* 237–50; D. McRae, "What is the Future of WTO Dispute Settlement?" (2004)

Settlement Body (DSB) started the review in late 1997, and held a series of informal discussions on the basis of proposals and issues that members identified. Although many members seemed to agree that improvements should be made to the understanding, the DSB could not reach a consensus on the results of the review. The deadline was extended to July 31, 1999, but there was no agreement. In the Doha Ministerial Declaration of November 20, 2001, again merely the following text could be agreed upon:

**13-027**

**Doha Ministerial Declaration of November 20, 2001**

**Dispute Settlement Understanding**[220]

> 30. We agree to negotiations on improvements and clarifications of the Dispute Settlement Understanding. The negotiations should be based on the work done thus far as well as any additional proposals by members, and aim to agree on improvements and clarifications not later than May 2003, at which time we will take steps to ensure that the results enter into force as soon as possible thereafter.

**13-028**    Furthermore, the Doha Declaration stated in para.47 that the negotiations regarding the DSU would not be part of the single undertaking—i.e. that they would not be tied to the overall success or failure of the other negotiations mandated by the declaration. Originally set to conclude by May 2003, in June 2007 the negotiations were continuing without a deadline. At the Hong Kong Ministerial Meeting of December 18, 2005 it was merely stated:

**13-029**

**Hong Kong Ministerial Meeting of December 18, 2005 (Statement)**

**DSU negotiations**

> 34. We take note of the progress made in the Dispute Settlement Understanding negotiations as reflected in the report by the Chairman of the Special Session of the Dispute Settlement Body to the Trade Negotiations Committee (TNC) and direct the Special Session to continue to work towards a rapid conclusion of the negotiations.

**13-030**    Prior to the Hong Kong Ministerial meeting, well over 80 WTO members had subscribed to more than 40 proposals, each of which contained several suggested changes, covering virtually all stages of the dispute settlement system. On May 16, 2003, the chairman of the negotiations circulated a draft legal text under his own responsibility.

Certain suggestions seem of lesser importance, for example the question

---

7 *Journal of International Economic Law* 3–21; B. Mercurio, "Improving Dispute Settlement in the World Trade Organization: The Dispute Settlement Understanding Review—Making it Work?" (2004) 38 *Journal of World Trade* 795–854; W. Weiss, "The reform of the DSU" (2004) 1(2) M.J.I.E.L. 97; and I. Garcia Bercero, "DSU reform—Why have negotiations to improve WTO dispute settlement failed so far and what are the underlying issues?", *The Journal of World Investment & Trade; Law, Economics, Politics*, 6 (2005) 6, 847–872.
220 Source: *http://www.wto.org*. (Accessed June 8, 2011).

of how to deal with inactive cases which remain dormant for several years without any indication that the complaining countries want to pursue these any further. In such cases, countries would be expected to withdraw their complaints formally.

The problem that the Appellate Body has sometimes to deal with cases where the original panel has not competed its analysis (due to judicial economy or different legal analysis) has led to the suggestion that the AB should be allowed to remand or refer a case back to the original panel if a factual issue arises at the appellate stage which had not been examined by the panel.

The problems regarding the compliance phase have led to new proposals on the sequencing (Art.21:5 in relation to Art.22 DSU). Here, some clarification regarding the procedural rules in cases when a member believes that another has failed to comply fully with the final rulings is necessary.

The issue of "amicus curiae briefs"[221] and thus access of civil society and NGOs to the dispute settlement mechanisms and transparency of the dispute settlement mechanism is more controversial. Despite the rulings by the AB, WTO parties remain split on a codification regarding the procedural status of these actors.

**Bilateral agreements**

The dispute settlement mechanisms in most bilateral or regional trade agreements are based on a traditional arbitration model: With regard to trade disputes, the specificities of the WTO dispute settlement mechanism (excluding the appellate phase) are often integrated into the working procedures of these arbitral tribunals to be established under the more recent agreements.[222] Bilateral trade agreements including investment provisions often provide in addition for a specific investment dispute settlement system (including investor-state arbitration) based on the traditional model found in most bilateral investment treaties.[223] This leads increasingly to the question of institutional overlap and parallel proceedings.[224]

**13-031**

**NAFTA Chapter 20, Section B—Dispute Settlement**[225]

**Article 2003: Cooperation**

The Parties shall at all times endeavor to agree on the interpretation and application of this Agreement, and shall make every attempt through cooperation and consultations to arrive at a mutually satisfactory resolution of any matter that might affect its operation.

**13-032**

---

[221] See above, para.13–007.
[222] See, for example, E.J. Cárdenas and G. Tempesta, "Arbitral awards under Mercosur's dispute settlement mechanism" (2001) 4 *Journal of International Economic Law* 337–66.
[223] See Ch.14, International Investment Law.
[224] See Ch.11 and above.
[225] Source: *http://www.nafta-sec-alena.org*. (Accessed June 8, 2011).

**Article 2004: Recourse to Dispute Settlement Procedures**

Except for the matters covered in Chapter Nineteen (Review and Dispute Settlement in Antidumping and Countervailing Duty Matters) and as otherwise provided in this Agreement, the dispute settlement provisions of this Chapter shall apply with respect to the avoidance or settlement of all disputes between the Parties regarding the interpretation or application of this Agreement or wherever a Party considers that an actual or proposed measure of another Party is or would be inconsistent with the obligations of this Agreement or cause nullification or impairment in the sense of Annex 2004.

**Article 2005: GATT Dispute Settlement**

1. Subject to paragraphs 2, 3 and 4, disputes regarding any matter arising under both this Agreement and the *General Agreement on Tariffs and Trade*, any agreement negotiated thereunder, or any successor agreement (GATT), may be settled in either forum at the discretion of the complaining Party.

2. Before a Party initiates a dispute settlement proceeding in the GATT against another Party on grounds that are substantially equivalent to those available to that Party under this Agreement, that Party shall notify any third Party of its intention. If a third Party wishes to have recourse to dispute settlement procedures under this Agreement regarding the matter, it shall inform promptly the notifying Party and those Parties shall consult with a view to agreement on a single forum. If those Parties cannot agree, the dispute normally shall be settled under this Agreement.

3. In any dispute referred to in paragraph 1 where the responding Party claims that its action is subject to Article 104 (Relation to Environmental and Conservation Agreements) and requests in writing that the matter be considered under this Agreement, the complaining Party may, in respect of that matter, thereafter have recourse to dispute settlement procedures solely under this Agreement.

4. In any dispute referred to in paragraph 1 that arises under Section B of Chapter Seven (Sanitary and Phytosanitary Measures) or Chapter Nine (Standards-Related Measures):

   (a) concerning a measure adopted or maintained by a Party to protect its human, animal or plant life or health, or to protect its environment, and

   (b) that raises factual issues concerning the environment, health, safety or conservation, including directly related scientific matters, where the responding Party requests in writing that the matter be considered under this Agreement, the complaining Party may, in respect of that matter, thereafter have recourse to dispute settlement procedures solely under this Agreement.

5. The responding Party shall deliver a copy of a request made pursuant to paragraph 3 or 4 to the other Parties and to its Section of the Secretariat. Where the complaining Party has initiated dispute settlement proceedings regarding any matter subject to paragraph 3 or 4, the responding Party shall deliver its request no later than 15 days thereafter. On receipt of such request, the complaining Party shall promptly withdraw from

participation in those proceedings and may initiate dispute settlement procedures under Article 2007.

6. Once dispute settlement procedures have been initiated under Article 2007 or dispute settlement proceedings have been initiated under the GATT, the forum selected shall be used to the exclusion of the other, unless a Party makes a request pursuant to paragraph 3 or 4.

7. For purposes of this Article, dispute settlement proceedings under the GATT are deemed to be initiated by a Party's request for a panel, such as under Article XXIII:2 of the *General Agreement on Tariffs and Trade 1947*, or for a committee investigation, such as under Article 20.1 of the Customs Valuation Code.

*Consultations*

## Article 2006: Consultations

1. Any Party may request in writing consultations with any other Party regarding any actual or proposed measure or any other matter that it considers might affect the operation of this Agreement.

2. The requesting Party shall deliver the request to the other Parties and to its Section of the Secretariat.

3. Unless the Commission otherwise provides in its rules and procedures established under Article 2001(4), a third Party that considers it has a substantial interest in the matter shall be entitled to participate in the consultations on delivery of written notice to the other Parties and to its Section of the Secretariat.

4. Consultations on matters regarding perishable agricultural goods shall commence within 15 days of the date of delivery of the request.

5. The consulting Parties shall make every attempt to arrive at a mutually satisfactory resolution of any matter through consultations under this Article or other consultative provisions of this Agreement. To this end, the consulting Parties shall:

    (a) provide sufficient information to enable a full examination of how the actual or proposed measure or other matter might affect the operation of this Agreement;

    (b) treat any confidential or proprietary information exchanged in the course of consultations on the same basis as the Party providing the information; and

    (c) seek to avoid any resolution that adversely affects the interests under this Agreement of any other Party.

*Initiation of Procedures*

## Article 2007: Commission—Good Offices, Conciliation and Mediation

1. If the consulting Parties fail to resolve a matter pursuant to Article 2006 within:

    (a) 30 days of delivery of a request for consultations,

    (b) 45 days of delivery of such request if any other Party has subsequently requested or has participated in consultations regarding the same matter,

(c) 15 days of delivery of a request for consultations in matters regarding perishable agricultural goods, or

(d) such other period as they may agree, any such Party may request in writing a meeting of the Commission.

2. A Party may also request in writing a meeting of the Commission where:

(a) it has initiated dispute settlement proceedings under the GATT regarding any matter subject to Article 2005(3) or (4), and has received a request pursuant to Article 2005(5) for recourse to dispute settlement procedures under this Chapter; or

(b) consultations have been held pursuant to Article 513 (Working Group on Rules of Origin), Article 723 (Sanitary and Phytosanitary Measures Technical Consultations) and Article 914 (Standards-Related Measures Technical Consultations).

3. The requesting Party shall state in the request the measure or other matter complained of and indicate the provisions of this Agreement that it considers relevant, and shall deliver the request to the other Parties and to its Section of the Secretariat.

4. Unless it decides otherwise, the Commission shall convene within 10 days of delivery of the request and shall endeavor to resolve the dispute promptly.

5. The Commission may:

(a) call on such technical advisers or create such working groups or expert groups as it deems necessary,

(b) have recourse to good offices, conciliation, mediation or such other dispute resolution procedures, or

(c) make recommendations, as may assist the consulting Parties to reach a mutually satisfactory resolution of the dispute.

6. Unless it decides otherwise, the Commission shall consolidate two or more proceedings before it pursuant to this Article regarding the same measure. The Commission may consolidate two or more proceedings regarding other matters before it pursuant to this Article that it determines are appropriate to be considered jointly.

*Panel Proceedings*

### Article 2008: Request for an Arbitral Panel

1. If the Commission has convened pursuant to Article 2007(4), and the matter has not been resolved within:

(a) 30 days thereafter,

(b) 30 days after the Commission has convened in respect of the matter most recently referred to it, where proceedings have been consolidated pursuant to Article 2007(6), or

(c) such other period as the consulting Parties may agree, any consulting Party may request in writing the establishment of an arbitral panel. The requesting Party shall deliver the request to the other Parties and to its Section of the Secretariat.

2. On delivery of the request, the Commission shall establish an arbitral panel.

3. A third Party that considers it has a substantial interest in the matter shall be entitled to join as a complaining Party on delivery of written notice of its intention to participate to the disputing Parties and its Section of the Secretariat. The notice shall be delivered at the earliest possible time, and in any event no later than seven days after the date of delivery of a request by a Party for the establishment of a panel.

4. If a third Party does not join as a complaining Party in accordance with paragraph 3, it normally shall refrain thereafter from initiating or continuing:

(a) a dispute settlement procedure under this Agreement, or

(b) a dispute settlement proceeding in the GATT on grounds that are substantially equivalent to those available to that Party under this Agreement, regarding the same matter in the absence of a significant change in economic or commercial circumstances.

5. Unless otherwise agreed by the disputing Parties, the panel shall be established and perform its functions in a manner consistent with the provisions of this Chapter. [. . .]

**Article 2012: Rules of Procedure**

1. The Commission shall establish by January 1, 1994 Model Rules of Procedure, in accordance with the following principles:

(a) the procedures shall assure a right to at least one hearing before the panel as well as the opportunity to provide initial and rebuttal written submissions; and

(b) the panel's hearings, deliberations and initial report, and all written submissions to and communications with the panel shall be confidential.

2. Unless the disputing Parties otherwise agree, the panel shall conduct its proceedings in accordance with the Model Rules of Procedure.

3. Unless the disputing Parties otherwise agree within 20 days from the date of the delivery of the request for the establishment of the panel, the terms of reference shall be:

"To examine, in the light of the relevant provisions of the Agreement, the matter referred to the Commission (as set out in the request for a Commission meeting) and to make findings, determinations and recommendations as provided in Article 2016(2)."

4. If a complaining Party wishes to argue that a matter has nullified or impaired benefits, the terms of reference shall so indicate.

5. If a disputing Party wishes the panel to make findings as to the degree of adverse trade effects on any Party of any measure found not to conform with the obligations of the Agreement or to have caused nullification or

impairment in the sense of Annex 2004, the terms of reference shall so indicate.

### Article 2013: Third Party Participation

A Party that is not a disputing Party, on delivery of a written notice to the disputing Parties and to its Section of the Secretariat, shall be entitled to attend all hearings, to make written and oral submissions to the panel and to receive written submissions of the disputing Parties.

### Article 2014: Role of Experts

On request of a disputing Party, or on its own initiative, the panel may seek information and technical advice from any person or body that it deems appropriate, provided that the disputing Parties so agree and subject to such terms and conditions as such Parties may agree.

### Article 2015: Scientific Review Boards

1. On request of a disputing Party or, unless the disputing Parties disapprove, on its own initiative, the panel may request a written report of a scientific review board on any factual issue concerning environmental, health, safety or other scientific matters raised by a disputing Party in a proceeding, subject to such terms and conditions as such Parties may agree.

2. The board shall be selected by the panel from among highly qualified, independent experts in the scientific matters, after consultations with the disputing Parties and the scientific bodies set out in the Model Rules of Procedure established pursuant to Article 2012(1).

3. The participating Parties shall be provided:

   (a) advance notice of, and an opportunity to provide comments to the panel on, the proposed factual issues to be referred to the board; and

   (b) a copy of the board's report and an opportunity to provide comments on the report to the panel.

4. The panel shall take the board's report and any comments by the Parties on the report into account in the preparation of its report.

### Article 2016: Initial Report

1. Unless the disputing Parties otherwise agree, the panel shall base its report on the submissions and arguments of the Parties and on any information before it pursuant to Article 2014 or 2015.

2. Unless the disputing Parties otherwise agree, the panel shall, within 90 days after the last panelist is selected or such other period as the Model Rules of Procedure established pursuant to Article 2012(1) may provide, present to the disputing Parties an initial report containing:

   (a) findings of fact, including any findings pursuant to a request under Article 2012(5);

   (b) its determination as to whether the measure at issue is or would be inconsistent with the obligations of this Agreement or cause nullification or impairment in the sense of Annex 2004, or any other determination requested in the terms of reference; and

(c) its recommendations, if any, for resolution of the dispute.

3. Panelists may furnish separate opinions on matters not unanimously agreed.

4. A disputing Party may submit written comments to the panel on its initial report within 14 days of presentation of the report.

5. In such an event, and after considering such written comments, the panel, on its own initiative or on the request of any disputing Party, may:

(a) request the views of any participating Party;

(b) reconsider its report; and

(c) make any further examination that it considers appropriate.

### Article 2017: Final Report

1. The panel shall present to the disputing Parties a final report, including any separate opinions on matters not unanimously agreed, within 30 days of presentation of the initial report, unless the disputing Parties otherwise agree.

2. No panel may, either in its initial report or its final report, disclose which panelists are associated with majority or minority opinions.

3. The disputing Parties shall transmit to the Commission the final report of the panel, including any report of a scientific review board established under Article 2015, as well as any written views that a disputing Party desires to be appended, on a confidential basis within a reasonable period of time after it is presented to them.

4. Unless the Commission decides otherwise, the final report of the panel shall be published 15 days after it is transmitted to the Commission.

*Implementation of Panel Reports*

### Article 2018: Implementation of Final Report

1. On receipt of the final report of a panel, the disputing Parties shall agree on the resolution of the dispute, which normally shall conform with the determinations and recommendations of the panel, and shall notify their Sections of the Secretariat of any agreed resolution of any dispute.

2. Wherever possible, the resolution shall be non-implementation or removal of a measure not conforming with this Agreement or causing nullification or impairment in the sense of Annex 2004 or, failing such a resolution, compensation.

### Article 2019: Non-Implementation-Suspension of Benefits

1. If in its final report a panel has determined that a measure is inconsistent with the obligations of this Agreement or causes nullification or impairment in the sense of Annex 2004 and the Party complained against has not reached agreement with any complaining Party on a mutually satisfactory resolution pursuant to Article 2018(1) within 30 days of receiving the final report, such complaining Party may suspend the application to

the Party complained against of benefits of equivalent effect until such time as they have reached agreement on a resolution of the dispute.

2. In considering what benefits to suspend pursuant to paragraph 1:

   (a) a complaining Party should first seek to suspend benefits in the same sector or sectors as that affected by the measure or other matter that the panel has found to be inconsistent with the obligations of this Agreement or to have caused nullification or impairment in the sense of Annex 2004; and

   (b) a complaining Party that considers it is not practicable or effective to suspend benefits in the same sector or sectors may suspend benefits in other sectors.

3. On the written request of any disputing Party delivered to the other Parties and its Section of the Secretariat, the Commission shall establish a panel to determine whether the level of benefits suspended by a Party pursuant to paragraph 1 is manifestly excessive.

4. The panel proceedings shall be conducted in accordance with the Model Rules of Procedure. The panel shall present its determination within 60 days after the last panelist is selected or such other period as the disputing Parties may agree. [. . .]

## THE TRADE POLICY REVIEW MECHANISM

**13-033**    The TPRM[226] is a permanent institution of the WTO, and responsibility for its administration vests with the Trade Policy Review Body[227] (TPRB). The TPRB is essentially the General Council of the WTO acting under a different framework.[228] The objectives of the TPRM are stated to be as follows[229]:

1. Improved adherence by all members to the WTO rules, disciplines and commitments.

---

[226] See GATT The Results of the Uruguay Round Of Multilateral Trade Negotiations 1994. The agreement on the TPRM is set out in Annex 3. See also, for example, R. Eglin, "Surveillance of balance-of- payments measures in the GATT (1987) 10 *The World Economy* 1–26; R. Blackhurst, "Strengthening GATT surveillance of trade-related policies", in E-U Petersmann and M. Hilf (eds), *The New GATT Round of Multilateral Trade Negotiations. Legal and Economic Problems* (1988) pp.123–55; V. Curzon-Price, "The GATT's New Trade Policy Review Mechanism" (1991) 14 *World Economy*, 227–38; S.P.C. Mavroidis, "Surveillance Schemes: The GATT's New Trade Policy Review Mechanism" (1992) 13 *Michigan Journal Of International Law* 374–414; Qureshi, (1996), Chs 3, 6, 10; J.S. Mah, "Reflection on the TPRM in the W.T.O." (1997) 31(5) J.W.T. 56; C. Hsiao, "Taiwan's first trade policy review in the World Trade Organization", *Chinese (Taiwan) Yearbook of International Law and Affairs*, 24.2006(2008), 185–348A. Ghosh, "Developing countries in the WTO Trade Policy Review Mechanism", *World trade review*, 9 (2010) 3, 419–455.

[227] See Arts III(4) and IV of the Marrakesh Agreement.

[228] See Arts III(4) and IV of the Marrakesh Agreement.

[229] See para.A of the Agreement establishing the TPRM, in Annex 3 of the Marrakesh Agreement.

2. Greater transparency in, and understanding of, trade policies and practices of members.

3. The enabling of collective appreciation and evaluation, in the framework of the WTO, of individual trade policies and practices and their impact on the functioning of the multilateral trading system.

These objectives are qualified by the stipulation that the TPRM is not to serve as a basis for the "enforcement" of specific WTO obligations or for dispute settlement procedures or to impose new policy commitments on members.

The objectives thus adumbrated and qualified may however be reformulated in a two-tiered fashion—namely, the objective of ensuring better implementation of the WTO code, (i.e. 1 and arguably also 3 above); and the objective of transparency (i.e. 2 and 3 above).

The Trade Policy Review Mechanism is a three-pronged institution. First, members have accepted the need for domestic transparency in their trade policy and practices. Domestic transparency involves the facilitation of, and mechanisms for, the endogenous review and scrutiny of a member's trade policies and practices. Thus, advance publicity of trade proposals, the soliciting of relevant interested group opinions and the establishment of independent non-governmental institutions to review governmental trade policies and practices would be the kind of domestic transparency measures contemplated. This domestic transparency requirement, however, is for the present not obligatory. Members have nevertheless undertaken to encourage and promote greater transparency in their own trading systems. Compliance with this undertaking is subject to WTO review. Secondly, the TPRB is to undertake an annual overview of the international trading environment. This review is to be based on an annual report prepared by the Director-General focusing on the activities of the WTO and significant policy issues pertaining to the international trading system. Thirdly, and most importantly, the establishment of a review procedure for the regular examination of individual member's trade policies and practices—i.e. the actual Trade Policy Review Mechanism.

### The TPRM framework

The criterion for the assessment of a member's foreign trade regime under the TPRM is the impact a member's trade policies and practices make on the multilateral trading order. The focus and function of the TPRM is intended to be an examination of the trade policies and practices of a member. This criterion is to be set, to the extent relevant, against the background of the wider economic and developmental needs, policies and objectives of the member concerned—including its external environment.    **13-034**

Every member is required to submit a full report (the Country Report) in relation to its trade policies and practices, when it is the subject of a review. The full reports are based on an agreed format, viz. the Outline Format for country reports.[230] The objective of the Outline Format is to ensure the eliciting of a certain level of essential detail that is both meaningful and readily accessible. The Outline Format in summary is divided into two parts, A and B, and an appendix. In Part A, titled "Trade policies and practices" the member is invited inter alia to provide information on the following:

1. Objectives of its trade policies.

2. A summary description of its import and export system and how it relates to the objectives stated in 1 above.

3. The domestic laws and regulations governing the application of trade policies.

4. The process of trade policy formulation and review.

5. Relevant international agreements.

6. The trade policy measures used by the member, e.g. tariffs, tariff quotas and surcharges, QRs, non-tariff measures, customs valuation, rules of origin, government procurement, technical barriers, safeguard action, anti-dumping actions, countervailing actions, export taxes and subsidies, free-trade zones, export restrictions, state-trading enterprises, foreign exchange controls related to imports and exports and any other measures covered by the General Agreement, its annexes and protocols.

7. Programmes in existence for trade liberalisation.

8. Prospective changes in trade policies and practices to the extent they can be made known.

Part B is titled and seeks information on "Relevant background against which the assessment of trade policies will be carried out: wider economic and developmental needs, external environment". The appendix comprises statistical and tabular information on e.g. trade flows of products in terms of their origin and destination.

In between reviews, the members are to provide brief reports when significant changes take place in their trade policies and practices. This is to be complemented by an annual update of statistical information provided by the members according to an agreed format.

**13-035** In addition to the full report, the WTO Secretariat draws up a report on its own account (the WTO Report), of the trade policies and practices of the member under review. This report is prepared by the Trade Policy Review Division of the WTO Secretariat on information available to it, and

---

[230] GATT document L/6552; and L/6552/Add.1 in relation to least-developed member countries. Approved on June 19–20, 1989.

that provided by members. The Secretariat is to seek clarification from the member concerned of its trade policies and practices.[231]

The WTO Report is based inter alia on two questionnaires drafted by the Trade Policy Review Division. The first is a basic questionnaire. The second is a more detailed one, drawing inter alia on information provided as a result of the first questionnaire. In addition to the questionnaires, staff from the WTO Secretariat also visit the capital of the country in order to gather information. There is no set format for the WTO Report. The Reports, however, normally contain six chapters and a summary of observations.[232]

Given the absence of a set format for the WTO Report, there is arguably a degree of latitude for the WTO Secretariat to set the agenda, or the orientation for the review. Thus, reviews of developing countries may particularly focus on external market access problems confronted by these countries. Commendable as this practice may be, it could be argued that such an orientation implies a judgement, which is really the TPRB's function. Although, the six chapters of the WTO Report are sent to the country under review for factual correction before it is circulated, it is still a matter of judgement whether this is a sufficient restraint on the WTO Secretariat in the crafting of the report. It may be that latitude for the WTO Secretariat is a *desideratum*; and may indeed facilitate for the country under review the "connivance" of the WTO in the inclusion of material which is politically expedient. The danger, however, is that international civil servants may get embroiled in the domestic politics of the country under review.

Every member is to be subject to a review but the frequency of the review differs as between members. Briefly, the criterion for the frequency of review is dependent on the impact the trade of the member has on the functioning of the "multilateral trading system". The impact is determined in terms of the member's share of the world trade in a representative period, and not its potential share.[233] Using this "impact" criterion, the first four trading entities (counting the EEC as one) in the league table are subject to review every two years; the next 16 every 4 years; and the rest every 6 years, save the least-developed countries for whom a longer period may be fixed. The TPRB may exceptionally, where changes in a member's trade policy impact significantly on the trade of other members, request an unscheduled review. In the case of members with a common external trade policy (e.g. a customs union) the

**13-036**

---

[231] See the agreement on the TPRM in Annex 3 of the Marrakesh Agreement.

[232] The chapters deal with the following topics: (1) the economic environment; (2) the trade policy regime, framework and objectives; (3) trade related aspects of the foreign exchange regime; (4) trade policies and practices by measure; (5) trade policy and practices by sector; and (6) trade disputes and consultations.

[233] See R. Blackhurst, "Strengthening GATT Surveillance of Trade-Related Policies", in Petersmann and Hilf (1998), p.151 where he states "a country's share in the contracting parties' total trade could be unusually small precisely because the country is very protectionist—in which case it could be argued that the country needs to be examined more frequently then indicated by its trade share alone. A more fundamental shortcoming is that the usual trade-share criterion fails to take into account the share of trade in domestic output."

review is to focus on all aspects of the common trade policies and practices, including the relevant trade policies and practices of the individual members.

The trade policy review is the responsibility of the TPRB. The TPRB is to conduct the review on the basis of the full report supplied by the member under review, and the report compiled by the WTO Secretariat. Both reports are confined to relevant information in relation to the foreign trade regime of the member under review. For every review two discussants are appointed, who introduce the discussion at the TPRB meeting. They are appointed by the Chair of the Council, in consultation with the member under review.[234] The discussants are normally trade delegates, but are supposed to act in their personal capacity. Members invite their representatives in the country under review, to comment on the WTO and Country Reports. Their observations are then sent to the country of origin of the representatives, before they finally arrive back to the delegate in Geneva. The nature of appraisal of country trade policies and practices is a function of national interests. Attendance at the reviews can therefore be low on occasions.

Upon the completion of the review by the TPRB, the reports by the member and the WTO secretariat, along with a summary record of the proceedings of the TPRB are published, and forwarded to the next regular Session of the Ministerial Conference to be noted.

## Key features

**13-037**     The Trade Policy Review Mechanism is an instrument of enforcement, no matter what the WTO members assert; despite denials by country trade officials[235]; and even though the agreement establishing the TPRM specifically states that the mechanism is not intended to serve as a basis for the enforcement of specific obligations, or for dispute settlement procedures. All the trade reviews published thus far contain in the preface the statement that the review exercise is not intended to serve as a basis for the enforcement of specific WTO or GATT obligations, or for dispute settlement procedures. Further, some of the country reports are also prefaced with such denials.[236]

These statements need to be construed with some circumspection. They are arguably self-serving, and tendered in a defensive posture, in order to shield their respective States from possible adverse consequences. There appears to be a "conspiracy of denial", where the enforcement attributes of the TPRM are concerned. Certainly, such a denial facilitates the eliciting of information and a freer discourse. Further, in reality, the establishment of the mechanism could only be initiated by nourishing this "denial". Thus, Roderick Abbott

---

[234] Para.C of the agreement on the TPRM in Annex 3 of the Marrakesh Agreement.

[235] See R. Abbott, "GATT and the Trade Policy Review Mechanism: Further Reflections on Earlier Reflections" (1993) *Journal of World Trade* 116–19.

[236] See, for example, statement made by representative of Uruguay at the Council Meeting in July 1992. GATT Trade Policy Review Mechanism—Uruguay Vol.2 at p.93.

states[237] inter alia: "if countries had thought that they would in any sense be facing a kind of tribunal. . .It is probable that there would have been no agreement to launch the exercise in the first place."

Now that the TPRM has arrived, and has functioned for some years, it may be time to explain to "Little Red Riding Hood what the function of the long teeth are"—albeit within the limits of the WTO system! At any rate whatever might be politically convenient, it cannot surely be appropriate to deny what in fact are the attributes of the behaviour of the actors being observed. The TPRM qua mechanism, can only be considered constructively if there is, as a starting premise, clarity as to its character. It can be conceived from an enforcement perspective in two respects. First, it has enforcement characteristics itself. Secondly, it facilitates enforcement.

The TPRM itself has enforcement characteristics for the following reasons. First, it is a compulsory exercise, in the sense that a member does not have the choice of opting out of the mechanism. Secondly, the whole process of the review comprises of approbation and disapprobation in terms of a normative framework comprising of legal as well as economic criteria. Thus, on the evidence there is a strong suggestion that the actors involved have couched their actions with reference to and within the framework of GATT and WTO. In this respect, the Reports and the discussion at the GATT Council Meeting are replete with allusions, either in defence or otherwise, to the GATT or the direction it is taking.[238] In addition, whilst the questionnaires sent by the GATT/WTO Secretariat in drafting the WTO Report are confidential, it is reasonable to assume that they facilitate free and frank questions being directed at the country under review. In the circumstances, conformity with the WTO code of country trade policies and practices is a concern of the TPRM, and is stated as such in the agreement establishing it.[239]

**13-038**

Thus, a facet of the TPRM is that it can be "*corrective*".[240] The "corrective" process derives from the fact that the TPRM is an invitation for the collective

---

[237] Abbott (1993), p.118.

[238] See, for example, in so far as GATT Reports are concerned: GATT Trade Policy Review—Uruguay at pp.99, 114, 137; GATT Trade Policy Review—Nigeria at p.39; GATT Trade Policy Review—Indonesia at pp.98 and 99; GATT Trade Policy Review—Thailand; GATT Trade Policy Review—Brazil at pp.76 and 122. In so far as Country Reports are concerned see for example GATT Trade Policy Review—Egypt at p.14; GATT Trade Policy Review—Bangladesh Vol.11 at p.54; GATT Trade Policy Review—Morocco at p.207; GATT Trade Policy Review—Uruguay at pp.96, 99 and 109; GATT Trade Policy Review—Nigeria at p.144; GATT Trade Policy Review—Thailand at pp.95, 110 and 119; GATT Trade Policy Review—Colombia at p.260; GATT Trade Policy Review—Brazil at pp.99, 101 and 116; GATT Trade Policy Review—Egypt at p.62.

[239] See para.A of the agreement on the TPRM in Annex 3 of the Marrakesh Agreement. The aims of the TPRM are spelled out as: (1) improved adherence by all contracting parties to GATT rules, disciplines and commitments; (2) greater transparency in, and understanding of, trade policies and practices of contracting parties; (3) the enabling of collective appreciation and evaluation by the contracting parties of individual trade policies and practices and their impact on the functioning of the multilateral trading system.

[240] See P. Van Dijk (ed.), *Supervisory Mechanisms in International Economic Organisations* (Kluwer Law International, 1984), p.11.

membership of the WTO to evaluate and appreciate the respective member's trade policies and practices. This has the effect of inculcating a corrective influence, within a particular normative framework. This process, albeit lacking in coercion, is disposed to having an impact on the course of State behaviour, even if in a given case it may not in fact have such an impact. In addition, particularly in the case of developing countries, the review exercises have precipitated an internal co-ordination of trade policy and practice; heightened consciousness in this field; and concentrated minds with respect to trade policy.

The seemingly innocuous "discourse" between the members involved in the review is an exercise in enforcement, even though it may partake of a broad-brush general enforcement approach, to which the Member State responds similarly by way of a broad and general "defensive" posture. However, the TPRM is not an enforcement mechanism through which specific WTO obligations are *thereby* enforced in a legal sense, as such. It is not an adjudicatory process, in as much as the pronouncements made in the TPRB, or by the TPRB, are not themselves to be construed as findings or binding recommendations.

13-039    Similarly, the TPRM affects State behaviour *ex ante*. It is a "*conditioning*" mechanism. It inculcates at the earliest possible moment a "WTO" approved pattern of behaviour—both through the impregnation of the national policy framework by substantive WTO trade prescriptions, as well as through the provision of conditions, including institutional, necessary for the evolution of WTO approved trade policies. The "conditioning "stems particularly from the probing of policy, policy formulation and the objectives of policies. Furthermore, the framework for this "conditioning" process is derived also, inter alia, from the general "psychoanalytical" imprint of the whole TPRM process. Thus, the WTO may be compared to the psychoanalyst, the member under review as the patient, and the Outline Country Format as the couch and the form that the "patient" has to occupy and fill. This "psychoanalysis" analogy, if accepted, carries with it the notion, inter alia, of infusing a particular trade policy approach to State behaviour. Thus, invitations to describe the objectives of national trade policy, the process of policy formulation, the domestic trade legislation and international agreements and their respective objectives, existing programmes for trade liberalisation and prospective changes in trade policies, cannot be mere objective descriptions without more—they are in fact descriptions made to the WTO through a mould already cast. This process of description involves not merely effusion but must also induce, in some measure, on the part of the member the subject of review, a prior orientation within the framework of the WTO code, which arises from the knowledge of having to account to a body with particular expectations, and from the influence of built-in prior suggestions of the institution in the mould of the TPRM. Thus, the process of description is not a mere contribution to transparency but rather its very proffering has the added consequence of having the potential to engender a degree of sensitivity on the part of the member to the ethos of the WTO code. As such the TPRM can be conditioning in its unveiling, as much as revealing.

The process of the TPRM can also lead to, or form a basis for, the enforcement of specific WTO obligations, or for dispute settlement, or impose new commitments on members.[241] Thus, information that is revealed in a TPRM exercise may be used by members as a basis for enforcement through the WTO dispute settlement procedures. The TPRM cannot have been intended to function as a process whereby upon revelation of a "misdemeanour", the member becomes "immune" from enforcement in respect of it. The TPRM does not accord absolution from trade sins. Indeed, members in actual reviews may state on record, that they reserve the right, or intend to take up, as the case may be, the matter further through the dispute settlement procedure.[242] Alternatively, prior pressure might conceivably be brought, that is prior to the actual review, to induce the member under review into giving unilateral commitments or undertakings in the TPRM exercise. Furthermore, there is nothing to preclude a member from subsequently invoking statements made in a review in relation to the State which made the representation. In addition, there is nothing to prevent the member itself under review to unilaterally undertake a binding commitment.[243]

This enforcement aspect is, however, dependent on the extent to which the review and transparency is thorough enough to identify all deviant behaviour. Some of the country reports thus far have been general rather then in depth; and not necessarily oriented towards highlighting possible deviant conduct. This is so even though adherence to the WTO code as much as transparency is the stated aim of the TPRM. This may in part be because in so far as the secretariat report is concerned the Trade Policy Review Division of the WTO is staffed mainly by non-lawyers.

Finally, the TPRM mechanism can also have a prescriptive trait or to borrow from a nomenclature[244] a potential "creative" function. This creative function may or may not be within the strict normative framework of the WTO. It derives, inter alia, from both the conditioning and corrective processes, which operate in an elastic fashion—as well as possibly from the ambiguity of the criteria for the review (discussed below).

### The criteria for the review

The agreement is not very transparent with respect to the criteria for the review. This much, however, cannot be denied from an interpretation of the language of the agreement and the intention of the negotiators, i.e. that the TPRM is not merely a mechanism to register national developments in

**13-040**

---

[241] See A.H. Qureshi, "The New GATT Trade Policy Review Mechanism" (1990) 24(3) *Journal of World Trade* 149.
[242] See, for example, GATT Trade Policy Review—Colombia at p.266.
[243] See Nuclear Tests Cases (1974) I.C.J. Reports.
[244] See Nuclear Tests Cases (1974) I.C.J. Reports.

trade policies, but also incorporates specifically the idea of "review", "assessment" and "evaluation". Conceptually, any form of "review", "assessment" and "evaluation" implies the existence of a framework against the background of which the review, assessment and evaluation would take place. There cannot be a review, indeed let alone mere monitoring, without the existence of some criteria. And there cannot be effective review and/or monitoring without some transparent criteria.

The normative structure of the criteria could in theory be multifarious encompassing legal, economic as well as political aspects. However, the competence of the WTO does not extend to what may be described as the "political" sphere.[245] A fortiori, the agreement on the TPRM can only refer to economic and/or legal criteria. Indeed this was the understanding of the negotiating group.

### The legal criteria

**13-041**    Insofar as the legal criteria are concerned the guidance is clear. Given that the TPRM is designed to improve adherence to WTO rules disciplines and commitments, the review must be processed against the background of the WTO code.

Although the purpose of the TPRM is stated to contribute to improved adherence by the members to the WTO code, this purpose is, it would seem, not immediate and/or exclusive. There is some lack of clarity in this respect—possibly deliberate. This derives from the fact that the function of the TPRM exercise is stated to be the examination of "the impact of a member's trade policies and practices on the multilateral trading system". The lack of clarity arises from the fact that there is no clear definition of what constitutes "the multilateral trading system". It could, for example, read as meaning "the multilateral juridical trading system" or it could be read as meaning "the de facto multilateral trading system" in its economic state. If the latter is the sense intended, then there is some tension between it and the objective of contributing to improved adherence to the WTO code. This is so, in as much as the suggestion that arguably may be read, is that the rule-oriented evaluation is in the immediate term to be "subordinated" to the evaluation in terms of the impact of the national trade policies and practices to the actual functioning of the international trading system, or to put it in another way, to the state of the "health" of the international trade. Thus, although violation of a rule may or may not have an impact on the health of the trading system (even if premised on the assumption that rule violation would eventually at any rate affect the "health" of international trade), conduct that comprises non-violation of a rule on the other hand may nevertheless have an impact on the "health" of the trading system. Whilst the two components may complement

---

[245] See, for example, F. Roessler, "The competence of GATT" (1987) 21(1) *Journal of World Trade* 73; and also J. Gold on political considerations in the context of the IMF in IMF *Pamphlet Series* No.32 at p.59.

each other, the difficulty arises when the "health of the international trade " is given a higher priority, or forms a qualification to the rule-based approach to evaluation, since the non-rule-based criterion is potentially a wider criterion.

The suggestion that this might well be the case arises from the following. First, in para.A of the agreement on the TPRM it is stated that the purpose of the TPRM is to "contribute" to improved adherence to the WTO code, etc. in order to achieve a smoother functioning of the multilateral trading system. The implication here is that ensuring rule compliance is not the direct and exclusive function of the TPRM, rather that rule compliance is a desideratum to the extent that it enables the smoother functioning of the multilateral trading system. Secondly, it is stated in the same paragraph that the TPRM will enable the evaluation of the "full range of the individual members' trade policies and practices [in the context of the WTO code] *and* their impact on the functioning of the multilateral trading system". Thus, the rule based approach to evaluation is *qualified* by the "and"—and the need to consider the "impact on the functioning of the multilateral trading system." Thirdly, it is specifically stated that the function (without more) of the TPRM is to examine the impact of a member's trade policies and practices on the "multilateral trading system". Finally, para.C of the agreement formulates the frequency of country review in the context of the impact on the functioning of the multilateral trading system of the member's trade policies and practices; the "impact" being specifically defined for this purpose in terms of the share of the world trade in a representative period.

Thus, to epitomise, the essential quest of the surveillance operation involved in the TPRM, based on an interpretation of the language of the agreement establishing the TPRM, relates to the real quality of the state of international trade, and only to that extent to rule adherence. This focus is a broad approach to rule adherence. It is an approach that would seem to be supported by some of the developed members during the negotiations, but not however by some of the developing members. It is not novel in the sense that the health oriented criterion reflects the existing Art.XXIII(1)(b) approach—namely that there is nullification or impairment of a benefit, if the attainment of any objective of the General Agreement is being impeded in the event of the application by another member of any measure, whether or not it conflicts with the provisions of the General Agreement. The difference between Art.XXIII and the criteria set out in the TPRM agreement is that in Art.XXIII, subpara.(a) stands on the same footing as subpara.(b), and is not qualified by subpara.(b).[246] The broad approach seems to be born out by the WTO review practices. Thus, questions on trade-related issues are raised in review exercises, for example trade-related competition policy and practice of the member under review,[247] even though there is no such code on competition policy and trade as yet.

---

[246] See Art.XXIII of the GATT 1994.
[247] See WTO Annual Report (1997), Ch.4.

Finally, the assessment under the framework of the WTO code, according to the TPRM agreement, is to be conducted "to the extent relevant" against the background of the wider economic and developmental needs, policies and objectives of the member as well as its external environment. It is not clear what is meant by "to the extent relevant" in terms of evaluating the trade policies and practices against the WTO code. Does it mean that, for example, the evaluation of the adherence to the WTO code should take into account these circumstances only to the extent that the WTO code itself allows for their recognition or is it contemplated that the rule-based evaluation should be against the background of a wider, more flexible framework?

### The economic criteria

**13-042**    Not only was the question of the pre-eminence of the economic criterion but so also was the precise scope of that criterion, the subject of differing emphasis, if not of view, during the negotiations in the FOG. Thus, some delegates from the developing countries, as was mentioned earlier, interpreted the review to take place in a narrow sense, i.e. only in terms of the WTO obligations as such; whereas some developed members took a wider view—namely that the total context of the trade policies and practices must be considered, including their rationale and relationship with the other economic policies. This divergence of perception is also discernable by a comparison of the legal and economic view points. Thus, Blackhurst echoing the standpoint of developed members asserts[248]:

"... the correspondence between GATT obligations and 'good' economic policies is close enough that surveillance based primarily on economic norms would never stray far from the General Agreement".

On the other hand, on an interpretation of the WTO code, it would appear that on the whole the WTO code is permissive, rather than intrusive. Its approach to the regulation of national trade policies is on the whole arguably minimalist.[249] Further, the remit of the WTO is only within the carefully defined parameters of the impact of domestic trade practice with international trade—to the extent that it forms a barrier to international trade, or is discriminatory in an international context. In short, the essence of the WTO code is simply that trade policies and practices must be transparent, non-discriminatory and they must be characterised by due process and proportionality. Provided these conditions are met a member is generally free to formulate its trade practices and policies as it wishes.

The difficulty with Blackhurst's view is as follows. There is in fact no

[248] Blackhurst (1988), p.148.
[249] E-U Petersmann at Conference on EC and US Trade Laws and the GATT organised by the College of Europe. September 1989; and also E-U Petersmann, "Strengthening the domestic legal framework of the GATT multilateral trade system," in Petersmann and Hilf (1988), pp.45 and 46.

necessary correspondence between the WTO code and "good" economic policies in the juridical sense. Further, it is questionable whether endowing them with such a linkage with the code is appropriate. "Good" economic policies may well result in compliance with the WTO code, but in terms of their juridical character they do not necessarily correlate. The normative framework of behaviour both in terms of domestic and International Law is determined with reference to the articulation of the norm. The letter of the law is on the whole the exclusive determinant of permissive or non-permissive behaviour. In interpreting that framework policy may well be taken into account—but that is distinct from asserting that the legal stipulation concerned also actually regulates all conduct that has a predisposition towards a conflict with that stipulation. Thus, the prohibition on murder is not a prohibition on brandishing a gun. Another prohibition on the brandishing of the gun is required. Similarly, a prohibition in relation to a gun is not a prohibition on verbal abuse. Another prohibition on verbal abuse is required. And finally, to labour the point somewhat, the prohibition on verbal abuse is not by itself an injunction to love.

The basis for the shift from rule-based surveillance alone to include policy-based surveillance cannot be solely on the assertion of this questionable relationship between "good economic policies" and the WTO code. This lack of juridical correspondence has the important consequence of precluding resort to a *carte blanche* economic criterion without more. The competence of the WTO would be exceeded if there were such resort to an economic criterion. The members are not to be presumed to have delegated such a level of external inquiry into their economic matters—albeit at the level of surveillance. Furthermore, in any event, an added difficulty is that it is not at all that clear what "good" economic policies are and whether there is indeed agreement about them.

What is the economic criterion, if any, that is contemplated in the TPRM agreement which may be resorted to for a collective appreciation and evaluation? What does the invocation of economic criteria involve? It would appear, prima facie, that the TPRM agreement is consonant with both the wider and narrower interpretations outlined above. However, before delving deeper, a distinction needs to be made between on the one hand *economic analysis* and the determination and proffering of *economic prescriptions*. The economic analysis is relevant in order to, for example, determine the causal relationship between declared national policy objectives of a member and the methodology employed towards achieving those objectives; the interaction of trade policy with fiscal and monetary policy; the effect of trade policy on other members. On the other hand, the need for economic solutions may give rise to the proffering of economic prescriptions which, for example, purport to be more efficient in terms of achieving the declared national objectives; in terms of the proper admixture of fiscal and monetary policies; in terms of a more favourable impact on the trade of other members; and in assisting the member in question to respect its commitments under the WTO code.

There is no difficulty with the provision of the economic analysis. This does indeed constitute the process of "appreciation, evaluation, review and assessment" by the collective membership, contemplated in the TPRM agreement. It should however be noted, as an addendum, that there may be some conflict in the process of evaluating trade policy instruments in terms of their declared national goals, and in the determination of their effects on the trade of other members—given that the two are not necessarily always synonymous. Thus, this conflict is alluded to implicitly by Blackhurst when he states[250]:

> "if it could be shown that a particular trade-related policy or set of policies was not only causing problems for trading partners, but was also not particularly effective or efficient in achieving the stated goals, the result is likely to be increased peer pressure on the country to revise the policy".

There is some difficulty however, it is suggested, in advocating the proffering of economic prescriptions within the framework of the TPRM. This is reinforced from the stipulation that the TPRM is not intended to serve as a basis for imposing new policy commitments on members. The status of such advice, if tendered, is therefore non-binding, even if not prohibited as such in the TPRM agreement. The point needs to be made and is not merely legalistic. This is because whilst the non-rule based approach to evaluation in the TPRM is designed to bring pressure to bear for the introduction of "good" trade policies—that is the extent of the scope of the TPRM mechanism. "Pressure" is not to translate into "intimidation". Furthermore, and significantly, the TPRM is not a licence to arrogate from the member in question the creative processes involved in the, albeit, "good" policy formulation, even if within the framework of the WTO code. The formulation of good policies and the choice of "good policies" within the framework of the WTO code is a function of the member under review.

## Some potential legal consequences arising from the TPRM

13-043    There are here primarily two points of note. First, to the extent that the TPRM mechanism involves evaluation of specific trade policy practices against the background of the WTO code by the TPRB, the practice could arguably involve or evolve into an interpretative process, given that the proceedings of the TPRB review will be taken note of by the next Session of the Ministerial Conference, the body in the WTO with interpretative jurisdiction.[251]

Secondly, whilst it is specifically stated that the TPRM mechanism is not intended to be a basis for the imposition of new policy commitments on members, there is nothing in the Outline Format or elsewhere which pre-

---

[250] See Blackhurst (1988), p.147.
[251] Art.IX of the Marrakesh Agreement. See also for example J. Jackson, *The World Trading System* (MIT, 1989), p.14 on the problems of interpretation under GATT.

cludes a member arguably from unilaterally undertaking a binding trade policy commitment. Thus, in the context of the drafting of the country report, particularly para.(A)(IV)(d) of the Outline Format, the member could for instance state:

> "The Government has also concluded that it is necessary to undertake a thorough going reform of the methods and instruments. . .The Government is planning to require. . .The Government has initiated the preparation of specific reforms. . .The Government will also consider. . .The Government will concentrate on encouraging. . .The Government will seek to provide the conditions necessary to ensure. . .The Government will seek to explore. . .".

This is the customary language of IMF Letters of Intent. It does not involve any specific enforceable (in the narrow sense) commitment or undertaking. The statements do not constitute positive undertakings. The statements are merely descriptive of a future course of conduct currently contemplated and not promissory.[252] However, there is no reason why the member might not tender the same in language comprising a binding undertaking. Thus, for example, it could state:

> "The government will undertake a thorough going reform of the methods and instruments. . .The Government will require. . .The Government will introduce the following reforms. . .The Government will. . .The Government will provide the conditions necessary. . .The Government will explore. . .".[253]

As a matter of General International Law the undertakings could, it is suggested, be binding if the promises tendered are intended to be legally binding.[254] This intention is not negated by the statement in the TPRM agreement that the TPRM is not intended to impose new policy commitments on members. A unilateral promise by a member intended to be legally binding does not constitute an imposition of a new commitment, rather it is the self-initiated voluntary undertaking of a new commitment.

## Conclusion

Some tentative observations may be made in relation to the effectiveness of the TPRM. First, insofar as the evaluation of the transparency engendered is concerned, to a certain extent this is a function of time—given that the review

**13-044**

---

[252] See this author, "The International Legal Theory of IMF Conditionality—An Alternative Approach". Ph.D thesis (available at the London School Of Economics, University of London library).

[253] In fact the US does make similar statements in its Country Report at p.105. It is stated inter alia: "The VRA program covering steel products. . .will be transitionally extended until March 31, 1992. However, the program will be liberalized so the import penetration of VRA countries is allowed to increase by one percentage point each year.At the conclusion of the new Steel Trade Liberalization, all voluntary arrangements will be terminated and the US steel industry will rely upon domestic trade laws to combat trade-distorting practices. . .".

[254] Nuclear Tests Case (1974) I.C.J. Reports, pp.253 and 267–8.

will be the subject of continued attention of the members, and indeed also of interested parties in the country reviewed. The evaluation is also dependent on the member involved, the nature of the country and secretariat reports, and the answers to questions posed during the TPRB meeting. Thus, a focus on a nation, for example the US, the trading policies and practices of which are the subject of considerable general attention any way, may not add as much to transparency as that engendered from a TPRM exercise of a lesser known trading nation.

The country reports have thus far been on the whole general, neutral, descriptive but comprehensive. That said however, in so far as the quality of the reports as a basis for the review of trade policies and practices by the TPRB, and the quality of the review of policy in the TPRB are concerned, these are matters for judgment that lie in the domain of the economist. It may be added, however, that the perspective of the reviews can be steeped in the trade official's background. Thus, it is interesting that in neither GATT nor Country Reports nor the discussion at the GATT Council have double taxation agreements been documented or commented upon, nor their impact on trade alluded to. It may be that such agreements are considered not to have a sufficiently direct impact on the flow of trade as opposed to investment decisions so as to warrant inclusion. This, however, may be a matter of judgement. Indeed, there may be a case for the inclusion of other issues as well.

Secondly, in so far as the evaluation of the "enforcement function" in the wider sense is concerned, this particularly can only be meaningfully undertaken in terms of the over all impact the TPRM makes in a long time-frame. Certainly, at any rate, forceful representations are made by the members during the review[255]—both in terms of rule and policy. The effectiveness of these has yet to be seen, and may well vary according to the stature of the member involved. Thus, it would be interesting to see if, in the long run, the TPRM evolves into an instrument that has more of an impact on the developing members, as it has the potential to.

**13-045**     In sum, in theory, the TPRM mechanism constitutes a significant attempt at surmounting the problem of adherence to the WTO code. As a mechanism, focus needs to be centred on its potential rather than its shortcomings. Doubtless it needs further fine tuning. Its launching has been described, albeit in GATT circles,[256] as a success. Presumably this is primarily a reference to the transparency function.

It is suggested that the following aspects of the TPRM need to be specially considered in any review of the mechanism. First, the information-gathering powers of the WTO need to be further strengthened. The Decision on Notification Procedures[257] under the Uruguay Round in this respect is welcome. In accordance with this Decision, members reaffirm their under-

---

[255] See GATT Focus 68 (February 1990) at p.13.
[256] See GATT Focus 68 (February 1990) at p.13.
[257] See The Results of the Uruguay Round Of Multilateral Trade Negotiations 1994.

taking to notify the WTO in relation to matters which affect the operation of the GATT 1994. The Decision also establishes the creation of the Central Registry of Notifications. The Central Registry is to keep members informed of their regular notification obligations, including unfulfilled regular notification obligations. There are, however, no sanctions attached to a failure to comply with notification requirements; nor, it would appear, any general express information-seeking authority. The Decision contemplates the strengthening of notification procedures. A Working Group is to be set up to review notification obligations and their compliance.

Secondly, there should be a general widening of the sources of information in the preparation of the WTO Secretariat Report. Thus, mechanisms should be set up so that members, as well as private parties, can in advance bring to the Secretariat's attention particular problems, which the Secretariat might take on board in its Report. If NGOs can make submissions to dispute settlement panels there is no reason why they cannot make submissions in the context of the TPRM. Further, the Secretariat might consider in the preparation of its Report, the commissioning of some of the work from outside.

Thirdly, it is understood that the Reports are often made available too late to the members. In this respect, a strict time schedule for the availability of the Reports may well be in point. An advance distribution of a summary of the principal issues prepared by the "discussants" may also be in order.[258]

Fourthly, the TPRB should be presented through the "discussants" with a **13-046** neutral and expert evaluation and elucidation of the two Reports. It is suggested the "discussants" need not necessarily be trade officials. One manner of ensuring neutrality could be by having one "discussant" from a developing State and another from a developed State. Generally, the "discussants" should take a more active role.

Fifthly, members should have the opportunity to ask questions and make observations through the "discussants" in an anonymous fashion. This practice of ensuring anonymity of the questioner member is a technique that is employed by the GATT and WTO in another context, i.e. as part of the process of negotiating accession to the GATT and WTO.[259] Further, wherever appropriate the "discussants" should take on board concerns of the developing countries.

Sixthly, sycophantic observations should be struck out. The ethos of the review process should be consciously de-politicised. The process of appreciation should be confined to where it might have a positive impact. Similarly, mechanisms should be placed so as to prevent the Country Report from degenerating into too much of a defensive exercise. In this respect the Outline Country Format perhaps needs to be considered again, so as to exclude or

---

[258] R.E. Abbott, Director DG 1.A. Commission of the European Communities (fax dated July 9, 1992 to the authors).
[259] G. Paterson, "The GATT: Categories, Problems and Procedures Of Membership" (1992) 1(7) *Columbia Business Law Review* 9.

inhibit substantial justification for the imposition of protectionist practices on external factors. In addition, the adversarial character of the review should be minimised.

Seventhly, the analytical framework of the Reports should be consistent, systematic, and exhaustive. Thus, there should be some form of legal appraisal as well. In the Country Reports the member should systematically justify its trade policies and practices in legal, economic and a general context.

Finally, there should be some form of a follow-up of the review. Thus, for example, members should be required to discuss the WTO review in their respective parliamentary forum. Some systematic observation of any follow-up action taken by the member under review should be made and recorded. Where from the review it is evident that trade policy and practice should be changed, but that the proposed changes cannot be made known, or are not made known, then the Director-General should be authorised to discuss those changes with the member on a confidential basis, somewhat as with the IMF surveillance over exchange-rate policy.[260]

---

[260] See for an account of the IMF practice, e.g. J. Gold, *Exchange Rates in International Law and Organization* (Chicago, American Bar Association, 1988), Ch.9.

# PART 4

# INTERNATIONAL LAW RELATING TO FACTOR MOVEMENT

### CHAPTER 14

# INTERNATIONAL INVESTMENT LAW

## GENERALLY

International investment law concerns itself with the direct (and to a lesser **14–001** extent) indirect or portfolio investment of foreign property abroad.[1] Its

[1] See, for example, B.A. Wortly, *Expropriation in Public International Law* (Cambridge: Cambridge University Press, 1959); G.M. White, *Nationalisation of Foreign Property* (London: Stevens & Sons, 1961); E.I. Nwogugu, *The Legal Problems of Foreign Investment in Developing Countries* (Manchester, Manchester University Press, 1965); C.F. Amerasinghe, *State Responsibility for Injuries to Aliens* (Oxford, Clarendon Press, 1967); G. Schwarzenberger, *Foreign Investment and International Law* (London, Stevens & Sons, 1969); A.A. Akinsanya, *The Expropriation of Multinational Property in the Third World* (New York, Praeger, 1980); American Law Institute, Restatement, Third, Foreign Relations Law of the United States (1987), para.712; D.C. Dicke (ed.), *Foreign Investment in the Present and a New International Economic Order* (Fribourg, Fribourg University Press, 1987); I. Brownlie, "Legal status of natural resources", 162 Recueil des Cours 245; R. Higgins, "The taking of property by the State: Recent developments in International Law" 176 Recueil des Cours 267; P.M. Norton, "A law of the future or law of the past? Modern Tribunals and the International Law of Expropriation" (1991) 85 A.J.I.L. 474; A. Mouri, *The International Law of Expropriation as Reflected in the work of the Iran-US Claims Tribunal* (Dordrecht, Martinus Nijhoff, 1994); G.T. Ellinides, "Foreign Direct Investment in Developing and Newly Liberalized Nations" (1995) 4 Journal of International Law and Practice 299–332; T.L. Brewer and S. Young, "Investment Policies in Multilateral and Regional Agreements: A Comparative Analysis, (1996) 5 Transnational Corporations 9–35; N. Schrijver, *Sovereignty over Natural Resources* (Cambridge, Cambridge University Press, 1997) Ch.6; P. Comeaux and N.S. Kinsella, *Protecting Foreign Investment under International Law: Legal Aspects of Political Risk* (Dobbs Ferry, Oceana Publishing, 1997); P.E. Comeaux, *Protecting Foreign Investment Under International Law* (Oceana, 1997). See more recently R.B. Doak, J. Crawford and M.W. Reisman, *Foreign Investment Disputes—Cases Materials and Commentary* (Kluwer Law International, 2005); N. Rubins and N.S. Kinsella, *International Investment, Political Risk, and Dispute Resolution: a Practitioner's Guide* (Dobbs Ferry: Oceana Publishing, 2005); *New Aspects of International Investment Law* (The Hague, Martinus Nijhoff, 2006), P. Muchlinski, F. Ortino and C. Schreuer (eds), *The Oxford Handbook of International Investment Law* (Oxford, Oxford University Press, 2008); D. Zachary, *The International Law of Investment Claims* (OUP, Oxford, 2009), J. Schokkaert and Y. Heckscher, *International Investments Protection: Comparative Law Analysis of Bilateral and Multilateral Interstate Conventions, Doctrinal Texts and Arbitral Jurisprudence Concerning Foreign Investments* (Bruylant, Bruxelles, 2009), A. Newcombe and L. Paradell, *Law and Practice of Investment Treaties: Standards and Treatment,* (Kluwer Law International, London, 2009); M. Sornarajah, M., *The International Law on Foreign Investment* (Cambridge, Cambridge University Press, 3rd edn, 2010), K. J.

principal participants involve the capital-exporting States (i.e. the home State of the investor) the capital-importing States (i.e. the host State), and the private foreign investors. Its main concerns are standards of treatment in the host State, especially investment protection and dispute settlement. At the same time, in recent years the globalization of the economy leads to more and more questions including market liberalisation (i.e. market access or establishments rights).

Traditionally, international investment law was particularly related to the capital flows from developed states to developing countries, but more recently all states try to attract important foreign investment flows and companies from emerging economies are increasingly important foreign investors be it in other emerging markets, developing countries or developed States.[2] Nevertheless, due to the traditional development dimension and the impact on sovereignty, the legal regime, such as it is remains controversial and no multilateral framework exists[3]—it remains therefore mainly bilateral at the level of treaty practice and related case-law from arbitration. There is still no comprehensive international legal framework governing the International Law of investment (be it in the WTO or elsewhere such as in the OECD or the World Bank)—due to the absence of a general consensus on many aspects. At the same time the number of bilateral treaties has been growing rapidly in recent decades and there are an increasing number of investment disputes (investor-state arbitration) that are subject to international scrutiny.

More particularly, at the level of general International Law, States have a general freedom to regulate the entry of foreign investment (pre-establishment), and a general discretion as to how they treat that investment post-entry (post-establishment).[4] However, this general discretion post-entry is qualified by the law on expropriation, and the question relating to the existence and content of an international minimum standard relating to the treatment of foreign investments and foreign investors. In the framework of general International Law, the primary normative pre-occupation has been the protection of foreign property against expropriation and treatment that is not "fair and equitable" or does not provide "full protection and security".[5]

---

Vandevelde, *Bilateral Investment Treaties—History, Policy, and Interpretation* (OUP, Oxford, 2010); J. W. Salacuse, *The Law of Investment Treaties* (OUP, Oxford, 2010).

[2] For details on international investment flows and their structure consult the annual World Investment Report published by UNCTAD,

[3] See A.A. Fatouros, "Towards an international agreement on foreign direct investment?" in OECD *Towards Multilateral Investment Rules* (1996) at p.50. For a developing country perspective see also K. Ekwueme, "A Nigerian perspective on a forward-looking multilateral agreement on investment", *The Journal of World Investment & Trade Law, Economics, Politics*, 7 (2006) 1, S.165–196

[4] See, for example, Fatouros (1996), p.53 and I. Shihata *The World Bank in a Changing World* (Dordrecht: Martinus Nijhoff, 1995), p.391, but more recently P. Dumberry, "Are BITs representing the "new" customary international law in international investment law?", *Penn State International Law Review*, 28 (2010) 4, 675–701. See also, for example, Art.2(a) of CERDS.

[5] See, for example, ICSID, *AAPL v Sri Lanka* (1991) or ICSID, *American Machine Tools v Zaire* (1997) 36 I.L.M. 1531. More recently also *Wena Hotels v Egypt* (2002) 41 I.L.M. 896;

At the treaty level, investment norms are to be found mainly in bilateral investment agreements, known as BITs.[6] Treaty-based norms are also to be found in some regional agreements which promote capital movement and grant rights of establishment, e.g. in the EU and NAFTA.[7] Some aspects of investment were also covered in the Fourth ACP (Lomé) Convention of 1992[8] which provided mainly for a framework for members to create a favourable environment for investment, and to enter into bilateral investment agreements.[9] The Economic Partnership Agreements (EPAs) that were promoted in recent years by the European Union to govern the future trade and investment relations between the EU and the ACP countries also contain some norms on investment although only few of them are already entered into force.[10] Other regional regimes include, for example, the Agreement among ASEAN Members for the Promotion and Protection of investments (1987); and the Agreement for Promotion, Protection and Guarantee of Investment, under the auspices of the Organisation of the Islamic Conference.[11] Amongst multilateral instruments of particular note are the GATS, TRIPS, and TRIMS within the WTO system which contains a limited number of rules relevant for investment although these agreements belong to the WTO system which has not officially endorsed investment questions.[12] At the sectoral level, a key instrument of note is the Energy Charter Treaty (ECT) 1994[13] dealing with the energy sector and in particular relations between European

**14–002**

*CME v Czech Republic* (2002, Stockholm Chamber of Commerce Rules) § 613 and *Lauder v Czech Republic* (2002 Stockholm Chamber of Commerce Rules) § 54. See also ICSID, *Middle East Shipping and Handling Co v Egypt* (2002).

[6] For a comprehensive overview on exiting BITs see UNCTAD, World Investment Instruments, online: *http:www.unctad.org.* (Accessed June 8, 2011). See also T. Begic, *Applicable Law in International Investment Disputes* (Eleven Internat. Publ., 2005). See also recently A. Lehavi, BITs and pieces of property, *The Yale Journal of International Law*, 36 (2011), 1, S. 115-166 and P. Dumberry, "Are BITs representing the "new" customary international law in international investment law?", *Penn State International Law Review*, 28 (2010) 4, 675–701.

[7] Certain older treaties, including the important group of 19th and 20th century Treaties on Friendship, Commerce and Navigation (or alternatively Establishment) often also include applicable norms. See for example ICJ, Case concerning Elettronica Sicula SpA (ELSI), *United States v Italy*, Judgment of July 10, 1989.

[8] See Arts 258 and 260 of the Lome Convention. See also the European Community Statement On Investment Protection Principles in the ACP States, Doc.ACP-CEE 2172/92 adopted by the Council on October 4, 1992.

[9] See WTO Annual Report (1996) at p.40.

[10] See Gus van Harten. Investment Provisions in Economic Partnership Agreements (Osgoode Hall Law School, York, 2008). On the EPAs in general, see Ch.11.

[11] Entered in force in 1988. See I ICSID Rev F.I.L.J. 407 (1986).

[12] See in this respect C.M. Correa, *Protecting Foreign Investment—implications of a WTO regime and policy options* (New Delhi, Zed Books, 2003) and D. Collins, "A new role for the WTO in international investment law", *Connecticut Journal of International Law*, 25.2009 (2010) 1, 1–35.

[13] See, for example, T.W. Wälde, "International Investment Under the 1994 Energy Charter Treaty—Legal, Negotiating and Policy Implications for International Investors within Western and Commonwealth of Independent States/Eastern European Countries" (1995) 29(5) *Journal of World Trade* 5–72; O.Q. Swaak-Goldman, "The Energy Charter Treaty and Trade—A Guide to the Labyrinth" (1996) 30(5) *Journal of World Trade* 115–64; T.W. Wälde, "Energy Charter Treaty-based Investment Arbitration—Controversial Issues" (2005) 5(3)

States and the member States of the former Soviet Union (USSR). These treaty instruments focus mainly on protection of foreign investment, non-discrimination, and the provision for dispute settlement. On the whole the treaty norms are scattered and non-comprehensive.

At the national level, there is now a general trend towards the reduction of barriers to the entry of foreign direct investment, although restrictions at the sectoral level are still maintained.[14] This was different in many developing states in the 1960s and 1970s when permanent sovereignty over natural resources was sometimes interpreted as on obstacle to the presence of foreign investors. Similarly, there is an increase in the reduction in post-entry interference.[15] Particularly, there is a growing practice of investors receiving MFN treatment,[16] fair and equitable treatment[17] and access to investor-state dispute settlement. These national regimes are often to be found in specifically enacted foreign investment legislation (known as investment codes[18]).

The general trends for a liberalised system at the national level are to be contrasted with the set-backs the development of international investment law has encountered at the international level. These comprise the failure of the international community to establish a code regulating the conduct of transnational corporations[19]; the failure of the international community to agree on a code of conduct on the transfer of technology for development

*The Journal of World Investment & Trade*, 373; C. Ribeiro (ed.), *Investment Arbitration and the Energy Charter Treaty* (Huntington, NY, Juris Publ., 2006).

[14] See WTO Annual Report (1996) at p.33.

[15] See WTO Annual Report (1996) at p.33.

[16] See WTO Annual Report (1996) at p.33. At the same time, the question whether this standard applies to all provisions of a BIT (e.g. including dispute settlement) has been treated differently by different arbitral tribunals in recent wars, following the arbitral award in *Emilio Agustín Maffezini v Kingdom of Spain*, ICSID Case No.ARB/97/7, Decision of the Tribunal on Objections to Jurisdiction, January 25, 2000, ICSID Review—(2001) 16(1) *Foreign Investment Law Journal*. See also L. Hsu, "MFN and Dispute Settlement—When the Twain Meet" (2006) 7(1) *The Journal of World Investment & Trade* 25–39. See below for details.

[17] There has been an intense discussion with regard to this standard under NAFTA Chapter 11, e.g. regarding Art.1105 (Minimum Standard) in *SD Myers v Canada*, Arbitral Award of November 13, 2000/October 21, 2001; *Pope & Talbot Inc v Canada* UNCITRAL (NAFTA), Award, April 10, 2001 and later *Mondev (Canada) v United States*, Arbitral Award of October 11, 2002 and *ADF v United States*, 2003. See also outside NAFTA ICSID, *Middle East Shipping and Handling Co. v Egypt* (2002). See also B. Choudhury, "Evolution or Devolution?—Defining Fair and Equitable Treatment in International Investment Law" (2005) 6(2) *The Journal of World Investment & Trade* 297. See below for details.

[18] Such legislation can be found in ICSID Investment Laws of the World, Oceana Publications. See, for example, J.D. Nolan, "A comparative analysis of the Laotian law on foreign investment, the World Bank guidelines on the treatment of foreign direct investment, and normative rules of international law on foreign direct investment", *Arizona Journal of International and Comparative Law*, 15 (1998) 2, 659–693.

[19] See the Draft UN Code of Conduct on Transnational Corporations (1983 and 1990 versions) Commission on Transnational Corporations, Report on the Special Session (March 7–18 and May 9–21, 1983) Official Record of the Economic and Social Council, 1883, Supplement No.7 (E/1983/17/Rev.1); and United Nations Economic and Social Council, Second Regular Session of 1990 (E/1990/94). See also, for example, P. Muchlinski, *Multinational Enterprises and the Law*, 2nd edn (Oxford, Oxford University Press, 2007).

purposes[20]; and the failure of the OECD in 1998 in establishing a Multilateral Agreement on Investment (MAI). However, these events have only served to intensify the need for a comprehensive multilateral agreement on investment.

At the same time, there continue to appear incidentally specific defensive reactions by governments in developing States and developed States against foreign investment. In recent times, this led to government interventions in developed states against the increasing number of take-overs and mergers affecting "national champions" or companies that are considered of be part of the domestic heritage.[21]

A central problem traditionally preoccupying the international community, particularly developed States, has been the treatment of investment of capital from private investors from developed States in developing States—although the problem is also a general one, regardless of the level of development of the State where the investment is taking place. In particular, one key question that has focused the mind of capital exporting countries has been the legality of governmental measures involving the expropriation of foreign property, and the measure of compensation upon such expropriation. Although nationalisation and expropriation are no longer in vogue in most economies, the concerns are still relevant in so far as the possibility of changes in economic planning exists, and in so far as expropriation can take different guises. The policies of Hugo Chavez in Venezuela, Evo Morales in Bolivia or the Government of Ecuador in 2006 reminded us of the continued risk of such policies in developing countries. Other recent examples include the expropriation of land owners and proposals to transfer a majority of shares in certain mining companies in Zimbabwe without compensation to nationals of that country in 2011. At the same time, the question whether certain government action, including a change of legislation, can violate the guarantees owed to investors is increasingly asked in all countries. Here the tension is normally conceived as being between the States' right to regulate and the fears of investors of "regulatory takings".[22] In addition the legitimate expectations of investors may suffer from specific action that the government or another state organ perceives as important for specific policy goals.

**14–003**

The General International Law framework has historically suffered from the tensions between the interests of the capital exporting, and those of the capital importing countries. The discernment of the law has thus been a complex, and sometimes controversial exercise. Examples are the tensions after the Mexican Revolution of 1910 or the Russian Revolution of 1917,

---

[20] See the UNCTAD Draft International Code of conduct on the transfer of technology (1985), UNCTAD Document TD/CODE TOT/47. See also for example M. Blakeney, *The Legal Aspects of the Transfer of Technology to Developing Countries* (Oxford, ESC, 1989).

[21] E.g. within the European Union—despite the free movement of capital—recently referred to as "economic patriotism", e.g. by former French Prime Minister Dominique de Villepin in 2005. See also S. Hindelang, *The free movement of capital and foreign direct investment.* (Oxford, New York [u.a.], Oxford Univ. Press, 2009) and J.A. Usher, "The evolution of the free movement of capital", *Fordham International Law* journal, 31 (2007/08) 5, S.1533–1570.

[22] Considered by some to be a a type of expropriation, see below.

the disputes between many newly independent States and former colonial powers after WW II and the discussions within the United Nations in the 1960s and 1970s. There has, however, since the 1990s been an acknowledged change in the law in this sphere, and consequentially some clarifications. The issues, however, are clear. What are the circumstances which can constitute expropriation? Can a State expropriate foreign property? If so, what are the circumstances in which it can expropriate? If it can expropriate, then is there an obligation to pay compensation, and if so, how much? If there is a prohibition on expropriation, and expropriation takes place, what is the measure of damages? Is there a specific minimum standard regarding the treatment of foreign investors and their investment? Are investors entitled to fair and equitable treatment, to full protection and security and the right to freely transfer their capital and related benefits out of the host country? Finally, what has been the impact, if any, of the numerous bilateral investment agreements, on the law of investment as it relates to expropriation?

## INTERNATIONALISATION OF INVESTMENT CONTRACTS

**14–004**  Individual investors have made a number of attempts at protecting their investment from the actions of the host State. These efforts have essentially been directed at internationalising[23] the contractual arrangement with the host State, so that the contractual relationship with the host State is not governed by its legal system. Such endeavours have been through contractual devices, including stabilisation, choice of law, and international arbitration clauses.[24] Stabilisation clauses[25] attempt to ensure that the future host State legislation does not result in changing the terms of the contract entered into by the host State with the investor, at the time of the entry of the investment.[26] Thus, essentially such clauses attempt at freezing the host State legislation as it related to the contract to the time when the investment agreement was entered into.[27] This type of guarantee is particularly common in agreements relating to natural resource (like petroleum production or mining).[28]

---

[23]  See Sornarajah (2010), p.289.
[24]  See below.
[25]  See below.
[26]  See for example Sornarajah (2010), p.281.
[27]  The leading arbitration awards from the 1970s and 1980s do include rulings in favour of the validity of stabilisation clauses: *Agip v Congo*; *BP v Libya*; *Liamco v Libya*, and *TOPCO v Libya*. However, the focus of the clauses was to ensure that the concession agreements were operative for the full term provided in the contract and so targeted expropriation (or a similar confiscatory measure) as the "event" to be prohibited. More recently the violation of a stabilisation clause was acknowledged in *CMS Gas Transportation Company v Argentine Republic*, Award of May 12, 2005 (ICSID).
[28]  See M.T.B. Coale, "Stabilization clauses in international petroleum transactions". *The Denver Journal of International Law and Policy*, 30 (2002) 2, S. 217-237 and T. J. Pate, "Evaluating stabilization clauses in Venezuela's strategic association agreements for heavy-crude extraction

At the same time it is highly controversial as it is often seen as a dangerous impediment for the State to take action in the future that is needed in the public interest or seems in the best interest of the population.[29] Stabilisation clauses, as a matter of domestic constitutional law, are problematic in that the legislator cannot normally bind itself to a private entity, irrevocably not to legislate otherwise. Further, the principle of permanent sovereignty over natural resources would undermine the binding character of such stabilisation clauses.[30]

**PETROLEUM AGREEMENT among THE REPUBLIC OF GHANA, GHANA NATIONAL PETROLEUM CORPORATION, KOSMOS ENERGY GHANA HC and THE E. O. GROUP IN RESPECT OF WEST CAPE THREE POINTS BLOCK OFFSHORE GHANA (DATED 22ND JULY 2004)**

14–005

§ 26.2 The State, its departments and agencies, shall support this Agreement and shall take no action which prevents or impedes the due exercise and performance of rights and obligations of the Parties hereunder. As of the Effective Date of this Agreement and throughout its term, the State guarantees Contractor the stability of the terms and conditions of this Agreement as well as the fiscal and contractual framework hereof specifically including those terms and conditions and that framework that are based upon or subject to the provisions of the laws and regulations of Ghana (and any interpretations thereof) including, without limitation, the Petroleum Income Tax Law, the Petroleum Law, the GNPC Law and those other laws, regulations and decrees that are applicable hereto. The State further represents and guarantees that the Contract Area is wholly within Ghana's territorial waters and is not subject to any dispute.

§ 26.3 This Agreement and the rights and obligations specified herein may not be modified, amended, altered or supplemented except upon the execution and delivery of a written agreement executed by the Parties. Any legislative or administrative act of the State or any of its agencies or subdivisions which purports to vary any such right or obligation shall, to the extent sought to be applied to this Agreement, constitute a breach of this Agreement by the State; provided, however, if the Petroleum (Exploration and Production) Law, 1984 (PNDCL 84) is amended or replaced (superseded), Contractor shall be entitled to enjoy and this Agreement (and any new petroleum agreement referred to herein) shall be deemed to include (or include — as applicable) the terms and conditions in such amendment or replacement law that favourably affect the rights and/or obligations of the Contractor under this Agreement.

in the Orinoco Belt". *University of Miami (Coral Gables, Fla.): The University of Miami Inter-American Law Review*, 40 (2009) 2, 347–381.

[29] See Sornarajah (2010) p.282.

[30] See and T.B. Hansen, "The Legal Effect Given Stabilization Clauses in Economic Development Agreements" (1988) 28 *Virginia Journal of International Law* 1015–41. See also *CMS Gas Transmission Company v Argentinian Republic*, ICSID Case No.ARB/01/8. Award of the Tribunal of May 12, 2005 and M. Burgstaller, "Nationality of Corporate Investors and International Claims against the Investor's Own State" (2006) 7(6) *The Journal of World Investment and Trade* 857. See also L. Cotula, "Stabilization clauses and the evolution of environmental standards in foreign investment contracts", *Yearbook of International Environmental Law*, 17 (2006), 111–138.

§ 26.4 Where a Party considers that a significant change in the circumstances prevailing at the time the Agreement was entered into, has occurred affecting the economic balance of the Agreement, the Party adversely affected thereby shall notify the other Parties in writing of the claimed change with a statement of how the claimed change has affected such economic balance or has otherwise affected relations between the Parties. The other Parties shall indicate in writing their reaction to such notification within a period of two (2) months after receipt of such notification. If such significant changes are established by the Parties to have occurred, the Parties shall meet to engage in negotiations and shall effect such changes in, or rectification of, these provisions as they may agree are necessary to restore the relative economic position of the Parties as at the date of this Agreement.

Choice-of-law clauses attempt at subverting the domestic law by referring, for example, to (public) International Law as the governing law.[31]

**14–006** **PETROLEUM AGREEMENT among THE REPUBLIC OF GHANA, GHANA NATIONAL PETROLEUM CORPORATION, KOSMOS ENERGY GHANA HC and THE E. O. GROUP IN RESPECT OF WEST CAPE THREE POINTS BLOCK OFFSHORE GHANA (DATED 22ND JULY 2004)**

§ 26.1 This Agreement and the relationship between the State and GNPC on one hand and Contractor on the other shall be governed by and construed with the laws of the Republic of Ghana consistent with such rules of international law as may be applicable, including rules and principles as have been applied by international tribunals.

International Arbitration[32] clauses ensure that disputes in relation to the contract are considered by neutral arbitrators. Particularly important are arbitrations between a host state and a foreign investor (investor-State arbitration).

**14–007** **PETROLEUM AGREEMENT among THE REPUBLIC OF GHANA, GHANA NATIONAL PETROLEUM CORPORATION, KOSMOS ENERGY GHANA HC and THE E. O. GROUP IN RESPECT OF WEST CAPE THREE POINTS BLOCK OFFSHORE GHANA (DATED 22ND JULY 2004)**

§ 24.1 Except in the cases specified in Article 26.4 any dispute or difference arising between the State and GNPC or either of them on one hand and Contractor on the other hand in relation to or in connection with or arising Out of any terms and conditions of this Agreement shall he resolved

---

[31] See A.F.M. Maniruzzaman, "State contracts and arbitral choice-of-law process and techniques", *Journal of International Arbitration*, 15 (1998) 3, S. 65–92 and J. Boghez, "The applicable law to state contracts. *Revista Română de Drept Internațional*, 8 (2009), 111–134 as well as T. Begic, *Applicable law in international investment disputes.* (Utrecht, Eleven Internat. Publ., 2005).

[32] See below.

> by consultation and negotiation, provided that if no agreement is reached within thirty (30) days after the date when either Party notifies the other that a dispute or difference exists within the meaning of this Article or such longer period specifically agreed to by the Parties or provided elsewhere in the Agreement, any Party shall have the right subject to Article 24.14 to have such dispute or difference settled through international arbitration, in accordance with the terms and provisions set forth below.

The critical question of course is whether these contractual devices are valid and successful in subverting the host State's legal system, where it relents on the contract.[33] Critics argue that the contractual devices which attempt to internationalise the contract are defective.[34] They argue that the contractual devices as such lack validity under International Law, and the breach of contract by the State does not result in international responsibility.[35] According to them, the contract between a private entity and a State is not an international agreement, and is not governed by International Law.[36] However, international responsibility arises where the State relents on its promise, if the State action constitutes a denial of justice, or the repudiation amounts to an act of expropriation.[37] At the same time, these devices are extremely common and at least when it comes to international arbitration and the choice of applicable law they have been regularly enforced by arbitral tribunals instituted thereunder.

## Bilateral Investment Treaties

These are essentially bilateral agreements, between capital exporting **14–008** and importing States, intended for the benefit and protection of national investors, investing in the State of the other party to the investment agreement. BITs[38] have featured critically in the development of international

---

[33] See S. Schwebel, "International Protection of Contractual Agreements" (1959) A.S.I.L. Proc. 273; F.A. Mann, "State contracts and State responsibility" (1960) 54 A.J.I.L. 572; R. Jennings, "State Contracts in International Law" (1961) 37 B.Y.I.L. 156 and S. Schwebel, "The Breach by a State of a Contract" in *Essays in Honour of Roberto Ago* (Milano: Giuffre, 1987).

[34] See Sornarajah (2010), p.284.

[35] See, for example, Brownlie (1998), p.550.

[36] See, for example, *Anglo-Iranian Oil Co Case* (1952) I.C.J. Reports.

[37] See, for example, Brownlie (1998), p.550.

[38] See, for example, UNCTAD Bilateral "Investment Treaties in the Mid-1990s (1998); R. Dolzer and M. Stevens, *Bilateral Investment Treaties* (The Hague, Martinus Nijhoff, 1995) and references therein; P.T. Mutchlinski, *Multinational Enterprises and The Law*, 2nd edn (2007). BITs are published by the ICSID in loose-leaf collection titled "Investment Promotion and Protection Treaties"; A.T. Guzman, "Why LDCs Sign Treaties That Hurt Them: Explaining the Popularity of Bilateral Investment Treaties" (1988) 38(4) *Virginia Journal of International Law* 639–88. See also A. Al Faruque, "Creating customary international law through bilateral investment treaties" (2004) 44(2) *The Indian Journal of International Law* 292–318 and P. Dumberry, "Are BITs representing the "new" customary international law in international investment law?", *Penn State International Law Review*, 28 (2010) 4, 675–701.

investment law—in demarcating the rights of investors and the obligations of host States in relation to those investors. In recent times they have not only acted as a principal driving force in ensuring investment protection and liberalisation in the investment field,[39] but have also acted as precedents for other investment regimes.[40] Some two-thirds of the approximately 1,160 BITs in the mid-nineties, were concluded in the 1990s, and involve the majority of States.[41] As of 2007 the UNCTAD has collected approximately 1,800 such treaties.[42] The success of BITs can be attributed to the scale of investment flows in recent times; and the fact that these arrangements on the whole have not undermined the discretion of the host State in investment matters—particularly in admission matters,[43] and in the pursuit of national economic policies.[44] In addition, most of today's Free Trade Agreements (FTAs)—despite their name—do not only cover trade in goods and services but also investment flows and a number of other disciplines. One of the earliest examples was certainly Chapter 11 of NAFTA (Investment) which entered into force in 1993. But today there are a very important number of bilateral agreements which include investment rules. In rare cases the negotiation of an FTA does not lead to the inclusion of a specific chapter on investment but a separate BIT.[45] At the same time, we see also trade agreements that do not include (comprehensive) rules on investment. This is particularly the case of the agreements negotiated by the European Union—at least in the past. Here, the lack of a far-reaching competence of the EU in this field led to very limited rules on investment in the otherwise very comprehensive and ambitious trade agreements concluded by the EU with an important number of States. Since the entry into force of the Lisbon Treaty on November 1, 2009 the EU enjoys also the power to negotiate investment agreements and this will lead to changes in the future negotiations—even if the exact scope of the new power and its implications for the many existing BITs of Member States with third States remain controversial.

---

[39]  See, for example, WTO Annual Report (1996).
[40]  E.g. the World Bank Guidelines.
[41]  WTO Annual Report (1996).
[42]  Available online at *http://www.unctad.org* (accessed June 8, 2011).
[43]  See, with regard to conditional admission, ICSID, *Azinian v Mexico* (1999) ARB (AF)/97/2 and ICSID, *Amco v Indonesia* (1988). See also S. Elshihabi, "The difficulty behind securing sector-specific investment establishment rights: the case of the Energy Charter Treaty", *The International Lawyer*, 35 (2001) 1, 137–158 and P. Juillard, "Freedom of establishment, freedom of capital movements, and freedom of investment", *ICSID Review*, 15 (2000) 1, 322–339.
[44]  ICSID, *Azinian v Mexico* (1999) ARB (AF)/97/2 at p.9.
[45]  This technique has for example sometimes been used by the EFTA States when they were unable to reach full consensus among them on the desirability of such rules and their exact wording. See, for example, the Agreement on Investment between the Republic of Korea and the Republic of Iceland, the Principality of Liechtenstein and The Swiss Confederation (Hong Kong, December 15, 2005) negotiated in parallel to the Free Trade Agreement between the EFTA States and the Republic of Korea signed on the same day at the same place.

**Treaty on the Functioning of the European Union—TITLE II COMMON COMMERCIAL POLICY**    **14-009**

Article 206 (ex Article 131 TEC): By establishing a customs union in accordance with Articles 28 to 32, the Union shall contribute, in the common interest, to the harmonious development of world trade, the progressive abolition of restrictions on international trade and on foreign direct investment, and the lowering of customs and other barriers.

Although generally similar in structure, there are also variations in content and wording of the BITs.[46] Broadly, the agreements focus on: (i) the scope of the application of the agreement (definition of investors and investments); (ii) the question of the admission of the investment; (iii) the standards of treatment post-entry, including investment protection; (iv) and the provision of dispute settlement processes in the event of a dispute between a foreign investor and the host State. Thus, the agreements concentrate mainly on the rights of the investor and the obligations of the host State,[47] rather than the obligations of the capital-exporting State, or indeed the obligations of the investor.[48]

COVERAGE

First, the coverage or scope of the application of investment agreements is    **14-010**
of particular importance. As they are today normally only of a bilateral (or regional) nature, they do only apply to investors and their investors of one of the Parties to the respective agreement. The investors covered can be either natural or legal persons and not all their activities in the other Party to the Agreement are investments that shall enjoy the protection of the agreement. This issue of coverage is usually dealt with in a separate part on definitions in these agreements.[49]

This leads first to the question of who is a national of the covered States. Most modern agreements simply rely on domestic law when it comes to natural persons and thereby try to avoid the discussions in general International Law with regard to dual citizens and the genuineness of nationality, as exemplified in the famous *Nottebohm* Case[50] of the International Court of Justice and many earlier arbitral awards. Sometimes dual citizens of the two contracting States are excluded from the protection (as it corresponds to many

---

[46] ICSID, *Azinian v Mexico* (1999) ARB (AF)/97/2 at p.35.
[47] See, for example, T. Brewer in *Towards Multilateral Investment Rules* (OECD, 1996), p.89.
[48] See, for example, the WTO Annual Report (1996) at p.35.
[49] See F. Ortino, (ed.), *Nationality and Investment Treaty Claims, Fair and Equitable Treatment in Investment Treaty Law, vol. 2 Investment Treaty Law* (London, BIICL, 2007) and *UNCTAD, Scope and definition* (New York, United Nations, 2011).
[50] ICJ, Nottebohm (*Liechtenstein v Guatemala*), Judgment of April 6, 1955. See J. Dolinger, "Nottebohm revisited", *Dimensão Internacional do Direito, 2000*, 141–186.

States' practice with regard to diplomatic protection). When it comes to legal persons however, the existence of various theories and diverging state practice with regard to the definition of its nationality normally leads to lengthy definitions in the BITs. The agreements normally use a combination of granting nationality based on the place of incorporation, the seat and the control by nationals of a Party. The latter is particularly important in view of the controversial acceptance of nationality of companies based solely on the fact that it is owned of controlled by nationals of that Party.[51]

**14–011**

**Agreement between Canada and the Hashemite Kingdom of Jordan for the Promotion and Protection of Investments entered into force on 14 December 2009**

SECTION A – DEFINITIONS

ARTICLE 1: Definitions

[...]

  (j)  enterprise means:

    (i)  any entity constituted or organized under applicable law, whether or not for profit, whether privately-owned or governmentally-owned, including any corporation, trust, partnership, sole proprietorship, joint venture or other association, and

    (ii)  a branch of any such entity;

  (k)  enterprise of a Party means an enterprise constituted or organized under the law of a Party, and a branch located in the territory of a Party and carrying out business activities there;

[...]

  (s)  investment of an investor of a Party means an investment owned or controlled directly or indirectly by an investor of such Party;

  (t)  investor of a Party means a Party, or a national or an enterprise of a Party, that seeks to make, is making or has made an investment. For greater certainty, it is understood that an investor "seeks to make an investment" only when the investor has taken concrete steps necessary to make said investment;

  (u)  investor of a non-Party means an investor other than an investor of a Party, that seeks to make, is making or has made an investment. For greater certainty, it is understood that an investor "seeks to make an investment" only when the investor has taken concrete steps necessary to make said investment;

[...]

---

[51] ICJ, Barcelona Traction, Light and Power Company, Limited (*Belgium v. Spain*) (New Application: 1962), Judgment of February 5, 1970. See P. M. Protopsaltis, "The challenge of the Barcelona Traction hypothesis", *The Journal of World Investment & Trade*, 11 (2010) 4, 561–599.

(w) national means a natural person who is a citizen or permanent resident of a Party, except that:

(i) natural person who is a dual citizen of Canada and the Hashemite Kingdom of Jordan shall be deemed to be exclusively a national of the Party of his or her dominant and effective nationality, and

(ii) a natural person who is a citizen of one Party and a permanent resident of the other Party shall be deemed to be exclusively a national of the Party of his or her citizenship;

In the case of the Hashemite Kingdom of Jordan "permanent resident" means a person who is legally entitled to reside in Jordan; [. . .]

In view of the increased use of subsidiaries and foreign companies to manage and control investments in third States or even in the home State of the original investor, the question whether such constructions and the use of the respective BITs are legitimate remains controversial. Some authors consider this to constitute "treaty shopping" and thus "an abuse of rights". In a number of cases arbitrators have come to the conclusion that such constructions used by third States nationals or domestic citizens are not sufficient to justify the investors' protection of a specific agreement. For example, in an arbitral award rendered in 2004 regarding the Case *Tokio Tokeles v Ukraine*[52] the Chairperson of the tribunal strongly dissented with the majority of the arbitrators as to whether company owned by Ukrainian investors but located in Poland could use the BIT between the two States to claim protection for its investments in Ukraine. While the majority used the broad definitions of the BIT to grant such protection, the Chairperson, Professor *Prosper Weil*, thought this was a frivolous use contrary to the idea of BITs and the general principles relating to diplomatic protection. Some agreements contain what is generally referred to as a "denial of benefits clause".[53]

**Energy Charter Treaty of 17 December 1994**                                    **14–012**

*ARTICLE 17 NON-APPLICATION OF PART III IN CERTAIN CIRCUMSTANCES*

Each Contracting Party reserves the right to deny the advantages of this Part to:

(1) a legal entity if citizens or nationals of a third state own or control such entity and if that entity has no substantial business activities in the Area of the Contracting Party in which it is organized; or

(2) an Investment, if the denying Contracting Party establishes that such

---

[52] ICSID Case No. ARB/02/18, Decision on Jurisdiction of 29 April 2004; see A. Alexeyev, "Tokios Tokelės vector", *The Journal of World Investment & Trade*, 9 (2008), 6, S. 519–549.

[53] See, for example, L. A. Mistelis and C. M. Baltag, "Denial of Benefits and Article 17 of the Energy Charter Treaty", in *Penn State Law Review* 113(2009), 1301 and P. M. Protopsaltis, "The challenge of the Barcelona Traction hypothesis", *The Journal of World Investment & Trade*, 11 (2010) 4, 561–599.

> Investment is an Investment of an Investor of a third state with or as to which the denying Contracting Party:
>
> (a) does not maintain a diplomatic relationship; or
>
> (b) adopts or maintains measures that:
>
>   (i) prohibit transactions with Investors of that state; or
>
>   (ii) would be violated or circumvented if the benefits of this Part were accorded to Investors of that state or to their Investments.

It is also controversial what activities can be considered as investments.[54] Here, it is in particular the question whether any activity by a foreigner leading to some financial interest (e.g. the conclusion of a simple sales agreement) shall be considered an investment by a foreign investor or whether a more restrictive approach should be taken. Many agreements contain very broad definitions basically considering an investment any asset having an economic value while others opt for more restrictive views. In particular with regard to the ICSID Convention which provides for a dispute settlement mechanism for investors the question has been discussed controversially. Many arbitral tribunals have come to the conclusion that an investment that entitles the respective investor to this mechanism is only present if four conditions are fulfilled (so-called *Salini* test[55]): a contribution of money or other assets of economic value; certain duration; an element of risk, and; a contribution to the host State's development. The validity of such a restrictive definition – especially if not contained in the underlying BIT – remains controversial. Traditionally portfolio investment was considered as being different from foreign direct investment and not worthy of protection by international investment law. This was justified with the fact that only the latter leads to control and in parallel to increased exposure. But many recent agreements blur this distinction.[56]

**14–013**

**Agreement between Canada and the Hashemite Kingdom of Jordan for the Promotion and Protection of Investments entered into force on 14 December 2009**

SECTION A – DEFINITIONS

ARTICLE 1: Definitions

---

[54] See J. Burda, "A new step towards a single and common definition of an investment?", *The Journal of World Investment & Trade*, 11 (2010) 6, 1085–1101 and P. Ranjan, Definition of investment in bilateral investment treaties of South Asian countries and regulatory discretion", *Journal of International Arbitration*, 26 (2009) 2, 217–235.

[55] Named after the award rendered on July 23, 2001 in the Case *Salini Construtorri S.p.A. and Italstrade S.p.A. v Morocco*, Jurisdiction, ICSID Case No. ARB/00/4 (Italy/Morocco BIT). See, for example, F. Yala, "The notion of "investment" in ICSID case law: a drifting jurisdictional requirement?", *Journal of International Arbitration*, 22 (2005) p, S. 105–126.

[56] See also M. Sornarajah, Portfolio investments and the definition of investment". *International Centre for Settlement of Investment Disputes:* ICSID review, 24.2009 (2010) 2, 516–520.

[. . .]

(r)  investment means:

   (i)  an enterprise,

   (ii)  shares, stocks and other forms of equity participation in an enterprise,

   (iii)  bonds, debentures, and other debt instruments of an enterprise,

   (iv)  a loan to an enterprise,

   (v)  notwithstanding subparagraphs (c) and (d) above, a loan to or debt security issued by a financial institution is an investment only where the loan or debt security is treated as regulatory capital by the Party in whose territory the financial institution is located,

   (vi)  an interest in an enterprise that entitles the owner to a share in income or profits of the enterprise,

   (vii)  an interest in an enterprise that entitles the owner to share in the assets of that enterprise on dissolution,

   (viii)  interests arising from the commitment of capital or other resources in the territory of a Party to economic activity in such territory, such as under

     a.  contracts involving the presence of an investor's property in the territory of the Party, including turnkey or construction contracts, or concessions, or

     b.  contracts where remuneration depends substantially on the production, revenues or profits of an enterprise;

   (ix)  intellectual property rights, and

   (x)  any other tangible or intangible, moveable or immovable, property and related property rights acquired in the expectation or used for the purpose of economic benefit or other business purpose, but "investment" does not mean,

   (xi)  claims to money that arise solely from

     a.  commercial contracts for the sale of goods or services by a national or enterprise in the territory of a Party to an enterprise in the territory of the other Party, or

     b.  the extension of credit in connection with a commercial transaction, such as trade financing, other than a loan covered by subparagraph (d) or (e), or

   (xii)  any other claims to money, that do not involve the kinds of interests set out in subparagraphs (a) to (j);

*Umbrella clauses* in BITs attempt to render any violation of a commitment made by the host State towards the foreign investor a violation of the BIT between the host State and the home State of the investor.[57] Such a

---

[57]  For example, 1967 OECD Draft Convention on the Protection of Foreign Property (Art.2): "Each Party shall at all times ensure the observance of undertakings given by it in relation to property of nationals of any other Party."

commitment can stem from a contractual provision whereby any breach of contract would trigger a treaty violation. Often the clauses refer to "observation of commitments". While the term "umbrella clauses" seems most common, such treaty devices are also referred to as *"pacta sunt servanda"* or "sanctity of contract" or "respect for contract" clauses. The validity[58] and scope[59] of such clauses has been disputed.

**14–014**

**Agreement between the Swiss Confederation and the Hashemite Kingdom of Jordan on the Promotion and Reciprocal Protection of Investments of 25 February 2001**

*Article 11 Other commitments*

1. If provisions in the legislation of either Contracting Party or rules of international law entitle investments by investors of the other Contracting Party to treatment more favourable than is provided by this Agreement, such provisions shall to the extent that they are more favourable prevail over this Agreement.

2. Each Contracting Party shall observe any obligation it has assumed with regard to investments in its territory by investors of the other Contracting Party.

ADMISSION OR ESTABLISHMENT

**14–015** In relation to the right of entry, there are mainly two approaches. The majority merely encourage the maintenance of a liberal admission policy. Generally the question of entry of investment is reserved in the final analysis to the

---

[58] See for commentaries more recently OECD Working Papers on International Investment, No.2006/3, Interpretation of the Umbrella Clause in Investment Agreements. Paris, October 2006 and C. Schreuer, "Travelling the BIT Route—Of Waiting Periods, Umbrella Clauses and Forks in the Road" (2004) 5(3) *The Journal of World Investment & Trade* 231 and T.W. Wälde, "The 'Umbrella' Clause on Investment Arbitration—A Comment on Original Intentions and Recent Cases" (2005) 6(2) *The Journal of World Investment & Trade* 183; W. Shan, "Umbrella clauses and investment contracts under Chinese BITs", *The Journal of World Investment & Trade*, 11 (2010) 2, 135–167; S. W. Schill, "Enabling private ordering; function, scope and effect of umbrella clauses in international investment treaties", *Minnesota Journal of International Law*, 18 (2009) 1, 1–97.

[59] See, for example, the different reasoning in *SGS Société Générale de Surveillance SA v Islamic Republic of Pakistan* (Case No.ARB/01/13), ICSID, Decision on Objections to Jurisdiction of August 6, 2003; (2003) 18 ICSID Rev.—F.I.L.J. 301; (2003) 42 I.L.M. 1290; (2005) 8 ICSID Rep. 406 and *SGS Société Générale de Surveillance SA v Republic of the Philippines* (Case No.ARB/02/6), ICSID, Decision of the Tribunal on Objections to Jurisdiction of January 29, 2004; (2005) 8 ICSID Rep. 518; Declaration by one of the arbitrators of January 29, 2004; (2005) 8 ICSID Rep. 568. See also ICISD; *Salini Costruttori spa et Italstrade v Kingdom of Morocco*, July 23, 2001 (Jurisdiction) (*BIT Italy—Morocco*). See also S.A. Alexandrov, "Breaches of Contract and Breaches of Treaty—The Jurisdiction of Treaty-based Arbitration Tribunals to Decide Breach of Contract Claims in SGS v. Pakistan and SGS v. Philippines" (2004) 5(4) *The Journal of World Investment & Trade* 555.

discretion of the host State. Such agreements may in the first instance grant a right of admission, but then subject it to the domestic legislation of the host State. The domestic legislation of the host State may contain restrictions, and be the subject of change from time to time. On the other hand, especially the BITS entered into by the US, although fewer, contain a stricter entry obligation. This approach is ensured through the application of the national, m-f-n, and the fair treatment standards, at the level of entry of investment, as well as post-entry. Such a formulation, however, is diluted by the inclusion of for example sectoral exemptions, and national and international security exemptions, including national public order.[60] Today the inclusion of market access guarantees (establishment rights) is also more common in the BITs of other States.

**Agreement between the Swiss Confederation and the Hashemite Kingdom**     **14–016**
**of Jordan on the Promotion and Reciprocal Protection of Investments of 25**
**February 2001**

**Article 3: Promotion, admission**

(1) Each Contracting Party shall in its territory promote as far as possible investments by investors of the other Contracting Party and admit such investments in accordance with its laws and regulations.

(2) When a Contracting Party shall have admitted an investment on its territory, it shall grant the necessary permits in connection with such an investment and with the carrying out of licensing agreements and contracts for technical, commercial or administrative assistance. Each Contracting Party shall, whenever needed, endeavour to issue the necessary authorisations concerning the activities of consultants and other qualified persons of foreign nationality.

**North American Free Trade Agreement (NAFTA) Article 1102: National Treatment**

1. Each Party shall accord to investors of another Party treatment no less favorable than that it accords, in like circumstances, to its own investors with respect to the establishment, acquisition, expansion, management, conduct, operation, and sale or other disposition of investments.

2. Each Party shall accord to investments of investors of another Party treatment no less favorable than that it accords, in like circumstances, to investments of its own investors with respect to the establishment, acquisition, expansion, management, conduct, operation, and sale or other disposition of investments.

3. The treatment accorded by a Party under paragraphs 1 and 2 means, with respect to a state or province, treatment no less favorable than the most favorable treatment accorded, in like circumstances, by that state or province to investors, and to investments of investors, of the Party of which it forms a part.

---

[60] See, for example, I. Shihata, *The World Bank in a Changing World* (Nijhoff, 1995), p.401–403.

> 4. For greater certainty, no Party may:
>
> (a) impose on an investor of another Party a requirement that a minimum level of equity in an enterprise in the territory of the Party be held by its nationals, other than nominal qualifying shares for directors or incorporators of corporations; or
>
> (b) require an investor of another Party, by reason of its nationality, to sell or otherwise dispose of an investment in the territory of the Party."

In addition to the focus on admission, the agreements generally contain post-entry obligations, involving the fair and equitable treatment of investors[61]; the provision for investors of the national treatment (NT) and MFN treatment[62]; the provision for investors to transfer payments internationally; protection against unlawful expropriation, including the payment of compensation; and the provision of dispute settlement processes, for both State disputes in relation to the agreement, as well as disputes between investors and the host State (investor-State arbitration).

## TREATMENT AND PROTECTION

**14–017** Even when the controversies between States regarding the proper treatment of foreign investors and their investment were more acute it was generally recognized that host states should not discriminate against and among foreign investors. As in other areas of international economic law this was usually expressed through the inclusion of a most-favoured-nation (MFN) clause and national treatment (NT) clause. They also are in line with the so-called Calvo Doctrine as developed in the 19th Century by the Argentinean *Carlos Calvo* (1824–1906) and very much in favour for long periods in most Latin-American States. He suggested that foreigners should be treated like domestic investors with respect to the treatment[63] (but also the availability of dispute settlement mechanisms).[64]

---

[61] See, for example, for recent examples on the discussion of this concept *CMS Gas Transmission Company v Argentinian Republic*, ICSID Case No.ARB/01/8. Award of the Tribunal of May 12, 2005, paras 273 et seq. See also *Azinian, Davitian & Baca v Mexico* ICSID Case No.ARB(AF)/97/2 (NAFTA) Award (English), November 1, 1999. See also C. Schreuer, "Fair and Equitable Treatment in Arbitral Practice" (2005) 6(3) *Journal of World Investment and Trade* 357.

[62] See especially on the scope of the MFN obligation *Maffezini v Spain* ICSID Case No.ARB/97/7 (*Argentina/Spain BIT*), Decision on objection to jurisdiction (English), January 25, 2000 and later decisions referring to this decision. See also J. Kurtz, "The MFN Standard and Foreign Investment—An Uneasy Fit?" (2004) 5(6) *The Journal of World Investment & Trade*, 861.

[63] See B. Juratowitch, "The relationship between diplomatic protection and investment treaties", *International Centre for Settlement of Investment Disputes: ICSID review*, 23.2008(2009) 1, 10–35

[64] See below.

**Agreement between the Swiss Confederation and the Hashemite Kingdom of Jordan on the Promotion and Reciprocal Protection of Investments of 25 February 2001**

**Article 4: Protection, treatment**

[. . .]

(2) Each Contracting Party shall in its territory accord investments and returns of investors of the other Contracting Party treatment not less favourable than that which it accords to investments or returns of its own investors or to investments or returns of investors of any third State, whichever is more favourable to the investor concerned.

(3) Each Contracting Party shall in its territory accord investors of the other Contracting Party, as regards the management, maintenance, use, enjoyment or disposal of their investments, treatment not less favourable than that which it accords to its own investors or investors of any third State, whichever is more favourable to the investor concerned.

(4) If a Contracting Party accords special advantages to investors of any third State by virtue of any existing or future agreement establishing a free trade area, a customs union or a common market or by virtue of any agreement on the avoidance of double taxation, it shall not be obliged to accord such advantages to investors of the other Contracting Party.

While the non-discrimination requirement regarding the treatment of foreign investors (be it with regard to nationals or third-country investors) was historically uncontroversial,[65], the exact scope of the MFN clause has led to considerable controversies. Here, the question as to whether it should allow an investor to import or borrow more favourable provision contained in other investment agreements by the host State is of primary importance. Normally each BIT is the outcome of a very specific negotiation process among two (or more) contracting States. While we have seen that the general structures are very similar, there are often differences with regard to the exact coverage and the wording of the treatment standards. Also, with regard to the available dispute settlement mechanisms, differences exist. It was in a now famous award in the Case *Maffezini v Spain*[66] that the question as to whether an Argentinean investor had to wait before he could submit his claim to arbitration (as foreseen in the directly applicable BIT between Spain and Argentina) or whether he had not to observe any waiting period (as foreseen in many other BITs concluded by Spain with

---

[65] See below on the specific requirements in the context of expropriation.
[66] *Emilio Agustin Maffezini v Kingdom of Spain* (ICSID Case No. ARB/97/7), Decision of the Tribunal on Objections to Jurisdiction, January 25, 2000. See R. Teitelbaum, "Who's afraid of Maffezini?", *Journal of International Arbitration*, 22 (2005) 3, 225–238 and A. R. Ziegler, "The Nascent international law on Most-Favoured-Nation (MFN) clauses in Bilateral Investment Treaties (BIT's)", *European Yearbook of International Economic Law*, 1 (2010), 77–101.

third States) was first addressed. While this tribunal interpreted the applicable MFN clause of the agreement as extending more favourable dispute settlement rules in BITs with third States to Argentinean investors, many writers and other arbitral tribunals dissented. The latter normally argued that this would undermine the specificity of each agreement and that MFN only applied to the treatment of the investor as such and not to more favourable provisions (especially regarding dispute settlement in other agreements). Later, this question was also asked in relation to the definition of investors and investments or the other treatment standards contained in BITs. As a consequence, some States have adapted their BITs as to limit the scope of the MFN clause (by excluding older BITs. Like in the case of Canada) or exclude certain areas (many countries have excluded dispute settlement provisions).

14–018      **Agreement between Canada and the Hashemite Kingdom of Jordan for the Promotion and Protection of Investments entered into force on 14 December 2009**

*ANNEX III Exceptions from Most-Favoured-Nation Treatment*

1. Article 4 [MFN treatment] shall not apply to treatment accorded under any bilateral or multilateral international agreement in force or signed prior to January 1, 1994.

2. Article 4 shall not apply to treatment by a Party pursuant to any existing or future bilateral or multilateral agreement:

   (a) establishing, strengthening or expanding a free trade area or customs union;

   (b) relating to:

      (i) aviation;

      (ii) fisheries; or

      (iii) maritime matters, including salvage.

3. For greater certainty, Article 4 shall not apply to any current or future foreign aid programme to promote economic development, whether under a bilateral agreement, or pursuant to a multilateral arrangement or agreement, such as the OECD Arrangement on Officially Supported Export Credits.

**US - Peru Trade Promotion Agreement, signed on April 12, 2006**

**Footnote to Article 10.4 (MFN):**

For greater certainty, treatment "with respect to the establishment, acquisition, expansion, management, conduct, operation, and sale or other disposition of investments" referred to in paragraphs 1 and 2 of Article 10.4 does not encompass dispute resolution mechanisms, such as those in Section B, that are provided for in international investment treaties or trade agreements.

A particularly important feature of most agreements is the so-called fair and equitable treatment (FET) clause.[67] This notion was included in many agreements relating to the treatment of foreigners since the late 18th century and has survived in this form until today. While the wording is very simple and straightforward its meaning has always been controversial as the extensive case law on it demonstrates. In view of this situation, the wording has hardly been changed over time and increasing case law has over time exemplified when a treatment is considered to be in violation of this standard. Furthermore, the FET clause is today normally thought of as being part of customary International Law but many agreements contain language that seems to be suggesting the required treatment under it should go beyond what is considered to be customary law (so-called minimum standard). Also, the interpretation of the terms "fair and equitable" by various arbitral tribunals over time have somewhat differed so that in recent times certain States have started to redefine the notion. In a very summary way it can be said that the treatment owed to foreign investors should not be incoherent and that legitimate expectations of the investors should be honoured, although the notion of "legitimate expectations" as such and what can be their basis is controversial in itself. One recent tribunal has claimed that the FET standard included "*the requirements of transparency, good faith, conduct that cannot be arbitrary, grossly unfair, unjust, idiosyncratic, discriminatory, lacking in due process or procedural propriety and respect of investor's reasonable and legitimate expectations*"[68]. But as many FET standards differ (slightly) in their wording it remains difficult to agree on a common notion. Some authors have also argued that the FET standard should make any breach of an international obligation (contained e.g. in another treaty like the WTO Agreement) a violation of the underlying BIT—but this is equally controversial and has been rejected by arbitrators and States in newer treaty models.

| | |
|---|---|
| **Agreement between the Swiss Confederation and the Hashemite Kingdom of Jordan on the Promotion and Reciprocal Protection of Investments of 25 February 2001** | **14–019** |

*Article 4: Protection, treatment*

(1) Investments and returns of investors of each Contracting Party shall at all times be accorded fair and equitable treatment and shall enjoy full protection and security in the territory of the other Contracting Party. Neither Contracting Party shall in any way impair by unreasonable or

---

[67] See G. Aguilar Alvarez, "Investments, fair and equitable treatment, and the principle of 'respect for the integrity of the law of the host state'", *Looking to the Future*, (2011), 579–605; R. Kläger, 'Fair and equitable treatment", *The Journal of World Investment & Trade*, 11 (2010) 3, 435–455; G. Cavazos Villanueva, *The fair and Equitable Treatment Standard in International Investment Law* (Ann Arbor, Mich., UMI, 2008).

[68] Sergei Paushok, *CJSC Golden East Company and CJSC Vostokneftegaz Company v. Mongolia*, UNCITRAL (Russia/Mongolia), Award on Jurisdiction and Liability, April 28, 2011, § 253.

discriminatory measures the management, maintenance, use, enjoyment, extension, or disposal of such investments.

**Agreement between Canada and the Hashemite Kingdom of Jordan for the Promotion and Protection of Investments (entered into force on 14 December 2009)**

*ARTICLE 5: Minimum Standard of Treatment*

1. Each Party shall accord to covered investments treatment in accordance with the customary international law minimum standard of treatment of aliens, including fair and equitable treatment and full protection and security.

2. The concepts of "fair and equitable treatment" and "full protection and security" in paragraph 1 do not require treatment in addition to or beyond that which is required by the customary international law minimum standard of treatment of aliens.

3. A determination that there has been a breach of another provision of this Agreement, or of a separate international agreement, does not establish that there has been a breach of this Article.

The notion of "full protection and security" is also contained in most agreements. While the exact difference to the FET standard is not fully settled it has most often been referred to in situations of armed conflict or civil strife. In these situations the use of physical force and the targeting of foreign investors by insurgents or mobs are particularly common. While the State is not considered to be responsible for all private actions like looting or attacks against foreign investors and their investment, it has certain obligations under this notion (which again is thought by most to be part of customary International Law) to provide them with the protection that seems possible and adequate in view of the situation.[69]

**14–020**     *Pantechniki S.A. Contractors & Engineers v. Republic of Albania*, **ICSID Case No. ARB/07/21 (Jan Paulsson, acting as sole arbitrator):**

In 1994, Pantechniki S.A. Contractors & Engineers (Pantechniki), a Greek company, entered into two contracts with Albania's General Road Directorate to perform construction work on bridges and roads in Albania. Pantechniki subsequently performed work under those contracts. In the spring of 1997, several major Albanian Ponzi schemes[70] collapsed, significantly affecting a large percentage of the Albanian population. Following the collapse of the schemes, violent riots ensued in many parts of the country, including the region where Pantechniki's work site was located. Pantechniki was forced to abandon its work site and repatriate its personnel, and its equipment and facilities were looted and destroyed. . . .

---

[69] See C. Schreuer, "Full Protection and Security", *Journal of International Dispute Settlement*, 1 (2010) 2, 353–369.

[70] A Ponzi scheme is a fraudulent investment operation that pays returns to separate investors, not from any actual profit earned by the organization, but from their own money or money paid by subsequent investors.

As to the full protection and security claim, arbitrator Paulsson determined that Albania had not acted negligently in failing to prevent the damage that Pantechniki suffered, and that the authorities were "powerless" given the scope of the unrest in the country. Thus, he dismissed this claim on the merits. Interestingly, arbitrator Paulsson indicated that the degree of "due diligence" required under the full protection and security standard might vary depending on the host state's level of development, and on socioeconomic or political conditions prevailing at the time of the investment.[71]

Another traditional fear of investors that is addressed in most BITs is the risk of being "locked in", i.e. incapable to repatriate the capital invested in the host state. The main reasons for this are restriction on the movement of capital.[72] This can be due to Government policies to avoid capital flight during economic crisis[73] or to foster domestic development. The repatriation of capital gains is sometimes also controversial as there may be a notion that they belong to the country where they were generated and thus should not be drained away to the country of the investor. In order to find a solution for the needs of the country to avoid economic problems relating to capital flows and the interest of the investor to maintain entrepreneurial freedom, most agreements include provision on the transfer of capitals.

**Agreement between the Swiss Confederation and the Hashemite Kingdom of Jordan on the Promotion and Reciprocal Protection of Investments of 25 February 2001**

**14–021**

**Article 5: Free transfer**

(1) Each Contracting Party shall grant the investors of the other Contracting Party the transfer without delay in a freely convertible currency of payments in connection with an investment, particularly, though not exclusively, of:

   (a) returns;

   (b) repayments of loans;

   (c) amounts assigned to cover expenses relating to the management of the investment;

   (d) royalties and other payments deriving from rights enumerated in Article 1, paragraph (2), letters (c), (d) and (e) of this Agreement;

   (e) the initial capital and additional contributions of capital necessary for the maintenance or development of the investment;

---

[71] Text taken from Marinn F. Carlson (Partner) and Joshua M. Robbins (Associate), Sidley Austin LLP, Sole arbitrator rejects claims against Albania, online: *http://arbitration.practical-law.com/0-422-4850.*

[72] See E. "Denza, Bilateral Investment Treaties and EU rules on free transfer", *European Law Review*, 35 (2010) 2, 263–274.

[73] See A. Kolo, "Investor protection vs host state regulatory autonomy during economic crisis", *The Journal of World Investment & Trade*, 8 (2007) 4, S. 457–503.

(f) the proceeds of the partial or total sale or liquidation of the investment, including possible increment values;

(g) payments arising out of the settlement of an investment dispute;

(h) earnings and other remuneration of personnel engaged from abroad in connection with an investment.

(2) Unless otherwise agreed with the investor, transfers shall be made at the rate of exchange applicable on the date of transfer pursuant to the exchange regulations in force of the Contracting Party in whose territory the investment was made.

**Agreement between Canada and the Hashemite Kingdom of Jordan for the Promotion and Protection of Investments (entered into force on 14 December 2009)**

ARTICLE 14 Transfers

1. Each Party shall permit all transfers relating to a covered investment to be made freely, and without delay, into and out of its territory. Such transfers include:

(a) contributions to capital;

(b) profits, dividends, interest, capital gains, royalty payments, management fees, technical assistance and other fees, returns in kind and other amounts derived from the investment;

(c) proceeds from the sale of all or any part of the covered investment or from the partial or complete liquidation of the covered investment;

(d) payments made under a contract entered into by the investor, or the covered investment, including payments made pursuant to a loan agreement;

(e) payments made pursuant to Articles 12 and 13; and

(f) payments arising under Section C.

2. Each Party shall permit transfers relating to a covered investment to be made in the convertible currency in which the capital was originally invested, or in any other convertible currency agreed by the investor and the Party concerned. Unless otherwise agreed by the investor, transfers shall be made at the market rate of exchange applicable on the date of transfer.

3. Notwithstanding paragraphs 1 and 2, a Party may prevent a transfer through the equitable, non-discriminatory and good faith application of its laws relating to:

(a) bankruptcy, insolvency or the protection of the rights of creditors;

(b) issuing, trading or dealing in securities;

(c) criminal or penal offences;

(d) reports of transfers of currency or other monetary instruments; or

(e) ensuring the satisfaction of judgments in adjudicatory proceedings.

4. Neither Party may require its investors to transfer, or penalize its

investors that fail to transfer, the income, earnings, profits or other amounts derived from, or attributable to investments in the territory of the other Party.

5. Paragraph 4 shall not be construed to prevent a Party from imposing any measure through the equitable, non-discriminatory and good faith application of its laws relating to the matters set out in subparagraphs (a) through (e) of paragraph 3.

6. Notwithstanding the provisions of paragraphs 1, 2 and 4, and without limiting the applicability of paragraph 5, a Party may prevent or limit transfers by a financial institution to, or for the benefit of, an affiliate of or person related to such institution, through the equitable, non-discriminatory and good faith application of measures relating to maintenance of the safety, soundness, integrity or financial responsibility of financial institutions.

7. Notwithstanding paragraph 1, a Party may restrict transfers of returns in kind in circumstances where it could otherwise restrict transfers under the WTO Agreement and as set out in paragraph 3.

## EXPROPRIATION

Expropriation (i.e. the deprivation by the State of foreign rights to property or its enjoyment[74]) can take various forms.[75] The process includes both direct expropriation; and indirect expropriation[76] where there is interference with the ownership of the property without being officially named as an expropriation covered by a specific law or decree. In the latter category, one distinguishes sometimes so-called "creeping expropriation" where a number of measures taken over time in their combined effect completely deprive the investor of his control over an investment.[77] Direct expropriation is often foreseen in the legislation of most states, e.g. for infrastructure projects or when in the general interest and normally involves the payment of due compensation. At the same time it can take the form of confiscation, requisition or nationalisation. Confiscation traditionally occurs when property is taken without compensation—in particular as a reaction to criminal behaviour by the owner. It is foreseen in most domestic criminal

**14–022**

---

[74] I. Brownlie, *Principles of Public International Law*, 5th edn (Oxford, Clarendon Press, 1998), p.534.

[75] See, for example, Sornarajah (2010), p.363; B.H. Weston, "Constructive takings under international law" (1975) 16 *Virginia J.I.L.* 103.

[76] See C. Knahr, "Indirect expropriation in recent investment arbitration", *Austrian Review of International and European Law*, 12.2007 (2010), 85–102 and M. Gutbrod, "Protection against indirect expropriation under national and international lagal systems", *Göttingen Journal of International Law*, 1 (2009) 2, 291–327.

[77] See P. Leon, "Creeping expropriation of mining investments", *Journal of Energy & Natural Resources Law*, 27 (2009) 4, 597–644.

legislations[78] but has also been used throughout history against certain groups of the population and foreigners.[79] Requisition usually takes place during armed conflict when the State is in need of certain goods and therefore takes private property available. It normally involves some form of compensation expect if the State cannot compensate in view of the economic situation or the urgency. In these cases it is normally foreseen that the compensation takes place once the State is in a position to pay it.[80] Nationalisation involves the taking of property as part of a government economic or social programme, normally involving a whole sector or even the economy as a whole.[81]

Indirect expropriation can take various forms, and has been defined, for example, as occurring when a State: "subjects alien property to taxation, regulation, or other action that is confiscatory, or that prevents, unreasonably interferes with, or unduly delays, effective enjoyment of an alien's property or its removal from the State's territory".[82] Sornarajah very helpfully groups the potential categories of indirect expropriation, which may give rise to international concern, for the purposes of exposition as follows[83]:

"(1) forced sales of property[84]; (2) forced sales of shares[85]; (3) indigenisa-

---

[78]  Brownlie (1998), p.534.
[79]  See *Center for Advanced Holocaust Studies (Washington, DC): Confiscation of Jewish property in Europe, 1933–1945.* (Washington, D.C., Center for Advanced Holocaust Studies, United States Holocaust Memorial Museum, 2003, and S. Petrén), "La confiscation des biens étrangers et les réclamations internationales aux quelles elle peut donner lieu". Recueil des cours / Académie de Droit International de La Haye, 109 (1963) 2, p. 492–571.
[80]  See, for example, Art.52 of the Convention (II) with Respect to the Laws and Customs of War on Land and its annex: Regulations concerning the Laws and Customs of War on Land. The Hague, July 29, 1899: Neither requisitions in kind nor services can be demanded from communes or inhabitants except for the necessities of the army of occupation. They must be in proportion to the resources of the country, and of such a nature as not to involve the population in the obligation of taking part in military operations against their country. These requisitions and services shall only be demanded on the authority of the commander in the locality occupied. The contributions in kind shall, as far as possible, be paid for in ready money; if not, their receipt shall be acknowledged. See also K. V. Okounev, "Guarantees against nationalisation, requisition and confiscation of foreign investments in Russia", *Svensk Juristtidning*, 83 (1998) 10, 837–843.
[81]  See G. Lagergren, *Five Important Cases on Nationalisation of Foreign Property,*. (Lund, Raoul Wallenberg Inst., 1988) and K. V. Okounev, "Guarantees against nationalisation, requisition and confiscation of foreign investments in Russia", *Svensk Juristtidning*, 83 (1998) 10, 837–843.
[82]  American Law Institute's Restatement on Foreign Relations Law of the United States (Vol.2, 1987) at p.200.
[83]  Sornarajah (2010), p.375. See more recently B. Kunoy, "Developments in Indirect Expropriation Case Law in ICSID Transnational Arbitration" (2005) 6(3) *The Journal of World Investment & Trade* 467 or Z.A. Al Qurashi, "Indirect Expropriation in the Field of Petroleum" (2004) 5(6) *The Journal of World Investment & Trade* 897.
[84]  As a result, for example, of threats by the State or its agents.
[85]  But subject to the rule in the *Barcelona Traction Case* (1970) I.C.J. Reports that only the State where a company has been incorporated can exercise diplomatic protection on behalf of the corporation under international customary law. See, however, P. M. Protopsaltis,

tion measures[86]; (4) exercising management control over the investment[87]; (5) inducing others to physically take over the property; (6) failure to provide protection when there is interference with the property of the foreign investor[88]; (7) administrative decisions which cancel licences and permits necessary for the foreign business to function within the State; (8) exorbitant taxation; (9) expulsion of the foreign investor contrary to international law; (10) acts of harassment such as the freezing of bank accounts, promoting of strikes, lockouts and labour shortages".

This category of indirect expropriation is neither exhaustive nor definitive; and needs to be examined against the background of what in International Law constitutes illegal expropriation, or expropriation giving rise to some form of reparation. More recently, other forms of government action that can reduce the value of an investment have been discusses under the heading of "measures tantamount to expropriation"[89] and often been described as "regulatory takings". The latter term stems originally from domestic law (especially in the United States) and relates to the question what kind of government action, including the adoption of new laws, leads to such interference with an investment that some form of compensation is due. The question is obviously controversial as the need to compensate can put the "right to regulate" of a State under pressure (e.g. in the area of environmental protection or the safeguard of certain human rights).[90]

---

"The challenge of the Barcelona Traction hypothesis", *The Journal of World Investment & Trade*, 11 (2010) 4, 561–599.

[86] Involving a gradual transfer of ownership from foreign interests local stakeholders.

[87] In this respect the discussion of the so-called "control principle" is particularly important; see ICJ, *Barcelona Traction Case, Belgium v Spain* (1970) I.C.J. Reports and ICSID; *Siemens AG v Argentine Republic*, ICSID Case No.ARB/02//8, Decision on Jurisdiction, August 3, 2004. See P. M. Protopsaltis, "The challenge of the Barcelona Traction hypothesis", *The Journal of World Investment & Trade*, 11 (2010) 4, 561–599.

[88] For example, where there is destruction of property as a consequence of civil strife or insurgency as a consequence of failure by the host State to protect the foreign property.

[89] See, for example, *Azinian v Mexico* (November 1, 1999); *Pope & Talbot v Canada* (June 26, 2000 interim award) or *Middle East Cement Shipping and Handling Co S.A v Arab Republic of Egypt* (ICSID Case No.ARB/99/6—April 12, 2002).

[90] See as important cases, especially under NAFTA, in this respect *Técnicas medioambientales (Tecmed) SA v United Mexican States*, ICSID (Additional Facility) Case ARB(AF)/00/2, Award of the Tribunal, May 29, 2003, para.114. and *Metalclad v United Mexican States*, ICSID (Additional Facility), ARB/AF/97/1, Award of the Tribunal, August 30, 2000; see also *Ethyl Corporation v Canada* UNCITRAL (NAFTA) Decision on Jurisdiction, June 24, 1998 and *Methanex Corp. v United States of America*, Arbitration under NAFTA and UNCITRAL, Final Award of the Tribunal, August 9, 2005, Section IV, Chapter D, para.6 et seq. Outside NAFTA see, for example, *Saluka v Czech Republic*, Award of March 17, 2006; see also M.A. Abdala, "Damage valuation of indirect expropriation in international arbitration cases (2003) 14(4) *The American Review of International Arbitration* 447–60. See also D. Clough, "Regulatory Expropriations and Compensation under NAFTA (2005) 6(4) *Journal of World Investment & Trade* 553 and S. R. Ratner, "Regulatory takings in institutional context", *American Journal of International Law*, 102 (2008) 3, 475–528.

**14–023**

**Foreign Affairs and International Trade (Canada): Official Information on the Case *Metalclad Corporation v. Mexico*, ICSID Case No. ARB(AF)/97/1 (NAFTA)**[91]

On August 30, 2000, the NAFTA Chapter 11 Tribunal in *Metalclad (USA) v. United Mexican States* found Mexico in breach of its Chapter 11 obligations. Mexico was ordered to pay US $16.7 million in compensatory damages to Metalclad ("the Investor"). This was the first final decision on the merits by a NAFTA Chapter 11 Tribunal that has ruled in favour of the investor.

The claim brought by Metalclad Inc., a publicly held U.S. company, alleged that Mexico's failure to grant it a municipal licence to operate its hazardous waste treatment facility and landfill site and the decree declaring the area where the facility and site were located an ecological zone, amounted to an expropriation without compensation, contrary to NAFTA Article 1110. [. . .].

The NAFTA rules allowed Mexico to seek a statutory review of the Tribunal's decision to the Canadian courts.

**Why was this case reviewed by the B.C. Supreme Court?**

Parties of a NAFTA Chapter 11 dispute can designate place of arbitration. As Vancouver was chosen for this case, the applicable Canadian legislation allows that the statutory review take place before a British Columbia court.

**Why did Canada intervene in the B.C. Supreme Court case?**

Recognizing that the *Metalclad* decision could have a persuasive impact on future tribunals, Canada chose to intervene in the *Metalclad* review. Canada's written submission argued that any interpretation of the NAFTA must promote the NAFTA's objectives and ensure governments possess flexibility to safeguard public interests.

Canada further argued that the NAFTA Tribunal incorrectly read into the Agreement obligations that federal governments are obligated to remove all doubt and uncertainty about all relevant legal requirements applicable to NAFTA investors.

**What did the B.C. Supreme Court rule?**

[. . .]

While Justice Tysoe found that there was no evidence of a violation of Article 1110 on account of events prior to the Ecological Decree, he held that the Tribunal's finding that Mexico had expropriated Metalclad's investment through issuance of the Ecological Decree was not patently unreasonable.

In upholding the Tribunal's finding that the Ecological Degree expropriated Metalclad's investment, Tysoe noted that, unless patently unreasonable, it was not for the B.C. Supreme Court to substitute its judgement for the Tribunal's judgement. As such, while Justice Tysoe noted that while the Tribunal had given "an extremely broad definition of expropriation for the purposes of Article 1110", it was not patently unreasonable.

Accordingly, the Award was not set aside in its entirety. The Court reduced the interest on damages, originally ordered to be paid to Metalclad, by 21 months and granted Metalclad 75% of its costs of the proceeding.

---

[91] Available at: *http://www.international.gc.ca/trade-agreements-accords-commerciaux/disp-diff/ Mun-metalclad.aspx?lang=en*. (Accessed June 8, 2011).

> **Does this decision mean NAFTA limits the rights of local governments to legislate and regulate in the public interest?**
>
> It should be noted that each NAFTA Chapter 11 case is very fact specific and does not set a binding precedent for future cases. Therefore one should not draw general conclusions based on the outcome of a particular case.
>
> Neither the Tribunal nor the Court in *Metalclad v. Mexico* call into question the right of a local government to regulate on environmental and public health grounds.
>
> The decision of the Tribunal in Metalclad found that changes to the rules by the state government, after Metalclad had been led to believe that it had all necessary authorisations and had invested a substantial amount in its operation (the plant was ready to open), were tantamount to expropriation. That is not the same as denying the right of government to regulate.
>
> The B.C. Supreme Court found that it could not review the Tribunal's finding that Mexico had expropriated Metalclad's investment through issuance of the Ecological Decree because that finding was not patently unreasonable.[ . . .]

In International Law a distinction is made between lawful and unlawful expropriation. Whereas lawful expropriation creates an obligation to pay compensation, unlawful expropriation creates an obligation to pay damages for the violation of the legal obligations relating to expropriation in International Law.[92] Lawful expropriation is said to occur when it is non-discriminatory and for a public purpose.[93] Some writers also include the requirement that the expropriation must not be arbitrary.[94] There is, however, some uncertainty as to the requirement of public purpose.[95] It is not mentioned in the Charter of Economic Rights and Duties of States (CERDS) of 1974, and has been queried as a requirement in the *Liamco* case.[96] In any event, it seems the determination of what constitutes public purpose is a matter essentially in the domain of the State concerned.[97] In addition, unlawful expropriation can occur not only where the taking is discriminatory, or possibly not for public purpose, but also in the following circumstances[98]: where there has been interference with the property of an international organisation, or property owned by a foreign State for official State purposes; where the seizure is contrary to promises made by the State resulting in estoppel; where the seizure results from crimes against humanity

---

[92] See, for example, Sornarajah (2010), p.447.
[93] See, for example, the 1962 General Assembly Resolution on Permanent Sovereignty Over Natural Resources; Certain German Interests in Polish Upper Silesia PCIJ, Series A, No.7, 1926, p.22. See also, for example, R. Higgins, *Problems and Process* (Oxford, Clarendon Press, 1994), p.142; Shrijver (1997), p.176; L.F. Oppenheim, *Oppenheim's International Law*, 9th edn (London, Longman, 1992), p.920 and more recently A. F. M. Maniruzzaman, "Expropriation of alien property and the principle of non-discrimination in international law of foreign investment: an overview", *Journal of Transnational Law & Policy*, 8 (1998) 1, 57–77.
[94] See, for example, Oppenheim (1992), p.920.
[95] See Shaw (1997), p.577; Brownlie (1998), p.547.
[96] (1981) 10 I.L.M. and Shaw (1997), p.577.
[97] See Brownlie (1998), p.547.
[98] See Brownlie (1998), p.541.

or genocide; where the expropriation is contrary to international agreements; where it is part of unlawful retaliations against another State. Thus, generally the distinction between lawful and unlawful expropriation is relatively clear.

The circumstances for a lawful expropriation must not only satisfy certain conditions, but need also to be accompanied by compensation. The precise measure of compensation has been the subject of some discourse, particularly in the recent past—the standpoints being polarised between the preferences of the majority developing States for the national treatment, and the minority developed States for an international standard. In a nutshell, developed States maintain that the standard of compensation should be such that prompt, adequate and effective compensation is given. "Prompt" refers to the timing of payment of compensation; it is sometimes replaced by the requirement that compensation should be without undue delay. "Adequate" refers to the amount of compensation, and is interpreted to mean full or fair market value.[99] Effective refers to the convertibility of the currency in which the compensation is made—including its transferability.[100] This is the "Hull formula", named after US Secretary of State Cordial Hull, who made such a claim in relation to Mexican expropriations in a letter to the Mexican Government in 1938.[101] On the other hand, capital-importing States have historically articulated a national standard of compensation applied to nationals and foreigners alike.[102] This view has progressed to an assertion in Art.2 of CERDS 1974 for appropriate compensation to be paid, taking into account relevant national laws of the expropriating State, and all the circumstances considered by it to be relevant.[103] According to critical authors, relevant considerations could include the situation where, for example the investor has recouped through profits his investment, or where the investment was actually harmful to the State.[104]

**14–024**    Authority for the Hull standard is claimed to rest in a number of sources. Thus, Professor Brownlie asserted that the standard has received considerable support from State practice, international tribunals and the majority of jurists in western countries.[105] On the other hand, it is asserted, for example by Sornarajah, that there is no basis neither under Customary International

---

[99] See, however, I. Marboe, "Compensation and Damages in International Law—The Limits of 'Fair Market Value'" (2006) 7(5) *The Journal of World Investment and Trade*, 723 et seq. See also D. Tamada, "Assessing damages in non-expropriation cases before international investment arbitration", *Japanese Yearbook of International Law*, 52.2009 (2010), 309–334 and A. J. H. Van der Walt, "The state's duty to pay 'just and equitable' compensation for expropriation", *The South African Law Journal*, 122 (2005) 4, 765–778.

[100] See, for example, Oppenheim (1992), p.921.

[101] M. Whitman, 8 *Digest of International Law* 657.

[102] Also known as the Calvo doctrine after the Argentinean lawyer Carlos Calvo, as mentioned above. See, for example, Brownlie (1998), p.538; Schrijver (1997), p.178.

[103] See Art.2(2) (c) of CERDS 1974 Contra Art.2 of CERDS with Art.4 of the 1962 GA Res on Permanent Sovereignty Over Natural Resources wherein the reference to compensation is "appropriate compensation, in accordance with the rules in force in the State taking such measures in the exercise of its sovereignty and in accordance with international law".

[104] See, for example, Sornarajah (2010), p.449.

[105] See Brownlie (1998), pp.536 and 537.

Law, or General Principles of Law, for a standard of full compensation.[106] Here only some of the main arguments are rehearsed. First, it is claimed that bilateral investment agreements commonly refer to the Hull formula. This treaty practice must, it is claimed, evidence State practice.[107] On the other hand, it has been pointed out that such attribution to the treaty practice is flawed, mainly for three reasons. First, the compensation standard in the treaty practice is not uniform, and in some reliance is placed on the national authority's valuation of the compensation. Secondly, the bilateral agreements are the result of negotiations—reflect compromises, or evidence power-premised negotiations. Thirdly, many of the same capital-importing States which have entered into bilateral investment agreements, at the multi-lateral level claim a different standard. Further, State practice generally does not reflect the full compensation standard. Thus, there is little evidence of full compensation having actually been paid in modern times. Indeed, the evidence is that States have negotiated in practice lump-sum agreements, which have fallen short of full compensation.[108] However, this view of the character of lump-sum agreements is not generally accepted,[109] on the grounds that they relate to specific situations, and are negotiated against the background of non-legal considerations.

Similarly, in the context of General Principles of Law, there have been raised arguments which militate against the Hull formula. First, the relevant principles such as unjust enrichment and acquired rights are equitable doctrines. They are relevant not just at the time of nationalisation, but at all material times during the whole relationship between the expropriating State, the capital exporting State and the investor—including particularly the time prior to nationalisation. Secondly, there is no universal practice of a right to property in national systems. Thirdly, national investment codes are not uniform in their prescription of a standard of compensation.[110]

In relation to international decisions in this field, the Iran-US Claim Tribunals have made an important contribution. However, the jurisprudence of the Tribunals is not supportive of the full compensation standard.[111] Finally, amongst jurists there is a tendency to reflect respective national interests. However, this is not general, and even amongst jurists from capital-exporting States, there are divergent views.[112]

In conclusion, there are two differing assessments of the General International Law position relating to the existence of the Hull formula. With **14–025**

---

[106] Sornarajah (2010), p.443.
[107] For example, Brownlie (1998), p.547 and Shaw (1997), p.581.
[108] Sornarajah (2010), p.451.
[109] See, for example, US Claims Tribunal in *Amoco International Finance Corporation v Iran* [1987] 15 Iran US CTR 189.
[110] Sornarajah (2010), p.414.
[111] Sornarajah (2010), p.435.
[112] See, for example, C. De Visscher, *Theory and Reality in International Law* (Princeton, Princeton University Press, 1968); C. Rousseau, *Droit International Public*, 10th edn (Paris, Dalloz, 1984); O. Schacter, "Compensation for expropriation" [1984] 78 A.J.I.L. 121.

respect to the national standard of compensation, as reflected in Art.2 of the 1974 CERDS, there are two standpoints as well. First, that it is merely *de lege ferenda*.[113] Secondly, that it is an "emergent principle applicable *ex nunc*".[114] Were the latter to be the case, such a principle of Customary International Law would not apply, according to Professor Brownlie, to the US and certain other Western governments, on the grounds that they have been persistent objectors.[115]

It is generally beginning to be accepted now that the opposing discourse is veering towards some form of a synthesis with respect to the question of compensation in relation to lawful expropriation. First, in the case of a large-scale nationalisation, as part of a programme of economic reform, compensation is to be with reference to the economic objectives of the nationalisation, and the economic viability of the economy as a whole.[116] The expectation of prompt and full compensation is not present.[117] This is grounded inter alia on the principle of self-determination, independence, sovereignty and equality.[118] However, where the investment at the invitation of the host State, is aborted through expropriation, before commencement of business, then the case for full compensation is diminished.[119] In the case of a one-off taking on a smaller scale, there is an expectation of full compensation.[120] In the case of lawful expropriation, the compensation relates to *damnum emergens*, i.e. actual loss.[121] It does not include *lucrum cessans*[122] (future losses). Finally, a certain limited and exceptional category of expropriation for public purposes, engaged in, for example, in the course of the exercise of police powers and defence measures, do not entail an expectation of compensation.[123]

In the case of unlawful expropriation, the State is liable for damages on the basis of *restitutio in integrum*, thus including consequential loss of profits[124] (i.e. *lucrum cessans*). Further, no valid title is recognised by foreign courts, as having been transferred.[125]

---

[113] See, for example, Brownlie (1998), p.545.

[114] Brownlie (1998), p.545.

[115] See, Brownlie, (1998), p.546. A norm of Customary International Law does not apply to a State which has objected to the norm in its formative stages.

[116] See, for example, Brownlie (1998), p.540; Shaw (1997), p.579; and Thomas W. Wälde and Bozu Sabahi, Compensation, Damages and Valuation, in Peter Muchlinski et al (eds.), *The Oxford Handbook of International Investment Law* (Oxford, OUP, 2008), p.1049.

[117] See *INA Corporation v The Islamic Republic of Iran* 8 Iran-US CTR, p.373 quoted by Shaw (1997), p.579.

[118] Brownlie (1998), p.539.

[119] See Wälde and Sabahi (2008), p.1078.

[120] See, for example, Brownlie (1998), p.540; Sornarajah (2010), p.409.

[121] See, for example, *Liamco Vase* 62 I.L.R. 140 at 201; and *AMCO v Islamic Republic of Iran* 83 I.L.R. 500. See also Higgins (1994), p.143.

[122] For example, Brownlie (1998), p.541. Contra Higgins (1994), p.142.

[123] See, for example, Brownlie (1998), p.540 and more recently B. Sabahi and N.J. Birch, "Comparative Compensation for Expropriation", *International Investment Law and Comparative Public Law*, 33 (2010), p.755–787.

[124] See *Chorzow Factory (Merits)*, PCIJ, Ser.A, No.17, p.29. See also, for example, Brownlie (1998), p.541.

[125] Brownlie (1998), p.541.

**Agreement between the Swiss Confederation and the Hashemite Kingdom of Jordan on the Promotion and Reciprocal Protection of Investments of 25 February 2001**

**Article 6: Expropriation**

(1) Neither of the Contracting Parties shall take, either directly or indirectly, measures of expropriation, nationalisation or any other measures having the same nature or the same effect against investments of investors of the other Contracting Party, unless the measures are taken in the public interest, on a non-discriminatory basis, and under due process of law, and provided that provisions be made for effective and adequate compensation. Such compensation shall amount to the market value of the investment expropriated immediately before the expropriatory action was taken or became public knowledge, whichever is earlier. The amount of compensation, interest included, shall be settled in a freely convertible currency and paid without delay to the person entitled thereto without regard to its residence or domicile.

(2) Due process of law includes, in particular, the right of an investor of a Contracting Party which claims to be affected by expropriation by the other Contracting Party to prompt review of its case, including the valuation of its investment and the payment of compensation in accordance with the provisions of this article, by a judicial authority or another competent and independent authority of the latter Contracting Party.

**AGREEMENT BETWEEN CANADA AND THE HASHEMITE KINGDOM OF JORDAN FOR THE PROMOTION AND PROTECTION OF INVESTMENTS (entered into force on 14 December 2009)**

*ARTICLE 13 Expropriation*

1. Neither Party shall nationalize or expropriate a covered investment either directly, or indirectly through measures having an effect equivalent to nationalization or expropriation (hereinafter referred to as "expropriation"), except for a public purpose, in accordance with due process of law, in a non-discriminatory manner and on prompt, adequate and effective compensation. For greater certainty, this paragraph shall be interpreted in accordance with Annex B.13(1) on the clarification of indirect expropriation.

2. Such compensation shall be equivalent to the fair market value of the expropriated investment immediately before the expropriation took place ("date of expropriation"), and shall not reflect any change in value occurring because the intended expropriation had become known earlier. Valuation criteria shall include going concern value, asset value including declared tax value of tangible property, and other criteria, as appropriate, to determine fair market value.

3. Compensation shall be paid without delay and shall be fully realizable and freely transferable. Compensation shall be payable in a freely convertible currency and shall include interest at a commercially reasonable rate for that currency from the date of expropriation until the date of payment.

4. The investor affected shall have a right, under the law of the Party making the expropriation, to prompt review, by a judicial or other independent authority of that Party, of its case and of the valuation of its investment in accordance with the principles set out in this Article.

5. The provisions of this Article shall not apply to the issuance of compulsory licenses granted in relation to intellectual property rights, or to the revocation, limitation or creation of intellectual property rights, to the extent that such issuance, revocation, limitation or creation is consistent with the WTO Agreement.

*Annex B.13(1) : Expropriation*

The Parties confirm their shared understanding that:

(a) Indirect expropriation results from a measure or series of measures of a Party that have an effect equivalent to direct expropriation without formal transfer of title or outright seizure;

(b) The determination of whether a measure or series of measures of a Party constitute an indirect expropriation requires a case-by-case, fact-based inquiry that considers, among other factors:

(i) the economic impact of the measure or series of measures, although the sole fact that a measure or series of measures of a Party has an adverse effect on the economic value of an investment does not establish that an indirect expropriation has occurred,

(ii) the extent to which the measure or series of measures interfere with distinct, reasonable investment-backed expectations, and

(iii) the character of the measure or series of measures;

(c) Except in rare circumstances, such as when a measure or series of measures are so severe in the light of their purpose that they cannot be reasonably viewed as having been adopted and applied in good faith, non-discriminatory measures of a Party that are designed and applied to protect legitimate public welfare objectives, such as health, safety and the environment, do not constitute indirect expropriation.

## DISPUTE SETTLEMENT

**14–027**    One of the most important features of modern investment law is that it provides most of the time for very efficient dispute settlement mechanisms directly available to the investors themselves against the host states, including international arbitration,[126] normally under ICSID[127] or alternative fora (e.g. International Chamber of Commerce, Stockholm Chamber of Commerce, Permanent Court of Arbitration etc.) with generally recognised procedures (UNICTRAL

---

[126] See E. Savarese, "Investment Treaties and the Investor's Right to Arbitration—Between Broadening and Limiting ICSID Jurisdiction" (2006) 7(3) *The Journal of World Investment & Trade* 407

[127] See below.

Arbitration Rules,[128] etc.). Until the mid-1990s only few disputes involving BITS had occurred[129] but since then this type of investment disputes has mushroomed and by today several hundreds of such cases have been published or are known as pending before international arbitral tribunals.[130] Normally the investor is given a choice to bring a claim to a domestic tribunal or one of various international arbitration procedures and fora. The agreements differ, however, with regard to the question as to whether these are exclusive alternatives or whether under certain circumstances these option can be used subsequently. Where the choice of one venue automatically excludes the others we speak normally of so-called "fork-in-the-road" clauses.[131] There is often a risk of parallel proceedings as in many cases the applicable rules are not clear or a variety of investors may use different BITs or proceedings to bring an action.[132] Where the enforcement of such awards is not already foreseen in the applicable Treaty (e.g. ICSID)[133] these arbitral awards are normally enforceable under the 1958 New York Treaty on Enforcement of Arbitral Awards, which has been ratified by an important number of States (e.g. awards rendered by specific institution applying the UNICTRAL rules). The enforcement of such awards is subject to all the known problems regarding the (partial) immunity of States against certain types of enforcement measures.[134]

---

**AGREEMENT BETWEEN CANADA AND THE HASHEMITE KINGDOM OF JORDAN FOR THE PROMOTION AND PROTECTION OF INVESTMENTS (entered into force on 14 December 2009)**                    14–028

*ARTICLE 22 Claim by an Investor of a Party on Its Own Behalf*

  1. An investor of a Party may submit to arbitration under this Section a claim that the other Party has breached an obligation under Articles 2 to

---

[128] UNCITRAL, the United Nations Committee on International Trade Law, has developed a set of procedural rules widely used in commercial arbitration but also between foreign investors and States; see, for example, D.D. Caron, L.M. Caplan and M. Pellonpää, *The UNCITRAL Arbitration Rules* (Oxford, Oxford University Press, 2006) Jan Paulsson, The Revised UNCITRAL Rules (Kluwer Law International, forthcoming February 2011).

[129] See, for example, WTO Annual Report (1996) at p.36.

[130] See, for example, T. Weiler, *International Investment Law and Arbitration—Leading Cases from ICSID, NAFTA Bilateral Treaties and Customariy International Law* (London: Cameron May, 2005).

[131] See C. H. Schreuer, Travelling the BIT Route: Of Waiting Periods, Umbrella Clauses and Forks in the Road, (2004) 5 *Journal of World Investment & Trade* 231 and P. Leon, "A fork in the investor-state road", *Journal of World Trade*, 42 (2008) 4, 671–690.

[132] A famous example for parallel proceedings are the various outcomes in the Case *Lauder/CME v Czech Republic*; see *CME Czech Republic B.V. v Czech Republic*, UNICTRAL (The Netherlands/Czech Republic BIT) Final Award, March 14, 2003 and *Lauder v Czech Republic*, UNCITRAL (United States/Czech Republic BIT), Final Award, September 3, 2001. For comments see F. de Ly, "Who wins and who loses in investment arbitation? Are investors and host states on a level playing field?", *The Journal of World Investment & Trade; Law, Economics, Politics*, 6 (2005) 1, 59–63.

[133] See below.

[134] See recently D. Chamlongrasdr, Foreign state immunity and arbitration (London, Cameron May, 2007 and C. Baltag, "Enforcement of arbitral awards against states", *The American Review of International Arbitration*, 19 (2008) 3/4, S. 391–414.

5, paragraph 6 (1), paragraph 6 (2), Articles 7 to 10 and Articles 12 to18, and that the investor has incurred loss or damage by reason of, or arising out of, that breach.

2. An investor may not make a claim if more than three years have elapsed from the date on which the investor first acquired, or should have first acquired, knowledge of the alleged breach and knowledge that the investor has incurred loss or damage.

*ARTICLE 23 Claim by an Investor of a Party on Behalf of an Enterprise*

1. An investor of a Party, on behalf of an enterprise of the other Party that is a juridical person that the investor owns or controls directly or indirectly, may submit to arbitration under this Section a claim that the other Party has breached an obligation under Articles 2 to 5, paragraph 6 (1), paragraph 6 (2), Articles 7 to 10 and Articles 12 to18, and that the enterprise has incurred loss or damage by reason of, or arising out of, that breach.

2. n investor may not make a claim on behalf of an enterprise described in paragraph 1 if more than three years have elapsed from the date on which the enterprise first acquired, or should have first acquired, knowledge of the alleged breach and knowledge that the enterprise has incurred loss or damage.

3. Where an investor makes a claim under this Article and the investor or a non-controlling investor in the enterprise makes a claim under Article 22 arising out of the same events that gave rise to the claim under this Article, and two or more of the claims are submitted to arbitration under Article 27, the claims should be heard together by a Tribunal established under Article 32, unless the Tribunal finds that the interests of a disputing party would be prejudiced thereby.

4. An investment may not make a claim under this Section.

**Agreement between the Swiss Confederation and the Hashemite Kingdom of Jordan on the Promotion and Reciprocal Protection of Investments of 25 February 2001**

*Article 9 Settlement of disputes between a Contracting Party and an investor of the other Contracting Party*

1. With a view to an amicable solution of disputes between a Contracting Party and an investor of the other Contracting Party and without prejudice to Article 10 of this Agreement, consultations will take place between the parties concerned.

2. If these consultations do not result in solution within six months from the date of the written request for consultations, the investor may submit the dispute either to the national jurisdiction of the Contracting Party in whose territory the investment has been made or to international arbitration. In the latter event the investor has the choice between either of the following:

   a) the international Center for Settlement of Investment Disputes (ICSID) instituted by the Convention on the Settlement of Investment Disputes between States and Nationals of other States, opened for signature at Washington, on 18 March 1956 (hereinafter the "Convention of Washington");

b) an ad hoc arbitral tribunal which unless otherwise agreed upon the parties to the dispute shall be established under the arbitration rules of the United Nations Commissions on International Trade Law (UNCITRAL);

c) arbitration in accordance with the Rules of Arbitration of the International Chamber of Commerce (ICC).

3. Each Contracting Party hereby consents to the submission of an investment dispute to international arbitration.

4. The Contracting Party which is a party to the dispute shall, at no time whatsoever during the settlement procedure or the execution of the sentence, raise as an objection the fact that the investor has received, by virtue of an insurance contract, a compensation covering the whole or part of the incurred damage.

5. A company which has been incorporated or constituted according to the laws in force in the territory of a Contracting Party and which, prior to the origin of the dispute, was under the control of nationals or companies of the other Contracting Party, shall, in accordance with Article 25 (2) (b) of the Convention of Washington, be treated as a company of the other Contracting Party.

6. Neither Contracting Party shall pursue through diplomatic channels a dispute submitted to international arbitration unless the other Contracting Party does not abide by any comply with the arbitral award.

7. The arbitral award shall be final and binding for the parties to the dispute and shall be executed according to national law.

ICSID

The ICSID Convention of 1965[135] provides the institutional and procedural  **14–029** framework[136] for the resolution of investment disputes.[137] The institution was sponsored by the World Bank under its mandate to promote private foreign investment for development purposes.[138] The Convention establishing the institution does not provide a code for investment regulation in International

---

[135] See The Convention on the Settlement of Investment Disputes Between States and Nationals of Other States 1965. See for example ICSID Basic Documents; Shihata (1991), Chs 9 and 10; Shihata (1995) Chs 11, 12, 13; A. Broches, *Selected Essays: World Bank, ICSID, and Other Subjects of Public and Private International Law* (Dordrecht: Martinus Nijhoff, 1995), Pt III; I. Shihata, *The World Bank in a Changing World* Vol.III (Dordrecht: Martinus Nijhoff, 2000), Chs 20–21; Christoph Schreuer with Loretta Malintoppi, August Reinisch and Anthony Sinclair, The ICSID Convention: A Commentary (Cambridge University Press, Cambridge, 2nd edn, 2009) and Yaraslau Kryvoi, The International Center for Settlement of Investment Disputes (Kluwer Law International, 2010).

[136] Broches (1995), p.165.

[137] ICSID Art.1.

[138] See IBRD Art. I.

Law. It is a conflict resolution mechanism in the investment field set up to facilitate and promote private international investment for economic development purposes.[139] The availability of an international conflict resolution mechanism provides for legal security and predictability for foreign investors.[140] In this vein, one of the key distinguishing features of the ICSID is that it provides a conflict resolution mechanism for investment disputes between private investors and States; and in this context places both private investors and States on an equal footing. The Convention was last revised in 2006.

The ICSID has jurisdiction in the following circumstances. First, generally the Convention applies to disputes arising as between the Contracting States of the Convention, and nationals of other Contracting States. Thus, the Convention does not apply as between Contracting States or as between private parties. Nor are the ICSID facilities available for disputes as between a national and his own State. Nationals include natural persons and juridical persons. Secondly, the facility is available in relation to any legal dispute arising directly out of a foreign investment.[141] Thirdly, the facility is available only as between Contracting States and nationals who have specifically given their consent for the dispute to be considered in the framework of the ICSID. Ratification of the Convention by itself is not enough as signifying consent for this purpose. Thus, the Convention, somewhat unlike the WTO dispute settlement mechanism, does not provide for a compulsory system of conflict resolution.[142] The consent must be given in writing. It may be proffered with respect to a specific dispute, or in advance with respect to a class of disputes.[143] A Contracting State may also indicate its consent to be subject to the jurisdiction of the mechanisms under the ICSID in its investment code. Foreign investors in turn can express their consent by accepting such a standing offer.[144] Further, the consent of the parties to the use of the ICSID facilities may also be found in contractual terms involving investments, and also in BITs. The consent once given in whatever form, however, cannot thereafter

---

[139] IBRD Art. I, see Preamble.

[140] The question whether an investor is truly "foreign" becomes controversial in times where the mobility of capital and the availability of foreign holding companies leads to situations where it is questionable whether the entity controlling a foreign company has the nationality of the host state; see, for example, *Tokios Tokelés v Ukraine*, ICSID Case No.ARB/02/18, Decision on Jurisdiction of April 29, 2004, especially the dissenting opinion of the President of the Tribunal. See also M. Burgstaller, "Nationality of Corporate Investors and International Claims against the Investor's Own State" (2006) 7(6) *The Journal of World Investment & Trade* 857 and R. Wisner and N. Gallus, "Nationality Requirements in Investor—State Arbitration" (2004) 5(6) *The Journal of World Investment & Trade* 927; P. Acconci, "Determining the Internationally Relevant Link between a State and a Corporate Investor—Recent Trends concerning the Application of the 'Genuine Link' Test" (2004) 5(1) *The Journal of World Investment & Trade* 139. See also the literature regarding the general debate on the definition of an investment, as quoted above.

[141] ICSID Art.25.

[142] See Broches (1995), p.165.

[143] ICSID Art.25.

[144] See, for example, Shihata (1995), p.435, and see also the Report of the World Bank Executive Directors on the Convention in Doc.ICSID/2.

be withdrawn.[145] In order to make the ICSID mechanism also available in cases between parties one of which is not a Contracting State or a national of a Contracting State, the ICSID Additional Facility Rules was created in 1978. This set of rules is very similar to the original ICSID rules, but contains a number of important differences such as the fact that the awards rendered thereunder are open to appeal in domestic courts.[146]

There are essentially two conflict resolution facilities available under the ICSID, namely the conciliation,[147] and the arbitration[148] processes. First, in relation to conciliation, any party may make a request to activate this process.[149] Upon such a request the conciliation is considered by a Conciliation Commission.[150] This Commission may consist of a sole conciliator, or an uneven number of conciliators appointed by the parties.[151] The conciliators may be chosen from a panel of conciliators. The Convention specifies the process involved in constituting this Commission. The Commission is to conduct the conciliation process in accordance with the Convention and the Conciliation Rules.[152] The function of the Commission is to clarify the issues, and to assist in bringing about a mutually acceptable settlement.[153] However, the Commission can only make non-binding recommendations.[154] Secondly, arbitration proceedings can be commenced at the request of any of the parties in writing.[155] The Arbitration Tribunal is to comprise of a sole arbitrator, or an uneven number of arbitrators appointed with the agreement of the parties.[156] The arbitrators may be chosen from a panel (list) of arbitrators but this is no requirement. If the Parties cannot agree on the arbitrators the Secretary-General of ICSID can intervene.[157] The arbitration is to be conducted in accordance with the Convention and the Arbitration Rules.[158]

The award of an ICSID Arbitral Tribunal is binding, and is not subject to appeal.[159] Further, the award is to be recognised as binding by all Contracting Parties; and the pecuniary obligations of the award can be enforced in the territory of any of the Contracting Parties, as if it was a final judgement of its own courts. However, upon an award being delivered, a party can: (i) request

**14–030**

---

[145] See Broches (1995), p.165.
[146] See A. Antonietti, "The 2006 amendments to the ICSID rules and regulations and the additional facility rules", *International Centre for Settlement of Investment Disputes: ICSID Review*, 21(2006) 2, 427–448.
[147] See IVSID Section 3.
[148] See ICSID Section IV.
[149] ICSID Art.28.
[150] ICSID Art.29.
[151] ICSID Art.29.
[152] ICSID Art.33.
[153] ICSID Art.34.
[154] ICSID Art.34.
[155] ICSID Art.36.
[156] ICSID Art.37.
[157] ICSID Art. 38.
[158] ICSID Art.44.
[159] ICSID Art.53.

an interpretation of the award[160]; or (ii) request for a revision of the award on the grounds of the discovery of a material fact[161]; or (iii) request an annulment of the award on the following grounds, viz. that the Tribunal was not properly constituted; that it exceeded its powers; that there was corruption involved; that there was a material departure from a fundamental rule of procedure; and on the grounds of a failure to state reasons for the award.[162]

The law that the Tribunal applies to the dispute is that law which the parties to the dispute have agreed should apply.[163] Where, however, the parties have not agreed upon the applicable law, the Tribunal applies the law of the Contracting State party to the dispute (including its conflict of laws) and relevant rules of International Law.[164] If the parties should so choose the Tribunal can also decide a dispute *ex aequo et bono*.[165]

Finally, both parties are to share the costs involved equally in the case of conciliation proceedings.[166] However, in the case of arbitration proceedings, unless agreed otherwise by the parties, the Tribunal shall decide upon the apportionment of the costs.[167]

14–031    ICSID Convention (excerpts)[168]

### CHAPTER II—Jurisdiction of the Centre

Article 25

(1) The jurisdiction of the Centre shall extend to any legal dispute arising directly out of an investment, between a Contracting State (or any constituent subdivision or agency of a Contracting State designated to the Centre by that State) and a national of another Contracting State, which the parties to the dispute consent in writing to submit to the Centre. When the parties have given their consent, no party may withdraw its consent unilaterally. [. . .]

Article 26

Consent of the parties to arbitration under this Convention shall, unless otherwise stated, be deemed consent to such arbitration to the exclusion of any other remedy. A Contracting State may require the exhaustion of local administrative or judicial remedies as a condition of its consent to arbitration under this Convention.

### CHAPTER III Conciliation Section 1 Request for Conciliation

---

[160] ICSID Art.50.
[161] ICSID Art.51.
[162] ICSID Art.52. See G. Verhoosel, "Annulment and enforcement review of treaty awards". *International Centre for Settlement of Investment Disputes: ICSID Review*, 23.2008(2009) 1, 119–154 and H. Smit, "Annulment and enforcement of international arbitral awards", *The American Review of International Arbitration*, 18 (2007) 3, 297–311.
[163] ICSID Art.42.
[164] ICSID Art.42. See, for example, Shihata (1995), Chs 12 and 22; and Broches (1995), Ch.7.
[165] ICSID Art.42.
[166] ICSID Art.61.
[167] ICSID Art.61.
[168] Source: *http://www.worldbank.org/icsid*. (Accessed June 8, 2011).

Article 28

(1) Any Contracting State or any national of a Contracting State wishing to institute conciliation proceedings shall address a request to that effect in writing to the Secretary-General who shall send a copy of the request to the other party.

## CHAPTER IV Arbitration Section I Request for Arbitration

Article 36

(1) Any Contracting State or any national of a Contracting State wishing to institute arbitration proceedings shall address a request to that effect in writing to the Secretary-General who shall send a copy of the request to the other party. [. . .]

## Section 3 Powers and Functions of the Tribunal

Article 41

(1) The Tribunal shall be the judge of its own competence.

(2) Any objection by a party to the dispute that that dispute is not within the jurisdiction of the Centre, or for other reasons is not within the competence of the Tribunal, shall be considered by the Tribunal which shall determine whether to deal with it as a preliminary question or to join it to the merits of the dispute.

Article 42

(1) The Tribunal shall decide a dispute in accordance with such rules of law as may be agreed by the parties. In the absence of such agreement, the Tribunal shall apply the law of the Contracting State party to the dispute (including its rules on the conflict of laws) and such rules of international law as may be applicable.

(2) The Tribunal may not bring in a finding of non liquet on the ground of silence or obscurity of the law.

(3) The provisions of paragraphs (1) and (2) shall not prejudice the power of the Tribunal to decide a dispute ex aequo et bono if the parties so agree.. . .

Article 52

(1) Either party may request annulment of the award by an application in writing addressed to the Secretary-General on one or more of the following grounds:

(a) that the Tribunal was not properly constituted;

(b) that the Tribunal has manifestly exceeded its powers;

(c) that there was corruption on the part of a member of the Tribunal;

(d) that there has been a serious departure from a fundamental rule of procedure; or

(e) that the award has failed to state the reasons on which it is based.

[. . .]

(6) If the award is annulled the dispute shall, at the request of either party, be submitted to a new Tribunal constituted in accordance with Section 2 of this Chapter.

**Section 6 Recognition and Enforcement of the Award**

Article 53

(1) The award shall be binding on the parties and shall not be subject to any appeal or to any other remedy except those provided for in this Convention. Each party shall abide by and comply with the terms of the award except to the extent that enforcement shall have been stayed pursuant to the relevant provisions of this Convention.

Article 54

(1) Each Contracting State shall recognize an award rendered pursuant to this Convention as binding and enforce the pecuniary obligations imposed by that award within its territories as if it were a final judgment of a court in that State. A Contracting State with a federal constitution may enforce such an award in or through its federal courts and may provide that such courts shall treat the award as if it were a final judgment of the courts of a constituent state.

(2) A party seeking recognition or enforcement in the territories of a Contracting State shall furnish to a competent court or other authority which such State shall have designated for this purpose a copy of the award certified by the Secretary-General. Each Contracting State shall notify the Secretary-General of the designation of the competent court or other authority for this purpose and of any subsequent change in such designation.

(3) Execution of the award shall be governed by the laws concerning the execution of judgments in force in the State in whose territories such execution is sought."

THE WORLD BANK GUIDELINES

**14–032**   The World Bank Guidelines[169] came into existence as a consequence of the request made to it in 1991 by a joint Ministerial Committee of the Development Committee of the Board of Governors of the IMF and the World Bank.[170] The Guidelines themselves are not binding. To the extent that they codify Customary International Law, qua such law they are binding. However, there appears to be some difference of opinion as to whether they

---

[169] The World Bank Guidelines On The Treatment Of Foreign Direct Investment (1992) 31 I.L.M 1363. See also J.D. Nolan, "A comparative analysis of the Laotian law on foreign investment, the World Bank guidelines on the treatment of foreign direct investment, and normative rules of international law on foreign direct investment", *Arizona Journal of International and Comparative Law*, 15 (1998) 2, 659–693.

[170] See, for example, I. Shihata, *The World Bank in a Changing World* (Dordrecht, Martinus Nijhoff, 1995), Vol.II, Ch.21.

in fact do that at all. Thus, according to I. Shihata, who was actually involved in the exercise, the Guidelines not only codify existing practices, but also aim at the progressive development of the law.[171] On the other hand, the view has been expressed that the Guidelines do not represent codification of Customary International Law but rather formulate generally acceptable international standards which support the objective of promoting foreign investment.[172]

The Guidelines avoided a focus on the conduct of investors because at the time of their formulation the UN Commission on Transnational Corporations was engaged in that endeavour.[173] Briefly, the Guidelines cover four main issues, viz. the entry of investment; the subsequent treatment of the investment; the protection of foreign investment (i.e. expropriation); and dispute settlement processes.

First, the Guidelines acknowledge the right of a State to regulate the admission of foreign investment.[174] The Guidelines, however, encourage liberalisation of investment, and suggest approaches to the maintenance of a liberal regime. Thus, the Guidelines invite States to have an open admission policy, subject to a restricted list of investment. Exceptionally, restrictions are permitted, for national security reasons; reservation of sectors in favour of nationals to further the State's economic development objectives, or the exigencies of its national interest; on account of public policy; and public health and the protection of the environment.[175] Further, the Guidelines recommend transparency, and the avoidance of unnecessary or unduly cumbersome and complicated procedural admission regulations.

Secondly, the subsequent post-admission treatment of the foreign investment[176] is subject to certain standards, viz. fair and equitable treatment; national treatment; MFN treatment; full protection of ownership rights; prompt issuance of necessary authorisations; permission for the transfer of necessary monies such as income, revenue and the repatriation of the proceeds of the investment; prevention of corrupt business practices; accountability and transparency in dealings with foreign investors. On the part of the capital exporting countries, the Guidelines impose an obligation not to obstruct the investment flows to developing countries.[177]

Thirdly, the Guidelines set out the circumstances in which expropriation can take place, namely for public purpose, without discrimination, and

---

[171] See Shihata (1995), p.588. He states: "the Guidelines were based, on the one hand, on general trends distilled from detailed surveys of treaties, laws, arbitral awards and other existing legal instruments and, on the other hand, on the practices and policies identified by the World Bank Group as being conducive to the evolution of an attractive investment environment. In this sense the guidelines do not merely codify accepted rules of international law but aim at progressively developing such rules."

[172] WTO Annual Report (1996), p.44.

[173] WTO Annual Report (1996), p.44.

[174] WTO Annual Report (1996), Guideline II.

[175] WTO Annual Report (1996), Guideline II. See in this respect L. Zarsky, *International Investment for Sustainable Development*, (Earthscan, 2004).

[176] WTO Annual Report (1996), Guideline III.

[177] WTO Annual Report (1996).

upon payment of appropriate compensation. "Appropriate" compensation is defined as "adequate, effective and prompt", and the Guidelines further elaborate on each of these components. In the event of comprehensive non-discriminatory nationalisations in the context of large scale social reforms, the compensation may be determined through negotiations, or failing that international arbitration.

Finally, in the event of a dispute the parties are to settle the dispute through negotiation, national courts, or through binding independent arbitration. The parties are encouraged where independent arbitration is invoked to use the facilities of the ICSID Convention.

**14–033**　　**World Bank Guidelines for the Treatment of Foreign Direct Investment (of 1991)[178]**

. . .

### III TREATMENT

1. For the promotion of international economic cooperation through the medium of private foreign investment, the establishment, operation, management, control, and exercise of rights in such an investment, as well as such other associated activities necessary therefore or incidental thereto, will be consistent with the following standards which are meant to apply simultaneously to all States without prejudice to the provisions of applicable international instruments, and to firmly established rules of customary international law.

2. Each State will extend to investments established in its territory by nationals of any other State fair and equitable treatment according to the standards recommended in these Guidelines.

3. (a) respect to the protection and security of their person, property rights and interests, and to the granting of permits, import and export licenses and the authorization to employ, and the issuance of the necessary entry and stay visas to their foreign personnel, and other legal matters relevant to the treatment of foreign investors as described in Section 1 above, such treatment will, subject to the requirement of fair and equitable treatment mentioned above, be as favorable as that accorded by the State to national investors in similar circumstances. In all cases, full protection and security will be accorded to the investor's rights regarding ownership, control and substantial benefits over his property, including intellectual property.

   (b) As concerns such other matters as are not relevant to national investors, treatment under the State's legislation and regulations will not discriminate among foreign investors on grounds of nationality.

4. Nothing in this Guideline will automatically entitle nationals of other States to the more favorable standards of treatment accorded to the nationals of certain States under any customs union or free trade area agreement.

---

[178] Source: *http://www.worldbank.org*. (Accessed June 8, 2011).

5. Without restricting the generality of the foregoing, each State will:

(a) promptly issue such licenses and permits and grant such concessions as may be necessary for the uninterrupted operation of the admitted investment; and

(b) to the extent necessary for the efficient operation of the investment, authorize the employment of foreign personnel. While a State may require the foreign investor to reasonably establish his inability to recruit the required personnel locally, e.g., through local advertisement, before he resorts to the recruitment of foreign personnel, labor market flexibility in this and other areas is recognized as an important element in a positive investment environment. Of particular importance in this respect is the investor's freedom to employ top managers regardless of their nationality.

6(1) Each State will, with respect to private investment in its territory by nationals of the other States:

(a) freely allow regular periodic transfer of a reasonable part of the salaries and wages of foreign personnel; and, on liquidation of the investment or earlier termination of the employment, allow immediate transfer of all savings from such salaries and wages;

(b) freely allow transfer of the net revenues realized from the investment;

(c) allow the transfer of such sums as may be necessary for the payment of debts contracted, or the discharge of other contractual obligations incurred in connection with the investment as they fall due;

(d) on liquidation or sale of the investment (whether covering the investment as a whole or a part thereof), allow the repatriation and transfer of the net proceeds of such liquidation or sale and all accretions thereto all at once; in the exceptional cases where the State faces foreign exchange stringencies, such transfer may as an exception be made in instalments within a period *which* will be as short as possible and will not in any case exceed five years from the date of liquidation or sale, subject to interest as provided for in Section 6 (3) of this Guideline; and

(e) allow the transfer of any other amounts to which the investor is entitled such as those which become due under the conditions provided for in Guidelines IV and V.

6(2) Such transfer as provided for in Section 6 (1) of this Guideline will be made (a) in the currency brought in by the investor where it remains convertible, in another currency designated as freely usable currency by the International Monetary Fund or in any other currency accepted by the investor, and (b) at the applicable market rate of exchange at the time of the transfer."

ATTEMPTS FOR A MULTILATERAL INVESTMENT AGREEMENT (MAI)

**14–034**   The need for a better international normative framework in the field of investment is generally accepted. Attempts to provide for a set of generally accepted rules of universal application go back to the 1970s. In 1974, the United Nations established the Programme on Transnational Corporations. Between 1974 and 1992, it was carried out by the United Nations Centre on Transnational Corporations (UNCTC). The UNCTC was the focal point, within the United Nations system, for all matters related to transnational corporations (TNCs) and foreign direct investment (FDI).

This need is grounded in economics, (for example because of the importance of investment to growth, productivity, competition, transfer of technology); the existence of barriers to foreign investment; and the unsatisfactory patchwork of investment rules. This need, however, is more deeply felt amongst developed countries,[179] and is motivated it has been contended, mainly to secure market access for investment.[180]

In particular, the case for a multilateral investment agreement[181] exists for a number of reasons. First, multilateralism is better than the current bilateral option. The need for reciprocity in a multilateral agreement is less pressing. All States, whether capital exporting or importing, have an interest in a multilateral arrangement. This is inter alia because a host State can also be an exporting State, either in future, or in particular respects. Secondly, a multilateral framework would facilitate binding commitments on the admission of investment. Most of the existing focus is on post-entry treatment of the investment.[182] Thirdly, the very existence of a multilateral agreement can strengthen the hand of the government in relation to domestic protectionist forces.

**14–035**   Finally, from an international perspective the multilateral approach facilitates policy coherence in the international investment sphere. Further, this coherence is facilitated not just in the field of investment, but also

---

[179] Contra UNCTAD World Investment Report (1996).

[180] A.V. Ganesan, "Strategic Options Available To Developing Countries With Regard To A Multilateral Agreement On Investment" UNCTAD Paper No.134 (1998).

[181] See, for example, WTO Annual Report (1996); UNCTAD World Investment Report: Investment, Trade and International Policy Arrangements (1996); P. Sauve, "Qs and As on Trade, Investment and the WTO" (1997) 31(4) *Journal of World Trade* 55–80; Z. Drabek, "A Multilateral Agreement on Investment: Convincing the sceptics", WTO Staff Working Paper ERAD-98-05 (June, 1998); *Towards Multilateral Investment Rules* (OECD, 1996); M. Daly, "Some Taxing Questions for the Multilateral Agreement on Investment (MAI)" (1997) 20(6) *The World Economy* 787–808; M. Daly, "Investment Incentives and the Multilateral Agreement on Investment" (1998) 32(2) *Journal of World Trade* 5–26; Y. Kodama, "The Multilateral Agreement on Investment and its Legal Implications for Newly Industrialising Economies" (1988) 32(4) *Journal of World Trade* 21–40; H. Perezcano, "Investment Protection Agreements—Should a Multilateral Approach Be Reconsidered?" (2003) 4(6) *The Journal of World Investment and Trade* 929.

[182] WTO Annual Report (1996), Ch.4, p.33.

generally in international economic policy formulation and the reinforcement of other internationally agreed economic policy objectives. In particular, the relationship between trade and investment is considered to be complementary.[183] Trade policy can have a significant impact on investments.[184] For example, on the one hand high tariffs can induce tariff jumping investments to service foreign markets.[185] Here tariffs are circumvented through establishing enterprises directly in the host State. However, such enterprises are generally geared only for the domestic host State market. On the other hand, low tariffs, especially if bound, can attract exported-orientated investments. Bound tariffs, unlike other trade policy instruments (and incentives), have the advantage that they cannot be withdrawn at the discretion of the host State.[186] In the same vein, regional trade agreements, for example the EC, stimulate investments as a consequence of the large market. Conversely, investment does not have a negative impact on the overall level of exports from the capital exporting country.[187] There is of course a positive impact of investment on the international trade of the host country.[188]

The barriers to investment are numerous and variegated. They include restrictions on the entry of investment; the screening of investments before entry; discrimination against foreign investment, and as between investors; restrictions on the type of ownership involved in the investment, e.g. compulsory joint venture requirements as a precondition of investment entry; restrictions on employment of foreigners; limitations on the availability of credit; expropriation of foreign investment; and performance requirements. Further, competition for foreign direct investment between countries can be unnecessary, wasteful, "unfair", and benefiting in the end mainly the multinational enterprises.[189]

The need for a better international investment regime is generally expressed in terms of a liberal investment framework, wherein governmental interference is minimal or non-existent.[190] Such a standpoint particularly accords with that of the OECD members, which are mainly capital exporting. The liberal framework involves, for example, freedom in the choice of the medium of investment (whether in the form of a joint venture, a subsidiary, or equity participation); national treatment in the choice of investment; the absence of performance requirements to promote economic or social objectives of the host State; market access; legal security and investor protection; transparency; and level playing fields between host countries,

---

[183] See, for example, WTO Annual Report (1996), Ch.4.
[184] WTO Annual Report (1996), p.18.
[185] WTO Annual Report (1996), p.16.
[186] WTO Annual Report (1996).
[187] WTO Annual Report (1996), p.21.
[188] WTO Annual Report (1996).
[189] Developed countries can easily outstrip developing countries in incentive competition, given their deep pockets.
[190] See, for example, R. Levey in *Towards Multilateral Investment Rules* (OECD, 1996), p.69.

so as to avoid harmful competition in the field of investment incentives; level playing fields for investors; and the provision of dispute settlement mechanisms.

**14–036** Such a liberal perception of an investment regime is not universally shared. However, the differences are not so much polarised as such, rather they are differences mainly in emphasis, in objectives, and in items for inclusion. Two aspects of this divergence are of particular note, and are symptomatic of the vested view points of the different parties. First, capital exporting countries prefer a wide definition of investment[191]—to include equity capital. On the other hand, investment is defined from the perspectives of host States as[192]:

> "involving a long-term relationship and reflecting a lasting interest and control of a resident entity in one economy (foreign direct investor or parent enterprise) in an enterprise resident in another economy (FDI enterprise or affiliate enterprise or foreign enterprise)".

Secondly, the developing perspective of an investment regime includes and emphasises the regulation of transnational corporations, and the provision of transfer of technology.[193]

These differences between the capital exporting and capital importing States need to be considered in the design of a multilateral investment agreement, against the background of General International Law investment norms, the relevant treaty practice (particularly BITs), and any directly relevant international efforts. In this context, the OECD MAI and the World Bank Guidelines[194] are of particular note.

**14–037** The OECD in mid-1995 formally launched negotiations for a Multilateral Agreement on Investment (MAI).[195] The OECD already had a track record in establishing codes in the investment field.[196] However, a number of considerations in particular gave an impetus to the negotiations—most of which are connected in one way or another, to the establishment of the WTO, in

---

[191] See, for example, ICSID, *Fedax v Venezuela*, July 11, 1997 (*BIT US—Venezuela*) or ICSID, *Ceskoslovenska obchodni banka, a.s. v Slovak Republic* (Case No.ARB/97/4) (Jurisdiction, May 24, 1999) 14 ICSID Rev. 251 and ICSID, *Mihalny v Sri Lanka*, March 15, 2002 (*BIT USA—Sri Lanka*).

[192] UNCTAD 1997.

[193] See, for example, UNCTAD Secretariat TD/B/COM.2/EM.3/2.

[194] See section immediately above.

[195] The text of the OECD MAI is available from the OECD website: *http://www.oecd.org*. See also C. Kirkpatrick and A.H. Qureshi, "The OECD Multilateral Agreement on Investment" (1998) Int.T.L.R 124–126. What follows on the OECD MAI draws from this article; C. Huiping, *OECD's Multilateral Agreement on Investment* (Kluwer Law International, 2002). For another developing country perspective see also K. Ekwueme, "A Nigerian perspective on a forward-looking multilateral agreement on investment", *The Journal of World Investment & Trade; Law, Economics, Politics*, 7 (2006) 1, 165–196.

[196] i.e. the Draft Convention on the Protection of Private Property (1967); the Declaration on International Investment and Multinational Enterprises (1976); the Codes of Liberalisation of Capital Movements and Current Invisible Operations.

January 1995.[197] First, the international economic order witnessed a substantial reduction in tariff barriers. This reduction heightened the international community's attention to non-tariff barriers. Non-tariff barriers have much in common with barriers to foreign direct investment. Secondly, the liberalisation of international trade in services through the GATS (General Agreement on Trade in Services) agreement also focused attention on non-tariff barriers. Non-tariff barriers also inhibit trade in services. Services require close attention to consumers. Thirdly, investment was placed on the multilateral agenda, through the WTO TRIMS Agreement. Fourthly, developed countries were somewhat disappointed with the "bottom-up approach" adopted in the Uruguay Round which allowed WTO members to opt into the GATS regime on a sector-by-sector basis as they wished.[198] On the other hand, the MAI was an opportunity for a more rapid approach to liberalisation through a "top-down" approach, which included at the outset all the sectors. Finally, there was a general awareness of the fact, that in the 1980s and 1990s, there was a spectacular growth in foreign investment, which outstripped the growth in international trade.

The negotiations were originally scheduled to complete in May 1997, then rescheduled to complete in April 1998. Towards the end of 1998, however, the OECD declared that the MAI negotiations had came to an unsuccessful halt, and no further progress has since been made in the OECD. The agenda for a multilateral investment agreement has, however, been set, and the issue will continue to be pressed in other fora—particularly the WTO.[199]

It is, however, useful to briefly review the draft OECD MAI, as the issues it raises will need to be considered in the context of any other negotiations. The draft OECD MAI purported to be a comprehensive agreement on foreign direct investment, aiming to deal with all economic sectors. Indeed the Director-General of the WTO likened the OECD attempt to "writing the constitution of a single global economy".[200] The OECD MAI dealt with both direct investment and portfolio investment. It concerned itself with all aspects of investment (including the establishment, acquisition, expansion, operation, management, maintenance, use and sale or other disposition of investments).

Essentially, it focused on three key aspects of investment. First, it sought    **14–038**
to ensure high standards for the liberalisation of investment regimes both pre-entry and post-entry of investment—whilst recognising the dictates of

---

[197] See, for example, M. Daly, "Some taxing questions for the Multilateral Agreement On Investment (MAI)" (1997) 20(6) *World Economy* 787–807.

[198] See M. Roy, "Implications for the GATS of Negotiations on a Multilateral Investment Framework—Potential Synergies and Pitfalls" (2003) 4(6) *The Journal of World Investment* 963.

[199] See also J. Kurtz, *A General Investment Agreement in the "WTO?"* (Harvard Law School, 2002) and E.C. Nieuwenhuys, *Multilateral Regulation of Investment* (Kluwer Law International, 2001).

[200] UNCTAD Press Release TAD/INF/PR/9628, October 8, 1996, available on *http://www.unctad.org.* (Accessed June 8, 2011).

sustainable development, environmental protection and labour standards.[201] This it did in particular by requiring: (1) the application of the national and the m-f-n standard to foreign investment; (2) transparency measures; (3) free movement of capital requirements; (4) prohibition of unnecessary performance requirements (such as local content requirements, export targets, nationality requirements for executives, members of boards of directors and employees); (5) liberal entry conditions (i.e. temporary entry, stay, and work permits) for investors and a certain category of labour (key personnel); (6) the maintenance of market conditions for investors, through national competition policy and open tendering procedures.

Secondly, the agreement sought to ensure high standards for investment protection, in particular from expropriation, and freedom of capital transfers. The agreement focused on both direct expropriations, and creeping/indirect expropriation. In the event of expropriation it must have been for a public purpose, and accompanied by prompt, adequate and effective compensation.

Thirdly, the agreement sought to make provision for an effective dispute settlement mechanism, through in particular binding arbitration between host State and investors, and between investor State and host State. Arbitration panels being empowered to award compensation and restitution.

In addition to these key features, the following points of the proposed agreement also deserve highlighting. First, the agreement had a host of exceptions e.g. allowing for deviations in circumstances necessitating the protection of human, animal, and plant life; for conservation purposes; for national security purposes in time of war; for membership of regional integration agreement. In addition, countries could add specific exceptions when becoming parties to the agreement, e.g. non-application in relation to particular sectors of the economy. Secondly, the agreement allowed for the use of safeguard measures, exceptionally and on a temporary basis. Thirdly, the agreement dealt with environmental protection and labour standards, preserving the host State's freedom to implement its environmental protection policies, and its own labour standards. However, the agreement prohibited the lowering of standards in the field of labour and environment in order to attract investment. Fourthly, the agreement prohibits the use of sanctions in the field of investment—in particular secondary boycotts of the kind contained in the US Helms-Burton and D'Amato Acts. Finally, a party could not withdraw within the first five years of its membership to the MAI. Further, the MAI regime would have applied for a period of 15 years in relation to investments made during the operation of the agreement prior to the notification of withdrawal. So, a State potentially could have been locked in for 20 years.

**14–039**        It will be apparent that the OECD MAI, aside from its procedural lapse in being undemocratic, given that developing countries were effectively

---

[201] See, for example, L. Zarsky, *International Investment for Sustainable Development* (Earthscan, 2004).

excluded in the negotiation process,[202] from the perspective of developing countries had a number of flaws. For example, the agreement prohibited: (1) local content in investment; (2) prohibited technology transfer requirements; (3) prohibited requirements of the hiring of local personnel; (4) encouraged dependence on foot loose and therefore unreliable foreign capital[203]; (5) changed the internationally accepted compensation rule in the case of expropriation of foreign property; (6) was silent on interest rates; (7) and finally, generally did not emphasise the obligations of the investors, particularly for example in the spheres of human rights, labour standards and environmental protection. In particular, the principal difference between the OECD MAI and the BITs that developing countries have mostly participated in is the national treatment standard at the pre-entry stage (right to establishment).

The OECD draft agreement was originally named the Multilateral Investment Agreement (MIA); but the US objected on the grounds that its acronym MIA could be read as Missing In Action![204] Its final acronym "MAI" in Italian means "never". This it appears has been its fate, as it has not materialised as an agreement. It would be unwise, however, for developing countries to say "never" to a multilateral process relating to investment. For developing countries, therefore, the critical concerns relate to the most appropriate forum for the consideration of multilateral rules on investment, and in particular the negotiating strategy to be adopted in future negotiations, so as to ensure their development objectives.

Now that the OECD appears to be out of the running as a forum, the candidates for the institutional peg for an international investment agreement appear to be the WTO or the World Bank Group. The WTO's credentials in the field of investment have been considered of particular note. Indeed, they have been characterised as being at the heart of the WTO.[205] Historically, the Havana Charter for the still-born ITO covered investment. In 1955 a resolution was passed under GATT on Investment for Economic Development which acknowledged that increased flow of capital achieved GATT objectives.[206] It is generally recognised that investment and trade are mutually supportive.[207] Existing WTO agreements impinge on investment issues—in particular the GATS, TRIPS, TRIMS, Agreement on Subsidies and Countervailing Measures, and the Agreement on Government Procurement.[208]

The World Bank Group was of course set up for development purposes,     **14–040**

---

[202] More than half of OECD investment takes place in developing countries; UNCTAD, World Investment Report 2006—FDI from Developing and Transition Economies: Implications for Development (Geneva, 2006).

[203] See, for example, N. Mabey, *Financial Times*, November, 4 1996.

[204] See *Financial Times*, June 2, 1997.

[205] See WTO Annual Report (1996), p.57. See also the work of the WTO Working Group on the Relationship between Trade and Investment.

[206] WTO Annual Report (1996), p.46.

[207] WTO Annual Report (1996), p.52.

[208] WTO Annual Report (1996), p.46.

and has much experience and expertise in the investment field. Indeed its focus on investment issues has been more direct, and in some ways it is the more natural seat for a multilateral investment agreement. The promotion of private foreign investment is a common purpose of the institutions of the World Bank Group.[209] In particular, the World Bank Group is involved in assisting its members in maintaining investment flows; in the provision of technical assistance, particularly to improve national investment codes[210]; and finally in being instrumental in the formulation of the 1992 World Bank Guidelines.

Critically, however the World Bank Group appears to lack the weight in terms of its capacity to enforce effectively a future international investment agreement. In the case of the WTO the institution has a relatively successful enforcement mechanism; particularly the dispute settlement mechanism, and significantly the cross-retaliation facility built into its implementation process. It is this fact that is likely to eclipse the World Bank Group in favour of the WTO. There is a danger that the World Bank Group will meet the same fate in the investment field, as WIPO in the intellectual property sphere. From a developing standpoint it should be noted that the World Bank Group's perspective of investment is "development" orientated, whereas that of the WTO is liberalisation.

Although not popularly discussed in the existing literature and debate, the institutional framework for a multilateral investment agreement need not necessarily have to be in terms of the WTO, or the World Bank Group. There are other possibilities, for example, a new World Investment Organisation. Alternatively, there can perhaps be a half-way house between a multilateral investment agreement, and the current bilateral system. This can be established through a multilaterally agreed model investment agreement, somewhat along the lines of double taxation agreements.[211] In the final analysis the institutional forum chosen for the negotiation of an international investment agreement may well influence the scope and coverage of the agreement.

14–041    At the centre of the concern for developing countries of course is the development dimension of any likely multilateral investment agreement. This is a perspective that is the subject of particular deliberation in UNCTAD[212]; although in 1996 the need for a multilateral investment was contested there-

---

[209] See Articles of Agreement of the institutions of the World Bank Group (e.g. Arts 1 (I) and (II) of the IBRD); and the preamble to *The World Bank Guidelines On The Treatment Of Foreign Direct Investment* (1992).

[210] Shihata (1995), p.64.

[211] According to Dolzer and Stevens (1995), pp.1–2 and 5, although the OECD 1967 Draft Convention on the Protection of Foreign Property failed to gain support as a formal instrument, it was recommended as a model agreement by the OECD, and indeed later played an important role in drafting of BITS negotiated by OECD members. Similarly, the Asian-African Legal Consultative Committee published a detailed model investment treaty with two variants in 1984 (see (1984) 23 I.L.M. 254).

[212] See the deliberations of the UNCTAD Trade and Development Board, Commission on Investment, Technology and Related Issues. See *http://www.unctad.org*. (Accessed June 8, 2011).

in.[213] Development is an important objective of investment agreements. To further this objective, the need to develop a strategy for the inclusion of development-friendly elements in an international investment agreement, has been advanced.[214]

As part of this development-friendly strategy a number of suggestions have been made. Here only a sense of some of the main points is referred to. In this context the work done by A.V. Ganeson in UNCTAD deserves particular attention. First, as part of his development-friendly strategy he suggests that the WTO is a suitable forum for an investment agreement, because of its bottom-up approach in GATS. However, within this WTO framework, he contends that the investment agreement should be "a stand-alone" agreement, with a separate dispute settlement machinery, devoid of cross-retaliation. Secondly, in terms of the actual content of the agreement, he points out in particular two critical issues, namely the definition of investment, and the according of the national treatment in the pre-establishment phase. This is because pre-establishment restrictions enable the pursuit of national objectives, and the definition of investment is connected with the level of foreign inflow.[215] Developing country concerns on pre-entry issues he states can be met through a list of exceptions; and/or the exclusion of the issue from the agenda for a number of years (e.g. 10 years). On the question of definition he points out that it is in the interest of developing countries to ensure a narrow definition—limited to direct investment.[216] Portfolio investment is less manageable, and more foot-loose. Thirdly, he stresses the need for the inclusion of certain "development-friendly" clauses, for example safeguard clauses; transition periods; and specific provisions ensuring the gradual integration of developing countries in the world economy. Fourthly, certain issues, for example, the need to strengthen domestic capacities, the control of anti-competitive practices, issues related to transfer of technology, national and cultural priorities, security considerations, the standard of behaviour of multinational enterprises in host countries, labour mobility, and disciplines in the field of investment incentives deserve special focus. Finally, in relation to performance requirements he suggests that developing countries may want to ensure that these do not go beyond TRIMS.[217]

To conclude the international economic order is in need of organisation in the field of investment. This need will itself tend towards order—commercial necessity being such. However, the critical questions relate to the timing, and the capacity of the international community to inject fairness in the emerging normative sphere of international investment law.

---

[213] UNCTAD World Investment Report (1996).
[214] UNCTAD September 1998, TD/B/COM.2/CRP.2. See particularly for example A.V. Ganesan, "Strategic options available to developing countries with regard to a multilateral agreement on investment" UNCTAD Paper No.134 (1998).
[215] Ganeson (1998).
[216] Excluding portfolio investment.
[217] Ganeson (1998).

## MIGA AND OTHER INVESTMENT GUARANTEE SCHEMES

**14-042**    MIGA[218] is part of an array of mechanisms to facilitate private investment in developing countries.[219] It was created as a member of the World Bank Group in 1988. A principal function of MIGA involves the giving of guarantees for non-commercial risks. The non-commercial risks involve losses as a consequence in particular of four events, viz. (i) host country restrictions of currency transfers; (ii) expropriation; (iii) breach or repudiation of contract by the host Government in circumstances where effective judicial processes are not available; and (iv) war and civil disturbances. In special circumstances the list of risks covered may be extended with the consent of the parties, and the Board of Directors of MIGA. Certain risk are expressly not covered, for example losses as a consequence of devaluation or depreciation; actions of the host government which have been consented to, and those which occur prior to the contract of guarantee.[220]

The guarantees for the non-commercial risks are available generally only in relation to certain types of investments; certain types of investors; and certain types of host States. The ambit of eligible investments is fairly wide, and includes for example equity and direct investment.[221] The investment however must be: (i) sound; (ii) contribute to the development of the host country; and (iii) be in conformity with the host country's laws, development objectives, and investment conditions.[222] The investors eligible for the protection of the guarantee generally comprise natural or juridical persons, who are nationals of another member country, other than the host State.[223] Finally, the reference to the eligible host countries is to developing member countries.[224] Further, the eligible host country must consent to the guarantee against the particular risks designated in any particular guarantee.[225]

The contract of guarantee between MIGA and the investor is governed by such terms as determined by MIGA.[226] In particular the organisation is to be run on a commercial basis.[227] Thus, the investor has to pay premiums for the benefit of the guarantee.[228] Disputes between holders of the guarantee and

---

[218] See, for example, I. Shihata, *MIGA and Foreign Investment* (Dordrecht, Martinus Nijhoff, 1988).

[219] See MIGA preamble and Art.2. See, for details, A. Ziegler and L.-P. Gratton, "Investment Insurance" in P. Muchlinski et al. (eds), *The Oxford Handbook of International Investment Law*, (OUP, Oxford, 2008), p.524–549; A. Tita, Investment insurance in international law", *The Journal of World Investment & Trade*, 11 (2010), 4, p.651–663

[220] MIGA Art.11.

[221] MIGA Art.12.

[222] MIGA Art.12.

[223] MIGA Art.13.

[224] MIGA Art.14.

[225] MIGA Art.15.

[226] MIGA Art.16.

[227] MIGA Art.25.

[228] MIGA Art.26.

MIGA, involving the contract of guarantee, are resolved through arbitration in accordance with the rules referred to in the contract.[229]

In addition to its guarantee operations, MIGA engages in investment promotion activities. These involve co-operation with investment related national agencies,[230] private insurers,[231] and generally the promotion of investment conditions in developing member countries.[232]

**MIGA Convention: Chapter I—Establishment, Status, Purposes and Definitions**[233]                                    **14–043**

*Article 1. Establishment and Status of the Agency*

(a) There is hereby established the Multilateral Investment Guarantee Agency (hereinafter called the Agency).

(b) The Agency shall possess full juridical personality and, in particular, the capacity to:

    (i) contract;

    (ii) acquire and dispose of movable and immovable property; and

    (iii) institute legal proceedings.

*Article 2. Objective and Purposes*

The objective of the Agency shall be to encourage the flow of investments for productive purposes among member countries, and in particular to develop member countries, thus supplementing the activities of the International Bank for Reconstruction and Development (hereinafter referred to as the Bank), the International Finance Corporation and other international development finance institutions.

To serve its objective, the Agency shall:

(a) issue guarantees, including coinsurance and reinsurance, against non-commercial risks in respect of investments in a member country which flow from other member countries;

(b) carry out appropriate complementary activities to promote the flow of investments to and among developing member countries; and

(c) exercise such other incidental powers as shall be necessary or desirable in the furtherance of its objective.

The Agency shall be guided in all its decisions by the provisions of this Article.

. . .

**Chapter III Operations**

*Article 11. Covered Risks*

---

[229] MIGA Art.58.
[230] MIGA Art.19.
[231] MIGA Art.21
[232] MIGA Art.23.
[233] Source: *http://www.miga.org*. (Accessed June 8, 2011).

(a) Subject to the provisions of Sections (b) and (c) below, the Agency may guarantee eligible investments against a loss resulting from one or more of the following types of risk:

(i) *Currency Transfer*

any introduction attributable to the host government of restrictions on the transfer outside the host country of its currency into a freely usable currency or another currency acceptable to the holder of the guarantee, including a failure of the host government to act within a reasonable period of time on an application by such holder for such transfer;

(ii) *Expropriation and Similar Measures*

any legislative action or administrative action or omission attributable to the host government which has the effect of depriving the holder of a guarantee of his ownership or control of, or a substantial benefit from, his investment, with the exception of non-discriminatory measures of general application which the governments normally take for the purpose of regulating economic activity in their territories;

(iii) *Breach of Contract*

any repudiation or breach by the host government of a contract with the holder of a guarantee, when (a) the holder of a guarantee does not have recourse to a judicial or arbitral forum to determine the claim of repudiation or breach, or (b) a decision by such forum is not rendered within such reasonable period of time as shall be prescribed in the contracts of guarantee pursuant to the Agency's regulations, or (c) such a decision cannot be enforced; and

(iv) *War and Civil Disturbance*

any military action or civil disturbance in any territory of the host country to which this Convention shall be applicable as provided in Article 66.

(b) Upon the joint application of the investor and the host country, the Board, by special majority, may approve the extension of coverage under this Article to specific non-commercial risks other than those referred to in Section (a) above, but in no case to the risk of devaluation or depreciation of currency.

(c) Losses resulting from the following shall not be covered:

(i) any host government action or omission to which the holder of the guarantee has agreed or for which he has been responsible; and

(ii) any host government action or omission or any other event occurring before the conclusion of the contract of guarantee.

*Article 12. Eligible Investments*

(a) Eligible investments shall include equity interest, including medium- or long-term loans made or guaranteed by holders of equity in the enterprise concerned, and such forms of direct investment as may be determined by the Board.

(b) The Board, by special majority, may extend eligibility to any other medium- or long-term form of investment, except that loans other than those mentioned in Section (a) above may be eligible only if they are related to a specific investment covered or to be covered by the Agency.

(c) Guarantees shall be restricted to investments the implementation of which begins subsequent to the registration of the application for the guarantee by the Agency. Such investments may include:

   (i) any transfer of foreign exchange made to modernize, expand, or develop an existing investment; and

   (ii) the use of earnings from existing investments which could otherwise be transferred outside the host country.

(d) In guaranteeing an investment, the Agency shall satisfy itself as to:

   (i) the economic soundness of the investment and its contribution to the development of the host country;

   (ii) compliance of the investment with the host country's laws and regulations;

   (iii) consistency of the investment with the declared development objectives and priorities of the host country; and

   (iv) the investment conditions in the host country, including the availability of fair and equitable treatment and legal protection for the investment.

*Article 13. Eligible Investors*

(a) Any natural person and any juridical person may be eligible to receive the Agency's guarantee provided that:

   (i) such natural person is a national of a member other than the host country;

   (ii) such juridical person is incorporated and has its principal place of business in a member or the majority of its capital is owned by a member or members or nationals thereof, provided that such member is not the host country in any of the above cases; and

   (iii) such juridical person, whether or not it is privately owned, operates on a commercial basis.

(b) In case the investor has more than one nationality, for the purposes of Section (a) above the nationality of a member shall prevail over the nationality of a non-member, and the nationality of the host country shall prevail over the nationality of any other member.

(c) Upon the join application of the investor and the host country, the Board, by special majority, may extend eligibility to a natural person who is a national of the host country or a juridical person which is incorporated in the host country or the majority of whose capital is owned by its nationals, provided that the assets invested are transferred from outside the host country.

*Article 14. Eligible Host Countries*

Investments shall be guaranteed under this Chapter only if they are to be made in the territory of a developing member country.

*Article 15. Host Country Approval*

The Agency shall not conclude any contract of guarantee before the host government has approved the issuance of the guarantee by the Agency against the risks designated for cover.

*Article 16. Terms and Conditions*

The terms and conditions of each contract of guarantee shall be determined by the Agency subject to such rules and regulations as the Board shall issue, provided that the Agency shall not cover the total loss of the guaranteed investment. Contracts of guarantee shall be approved by the President under the direction of the Board."

**14–044** Many States and groupings of states also provide for institutions available for the insurance of investment risks. The United States and other major capital-exporting countries developed early on national investment insurance programmes, which were supplemented later by private political risk insurance systems. These national and private mechanisms, essentially instruments belonging to the most advanced countries created to favour their national enterprises on the world marketplace, were later completed by regional and international schemes. The protection of investment becomes a prerequisite and a sine qua non condition to the promotion of international investment.[234] National investment guarantee mechanisms were implemented as an answer to enterprises' fear of committing themselves on spending large amounts of money to invest in regions of the world that were not always stable. An interesting example of such a mechanism is the Overseas Private Investment Corporation (OPIC), created by the United States Government in 1971. Considered to be the first international guarantee organisation (and still the only regional one), the Inter-Arab Investment Guarantee Corporation was equally created in 1971.[235]

---

[234] "[C]'est de la solidité de la protection que dépend l'efficacité de la promotion." (D. Carreau and P. Juillard, *Droit International Économique*, 2nd edn (Paris, Dalloz, 2005), para.1109.) See also J.-P. Laviec, *Protection et promotion des investissements, Étude de Droit International Économique* (PUF, 1985).

[235] For details see Ziegler and Gratton (2008).

### CHAPTER 15

# INTERNATIONAL MOVEMENT OF LABOUR AND LABOUR STANDARDS

## GENERALLY

The (free) movement of labour has always been an important factor for eco-    **15-001**
nomic development.[1] The immigration of huge groups of workers and settlers
in the 18th and especially the 19th century has made possible the growth of
economies such as the United States, Canada and Australia, but also many
Latin American countries. Not only workers moved between nation states
but also many persons who came with smaller or bigger amounts of capital
in order to establish their own business and thereby often create the foundations for important companies and the development of specific sectors of the
economy.[2] While this development was in the beginning closely related to
the colonisation of these territories, today the phenomenon of migration is
of increasing importance for the global economy. From a purely economic
point of view labour, including both unskilled and skilled workers, is an
important input into the economic production process of both goods and
services. Where it is not sufficiently available, the capital involved in this
process will be used inefficiently. Productivity increases may lead to changing
ratios between labour and capital inputs, but there will always be limits on
the substitutability. Furthermore the specific knowledge of certain workers
(engineering, information technology, medicine etc.) may be seen as a contribution to the knowledge base of an economy just as the transfer of technology as such.

Especially in view of the lack of trained workers in certain States or the
ageing societies of most developed States, migration is becoming increasingly
important. This contrasts strikingly with the legal regulation of migration.

---

[1] See M. Trebilcock and R. Howse, *Regulation of International Trade*, 3rd edn (London:
Routledge, 2005), Ch.19 and M. Trebilcock, "The Law and Economics of Immigration
Policy" (2003) 5 *American Law and Economics Review* p.271; J.P. Trachtman, The interna-
tional law of economic migration (Kalamazoo, Mich, W.E. Upjohn Institute for Employment
Research, 2009).

[2] See Ch.14.

While the absence of rules allowed for the massive migration flows of the 19th and early 20th century to the new world, the economic crisis of the 1920s (and the massive unemployment resulting from it) led in many countries to restriction of immigration flows. Only few countries apply an active immigration policy and even they normally limit immigration to certain types of labour which are in high demand (e.g. Australia, Canada, etc.). The fears of unemployment and xenophobic attitudes have generally blocked any attempt to liberalise the flow of workers across borders internationally. Unlawful migration between developing States and developed nations has therefore become of paramount importance, apart from the migratory flows due to humanitarian crisis and conflicts. Nevertheless, current demographic developments (retired persons constituting an increasing part of the population) in countries like Japan, Germany, Italy and even China make it very likely that they will have to change their attitude towards migration in the very near future.[3]

At least with regard to developing countries, the International Organization for Migration (IOM) plays an important role in this respect. It is an international organization established in 1951 that is committed to the principle that humane and orderly migration benefits migrants and society. This requires important activities in the area of the treatment of refugees and internally displaced persons. In 2011 the IMO had more than 3,000 field staff working in more than 2,800 projects.

**15-002**    Due to the political resistance in many countries the work relating to the opening of labour markets is rather limited in the four broad areas of migration management: Migration and development, facilitating migration, regulating migration, and forced migration. Many developing countries rely heavily on the remittances sent home by their migrant workers.[4] Only regionally (e.g. European Union, Nordic Labour Market, etc.) has the free movement of persons been successfully regulated in international treaties. Other agreements try to facilitate the migration of workers through less far-reaching mechanisms, as is the case in Mercosur where nationals of member States are entitled to obtain a (temporary) work permit.

There are incidental rules in trade and investment agreements, but their scope is necessarily limited. In particular, the question of labour migration remains highly controversial in the context of the WTO although the temporary presence of natural persons to provide services[5] and key personnel for trade and investment operations (also referred to as Business Persons)[6] are generally considered as international economic relations. Apart from the mere opening of the national territory for the permanent or temporary

---

[3] See Philip Martin, Manolo Abella and Christiane Kuptsch, *Managing Labor Migration in the Twenty-First Century* (Yale University Press, 2006) and *United Nations, World population monitoring* (New York, United Nations, 2009).

[4] See *Economic implications of remittances and migration*. Washington, DC: IBRD, 2006.

[5] See mode three of the four modes to supply services in the framework of the GATS (and many free trade agreements) as described in Ch.12.

[6] See below.

presence of foreign workers, service suppliers or investors, a comprehensive integration of labour markets normally also requires rules on the admission of family members, recognition of qualifications (diplomas, etc.)[7] and social security schemes, etc. This is a highly ambitious approach and is normally found only in agreements establishing an internal market for labour, such as it is the case in the European Union.[8]

There exist occasionally less ambitious agreements between countries which rely heavily on remittances by their emigrants (Philippines, etc.) and countries with an important foreign work force (many Gulf states) regulating certain aspects of labour migration between the Parties (Labour agreements).[9]    **15-003**

Apart from migratory flows, the working conditions and social standards are often discussed in the context of international trade and investment. The main issue concerns normally the question where the existing standard in a State (national law) should be taken into account when regulating trade and investment flows. It is argued that differences in domestic regulation could distort these flows or are leading to a frivolous "race to the bottom" of such standard where the result of production can easily cross borders. Terms like "social dumping" characterise this discussion. Apart from human rights considerations they influence attempts to harmonise social standards and labour laws internationally, e.g. under the auspices of the International Labour Organization (ILO).

Finally, the important migratory flows in economic sectors like care or health services can also have negative influences on the home market. As a result of this, the World Health Organization has unanimously adopted the Global Code of Practice on the International Recruitment of Health Personnel at the 63rd World Health Assembly held in May 2010. The Code, not binding on the Member States, provides "an ethical framework to guide Member States in the recruitment of health workers." The Code is primarily meant to address the shortage of health workers in developing countries. The Code encourages Member States to work together in "sustain[ing] health human resources development and training," and asks the Member States to "discourage active recruitment of health personnel from developing countries facing critical shortages of health workers."[10]

---

[7] See, for examples from outside Europe, L. Hawthorne, "Qualifications Recognition Reform for Skilled Migrants in Australia", *International Migration*, 40 (2002) 6, pp.55–91

[8] See below.

[9] See, for example, the Memorandum of Understanding signed between the Philippines and the United Arab Emirates (UAE) on April 11, 2007 the Japan–Philippines Economic Partnership Agreement (JPEPA), including an important part on the movement of labour (Filipino nurses and other care-givers working in Japan's welfare institutions), signed on September 9, 2006. See J. Dwyer, "What's wrong with the global migration of health care professionals?", *Hastings Center: The Hastings Center Report*, 37 (2007), 5, pp.36–43

[10] A.L. Taylor and L.O. Gostin, "International recruitment of health personnel" (2010) 375(9727) *The Lancet* pp.1673–1675.

## Movement of Labour

**15-004**   Customary International Law leaves States with complete freedom regarding the admission of foreigners, with the exception of certain humanitarian admission (e.g. refugees).[11] With regard to the admission of foreigners to the domestic labour market, most States have instituted important barriers to protect the domestic work force from competition, even if in times of economic growth this can lead to shortages with regard to certain types of (skilled) workers. In many countries the treatment of refugees dominates the political and legal debate while economic integration as a tool for growth and economic cooperation is of a secondary nature. Even where international treaties address the access to gainful employment they often remain purely hortatory in this respect.

> **United Nations Convention relating to the Status of Refugees, adopted on 25 July 1951. Chapter III: Gainful Employment:**
>
> Article 17 Wage-Earning Employment
>
> 1. The Contracting State shall accord to refugees lawfully staying in their territory the most favourable treatment accorded to nationals of a foreign country in the same circumstances, as regards the right to engage in wage-earning employment.
>
> 2. In any case, restrictive measures imposed on aliens or the employment of aliens for the protection of the national labour market shall not be applied to a refugee who was already exempt from them at the date of entry into force of this Convention for the Contracting State concerned, or who fulfils one of the following conditions:
>
>    (a) He has completed three years' residence in the country;
>
>    (b) He has a spouse possessing the nationality of the country of residence. A refugee may not invoke the benefits of this provision if he has abandoned his spouse;
>
>    (c) He has one or more children possessing the nationality of the country of residence.
>
> 3. The Contracting States shall give sympathetic consideration to assimilating the rights of all refugees with regard to wage-earning employment to those of nationals, and in particular of those refugees who have entered their territory pursuant to programmes of labour recruitment or under immigration schemes.
>
> Article 18 Self-Employment
>
> The Contracting States shall accord to a refugee lawfully in their territory treatment as favourable as possible and, in any event, not less favourable than that accorded to aliens generally in the same circumstances, as regards the

---

[11]   United Nations Convention relating to the Status of Refugees, adopted on July 25, 1951.

right to engage on his own account in agriculture, industry, handicrafts and commerce and to establish commercial and industrial companies.

Article 19 Liberal Professions

1. Each Contracting State shall accord to refugees lawfully staying in their territory who hold diplomas recognized by the competent authorities of that State, and who are desirous of practicing a liberal profession, treatment as favourable as possible and, in any event, not less favourable than that accorded to aliens generally in the same circumstances.

2. The Contracting States shall use their best endeavours consistently with their laws and constitutions to secure the settlement of such refugees in the territories, other than the metropolitan territory, for whose international relations they are responsible.

Regionally, the integration of labour markets has been achieved by a number **15-005** of countries.[12] Most famously the European Union (EU) has built its concept of a Common Market (now called the Internal Market) on the free movement of workers which was later developed into a fully fledged right to move across borders for all citizens of the European Union.[13] For workers, this freedom has existed since the foundation of the European Economic Community in 1957. It is still laid down in Art.45 of the Treaty on the Functioning of the European Union (TFEU) and it entails: the right to look for a job in another Member State, the right to work in another Member State, the right to reside there for that purpose, the right to remain there, and the right to equal treatment in respect of access to employment, working conditions and all other advantages which could help to facilitate the worker's integration in the host Member State. Certain rights are extended to family members of the worker. They have, in particular, the right to live with the worker in the host Member State and the right to equal treatment as regards for example education and social advantages. Some members of the family have also the right to work there.[14] Today these freedoms are an integrative part of the EU policy regarding European citizenship which can no longer be considered of a purely economic nature.[15] Other examples for economic integration approaches

[12] See, for example, A. Adepoju, "Fostering free movement of persons in West Africa" (2002) 40 *International Migration* pp.3–28; S. Nonnenmacher, "Free movement of persons in the Caribbean Community". *International migration law*, (2007), pp.387–401 or C.J. Cassise, "The European Union v. the United States under the NAFTA" (1996) 46(4) *Syracuse Law Review* 1343–79.

[13] The European Community has included similar provision in agreements with third states, such as in the European Economic Area (EEA) Agreement, the Association Agreement with Turkey or in a bilateral agreement with Switzerland; See also J. Peixoto, "Migration and policies in the European Union" (2001) 39(1) *International Migration* 33–61.

[14] See, for example, N. Rogers and R. Scannell, *Free Movement of Persons in the Enlarged European Union* (Sweet and Maxwell, 2005), E. Spaventa, *Free movement of persons in the European Union*. (The Hague, Kluwer Law International, 2007); F. Weiss, *Free Movement of Persons within the European Community* (Kluwer Law International, 2nd edn, 2007).

[15] Article 9 of the Treaty on European Union: "In all its activities, the Union shall observe the principle of the equality of its citizens, who shall receive equal attention from its institutions, bodies, offices and agencies. Every national of a Member State shall be a citizen of the Union. Citizenship of the Union shall be additional to and not replace

include the creation of a Nordic labour market[16] by the Nordic countries or co-operation between Australia and New Zealand.[17] Also the Mercosur States have liberalised the movement of workers between the member States as well Bolivia and Chile. In the Treaty of Brazilia of December 6, 2002 a scheme is foreseen to provide all nationals with temporary work permits (upon fulfilment of certain conditions) and to allow them to migrate with their family members and eventually to apply for permanent residency. They refer to a Common Area of Free Residence including the right to work (*Área de Libre Residencia con derecho a trabajar*).[18]

**Treaty on the Functioning of the European Union (TFEU) TITLE IV—FREE MOVEMENT OF PERSONS, SERVICES AND CAPITAL[19]**

**CHAPTER 1: WORKERS**

Article 45 (ex Article 39 TEC)

1. Freedom of movement for workers shall be secured within the Union.

2. Such freedom of movement shall entail the abolition of any discrimination based on nationality between workers of the Member States as regards employment, remuneration and other conditions of work and employment.

3. It shall entail the right, subject to limitations justified on grounds of public policy, public security or public health:

   (a) to accept offers of employment actually made;

   (b) to move freely within the territory of Member States for this purpose;

   (c) to stay in a Member State for the purpose of employment in accordance with the provisions governing the employment of nationals of that State laid down by law, regulation or administrative action;

   (d) to remain in the territory of a Member State after having been

---

national citizenship". See also S. Currie, "'Free' movers? The post-accession experience of accession-8 migrant workers in the United Kingdom", (2006) 31(2) *European Law Review* 207–229.

[16] The Nordic Council of Ministers' co-operation in the labour market field has been based on the agreement for a common Nordic Labour Market since 1954, and in the work environment field on the Nordic Convention on the Working Environment since 1989.

[17] Especially the Trans-Tasman Travel Arrangement (TTTA) as announced in 1973, allowing their citizens to live in each other's territories indefinitely and take on most employment; interestingly, the TTTA is not expressed in the form of any binding bilateral treaty between New Zealand and Australia, but rather is a series of immigration procedures applied by each country and underpinned by joint expressions of political support (Source: New Zealand Ministry of Foreign Affairs and Trade, *http://www.mfat.govt.nz/Foreign-Relations/Australia/0-trans-tasman-travel.php*. (Accessed June 8, 2011)).

[18] Agreement on Residence for Nationals of Mercosur Member States as well as Bolivia and Chile (Acuerdo sobre Residencia para Nacionales de los Estados Partes del MERCOSUR, Bolivia y Chile), Brasilia, December 6, 2002.

[19] Source: Official Journal of the European Union, C83 of 30 March 2010, 47.

employed in that State, subject to conditions which shall be embodied in regulations to be drawn up by the Commission.

4. The provisions of this Article shall not apply to employment in the public service.

Article 46 (ex Article 40 TEC)

The European Parliament and the Council shall, acting in accordance with the ordinary legislative procedure and after consulting the Economic and Social Committee, issue directives or make regulations setting out the measures required to bring about freedom of movement for workers, as defined in Article 45, in particular:

(a) by ensuring close cooperation between national employment services;

(b) by abolishing those administrative procedures and practices and those qualifying periods in respect of eligibility for available employment, whether resulting from national legislation or from agreements previously concluded between Member States, the maintenance of which would form an obstacle to liberalisation of the movement of workers;

(c) by abolishing all such qualifying periods and other restrictions provided for either under national legislation or under agreements previously concluded between Member States as imposed on workers of other Member States conditions regarding the free choice of employment other than those imposed on workers of the State concerned;

(d) by setting up appropriate machinery to bring offers of employment into touch with applications for employment and to facilitate the achievement of a balance between supply and demand in the employment market in such a way as to avoid serious threats to the standard of living and level of employment in the various regions and industries.

## LABOUR MOVEMENTS

In the context of the multilateral trading system, the issue of migration had **15-006** to be discussed with the integration of services into the WTO. While a comprehensive regulation of migratory flows is obviously politically impossible, the concept of service supply through temporary presence on the territory of another Member State leads to the addressing the issue. Mode 4 of the GATS defines supply of a service "as by a service supplier of one Member, through presence of natural persons of a Member in the territory of any other Member". A specific annex makes clear that this particular aspect of the trade in services is intended to be of limited scope, especially limiting the access to a market to temporary presence.

**15-007**    **Annex on Movement of Natural Persons Supplying Services under the Agreement (GATS)[20]**

1. This Annex applies to measures affecting natural persons who are service suppliers of a Member, and natural persons of a Member who are employed by a service supplier of a Member, in respect of the supply of a service.

2. The Agreement shall not apply to measures affecting natural persons seeking access to the employment market of a Member, nor shall it apply to measures regarding citizenship, residence or employment on a permanent basis.

3. In accordance with Parts III and IV of the Agreement, Members may negotiate specific commitments applying to the movement of all categories of natural persons supplying services under the Agreement. Natural persons covered by a specific commitment shall be allowed to supply the service in accordance with the terms of that commitment.

4. The Agreement shall not prevent a Member from applying measures to regulate the entry of natural persons into, or their temporary stay in, its territory, including those measures necessary to protect the integrity of, and to ensure the orderly movement of natural persons across, its borders, provided that such measures are not applied in such a manner as to nullify or impair the benefits accruing to any Member under the terms of a specific commitment."[21]

**15-008**    Despite the limited scope of the movement of natural persons under the GATS, the commitments made by WTO members under mode 4 GATS remain very poor which is normally due to the domestic constraints on governments in view of fears of massive immigration. At the same time, developing countries especially have asked during the Doha Round of multilateral trade negotiations that WTO members make more commitments in this respect.[22] In view of the general problems of finding mutually acceptable solutions on market access in the services sector, the discussions regarding better temporary access for natural persons remained very basic.[23] Some countries have also entered trade-related obligations with respect to

---

[20] Source: *http://www.wto.org*. (Accessed June 8, 2011).

[21] The sole fact of requiring a visa for natural persons of certain members and not for those of others shall not be regarded as nullifying or impairing benefits under a specific commitment. See C. Fresnedo de Aguirre, "Circulación de personas físicas y capacidad para contratar en el Mercosur", *Estudios en memoria de Eduardo Jiménez de Aréchaga*, 2000, pp.155–200.

[22] See P. Bhatnagar, "Regional arrangements for mode 4 in the services trade" (2005) 4(2) *World Trade Review* pp.171–99, E. Guild, "The movement of natural persons and the GATS" (1999) 4(3) *European Foreign Affairs Review* pp.395–415; and D. Persin, "Free movement of labour". *Journal of World Trade*, 42 (2008), 5, pp.837–864; T. Broude "The WTO/GATS Mode 4, international labor migration regimes and global justice", *Cosmopolitanism in context*, (2010), pp.75–105; M. Klein Solomon, "GATS Mode 4 and the mobility of labour", *International Migration Law*, (2007), pp.107–127.

[23] See T. Broude, "The WTO/GATS Mode 4, international labor migration regimes and global justice", *Cosmopolitanism in Context*, (2010), ss.75–105.

certain types of temporary entry of foreigners, especially business visitors.[24] Typical examples are the obligations entered into by NAFTA States or by the members of other agreements modelled after NAFTA (e.g. the bilateral Canada–Chile Free Trade Agreement (CCFTA).[25]

| **Chapter Sixteen: Temporary Entry for Business Persons (NAFTA)[26]** | **15-009** |

*"Article 1601: General Principles*

Further to Article 102 (Objectives), this Chapter reflects the preferential trading relationship between the Parties, the desirability of facilitating temporary entry on a reciprocal basis and of establishing transparent criteria and procedures for temporary entry, and the need to ensure border security and to protect the domestic labor force and permanent employment in their respective territories.

*Article 1602: General Obligations*

1. Each Party shall apply its measures relating to the provisions of this Chapter in accordance with Article 1601 and, in particular, shall apply expeditiously those measures so as to avoid unduly impairing or delaying trade in goods or services or conduct of investment activities under this Agreement.

2. The Parties shall endeavor to develop and adopt common criteria, definitions and interpretations for the implementation of this Chapter.

*Article 1603: Grant of Temporary Entry*

1. Each Party shall grant temporary entry to business persons who are otherwise qualified for entry under applicable measures relating to public health and safety and national security, in accordance with this Chapter, including the provisions of Annex 1603.

2. A Party may refuse to issue an immigration document authorizing employment to a business person where the temporary entry of that person might affect adversely:

   (a) the settlement of any labor dispute that is in progress at the place or intended place of employment; or

   (b) the employment of any person who is involved in such dispute.

3. When a Party refuses pursuant to paragraph 2 to issue an immigration document authorizing employment, it shall:

   (a) inform in writing the business person of the reasons for the refusal; and

---

[24] See E. G. Yost, "The North American Free Trade Agreement: Chapter sixteen, 'temporary entry for business persons'", *The North American Free Trade Agreement: a new frontier in international trade and investment in the Americas*, pp.247–267.

[25] See also C.J. Cassise, "The European Union v the United States under the NAFTA" (1996) 46 *Syracuse Law Review* 4 pp.1343–1379; E. M. Worrell, "Free trade, free migration", *Temple International and Comparative Law Journal*, 23 (2009), 1, pp.113–142.

[26] Source: *http://www.nafta-sec-alena.org*. (Accessed June 8, 2011).

(b) promptly notify in writing the Party whose business person has been refused entry of the reasons for the refusal.

4. Each Party shall limit any fees for processing applications for temporary entry of business persons to the approximate cost of services rendered."

Similar provision can be found in many bilateral investment treaties (BIT)[27] of combined trade and investment agreements, where the temporary presence of so called investors and so-called "key personnel" is a very common feature. Normally, they only apply to the persons as such but modern life styles increasingly lead to questions regarding a temporary entry permit for family members.

**15-010**

**Examples:**

**Agreement between the Government of Australia and the Government of the Argentine Republic on the Promotion and Protection of Investments, and Protocol (Canberra, 23 August 1995)**

*Article 6 Entry and sojourn of personnel*

1. A Contracting Party shall, subject to its laws and regulations relating to the entry and sojourn of non-citizens, permit natural persons who are investors of the other Contracting Party and personnel employed by companies or legal persons of that other Contracting Party to enter and remain in its territory for the purpose of engaging in activities connected with investments.

2. A Contracting Party shall, subject to its laws and regulations, permit investors of the other Contracting Party who have made investments in the territory of the first Contracting Party to employ within its territory key technical and managerial personnel of their choice regardless of citizenship.

**Agreement on Investment between the Republic of Korea and the Republic of Iceland, the Principality of Liechtenstein and The Swiss Confederation (Hong Kong, 15 December 2005)**

*ARTICLE 8 Key Personnel*

[. . .]

3. Each Party shall, subject to its laws and regulations, grant temporary entry and stay and provide any necessary confirming documentation to the spouse and minor children of a natural person who has been granted temporary entry, stay and authorisation to work in accordance with paragraphs 1 and 2; the spouse and minor children shall be admitted for the period of the stay of that person.

---

[27] See M. Panizzon, "International law of economic migration: a ménage à trois?", *Journal of World Trade*, 44 (2010), 6, pp.1207–1252.

## HARMONISATION OF LABOUR LAW AND SOCIAL STANDARDS

A main argument against the inclusion of social standards and labour rights **15-011** in trade and investment agreements is the existence of a different set of rules particularly designed to improve labour rights at the global and regional level. Since the beginning of the 20th century there have been multilateral efforts to define minimum standards at the global level especially related to the work of the International Labour Organization (ILO).[28]

The ILO was founded in 1919, in the wake of a World War, to pursue a vision based on the premise that universal, lasting peace can be established only if it is based upon decent treatment of working people. Its first constitution was part of the Treaty of Versailles of 1919.[29] The ILO became the first specialised agency of the UN in 1946. Today, the International Labour Organization (ILO) is devoted to advancing opportunities for women and men to obtain decent and productive work in conditions of freedom, equity, security and human dignity. Its main aims are to promote rights at work, encourage decent employment opportunities, enhance social protection and strengthen dialogue in handling work-related issues.

The ILO achieves this goal mostly by drawing up and overseeing international labour standards. Working with its 178 Member States, the ILO seeks to ensure that labour standards are respected in practice as well as principle. By the end of 2006, the ILO had adopted 187 Conventions and 198 Recommendations covering a broad range of subjects: freedom of association and collective bargaining, equality of treatment and opportunity, abolition of forced and child labour, employment promotion and vocational training, social security, conditions of work, labour administration and labour inspection, prevention of work-related accidents, maternity protection, and the protection of migrants and other categories of workers such as seafarers, nursing personnel or plantation workers.

Of the ILO conventions eight have been declared as being of fundamental importance as so-called fundamental ILO conventions.[30] By referring to four core issues of international labour relations (freedom of association, the right to organise and collective bargaining; non-discrimination; prohibition of

---

[28] See above para.15–004 for the creation of a linkage between trade, investment and ILO labour standards in bilateral agreements.

[29] See H.G. Bartolomei de la Cruz, *The International Labor Organization* (Boulder, Col., Westview Press, 1996) or O. Junlin, "The international labour organization's role in nationalizing the international movement to abolish child labor" (2006) 7 *Chicago Journal of International Law* 337–49; G. Rodgers, Gerry, *The International Labour Organization and the quest for social justice,* 1919–2009. (Ithaca, NYILR Press, 2009).

[30] These eight ILO Conventions are: Freedom of Association and Protection of the Right to Organize Convention, 1948 (No.87); Right to Organize and Collective Bargaining Convention, 1949 (No.98); Forced Labour Convention, 1930 (No.29); Abolition of Forced Labour Convention, 1957 (No.105); Discrimination (Employment and Occupation) Convention, 1958 (No.111); Equal Remuneration Convention, 1951 (No.100); Minimum Age Convention, 1973 (No.138); Worst Forms of Child Labour Convention, 1999 (No.182).

forced labour; and prohibition of child labour), the 1998 ILO Declaration on Fundamental Principles and Rights at Work stresses the importance of Members ratifying the corresponding eight conventions.[31]

**15-012**    **ILO Declaration on Fundamental Principles and Rights at Work, 86th Session, Geneva, June 1998[32]**

Whereas the ILO was founded in the conviction that social justice is essential to universal and lasting peace;

Whereas economic growth is essential but not sufficient to ensure equity, social progress and the eradication of poverty, confirming the need for the ILO to promote strong social policies, justice and democratic institutions;

Whereas the ILO should, now more than ever, draw upon all its standard-setting, technical cooperation and research resources in all its areas of competence, in particular employment, vocational training and working conditions, to ensure that, in the context of a global strategy for economic and social development, economic and social policies are mutually reinforcing components in order to create broad-based sustainable development;

Whereas the ILO should give special attention to the problems of persons with special social needs, particularly the unemployed and migrant workers, and mobilize and encourage international, regional and national efforts aimed at resolving their problems, and promote effective policies aimed at job creation;

Whereas, in seeking to maintain the link between social progress and economic growth, the guarantee of fundamental principles and rights at work is of particular significance in that it enables the persons concerned, to claim freely and on the basis of equality of opportunity, their fair share of the wealth which they have helped to generate, and to achieve fully their human potential;

Whereas the ILO is the constitutionally mandated international organization and the competent body to set and deal with international labour standards, and enjoys universal support and acknowledgement in promoting Fundamental Rights at Work as the expression of its constitutional principles;

Whereas it is urgent, in a situation of growing economic interdependence, to reaffirm the immutable nature of the fundamental principles and rights embodied in the Constitution of the Organization and to promote their universal application;

The International Labour Conference

1. Recalls:

   (a) that in freely joining the ILO, all Members have endorsed the principles and rights set out in its Constitution and in the Declaration of Philadelphia, and have undertaken to work towards attaining the overall objectives of the Organization to the best of their resources and fully in line with their specific circumstances;

---

[31] See P. Alston "'Core labour standards' and the transformation of the international labour rights regime" (2004) 15(3) *European Journal of International* Law 457–521 and B.A. Langille, "Core labour rights—The true story (reply to Alston)", *European Journal of International Law*, 16 (2005) 3, ss.409–437.

[32] Source: *http://www.ilo.org*. (Accessed June 8, 2011).

(b) that these principles and rights have been expressed and developed in the form of specific rights and obligations in Conventions recognized as fundamental both inside and outside the Organization.

2. Declares that all Members, even if they have not ratified the Conventions in question, have an obligation arising from the very fact of membership in the Organization to respect, to promote and to realize, in good faith and in accordance with the Constitution, the principles concerning the fundamental rights which are the subject of those Conventions, namely:

(a) freedom of association and the effective recognition of the right to collective bargaining;

(b) the elimination of all forms of forced or compulsory labour;

(c) the effective abolition of child labour; and

(d) the elimination of discrimination in respect of employment and occupation.

3. Recognizes the obligation on the Organization to assist its Members, in response to their established and expressed needs, in order to attain these objectives by making full use of its constitutional, operational and budgetary resources, including, by the mobilization of external resources and support, as well as by encouraging other international organizations with which the ILO has established relations, pursuant to article 12 of its Constitution, to support these efforts:

(a) by offering technical cooperation and advisory services to promote the ratification and implementation of the fundamental Conventions;

(b) by assisting those Members not yet in a position to ratify some or all of these Conventions in their efforts to respect, to promote and to realize the principles concerning fundamental rights which are the subject of these Conventions; and

(c) by helping the Members in their efforts to create a climate for economic and social development.

4. Decides that, to give full effect to this Declaration, a promotional follow-up, which is meaningful and effective, shall be implemented in accordance with the measures specified in the annex hereto, which shall be considered as an integral part of this Declaration.

5. Stresses that labour standards should not be used for protectionist trade purposes, and that nothing in this Declaration and its follow-up shall be invoked or otherwise used for such purposes; in addition, the comparative advantage of any country should in no way be called into question by this Declaration and its follow-up."

## TRADE, INVESTMENT AND SOCIAL STANDARDS

While the migratory flows permitted or conceded in international economic law remain very limited, the questions relating to the effects of trade and investment flows on the working conditions in other countries are of growing concern to labour unions and NGOS in many countries. In a globalised     **15-013** economy, where investment flows are very mobile and where the production of goods and even services (e.g. computer programming) can be easily shifted to other states, the role of social standards and labour laws (as important factors affecting investment decision) is increasingly controversial.[33] A similar question obviously takes place relating to the protection of the environment and to a certain extent cultural diversity.

Traditionally, the multilateral trading system of the GATT (and now the WTO) has tried to eliminate this discussion from the liberalisation negotiations.[34] More recently the question has surfaced whether the social standards observed in a country should be taken into account when regulating the entry of goods. The issue is normally discussed as part of the discussion on whether processes and production methods (PPM) can affect the quality of a good and therefore be a basis for product differentiation at the border (including

[33] See E. De Wet, "Labour standards in the globalized economy: The inclusion of a social clause in the General Agreement on Tariffs and Trade/World Trade Organization", Discussion Paper, DP/76/1994 (ILO, International Institute for Labour Studies, Geneva, 1994); D. Ehrenberg, "The Labor Link: Applying the International Trading System to Enforce Violations of Forced and Child Labor" (1995) 20(2) *The Yale Journal of International Law* 361–417; J.A. De Castro, "Trade and Labour Standards: Using the wrong instruments for the rights cause", UNCTAD, Discussion Paper, No.99 (May 1995); A. Sapire, "The interaction between labour standards and international trade policy" (1995) 18(6) *The World Economy* 791–803; OECD, Trade and Labour Standards. A Review of the Issues (Paris, Organization for Economic Cooperation and Development, 1995); WTO, Singapore Ministerial Declaration (Ministerial Conference, Singapore December 9–13, 1996), WT/MIN(96)/DEC, December 18, 1996; P. Waer, "Social clauses in international trade—the debate in the European Union" (1996) 30(4) J.W.T. 25–42; D. Rodrik, *Labor Standards in International Trade: Do they matter and what do we do about them?* (Washington, Overseas Development Council, 1996); H. Ward, "Common but Differentiated Debates: Environment, labour and the World Trade Organization" (1996) 45 *International and Comparative Law Quarterly* 592–632; F. Weiss, "Internationally Recognized Labour Standards and Trade" (1996) *Legal Issues of European Integration* 161–78; B. Langille, "Eight ways to think about international labour standards" (1997) 31(4) J.W.T. 27–54; J.S. Mai, "Core labour standards and export performance in developing countries" (1997) 20(6) *The World Economy* 773–785; N. Haworth and S. Hughes, "Trade and International Labour Standards: Issues and Debates over a Social Clause" (1997) 39(2) *The Journal of Industrial Relations* 179–95; K.E. Maskus, "Should Core Labour Standards Be Imposed Through International Trade Policy", Policy Research Working Paper, 1817, The World Bank Development Research Group, August 1997; S.S. Golub, 'International labor standards and international trade", IMF Working Paper WP/97/37 (Washington D.C, April, 1997); E-U Petersmann, "The WTO constitution and human rights" (2000) 3 *Journal of International Economic Law* 19–25; T. Cottier, "Trade and Human Rights: A Relationship to Discover" (2002) 5 *Journal of International Economic Law* 111–32; P. Macklem, "Labour Law Beyond Borders" (2002) 5 *Journal of International Economic Law* 605–45; C. Lopez-Hurtado, "Social Labelling and WTO Law" (2002) 5 *Journal of International Economic Law* 719–46; C. Thomas, "Trade-Related Labor and Environment Agreements?" (2002) 5 *Journal of International Economic Law* 791–819; H.-M. Wolffgang, "Core labour standards in world trade law" (2002) 36(5) J.W.T. 883–901; C. McCrudden and A. Davies, "A perspective on trade and labor rights" (2003) 3 *Journal of International Economic Law* 43–62; C. Kaufmann, *Globalisation and Labour Rights: the Conflict between Core Labour Rights and International Economic Law* (Hart Publishing, 2007).

[34] See T. Greven, "Social Standards in Bilateral and Regional Trade and Investment Agreements—Instruments, Enforcement, and Policy Options for Trade Unions" (Dialogue on Globalization: Occasional Papers No.16, Geneva 2005) and OECD, International trade and core labour standards (Paris, 2000).

prohibitions of entry).[35] One clear example of such a consideration can be found in the GATT 1947 itself (Art.XX (e)).

**Article XX: General Exceptions (GATT)[36]**

Subject to the requirement that such measures are not applied in a manner which would constitute a means of arbitrary or unjustifiable discrimination between countries where the same conditions prevail, or a disguised restriction on international trade, nothing in this Agreement shall be construed to prevent the adoption or enforcement by any contracting party of measures:

[...]

(e) relating to the products of prison labour;

...

Otherwise the parties of the GATT and regional and bilateral trade agreements have had a tendency to accept that social standards may differ and should not be a basis for trade restrictions and differential treatment. This is less controversial between countries where essentially the same social standards prevail, while it causes more controversies between developing countries and developed countries. At the 1996 Singapore Ministerial Conference, members defined the WTO's role on this issue, identifying the International Labour Organization (ILO)[37] as the competent body to negotiate labour standards. There is no work on this subject in the WTO's Councils and Committees. However the secretariats of the two organisations work together on technical issues under the banner of "coherence" in global economic policy-making.[38] The issue was also raised at the Seattle Ministerial Conference in 1999, but with no agreement reached. The 2001 Doha Ministerial Conference reaffirmed the Singapore declaration on labour without any specific discussion.

**15-014**

**1996 Singapore Ministerial Declaration (WTO)[39]**

**15-015**

"*Core Labour Standards*

4. We renew our commitment to the observance of internationally recognized core labour standards. The International Labour Organization (ILO) is the competent body to set and deal with these standards, and we affirm our support for its work in promoting them. We believe that economic growth and development fostered by increased trade and further trade liberalization contribute to the promotion of these standards. We reject the use of

---

[35] See A. Giansanti, "La tutela di interessi non economici nel sistema OMC", *Editoriale Scientifica*, (2008).

[36] Source: *http://www.wto.org*. (Accessed June 8, 2011).

[37] See above para.15–010.

[38] See, for example, "Trade and Employment: Challenges for Policy Research. A Joint Study of the International Labour Office and the Secretariat of the World Trade Organization", Geneva: World Trade Organization and International Labour Office, 2007.

[39] Source: *http://www.wto.org*. (Accessed June 8, 2011).

> labour standards for protectionist purposes, and agree that the compara-
> tive advantage of countries, particularly low-wage developing countries,
> must in no way be put into question. In this regard, we note that the WTO
> and ILO Secretariats will continue their existing collaboration."

**15-016**   As a result there is a tendency in certain countries to ask for the inclusion of
social clauses into their bilateral trade and investment agreements even if this
is criticised as ineffective and inappropriate by many observers. At the same
time countries may feel under pressure to unilaterally adopt revised labour
and social standards as a prerequisite to entering into negotiations with
trading partners demanding them. Here it is very common to refer to internationally recognised labour standards, or the basic principles at work outlined
in the ILO Declaration in 1998, such as the freedom for setting up associations, organising and building a collective labour agreement, or the principles
on no forced labour, on working hours and safety labour.[40] It seems that
increasingly trading partners demand such preliminary or parallel amendments of domestic laws as a condition for the conclusion or entry into force
of FTAs.[41] As a corollary this allows the agreements as such to refer only to
an obligation to enforce the domestic labour laws. Peru and Columbia have
recently engaged in important revisions of their domestic legislation prior to
concluding FTAs with the United States.[42]

**15-017**   **NORTH AMERICAN AGREEMENT ON LABOR COOPERATION (14
September 1993)**

PART TWO: OBLIGATIONS

*Article 2: Levels of Protection*

Affirming full respect for each Party's constitution, and recognizing the right
of each Party to establish its own domestic labor standards, and to adopt or
modify accordingly its labor laws and regulations, each Party shall ensure that
its labor laws and regulations provide for high labor standards, consistent
with high quality and productivity workplaces, and shall continue to strive to
improve those standards in that light.

Article 3: Government Enforcement Action

1.  Each Party shall promote compliance with and effectively enforce its
    labor law through appropriate government action, subject to Article 42,
    such as:

    (a)  appointing and training inspectors;

---

[40] See Robert G. Finbow, *The Limits of Regionalism: NAFTA's Labour Accord* (Ashgate, 2006).
[41] See C. Granger, "Core labour standards in trade agreements", *Journal of World Trade*, 40
(2006), 5, pp.813–836.
[42] See A.R. Schmidt, "A new trade policy for America", *Indiana International & Comparative
Law Review*, 19 (2009), 1, pp.167–201; R. Dombois, "Transnational labor regulation in the
NAFTA—a problem of institutional design?", *The International Journal of Comparative
Labour Law and Industrial Relations*, 19 (2003) 4, pp.421–440 and N.L. Grimm, "The North
American Agreement on Labor Cooperation and its effects on women working in Mexican
maquiladoras", *American University Law Review*, 48 (1998) 1, pp.179–227.

(b) monitoring compliance and investigating suspected violations, including through on-site inspections;

(c) seeking assurances of voluntary compliance;

(d) requiring record keeping and reporting;

(e) encouraging the establishment of worker-management committees to address labor regulation of the workplace;

(f) providing or encouraging mediation, conciliation and arbitration services; or

(g) initiating, in a timely manner, proceedings to seek appropriate sanctions or remedies for violations of its labor law.

2. Each Party shall ensure that its competent authorities give due consideration in accordance with its law to any request by an employer, employee or their representatives, or other interested person, for an investigation of an alleged violation of the Party's labor law. . .

**United States—Peru Trade Promotion Agreement (12 April 2006)**

Chapter Seventeen: Labor

*Article 17.1: Statement of Shared Commitments*

The Parties reaffirm their obligations as members of the International Labor Organization (ILO).

*Article 17.2: Fundamental Labor Rights*[43]

1. Each Party shall adopt and maintain in its statutes and regulations, and practices thereunder, the following rights, as stated in the ILO Declaration on Fundamental Principles and Rights at Work and its Follow-Up (1998) (ILO Declaration):[44]

(a) freedom of association;

(b) the effective recognition of the right to collective bargaining;

(c) the elimination of all forms of compulsory or forced labor;

(d) the effective abolition of child labor and, for purposes of this Agreement, a prohibition on the worst forms of child labor; and

(e) the elimination of discrimination in respect of employment and occupation.

2. Neither Party shall waive or otherwise derogate from, or offer to waive or otherwise derogate from, its statutes or regulations implementing paragraph 1 in a manner affecting trade or investment between the Parties, where the waiver or derogation would be inconsistent with a fundamental right set out in that paragraph.

---

[43] To establish a violation of an obligation under Art.17.2.1 a Party must demonstrate that the other Party has failed to adopt or maintain a statute, regulation, or practice in a manner affecting trade or investment between the Parties.

[44] The obligations set out in Art.17.2, as they relate to the ILO, refer only to the ILO Declaration.

*Article 17.3: Enforcement of Labor Laws*

1. (a) A Party shall not fail to effectively enforce its labor laws, including those it adopts or maintains in accordance with Article 17.2.1, through a sustained or recurring course of action or inaction, in a manner affecting trade or investment between the Parties, after the date of entry into force of this Agreement.

   (b) A decision a Party makes on the distribution of enforcement resources shall not be a reason for not complying with the provisions of this Chapter. Each Party retains the right to the reasonable exercise of discretion and to bona fide decisions with regard to the allocation of resources between labor enforcement activities among the fundamental labor rights enumerated in Article 17.2.1, provided the exercise of such discretion and such decisions are not inconsistent with the obligations of this Chapter.3

2 Nothing in this Chapter shall be construed to empower a Party's authorities to undertake labor law enforcement activities in the territory of another Party.

The United States and the European Union have also included human rights considerations, including specific labour rights as contained in specific ILO Convention,[45] into their GSP schemes[46] under the GATT/WTO:

**15-018**

**COUNCIL REGULATION (EC) No.980/2005 of June 27, 2005 applying a scheme of generalised tariff preferences[47]**

SECTION 2 Special incentive arrangement for sustainable development and good governance

*Article 8*

1. Common Customs Tariff ad valorem duties on all products listed in Annex II which originate in a country included in the special incentive arrangement for sustainable development and good governance shall be suspended. . ...

*Article 9*

1. The special incentive arrangement for sustainable development and good governance may be granted to a country which:

   (a) has ratified and effectively implemented the conventions listed in Part A of Annex III, and

   (b) has ratified and effectively implemented at least seven of the conventions listed in Part B of Annex III, and. . .

---

[45] See above para.15–012.
[46] See Ch.12 and in particular U. Turksen, "The WTO law and the EC's GSP+ Arrangement", *Journal of World Trade*, 43 (2009), 5, pp.927–968.
[47] [2005] O.J. L169/1.

***ANNEX III* Conventions referred to in Article 9 PART A**

**Core human and labour rights UN/ILO Conventions**

1. International Covenant on Civil and Political Rights

2. International Covenant on Economic, Social and Cultural Rights

3. International Convention on the Elimination of All Forms of Racial Discrimination

4. Convention on the Elimination of All Forms of Discrimination Against Women

5. Convention against Torture and other Cruel, Inhuman or Degrading Treatment or Punishment

6. Convention on the Rights of the Child

7. Convention on the Prevention and Punishment of the Crime of Genocide

8. Convention concerning Minimum Age for Admission to Employment (No 138)

9. Convention concerning the Prohibition and Immediate Action for the Elimination of the Worst Forms of Child Labour (No 182)

10. Convention concerning the Abolition of Forced Labour (No 105)

11. Convention concerning Forced or Compulsory Labour (No 29)

12. Convention concerning Equal Remuneration of Men and Women Workers for Work of Equal Value (No 100)

13. Convention concerning Discrimination in Respect of Employment and Occupation (No 111)

14. Convention concerning Freedom of Association and Protection of the Right to Organise (No 87)

15. Convention concerning the Application of the Principles of the Right to Organise and to Bargain Collectively (No 98)

16. International Convention on the Suppression and Punishment of the Crime of Apartheid.

CHAPTER 16

# INTERNATIONAL FISCAL LAW: RELIEF FROM DOUBLE TAXATION

## INTRODUCTION

The object of this chapter is to outline the fundamentals of International **16-001**
Fiscal Law (IFL) with specific reference to international relief from double
taxation. To this end the first section focuses on IFL and policy. Section two
explains the problem of double taxation. This is followed by a consideration
of the different systems of relieving double taxation, with a particular focus
on relief of double taxation of international business income, in terms of the
material set out. The penultimate section focuses on enforcement of double
taxation relief accorded in international agreements and generally international co-operation in fiscal matters. The final section looks at the UN work
in double taxation relief and in particular the differences in the OECD and
UN approaches to relieving the burden of double taxation. It is not possible
to give here an exhaustive analysis of double taxation relief provisions set out
in double taxation agreements.

## INTERNATIONAL FISCAL LAW AND DOUBLE TAXATION RELIEF

The problem of double taxation and the manner of according relief for **16-002**
double taxation is a core preoccupation of IFL.[1] IFL generally and double

---

[1] For general works in international taxation see, for example, S. Picciotto, *International
Business Taxation* (Weidenfeld & Nicolson, 1992); A.H. Qureshi, The *Public International
Law of Taxation: Text, Cases & Materials* (Graham and Trotmann/Nijhoff, 1994); B.J.
Arnold and M.J. McIntyre, *International Tax Primer* (Kluwer Law International, 2002); R.
Rohatgi, *Basic International Taxation*, 2nd edn (Richmond Law and Tax, 2005); A. Miller,
*Principles of International Taxation* (Totell Publishing, 2006); P. Baker, *Double Taxation
Conventions and International Tax Law* (Sweet and Maxwell, looseleaf); A. Amatucci, et al.
(eds) *International tax law* (Alphen aan den Rijn, Kluwer Law International, 2006); R.S. Avi-
Yonah, *International Tax as International Law, an Analysis of the International Tax Regime,*
(Cambridge, Cambridge University Press, 2007); C. van, Raad, *Materials on International and*

taxation relief[2] specifically form very much an aspect of International Economic Law—concerned as they are with how national taxation affects cross border trade transactions in goods and services and factor movements in labour and capital investment. Traditionally, however, IFL has generally been regarded as a discreet branch of law in its own right. One particular reason being that this has historically been an autonomous branch of law that generally requires a specific background in taxation. Moreover, in most international economic organisations regulatory compliance in the sphere of taxation has tended in the past to be at the margins, if at all. However, the challenges of globalisation and increased awareness of different policy interactions both at the national and international levels, make such fiscal policy isolation increasingly untenable. Indeed, the normative frameworks of international trade, investment and development are beginning to configure the interface between their respective spheres and IFL.

At its core IFL is concerned with the challenges of coordinating national and international efforts in taxing incoming and outgoing cross-border transactions. Globalisation and modern exigencies have meant that IFL is also concerned with reinforcing national efforts at ensuring the integrity and efficacy of national tax systems including the attainment of globally agreed objectives. The attainment of the core functions of IFL have historically been underpinned in varying degrees by principles of neutrality and equity.[3] More particularly, the macro level challenges that confront the international fiscal order may be summarised as follows. First and foremost, a primary and traditional goal is the elimination of double taxation. This is because double taxation creates an unjust burden on the taxpayer and creates obstacles to international flows of trade in goods and services, investment, labour and the transfer of technology. Second, of note is the practice of tax discrimination in national systems particularly tax incentives to attract foreign investment. Such practices create and contribute to distortions in trade and investment decisions. Thus, a number of the cases in the WTO have involved both questions of tax discrimination and tax subsidies.[4] By the same token the EU

---

*EC Tax Law*, 9th edn (Leiden, International Tax Center Leiden, 2009); P. Harris & D. Oliver, *International Commercial Tax*, (Cambridge University Press, 2010).

[2] For specific works on double taxation see for example P. Baker, *Double Taxation Conventions and International Tax Law* (London, Sweet and Maxwell, looseleaf); K. Vogel, *Double Taxation Conventions,* 3rd edn (Kluwer, 1997); M. Rasmussen *International Double Taxation* (Kluwer Law International, 2011); OECD Model Tax Convention; UN Model Double Taxation Convention.

[3] See for example K. Vogel, "Worldwide vs source taxation of income—a review and re-evaluation of arguments" (1988) 10 *INTERTAX* 310–320.

[4] See, for example, GATT Panel Report (1976): Income Tax Practices Maintained by France, Belgium, Netherlands, *BISD*, 23 Supplement; GATT Panel Report (1976) DISC case, *BISD*23rd Supplement; WTO Appellate Body Report, United States—Tax Treatment for "Foreign Sales Corporations", WT/DS108/AB/R (2000); United States—Tax Treatment for "Foreign Sales Corporations", Recourse to Art.21.5 of the DSU by the European Communities, WT/DS108/AB/RW, 2000. See also secondary literature, for example, J. Fisher-Zernin, "GATT versus Tax Treaties? The basic conflicts between international taxation methods and the rules and concepts of GATT" (1987) 3 J.W.T. 21 at 39–62; L. Eden,

and the OECD have been particularly concerned with the phenomenon of "harmful" tax competition among taxing authorities with respect to international financial flows; and thus have introduced responses to counter the harmful use of tax incentives intended to distort investment flows especially into tax havens.[5] The OECD efforts at combating harmful tax competition are

"Free trade, tax reform, and transfer pricing" (1991) *Canadian Tax Journal* 96–112; A. Qureshi, *The Public International Law of Taxation* (1994), Ch.5; A. Qureshi, "Trade related aspects of international taxation—a new WTO code of conduct?" (1996) 30 J.W.T. 161–194 April Issue; D. Hughes, "Withholding taxes & the Most Favoured Nation Clause" (1997) 51 B.I.F.D. 126; R. Green, "Anti-legalistic approaches to resolving disputes between governments: A comparison of the international tax and trade regimes" (1998) 23(1) *Yale Journal of International Law*, 79–139; R.H.C. Luja, "WTO Agreements versus the EC Fiscal Aid Regime: Impact on Direct Taxation" (1999) 27 *INTERTAX* 207–225; L. Bao, "The WTO Accession & Tax Policy Options in China" (2001) 29 *INTERTAX* 283; A. Qureshi and R. Grynberg, "United States Tax Subsidies Under Domestic International Sales Corporation, Foreign Sales Corporation and Extraterritorial Income Exclusion Act Legislation Within the Framework of the World Trade Organization" (2002) 36 J.W.T. 978–992; L. Bao, "Economic globalization, WTO & Tax Reform in China", 29 *INTERTAX* 341; K.E. Sorensen, "Direct taxation and WTO Agreements", E.T. Vol.42; No.6/7, p.206; P.R. McDaniel, "The impact of trade agreements on tax systems"(2002) 30 *INTERTAX* 166; J.B. Gross, "OECD defensive measures against harmful tax competition: legality under WTO" (2003) 11 *INTERTAX* 390; G. Cappadona, "WTO, GATT, tax treaties and international taxation: the effects of their interactions and the possibilities of conflict" (2004) IV(4) *Dritto e Pratica Tributaria Internazionale Padova* 457–532; M. Daly, The WTO and Direct Taxation, WTO Discussion Paper No.9 (June 2005); J. Bourgeois, "WTO and Direct Taxation In and Out", Ch.6 in *Trade Law Experienced: Pottering About in the GATT and WTO* (London, Cameron May, 2005); D. Durrschudct, "Tax treaties and most-favoured nation treatment, particularly within the EU" (2006) B.I.F.D. 202–214; J. Herdin-Winter (ed.), *The Relevance of WTO Law for Tax Matters* (Linde, 2006); Waincymer, J, "International tax and international trade policy objectives" in *A vision of taxes within and outside European borders: Festschrift in honor of Prof. Dr. Frans Vanistendael* (Alphen aan den Rijn, Kluwer Law International, 2008).

[5] See, for example, Harmful Tax Competition: An emerging Global Issue (OCED, 1998); Towards Global Tax Co-operation (OCED, 2000); The OECD's Project on Harmful Tax Practices (OCED, 2001); Guidance in Applying the 1998 Report to Preferential Tax Regimes (OCED, 2004); Towards tax co-ordination in the European Union (EU, 1997). See also secondary literature, for example, A. Easson, "Tax Competition and Investment Incentives" (1997) 2(2) *The EC Tax Journal* 65; C. Pinto, "EU and the OECD to fight harmful tax competition. Has the right path being undertaken?" (1998) 26(12) *INTERTAX* 386; T. Rosenbuj, "Harmful tax competition" (1999) *INTERTAX* 316; European Taxation—Special issue on Harmful Tax Competition, Vol.40, No.3, Sept 2000, p.399–439; E. Osterweil, "OECD Report on Harmful Tax Competition and the European Union code of conduct compared" (1999) 39(6) E.T.; J.M. Weiner, "OECD Project on Harmful Tax Practices marks fifth year" (2003) 31(3) *Tax Notes* 233–8; J.B. Gross, "OECD Defensive Measures against Harmful Tax Competition Legality under WTO" (2003) 31(11) *INTERTAX* 390 at 395; I. Hotbauer, "To what extent does the OECD Harmful Tax Competition Project violate the most-favoured-nation obligations under the WTO law" (2004) 44(a) E.T. 400–3; M Littlewood, "Tax Competition", *Michigan Journal of International Law*, 26:1 (2004),411-487; A.J. Easson, "Harmful tax competition: an evaluation of the OECD initiative" (2004) 34(101) *Tax Note International* 1037–77; P. Baker, "The World-wide response to the harmful tax competition campaigns (updated to April 2004)", 111(2) *GITC Review* 1–42; B.J. Kiekebeld, *Harmful Tax Competition in the European Union: code of conduct, countermeasures and EU Law* (Kluwer, 2004); A.J. Eason, "Harmful Tax Competition: an evaluation of the OECD initiative" (2004) 34(10) *Tax Notes* 1037–77; L.C. McLure, "Will the OECD initiative on harmful tax competition help developing and transition countries?" (2005) 59(3) B.I.F.D. 90–8; R. Tealher, *The Benefits of Tax Competition* (London: Institute of Economic Affairs, 2005); M.F. Ambrosano, et al., "Eliminating harmful tax practices in tax havens: defensive measures by

now orchestrated through the OECD based Global Forum on Transparency and Exchange and Information for Tax Purposes, essentially as a drive for good governance in tax matters[6] viz., transparency and exchange of information. Third, international tax evasion and avoidance,[7] for example through transfer pricing, particularly consequent upon the liberalisation of trade and investment, along with the phenomenon of globalisation, have created the need for increased co-operation in the enforcement of national and international fiscal norms. Both developing and developed countries lose revenue from tax planning and evasion that can be quantified in billions of dollars per year. According to a Norwegian study illegal outflows of finances from developing countries amounted in 2006 to $64 to $979 billion—some seven times the inflow into these countries of official aid.[8] In the case of developed countries one estimate for revenue loss for the United States is 100 billion dollars per year.[9] Fourth, developing countries face a plethora of national taxation problems, for example in the design and enforcement of their tax systems, that arise from the phenomenon of development and that call for special international assistance.[10] Developing countries need to raise tax revenue.[11] In the same vein the impact of the particular orientation of the international fiscal system, including the manner of according double taxation relief in double taxation agreements, on the development of developing countries, is of international concern. Thus, it is to be noted that only relatively recently "taxation and development" have found a setting in the OECD agenda—the

---

major EU countries and Tax Haven Reforms" (2005) 53(3) *Canadian Tax Journal* 685–719; J. Dabner, "To join the international tax cartel or not? How should Asia respond to the OECD's harmful tax regimes projected?" (2005) 11(3) *New Zealand Journal of Taxation Law and Policy* 299–313; R. Teather, *The Benefits of Tax Competition* (The Institute of Economic Affairs, 2005); L. Cerioni, "Harmful tax competition revisited: why not a purely legal perspective under EU law?" (2005) 45 E.T. 267–8; A. Nov, "Tax competition: an analysis of the fundamental arguments" (2005) 37(4) *Tax Notes International* 323–53; N. Bridgland, "The EU code of conduct to eliminate harmful or potential harmful business tax regimes: the future" (2006) 8(1) *Tax Planning International* 8–11; OECD Implementing the Tax Transparency Standards: A Handbook for Assessors and Jurisdictions (2010); OECD: The Global Forum On Transparency And Exchange Of Information For Tax Purposes, A Background Information Brief: 20 April 2011; OECD: Tackling Aggressive Tax Planning Through Improved Transparency And Disclosure. Report On Disclosure Initiatives (February 2011).

6    See European Commission Communication on Promoting Good Governance in Tax Matters. European Commission COM (2009) 201.

7    See on concepts of tax evasion and tax avoidance for example UN *Manual for the Negotiation of Bilateral Tax Treaties between Developed and Developing Countries*, ST/ESA/PAD/SER.E/37,2003 pp.33–52.

8    Norwegian Government Commission Report "Tax Havens and Development", June 2009.

9    See OECD at *http://www.oecd.org/findDocument/0,3770,en_2649_33767_1_119832_1_1_1,00.html*. (Accessed June 8, 2011).

10   See the work of the UN Experts on International Tax Cooperation in Tax Matters *http://www.un.org/esa/ffd/ffdtaxation.htm*. (Accessed June 8, 2011). See also for example V. Thuronyi, *Tax Law design and Drafting* (Kluwer Law International, 2000).

11   See OECD Current Tax Agenda April 2011; and Communication from the Commission to the European Parliament, the Council and the European Economic and Social Committee *Tax and Development* Cooperating with Developing Countries on Promoting Good Governance in Tax Matters SEC(2010)426 Brussels, April 2010.

OECD being a key institution in the development of IFL, albeit an organisation concerned with its primarily developed country membership. Fifth, of note are the fiscal challenges that accompany modern technology. A key phenomenon here is the taxation of electronic commerce.[12]

Finally, insights into some of the contemporary fiscal challenges can be fathomed from the preoccupations of the OECD.[13] Not only is the importance of improving revenue collection in developing countries for growth and poverty reduction recognised but so is its importance for developed countries to improve economic performance in the light of the recent financial crisis through growth oriented taxation. Moreover, the importance of taxation to achieve multilateral goals, such as environmental protection (green taxes) and the fight against corruption are also recognised. The OECD perception of contemporary international tax problems requiring international co-operation is not very different from that espoused by the UN Committee of Experts on International Cooperation in Tax Matters, a subsidiary body of the Economic and Social Council, focusing on international tax matters particularly in terms of developing countries.[14] Of note however is the allusion to corporate social responsibility in the framework of taxation by the UN Committee of Experts. This alignment of perceptions is not very surprising as the work of the UN in taxation often takes its cue from the work of the OECD in taxation.

**A/RES/65/1 19th October 2010 Resolution adopted by the UN General Assembly 65/1.**                                  **16-003**

**Keeping the promise: united to achieve the Millennium Development Goals**

*The General Assembly*

*Adopts* the following outcome document of the High-level Plenary Meeting of the General Assembly on
the Millennium Development Goals at its sixty-fifth session:

. . .

---

[12] See *http://www.oecd.org* (accessed June 8, 2011) for work in the OECD on Taxation and Electronic Commerce.

[13] See OECD Current Tax Agenda April 2011: "• How to reduce tax barriers to cross border trade and investment? • How can the administrative aspects of transfer pricing be improved? • How to design tax systems that are competitive, restore growth, reduce inequality, spur innovation, stimulate employment, and achieve fiscal consolidation? • How can tax measures be used to address climate change? • What is the right mix of direct and indirect taxes? • How can developing countries improve their tax systems so as to mobilise domestic resources? • How can taxpayer services be improved? • How can inter-agency collaboration help governments deter, detect and deal with financial crimes more effectively? • How can administrative co-operation among revenue bodies be improved to tackle international tax evasion? • How to implement the international standards of transparency and effective exchange of information for tax purposes?" *http://www.oecd.org/dataoecd/38/17/1909369.pdf* (accessed June 8, 2011).

[14] See UN Economic and Social Council: Strengthening of institutional arrangements to promote international cooperation in tax matters, including the Committee of Experts on International Cooperation in Tax Matters, E/2011/76 March 2011.

> Millennium Development Goal 8 — Develop a global partnership for development
>
> 78. We commit ourselves to accelerating progress in order to achieve Millennium
>
> Development Goal 8, including by:
>
> (*i*) Enhancing and strengthening domestic resource mobilization and fiscal space, including, where appropriate, through modernized tax systems, more efficient tax collection, broadening the tax base and effectively combating tax evasion and capital flight. While each country is responsible for its tax system, it is important to support national efforts in these areas by strengthening technical assistance and enhancing international cooperation and participation in addressing international tax matters. We look forward to the upcoming report by the Secretary-General examining the strengthening of institutional arrangements to promote international cooperation in tax matters;
>
> **EU Commission Communication 2010:**
>
> 1. STRENGTHENING GOOD GOVERNANCE IN TAX MATTERS IN DEVELOPING COUNTRIES: In many developing countries, the sustainable provision of public services that is necessary to achieve and maintain the Millennium Development Goals (MDG) requires an increase in domestic revenue. Their tax-to-GDP ratio ranges between 10 to 20% as opposed to 25 to 40% in developed countries. Increasing domestic revenue not only creates additional space for supporting MDG-related spending, it also allows a country to assume ownership for its policy choices.[15]

**16-004**  Many of the challenges that confront the international tax order are underpinned by the fundamental question of how transnational fiscal facts should be taxed between States. In particular whether the source country, where the revenue is generated, has priority in taxation; or whether the residence country, where the taxpayer is resident or a national of, can tax on a worldwide basis? In legal analysis the question of the allocation of fiscal jurisdiction as between States under International Law has been mainly framed in terms of the existence of the requirement or otherwise of a reasonable connection between the taxing State and the taxpayer.[16] From the perspective of international tax policy discourse however this fundamental question is much more complex. First, although the tax policy discourse is primarily informed by considerations of equity and neutrality there is an underlying assumption that there are universally agreed goals for the international tax order. Thus, there is no comprehensive multilateral agreement on taxation. The international institutions that focus on taxation are disparate, and there

---

[15]  Commission to the European Parliament, the Council and the European Economic and Social Committee *Tax and Development* Cooperating with Developing Countries on Promoting Good Governance in Tax Matters SEC(2010)426 Brussels, April 2010.

[16]  See Ch.3 on Jurisdiction.

does not appear to be consensus for one single institution for international tax co-operation. The existing international arrangements for international co-operation revolve mainly around the OECD and the UN Committee of Experts on International Cooperation in Tax Matters; along with technical assistance and policy input through the Bretton Woods and related institutions; including regional groupings of tax administrators. Moreover, the normative framework of international taxation, such as it is, is also sourced variously. It is the case though that the principles of equity and neutrality underpin most major tax systems, although the precise nature, scope and content of these is the subject of some contention. Moreover, they are reinforced by the underlying principles upon which the world trading system is set viz., liberal trade, the power of the market and in some measure the development goals of developing countries. In particular, the need to avoid double taxation and the avoidance of non-taxation through co-operation between taxing authorities forms a basic goal of tax treaties.[17] Not all principles that underpin the domestic tax system are mirrored internationally though, as for instance redistribution. The principle of redistribution in some measure assumes a guiding force and a common good. Second, the concepts of the residence of the taxpayer and source of the income- or gain-generating activity are not necessarily self-evident, although at some level identifiable. In particular, modern technology in the form of e-commerce makes it increasingly difficult to connect with either source or residence. Finally, the discourse on the appropriate criteria for the allocation of fiscal jurisdiction as between States is set against various standpoints, viz. national, global, residence State, source State, and the individual. Indeed, the particular nature of the income and gain itself may also be a factor in the equation. Moreover, although the discourse on allocation of fiscal jurisdiction among States has traditionally been focused in terms of the residence or the source States, these locations are not necessarily exclusive or indeed exhaustive. Thus, other grounds are the principle of nationality and the principle of origin or economic location.[18] To conclude, the question where is the appropriate locus of fiscal jurisdiction with respect to transnational fiscal facts, is accompanied by a set of assumptions, sometimes conflicting goals and technological challenges.

It is against this background that the international tax policy discourse needs to be considered. First, the notion of equity as between States, and in terms of the individual taxpayer—namely inter-nation equity and inter-individual equity—need to be considered. Inter-nation equity is difficult to define. It involves, however, determining what is the appropriate share of the transnational revenue as between States.[19] Thus it engages questions such as what is the appropriate source State entitlement? What are the services rendered by the State? Is the State policy non-discriminatory as between

---

[17] See, for example, Arnold and McIntyre (2002), p.6.
[18] See General Report citing Kemmeren at p.84.
[19] See, for example, Arnold and McIntyre (2002), p.4.

States? Is the State fiscal policy based on reciprocity and equality as between States? All of these factors are underpinned by considerations of fairness/ justice. Individual equity on the other hand involves the notion of equality of tax treatment of taxpayers in source and residence States, and within the taxing State. Individual equity may be based either on "the benefit rule or the ability-to-pay rule".[20] Thus, individual equity engages the relationship between the State and the taxpayer, in particular in terms of the actual or potential benefits derived from the State; and the due regard taken into account by the State in fiscal policy to the economic capacity to pay taxes. Furthermore, in traditional tax discourse equity is considered as involving both the notions of vertical and horizontal equity. Vertical equity calls for taxpayers with different capacities to share the burden of taxation according to their different capacities. On the other hand, the notion of horizontal equity implies equality as between different taxpayers in similar circumstances. Generally, in practice fiscal policy focuses more on the ability to pay.[21]

**16-005**     Second, of note is the notion of neutrality in international taxation. This is concerned with enhancing efficiency and fairness in competition with respect to cross-border transactions,[22] such that the market system is not hindered by governmental action. Neutrality in circumstances of different national tax systems is difficult to achieve, and is therefore essentially a relative concept. In international tax neutrality has two facets, viz. capital export neutrality (CEN) and capital import neutrality (CIN). Capital export neutrality is concerned with ensuring that outflows of capital from a State are not informed by tax considerations,[23] i.e. the taxpayer pays the same tax whether the investment is within or outside the State. Capital import neutrality involves the circumstance where the investment is subjected to the same tax regardless of its origin. Thus, it involves ensuring that investment outflows share the same burden of taxation in a foreign jurisdiction as all the other investors in that jurisdiction.[24] Economists are challenged by the question which of these two principles should take priority, or what the balance as between the two principles should be—although without much agreement.[25] However, it is generally recognised that complete neutrality in terms of taxation and multistate taxation are difficult to achieve. Be that as it may the principle of capital import neutrality favours the source State as it involves the residence State exempting revenue in the source State. Not surprisingly in the OECD there is a preference for capital export neutrality, although multinational companies

---

[20] See, for example, A. Schindel and A. Atchabahian, "Source and residence: new configuration of their principles" General Report *Cahiers de Droit Fiscal International* Vol.90a 2005 IFA, p.31.

[21] Schindel and Atchabahian (2005), p.31.

[22] See, for example, Arnold and McIntyre (2002), pp.5–6.

[23] See, for example, Arnold and McIntyre (2002), pp.5–6.

[24] See, for example, Arnold and McIntyre (2002), p.6.

[25] See, for example, Arnold and McIntyre (2002), p.6.

in OECD residence States have been advocating a shift to CIN in order to strengthen their international competitiveness.[26]

The notion of neutrality is also concerned with ensuring the elimination of tax discrimination.[27] In this context tax incentives are of significance. Tax incentives are particularly dear to developing States, as a mechanism to attract investment. The OECD has responded to some forms of tax incentives by characterising them as "harmful tax competition",[28] along with a system of retaliation for such genre of competition.

Third, although most analysis of the international tax order tends to draw from the criteria of equity and neutrality, States are also heavily informed by fiscal sovereignty in the choice of their international tax systems.[29] The national perspective has a dimension in the business of attracting foreign investment, in protecting the internal value system of the State, and in protecting the domestic revenue base from being undermined. Fourth, the allocation of fiscal revenue as between residence and source states and indeed generally as between States must also take cognisance of the development goals and particular circumstances of developing nations. Thus, developing States feel the need to embrace tax incentives to attract foreign investment, and generally require an international tax system that is more source based. For example, the credit method of relieving double taxation found in most double taxation agreements undermines reduction of taxes in developing countries.[30] Finally, the international tax system also needs to be structured such that it is administratively manageable, simple, certain and transparent. This is a focus on good governance in taxation. In this respect developing countries need technical assistance, particularly in the design and implementation of effective tax enforcement systems.

In conclusion, the main reasons for a system of allocation of fiscal jurisdiction, in the light of the considerations set out above, that favour the source State have been aptly summarised as follows[31]:

**Angel Schindel and Adolfo Atchabahian, "Source and residence: new configuration of their principles" General Report** *Cahiers de droit fiscal international* Vol.90a 2005 IFA, p.30 (Footnotes omitted)

"(a)  Most appropriate and logical criterion under the sovereignty principle: the        **16-006**
        source principle, as an attribute of primary and in some cases exclusive
        taxing powers, rests on an adequate allocation of taxing claims at an inter-
        national level, as it allows each state to pursue its own tax policy in line
        with, and with respect for, other states; it asserts in the tax field the principle
        of sovereign equality of nations, and the notion, widely accepted from the

---

[26] See, for example, General Report at p.36.
[27] See, for example, Avv. Pietro Adonnino, *Non-discrimination rules in international taxation* General Report, *Cahiers de Droit Fiscal International* Vol.78b (1993).
[28] See further below on harmful tax competition.
[29] See, for example, Bird IBFD 1978. See also T, Rixen, *The Political Economy of International Tax Governance* (New York, Palgrave Macmillan, 2008).
[30] See further below.
[31] See the seminal work of K. Vogel, "Worldwide vs source taxation of income—a review and re-evaluation of arguments" (1988) *INTERTAX*.

theoretical and conceptual standpoint, that the primary taxing authority should be exercised by the source country.

(b) Fosters international competition: since the costs of production structures, particularly labour costs, vary between countries, except in economic unions where they tend to converge, source-based taxation allows compensatory relief through less burdensome tax systems.

(c) Ease of administration and lower administration costs: the proximity of the source to the taxing state makes tax administration easier. Information exchange requirements are less stringent as it is difficult to extend examination powers beyond the borders of each country.

(d) Incentive to improve the productivity of government expenditure: Vogel has held that source-based taxation provides an incentive to investment in countries where the relation between taxes and public goods is more beneficial to the investor; hence, 'source'-based taxation provides an incentive for government to cut inefficient or low productivity public expenditure.

(e) Eliminates the need for DTCs: from a theoretical and hypothetical framework, it has been argued that, should all countries adopt source-based taxation on an exclusive basis, there would be no need for DTCs because income would be levied only once in the source country."

**16-007**   On the other hand, the main considerations in the discourse with respect to fiscal jurisdiction based on residence have been aptly summarised as follows[32]:

**16-008**   "Advantages:

(a) It adheres, to a greater extent, to the principle of horizontal equity in that it allows the personal circumstances of the taxpayer to be taken into account, and in doing so, it does not hinder the application of tax progressivity.

(b) It neutralises harmful tax competition by "tax havens", that is, low-or zero-tax jurisdictions.

Disadvantages:

(a) It is complex from the tax administration viewpoint. Its widespread application calls for a certain coordination in drafting rules, as well as the exchange of information.

(b) Since countries are not expected to relinquish the simultaneous application of source-based taxation in order to avoid double taxation, DTC or unilateral relief rules become essential.

(c) It ignores the differential cost structure of factors among countries, which tends to neutralise the relative advantages that would derive therefrom.

(d) It overlooks the risks and difficulties faced by investors abroad."

**16-009**   To sum up the case as between the source and residence States—while opinions are to be found entrenched in both quarters—and whereas conceptually the prior authority of the source State is acknowledged—in practice the fiscal authority of the State of residence has prevailed.[33] However, it is maintained "from the point

---

[32] Angel Schindel and Adolfo Atchabahian, "Source and residence: new configuration of their principles", General Report *Cahiers de Droit Fiscal International*, Vol.90a 2005 IFA, p.31.

[33] Schindel and Atchbahian (2005), p.39.

of view of international equity, efficiency, exclusive or predominant taxation at source is shaping up as the most reasonable basis for taxation".[34]

## THE PROBLEM OF DOUBLE TAXATION

Double taxation is defined in the OECD[35] Model Convention as:                **16-010**

". . . the imposition of comparable taxes in two (or more) States on the same taxpayer in respect of the same subject-matter and for identical periods."

In the UN Model Tax Convention[36] it is defined similarly as:

". . . the imposition of similar taxes in two or more States on the same taxpayer in respect of the same base. . .".

In both Model Conventions however double taxation is not defined in the actual Articles or the Commentaries attached to the Articles.[37] It will be observed also that though the OECD and UN definitions are similar, they are not identical in that "similar" arguably has a wider sense than "comparable". Be that as it may, this conception of double taxation is nevertheless considered a description of juridical double taxation in the context of the OECD and UN Model Conventions respectively. Juridical double taxation is to be distinguished from economic double taxation which is much broader in scope. Economic double taxation:

". . . describes the phenomena of an income flow being subjected to more than one charge to tax under the same domestic tax system".[38]

In the OECD Model Convention economic double taxation is described variously as follows[39]:

". . . where two different persons are taxable in respect of same income and capital".

A classic example of the occurrence of economic double taxation is where    **16-011** the profits of a corporate enterprise are subjected to corporation tax, and

---

[34] Schindel and Atchbahian (2005), p.40.
[35] Defined in the Introduction to the OECD Model Tax Convention on Income and on Capital (hereinafter referred to as the OECD Model).
[36] Defined in the Introduction to the UN Model Double Taxation Convention Between Developed and Developing Countries (hereinafter referred to as the UN Model).
[37] See Arnold and McIntyre (2002).
[38] See, for example, J.D.R. Adam and J. Whally, *The International Taxation of Multinational Enterprises* (Associated Business Programmes Ltd, 1977), p.41.
[39] See, for example, Art.1 para.23; Art.9 para.5; Art.10 para.40 and Art.11 para.1 of the OECD Model.

thereafter a dividend distribution to shareholders is made from those taxed profits, and the taxpayer is further subject to income tax on the dividends received. In such circumstances the same income flow would have been the subject of double taxation[40] once at the level of the corporation and on another occasion at the level of the shareholder. This flow of income when it occurs across different jurisdictions, for example dividend flows from a subsidiary to a parent company located in a different jurisdiction and thereafter from the parent company to its shareholders, will result in the same income being subjected to tax on four occasions across two jurisdictions. This international dimension raises the problem of according double taxation relief for the underlying taxation (or indirect tax) accompanying the income flow. It will be noted the scope of juridical double taxation does not cover such underlying double taxation given that there is more than one taxpayer and the taxes are not necessarily the same. The reason why juridical double taxation is not coterminous with economic double taxation is because of the potential open-ended character of what can constitute economic double taxation; along with the policy decision of some States not to accord double taxation for all or certain types of economic double taxation.[41]

The causes of double taxation are varied. They are set however mainly in the differences in the national approaches to taxation. Thus, some States claim full or unlimited tax jurisdiction with respect to all or certain types of income. Such jurisdictions claim to tax on the basis of the residence or nationality of the taxpayer over all the taxpayer's income wherever arising (i.e. residence or worldwide). On the other hand, some States claim a limited jurisdiction taxing only income arising within its territory (source-based jurisdiction). This residence–source conflict is one of the primary causes of double taxation. Although it should be noted that in practice States adopt a mixture of connecting factors to base jurisdiction.[42] Other causes of double taxation rooted in jurisdictional conflicts arise from the differences in the conceptions of the different connecting factors[43] upon which to base taxation.[44] For example there may be different criteria for residence,[45] or conceptions of source[46] or its scope as between different States. Thus, whereas two States may purport to base their jurisdiction to tax on the basis of residence or source, because of different conceptions of residence

---

[40] See Art.10 para.40 of the OECD Model Convention.

[41] See, for example, Arnold and McIntyre (2002), p.30.

[42] See, for example, General Report at p.40.

[43] For example, nationality, residence, domicile, source of income. Connecting factors are the links which form the connection between the taxpayer and the taxing State.

[44] For example, the use by one jurisdiction of residence and worldwide income and the other the source of the income.

[45] For example, in the case of a corporation residence based on incorporation in one jurisdiction and residence based on place of management in another.

[46] For example, source defined in terms of the residence of the debtor in one State and in another in terms of the place of payment of the interest.

or source, both States end up claiming fiscal jurisdiction (i.e. residence–residence or source–source conflicts). Double taxation can also arise as a result of differences other than jurisdictional conflicts *stricto sensu*. For example, as a result of differences in the characterisation of the particular taxable income or gain resulting in conflicting claims to jurisdiction[47]; differences in the characterisation of different taxable entities[48]; differences in the valuation of internationally transacted goods and services as a consequence of transfer pricing practices; differences in interpreting provisions in double taxation agreements; and differences in accounting practices, for example the computation of the taxable base of multinational enterprises through the use of the unitary and separate accounting methods respectively, in different jurisdictions.[49]

## SYSTEMS FOR RELIEVING DOUBLE TAXATION

Systems for the relief of double taxation can be found in a national setting, offered on a unilateral basis; as well as a consequence of bilateral or regional initiatives, founded in international agreements. For example relief for double taxation is accorded on a unilateral basis in the UK to a person resident in the UK for foreign taxes on income and gains, where relief for such double taxation is not covered in an international agreement.[50] Most double taxation relief is however accorded under double taxation agreements (DTA) and is essentially aimed at direct taxes. By the end of 2009 there were some 2,894 double taxation agreements.[51] In 2006 some 39 per cent of the DTA were between developed and developing countries, and 29 per cent among developed countries.[52] According to the OECD there are some 350 double taxation agreements between OECD Member countries and over 1,500 worldwide that are based on the OECD Model Tax Convention.[53]

**16-012**

Most double taxation agreements are either based on the OECD Model

---

[47] For example, characterising a payment in one State as an item of employment income, and in another as an item of royalty.

[48] For example, one State recognising an entity as a partnership and the other not so recognising it.

[49] See, for example, A. H. Qureshi "Unitary taxation and general international law." *Bulletin for International Fiscal Documentation*, Feb. 1987, Vol.41, pp. 56—64 and 88; Reuven S Avi-Yonah, *International Tax as International* Law, (CUP, 2007), pp.102–123; and M. J. McIntyre, "Design of a National Formulary Apportionment Tax System" (1991) in A. H. Qureshi and Xuan Gao (eds) *International Economic Law: Critical Concepts in Law* (Routledge, 2010) Vol.VI.

[50] See INTM161300 & INTM161030—UK residents with foreign income or gains: double taxation relief. See *http://www.hmrc.gov.uk/manuals/intmanual/INTM161030.htm*. (Accessed June 8, 2011).

[51] See UNCTAD, WIR 2010.

[52] See UNCTAD, *International Investment Arrangements: Trends and Emerging Issues* (2006).

[53] *http://www.oecd.org*. (Accessed June 8, 2011).

Tax Convention[54] or the UN Model Double Taxation Convention.[55] However, individual States also have their own model tax conventions, as for instance the United States.[56] Model double taxation conventions are not themselves international agreements but rather provide a basis or model for the negotiation of an actual agreement. Where States have their own model, in effect this is a declaration in advance of the terms upon which they would negotiate a double taxation agreement. On the other hand some States prefer not to disclose their hand in advance in the negotiations and therefore do not have individual model conventions.

Given the fact that a double taxation agreement involves the allocation of fiscal jurisdiction as between States, as this is a manner of avoiding conflicts of jurisdictional claims, the orientation of a double taxation model will be informed by the nature of the flow of income and capital across respective jurisdictions. Thus, since developing countries at any rate traditionally have generally been importers of investment flows, the orientation of a double taxation agreement that would best suit them would be one which favours more source country jurisdiction. On the other hand, capital exporting countries prefer to base their jurisdiction on residence so as to be able to claw back the capital export flows from their jurisdictions. This classical divide between capital exporting and importing countries however has been impacted upon by globalisation such that the picture is more one of countries having differing hybrid flows.[57] The UN and OECD Model tax conventions reflect generally a source and residence orientation respectively. The UN Model has been negotiated under the auspices of the United Nations and is a model designed for double taxation agreements as between developing and developed States. On the other hand the OECD Model primarily was intended to reflect the interests of developed States and therefore forms the basis for an agreement as between developed States. However, the UN Model in large part is itself modelled on the OECD Model and it is estimated that some 90 per cent of its text is based on the OECD Model.[58]

**16-013**    Both models, although primarily focused on relieving double taxation, touch upon other aspects of international taxation, for example, discriminatory taxation and exchange of information. It needs to be noted though that in this respect the OECD Model is much more open in its scope. In fact, the OECD Model has been very much in the lead in the development of international fiscal law generally, as well as particularly in adapting methods of relieving double taxation to the exigencies of globalisation and modern developments in technology and communications.

Broadly, the structure of agreements based on both the OECD and UN

---

[54] *http://www.oecd.org/dataoecd/25/24/47213736.pdf.* (Accessed June 8, 2011).
[55] *http://unpan1.un.org/intradoc/groups/public/documents/un/unpan002084.pdf.* (Accessed June 8, 2011).
[56] United States Model Income Tax Convention of November 15, 2006.
[57] See, for example, Schindel and Atchabahian (2005), p.25.
[58] Tax Sparing; A Reconsideration (OECD, 1998).

Model is the same. The double taxation agreements apply to persons "resident" in one or both of the Contracting States.[59] "Residence" is defined with reference to the domestic law of the Contracting State.[60] The taxes for which double taxation relief is available are income and capital taxes.[61] Double taxation relief does not cover other taxes, for example, indirect taxes or inheritance tax.

## METHODS OF RELIEVING DOUBLE TAXATION

There are generally four main methods of relieving double taxation that may     **16-014**
be accorded unilaterally or through agreement. In practice a combination of these methods may be availed of. In the case of double taxation agreements, in the first instance the general approach is to co-ordinate the allocation of fiscal jurisdiction between the source and the residence States as a way of avoiding or reducing conflicts of fiscal jurisdiction. This co-ordination is accompanied further by the application of either the credit or the exemption methods of relieving double taxation.

### Allocating jurisdiction

The allocation of jurisdiction to tax to the various items of income and gains     **16-015**
as between source and residence States respectively is negotiated through double taxation agreements. This is the general approach adopted in most double taxation agreements to eliminate or reduce double taxation. In practice, some items of income, however, are more conveniently taxed either in the residence State or the source State. Jurisdiction is allocated either to the exclusive jurisdiction of the source or the residence State. Prime examples of exclusive source jurisdiction are income from immovable property[62]; and the business profits of a Permanent Enterprise[63] located in the source State. The Models use the concept of Permanent Establishment[64] which essentially establishes the level of necessary presence in the source State so as to establish source State jurisdiction. Thus, the branch of an enterprise in a resident State that is located in a source State is considered to be a Permanent Establishment. A good example of exclusive residence State jurisdiction is the business profits of a resident enterprise.[65] Where, however, the jurisdiction negotiated is not exclusive to either, in other words where there is concurrent

---

[59] See Arts 1 of the OECD Model and UN Model respectively.
[60] See Arts 4 of the OECD and UN Model Conventions respectively.
[61] See Arts 2 of the OECD and UN Model Conventions respectively.
[62] See Arts 6 of the UN and OECD Models respectively.
[63] See Arts 7 and 5 of the UN and OECD Models respectively.
[64] See, for example, J. Sasseville & A.A. Skaar, *Is there a Permanent Establishment?* General Report, *Cahiers de Droit Fiscal International*, 94a (2009).
[65] See Arts 7 of the OECD and UN Models respectively.

jurisdiction, in those circumstances, the amount of tax that the source State can tax is limited. For example in the case of dividends and interest payments from a source country to persons in the resident State there is a limit to the tax (withholding tax) that the source country can levy on the dividends and interest payments made to persons in the resident State.[66] Where the items of income are not specifically allocated to any jurisdiction the resident State has jurisdiction in a sense almost by default.[67]

To relieve double taxation and also to deal with tax evasion, the Models co-ordinate the manner in which the prices of goods and services as between related parties across different jurisdictions are calculated, as well as attribute appropriate profits as between related parties across different jurisdictions. This is done through the adoption of the arm's length principle wherein transactions as between related parties are evaluated in accordance with the manner in which independent parties in the same circumstances would engage in those transactions.[68] In other words, the market price is used by relevant taxing authorities to determine the value of the transactions as between related parties in the different jurisdictions. In addition, anti-tax avoidance provisions are to be found scattered in other provisions. One particular mechanism is to ensure that the recipient of a particular payment is actually the beneficial owner.[69]

**Extracted from OECD Model Tax Convention:**

**Article—5 PERMANENT ESTABLISHMENT**[70]

**16-016**

1. For the purposes of this Convention, the term 'permanent establishment' means a fixed place of business through which the business of an enterprise is wholly or partly carried on.

2. The term 'permanent establishment' includes especially:

    *a)* a place of management;

    *b)* a branch;

    *c)* an office;

    *d)* a factory;

    *e)* a workshop, and

    *f)* a mine, an oil or gas well, a quarry or any other place of extraction of natural resources.

3. A building site or construction or installation project constitutes a permanent establishment only if it lasts more than twelve months.

---

[66] See Arts 10 and 11 of the OECD and UN Models respectively.
[67] See Arts 21 of the OECD and UN Models respectively.
[68] See Arts 7 and 9 of the OECD and UN Models respectively. See also the Transfer Pricing Guidelines (1995 as updated).
[69] See, for example, Arts 10, 11 and 12 of the OECD and UN Models respectively.
[70] Source: *http://www.oecd.org*. (Accessed June 8, 2011).

4. Notwithstanding the preceding provisions of this Article, the term 'permanent establishment' shall be deemed not to include:

   *a)* the use of facilities solely for the purpose of storage, display or delivery of goods or merchandise belonging to the enterprise;

   *b)* the maintenance of a stock of goods or merchandise belonging to the enterprise solely for the purpose of storage, display or delivery;

   *c)* the maintenance of a stock of goods or merchandise belonging to the enterprise solely for the purpose of processing by another enterprise;

   *d)* the maintenance of a fixed place of business solely for the purpose of purchasing goods or merchandise or of collecting information, for the enterprise;

   *e)* the maintenance of a fixed place of business solely for the purpose of carrying on, for the enterprise, any other activity of a preparatory or auxiliary character;

   *f)* the maintenance of a fixed place of business solely for any combination of activities mentioned in subparagraphs *a)* to *e)*, provided that the overall activity of the fixed place of business resulting from this combination is of a preparatory or auxiliary character.

5. Notwithstanding the provisions of paragraphs 1 and 2, where a person —other than an agent of an independent status to whom paragraph 6 applies—is acting on behalf of an enterprise and has, and habitually exercises, in a Contracting State an authority to conclude contracts in the name of the enterprise, that enterprise shall be deemed to have a permanent establishment in that State in respect of any activities which that person undertakes for the enterprise, unless the activities of such person are limited to those mentioned in paragraph 4 which, if exercised through a fixed place of business, would not make this fixed place of business a permanent establishment under the provisions of that paragraph.

6. An enterprise shall not be deemed to have a permanent establishment in a Contracting State merely because it carries on business in that State wwthrough a broker,general commission agent or any other agent of an independent status, provided that such persons are acting in the ordinary course of their business.

7. The fact that a company which is a resident of a Contracting State controls or is controlled by a company which is a resident of the other Contracting State, or which carries on business in that other State (whether through a permanent establishment or otherwise), shall not of itself constitute either company a permanent establishment of the other.[71]

## Article—7 BUSINESS PROFITS

1. Profits of an enterprise of a Contracting State shall be taxable only in that State unless the enterprise carries on business in the other Contracting State through a permanent establishment situated therein.

**16-017**

[71] Extracted from OECD Model Tax Convention.

If the enterprise carries on business as aforesaid, the profits that are attributable to the permanent establishment in accordance with the provisions of paragraph 2 may be taxed in that other State.

2. For the purposes of this Article and Article [23A] [23B], the profits that are attributable in each Contracting State to the permanent establishment referred to in paragraph 1 are the profits it might be expected to make, in particular in its dealings with other parts of the enterprise, if it were a separate and independent enterprise engaged in the same or similar activities under the same or similar conditions, taking into account the functions performed, assets used and risks assumed by the enterprise through the permanent establishment and through the other parts of the enterprise.

3. Where, in accordance with paragraph 2, a Contracting State adjusts the profits that are attributable to a permanent establishment of an enterprise of one of the Contracting States and taxes accordingly profits of the enterprise that have been charged to tax in the other State, the other State shall, to the extent necessary to eliminate double taxation on these profits, make an appropriate adjustment to the amount of the tax charged on those profits. In determining such adjustment, the competent authorities of the Contracting States shall if necessary consult each other.

4. Where profits include items of income which are dealt with separately in other Articles of this Convention, then the provisions of those Articles shall not be affected by the provisions of this Article.[72]

## Article—9 ASSOCIATED ENTERPRISES

**16-018**    Where

*a)* an enterprise of a Contracting State participates directly or indirectly in the management, control or capital of an enterprise of the other Contracting State, or

*b)* the same persons participate directly or indirectly in the management, control or capital of an enterprise of a Contracting State and an enterprise of the other Contracting State, and in either case conditions are made or imposed between the two enterprises in their commercial or financial relations which differ from those which would be made between independent enterprises, then any profits which would, but for those conditions, have accrued to one of the enterprises, but, by reason of those conditions, have not so accrued, may be included in the profits of that enterprise and taxed accordingly.

2. Where a Contracting State includes in the profits of an enterprise of that State—and taxes accordingly—profits on which an enterprise of the other Contracting State has been charged to tax in that other State and the profits so included are profits which would have accrued to the enterprise of the first-mentioned State if the conditions made between the two enterprises had been those which would have been made between independent enterprises, then that other State shall make an appropriate adjustment to the amount of the tax charged therein on those profits. In determining such adjustment, due regard shall be had to the other

---

[72] Extracted from OECD Model Tax Convention.

provisions of this Convention and the competent authorities of the Contracting States shall if necessary consult each other.

## Article—10 DIVIDENDS

1. Dividends paid by a company which is a resident of a Contracting State to a resident of the other Contracting State may be taxed in that other State.

**16-019**

2. However, such dividends may also be taxed in the Contracting State of which the company paying the dividends is a resident and according to the laws of that State, but if the beneficial owner of the dividends is a resident of the other Contracting State, the tax so charged shall not exceed:

   *a)* 5 per cent of the gross amount of the dividends if the beneficial owner is a company (other than a partnership) which holds directly at least 25 per cent of the capital of the company paying the dividends;

   *b)* 15 per cent of the gross amount of the dividends in all other cases.

   The competent authorities of the Contracting States shall by mutual agreement settle the mode of application of these limitations. This paragraph shall not affect the taxation of the company in respect of the profits out of which the dividends are paid.

3. The term 'dividends' as used in this Article means income from shares, 'jouissance' shares or 'jouissance' rights, mining shares, founders' shares or other rights, not being debt-claims, participating in profits, as well as income from other corporate rights which is subjected to the same taxation treatment as income from shares by the laws of the State of which the company making the distribution is a resident.

4. The provisions of paragraphs 1 and 2 shall not apply if the beneficial owner of the dividends, being a resident of a Contracting State, carries on business in the other Contracting State of which the company paying the dividends is a resident through a permanent establishment situated therein and the holding in respect of which the dividends are paid is effectively connected with such permanent establishment. In such case the provisions of Article 7 shall apply.

5. Where a company which is a resident of a Contracting State derives profits or income from the other Contracting State, that other State may not impose any tax on the dividends paid by the company, except insofar as such dividends are paid to a resident of that other State or insofar as the holding in respect of which the dividends are paid is effectively connected with a permanent establishment situated in that other State, nor subject the company's undistributed profits to a tax on the company's undistributed profits, even if the dividends paid or the undistributed profits consist wholly or partly of profits or income arising in such other State.

## Article—11 INTEREST

1. Interest arising in a Contracting State and paid to a resident of the other Contracting State may be taxed in that other State.

**16-020**

2. However, such interest may also be taxed in the Contracting State in

which it arises and according to the laws of that State, but if the beneficial owner of the interest is a resident of the other Contracting State, the tax so charged shall not exceed 10 per cent of the gross amount of the interest. The competent authorities of the Contracting States shall by mutual agreement settle the mode of application of this limitation.

3. The term 'interest' as used in this Article means income from debt-claims of every kind, whether or not secured by mortgage and whether or not carrying a right to participate in the debtor's profits, and in particular, income from government securities and income from bonds or debentures, including premiums and prizes attaching to such securities, bonds or debentures. Penalty charges for late payment shall not be regarded as interest for the purpose of this Article.

4. The provisions of paragraphs 1 and 2 shall not apply if the beneficial owner of the interest, being a resident of a Contracting State, carries on business in the other Contracting State in which the interest arises through a permanent establishment situated therein and the debt-claim in respect of which the interest is paid is effectively connected with such permanent establishment. In such case the provisions of Article 7 shall apply.

5. Interest shall be deemed to arise in a Contracting State when the payer is a resident of that State. Where, however, the person paying the interest, whether he is a resident of a Contracting State or not, has in a Contracting State a permanent establishment in connection with which the indebtedness on which the interest is paid was incurred, and such interest is borne by such permanent establishment, then such interest shall be deemed to arise in the State in which the permanent establishment is situated.

6. Where, by reason of a special relationship between the payer and the beneficial owner or between both of them and some other person, the amount of the interest, having regard to the debt-claim for which it is paid, exceeds the amount which would have been agreed upon by the payer and the beneficial owner in the absence of such relationship, the provisions of this Article shall apply only to the last-mentioned amount. In such case, the excess part of the payments shall remain taxable according to the laws of each Contracting State, due regard being had to the other provisions of this Convention.

### Article—12 ROYALTIES

16-021

1. Royalties arising in a Contracting State and beneficially owned by a resident of the other Contracting State shall be taxable only in that other State.

2. The term 'royalties' as used in this Article means payments of any kind received as a consideration for the use of, or the right to use, any copyright of literary, artistic or scientific work including cinematograph films, any patent, trade mark, design or model, plan, secret formula or process, or for information concerning industrial, commercial or scientific experience.

3. The provisions of paragraph 1 shall not apply if the beneficial owner of the royalties, being a resident of a Contracting State, carries on business in the other Contracting State in which the royalties arise through a permanent establishment situated therein and the right or property in

respect of which the royalties are paid is effectively connected with such permanent establishment. In such case the provisions of Article 7 shall apply.

4. Where, by reason of a special relationship between the payer and the beneficial owner or between both of them and some other person, the amount of the royalties, having regard to the use, right or information for which they are paid, exceeds the amount which would have been agreed upon by the payer and the beneficial owner in the absence of such relationship, the provisions of this Article shall apply only to the last-mentioned amount. In such case, the excess part of the payments shall remain taxable according to the laws of each Contracting State, due regard being had to the other provisions of this Convention.

Relief from double taxation through the allocation of fiscal jurisdiction is further co-ordinated and reinforced by requiring the residence State to accord relief through either the credit or the exemption methods where the State of source has exclusive or limited jurisdiction.

## Credit Method

In the credit method tax due in one State can be offset by tax paid by the same taxpayer on the same income or gain in the other State. Thus, normally the State of residence would give a tax credit against tax due for the tax paid in the source State on the foreign source income or gain. There are two versions of the credit method: credit with limit (ordinary credit) and full credit. The credit with limit affords a credit only up to the amount of taxation on the foreign source income or gain, which would otherwise be taxable in the "residence" State giving the tax credit. So no refund of tax is given, and the credit cannot be offset against other taxes due[73]; although some States allow for the credit to be carried forward and back.[74] In the circumstances, the foreign source income or gain bears an effective tax rate that is the higher as between the foreign and domestic tax rates.[75]

**16-022**

### ARTICLE—23 B CREDIT METHOD[76]

1. Where a resident of a Contracting State derives income or owns capital which, in accordance with the provisions of this Convention, may be taxed in the other Contracting State, the first-mentioned State shall allow:

   *a)* as a deduction from the tax on the income of that resident, an amount equal to the income tax paid in that other State;

   *b)* as a deduction from the tax on the capital of that resident, an amount equal to the capital tax paid in that other State.

**16-023**

---

[73] See, for example, Arnold and McIntyre (2002), p.36.
[74] Rohatgi (2005), p.210.
[75] Rohatgi (2005), p.210.
[76] Source: *http://www.oecd.org*. (Accessed June 8, 2011).

> Such deduction in either case shall not, however, exceed that part of the income tax or capital tax, as computed before the deduction is given, which is attributable, as the case may be, to the income or the capital which may be taxed in that other State.
>
> 2. Where in accordance with any provision of the Convention income derived or capital owned by a resident of a Contracting State is exempt from tax in that State, such State may nevertheless, in calculating the amount of tax on the remaining income or capital of such resident, take into account the exempted income or capital.[77]

**16-024**　In practice, most developed States, particularly common law countries,[78] use the ordinary credit method. The credit method is said to conform to capital export neutrality, as it is neutral in terms of the decision to invest within or outside the State. However, its operation is accompanied by a number of compliance and administrative issues. These have been summarised as follows:

> - What foreign taxes are creditable?
>
> - How should the limitations on the credit be calculated? On a source-by-source or item-by-item basis? On a country-by-country basis? Or on an overall basis, with various special rules applicable to certain types of income? Or some combination of these methods?
>
> - What rules should be adopted for determining the source of income and deductions?
>
> - Should a credit be allowed for the underlying foreign taxes paid by a foreign affiliate on its income out of which it pays dividend?[79]

### Credit Method and Tax Sparing

One specific concern from a development perspective relates to the fact that the credit method can undermine the efforts of developing countries in attracting foreign investment through tax incentives. Under the credit method the tax reductions given in the source developing country can result in a commensurate increase in the tax revenue share of the residence developed State. So as not to undermine the tax incentives accorded by other States, in particular developing countries in pursuit of their development objectives, a practice has developed among some States of establishing a tax-sparing mechanism, either unilaterally or on a bilateral basis.

> "Most Member countries have traditionally viewed tax sparing as part of the foreign aid policy and granted it with a view to promoting industrial, commercial, scientific, or other development in developing countries. Some

---

[77] Extracted from OECD Model Tax Convention. Article 23A of the UN Model is the same.
[78] Rohatgi (2005), p.209.
[79] Reprinted with the permission of Wolters Kluwer Law of Business, from Arnold and McIntyre, *International Tax Primer*, 2nd edn, p.38 (2002).

Member countries have granted tax sparing as a matter of tax policy. This policy has partly been prompted by a fear that a consistent application of the credit method would put their resident investors at a competitive disadvantage compared to local or other foreign investors able to fully benefit from tax incentives in the host country."[80]

Tax sparing involves "constructing" a phantom payment of tax in the developing or source State, in circumstances where it has actually not been paid as a consequence of a tax reduction or incentive. This deemed payment of tax in the source State would be constructed on the basis of what would normally have been taxed were it not for the tax incentive or reduction in order to attract investment.

**EXAMPLE[81]**

Company A that is a resident of country X establishes subsidiary S in country Y. S derives 100 in net income during its first year of operation. The income tax rate in country Y is 30 per cent. Because of applicable tax incentive legislation in country Y, S pays no income tax during the first five years of operation. Accordingly, the taxes spared in year 1 by S in country Y amount to 30.

In year 2, S pays 50 of its net income in dividends to A in country X. The corporate income tax rate in country X is 40 per cent. There is no tax at source on outward dividends in country Y. Country X taxes foreign dividends at the full corporate income tax rate, but allows a credit for foreign taxes paid, including corporate income tax paid by foreign subsidiaries on income out of which the dividends are paid (the "underlying tax" on the income distributed). Since no tax has been levied in country Y on the distributed income, A will pay 20 in corporate income tax on the dividends in country X (40 per cent out of 50).

However, if the effective tax in country Y was not zero, for example because of a withholding tax of 15 per cent, A will pay 12.50 in corporate income tax on the dividends in country X (25 per cent out of 50)."

**16-026**

**OECD[82]**

"In the case of a credit country, tax sparing provisions basically enable the investor to obtain a foreign tax credit for the taxes that have been 'spared' (*i.e.* not actually paid) under the incentive regime of the source country."

**Example of a tax sparing provision: Pakistan–US (1957)—Article XV**

"For the purposes of this credit there shall be deemed to have been paid by a United States domestic corporation the amount by which such Pakistan taxes (other than the business profits tax) have been reduced under the provisions of section 15B of the Income Tax Act, 1922 (XI of 1922) as in effect on the date of the signature of the present Convention: . . .

(Not ratified by the US because of US Senate rejection of this tax sparing provision.)

---

[80] Tax Sparing; A Reconsideration (OCED, 1998), *http:// www.oecd.org*. (Accessed June 8 2011).
[81] Tax Sparing; A Reconsideration (OECD, 1998), *http:// www.oecd.org*. (Accessed June 8 2011).
[82] Tax Sparing; A Reconsideration (OECD, 1998), *http:// www.oecd.org*. (Accessed June 8 2011).

**16-027**    Tax-sparing provisions have been in existence for some four decades in the bilateral treaty practice of States,[83] and can vary, for example, according to the category of tax payer, the income in question, the deemed paid tax, and the type of countries eligible.[84] In some cases the tax-sparing provisions are accompanied by anti-abuse provisions. However, among developed States the United States has been consistent in not according tax sparing.[85]

The general view among OECD members is that "the provisions of tax sparing in treaties is not an effective way to provide foreign investment and to promote national economic goals".[86] Several reasons for this position have been advanced.[87] First to note is the drain on the economy of the resident or tax-sparing State. This has increased in the light of globalisation and the consequent increased cross-border flows. Tax sparing was developed at a time when cross-border flows were not substantial and restricted. Second, affording direct financial aid is relatively more transparent than the tax-sparing mechanism. Thus, it is not possible to accurately quantify the value of tax sparing as compared with direct aid. Further, direct aid carries with it the advantage that it can be accompanied with conditions, and the donor can influence what it is spent on. Third, tax sparing can unduly encourage investors to repatriate their profits from developing or source countries to take advantage of all the tax sparing in the residence State. Fourth, it does not necessarily follow that the credit or tax incentive matrix results in an increase in the revenue of the residence State. This is because there may not be any tax due in the country of residence or one that would occur in the future only. Moreover, not according tax sparing does not undermine the force of attraction for the investment of the tax reduction.

> "Investment decisions taken by international investors resident in credit countries are rarely dependent on or even influenced by the existence or absence of tax sparing provisions in treaties."[88]

**16-028**    Fifth, tax sparing results in complex legislation and administration. Finally, there are several difficulties with the very practice of tax incentives to induce investment flows. First, it appears generally accepted that tax inducements are not an effective mechanism for attracting investment. Indeed, they distort investment and can attract the wrong kind of inward flow of capital or foot-loose investment. Moreover, the practice of

---

[83]  Tax Sparing; A Reconsideration (OECD, 1998).
[84]  Tax Sparing; A Reconsideration (OECD, 1998).
[85]  Tax Sparing; A Reconsideration (OECD, 1998).
[86]  Tax Sparing; A Reconsideration (OECD, 1998).
[87]  See Tax Sparing; A Reconsideration (OECD, 1998).
[88]  Tax Sparing; A Reconsideration (OECD, 1998), *http:// www.oecd.org*. (Accessed June 8, 2011).

tax incentives induces tax competition among States. Thus, Arnold and McIntyre observe[89]:

"The general conclusion to be drawn from the voluminous tax literature dealing with tax incentives is that the costs of tax incentives are typically large, the benefits are always uncertain, and only rarely to the potential benefits justify the likely costs."

Second, tax incentives encourage lobbying in other sectors not covered by the tax incentives for similar treatment. Third, the tax sparing/tax incentives matrix leads to tax planning to take advantage of the incentives, as well as the tax sparing—through the use of conduit entities and shopping into the right double taxation agreement. For example, tax sparing provides an incentive for affiliated companies to engage in transfer pricing—in particular shifting profits into the developing or source State to benefit from the tax incentive while also having a presence in the residence State to take advantage of the tax sparing. Finally, tax sparing provides incentives for residence States to maintain high rates of tax so as to facilitate an increased tax-sparing credit benefit for residence investors investing abroad. Equally, the lack of tax sparing can induce higher taxes in the developing or source State.

**Exemption Method**

In this case the taxpayer is exempt from taxation from either the source or the residence State completely. Thus the exemption method can either be on an origin or destination basis—where origin refers to exemption in the State of source of income or gain, and "destination" refers to exemption in the residence of tax payer. However, normally under the exemption method the residence State exempts from taxation the foreign source income or gain. Thus the fiscal jurisdiction of the source State is maintained. The exemption method involves the territorial principle of taxation, as it entails recognition of the exclusive fiscal competence of the source State.[90] With the exemption method the problems associated with the application of the credit method with respect to tax incentives do not occur. Moreover, as it is consistent with the integrity of the source basis of taxation, from the viewpoint of appropriateness of fiscal jurisdiction, it has many positive attributes. However, in practice very few States adhere to it in full—one example is Hong Kong.[91] In practice the exemption method is confined to particular types of income or gain, for example business income.[92]

The exemption method comes mainly in two forms: (1) the full exemption,

**16-029**

---

[89]  Tax Sparing; A Reconsideration (OECD, 1998), p.52.
[90]  See, for example, General Report at p.43.
[91]  See Arnold and McIntyre (2002), p.33.
[92]  See Arnold and McIntyre (2002), p.33.

where the foreign source income or gain is fully exempt from residence tax; and (2) the exemption with progression method. In some States, however, the exemption is only available with respect to foreign income or gain that is subject to tax at a comparable rate.[93] Under the exemption with progression, the foreign sourced income or gain is added on to the income or gain in the residence State, in order to determine the applicable rate of tax to the residence State income or gain. The foreign source income or gain is not however the subject of taxation.

### ARTICLE—23 A EXEMPTION METHOD

1. Where a resident of a Contracting State derives income or owns capital which, in accordance with the provisions of this Convention, may be taxed in the other Contracting State, the first- mentioned State shall, subject to the provisions of paragraphs 2 and 3, exempt such income or capital from tax.

2. Where a resident of a Contracting State derives items of income which, in accordance with the provisions of Articles 10 and 11, may be taxed in the other Contracting State, the first-mentioned State shall allow as a deduction from the tax on the income of that resident an amount equal to the tax paid in that other State. Such deduction shall not, however, exceed that part of the tax, as computed before the deduction is given, which is attributable to such items of income derived from that other State.

3. Where in accordance with any provision of the Convention income derived or capital owned by a resident of a Contracting State is exempt from tax in that State, such State may nevertheless, in calculating the amount of tax on the remaining income or capital of such resident, take into account the exempted income or capital.

4. The provisions of paragraph 1 shall not apply to income derived or capital owned by a resident of a Contracting State where the other Contracting State applies the provisions of this Convention to exempt such income or capital from tax or applies the provisions of paragraph 2 of Article 10 or 11 to such income.[94]

16-030    Generally, the exemption method is simpler to administer and successfully eliminates double taxation that arises as a consequence of source–residence conflict.[95] However, it is contrary to the principle of CEN, in that where the foreign source income taxation is lower, resident investors who invest abroad as opposed to within the territory are favoured. Normally, the exemption method is preferred by civil law systems, and by countries[96] which favour a

---

[93] See, for example, Rohatgi (2005), p.209.
[94] Extracted from OECD Model Tax Convention. Article 23 A of the UN Model is similar. However, its para.2 has no reference to Art.10, and there is no para.4.
[95] Arnold and McIntyre (2002), p.34.
[96] See, for example, Rohatgi (2005), p.209.

territorial system of taxation. Generally, in theory the exemption method is highly regarded.[97]

Both the UN and the OECD Models make optional the availability of the exemption and the credit methods. This option is available to the resident contracting State. Both prescribe the ordinary credit method and also allow for the use of the exemption with progression.

### Deduction Method

Finally, to complete the picture the deduction method of relieving double tax- **16-031** ation needs to be noted—although it is not a method for relieving double taxation that is endorsed in either the OECD or the UN Models. This is because it is considered to be the least effective in relieving double taxation, as compared to the credit and exemption methods. Moreover, it is not neutral in terms of investment decisions, as it favours domestic investment thus undermining the principle of CEN.[98] The use of the deduction method results in the application of a combined rate higher than that applied to the domestic source income or gain.[99] Under the deduction method the foreign tax paid is allowed as a deduction from the taxable profits of the residence State. In the credit method the foreign tax is credited against the tax due in the residence State. Generally the method is used by some States in a limited form as an option where the standard forms of relieving double taxation are not available.[100]

### ENFORCEMENT OF DOUBLE TAXATION RELIEF AND CO-OPERATION IN FISCAL MATTERS

Enforcement of double taxation relief and co-operation between tax authori- **16-032** ties generally are intertwined in double taxation agreements. Double taxation agreements serve both to relieve double taxation and provide a medium for tax authorities for co-operation with respect to both domestic tax issues as well as international tax matters. In particular, the agreements provide co-operative measures to address tax evasion. In this context the following questions are of particular note:

- How double taxation agreements are interpreted?

- What dispute settlement mechanisms are available?

- How do tax authorities exchange information about tax payers?

[97] See General Report at p.43.
[98] See, for example, Arnold and MacIntyre (2002), p.32.
[99] See, for example, Arnold and MacIntyre (2002), p.32.
[100] See, for example, Arnold and MacIntyre (2002), p.32.

- What mechanisms are available to assist in the recovery of tax owed by a taxpayer in another jurisdiction?

### Interpreting double taxation agreements

16-033    Double taxation agreements are international agreements. Therefore Arts 31–33 of the Vienna Convention on the Law of Treaties 1969 (VC) apply. The double taxation agreements contain a general definition provision.[101] However, since a general definition provision cannot possibly define all terms, the agreements specifically contain a reference mechanism to the domestic law of the Contracting State, for the interpretation of terms not found expressly defined in the agreement.[102] This provision is not transparent as to the particular Contracting State whose domestic law is to inform the interpretation.

> "2. As regards the application of the Convention at any time by a Contracting State, any term not defined therein shall, unless the context otherwise requires, have the meaning that it has at that time under the law of that State for the purposes of the taxes to which the Convention applies, any meaning under the applicable tax laws of that State prevailing over a meaning given to the term under other laws of that State."[103]

In addition, both Models are accompanied by extensive Commentary. The Commentary is specifically intended to assist in the interpretation of the provisions of the text of the Models.[104] Since the OECD Model Commentary is constantly being revised the question is posed as to whether later changes to commentary inform double taxation agreements agreed to prior to the changes. The OECD Model in this respect specifically makes clear those later changes to Commentary inform also pre-dated double taxation agreements. There has been extensive analysis of the problems of interpreting double taxation agreements—including the vexed question as to how the Commentary fits into the scheme of Arts 31–32 of the VC.[105]

---

[101]  See Arts 3 of the OECD and the UN Models respectively.
[102]  See Arts 3(2) of the OECD and UN Models respectively.
[103]  Source: OECD Model Tax Convention.
[104]  OECD Model Introduction para.33.
[105]  See, for example, IFA, "The interpretation of double taxation conventions" (1960) 42 *Cahier de Droit Fiscal International*; A.F. Jones et al., "The interpretation of tax treaties with particular reference to article 3(2) of the OECD Model" (1984) B.T.R. 14, 90, 545; K. Vogel, "Double Tax Treaties and Their Interpretation" (1986) 4 *International Tax and Business Lawyer*, 4; IFA, "Interpretation of tax treaties" (1986) B.I.F.D. 75; "IFA Interpretation of double taxation conventions" in *Cahiers de Fiscal International* (Deventer, Kluwer, 1993) Vol.LXXVIIIA; A. Jones and F. John "Qualification conflicts: The meaning in article 3(2) of the OECD Model" in H. Bersse, *Festschrift fur Karl Beusch* (1993), ss. 43–62; H.J. Ault, "The role of the OECD commentaries in the interpretation of tax treaties" in H.H. Alpert and K.V. Raad, *Essays on International Taxation* (Kluwer Law International, 1993), p.61; P. Van Raad, "Interpretation & Application of Tax Treaties by Tax Courts" (1996) 36 *European Taxation* 3; K. Vogel, "The influence of the OECD Commentaries on Treaty Interpretation" (2000) 54(12) B.I.F.D. (and M.J. Ellis in same volume); F. Englen,

### International tax disputes: Mutual Agreement Procedure

Disputes as between the taxpayer and a tax authority (known as the **16-034** Competent Authority (CA)) and as between Competent Authorities, with respect to the double taxation agreement, are decided through a dispute settlement system known as the Mutual Agreement Procedure (MAP).[106] There are a number of problems with the MAP. The main weakness of the system however is that it does not impose any obligation on the part of the CA to resolve the dispute. Moreover, the taxpayer has limited rights under the procedure, for example, no participatory rights in the proceedings. There is also no appeal process. In 2008, in response to some of the criticisms of the MAP,[107] the OECD included an arbitration facility integral to the MAP system with respect to unresolved issues between the Competent Authorities.

The OECD has also now compiled statistics of the user of MAP in OECD countries, as well as non-OECD countries willing to participate in the provision of statistics, of cases under MAP.[108] Accordingly, in 2009 there were some 3,219 MAP cases in OECD countries in contrast to some 2,352 cases

"Interpretation of Tax Treaties Under International Law" (2004) 7 B.I.F.D; D. Ward, "The role of the Commentaries on the OECD Model in the Tax Treaty Interpretation Process" (2006) 3 *Bulletin for International Taxation* 97–102 (see also Response by Prof M.J. Ellis, pp.103–4); H. Pijit, "The OECD Commentary as a Source of International Law and the role of the judiciary" (2006) 5 *European Taxation* 216–24; M.N. Kandev, 'Tax treaty interpretation: determining domestic meaning under article 3(2) of the OECD Model' in *Canadian tax journal = Revue fiscale canadienne*. Toronto. Vol.55 (2007), no.1; pp.31–71; J.A. Becerra, *Interpretation and application of tax treaties in North America*, (Amsterdam, I.B.F.D., 2007); S. Douma & F. Engelin (eds) *The legal status of the OECD Commentaries* (Amsterdam, I.B.F.D., 2008); M. Schilcher, & P. Weninger, (eds), *Fundamental issues and practical problems in tax treaty interpretation* (Wien, Linde, 2008); E. Baistrocchi, "The use and interpretation of tax treaties in the emerging world: theory and implications", *British Tax Review*. London. (2008), no.4; pp.352–39.1; B.J. Arnold, "The interpretation of tax treaties: myth and reality", *Bulletin for International Taxation*. Amsterdam. Vol.64 (2010), no.1; pp.2–15; A. Ward, "The use of OEEC–OECD historical documents in interpreting tax treaties", P. Baker et al. (eds) *Tax polymath: a life in international taxation: essays in honour of John F. Avery Jones*. (Amsterdam, I.B.F.D., 2010), pp.3–18.

[106] See Arts 25 of the OECD and UN Models respectively. Avery-Jones, "The legal nature of the Mutual Agreement Procedure under the OECD Model Convention" (1979) B.T.R. 333; (1980) B.T.R. 21; IFA, *Mutual Agreement Procedure and Practice* (Deventer, Kluwer, 1981) 66 *Cahier de Droit Fiscal International*; Z.D. Altman, *Dispute Resolution under Tax Treaties IBFD Doctoral Series* Vol.11 (2006); *Improving the Resolution of Tax Treaty Disputes* (OECD, 2007); OECD: *Manual on Effective Mutual Agreement Procedures (MEMAP)*; C. Burnett, "International tax arbitration", *Australian tax review*. Pyrmont. Vol.36 (2007), no.3; pp.173–190; H.J. Ault, & J. Sasseville, "2008 OECD Model: the new arbitration provision" *Bulletin for international taxation*. Amsterdam. Vol.63 (2009), no.5/6; pp.208–215; L. Loureiro, Nobrega e Silva "Mutual agreement procedure: preventing the compulsory jurisdiction of the international Court of Justice?" *INTERTAX*. Alphen aan den Rijn. Vol.37 (2009), no.10; pp.529–544 "Mutual agreement procedure: preventing the compulsory jurisdiction of the international Court of Justice?" *INTERTAX*. Alphen aan den Rijn. Vol.37 (2009), no.10; pp.529–544.

[107] OECD: *improving the resolution of tax treaty disputes* (2007).

[108] See OECD: *Country Mutual Agreement Procedure Statistics* at *www.oecd.org*. (Accessed June 8, 2011).

in 2006. The highest number of cases in 2009 under the MAP involved the United States with some 724 cases, followed by Germany (543), Belgium (265), France (233), Canada (206), Switzerland (143) and the UK and Austria (120 respectively). Although there is an overall rise in cases between 2006 and 2009 in the OECD countries, in some countries the number of cases during the period has been stable. The rise has been particularly pronounced in the cases of the United States, Switzerland and Belgium.

## ARTICLE—25 MUTUAL AGREEMENT PROCEDURE[109]

**16-035**

1. Where a person considers that the actions of one or both of the Contracting States result or will result for him in taxation not in accordance with the provisions of this Convention, he may, irrespective of the remedies provided by the domestic law of those States, present his case to the competent authority of the Contracting State of which he is a resident or, if his case comes under paragraph 1 of Article 24, to that of the Contracting State of which he is a national. The case must be presented within three years from the first notification of the action resulting in taxation not in accordance with the provisions of the Convention.

2. The competent authority shall endeavour, if the objection appears to it to be justified and if it is not itself able to arrive at a satisfactory solution, to resolve the case by mutual agreement with the competent authority of the other Contracting State, with a view to the avoidance of taxation which is not in accordance with the Convention. Any agreement reached shall be implemented notwithstanding any time limits in the domestic law of the Contracting States.

3. The competent authorities of the Contracting States shall endeavour to resolve by mutual agreement any difficulties or doubts arising as to the interpretation or application of the Convention. They may also consult together for the elimination of double taxation in cases not provided for in the Convention.

4. The competent authorities of the Contracting States may communicate with each other directly, including through a joint commission consisting of themselves or their representatives, for the purpose of reaching an agreement in the sense of the preceding paragraphs.

5. Where,

   a) under paragraph 1, a person has presented a case to the competent authority of a Contracting State on the basis that the actions of one or both of the Contracting States have resulted for that person in taxation not in accordance with the provisions of this Convention, and

   b) the competent authorities are unable to reach an agreement to resolve that case pursuant to paragraph 2 within two years from the presentation of the case to the competent authority of the other Contracting State, any unresolved issues arising from the case shall be submitted to arbitration if the person so requests.

---

[109] Source: *http://www.oecd.org*. (Accessed June 8, 2011).

> These unresolved issues shall not, however, be submitted to arbitration if a decision on these issues has already been rendered by a court or administrative tribunal of either State. Unless a person directly affected by the case does not accept the mutual agreement that implements the arbitration decision, that decision shall be binding on both Contracting States and shall be implemented notwithstanding any time limits in the domestic laws of these States. The competent authorities of the Contracting States shall by mutual agreement settle the mode of application of this paragraph 1

1. In some States, national law, policy or administrative considerations may not allow or justify the type of dispute resolution envisaged under this paragraph. In addition, some States may only wish to include this paragraph in treaties with certain States. For these reasons, the paragraph should only be included in the Convention where each State concludes that it would be appropriate to do so based on the factors described in paragraph 65 of the Commentary on the paragraph. As mentioned in paragraph 74 of that Commentary, however, other States may be able to agree to remove from the paragraph the condition that issues may not be submitted to arbitration if a decision on these issues has already been rendered by one of their courts or administrative tribunals.[110]

## Exchange of Information

Information about a tax payer's affairs is important to preserve the integrity of a country's tax system and to enable it to effectively enforce its international taxation.[111] In particular, exchange of information as between tax authorities about taxpayers is necessary for the correct application of double taxation agreements (DTAs).[112] For example, exchange of information is needed for the implementation of the arm's length pricing mechanism as between associated enterprises operating from different jurisdictions. The existing international framework for the exchange of information is rooted in Art.26 of the OECD and UN Models, along with the 1998 OECD Report on Harmful Tax Competition which identified lack of effective exchange of information as a key element in the determination of "harmful tax competition" within tax havens and harmful preferential regimes.[113]

**16-036**

> **Box I (Source: OECD Harmful Tax Competition Report: An Emerging Global Issue (1998))**
>
> **KEY FACTORS IN IDENTIFYING TAX HAVENS FOR THE PURPOSES OF THIS REPORT**

---

[110] Extracted from OECD Model Tax Convention.
[111] Source: *www.oecd.org.* (Accessed June 8, 2011).
[112] See Commentary to Art.26 of the OECD Model Tax Convention.
[113] See, for example, 1998 Report on Harmful Tax Competition (OECD, 1998); Harmful Tax Practices Report (OECD, 2001).

### *a)* No or only nominal taxes

No or only nominal taxation on the relevant income is the starting point to classify a jurisdiction as a tax haven.

### *b)* Lack of effective exchange of information

Tax havens typically have in place laws or administrative practices under which businesses and individuals can benefit from strict secrecy rules and other protections against scrutiny by tax authorities thereby preventing the effective exchange of information on taxpayers benefiting from the low tax jurisdiction.

### *c)* Lack of transparency

A lack of transparency in the operation of the legislative, legal or administrative provisions is another factor in identifying tax havens.

### *d)* No substantial activities

The absence of a requirement that the activity be substantial is important since it would suggest that a jurisdiction may be attempting to attract investment or transactions that are purely tax driven."

**"Box II (Source: OECD Harmful Tax Competition Report: An Emerging Global Issue (1998))**

**KEY FACTORS IN IDENTIFYING AND ASSESSING HARMFUL PREFERENTIAL TAX REGIMES FOR THE PURPOSES OF THIS REPORT**

### *a) No or low effective tax rates*

A low or zero effective tax rate on the relevant income is a necessary starting point for an examination of whether a preferential tax regime is harmful. A zero or low effective tax rate may arise because the schedule rate itself is very low or because of the way in which a country defines the tax base to which the rate is applied. A harmful preferential tax regime will be characterised by a combination of a low or zero effective tax rate and one or more other factors set out in this Box and, where relevant, in this section.

### *b) 'Ring fencing' of regimes*

Some preferential tax regimes are partly or fully insulated from the domestic markets of the country providing the regime. The fact that a country feels the need to protect its own economy from the regime by ring-fencing provides a strong indication that a regime has the potential to create harmful spillover effects. Ring-fencing may take a number of forms, including:

- – a regime may explicitly or implicitly exclude resident taxpayers from taking advantage of its benefits.

- – enterprises which benefit from the regime may be explicitly or implicitly prohibited from operating in the domestic market.

### *c) Lack of transparency*

The lack of transparency in the operation of a regime will make it harder for the home country to take defensive measures. Non-transparency may arise from the way in which a regime is designed and administered. Non-transparency is a broad concept that includes, among others, favourable application of laws and regulations, negotiable tax provisions, and a failure to make widely available administrative practices.

### d) Lack of effective exchange of information

The lack of effective exchange of information in relation to taxpayers benefiting from the operation of a preferential tax regime is a strong indication that a country is engaging in harmful tax competition.

Briefly, the OECD conception of harmful tax practices announced in 1998 **16-037** embraces two circumstances viz., tax havens and harmful preferential tax regimes concerned with mobile financial flows, such as portfolio investment, excluding investment in "plant, building and equipment."[114] Two common features in the criteria for identifying these harmful tax practices involve "lack of transparency and effective exchange of information". Additionally, a tax haven is defined with reference to the tax rates and the kind of activity in the tax haven, whereas preferential regimes are defined essentially as involving "targeted tax incentives".[115] The OECD response to such practices involves recommending member countries to introduce domestic tax legislation to counteract such practices, for example, legislation relating to Controlled Foreign Corporations; and the introduction of countermeasures, ranging from fiscal measures such as the denial of tax deductions for payments made into tax havens, imposition of withholding taxes on payments made to jurisdictions engaged in harmful tax practices, to possible non-fiscal sanctions. However, the current response to the elimination of the harmful tax practices has evolved essentially into a requirement for transparency and effective exchange of information systems. Indeed, not only does there seem to be a change in response but rather the response itself is emphasised in terms of a different agenda, namely tax avoidance and evasion.

The OECD "harmful tax competition" has been the subject of much criticism. The objections include lack of clarity in terms of the definition of harmful tax competition, the assumption that the practices identified are harmful, and the presumption of engaging in the fiscal affairs of another jurisdiction.[116] However, whatever may be the state of the OECD campaign now on harmful tax competition, its significance lies not merely in its contribution to international fiscal transparency and effective exchange of information, but also in its introduction in the IFL lexicon of a fundamental concept, namely the notion of fair competition among fiscal authorities with respect to taxation.

In the circumstances, the current efforts at ensuring transparency in taxation and effective exchange of information as between tax authorities, encompass the following regimes:

---

[114] See OECD 1998 Report on Harmful Tax Competition.
[115] M. Littlewood, "Tax Competition", *Michigan Journal of International Law*, 26:1 (2004), 411–487 at p.164.
[116] See, for example, M. Littlewood (2004).

- Article 26 of the OECD and UN Models respectively as set out in DTAs

- Agreement on exchange of Information on Tax Matters 2002

- Multilateral Convention on Mutual Administrative Assistance in Tax Matters 1988 (as amended by 2010 Protocol)[117]

- The Global Forum on Transparency and Exchange and Information for Tax Purposes.[118]

Double taxation agreements are generally accompanied with exchange of information systems.[119] The provisions on exchange of information in double taxation agreements also serve to facilitate the correct application of national taxes covered under the DTA, and generally to prevent tax avoidance and evasion.[120] Exchange of information is not confined to the taxes covered by DTAs, nor to information about resident taxpayers only. Thus, information relating to indirect taxes is covered. The exchange of information between tax authorities on taxpayer circumstances is accompanied by certain safeguards to protect the taxpayer's trade interests including national interests. Thus, only foreseeable relevant information can be requested. Furthermore, trade secrets are protected and the information passed may be used normally only by the tax authorities. Moreover, there is a condition of reciprocity in the mechanisms used for obtaining information. Thus, a State may be refused information upon a request which involves use of powers which the requesting State itself does not posses under its domestic law.

---

[117] Current signatories May 2011 (Source: OECD): Denmark, Finland, Iceland, Italy, France, Netherlands, Norway, Sweden, Ukraine, United Kingdom, United States, Korea, Mexico, Portugal and Slovenia.

[118] OECD: The Global Forum on Transparency and Exchange of Information for Tax Purposes: A Background Information Brief (May 2011); OECD: Implementing the Tax Transparency Standards: A Handbook for Assessors and Jurisdictions (2010).

[119] See Art.26 of the OECD and UN Models respectively. See also, for example, IFA, "International mutual assistance through exchange of information", *Cahier De Droit Fiscal International* Vol.LXXVb (1990); *Tax information exchange between OECD Member Countries*, A Report by the Committee on Fiscal Affairs (OECD, 1994); G. Prats et al., "Exchange of information Under Article 26 of the UN Model Tax Convention" (1999) 53(12) B.I.F.D. 541–548. Manual on the Implementation of Exchange of Information Provisions for tax Purposes (OECD, 2006); M.J. McIntyre, "Identifying the new international standard for effective information exchange" *Tax treaties: building bridges between law and economics.* Amsterdam, IBFD, 2010; pp.481–516; A.C.M. Schenk-Geers, *International exchange of information and the protection of taxpayers*, (Alphen aan den Rijn: Kluwer Law International, 2009); T. Anamourlis, & L. Nethercott, "An overview of tax information exchange agreements and bank secrecy", *Bulletin for International Taxation.* Amsterdam. Vol.63 (2009), no.12; pp.616–621;

[120] See Commentary to Art.26 of the OECD Model Tax Convention.

## ARTICLE—26 EXCHANGE OF INFORMATION

1. The competent authorities of the Contracting States shall exchange such information as is foreseeably relevant for carrying out the provisions of this Convention or to the administration or enforcement of the domestic laws concerning taxes of every kind and description imposed on behalf of the Contracting States, or of their political subdivisions or local authorities, insofar as the taxation thereunder is not contrary to the Convention. The exchange of information is not restricted by Articles 1 and 2.

    **16-038**

2. Any information received under paragraph 1 by a Contracting State shall be treated as secret in the same manner as information obtained under the domestic laws of that State and shall be disclosed only to persons or authorities (including courts and administrative bodies) concerned with the assessment or collection of, the enforcement or prosecution in respect of, the determination of appeals in relation to the taxes referred to in paragraph 1, or the oversight of the above. Such persons or authorities shall use the information only for such purposes. They may disclose the information in public court proceedings or in judicial decisions.

3. In no case shall the provisions of paragraphs 1 and 2 be construed so as to impose on a Contracting State the obligation:

    a) to carry out administrative measures at variance with the laws and administrative practice of that or of the other Contracting State;

    b) to supply information which is not obtainable under the laws or in the normal course of the administration of that or of the other Contracting State;

    c) to supply information which would disclose any trade, business, industrial, commercial or professional secret or trade process, or information the disclosure of which would be contrary to public policy (ordre public).

4. If information is requested by a Contracting State in accordance with this Article, the other Contracting State shall use its information gathering measures to obtain the requested information, even though that other State may not need such information for its own tax purposes. The obligation contained in the preceding sentence is subject to the limitations of paragraph 3 but in no case shall such limitations be construed to permit a Contracting State to decline to supply information solely because it has no domestic interest in such information.

5. In no case shall the provisions of paragraph 3 be construed to permit a Contracting State to decline to Supply information solely because the information is held by a bank, other financial institution, nominee or person acting in an agency or a fiduciary capacity or because it relates to ownership interests in a person.[121]

The Agreement on Exchange of Information on Tax Matters established by the OECD Global Forum Working Group on Effective Exchange of Information comprises two agreements. One is a model bilateral agreement

[121] Extracted from OECD Model Tax Convention.

which States can use to enter into a bilateral agreement and another is a multilateral agreement which States can become parties to with the option of specifying which countries they want to be bound with under the agreement. The number of States which have signed specific Tax Information Exchange Agreements (TIEAs) has recently risen very significantly. Thus, in 2008 there were some 44 TIEAs, whereas in May 2011 there were some 468; and if new DTA are included the number of agreements in total rose to some 600.[122] The agreements reflect the appropriate standards for exchange of information that countries ought to have both within and outside the OECD; and involve non-OECD countries as well. Briefly, the agreements contain, inter alia, provision for exchange of information upon request, provision for tax examinations abroad and include a Mutual Agreement Procedure for any differences that may arise in the context of the provision of information. The agreements also contain certain safeguards, for example, to protect trade secrets and confidentiality.

International and regional arrangements on assistance in the collection of tax matters also contain systems for exchange of information.[123] One notable one is the Convention on Mutual Administrative Assistance in Tax Matters jointly established by the Council of Europe and the OECD. It was opened for signature in 1988 and amended via a Protocol in May 2010, in order to update it, to facilitate banking information, and to ensure its availability for signature to non-OECD countries. The Protocol was due to come into effect in June 2011. The Convention provides for administrative co-operation in tax matters including exchange of information and recovery of foreign tax claims. Not many States however are parties to it although the Protocol has been signed by some 20 States.

The establishment of the Global Forum on Transparency and Exchange and Information for Tax Purposes (the Global Forum) has been underpinned by the efforts of the G20, in particular its concern to combat international tax evasion and the implementation of international standards of transparency and exchange of information.[124] The Global Forum has some 101 members and this membership is not confined to OECD members.[125] Although its roots are set in the ad hoc Global Forum set up by the OECD in 2000, it was reorganised in 2009 with a wider membership along with a set mandate.[126] It has a Secretariat that is based in the OECD's Centre for Tax Policy and Administration. Its current mandate is to implement certain standards on

---

[122] OECD: The Global Forum on Transparency and Exchange of Information for Tax Purposes: A Background Information Brief (May 2011).

[123] For example, the Joint Council of Europe/OECD Convention on Mutual Administrative Assistance in Tax Matters 1988.

[124] OECD: The Global Forum on Transparency and Exchange of Information for Tax Purposes: A Background Information Brief (May 2011).

[125] OECD: The Global Forum on Transparency and Exchange of Information for Tax Purposes: A Background Information Brief (May 2011).

[126] OECD: The Global Forum on Transparency and Exchange of Information for Tax Purposes: A Background Information Brief (May 2011).

transparency and exchange of information through a system of peer review involving both members and non-members. The review focuses both on the relevant domestic laws and exchange of information agreements as well as their effectiveness in practice. Thus, Phase One of the review focuses on the domestic law and relevant international agreements, whereas Phase Two focuses on the implementation of the standards of transparency and exchange of information. The standards of transparency and exchange of information are essentially those to be found in Art.26 of the OECD Model and the Agreement on Exchange of Information 2002.[127] All jurisdictions are encouraged to enter into TIEAs. The recent increase in the number of TIEAs is essentially attributable to the work and efforts of the Global Forum. All members of the Forum are subject to the review as are any non-members considered of interest. Non-members not co-operating will be evaluated on the best information available. The review process is overseen by a 30-member Peer Review Group. The review process involves a report and judgements about compliance in terms of ratings viz., whether the jurisdiction is compliant, largely compliant, partially compliant, or not compliant.[128] In the event of non-compliance members individually decide how to respond in order to enforce their taxation. The G20 has agreed to stand ready to take action against non-cooperative jurisdictions.[129]

## THE 10 ESSENTIAL ELEMENTS OF TRANSPARENCY AND EXCHANGE OF INFORMATION FOR TAX PURPOSES[130]

### A  AVAILABILITY OF INFORMATION                                      16-039

**A.1.** Jurisdictions should ensure that ownership and identity information for all relevant entities and arrangements is available to their competent authorities.

**A.2.** Jurisdictions should ensure that reliable accounting records are kept for all relevant entities and arrangements.

**A.3.** Banking information should be available for all account-holders.

### B  ACCESS TO INFORMATION

**B.1.** Competent authorities should have the power to obtain and provide information that is the subject of a request under an EOI agreement from any person within their territorial jurisdiction who is in possession or control of such information.

---

[127] OECD: The Global Forum on Transparency and Exchange of Information for Tax Purposes: A Background Information Brief (May 2011).
[128] OECD: The Global Forum on Transparency and Exchange of Information for Tax Purposes: A Background Information Brief (May 2011).
[129] See G20 Declaration: Strengthening the Financial System London, UK April 2, 2009 cited in OECD: The Global Forum on Transparency and Exchange of Information for Tax Purposes: A Background Information Brief (May 2011).
[130] Source: OECD: The Global Forum on Transparency and Exchange of Information for Tax Purposes: A Background Information Brief (May 2011).

**B.2.** The rights and safeguards that apply to persons in the requested jurisdiction should be compatible with effective exchange of information.

### C  EXCHANGING INFORMATION

**C.1.** EOI mechanisms should provide for effective exchange of
information.

**C.2.** The jurisdictions' network of information exchange mechanisms
should cover all relevant partners.

**C.3.** The jurisdictions' mechanisms for exchange of information should
have adequate provisions to ensure the confidentiality of information received.

**C.4.** The exchange of information mechanisms should respect the rights
and safeguards of taxpayers and third parties.

**C.5.** The jurisdiction should provide information under its network of
agreements in a timely manner.

In conclusion, it will be noted that the system of exchange of information
serves a number of purposes and is neither confined to DTAs or OECD
members alone. Moreover, the system of peer review for systems of exchange
of information could well be the precursor of a more comprehensive system
of country fiscal surveillance.

### Assistance in the collection of taxes

**16-040**   Generally, States do not assist in the recovery of national tax claims as a
matter of public policy. The kind of assistance relevant here comprises assistance in the recovery of a tax claim; measures of conservancy, for example
freezing of a taxpayer's assets; and the servicing of legal documents on
the taxpayer. This historical State practice of not assisting in the recovery

of tax claims, stemming as it does from an erroneous equation of revenue laws with penal laws, has been criticised as being unwarranted in this era of globalisation.[131] There are however some international arrangements albeit with a limited number of State parties[132]; as well as regional arrangements to facilitate assistance as between States in the recovery of revenue claims.[133] Moreover, the OECD Model provides for the option for States to negotiate a framework in double taxation agreements to facilitate recovery of national tax claims against tax payers on a reciprocal basis.[134] This is also the case now with the UN Model.[135]

## THE UN AND INTERNATIONAL CO-OPERATION IN TAX MATTERS

International tax policy and practice has been led essentially by developed States through the OECD. Developing States have not been able to take a similar lead through a comparable institutional structure.[136] However, the developing perspective on international tax issues has been able to find its voice somewhat through the United Nations Committee of Experts on International     **16-041**

---

[131] See B.A. Silver, "Modernizing the Revenue Rule: The Enforcement of Foreign Tax Judgements" (1992) 22 *GA.J.Int'L & Comp.*

[132] OECD Model Convention for Mutual Administrative Assistance in the Recovery of Tax Claims 1981 (note: no agreements have been based on this Model); Joint Council of Europe/OECD Convention on Mutual Administrative Assistance in Tax Matters 1988.

[133] Commission Communication, dated May 31, 2006, to the Council, the European Parliament and the European Economic and Social Committee concerning the need to develop a co-ordinated strategy to improve the fight against fiscal fraud (COM(2006) 254; Council Regulation (EC) No.2073/2004 of November 16, 2004 on administrative co-operation in the field of excise duties; Council Regulation (EC) No.1798/2003 of October 7, 2003 on administrative co-operation in the field of value added tax and repealing Regulation (EEC) No.218/92; Council Directive 76/308/EEC of March 15, 1976 on mutual assistance for the recovery of claims resulting from operations forming part of the system of financing the European Agricultural Guidance and Guarantee Fund, and of agricultural levies and customs duties, and in respect of value-added tax; Council Directive 77/799/EEC of December 19, 1977 concerning mutual assistance by the competent authorities of the Member States in the field of direct taxation and taxation of insurance premiums; May 26, 2008 (Council Directive 2008/55/EC);European Convention on Mutual Assistance in Criminal Matters; Nordic Mutual Assistance Convention on Mutual Administrative Assistance in Tax Matters (1989); Commission Regulation (EC) 1179/2008). See also February 2, 2009 proposal for a new Council Directive on mutual assistance for the recovery of taxes COM/2009/28. M. Vascego & S. Van, Thiel, "Council adopts new directive on mutual assistance in recovery of tax and similar claims", *European Taxation* Vol.5 (2010), no.6, pp.23–237.

[134] See Art.27 of the OECD Model.

[135] See Finalised Text as Agreed by Committee of Experts on International Cooperation in Tax Matters, at its Second Session, Geneva, October 30–November 3, 2006 Assistance in the Collection of Taxes (Art.27) and its Commentary at *http://www.un.org/esa/ffd/tax/Art27_MutualAssistance.pdf.* (Accessed June 8, 2011).

[136] See Global Economic Governance International Taxation, Investment & Financing for Development at *http://www.southcentre.org/GGDP/newGEG_IntTaxInvFFD.htm.* (Accessed June 8, 2011).

Cooperation in Tax Matters. This Committee (UN Tax Committee) is a subsidiary organ of the UN Economic and Social Council. This UN Tax Committee is the predecessor of the UN Ad Hoc Group of Experts on Tax Treaties between Developed and Developing Countries, which was established in 1968; and was responsible for the 1980 UN Model Double Taxation Convention between developed and developing countries. This Model was revised in 2001,[137] with an update due to be completed in 2011.[138] The UN Tax Committee's mandate is broader so as to focus not just on double taxation relief but also generally on international co-operation in tax matters,[139] with particular focus on developing countries and countries with economies in transition. The 1980 Model was accompanied by a Manual which was revised in 2003.[140] Its purpose "is primarily meant as a training material explaining the process and purpose of negotiation of bilateral tax treaties, as well as the fundamentals of international taxation and international tax evasion and avoidance".[141] Although there has not been substantial academic focus and research[142] on the UN Model and the development perspective of international taxation, the UN Manual is a valuable source of explanation and analysis.

The UN Model is the subject of political compromise between developed and developing countries. It takes its cue essentially from the OECD Model. Moreover, the mode of its development is slower. Thus, whereas the OECD

---

[137] Can be accessed at *http://www.un.org/esa/ffd/Taxation/index.htm*. (Accessed June 8, 2011).

[138] See UN Economic and Social Council: Strengthening of institutional arrangements to promote international cooperation in tax matters, including the Committee of Experts on International Cooperation in Tax Matters. Report of the Secretary-General, E/2011/76 (March 2011).

[139] See *http://www.un.org/esa/ffd/Taxation/ffdtaxationoverview.htm*. (Accessed June 8, 2011).

[140] *Manual for the Negotiation of Bilateral Tax Treaties Between Developed and Developing Countries* (New York, 2003), p.215.

[141] See Forword to the Manual.

[142] See, however, S. Surrey, "United Nations Group of Experts and the Guidelines between Developed and Developing Countries" (1978) 19 *Harv Int. L.J.* 1–65; S. Surrey, *United Nations Convention for Tax Treaties Between Developed and Developing Countries—A description and analysis* (I.B.F.D., 1980); H.G. Goldberg, "Conventions for the elimination of international double taxation: Towards a developing country model" (1983) 15(3) *Law and Policy in International Business* 833–909; C. Van Raad, *Model income tax treaties: a comparative presentation of the texts of the Model Double Taxation Conventions on Income and Capital of the OECD, 1963 & 1977, UN, 1980 & US 1980* (Deventer, Kluwer, Law International, 1990); R.T. Bartlett, "The making of double taxation agreements"(1991) B.T.R. 76; R.J. Vann, "A model tax treaty for the Asian-Pacific Region?" (1991) 45 *B.I.F.D.* 99; IFA, *Double Taxation treaties between industrialised and developing countries, the OECD and UN Models—a comparison* (Deventer, Kluwer Law and Taxation, 1992); Willen and Wijner et al., "The UN Model in Practice" (1997) 51 B.I.F.D. 574; W.F.G. Wijren, "Towards a new UN Model?" (1998) 3 B.I.F.D; G. Prats et al., "Exchange of information under Article 26 of the UN Model Tax Convention" (1999) 53(12) B.I.F.D. 541–548; E. van der Bruggen, "A preliminary look at the new UN Model Double Tax Convention" (2002) 2 B.T.R. 119–34; E.V. Bruggen, "A preliminary look at the new UN Model Tax Convention" (2002) 2 B.T.R. 119–34; B. Kosters, "The UN Model Tax Convention and its recent developments" (2004) 10(1/2) *Asia-Pacific Tax Bulletin* 4–12; T.J. Glistan, "Electronic commerce and the UN Model Double Taxation Convention" (2004) 32(8/9) *INTERTAX* 387. Lennard, M. "The UN Model Tax Convention as compared with the OECD Model Tax Convention: current points of difference and recent developments," *Asia-Pacific Tax Bulletin*. Vol.15 (2009), no.1; pp. 4–11.

Model is perambulatory in the sense that it is constantly being developed and changed in response to developments in international economic relations and technology, the UN Model is less adept at responding to changes. Further, the differences between the Models arguably are of detail rather than of substance as such. This "duplication" has prompted a focus on the international institutional arrangements for co-operation in tax matters and on the need to strengthen the UN Committee qua an intergovernmental organisation.[143] Be that as it may the UN Model is, according to the UN, "heavily relied upon by developing countries in tax treaty negotiations".[144]

The differences in the Models orientate the UN Model more in favour of the source State. In particular the main differences[145] thus are to be found in the definition of a Permanent Establishment, and the profits that can be attributed to it. Moreover, for royalties there is no exclusive jurisdiction for the residence State; and the limits on the source State taxes on dividend and interest payments have been left open, to be negotiated between the parties.

16-042

7. The United Nations Model Convention represents a compromise between the source principle and the residence principle. However, it gives more weight to the source principle than does the OECD Model Convention, which contains a more restrictive definition of a permanent establishment and, in the areas of shipping profits, dividends, interest and royalties, relies more strongly on taxation at source at relatively lower rates or sometimes exclusive taxation by the country of residence. (The allocation of greater taxing power to the source country in the United Nations Model Convention does not mean that the withholding tax rates in the OECD Model Convention on dividends, interest or royalties are too low as a matter of principle and that the Contracting States should always strive for higher rates). As a correlative to the principle of taxation at source, the articles of the United Nations Model Convention are predicated on a recognition by the source country that taxation of income from foreign capital: (1) should take into account expenses allocable to the earnings of that income so that such income is taxed on a net basis; (2) should not be imposed at so high a rate as to unduly discourage investment; and (3) should take into account the appropriateness of a sharing of revenue with the country providing the capital. In addition, the United Nations Model Convention embodies the idea that it would be appropriate for the residence country to extend a measure of relief from double taxation through either foreign tax credit or exemption, as in the OECD Model Convention."[146]

**"UN Model Article 5 PERMANENT ESTABLISHMENT**

---

[143] See UN Economic and Social Council: Strengthening of institutional arrangements to promote international cooperation in tax matters, including the Committee of Experts on International Cooperation in Tax Matters. Report of the Secretary-General, E/2011/76 (March 2011).

[144] See para.34 E/2011/76 (March 2011).

[145] See for example Arts 2, 4, 5, 7, 9, 10, 11, 13 and 18 of the UN Model.

[146] Source: Manual for the Negotiation of Bilateral Tax Treaties between Developed and Developing Countries 2003, *http://www.un.org*. (Accessed June 8, 2011).

**16-043**

1. For the purposes of this Convention, the term 'permanent establishment' means a fixed place of business through which the business of an enterprise is wholly or partly carried on.

2. The term 'permanent establishment' includes especially:

   (a) A place of management;

   (b) A branch;

   (c) An office;

   (d) A factory;

   (e) A workshop;

   (f) A mine, an oil or gas well, a quarry or any other place of extraction of natural resources.

3. The term 'permanent establishment' also encompasses:

   (a) A building site, a construction, assembly or installation project or supervisory activities in connection therewith, but only if such site, project or activities last more than six months;

   (b) The furnishing of services, including consultancy services, by an enterprise through employees or other personnel engaged by the enterprise for such purpose, but only if activities of that nature continue (for the same or a connected project) within a Contracting State for a period or periods aggregating more than six months within any twelve-month period.

4. Notwithstanding the preceding provisions of this article, the term 'permanent establishment' shall be deemed not to include:

   (a) The use of facilities solely for the purpose of storage or display of goods or merchandise belonging to the enterprise;

   (b) The maintenance of a stock of goods or merchandise belonging to the enterprise solely for the purpose of storage or display;

   (c) The maintenance of a stock of goods or merchandise belonging to the enterprise solely for the purpose of processing by another enterprise;

   (d) The maintenance of a fixed place of business solely for the purpose of purchasing goods or merchandise or of collecting information, for the enterprise;

   (e) The maintenance of a fixed place of business solely for the purpose of carrying on, for the enterprise, any other activity of a preparatory or auxiliary character.

   (f) The maintenance of a fixed place of business solely for any combination of activities mentioned in subparagraphs (a) to (e), provided that the overall activity of the fixed place of business resulting from this combination is of a preparatory or auxiliary character.

5. Notwithstanding the provisions of paragraphs 1 and 2, where a person—other than an agent of an independent status to whom paragraph 7 applies—is acting in a Contracting State on behalf of an enterprise of the other Contracting State, that enterprise shall be deemed to have a

permanent establishment in the first-mentioned Contracting State in respect of any activities which that person undertakes for the enterprise, if such a person:

(a) Has and habitually exercises in that State an authority to conclude contracts in the name of the enterprise, unless the activities of such person are limited to those mentioned in paragraph 4 which, if exercised through a fixed place of business, would not make this fixed place of business a permanent establishment under the provisions of that paragraph; or

(b) Has no such authority, but habitually maintains in the first-mentioned State a stock of goods or merchandise from which he regularly delivers goods or merchandise on behalf of the enterprise.

6. Notwithstanding the preceding provisions of this article, an insurance enterprise of a Contracting State shall, except in regard to re-insurance, be deemed to have a permanent establishment in the other Contracting State if it collects premiums in the territory of that other State or insures risks situated therein through a person other than an agent of an independent status to whom paragraph 7 applies.

7. An enterprise of a Contracting State shall not be deemed to have a permanent establishment in the other Contracting State merely because it carries on business in that other State through a broker, general commission agent or any other agent of an independent status, provided that such persons are acting in the ordinary course of their business. However, when the activities of such an agent are devoted wholly or almost wholly on behalf of that enterprise, and conditions are made or imposed between that enterprise and the agent in their commercial and financial relations which differ from those which would have been made between independent enterprises, he will not be considered an agent of an independent status within the meaning of this paragraph.

8. The fact that a company which is a resident of a Contracting State controls or is controlled by a company which is a resident of the other Contracting State, or which carries on business in that other State (whether through a permanent establishment or otherwise), shall not of itself constitute either company a permanent establishment of the other.

The UN Committee has proposed changes to its commentary to Art.5.[1]

## Conclusion

The development of international fiscal law has been skewed by its historical legislative *modus operandi*. The development of IFL has traditionally been anchored in the normative efforts to combat double taxation and new challenges are being dealt with through that normative framework—in some ways as appendages. Thus it is not possible to bring general fundamental

**16-044**

---

[1] UN E/C.18/2010/6.

changes in the international tax order given that it is set against a widespread bilateral system ostensibly and mainly aimed at relieving double taxation.[2] This has led one critique to conclude that the bilateralism based on the Model systems is "increasingly inefficient, irrelevant and inflexible".[3] "Inefficient", for example because double taxation relief is afforded according to types of income and capital which encourages tax planning through artificial re-characterisation of income and capital types.[4] By the same token, differences between double taxation agreements have led to the practice of treaty shopping, to take advantage of the differences in the different double taxation agreements or the lack of them. "Irrelevant", because the double taxation agreements are not able to respond effectively to "emerging tax issues"—for example, in the sphere of tax avoidance and evasion, and electronic commerce.[5] "Inflexible", because of the difficulties posed in bringing about general changes to the entrenched bilateralism.[6] These observations made over a decade ago still have a resonance. Moreover, the principal drivers in the development of International Fiscal Law have been developed States, and the imprint of the practices of multinational corporations. The need to focus on this sphere from the standpoint of development is only now beginning at the political level.[7] The realisation that aid has a relationship with domestic revenue capacity in developing countries has raised development and taxation on the agenda of the OECD. Finally, the relatively discreet and bilateral nature of international taxation has meant that it has tended to be somewhat removed from other spheres of international economic relations. Therefore, there is a question as to how well it is co-ordinated with the other dimensions of international economic relations—namely international trade, investment, patterns of labour movement and development.

In the circumstances some of the fundamental questions with respect to IFL from a legal perspective may be conceived of as follows. First, of note is that the traditional definition of IFL is being stretched such that its scope is beginning to focus on the national tax system which traditionally has been considered within the domestic jurisdiction of the State. Thus, the UN and the OECD focus on strengthening domestic tax systems in particular in terms of its efficiency. Secondly, with respect to the source and residence discourse the legal challenge centres around discerning State practice and treaty practice, for trends either way. At the policy level, here the discourse beyond traditional "equity and neutrality" to include, for instance, distributive

---

[2]  See, for example, R.J. Vann, "A Model Tax Treaty for the Asian-Pacific Region?" (1991) 45 B.I.F.D. 99.
[3]  Vann (1991), p.100.
[4]  Vann (1991), p.103.
[5]  Vann (1991), p.107.
[6]  Vann (1991), p.110.
[7]  In 2010 the OECD set up an informal Task Force on Tax and Development. See Co-chairs Joint Statement Joint Meeting on Tax and Development Between the Committee on Fiscal Affairs (Cfa) and the Development Assistance Committee (Dac) January 27, 2010 at *http://www.oecd.org/dataoecd/7/36/44493096.pdf.* (Accessed June 8, 2011).

justice as between States in the design of the international fiscal order and its orientation deserves further examination.[8] Thirdly, a key effort in combating tax evasion and avoidance as well as "harmful tax competition" has involved the OECD in peer pressure and counter measures. The brandishing of States engaged in harmful tax practices and the consequent pressure on them to change legislation in terms of transparency and disclosure requirements invites scrutiny of such an effort from the stand-point of Public International law, in particular sovereignty and non-intervention principles. Similarly the place of the traditional "revenue rule" of not enforcing foreign tax claims in the event of tax evasion in modern international economic relations is beginning to be undermined through treaty efforts. Fourthly, the impact of the vast network of DTAs on customary international fiscal law must surely call for analysis. Is there, for instance, an obligation under customary International Law not to double tax? Fifthly, non-discrimination provisions in international agreements, including DTAs, BITs, the WTO and regional integration agreements, raise questions of scope and interpretation and indeed relationships inter-se. Sixthly, the manner of calculating multijurisdictional company profits in terms of Public International Law and fiscal jurisdiction remains a question on the IFL agenda. Finally, an overarching consideration of course is how far in real terms the traditional freedom in fiscal jurisdiction and sovereignty has now been re-defined through the bilateral and multilateral efforts of the OECD, the UN and also the IMF and the WTO.

---

[8]   I am grateful to Ajay Kumar for highlighting this to me.

# INTERNATIONAL DEVELOPMENT LAW

CHAPTER 17

# INTERNATIONAL DEVELOPMENT LAW

INTRODUCTION[1]

International development law (IDL) covers a number of spheres. Indeed,  **17-001**
it covers as many spheres as there are ways of facilitating development viz.,
development through trade; development through investment; development through financing; development through efficient and growth related

[1] See, for example, M. Flory, *Droit International Du Development* (Paris: Presses Universitaires de France, 1977); A. Pellet, *Le Droit International Du Development* (Paris:,Presses Universitaires de France, 1978); B.O. de Rivero, *New Economic Order & International Development Law* (Oxford: Pergamon, 1980); R.P. Anand, *International Law and the Developing Countries; Confrontation or Cooperation?* (New Delhi, Banyan Publications, 1986); F. Snyder and P. Slinn, *International Law of Development: Comparative Perspectives* (1987); P. de Waart et al. (eds), *International Law & Development* (Dordrecht, Boston, London, Martinus Nijhoff, 1988); D.D. Bradlow, "Differing conceptions of development and the content of International Development Law", *South African Journal of Human Rights,* 21:1 (2005), 47–85; F.V. Garcia-Amador, *The Emerging International Law of Development* (New York, Oceana Publications, 1990); S.R. Chowdry, *The Right to Development in International Law* (Dordrecht, Martinus Nijhoff, 1992); M. Bulajic, *Principles of International Development Law,* 2nd revised edn (Dordrecht, London, Martinus Nijhoff, 1992); A. Carty (ed.), *Law and Development* (1992); B.G. Ramcharan, *The Concept of Protection in the International Law of Human Rights* (Dordrecht, Martinus Nijhoff, 1993); W. Lang, *Sustainable Development and International Law* (Boston, Graham and Trotman/Martinus Nijhoff, 1995); E. Kwakwa, "Emerging International Development Law and Traditional International Law—Congruence or Cleavage?" (1997) 17 *Georgia Journal of International and Comparative Law* 431–55; A. Lindroos, *The Right to Development* (H Forum Luris, 1999); A.E. Boyle and D. Freestone (eds), *The International law and Sustainable Development: Past Achievements and Futire Challenges* (Oxford, Oxford University Press, 1999); M.-C. Seggar, Cordonier, *Sustainable Development Law: Principles, Practices and Prospects* (Oxford, Oxford University Press, 2004); M.-C. Seggar and C. Weermantry, *Sustainable Justice: Reconciling Economic, Social and Environmental Law* (Leiden, Martinus Nijhoff, 2004); N. Schrijver and F. Weiss (eds), *International Law and Sustainable development: Principles and Practice* (Boston and Leiden, Martinus Nijhoff, 2004); M.W. Gehring and M.-C. Cordoner Segger, *Sustainable Development—World Trade Law* (London, Kluwer Law International, 2005); D. French, *International Law and Policy of Sustainable Development* (Manchester, Manchester University Press, 2005); N. Schrijver, *The evolution of sustainable development in international law: Inception, maning and status* (2008); R. Sarkar *International Development Law: Rule of Law, Human Rights, & Global Finance,* (Oxford University Press, 2009); M-C Cordoner Segger, M.W. Gehring and A. Newcombe *Sustainable development in World Investment Law,* (Kluwer Law International, 2010).

taxation; and development in the framework of sustainable development. Further, the goal of development can be realised both at the domestic level, as well as through international efforts. Thus, IDL straddles both domestic and International Law. Here only the Public International Law aspects of development are considered. Within the Public International Law framework IDL can be defined as "the branch of international law that deals with the rights and duties of states and others involved in the development process".[2] Thus, the focus here is on the international institutions and mechanisms which facilitate or pertain to development. From this perspective, development issues are mainly concerned with the development of "developing states". However, development is also of general concern to the international community at large, preoccupying the attention of all nations. This is mainly for three reasons. First, International Economic Law (IEL) has a welfare dimension. IDL is this dimension. Thus, the relationship between poverty elimination and international peace and security and the welfare of the international community is acknowledged.[3] Secondly, the fact of the globalised economy, and the foreign origins of some of the processes facilitating development, both necessitate and generate international concern.[4] Thirdly, development concerns are not merely voluntary but rather their basis is set in justice.[5] Development involves re-distribution against the background of arbitrarily distributed world resources. In such circumstances Rawl's intellectual apparatus of the "veil of ignorance" for the construction of a world order for States calls for redistribution of the world's scarce resources not as a matter of "consent" but as a matter of obligation set in justice. Moreover, Rawl's differential principle involves special treatment for the least developed States. Fourthly, in an inter-dependent globalised world the scope of State self-interest stretches to encompass an international dimension. Thus, famine in another State can involve immigration from that State. Finally, development is a fundamental objective of IEL[6]; and as such it is of concern and an aspiration for all nations, and at all times.

Historically, in international economic relations the notion of develop-

---

[2] D.D Bradlow, "Differing conceptions of development and the content of International Development Law", *South African Journal of Human Rights*, 21:1 (2005), 47–85.

[3] See United Nations Millennium Declaration (2000) and Monterrey Consensus of the International Conference on Financing for Development (2002).

[4] See United Nations Millennium Declaration (2000) and Monterrey Consensus of the International Conference on Financing for Development (2002).

[5] See J. Rawls *Theory of Justice*, (Harvard University Press: 1971); P. Van Parijs, "International Distributive Justice", in R.E.Goodin et al.(eds), *A Companion to Contemporary Political Philosophy*, Vol–2, (OUP, 2007); F.Garcia, "Global Justice and the Bretton woods Institutions", J.I.E.L., 10 3 2007 pp.461–81.

[6] See United Nations Millennium Declaration (2000) and Monterrey Consensus of the International Conference on Financing for Development (2002) and see, for example, Van Themaat, *The Changing Structure of International Economic Law* (1981) and F.V. Garcia-Amador (1990), p.41.

ment has been associated with economic development.[7] Thus, developing countries have been preoccupied with such issues as preferential treatment in trade, stable commodity prices, nationalisation, access to capital and good governance in international economic institutions.[8] However, over time conceptions of development have evolved and indeed differ. The differences in conceptions of development inform the content of IDL.[9] Thus, IDL has evolved from the grips of colonialism to the liberating movement of the New International Economic Order[10]; from that reaction, to the more all encompassing notion of sustainable development. Today there is increasing emphasis on poverty elimination at the practical level[11]; and the realisation of fundamental human freedoms[12] and international distributive justice[13] at the ideological level. Thus, there has been a movement away from the historical economic focus to a more holistic approach to development.[14] The extent of this movement, and therefore our understanding of the content of IDL, depends as Daniel Bradlow very aptly put it "to a large extent on one's view of the relationship between economic growth and the social (including human rights), environmental, political, and cultural aspects of the development process."[15] Moreover, the means to achieve development whether in the economic or holistic sense are not necessarily universally agreed.

IDL has not traditionally been covered well, if at all, in standard IEL textbooks[16]; nor indeed in a coherent fashion within IEL. Further, given

---

[7] D.D. Bradlow, "Differing conceptions of development and the content of International Development Law", *South African Journal of Human Rights,* 21:1 (2005), 47–85

[8] D.D. Bradlow.

[9] D.D. Bradlow. "Differing conceptions of development and the content of International Development Law", *South African Journal of Human Rights,* 21:1 (2005), 47–85.

[10] See the Declaration on the establishment of a New International Economic Order (NIEO) (Res 3201 (S-VI)) May 1974; the Programme of Action (for the establishment of a NIEO) (Res 3202 (S-VI)) May 1974; the Charter of Economic Rights and Duties of States (Res 3281 (XXIX)) December 1974. See also, for example, K. Hossain (ed.), *Legal Aspects of the New International Economic Order* (London, Francis Pinter, 1980); N. Horn, "Normative problems of a New International Economic Order", *JWT,* 16:4 (1982), 338–351; Hossain and Chowdhury (eds), *Permanent sovereignty over natural resources in International law* (London, Francis Pinter, 1984); Makarczyk, *Principles of a New International Economic Order* (Dordrecht, Martinus Nijhoff, 1988); and Opperman and Petersmann (eds), *Reforming the International Economic Order* (Berlin, Duncker and Humblot, 1987); A.H. Qureshi "Critical Concepts in the New International Economic Order and its Impact on the Development of International Economic Law—A Tribute to the Call for a NIEO", *Manchester Journal of International Economic Law,* December 2010.

[11] See United Nations Millennium Declaration (2000) and Monterrey Consensus of the International Conference on Financing for Development (2002).

[12] See, for example, Amartya Sen, *Development as Freedom,* (OUP, 1999).

[13] See, for example, John Rawls, *Theory of Justice* (1971); P. Van Parijs, "International Distributive Justice", in R.E. Goodin et al. (eds), *A Companion to Contemporary Political Philosophy, Vol.2,* (OUP, 2007); F. Garcia, "Global Justice and the Bretton woods Institutions", J.I.E.L., 10, 3, 2007 pp.461–481.

[14] D.D. Bradlow.

[15] D.D. Bradlow.

[16] J.H. Jackson, W.J. Davey and A.O. Sykes, *Legal Problems of International Economic Relations: Cases, Materials and Text on the National and International Regulation of Transnational Economic Relations,* 4th edn (St. Paul: West Group, 2002); I. Seidl-Hohenveldern, *International*

that a noticeable portion of IDL is dependent upon sources such as soft law and General International Law, there is an absence of both a systematic appraisal of the status of soft law instruments and State practice relevant to the development sphere. Indeed, the development of IDL might be said to be informed by the legislative vessel afforded to it within IEL. For example, IDL begs some fundamental questions—what is a "developing State"? Is there an obligation to accord special and differential treatment to developing countries in international economic relations? Yet in the Anglophone literature there has been insufficient focus on the practice of States and International Economic Organisations in relation to these questions.[17] Nor it seems is there a sufficient political will to address in a legislative manner such fundamental questions that underpin IDL. In the Doha Round both these fundamental questions remain largely unanswered and may be said to have hampered the progress of the Round.

17-002      In short, IDL suffers from a lack of a proper constitutional and institutional framework in the international sphere, although at the institutional level, development financing has found a ready peg with the World Bank Group. Thus, the World Bank has been described by Ibrahim Shihata[18] as the premier development institution.[19] Others have similarly crowned it, although the strictly correct description of the World Bank Group is that it is a premier institution for *financiering* for development, and not development par excellence.[20] At the regional level of particular note are development banks.[21]

Other institutions and programmes involved with the development enterprise as defined by the Millennium Development Goals (MDGs), are collectively referred to as the United Nations Development Group (UNDG). The UNDG comprises "32 UN funds, programmes, agencies, departments, and offices."[22] These include UNDP, UNICEF, UNFPA, WFP, OHCHR, UNIFEM, UNOPS, UNAIDS, UN Habitat, UNODC, WHO, DESA, IFAD, UNCTAD, UNESCO, FAO, UNIDO, ILO, UNDPI, OHRLLS, SRSGCAC, UNEP, UNHCR, OSAA, UNWTO, WMO, ITU, and the

---

*Economic Law*, 3rd rev. edn (The Hague, London, Kluwer Law International, 1999); A.F. Lowenfeld, *International Economic Law* (Oxford, Oxford University Press, 2008).

[17] See, on definition of developing countries, for example, G. Verdirame, "The definition of developing countries under GATT and other International Law" (1996) 39 *German Yearbook of International Law* 164–97 at p.166; Fan Cui, "Who are the developing countries in the WTO?", *The Law and Development Review*, 1:1 (2008), 121-152. And see, on differential treatment, for example, P. Cullet, "Differential Treatment in International Law: Towards a New Paradigm of Inter-state Relations" (1999) 10(3) E.J.I.L. 549–82.

[18] Senior Vice-President and General Council of the World Bank.

[19] See I. Shihata, *The World Bank in a Changing World* Vol.II (The Hague, London, Martinus Nijhoff, 1995), p.34.

[20] See A.H. Qureshi "International Trade for Development: the WTO as a Development Institution?" 43:1 *Journal of World Trade*, (February 2009) p.173–188.

[21] See *http://www.undg.org/index.cfm?P=13*. (Accessed June 8, 2011). For example, the Inter-American Development Bank, the African Development Bank, the Asian Development Bank, Islamic Development Bank.

[22] See *www.undg.org*. (Accessed June 8, 2011).

World bank, INFIP, OCHA, (as Observers). The UNDG takes its cue from a mandate that is regularly informed by a "Comprehensive Policy Review of operational activities for development of the United Nations system," under a General Assembly resolution.[23] This Comprehensive Policy Review, initially since 1989, took place on a triennial basis (TCPR), but since 2008[24] will take place on a quadrennial basis (QCPR). The Comprehensive Policy Reviews provide policy orientation for development co-operation along with institutional coherence and co-ordination in international and national development efforts. Moreover, the reviews serve "as an important instrument for the monitoring and the assessment of UN development operations."[25] It is fair to observe, however, that these reviews appear to be programmatic, aspirational and hortatory—without binding content. Thus, in the 2008 Comprehensive Policy Review the General Assembly[26]:

> "*Urges* donor countries and other countries in a position to do so to substantially increase their voluntary contributions to the core/regular budgets of the United Nations development system, in particular its funds, programmes and specialized agencies, and to contribute on a multi-year basis, in a sustained and predictable manner;"

Moreover, unlike the international trade and monetary spheres which have clear basic constitutional regimes underpinning them set within a clear institutional framework, IDL does not have such a coherent system underlying it. The executive, legislative and judicial processes in IDL are to be found fragmented, if at all. Further, much of IDL is to be found in soft law (particularly in the form of UN resolutions), in General International Law and in bilateral treaty arrangements. There is no one multilateral regime which covers the gambit of development issues. In some measure development concerns are integrated in international trade and monetary law. However, a substantial part of IEL is also exclusively concerned with development issues. This fragmented constitutional and normative character of IDL makes it a particularly difficult branch of IEL. The difficulty is exacerbated in particular by the differing perspectives on the ways of facilitating development. Thus, from a legal perspective, a principal challenge is to discern the law from the aspiration of nation States. From an economic perspective, a principal quest is to fathom the optimum way or ways to facilitate development; both against as well as despite the political realities of our times.

In sum, the normative framework of development can be analysed as performing and having the following characteristics and functions. First, it is marked by the traditional model of rights and responsibilities. These rights and responsibilities can rest both on the developed and the developing **17-003**

---

[23] *www.undg.org.* (Accessed June 8, 2011).
[24] For the 2008 TCPR see UNGA Resolution 62/208.
[25] *www.undg.org.* (Accessed June 8, 2011).
[26] See para.19 of GA Resolution 62/208.

members of the international community. Thus, the protection of foreign investment, the regulation of foreign investment, the regulation of multi-national corporations, sustainable development and economic sovereignty fall under this traditional normative model. Importantly here, however, is the absence of an obligation to assist in development—although this negative is increasingly under challenge. Secondly, there are the co-operative or facilitative frameworks. Here are to be found the structures of development assistance; technology transfer; commodity arrangements; and preferential treatment in trade. Arguably the resources here can be inadequate with stringent conditions and questionable governance structures. Thirdly, there is the integrationist framework. Here the mechanisms which facilitate the full participation and inclusion of development and developing States in the international economy are germane, e.g. participating in international economic organisations, the sharing of international responsibilities, and the mainstreaming of development goals in the operations of international economic organisations. This effort is mainly aspirational although the UN Comprehensive Policy Review is to be noted. Fourthly, there is the externally orientated regulatory framework which aims at setting standards and structure within the domestic economy so as to ensure unhindered development. Recent efforts have involved bestowing ownership of such frameworks at the country level. Examples here would be good governance in domestic policy making and implementation, balance of payments adjustments and elimination of poverty. Finally, there are the communal frameworks which ensure that the resources that are common to mankind, for example, the deep sea bed, are shared by the international community as a whole. In each of these different spheres and endeavours the normative content may be hard, soft or indeed even aspirational.

In learning IDL a number of precautionary lenses need to be worn. First, this is a branch of IEL that can be politicised, and polarised along the lines of developing and developed States. This complexion can descend even to the level of publicists. Therefore, in understanding IDL it is important not to rely uncritically on writers from only one sphere of the international economy. Secondly, particularly where development issues or perspectives are enmeshed with the rest of IEL, there is a dearth of analysis from writers from developing States. Further, development issues are often selectively treated in standard works of International Law originating in developed States. Thus, the topic of investment protection and environmental law features in standard International Law text-books.[27] These are issues dear to developed States. However, the rest, indeed arguably the core of development law, is ignored. Thirdly, because it is easy to be emotive about development, there is a danger in being swayed by the programmatic character of some

---

[27] See, for example, M. Shaw, *International Law*, 6th edn (Cambridge, Cambridge University Press, 2008); I. Brownlie, *Principles of Public International Law*, 6th edn (Oxford, Oxford University Press, 2003).

of its content, in ones appraisal of its legal content. Finally, although the NIEO movement has a historical setting, and requires careful consideration in the determination of its contribution to the development of IEL, it can be commended as a tool for the appraisal of IDL—although by no means an exclusive one.[28] Since development is mainly a developing phenomenon, what better tool of appraisal than the developing spectacles.

Some aspects of development have already been alluded to in other chapters, for example, in the chapters dealing with economic sovereignty, international monetary and financial relations, world trade, international investment and taxation. Here, the main focus is on some of the fundamental legal principles underpinning IDL and on international development assistance[29] as key spheres in the development strategy of particular interest to developing and developed States respectively. What have not been focused on are areas where the legal framework particularly is somewhat weak.[30]

## FUNDAMENTAL CONCEPTS AND PRINCIPLES

The participants of IDL comprise of States and international organisations, particularly international economic organisations. **17-004**

There is no definition of a development institution as such in International Law.[31] International organisations are not defined functionally. However they have core functions and are categorised accordingly for various purposes. Legal issues in relation to international organisations arise in the context of specific exercises of powers which raise questions of authority/mandate and competence. These questions are determined through the process of interpretation of the relevant treaty text. In this process of treaty interpretation, and as a consequence of the principle of speciality,[32] the defining features of

---

[28] See A.H. Qureshi "Critical Concepts in the New International Economic Order and its Impact on the Development of International Economic Law—A Tribute to the Call for a NIEO" in *Manchester Journal of International Economic Law*, December 2010.

[29] See Ch.18.

[30] On the international regulatory framework pertaining to Transfer of Technology see, for example, M. Blakenely, *Legal aspects of the transfer of technology to developing countries* (Oxford, ESC, 1989). On Commodity Agreements see, for example, K.-U.-R. Khan, *The Law & Organisation of International Commodity Agreements* (The Hague, London, Martinus Nijhoff, 1982). On Multinational Corporations see, for example, P. Muchlinski, *Multinational Enterprises and the Law* (Oxford, Oxford University Press, 2nd edn 2007).

[31] This and the next three paragraphs derive from the article A.H. Qureshi "International Trade for Development: the WTO as a Development Institution?" 43:1 *Journal of World Trade*, (February 2009) pp.173–188.

[32] Legality of the Use by a State of Nuclear Weapons in armed conflict 1996 (Preliminary Objections): "In the opinion of the Court, to ascribe to the WHO the competence to address the legality of the use of nuclear weapons 'even in view of their health and environmental effects' would be tantamount to disregarding the principle of speciality; for such competence could not be deemed a necessary implication of the Constitution of the Organization in the light of the purposes assigned to it by its member States. Para 26: It follows from the various

the organization may provide an insight into the particular question of competence at issue. However, although every international economic organization may have identifiable core competencies which inform its character and provide a label, there is the need for some caution here. Labels can be useful for some purposes, but they can also serve to blind and obscure. Thus, the mandates of international economic organizations can be complex and nuanced.[33] They may well be multifaceted, such that the organization can be described as exuding differing attributes and characteristics in varying degrees.

In the same vein, international economic organisations possess international personality. This personality is accompanied by responsibilities. International organisations are subject to International Law. It may or may not be that there is an enforceable obligation in International Law, for all subjects of International Law, in particular in the economic sphere, to take cognizance of the development condition and imperative. However, international organisations operate within the international economic order. As such, the spirit and the endeavour of that order must at least provide some sort of a context within which international organisations can formulate their normative responses to international economic problems.

17-005     A survey of the objects and purposes of the principal international economic organisations would reveal similarities[34] in terms of development and development related goals. A survey of the family of international development agencies (e.g. the UN Development Group) would reveal the same. The UN Development Group includes different development agencies concerned with disparate facets of development—for example, human rights (UNHCHR), refugees (UNHCR), labour standards (ILO), environment (UNEP), welfare of children (UNICEF), welfare of women (UNIFEM),

---

instruments mentioned above that the WHO Constitution can only be interpreted, as far as the powers conferred upon that Organization are concerned, by taking due account not only of the general principle of speciality, but also of the logic of the overall system contemplated by the Charter. If, according to the rules on which that system is based, the WHO has, by virtue of Article 57 of the Charter, 'wide international responsibilities', those responsibilities are necessarily restricted to the sphere of public 'health' and cannot encroach on the responsibilities of other parts of the United Nations system. And there is no doubt that questions concerning the use of force, the regulation of armaments and disarmament are within the competence of the United Nations and lie outside that of the specialized agencies. Besides, any other conclusion would render virtually meaningless the notion of a specialized agency; it is difficult to imagine what other meaning that notion could have if such an organization need only show that the use of certain weapons could affect its objectives in order to be empowered to concern itself with the legality of such use. It is therefore difficult to maintain that, by authorizing various specialized agencies to request opinions from the Court under Article 96, paragraph 2, of the Charter, the General Assembly intended to allow them to seize the Court of questions belonging within the competence of the United Nations."

[33] See, for example, David Vines, "The WTO in Relation to the Fund and the Bank: Competencies, Agendas and Linkages", in *The WTO as an International Organization*, ed. A.O. Krueger (University of Chicago Press, 1998), 61.

[34] See, for example, G.P. Sampson, "Greater Coherence in Global Economic Policymaking: A WTO Perspective", in *The WTO as an International Organization*, ed. A.O. Krueger (University of Chicago Press, 1998), 259.

food (WFP), aids (UNAIDS), drugs (UNODC), trade and development (UNCTAD), development funding (World Bank Group). This grouping and co-ordination of development efforts, is an articulation of the fact that there is a "panorama of development policies", of which trade is integral.[35] It is also illustrative that the development agencies in different spheres avail themselves of different mechanisms in the operation and implementation of their development role. Thus, in the UN Development Group are agencies which engage in the development process in their respective sphere through financial aid, technical assistance, standard setting, and the provision of a forum for discussion and negotiation. In sum, there are differences in the core competencies and functions of these agencies found in the UN development group. There is thus no archetypal development agency at the functional level as such.

However, the key focus of IDL centres around developing countries in the broad sense. In many respects IDL and IEL generally, in the distribution of rights and duties, differentiates between States according to the level of their development. This normative disparity arises in the economic relations between States in the discharge of international economic responsibilities and in the costs and benefits arising from membership to international economic organisations. Thus, the benefits of being categorised as a least developed country fall mainly in three areas: multilateral trade; finance for development; and technical assistance.[36] Further, this differentiation takes into account the graduated character of the phenomenon of developing, distinguishing for example, between developing[37] and least-developed countries. Thus, the UN Committee for Development has been authorised by the UN General Assembly to identify which countries are least developed and which have graduated from being least developed to a higher level of development.[38] However, as a matter of General International Law it has been contended that there is no obligation on the part of developed States to recognise the condition of a State as being one of a developing country.[39] This proposition however may need now to be considered more rigorously. Further, in International Law it is claimed that there is no general definition of what is a developing country.[40] States and international economic organisations use their own definitions.[41] Thus, in the WTO self-designation is the primary method, whereas in the UN in relation to less developed countries a list-based approach is adopted based on certain criteria. There are several

---

[35] See, for example, A. Keck & P. Low, "Special and Differential Treatment in the WTO: Why, When and How?", Staff Paper ERSD-2004-03 May, 2004, 9.

[36] See UN Economic & Social Council E/2001/94 para.6.

[37] Also referred to as less developing. See EU-LDC Network website.

[38] UN Economic & Social Council E/2001/94

[39] G. Verdirame, "The definition of developing under GATT and other International Law" (1996) *German Yearbook of International Law* p.195; Fan Cui, "Who are the developing countries in the WTO?", *The Law and Development Review*, 1:1 (2008), 121–152.

[40] See, for example, Garcia-Amador (1990), p.58. See also G. Verdirame (1996), p.195.

[41] See G. Verdirame (1996), for example.

possible reasons for this lack of consensus and uniform practice.[42] First, there are different types of developing countries with different needs and interests. Secondly, the concept of development is dynamic and complex. Finally, there may be political advantage in obfuscation.

17-006     Be that as it may, there are several factors that can be relevant in evaluating the condition of development for the purposes of defining a developing country. Indeed, conceptions of development as well as the purpose and context of defining can inform the definition. The considerations that have featured and been mooted include[43] first, economic based criteria such as national income viz., Gross Domestic Product or Gross National Income, and the UN Economic Vulnerability Index which reflects economic structure, e.g. share of manufacturing and services in GDP/export instability. Secondly, social aspects of development to include, for example, Amartya Sen's conception of development as basic human freedoms, the UN Human Assets Index (HAI) to reflect human quality and human assets, for example, calorie intake/ child mortality/secondary school enrolment/adult literacy; and the Friends of Earth: Happy Planet Index compiled to reflect human well-being and environmental impact. And finally, country size has also been a consideration.

With respect to least-developed countries the UN definition of "Least-Developed Countries" (LDCs)[44] is widely used, including by the WTO albeit for a specific purpose.[45] However, it is to be noted that the International Development Association's definition of a least-developed country, also used by the IMF,[46] is at variance with the UN criteria.[47]

In conclusion, however, some common practice can be discerned.[48] First, there is sufficient evidence of at least a three-tiered category of development in which States fall—viz. developed, developing and least developed.[49] It is to be noted though that the Doha Round of multilateral trade negotiations have stalled as a consequence of a lack of a clear recognition of another category, namely the emerging economies such as China, Brazil and India.

---

[42] See Fan Cui, "Who are the developing countries in the WTO?", *The Law and Development Review*, 1:1 (2008), 121–152.

[43] See Fan Cui, "Who are the developing countries in the WTO?", *The Law and Development Review*, 1:1 (2008), 121–52.

[44] See the UN Committee for Development Planning's work as endorsed by the UN General Assembly (GA Res.2768 (XXVI) of November 18, 1971); and the revised criteria endorsed by the GA in 1991 (GA Res.46/206 of December 20, 1991). For a comprehensive assessment of the definition of least-developed States see UN Committee for Development Policy: *Handbook on the Least Developed Country Category: Inclusion, Graduation and Special Support Measures.* (UN, 2008).

[45] The UN definition of Least-Developed Countries is adopted in Annex VII of the WTO Agreement on Subsidies.

[46] See The Chairman's Summing Up at the Conclusion of the Discussion on Special Disbursement Account Executive Board Meeting 86/56—March 26, 1986 in IMF *Selected Decisions*, 22nd Issue, p.336. See low-income countries: Decision No.8240-(86/56) SAF March 26, 1986, as amended. Note IMF uses the description low income countries.

[47] Verdirame (1996), p.195.

[48] Verdirame (1996), p.195.

[49] Verdirame (1996), p.194.

Secondly, the stages of development are such that States can graduate from a category.[50]

**UN Composition of macro geographical (continental) regions, geographical sub-regions, and selected economic and other groupings[51]**

"There is no established convention for the designation of 'developed' and 'developing' countries or areas in the United Nations system. In common practice, Japan in Asia, Canada and the United States in northern America, Australia and New Zealand in Oceania, and Europe are considered 'developed' regions or areas. In international trade statistics, the Southern African Customs Union is also treated as a developed region and Israel as a developed country; countries emerging from the former Yugoslavia are treated as developing countries; and countries of eastern Europe and of the Commonwealth of Independent States (code 172) in Europe are not included under either developed or developing regions."

17-007

**World Bank Definitions[52] :**

"**Developed countries (industrial countries, industrially advanced countries).** High-income countries, in which most people have a high standard of living. Sometimes also defined as countries with a large stock of physical capital, in which most people undertake highly specialized activities. According to the World Bank classification, these include all high-income economies except Hong Kong (China), Israel, Kuwait, Singapore, and the United Arab Emirates. Depending on who defines them, developed countries may also include middle-income countries with transition economies, because these countries are highly industrialized. Developed countries contain about 15 percent of the world's population. They are also sometimes referred to as 'the North'.

**Developing countries.** According to the World Bank classification, countries with low or middle levels of GNP per capita as well as five high-income developing economies—Hong Kong (China), Israel, Kuwait, Singapore, and the United Arab Emirates. These five economies are classified as developing despite their high per capita income because of their economic structure or the official opinion of their governments. Several countries with transition economies are sometimes grouped with developing countries based on their low or middle levels of per capita income, and sometimes with developed countries based on their high industrialization. More than 80 percent of the world's population lives in the more than 100 developing countries.

**Low-income countries.** Classified by the World Bank in 1997 as countries whose GNP per capita was $755 or less in 1999.

**Least developed countries.** Low-income countries where, according to the United Nations, economic growth faces long-term impediments- such as structural weaknesses and low human resources development. A category used to guide donors and countries in allocating foreign assistance."

"Eligibility for IDA support depends first and foremost on a country's relative poverty, defined as GNI per capita below an established threshold and updated annually (in fiscal year 2011: US$1,165).[53]

17-008

---

[50] Verdirame (1996), p.194. See also World Bank Group practice and GATT 1994.
[51] http://unstats.un.org/unsd/methods/m49/m49regin.htm. (Accessed June 8, 2011).
[52] http://www.worldbank.org/depweb/english/beyond/global/glossary.html. (Accessed June 8, 2011).
[53] Source: http://www.worldbank.org. (Accessed June 8, 2011).

**What are the least developed countries?**[54]

Forty-nine countries are currently designated by the United Nations as 'least developed countries' (LDCs). These are: Afghanistan, Angola, Bangladesh, Benin, Bhutan, Burkina Faso, Burundi, Cambodia, the Central African Republic, Chad, the Comoros, the Democratic Republic of the Congo, Djibouti, Equatorial Guinea, Eritrea, Ethiopia, the Gambia, Guinea, Guinea-Bissau, Haiti, Kiribati, the Lao People's Democratic Republic, Lesotho, Liberia, Madagascar, Malawi, Maldives, Mali, Mauritania, Mozambique, Myanmar, Nepal, Niger, Rwanda, Samoa, Sao Tome and Principe, Senegal, Sierra Leone, the Solomon Islands, Somalia, Sudan, Timor-Leste, Togo, Tuvalu, Uganda, the United Republic of Tanzania, Vanuatu, Yemen and Zambia.

The list of LDCs is reviewed every three years by the United Nations Economic and Social Council

(ECOSOC), in the light of recommendations by the Committee for Development Policy (CDP). The following three criteria were used by the CDP in the latest review of the list of LDCs, which took place in March 2009:

(a) a **'low-income'** criterion, based on a three-year average estimate of the gross national income (GNI) per capita, with a threshold of $905 for possible cases of addition to the list, and a threshold of $1,086 for graduation from LDC status;

(b) a **'human assets weakness'** criterion, involving a composite index (the Human Assets Index) based on indicators of: (i) nutrition (percentage of the population that is undernourished); (ii) health (child mortality rate); (iii) school enrolment (gross secondary school enrolment rate); and (iv) literacy (adult literacy rate);

and

(c) an **'economic vulnerability'** criterion, involving a composite index (the Economic Vulnerability Index) based on indicators of: (i) natural shocks (index of instability of agricultural production; share of the population made homeless by natural disasters); (ii) trade shocks (an index of instability of exports of goods and services); (iii) exposure to shocks (share of agriculture, forestry and fisheries in GDP; index of merchandise export concentration); (iv) economic smallness (population in logarithm); and (v) economic remoteness (index of remoteness).

For all three criteria, different thresholds are used for identifying cases of addition to, and cases of graduation from, the list of LDCs. A country will qualify to be added to the list if it meets the addition thresholds on all three criteria and does not have a population greater than 75 million. Qualification for addition to the list will effectively lead to LDC status only if the government of the relevant country accepts this status. A country will normally qualify for graduation from LDC status if it has met graduation thresholds under at least two of the three criteria in at least two consecutive triennial reviews of the list. However, if the GNI per capita of an LDC has risen to a level at least double that of the graduation threshold, the country will be

---

[54] UNCTAD: THE LEAST DEVELOPED COUNTRIES REPORT: *Towards a New International Development Architecture for LDCs* 2010 (*http://www.unctad.org/en/docs/ldc2010_en.pdf*. (Accessed June 8, 2011)).

deemed eligible for graduation regardless of its performance under the other two criteria.

Only two countries have so far graduated from LDC status: Botswana in December 1994, and Cape Verde in December 2007. In March 2009, the CDP recommended the graduation of Equatorial Guinea. This recommendation was endorsed by ECOSOC in July 2009 (resolution 2009/35), but the General Assembly had not, by September 2010, confirmed this endorsement. Also in September 2010, the General Assembly, giving due consideration to the unprecedented losses which Samoa suffered as a result of the Pacific Ocean tsunami of 29 September 2009, decided to defer to 1st January 2014 the graduation of that country. In accordance with General Assembly resolution 60/33, Maldives is expected to graduate from LDC status on 1st January 2011.

After a CDP recommendation to graduate a country has been endorsed by ECOSOC and the General Assembly, the graduating country is granted a three-year grace period before graduation effectively takes place. This grace period, during which the country remains an LDC, is designed to enable the graduating State and its development and trade partners to agree on a 'smooth transition' strategy, so that the possible loss of LDC specific concessions at the time of graduation does not disrupt the socio-economic progress of the country.

Development has been defined as the process which facilitates for every **17-009** human person and all peoples the enjoyment of economic, social, cultural and political development.[55] Thus development is a comprehensive process, aimed at the improvement of the entire population, and all individuals.[56] It is a fundamental goal of the international community, and is a clearly stated objective of the UN. The UN is enjoined in its Charter to promote higher standards of living, full employment, and generally conditions for economic, social and development progress.[57]

This open-ended concept of development has now been given a more concrete content by the international community in the form of the UN General Assembly Resolution—the Millennium Declaration.

## THE MILLENNIUM DEVELOPMENT GOALS and the United Nations Role[58]

In September 2000, at the United Nations Millennium Summit, world leaders **17-010** agreed to a set of time bound and measurable goals and targets for combating poverty, hunger, disease, illiteracy, environmental degradation and discrimination against women. Placed at the heart of the global agenda, they are now called the Millennium Development Goals (MDGs). The Summit's Millennium Declaration also outlined a wide range of commitments in human rights, good governance and democracy.

At the International Conference on Financing for Development in

---

[55] Art.1 of the Declaration on the Right to Development (1986).
[56] Preamble to the Declaration on the Right to Development (1986).
[57] Art.55 of the UN Charter.
[58] Extracts from the UN Fact Sheet on Implementing the Millennium Declaration 2002 UN Resolution adopted by the General Assembly 55/2. United Nations Millennium Declaration, http://www.un.org. (Accessed June 8, 2011).

Monterrey, Mexico, earlier this year, leaders from both developed and developing countries started to match these commitments with resources and action, signalling a global deal in which sustained political and economic reform by developing countries will be matched by direct support from the developed world in the form of aid, trade, debt relief and investment.

The MDGs provide a framework for the entire UN system to work coherently together towards a common end. The UN Development Group (UNDG) will help ensure that the MDGs remain at the centre of those efforts. . .

## MILLENNIUM DEVELOPMENT GOALS TO BE ACHIEVED BY 2015

- **HALVE EXTREME POVERTY AND HUNGER**

  1.2 billion people still live on less than $1 a day. But 43 countries, with more than 60 per cent of the world's people, have already met or are on track to meet the goal of cutting hunger in half by 2015.

- **ACHIEVE UNIVERSAL PRIMARY EDUCATION**

  113 million children do not attend school, but this goal is within reach; India, for example, should have 95 per cent of its children in school by 2005.

- **EMPOWER WOMEN AND PROMOTE EQUALITY BETWEEN WOMEN AND MEN**

  Two-thirds of the world's illiterates are women, and 80 per cent of its refugees are women and children.

  Since the 1997 Microcredit Summit, progress has been made in reaching and empowering poor women, nearly 19 million in 2000 alone.

- **REDUCE UNDER-FIVE MORTALITY BY TWOTHIRDS**

  11 million young children die every year, but that number is down from 15 million in 1980.

- **REDUCE MATERNAL MORTALITY BY THREEQUARTERS**

  In the developing world, the risk of dying in childbirth is one in 48. But virtually all countries now have safe motherhood programmes and are poised for progress.

- **REVERSE THE SPREAD OF DISEASES, ESPECIALLY HIV/AIDS AND MALARIA**

  Killer diseases have erased a generation of development gains. Countries like Brazil, Senegal, Thailand and Uganda have shown that we can stop HIV in its tracks.

- **ENSURE ENVIRONMENTAL SUSTAINABILITY**

  More than one billion people still lack access to safe drinking water; however, during the 1990s, nearly one billion people gained access to safe water and as many to sanitation.

- **CREATE A GLOBAL PARTNERSHIP FOR DEVELOPMENT, WITH TARGETS FOR AID, TRADE AND DEBT RELIEF**

  Too many developing countries are spending more on debt service than on social services. New aid commitments made in the first half of 2002 alone, though, will reach an additional $12 billion per year by 2006.

By the same token, in 2010 UNCTAD has tried to give more specific content to the concept of development through its call for a new international development architecture (NIDA) for the LDCs.

### PILLARS, PRINCIPLES AND PROCESSES OF THE PROPOSED NIDA[59]

**17-011**

As stated in the introduction to this overview, UNCTAD is calling for a new international development architecture (NIDA) for the LDCs to foster new, more inclusive development paths. The Report proposes a conceptual framework for the NIDA, including its objectives, the key principles which should inform its design and its major pillars. It also proposes key elements of a positive agenda for action in the creation of the NIDA, identifying priority areas. These are intended to be catalytic rather than exclusive.

Within both the global economic regimes and the South-South development cooperation framework, the Report identifies five major pillars which require reforms to constitute the NIDA. These are:

- The international financial architecture, including the aid and debt relief regime as well as regimes affecting private capital flows, both into LDCs by non-residents and out of LDCs by residents;

- The multilateral trade regime;

- An international commodity policy;

- An international knowledge architecture which enables access to, and use and generation of knowledge, including technology transfer and acquisition; and

- A regime for climate change adaptation and mitigation.

A new generation of special ISMs for the LDCs would be elaborated within each of these pillars. The resulting new architecture should thus be able to influence and shape economic behaviour of all agents operating in the domains of finance, trade, commodities, technology, and climate change adaptation and mitigation in order to achieve the basic objectives of the NIDA.

It is proposed that the overall design of the NIDA for LDCs be based on eight fundamental principles, as follows:

(i) Enable new, more inclusive development paths in LDCs based on the development of productive capacities, the associated expansion of productive employment and improvement in the well-being of all people;

(ii) Foster and support country ownership of national development strategies and enhance the space for development policy;

(iii) Facilitate LDCs' strategic integration into the global economy in line with their development needs and capacities, including through a better balance between external and domestic sources of demand;

---

[59] Edited Extract from Unctad: the Least Developed Countries Report: Towards a New International Development Architecture for LDCs (2010).

(iv) Redress the balance between the role of the market and the State. The State should play a more significant role in guiding, coordinating and stimulating the private sector towards the achievement of national development objectives;

(v) Promote greater domestic resource mobilization in LDCs with a view to reducing aid dependence;

(vi) Promote greater policy coherence between the different domains of trade, finance, technology, commodity and climate change mitigation and adaptation, and also between the global economic and trade regimes and the ISMs;

(vii) Support South-South cooperation as a strong complement to North-South cooperation;

(viii) Foster more democratic and universal participation in the global system of governance by giving greater voice and representation to LDCs.

A key feature of the proposed new architecture is an integrated policy approach which embeds international support mechanisms targeted at LDCs within both global economic regimes and South-South development cooperation. Some might argue that with the increasing differentiation of the world economy, the development dimension of global economic regimes should focus exclusively on the poorest countries, particularly the LDCs. However, this approach is analytically flawed and is rejected here, as there are major drawbacks to treating international support measures for LDCs as a substitute for systemic reforms.

Such a narrow approach would have unintended effects. Firstly, it is clear from the experience of the past 30 years that the problem is not just the weak growth performance of the poorest countries, but also the fact that some developing countries which are a slightly more advanced than the LDCs have experienced growth failures which have pushed them down into the LDC group. Secondly, it is necessary to view the global development process in dynamic terms: if the more advanced developing countries are not able to deepen their industrialization and move up the technological ladder and out of the simple products being exported by the poorer countries, it will be difficult for the poorest countries to develop. As noted in the *LDC Report 2002*: "To the extent that the more advanced developing countries meet a glass ceiling which blocks their development, there will be increasing competition between the LDCs and other developing countries." In this situation, special international support mechanisms ISMs for the LDCs could accelerate the graduation of some of these countries from the LDC category. However, at the same time, some other developing countries that are just above the LDC threshold might experience such weak economic performance as to risk entering the LDC category. Thus, although the special measures might provide benefits for some LDCs, their effect globally would be counterproductive.

The Report therefore advocates a mix of more developmental and coherent global economic regimes for *all* developing countries, including LDCs, along with special measures targeted to address the specific handicaps and vulnerabilities of the LDCs. As the more advanced developing countries move up the development ladder, LDCs could move into the production of goods and services that were formerly but can no longer be competitively produced in those more advanced developing countries. This process should be facilitated by South-South development cooperation aimed at reinforcing the mutually supportive economic relationships between the more advanced and the least developed developing countries. Finally it is important for the LDCs to have a greater voice and representation in global governance. Although the Report does not deal with this issue, it is critical to the process of creating a NIDA for LDCs.

Further, the process of development has been ascribed, under General International Law, as a right of States to development.[60]

**Declaration on the Right to Development (Adopted by General Assembly resolution 41/128 of December 4, 1986)[61]**                                    17-012

Proclaims the following Declaration on the Right to Development:

**Article 1**

1. The right to development is an inalienable human right by virtue of which every human person and all peoples are entitled to participate in, contribute to, and enjoy economic, social, cultural and political development, in which all human rights and fundamental freedoms can be fully realized.

2. The human right to development also implies the full realization of the right of peoples to self-determination, which includes, subject to the relevant provisions of both International Covenants on Human Rights, the exercise of their inalienable right to full sovereignty over all their natural wealth and resources.

**Article 2**

1. The human person is the central subject of development and should be the active participant and beneficiary of the right to development.

2. All human beings have a responsibility for development, individually and collectively, taking into account the need for full respect for their human rights and fundamental freedoms as well as their duties to the community, which alone can ensure the free and complete fulfilment of the human being, and they should therefore promote and protect an appropriate political, social and economic order for development.

3. States have the right and the duty to formulate appropriate national development policies that aim at the constant improvement of the well-being of the entire population and of all individuals, on the basis of their active, free and meaningful participation in development and in the fair distribution of the benefits resulting therefrom.

---

[60] See Separate opinion of Vice-President Weeramantry in Case concerning Gabcikovo-Nagymaros Project (Hungary/Slovakia) (1997) I.C.J. Reports; Declaration on the right to development (annex to UN Res. 41/128 (1986); Principle 3 of the Rio Declaration. See also for example R.J. Dupuy (ed.), *The Right to Development at the International Level* (Hague Academy of International Law, 1979); Chowdry (ed.) (1992); Garcia-Amador (1990), Ch.2; N. Schrijver, *Sovereignty over natural resources* (Cambridge, Cambridge University Press, 1997); Isabella D. Bunn, "The right to development: Implications for international economic law", *American University International Law Review*, 15:6 (2000), 1425–1467. See also Ch.2 above.

[61] Source: *http://www.un.org*. (Accessed June 8, 2011).

## Article 3

1. States have the primary responsibility for the creation of national and international conditions favourable to the realization of the right to development.

2. The realization of the right to development requires full respect for the principles of international law concerning friendly relations and co-operation among States in accordance with the Charter of the United Nations.

3. States have the duty to co-operate with each other in ensuring development and eliminating obstacles to development. States should realize their rights and fulfil their duties in such a manner as to promote a new international economic order based on sovereign equality, interdependence, mutual interest and co-operation among all States, as well as to encourage the observance and realization of human rights.

## Article 4

1. States have the duty to take steps, individually and collectively, to formulate international development policies with a view to facilitating the full realization of the right to development.

2. Sustained action is required to promote more rapid development of developing countries. As a complement to the efforts of developing countries, effective international co-operation is essential in providing these countries with appropriate means and facilities to foster their comprehensive development.

## Article 5

States shall take resolute steps to eliminate the massive and flagrant violations of the human rights of peoples and human beings affected by situations such as those resulting from apartheid all forms of racism and racial discrimination, colonialism, foreign domination and occupation, aggression, foreign interference and threats against national sovereignty, national unity and territorial integrity, threats of war and refusal to recognize the fundamental right of peoples to self-determination.

## Article 6

1. All States should co-operate with a view to promoting, encouraging and strengthening universal respect for and observance of all human rights and fundamental freedoms for all without any distinction as to race, sex, language or religion.

2. All human rights and fundamental freedoms are indivisible and interdependent; equal attention and urgent consideration should be given to the implementation, promotion and protection of civil, political, economic, social and cultural rights.

3. States should take steps to eliminate obstacles to development resulting from failure to observe civil and political rights, as well as economic social and cultural rights.

## Article 7

All States should promote the establishment, maintenance and strengthening of international peace and security and, to that end, should do their utmost to achieve general and complete disarmament under effective international control, as well as to ensure that the resources released by effective disarmament measures are used for comprehensive development, in particular that of the developing countries.

**Article 8**

1. States should undertake, at the national level, all necessary measures for the realization of the right to development and shall ensure, inter alia, equality of opportunity for all in their access to basic resources, education, health services, food, housing, employment and the fair distribution of income. Effective measures should be undertaken to ensure that women have an active role in the development process. Appropriate economic and social reforms should be carried out with a view to eradicating all social injustices.

2. States should encourage popular participation in all spheres as an important factor in development and in the full realization of all human rights.

**Article 9**

1. All the aspects of the right to development set forth in the present Declaration are indivisible and interdependent and each of them should be considered in the context of the whole.

2. Nothing in the present Declaration shall be construed as being contrary to the purposes and principles of the United Nations, or as implying that any State, group or person has a right to engage in any activity or to perform any act aimed at the violation of the rights set forth in the Universal Declaration of Human Rights and in the International Covenants on Human Rights.

**Article 10**

Steps should be taken to ensure the full exercise and progressive enhancement of the right to development, including the formulation, adoption and implementation of policy, legislative and other measures at the national and international levels.

The right to development, however, can be in competition with international **17-013** environmental standards; thus necessitating the integration of environmental concerns with development. This integration has found expression in the concept of sustainable development. This has been acknowledged by the International Court of Justice as follows:

"This need to reconcile economic development with protection of the environment is aptly expressed in the concept of sustainable development."[62]

However, despite this judicial acknowledgement of the *concept* (contra principle) of sustainable development, its status under International

---

[62] Case concerning Gabcikovo-Nagymaros Project (*Hungary/Slovakia*) (1997) I.C.J. Reports 7 at 78.

Law is somewhat unclear. Certainly, Judge Weeramantry in the Case Concerning the Gabcikovo-Nagymaros Project concluded that the principle of sustainable development was a norm of Customary International Law.[63] However, this conclusion has been criticised and doubted.[64] In particular, on the basis that the majority decision acknowledged only *the need* to reconcile the tension between development and the environment through *the concept* of sustainable development. Moreover, it is contended that there is insufficient evidence of State practice and *opinio juris* establishing the claim that the principle is one of Customary International Law.

Nevertheless, despite this analysis by international scholars of the status in International Law of the principle of sustainable development, it is the case that the principle has featured in a number of judicial pronouncements, and several international instruments.[65] Moreover, the principle of sustainable development is to be found underpinning the work of a number

---

[63] See Separate opinion of Vice-President Weeramantry in Case concerning Gabcikovo-Nagymaros Project (*Hungary/Slovakia*) (1997) I.C.J. Reports.

[64] See P.N. Okowa, "Case concerning the Gabcikovo-Nagymaros Project (Hungary/Slovakia)" (1998) 47 I.C.L.Q. 688–697, and P.N. Okowa, "Procedural obligations in International Environmental Agreements" (1996) B.Y.I.L. 275–336; V. Lowe, "Sustainable Development and Unsustainable Arguments" in Boyle and Freestone (eds) (Oxford, Oxford University Press, 1999), p.20; Birnie and Boyle, *International Law and the Environment*, 2nd edn (Oxford, Oxford University Press, 2002), p.95; D. French, *International Law and Policy of Sustainable Development* (Manchester: Manchester University Press, 2005), p.51; C. Voigt, *Sustainable Development as a Principle of International Law* (Martinus Nijhoff, 2009), N. Schrijver, *The Evolution of Sustainable Development in International Law* (Martinus Nijhoff, 2008).

[65] Case concerning the Gabcikovo-Nagymaros Project (*Hungary/Slovakia*) (1997) I.C.J. Reports of the United States—Import Prohibition of Certain Shrimp And Shrimp Products, Report of the Appellate Body (1998). For multilateral treaties where it has been mentioned, see, for example, the UN Framework Convention on Climate Change (1992), and the Convention on Biological Diversity (1992); UN Convention to combat desertification (1994). For declarations where it has been referred to, see, for example, the: (1) Report of the UN Conference on Human Environment, Stockholm, 1972; (2) UN Conference on Environment and Development, Rio de Janeiro (1992) (see Agenda 21 and the Rio Declaration on Environment and Development); the Copenhagen Declaration (1995); and the Johannesburg Declaration on Sustainable Development (2002). See also, for example, Munro and Lammers (eds), *Environmental Protection and Sustainable Development: Legal Principles and Recommendations* (London, Graham & Trotman, 1986); P. Sands, "International Law in the field of sustainable development" (1994) 65 B.Y.I.L. 303; W. Lang (ed.), *Sustainable Development in International Law* (London, Graham & Trotman/Martinus Nijhoff, 1995); N. Schrijver, *Sovereignty over Natural Resources* (Cambridge, Cambridge University Press, 1997); D. Shanmaganath, "Status of Sustainable Development as a Principle of National and International Law: the Indian Approach" (1997) 9 *Journal of Environmental Law* 387–402; Contra I. Brownlie who considers the principle as problematic and is himself equivocal as to its legal character acknowledging only that it has been proffered as an emergent principle (See I. Brownlie, *Principles of Public International Law*, 5th edn (Oxford, Oxford University Press, 1998), p.287; P. Birnie and A. Boyle, *International Law and the Environment*, 2nd edn (Oxford, Oxford University Press, 2002).

of international economic organisations,[66] e.g. the WTO,[67] NAFTA,[68] and the EU.[69] Indeed, the UN Commission on Sustainable Development was established by the General Assembly in December 1992 to review the progress in the implementation of the international agenda on sustainable development. Further, significantly for IDL, a number of key international development agencies, such as the World Bank, the Asian Development Bank, the African Development Bank, and the European Bank for Reconstruction and Development subscribe to the principle of sustainable development.[70]

"Sustainable development" is a broad and evolving term embracing development and environmental objectives, as well as the protection of civil and political rights.[71] In its nascent phase it was more focused on development and the environment.[72] In later international instruments, however, there is evidence of a third dimension, namely social development.[73] Thus, the three interdependent pillars of sustainable development have been described as comprising "economic development, social development and environmental protection".[74] Social development embraces human rights and good governance.[75]

The principle of sustainable development has been stated to include the **17-014** principles of the "trusteeship of earth resources, inter-generational rights, protection of flora and fauna, respect for land, maximisation of the use of natural resources while preserving their regenerative capacity, and the principle that development and environmental protection should go hand in hand".[76] These principles derive from various spheres of International Law, including "human rights, State responsibility, environmental law, economic

---

[66] Separate Opinion of Vice-President Weeramantry, Gabcikovo-Nagymaros Project (Hungary/Slovakia) ICJ (1997).
[67] See the preamble to the Marrakesh Agreement Establishing the WTO. See also the WTO Appellate Report on the *Shrimps* Case (1998).
[68] See preamble to NAFTA.
[69] Art.2 of the ECT.
[70] Separate Opinion of Vice-President Weeramantry.
[71] For example, P. Sand, "International Law in the Field of Sustainable Development" (1994) 65 B.Y.I.L. 303.
[72] See French (2005), p.22.
[73] French (2005), p.22 and para.2 of The Plan of Implementation adopted in Johannesburg 2002.
[74] French (2005), p.22.
[75] French (2005), p.22 and paras 5 and 4 of The Plan of Implementation adopted in Johannesburg 2002.
[76] Separate Opinion of Vice-President Weeramantry. See also for example N. Schrijver (1997), p.336. See also M.C.W. Pinto at p.18 in F. Weiss et al. (eds), *International Economic Law with a Human Face* (The Hague, Kluwer, 1998) where he lists the principles as comprising: the right to development; the rights to a healthy environment, the eradication of poverty; equity; sovereignty over natural resources; sustainable use of natural resources; prevention of environmental harm; the precautionary principle; differentiated responsibilities; special treatment; common heritage; cooperation in relation to trans boundary resources; good governance at national and international level; conflict resolution mechanisms. These principles are based on the work undertaken by an Expert Group convened to advise the UN Commission on Sustainable Development in September 1995.

and industrial law, equity, territorial sovereignty, abuse of rights, good neighbourliness".[77]

At its core four elements can be identified in the notion of sustainable development—each with varying degrees of legal validity.[78] These comprise the principle of inter-generational equity; the sustainable use of natural resources; the equitable use of natural resources, such that the needs of other States are taken into account; and the principle of integration—requiring the integration of environmental concerns with development plans.[79] Amongst all of these, the principle of integration is considered to be the strongest in its legal pedigree.[80] Other principles of note, particularly in the context of the environment include: the principle of good neighbourliness and international co-operation, principle of preventative action, the precautionary principle, and the "polluter pays" principle.[81] Of particular relevance to the developing countries is the principle of common but differentiated responsibility. This implies that in the application of environmental standards, it is necessary to take into account the economic, social and other circumstances of the country.[82] However, the principle of common but differentiated responsibility also has a general role in IEL. Thus, Philip Sand asserts that this principle is rooted in IEL.[83] This principle is followed in the WTO, and to a certain extent in the IMF and the World Bank Group.[84] For example, weighted voting is not merely about voting rights, but also about obligations relating to subscriptions to the organisations. This responsibility is graduated according to economic development. On the other hand, however, there is no positive right for the redistribution of wealth amongst nations. The concept of fairness, however, has entered the international economic agenda, particularly since the 1974 General Assembly Declaration on the Establishment of a NIEO.[85] Moreover, of late redistribution as a matter of justice has been called for based on Rawl's theory of justice.[86] Finally, the principle of good governance, specially participatory democracy and due process, although pertinent to the peculiar circumstances of developing

---

[77] Separate opinion of Vice-President Weeramantry in Gabcikovo-Nagymaros Project (Hungary/Slovakia) ICJ Report (1997).

[78] P. Sand in Lang (ed.) (1999), p.60.

[79] P. Sand in Lang (ed.) (1999).

[80] P. Sand in Lang (ed.) (1999). See also the WTO *Shrimps* Case and the Separate Opinion of Vice-President Weeramantry.

[81] See for example P. Sand in Lang (ed.) (1999), p.62.

[82] See also, for example, the WTO *Shrimps* Case (1998).

[83] See P. Sand in Lang (ed.) (1999), p.64.

[84] See, for example, W.D. Verwey, *The Principle of Preferential Treatment for Developing Countries and Particularly Needy Sub-groups among them in the Practice of States and Intergovernmental Organizations* in UN Doc.UNITAR/DS/S at 24–35 (August 15, 1982).

[85] See T.M. Franck, *Fairness in International Law And Institutions* (New York, Oxford University Press, 1995).

[86] See Phillipe van Parjis, "International Distributive Justice" in R.E. Goodin, P. Petit and T. Pogge (eds), *A Companion to Contemporary Political Philosophy,* Vol.2, (OUP, 2007, pp.638–652.); F.J. Garcia, "Global Justice and the Bretton Woods Institutions", J.I.E.L., 10:3 (2007), 461–481.

countries, is also of general relevance.[87] Thus, the IMF, the World Bank and the WTO have established codes of conduct in this field which they expect members to implement.

However, despite the identification of some of the principles, there is no clear legal definition under International Law of "sustainable development".[88] The all encompassing, and open-textured nature[89] of the concept, robs it somewhat of the facility of clear representation and ready use. Nevertheless, as a mechanism for resolving the often conflicting strains in IEL, as well as ensuring a balanced growth of the international economy, it has begun to serve its purpose, and been invoked in international judicial fora.[90] Further, given that it is in fact a compendium of principles, the principles being drawn need to be evaluated for their legal nature—for the pot of sustainable development can contain varying degrees of legal virtue, viz. hard law, soft law as well as controversial aspirations.[91] Not all of the principles embracing sustainable development have found their way into the corpus of IEL.

Finally, two points need to be made about the principle of sustainable **17-015** development. First, it appears to be weak in its emphasis and concern on inter-nation equity, particularly in its legal content. Secondly, and following on any principle that is a compendium of principles, and at that not clearly defined, lends itself for exploitation by vested interests. In an international economic system that is underpinned by economic power the emphasis on the particular principles may become unbalanced. Finally, the sustainable movement is symptomatic of a particular condition of mankind, (specially the key economic shapers of the international economy), in not being able to address exclusively and effectively questions that seemingly are unconnected to vested interests, in this instance development. There is a short concentration span, sometimes even accompanied by irritation, when development issues are raised and advocated. This is manifest not merely at the level of the States, but also at the level of jurists. In some measure, sustainable development serves to maintain everybody's attention. In that sense it serves a positive purpose. Although it may be regarded as a second best approach to development issues, which deserve attention in their own right.

---

[87] See Franck (1995).
[88] See P. Sand, "International Law in the field of sustainable development: emerging legal principles" in Lang, *Sustainable Development and International Law* (1995), p.58.
[89] P. Sand in Lang (ed.) (1999), p.56.
[90] viz., the WTO *Shrimps* case and the ICJ case concerning Gabcikovo-Nagymaras Project.
[91] P. Sand in Lang (ed.) (1999), p.54. See also M.C.W. Pinto, "The legal context: concepts, principles, standards and institutions" in F. Weiss, E. Denters and P. de Waart (eds), *International Economic Law With A Human Face* (The Hague, Kluwer Law International 1998).

**REPORT OF THE UNITED NATIONS CONFERENCE ON ENVIRONMENT AND DEVELOPMENT**[92]

(Rio de Janeiro, 3–14 June 1992) Annex I

RIO DECLARATION ON ENVIRONMENT AND DEVELOPMENT

**17-016**  The United Nations Conference on Environment and Development, Having met at Rio de Janeiro from 3 to 14 June 1992, Reaffirming the Declaration of the United Nations Conference on the Human Environment, adopted at Stockholm on 16 June 1972, a/ and seeking to build upon it, With the goal of establishing a new and equitable global partnership through the creation of new levels of cooperation among States, key sectors of societies and people, Working towards international agreements which respect the interests of all and protect the integrity of the global environmental and developmental system, Recognizing the integral and interdependent nature of the Earth, our home, Proclaims that:

**Principle 1:** Human beings are at the centre of concerns for sustainable development. They are entitled to a healthy and productive life in harmony with nature.

**Principle 2:** States have, in accordance with the Charter of the United Nations and the principles of international law, the sovereign right to exploit their own resources pursuant to their own environmental and developmental policies, and the responsibility to ensure that activities within their jurisdiction or control do not cause damage to the environment of other States or of areas beyond the limits of national jurisdiction.

**Principle 3:** The right to development must be fulfilled so as to equitably meet developmental and environmental needs of present and future generations.

**Principle 4:** In order to achieve sustainable development, environmental protection shall constitute an integral part of the development process and cannot be considered in isolation from it.

**Principle 5:** All States and all people shall cooperate in the essential task of eradicating poverty as an indispensable requirement for sustainable development, in order to decrease the disparities in standards of living and better meet the needs of the majority of the people of the world.

**Principle 6:** The special situation and needs of developing countries, particularly the least developed and those most environmentally vulnerable, shall be given special priority. International actions in the field of environment and development should also address the interests and needs of all countries.

**Principle 7:** States shall cooperate in a spirit of global partnership to conserve, protect and restore the health and integrity of the Earth's ecosystem. In view of the different contributions to global environmental degradation, States have common but differentiated responsibilities. The developed countries

---

[92] Report of the United Nations Conference on the Human Environment, Stockholm, June 5–16, 1972 (United Nations publication, Sales No.E.73.II.A.14 and corrigendum), Ch.I, *http://www.un.org*. (Accessed June 8, 2011).

acknowledge the responsibility that they bear in the international pursuit of sustainable development in view of the pressures their societies place on the global environment and of the technologies and financial resources they command.

**Principle 8:** To achieve sustainable development and a higher quality of life for all people, States should reduce and eliminate unsustainable patterns of production and consumption and promote appropriate demographic policies.

**Principle 9:** States should cooperate to strengthen endogenous capacity-building for sustainable development by improving scientific understanding through exchanges of scientific and technological knowledge, and by enhancing the development, adaptation, diffusion and transfer of technologies, including new and innovative technologies.

**Principle 10:** Environmental issues are best handled with the participation of all concerned citizens, at the relevant level. At the national level, each individual shall have appropriate access to information concerning the environment that is held by public authorities, including information on hazardous materials and activities in their communities, and the opportunity to participate in decision-making processes. States shall facilitate and encourage public awareness and participation by making information widely available. Effective access to judicial and administrative proceedings, including redress and remedy, shall be provided.

**Principle 11:** States shall enact effective environmental legislation. Environmental standards, management objectives and priorities should reflect the environmental and developmental context to which they apply. Standards applied by some countries may be inappropriate and of unwarranted economic and social cost to other countries, in particular developing countries.

**Principle 12:** States should cooperate to promote a supportive and open international economic system that would lead to economic growth and sustainable development in all countries, to better address the problems of environmental degradation. Trade policy measures for environmental purposes should not constitute a means of arbitrary or unjustifiable discrimination or a disguised restriction on international trade. Unilateral actions to deal with environmental challenges outside the jurisdiction of the importing country should be avoided. Environmental measures addressing transboundary or global environmental problems should, as far as possible, be based on an international consensus.

**Principle 13:** States shall develop national law regarding liability and compensation for the victims of pollution and other environmental damage. States shall also cooperate in an expeditious and more determined manner to develop further international law regarding liability and compensation for adverse effects of environmental damage caused by activities within their jurisdiction or control to areas beyond their jurisdiction.

**Principle 14:** States should effectively cooperate to discourage or prevent the relocation and transfer to other States of any activities and substances that cause severe environmental degradation or are found to be harmful to human health.

**Principle 15:** In order to protect the environment, the precautionary approach shall be widely applied by States according to their capabilities. Where there are threats of serious or irreversible damage, lack of full scientific certainty shall not be used as a reason for postponing cost-effective measures to prevent environmental degradation.

**Principle 16:** National authorities should endeavour to promote the internalization of environmental costs and the use of economic instruments, taking into account the approach that the polluter should, in principle, bear the cost of pollution, with due regard to the public interest and without distorting international trade and investment.

**Principle 17:** Environmental impact assessment, as a national instrument, shall be undertaken for proposed activities that are likely to have a significant adverse impact on the environment and are subject to a decision of a competent national authority.

**Principle 18:** States shall immediately notify other States of any natural disasters or other emergencies that are likely to produce sudden harmful effects on the environment of those States. Every effort shall be made by the international community to help States so afflicted.

**Principle 19:** States shall provide prior and timely notification and relevant information to potentially affected States on activities that may have a significant adverse transboundary environmental effect and shall consult with those States at an early stage and in good faith.

**Principle 20:** Women have a vital role in environmental management and development. Their full participation is therefore essential to achieve sustainable development.

**Principle 21:** The creativity, ideals and courage of the youth of the world should be mobilized to forge a global partnership in order to achieve sustainable development and ensure a better future for all.

**Principle 22:** Indigenous people and their communities and other local communities have a vital role in environmental management and development because of their knowledge and traditional practices. States should recognize and duly support their identity, culture and interests and enable their effective participation in the achievement of sustainable development.

**Principle 23:** The environment and natural resources of people under oppression, domination and occupation shall be protected.

**Principle 24:** Warfare is inherently destructive of sustainable development. States shall therefore respect international law providing protection for the environment in times of armed conflict and cooperate in its further development, as necessary.

**Principle 25:** Peace, development and environmental protection are interdependent and indivisible.

**Principle 26**: States shall resolve all their environmental disputes peacefully and by appropriate means in accordance with the Charter of the United Nations.

**Principle 27:** States and people shall cooperate in good faith and in a spirit of partnership in the fulfillment of the principles embodied in this Declaration and in the further development of international law in the field of sustainable development."

### World Summit on Sustainable Development, Johannesburg, South Africa 2002[93]

"Johannesburg Plan of Implementation

I. Introduction

1. The United Nations Conference on Environment and Development, held in Rio de Janeiro in 1992,[94] provided the fundamental principles and the programme of action for achieving sustainable development. We strongly reaffirm our commitment to the Rio principles,[95] the full implementation of Agenda 212 and the Programme for the Further Implementation of Agenda 21.[96] We also commit ourselves to achieving the internationally agreed development goals, including those contained in the United Nations Millennium Declaration[97] and in the outcomes of the major United Nations conferences and international agreements since 1992.

   **17-017**

2. The present plan of implementation will further build on the achievements made since the United Nations Conference on Environment and Development and expedite the realization of the remaining goals. To this end, we commit ourselves to undertaking concrete actions and measures at all levels and to enhancing international cooperation, taking into account the Rio principles, including, inter alia, the principle of common but differentiated responsibilities as set out in principle 7 of the Rio Declaration on Environment and Development.[98] These efforts will also promote the integration of the three components of sustainable development—economic development, social development and environmental protection—as interdependent and mutually reinforcing pillars. Poverty eradication, changing unsustainable patterns of production and consumption and protecting and managing the natural resource base of economic and social development are overarching objectives of, and essential requirements for, sustainable development.

3. We recognize that the implementation of the outcomes of the Summit should benefit all, particularly women, youth, children and vulnerable

---

[93] Source: *http://www.un.org*. (Accessed June 8, 2011).

[94] Report of the United Nations Conference on Environment and Development, Rio de Janeiro, June 3–14, 1992 (United Nations publication, Sales No.E.93.I.8 and corrigenda).

[95] Report of the United Nations Conference on Environment and Development, Rio de Janeiro, June 3–14, 1992 (United Nations publication, Sales No.E.93.I.8 and corrigenda), Vol.I: Resolutions Adopted by the Conference, resolution 1, annexes I and II.

[96] General Assembly resolution S-19/2, annex.

[97] General Assembly resolution 55/2.

[98] Report of the United Nations Conference on Environment and Development, Rio de Janeiro, June 3–14, 1992 (United Nations publication, Sales No.E.93.I.8 and corrigenda), Vol.I: Resolutions Adopted by the Conference, resolution 1, annex I.

groups. Furthermore, the implementation should involve all relevant actors through partnerships, especially between Governments of the North and South, on the one hand, and between Governments and major groups, on the other, to achieve the widely shared goals of sustainable development. As reflected in the Monterrey Consensus,[99] such partnerships are key to pursuing sustainable development in a globalizing world.

4. Good governance within each country and at the international level is essential for sustainable development. At the domestic level, sound environmental, social and economic policies, democratic institutions responsive to the needs of the people, the rule of law, anti-corruption measures, gender equality and an enabling environment for investment are the basis for sustainable development. As a result of globalization, external factors have become critical in determining the success or failure of developing countries in their national efforts. The gap between developed and developing countries points to the continued need for a dynamic and enabling international economic environment supportive of international cooperation, particularly in the areas of finance, technology transfer, debt and trade and full and effective participation of developing countries in global decision-making, if the momentum for global progress towards sustainable development is to be maintained and increased.

5. Peace, security, stability and respect for human rights and fundamental freedoms, including the right to development, as well as respect for cultural diversity, are essential for achieving sustainable development and ensuring that sustainable development benefits all.

6. We acknowledge the importance of ethics for sustainable development and, therefore, emphasize the need to consider ethics in the implementation of Agenda 21.

(Paragraphs 7–170 omitted here.)

[99] Report of the International Conference on Financing for Development, Monterrey, Mexico, March 18–22, 2002 (United Nations publication, Sales No.E.02.II.A.7), Ch.I, resolution 1, annex.

CHAPTER 18

# INTERNATIONAL DEVELOPMENT ASSISTANCE—AND THE WORLD BANK GROUP[1]

## GENERALLY

International development assistance can take a number of forms. Chiefly, **18-001** though, the mechanisms comprise of aid; loans; debt relief; measures to encourage or facilitate investment, for example loan guarantees; the provision of conflict resolution mechanisms; and finally technical assistance. The sources of such flows can be States disbursing bilateral aid; international economic organisations viz., the World Bank Group, the IMF, regional development banks, UN agencies; and private enterprises. Indeed, according

---

[1] See the Articles of Agreement of the IBRD, IDA, IFC, MIGA and ICSID; *Decisions of the Executive Directors under Article IX of the Articles of Agreement on questions of interpretation of the Articles of Agreement* IBRD (1991); *Proceedings and documents*, United Nations Monetary and Financial Conference, Bretton Woods, New Hampshire, 1944 (1948) 2 Volumes, Washington DC, Dept of State Publication; and *http://www.worldbank.org.* (Accessed June 8, 2011). See also, for example, G.R. Delaume, *Legal Aspects of International Lending and Economic Development Financing* (Dobbs Ferry, Oceana Publications, 1967); E.S. Mason and R.E. Asher, *The World Bank Since Bretton Woods* (Washington, Brookings Institution, 1973); L. Lazar, *Transnational Economic and Monetary Law* (Dobbs Ferry, Oceana Publications, 1977) Book 3, Ch.9; C. Payer, *The World Bank: A Critical Analysis* (New York: Monthly Review Press,1982); H.G. Petersmann, "The operations of the World Bank and the evolution of its institutional functions since Bretton Woods (1944–84)" (1983) G.Y.I.L. 26; H. Bretaudeau, *La Banque Mondiale* (Paris, PUF, 1986); I. Shihata, *MIGA and Foreign Investment: The Origins, Operations, Policies and Basic Documents of the Multilateral Investment Guarantee Agency* (Dordrecht, Boston, Lancaster: Martinus Nijhoff, 1988); I. Shihata, *The World Bank in a Changing World* (Dordrecht, Martinus Nijhoff, 1991); B.S. Brown, *The United States and the Politicization of the World Bank: Issues of International Law and Policy* (Kegan Paul International, 1992); S.K. Chatergee, "The World Bank" in H. Fox (ed.), *Economic Law And Developing States* (1992); I. Shihata, *The World Bank in a Changing World* (The Hague, Martinus Nijhoff, 1995), Vol.II; A. Broches, *World Bank, ICSID, and other Subjects of Public and Private International Law* (Martinus Nijhoff, 1995); J.M. Griesgraber (ed.), *The World Bank—Lending on a Global Scale* (London, Pluto Press with Center of Concern, 1996); I. Shihata, *The World Bank in a Changing World* (Martinus Nijhoff, 2000), Vol.III; P.K. Nevitt and F. Fabozzi. *Project Financing*, 7th edn (London, Euromoney Books, 2000); C.L. Gilbert and D. Vines, *The World Bank: Structure and Policies* (Cambridge, Cambridge University Press, 2000).

to one World Bank Report[2] there are now over 150 agencies involved in development assistance including increasing "South–South exchanges of financial resources." This has led to the following observation being made[3]:

> "While this expanding roster of participants has brought additional resources, and new ideas, expertise, and approaches to address global development challenges, it has also brought risks of aid fragmentation, loss of efficiency, and mismatch with country priorities. These problems are most acute in fragile and conflict-affected countries where fragmentation and international agendas can overwhelm government capacity to set priorities and coordinate international assistance, underscoring the need for harmonization and alignment of aid programs."

The object of development assistance need not directly be the State. Rather, it may be the private sector. Further, the assistance may involve a single entity, or a combination of international and private entities. In addition the assistance may be directed at the economy as a whole; or relate to a specific project, or sector of the economy.[4] This cocktail of assistance measures, donors and beneficiaries, makes this branch of international development law complicated, detailed in character, and straddling International Law and domestic law.

The Monterrey Consensus[5] is one relatively recent effort at promoting co-ordination and coherence in the international financing for development. The Monterrey Consensus is the result of the Conference on Financing for Development held on March 19–22, 2002 between some developed and developing countries. The Conference was preceded by two years of negotiations between the participants in the conference. However, the Consensus is essentially non-binding and contains various hortatory declarations. It is nevertheless an attempt at approaching development financing in a comprehensive manner. Moreover, it is accompanied by an apparatus for its implementation.[6]

---

[2] World Bank: "New World, New World Bank Group: (I) Post-Crisis Directions," para.6, 2010 (DC2010-0003).

[3] World Bank: "New World, New World Bank Group: (I) Post-Crisis Directions," para.7, 2010 (DC2010-0003).

[4] Focusing on a particular sector of the economy.

[5] See UN *Report of the International Conference on Financing for Development*, Monterrey, Mexico 18022 March 2002 A/CONF.198/11. See also, for example, I. Haque and R. Burdescu, "Monterrey Consensus on Financing for Development: Response Sought from International Economic Law", (2004) 27 *B.C. Int'l. & Comp. 2 Rev.* 219; and A.H. Bouab, "Financing for development: The Monterrey Consensus" in *Michigan Journal of International Law*, 26:1 (2004), pp.359–369.

[6] See para.69 of the Monterrey Consensus. See also reports of the UN Secretary-General on the International Financial System and Development; External Debt Crisis and Development and International Trade and Development, the note by the Secretary-General on Coherence, Coordination and Cooperation in the context of the implementation of the Monterrey Consensus and the 2005 World Summit Outcome (E/2006/48), and the summary by the President of the Economic and Social Council of the special high-level meeting of the Council with the Bretton Woods institutions, the World Trade Organization and the United Nations Conference on Trade and Development (A/61/81–E/2006/73). See *http:www.un.orglesalffd.* (Accessed June 8, 2011).

The Monterrey Consensus is aimed mainly at progressing with the **18-002** Millennium Development Goals, and developing consensus on the mobilisation of financial resources for development as well as the appropriate conditions for development along with the reception of development resources. The Conference focused on the various sources of funding. At its core, the Monterrey Consensus embraces certain "leading actions", viz. (1) mobilising domestic financial resources for development (this focuses on the internal domestic conditions necessary to facilitate investment, for example, coherent macroeconomic policies, good governance, fighting corruption, national infrastructure); (2) mobilising international resources for development including foreign direct investment (here the focus is on domestic conditions to attract investment, for example, investment protection, avoidance of double taxation, fair competition; the promotion and facilitation by national, regional and international institutions of private foreign investment; corporate responsibility; introduction of new private and public sector financing mechanisms); (3) international trade as an engine for development (here the focus is on promoting a rule-based, open, non-discriminatory and equitable trading system along with the implementation of the Doha Agenda); (4) increasing international financial and technical co-operation for development (here the focus is on official development assistance (ODA), national ownership of development plans and good governance, recognition of the need by developed nations to increase ODA to developing countries with a target of 0.7 per cent of gross national product (GNP) and 0.15 to 0.20 per cent of GNP of developed countries to least-developed countries, increasing the efficacy of ODA); and (5) external debt (here the focus is on sustainable debt financing, sound national macroeconomic policies, flexibility with respect to the eligibility criteria for the Heavily Indebted Poor Countries Initiative); addressing systemic issues: enhancing the coherence and consistency of the international monetary, financial and trading systems in support of development (focus on such matters as the improvement of global economic governance and the strengthening of the United Nations leadership in promoting development; national co-ordination between relevant Ministries, reform of the international financial architecture, including effective participation of developing countries in international economic decision-making; improved co-ordination between international economic institutions, the role of IMF in surveillance and conditionality). In short, the consensus focuses both on the internal efforts of the target beneficiaries of development assistance as well as improved co-ordination at the international level and from the international level—including effective participation of developing countries in international economic decision-making. Most significantly, the Consensus does not involve a pledge on a quantified amount of increased financial flows for development. It is focused more on policy and institutional reform and co-ordination. In particular it is arguably more focused on the efforts of the target beneficiaries.

In sum, the Monterrey Consensus has a function, albeit in soft terms in co-ordinating development assistance through the World Bank Group, in informing as to the nature of the development assistance and the apparatus through which it is imparted. A further wider context within which the World Bank Group development assistance is set in the UNDG Comprehensive Policy Review of operational activities for development of the United Nations system referred to in Ch.17.

**Monterrey Consensus of the International Conference on Financing for Development[7]**

**18-003**

The International Conference on Financing for Development

Having met in Monterrey Mexico, from 18 to 22 March 2002,

1. Adopts the Monterrey Consensus of the International Conference on Financing for Development, which is annexed to the present resolution:

2. Recommends to the General Assembly that it endorse the Monterrey Consensus as adopted by the Conference.

**I. Confronting the challenges of financing for development: a global response**

1. We the heads of State and Government, gathered in Monterrey, Mexico, on 21 and 22 March 2002, have resolved to address the challenges of financing for development around the world, particularly in developing countries. Our goal is to eradicate poverty, achieve sustained economic growth and promote sustainable development as we advance to a fully inclusive and equitable global economic system.

2. We note with concern current estimates of dramatic shortfalls in resources required to achieve the internationally agreed development goals, including those contained in the United Nations Millennium Declaration.

3. Mobilizing and increasing the effective use of financial resources and achieving the national and international economic conditions needed to fulfil internationally agreed development goals, including those contained in the Millennium Declaration, to eliminate poverty, improve social conditions and raise living standards, and protect our environment, will be our first step to ensuring that the twenty-first century becomes the century of development for all.

4. Achieving the internationally agreed development goals, including those contained in the Millennium Declaration, demands a new partnership between developed and developing countries. We commit ourselves to sound policies, good governance at all levels and the rule of law. We also commit ourselves to mobilizing domestic resources, attracting international flows, promoting international trade as an engine for development, increasing international financial and technical cooperation for development, sustainable debt financing and external debt relief, and enhancing the coherence and consistency of the international monetary, financial and trading systems.

5. The terrorist attacks on 11 September 2001 exacerbated the global

---

[7] Source: *http://www.un.org*. (Accessed June 8, 2011).

economic slowdown, further reducing growth rates. It has now become all the more urgent to enhance collaboration among all stakeholders to promote sustained economic growth and to address the long-term challenges of financing for development. Our resolve to act together is stronger than ever.

6. Each country has primary responsibility for its own economic and social development, and the role of national policies and development strategies cannot be overemphasized. At the same time, domestic economies are now interwoven with the global economic system and, inter alia, the effective use of trade and investment opportunities can help countries to fight poverty. National development efforts need to be supported by an enabling international economic environment. We encourage and support development frameworks initiated at the regional level, such as the New Partnership for Africa's Development and similar efforts in other regions.

7. Globalization offers opportunities and challenges. The developing countries and countries with economies in transition face special difficulties in responding to those challenges and opportunities. Globalization should be fully inclusive and equitable, and there is a strong need for policies and measures at the national and international levels, formulated and implemented with the full and effective participation of developing countries and countries with economies in transition to help them respond effectively to those challenges and opportunities.

8. In the increasingly globalizing interdependent world economy, a holistic approach to the interconnected national, international and systemic challenges of financing for development—sustainable, gender-sensitive, people-centred development—in all parts of the globe is essential. Such an approach must open up opportunities for all and help to ensure that resources are created and used effectively and that strong, accountable institutions are established at all levels. To that end, collective and coherent action is needed in each interrelated area of our agenda, involving all stakeholders in active partnership.

9. Recognizing that peace and development are mutually reinforcing, we are determined to pursue our shared vision for a better future, through our individual efforts combined with vigorous multilateral action. Upholding the Charter of the United Nations and building upon the values of the Millennium Declaration, we commit ourselves to promoting national and global economic systems based on the principles of justice, equity, democracy, participation, transparency, accountability and inclusion.

## II. Leading actions

A. Mobilizing domestic financial resources for development

(Paragraphs 10–19 omitted)

B. Mobilizing international resources for development: foreign direct investment and other private flows

(Paragraphs 20–25 omitted)

C. International trade as an engine for development

(Paragraphs 26–38 omitted)

D. Increasing international financial and technical cooperation for development

(Paragraphs 39–46 omitted)

E. External debt

(Paragraphs 47–51 omitted)

F. Addressing systemic issues: enhancing the coherence and consistency of the international monetary, financial and trading systems in support of development

(Paragraphs 52–67 omitted)

### III. Staying engaged

68. To build a global alliance for development will require an unremitting effort. We thus commit ourselves to keeping fully engaged, nationally, regionally and internationally, to ensuring proper follow-up to the implementation of agreements and commitments reached at the present Conference, and to continuing to build bridges between development, finance, and trade organizations and initiatives, within the framework of the holistic agenda of the Conference. Greater cooperation among existing institutions is needed, based on a clear understanding and respect for their respective mandates and governance structures.

(Paragraphs 69–73 omitted)

## WORLD BANK GROUP

**18-004** The World Bank Group plays an important role in development assistance such that it is generally described as the "premier development institution" in international economic relations. Its establishment is rooted in the Bretton Woods Conference,[8] alongside the creation of the IMF. It was envisaged as one of the three pillars[9] of the international economic system, focusing at the outset on the financing of post-war reconstruction and development. The International Bank for Reconstruction and Development (IBRD), known as the World Bank, came into being in 1946. Subsequently, other institutions were created alongside it, viz. the International Development Association (IDA) in 1960; the International Finance Corporation (IFC) in 1965[10]; the International Centre for Settlement of Investment Disputes (ICSID) opera-

---

[8] UN Monetary and Financial Conference, Bretton Woods, New Hampshire, USA (1944).
[9] The other being the IMF dealing with monetary matters, and the abortive ITO dealing with trade issues.
[10] Contra Chatergee (1992), p.119 where he states it was established in 1965. This may be a typing error however.

tional in 1966[11]; and the Multilateral Investment Agency (MIGA) established in 1988.[12] Together these institutions are known as the World Bank Group.[13]

An exposition of the World Bank Group from a legal perspective by an outsider is fraught with difficulties. This is because the existing legal appraisal is not systematic or sufficient. Some of the existing contribution, the value of which is acknowledged, flows mainly from I. Shihata, the General Counsel of the World Bank, and other similarly placed individuals from the Legal Department in the past. As with the IMF such contributions need to be critically assessed, so as to understand the extent to which they are justifying appraisals of the activities of the Bank. Further, there is a certain lack of transparency in the "law" of the World Bank Group despite recent transparency measures. Generally, the legal material that is publicly available is as follows[14]: (i) the Articles of Agreement and By-Laws; (ii) the Agreements with other international organisations; (iii) loan and credit agreements registered with the UN; the proceedings of the World Bank Administrative Tribunal relating to staff employment matters. In addition, the World Bank website has useful information—particularly of note is the World Bank's Operational Manual. However, the proceedings of the Board of Executive Directors are confidential; and the decisions of the Executive Board are not readily available[15]—particularly because they have not been systematically set out in any one source, as they have been in the IMF Selected Decisions series.[16] Important decisions of the Executive Board however are announced through press releases. It is understood that the decisions of the Executive Board are often succinct, merely approving or referring to staff papers. Thus, because these decisions are not specifically drafted for the Board to pass as such, the Board decision is to be found in both the staff paper, and the reference in the Decision to it. This *modus operandi* is somewhat inelegant and raises questions of transparency, and generally good governance within the World Bank Group. The Executive Board of the World Bank has approved in 2009 a new Policy on Access to Information which became effective in July 2010. This policy is said to represent a fundamental shift in the World Bank's approach to transparency and includes an opening up of access to relevant Board proceedings.[17] It remains to be seen how the law of the World Bank Group will become more accessible and systematically set out within this new shift in policy.

At the outset it should be noted that many of the legal issues and problems (and therefore the legal analysis) in relation to the World Bank Group are

---

[11] ICSID is dealt with in Ch.15 on International Investment Law.

[12] MIGA is dealt with in Ch.15 on International Investment Law.

[13] The Articles of Agreement of the World Bank Group are available at the World Bank website.

[14] See World Bank Policy on Disclosure of Information 1994 published in Shihata (1995).

[15] See, however, the World Bank website.

[16] H. Cisse, Legal Counsel World Bank telephone conversation November 9, 1998.

[17] See World Bank Press Release No: 2010/214/OPCS

common within the Group, and mirror in some senses those of the IMF.[18] Thus, in relation to questions, for example as to the legal character of the relations between the institutions of the World Bank Group and Member States and private parties; the binding character of terms and conditions attached to financial assistance; and the mechanisms (or lack of them) to ensure that the institutions are not exceeding their mandate—these are all matters wherein the analysis in relation to IMF operations can be pertinent by analogy[19]; as indeed the conclusions in relation to one of the institutions of the Group can be relevant in relation to the other institutions. For example, where the power to interpret the Articles and the power to give assistance coincide, as they do in the World Bank Group, as indeed in the IMF, the same problems and considerations ensue as in the IMF, in relation to the application of the doctrine of *ultra vires*.

## THE FUNCTIONS OF THE WORLD BANK GROUP

**18-005**  The functions of the IBRD are informed by its purposes, which are stated to be as follows[20]:

"(i) To assist in the reconstruction and development of territories of members, including the restoration of economies destroyed or disrupted by war, the reconversion of productive facilities to peacetime needs and the encouragement of the development of productive facilities and resources in less developed countries.

(ii) To promote in the long run the balanced growth of international trade and the maintenance of equilibrium in balance of payments, and to assist in raising productivity, the standard of living and conditions of labour."

Two things are to be noted in relation to these objectives. First, the war time reconstruction role has historical origins. Secondly, the essential conditions aimed at, relate to the development objective. These development objectives are to be achieved, mainly in a four-fold manner through, viz[21]:

"(i) the facilitation of investment of capital;

(ii) the promotion of private investment by means of guarantees or participation in loans and other investments made by private investors;

(iii) the supplementing of private investment by the Bank, out of its own capital, through funds raised by it, and through other resources, on suitable conditions;

(iv) the encouragement of international investment."

**18-006**  These functions are to be carried out within the normative framework of

---

[18] For this reason the analysis here is not as extensive as it is in Pt 2: International Monetary Law.

[19] See chapters on International Monetary Law.

[20] See IBRD Art.I.

[21] IBRD Art.I.

the World Bank—particularly in a manner so as to ensure[22] that the Bank's financial operations are directed at useful and urgent projects; and with due regard to the effect of international investment on business conditions in the territories of members.

The purposes of the IDA are as follows[23]:

"(i) To promote economic development, increase productivity and standards of living in less-developed countries of its membership;
(ii) To further the developmental objectives of the IBRD."

These purposes, specifically directed at the less-developed members, are to be achieved particularly through the availability of finance on more flexible and less onerous terms than those available through conventional loans.

The IFC, MIGA and the ICSID are more orientated towards the assistance of the private sector. Thus, the purpose of the IFC is to[24] further economic development through the encouragement of productivity of private enterprises in member countries, and thereby to supplement the efforts of the IBRD. This purpose is performed through[25]:

**18-007**

"(i) financing, in association with private investors, the establishment and growth of productive private enterprises, without guarantee of repayment by the member government concerned, where sufficient private capital is not available on reasonable terms;
(ii) bringing together investment opportunities, domestic and foreign private capital, and experienced management;
(iii) creating conditions for the flow of investment in member countries."

The objective of MIGA is to[26] encourage the flow of private investments for productive purposes among member countries, in particular developing member countries. This is achieved mainly through[27]:

"(i) issuing guarantees against non-commercial risks for investments flowing from other member countries;
(ii) engaging in complementary activities to encourage the flow of investments in developing country members."

The purpose of the ICSID is to provide facilities for conciliation and arbitration of investment disputes between Contracting States and nationals of other Contracting States.[28]

In summary, the principal collective functions of the World Bank Group in furtherance of economic development are to:

(1) make available financial resources to governments;

---

[22] IBRD Art.I.
[23] See IDA Preamble and Art.I.
[24] IFC Art.I.
[25] IFC Art.I.
[26] See MIGA Preamble and Art.2.
[27] MIGA Preamble and Art.2.
[28] See ICSID Art.1(2).

(2) make available financial resources to private enterprises;

(3) stimulate and trigger investment flows for development purposes; for example through the provision of guarantees for non-commercial risks; through the generation of appropriate development institutions and norms; and

(4) provide security and predictability to foreign investors engaging with foreign governments, through the availability of conciliation and arbitration mechanisms.

It will be noted that the aims of the disparate institutions of the World Bank Group are the same, complementary and reinforcing; although the manner of achieving those aims are somewhat different. In the light of this there is close co-operation between the institutions.[29]

The World Bank Group is prohibited from taking political considerations into account in its decision-making processes.[30] The prohibition is expressly stated, and relates to both interference in domestic political affairs, as well as being influenced by the political character of the member. Only economic considerations are to be taken into account. However, it is not very clear how this objective is actually implemented.

**Article IV SECTION 10 of the Articles of Agreement of the IBRD.[31]**

18-008     **Political Activity Prohibited**

The Bank and its officers shall not interfere in the political affairs of any member; nor shall they be influenced in their decisions by the political character of the member or members concerned. Only economic considerations shall be relevant to their decisions, and these considerations shall be weighed impartially in order to achieve the purposes stated in Article I.

INSTITUTIONAL ASPECTS OF THE WORLD BANK GROUP

18-009     Generally, the institutional aspects of the World Bank Group mirror somewhat the IMF model, and of each other within the Group. However, given that it is a kind of a bank, its institutional structure also resembles that of a corporation, with, for example, a capital stock, to which the members subscribe shares.[32] The institution, it will be noted, does not completely conform to a traditional notion of a Bank, in that it does not receive deposits, and a substantial part of its subscribed capital is not paid in.[33] Further, some of the

---

[29] See for example IBRD Art.V s.8; IFC Art.IV s.7; IDA Art.VI s.6; MIGA Art.35.
[30] See IBRD Art.IV s.10; IFC Art.III s.9; IDA Art.V s.6; IDA; MIGA Art.34.
[31] Source: *http://www.worldbank.org*. (Accessed June 8, 2011).
[32] See L. Forget in Shihata (1995), Appendix V.
[33] See Masan and Asher (1973), p.12.

institutions of the Group have been likened to a subsidiary of the Bank.[34] Finally, although legally an international organisation, the ICSID is essentially a dispute settlement facility. It does not have the full trappings of an organisation.[35]

More specifically, the following institutional aspects of the World Bank Group are of particular note. First, membership generally to the Group is directly[36] or indirectly[37] linked to membership of the IMF and the IBRD, and is consequently limited to States. Like the IMF and the WTO, membership is near universal. In the IDA there are two formal categories of members viz., Pt I members which are the industrialised countries, and the Pt II members comprising the middle- and low-income members.[38] Membership to the IBRD ceases when a member ceases to become a member of the IMF.[39] And membership in the IFC,[40] and IDA,[41] ceases when a member ceases to be a member of the IBRD. In the case of MIGA, whereas membership is linked to participation in the IBRD, there does not appear any equivalent provision on cessation, when a member ceases to be a member of the IBRD. In the case of the ICSID there are no cessation provisions which are triggered as a consequence of a member ceasing to be a member of the Bank.

Secondly, the IBRD,[42] IFC,[43] IDA[44] and MIGA[45] have a Board of Governors, Executive Board and a President. In the case of the ICSID there is an Administrative Council and a Chairman.[46] The ICSID is located in Washington at the headquarters of the World Bank. The governors, directors and the president of the IBRD are *ex officio* members of the IDA and IFC. MIGA governors and directors however are appointed separately.[47] In the case of the ICSID the Bank governors and the President act *ex officio* as members of the Administrative Council and its chairman respectively. The governors are appointed by each member. The Board of Governors have all the powers, and meet annually. It is a large body and therefore is better adapted to ratifying proposals than initiating them.[48] However, many of these powers have been delegated to the Board of Directors,[49] with the exception of those specifically reserved for the Governors under

[34] See, for example, Lazar (1977), 3-9-064 where he likens the IFA to a subsidiary of the Bank.
[35] See, for example, Mason and Asher (1973), p.82.
[36] See IBRD Art.II.
[37] See IFC Art.II; IDA Art.II; MIGA Art.4; ICSID Art.67.
[38] Mason and Asher (1973), p.81, and see IDA Art.II.
[39] IBRD Art.VI, s.3.
[40] Art.V s.3.
[41] Art.VII s.3.
[42] IBRD Art.V.
[43] IFC Art.IV.
[44] IDA Art.VI.
[45] MIGA Art.30.
[46] ICSID Ch.1, s.2.
[47] MIGA Ch.V; and see Shihata (1995), Appendix V at p.741.
[48] See Mason and Asher (1973), p.63.
[49] Mason and Asher (1973), p.63.

the Articles, for example, appeals from decisions of the Executive Board on questions of interpretation, suspension of members and amendments. There are currently 25 executive directors in total.[50] Five of the directors are appointed by the members with the highest share or contribution,[51] and the rest are elected.

Thirdly, there is a system of weighted voting in operation at the IBRD,[52] IDA,[53] IFC,[54] and MIGA.[55] Thus, every member is allocated an initial basic vote, plus votes linked to its share of the capital,[56] or its paid in fund.[57] Voting in the ICSID is, however, on the basis of one vote per one member.[58] Generally, decisions are arrived at through a majority vote when voting takes place.[59] In practice decisions are arrived at through consensus as in the WTO.[60]

**IBRD Article V SECTION 3. Voting[61]**

18-010

(a) Each member shall have two hundred fifty votes plus one additional vote for each share of stock held.

(b) Except as otherwise specifically provided, all matters before the Bank shall be decided by a majority of the votes cast.

Fourthly, the Board of Directors are responsible for the daily management of the functions of their respective institutions, which include all matters of operational policy and approval of loans.[62] However, it is to be noted that the Board of Directors can end up taking their cue in many respects from the staff and the President. For example the Board can be reduced to authorising and legitimising the activities of the staff.[63] Thus, if the management of the institution is not satisfied with a proposal it may never reach the Board of Directors.[64] As in the IMF the elected directors cannot split the votes of the constituency of the membership which voted them in. Further it is not clear, as in the IMF, whether the Executive Directors are representatives, or

---

[50] See www.worldbank.org. (Accessed June 8, 2011). See also, for example, I. Shihata in R.C. Effros (ed.) (Washington: International Monetary Fund, 1998), Vol.5.

[51] For example, IBRD Art.V.

[52] IBRD Art.V, s.3.

[53] IDA Art.VI s.3.

[54] IFC Art.IV s.3.

[55] MIGA Art.39.

[56] For example, IBRD Art.V s.3; and IFC Art.IV s.3.

[57] IDA Arts III and VI.

[58] ICSID Art.7.

[59] See, for example, IBRD Art.5 s.3.

[60] See, for example, A. Broches, "Development of International Law by the International Bank of Reconstruction and Development" in *Proceedings of the American Journal of International Law* (1965).

[61] Source: http://www.worldbank.org. (Accessed June 8, 2011).

[62] Shihata (1995), Appendix V at p.744.

[63] Mason and Esher (1973), p.63.

[64] Mason and Asher (1973), p.90.

owe allegiance to the Bank.[65] They are paid by the Bank. Decision-making in the World Bank group suffers therefore from some of the same criticisms as directed at the IMF.

Fifthly, the interpretation mechanisms of the IBRD,[66] IFC,[67] IDA,[68] and MIGA[69] are similar to that of the IMF. Thus, questions of interpretation are to be raised with the Board of Directors, and can be further pursued with the Board of Governors whose decision, however, is final. The system in the World Bank Group, as in the IMF and the WTO, has internalised the process of interpretation, allowing policy-making organs of the World Bank Group to be involved in the interpretative processes. This gives the organs of the World Bank Group considerable latitude, and one that has been considered as being broader than what a judicial authority would have.[70] However, this power of interpretation is subject to the express language of the text of the agreement. Within those parameters, however, the legal advisers of the World Bank Group have emphasised that limitations on the freedom of action of the Bank cannot be read in the Articles, except where expressly stated or found by necessary implication.[71] As in the IMF not many formal interpretative decisions have transpired in the practice of the World Bank Group—the last one being in 1986.[72] Most questions of interpretation are settled implicitly[73] or through "concurring with the interpretation submitted to them by the General Counsel of the Bank".[74] The General Counsel's role can thus be critical in the process of interpretation.

## IBRD Article IX: Interpretation[75]

(a) Any question of interpretation of the provisions of this Agreement arising between any member and the Bank or between any members of the Bank shall be submitted to the Executive Directors for their decision. If the question particularly affects any member not entitled to appoint an Executive Director, it shall be entitled to representation in accordance with Article V, Section 4 (h).

(b) In any case where the Executive Directors have given a decision under (a) above, any member may require that the question be referred to the Board of Governors, whose decision shall be final. Pending the result of the reference to the Board, the Bank may, so far as it deems necessary, act on the basis of the decision of the Executive Directors.

18-011

---

[65] Mason and Asher (1973), p.91.
[66] IBRD Art.IX.
[67] IFC Art.VIII.
[68] IDA Art.X.
[69] MIGA Art.56.
[70] Shihata (1995), p.78.
[71] Shihata (1995), p.79.
[72] See www.worldbank.org. (Accessed June 8, 2011). Shihata (1995), p.743.
[73] Mason and Asher (1973), p.90.
[74] See www.worldbank.org. (Accessed June 8, 2011).
[75] Source: http://www.worldbank.org. (Accessed June 8, 2011).

Sixthly, the respective constitutions of the institutions of the World Bank Group contain provisions for amendment[76]; and special voting majorities for certain types of amendments.[77] However, few amendments have taken place thus far.[78] The World Bank it seems has evolved through "breeding" other institutions, rather than developing through major overhauls. Indeed, the "breeding" approach was engaged in so as to forestall the possibility of a floodgate of controversial amendments to the Bank Articles of Agreement.[79]

Seventhly, there are no specific mechanisms for dispute resolution as such in the Articles of Agreement establishing the IBRD, IDA, and IFC. However, MIGA has a specific procedure for disputes between members.[80] In relation to disagreements between a member that has withdrawn these are to be dealt with through arbitration. Finally, in so far as disputes between the Bank and borrowers are concerned—these are settled by negotiation, and if this does not result in a solution, through arbitration. Bank loan agreements provide for such a dispute settlement mechanism.[81] In practice most disputes have been resolved through negotiation.[82] With respect to disputes internally as it concerns staff in their work environment the World Bank has a Conflict Resolution System which encompasses Ombuds Services, Mediation Services, Peer Review Services and Respectful Workplace Advisors.[83]

**18–012**      Further, of particular note is the establishment of the World Bank Inspection Panel by the IBRD and the IDA[84] of a grievance redress mechanism for private parties. Under the Inspection Panel system, an affected party in the territory of the borrower (which must be a community of persons, e.g. an organisation, association, society or grouping of individuals), or its representative, or an Executive Director, may request an inspection where:

> "its rights or interests have been or are likely to be directly affected by an action or omission of the Bank as a result of a failure of the Bank to follow its operation policies and procedures with respect to the design, appraisal and/or implementation of a project financed by the Bank (including situations where the Bank is alleged to have failed in its follow-up on the borrower's obligations under loan agreements

---

[76] IBRD Art.VIII; IFC Art.VII; IDA Art.IX; MIGA Chap.X; ICSID Art.IX.

[77] See, for example, IBRD Art.VIII and Art.VI s.1 in relation to a member's right to withdraw.

[78] For example, only two amendments have taken place thus far in the case of the IBRD, viz. 1965 and 1989 in relation to two specific issues.

[79] Mason and Asher (1973), p.79.

[80] MIGA Art.57.

[81] Shihata (1995), p.294.

[82] Shihata (1995), p.294.

[83] See *www.worldbank.org*. (Accessed June 8, 2011).

[84] See Resolution of the Executive Directors establishing the Inspection Panel (No.93-10 for the IBRD and 93-6 for IDA) circulated as document No.Sec M93-988 IBRD and Sec M93-313 IDA September 93. See also for example Shihata (1995), Ch.7; I. Shihata, *The World Bank Inspection Panel* (New York, Oxford University Press, 1994); I. Shihata, *The World Bank Inspection Panel: IN Practice* (Oxford, Oxford University Press, 2000); D. Clark et al. (eds), *Demanding Accountability: Civil Society and the World bank Inspection Panel* (Rowman & Littlefield Publishers Inc, 2003); G. Alfredsson and R. Ring (eds), *The Inspection Panel of the World Bank: A Different Complaints Procedure*, (Martinus Nijhoff, 2001); *Accountability at the World Bank: The Inspection Panel 10 Years On* (World Bank, 2003).

with respect to such policies and procedures) provided in all cases that such failure has had, or threatens to have, a material adverse effect".[85]

Thus, there must be an affected party, which has suffered or might suffer material damage, from a serious failure by the Bank.[86] Further, the complaint must have been first put to the Management of the Bank. The Inspection Panel comprises impartial individuals from three Bank member countries.[87] The recommendations of the Panel are made to the Executive Board.

The following observations may be made about the Inspection Panel system. First, the Inspection Panel system does not partake of judicial proceedings. It is considered to be an independent administrative review.[88] The recommendations do not have the character of a decision. Secondly, the Inspection Panel system is not concerned with disputes with the borrower. Finally, it will be observed that the Inspection Panel system is a mechanism which provides for a degree of transparency and accountability. It gives non-governmental organisations and citizens in a borrowing country an opportunity for participation; and above all for the affected parties of international actions, a direct form of remedy. Between 1994–2010 there were some 70 requests for Inspection Panels. The Inspection Panel mechanism may well have a useful role to play in the operations of other international economic organisations—including particularly the IMF.

Eighthly, all the institutions of the World Bank Group enjoy separate international legal personality, and the normal privileges and immunities enjoyed by international organisations.[89] However, in view of the fact that some of the key organs of some of the institutions share the same de facto identity in a different hat, this independent legal personality, albeit de jure does become somewhat cosmetic. Further, because the World Bank Group has dealings with the private sector, and relies on it in some circumstances, the immunity from legal process that it possesses in the territories of its member countries is limited. This is to facilitate interaction with the private sector.[90]

**18-013**

Ninthly, the Bank is a specialised agency of the UN, and has entered into an agreement with the UN establishing that relationship. Under the agreement the Bank pays due regard to UN Security Council decisions.[91] Further, the World Bank Group are to co-operate with other related international economic organisations, and give due consideration to the recommendations made.[92] The World Bank Group's closest relation is of course the IMF,

---

[85] Para.12 of the Resolution Establishing the World Bank Inspection Panel (1993).
[86] Resolution Establishing the World Bank Inspection Panel (1993), para.13; and Shihata (1995), Ch.7.
[87] Resolution Establishing the World Bank Inspection Panel (1993), para.2.
[88] Shihata (1995), p.290.
[89] IBRD Art.VII.
[90] See, for example, Broches (1995), Pt 1.
[91] Shihata (1995), p.747.
[92] For example, IBRD Art.V s.8.

and the institutions have tried to design ways of collaborating specially in the context of the Enhanced Structural Adjustment Facility and the HIPC initiative.[93] The main distinction between the IMF and the World Bank Group is that the IMF has mainly a short-term economic focus, whereas the World Bank Group has a long-term resource allocation and economic development stand.[94]

The authority to co-operate with relevant international economic organisations has been interpreted as not excluding co-operation with NGOs, in so far as the IBRD and the IDA are concerned.[95] However, this co-operation is done in a manner consistent with the policies of the borrowing country's attitude towards the NGO, and with its knowledge.[96] To encourage such co-operation a number of institutional measures have been set up. A NGO–World Bank Committee has been established[97] to facilitate a dialogue between the World Bank and NGOs; the NGOs have access to the Inspection Panel system; and a Public Information Centre has been established to enable the better dissemination of information.[98] NGOs are involved in many aspects of project lending,[99] and can be useful in identifying and assisting at grass-root level the problems associated with a project proposal, and its implementation. NGOs can themselves be recipients of grants[100] from the World Bank through a variety of Bank sources.[101] Although there is no formal authority in the Articles, the Bank is understood to have this authority to give grants as a consequence of practice, implied powers, and an interpretation of the Executive Directors in 1964.[102]

**18-014**    Tenthly, in general each member has to subscribe to a certain number of shares[103] of the capital stock; or subscribe funds[104]; or in the case of the ICSID, make payments to meet the expenses of the ICSID. The amounts in question are determined by the institutions, and reflect the member's IMF quota.[105] In the case of the Bank only a small proportion of its capital is actually paid up, which is at the time of subscription. The rest is callable.[106]

---

[93] See above Pt 2.
[94] See M. de Vries, *IMF 1966–1971*, Vol.I at pp.610–16.
[95] See Shihata (1995), p.238.
[96] Shihata (1995), p.238; and World Bank Operational Manual, Operational Directive (OD), 14.70, Involving NGOs in Bank-supported Activities, at para.1 (August 1989). This, however, may well undermine the NGO effort where the NGO policies conflict with that of the government.
[97] Shihata (1995), p.241.
[98] Shihata (1995), p.243.
[99] Shihata (1995), Ch.6.
[100] Contra loans.
[101] Shihata (1995), p.268. I. Shihata lists for the Bank's Special Grants programme; Consultancy Trusts Funds; the Project Preparation Facility, the Institutional Development Fund, the Global Environment Facility.
[102] Shihata (1995), p.268.
[103] IBRD Art.II s.3; IFC Art.II s.3; MIGA Art.6.
[104] IDA Art.II s.1.
[105] Shihata (1995), Appendix V at p.741.
[106] IBRD Art.II.

The paid-in portion is divided into that which is paid in the member's own currency and the rest in "gold or United States dollars".[107] The Bank thus funds a large proportion of its lending, not through its subscribed capital, but rather through borrowing in the international capital markets, through the issue of highly rated bonds (debt securities).[108] The Bank's callable capital (i.e. the unpaid portion of its capital subscription) acts somewhat like a security for the Bank's borrowing.[109] In fact the IBRD is "one of the largest international borrowers in the world".[110] In addition, the Bank also raises funds in other ways, for example, by selling portions of its loans to commercial banks.[111] In the case of the ICSID the expense contributions are in proportion to subscriptions to the capital stock of the Bank. MIGA's income is also supplemented by its premium and investment income. In the case of the IFC, the IBRD may make loans to it.[112] In the case of the IDA, it relies, in addition to its subscriptions, on voluntary contributions by donor countries on a periodical basis. In addition, generally the institutions can borrow from official and private sources—including the capital markets.

**18-015**

"There are six main reasons for the high degree of quality of World Bank debt instruments. First, World Bank debt is backed by the Bank's 187 sovereign shareholders. Second, the World Bank follows highly prudent financial policies that restrict its lending to a maximum of one dollar in loans per one dollar of total capital - the current ratio is as low as 47 cents in loans per one dollar of capital. The financial leverage is equally low as the World Bank's borrowings currently account for about 55% of its total capital. Third, the World Bank has achieved an annual operating income of above US$1 billion for over 15 years. Fourth, the World Bank maintains a highly liquid asset base in order to be flexible in the timing of its new debt issuance. Fifth, the World Bank's prudent lending policies, loan concentration limits ensure the high quality of the World Bank's loan portfolio. And finally, the World Bank only lends to sovereigns and sovereign-guaranteed projects and is recognized by the major rating agencies to enjoy a preferred creditor status with its borrower shareholders."[113]

Finally, the World Bank Group is serviced by an Independent Evaluation Group (IEG) originally established in 1973. The IEG is independent of the World Bank Group and is responsible for the "assessment of the relevance, efficacy, and efficiency of World Bank Group operational programmes and

---

[107] See IBRD Art.II. This has been interpreted by the EB in terms of SDR's. See Shihata (1995), "The standard of value of the Bank's capital after the demise of the Gold Dollar" (Ch.2).

[108] "In *finance*, a *bond* is a *debt security*, in which the authorised issuer owes the holders a debt and is obliged to repay the principal and interest (the *coupon*) at a later date, termed maturity." From *Wikipedia, the free encyclopedia*, (*http://wikipedia.org*. (Accessed June 8, 2011)).

[109] See, for example, A. Broches, *Selected Essays: World Bank, ICSID, and Other Subjects of Public and Private International Law* (Dordrecht, Martinus Nijhoff, 1995), Pt I.

[110] See *http://treasury.worldbank.org/Services/Capital-Markets/FAQs.html#1*. (Accessed June 8, 2011).

[111] See *http://treasury.worldbank.org/Services/Capital-Markets/FAQs.html#1*. (Accessed June 8, 2011).

[112] IBRD Art.III s.6.

[113] Source: *http://treasury.worldbank.org/cmd/html/faq_english.html*. (Accessed June 8, 2011).

activities, and their contribution to development effectiveness".[114] It will be noted that unlike the IMF the World Bank has enjoyed a longer history of such an institutionalised independent evaluation system.

Like the IMF, the World Bank Group has also undergone recent governance reforms in 2008 and 2010 in order to enhance the voice and participation of developing and transition countries in decision-making of the World Bank Group.[115] This has involved a phased increase in voting shares of developing and transition economies in the IBRD,[116] IFC[117] and IDA[118]; reforming the shareholding principles in the World Bank Group, for example, by taking into account not only economic weight in the world economy as with the IMF quotas but also contributions made to the World Bank Group and principles of equity; and finally, by adding a third Executive Board Director from Africa. These reforms have been coupled with an increase in the capital resources of the World Bank Group.

However, the World Bank Group governance seems to have escaped the kind of scrutiny that the recent financial crisis precipitated in terms of the IMF. Nevertheless, of note are the observations of the Director General of the World Bank Independent Evaluation Group made in 2007[119] with respect to three areas of particular focus that the Executive Directors should take on board. First, there should be a review of the selection and mandate of the President and Senior Management given, in particular, the current non-transparent criteria and restricted nomination process for the post of the President. Similar observations have been made with respect to the IMF. Secondly, there is a need to review the role and function of the Executive Board particularly in terms of its relationship with the management. Similar observations have been made in relation to the IMF. Finally, there is the need for greater internal safeguards and checks and balances including accountability, transparency and whistleblower protection. Similar observations have been made in relation to whistleblowers in the IMF.

---

[114] See Mandate of the Director-General Evaluation: *http://www.worldbank.org/ieg/index.html.* (Accessed June 8, 2011).

[115] See World Bank: World Bank Group Voice Reform: Enhancing Voice and Participation of Developing and Transition Countries in 2010 and Beyond (DC 2010-0006: April 19, 2010)

[116] This would increase voting power of developing and transition economies to about 50%. See World Bank Group Voice Reform 2010.

[117] This would involve an increase from 33.4% to around 38.5–41%. See World Bank Group Voice Reform 2010.

[118] This would involve an increase from around 40% to approximately 46%. See World Bank Group Voice Reform 2010.

[119] See The World Bank Group's Governance: Issues for Review From the Director General, Evaluation to the Executive Directors, May 25, 2007 at *http://www.worldbank.org/ieg/issues_for_review.pdf.* (Accessed June 8, 2011).

## The Financial Operations of the World Bank Group

The financial operations of the World Bank Group are two-dimensional, viz. the revenue raising operations of the organisation on the one hand, and on the other its financial assistance to its members. Here the emphasis will be on the financial assistance. As the assistance by the World Bank Group is at two levels, namely States and individuals, the particular financial operations of the World Bank Group need to be considered individually.

**18-016**

---

**"Fund Generation[120]**

IBRD lending to developing countries is primarily financed by selling AAA-rated bonds in the world's financial markets. While IBRD earns a small margin on this lending, the greater proportion of its income comes from lending out its own capital. This capital consists of reserves built up over the years and money paid in from the Bank's 185 member country shareholders. IBRD's income also pays for World Bank operating expenses and has contributed to IDA and debt relief.

IDA is the world's largest source of interest-free loans and grant assistance to the poorest countries. IDA's funds are replenished every three years by 40 donor countries. Additional funds are regenerated through repayments of loan principal on 35-to-40-year, no-interest loans, which are then available for re-lending. IDA accounts for more than 40% of our lending".

**18-017**

---

### The IBRD and the IDA[121]

In practice, both of these organisations focus mainly, although not exclusively, in imparting financial assistance in the form of loans,[122] the facilitation of loans, and the proffering of guarantees to Member States.[123] However, in the case of the IBRD, where the lending is to an individual party, the member in whose territory the loan is being made needs to guarantee the repayment of the principal and interest.[124] In the case of the IDA, although the organisation is authorised to finance private individuals, such financing may also be expected to be accompanied by a governmental repayment guarantee.[125] However, because IDA loans are for very long periods (between 35 to 40

**18-018**

---

[120] www.worldbank.org. (Accessed June 8, 2011).
[121] See, in particular, *The World Bank's Operational Manual* available on the World Bank website. See also, for example, P. Benoit, *The World Bank Group's Financial Instruments for Infrastructure* (January 1997) also on the World Bank website.
[122] See IDA Arts I and V s.2(c); and IBRD Arts I and III s.4.
[123] IBRD Art.IV s.1; and IDA Art.V s.2.
[124] IBRD Art.III s.4.
[125] See IDA Art.l2 V s.2.

years) and on highly concessional terms, such financing in practice is unlikely to take place.[126]

In many respects similar in their handling of financial assistance, the IBRD and the IDA differ in one important respect in relation to their clientele—namely in relation to the kind of eligible Member States which can benefit from their financial operations. In the first instance, the members eligible for IBRD financial assistance are those members who cannot elsewhere obtain such assistance under conditions which in the opinion of the Bank are reasonable.[127] These are middle-income countries. This requirement under the IBRD Articles is considered to be the legal basis for the Bank's "graduation policy". Essentially, under this requirement member countries become ineligible to use the IBRD resources as their creditworthiness improves.[128] Briefly, a member country's position is reviewed upon its attaining a certain level of per capita income GNI.[129] Under the review the Bank focuses on access to capital markets on reasonable terms, and the development of key economic and social institutions relevant for development in the member's territory.[130] On the other hand, in relation to the IDA its clientele are confined to the less-developed member countries,[131] which are unable to have access to private capital, on terms which are reasonable for them.[132]

Normally, the IDA practice in lending reflects that of the IBRD.[133] Generally, the loans are for the purposes of financing projects for reconstruction or development,[134] for example, the building of dams or power stations. These are known as hard projects.[135] The Bank also lends for soft projects, for example education and family planning.[136] The project financing takes place under a framework (i.e. the project cycle). The processes involved in the project cycle, involving both the borrower and the Bank, comprise the project identification; appraisal; negotiation and approval; implementation and supervision; and post-evaluation.[137]This kind of lending now comes under the Bank's investment operations and is referred to as investment lending.

**18-019**     However, under special circumstances loans for purposes other than

---

[126] See Shihata (1995), p.349.

[127] See IBRD Art.III s.4(ii).

[128] Shihata (1995), p.750.

[129] Shihata (1995), p.750. For fiscal year 2005 US $5,295 per capita income initiates IBRD graduation process, although countries with a higher per capita income are able to borrow under special circumstances (See Annual Report 2005 at World Bank website).

[130] See Shihata (1995) and World Bank Annual Report 2005.

[131] See IDA preamble; and Arts I and V s.1(a). Operational cut-off for IDA eligibility for FY07 is $1,025 (2005 GNI per capita). See World Bank website. See World Bank *Annual Report* (2006).

[132] IDA Art.V s.1(c).

[133] Shihata (1995), p.749.

[134] See IBRD Art.III s.4(vii) and IDA Art.V s.1(b).

[135] See, for example, H.N. Scott in R.C. Effros (ed.), *Current Legal Issues Affecting Central Banks* (Washington: International Monetary Fund, 1994), Vol.2 at p.10.

[136] See, for example, H.N. Scott in R.C. Effros (ed.), *Current Legal Issues Affecting Central Banks* (Washington: International Monetary Fund, 1994), Vol.2 at p.10.

[137] See, for example, H. Bretaudeau, Ch.VII; and Chatergee (1992), p.128.

projects can also be made. The determination of what constitutes "special circumstances" is made by the Executive Boards.[138] This exception of "special circumstance" has been interpreted liberally,[139] to disburse loans and guarantees, in particular for example for structural and sectoral adjustment purposes.[140] The Bank introduced in 1980 Structural Adjustment Loans (SAL), and in 1984 Sectoral Adjustment Loans (SECALs).[141] Structural adjustment loans aim at reforming the fundamentals of the economy, or aspects of it, and at dealing with balance of payments disequilibrium; whereas sectoral adjustment loans focus on particular sectors of the economy, for example the energy sector. The Bank embarked on widening its focus from projects to sectoral and structural issues because of the realisation of the need to focus on the broader economic context within which projects were being financed.[142] In this vein the Bank also crafted hybrid loans, with a combined sectoral and structural focus.[143] In addition, the Bank has interpreted its Articles of Agreement, on the basis of the existence of implied powers, to be able to disburse loans for debt and debt-service reduction, where this was a necessary condition for development.[144] In this context, the Executive Directors adopted policies and guidelines in 1989.[145] However, such loans can only be facilitated if they materially increase investment in the borrowing member country, beyond the mere reduction of the debts.[146] Such funding had to be in the framework of a SAL.[147] This kind of lending has now been rationalised and falls under the Bank's development policy operations.

In sum, as of 2004, with respect to both the IBRD and IDA, the various loan and credit facilities offered by the two institutions have now been simplified. The IBRD and the IDA now offer only two forms of loans and credits, viz. Investment Loans and Development Policy loans. The Development Policy Lending replaces adjustment lending, viz. sectoral adjustment loans, structural adjustment loans and poverty-reduction support credit.[148] The investment loans model is currently under review as the current model of

---

[138] Shihata (1995), p.751.
[139] Shihata (1995), p.8.
[140] Shihata (1995), p.8.
[141] Shihata (1995), p.25.
[142] See, for example, H.N. Scott in R.C. Effros (ed.), *Current Legal Issues Affecting Central Banks* Vol.2 at p.10.
[143] See, for example, H.N. Scott in R.C. Effros (ed.), *Current Legal Issues Affecting Central Banks* Vol.2 at p.12.
[144] See, for example, H.N. Scott in R.C. Effros (ed.), *Current Legal Issues Affecting Central Banks* Vol.2 at p.14. See also Shihata (1995), p.27.
[145] Shihata (1995), p.759.
[146] Shihata (1995), p.15.
[147] Shihata (1995), p.16.
[148] See *http://web.worldbank.org/WBSITE/EXTERNAL/NEWS/0,,contentMDK:20237378~menuPK:34457~pagePK:64003015~piPK:64003012~theSitePK:4607,00.html.* (Accessed June 8, 2011).

lending is not responsive to country needs and is considered overburdened with "internal rule based processes and requirements". [149]

### "Investment Operations[150]

**18-020**    Investment loans, credits and grants provide financing for a wide range of activities aimed at creating the physical and social infrastructure necessary to reduce poverty and create sustainable development. Over the past two decades, investment operations have, on average, accounted for 75 to 80 percent of the Bank's portfolio.

The nature of investment operations has changed over time. Originally focused on hardware, engineering services, and bricks and mortar, investment lending and grants have come to focus more on institution building, social development, and improving the public policy infrastructure needed to strengthen private sector activity.

### Development Policy Operations[151]

Development Policy operations provide rapid financial assistance to allow countries to deal with actual or anticipated development financing requirements of domestic or external origins. They typically support the achievement of a set of development results through a medium-term program of policy and institutional actions consistent with a country's economic and sectoral policies.

In Fiscal Year 2008, IDA and IBRD development policy operations accounted for 27 percent of total Bank commitments; in Fiscal Year 2009 they were at 40 percent as the Bank supported countries in their response to the financial crisis.

Development Policy operations can be stand-alone operations or more frequently be part of a programmatic series of operations. In programmatic operations, the Bank supports the implementation of a medium-term program of policy reforms through a series of annual operations, each of which is disbursed against a mutually agreed set of policy and institutional actions. In low-income countries where a national poverty reduction strategy (PRS) has been officially adopted by the government and where a Development Policy series supports PRS implementation, Development Policy operations may also be called Poverty Reduction Support Credits (PRSCs). They typically consist of a programmatic series of three annual operations."

**18-021**    Finally, in so far as the modalities of the lending is concerned, the institutions can either make direct loans (known as A loan), or facilitate lending, through the participation of the private sector (loan syndication programme known as B Loan).[152] Where the financing (whether in the form of loan or guarantee) involves directly the Member State and the institutions of the World Bank Group, the instrument is an international agreement governed by International Law.[153] As such, the loan and guarantee agreements are

---

[149] See World Bank Operations and Country Services: Investment Lending Reform: Concept Note (2009).
[150] Source: *http://www.worldbank.org*. (Accessed June 8, 2011).
[151] Source: *http://www.worldbank.org*. (Accessed June 8, 2011).
[152] Shihata (1995), p.758.
[153] See, for example, Broches (1995), Pts I and II.

registered with the Secretariat of the UN under Art.102 of the UN Charter. Where the financing involves a relationship between the institutions of the World Bank Group and private parties, however, the agreements in question are not international agreements governed by International Law.[154] Thus, where a loan is made to a private party under guarantee by the member country in question, the loan agreement itself, whilst partaking of an international character, is not an international agreement governed by International Law.[155]

The general conditions, in addition to the ones already mentioned, under which financing is made available are set out in the Articles of Agreement of the IBRD and the IDA.[156] The principal considerations of note are as follows. First, and foremost, generally the financing must be for productive, reconstruction and development purposes,[157] and in order to promote private foreign investment.[158] This would exclude loans for military purposes. Secondly, the total of loans and guarantees made must not be such as to exceed 100 per cent of the unimpaired subscribed capital, reserves and surplus of the IBRD.[159] Thirdly, the IBRD must act prudently, both in the interests of the borrower, and the membership as a whole.[160] Further, the Bank must pay due regard to the borrower being able to meet its obligations. The practice of the Bank is to carry out regular reviews of creditworthiness of members in terms of their eligibility as Bank borrowers.[161] Fourthly, the IBRD terms and conditions with reference to rates, charges and repayment schedules and compensation should be reasonable and suitable.[162] The IBRD charges interest and commission on its guarantees.[163] The Articles set out the circumstances of such charges.[164] In the case of the IDA, such terms are of a concessional nature.[165] Fifthly, financing for projects that a member does not consent, shall not be provided.[166] Sixthly, the assistance is to be made available only upon the recommendation of a loan committee.[167] This committee will have a nominee of the beneficiary member, and members of the technical staff of the respective Bank institutions. Seventhly, the loans by the Bank are to contain a negative pledge clause, preventing a member from giving other creditors priority over the Bank's interests.[168] Finally, both the IBRD and the IDA are

---

[154] See, for example, Broches (1995), Pts I and II.
[155] See, for example, Broches (1995), Pts I and II.
[156] See, for example, IBRD Art.III and IDA Art.V.
[157] See IBRD Art.I and IDA Art.V.
[158] IBRD Art.I and IDA Art.I.
[159] IBRD Art.III s.3.
[160] IBRD Art.III s.4 (v).
[161] Shihata (1995), p.751.
[162] Shihata (1995), p.751.
[163] IBRD Art.IV ss.4 and 5.
[164] IBRD Art.IV ss.4 and 5.
[165] IDA Art.1.
[166] IDA Art.V.
[167] IBRD Art.III s.4 and IDA Art.V.
[168] See, for example, Shihata (1995), p.759.

not to interfere as to whether the financing is to be spent in the territory of any particular member or members.[169] Thus, the necessary purchases for goods and services for the purposes of the project can be made from any member country. In addition to the stipulations under the respective constitutions of the IBRD and the IDA, the loan/guarantee agreements also incorporate, by reference; standard terms set out in General Conditions.[170]

### IBRD Articles of Agreement III[171]

#### SECTION 1. Use of Resources

18-022

(a) The resources and the facilities of the Bank shall be used exclusively for the benefit of members with equitable consideration to projects for development and projects for reconstruction alike.

#### SECTION 4. Conditions on which the Bank may Guarantee or Make Loans

The Bank may guarantee, participate in, or make loans to any member or any political sub-division thereof and any business, industrial, and agricultural enterprise in the territories of a member, subject to the following conditions:

(i) When the member in whose territories the project is located is not itself the borrower, the member or the central bank or some comparable agency of the member which is acceptable to the Bank, fully guarantees the repayment of the principal and the payment of interest and other charges on the loan.

(ii) The Bank is satisfied that in the prevailing market conditions the borrower would be unable otherwise to obtain the loan under conditions which in the opinion of the Bank are reasonable for the borrower.

(iii) A competent committee, as provided for in Article V, Section 7, has submitted a written report recommending the project after a careful study of the merits of the proposal.

(iv) In the opinion of the Bank the rate of interest and other charges are reasonable and such rate, charges and the schedule for repayment of principal are appropriate to the project.

(v) In making or guaranteeing a loan, the Bank shall pay due regard to the prospects that the borrower, and, if the borrower is not a member, that the guarantor, will be in position to meet its obligations under the loan; and the Bank shall act prudently in the interests both of the particular member in whose territories the project is located and of the members as a whole.

(vi) In guaranteeing a loan made by other investors, the Bank receives suitable compensation for its risk.

---

[169] IBRD Art.III s.V; IDA Art.V s.I.

[170] Shihata (1995), p.755. See the IBRD's General Conditions Applicable to Loan and Guarantee Agreements; and the IDA's General Conditions Applicable to Development Credit Agreements. See also The World Bank Operational Manual at www.worldbank.org. (Accessed June 8, 2011).

[171] Source: http://www.worldbank.org. (Accessed June 8, 2011).

(vii) Loans made or guaranteed by the Bank shall, except in special circumstances, be for the purpose of specific projects of reconstruction or development."

**IBRD Article IV SECTION 1. Methods of Making or Facilitating Loans**          18-023

"(a) The Bank may make or facilitate loans which satisfy the general conditions of Article III in any of the following ways:

   (i) By making or participating in direct loans out of its own funds corresponding to its unimpaired paid-up capital and surplus and, subject to Section 6 of this Article, to its reserves. 2.          Section added by amendment effective December 17, 1965.

   (ii) By making or participating in direct loans out of funds raised in the market of a member, or otherwise borrowed by the Bank.

   (iii) By guaranteeing in whole or in part loans made by private investors through the usual investment channels.

(b) The Bank may borrow funds under (a) (ii) above or guarantee loans under (a) (iii) above only with the approval of the member in whose markets the funds are raised and the member in whose currency the loan is denominated, and only if those members agree that the proceeds may be exchanged for the currency of any other member without restriction."

**IDA Article V: Operations**

**"SECTION 1. Use of Resources and Conditions of Financing**          18-024

(a) The Association shall provide financing to further development in the less-developed areas of the world included within the Association's membership.

b) Financing provided by the Association shall be for purposes which in the opinion of the Association are of high developmental priority in the light of the needs of the area or areas concerned and, except in special circumstances, shall be for specific projects.

(c) The Association shall not provide financing if in its opinion such financing is available from private sources on terms which are reasonable for the recipient or could be provided by a loan of the type made by the Bank.

(d) The Association shall not provide financing except upon the recommendation of a competent committee, made after a careful study of the merits of the proposal. Each such committee shall be appointed by the Association and shall include a nominee of the Governor or Governors representing the member or members in whose territories the project under consideration is located and one or more members of the technical staff of the Association. The requirement that the committee include the nominee of a Governor or Governors shall not apply in the case of financing provided to a public international or regional organization.

(e) The Association shall not provide financing for any project if the member in whose territories the project is located objects to such financing, except that it shall not be necessary for the Association to assure itself that individual members do not object in the case of financing provided to a public international or regional organization.

(f) The Association shall impose no conditions that the proceeds of its financing shall be spent in the territories of any particular member or members. The foregoing shall not preclude the Association from complying with any restrictions on the use of funds imposed in accordance with the provisions of these Articles, including restrictions attached to supplementary resources pursuant to agreement between the Association and the contributor.

(g) The Association shall make arrangements to ensure that the proceeds of any financing are used only for the purposes for which the financing was provided, with due attention to considerations of economy, efficiency and competitive international trade and without regard to political or other non-economic influences or considerations.

(h) Funds to be provided under any financing operation shall be made available to the recipient only to meet expenses in connection with the project as they are actually incurred.

**SECTION 2. Form and Terms of Financing**

(a) Financing by the Association shall take the form of loans.

18-025  Development Policy Lending is authorised under the "special circumstances" provisions in the IBRD and IDA Articles of Agreement.[172] Since the World Bank's involvement in adjustment lending, the Bank has had to be involved in Conditionality. Investment Lending (project lending) does not normally involve Conditionality. The Bank's Conditionality has been explained in the *Review of World Bank Conditionality* (2005).[173] This Review also contains a background paper titled *Legal Aspects of Conditionality in Policy-Based Lending* prepared by the Legal Vice Presidency of the World Bank (Legal Opinion). The main points of the Review and the legal opinion may be summarised as follows. As a preliminary it is noted that there is no legal definition of the World Bank Conditionality found expressly in the Articles of the IBRD or the IDA.[174] The Bank's guidance on adjustment lending was codified in December 1992 in the Operative Directive (OD) 8.60. In August 2004, new guidance on policy-based lending was formulated through Operational Policy OP 8.60.[175] Paragraph 13 of the OP 8.60 sets out certain essential requirements relating to World Bank Conditionality as follows:[176]

---

[172] IBRD Art.III s.40 (vii) and IDA Art.V, s.1 (9b).

[173] In 2007 there was another review of bank operations leading to another report titled: Conditionality in Development Policy Lending (2007).

[174] See para.2 of *Legal Aspects of Conditionality in Policy-Based Lending* prepared by the Legal Vice Presidency of the World Bank (Background Paper 2 prepared by H. Cisse and V. Raghavan) found in the *Review of World Bank Conditionality* (2005).

[175] Background Paper 2, above, para.7.

[176] Background Paper 2, above, para.8. And see OP 8.60—Development Policy Lending in World Bank Operational Policies at *www.worldbank.org*. (Accessed June 8, 2011).

"13. *Conditions.* The Bank determines which of the agreed policy and institutional actions by the country are critical for the implementation and expected results of the program supported by the development policy loan. The Bank makes the loan funds available to the borrower upon maintenance of an adequate macroeconomic policy framework, implementation of the overall program in a manner satisfactory to the Bank, and compliance with these critical program conditions. The Bank seeks to harmonize these conditions with other development partners in consultation with the country." (Footnotes omitted).

In addition, the 2005 review identifies certain good practice principles governing the formulation of conditionality as follows: ownership; harmonisation; customisation; criticality; and transparency and predictability. In substance, these mirror the IMF Guidelines on Conditionality.

**Source: Review of World Bank Conditionality September 2005[177]**    **18-026**

**Table 1. Good Practice Principles**

| | |
|---|---|
| Ownership | *Reinforce country ownership.* |
| Harmonization | *up-front with the government and other financial partners on a coordinated accountability framework.* |
| Customization | *the accountability framework and modalities of Bank support to country circumstances.* |
| Criticality | *only actions critical for achieving results as conditions for disbursement.* |
| Transparency and Predictability | *transparent progress reviews conducive to predictable and performance-based financial support.* |

In addition to these Good Practice Principles, political conditions are prohibited.[178] Further guidance on World Bank Conditionality formulation is to be found in the Legal Opinion included in the 2005 World Bank Review. This mainly stipulates that the imposition of conditions should take into account the capacity of the member to implement the conditions, the member's constitution and its ability to bring legislative changes.[179] Furthermore, conditions that compromise the member's negotiating stand in international trade negotiations should be avoided as should cross-conditions.[180]

   The conditions can only involve economic considerations.[181] Economic considerations have been interpreted to include good governance,[182] and macro-economic conditions, such as trade liberalisation, exchange rate adjustments, fiscal policy reform and price reform.[183] The borrower's undertakings are contained in its letter, which is referred to as the Letter of

**18-027**

---

[177] Source: *http://www.worldbank.org.* (Accessed June 8, 2011).
[178] See IDA Art.V s.6 and IBRD Art.IV. See also *Legal Aspects of Conditionality* (2005), para.51.
[179] *Legal Aspects of Conditionality* (2005), para.56.
[180] *Legal Aspects of Conditionality* (2005), paras 59 and 64.
[181] For example IBRD Art.IV s.10.
[182] Shihata (1995), p.754.
[183] See, for example, Scott in Effros (ed.) (1998), p.10.

Development Policy. The terms of this letter are referred to in the loan agreement.[184] In addition, all financing undergoes environmental impact evaluation.[185]

The mandate for World Bank Conditionality, despite the absence of explicit reference to it in the IBRD and IDA Articles, is explained as follows. First, it is maintained that the "special circumstances" under which policy-based lending is authorised, are accompanied by a wide degree of discretion to set development policy conditions.[186] Secondly, all IDA and IBRD lending must be in accordance with the purposes[187] of the two institutions. These purposes leave ample discretion as to how the purposes are to be achieved.[188] In particular, the injunction for the lending to facilitate "productive purposes" is interpreted as a mandate for the imposition of conditions in order to ensure productive purposes.[189] Thirdly, both the IBRD and the IDA mandate the imposition of appropriate terms to be imposed in loans.[190] Although these terms are mainly directed at the financial and credit aspects of the loans this reference does not exclude the imposition of macroeconomic conditions.[191]

**18-028**     Unlike the IMF the World Bank loans are in legal analysis loans. They are set in the form of an international agreement in the case of the IBRD and the IDA. However, the World Bank Conditionality is generally not considered to be contractually enforceable under the international agreement.[192] The rationale for this is set out as follows[193]:

> "39.  There are several reasons for such a position. First, it is within the sovereign prerogative of a member state whether or not to take the critical policy and institutional actions that constitute conditions for disbursing a policy-based loan. Some of these actions may entail delicate and sensitive domestic considerations and involve internal decision making, including parliamentary approval. It would be unwise and inappropriate for the Bank to be seen as influencing or interfering with these processes. Second, treating a borrower's failure to implement a policy action as a breach of a legal obligation owed to the Bank could create significant financial repercussions for the country. Aside from negative consequences for future Bank and other donor support, the borrower's standing in international financial markets could be seriously affected." (Footnotes omitted.)

In practice, the Bank has set its parameters for enforcement like the IMF through, for example, prior actions, tranche-release conditions, triggers

---

[184]  Scott in Effros (ed.) (1998), p.10.
[185]  Shihata (1995), p.32.
[186]  *Legal Aspects of Conditionality* (2005), para.23.
[187]  See Art.1 of IBRD and Art.1 of the IDA.
[188]  *Legal Aspects of Conditionality* (2005), para.28.
[189]  *Legal Aspects of Conditionality* (2005), para.31.
[190]  *Legal Aspects of Conditionality* (2005), para.32 and Arts 1 of IBRD and IDA and Art.V s.2(b) of the IDA.
[191]  *Legal Aspects of Conditionality* (2005), para.33.
[192]  *Legal Aspects of Conditionality* (2005), para.38.
[193]  *Legal Aspects of Conditionality* (2005), para.39.

and benchmarks and further suspension of disbursements. In particular, the disbursements of the loans are spread, thus facilitating suspension of further disbursements in the event of a default or non-compliance. The availability of the loan through different tranches is of particular note to ensure compliance with the conditions set. Moreover, in the event of default the Articles describe the options available.[194] The Articles give the institutions the authority to ensure arrangements for the proper use by the borrower of the funds, including its efficient and economic use.[195] Thus, the financial agreements normally contain provisions ensuring the Bank's access to the project; the availability of relevant information; consultation clauses; and clauses ensuring the Bank's priority over other creditors.[196] The ultimate sanction at the disposal of the Bank is of course the suspension of membership.[197]

## IFC[198]

Principally, the IFC provides funding for private enterprises at market rates. This financing of the private sector can take any appropriate form—including loans, equity investment and the underwriting of portfolio investments. Further, the IFC also facilitates financing through the mobilisation of loans from the private sector.[199] The IFC has a "B" loan programme from which it lends to private enterprises (in addition from its own funds i.e. the "A" Loan).[200] Under the "B" loan programme the IFC mobilises funds from the commercial banking sector by selling to the commercial banks participation in the "B" loan, through participation agreements with the banks.[201] On record in the contract, however, the IFC is the lender in relation to the private borrower.[202] In this manner the investment of the commercial banks avails itself of some of the privileges that the IFC enjoys, including immunity from taxation.[203] Further, this financing in the private sector comprises mainly of private sector project financing—including

**18-029**

---

[194] See, for example, IBRD Art.IV s.7.

[195] See IBRD Art.III and IDA Art.V.

[196] See, for example, Shihata (1995), p.755.

[197] See, for example, IBRD Art.V s.7 and IDA Art.VII.

[198] See Article of Agreement of the IFC. See also, for example, D.L. Khairallah, "Developments at the IFC" Ch.3 in R. Effros (ed.), *Current Legal Issues Affecting Central Banks*, IMF (1996), Vol.3; J.A. Sullivan, "Developments at the IFC", Ch.3 in R. Effros (ed.), *Current Legal Issues Affecting Central Banks*, IMF (1997), Vol.4; and M. Aizawa, "Developments at the IFC" Ch.3 in R. Effros (ed.), *Current Legal Issues Affecting Central Banks*, IMF (Washington: International Monetry Fund, 1998), Vol.5.

[199] See IFC Art.III. See also, for example, Aizawa (1998), p.50.

[200] Aizawa (1998), p.50.

[201] Aizawa (1998), p.50.

[202] Aizawa (1998), p.50.

[203] IFC Art.VI and Aizawa (1998), p.50.

infrastructure projects. Infrastructure projects are projects involving the building of the infrastructure of a country, e.g. the building of highways and ports, where the Government of the country mobilises private participation.

The criteria against which the IFC is allowed to engage in its investments and financing are as follows. First and foremost, the investment must be in productive private enterprises. The Government may, however, have a minority shareholding in the private enterprise.[204] The financing must be undertaken on sound commercial grounds. Thus, the investment must be such that the IFC can recoup its capital. Secondly, the investment must benefit the local economy, and should satisfy environmental considerations.[205] Thirdly, the financing must be for undertakings which do not have available sufficient private capital on reasonable terms.[206] Fourthly, the financing must not enjoy the benefit of a governmental repayment guarantee.[207] Finally, the financing of an enterprise in a member country must be with the consent of that member country.[208]

In addition to the specification of criteria determining the question of the involvement of the IFC in any private investment, there are also set conditions which determine the actual manner of its involvement. Thus, first, the IFC cannot dictate where the proceeds of the investment are to be further invested.[209] Secondly, the IFC's involvement in the investment should be like that of a silent partner in a business adventure, without involvement in the management of the enterprise.[210] Thirdly, the IFC is required to maintain a diverse portfolio of investment, and to revolve its funds through the sale of investments to the private sector when appropriate upon satisfactory terms.

**18-030**    In addition to its funding operations, the IFC encourages promotional activities in the private sector. This it does through a variety of methods. Of particular note is the joint participation of the IFC with the IBRD in an advisory service—namely the Foreign Investment Advisory Service—which advises on foreign investment laws.[211] Further, the IFC provides technical assistance, particularly in such matters as privatisation,[212] and in the development of capital markets.[213]

---

[204] Aizawa (1998), p.50; IFC Art.III.
[205] IFC Art.I and see also J.A. Sullivan (1997), p.35.
[206] IFC Art.I.
[207] IFC Art.I.
[208] IFC Art.I.
[209] IFC Art.I.
[210] IFC Art.I.
[211] Aizawa (1998), p.52.
[212] Aizawa (1998), p.52.
[213] Aizawa (1998), p.52.

## IFC ARTICLE III[214]        **18-031**

*Operations*

*SECTION 1. Financing Operations*

The Corporation may make investments of its funds in productive private enterprises in the territories of its members. The existence of a government or other public interest in such an enterprise shall not necessarily preclude the Corporation from making an investment therein.

### SECTION 2. Forms of Financing[3]

The Corporation may make investments of its funds in such form or forms as it may deem appropriate in the circumstances.

> [3] Amended September 21, 1961. Original text: (a) The Corporation's financing shall not take the form of investments in capital stock. Subject to the foregoing, the Corporation may make investments of its funds in such form or forms as it may deem appropriate in the circumstances, including (but without limitation) investments according to the holder thereof the right to participate in earnings and the right to subscribe to, or to convert the investment into, capital stock. (b) The Corporation shall not itself exercise any right to subscribe to, or to convert any investment into, capital stock.

### SECTION 3. Operational Principles

The operations of the Corporation shall be conducted in accordance with the following principles:

(i) *the Corporation shall not undertake any financing for which in its opinion sufficient private capital could be obtained on reasonable terms;*

(ii) *the Corporation shall not finance an enterprise in the territories of any member if the member objects to such financing;*

(iii) *the Corporation shall impose no conditions that the proceeds of any financing by it shall be spent in the territories of any particular country;*

(iv) *the Corporation shall not assume responsibility for managing any enterprise in which it has invested and shall not exercise voting rights for such purpose or for any other purpose which, in its opinion, properly is within the scope of managerial control;*[4]

> [4] Amended September 21, 1961. Original text: (iv) The Corporation shall not assume responsibility for managing any enterprise in which it has invested;

(v) *the Corporation shall undertake its financing on terms and conditions which it considers appropriate, taking into account the requirements of the enterprise, the risks being undertaken by the Corporation and the terms and conditions normally obtained by private investors for similar financing;*

(vi) *the Corporation shall seek to revolve its funds by selling its investments to private investors whenever it can appropriately do so on satisfactory terms;*

(vii) *the Corporation shall seek to maintain a reasonable diversification in its investments.*

---

[214] Source: *http://www.worldbank.org.* (Accessed June 8, 2011).

### SECTION 4. Protection of Interests

Nothing in this Agreement shall prevent the Corporation, in the event of actual or threatened default on any of its investments, actual or threatened insolvency of the enterprise in which such investment shall have been made, or other situations which, in the opinion of the Corporation, threaten to jeopardize such investment, from taking such action and exercising such rights as it may deem necessary for the protection of its interests.

### SECTION 5. Applicability of Certain Foreign Exchange Restrictions

(Omitted.)

### SECTION 6. Miscellaneous Operations

In addition to the operations specified elsewhere in this Agreement, the Corporation shall have the power to:

(i) *borrow funds, and in that connection to furnish such collateral or other security therefore as it shall determine; provided, however, that before making a public sale of its obligations in the markets of a member, the Corporation shall have obtained the approval of that member and of the member in whose currency the obligations are to be denominated; if and so long as the Corporation shall be indebted on loans from or guaranteed by the Bank, the total amount outstanding of borrowings incurred or guarantees given by the Corporation shall not be increased if, at the time or as a result thereof, the aggregate amount of debt (including the guarantee of any debt) incurred by the Corporation from any source and then outstanding shall exceed an amount equal to four times its unimpaired subscribed capital and surplus;*[5] [5] Last clause added by amendment effective September 1, 1965.

(ii) *invest funds not needed in its financing operations in such obligations as it may determine and invest funds held by it for pension or similar purposes in any marketable securities, all without being subject to the restrictions imposed by other sections of this Article;*

(iii) *guarantee securities in which it has invested in order to facilitate their sale;*

(iv) *buy and sell securities it has issued or guaranteed or in which it has invested;*

(v) *exercise such other powers incidental to its business as shall be necessary or desirable in furtherance of its purposes.*

# INDEX